IAAP Handbook of Applied Psychology

Wiley-Blackwell IAAP Handbooks of Applied Psychology

Made up of new essays from leading researchers and theorists, each IAAP Handbook of Applied Psychology gives a complete and incisive overview of a major area of applied psychology and sets an agenda for future research. Individually each Handbook represents the state of current thinking in a particular field. As a whole, the Handbooks set out what the study of applied psychology has achieved to date and survey its most productive present concerns.

Published

IAAP Handbook of Applied Psychology
Edited by Paul R. Martin, Fanny M. Cheung, Michael C. Knowles, Michael Kyrios, Lyn Littlefield, J. Bruce Overmier, and José M. Prieto

IAAP Handbook of Applied Psychology

Edited by Paul R. Martin, Fanny M. Cheung,
Michael C. Knowles, Michael Kyrios,
Lyn Littlefield, J. Bruce Overmier, and
José M. Prieto

WILEY-BLACKWELL
A John Wiley & Sons, Ltd., Publication

This edition first published 2011

Blackwell Publishing was acquired by John Wiley & Sons in February 2007. Blackwell's publishing program has been merged with Wiley's global Scientific, Technical, and Medical business to form Wiley-Blackwell.

Registered Office
John Wiley & Sons Ltd, The Atrium, Southern Gate, Chichester, West Sussex, PO19 8SQ, United Kingdom

Editorial Offices
350 Main Street, Malden, MA 02148-5020, USA
9600 Garsington Road, Oxford, OX4 2DQ, UK
The Atrium, Southern Gate, Chichester, West Sussex, PO19 8SQ, UK

For details of our global editorial offices, for customer services, and for information about how to apply for permission to reuse the copyright material in this book please see our website at www.wiley.com/wiley-blackwell.

Library of Congress Cataloging-in-Publication Data

IAAP handbook of applied psychology / edited by Paul R. Martin ... [et al.].
p. cm. – (Wiley-Blackwell IAAP handbooks of applied psychology)
Includes bibliographical references and index.
ISBN 978-1-4051-9331-3 (hbk. : alk. paper)
1. Psychology, Applied. I. Martin, Paul R., 1951-
BF636.I23 2011
158–dc22

2010042201

A catalogue record for this book is available from the British Library.

This book is published in the following electronic formats: ePDFs 9781444395136; Wiley Online Library 9781444395150; ePub 9781444395143

Set in 10/12.5 pt Galliard by Toppan Best-set Premedia Limited
Printed and bound in Singapore by Markono Print Media Pte Ltd

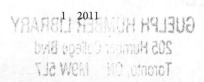

1 2011

Contents

About the Editors

Paul R. Martin is Professor and Head of the School of Psychology at Griffith University, Queensland, Australia. He is a Fellow of the British Psychological Society, an Honorary Fellow of the Australian Psychological Society (APS), and a Fellow of the International Association of Applied Psychology. He was President of the 27th International Congress of Applied Psychology. He completed his undergraduate studies at the University of Bristol, his clinical training through the Oxfordshire Regional Health Authority, and his doctorate at the University of Oxford. He held appointments at the Universities of Oxford, Western Australia, New England, RMIT, and Monash University before commencing his current appointment in 2011. He has held a number of professional leadership positions including National President of the Australian Behaviour Modification Association, and Director of Science and then President of the APS. His main research interest has been headache and migraine, with subsidiary interests in stress, depression (including postnatal depression), and social support. He has authored/edited eight books and over 120 journal articles.

Fanny M. Cheung is Chair Professor of Psychology and Director of the Hong Kong Institute of Asia Pacific Studies at the Chinese University of Hong Kong. Cheung received her BA from the University of California at Berkeley and her PhD from the University of Minnesota. Her research interests include cross-cultural personality assessment and gender equality. She was the Founding Chairperson of the Equal Opportunities Commission of the Hong Kong Government. A Fellow of the American Psychological Association and the Association of Psychological Science, she is currently a member of the Board of Directors of the International Association of Applied Psychology and President-Elect of the International Testing Commission.

Michael C. Knowles (MCom (Qld), PhD (Edin)) has lectured at Edinburgh University, Monash University, the Sloan School of Management at the Massachusetts Institute of Technology, the Wharton School of Management at the University of Pennsylvania, and throughout many countries in Southeast Asia. He is a former Director of the MBA Programs Division, Faculty of Business and Economics, Monash University, Melbourne, Australia. He has been employed in, undertaken research into, or consulted for private companies, the civil service, and military and religious organizations. He has published widely and his principal teaching area is organizational behavior. He is a past President of the Australian Psychological Society and is currently President of the International Association of Applied Psychology. His awards include a Faculty Award for Excellence in Teaching at Monash University, the Elton May Award of the Australian Psychological Society for Outstanding Contributions to Industrial/Organizational Psychology, and the First Annual Award of the American Psychological Association for Distinguished Contributions to Global Psychology.

Michael Kyrios is an academic clinical psychologist who holds the chair in Psychology at Swinburne University of Technology where he is Director of the Brain and Psychological Sciences Research Centre and Chair of the National eTherapy Centre executive committee. He has been a chief investigator on grants in the study of obsessive-compulsive and spectrum disorders, depression in primary care, and mood disorders in medical conditions. He is a Fellow of the Australian Psychological Society, inaugural Chair of the Special Interest Group in Psychology and Cultures, a previous national chair of the College of Clinical Psychologists, and works closely with other professions and mental health consumer groups in the dissemination of psychological knowledge. He was Chair of the Scientific Program Committee for the 2010 International Congress of Applied Psychology, and will chair the scientific program for the World Congress of Behavioral and Cognitive Therapies in 2016.

Lyn Littlefield (OAM, FAPS, FAICD, FAIM, BSC, DipEd, BBSc(Hons), MPsych, PhD) is the Executive Director of the Australian Psychological Society (APS), the peak national professional body for psychologists in Australia. Lyn also holds an appointment as a professor of Psychology at La Trobe University, where she was previously the head of the School of Psychological Science and established the first professional doctorate in Clinical Child, Adolescent, and Family Psychology in Australia. In parallel with her academic career, she has worked as a clinical psychologist for over 20 years and established a research, development, and training center for the Victorian State government. She has led numerous research and evaluation projects, written books, practice manuals, papers, and articles and delivered over 100 conference presentations. Lyn is a Fellow of the Australian Psychological Society, the Australian Institute of Company Directors, and the Australian Institute of Management. She won a Medal of the Order of Australia "for service to the welfare of children and families, … and the development and advancement of training and education in the field of child, adolescent and family psychology."

J. Bruce Overmier is Professor of Psychology, Neuroscience, and Cognitive Science at the University of Minnesota, past officer of several major psychological organizations and President of the International Union of Psychological Science. Overmier's research spans specialties of learning, memory, stress, psychosomatic disorders, and their biological substrates. Author of some 200 publications, he teaches both undergraduate and graduate students. Occasionally, Overmier publishes with his wife, Judith Ann Overmier, who is a Professor Emeritus of Library and Information

Science at the University of Oklahoma. An example of their joint work is *Psychology: IUPsyS Global Resource* (editions 1–5), a CD-ROM reference tool in international psychology.

José M. Prieto has been head of the Department of Individual Differences and Work Psychology, Complutense University of Madrid. His field of expertise is personnel psychology, and his research areas are: personnel selection, multivariate analysis in personnel assessment, training and development, self-development programs, and Zen meditation. He is past Secretary General of the IAAP (1998–2006), and is now online communication officer. Prieto lectures in English, French, Spanish, and Italian, and his publications are mainly in Spanish and English. He was the founder of Revista de Psicología del Trabajo y de las Organizaciones in Spain and a member of the European Network of Organizational Psychology (1984–2005). He was also the Spanish delegate to IUPSYS and EFPA for two decades. He has had four books of poetry already published. Prieto is a practitioner of Zen and Qigong as a survival kit for a healthy life style into old age.

About the Contributors

Charles Abraham is a social and health psychologist. His research focuses on identifying modifiable psychological antecedents of behavior and designing and testing interventions to change these antecedents and promote health-related behaviors. He has investigated condom use, physical activity, healthy eating and alcohol consumption. He was the founding chair of the Division of Health Psychology in the UK and played a key role in developing training programs for UK Health Psychologists. He has served as a coeditor of *Psychology & Health* and as a consultant in the UK Department of Health and the National Institute for Health and Clinical Excellence.

Gerrit Antonides is a professor of Economics of Consumers and Households at Wageningen University and senior fellow of the Mansholt Institute at Wageningen, the Netherlands. He obtained his MD in psychology from the University of Utrecht and his PhD in economics from Erasmus University Rotterdam. He has published in the areas of economic psychology, consumer behavior and behavioral economics. He serves as an editor of the *Journal of Economic Psychology*, and as a board member of the International Association for Research on Economic Psychology (IAREP) and the Society for the Advancement of Behavioral Economics (SABE).

Faedra R. Backus, a doctoral student in Counseling Psychology at Boston College, received her MA in Mental Health Counseling from Boston College and her BA in Psychology and Educational Studies from Colgate University. Her current research interests include the psychology of working, school-to-work transitions, gender role socialization, and men's health behaviors.

Chiwoza R. Bandawe is a Malawian clinical psychologist with the University of Malawi, College of Medicine. He obtained his PhD in 2000 from the University of Cape Town, South Africa where he also served as Senior Lecturer in Psychology between 2004 and 2007. In his mission to promote mental health literacy in Malawi, he has been a keen newspaper columnist since 1996 as well as giving numerous interviews to the media. He facilitates numerous psychosocial workshops and seminars for organizations, communities, and groups. He is the author of three books and has published in several academic journals as well as authoring and coauthoring several book chapters. His research interests include understanding various aspects of applied indigenous social psychology and practical mental health.

David Bartram, BA, DPhil, CPsychol, CSc, FBPsS, is President IAAP Division 2 (Assessment and Evaluation). He is Research Director for SHL Group Ltd. Prior to that he was Dean of the Faculty of Science and the Environment, and Professor of Psychology in the Department of Psychology at the University of Hull. He is Past-President and a current Council Member of the ITC. He is the Convenor of the EFPA Standing Committee on Tests and Testing and a member and past Chair of the British Psychological Society's Steering Committee on Test Standards. He was appointed Special Professor in Occupational Psychology and Measurement at the University of Nottingham in 2007.

Catherine Robina Bateman Steel is a lecturer at the School of Public Health and Community Medicine at the University of New South Wales, and is an Australian Faculty of Public Health Medicine Trainee. She is a medical doctor with a degree in Medical Anthropology and a masters in Public Health in Developing Countries from the London School of Hygiene and Tropical Medicine. She has a long-term interest in international public health and helped to set up the International Health and Medical Education Centre at UCL in London. She has clinical experience in a variety of hospital roles, in particular psychiatry, in the UK and Australia. Her research experience includes investigating the mental health effects of detaining asylum seekers in Australia, an extensive period in East Timor managing an epidemiological mental health study, and more recently investigating healthcare-seeking behavior in East Timor. Her research interests are in international health, vulnerable and marginalized populations particularly refugees and asylum seekers, cross-cultural health, mental health, mixed methods research particularly the intersection of anthropological and epidemiological methods, the research–service interface, and the ethics of international health research and intervention.

Bridget K. Biggs, PhD, LP, is a senior associate consultant in the Department of Psychiatry and Psychology at the Mayo Clinic, Rochester, Minnesota, USA. She contributed to this volume while an assistant professor in the Clinical Child Psychology Program at the University of Kansas, Lawrence, Kansas, USA. Her research interests include the role of peer relations for the emotional and physical health of children and adolescents and the development and evaluation of multidisciplinary interventions.

David L. Blustein is a professor in the Department of Counseling, Developmental, and Educational Psychology at Boston College. He is a fellow of Division 17 (Counseling Psychology) of the American Psychological Association and he has received the Division 17 Early Career Scientist-Practitioner Award and the John Holland Award for Outstanding Achievement in Personality and Career Research. He has published in the areas of career development, work-based transitions, work and interpersonal functioning, and the psychology of working. He also has published a book entitled *The Psychology of Working: A New Perspective for Career Development, Counseling, and Public Policy.*

Lyle E. Bourne, Jr. (PhD, University of Wisconsin, 1956) is Professor of Psychology (Emeritus), Department of Psychology, University of Colorado at Boulder. His general research interests lie in cognitive psychology, with ancillary work in clinical, biological, and social psychology. Currently, his primary focus is human learning and memory for facts and skills, with the aim of assessing the effectiveness of various training methods. He has collaborated on the development of quantitative, computational and neurophysiological models of cognitive processes.

José J. Cañas has a BA in Psychology from the University of Granada, Spain, and a PhD in Experimental Psychology from the University of South Florida, USA. He is currently Professor of Ergonomics at the University of Granada. His teaching and research activities have been focused on the psychological aspects of the interaction of humans and artefacts. He has conducted research projects on mental models, complex and dynamic problem solving, and psychological aspects of interface design for the disabled. He has published several books on Ergonomics, and his research has been published in prestigious journals such as the *International Journal of Human-Machine Studies* and *Ergonomics.*

Stuart C. Carr is Professor of Psychology at Massey University in New Zealand, where he coordinates the interdisciplinary Poverty Research Group. Author of several leading volumes on the psychology of poverty reduction, Stuart is a cofounder of the Global Task Force for Humanitarian Work Psychology. He is the lead researcher in Project ADDUP, focusing on remuneration disparity in aid and development work, and its impact on development work performance. Other projects include the Global Special Issue on Psychology and Poverty Reduction, an online support network for psychologists in poverty reduction, "Povio," and co-editing the participating *Journal of Pacific Rim Psychology.*

Christine Catraio is a doctoral candidate in counseling psychology at Boston College. She received her masters degree in counseling psychology at Boston College. Her research interests include career development, gender issues, and multicultural counseling.

Maria T. N. Coutinho, MA, is a doctoral student in Counseling Psychology at the Lynch School of Education at Boston College. Maria is currently completing her pre-doctoral internship at the Cambridge Health Alliance in the combined child/adult outpatient track. Maria's interests include the intersection of vocational and ethnic identities, particularly as they pertain to the experiences of immigrants. Additional research interests include the work experience of women, and low-income populations. Maria's clinical interests include child and family treatment and the collaboration of systems (schools and community agencies) in the provision of mental health services to children and families.

Karen Dugganis a researcher and project manager at Manchester Metropolitan University (MMU) and works on participative community projects in partnership with educational institutions and community organizations. She is particularly interested in addressing social inequalities and facilitating social and transformational change through collective action. Her special interest and research focus is in exploring innovative and creative ways to widen participation into and through the Higher Education system by using Community Psychology approaches to explore diversity and achievement. Karen is working on a part-time PhD in community psychology at MMU.

Rocío Fernández-Ballesteros (PhD Political and Social Sciences, Dip Sociology, Dip Psychology) is a clinical psychologist. Since 1979, she has been Professor of Psychology, Autonomous University of Madrid. She was Chair of the Department of Psychodiagnosis and Measurement (1980–1983), First Dean, Faculty of Psychology (1983–1987), and Director, Masters program in Social Gerontology (1990–2005). Since 2004, she has been Director, University Program for Older Persons. She was President, IAAP Divison 2 (Psychological Assessment, 1990–1994) and Division 7 (Applied Gerontology, 2002–2006), and Executive Committee Member (1990–2006). She is a Fellow member, Gerontological Society of America, and is founder and former President, European Association of Psychological Assessment (EAPA, 1992–1999). Fernández-Ballesteros is also founder and former Editor-in-Chief, *European Journal of Psychological Assessment* (EJPA) (1985–2005), Associate/Consulting Editor, 20 national and international journals, and consultant, advisor and/or evaluator of international organizations (UN, UNESCO, WHO). She is the author of 26 books and 250 research articles (in Spanish, English, Italian, and German). Fernández-Ballesteros has won the Aristotle Prize (EFPA, 2005), Distinguished Award (IAAP, 2006), Huarte de San Juan Award (COP-CyL, 2009), and Honorary Award (COP-Madrid, 2009).

Cynthia D. Fisher (MS, PhD Purdue) is Professor of Management at Bond University. She is the author of articles on employee attitudes and work behavior, performance appraisal and feedback, employee socialization, and emotions at work. Her research has been supported by the Office of Naval Research in the United States and by the Australian Research Council. She has served on the editorial boards of the *Academy of Management Review*, *Organizational Behavior and Human Decision Processes*, the *Journal of Applied Psychology*, and the *Journal of Organizational Behavior*. She is a Fellow of the Society for Industrial and Organizational Psychology.

David Fontana was Distinguished Visiting Fellow at Cardiff University and Visiting Full Professor of Transpersonal Psychology at Liverpool John Moores University. A Fellow of the British Psychological Society, he was the author of over 45 books translated into 26 languages. He was formerly Chair of the Transpersonal Psychology Section of the British Psychological Society, which he was instrumental in founding. Eastern and Western spiritual traditions and psycho-spiritual development were a major feature of his work, and among his most recently published books are *Psychology, Religion and Spirituality* and *Is There an Afterlife?*

María Paz García-Vera has a PhD in clinical psychology from Complutense University of Madrid. She is a tenured-professor at the Department of Personality, Assessment and Clinical Psychology of the Complutense University of Madrid and Director of the University Psychology Clinic of this university. Her research interests include psychological treatment of tobacco addiction, essential arterial hypertension, and psychopathological consequences of terrorist attacks. She has coedited *Ayuda psicológica a las víctimas de atentados y catástrofes* ("Psychological support for victims of terrorist attacks and catastrophes"; Complutense Press, 2008) and has authored or co-authored more than 50 scientific papers, including chapters in books and journal articles.

Janel Gauthier PhD, is Professor of Psychology at Laval University in Canada, Secretary-General of the International Association of Applied Psychology (IAAP), and Canadian Delegate to the General Assembly of the International Union of Psychological Science (IUPsyS). He is also a past-president and a fellow of the Canadian Psychological Association (CPA), and a recipient of the CPA Award for Distinguished Contributions to the International Advancement of Psychology. He chaired the international Joint Ad Hoc Committee which developed the *Universal Declaration of Ethical Principles for Psychologists* adopted unanimously by the IUPsyS General Assembly and the IAAP Board of Directors in Berlin in 2008.

Robert Gifford is Professor of Psychology and Environmental Studies at the University of Victoria. Elected Fellow of the American Psychological Association, the Canadian Psychological Association, the Association for Psychological Science, he was given a Career Award from the Environmental Design Research Association. He is the author of over 85 refereed scientific publications and four editions of *Environmental Psychology: Principles and Practice.* He is the editor of the *Journal of Environmental Psychology*, was President of the American Psychological Association's Population and Environment Division, and is the current President of the Environmental Psychology division of the International Association of Applied Psychology.

A. Ian Glendon (PhD, School of Psychology, Griffith University, Gold Coast, Australia) previously held full-time or visiting positions at universities in Beijing, Birmingham, Brisbane, Edinburgh, Hong Kong, and Manchester. His research interests include transportation psychology, driver stress/behavior, safety/risk management, and safety culture/climate. His over 100 publications include five books. He has consulted for over 60 clients on safety auditing, safety culture/climate analysis, injury/incident analysis, task analysis, and human error/reliability analysis. He is a registered psychologist in Queensland, a Chartered Fellow of the Institution of Occupational Safety and Health, a Chartered Occupational Psychologist (UK), and President (2006–2010) of IAAP's Traffic and Transportation Psychology Division.

Perilou Goddard is Professor of Psychological Science at Northern Kentucky University, where she was the recipient of the Frank Sinton Milburn Award for outstanding professor in 1999. She earned her PhD in clinical psychology from Indiana

University in 1987. Her research interests focus on attitudes toward drug policy issues in the US and other countries.

Ronald K. Hambleton holds the title of Distinguished University Professor and is Executive Director of the Center for Educational Assessment at the University of Massachusetts Amherst. He earned a BA in 1966 from the University of Waterloo in Canada with majors in mathematics and psychology, and an MA in 1968 and PhD in 1969 from the University of Toronto with specialties in psychometric methods and statistics. He has been teaching graduate-level courses in educational and psychological testing, item response theory and applications, classical test theory models and methods, and offers seminar courses on applied measurement topics at UMass since 1969. He is the author or coeditor of nine books and has published many papers on topics related to item response theory and applied measurement issues such as test adaptation methodology, score reporting, criterion-referenced assessment, detection of item bias, and computer-based testing.

Xiaoqi Han is a second-year PhD student in the marketing department of University of Cincinnati. Her research interest is consumer information processing, consumer inference and consumer judgment under limited information (Omission Neglect).

Alice F. Healy received her doctorate from Rockefeller University and was on the faculty of Yale University before joining the faculty of the University of Colorado, Boulder, where she is currently College Professor of Distinction and Director of the Center for Research on Training. She has served as Chair of the Society of Experimental Psychologists and of the Psychology Section of the AAAS, President of the Rocky Mountain Psychological Association and of the Experimental Psychology Division of the APA, and Editor of *Memory & Cognition*. She has published over 190 articles and chapters and is author or editor of seven books.

Yo Jackson is a licensed, board-certified clinical child psychologist specializing in trauma, resilience, and diversity issues in children. She is an associate professor at the University of Kansas, a core faculty member of the Clinical Child Psychology Program, appointed in both the Psychology and Applied Behavioral Science Departments. She has published numerous articles and conducts several research projects on the factors that make children resilient after exposure to stress, the development of interventions for children exposed to major life events and trauma, the role of protective factors in promoting adaptive behavior in children, and developing models of competence in children exposed to multiple stressors. Her research involves investigating both typical schoolchildren as well as special populations, such as children exposed to maltreatment. She also conducts research on multicultural issues and the role of acculturation on mental health.

Christina Weyer Jamora, PhD, works at San Francisco Clinical Neurosciences as a neuropsychologist, psychotherapist, and researcher. She is also an associate clinical professor in the Department of Psychiatry at the University of California, San Francisco and neuropsychologist in the Department of Neurosurgery at San Francisco General

Hospital, a Level 1 trauma center. She completed her Bachelor's Degree in nursing with a minor in psychology at Indiana University. She worked as a psychiatric registered nurse at Langley Porter at the University of California, San Francisco. She completed her PhD in clinical psychology at the California School of Professional Psychology, San Francisco. She completed an internship at Jersey Shore University Medical Center and two years of postdoctoral training in neuropsychology at San Francisco Clinical Neurosciences under the direction of Ronald Ruff and San Francisco General Hospital. She currently splits her time between working in neurosurgery at San Francisco General Hospital and private practice providing psychotherapy and cognitive rehabilitation. She also serves as the president of the board of trustees for the Marin Brain Injury Network. Her current research interests focus on traumatic brain injury, cognitive rehabilitation, and therapeutic assessment.

Carolyn Kagan is Professor of Community Social Psychology and a registered Counseling Psychologist and qualified social worker. She is Director of the Research Institute for Health and Social Change at Manchester Metropolitan University, UK, where the first action learning UK Masters program in community psychology is based. Much of her work concerns the wellbeing of those marginalized by the social system, and the ways this can be enhanced or obstructed through participation. Her work has contributed to UK and international service and policy. Her most recent work includes arts for health, urban regeneration, forced labor and university–community engagement. See www.compsy.org.

Frank R. Kardes is the Donald E. Weston Professor of Marketing at the College of Business at the University of Cincinnati. He is a recipient of the Distinguished Scientific Achievement Award of the Society for Consumer Psychology, and a fellow of several professional societies. He was an editor of the *Journal of Consumer Psychology*, *Advances in Consumer Research*, and the *Handbook of Consumer Psychology*, and is currently an associate editor of the *Journal of Consumer Research* and the *Journal of Consumer Psychology*.

Paul Kennedy is Professor of Clinical Psychology at the University of Oxford, and Trust Head of Clinical Psychology based at the National Spinal Injuries Centre, Stoke Mandeville Hospital. He has published over 90 scientific papers for peer-reviewed journals, and has written and edited a number of books on clinical health psychology and physical disability. He is founding chair of both the Multidisciplinary Association of Spinal Cord Injury Professionals and the European Spinal Psychologists Association. In 2002 he was awarded the Distinguished Service Award by the American Association of Spinal Cord Injury Psychologists and Social Workers, and in 2005 he was awarded a visiting fellowship to Australia by the New South Wales Ministry of Science and Medical Research. He is an enthusiastic scientist practitioner who enjoys the interplay between service provision, research, and training.

Gerjo Kok is a social psychologist with an MSc and PhD from the University of Groningen. He was professor of health promotion and chair of the Department of Health Promotion at Maastricht University between 1984 and 1998. He was appointed the endowed professor for Aids prevention and health promotion 1992–2004. Since 1998 Gerjo Kok has been professor of applied psychology at Maastricht. From 1998 to 2006 he was also dean of the School of Psychology and Neuroscience there. His publications concern the application of social psychological theory to planned behavior change. He is coauthor of *Planning Health Promotion Programs: An Intervention Mapping Approach*, 2006.

Mark M. Leach PhD, is a professor and Director of Training of the Counseling Psychology program at Louisville. He is an associate editor of the APA journal *Psychology of Religion and Spirituality*, serves on other editorial boards, is Tri-Chair of the International Section of Division 17 (Counseling Psychology), and on the executive committee of Division 16 (Counseling Psychology) of the International Association of Applied Psychology. He is a Fellow of APA. He has authored or coedited four books and has numerous publications. His primary research interests include forgiveness, international counseling issues, spirituality and religion, comparative ethics, and culture and suicide.

Frederick T. L. Leong, PhD, is Professor of Psychology at Michigan State University and serves as the Director of the Center for Multicultural Psychology Research. He has authored or coauthored over 120 articles in various psychology journals, 80 book chapters, and edited or coedited 10 books. He is a Fellow of the APA and APS. He is the Founding Editor of the *Asian American Journal of Psychology*. His major clinical research interest centers around culture and mental health and cross-cultural psychotherapy and his I-O research is focused on cultural and personality factors related to career choice, work adjustment, and occupational stress.

Aleksandra Luszczynska, PhD, professor of psychology, works at Warsaw School of Social Sciences and Humanities (Warsaw, Poland) and in the Trauma, Health, & Hazards Center, University of Colorado (Colorado Springs, USA). From 2010 to 2014 she will serve as President of the Health Psychology Division, IAAP. Currently, she is chief editor of *Anxiety, Stress, & Coping*. Her research interests comprise theory-based interventions aiming at health behavior change and psychosocial resources affecting quality of life. She is author of over 50 publications in journals such as *Health Psychology*, *Rehabilitation Psychology*, or *Psychology and Health*.

Girishwar Misra is a professor of applied social psychology at the University of Delhi, India. He has been a Fulbright fellow at Swarthmore College, Philadelphia and Michigan University, visiting professor at the University of the Ruhr, Bochum, Germany, and an ESRC Fellow at Sussex University, UK. He has published widely on deprivation, self-processes, emotions, and well-being. His publications include *Applied Social Psychology in India*, *Perspectives on Indigenous Psychology*, *Psychology and Societal Development*, *Psychological Perspectives on Stress and Health*, *Psychology of Poverty and Disadvantages*, *Rethinking Intelligence*, and *Psychology in India: Advances in Research*. He is editor of *Psychological Studies* published by Springer.

Kerri A. Murphy is a fifth-year doctoral student in Counseling Psychology at Boston College. She received her BA in Psychology from the University of Michigan before returning to Boston to pursue her Master's degree in mental health counseling at Boston College. Her research interests include career and identity development, mentoring, and the potency of work to promote or inhibit young adults' psychological and physical health and school engagement. As a graduate student, she has worked clinically and vocationally with students at MIT, Tufts University, and Emerson College and will be completing her APA internship at Suffolk University during 2009–2010.

Peter Nenniger is a full professor of education and co-director at the Centre for Educational Research of the University of Koblenz-Landau (Germany). He graduated in 1970 in psychology and, after post-graduate studies in Aix-en-Provance (France), received his PhD in psychology and education 1977 at the University of Mannheim (Germany) and obtained his habilitation in education in 1984 at the University of Freiburg (Germany). From 1977 to 1985 he was assistant professor at the University of Freiburg, from 1985 to 1992 associate professor at the University of Kiel, since 1992 he has been full professor at University of Koblenz-Landau and from 1986 to 2000 he was visiting professor at the University of Basle (Switzerland). He served as a consultant to several parliamentary, governmental, and scientific committees in Finland, France, Germany, Switzerland, and the European Union, is editor of *Empirische Pädagogik* and is currently liaison officer of the German Research Foundation and President-in-office of Division 5 of the International Association of Applied Psychology (IAAP). He has published widely in international journals and been a keynote speaker at national and international conferences.

Thomas Oakland, PhD, ABPP, ABPN, is a professor within the school psychology program at the University of Florida. He is President of the International Foundation for Children's Education, President Elect of the International Association of Applied Psychologists' Division of Psychological Assessment and Evaluation, and past–president of the International School Psychology Association and the International Test Commission. He has worked in more than 45 countries. He holds honorary status as Professor of Psychology at the Iberoamerican University in San Jose, Costa Rica, the University of Hong Kong, and the Universidade Lusíada do Porto, Portugal. He received the American Psychological Association's 2003 Award for Distinguished Contributions to the Advancement of Psychology Internationally.

Ronan O'Carroll is Professor of Psychology at the University of Stirling, UK. He has previously held the posts of Senior Scientist at the MRC Brain Metabolism Unit in Edinburgh and Professor of Psychology at the University of St Andrews. He is a practicing clinical-, health-, and neuro-psychologist. He has research interests in adherence to medication, organ transplantation, and prediction of outcome following medical and surgical interventions. He is currently associate editor of the *British Journal of Health Psychology* and the *British Journal of Clinical Psychology* and is on the editorial board of *Psychology and Health*. He has published over 140 papers in peer-reviewed journals.

James R. P. Ogloff, JD, PhD, FAPS, trained as a lawyer and psychologist, and is Foundation Professor of Clinical Forensic Psychology, Monash University; Director of the Centre for Forensic Behavioural Science; and Director of Psychological Services, Victorian Institute of Forensic Mental Health. He has given invited addresses or workshops in countries around the world. He is a fellow of the Canadian, American, and Australian psychological societies. He is the president of the Australian and New Zealand Association of Psychiatry, Psychology, and Law, past-president of the Canadian Psychological Association, and past-president of the American Psychology Law Society. He has published 14 books/monographs and 190 scholarly articles and book chapters.

Susannah B. F. Paletz received her PhD in social psychology at the University of California, Berkeley, in December 2003. Her dissertation was on implicit theories of creativity in China, Japan, and the United States. She was then a research psychologist at NASA Ames Research Center where she worked with the distributed decision-making laboratory and the award-winning human–computer interaction laboratory. Since September 2008 she has been a postdoctoral research associate at the University of Pittsburgh, studying relationships between social and cognitive variables in teamwork. Her research applies social psychological methods and theory to teamwork, creativity, and culture, particularly in science, engineering, and aviation.

Janak Pandey, currently Vice-Chancellor of the Central University of Bihar, was until recently Professor and Head of the Advanced Centre of Psychology and the Centre of Behavioural and Cognitive Sciences at the University of Allahabad, India. His PhD in social psychology is from the Kansas State University where he was on a Fulbright Scholarship. He is an honorary Fellow and past President of the International Association for Cross-Cultural Psychology and a member of the Executive of the IUPsyS and of the Board of the IAAP. He has published extensively in the areas of social influence processes and on issues related to economic and environmental stressors. He edited reviews of two rounds of psychological research in India leading to six volumes.

José M. Peiró is currently Professor of Work and Organizational (W&O) Psychology at the University of Valencia. He is Director of the Research Institute of Human Resources Psychology, Organizational Development and Quality of Working life (IDOCAL). He is also President of Division 1: Organizational Psychology of IAAP, a past-president of the EAWOP and fellow member of SIOP and the EAOHP. He was former associate editor of the *European Journal of Work and Organizational Psychology*. He has published articles in scientific journals on occupational stress, psychosocial risk prevention at work, absenteeism, training in organizations, organizational climate, team work, and customer satisfaction in service organizations.

Kaiping Peng is a tenured faculty member at the Department of Psychology of the University of California at Berkeley. He received his PhD in Social Psychology from the University of Michigan in 1997. He is currently the chair of the Department of Psychology at Tsinghua University in China as well the head of social/personality psychology at the University of California, Berkeley. He also directs the Culture and Cognition Lab and the Berkeley Program of Psychological Studies in China there. He has published nine books and over a hundred articles on cultural and social psychology.

Kathryn Nicholson Perry, PhD, is presently lecturer and placement coordinator on the Master of Psychology (Clinical) course at the University of Western Sydney. She completed her undergraduate and clinical psychology training in the UK, and completed her PhD in the Faculty of Medicine, University of Sydney on psychological aspects of spinal cord injury (SCI) pain. She has worked in both clinical and research roles in clinical health and rehabilitation psychology, most recently on the development of a psychosocial strategy for people with SCI. She is the National Convenor of the Australian Psychological Society Rehabilitation Psychology Interest Group.

Keith J. Petrie holds a personal chair at the University of Auckland in health psychology. Over the past 10 years he has been a key figure in developing the field of health psychology in New Zealand. His primary research focus involves how patients construct beliefs about their illness and how these influence coping, adherence to treatment, and recovery from illness. He and his research group are known internationally for constructing new methods for measuring patients' perceptions of illness and developing early intervention programs designed to change patients' illness perceptions. He also does research in the area of psycho-immunology and fatigue.

Jean L. Pettifor over her career has been a practitioner, teacher, and researcher as well as serving in many positions in psychology organizations provincially, nationally, and internationally. She is best known for her continuing focus on quality in practice and value-based ethical decision-making for psychologists. Her extensive publications reflect the search for universal ethical principles. Her university degrees include BA (University of Saskatchewan); BEd, MA, MEd (University of Alberta); and PhD (Clinical Psychology, Wayne State University). Among her many awards is the Honorary Degree of Doctor of Laws (Athabasca University). She is a mentor and role model for hundreds of students.

Bruce E. Pfeiffer is an assistant professor of Marketing at the Whittemore School of Business and Economics at the University of New Hampshire. His research interests include consumer information processing, consumer judgment and decision-making, consumer inference formation, omission neglect, persuasion, attitude formation and polarization, temporal construal, and affect. He is a member of the American Marketing Association, the Association for Consumer Research, and the Society for Consumer Psychology. His CV is available at http://wsbe.unh.edu/node/12563.

Martin Pinquart is Professor for developmental psychology at the Philipps University of Marburg, Germany. His research interests focus on developmental regulation, effects of social change on human development, and geropsychology. He has been the secretary of the Task Force for Geropsychology of the European Federation of Psychologists' Associations (EFPA) from 2003 to 2009.

Joseph P. Reser is an Emeritus Reader in Social and Environmental Psychology at the University of Durham, and Adjunct Professor at Griffith University (Psychology) and at the University of Queensland (Architecture). He is an environmental and social psychologist with research, teaching, and consulting experience across Australia, and has held academic appointments at universities in the United States, Canada, the UK, and Australia. Joseph is a Fellow of the Australian Psychological Society, Chair of the Australian Psychological Society Disaster Preparedness and Response Advisory Group, a member of the Australian National Mental Health Disaster Taskforce Expert Advisory Group, and a member of the Editorial Advisory Board of the *Journal of Environmental Psychology.*

Michael Richards is just beginning his studies in community psychology as a PhD student at Manchester Metropolitan University (MMU), UK. He has recently completed his Master's degree in Community Psychology from MMU. Much of his work concerns marginalized young men in Manchester, UK where life expectancy for men can be up to 10 years lower than elsewhere in the country. He works on themes related to masculinity, sexual health, and relationships and is particularly interested in using action research in his work.

Michael C. Roberts PhD, ABPP, is Professor and Director of the Clinical Child Psychology Program at the University of Kansas. He holds diplomas in Clinical Psychology and Clinical Child and Adolescent Psychology. He has published close to 200 journal articles and book chapters, and 19 books including *Handbook of Pediatric Psychology*, *Handbook of Clinical Child Psychology*, and *Handbook of Evidence-Based Therapies for Children and Adolescents.* His areas of research and publications include professional issues, therapeutic outcomes and program evaluation, mental health and service delivery, and pediatric psychology. He is the editor of *Professional Psychology: Research and Practice.*

Victoria L Roberts is a PhD candidate at the Melbourne Business School at the University of Melbourne. She conducts research on ethical leadership and the effect of situation contingent units of personality on ethical outcomes at work. She received a Master of Philosophy in Business and Economics from the University of Sydney for her research in the effect of identity relevant feedback on performance and learning. Victoria is currently a member of the Accelerated Learning Laboratory at the Melbourne Business School.

Robert A. Roe is Emeritus-Professor of Organizational Theory and Organizational Behavior at Maastricht University, the Netherlands. He studied psychology and obtained his doctorate at the University of Amsterdam. He was Professor of Work and Organizational Psychology in Delft, Tilburg, and Nijmegen, Director of the Work and Organization Research Center in Tilburg, Director of the Netherlands Aeromedical Institute, and founding President of the European Association of Work and Organizational Psychology. He is currently President of the European Federation of Psychology Associations. His publications cover a broad range of topics in work and organizational psychology.

Ronald Ruff PhD, ABPP, works at San Francisco Clinical Neurosciences as a neuropsychologist, psychotherapist, and researcher, and he is a clinical professor in the Department of Psychiatry at the University of California San Francisco. He completed his PhD at the University of Zurich and 2 years of postdoctoral studies at the University of Oxford and University of Stanford. Thereafter, he was involved in multiple research studies with traumatic brain injured patients (TBI) at the University of California San Diego for 10 years. In 1990, he relocated to San Francisco, where he worked as a clinician with TBI patients in the Department of Rehabilitation at St. Mary's Medical Center. He is currently in private practice and his research interests include test development (he has published four widely used neuropsychological tests), studies with TBI populations (he has published over 100 articles and book chapters), and developing cognitive rehabilitation programs. He is on the editorial board of neuropsychological journals, and he has been invited to lecture in both the US and internationally. He is a fellow of the American Psychological Association and the National Academy of Neuropsychology (NAN). He is a past member of the California Board of Psychology and past President of NAN.

Jesús Sanz has a PhD in clinical psychology from Complutense University of Madrid. He is currently a tenured professor at the Department of Personality, Assessment and Clinical Psychology of the Complutense University of Madrid and Vice-Dean for Studies, Educational Innovation, and the European Higher Education Area of the Faculty of Psychology of this university. His research interests include cognitive factors in depression, psychometric assessment of anxiety and depression, the basic structure of personality, and the role of personality and psychological treatments in essential arterial hypertension. He has authored or co-authored more than 90 scientific papers, including chapters in books and journal articles, on those topics.

Mark L. Savickas is Professor of Behavioral Sciences at the Northeastern Ohio Universities College of Medicine and an adjunct professor of Counseling at Kent State University in the USA as well as a visiting professor at Vrije University in Belgium and Loughborough University in England. He has authored over a hundred articles and chapters on vocational psychology. He is a fellow of the American Psychological Association, American Counseling Association, Association for Psychological Science, and the National Career Development Association. He has received honorary doctorates from the University of Lisbon (Portugal) and the University of Pretoria (South Africa).

Herman P. Schaalma, PhD is a social psychologist and health scientist working in the field of the planned development, implementation, and evaluation of theory- and evidence-based health promotion programs, with a focus on sexual health and AIDS prevention. Since 2005 he has been associate professor at the Department of Work

& Social Psychology, Faculty of Psychology & Neuroscience, Maastricht University. Since May 2006 he has held the endowed chair for AIDS prevention with a special focus on developing culturally sensitive prevention programs.

Marcia J. Scherer PhD, MPH, is President of the Institute for Matching Person and Technology, USA; Professor of Physical Medicine and Rehabilitation, University of Rochester Medical Center; author of the books *Living in the State of Stuck: How Assistive Technology Impacts the Lives of People with Disabilities* and *Connecting to Learn: Educational and Assistive Technology for People with Disabilities*; and editor of the journal *Disability and Rehabilitation: Assistive Technology*. She is Fellow of the American Psychological Association, American Congress of Rehabilitation Medicine, and the Rehabilitation Engineering and Assistive Technology Society of North America (RESNA).

Asiya Siddiquee is a lecturer in psychology at Manchester Metropolitan University (MMU). Her research interests include information communication technologies, marginalization and community psychology, with an emphasis on the experiences of people from minority ethnic groups. Her interest with community psychology began as an undergraduate at MMU, and her doctoral research entitled "A Community Psychology Approach to Investigating the Impact of the Internet" was completed in 2006.

Zachary Steel is a clinical psychologist and senior lecturer at the Centre for Population Mental Health Research at the School of Psychiatry, University of NSW, Australia. He has published widely on the mental health and well-being of asylum seekers in the community and in immigration detention. This research has played an important role in providing a scientific foundation for informed critique of harsh government policies on asylum seekers. His other research interests include the long- term effects of trauma on refugee and conflict-affected populations, the development of culturally informed psychiatric epidemiology, and clinical interventions in complex emergencies.

Ric G. Steele PhD, ABPP (Clinical Child Psychology Program, University of Kansas) has published approximately 75 journal articles and book chapters, and several handbooks on youth health and mental health issues. Steele's research examines the promotion of physical and mental health across a spectrum of health categories, with particular attention to the promotion of weight-related health. Steele is an Associate Editor for the *Journal of Child and Family Studies*, and is on the editorial boards of the *Journal of Pediatric Psychology*, the *Journal of Clinical Child and Adolescent Psychology*, *Children's Health Care*, and *Professional Psychology: Research and Practice*.

Linda Steg is Professor of Environmental Psychology at the University of Groningen. Her research focuses on measuring, explaining, and changing environmentally significant behavior, in particular household energy use and car use. She is particularly interested in the role of values, norms, and moral concerns. She is a Fellow of the Energy Delta Research Centre of the University of Groningen, president-elect of

Division 4 "Environmental Psychology", and treasurer of Division 13 "Traffic and Transport Psychology" of the International Association of Applied Psychology (IAAP). Moreover, she coordinates the sustainability network of the International Association of People-Environment Studies (IAPS).

William Stiers, PhD, ABPP (RP) completed his doctoral degree in Counseling Psychology at Northwestern University in the United States. After working as a Senior Research Health Scientist at the U.S. Department of Veterans Affairs, he then completed a two-year clinical post-doctoral fellowship in Rehabilitation Psychology and Neuropsychology at the University of Michigan, and Dr. Stibecame board-certified in Rehabilitation Psychology. He was President of the American Psychological Association, Division of Rehabilitation Psychology, and serves as an examiner for board certification in Rehabilitation Psychology. He is now in the Department of Physical Medicine and Rehabilitation at Johns Hopkins University School of Medicine.

Peter C. Terry, PhD, FBASES, MAPS, is Professor of Psychology at the University of Southern Queensland. He is one of the most experienced applied sport psychologists in the world. Over the past 25 years he has provided support to more than 1,500 international and professional performers, including Olympic medalists in nine sports. Peter has been team psychologist at eight Olympic Games and 80 other major international events. Author of more than 170 publications, he is a Fellow of the British Association of Sport and Exercise Sciences and past-President of the Australian Psychological Society's College of Sport Psychologists.

Lois E. Tetrick received her doctorate in industrial and organizational psychology from Georgia Institute of Technology in 1983. She is currently the Director of the Industrial and Organizational Psychology Program at George Mason University. She is editor of the *Journal of Occupational Health Psychology* and is the co-editor with James C. Quick of the *Handbook of Occupational Health Psychology* and *Health and Safety in Organizations* with David Hofmann. She is a fellow of the European Academy of Occupational Health Psychology, the American Psychological Association (APA), the Society for Industrial and Organizational Psychology (SIOP), and the Association for Psychological Science. She served as president of SIOP 2007–2008, chair of the Human Resources Division of the Academy of Management 2001–2002, SIOP representative on the APA Council of Representatives 2003–2005, and a member of the APA Board of Scientific Affairs 2006–2009. Her research interests are occupational health and safety, occupational stress, the work–family interface, and exchange relationships between employees and their organizations such as reflected in psychological contracts.

Boris B. Velichkovsky graduated with highest honors from the Free University of Berlin in linguistics, psychology, and computer science. In 2007, he received his PhD from the Institute of Psychology of the Russian Academy of Sciences. He is currently senior teacher at the Department of Psychology of Moscow State University and the Head of the Department of Cognitive-Affective Processes in the Institute of Cognitive Studies of the Russian National Research Center, the "Kurchatov Institute." His main research interests include topics of individual differences in cognitive control and stress resistance, memory, linguistic influences on cognitive processing, as well as human–computer interaction.

Boris M. Velichkovsky received his education at Moscow State Lomonossow-University (psychology) and Berlin Humboldt-University (physics). In 1990, he became professor of the Department of Neuropsychology at the University of Bielefeld (Germany). Following a NSERC professorship at the University of Toronto, he assumed his current position of director of the Psychology Institute III, Dresden University of Technology. His research interests are related to human visual cognition and to a combination of methods derived from domains of nanotechnology, information technology, biotechnology, and cognitive science. He coordinates a number of international and national research projects. He is also a member of several professional boards.

John Weinman is Professor of Psychology applied to Medicine at the Institute of Psychiatry in King's College London. He is a Fellow of the BPS, EHPS, and ABMR and Academician of the Academy of Social Sciences. He was founding editor of *Psychology and Health: an International Journal* and has published widely in the field of health psychology. He has played a major role in the development of health psychology in the UK and Europe. His main research areas are cognition and health; adherence to medical treatment; stress, wound healing and recovery from surgery; self-regulation in chronic illness.

Jennifer Whelan is currently a post-doctoral research associate at the Melbourne Business School's Accelerated Learning Laboratory. She received her PhD in social psychology at the University of Melbourne in 2007 and conducted post-doctoral research on implicit self-esteem and self-regulation. Her research ranges across psychological essentialism, national identity, stereotyping and prejudice, and culture. Her current research interests include dynamic personality processes, ethical leadership and moral psychology.

G. Terence Wilson received his BA (Hons) degree from Witwatersrand University in Johannesburg, South Africa, and his PhD from the State University of New York at Stony Brook. He is currently the Oscar K. Buros Professor of Psychology at Rutgers University, USA. He has coauthored or edited several books, published numerous scientific articles, and is the editor of *Behaviour Research and Therapy.* A former President of the Association for Advancement of Behavior Therapy, he has received several honors and awards for distinguished contributions to clinical psychology. He is a member of the American Psychiatric Association's Work Group for eating disorders for DSM-V.

Robert E. Wood is Professor of Management at Melbourne Business School and Director of the Accelerated Learning Laboratory (ALL). His research studies how motivational and cognitive processes interact to influence learning and performance on complex tasks, such as managerial problem solving, ethics, and leadership. His research publications appear in many leading international journals. On the practitioner side, he has served on many boards and regularly delivers industry-training programs. He was editor of *Applied Psychology an International Review*, and has served on the editorial boards of most leading scholarly journals in management and organizational psychology.

Preface

The origins of this Handbook go back to the successful bid by the Australian Psychological Society (APS) to host the 27th International Congress of Applied Psychology (ICAP) on behalf of the International Association of Applied Psychology (IAAP), in Melbourne in July, 2010. The bid was led by the APS President at that time (Paul Martin) and the APS Executive Director (Lyn Littlefield), and they wanted the 27th ICAP to stand out and to have an impact beyond the event itself. This led to discussions with publishers with respect to bringing out a volume in association with the Congress. Agreement was reached with Blackwell (subsequently Wiley-Blackwell) to produce an international handbook that would cover the whole spectrum of applied psychology. The goal was to track down leading authorities in each of the domains of applied psychology, and invite them to complete two complementary tasks: write chapters for the Handbook; and deliver state-of-the-art addresses at the Congress.

The link between IAAP and the Handbook was there from the beginning as ICAP is the Congress of IAAP. As the project progressed, however, the Handbook evolved into the *IAAP Handbook of Applied Psychology.* Distinguished psychologists from different continents were invited to join the original Australian editors to ensure that the editorial group was international and had the range of expertise and knowledge necessary for successful completion of this wide-ranging task.

The Handbook was designed to provide a critical overview of applied psychology. Each chapter would focus on one field of applied psychology, and the goal was to provide the reader with a stimulating overview of the field highlighting key research findings. The chapters would be a combination of historical overview, practical examples, and state-of-the-art findings. The chapters would adopt an international perspective, and would include topics such as:

- Defining the field, scope of the field (e.g., speciality areas), what do academics/practitioners do in this field, and where do they do it?
- Trends in the field and key developments.
- Challenges on the one hand and opportunities on the other, for applied psychology in this field.

- Future developments in the field—what needs to happen in terms of the research literature and practice?

The structure of the Handbook took into account the 17 Divisions of IAAP but the larger Divisions gave rise to multiple chapters, and additional chapters were added to provide the comprehensive coverage of applied psychology that was the goal of the Handbook. The names of prospective authors were solicited from a number of sources including the Divisions of IAAP and the professional Colleges of APS. Most individuals approached to be authors accepted their invitations, and the Handbook finished up with 78 editors and authors from 11 countries. All contracted chapters were submitted except for the one on "political psychology."

We are deeply grateful to all the authors who have written what we believe are excellent chapters. We would like to thank the reviewers of the original proposal who helped shape the structure and content of the Handbook. We would also like to acknowledge Wiley-Blackwell who were always constructive and supportive throughout this marathon project.

Paul R. Martin on behalf of the Editors: Fanny M. Cheung, Michael C. Knowles, Michael Kyrios, Lyn Littlefield, J. Bruce Overmier, and José M. Prieto.

Part I
Professional Psychology

1

Clinical Child Psychology

Research and Practice Applications

Michael C. Roberts, Bridget K. Biggs, Yo Jackson, and Ric G. Steele

> Mental and behavioural problems during childhood and adolescence are a serious public-health concern. About half of all lifetime mental disorders begin before the age of 14 years. Worldwide prevalence rates for child and adolescent mental disorders are around 20% with similar types of disorders across cultures…the gap in mental-health services for children and adolescents with mental disorders is evident in virtually all countries at a time when the need has never been greater. (Belfer & Saxena, 2006, p. 551)

Clinical child psychology as a research and practice specialty of applied psychology seeks to investigate and remediate mental health problems for children, adolescents, and their families. Aspects of clinical child psychology are found in different countries with a broad range of populations, settings, problems, assessment, and intervention techniques. As noted in one definition,

> The research and practices of Clinical Child Psychology are focused on understanding, preventing, diagnosing, and treating psychological, cognitive, emotional, developmental, behavioral, and family problems of children. Of particular importance to clinical child and adolescent psychologists is a scientific understanding of the basic psychological needs of children and adolescents and how the family and other social contexts influence socio-emotional adjustment, cognitive development, behavioral adaptation, and health status of children and adolescents. (Clinical Child Psychology Formal Specialty Definition, 2005)

Several efforts and developments in the United States, as one example of formalizing the clinical child psychology specialty, include recognition as a specialty in professional psychology by the American Psychological Association (APA: Commission for the Recognition of Specialties and Proficiencies in Professional Psychology, 2009),

IAAP Handbook of Applied Psychology, First Edition. Edited by Paul R. Martin, Fanny M. Cheung, Michael C. Knowles, Michael Kyrios, Lyn Littlefield, J. Bruce Overmier, and José M. Prieto.

establishment of board certification (American Board of Clinical Child and Adolescent Psychology, 2009), formation of divisions within APA (e.g., Society of Clinical Child and Adolescent Psychology, 2009; Society of Pediatric Psychology, 2009a), and development of accredited doctoral training programs providing substantiated training (e.g., University of Kansas Clinical Child Psychology Program; University of Denver Child Clinical Psychology Program). Other countries have also begun a process of developing their clinical child and adolescent psychology components (e.g., Australia, New Zealand, and England), but, in some countries, these types of specialists in child and adolescent mental health services are virtually nonexistent. The emergence of clinical child psychology as a specialty field is documented by numerous international professional journals devoted to its primary topics (e.g., *Child and Adolescent Mental Health*; *Clinical Child and Family Psychology Review*; *Clinical Child Psychology and Psychiatry*; *Developmental Psychopathology*; *Journal of Abnormal Child Psychology*; *Journal of Child Psychology and Psychiatry*; *Journal of Clinical Child and Adolescent Psychology*; and *Journal of Pediatric Psychology*).

Range of topics and problems for clinical child psychology

Clinical child psychologists provide services and conduct research on a range of problems and psychological concerns such as (a) infants born preterm, medically ill, or exposed to drugs; (b) youth with serious emotional disturbances such as schizophrenia and developmental disorders such as autism and mental retardation; (c) children with behavior and psychological disorders such as attention deficit/hyperactivity, oppositional defiant or conduct disorders, anxiety, or depression; (d) children adjusting to life changes such as divorce, death, relocation, or remarriage; (e) children coping with trauma of disasters, war, terrorism, or community/family violence (including child physical and sexual abuse); (f) children living with physical illnesses, adhering to medical regimens, or coping with pain; (g) children with cognitive deficits and school performance problems; (h) adolescents with delinquency and high-risk behaviors of substance abuse or sexual behaviors; and (i) children in poverty and without adequate health care. Of course this list is illustrative at best, not comprehensive (see also Ollendick & Schroeder, 2003; Roberts & Steele, 2009; Walker & Roberts, 2001). The epidemiology and range of children's mental health problems appears to be similar for developing and developed areas of the world (Belfer & Rodhe, 2005).

Settings in which clinical child psychologists function

The settings in which clinical child psychological researchers and practitioners conduct their work include a diverse range of models, facilities, and units to organize services.

Mental health centers. In some countries, clinical child specialists primarily practice within a national health service in governmental units for child and adolescent mental health services. Similarly, in the US, mental health services are most commonly available through the public sector in a system of community mental health centers and child guidance clinics (Smith-Boydston, 2005). Responsive to cultural and community needs, these outpatient centers often involve teams of mental health professionals. Through concepts of "system of care" and treating individuals in the "least restrictive environment" (e.g., community-based services), professionals collaborate with agencies for social welfare, juvenile justice, alcohol and drug treatment, health care, and with schools. Outpatient services may include individual, group, or family therapy. Community outreach services may also be provided for school-based preventive programs or in-home interventions such as multisystemic treatment.

Schools. When children in educational settings display psychological problems that require intensive intervention to enhance developmental and educational outcomes, clinical child psychologists frequently consult, assess, and intervene with problems of behavior management and academic performance. For example, psychological services for children with serious emotional disturbances may be provided through school-based programs such as therapeutic classrooms or day treatment programs (Roberts, Jacobs, Puddy, Nyre, & Vernberg, 2003). School psychologists may also provide services for psychoeducational needs of children in educational settings (Lee & Jamison, 2005), but not all countries differentiate the specialties.

Children's hospitals and medical settings. Pediatric psychologists, as a subspecialty in clinical child psychology, provide clinical services for children through hospitals and outpatient clinics specializing in the care of children and adolescents. Their practice includes inpatient and outpatient modalities based in medical settings that address concerns related to health care and medical illness (Roberts & Steele, 2009). These services may be indirect (e.g., through consultation and collaboration with physicians and nurses) or direct interventions (i.e., involving the child or family), and focus on issues such as adjustment to disease, medical adherence, pain control, behavior management, health promotion, and problem prevention. In addition to children's hospitals, university-based medical centers frequently employ psychologists to provide services and investigate these phenomena in departments of pediatrics or departments of psychiatry. Psychologists conduct significant clinical research on pediatric psychosocial issues.

Inpatient treatment centers. In providing the most intensive form of intervention for severe disorders, clinical child psychologists work with a team of professionals in inpatient settings that include government-subsidized psychiatric hospitals and independent residential or inpatient treatment facilities. These centers often face the most acute challenges of psychosocial impairment and potential harm to self or others (Vargas & de Dios Brambila, 2005). Some centers focus on short-term stays of less than two weeks for stabilization while others allow longer-term residential care. Clinical child psychologists provide assessment and diagnostic services in addition to direct psychotherapy through individual and group modalities.

Private practice. In some countries, such as in the US, a sizeable number of child specialists in outpatient private practice receive reimbursement from health insurance plans or from personal payments by parents for providing psychological assessment and treatment services (Landolf, 2005). The private practitioner frequently works with the parents or family and consults with other professionals such as teachers or physicians. This model requires entrepreneurship and may be subject to limitations on reimbursement for certain activities or parental ability to self-pay. Although many work in individual private practices, psychologists and other mental health professionals may work together in groups in these settings for financial reasons and to coordinate different aspects of care (e.g., with social workers and psychiatrists).

University and research settings. Clinical child and pediatric psychologists serve on faculties of universities and colleges where they conduct research, teach, and supervise baccalaureate and doctoral trainees. University-based researchers investigate the full gamut of topics in child development, psychopathology, psychological interactions with physical health, and effective interventions to improve the quality of life for children and their families. Grants often support scientific activities. Research institutes, funded by philanthropies or grants, provide another setting in which child-oriented investigators work in teams to improve understanding of such issues as the etiology and course of developmental psychopathology or the organization and impact of mental health service delivery.

Trends and Key Developments in Clinical Child Psychology

Developmental psychopathology

As a field concerned with identifying and treating emotional, behavioral, and developmental disorders in childhood and adolescence, clinical child psychology is naturally concerned with how these disorders emerge and progress. In this regard, the thinking of clinical child psychologists is greatly influenced by the field of developmental psychopathology, defined as "the study of the origins and course of individual patterns of behavioral maladaptation" (Sroufe & Rutter, 1984, p. 18). Rutter and Sroufe (2000; see also Sroufe & Rutter, 1984) described the developmental psychopathology perspective in terms of the field's view on three key issues: (a) causal processes, (b) development, and (c) continuities and discontinuities between psychopathology and normality. Regarding causal processes, the field of developmental psychopathology aims to understand how risk and protective mechanisms operate and lead to either disorder or adjustment and the factors that influence the course of pathological processes after they first surface. Psychopathology is viewed as emerging from a complex interplay of multiple genetic, biologic, and environmental factors and transactions between an individual and the environment that unfold in a chain of effects over time (Rutter & Sroufe, 2000). The connection to clinical child psychology is quite intuitive: by identifying the factors and processes that give rise to disorder versus adjustment, developmental psychopathological research identifies potential targets for prevention and treatment for anxiety, depression, oppositional and anti-social behavior, and other childhood problems.

A focus on development is central to both clinical child psychology and developmental psychopathology. A central tenet of developmental psychopathology is that knowledge of typical development is needed to understand the emergence of disorder and, conversely, that understanding the development of psychopathology sheds light on basic developmental processes (Cicchetti, 1984). Although development implies change, development also includes continuity and coherence, as many aspects of the individual remain constant over time, and current behaviors and circumstances are connected to the individual's past and future. Attention to the developmental periods and their associated challenges and milestones are particularly germane to clinical child psychology. Treatments may need to address not only the presence of a disorder, but also the areas of development affected by the disorder. Further, the clinical child psychologist is mindful of development as it relates to the emerging skills of the child and the child's ability to benefit from a particular treatment modality.

The third central concept identified as by Rutter and Sroufe (2000) is the notion that there are both continuities and discontinuities between normality and psychopathology. That is, psychopathology, in some senses can be represented as an extreme of a characteristic present in normal existence. Conversely, psychopathology may represent a complete departure from typical development. The practice of clinical child psychology often necessitates a categorical view of psychopathology; psychologists often determine whether the presenting symptoms meet criteria for a disorder (i.e., for billing/insurance reimbursement purposes). Nonetheless, clinical child psychologists are aware that symptoms and behavior frequently occur along a continuum of severity. In addition, they are aware of consistencies and changes in the presentation of disorders across development. Calls for diagnostic systems that more strongly reflect developmental changes are illustrative of this awareness.

Evidence-based practice

The evidence-based practice movement in clinical child psychology strives to provide child and adolescent services that have adequate scientific support for their use. This movement is not unique to the field of clinical child psychology, because science-informed approaches to assessment, diagnosis, and treatment are emphasized by other professions including medicine, public health, and social work (Roberts & James, 2008). Although the term "evidence-based practice" and related terms including "empirically supported treatments" are relatively new, the notion of integrating science and practice is consistent with the longer-standing tradition of training doctoral level psychologists in both research and practice in many developed countries (APA Presidential Task Force on Evidence-Based Practice, 2006; Charman & Barkham, 2005).

The common thread in the messages of the evidence-based practice movement around the globe is that clinical practice should be based on evidence of what works from carefully designed and reviewed scientific study (see, for example, APA Presidential Task Force, 2006, in the US; Charman & Barkham, 2005, in Australia; and the World Health Organization, 2005). Most definitions of evidence-based practice (EBP) are based on empirically supported treatments (ESTs) and often mention the use of psychometrically sound assessment techniques. ESTs are typically defined as including a clear description of intervention procedures in a treatment manual and empirical evidence demonstrating the treatment's efficacy over a control or alternative treatment condition, with randomized controlled trials (RCTs) often held as the gold standard. Peer-reviewed publications summarizing evidence-based practice specific to clinical child and adolescent psychology include special issues and sections on psychosocial treatments (Lonigan, Elbert, & Johnson, 1998; Silverman & Hinshaw, 2008), evidence-based assessment (Mash & Hunsley, 2005), and special issues on assessment and treatment in pediatric psychology (Cohen et al., 2008; and Spirito, 1999; respectively). A growing number of edited books on EBP with children and adolescents have also been published (e.g., Carr, 2000; Hibbs & Jensen, 2005; Fonagy, Target, Cottrell, Phillips, & Kurtz, 2002; Mash & Barkley, 2007; Steele, Elkin, & Roberts, 2008). The report of the American Psychological Association Task Force on Evidence-Based Practice for Children and Adolescents (2008) also provides applications of EBP to clinical child and adolescent psychology.

As in other fields of professional psychology, the EBP movement in clinical child psychology has stirred some controversy. Criticisms of EBP include claims that manuals promote a "cookbook" approach to treatment without adequate attention to individual client characteristics and that the EBP movement places too great an emphasis on RCTs, which some claim to weigh internal validity too strongly over generalizability to populations commonly seen in clinics (see Roberts & James, 2008). Proponents of EBP addressed such criticisms by stressing that, while manuals should provide clear guidance on the core elements of a treatment, their implementation requires clinical judgment and can be tailored for the characteristics of an individual client. This "flexibility within fidelity," as termed by Kendall and Beidas (2007), is particularly important in working with children and adolescents, among whom there is great variability across development.

The criticisms of ESTs and EBPs have also been implicitly or explicitly addressed in the various descriptions of EBP. For example, in the United States, clinical expertise and patient characteristics, culture, and preferences are explicitly included with research-based evidence as the "three pillars" of EBP (APA Presidential Task Force on Evidence-Based Practice, 2006). To address criticisms related to over-reliance on the "top-down" approach of RCTs, some have advocated for efforts to study outcomes related to clinical practice in the community as a way to build the evidence base "from the bottom up" (Charman & Barkham, 2005; WHO, 2005).

Although defining the criteria for empirically supported treatments has not been without controversy, defining clinical expertise has lagged behind and proven to be more elusive. Recent definitions have included "competence attained by psychologists through education, training, and experience that results in effective practice" (APA Presidential Task Force on Evidence-based Practice, 2006, p. 275). Currently underway are efforts to enumerate domains of competence (e.g., assessment, treatment and cultural sensitivity) as well as the specific experiences and skills needed to learn and demonstrate competence in each domain at various levels of competency. Efforts to define how one should integrate client characteristics and preferences into evidence-based practice have been less formalized.

Cultural competence

Clinical child psychology, like most clinical fields, has begun to recognize the importance of culture in the lives of youth. Because youth of different ethnic origins will likely outnumber Caucasian youth in the US by the year 2023 (US Census, 2004) and because, internationally, the number of youth with non-European ethnicities is greater than the number of youth with European heritages, the need for attention to the mental health needs of youth from diverse backgrounds is sorely needed. Signs of hope that the field is responding to the need suggest that not only do clinical child psychologists understand the importance of attending to the psychological health of children, but that a new generation of professionals is emerging who have been trained to integrate the knowledge base on the role of culture into their research and practice endeavors. For example, in 1982, 60% of accredited clinical programs in the US did not offer a course on multicultural issues and no program required such a course in their model of training (Bernal & Padilla, 1982). In 1995 however, the American Psychological Association Committee on Accreditation mandated that diversity issues be addressed in a required course as well as being incorporated into courses in the general clinical curriculum. To date, all accredited clinical programs in the US, including clinical child programs, have courses devoted to presenting the issues relevant to the multicultural world of youth. To understand the multicultural competence trend in clinical child psychology, it is important to understand not only how these professionals are trained, but also the professional mandates and guidelines, and the operation of these requirements into the practice and science of clinical child psychology. Diversity issues or multicultural skills in clinical child psychology can mean many things, and the definition of culture and cultural competence for clinical child professionals has had many iterations. These terms need to be clarified so that professionals agree on the terms and clinical training and practice can assess and evaluate knowledge and practice of multicultural competencies (Giannet, 2003). In its most simple form, cultural competence is defined as the ability to provide professional services cross-culturally (Sue & Sue, 2008). To do so means that the psychologist understands (a) his or her own cultural values and biases, (b) the worldview and values of the target population, and (c) how to adapt clinical and research approaches to the culture of the target population.

Professional mandates and guidelines. In 2003, two significant developments in the US addressed the needs of multicultural populations and clinical child service providers. First, the Ethical Principles and Code of Conduct published by the American Psychological Association took effect (APA, 2002). The new ethical code made it clear that to provide ethical services is to respect and be aware of cultural differences and to incorporate cultural information into practice and service (i.e., in interpreting test data and establishing boundaries of competence). Second, the Guidelines on Multicultural Education, Training, Research, Practice, and Organizational Change for Psychologists were published by APA's Office of Ethnic Minority Affairs (APA, 2003). This document provides six guidelines that "reflect the knowledge and skills needed for the profession in the midst of dramatic historic sociopolitical changes in U.S. society, as well as needs from new constituencies, markets, and clients" (p. 5).

The document specifically mentions services to children, youth, and families as a part of the need for culturally appropriate psychological services. These recent efforts suggest that the field is changing from a monocultural perspective to a more multicultural one that appreciates the meaningful differences and complexity that culture brings to clinical science and practice (Pack-Brown & Williams, 2003).

Practice implications. As a result of professional mandates and guidelines, the field of clinical child psychology has begun to address the need for cultural competence in several ways. First, as mentioned before, training programs are incorporating multicultural information in their curricula. Moreover, in an effort to create competency standards for clinical practice, the Association of Directors of Psychology Training Clinics (2009) produced a report detailing practicum competencies. Specifically, this document spells out in one of their 11 standard clinical competencies that trainees and practitioners need to have knowledge of themselves in the context of diversity and how their own culture impacts treatment, knowledge of how culture impacts the treatment relationship, and the ability to work effectively with diverse others in assessment, treatment, and consultation. As psychology training programs begin to address these competencies, the field is moving beyond general definitions of cultural competence to delineate specific skills, attitudes, and behaviors that constitute culturally competent practice.

Professional implications. Research in clinical child psychology has also seen an increase in professional standards and the dawn of an era of a rethinking of research methods as they apply to cultural issues. Clearly, science cannot inform practice if science is not following a shared value toward more cultural application and utility of research findings. Clinical child psychology researchers are beginning to adjust their approaches to address questions that are not only relevant to cultural issues (i.e., cultural adaptations and empirically based practice), but also beginning to focus on the very nature of the operation of culture in the mental health of children of color. Although the same emphasis has not been placed on other kinds of diversity (i.e., religious, linguistic, or sexual), some change can be observed, not only in the research questions, but also in the greater numbers of children of color included in research, and in the ways that research is designed and the findings interpreted for youth of color. For example, in the *Journal of Clinical Child and Adolescent Psychology* from 2000 to 2008, 27 articles were published directly related to populations of ethnic minority youth and their mental health needs. This is in contrast to only 17 similar kinds of articles published in the decade prior, suggesting a significant increase in the number of scholarly articles related to culture. Although this journal is not the only one publishing important work on culture and clinical child issues, the example above does suggest that ethnic minority youth issues are getting more attention in research.

Internationally, signs that research is invested in the mental health needs of youth are abundant. International journals consistently publish work on youth from various ethnic backgrounds along with topics that may see little attention in U.S. populations. For example, clinical child research includes studies such as on adjustment after exposure to terror attacks among Palestinian children (Punamaki, Qouta, & El-Sarraj, 2001), the effects of war on youth (Ronen, Rahav, & Rosenbaum, 2003), coping with HIV/AIDS within the cultural context of South Africa (Cook & Du Toit, 2005), and the sociological context of *ijima* (bullying) in Japan (Ruiz & Tanaka, 2001).

Psychopharmacology

Considerable variability exists across countries in the use of pharmacological treatments for children's mental health conditions (Clavenna, Rossi, DeRosa, & Bonati, 2007; Vittiello, 2008). As described in more detail by Vittiello, the observed differences in prescription rates across countries probably reflect differences in cultures and cultural values, healthcare systems, clinical practice and treatment guidelines, pharmaceutical marketing, and regulations on the distribution and prescription of pharmacologic agents. Despite the overall differences by country or culture, the past two decades have witnessed a sharp increase in the rates of psychotropic medication prescriptions issued for children and adolescents in a number of industrialized nations, including several in the European Union, Canada, and the United States (Clavenna et al., 2007; Mitchell et al., 2008; Olfson, Blanco, Liu, Moreno, & Laje, 2006; Parks Thomas, Conrad, Casler, & Goodman, 2006). Similar to the differences in base rates, these observed changes in prescription rates may reflect changing guidelines for diagnosis and treatment, changes in regulations governing the use of these medications in youths, new findings regarding the safety of some medications, and the development of newer (and sometimes safer) pharmaceutical agents (Clavenna et al., 2007; Parks Thomas et al., 2006; Vittiello, 2008).

Although the literature on pediatric psychopharmacology has lagged behind the adult literature (Brown, Daly, Carpenter, & Cohen, 2009), a number of large clinical trials have recently begun to evaluate the efficacy and safety of pharmacological treatments for children and youth. For example, several large-scale evaluations have compared pharmacological treatment to cognitive-behavioral treatment (CBT) and combined therapies for Attention Deficit Hyperactivity Disorder (ADHD; MTA Cooperative Group, 1999a, 1999b), anxiety disorders (including Separation Anxiety Disorder, Generalized Anxiety Disorder, and Social Phobia; Walkup et al., 2008), Obsessive-Compulsive Disorder (OCD; Pediatric OCD Treatment Study [POTS] Team, 2004), and depression (Treatment of Adolescent Depression Study [TADS] Team, 2004). These major studies, as well as a number of other studies on the efficacy and/or safety of pharmacological therapies for a wider range of disorders and conditions are reviewed by Brown et al. (2009) and by the APA Working Group on Psychoactive Medications for Children and Adolescents (APA Working Group, 2006).

A growing body of evidence documents that some pharmacologic treatments can be effective for some mental health conditions in some children and adolescents (APA Working Group, 2006; Brown et al., 2009). Estimated effect sizes for pharmacological treatments of children and adolescents' mental health conditions vary widely, from nonsignificant to large, depending on the condition, comorbid diagnoses, and whether the pharmacotherapy was delivered in combination with psychological treatments (APA Working Group, 2006). For example, fairly robust evidence exists for the use of stimulant medication for children and adolescents with ADHD combined with behavioral therapy for initial symptom reduction (MTA Cooperative Group, 1999a, 1999b). Similarly, serotonin specific reuptake inhibitors (SSRIs, e.g., fluoxetine) have shown moderately significant effects on depression (Usala, Clavenna, Zuddasa, & Bonati, 2008), particularly when delivered with CBT (APA Workgroup, 2006). However, few studies have examined the long-term efficacy (or side effects) of pharmacological treatment for mental health conditions (APA Working Group, 2006; Brown et al., 2009), so the relative long-term risk/benefit ratio of many psychoactive medications remains uncertain.

As suggested by the above discussion, a number of issues should be weighed before considering pharmacotherapy as a treatment option. These include (a) the strength of evidence for the efficacy of the medication; (b) the likelihood and significance of possible side effects; and (c) the incremental benefit of medication over other available treatment options. Indeed, with these concerns in mind, the APA Working Group (2006) recommended a conservative approach to the use of medications when effective or efficacious psychological treatments are available. Specifically, they noted that:

> For most of the disorders reviewed [in this report], there are psychosocial treatments that are solidly grounded in empirical support as stand-alone treatments. Moreover, the preponderance of available evidence indicates that psychosocial treatments are safer than psychoactive medications. Thus, it is our recommendation that in most cases, psychosocial interventions be considered first. The acute and long-term safety and efficacy data that are available for each disorder will be central to this determination. (p. 174)

Not only do clinical child psychologists consult with physicians over psychoactive medications, but also, in the US, some states have authorized psychologists with special training to prescribe medication for mental health disorders.

Pediatric psychology

As noted above, the term "clinical child psychology" encompasses activities in a number of contexts, among which is the intersection of the physical and mental health of children and adolescents known as "pediatric psychology" or "child health psychology." As defined by the Society of Pediatric Psychology (SPP, 2009b), "pediatric psychology is an integrated field of science and practice in which the principles of psychology are applied within the context of pediatric health." Reflecting research, practice, advocacy, and service areas, pediatric psychologists promote the health and development of children, adolescents, and their families across the continuum of health risk categories (i.e., healthy children, children at risk of disease, and children with diagnosed medical conditions).

The argument could be made that pediatric psychology has existed as long as clinical child psychology and clinical psychology have (Aylward, Bender, Graves, & Roberts, 2009; Walker, 1988). The Society of Pediatric Psychology was formed in 1969 (Aylward et al., 2009) and eventually recognized as a separate APA Division (in 2000) with a respected *Journal of Pediatric Psychology* (*JPP*; in 1976). Guidelines for training pediatric psychologists have been provided (Drotar, 1985; Spirito et al.,

2003). As noted by Kazak (2000) and more recently by Aylward et al., the subspecialty of pediatric psychology has achieved a clear position within psychology, with an identifiable and influential research base and scope of practice.

In terms of both research and practice, pediatric psychology is concerned with the psychosocial, developmental, and contextual factors associated with the etiology, course, and outcomes of medical conditions in children and adolescents, as well as the assessment and treatment of behavioral and emotional problems associated with illness, injury, or disability (SPP, 2009b). As noted by Aylward and colleagues (2009), the field addresses a wide range of chronic illnesses, such as asthma, cancer, diabetes, obesity, pediatric sleep problems, and sickle cell disease. Although, at times, there has been disagreement about specific content areas within pediatric psychology (Roberts & Steele, 2009), a broad view of the field is generally espoused by the SPP and *JPP*. This broad view includes prevention of illnesses and injury in children and adolescents, as well as promotion of optimal health and wellbeing, improvement of health care delivery systems, and advocacy for public policies that benefit children, adolescents, and families (SPP, 2009b).

Consistent with the general training recommendations for psychologists working with children, adolescents, and families (see Roberts et al., 1998), specialty training for pediatric psychologists begins with the broad and general principles common to professional psychology training programs. However, because of the unique needs and circumstances of children and adolescents, these broad and general principles must be considered in a developmental context for maximum benefit to the intended recipients of services (i.e., children, youths, and families; see Roberts, 2006). Characteristics of training programs for the subspecialty (Spirito et al., 2003) include training in a variety of interdisciplinary settings (including primary care) that allow trainees to gain exposure to and experience with intervention, assessment, and research methods applicable to children and families. Within these various settings, Spirito and colleagues recommended that trainees gain exposure to and experience with the range of professional roles and services that pediatric psychologists perform. Finally, they recommended specialized training with regard to the unique ethical and legal issues applicable to children and families, as well as training with regard to disease processes and medical management of pediatric medical conditions.

Challenges and Opportunities for Applied Psychology in Clinical Child and Adolescent Psychology

Evidence-based practice in the "real world"

Despite the gains that have been made through research in identifying assessment and treatment approaches that can be successful in treating childhood mental health problems, a number of authors have noted a gap between the evidence base amassed by research and professional practice with treatment of children and adolescents (Higa & Chorpita, 2008; Silverman & Hinshaw, 2008; Weisz, Chu, & Polo, 2004).

A number of barriers to the adoption of EBPs have been noted. First, multiple, complex, and sometimes conflicting definitions and taxonomies of EBP make it difficult for clinicians to know which approaches have adequate support for their use (Higa & Chorpita, 2008; Proctor et al., 2007; Weisz et al., 2004). Second, some have argued that the criteria for empirical support is so strict that, for some problems and individuals, there is no treatment that meets the given criteria, perhaps mitigating the confidence that clinicians have in a particular treatment (Higa & Chorpita, 2008). Third, when there are multiple treatments identified as EBP, there may be little guidance available on which treatment to select for whom and under what conditions (Higa & Chorpita, 2008). Fourth, even if there were consensus on what constitutes EBP, much more work needs to be done in dissemination. Not only do clinicians need to be aware of the most up-to-date EBPs, they also need training on their implementation, which takes time and resources (Higa & Chorpita, 2008; Proctor et al., 2007). Although training in EBPs is associated with clinicians' use of EBPs, favorable attitudes toward EBPs among clinicians, their work places, and their colleagues are also uniquely predictive of their use (Nelson & Steele, 2007). Therefore, developers and disseminators of EBPs need to be sensitive to the views of clinicians in the community and to the social contexts in which they work (Higa & Chorpita, 2008; Smith-Boydston & Nelson, 2008). Providing evidence of the success of a treatment in highly controlled clinical trials may not be adequately persuasive to practitioners, as the most highly rated factors influencing clinicians' use of EBPs include studies of a treatment's effectiveness in "real world" contexts, perceived flexibility of the treatment, and appeal to colleagues and clients (Nelson & Steele, 2008).

Research has only just begun to identify some of the barriers to and facilitators of the use of EBPs and very little of that work has focused specifically on the assessment and treatment of children and adolescents. As the field moves forward, it is faced with the challenge of evaluating what methods of dissemination work best and whether dissemination of EBPs actually leads to improved outcomes in the community (Weisz et al., 2004). Proposed models to guide this work include Weisz's deployment-focused model (Weisz et al., 2004) and the multilevel contextual model proposed by Schoenwald and Hoagwood (2001). Both models emphasize attention to the context of service delivery in the development and evaluation of assessment and treatment methods. Also, to increase the chances that youth will receive the treatments best suited for their specific needs, individual characteristics, and circumstances, further work is needed to develop and disseminate effective means of assessment to match clients to treatments, to promote the practice of ongoing assessment to inform treatment (Weisz et al., 2004), and to identify the moderators and mediators of effective clinical practice so clinicians know what works for whom, under what circumstances, and how to aid in treatment planning (Silverman & Hinshaw, 2008). Finally, data on the financial costs and benefits of assessment and treatment approaches may be useful to program and center directors and others who influence the adoption of EBPs (Proctor et al., 2007).

Training issues/competencies

Although clinical child and adolescent psychology has been practiced for many decades, specific guidelines for training and for assessing professional competencies have emerged more recently. Recognizing the lack of standards for training psychologists to work with youths and families, in 1981 Division 37 of the American Psychological Association commissioned a task force to develop guidelines to assist training programs develop specific curricula and practical experiences to ensure the competency of psychologists working with children, youth, and families (Roberts, Erickson, & Tuma, 1985). Building on this work, a subsequent task force commissioned by the U.S. National Institute of Mental Health (NIMH) produced a model for training psychologists to provide services for children and adolescents (Roberts et al., 1998), and the APA Practice Directorate established a task force commissioned to review and update existing recommendations for training (see La Greca & Hughes, 1999). Consistent with these initiatives, APA Division 54 (Society of Pediatric Psychology) later produced recommendations for specialty training in pediatric (child health) psychology (Spirito et al., 2003).

As noted by La Greca and Hughes (1999) and Prinstein and Roberts (2006), these various groups voiced consistent recommendations about specialty training for psychologists who work with children, adolescents, and families. These recommendations included (a) the necessity of developmentally oriented coursework and practicum experiences; (b) a faculty with specific expertise in treatment and research with children, families, and youth; (c) opportunities for exposure to and experience with children, families, and youth in the range of professional roles (e.g., clinical services and research); (d) exposure to and experience with multisystemic models of intervention; and (e) mechanisms to assess specific competencies related to working with children, adolescents, and families.

Beyond training recommendations, these various groups identified a number of challenges that the specialty area would have to address to realize its promise to enhance treatment options for children, youth, and families. Among these challenges were listed (a) the need for recognition and representation on relevant accrediting bodies; (b) acceptance of the standards for specialty training by "general" programs; (c) delineation (and valid means of assessing) core competencies; and (d) recognition of specialty practice areas by licensing boards (La Greca & Hughes, 1999; Roberts et al., 1985).

Although there is some evidence that the specialty area of clinical child and adolescent psychology has been recognized by the field at large (La Greca & Hughes, 1999; Prinstein & Roberts, 2006), several of the challenges previously identified still remain. Among these are how best to document that the unique training needs of psychologists who serve children, adolescents, and families are met in the context of largely adult-focused clinical training programs; how to enforce standards for minimal training experiences for psychologists who wish to work with these populations; and how child-oriented training programs can work with accrediting bodies that typically operate within a "general" or "adult-oriented" program model (Prinstein & Roberts, 2006). As evidenced by a number of programs that have overcome these challenges successfully (see Roberts, 2006), these hurdles are not insurmountable, and progress is being made, particularly with regard to programs meeting the training needs of clinical child and adolescent psychologists and programs working with accrediting bodies to resolve the tension between broad and general training needs and specialization.

The field at large has become increasingly aware of the need for more comprehensive models for assessment of professional competencies (Kaslow et al., 2007; Roberts, Borden, Christiansen, & Lopez, 2005). The field has historically endorsed the assessment of entry-level professional competencies (Rubin et al., 2007), and Roberts and colleagues (1998) have articulated specific "exit criteria" (p. 299) for trainees at various levels (e.g., after completion of graduate training, internship, and post-doctoral training). However, assessment of competencies after licensure (i.e., post-entry-level) has remained more controversial (Roberts et al., 2005). Contributing to the controversy are questions regarding which competencies should be assessed, how frequently to assess them, and what form the assessments should take (e.g., Kaslow et al., 2007).

Within the context of the evidence-based practice movement, the issue of ongoing periodic assessment of competencies becomes increasingly important. Because the evidence base for psychological treatments for children, youths, and families continues (and will continue) to expand, mental health professionals must engage in continuing education to stay abreast of the current treatment literature (Long, 2008; Ollendick, 1984). A survey of practicing psychologists revealed that a majority of those sampled generally agreed that continuing education should be mandatory for licensure (Sharkin & Plageman, 2003). However, when participants were asked how frequently continuing education programs improve their practice as clinicians, responses were mixed. Consistent with this finding, a meta-analysis of the impact of formal continuing medical education programs for physicians revealed modest effect sizes (Davis et al., 1999), with higher effect sizes reserved for more interactive programs. These types of study suggest that efforts to provide continuing education to mental health professionals should employ more interactive approaches (e.g., perhaps including role-playing or supervision), and should be assessed for efficacy in terms of the professionals' resulting competencies.

Internationally, issues of training, dissemination, and implementation of best practices in treating children, adolescents, and their families are increasingly becoming articulated. For example, Belfer and Saxena (2006) presented:

> Training adequate numbers of providers capable of using the latest findings about child and adolescent mental-health disorders to implement effective treatments is a challenge faced in all countries. Most relevant is the absence of standards for training, the failure to use potential resources, and the inability to implement supplemental training for those who already have access to children potentially in need. Standards for training are non-existent in many areas of the world and lack enforcement in many others. (p. 552)

Future Developments

As the knowledge bases expand, demographics shift, and empirical evidence confirms new information, clinical child psychology will evolve. The mental health needs of children and adolescents require ongoing attention so that societies around the world can continue to grow and prosper. The clinical child psychologist needs a multidimensional set of skills to meet this challenge. Professionals in the field have expanded their roles and what constitutes the work of a clinical child psychologist can take many forms. The following discussion is but a short list of important emerging topics for the field and next steps for research and practice.

Diagnostic developments

Determining the nature and form of mental illness in youth is one of the important functions for clinical child psychologists. To this end, professionals use two main tools for the general classification and organization of mental illnesses: The International Classification of Diseases (ICD-10) and the Diagnostic and Statistical Manual (DSM-IV). These classification and diagnostic systems are similar. The DSM is a proprietary product of the American Psychiatric Association and widely used in the US (although "cross-walk" translations of DSM diagnoses to ICD categories are required for reimbursement and data reporting). The ICD is widely available through the World Health Organization website and publications (World Health Organization, 2009). The ICD is mandated for use in member nations. The ICD chapters include classifications for mental and behavioral disorders including ones primarily for childhood and adolescence. Both systems are currently in the process of revision and work groups are meeting to present and discuss the latest evidence regarding the nature and form of mental illness. Issues under discussion involve developmental considerations such as continuity of child and adult disorders, clinical utility and research criteria, categories versus dimensions of diagnoses, multicultural perspectives, gender relationships, and disability and impairment related to psychopathological disorders. Clinical child psychologists and psychiatrists are involved in the process around the world.

Treatment developments

Research on the development of interventions for youth in the US has over the past 15 years focused primarily on the creation, evaluation, and dissemination of empirically based treatments (EBTs) (Steele, Elkin, & Roberts, 2008). The research on EBTs suggests that approaches such as cognitive-behavioral treatment and interpersonal therapy are effective in reducing depressive symptoms and that cognitive-behavioral treatments are effective in treating anxiety-related disorders. For externalizing problems, behavioral management training and behavioral therapy have produced effective improvements in the functioning of youth with conduct-related disorders. The next frontier for this promising line of research will be to address the applicability of known approaches to a wide variety of youth representing different cultural groups, to develop effective and systematic methods for dissemination of knowledge, and to continue to expand treatment for youth who present with multiple kinds of psychopathology.

Many countries are developing their own approaches to the prevention and treatment of mental health problems (Verhulst et al., 2003). For example, a large-scale violence prevention and intervention program was created in Medellin, Colombia, to address the risk of aggression in 8,900 youth (Duque, Klevens, Ungar, & Lee, 2005). Using weekly home visits and parenting workshops the authors sought to improve communication, supervision, and consequences for youth who had significant markers of risk for externalizing problems. A recent survey of the literature reveals that intervention efforts to reduce or prevent the development of psychological problems is evident in many developed countries and that systematic approaches to treatment are less clear in underdeveloped countries.

In addition to the need for more research on treatment, it is important to remember that a psychological approach for understanding and remediating mental health treatment is not universally accepted around the world. Recently, *The Lancet* created a global mental health group and, in a series of papers over the past year, has detailed the epidemiological rates of mental illness and the need for effective mental health treatment around the world (Lancet Global Mental Health Group, 2007). Moreover, this group is charged with increasing awareness of global mental health issues as well as addressing accessibility to treatment for psychological conditions worldwide. Patel, Flisher, Hetrick, and McGarry (2007) summarized the epidemiological evidence of mental disorder in youth and found that, taken together, the worldwide estimates suggest that at least one out of every four to five young people will experience a mental disorder in any given year. Although data are not available yet to determine the rates in less developed countries, the available evidence suggests that the necessity for treatment is great and future research must address the global as well as the local need.

Serious emotional disturbances

Children and adolescents with serious emotional disturbance (SED) are among the most challenging for families, schools, and psychologists (Jacobs, Randall, Vernberg, Roberts, & Nyre, 2005). These children present with severe impairments in psychological and behavioral functioning, with impact on scholastic achievement. They may exhibit a complex set of behaviors including disruptive behavior disorders, anxiety and mood disorders, psychosis, post-traumatic stress disorder, and cognitive/learning problems. They may receive concurrent multiple diagnostic labels and psychotropic medications. Children with SED are involved with many agencies such as law enforcement and juvenile justice, child protection and welfare, and mental and medical health. These youth often receive no or inadequate services in community or school settings.

Greater attention has been given in clinical child psychology to children with less severe problems than to those with poorer prognoses. Children with SED will confront their societies over time with more demanding behaviors. Research is urgently needed into etiological factors and preventive interventions. More scientific investigation must help create effective psychotherapeutic interventions in schools, outpatient and inpatient settings, and health care settings. A research agenda is needed into the effectiveness of psychoactive medication for the constellation of diagnoses subsumed in the SED category (Brown et al., 2008). Finally, clinical child psychologists need to investigate the optimal organization of service delivery for comprehensive attention to the needs of children with SED and their families (e.g., McDougall, Worrall-Davies, Hewson, Richardson, & Cotgrove, 2008).

Trauma/war/terrorism

Exposure to trauma is not unique to youth, but clearly the research supports the notion that youth are especially vulnerable to its effects (Kelleher et al., 2008). Exposure to violence is considered a public health issue and organizations like the Centers for Disease Control and the World Health Organization (WHO) have been on the forefront of the effort to address the impact of experiences like abuse, terrorism, and exposure to war in youth. Research and intervention efforts are primarily organized into: (a) etiology and surveillance of violence, (b) development of prevention programs, and (c) dissemination of best practices for prevention and treatment. In 2002, the WHO published the *World Report on Violence and Health* (Krug, Dahlberg, Mercy, Zwi, & Lozano, 2002) suggesting that not only is violence around the world increasing, but that the effects on the world's youth suggest a growing epidemic of physical and mental health problems.

Future research needs to be vigilant regarding the study of trauma and youth health outcomes. Beyond documenting the rates of pathology associated with trauma, research is beginning to address and develop models of the relations between exposure to trauma and outcomes (Jackson, Kim, & Delap, 2007) so that the specific mechanisms that create and maintain pathology can be identified. Scientific testing of these models could identify mechanisms underlying the trauma-outcome link that could be fruitful targets for helping youth cope effectively with trauma.

Interdisciplinary research and practice

As recognized by leaders in National Institutes of Health (2007: p. 1) in the US, "scientific progress often comes at the interface of traditional boundaries." Similarly, there is growing recognition that the best care of children and adolescents often necessitates effective multidisciplinary collaboration. These trends portend increasing need and opportunity for clinical child psychologists to collaborate with professionals from other disciplines in their research and practice. The growing emphasis on interdisciplinary research and practice is indicated by a number of recent developments such as the evaluation of multimodal treatments. Clinical child psychologists and other professionals must work together to evaluate psychosocial and pharmaceutical treatments alone and in combination. In the treatment of some youth, interdisciplinary care often extends beyond mental health professionals. The distinctive rise of subspecialty research and practice areas within clinical child psychology represents further evidence of the growing importance of interdisciplinary work. For example, the subspecialty area of pediatric psychology stands at the interface of children's physical and mental health. As professionals who study and treat youth with health concerns, the work of pediatric psychologists necessitates collaboration with pediatricians and other health professionals, including nurses, nutritionists, and child life specialists. Similarly, the emerging fields of genomics (Tercyak, 2009) and clinical child neuroscience (South, Wolf, & Herlihy, 2009) represent specialty areas that are only possible through collaboration among professionals from a variety of fields including clinical psychology, developmental psychology, genetics, neurology, medicine, and bio-engineering.

Psychopharmacology

Several challenges lie ahead for the practice of professional psychology, particularly as it relates to psychopharmacology. At the most basic level, additional research is needed to investigate the long-term efficacy and safety of pharmacological treatments for mental health disorders in children and adolescents (Brown et al., 2009), including investigations of the impact of pharmacotherapy on adaptive functioning and quality of life, and the safety, efficacy, and use of pharmacotherapy within diverse populations (APA Working Group, 2006). Further, comparisons between pharmacological and psychological treatments have typically been limited to tightly controlled efficacy studies, many of which do not assess the impact of the treatments as they are delivered in "real world" conditions. Effectiveness studies, which allow greater degrees of external validity, are needed to determine whether apparent treatment gains are realized when delivered under more typical clinical conditions.

As noted above, the use of pharmacotherapy for mental disorders is increasing in a number of (particularly Western) nations (e.g., Clavenna et al., 2007; Olfson et al., 2006; Mitchell et al., 2008; Parks et al., 2006). However, the field is also seeing a two point five- to eightfold increase in polypharmacy, or the practice of prescribing more than one medication to treat a disorder (Bhatara, Feil, Hoagwood, Vitiello, & Zima, 2004). Unfortunately, the research support for the use of polypharmacy with youth is scant and it is nonexistent regarding support for the use of more than two psychotropic medications concurrently (Safer, Zito, & dos Reis, 2003). Perhaps of greater concern, 45% of the medications prescribed for the treatment of emotional or behavioral problems in youth are not approved for use with children in the US (Naylor et al., 2007). Clearly, more research is necessary on the use of psychotropic medications with youth. Monitoring of short-term improvements must be paired with assessment of long-term effects on youth whose development may be more sensitive to the effects of medications.

At a different level, research is needed to evaluate practice patterns and sequencing of psychoactive medications relative to other modes of therapy. For example, Pelham (2008) recently reported that in samples of children with ADHD, receipt of medication prior to behavior therapy reduced participants' willingness to engage in therapy. Conversely, receiving behavior therapy first reduced participants' interest in receiving medication for symptom relief. The implication is that "multimodal treatments" for ADHD may be undermined by the relative timing of the pharmacologic and/or psychosocial components of the intervention. Whether and how this principle applies to other conditions and medications remains to be seen.

Professional psychology in Canada, the UK, and the US continues to struggle with the issue of prescription privileges for psychologists (RxP; Brehm, 2008; Lavoie & Barone, 2006), with convincing arguments on both sides. Although such a course is controversial, the APA Council of Representatives has adopted a general training curriculum for postdoctoral training in psychopharmacology, and the APA's College of Professional Psychology has created an examination to be used in the evaluation of candidates' competencies to prescribe medications (APA Practice Organization, 2007). Some jurisdictions in the US (i.e., the US Military, New Mexico, and Louisiana) currently grant limited RxP, and legislation to allow RxP has been introduced in at least 20 other states in the US. Consistent with the need for research into the long-term outcomes resulting from psychoactive medications, research is needed to determine the degree to which RxP positively impact patient/client outcomes, particularly among children and adolescents.

This movement toward prescription privileges has been controversial. Regardless of where individual psychologists stand on the prescription privilege issue, a solid working knowledge of psychopharmacologic treatments is important for mental health professionals (APA Working Group, 2006; Brown et al., 2009). Because their traditional scope of practice typically involves assessment of children's functioning in multiple contexts (i.e., family/home, school and peer), clinical child and adolescent psychologists are uniquely poised to improve upon multimodal treatment and assessment of children's symptoms. In addition, mental health professionals who are familiar with the current treatment literature on psychoactive medications will be better able to help families make informed decisions about treatment options (APA Working Group, 2006).

Conclusions

Although our description of clinical child psychology has largely drawn on examples in the U.S. developments, we have tried to make clear that worldwide mental health needs of children, adolescents, and their families are enormous. International developments in clinical child psychology are invigorating in terms of the science and practice of applied psychology, but are uneven in availability. Formalization of the roles and functions of this specialty are progressing in different stages. The value of applied child psychology perspectives is becoming recognized in a diversity of settings for a range of presenting behavior problems. Further development of understanding of developmental psychopathology and evidence-based practice will be important foci for clinical child psychologists globally.

References

American Board of Clinical Child and Adolescent Psychology. (2009). Homepage. Retrieved November 30, 2010 from www.clinicalchildpsychology.com/

American Psychological Association (APA). (2002). Ethical Principles and Code of Conduct. *American Psychologist*, *57*, 1060–1073.

American Psychological Association. (2003). Guidelines on multicultural education, training, research, practice, and organizational change for psychologists. *American Psychologist*, *58*, 377–402.

American Psychological Association Practice Organization. (2007). *PEP Performance: Postdoctoral psychopharmacological training programs: 2000–2007*. Washington, DC: APA Practice Organization.

American Psychological Association Presidential Task Force on Evidence-Based Practice. (2006). Evidence-based practice in psychology. *American Psychologist*, *61*, 271–285.

American Psychological Association Task Force on Evidence-Based Practice for Children and Adolescents. (2008). Disseminating evidence-based practice for children and adolescents: A systems approach to enhancing care. Washington, DC: American Psychological Association. Retrieved January 11, 2009 from www.apa.org/pi/cyf/evidence.html

American Psychological Association Working Group on Psychoactive Medications for Children and Adolescents. (2006). *Report of the working group on psychoactive medications for children and adolescents. Psychopharmacological, psychosocial, and combined interventions for childhood disorders: Evidence base, contextual factors, and future directions.* Washington, DC: American Psychological Association.

Association of Directors of Psychology Training Clinics. (2009). Homepage. Retrieved February 11, 2009 from www.adptc.org/?module-Home.

Aylward, B. S., Bender, J. A., Graves, M. M., & Roberts, M. C. (2009). Professional issues: Historical developments and trends in pediatric psychology. In M. C. Roberts & R. G. Steele (Eds.), *Handbook of pediatric psychology* (4th ed.). New York: Guilford.

Belfer, M. L., & Saxena, S. (2006). WHO Child Atlas Project. *The Lancet, 367*, 551–552.

Belfer, M. L., & Rohde, L. A. (2005). Child and adolescent mental health in Latin America and the Caribbean: Problems, progress, and policy research. *Revista Panamericana de Salud Pública, 18*, 359–365.

Bernal, M. E., & Padilla, A. M. (1982). Status of minority curricula and training in clinical psychology. *American Psychologist, 37*, 780–787.

Bhatara, V, Feil, M., Hoagwood, K., Vitiello, B., & Zima, B. (2004). National trends in concomitant psychotropic medication with stimulants in pediatric visits: Practice versus knowledge. *Journal of Attention Disorders, 7*, 217–226.

Brehm, S. S. (2008). The future of psychology and APA. *American Psychologist, 63*, 337–344.

Brown, R. T., Antonuccio, D. O., DuPaul, G. J., Fristad, M. A., King, C. A., Leslie, L. K., ... Vitiello, B. (2008). *Childhood mental health disorders: Evidence base and contextual factors for psychosocial, psychopharmacological, and combined interventions.* Washington, DC: American Psychological Association.

Brown, R. T., Daly, B. P., Carpenter, J. L., & Cohen, J. (2009). Pediatric pharmacology and psychopharmacology. In M. C. Roberts & R. G. Steele (Eds.), *Handbook of pediatric psychology* (4th ed.). New York: Guilford.

Carr, A. (Ed.). (2000). *What works with children and adolescents? A critical review of psychological interventions with children, adolescents and their families.* Florence, KY: Taylor & Frances/Routledge.

Charman, D., & Barkham, M. (2005). Psychological treatments: Evidence-based practice and practice-based evidence. *InPsych Highlights.* Retrieved November 30, 2010 from www.psychology.org.au/publications/inpsych/treatments.

Cicchetti, D. (1984). The emergence of developmental psychopathology. *Child Development, 55*, 1–7.

Cohen, L. L., La Greca, A. M., Blount, R. L., Kazak, A. E., Holmbeck, G. N., & Lemanek, K. L. (2008). Introduction to special issue: Evidence-based assessment in pediatric psychology. *Journal of Pediatric Psychology, 33*(9), 911–915.

Clavenna, A., Rossi, E., DeRosa, M., & Bonati, M. (2007). Use of psychotropic medications in Italian children and adolescents. *European Journal of Pediatrics, 166*, 339–347.

Clinical Child Psychology Formal Specialty Definition. (2005). Specialties Fact Sheet Council of Specialties. Retrieved November 30, 2010 from cospp.org/specialties/clinical-child-psychology

Commission for the Recognition of Specialties and Proficiencies in Professional Psychology. (2009). The historical roots of CRSPPP and its mission to recognize specialties and proficiencies in professional psychology. Retrieved December 12, 2010 from www.apa.org/ed/graduate/specialize/history.aspx

Cook, P., & Du Toit, L. (2005). Overcoming adversity with children affected by HIV/AIDS in the indigenous South African cultural context. In M. Ungar (Ed.), *Handbook of working with children and youth* (pp. 247–262). Thousand Oaks: Sage.

Davis, D., O'Brien, M. A., Freemantle, N., Wolf, F. M., Mazmanian, P., & Taylor-Vaisey, A. (1999). Impact of formal continuing medical education: Do conferences, workshops, rounds, and other traditional continuing education activities change physician behavior or health care outcomes? *JAMA*, *282*(9), 867–874.

Drotar, D. (1985). Integrating pediatric and clinical child psychology: Perspectives in clinical training. In J. M. Tuma (Ed.), *Proceedings: Conference on training clinical child psychologists* (p. 69–73). Washington DC: Section on Clinical Child Psychology, American Psychological Association.

Duque, L. F., Klevens, J., Ungar, M., & Lee, A. W. (2005). Violence prevention programming in Colombia. In M. Ungar (Ed.), *Handbook for working with children and youth* (pp. 455–471). Thousand Oaks: Sage.

Fonagy, P., Target, M., Cottrell, D., Phillips, J., & Kurtz, Z. (2002). *What works for whom? A critical review of treatments for children and adolescents.* New York: Guilford.

Giannet, S. (2003). Cultural competence and professional psychology training: Creating the architecture for change. *Journal of Evolutionary Psychology*, *24*, 117–128.

Hibbs, E. D., & Jensen, P. S. (Eds.) (2005). *Psychosocial treatments for child and adolescent disorders: Empirically based strategies for clinical practice* (2nd ed.).Washington, DC: American Psychological Association.

Higa, C. K., & Chorpita, B. F. (2008). Evidence-based therapies: Translating research into practice. In R. G. Steele, T. D. Elkin, & M. C. Roberts (Eds.), *Handbook of evidence-based therapies for children and adolescents: Bridging science and practice* (pp. 45–61). New York: Springer.

Jackson, Y., Kim, K., & Delap, C. (2007). Mediators of control beliefs, stressful life events, and behavioral outcome: The role of appraisal and social support. *Journal of Traumatic Stress*, *20*, 147–160.

Jacobs, A. K., Randall, C., Vernberg, E. M., Roberts, M. C., & Nyre, J. E. (2005). Providing services within a school-based intensive mental health program. In R. G. Steele & M. C. Roberts (Eds.), *Handbook of mental health services for children, adolescents, and families* (pp. 47–61). New York: Kluwer/Plenum Academic.

Kaslow, N. J., Rubin, N. J., Bebeau, M. J., Leigh, I. W., Lichtenberg, J. W., Nelson, P. D., … Smith, I. L. (2007). Guiding principles and recommendations for the assessment of competence. *Professional Psychology: Research and Practice*, *38*(5), 441–441.

Kazak, A. (2000). The *Journal of Pediatric Psychology*: A brief history (1969–1999). *Journal of Pediatric Psychology*, *25*, 463–470.

Kelleher, I., Harley, M., Lynch, F., Arseneault, L., Fitzpatrick, C., & Cannon, M. (2008). Associations between childhood trauma, bullying and psychotic symptoms among a school-based adolescent sample. *British Journal of Psychiatry*, *193*, 378–382.

Kendall, P., & Beidas, R. (2007). Smoothing the trail for dissemination of evidence-based practices for youth: Flexibility within fidelity. *Professional Psychology: Research and Practice*, *38*(1), 13–20.

Krug, E. G., Dahlberg, L. L., Mercy, J. A., Zwi, A. B., & Lozano, R. (2002). *World report on violence and health.* Geneva: WHO.

La Greca, A. M., & Hughes, J. N. (1999). United we stand, divided we fall: The education and training needs of clinical child psychologists. *Journal of Clinical Child Psychology*, *28*(4), 435–435.

Lancet Global Mental Health Group. (2007). Scale up services for mental disorders: A call for action. *The Lancet*, *370*, 1241–1252.

Landolf, B. M. (2005). Outpatient-private practice model. In R. G. Steele & M. C. Roberts (Eds.), *Handbook of mental health services for children, adolescents, and families* (pp. 111–131). New York: Springer.

Lavoie, K. L., & Barone, S. (2006). Prescription privileges for psychologists: A comprehensive review and critical analysis of current issues and controversies. *CNS Drugs, 20*, 51–66.

Lee, S. W., & Jamison, T. R. (2005). School psychology services. In R. G. Steele & M. C. Roberts (Eds.), *Handbook of mental health services for children, adolescents, and families* (pp. 31–45). New York: Springer.

Long, N. (2008). Editorial: Closing the gap between research and practice—the importance of practitioner training. *Clinical Child Psychology and Psychiatry, 13*(2), 187–190.

Lonigan, C. J., Elbert J. C., & Johnson, S. B. (1998). Empirically supported psychosocial interventions for children: An overview. *Journal of Clinical Child Psychology, 27*, 138–145.

Mash, E. J., & Barkley, R. A. (2007). *Assessment of childhood disorders* (4th ed.). New York: Guilford Press.

Mash, E., & Hunsley, J. (2005). Evidence-based assessment of child and adolescent disorders: Issues and challenges. *Journal of Clinical Child and Adolescent Psychology, 34*(3), 362–379.

McDougall, T., Worrall-Davies, A., Hewson, L., Richardson, G., & Cotgrove, A. (2008). Tier 4 Child and Adolescent Mental Health Services (CAMHS)-Inpatient care, day services and alternatives: An overview to Tier 4 CAMHS provision in the UK. *Child and Adolescent Mental Health, 13*, 173–180.

Mitchell, B., Carleton, B., Smith, A., Prosser, R., Brownell, M., & Kozyrskyj, A. (2008). Trends in psychostimulant and antidepressant use by children in 2 Canadian provinces. *La Review Canadienne de Psychiatrie, 53*, 152–159.

MTA Cooperative Group. (1999a). Fourteen-month randomized clinical trial of treatment strategies for attention deficit/hyperactivity disorder. *Archives of General Psychiatry, 56*, 1073–1086.

MTA Cooperative Group. (1999b). Moderators and mediators of treatment response for children with attention deficit/hyperactivity disorder. *Archives of General Psychiatry, 56*, 1088–1096.

National Institutes of Health (and Department of Health and Human Services). (2007, November). Report of Trans-National Institutes of Health Research Conducted in Fiscal Year 2007: Report to Congress. Retrieved November 30, 2010, from http://dpcpsi.nih.gov/collaboration/2007_Report_of_Trans-NIH_Research.pdf.

Naylor, M. W., Davidson, C. V., Ortega-Piron, D. J., Bass, A., Gutierrez, A., & Hall, A. (2007). Psychotropic medication management for youth in state care: Consent, oversight, and policy considerations. *Child Welfare, 86*, 175–192.

Nelson, T. D., & Steele, R. G. (2007). Predictors of practitioner self-reported use of evidence-based practices: Practitioner training, clinical setting, and attitudes toward research. *Administration and Policy in Mental Health and Mental Health Services Research, 34*, 319–330.

Nelson, T. D., & Steele, R. G. (2008). Influences on practitioner treatment selection: Best research evidence and other considerations. *Journal of Behavioral Health Services and Research, 35*, 170–178.

Olfson, M., Blanco, C., Liu, L., Moreno, C., & Laje, G. (2006). National trends in the outpatient treatment of children and adolescents with antipsychotic drugs. *Archives of General Psychiatry, 63*, 679–685.

Ollendick, T. H. (1984). Training in clinical child psychology: The role of continuing education. *Journal of Clinical Child Psychology, 13*(1), 90–91.

Ollendick, T. H., & Schroeder, C. S. (2003). (Eds.). *Encyclopedia of clinical child and pediatric psychology*. New York: Kluwer/Plenum.

Pack-Brown, S. P., & Williams, C. B. (2003). *Ethics in a multicultural context*. Thousand Oaks, CA: Sage.

Parks Thomas, C., Conrad, P., Casler, R., & Goodman, E. (2006). Trends in the use of psychotropic medications among adolescents, 1994–2001. *Psychiatric Services*, *57*, 63–69.

Patel, V., Flisher, A. J., Hetrick, S., & McGarry, P. (2007). Mental health of young people: A global public-health challenge. *The Lancet*, *369*, 1302–1313.

Pediatric OCD Treatment Study Team. (2004). Cognitive behavioral therapy, sertraline, and their combination for children and adolescents with obsessive-compulsive disorder: The Pediatric OCD Treatment Study (POTS) randomized controlled trial. *Journal of the American Medical Association*, *292*, 1969–1976.

Pelham, W. E. (2008, October). Life in ADHD intervention after the MTA: Treatment modality combinations, components, sequences and doses. Paper presented at the Kansas Conference on Clinical Child and Adolescent Psychology, Lawrence, KS, USA. Retrieved November 30, 2010 from www2.ku.edu/~clchild/conference/Pelham.pdf.

Prinstein, M. J., & Roberts, M. C. (2006). The professional adolescence of clinical child and adolescent psychology and pediatric psychology: Grown up and striving for autonomy. *Clinical Psychology: Science and Practice*, *13*, 263–268.

Proctor, E. K., Knudsen, K. J., Fedoravicius, N., Hovmand, P., Rosen, A., & Perron, B. (2007). Implementation of evidence-based practice in community behavioral health: Agency director perspectives. *Administration and Policy in Mental Health and Mental Health Services Research*, *34*, 479–488.

Punamaki, R. L., Qouta, S., & El-Sarraj, E. (2001). Resiliency factors predicting psychological adjustment after political violence among Palestinian children. *International Journal of Behavioral Development*, *25*, 256–267.

Roberts, M. C. (2006). Essential tension: Specialization with broad and general training in psychology. *American Psychologist*, *61*(8), 862–870.

Roberts, M. C., Borden, K. A., Christiansen, M. D., & Lopez, S. J. (2005). Fostering a culture shift: Assessment of competence in the education and careers of professional psychologists. *Professional Psychology: Research and Practice*, *36*, 355–361.

Roberts, M. C., Carlson, C. I., Erickson, M. T., Friedman, R. M., La Greca, A. M., Lemanek, K. L., ... Wohlford, P. F. (1998). A model for training psychologists to provide services for children and adolescents. *Professional Psychology: Research and Practice*, *29*(3), 293–299.

Roberts, M. C., Erickson, M. T., & Tuma, J. M. (1985). Addressing the needs: Guidelines for training psychologists to work with children, youth, and families. *Journal of Clinical Child Psychology*, *14*, 70–79.

Roberts, M. C., Jacobs, A. K., Puddy, R. W., Nyre, J. E., & Vernberg, E. M. (2003). Treating children with serious emotional disturbances in schools and community: The Intensive Mental Health Program. *Professional Psychology: Research and Practice*, *34*, 519–526.

Roberts, M. C., & James, R. L. (2008). Empirically supported treatments and evidence-based practice for children and adolescents. In R. G. Steele, T. D. Elkin, & M. C. Roberts (Eds.), *Handbook of evidence-based therapies for children and adolescents: Bridging science and practice* (pp. 9–24). New York: Springer.

Roberts, M. C., & Steele, R. G. (2009). Preface. In M. C. Roberts & R. G. Steele (Eds.), *Handbook of pediatric psychology* (4th ed.). New York: Guilford.

Ronen, T., Rahav, G., & Rosenbaum, M. (2003). Children's reactions to war situations as a function of age and sex. *Anxiety, Stress, and Coping: An International Journal*, *16*, 59–69.

Rubin, N. J., Bebeau, M., Leigh, I. W., Lichtenberg, J. W., Nelson, P. D., Portnoy, S., ... Kaslow, N.J. (2007). The competency movement within psychology: An historical perspective. *Professional Psychology: Research and Practice, 38*, 452–462.

Ruiz, F., & Tanaka, K. (2001). The ijime phenomenon and Japan: Overarching considerations for cross-cultural studies. *Psychologia: An International Journal of Psychology in the Orient, 44*(2), 128–138.

Rutter, M. & Sroufe, L. A. (2000). Developmental psychopathology: Concepts and challenges. *Development and Psychopathology, 12*, 265–296.

Safer, D. J., Zito, J. M., & dos Reis, S. (2003). Concomitant psychotropic medication for youth. *American Journal of Psychiatry, 160*, 438–449.

Schoenwald, S. K., & Hoagwood, K. (2001). Effectiveness, transportability, and dissemination of interventions: What matters when? *Psychiatric Services, 52*(9), 1190–1197.

Sharkin, B. S., & Plageman, P. M. (2003). What do psychologists think about mandatory continuing education? A survey of Pennsylvania practitioners. *Professional Psychology: Research and Practice, 34*(3), 318–323.

Silverman, W. K., & Hinshaw, S. P. (2008). The second special issue on evidence-based psychosocial treatments for children and adolescents: A ten year update. *Journal of Clinical Child and Adolescent Psychology, 37*(whole issue #1).

Smith-Boydston, J. M. (2005). Providing a range of services to fit the needs of youth in community mental health centers. In R. G. Steele & M. C. Roberts (Eds.), *Handbook of mental health services for children, adolescents, and families* (pp. 103–116). New York: Springer.

Smith-Boydston, J. M., & Nelson, T. D. (2008). Adoption of evidence-based treatments in community settings: Obstacles and opportunities. In R. G. Steele, T. D. Elkin, & M. C. Roberts (Eds.), *Handbook of evidence-based therapies for children and adolescents: Bridging science and practice* (pp. 521–536). New York: Springer.

Society of Clinical Child and Adolescent Psychology. (2009). Division 53 of American Psychological Association. Retrieved November 30, 2010 from www.clinicalchildpsychology.org/

Society of Pediatric Psychology. (2009a). Division 54 of American Psychological Association. Retrieved November 30, 2010 from www.societyofpediatricpsychology.org/

Society of Pediatric Psychology. (2009b). Who we are. Accessed on January 9, 2009 from www.societyofpediatricpsychology.org/~division54/who/index.shtml.

South, M., Wolf, J., & Herlihy, L. (2009). New directions: Translating clinical child neuroscience to practice. In M. C. Roberts & R. G. Steele (Eds.), *Handbook of pediatric psychology* (4th ed., pp. 737–754). New York: Guilford.

Spirito, A. (1999). Introduction to special series on empirically supported treatments in pediatric psychology. *Journal of Pediatric Psychology, 24*(2), 87–90.

Spirito, A., Brown, R. T., D'Angelo, E. J., Delamater, A. M., Rodrigue, J. R., & Siegel, L. J. (2003). Training pediatric psychologists for the 21st century. In M. C. Roberts (Ed.), *Handbook of pediatric psychology* (3rd ed., pp. 19–31). New York: Guilford.

Sroufe, L. A., & Rutter, M. (1984). The domain of developmental psychopathology. *Child Development, 55*, 17–29.

Steele, R. G., Elkin, T. D., & Roberts, M. C. (Eds.). (2008). *Handbook of evidence-based therapies for children and adolescents: Bridging science and practice.* New York: Springer.

Sue, D. W., & Sue, D. (2008). *Counseling the culturally diverse.* Hoboken, NJ: Wiley.

Treatment for Adolescent Depression Study (TADS) Team. (2004). Fluoxetine, cognitive-behavioral therapy, and their combination for adolescents with depression. *Journal of the American Medical Association, 292*, 807–820.

Tercyak, K. P. (2009). Genetics and genetic testing. In M. C. Roberts & R. G. Steele (Eds.), *Handbook of pediatric psychology* (4th ed.). New York: Guilford.

Usala, T., Clavenna, A., Zuddasa, A., & Bonati, M. (2008). Randomised controlled trials of selective serotonin reuptake inhibitors in treatment depression in children and adolescents: A systematic review and meta-analysis. *European Neuropsychopharmacology*, *18*, 62–73.

U. S. Census. (2004). Hispanic and Asian Americans increasing faster than overall population. Accessed August 15, 2008 from www.census.gov/Press-Release/www/releases/archives/race/001839.html.

Vargas, L. A., & de Dios Brambila, A. (2005). Inpatient treatment models. In R. G. Steele & M. C. Roberts (Eds.), *Handbook of mental health services for children, adolescents, and families* (pp. 133–149). New York: Springer.

Verhulst, F. C., Achenbach T. M., van der Ende, J., Erol, N., Lambert, M. C., Leung, P. W. L., … Zubrick, S. R. (2003). Comparisons of problems reported by youths from seven countries. *American Journal of Psychiatry*; *160*, 1479–1485.

Vittiello, B. (2008). An international perspective on pediatric psychopharmacology. *International Review of Psychiatry*, *20*, 121–126.

Walker, C. E. (1988). Presidential address: The future of pediatric psychology. *Journal of Pediatric Psychology*, *13*, 465–478.

Walker, C. E., & Roberts, M. C. (Eds.). (2001). *Handbook of clinical child psychology* (3rd ed.). New York: Wiley.

Walkup, J., Albano, A. M., Piacentini, J., Birmaher, B., Compton, S. N., Sherrill, J. T., et al. (2008). Cognitive behavioral therapy, sertraline, or a combination in childhood anxiety. *The New England Journal of Medicine*, *359*(26), 2753–2766.

Weisz, J. R., Chu, B. C., & Polo, A. J. (2004). Treatment dissemination and evidence-based practice: Strengthening intervention through clinician–researcher collaboration. *Clinical Psychology: Research & Practice*, *11*, 300–307.

World Health Organization (2005). Promoting mental health: Concepts, emerging evidence, practice. Retrieved November 30, 2010 from www.who.int/mental_health/evidence/en/promoting_mhh.pdf

World Health Organization. (2009). Home page. Retrieved November 30, 2010 from www.who.int/classifications/icd/en/.

2

Clinical Psychology

Adult

G. Terence Wilson

The focus in this chapter[1] is on the recent history and current status of clinical psychology in North America and the United Kingdom. Advances in these countries have been significantly influenced by the research of clinical psychologists across Europe and other countries such as Australia and New Zealand. In turn, developments in North America and the UK have had an important bearing on clinical research and practice elsewhere in the world.

Historical Overview

Modern clinical psychology was an outgrowth of World War II and its aftermath. In countries in Western Europe the major influence was the development of mental health facilities to meet the widespread challenges faced by the different health authorities in the wake of the war. In Eastern Europe clinical psychology only began to emerge in the 1980s after changes in political systems that had been critical of the field (Lunt, 2001). In the United States the United States Public Health Service and the Veterans Administration (VA) aggressively supported the funding of doctoral programs in clinical psychology in order to expand the pool of mental health professionals. Prior to the war the role of psychologists in the US and elsewhere had been restricted to assessment—the administration and scoring of objective personality tests and projective tests such as the Rorshach. Psychotherapy itself was the exclusive province of psychiatry. The war abruptly changed this dominance of psychiatry in the US as clinical psychologists were pressed into service to help provide an increasing need for mental health services.

IAAP Handbook of Applied Psychology, First Edition. Edited by Paul R. Martin, Fanny M. Cheung, Michael C. Knowles, Michael Kyrios, Lyn Littlefield, J. Bruce Overmier, and José M. Prieto.

The defining development in the field of clinical psychology took place in 1949, at the University of Colorado in Boulder. A two-week conference resulted in the formulation of a single model for the training of graduate students as clinical psychologists—the scientist-practitioner or Boulder model as it came to be known. The model "specified core clinical skills; required practicum work; required a full-year internship; and mandated research training and a research dissertation" (Benjamin, 2005, p. 18). The model was a grand compromise calculated to placate academics and clinical practitioners alike and so unify the field of psychology as McFall (2006) has noted. Clinical psychologists would be trained to be both scientists, expert in the conduct of research, as well as professionals, practitioners skilled in the administration of psychological tests and psychotherapy.

It would be difficult to overstate the impact of the scientist-practitioner model on clinical psychology. It remains the dominant model of clinical training in psychology in North America (Benjamin, 2005), as well as the UK and parts of Europe such as the Nordic countries (Lunt, 2001). Nevertheless, dissatisfaction with the scientist-practitioner model was not long in coming in the US. In many ways the compromise at Boulder had merely papered over the cracks between scientists and professionals. The former saw practitioner training as undermining a focus on research, whereas the latter complained that the model did not provide for adequate training in the application of psychology and produced too limited a number of practitioners. In 1970 the first freestanding (i.e., not part of a university) school of professional psychology was founded in California by Nicholas Cummings. In short order this was followed by another landmark conference, this time at Vail Colorado, which endorsed the scholar-practitioner model of clinical training (Korman, 1974). The model had its own degree—the doctor of psychology (Psy.D.)—the goal of which was to minimize research training and devote substantially more time to training in professional practice.

The 1970s witnessed the rapid growth of clinical psychology. The long-standing battle with psychiatry was won: by the end of the decade clinical psychologists had attained parity with psychiatrists and were the chief providers of psychotherapy. Within the field of psychology as a whole the clinical practitioners ascended to a position of dominance as they gained control of the governance of the American Psychological Association (APA) that had hitherto been primarily the preserve of distinguished academic psychologists. The APA became increasingly committed to the guild issues that were the concern of practitioners who now constituted the largest majority of its members. Unable to find a workable compromise, many academic/scientific psychologists left the APA and founded a new organization—the American Psychological Society (which is now called the Association for Psychological Science [APS])—dedicated to advancement of scientific psychology in teaching, research, and clinical applications. Little wonder then that this period has been called the golden age of clinical psychology. The increase in Psy.D. training programs proved to be remarkable. Benjamin (2005) has observed that by 1997 schools of professional psychology offering the Psy.D. were producing twice as many graduates in clinical psychology as the more traditional university-based programs.

Contemporary Trends: Clinical Research

The aftermath of World War II also witnessed the end of the psychoanalytic hegemony of psychotherapy that had previously existed. The development of theoretically and clinically diverse alternatives to psychoanalytic and psychodynamic models of treatment began to change the face of the field. One example was the founding and growth of behavior therapy, which in its early days was defined as the application of learning or conditioning theory to the treatment of clinical problems. The guiding philosophy of this approach was behaviorism, and its foundations rested on the application of principles that had been formulated in basic psychological research in animal conditioning laboratories, arguably the most important element of experimental psychology in the 1940s and 1950s. Another prominent example was Carl Rogers's (1951) client-centered therapy. This was but one illustration of a growing humanistic trend in clinical psychology, an approach that differed in fundamental ways from both the psychoanalytic and behavioristic traditions. Contrary to the deterministic traditions of psychoanalysis and behaviorism, client-centered therapy relies upon the patient's personal resources for growth and self-actualization in spite of environmental limitations and challenges (Raskin, Rogers, & Witty, 2008).

Clinical psychologists not only were the founders and early proponents and practitioners of different forms of psychological treatment in the wake of the war, but they also began to adapt their methodological expertise to conducting research on different forms of psychotherapy. Of all these developments in clinical research the one that has had the most profound impact on the field has been behavior therapy (more typically referred to as cognitive behavior therapy today). It is important nonetheless to remember that Rogers was a pioneer in conducting research on psychotherapy especially what would be called process research on the content of therapy sessions (Raskin et al., 2008). To illustrate the advances in research on psychological treatments and their effectiveness the following section summarizes the evidence regarding four major contemporary therapeutic approaches.

Cognitive Behavioral Therapy (CBT)

Behavior therapy originally entailed the application of classical and operant conditioning principles to psychiatric disorders. In the 1970s behavior therapy incorporated cognitive principles and procedures and quickly came to be known as cognitive behavioral therapy (CBT) as the discipline of psychology as a whole "went cognitive." A driving force behind the development of CBT was the influence of Bandura's (1969) social learning theory, which later would become relabeled as social cognitive theory. In addition to the traditional behavioristic emphasis on environmental determinants of behavior, this approach focused actively on unobservable cognitive and affective processes involved in the development, maintenance, and modification of behavior and clinical disorders (Bandura, 2004). In parallel fashion to this conceptual broadening of the field, its therapeutic models and strategies were enriched by the adaptation and adoption of the overlapping cognitive therapies of Ellis and Beck respectively. The field of applied behavior analysis, which is the outgrowth of

Skinnerian operant conditioning principles and procedures, continues to flourish as a treatment particularly for children with problems such as developmental disabilities. No simple definition of contemporary CBT is possible. The broad rubric encompasses different theoretical perspectives and distinctive albeit overlapping therapeutic techniques and strategies.

Conceptual developments. CBT is an evolving system of psychological treatment. The most recent theoretical development has been dubbed the "third wave" of behavior therapy (Hayes, Follette, & Linehan, 2004). The three most prominent forms of this approach are Dialectical Behavior Therapy (DBT) (Linehan, 1993), Acceptance and Commitment Therapy (ACT) (Hayes, Luoma, Bond, Masuda, & Lillis, 2006), and mindfulness-based cognitive therapy (Segal, Teasdale, & Williams, 2004). Collectively, these treatments have overlapping conceptual and technical foundations. Common principles include the following: (a) a focus on acceptance as well as behavioral change, and the relationship between the two. This is the seminal dialectic of DBT; (b) the emphasis on function rather than content of thought and beliefs; (c) the importance of metacognitive awareness (Segal et al., 2004). Rather than trying to change the content of beliefs, or challenge their validity, the focus is on the patient's relationships to dysfunctional thoughts and feelings; (d) the emphasis on reducing experiential avoidance, namely, accepting negative thoughts and feelings instead of suppressing, challenging, or otherwise trying to block or eliminate them.

Disagreement currently exists regarding the efficacy of elements of this "third wave" of behavior therapy (Ost, 2008). Nevertheless, DBT has proven to be an effective treatment for borderline personality disorder, mindfulness-based cognitive therapy for depression has yielded promising preliminary findings, and ACT is being evaluated in the treatment of a wide range of clinical problems (Hayes et al., 2004).

Some proponents of these treatments have suggested that they represent a qualitatively different approach from CBT in general. The more common view, however, is that they are part of the continuing evolution of CBT. Domains of overlap between traditional behavior therapy and CBT are clearly apparent. For example, the emphasis on function rather than content has always been a core principle of behavioral psychology and therapy. Furthermore, although the cognitive restructuring that characterizes Beck's cognitive therapy is aimed at challenging and disputing thoughts and beliefs, cognitive therapy also originally included the intervention of "decentering" that is akin to the concept of metacognitive awareness (Beck, Rush, Shaw & Emery, 1979).

Efficacy and effectiveness research. Clinical research on CBT rapidly expanded into all areas of the treatment of clinical disorders. Operationally explicit and replicable treatment protocols were increasingly applied to specific clinical disorders that had been reliably described in another landmark development, namely, the publication of DSM-III in 1980 (American Psychiatric Association, 1980). In marked contrast to the small, single investigator-based studies of the 1960s and early 1970s, CBT treatments increasingly have been put to the test in methodologically sophisticated, adequately powered, multisite investigations. The result is that CBT treatments dominate a number of what are widely considered to be empirically supported treatments (e.g., Chambless & Ollendick, 2001; Nathan & Gorman, 2007). CBT treatments are also the interventions most commonly identified by the National Institute for Clinical Excellence (NICE) guidelines in the UK. The latter are arguably the most comprehensive, rigorous, interdisciplinary, and transparent treatment guidelines available.

The bulk of the research to date, on CBT and other therapies, has been in the form of efficacy studies—the goal of which is to develop and evaluate evidence-based treatments under tightly controlled conditions with considerations of the internal validity of the research paramount. Thus CBT treatments have been shown to be more effective than wait-list and attention-placebo control conditions. The former controls for the passage of time, the latter for patients' expectations about being in treatment, undergoing repeated assessment, and having comparable contact with clinic personnel (e.g., Goldstein, de Beurs, Chambless, & Wilson, 2000). All of these factors are capable of changing behavior in specific contexts and therefore it is important to show that they alone cannot account for the efficacy of the treatment method in question.

A still more stringent research design that has been used pits the CBT treatment against supportive psychotherapy (SPT) (e.g., Walsh et al., 1997). In this design SPT controls for the role of the therapist-patient relationship in evaluating the effects of the specific treatment. Given the importance attached to the latter in the traditional psychotherapy literature (see below), the superiority of a specific treatment over SPT provides potent evidence of specific therapeutic effects.

The most compelling evidence for the efficacy of specific CBT treatments comes from well-controlled comparisons with state-of-the-art pharmacological therapy. Over the past 30 years empirically supported psychological treatments have been developed for a range of psychiatric disorders, including depression, anxiety disorders, and eating disorders. Research suggests that certain CBT treatments are as effective, or more effective, than the leading pharmacological treatments for these conditions (Hollon, Stewart, & Strunk, 2005; Wilson & Shafran, 2005).

The goal of effectiveness studies is to extend and adapt treatments to routine clinical service settings. The emphasis is on external as opposed to internal validity. Contrary to the claims of critics (e.g., Westen, Novotny, & Thompson-Brenner, 2004), accumulating evidence indicates that the effects of CBT treatments from efficacy trials can and typically do generalize to routine clinical service settings (e.g., Stewart & Chambless, 2009; Stirman, DeRubeis, Crits-Christoph, & Brody, 2003; Whaley & Davis, 2007).

Innovations in treatment outcome research are increasingly addressing issues such as cost-effectiveness. The evidence on evidence-based psychological treatments in general thus far is very promising (e.g., Baker, McFall, & Shoham, 2009), and this dimension of outcome may well represent a significant advantage for psychological treatment over pharmacotherapy.

Other innovations feature the use of such cost-effective and globally disseminable interventions as guided self-help and internet-based CBT. The potential of guided self-help can be illustrated by its success in the treatment of eating disorders (Latner & Wilson, 2007). For example, in the UK, Schmidt et al. (2007) compared family therapy with guided self-help based on cognitive–behavioral principles (CBTgsh) in the treatment of adolescents with bulimia nervosa and related eating disorders. Both treatments resulted in significant improvement in binge eating and purging at the end of treatment (6 months) and at 12-month follow-up. Moreover, CBTgsh was associated with greater acceptability and lower cost than family therapy.

Internet-delivered treatment has been defined as "a therapy that is based on self-help books, guided by an identified therapist who gives feedback and answers to questions, with a scheduling that mirrors face-to-face treatment, and which can also include interactive online features" (Andersson et al., 2008, p. 164). Results of internet-based CBT interventions show that it is effective with at least a subset of patients with anxiety and mood disorders, and other health problems including headaches, insomnia, and pain (Andersson, 2009). It appears that the involvement of an online therapist is important in facilitating adherence to treatment and its success. In view of its cost-effectiveness and global capabilities, this treatment modality is likely to feature prominently in the future of psychological treatment.

Alternative forms of psychological treatment

CBT is not the only form of psychological treatment to have received empirical support in the light of advances in treatment outcome research.

Interpersonal psychotherapy (IPT). Originally developed by Klerman, Weissman, Rounsaville, & Chevron (1984), IPT is a structured, manual-based treatment that can be implemented on an individual or group basis. The primary emphasis is on helping patients identify and modify current interpersonal problems that are hypothesized to be maintaining the target clinical disorder. Interpersonal problem areas are identified in four social domains: grief, role disputes, role transitions, and interpersonal deficits. The treatment is both nondirective and noninterpretive.

Findings from RCTs have established that IPT is an effective treatment for adolescent and adult depression. It is superior to TAU in treating depressed adolescents in school-based health clinics (Mufson et al., 2007), and significantly augments pharmacological therapy in severely depressed patients (Schramm et al., 2007). Initially developed specifically to treat depression, IPT has been modified so that it is now also a treatment for the eating disorders bulimia nervosa and binge eating disorder (BED). RCTs have shown that IPT is effective (NICE, 2004). In the case of overweight or obese patients with BED, IPT is equal to CBT and significantly superior to behavioral weight-loss treatment at 2-year follow-up (Wilson, Wilfley, Agras, & Bryson, 2010).

Family therapy. Another widely used modality of psychological treatment is family therapy that has, selectively, been shown to be effective. In their review of empirically supported treatments, Baker et al. (2009) identified family treatment, based on the principles of either behavior therapy or structural family-systems therapy, as a consistently effective means of decreasing rehospitalization rates for patients with schizophrenia who had also been treated with pharmacotherapy.

As with other broad categories of therapeutic systems, family therapy comprises different methods with dissimilar theoretical foundations. Outcomes vary as a function of which specific form of family therapy is evaluated. Developed in the UK, the Maudsley model of family therapy has been shown to be effective in the treatment of adolescent patients with anorexia nervosa. The approach is very different from traditional forms of family therapy typically used in the US. Structured and manual-based, the treatment involves 10 to 20 family sessions spaced over 6 to 12 months (Lock, le Grange, Agras, & Dare, 2001). The recommended "conjoint" format specifies that all family members should be seen together. In the first phase of treatment, parents are directed to take complete control over their child's eating and weight, and coached in the requisite skills for so doing. Parental control and authority is then gradually reduced as the adolescent begins to improve. In the later stages of therapy, the adolescent's right to age-appropriate autonomy is explicitly linked to the resolution of the eating disorder.

Anorexia nervosa is notoriously difficult to treat. The significance of this model of family therapy is that it appears to be the most promising treatment available for adolescent patients (Wilson, Grilo, & Vitousek, 2007). Nevertheless, whether the positive results to date are a function of the specific treatment or simply due to the focus on adolescents who are known to have a better prognosis than more chronic cases, remains to be determined.

Psychodynamic therapy. In contrast to other psychological therapies, there has been relatively little empirical research on the efficacy of psychodynamic therapy. RCTs comparing psychodynamic treatments to control conditions such as attention or pill placebos, TAU, or specific pharmacological therapies as is the custom with CBT and IPT, are almost nonexistent. Proponents of psychodynamic therapy are quick to point out that the absence of this sort of empirical evidence does not mean that the therapy is necessarily ineffective. As true as this counter might be, the onus is on protagonists to provide empirical evidence of efficacy. The need to rigorously evaluate all alternative psychological therapies is underscored by findings indicating that at least some treatments naturalistically delivered by practicing clinicians in representative treatment settings do not appear to be effective (e.g., Weisz, Weersing, & Henggeler, 2005).

Are some psychological treatments more effective than others?

Traditional psychotherapists frequently respond to the growth of empirically supported treatments by dismissing or minimizing the clinical relevance of the sort of research evidence summarized above. They argue that demonstrating the superiority of CBT over a pill placebo or some form of "bland pseudotherapy" control condition (Holmes, 2002) is insufficient. Rather, they have called for comparisons of current empirically supported treatments with what they deem to be a bona fide alternative form of psychotherapy. When these comparisons are made, critics contend that CBT and other empirically supported treatments are not superior to traditional psychodynamic therapies. According to this view, all forms of psychotherapy are equally effective—the Dodo Bird verdict first issued by Luborsky, Singer, & Luborsky (1975): "everyone has won, and all must have prizes."

Proponents of this position rely heavily on the use of meta-analyses of existing studies. A meta-analysis is a quantitative method for summarizing and evaluating large numbers of independent studies using accepted statistical techniques. For example, an effect size index is derived for each study and then compared across the entire range of studies. First used by Smith and Glass (1977) and Smith, Glass, and Miller (1980) for evaluating the effects of psychotherapy, meta-analysis was presumed to overcome the inherent limitations of so-called "literary reviews" of evidence, which were subject to the individual reviewer's personal biases and preconceptions. Instead, meta-analysis, in principle, allows for both more thorough and more comprehensive reviews of bodies of literature.

Beginning with the Smith and Glass (1977) paper, various meta-analyses have shown few if any differences in outcome across different forms of psychological treatment. In turn, the use of meta-analyses has attracted strong criticism from advocates of using rigorous methodological standards such as those adopted in the NICE guidelines to assess therapeutic efficacy. It has been argued that the meta-analyses that have been published are often methodologically flawed in several ways. Two examples may be cited. First, they are not necessarily comprehensive reviews. Indeed, Wilson and Rachman (1983) pointed out that the original Smith et al. (1980) meta-analysis omitted numerous relevant studies and introduced demonstrable biases in what was selected for review. A telling illustration of this problem is a recent meta-analysis claiming that all bona fide treatments of PTSD are equally effective (Benish, Imel, & Wampold, 2008). This assertion is contradicted by seven other meta-analyses which, as Ehlers et al. (2010) noted, had concluded that trauma-focused psychological treatments (e.g., CBT) are more effective than treatments that do not focus specifically on patients' memories of trauma. Ehlers et al. explain the discrepancy by showing how Benish et al. (2008) exercised marked selectivity (bias) in excluding certain studies based on their arbitrary and questionable definition of "bona fide treatment." To avoid these controversies in the future Ehlers et al. have called for "transparency in reporting exclusions in meta-analyses" and suggest that "bona fide treatments should be defined on empirical and theoretical grounds rather than by judgments of the investigators' intent."

A second problem is that meta-analyses often include poor-quality studies with major methodological limitations, ranging from small sample sizes, inadequate outcome measures, failure to use intent-to-treat analyses, and lack of evidence of treatment integrity. Certainly there have been proponents of meta-analysis who would recommend excluding methodologically inferior studies (Strube & Hartmann, 1982), but this is not always the case. Bad research can lead to false conclusions with adverse consequences. In a study of standard counseling services in the National Health System in the UK, Stiles, Barkham, Mellor-Clark, & Connell (2007) concluded that these different forms of treatment were not only equally effective but also yielded outcomes comparable to those obtained in RCTs of empirically supported treatments. In response, Clark et al. (2008) showed that the findings were essentially uninterpretable. First, there was no randomization to treatments. Second, Stiles et al. (2007) included only "completers" in their analysis—patients who complete both pre- and post-treatment measures. Subsequent research by Clark, Fairburn, & Wessely (2009) has established that patients who drop out of treatment in this setting have fared worse than those who continue. Hence the outcome is overstated by Stiles et al. Third, no evidence is provided that any of the treatments was competently administered (see below). Stiles et al. assumed the validity of the Dodo Bird verdict and claimed their results were consistent with this much contested judgment.

It was hoped that meta-analysis would resolve controversies regarding therapeutic efficacy because of its potentially objective and quantitative nature. In reality it has contributed yet another dimension to the long-standing controversy. We should not be surprised. As early as 1982 Strube and Hartmann observed that meta-analysis "requires a series of complex, sometimes arbitrary decisions and sensitivity to a variety of vexing problems" (p. 130) before the computer objectively integrates or disaggregates the data. Given this reality, the rigor of meta-analysis can be more illusory than real, and it is clear that "inevitable dilemmas similar to those faced by the 'literary reviewer' must be faced by the meta-analysts" (Wilson & Rachman, 1983, p. 55).

Meta-analyses undoubtedly have a place in the future evaluation of treatment outcome. Nevertheless, they are no substitute for large-scale, randomized clinical trials with sufficient power and precision to unambiguously evaluate treatment efficacy. Hennekens and DeMets (2009) have recently illustrated how a single well-controlled RCT produced results—with significant patient health implications—at odds with several meta-analyses of smaller, less well-controlled studies in the treatment of myocardial infarction.

It is easy to understand the demand that empirically supported treatments be compared directly with alternative therapies. Hence the importance of a number of well-controlled studies that have compared CBT treatments with pharmacological therapies. Believers in the Dodo Bird verdict tend to ignore this growing body of research. Comparing different psychological treatments with each other in high-quality studies poses particular challenges. A major sticking point is treatment integrity, namely, the degree to which each treatment was delivered in a competent fashion consistent with its conceptual underpinnings. One of many examples is the Bhar and Beck (2009) critique of a meta-analytic review claiming to show that short-term psychoanalytic psychotherapy is as effective as CBT (Leichsenring et al., 2004). Bhar and Beck point out that it is unknown to what degree studies of CBT were administered in a competent fashion by suitably trained therapists—the issue of treatment integrity.

Ultimately the best means of overcoming this problem is what has been called "adversarial collaboration" in which experts in different psychological treatments work together in a single study in which they vouch for the integrity of their respective therapies in a comparative outcome study. A promising example is the comparative study pitting schema-focused therapy against transference-focused psychotherapy in the Netherlands (Giesen-Bloo et al., 2006). A key element of this multisite study was that experts in both therapies conducted the training of therapists in the respective treatments. The results through three years showed that SFT was significantly more effective than TFP in reducing borderline personality specific psychopathology and improving a number of other measures including quality of life and neuroimaging assessment of emotion regulation. This impressive study may set a standard for future comparative outcome studies to emulate.

Therapists and therapies

Psychotherapists who subscribe to the view that all treatments are equally effective explain the hypothesized phenomenon by arguing that common factors among different treatments are more potent than any specific therapy component (e.g., Messer & Wampold, 2002). Furthermore, the overridingly most powerful factor is said to be the therapists themselves and the therapeutic alliance they develop with their patients. This is one of the most persistent and widely shared assumptions among traditional psychotherapists. In its more extreme form the contention is that specific treatments are essentially irrelevant provided that the therapist has the appropriate expertise.

Objections to this article of faith are many. One is that the "common factor" finding derives mostly from flawed research—the study of weak if not ineffective treatments or substandard implementation of effective treatments. Consensus exists that the therapist is important in the administration of effective treatment and under these circumstances the therapist's influence will be maximized. Second, it is at odds with robust findings of well-controlled RCTs showing no therapist effects in studies demonstrating the superiority of one treatment over another (e.g., Loeb et al., 2005). In these studies all therapists are trained to a high level of competence in the implementation of both treatments under investigation. Hence differences between treatments can be unambiguously attributed to specific treatment effects of the therapies.

Other sources of evidence point to the efficacy of specific treatments. For example, therapists obtain improved outcomes as they become more competent in cognitive therapy for depression (DeRubeis, Hollon, et al., 2005). In contrast, the evidence shows that therapists do not achieve better results through experience per se (Bickman, 1999; Dawes, 2004). Therapist factors are not necessarily "nonspecific" as the common processes belief dictates. Detailed analysis of the Giesen-Bloo et al. (2006) study summarized above showed that the "type of treatment differentially affects the quality and development of the therapeutic alliance" and that "the therapeutic relationship and specific techniques interact with and influence one another" in producing change in SFT (Spinhoven, Giesen-Bloo, van Dyck, Kooiman, & Arntz, 2007). Finally, the "common factors" view flies in the face of rigorous evidence-based guidelines (e.g., NICE) as well as rapidly developing forms of effective guided self-help and internet-based interventions as noted above.

The oft-cited correlation between measures of the therapeutic alliance and treatment outcome cannot disentangle cause from consequence (DeRubeis, Brotman, & Gibbons, 2005). We need studies that examine temporal relationships in the interaction between the therapeutic relationship and change on outcome measures. Preliminary research of this nature indicates that the therapeutic relationship does not mediate outcome in studies of CBT (DeRubeis, Brotman, et al., 2005), but that it may in other psychotherapies such as brief dynamic therapy (Barber, Connolly, Crits-Christoph, Gladis, & Siqueland, 2000).

In summarizing the "common factors" view, Messer and Wampold (2002, p. 23) stated that "Because more variance is due to therapists than the nature of treatment, clients should seek the most competent therapist possible (which is often well known within a local community of practitioners) rather than choosing a therapist by expertise in empirically-supported treatments." The opposing view would be to counsel patients to consult well-trained therapists capable of competently implementing empirically supported treatments. An important RCT on the treatment of borderline personality disorder has put these two competing viewpoints to a rigorous empirical test. Linehan et al. (2006) compared DBT with what was called community treatment by experts (CTBE). DBT was administered by less experienced therapists including graduate students in clinical psychology. CTBE was carried out by therapists nominated by community mental health leaders for their ability to work successfully with difficult-to-treat patients. The CTBE supervision group during the study was led by the director of the Seattle Psychoanalytic Society and Institute and therapists were allowed to use their preferred (non-CBT and non-DBT) approach. Among other outcome measures the DBT treatment resulted in half as many suicide attempts and self-injurious acts, and significantly fewer psychiatric hospitalizations than the CTBE condition.

Contemporary Trends: Clinical Practice

The so-called golden age of clinical psychology in the US proved to be short-lived, as the field has had to confront both internal and external forces that continue to pose serious challenges to the field. I begin with the internal dissension and controversy within clinical psychology.

In 1995, a group of academic clinical psychologists under the leadership of Richard McFall founded the Academy of Psychological Clinical Science (APCS), an association of U.S. and Canadian doctoral training programs in clinical and health psychology. They proposed yet a third approach to clinical training—the clinical scientist model (McFall, 2006). The model seeks to unify research and practice within the framework of psychology as an applied science. Training in clinical science, as opposed to specialized practitioner training, would be the central goal of all doctoral level training in psychology. Within 10 years the Academy comprised 54 member programs—45 university-based Ph.D training programs (primarily from many of the most distinguished and highly rated psychology departments in North America) and nine predoctoral internship programs.

The debate among the respective merits of the different models of clinical training shows no sign of abating. Critics of the Psy.D. point out that admission to these programs is significantly less selective than those of Ph.D programs, that Psy.D. graduates of these programs receive inferior training in applied science, and that they perform less well on a standardized test that is part of the licensing exam (McFall, 2006). Critics of the clinical science model argue that it devalues the importance of clinical practice and fails to prepare graduates adequately for the wide-ranging demands of practice (Peterson, 1996, 2003). The clinical scientist model requires clinicians to be scientists who contribute accumulating knowledge to the field. No distinction is drawn between science and practice. Critics argue that this is unrealistic. Producing well-trained practitioners who are intelligent consumers of science is what other health care professions such as medicine and nursing do (Cummings cited in Yalom, 2009).

Recent events indicate that the controversy over relative emphases on science and practice in clinical training is likely to be taken to an even higher level. The trigger is the launching by APCS in 2007 of a new accreditation system—the Psychological Clinical Science Accreditation System (PCSAS)—for competence in psychological clinical science. To this day accreditation of all clinical psychology training programs, Ph.D. and Psy.D. alike, is conducted by the APA which accordingly exercises the ultimate control over clinical training and subsequent licensing for clinical practice. The APCS and other critics have faulted the APA accreditation system on a number of counts, including an insufficient commitment to scientific training and unwarranted interference in doctoral programs' curricula and degree requirements that regulatory demands entail. A central element in this debate is the failure of the current system to require specific training and competence in empirically-supported treatments (Baker et al., 2009), a transcendent issue to which I now turn.

Evidence-based treatment

As described earlier in this chapter, the past 30 years has seen the development and evaluation of a number of empirically supported psychological treatments, primarily forms of CBT, for a range of clinical disorders in children and adults (e.g., Baker et al., 2009; NICE, 2004a, 2004b). It is also the case that these treatments are not widely implemented in routine clinical service either in North America or Europe (Shafran et al., 2009). Nevertheless, one outstanding exception to this situation is a revolutionary development taking place in the expansion of evidence-based psychological therapy in the UK (Clark et al., 2009).

Increasing Access to Psychological Therapy (IAPT). In 2007 the UK government announced the funding of a major expansion in the provision of psychological treatment services known as Improving Access to Psychological Therapy (IAPT). The unprecedented investment would be devoted to training and employing at least 3,600 new psychological therapists offering evidence-based treatment within the first three years. Two developments, in particular, were behind this change in public policy. The first was the publication between 2004 and 2007 of clinical guidelines by NICE documenting the efficacy of specific psychological therapies (mainly CBT) for depression and anxiety disorders. The second was a detailed economic analysis arguing that these treatments would largely pay for themselves by reducing welfare benefits and medical costs on the one hand, and increasing revenue through improved work productivity on the other (Layard et al., 2006).

The results from two initial demonstration sites are now available and the news is good (Clark et al., 2009). Using a stepped-care approach in which "low-intensity" interventions (e.g., guided self-help) were implemented where appropriate before moving to "high-intensity" treatments, large numbers of patients were treated. A session-by-session outcome monitoring system proved feasible and resulted in an unusually complete data set. The clinical outcomes were favorable and in line with expectations based on the NICE recommendations. Roughly 55% of patients were rated as recovered, and largely maintained their improvements at 10 month follow-up. The promising findings of the IAPT initiative thus far go well beyond enhancing the well-being of patients receiving these services. Of theoretical and practical significance is that it shows that the findings of controlled research (RCTs) can indeed be generalizable to routine clinical practice contrary to the many critics of research-based treatment (e.g., Westen et al., 2004). In this connection it is also noteworthy that the outcomes were comparable across different ethnic groups. As noted above, a priority for clinical research in the US is to demonstrate its relevance and applicability to racially and culturally diverse populations of patients. In the event that this ground-breaking initiative continues to succeed it is likely to influence clinical services in other parts of the world. For example, as noted by Rachman and Wilson (2008, p. 294), "in 2006 Australia introduced a scheme to provide better access to psychological treatment: 'It is recommended that cognitive behaviour therapy be provided' or any other evidence-based psychological treatment, as deemed relevant (www.psy.org.au/medicare/)."

Despite its apparent success, the IAPT initiative has not been without some critics in the UK. It has been in the US, however, that opposition to this sort of endorsement and implementation of empirically supported treatments based on NICE guidelines has been most concerted.

Opposition to manual-based, empirically supported treatments. As noted earlier, the relatively rapid emergence of RCTs showing the efficacy of specific (mainly CBT) treatments has been met with a range of objections such as the claim that tightly controlled research studies have little if any relevance to clinical practice in the "real world," that all forms of psychotherapy are equally effective, and that it is the contribution of the therapist per se that is most important. Not surprisingly, given these widely shared sentiments, the APA does not require doctoral programs in clinical psychology to include training in empirically supported treatments, a major reason for the development of the PCSAS (Baker et al., 2009). For example, in their national survey of training in psychotherapy across different disciplines, Weissman et al. (2006) reported that only 20% of Psy.D. programs required clinical supervision in CBT, the dominant evidence-based treatment. Interestingly, psychiatry was more likely to mandate supervision in CBT than psychology training programs as a whole.

In a recent move the APA has embraced the concept of "evidence-based practice" (EBP) (APA Presidential Task Force on Evidence-Based Practice, 2006). The concept is defined as "the integration of the best available research with clinical expertise in the context of patient characteristics, culture, and preferences" (p. 284). The problem with the APA position is that the choice of treatment ultimately depends on the clinical judgment of the individual practitioner who is supposed to integrate these three different sources of information in formulating a treatment plan. Extensive research dating back to Meehl's (1986) classic book on actuarial versus clinical judgment has clearly revealed the limitations of subjective clinical judgment of precisely the sort elevated to such an important status in the APA scheme of EBP. The remarkably consistent evidence on this issue can be summarized as follows: "In predicting behavior, highly trained clinical experts who assess all available information, and integrate it based on their own understanding of the details of the individual case, do no better and usually worse than actuarial prediction" (Dawes, Faust, & Meehl, 1989, p. 1670). Surveys have shown that therapists often choose components of evidence-based treatment manuals based on their clinical experience or subjective preference, hence omitting or diluting what may be the most effective therapeutic elements of the treatment package (von Ranson & Robinson, 2006; Waller, 2009). It is precisely these well-documented limitations in decision making and case formulation that necessitate the type of treatment guidelines exemplified by the NICE recommendations, but which are eschewed by the APA and similar traditional clinical positions (Dawes, 1994; Wilson, 1996).

Proponents of a scientifically based approach to treatment argue that we must differentiate between types of evidence, and assign primary value to empirical research (i.e., RCTs). Illustrating this view, Wilson and Shafran (2005) advocated that "where sufficient evidence exists to allow a general recommendation, the best practice must be to implement the treatment that enjoys the most empirical support rather than invoke subjective judgment" (p. 81). In stark contrast, the APA position scheme deliberately does not assign priority value to empirical research in clinical decision making. As Wampold, Goodheart, and Levant (2007) have stated, the APA report does not "privilege certain types of evidence." The battle lines are clearly drawn. Whereas the APA position allows the preservation of the status quo, the scientific approach represented in the IAPT and promoted by the APCS and other groups calls for radical change in the overall training of therapists and clinical practice.

Managed care

I turn now to some of the external influences that have so heavily impacted the profession of clinical psychology in the US. The advent and expansion of managed care in the 1980s changed the practice of psychotherapy in the US. Managed care is a system with cost containment as its principal goal and its effects have been dramatic. It has reduced mental health's overall share of the money spent on health care, limited the number of therapy sessions that insurance companies would reimburse, and lowered fees for service (Karon, 1995). Despite these relatively less favorable working conditions for clinical psychologists providing psychotherapy than in previous years, there has been no drop in demand for clinical training especially in Psy.D. programs (see below). However, one of the consequences of managed care and reduced reimbursement for psychotherapy was the proliferation of professionals from other disciplines seeking to offer psychotherapy. Writing in 2005, Benjamin predicted that "Master's-level practitioners, under a variety of labels (e.g., licensed professional counselors, mental health counselors, marriage and family therapists) will become the dominant providers of psychotherapy" (p. 25). That is already the case. The demand for doctoral-level clinical psychologists as providers of psychotherapy has declined and shows no sign of recovering. Competition for providing psychotherapy is fierce, not the least from social workers. Weissman et al. (2006) reported that together with clinical psychology, social work has the largest number of students in training to provide psychotherapy who are also, with Psy.D. graduates, the least likely to be skilled in evidence-based treatments.

The loss of their former pre-eminence in the provision of psychotherapy left clinical psychologists with the need to redefine their professional identity. The result has been continued dissension and debate within the field. One option favored by the APA leadership has been to try to obtain prescription privileges for clinical psychologists through legislative reform in the various states in the US (DeLeon, Sammons, & Sexton, 1995). This policy decision sparked a major ongoing controversy within the field. Opponents have argued that this attempt to "medicalize" psychology would only harm the training of competent clinical psychologists. The concern is that the necessary psychological knowledge and skills in the application of that knowledge would necessarily be short-changed given the time that would be need to be devoted to coursework and practice in pharmacotherapy. Critics have also pointed out that it is no longer psychiatrists who typically prescribe medication for psychological disorders, but primary care physicians. In short, the job market for writing prescriptions no longer seems as inviting as it once was.

An alternative response to managed care and its impact on clinical practice is to improve doctoral training in clinical psychology along the lines articulated by the APSC. According to this view, what makes clinical psychology distinctive and ultimately of professional value is its basis in the discipline of scientific psychology. No other discipline can provide comparably sophisticated education and training in psychological science and its applications. Training clinical psychologists to be competent and versatile providers of evidence-based treatment would be the course of action most likely to make them and their skills indispensable within the broader framework of health care. A key feature of this proposal is that evidence-based treatments are cost-effective as discussed earlier in this chapter. The model here would be the IAPT initiative in the UK that is calculated to pay for itself in providing greatly improved mental health services to the population.

Future Developments

Although effective treatments are now available for a range of different clinical disorders, the need remains to develop still more effective interventions that will benefit individuals for whom current methods do not work. Central to this task will be increasingly sophisticated research on mechanisms and moderators of therapeutic change.

Mechanisms of therapy outcome

Understanding mechanisms of change, namely, how treatments achieve their effects, will enable clinicians to focus more directly on and refine active therapeutic components of treatment protocol (Murphy, Cooper, Hollon, & Fairburn, 2009). Importantly, inactive or redundant components can be eliminated (Kraemer, Wilson, Fairburn, & Agras, 2002). The result would be treatment that is both more effective and more efficient.

Integrating different treatments. Increasingly, evidence-based psychological treatments such as CBT are being used in combination with pharmacological therapies. "Psychotherapy integration," in which different psychological treatments would be combined (integrated), continues to have considerable and widespread appeal to practitioners. In both cases it would seem essential to identify the mechanisms of change in the different psychological and pharmacological treatments to facilitate the desired synergistic or additive effect. Absent this understanding, it is possible that the treatments might simply prove redundant or, worse, undermine one another's efficacy. For example, therapists commonly report an eclectic orientation in which they combine CBT techniques with other therapies including psychodynamic therapy. The effectiveness of this strategy is unknown. Simply culling specific techniques from total CBT treatment protocols is unlikely to be as effective as competently administered, manual-based CBT protocols.

Integrating psychological treatment with medication also poses potential problems. For example, combining CBT with medication in the treatment of anxiety disorders has yielded mixed results. Major controlled studies have shown both beneficial (e.g., Walkup et al., 2009) or adverse effects of the combination (e.g., Barlow, Gorman, Shear, & Woods, 2000). An intriguing exception to the atheoretical or trial-and-error integration of treatments has been combining exposure treatment for anxiety disorders with the drug D-cycloserine. The latter is an agonist at the receptors in the brain where extinction learning has been shown to occur. In short, both the drug and behavioral (exposure) treatments appear to be acting in concert via the same brain mechanisms. Initial results of this combined treatment suggest that it is significantly more efficient than exposure treatment alone (Hofmann, 2007). This translational research stands as an instructive example of the potential benefits of incorporating future advances in neuroscience in psychological treatment

Comorbidity. The traditional approach to addressing complex cases with psychiatric comorbidity has been to expand treatment, to use more techniques aimed at the co-occurring problems. A classic example of this strategy is Lazarus's (1981) multimodal therapy. Multifaceted treatment packages might well be necessary to address certain complex clinical disorders, but the identification of mechanisms of change might provide an alternative approach at least in some instances. For example, Craske et al. (2007) found that a single targeted CBT treatment for panic disorder yielded more positive influences on co-occurring anxiety disorders than multiple treatments aimed at the comorbidities. The authors of this study hypothesized that the single treatment targeted the core underlying mechanism maintaining the related problems.

Moderators of therapy outcome

Treatment outcomes would be significantly enhanced if we could match treatments to specific problems in particular patients. Knowledge of nonspecific predictors of treatment outcome let alone the interaction of patient subtypes with different treatments (moderators) is limited (Kraemer et al., 2002), although increasingly well-designed studies have begun to target the identification of both predictor and moderator variables. Two examples from the treatment of depression can illustrate the practical value of moderators of change.

In the first, evidence exists showing that, in general, both CBT and IPT are effective treatments for depression. However, in two comparative studies of these therapies, CBT proved superior to IPT in patients with a comorbid personality disorder (Joyce et al., 2007), with greater adult attachment insecurity (McBride et al., 2006), and greater severity of depression (Luty et al., 2007). In the second, a large, multi-site RCT showed that on the whole CBT was as effective as antidepressant medication (ADM) at post-treatment (DeRubeis, Hollon, et al., 2005). CBT was significantly more effective in those patients with histories of taking ADM (Leykin et al., 2007) and in those who were unemployed and reported high levels of negative life events prior to treatment (Fournier et al., 2009). However, ADM was superior to CBT in patients with a comorbid personality disorder (Fournier et al., 2006). Clearly these findings must be regarded as preliminary pending subsequent replication. Nevertheless, they show how research of this sort would provide important practical information for making critical treatment choices.

Practitioners want to know if a specific treatment is the most effective for a particular patient. Yet as Kraemer, Frank, and Kupfer (2006) point out, this is an unanswerable question: "the best science can do is provide evidence for how well a given treatment works for a study population that shares with a given patient the same characteristics pertinent to the success of the treatment" (p. 1286). There can be no shortcut via the analysis of individual case studies as has too often been the case in traditional psychotherapies. Large-scale studies with adequate statistical power for examining hypothesized moderators will be necessary.

Dissemination and implementation

Existing evidence-based treatments are not being adopted and implemented in routine clinical practice. Moreover, even when patients do receive these treatments they are delivered in a less than optimal or competent manner (Shafran et al., 2009). The director of the National Institute of Mental Health (NIMH) in the US highlighted this problem in the following statement: "We have powerful, empirically-supported psychosocial interventions, but they are not widely available. ... A serious deficit exists in training for empirically-supported psychosocial interventions. ... Translational research will need to focus not only on 'bench to bedside' but also on 'bedside to practice' " (Insel, 2009).

With few exceptions, research on psychological treatments has focused on its efficacy and effectiveness as summarized earlier in this chapter. There is now a pressing need to undertake research on dissemination and implementation. The former has been defined as the targeted distribution of treatments, the latter as the strategies required to integrate evidence-based treatments within diverse clinical service settings (Proctor et al., 2009). The chief concerns of implementation are not patient outcomes per se, but the acceptability, feasibility, sustainability, and cost of the treatment within the service setting.

Barriers to dissemination and implementation. One barrier is that too few clinicians are being trained in how to implement effective treatments, many of which are relatively recent developments. The need is to identify and assess competency levels required for therapists to implement empirically supported treatments effectively. We must develop effective and efficient methods of training and supervision that would be feasible for widespread use. Dissemination that requires labor-intensive training followed by ongoing supervision will be limited by the availability of relevant experts in these treatments. Web-based training and supervision is beginning to be investigated as a feasible yet effective alternative to traditional modes of training (Cucciare, Weingardt, & Villafranca, 2008).

A second barrier is the nature of the treatment itself. Less complex treatments require less training. Guided self-help, computer-based, and similar "low-intensity" interventions enjoy obvious advantages in this respect (Greist, 2008). Computer-based self-help programs or clinician-assisted internet-based programs, which have been shown to be effective in treating anxiety and depression as summarized above (Andersson, 2009), by their very nature lend themselves to improving dissemination and global implementation (Andrews & Titov, 2009). Hayes (2004, p. 2) has criticized the proliferation of treatment manuals aimed at specific clinical disorders, arguing that "such a 'brute force' empirical approach makes it increasingly difficult to teach what is known or to focus on what is essential." The counter to this objection has been the increasing development of transdiagnostic treatments that treat similar disorders using interventions that may target core underlying processes common to a range of diagnostic categories (e.g., Craske et al., 2009; Fairburn, 2008). These treatments offer greater flexibility in the pacing and content of treatment while still providing structure. By being "therapist-friendly" the goal is also to make them more feasible and acceptable in routine clinical practice.

A third barrier has been the typically strained relationship between researchers and practitioners as described in the historical overview in this chapter. Westen et al. (2005) have observed that "clinicians do not want to be disseminated on" (p. 431). Researchers need to find a more constructive and collaborative means of working with practitioners than has traditionally been the case. One such model is the community-partnership approach involving a "collaborative, cyclical and iterative process" between researchers and practitioners (Becker, Stice, Shaw, & Woda, 2009). A revealing illustration of the likely benefits of this model is provided by Andrews and Titov (2009) in Australia. Despite accumulating research evidence on the effectiveness of a psychological treatment for stuttering, the uptake of this approach among speech pathologists, who dominated clinical services in this area, was minimal. The situation changed and the program was more broadly implemented when speech pathologists themselves began to research and modify the treatment.

As appealing as the prospect of partnering with practitioners might be for clinical researchers, in general the still unanswered question, as Proctor et al. (2009) pose, is to what extent can this collaboration encourage local adaptation of research-based treatments, thereby improving adoption and implementation, without compromising effectiveness?

Concluding Comments

It was only 50 years ago that the landmark meeting in Boulder, Colorado, produced the original blueprint for what was to become the science and practice of clinical psychology not just in the US but around the world. The field has flourished in ways that those pioneers of clinical psychology perhaps could not have fully imagined. For all the internecine disputes about the optimal model of training and the continuing controversies over the right balance between research and practice, clinical psychology has emerged as a dominant force in the politics and provision of mental health services in the US and the UK. Other countries seem poised to follow in the same footsteps.

The concept of evidence-based practice of psychological therapy, derived from the earlier advances in evidence-based medicine, is now widely embraced although the details are still hotly debated in the US and elsewhere as discussed earlier in this chapter. With very few exceptions, it has been clinical psychologists who have developed, implemented, and evaluated evidence-based treatments such as CBT. Continuing innovations in treatment (e.g., the "third wave" of behavior therapy) are the work of clinical psychologists. These psychological treatments are proving as effective, if not more so in some instances, than the pharmacological therapies that are the mainstay of psychiatry. Importantly, they may also be more cost-effective in the long run.

The influential role of clinical psychology is likely to extend beyond mental health to health care in general (Benjamin, 2005). The same principles and procedures of evidence-based therapy that are effective in treating traditional psychiatric disorders have already been shown to be effective in improving the lives of patients with wide-ranging medical problems and illnesses, including pain management, cardiovascular disease, gastrointestinal disorders, headaches, HIV/AIDS, and sleep disorders such as insomnia. The special issue of the *Journal of Consulting and Clinical Psychology* in June 2002 provided an instructive summary of many of the advances in what has come to be known as behavioral medicine. No less a visionary than Nicholas Cummings (see Yalom, 2009) has sketched out the future contributions that clinical psychologists have to make to overall health care beyond its traditional purview, and how this might happen.

Underpinning these applications of clinical psychology to both mental health and health care in general is the field's grounding in the discipline of scientific psychology (McFall, 2006; Peterson, 2003). In the ultimate analysis, this is the distinctive strength of clinical psychology and the platform for integrating the groundbreaking advances in behavioral and cognitive neuroscience into clinical applications in the future.

Note

1 I am grateful to Rebecca Greif for her critical reading of this chapter.

References

American Psychiatric Association. (1980). *Diagnostic and statistical manual of mental disorders.* Washington, DC: American Psychiatric Association.

Andersson, G. (2009). Using the internet to provide cognitive behaviour therapy. *Behaviour Research and Therapy, 47*, 175–180.

Andersson, G., Bergström, J., Holländare, F., Carlbring, P., Kaldo, V., & Ekselius, L. (2005). Internet-based self help for depression: A randomised controlled trial. *British Journal of Psychiatry, 187*, 456–461.

Andrews, G. & Titov, N. (2009). Hit and miss: Innovation and the dissemination of evidence based psychological treatments. *Behaviour Research and Therapy 47*, 974–979.

APA Presidential Task Force on Evidence-Based Practice. (2006). Evidence-based practice in psychology. *American Psychologist, 61*, 271–285.

Baker, T., McFall, R., & Shoham, V. (2009). Current status and future prospects of clinical psychology: Toward a scientifically principled approach to mental and behavioral health care. *Psychological Science in the Public Interest, 9*, 67–103.

Bandura, A. (1969). *Principles of behavior modification.* New York: Holt.

Bandura, A. (2004). Swimming against the mainstream: The early years from chilly tributary to transformative mainstream. *Behaviour Research and Therapy, 42*, 613–630.

Barber, J. P., Connolly, M. B., Crits-Christoph, P., Gladis, & Siqueland, L. (2000). Alliance predicts patients' outcome beyond in-treatment change in symptoms. *Journal of Consulting and Clinical Psychology, 68*, 1027–1032.

Barlow, D. H., Gorman, J. M., Shear, M. K., & Woods, S. W. (2000). Cognitive-behavioral therapy, imipramine, or their combination for panic disorder. *Journal of the American Medical Association, 283*, 2529–2536.

Beck, A. T., Rush, J., Shaw, B., & Emery, G. (1979). *Cognitive therapy of depression.* New York: Guilford Press.

Becker, C. B., Stice, E., Shaw, H., & Woda, S. (2009). Use of empirically supported interventions for psychopathology: can the participatory approach move us beyond the research-to-practice gap? *Behaviour Research and Therapy, 47*, 265–274.

Benish, S. G., Imel, Z. E., & Wampold, B. E. (2008). The relative efficacy of bona fide psychotherapies for treating post-traumatic stress disorder: A meta-analysis of direct comparisons. *Clinical Psychology Review, 28*, 746–758.

Benjamin, L. T. (2005). A history of clinical psychology as a profession in America (and a glimpse at its future). *Annual Review of Clinical Psychology, 1*, 1–30.

Bhar, S. S., & Beck, A. T. (2009) Treatment integrity of studies that compare short-term psychodynamic psychotherapy with cognitive-behavior therapy. *Clinical Psychology: Science and Practice, 16*, 370–378.

Bickman, L. (1999). Practice makes perfect and other myths about mental health services. *American Psychologist, 54*, 965–978.

Chambless, D. L. & Ollendick, T. H. (2001). Empirically supported psychological interventions: Controversies and evidence. *Annual Review of Psychology, 52*, 685–716.

Clark, D., Layard, R., Smithies, R., Richards, D.A., Suckling, R., & Wright, B. (2009). Improving access to psychological therapy: Initial evaluation of two UK demonstration sites. *Behaviour Research and Therapy, 47*, 910–920.

Clark, D. M., Fairburn, C. G., & Wessely, S. (2008). Psychological treatment outcomes in routine NHS services: A commentary on Stiles et al. (2007). *Psychological Medicine, 38*, 629–634.

Craske, M. G., Farchione, T. J., Allen, L. B., Barrios, V., Stoyanova, M., & Rose, R. D. (2007). Cognitive behavioral therapy for panic disorder and comorbidity, more of the same or less of more? *Behaviour Research and Therapy, 45*, 1096–1109.

Craske, M. G., Roy-Byme, P. P., Stein, M. B., Sullivan, G., Sherbourne, C. & Bystritsky, A. (2009). Treatment for anxiety disorders: Efficacy to effectiveness to implementation. *Behaviour Research and Therapy, 47*, 931–937.

Cucciare, M. A., Weingardt, K. R., & Villafranca, S. (2008). Using blended learning to implement evidence-based psychotherapies. *Clinical Psychology: Science and Practice, 15*, 299–307.

Dawes, R. M. (1994). *House of cards: Psychology and psychotherapy built on myth.* New York: Free Press.

Dawes, R. M., Faust, D., & Meehl, P. (1989) Clinical versus actuarial judgment. *Science, 243*, 1668–1674.

DeLeon, P. H., Sammons, M. T., & Sexton, J. L. (1995). Focusing on society's real needs: Responsibility and prescription privileges? *American Psychologist, 50*, 1022–1032.

DeRubeis, R. J., Brotman, M. A., & Gibbons, C. J. (2005). A conceptual and methodological analysis of the nonspecifics argument. *Clinical Psychology: Science and Practice, 12*, 174–183.

DeRubeis, R. J., Hollon, S. D., Amsterdam, J. D., Shelton, R. C., Young, P. R., Salomon, R. M., O'Reardon, J. P., Lovett, M. L., Gladis, M. M., Brown, L. L., & Gallop, R. (2005). Cognitive therapy vs. medications in the treatment of moderate to severe depression. *Archives of General Psychiatry, 62*, 409–416.

Ehlers, A., Bisson, J., Clark, D. M., Creamer, M., Pilling, S., Richards, D., Schnurr, P., Turner, S., & Yule, W. (2010). Do all psychological treatments really work the same in posttraumatic stress disorder? *Clinical Psychology Review, 30*, 269–276

Fairburn, C. G. (2008). *Cognitive behavioural therapy and the eating disorders.* New York: Guilford Press.

Fournier, J. C., DeRubeis, R. J., Shelton, R. C., Gallop, R., Amsterdam, J. D., & Hollon, S. D. (2008). Antidepressant medications v. cognitive therapy in people with depression with or without personality disorder. *British Journal of Psychiatry, 192*, 124–129.

Fournier, J. C., DeRubeis, R. J., Shelton, R. C., Hollon, S. D., Amsterdam, J. D., & Gallop, R. (2009). Prediction of response to medication and cognitive therapy in the treatment of moderate to severe depression. *Journal of Consulting and Clinical Psychology, 77*, 775–787.

Giesen-Bloo, J., van Dyck, R., Spinhoven, P., van Tilburg, W., Dirksen, C., van Asselt, T. et al. (2006). Outpatient psychotherapy for Borderline Personality Disorder. *Archives of General Psychiatry, 63*, 649–658.

Goldstein, A. J., deBeurs, E., Chambless, D. L., & Wilson, K. A. (2000). EMDR for panic disorder with agoraphobia: Comparison with waiting list and credible attention-placebo control condition. *Journal of Consulting and Clinical Psychology, 68*, 947–956.

Greist, J. (2008). A promising debut for computerized therapies. *American Journal of Psychiatry, 165*, 793–795.

Hayes, S. C. (2004). Acceptance and commitment therapy and the new behavior therapies: Mindfulness, acceptance, and relationship. In S. C. Hayes, V. M. Follette, & M. Linehan, (Eds.), *Acceptance, mindfulness, and behavior change* (pp. 1–29). New York: Guilford Press.

Hayes, S. C., Follette, V., & Linehan, M. M. (Eds.) (2004) *Mindfulness and acceptance: Expanding the cognitive-behavioral tradition.* New York: Guilford Press

Hayes, S. C., Luoma, J. B., Bond, F. W., Masuda, A., & Lillis, J. (2006). Acceptance and commitment therapy: Model, processes and outcomes. *Behaviour Research and Therapy, 44*, 1–25.

Hennekens, C. H., & DeMets, D. (2009). The need for large-scale randomized evidence without undue emphasis on small trials, meta-analyses, or subgroup analyses. *Journal of the American Medical Association, 302*, 2361–2362.

Hofmann, S. (2007). Enhancing exposure-based therapy from a translational research perspective. *Behaviour Research and Therapy, 45*, 1987–2001.

Hollon, S. D., Stewart, M. O., & Strunk, D. (2006). Enduring effects for cognitive behavior therapy in the treatment of depression and anxiety. *Annual Review of Psychology, 57*, 11.1–11.31.

Holmes, J. (2002). All you need is cognitive behavioural therapy? *British Medical Journal, 342*, 288–291.

Insel, T. R. (2009). Translating scientific opportunity into public health impact: A strategic plan for research on mental illness. *Archives of General Psychiatry, 66*, 128–133.

Joyce, P. R., McKenzie, J. M., Carter, J. D., Rae, A. M., Luty, S. E., Frampton, C. M. A., & Mulder, R. (2007). Temperament, character and personality disorders as predictors of response to interpersonal psychotherapy and cognitive-behavioural therapy for depression. *British Journal of Psychiatry, 190*, 503–508.

Karon, B. P. (1995). Provision of psychotherapy under managed health care: a growing crisis and national nightmare. *Professional Psychology: Research and Practice, 26*, 5–9.

Klerman, G. L., Weissman, M., Rounsaville, B., & Chevron, E. (1984). *Interpersonal psychotherapy of depression*. New York: Basic Books.

Korman, M. (1974). National conference on levels and patterns of professional training in psychology: The major themes. *American Psychologist, 29*, 441–449.

Kraemer, H., Wilson, G. T., Fairburn, C. G., & Agras, W. S. (2002). Mediators and moderators of treatment effects in randomized clinical trials. *Archives of General Psychiatry, 59*, 877–883.

Kraemer, H. C., Frank, E., & Kupfer, D. J. (2006). Moderators of treatment outcomes. *Journal of the American Medical Association, 296*, 1286–1288.

Latner, J., & Wilson, G. T. (Eds.) (2007). *Self-help for obesity and eating disorders*. New York: Guilford Press.

Layard, R., Bell, S., Clark, D. M., Knapp, M., Meacher, M., Priebe, S., ... Wright, B. (2006). *The depression report: A new deal for depression and anxiety disorders*. London School of Economics. Available at http://cep.1se.ac.uk Centre for Economic Performance Report.

Lazarus, A. A. (1981). *The practice of multimodal therapy*. New York: McGraw-Hill.

Leichsenring, F., Salzer, S., Jaeger, U., Kächele, H., Kreische, R., Leweke, F., ... Leibing, E. (2009). Short-term psychodynamic psychotherapy and cognitive-behavioral therapy in generalized anxiety disorder: A randomized, controlled trial. *American Journal of Psychiatry, 166*, 875–881.

Leykin, Y., Amsterdam, J. D., DeRubeis, R. J., Gallop, R., Shelton, R. C., & Hollon, S. D. (2007). Progressive resistance to SSRI but not to cognitive therapy in the treatment of major depression. *Journal of Consulting and Clinical Psychology, 75*, 267–276.

Linehan, M. M. (1993). *Skills training manual for treating borderline personality disorder*. New York: Guilford Press.

Linehan, M. M., Comtois, K. A., Murray, A. M., Brown, M. Z., Gallop, R. J., Heard H. L., ... Lindenboim, N. (2006). Two-year randomized trial and follow-up of dialectical behavior therapy vs. therapy by experts for suicidal behaviors and borderline personality disorder. *Archives of General Psychiatry, 63*, 757–766.

Lock, J., le Grange, D., Agras, W. S., & Dare, C. (2001). *Treatment manual for anorexia nervosa: A family-based approach*. New York: Guilford Press.

Loeb, K. L., Wilson, G. T., Labouvie, E., Pratt, E. M., Hayaki, J., Walsh, B. T., Agras, W. S., & Fairburn, C. G. (2005). Therapeutic alliance and treatment adherence in two interventions for bulimia nervosa: A study of process and outcome. *Journal of Consulting and Clinical Psychology, 73*, 1097–1106.

Luborsky, L., Singer, B., & Luborsky, L. (1975). Comparative studies of psychotherapies: Is it true that "everyone has won and all must have prizes"? *Archives of General Psychiatry, 32*, 995–1008.

Lunt, I. (2001). History of clinical psychology in Europe. In N. J. Smelser, & P. B. Baltes (Eds.), *International Encyclopedia of the Social and Behavioral Sciences* (pp. 2025–2029). Oxford: Elsevier.

Luty, S. E., Carter, J. D., McKenzie, J. M., Rae, A. M., Frampton, C. M. A., Mulder, R. T., & Joyce, P. R. (2007). Randomised controlled trial of interpersonal psychotherapy and cognitive-behavioural therapy for depression. *British Journal of Psychiatry*, *190*, 496–502.

McBride, C., Atkinson, L., Quilty, L. C., & Bagby, R. M. (2006). Attachment as moderator of treatment outcome in major depression: A randomized control trial of interpersonal psychotherapy versus cognitive behavior therapy. *Journal of Consulting and Clinical Psychology*, *74*, 1041–1054.

McFall, R. M. (2006). Doctoral training in clinical psychology. *Annual Review of Clinical Psychology*, *2*, 21–49.

Meehl, P. (1986). The causes and effects of my disturbing little book. *Journal of Personality Assessment*, *50*, 370–375.

Messer, S. B., & Wampold, B. E. (2002). Let's face facts: Common factors are more potent than specific therapy ingredients. *Clinical Psychology: Science and Practice*, *9*, 21–25.

Mufson, L., Dorta, K. P., Wickramaratne, P., Nomura, Y., Olfson, M. & Weissman, M. M. (2004). A randomized effectiveness trial of interpersonal psychotherapy for depressed adolescents. *Archives of General Psychiatry*, *61*, 577–584.

Murphy, R., Cooper, Z., Hollon, S. D., & Fairburn, C. G. (2009). How do psychological treatments work? Investigating mediators of change. *Behaviour Research and Therapy.*

Nathan, P. E., & Gorman, J. (2007). *Treatments that work* (3rd ed.). New York: Oxford University Press.

NICE. (2004a). *Depression: Management of depression in primary and secondary care (clinical guide 23)*. London, UK: National Institute for Clinical Excellence.

NICE. (2004b). *Anxiety: Management of anxiety (panic disorder, with and without agoraphobia, and generalized anxiety disorder) in adults in primary, secondary and community care (clinical guidance 22)*. London, UK: National Institute for Clinical Excellence.

Ost, L. G. (2008). Efficacy of the third wave of behavioral therapies: A systematic review and meta-analysis. *Behaviour Research and Therapy*, *46*, 296–321.

Peterson, D. R., (1996). Making psychology indispensable. *Applied and Preventative Psychology*, *5*, 1–8.

Peterson, D. R., (2003). Unintended consequences: Ventures and misadventures in the education of professional psychologists. *American Psychologist*, *58*, 791–800.

Proctor, E. K., Landsverk, J., Aarons, G., Chambers, D., Glisson, C., & Mittman, B. (2009). Implementation research in mental health services: An emerging science with conceptual, methodological, and training challenges. *Administration and Policy in Mental Health*, *36*, 24–34.

Rachman, S., & Wilson, G. T. (2008). Commentary. *Behaviour Research and Therapy*, *46*, 293–295.

Raskin, N. J., Rogers, C., & Witty, M. C. (2008). Client-centered therapy. In R. J. Corsini & D. Wedding (Eds.), *Current psychotherapies* (8th ed., pp. 141–186). California: Thomson Brooks/Cole.

Rogers, C. (1951). *Client-centered therapy*. Boston: Houghton Mifflin.

Schmidt, U., Lee, S., Beecham, J., Perkins, S., Treasure, J., Yi, I., Winn, S., … Eisler, I. (2007). A randomized controlled trial of family therapy and cognitive-behavioral guided self-care for adolescents with bulimia nervosa or related disorders. *American Journal of Psychiatry*, *164*, 591–598.

Schramm, E., van Calker, D., Dykierek, P., Lieb, K., Kech, S., Zobel, D., Leonhart, R., & Berger, M. (2007). An intensive treatment program of interpersonal psychotherapy plus pharmacotherapy for depressed inpatients: Acute and long-term results. *American Journal of Psychiatry, 164*, 768–777.

Segal, Z. V., Teasdale, J. D., & Williams, M. (2004). Mindfulness-based cognitive therapy: Theoretical rationale and empirical status. In S. C. Hayes, V. M. Follette, & M. M. Linehan (Eds.). *Mindfulness and acceptance: Expanding the cognitive-behavioral tradition* (pp. 45–65). New York: Guilford Press.

Shafran, R., Clark, D. M., Fairburn, C. G., Arntz, A., Barlow, D. H., Ehlers, A., … Wilson, G. T. (2009). Mind the gap: Improving the dissemination and implementation of CBT. *Behaviour Research and Therapy, 47*, 902–909.

Smith, M. L., & Glass, C. V. (1977). Meta-analysis of psychotherapy outcomes studies. *American Psychologist, 32*, 752–760.

Smith, M. L., Glass, G. V., & Miller, T. (1980). *The benefits of psychotherapy*. Baltimore, Md.: Johns Hopkins University Press.

Spinhoven, P., Giesen-Bloo, J., van Dyck, R., Kooiman, K., & Arntz, A. (2007). The therapeutic alliance in schema-focused therapy and transference-focused psychotherapy in borderline personality disorder. *Journal of Consulting and Clinical Psychology, 75*, 104–115.

Stewart, R., & Chambless, D. (2009). Cognitive-behavioral therapy for adult anxiety disorders in clinical practice: A meta-analysis of effectiveness studies. *Journal of Consulting and Clinical Psychology, 77*, 595–606.

Stiles, W. B., Barkham, M., Mellor-Clark, J., & Connell, J. (2007). Effectiveness of cognitive-behavioural, person-centred, and psychodynamic therapies in UK primary care routine practice: replication in a larger sample. *Psychological Medicine*. Published online: 10 September 2007. doi:10.1017/S0033291707001511.

Stirman, S. W., DeRubeis, R. J., Crits-Christoph, P., & Brody, P. E. (2003). Are samples in randomized controlled trials of psychotherapy representative of community outpatients? *Journal of Consulting and Clinical Psychology, 71*, 963–972.

Strube, M. J., & Hartmann, D. P. (1982). A critical appraisal of meta-analysis. *British Journal of Clinical Psychology, 21*, 129–140.

von Ranson, K. M., & Robinson, K. E. (2006). Who is providing what type of psychotherapy to eating disorder clients? A survey. *International Journal of Eating Disorders, 39*, 27–34.

Walkup, J. T., Albano, A. M., Piacentini, J., Birmaher, B., Compton, S. N., Sherrill, J. T. et al. (2008). Cognitive behavioural therapy, sertraline, or a combination in childhood anxiety. *The New England Journal of Medicine, 359*, 2753–2766.

Waller, G. (2009). Evidence-based treatment and therapist drift. *Behaviour Research and Therapy, 47*, 119–127.

Walsh, B. T., Wilson, G. T., Loeb, K. L., Devlin, M. J., Pike, K. M., Roose, S. P., Fleiss, J., & Waternaux, C. (1997). Medication and psychotherapy in the treatment of bulimia nervosa. *American Journal of Psychiatry, 154*, 523–531.

Wampold, B. E., Goodheart, C. D., & Levant, R. F. (2007). Clarification and elaboration on evidence-based practice in psychology. *American Psychologist, 62*, 616–618.

Weissman, M. M., Verdeli, H., Gameroff, M. J., Bledsoe, S. E., Betts, K., Mufson, L. … Wickramaratne, P. (2006). National survey of psychotherapy training in psychiatry, psychology, and social work. *Archives of General Psychiatry, 63*, 925–934.

Weisz, J. R., Weersing, V. R., & Henggeler, S. W. (2005). Jousting with straw men: Comment on Westen, Novotny, and Thompson-Brenner (2004). *Psychological Bulletin, 131*, 418–426.

Westen, D., Novotny, C. M., & Thompson-Brenner, H. (2004). The empirical status of empirically supported psychotherapies: assumptions, findings, and reporting in controlled clinical trials. *Psychological Bulletin*, *130*, 631–663.

Westen, D., Novotny, C. M., & Thompson-Brenner, H. (2005). EBP + EST: reply to Crits-Christoph et al. (2005) and Weisz et al. (2005). *Psychological Bulletin*, *131*, 427–433.

Whaley, A., & Davis, K. (2007). Cultural competence and evidence-based practice in mental health services: A complementary perspective. *American Psychologist*, *62*, 563–574.

Wilson, G. T. (1996). Manual-based treatments: The clinical application of research findings. *Behaviour Research and Therapy*, *34*, 295–315.

Wilson, G. T., Grilo, C., & Vitousek, K. (2007). Psychological treatment of eating disorders. *American Psychologist*, *62*, 199–216.

Wilson, G. T., & Rachman, S. (1983). Meta-analysis and evaluation of psychotherapy outcome: Limitations and liabilities. *Journal of Consulting and Clinical Psychology*, *51*, 54–64

Wilson, G. T. & Shafran, R. (2005). Eating disorders guidelines from NICE. *The Lancet*, *365*, 79–81.

Wilson, G. T., Wilfley, D. E., Agras, W. S., & Bryson, S. W. (2010). Psychological treatments for Binge Eating Disorder. *Archives of General Psychiatry*, *67*, 94–101.

Yalom, V. (2009). Featured interview with Nick Cummings, PhD. Retrieved from www.psychotherapy.net/interview/Nick_Cummings.

3

Clinical Health Psychology

John Weinman, Ronan O'Carroll,
and Keith J. Petrie

Health psychology is a broad field that focuses on the role of psychological processes in health, illness, and healthcare delivery. In recent years it has used its research base for developing psychological interventions designed to influence a wide range of health-related outcomes for both preventing and controlling chronic physical health problems (Leventhal, Weinman, Leventhal, & Phillips, 2008).

The term "clinical health psychology" is usually applied to the area of health psychology that is concerned with understanding psychological responses of patients with physical health problems, and with the application of psychological interventions in clinical settings. Traditionally its practitioners have a background training in clinical psychology but have chosen to concentrate their research and practice on behavioral aspects of physical health. However, as professional training in health psychology has progressed in recent years, there are now interventions which have been developed and implemented by psychologists who have emerged from training in health psychology (Michie & Abraham, 2004).

In this chapter we will provide a selective overview of three core themes in clinical health psychology research and practice. In the first section, the focus will be on processes involved in symptom perception and the ways in which these influence patients' help-seeking behavior and responses to early diagnostic investigations. The second section will examine the ways in which patients respond to illness and the efficacy of psychological interventions designed to improve both psychological and medical outcomes. The final section is concerned with psychological aspects of treatment, and on the extent to which patients adhere and respond to their treatment.

IAAP Handbook of Applied Psychology, First Edition. Edited by Paul R. Martin, Fanny M. Cheung, Michael C. Knowles, Michael Kyrios, Lyn Littlefield, J. Bruce Overmier, and José M. Prieto.

A unifying model

Health psychology research and practice draws upon a wide range of models for explaining and changing health-related behavior (Conner & Norman, 2005) but only a subset of these has been consistently applied in clinical settings. Although this chapter examines a range of psychological processes from symptom perception to illness coping, there is a theoretical approach that unifies many of its themes, particularly from the patient's perspective. This is the self-regulatory approach, which proposes that, as health threats and illnesses pose a challenge to the self-system and to an individual's key goals, people actively attempt to make sense of these threats in order to minimize their impact. While Carver & Scheier (1998) have provided a generic model of self-regulation, the most widely used model, which has been used in clinical health psychology, is the Common-Sense Model of Self-Regulation (CS-SRM) developed by Leventhal and colleagues (Leventhal et al., 1984). This provides a framework for explaining how the individual attempts to make sense of a health threat by developing both cognitive and emotional representations that then activate behavioral responses (e.g., deciding to seek medical help; following medical advice, etc.).

The individual's initial representations of a health problem (e.g., "my stomach ache is a temporary problem brought on by something specific such as overeating") give rise to specific coping procedures (e.g., not eating; taking antacids), which are then appraised for their effectiveness. If the appraisal process indicates that the mode of coping is not working, then another coping procedure may be selected or the individual may change their perception of the nature of the problem (e.g., "this stomach pain has lasted for the whole day and has not responded to indigestion medication—it must be something more serious") and their response to it (e.g., deciding to seek medical help). At the core of this approach is the individual's own understanding or representation of their problem, and this consists of a number of related beliefs about its nature (Leventhal et al., 1984). Thus, on experiencing a new symptom, the individual will typically provide a label or description and will link this with other symptoms that they are experiencing. These aspects constitute their perceived *identity* of the problem, and this is typically linked with a *causal* explanation, as well as expectations about how long the problem will last (*timeline*), its likely effects (*consequences*), and the extent to which it is amenable to *cure* or *control* by the individual and others such as health care staff. These representations will influence how the individual responds to the initial symptoms and to the results of any subsequent investigation, as well as their evaluation of the appropriateness and efficacy of recommended treatment or advice, as will be described in more detail in different sections below.

Response to Symptoms and Investigations

Symptom perception

Suffering from physical symptoms is a common experience for most people. Studies show that the majority of people suffer from at least one symptom at any given time

(Hannay, 1978; Pennebaker & Skelton, 1978). Mostly these are minor complaints and are not signs of a serious illness. However, common symptoms such as musculoskeletal pain, headache, cough, and nasal congestion are a major cause of reduced functioning and absenteeism from the workplace (Kroenke & Harris, 2001).

While symptoms are often a result of underlying physiological changes, psychological factors also play an important role in both the noticing of symptoms and seeking medical help for the complaint (Eriksen & Ihleback, 2002). Symptom reporting is strongly influenced by attentional factors, cognitive schemas that cause individuals to focus on or expect particular physical sensations, as well as emotional states. In the next section each of these factors is examined in more detail.

A powerful way to influence the noticing of symptoms is to manipulate an individual's attentional focus. Psychologists have found that when an individual's attention is directed away from the external environment and towards the self, the person is more likely to notice symptoms. For example, in one study of individuals exercising on a treadmill, researchers played either an amplification of the participant's breathing or street sounds. The results showed that participants who were played sounds of their own breathing reported more symptoms than the group played street sounds (Pennebaker & Lighter, 1980).

Studies also show that when the environment is lacking in stimulation or interest, individuals turn their attention inwards and are more likely to notice symptoms. This helps explain why people cough more in the boring parts of movies or lectures (Pennebaker, 1980). Epidemiological evidence concerning who is more likely to report symptoms is also supportive of this process. Individuals who live alone, are socially isolated, and who work in the house as opposed to in paid employment tend to report more symptoms (Feder et al., 2001; Pennebaker, 1982). The role of attentional factors in symptom reporting has been explained by the competition for cues theory, which proposes that, as the number and salience of external cues increase, attention to internal stimuli will decrease and, conversely, as the environment becomes less demanding of attention then focus on internal cues will increase (Pennebaker, 1982; Pennebaker & Lighter, 1980). For example, common pain such as toothache is often reported as feeling worse during the night when there is a reduction in external cues.

Along with attentional focus, the way individuals cognitively organize and interpret physiological sensations can have a strong influence on symptom reporting, and the CS-SRM, outlined in the opening section of this chapter, provides an explanatory framework for this. In general, individuals search for information that is consistent with a prevailing schema and disregard information that does not fit. Schemas can be activated quite quickly by giving someone a diagnosis. For example, Croyle and Sande (1988) had participants complete a medical test and then diagnosed some with a completely fictitious illness. Those given an erroneous disease reported more symptoms that they had been told were associated with the condition than did participants who were told they did not have the condition.

Schemas can also influence symptom reporting through existing beliefs or expectations. For example in a multicenter aspirin trial, one of the three centers inadvertently left off information on the consent form about possible gastrointestinal side effects of the drug. The centers where the possible gastrointestinal side effects were given had six times as many participants withdraw from the study due to these symptoms compared to the center that did not include these side effects on the consent form (Myers, Cairns, & Singer, 1987). In other studies perceived sensitivity to mobile phones is associated with the reporting of physical symptoms (Rubin, Cleare, & Wessely, 2008), even though in double blind trials individuals who believe they are sensitive to the effects of electromagnetic fields from mobile phones cannot reliably detect the presence of such radiation (Roosli, 2008). Similarly, people's beliefs that their health is threatened by aspects of modern life such as radiation, genetically modified food, and pollution were more likely to report symptoms following an aerial spray programme designed to eradicate a moth than individuals with low levels of modern health worries (Petrie et al., 2005).

More dramatic examples of the influence of cognitive schemas on symptom reporting are seen in incidents of mass psychogenic illness. In such incidents a large number of people suddenly become unwell, often in response to an unusual environmental event such as an odor or believing that they have been bitten by an insect. A mass psychogenic illness is typically characterized by a rapid increase in cases complaining of nonspecific symptoms such as headache, cough, abdominal pain, and nausea. Symptoms often seem to spread between individuals by line of sight rather than through direct contact and typically resolve relatively quickly. There are hundreds of examples of mass psychogenic illness through history often with a colorful and dazzling array of perceived causes (Evans & Bartholomew, 2009) and often reflecting the social concerns and beliefs of the time (Bartholomew & Wessely, 2002).

The way in which symptoms are perceived has also been shown to play an important role in influencing whether someone decides to seek medical help and how quickly they do so. There is now consistent evidence showing that if patients experience "atypical" symptoms of a potentially serious condition (i.e., those that they would not normally associate with the condition), then they are less likely to believe it is a serious problem and, as a result, are much more likely to delay in seeking help. One medical condition where this type of delay can have serious consequences is myocardial infarction (MI) since the mismatch between patients' pre-existing MI schemas and the symptoms that they experience has been found to be a key factor in patient delay (Horne, James, Petrie, Weinman, & Vincent, 2000; Johansson, Stromberg, & Swahn, 2004). Similarly, but over a longer time period, mismatches between patients' symptoms and their illness schema have also been associated with delay in seeking help in women with breast cancer (Bish, Ramirez, Burgess, & Hunter, 2005). In both these conditions, delay results in a poorer clinical outcome.

Another important factor influencing both the reporting of symptoms and seeking medical care is the patient's emotional state at the time. High trait anxiety and health anxiety have been found to be associated with an increased focus on internal bodily states, which leads to more symptoms being detected and reported (Watson & Pennebaker, 1989). Many patients who do not have significant medical illness but consistently seek medical care for reassurance about their symptoms tend to be high in trait anxiety (Potts & Bass, 1995) and often catastrophize about symptoms (Petrie, Moss-Morris, & Weinman, 1995). Highly anxious patients also tend to be less likely to make normalizing attributions about the causes of common somatic symptoms than other people (Sensky, MacLeod, & Rigby, 1996), and to be more pessimistic about symptoms (Page et al., 2004).

In summary, reports of physical symptoms are strongly influenced by psychological factors, such as attentional focus, cognitive schemas, and emotions. In the next section we look at how these factors can influence the extent to which patients are reassured by the results of diagnostic tests and other related communication in the clinical setting.

Reassurance

Reassurance can be defined as communication between a doctor and patient that is intended to allay the patient's health-related concerns. It is a central part of many medical consultations, and reassuring patients who believe that they are ill is one of the most common interventions provided by doctors. Unfortunately, research shows that in many medical encounters the reassurance provided by doctors is ineffective in reducing patient worry about their health and a large number of patients remain unnecessarily concerned about symptoms following a negative diagnostic test and a reassuring message (Howard & Wessely, 1996; McDonald, Daly, Jelinek, Panetta, & Gutman, 1996).

Reassurance failure leads to unnecessary investigations, inappropriate use of medication, and disability. For example, while chest pain is a common presenting symptom complaint in primary and secondary medical care, the incidence of ischaemic heart disease in general practice patients presenting with a new episode of chest pain is low, and in the majority of cases no identified organic basis for chest pain complaints can be found (Bass, 1991). Follow-up studies show that the reassurance message is often ineffective and patients without significant disease continue to be high users of health care services and report that they cannot perform low or moderately intensive activities "because of my heart" (Lavey & Winkle, 1979; Papanicolaou et al., 1986). Moreover, between 30 and 70% continue to take cardiac medication, and most remain convinced that they have cardiac illness (Lantinga et al., 1988; Potts, & Bass, 1993). Many patients will seek further care and inappropriate investigations because of continued worry about symptoms.

Research has consistently found that a significant proportion of patients fail to be reassured despite receiving normal results. The numbers vary between studies but the proportion of patients not reassured is typically between 30 and 60% (Channer, James, Papouchado, & Rees, 1987; Howard & Wessely, 1996). Also, while many patients' worry is reduced immediately following testing and communication from the doctor about the test results, as time goes on, patients typically become less reassured and often return to levels of anxiety similar to prior to testing (Lucock, Morley, White, & Peake, 1997; McDonald et al.,1996).

The lack of impact of the reassurance message in medical consultations is due to a number of factors, including the influence of medical testing on health perceptions, as well as both patient and doctor variables. The process of being referred for medical testing can, in itself, make feelings of illness vulnerability more salient to patients and can serve to reinforce the patient's belief that there is something seriously wrong with their health. Several studies have found evidence that investigations may not always be useful in reassuring patients, but rather cause harm by creating anxiety and encouraging the patient's illness beliefs (Howard et al., 2005; Peters, 1991).

Both patient and doctor factors also contribute to poor reassurance outcomes. Patients' illness perceptions have been found to be important determinants of reassurance immediately following the investigation and at further follow-up following a stress exercise cardiac test (Donkin et al., 2006). Those patients who had already developed ideas that their illness was going to last a long time were the least reassured following exercise testing. Another factor that is likely to be important in this process is the delay involved, either before the diagnostic test is undertaken or before reassurance is received after testing. A long delay allows more time for negative illness beliefs to become established (Nijher, Weinman, Bass, & Chambers, 2001). This may include negative or catastrophic ideas about symptoms, as well as a reduction in work hours or leisure activities. All of these factors make subsequent reassurance considerably more difficult (Petrie et al., 1995).

Poor medical knowledge and the previous experience of medical misdiagnosis can also undermine successful reassurance. For example, patients undergoing echocardiography for chest pain symptoms or a benign heart murmur were not reassured even though heart disease was ruled out by a normal test result. Later interviews with the patients revealed that many lacked the important understanding that a murmur or symptoms could continue even though there was no heart pathology. Patients with a better understanding had reduced anxiety about their symptoms (McDonald et al., 1996). A recent study found that the ability of patients to identify even major body parts, like the heart, lung, or kidney, is quite limited and, interestingly, no better in patients with organ-specific pathology—such as renal patients identifying the location of the kidney (Weinman, Yusuf, Berks, Rayner, & Petrie, 2009). This lack of basic medical knowledge means patients are often unable to understand the significance or meaning of a negative test.

High anxiety has been associated with lower levels of reassurance in a number of clinical studies including women undergoing bone screening for osteoporosis (Rimes & Salkovskis, 2002), exercise stress testing for chest pain (Channer et al., 1987), and in patients with severe headaches following a neurological consultation (Fitzpatrick & Hopkins, 1981). Anxiety probably undermines reassurance by influencing patients' interpretation statements of likelihood or probability from clinicians. Most reassurance messages contain probability statements and how patients respond to statements such as "I think it is very unlikely that you have bowel cancer" depends on the level of probability that the patient assigns to the phrase "very unlikely." A recent study in a group of patients with a history of unexplained medical complaints found these patients overestimated the likelihood of an illness when listening to a tape recording of a medical report compared to control patients (Rief, Heitmuller, Reisberg, & Ruddel, 2006).

Doctors can also contribute to poor reassurance. An important consideration here is the differing drivers of behavior in doctors and patients. The major consideration for doctors following the presentation of abnormal symptoms is the ruling out of significant pathology; for patients, the focus is more likely to be on an explanation of why the symptoms have occurred or on receiving treatment to reduce symptoms. Symptoms that cannot be explained raise the concern in the doctor that they may be missing important pathology. This can push doctors towards further investigations, which may weaken any concurrent reassurance message (Turner, 2001). Negative investigations may also fail to reassure patients simply because the doctor continues to prescribe medication for the condition and this communicates an ambiguous (mixed) message to the patient regarding their health (Howard et al., 2005).

Some researchers have commented that reassurance is the most widely used, but poorly understood intervention in medicine (Bass, 1990). It is clear from the available research that patients who are not reassured following negative medical investigations are a major source of cost for health systems because they continue to attend medical appointments at high rates, have further medical investigations, and undertake procedures that have a high risk of iatrogenic harm (Page & Wessely, 2003; Reid, Wessely, Crayford, & Hotopf, 2002). There is a pressing need to develop effective psychological interventions to improve reassurance.

Improving reassurance

There have been very few investigations of interventions designed to improve reassurance in medical consultations and randomized controlled trials in this area are rare, despite calls for more such studies (Howard, 1996). Basic information about reassurance is lacking. For example, while diagnostic tests are often ordered as a means of reassuring patients, the results are equivocal as to whether tests do actually reassure patients (Howard et al., 2005; Sox, Margulies, & Sox, 1981).

Most previous studies that have attempted to improve reassurance have done so by increasing the dose of reassurance following the medical investigation. However, this approach does not seem to be successful in reducing symptom concerns. In two studies patients who had previously been reassured by their cardiologist that they did not have cardiac disease but still had symptoms were recruited from general practices (Klimes, Mayou, Pearce, Coles, & Fagg, 1990) or from a cardiology clinic (Mayou et al., 1997). The patients were randomized to 10 hours of cognitive behavioral therapy (CBT) or standard care. CBT was successful in reducing symptoms and improving activity, however, recruitment was difficult as patients were reluctant to be involved in a psychological treatment for what they saw as a "physical" problem. A further study with noncardiac chest pain patients using a brief one-hour intervention following negative results with a booklet and personal follow-up was also unappealing to many patients and did not show any efficacy (Sanders et al., 1997).

While increasing the intensity of the reassurance message may appear logical, by the time patients undergo medical tests many have already developed negative ideas and beliefs about their symptoms, and thus reassurance messages are much less effective (Donkin et al., 2006). Patients' established negative beliefs about their symptoms limit their ability to assimilate reassuring messages that are inconsistent with their personal view of the seriousness of their condition (Nijher et al., 2001). Furthermore, patients' levels of health anxiety and pre-existing negative ideas about their symptoms may mean negative results are reinterpreted in a threatening manner when filtered through higher anxiety and negative illness perceptions. An earlier study of patients with noncardiac chest pain has noted that many patients were unprepared for the possibility of negative findings and lacked a context in which to interpret such results (Sanders et al., 1997).

A new approach has investigated whether giving patients information about the diagnostic test and the meaning of a negative result *prior* to undergoing the investigation would strengthen the reassuring message from the doctor, by giving the patient both a context and a mental schema to help make sense of the diagnostic result. A recent clinical trial found that one month after the test, patients who had received the prior information about the diagnostic test and a brief discussion about the meaning of normal results had significantly fewer complaints of chest pain, were less worried that there was something seriously wrong with their heart, and fewer of them were taking cardiac medication. At one month, patients in the standard care control group were still worried about their health and the majority were not reassured by the investigation (Petrie et al., 2007).

So far in this chapter, we have focused on the role of psychological processes in the early stages of the healthcare process. Once patients have been diagnosed with a specific condition, there is growing evidence that the impact of this will also be influenced by many of the cognitive and emotional processes which affect behavorial responses to symptoms and investigation. We now turn to a consideration of these factors.

Cognitive, Emotional, and Behavioral Response to Illness

When confronted with the diagnosis of a new illness, individuals have to deal with the fact that their state of health and/or bodily functions have changed for the worse, with the possibility that they may not recover to their premorbid level of functioning. Moos and Schaefer (1984) proposed that a diagnosis can be considered a crisis when it involves changes in identity (carer to patient), location (home to hospital), role (independent to passive), or social support (social to isolated) and changes in the future (with career or life plans now uncertain). Adaptation to this new information and illness state obviously varies with disease. For some conditions (MI or stroke), there will be an abrupt, sudden onset whereas in others, such as diabetes, there may be no symptomatic change and the diagnosis may be an unexpected consequence of a routine blood or urine test. Getting used to this new role may require a number of adjustments and adaptations. Patients may need to learn how to cope with their symptoms and/or to deal with the changes required to manage their condition (e.g., dietary change, exercise change, and adherence to medical advice and treatment: Petrie and Reynolds, 2007). Individuals vary in how well they adapt to or cope with this new role. Broad categories of coping have been identified, including approach coping (e.g., adhering to medical advice, lifestyle change) versus avoidance coping (e.g., denial), and emotion- versus problem-focused coping. Some individuals act as if their status is unchanged, whereas others may actively and enthusiastically engage with their new role in an attempt to manage their condition as effectively as possible. As was outlined at the beginning of this chapter, the CS-SRM proposes that individuals evaluate the effectiveness of their chosen coping strategy and then determine whether to continue or to change it. Moreover, the quality of social support that an individual receives can be critical in determining the degree of adaptation to the new role. Chronic illness can place a considerable burden on the individual and their family, and can have a significant impact on the quality of life of both.

Depression and outcome in illness

Depression has been shown to be an important determinant of outcome in many chronic illnesses. Pressure of space precludes a full review, and the interested reader is referred to Steptoe (2007). The relationship between depression and coronary heart disease (CHD) and cancer will be briefly reviewed next.

Depression and prognosis in cardiac patients. Frasure-Smith et al. (1993) published a seminal study of patients who were followed up for six months after a myocardial infarction (MI). After controlling for the effects of left ventricular dysfunction and previous MI, major depression was associated with a fourfold increase in mortality. A larger scale 5-year follow-up study showed that increased risk was observed, not only in those diagnosed with major depression, but depression symptoms had a dose-response relationship with cardiac mortality. The risk associated with depression was independent of, and of a similar magnitude as either having a previous MI or having diabetes or ventricular dysfunction (Lesperance, Frasure-Smith, Talajic, & Bourassa, 2002). There is increasing interest in the association of negative affectivity with social inhibition in cardiac patients. This comorbidity is termed the "distressed personality type," or Type D. In a 6- to 10-year follow-up of CHD patients, after controlling for biomedical factors, those classified as Type D had a fourfold risk of cardiac mortality (Denollet, Pedersen, Vrints, & Conraads, 2006).

Depression/negative affectivity is common in cardiac patients, with estimates of major depressive disorder of about 15% in patients following acute myocardial infarction (Lett, Sherwood, Watkins, & Blumenthal, 2007). Most of the studies reporting a risk associated with depression have been conducted in patients hospitalized following myocardial infarction and have reported large effect size, comparable in magnitude to or greater than traditional risk factors and suggest that the presence of depression confers about 2.5 times the risk of mortality (Barth, Schumacher, & Herrmann-Lingen, 2004; van Melle et al., 2004). A key issue relates to the criticism that depression may merely represent a marker for disease severity and it is this disease severity which ultimately is responsible for increased risk. However, depression appears to confer a unique risk above and beyond any such association (Lett et al., 2007).

A number of plausible mechanisms linking depression and coronary artery disease have been proposed, including poor treatment adherence (see next section), alterations in the autonomic nervous system and hypothalamic pituitary adrenal access functioning, platelet activation, and inflammation (Lett et al., 2004). Depression/Type D may also be associated with more unhealthy behaviors (e.g., smoking, lack of exercise, poor diet; Williams et al., 2008) and/or increased cardiac output under conditions of stress (Williams, O'Connor, & O'Carroll, 2009). Atherosclerosis may also lead to physiological changes associated with the development of depression (Lesperance & Frasure-Smith, 2007).

It is important to distinguish between depression as a risk factor for subsequent coronary heart disease and the identification of new-onset depression in patients who have pre-existing coronary heart disease (e.g., post MI), and whether the presence of depression influences prognosis. Dickens et al. (2008) distinguished between those who were depressed before their MI (pre-MI depression) and those who developed depression in the 12 months after MI (new-onset depression). Cardiac death during 8-year follow-up was predicted by new-onset depression, whereas pre-MI depression did not convey any additional risk of cardiac mortality.

Treating depression in CHD. Over the past 10 years a number of large-scale studies have attempted to treat depression in MI patients in an attempt to improve outcomes. The results of these studies have been disappointing. In the SADHART study, the antidepressant sertraline had no significant effect relative to placebo on the primary outcome, change from baseline in left ventricular ejection fraction. There was a significant improvement in clinical global impression scale, but not on the Hamilton Depression Rating Scale (HRSD) (Glassman et al., 2002). The ENRICHD trial randomized nearly 2,500 patients with depression after MI to usual medical care or CBT-based psychosocial interventions. At 6-month follow-up there was no significant difference in event-free survival between usual care and psychosocial intervention. There was a small improvement in psychosocial outcome at 6 months favouring treatment, a 2-point difference on the HRSD (Berkman et al., 2003). Finally, in the MIND-IT trial, MI patients with depression were randomly allocated to antidepressant treatment versus treatment as usual. At 18 months there was no difference between intervention and control groups either on mean BDI score or presence of ICD-10 depression and the cardiac event rate was similar between the groups—14% in the intervention group and 13% in the control group (van Melle et al., 2007). Taken together, the results of these recent large-scale treatment trials are disappointing, and provide no evidence that treating depression in MI patients improves medical outcomes. The CREATE trial compared the antidepressant citalopram with interpersonal psychotherapy in depressed patients with established coronary artery disease. Citalopram proved superior to placebo at 12 weeks with a 3-point HRSD difference. However, there was no evidence of a beneficial effect of IPT over clinical management, (Lesperance et al., 2007).

In a recent systematic review of the evidence, Thombs et al. (2008) concluded that depression treatment with medication or cognitive behavioral therapy in patients with cardiovascular disease is associated with modest improvement in depressive symptoms, but results in no improvement in cardiac outcomes. A striking finding from these trials is that there is often a significant but only a very modest difference in depression outcome between antidepressant and placebo conditions, and it is thus very difficult to demonstrate that effective treatment of depression improves survival. The cardiac–depression trials to date have been significantly underpowered to demonstrate a small effect on cardiac events or survival (Carney & Freedland, 2007a). Furthermore, in antidepressant trials of *noncardiac* depressed patients, recent evidence points to a striking placebo response, and relatively small differences between active and placebo treatment, particularly in mild/moderate depression (Kirsch et al., 2008). Despite this, Carney and Freedland (2007b) recommend that depressed patients should be identified and treated in order to improve their psychological adjustment, well-being, and quality of life, regardless of whether such treatment can improve medical outcomes.

Depression and cancer. While the prevalence of depression in cancer patients is more common than in the general population, it is only as common as, or a little more common than, in general medical patients (Simon, Palmer, & Coyne, 2007). There are clear problems in the identification of depression in cancer patients as there may be significant overlap between depressive symptoms and the symptoms of cancer and its treatment. Even though there are few randomized-controlled trials of treatments for depression in patients with cancer, they have been shown to respond to several classes of antidepressants (Evans et al., 2005). Sheard and Maguire (1999) published a meta-analysis on the effects of psychological interventions on depression in cancer patients and, after removing outliers with design flaws, the treatment effect size was a very modest 0.19. More promising data were provided by Nezu, Nezu, Felgoise, McClure, and Houts (2003) who showed that problem-solving therapy significantly reduced distress. Recently, Strong et al. (2008) randomly allocated 200 outpatients with cancer and depression to treatment as usual, or nurse-led problem-solving therapy. A significant treatment effect was observed sustained at 6- and 12-month follow-up.

Cognitive Behavioral Interventions

There is now unequivocal evidence that health behaviors are powerful determinants of subsequent morbidity and mortality. For example, Khaw et al. (2008) followed up 20,000 UK individuals over 13 years and recorded smoking, physical inactivity, high alcohol intake, and low fruit and vegetable consumption at baseline. The four health behaviors combined predicted a fourfold difference in mortality risk, which was equivalent to dying 14 years younger if one engaged in the four unhealthy behaviors at baseline. A very brief review of notable health behavior interventions will now be presented, divided into secondary or tertiary interventions. (For primary interventions, see Chapter 4 on Health Promotion).

Secondary interventions

One of the most impressive health behavior interventions in this area was conducted in Finland by Tuomilehto et al. (2001). They identified people who were at high risk of developing Type 2 diabetes (overweight with impaired glucose tolerance). They were randomly assigned to an intensive lifestyle intervention (which included personalized nutritional and dietary advice and supervised exercise) versus a control condition of oral and written advice about diet and exercise. Significant differences emerged in dietary change and exercise, resulting in a reduction in relative risk of developing diabetes in the intervention group (11% versus 23%). At 8-year follow-up there was still a highly protective effect from the intervention in preventing diabetes, with a 36% reduction in relative risk (Lindstrom et al., 2006). Lifestyle interventions are at least as effective as drug treatment aimed at preventing or delaying the development of Type 2 diabetes (Gillies et al., 2007; Knowler at al., 2002). However, an important negative finding was reported by Kinmonth et al. (2008), who recruited a large sample of UK sedentary adults who were at risk of developing Type 2 diabetes. Patients were randomized to a brief advice/motivational leaflet or a 1-year theory-based behavior change programme, aimed at increasing physical activity. The intervention took a self-regulatory approach, focusing on goal setting, action planning, self-monitoring, using rewards, etc. However, no significant differences in physical activity, clinical, or biochemical measures resulted as a consequence of the 1-year intervention. The authors concluded that "Our findings suggest that approaches based on personal education and individual behavior change alone are unlikely to increase physical activity in an environment where there are plentiful inducements to keep still" (Kinmonth et al., 2008, p. 47). This highlights the importance of environmental factors, which many individual-focused psychological interventions tend to ignore. Given the pandemic predictions regarding the global increase in Type 2 diabetes, with associated morbidity and mortality costs, further rigorous evaluation of health-behavior change in high-risk populations is urgently required.

Many of the challenges found in trying to persuade "at risk" individuals to change their behavior or take preventive medication to avoid progression to full-blown disease are very similar to those aimed at improving treatment adherence in patients with definite health problems (see section 3, below).

Tertiary interventions

A range of approaches have been developed for helping patients manage or cope with chronic health problems. Here we first describe approaches to facilitate self-management, followed by an outline of more specific interventions for patients with heart disease and cancer.

Chronic disease self-management interventions. Lorig and colleagues developed an important self-care approach involving lay tutors for arthritis patients. The programme reduced pain and disability, improved quality of life, and reduced utilization of medical services (Lorig & Holman, 2003). These self-management programmes are based on Bandura's social cognitive theory, and focus on self-efficacy as a prerequisite for behavior change. Typically the 6-session program covers relaxation techniques, action planning, problem solving, symptom management, etc. Many health services round the world have now adopted this lay-led "expert patient" model in the hope that it will deliver cost-effective health gains. An early evaluation of the self-management programs in the UK however, revealed that, while the interventions improved participants' self-efficacy, self-rated health, and frequency of exercise, there was no improvement in symptoms, health-related quality of life, or, crucially, health care utilization (Foster, Taylor, Eldridge, Ramsay, & Griffiths., 2007). This has led some critics to question whether these programmes could be made more effective by incorporating slots for clinicians to teach disease management skills (Griffiths Foster, Ramsay, Eldridge, & Taylor, 2007). An example is provided by Davies et al. (2008), who reported on the outcome of the DESMOND trial, a large RCT where patients with newly diagnosed Type 2 diabetes were randomly allocated to usual care versus a 6-hour structured group education program led by two trained health care professionals. The intervention was based on the CS-SRM, dual-process theory and social learning theory and focused on patient empowerment and lifestyle factors such as food choice, physical activity, and cardiovascular risk factors. The intervention resulted in greater reductions in weight, smoking, and depression at 12-month follow-up. However, there was no differential change in Haemoglobin A1c or physical activity levels at 12 months. The general area of self-management and behavioral interventions has recently been well reviewed (Newman, Steed, & Mulligan, 2009).

Psychological rehabilitation interventions in MI patients. Since there is now considerable evidence that psychological factors, particularly patients' cognitions and emotions, can impact strongly on the recovery of MI patients, a number of interventions have been developed from these findings. For example, Lewin, Robertson, Cay, Irving, and Campbell (1992) evaluated a home-based, self-help rehabilitation program versus usual care in MI patients. The intervention was delivered using the *Heart Manual* which contained six weekly sections covering education, stress management, advice for dealing with intrusive distressing thoughts, and psychological problems commonly experienced by post-MI patients. At 1-year follow-up, psychological adjustment was significantly better in the intervention group, and they had significantly less contact with their GP and fewer were readmitted to hospital. A similar study used a 5-week, home-based, workbook-based intervention with stroke patients, aimed at improving outcomes by changing cognitions about control. At 6-month follow-up, the intervention group showed significantly better disability recovery than those in the control group (Johnston et al., 2007). Cardiac rehabilitation interventions that incorporate personalized action plans and coping plans have also been shown to lead to a twofold increase in rates of weekly exercise (Sniehotta et al., 2005; Sniehotta, Scholz, & Schwarzer, 2006).

Given the widespread popularity of the CS-SRM of illness, it is striking how few treatment trials have been published where an attempt has been made to manipulate illness perceptions to therapeutic effect. There have been a huge number of cross-sectional and longitudinal observational studies that have used the CS-SRM to demonstrate clear associations between illness perceptions and a wide number of patient outcomes (see meta-analysis by Hagger and Orbell (2003). However, cross-sectional and longitudinal designs cannot establish causality, and randomized trials are fundamental to establishing the utility of the model in improving patient outcomes. Petrie, Cameron, Ellis, Buick, and Weinman (2002) argued that following MI, specific dysfunctional illness perceptions should be identified and modified at an early stage in order to optimize rehabilitation outcomes. They conducted a brief 3-session intervention, which focused on eliciting and challenging MI patients' illness beliefs and personalized action plans were developed collaboratively. Patients in the intervention group reported they were better prepared for leaving hospital and returned to work quicker than those in the control group (Petrie et al., 2002). These findings were replicated by Broadbent, Ellis, Thomas, Gamble, and Petrie (2009b) in an intervention consisting of four half-hour sessions, including one session with both the patient and their spouse, exploring the spouse's causal perceptions and exploring and normalizing concerns about going home. At 6 months, patients in the intervention group demonstrated positive changes in both causal attribution and understanding of their MI, and had a faster and more successful return to work. In an accompanying paper, (Broadbent, Ellis, Thomas, Gamble, & Petrie, 2009a) reported that the spouses in the intervention arm had higher illness understanding, lower concern, stronger causal attributions to hereditary factors, and fewer questions about their partner's heart condition compared to the control group. At 3-month follow-up spouses in the intervention group were also less worried about the illness.

Cognitive behavioral interventions in breast cancer patients. Cognitive behavioral interventions are also effective in reducing distress amongst people who have undergone medical treatment for cancer. A particularly impressive example is Cognitive Behavioral Stress Management (CBSM) in breast cancer patients. Therapist and participant CBSM treatment manuals have been published by the APA (Antoni, 2002a, 2002b). A 10-week CBSM group intervention has been shown to reduce emotional distress, emotional thoughts about cancer and interpersonal disruption for up to one year in women being treated for stage one to three breast cancer (Antoni et al., 2006b). The CBSM effects appeared to be mediated by women's perceived ability to relax (Antoni et al., 2006a). Women with breast cancer who perceive their partners to be unsupportive benefit more from a couple-focused group intervention (Manne et al., 2005). Furthermore, breast cancer patients with higher initial levels of cancer related stress show greatest reductions in depression and fatigue (Andersen et al., 2004).

Reducing stress could conceivably influence tumor growth activities via mechanisms that include effects on the HPA axis and on immune function (e.g., lymphocyte proliferation and TH1 cytokine production). However, there are relatively few studies in this area which have demonstrated reliable effects on physiological indictors. McGregor and Antoni (2009) propose that future studies should focus more on stress-tumor pathways (e.g., the neuroendocrine processes that promote tumor growth and metastasis), and that these studies should involve larger cohorts, followed up over longer periods of time in order to properly test the effects of psychological interventions on health.

However, whether psychosocial interventions can influence longer-term health outcomes, such as mortality, cancer recurrence, or disease-free intervals is a hotly controversial area (Coyne, Stefanek, & Palmer, 2007). One would have to demonstrate a plausible link between the psychosocial intervention and a biological mechanism affecting tumor growth or metastasis. Greer, Morris, and Pettingale (1979) initially reported an association between denial, helplessness/hopelessness, fighting spirit, and survival in a group of early-stage breast cancer patients. The "fighting spirit" finding attracted widespread attention, with resulting concerns that a belief was being created that "brave and good people defeat cancer and that cowardly and undeserving people allow it to kill them" (Diamond, 1998, p. 52). Watson, Homewood, Haviland, and Bliss (2005) showed that high fighting spirit conferred no survival advantage, but helplessness/hopelessness remained a poor prognostic indicator at 10-year follow-up. A controversial study, (with over 1,000 citations to date) was reported by Spiegel, Bloom, Kraemer, and Gottheil (1989), who evaluated the effect of a psychosocial intervention on survival in patients with metastatic breast cancer. The intervention consisted of weekly supportive group therapy with self-hypnosis for pain. At 10-year follow-up, survival time was doubled in the intervention group versus the control group. However, there have been several failures to replicate this finding, and independent analyses have suggested that while there was a difference in mean, there was no difference in median survival (Edwards, Hailey, & Maxwell, 2004), and that the patients in the control arm had a worse prognosis than would normally be expected (Fox, 1998).

Simon, Palmer, and Coyne (2007) conclude that the evidence that depression causes cancer or accelerates its progression, or that interventions for depression improve survival is largely absent or negative. They contrast this with the robust prognostic value for depression in cardiovascular disease and argue that in the absence of credible evidence, continued claims that psychological interventions promote survival in cancer patients could prove damaging to the field: "When strong claims about the role of depression in cancer ultimately need to be abandoned, it would seem to be an undignified retreat to claim that the usefulness of detecting and treating depression based on the 'mere' benefits for wellbeing or quality of life. An unwarranted strong claim thus could rob the credibility of what had always been a reasonable claim" (Simon et al., 2007, p. 228).

Treatment Behavior

Just as patients have been found to vary greatly in their response to symptoms and illness, they also react to their treatment in a range of ways, which can have very significant effects on clinical outcomes. Two major areas of patient behavioral variation are seen in the extent to which patients adhere to their prescribed treatment, and in the nonspecific positive (placebo) and negative (nocebo) effects of the treatment on clinical outcome. A brief, selective overview of research on these two areas is now presented.

Adherence to treatment

The extent to which the patient adheres to the advice or treatment offered in health-care consultations has been widely studied. Most medical consultations result in the prescription of treatment or advice, and the use of medicines is a key aspect of the self-management of most chronic illnesses. However, many patients fail to do this and, provided that there is a good evidence base for the efficacy of the treatment, low rates of adherence to recommended treatment are a major problem in chronic physical illnesses (WHO, 2003). The levels of reported medication nonadherence vary greatly, but there is a consensus that around 50% of patients with chronic health problems do not adhere appropriately to their prescribed treatment (Haynes, Ackloo, Sahota, McDonald, & Yao, 2009; WHO, 2003). Even patients who have experienced major health problems, such as MI and Chronic Obstructive Pulmonary Disease (COPD), show low levels of uptake of rehabilitation programs (Cooper, Jackson, Weinman, & Horne, 1999; Fischer et al., 2009) as well as considerable variation in the adoption of recommended behavioral changes. Patients fail to follow medical advice or treatment for a number of reasons, and these can be broadly categorized as either *intentional* or *unintentional.*

Unintentional nonadherence can be due to such factors as forgetting, and inability to follow treatment instructions because of a lack of understanding or physical problems such as poor eyesight or impaired manual dexterity. Moreover, if the quality of medical communication is poor and patients receive information that is difficult to understand or recall, this makes it less likely that treatment will be adhered to (Ley, 1988). Cognitive impairment is also associated with poor adherence, even very mild cognitive impairment in healthy elderly people has a detrimental impact on medication adherence (Hayes, Larimer, Adami, & Kaye, 2009). Another possible cause of unintentional nonadherence that has been identified recently is the patient's level of executive function or planning ability. Taking one or more medications and/or changing lifestyle on a regular basis requires self-regulatory skills on the part of the individual and there is now evidence that individual variation in these skills can have an impact on successful adherence. For example, Hall and colleagues have shown that individual differences in executive function, as assessed on a computer-based task, predicted subsequent levels of dietary behavior and physical activity in a student sample (Hall, Fong, Epp, & Elisa, 2008). Relatedly, in a clinical study of adherence to cholesterol lowering medication, Stilley, Sereika, Muldoon, Ryan, and Dunbar-Jacob, (2004) found that similar aspects of cognitive processing ability as well as the personality trait of conscientiousness explained significant variance in electronically metered medication use.

Intentional nonadherence arises when the patient makes a strategic decision not to take the treatment as instructed. For example, hypertensive patients, who believe that they can judge when their blood pressure is high by the presence of symptoms such as stress or headache, have been found to take their medication only when these symptoms are experienced (Meyer, Leventhal, & Gutmann, 1985). From a CS-SRM perspective, the level of treatment adherence may be indicative of a strategic coping response which is entirely consistent with the patient's perception of their problem. Thus patients with asthma who perceive their condition as cyclical in nature are less likely than those with a more chronic time-line representation to adhere to their medication over a long period of time (Horne & Weinman, 2002; Halm, Mora, & Leventhal, 2006).

Even though selected personality variables, such as conscientiousness (e.g., Stilley et al., 2004), have been associated with treatment adherence, research has moved away from attempts to identify stable trait factors which characterize the nonadherent patient to achieving a greater understanding of how and why patients decide to take some treatments and not others. A range of psychological theories have been used to explain intentional nonadherence (Horne & Weinman, 1998) but the CS-SRM provides a particularly useful framework. As was discussed earlier, symptom perception influences illness representations and adherence as a coping behavior, but patients' beliefs about their symptoms are often erroneous and this can result in poor control of symptoms and illness (Leventhal, Diefenbach, & Leventhal, 1992). In addition to acknowledging the role of patients' beliefs about their illness, current adherence research has shown that patients hold views about their treatment and that these seem to play a critical role in influencing levels of intentional nonadherence (Horne, 2003). This research has revealed two broad factors describing people's beliefs about their prescribed medicines: their perceived *necessity* for maintaining health and their *concerns* based on worries about possible dependence or harmful long-term effects. Patients with stronger concerns based on beliefs about the potential for long-term effects and dependence reported lower adherence rates, whilst those with stronger beliefs in the necessity of their medication reported greater adherence to medication regimen (Horne & Weinman, 1999). This work points to the importance of accessing patients' beliefs as a prerequisite of any intervention designed to increase medication adherence (see below).

A common barrier to treatment adherence is that the patient and the health provider do not share the same model of their condition and its treatment. This is particularly the case where the treatment does not seem to make sense to the patient. In many cases medical staff are unaware of patients' ideas about their condition as staff rarely ask patients about their own ideas in routine consultations. The following clinical case example may prove illustrative. Intermittent claudication (IC) is a condition where atheromatous material leads to blocking of blood vessels in the legs, which leads to significant pain and disability. Exercise such as walking is recommended to improve revascularization in the leg and to combat muscle wastage. However many IC patients do not exercise because of the pain it provokes. Cunningham (2010) conducted qualitative interviews with IC patients regarding their reasons for not exercising. One elderly man explained that he believed that his leg pain was caused by walking his dogs in long, wet grass. The doctor's treatment advice (that he should engage in regular walking) was clearly at odds with the patient's illness belief regarding its causation. It is thus easy to understand why this individual did not adhere to treatment advice to walk as, from the patients' perspective, this was what had caused his condition in the first place! This is an important area for intervention. An example is provided by Karamanidou, Weinman, and Horne (2008), who compared the effect of a CS-SRM-based psycho-educational intervention versus standard care control on knowledge of phosphate control and beliefs about phosphate binding medication (PBM) in patients with end-stage renal disease. Although PBM is crucial for reducing the risk of cardiovascular events caused by elevated phosphate levels, adherence is poor as the treatment is poorly understood by patients and has no noticeable effects on symptoms. The intervention included a simple demonstration using a plastic container to represent the patient's stomach, and phosphate solution was poured in to represent high-phosphate food. PBM was then introduced, and patients were asked to describe what they saw, as they observed the medication binding and solidifying—thus providing a simple concrete image of the mode of action of PBM. The intervention was successful in improving knowledge, treatment coherence, medication outcome efficacy beliefs, and general understanding of treatment, an effect which was sustained through to 4-month follow-up. Further studies of this kind are important in order to provide patients with a coherent model of the fit between their condition and the recommended treatment so as to provide convincing reasons for the need to adhere to it.

Another factor that has been consistently linked with lower adherence rates in a wide range of health problems is depression, which may be one reason for the adverse effects of depression on illness outcome that were described in the previous section. In a meta-analytic review of the effects of anxiety and depression on adherence, DiMatteo, Lepper, and Croghan (2000) found that whereas anxiety was not consistently associated with adherence, the odds are three times greater that depressed patients would be nonadherent with medical treatment compared with those who are not depressed. Although this review is only based on observational studies, which preclude a causal explanation, depression may well affect both intentional and unintentional aspects of nonadherence by influencing planning/executive processes as well as overall motivation to follow advice or treatment.

Interventions to improve treatment adherence

Given the extent and the seriousness of the adherence problem in healthcare delivery (WHO, 2003), there have been many attempts to develop interventions to remedy the situation. The nature and efficacy of these have been summarized and reviewed in Cochrane reviews (Haynes, Ackloo, Sahota, McDonald, & Yao, 2009). In the most recent of these, they note that many types of intervention have been used, from quite simple changes in the dosage regimen and the use of reminders to more complex interventions involving patient instructions, counseling, incentives, and various psychological therapies. Despite their best efforts to identify the most effective approaches, they comment that this field of research is still quite poor in terms of quality and clear evidence of efficacy. In general, the studies are marred by quite small sample sizes and limited measurement of both behavioral and clinical outcomes. Thus they conclude that "high priority should be given to fundamental and applied research concerning innovations to assist patients to follow medication prescriptions for long-term medical disorders" (Haynes et al., 2009, p. 2).

One reason why the majority of interventions fail to show consistent significant effects is because they have not been based on a sound theoretical understanding of why patients do not adhere to a particular treatment. It has become clear that successful interventions will need to address both the motivational (i.e., intentional) and volitional (i.e., unintentional) aspects of nonadherence in ways which make sense to the patient (e.g., see Horne & Weinman, 2004). In general, researchers have focused their efforts more on the unintentional aspects by providing better instructions, reminders, or prompts, but, in failing to address the important motivational issues, they are unlikely to produce long-term changes in adherence behavior. Changing patient behavior remains a major challenge for clinical health psychology and some of the examples of innovative interventions provided earlier in this chapter show the direction in which this work should go.

Adherence and outcome

The cumulative research evidence on intentional nonadherence has highlighted two important factors. First, any treatment is clearly not a neutral, external stimulus since patients have been shown to have clear beliefs and expectations about both medical treatments in general and the specific treatments that they have been prescribed. Second, these beliefs play an important role in determining the extent to which treatments are adhered to. Since beliefs can play such a strong role in adherence behavior, it has also been proposed that they could have a strong influence on the effectiveness of a treatment. This could simply be because patients with positive beliefs are more likely to take sufficient quantities of their medication to guarantee a therapeutic response. In meta-analyses, Dimatteo, Giordani, & Lepper (2002) have shown a reasonably strong association between level of patient adherence and clinical outcome across a wide range of medical problems, and more recently Simpson et al. (2006) showed that, in adherent patients, the risk of mortality was about half of that found in nonadherent patients. However, this relationship between adherence and outcome cannot be entirely due to the biological effects of the medication since a very similar relationship has been found between adherence to an inert (placebo) substance and therapeutic outcome, including mortality (Simpson et al., 2006). For example in a large placebo-controlled trial of antihypertensive medication in cardiac patients, Horwitz and Horwitz (1993) showed that those who were adherent to a placebo treatment had a significantly better clinical outcome than nonadherent patients. Moreover, the difference in outcome between adherent and nonadherent patients was very similar to those who were in the active treatment arm of the study. Thus the beliefs that serve to motivate patients to take their treatment also seem to be associated with a better response to treatment, regardless of whether it has any pharmacologically active ingredients, and these effects can be understood as placebo or nonspecific responses to treatment. Although more adherent patients are also more likely to engage in other health protective behaviors, it is important to note that this was controlled for in the Horwitz and Horwitz study.

Placebo effects in treatment. It has been long acknowledged that many patients will show clinical improvements after being given an inert substance in the form of a "dummy" pill that looks like an active medication. This is seen most clearly in the responses of patients in the placebo arm of a clinical trial, such as that described by Horwitz and Horwitz (1993) above. These effects are seen across a wide range of treatment settings including different types of medication and even surgery (e.g., McCrae et al., 2004). As well as responding positively to inactive treatments, many studies have also shown that patients' responses to active treatments can be enhanced if they have positive expectancies, which may be due to the way in which the treatment is introduced by the doctor in clinical settings (Benedetti, 2002) or in more controlled experimental or clinical studies (e.g., Price, 2001). For this reason, these different types of placebo response are sometimes known as nonspecific treatment effects.

There are now many studies of these effects and it is beyond the scope of this article to provide a comprehensive overview. Many excellent reviews exist (e.g., Price, Finniss, & Benedetti, 2008) and there are systematic reviews and meta-analysis for specific treatments or conditions (e.g., Moncrieff, Wessely, & Hardy, 2004; Sysko & Walsh, 2007). Research to date has not only established the extent and magnitude of these effects but has also attempted to elucidate the underlying psychological processes and neurobiological mechanisms.

A number of psychological mechanisms have been put forward to explain how these nonspecific treatment effects may occur. Older studies tended to look for more dispositional explanations by trying to characterize placebo responders and nonresponders, but more recent work has acknowledged two distinct but potentially overlapping explanations. The first is based on principles of classical conditioning, whereby the pairing of neutral stimuli in the treatment environment (e.g., the administration of a pill) with an unconditioned stimulus (the active medication) results in a conditioned response (i.e., a therapeutic response to a placebo pill, which resembles previously effective treatments). These effects have been found in animal and human studies, and seem to be mediated by unconscious processes (see Stewart Williams and Podd, 2004).

The second explanatory mechanism is based on the expectations that the patients have about the "treatment" which they are being given. These expectancies can be either investigated as pre-existing variations in patients' beliefs or can be modified in the clinical context. An excellent example of this is the work of Linde et al. (2007) who reported the findings from randomized controlled trials in which they compared real and sham acupuncture for pain relief for four different clinical problems. Prior to starting treatment, patients were asked about their general beliefs about acupuncture and their specific treatment expectations. The results showed that those with stronger expectations experienced greater benefit regardless of whether they had received the real or sham treatment. Similarly, in their double-blind study of real versus sham surgical transplantation of embryonic dopamine neurons in patients with Parkinson's disease, McRae et al. (2004) reported that it was those patients who thought they had received the transplant who showed better outcomes. In addition to influencing a wide range of medical outcomes, there is also now evidence that expectancy effects can produce positive changes in cognitive functioning (Oken et al., 2008).

The extent to which patients' beliefs or expectancies about their treatment can influence clinical outcome have also been demonstrated in the use of the so-called "open–hidden" treatment paradigm. Here all patients receive the same active treatment but not all are aware that it is being administered, which provides a comparison between the effect of the drug alone and the additional expectancy-based, placebo effects. The significantly greater effect of the open administration of a treatment again provides powerful evidence for the influence of the nonspecific treatment effects, which are activated by patient expectancies (Colloca, Lopiano, Lanotte, & Bennedetti, 2004). It has also been found that more significant changes in brain metabolic activity are found in patients who were expecting to receive an active treatment injection compared with those expecting a placebo, even though both were given the active treatment (Volkow et al., 2003). There are now a growing number of brain imaging and other related studies, which are beginning to provide evidence about the neurobiological mechanisms which might be mediating these effects (Finniss & Benedetti, 2005).

Nocebo effects in treatment. Just as patients have been found to experience and report more positive effects from an active or inert treatment if they have positive expectancies about it, they can also show negative effects, such as side-effects, which do not seem to be due to the treatment. Again, these can be most easily observed in the placebo arm of a clinical trial, where between a fifth and a quarter of participants have been reported to spontaneously report side-effects (e.g., Rosenzweig,

Brohier, & Zipfel, 1993). In studies of patients in clinical trials of treatments for largely asymptomatic conditions, such as hypertension, very similar levels of these side-effects are found in both the active and placebo conditions (Preston, Materson, Reda , & Williams, 2000).

In a thoughtful review of nocebo effects, Barsky, Saintfort, Rogers, and Borus (2002) report that 25% of patients on placebo treatment will spontaneously detail negative side-effects and that even higher rates are found if patients are specifically asked about these. The sorts of factors, which have been put forward to explain placebo effects have also been proposed to account for nonspecific side-effects. These side-effects are found in both the active and placebo conditions (e.g., Preston et al., 2000). These "nocebo" effects can be understood in terms of many of the processes involved in symptom perception, described in the first section of this chapter. Variations in symptom perception due to general or specific health anxiety can influence the extent to which patients attend to and report side-effects. Negative expectations about treatment can be based on past experience or on contextual factors, such as the way in which information about side-effects is provided prior to treatment (Flaten, Simonsen, & Olsen, 1999; Myers et al., 1987). Past experience may serve to increase side-effects either via the activation of schema and related expectancies or through the process of classical conditioning. For example, many cancer patients undergoing chemotherapy can develop a conditioned nausea response, which can be elicited when they enter the treatment setting because of the association with the nausea experienced previously during treatment. This anticipatory nausea and vomiting has been successfully managed with psychological interventions (Morrow & Doblin, 1988).

Since patients on active treatment can also develop these nonspecific side-effects, this may result in patients abandoning effective and potentially life-saving treatments prematurely. Indeed, as was discussed earlier, these side-effects may result in generating the concerns about treatment which are known to be associated with low adherence (Horne, 2003). Barsky et al. (2002) discuss a number of strategies for both explaining these side-effects to patients and for helping them tolerate them long enough to obtain the therapeutic benefits arising from better adherence.

Summary and Conclusions

In this chapter we have provided a selective, state of the art overview of the field of clinical health psychology. It is a fast-growing area of research and practice, which attempts to broaden existing models of health and disease and, in doing so, is beginning to generate interesting insights into the complex interaction between mind and body. While there is considerable evidence that psychological factors have a significant influence on the outcome of all major physical health problems, there has been less progress in developing effective psychological interventions for improving illness coping and treatment adherence as a basis for improving both morbidity and mortality. However, it is important not to focus exclusively on biomedical or disease-related outcomes when evaluating the efficacy of psychological interventions. As Kaplan (2000) has pointed out, when working with patients with physical health problems, psychological outcomes are of equal or possibly greater importance, and the contribution of psychological interventions for achieving improvements in mood and quality of life should not be undervalued. As clinical health psychology progresses, we will not only be able to gain a much better understanding of how psychological processes influence health outcomes but it will also be possible to use this knowledge to develop more effective psychological interventions in the clinical setting.

References

Andersen, B. L., Farrar, W. B., Golden-Kreutz, D. M., Glaser, R., Emery, C. F., Crespin, T. R. ... Carson, W. E., III (2004). Psychological, behavioral, and immune changes after a psychological intervention: a clinical trial. *Journal of Clinical Oncology*, *22*, 3570–3580.

Antoni, M. (2002a). *Stress management intervention for women with breast cancer: training manual.* Washington: American Psychological Association.

Antoni, M. (2002b). *Stress management intervention for women with breast cancer: participant's workbook.* Washington: American Psychological Association.

Antoni, M., Lechner, S. C., Kazi, A., Wimberly, S. R., Sifre, T., Urcuyo, K. R., ... Carver, C. S. (2006a). How stress management improves quality of life after treatment for breast cancer. *Journal of Consulting and Clinical Psychology*, *74*, 1143–1152.

Antoni, M., Wimberly, S. R., Lechner, S. C., Kazi, A., Sifre, T., Urcuyo, K. R., ... Carver, C. (2006b). Reduction of cancer-specific thought intrusions and anxiety symptoms with a stress management intervention among women undergoing treatment for breast cancer. *The American Journal of Psychiatry*, *163*, 1791–1797.

Barsky, A., Saintfort, R., Rogers, M. P., & Borus, J. F. (2002). Nonspecific medication side-effects and the nocebo phenomenon. *Journal of the American Medical Association*, *287*, 622–627

Barth, J., Schumacher, M., & Herrmann-Lingen, C. (2004). Depression as a risk factor for mortality in patients with coronary heart disease: a meta-analysis. *Psychosomatic Medicine*, *66*, 802–813.

Bartholomew, R. E., & Wessely, S. (2002). Protean nature of mass sociogenic illness. *British Journal of Psychiatry*, *100*, 300–306.

Bass, C. (1990). *Somatization: physical symptoms and psychological illness.* Oxford: Blackwell.

Bass, C. M. (1991). Unexplained chest pain and breathlessness. *Medical Clinics of North America*, *75*, 1157–1173.

Benedetti, F. (2002). How the doctor's words affect the patient's brain. *Evaluation & the Health Professions*, *25*, 369–386.

Benedetti et al. (2005)

Berkman, L. F., Blumenthal, J., Burg, M., Carney, R. M., Catellier, D., Cowan, M. J., ... Raczynski, J. M. (2003). Effects of treating depression and low perceived social support on clinical events after myocardial infarction: the Enhancing Recovery in Coronary Heart Disease Patients (ENRICHD) randomized trial. *Journal of the American Medical Association*, *289*, 3106–3116.

Bish, A., Ramirez, A., Burgess, C., & Hunter, M. (2005). Understanding why women delay in seeking help for breast cancer symptoms. *Journal of Psychosomatic Research*, *58*, 321–326.

Broadbent, E., Ellis, C. J., Thomas, J., Gamble, G., & Petrie, K. J. (2009a). Can an illness perception intervention reduce illness anxiety in spouses of myocardial infarction patients? A randomized controlled trial. *Journal of Psychosomatic Research*, *67*, 11–15.

Broadbent, E., Ellis, C. J., Thomas, J., Gamble, G., & Petrie, K. J. (2009b). Further development of an illness perception intervention for myocardial infarction patients: a randomized controlled trial. *Journal of Psychosomatic Research*, *67*, 17–23.

Carney, R. M., & Freedland, K. E. (2007a). Does treating depression improve survival after acute coronary syndrome? Invited commentary on effects of antidepressant treatment following myocardial infarction. *British Journal of Psychiatry*, *190*, 467–468.

Carney, R. M., & Freedland, K. E. (2007b). The management of depression in patients with coronary heart disease. In A. Steptoe (Ed.), *Depression and physical illness.* Cambridge: Cambridge University Press.

Carver, C. S., & Scheier, M. F. (1998). *On the self-regulation of behavior.* New York: Cambridge University Press.

Channer, K. S., James, M., Papouchado, M., & Rees, J. R. (1987). Failure of a negative exercise test to reassure patients with chest pain. *Quarterly Journal of Medicine*, *63*, 315–322.

Colloca, L., Lopiano, L., Lanotte, M., & Bennedetti, F. (2004). Overt versus covert treatment for pain, anxiety and Parkinson's disease. *Lancet Neurology*, *3*, 679–684.

Conner, M., & Norman, P. (2005). *Predicting health behaviour: Research and practice with social cognition models* (2nd ed.). Buckingham, UK: Open University Press.

Cooper, A., Jackson, G., Weinman, J., & Horne, R. (2002). Factors associated with cardiac rehabilitation attendance: A systematic review of the literature. *Clinical Rehabilitation*, *16*, 541–552.

Coyne, J. C., Stefanek, M., & Palmer, S. C. (2007). Psychotherapy and survival in cancer: The conflict between hope and evidence. *Psychology Bulletin*, *133*, 367–394.

Croyle, R. T., & Sande, G. N. (1988). Denial and confirmatory search: Paradoxical consequences of medical diagnosis. *Journal of Applied Social Psychology*, *18*, 473–490.

Cunningham, M. (2010). *The role of psychological factors in relation to outcome in intermittent claudication* (Unpublished doctoral dissertation). Psychology Department, University of Stirling.

Davies, M. J., Heller, S., Skinner, T. C., Campbell, M. J., Carey, M. E., Cradock, S., … Khunti, K. (2008). Effectiveness of the diabetes education and self management for ongoing and newly diagnosed (DESMOND) programme for people with newly diagnosed type 2 diabetes: cluster randomised controlled trial. *British Medical Journal*, *336*, 491–495.

Denollet, J., Pedersen, S. S., Vrints, C. J., & Conraads, V. M. (2006). Usefulness of type D personality in predicting five-year cardiac events above and beyond concurrent symptoms of stress in patients with coronary heart disease. *American Journal of Cardiology*, *97*, 970–973.

Diamond, J. (1998). *Because cowards get cancer too.* Vermilion: London.

Dickens, C., McGowan, L., Percival, C., Tomenson, B., Cotter, L., Heagerty, A., & Creed, F. (2008). New onset depression following myocardial infarction predicts cardiac mortality. *Psychosomatic Medicine*, *70*, 450–455.

DiMatteo, M. R., Giordani, P. J., & Lepper, H. S. (2002). Patient adherence and medical treatment outcomes: a meta-analysis. *Medical Care*, *40*, 794–811.

DiMatteo, M. R., Lepper, H. S., & Croghan, T. W. (2000). Depression is a risk factor for noncompliance with medical treatment. *Archives of Internal Medicine*, *160*, 2101–2107.

Donkin, L., Ellis, C. J., Powell, R., Broadbent, E., Gamble, G., & Petrie, K. J. (2006). Illness perceptions predict reassurance following a negative stress testing result. *Psychology and Health*, *21*, 421–430.

Edwards, A. G., Hailey, S., & Maxwell, M. (2004). Psychological interventions for women with metastatic breast cancer. *Cochrane Database of Systematic Reviews*: CD004253.

Eriksen, H. R., & Ihlebaek, C. (2002). Subjective health complaints. *Scandinavian Journal of Psychology, 43*, 101–103.

Evans, D. L., Charney, D. S., Lewis, L., Golden, R. N., Gorman, J. M., Krishnan, K. R., ... Valvo, W. J. (2005). Mood disorders in the medically ill: Scientific review and recommendations. *Biological Psychiatry, 58*, 175–189.

Evans, H., & Bartholomew, R. (2009). *Outbreak: The encyclopedia of extraordinary social behavior.* San Antonio, TX; Anomalist Books.

Feder, A., Olfson, M., Gameroff, M., Fuentes, M., Shea, S., Lantigua, R. A., & Weissman, M. M. (2001). Medically unexplained symptoms in an urban general medicine practice. *Psychosomatics, 42*, 261–268.

Finniss, D. G., & Benedetti, F. (2005). Mechanisms of the placebo response and their impact on clinical trials and practice. *Pain, 114*, 3–6.

Fischer, M., Scharloo, M., Abbink, J. J., van't Hul, A. J., van Ranst, D., Rudolphus, A., ... Kaptein A. A. (2009). Dropout and attendance in pulmonary rehabilitation: The role of clinical and psychosocial variables. *Respiratory Medicine, 103*, 1564–1571.

Fitzpatrick, R., & Hopkins, A. (1981). Referrals to neurologists for headaches not due to structural disease. *Journal of Neurology, Neurosurgery & Psychiatry, 44*, 1061–1067.

Flaten, M. A., Simonsen, T., & Olsen, H. (1999). Drug-related information generates placebo and nocebo responses that modify the drug response. *Psychosomatic Medicine, 61*, 250–255.

Foster, G., Taylor, S. J., Eldridge, S. E., Ramsay, J., & Griffiths, C. J. (2007). Self-management education programmes by lay leaders for people with chronic conditions. *Cochrane Database of Systematic Reviews*: CD005108.

Fox, B. H. (1998). A hypothesis about Spiegel et al.'s 1989 paper on psychosocial intervention and breast cancer survival. *Psycho-Oncology, 7*, 361–370.

Frasure-Smith, N., Lesperance, F., & Talajic, M. (1993). Depression following myocardial infarction. Impact on 6-month survival. *Journal of the American Medical Association, 270*, 1819–1825.

Gillies, C. L., Abrams, K. R., Lambert, P. C., Cooper, N. J., Sutton, A. J., Hsu, R.T., & Khunti, K. (2007). Pharmacological and lifestyle interventions to prevent or delay type 2 diabetes in people with impaired glucose tolerance: Systematic review and meta-analysis. *British Medical Journal , 334*, 299–302.

Glassman, A. H., O'Connor, C. M., Califf, R. M., Swedberg, K., Schwartz, P., Bigger, J. T., Jr., ... McIvor, M. (2002). Sertraline treatment of major depression in patients with acute MI or unstable angina. *Journal of the American Medical Association, 288*, 701–709.

Greer, S., Morris, T., & Pettingale, K. W. (1979). Psychological response to breast cancer: effect on outcome. *Lancet, 2*, 785–787.

Griffiths, C., Foster, G., Ramsay, J., Eldridge, S., & Taylor, S. (2007). How effective are expert patient (lay led) education programmes for chronic disease? *British Medical Journal, 334*, 1254–1256.

Hagger, M. S., & Orbell, S. (2003). A meta-analytic review of the common-sense model of illness representations. *Psychology & Health, 18*, 141–184.

Hall, P. A., Fong, G. T., Epp, L. J., & Elisa, L. J. (2008). Executive function moderates the intention–behaviour link for physical activity and dietary behaviour. *Psychology & Health, 23*, 309–326.

Halm, E. A., Mora, P., & Leventhal, H. (2006). No symptoms, no asthma: The acute episodic disease belief is associated with poor self-management among inner city adults with persistent asthma. *Chest, 129*, 573–580.

Hannay, D. R. (1978). Symptom prevalence in the community. *Journal of the Royal College of General Practitioners, 28*, 492–499.

Hayes, T. L., Larimer, N., Adami, A., & Kaye, J. A. (2009). Medication adherence in healthy elders: small cognitive changes make a big difference. *Journal of Aging and Health, 21*, 567–80.

Haynes, R. B., Ackloo, E., Sahota, N., McDonald, H. P., & Yao, X. (2009). Interventions for enhancing medication adherence. *Cochrane Database of Systematic Reviews*, Issue 2, Art No.: CD000011.DOI: 10.1002/14651858.CD000011.pub3.

Horne, R. (2003). Treatment perceptions and self-regulation. In L. D. Cameron & H. Leventhal (Eds.), *The self-regulation of health and illness behavior* (pp. 138–153). London: Routledge.

Horne, R., James, D., Petrie, K., Weinman, J., & Vincent, R. (2000). Patients' interpretation of symptoms as a cause of delay in reaching hospital in acute myocardial infarction. *Heart, 83*(4), 388–393.

Horne, R., & Weinman, J. (1998). Predicting treatment adherence: An overview of theoretical models. In L. Myers & K. Midence (Eds.), *Adherence to treatment in medical conditions* (pp. 25–50). London: Harwood Academic.

Horne, R., & Weinman, J. (1999). Patients' beliefs about prescribed medicines and their role in adherence to treatment in chronic physical illness. *Journal of Psychosomatic Research, 47*, 6, 555–567.

Horne, R., & Weinman, J. (2002). Self-regulation and self-management in asthma: Exploring the role of illness perceptions and treatment beliefs in explaining nonadherence to preventer medication. *Psychology and Health. 17*, 17–33.

Horne, R., & Weinman, J. (2004). The theoretical basis of concordance and issues for research. In C. Bond (Ed.), *Concordance* (pp. 119–146). London: Pharmaceutical Press.

Horwitz, R. I., & Horwitz, S. M. (1993). Adherence to treatment and health outcomes. *Archives of Internal Medicine, 153*, 1863–1868.

Howard, L. (1996). Telling patients there is nothing wrong: Randomised controlled trials are needed. *British Medical Journal, 313*, 1210.

Howard, L., & Wessely, S. (1996). Reappraising reassurance: The role of investigations. *Journal of Psychosomatic Research, 41*, 307–311.

Howard, L., Wessely, S., Leese M., Page, L., McCrone, P., Husain, K., Tong, J., & Dowson A. (2005). Are investigations anxiolytic or anxiogenic? A randomised controlled trial of neuroimaging to provide reassurance in chronic daily headache. *Journal of Neurology Neurosurgery and Psychiatry, 76*, 1558–1564.

Johansson, I., Stromberg, A., & Swahn, E. (2004). Factors related to delay times in patients with suspected myocardial infarction. *Heart & Lung, 33*, 291–300

Johnston, M., Bonetti, D., Joice, S., Pollard, B., Morrison, V., Francis, J. J., & MacWalter, R. (2007). Recovery from disability after stroke as a target for a behavioural intervention: results of a randomized controlled trial. *Disability Rehabilitation, 29*, 1117–1127.

Kaplan, R. M. (2000). Behavior as the central outcome in health care. *American Psychologist, 45*, 1211–1220.

Karamanidou, C., Weinman, J., & Horne, R. (2008). Improving haemodialysis patients' understanding of phosphate-binding medication: A pilot study of a psycho-educational intervention designed to change patients' perceptions of the problem and treatment. *British Journal of Health Psychology, 13*, 205–214.

Khaw, K. T., Wareham, N., Bingham, S., Welch, A., Luben, R., & Day, N. (2008). Combined impact of health behaviours and mortality in men and women: the EPIC-Norfolk prospective population study. *PLoS Medicine 5*, e12.

Kinmonth, A. L., Wareham, N. J., Hardeman, W., Sutton, S., Prevost, A. T., Fanshawe, T., … Griffin, S. J. (2008). Efficacy of a theory-based behavioural intervention to increase physical activity in an at-risk group in primary care (ProActive UK): A randomised trial. *Lancet*, *371*, 41–48.

Kirsch, I., Deacon, B. J., Huedo-Medina, T. B., Scoboria, A., Moore, T. J., & Johnson, B. T. (2008). Initial severity and antidepressant benefits: A meta-analysis of data submitted to the Food and Drug Administration. *PLoS Medicine*, *5*, e45.

Klimes, I., Mayou, R. A., Pearce, M. J., Coles, L., & Fagg, J. R. (1990). Psychological treatment for atypical noncardiac chest pain: A controlled evaluation. *Psychological Medicine*, *20*, 605–611.

Knowler, W. C., Barrett-Connor, E., Fowler, S. E., Hamman, R. F., Lachin, J. M., Walker, E. A., & Nathan, D. M. (2002). Reduction in the incidence of type 2 diabetes with lifestyle intervention or metformin. *New England Journal of Medicine*, *346*, 393–403.

Kroenke, K., & Harris, L. (2001). Symptoms research: a fertile field. *Annals of Internal Medicine*, *134*, 801–802.

Lantinga, L. J., Sprafkin, R. P., McCroskery, J. H., Baker, M. T., Warner, R. A., & Hill, N. E. (1988). One-year psychosocial follow-up of patients with chest pain and angiographically normal coronary arteries. *American Journal of Cardiology*, *62*, 209–213.

Lavey, E. B., & Winkle, R. A. (1979). Continuing disability in patients with chest pain and normal coronary arteriograms. *Journal of Chronic Disease*, *32*, 191–196.

Lesperance, F., & Frasure-Smith, N. (2007): Depression and heart disease. *Cleveland Clinical Journal of Medicine*, *74* Suppl. 1: S63–66.

Lesperance, F., Frasure-Smith, N., Koszycki, D., Laliberte, M. A., van Zyl, L. T., Baker, B., ... Guertin, M. -C. (2007). Effects of citalopram and interpersonal psychotherapy on depression in patients with coronary artery disease: The Canadian Cardiac Randomized Evaluation of Antidepressant and Psychotherapy Efficacy (CREATE) trial. *Journal of the American Medical Association*, *297*, 367–379.

Lesperance, F., Frasure-Smith, N., Talajic, M., Bourassa, M. G. (2002). Five-year risk of cardiac mortality in relation to initial severity and one-year changes in depression symptoms after myocardial infarction. *Circulation*, *105*, 1049–1053.

Lett, H. S., Blumenthal, J. A., Babyak, M. A., Sherwood, A., Strauman, T., Robins, C., & Newman, M. F. (2004). Depression as a risk factor for coronary artery disease: evidence, mechanisms, and treatment. *Psychosomatic Medicine*, *66*, 305–315.

Lett, H. S., Sherwood, A., Watkins, A., & Blumenthal, J. (2007). Depression and prognosis in cardiac patients. In: A. Steptoe (Ed.), *Depression and Physical Illness* (pp. 87–108). Cambridge: Cambridge University Press.

Leventhal, H., Diefenbach, M., & Leventhal, E. A. (1992). Illness cognition: Using commonsense to understand treatment adherence and affect cognition interactions. *Cognitive Therapy & Research*, *16*, 143–163.

Leventhal, H., Nerenz, D. R., & Steele, D. J. (1984). Illness representations and coping with health threats. In A. Baum, S. E. Taylor, & J. E. Singer (Eds.), *Handbook of Psychology and Health, Volume IV : Social Psychological Aspects of Health* (pp. 219–252). Hillsdale, NJ: Lawrence Erlbaum Associates.

Leventhal, H., Weinman, J., Leventhal, E. A., & Phillips, L. A. (2008). Health Psychology: The search for pathways between behaviour and health. *Annual Review of Psychology*, *59*, 477–505.

Lewin, B., Robertson, I. H., Cay, E. L., Irving, J. B., & Campbell, M. (1992). Effects of self-help post-myocardial-infarction rehabilitation on psychological adjustment and use of health services. *Lancet*, *339*, 1036–1040.

Ley, P. (1988). *Communicating with patients: Improving communication, satisfaction and compliance.* London: Croom Helm.

Linde, K., Witt, C. M., Streng, A., Weidenhammer, W., Wagenpfeil, S., Brinkhaus, B., Willich, S., & Melchart, D. (2007). The impact of patient expectations on outcomes in four randomized controlled trials of acupuncture in patients with chronic pain. *Pain, 128*, 264–271.

Lindström, J., Ilanne-Parikka, P., Peltonen, M., Aunola, S., Eriksson, J. G., Hemiö, K., … Tuomilehto, J. (2006). Sustained reduction in the incidence of type 2 diabetes by lifestyle intervention: Follow-up of the Finnish Diabetes Prevention Study. *Lancet, 368*, 1673–1679.

Lorig, K. R., & Holman, H. (2003). Self-management education: History, definition, outcomes, and mechanisms. *Annals of Behavioral Medicine, 26*, 1–7.

Lucock, M. P., Morley, S., White, C., & Peake, M. D. (1997). Responses of consecutive patients to reassurance after gastroscopy: Results of self administered questionnaire survey. *British Medical Journal, 315*, 572–575.

Manne, S. L., Ostroff, J. S., Winkel, G., Fox, K., Grana, G., Miller, E., … Frazier, T. (2005). Couple-focused group intervention for women with early stage breast cancer. *Journal of Consulting and Clinical Psychology, 73*, 634–646.

Mayou, R. A., Bryant, B. M., Sanders, D., Bass, C., Klimes, I., & Forfar, C. (1997). A controlled trial of cognitive behavioural therapy for noncardiac chest pain. *Psychological Medicine, 27*, 1021–1031.

McDonald, I. G., Daly, J., Jelinek, V. M., Panetta, F., & Gutman, J. M. (1996). Opening Pandora's box: The unpredictability of reassurance by a normal test result. *British Medical Journal, 313*, 329–332.

McGregor, B. A., & Antoni, M. H. (2009). Psychological intervention and health outcomes among women treated for breast cancer: a review of stress pathways and biological mediators. *Brain, Behavior, and Immunity, 23*, 159–166.

McRae, C., Cherin, E., Yamazaki, G., Diem, G., Vo, A. H., Russell, D., … Freed, C. R. (2004). Effects of perceived treatment on quality of life and medical outcomes in a double-blind placebo surgery trial. *Archives of General Psychiatry, 61*, 412–420.

Meyer, D., Leventhal, H., & Gutmann, M. (1985). Common-sense models of illness : the example of hypertension. *Health Psychology, 4*, 115–135.

Michie, S., & Abraham, C. (Eds.). (2004). *Health psychology in practice.* Oxford: BPS Blackwell.

Moncrieff, J., Wessely, S., & Hardy, R. (2004). Active placebos versus antidepressants for depression. *Cochrane Database of Systematic Reviews*, (1): CD003012.

Moos, R. H., & Schaefer, J. A. (1984). The crisis of physical illness: An overview and conceptual approach. In R. H. Moos (Ed.), *Coping with physical illness: New perspectives* (pp. 3–25). New York: Plenum.

Morrow, G. R., & Doblin, P. L. (1988). Anticipatory nausea and vomiting in cancer patients undergoing chemotherapy treatment : prevalence, etiology and behavioral interventions. *Clinical Psychology Review, 8*, 517–556.

Myers, M. G., Cairns, J. A., & Singer, J. (1987). The consent form as a possible cause of side effects. *Clinical Pharmacology and Therapeutics, 42*, 250–253.

Newman, S., Steed, L., & Mulligan, K. (Eds.). (2009). *Chronic physical illness: self-management and behavioural interventions.* Maidenhead, UK: Open University Press.

Nezu, A. M., Nezu, C. M., Felgoise, S. H., McClure, K. S., & Houts, P. S. (2003). Project Genesis: Assessing the efficacy of problem-solving therapy for distressed adult cancer patients. *Journal of Consulting and Clinical Psychology, 71*, 1036–1048.

Nijher, G., Weinman, J., Bass, C., & Chambers, J. (2001). Chest pain in people with normal coronary arteries. *British Medical Journal, 323*, 1319–20.

Oken, B., Flegal, K., Zajdel, D., Kishiyama, S., Haas, M., & Peters, D. (2008). Expectancy effect: impact of pill administration on cognitive performance in healthy seniors. *Journal of Clinical and Experimental Neuropsychology, 30*, 7–17.

Page, L. A., Howard, L. M., Husain, K., Tong, J., Dowson, A. J., Weinman, J., & Wessely, S. (2004). Psychiatric morbidity and cognitive representations in chronic daily headache. *Journal of Psychosomatic Research*, *57*, 549–555.

Page, L. A., & Wessely, S. (2003). Medically unexplained symptoms: exacerbating factors in the doctor-patient encounter. *Journal of the Royal Society of Medicine*, *96*, 223–227.

Papanicolaou, M. N., Califf, R. M., Hlatky, M. A., McKinnis, R. A., Harrell, F. E., Mark, D. B., ... & Pryor, D. B. (1986). Prognostic implications of angiographically normal and insignificantly narrowed coronary arteries. *American Journal of Cardiology*, *58*, 1181–1187.

Pennebaker, J. W. (1980). Perceptual and environmental determinants of coughing. *Basic and Applied Social Psychology*, *1*, 83–91.

Pennebaker, J. W. (1982). *The psychology of physical symptoms*. New York: Springer-Verlag.

Pennebaker, J. W., & Lightner, J. M. (1980). Competition of internal and external information in an exercise setting. *Journal of Personality and Social Psychology*, *39*, 165–174.

Pennebaker, J. W., & Skelton, J. A. (1978). Psychological parameters of physical symptoms. *Personality and Social Psychology Bulletin*, *4*, 524–530.

Peters, A. A. W. (1991). A randomized clinical trial to compare two different approaches in women with chronic pelvic pain. *Obstetrics and Gynaecology*, *77*, 740–741.

Petrie, K. J., Broadbent, E. A., Kley, N., Moss-Morris, R., Horne, R., & Rief, W. (2005). Worries about modernity predict symptom complaints after environmental pesticide spraying. *Psychosomatic Medicine*, *67*, 778–782.

Petrie, K. J., Cameron, L. D., Ellis, C. J., Buick, D., & Weinman, J. (2002). Changing illness perceptions after myocardial infarction: an early intervention randomized controlled trial. *Psychosomatic Medicine*, *64*, 580–586.

Petrie, K. J., Moss-Morris, R., & Weinman, J. (1995). The impact of catastrophic beliefs on functioning in chronic fatigue syndrome. *Journal of Psychosomatic Research*, *39*, 31–37.

Petrie, K. J., Muller, J. T., Schirmbeck, F., Donkin, L., Broadbent, E., Ellis, C. J., ... Rief, W. (2007). Effect of providing information about normal test results on patients' reassurance: randomised controlled trial. *British Medical Journal*, *334*, 352–355.

Petrie, K., & Reynolds, L. (2007). Coping with chronic illness. In S. Ayers, A. Baum, C. McManus, S. Newman, K. Wallston, J. Weinman, & R. West (Eds.), *The Cambridge handbook of psychology, health and medicine* (pp. 46–50). Cambridge: Cambridge University Press.

Potts, S. G., & Bass, C. M. (1993). Psychosocial outcome and use of medical resources in patients with chest pain and normal or near-normal coronary arteries: A long term follow-up study. *Quarterly Journal of Medicine*, *86*, 583–593.

Preston, R. A., Materson, B. J., Reda , D. J., & Williams, D. W. (2000). Placebo-associated blood pressure response and averse effects in the treatment of hypertension. *Archives of Internal Medicine*, *160*, 1449–1454.

Price, D. D. (2001). Assessing placebo effects without placebo groups: An untapped possibility? *Pain*, *90*, 201–203.

Price, D. D., Finniss, D. G., & Benedetti, F. (2008). A comprehensive review of the placebo effect: Recent advances and current thought. *Annual Review of Psychology*, *59*, 565–590.

Reid, S., Wessely, S., Crayford, T., & Hotopf, M. (2002). Frequent attenders with medically unexplained symptom: Service use and costs in secondary care. *British Journal of Psychiatry*, *180*, 248–253.

Rief, W., Heitmuller, A. M., Reisberg, K., & Ruddel, H. (2006). Why reassurance fails in patients with unexplained medical symptoms—An experimental investigation of remembered probabilities. *PLoS Medicine*, *3*, e269. DOI: 10.1271/journal.pmed.0030269.

Rimes, K. A., & Salkovskis, P. M. (2002). Prediction of psychological reactions to bone density screening for osteoporosis using a cognitive-behavioural model of health anxiety. *Behaviour Research and Therapy*, *40*, 359–381.

Roosli, M. (2008). Radiofrequency electromagnetic field exposure and nonspecific symptoms of ill health: a systematic review. *Environmental Research*, doi:10.1016/j.envres.2008.1002.1003.

Rosenzweig, P., Brohier, S., & Zipfel, A. (1993). The placebo effect in healthy volunteers: influence of experimental conditions on the adverse events profile during phase 1 studies. *Clinical Pharmacology Therapy*, *54*, 578–583.

Rubin, G. J., Cleare, A. J., & Wessely, S. (2008). Psychological factors associated with self-reported sensitivity to mobile phones. *Journal of Psychosomatic Research*, *64*, 1–9.

Sanders, D., Bass, C., Mayou, R. A., Goodwin, S., Bryant, B. M., & Tyndel, S. (1997). Noncardiac chest pain: why was a brief intervention apparently ineffective. *Psychological Medicine*, *27*, 1033–1040.

Sensky, T., MacLeod, A. K., & Rigby, M. E. (1996). Causal attributions about common somatic sensations among frequent general practice attenders. *Psychological Medicine*, *26*, 641–646.

Sheard, T., & Maguire, P. (1999). The effect of psychological interventions on anxiety and depression in cancer patients: results of two meta-analyses. *British Journal of Cancer*, *80*, 1770–1780.

Simon, L., Palmer, S. C., & Coyne, J. C. (2007). Cancer and depression. In A. Steptoe (Ed.), *Depression and physical illness.* Cambridge: Cambridge University Press.

Simpson, S. H., Eurich, D. T., Majumdar, S. R., Padwal, R. S., Tsuyuki, R. T., Varney, J., & Johnson, J. A. (2006) A meta-analysis of the association between adherence to drug therapy and mortality. *British Medical Journal*, *333*, 15.

Sniehotta, F. F., Scholz, U., Schwartzer, R., Fuhrmann, B., Kiwus, U., & Voller, H. (2005). Long-term effects of two psychological interventions on physical exercise and self-regulation following coronary rehabilitation. *International Journal of Behavioral Medicine*, *12*, 244–255.

Sniehotta, F. F., Scholz, U., & Schwarzer, R. (2006). Action plans and coping plans for physical exercise: A longitudinal intervention study in cardiac rehabilitation. *British Journal of Health Psychology*, *11*, 23–37.

Sox, H. C., Margulies, I., Sox, C. H. (1981). Psychologically mediated effects of diagnostic tests. *Annals of Internal Medicine*, *95*, 680–685.

Spiegel, D., Bloom, J. R., Kraemer, H. C., & Gottheil, E. (1989). Effect of psychosocial treatment on survival of patients with metastatic breast cancer. *Lancet*, *2*, 888–891.

Steptoe, A. (Ed.) (2007). *Depression and physical illness.* Cambridge: Cambridge University Press.

Stilley, C. S., Sereika, S., Muldoon, M. F., Ryan, C. M., & Dunbar-Jacob, J. (2004). Psychological and cognitive functioning: predictors of adherence with cholesterol lowering treatment. *Annals of Behavioral Medicine*, *27*, 117–124.

Stewart-Williams, S., & Podd, J. (2004). The placebo effect : dissolving the expectancy versus conditioning debate. *Psychological Bulletin*, *130*, 324–340.

Strong, V., Waters, R., Hibberd, C., Murray, G., Wall, L., Walker, J., … Sharpe, M. (2008). Management of depression for people with cancer (SMaRT oncology 1): A randomised trial. *Lancet*, *372*, 40–48.

Sysko, R., & Walsh, B. T. (2007). A systematic review of placebo response in studies of bipolar mania. *Journal of Clinical Psychiatry*, *68*, 1213–1217.

Thombs, B. D., de Jonge, P., Coyne, J. C., Whooley, M. A., Frasure-Smith, N., Mitchell, A. J., … Ziegelstein, R. C. (2008). Depression screening and patient outcomes in cardiovascular care: A systematic review. *Journal of the American Medical Association, 300*, 2161–2171.

Tuomilehto, J., Lindström, J., Eriksson, J. G., Valle, T. T., Hämäläinen, H., Ilanne-Parikka, P., … Uusitupa, M. (2001). Prevention of type 2 diabetes mellitus by changes in lifestyle among subjects with impaired glucose tolerance. *New England Journal of Medicine, 344*, 1343–1350.

Turner, J. (2001). Medically unexplained symptoms in secondary care. *British Medical Journal, 322*, 745–746.

van Melle, J. P., de Jonge, P., Honig, A., Schene, A. H., Kuyper, A. M., Crijns, H. J., … Ormel, J. (2007). Effects of antidepressant treatment following myocardial infarction. *British Journal of Psychiatry, 190*, 460–466.

van Melle, J. P., de Jonge, P., Spijkerman, T. A., Tijssen, J. G., Ormel, J., van Veldhuisen, D. J., … van den Berg, M. P. (2004). Prognostic association of depression following myocardial infarction with mortality and cardiovascular events: A meta-analysis. *Psychosomatic Medicine, 66*, 814–822.

Volkow, N. D., Wang, G. J., Ma, Y., Fowler, J. S., Zhu, W., Maynard, L., … Swanson, J. M. (2003). Expectation enhances the regional brain metabolic and the reinforcing effects of stimulants in cocaine abusers. *Journal of Neuroscience, 23*, 11461–11468.

Watson, D., & Pennebaker, J. W. (1989). Health complaints, stress, and distress: Exploring the central role of negative affectivity. *Psychological Review, 96*, 234–254.

Watson, M., Homewood, J., Haviland, J., & Bliss, J. M. (2005). Influence of psychological response on breast cancer survival: 10-year follow-up of a population-based cohort. *European Journal of Cancer, 41*, 1710–1714.

Weinman, J., Yusuf, G., Berks, R., Rayner, S., & Petrie, K. J. (2009). How accurate is patients' anatomical knowledge?: A cross-sectional questionnaire study of six patient groups and a general public sample. *BMC Family Practice, 10*, 43. doi:10.1186/1471-2296-10-43.

Williams, L., O'Connor, R. C., Howard, S., Hughes, B. M., Johnston, D. W., Hay, J. L., … O'Carroll, R. E. (2008). Type-D personality mechanisms of effect: The role of health-related behavior and social support. *Journal of Psychosomatic Research, 64*, 63–69.

Williams L, O'Connor R. C., O'Carroll R. E. (2009). Type D personality and cardiac output in response to stress. *Psychology & Health, 24*, 489–500.

World Health Organization. (2003). *Adherence to long-term therapies: Evidence for action.* Geneva: World Health Organization.

4

Health Promotion

Charles Abraham, Gerjo Kok, Herman P. Schaalma, and Aleksandra Luszczynska

Identifying Determinants of Health: A Social Ecological Perspective

What shapes health? In many developing countries the primary determinants are economic. Poverty deprives people of shelter, clean water, and nutrition and creates environments conducive to outbreaks of infectious diseases. Consequently, for much of the world's population the foundations of health promotion are transfers of (a) resources from rich countries to poor people and (b) skills and technologies from industrial countries to empower poorer people to be self-sufficient and create the resources they need to nurture health.

In affluent countries, increased national wealth (e.g., gross national product) does not result in reduced population morbidity or increased longevity. In this context, health is better predicted by individuals' position within socio-economic hierarchies, than the wealth of their nation. More equally distributed wealth is associated with better population health in affluent societies, as evidenced by associations between economic equality and longevity in cross-national studies. The contrast in this relationship between wealth and health in poor and rich countries has been called the "epidemiological transition" (Wilkinson, 1996).

Health and health-related behavior patterns are embedded in legislative and social contexts. Legislative and executive actions of governments are assumed to influence health promotion by developing health infrastructure, information policies, economic policies (e.g., taxation, subsidies, and economic incentives), environmental policies (including altering the physical environment), and social policies (intervening in social-economic environments by addressing social disparities; Gostin 2004; Perdue, Mensah, Goodman, & Moulton, 2005).

IAAP Handbook of Applied Psychology, First Edition. Edited by Paul R. Martin, Fanny M. Cheung, Michael C. Knowles, Michael Kyrios, Lyn Littlefield, J. Bruce Overmier, and José M. Prieto.

Taxation, employment law, benefit systems and legislation governing the sale and advertising of food and drugs all affect health through, amongst other routes, their impact on people's access to resources, the stress people experience in their everyday lives, and the behavioral choices with which they are faced. For example, many European countries have banned smoking in public places and legislated for sanctions against those who sell tobacco to children. Such action is likely to shift smoking patterns over time and create new normative expectations in subsequent generations, thereby having at least as great an impact on public health as individual smoking cessation programs. Legislative interventions can have immediate effects. For example, Sargent, Shepard, and Glantz (2004) found that myocardial infarction admissions to a hospital in Montana, USA fell significantly over six months during a smoking ban in public places, while at the same time, surrounding areas (without a smoking ban) experienced nonsignificant increases. Thus formulation of national and international policy and legislation plays a primary role in public health promotion, impacting directly on people's health and creating the context in which other health promotion activities can develop.

As well as intervention at national and international levels health promotion may focus on community development. Community development interventions seek to involve people in a geographically defined area in identifying local needs and assets and facilitating action to create or acquire new resources, skills and/or behavior patterns. Such interventions may focus on the empowerment and education of local people in order that they understand and can provide health-related advice (including the use of available media such as the internet). Alternatively, they can actively promote health-related behaviors such as buying and consuming fruit and vegetables and involve campaigns to establish local fresh-produce markets and/or the provision of vouchers to make healthier products more affordable. They might, instead, focus on skills development. For example, they could train local people to run and facilitate groups for those with chronic illnesses. Some community interventions are much more comprehensive and target a range of health-related behavior patterns. For example, the North Karelia Project, which began in Finland in 1972, included education on smoking, diet, and hypertension. The project employed widely distributed leaflets, radio and television slots, and education in local organizations. Voluntary sector organizations, schools, and health and social services were involved and training was provided in various contexts. The intervention included the education of school students about the health risks of smoking and the social influences that lead young people to begin smoking as well as skills training for students in how to resist such social influences. This comprehensive intervention was found to be effective by evaluations using a range of indices including reduction in smoking and serum cholesterol levels. For example, 15 years later, smoking prevalence was 11% lower amongst intervention participants compared to controls (Vartiainen, Paavola, McAlister, & Puska, 1998).

In a review of evaluations of comprehensive community interventions (including the North Karelia Project), Hingson and Howland (2002) found that greater effectiveness was observed when interventions: (1) targeted behaviors with immediate health consequences such as alcohol misuse or sexual risk taking; (2) targeted young people to prevent uptake of health-risk behaviors; (3) combined environmental and institutional policy change with theory-based behavior change interventions; and (4) involved communities themselves in intervention design.

Organizational rules, norms, and resources may create stress and impede health behavior change. They are, therefore, often targeted both in community interventions and in single-organization or worksite interventions. Worksite interventions may aim to integrate physical activity into employees' days including exercise breaks and promotion of walking and stair use or change the availability of healthy food and/or how food is labelled (e.g., Engbers, van Poppel, Chin, Paw, & van Mechelen, 2005). Worksite interventions focusing on exercise have been found to be effective in increasing physical activity and fitness as well as promoting weight loss amongst participants (Abraham & Graham-Rowe, 2009; King, Carl, Birkel, & Haskell, 1988).

Health promotion involves interventions at many different levels, from individual-level interventions focusing on health-related cognitions, emotions, and behavior patterns, through family and group interventions, organizational change intervention, and whole-community interventions, and even to national and international legislation. Kok, Gottlieb, Commers, and Smerecnik (2008) endorsed this multilevel approach in the "social ecological" model of change (see Figure 4.1).

The socioecological model mirrors other frameworks that seek to integrate macro-level environmental policies (applied at regional or national level), meso-level environmental policies and promotion programs, and micro-level health promotion programs. These frameworks are often developed to facilitate specific health interventions such as obesity reduction (Sacks, Swinburn, & Lawrence, 2008; Stirling, Lobstein, Millstone, & the PorGrow Research Team, 2007). Stakeholders at the meso level include schools and work organizations, community groups, health-related

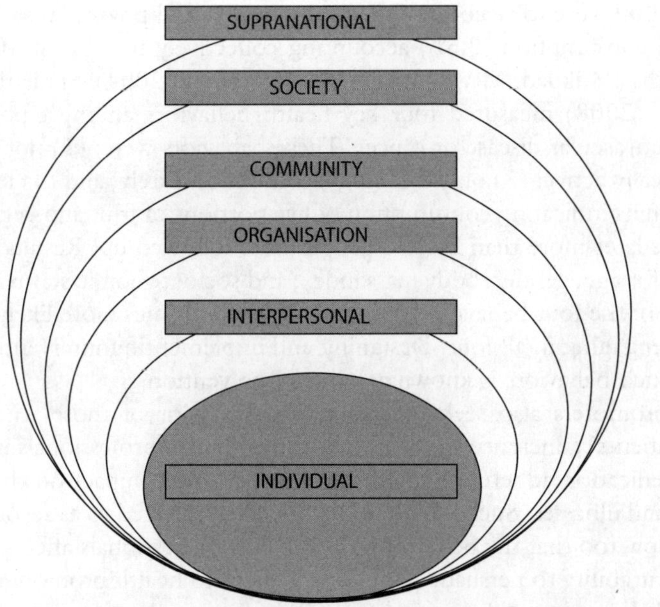

Figure 4.1. Levels of behavior change intervention (Kok et al., 2008)

institutions, manufacturers and distributors of related goods and health systems, and health providers. These stakeholders may develop their own health promotion interventions or provide the venue for application of interventions. Integrating interventions at macro, meso, and micro levels is likely to be much more effective than applying separate interventions at one or more levels (National Institute of Health and Clinical Excellence, 2007).

Health is shaped by genetic inheritance, social structure, wealth and by what we do. Behavior change is often the primary aim of health promotion (at various levels) because behavior can be modified and because change in behavior patterns has the potential to make substantial differences to public health. Behavior determines the prevalence of infectious diseases such as HIV spread, hepatitis C, human papilloma virus, and malaria. In addition, in affluent societies where, for the majority of the population, the threat of infant death and death due to infectious diseases has been minimized, behavior patterns are important to the prevalence of serious degenerative illnesses such as heart disease, stroke, various cancers (including lung cancer), and diabetes. It is estimated that half of all cancers are preventable (Cancer Research UK, 2009), yet the prevalence and incidence of cancers and diabetes are increasing worldwide due to reduced levels of physical activity and increasing average weight. For example, it is predicted that 380 million people will have diabetes by 2025 (International Diabetes Federation, 2009).

Health promotion designed to change behavior patterns may target different types of health-related behavior. Primary prevention focuses on reducing health risk behaviors—for example, the Alameda County study, which followed nearly 7,000 people over 10 years and showed that sleep, exercise, drinking alcohol, and eating habits predict mortality (Belloc & Breslow, 1972). The association between such "health risk" behaviors and health remains evident. The leading causes of death in the US in 2000 were tobacco use (18.1%), poor diet and physical inactivity (16.6%), and alcohol consumption (3.5%) accounting collectively for almost 40% of all premature deaths (Mokdad, Marks, Stroup, & Gerberding, 2004). Similarly, in the UK, Khaw *et al.* (2008) measured four key health behaviors amongst people with no known cardiovascular disease or cancer. These behaviors were: (1) not smoking; (2) being physically active; (3) only drinking alcohol moderately; and (4) levels of blood plasma vitamins indicating consumption of five portions of fruit and vegetables a day. Eleven years later more than 20,000 people were followed up. Results showed that, controlling for age, gender, body mass index, and socioeconomic status, those engaging in none of the four behaviors were more than four times more likely to have died than those engaging in all four. Designing and implementing interventions designed to change such behaviors is known as primary prevention.

Health promoters also seek to change the behavior of those who are ill. For example, patients' adherence to the advice of health care professionals including self-care and medication adherence advice can have a critical impact on the progression of diseases and illnesses. Such interventions are often referred to as secondary prevention. We know too that the behavior of health care professionals affects public health through their ability to persuade patients to adhere to health promotion recommendations and through good practice, including, for example, limiting the spread of disease by infection-control behaviors and consistent, evidence-based prescribing.

As people live longer lives in affluent countries they are more likely to develop long-term physical illness (LTI) such as hypertension, asthma, diabetes, coronary heart disease, stroke, chronic obstructive pulmonary disease, cancer, heart failure, chronic pain, and epilepsy (Department of Health, 2008). In the absence of medical cures, the challenge for people with LTIs is to adapt to their illness, adopting the most effective coping strategies including social support seeking and maintenance of high confidence, or self-efficacy, in managing their illness. Differences in coping responses can enhance quality of life (QoL) and longevity. For example, Moskowitz, Epel, and Acree (2008) found that positive affect, including "enjoying life," was associated with mortality amongst people with diabetes and people over 65, and especially those reporting higher levels of stress. Interventions designed to promote coping with illness or minimize the effects of established illness, rather than prevent illness, are often referred to as tertiary prevention.

The importance of psychological adaptation, resilience, positive affect, and the availability of social support for those with LTIs emphasizes that health is more than an absence of medical conditions. As the World Health Organization defines it, health is "a state of complete physical, mental and social well-being and not merely the absence of disease or infirmity" (WHO, 1948).

This definition challenges those engaged in health promotion to identify, assess and intervene to shape determinants of "physical, mental and social well being." This definition, combined with a social ecological perspective emphasizing the importance of multiple levels of intervention including at the international, national, community, organizational, and individual levels, creates a very broad canvas of intervention possibilities for those working towards health promotion.

Useful Guidance for Health Promoters

The National Institute for Health and Clinical Excellence (NICE), which advises on best practice and cost-effectiveness in the UK National Health Service, has published guidance on how to promote health behavior change (NICE, 2007). This guidance acknowledges that interventions need to be undertaken at individual, community, and population levels and articulates key principles of intervention design and management relevant to each level. The guidance emphasizes the importance of planning and evaluation, including cost-effectiveness. It also emphasizes the need for careful analyses of the determinants of health. An eight page summary can be downloaded at http://guidance.nice.org.uk/PH6.

Corresponding to the social ecological perspective outlined above, the NICE (2007) guidance underlines the importance of assessing and intervening to change the social context in which health-related behavior develops and is sustained. This may involve health promoters in attempting to remove social or financial barriers that make it difficult for people to make positive changes in their lives. Thus health promotion also involves social policy development focusing on ways to alleviate local poverty, and limited employment and educational opportunities.

The NICE guidance emphasizes the importance of high-quality, evidence-based training for health promoters to design, evaluate, and deliver interventions. In particular, the guidance notes that specialist training is required to ensure that health promotion teams are able to competently

1. identify and assess evidence related to behavior change;
2. understand evidence relating to psychological, social, economic and cultural determinants of behavior;
3. interpret relevant data on local or national needs and characteristics;
4. design and plan, implement and evaluate interventions; and
5. work in partnership with members of the target population(s) and those with local knowledge.

This implies that health promotion teams need to assemble a sophisticated set of competencies and that workforce training in health promotion must ensure that practitioners have, maintain, and update these key competencies.

Planning Health Promotion

Effective health promotion depends on understanding which determinants of health (including behavior) need to be changed and then effectively intervening to change these. Changing key determinants relies on understanding the causal and regulatory processes underpinning those determinants. For example, if the problem is obesity and the primary determinant is higher-than-needed calorie intake, then a variety of underpinning processes including regulation of food producers and individual eating motivation need to be considered in order to design effective interventions. In most cases this necessitates detailed, evidence-based planning. Failures to apply research-based models of multilevel causal processes and inadequate planning are common reasons for the failure of health promotion initiatives.

The Predisposing, Reinforcing, and Enabling Constructs in Educational/Environmental Diagnosis and Evaluation (PRECEDE) approach emphasizes the importance of problem analysis prior to intervention (Green, Kreuter, Deeds & Partridge, 1980). This approach has been combined with the Policy, Regulatory, and Organization Constructs in Educational and Environmental Development (PROCEED) model (Green & Kreuter, 2005) which highlights the importance of social and environmental determinants of health and health behavior. The combined PRECEDE-PROCEED framework is widely applied in health promotion planning and is depicted in Figure 4.2.

The PRECEDE-PROCEED framework includes a series of planning phases. It proposes that health promotion should begin with (1) an assessment of the quality of life (QoL) of the target group, whether this is a community or a country, and (2) an epidemiological analysis of health problems and their relevance. This initial focus on QoL echoes the breadth of the WHO definition of health and emphasizes that health is valuable because it maximizes quality of life and longevity (Kaplan, 1990). This first phase of analysis should clarify how health is linked to QoL within the group and should identify change targets including individuals, organizations, policies, and legislation.

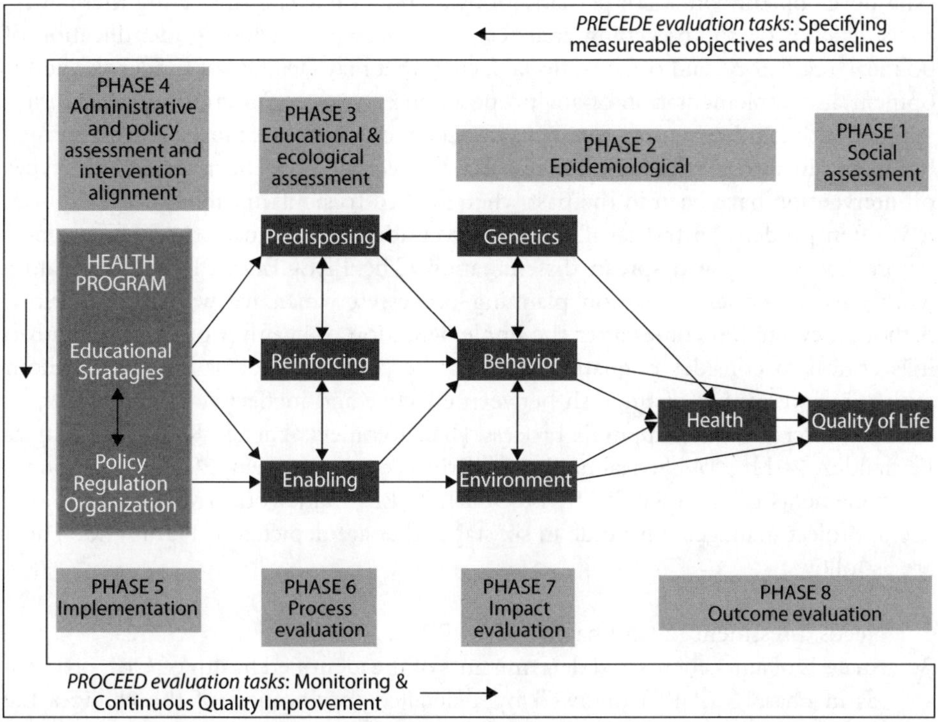

Figure 4.2. The PRECEDE-PROCEED model for health program planning (Green & Kreuter, 2005)

The next planning phase includes identification of the behavioral, social, and environmental factors that shape the health problem of interest. This phase should establish whether the health problem is linked to specific behaviors, and, if it is, to whose behaviors. In addition, social, environmental, or legislative changes that are needed should be identified as well as the decision-makers responsible for those changes.

Next, the model advises health promoters to focus on needs assessment, examining determinants of the behavioral and environmental antecedents of health or quality-of-life concerns. This assessment should identify determinants that must be changed in order to initiate and sustain the behavioral and environmental change. For example, in relation to individual behavior three categories of determinants are defined. Predisposing factors refer to cognitive antecedents that provide a rationale or motivation for behavior (e.g., knowledge, attitudes, values, and goal priorities). Enabling factors are social and psychological factors that facilitate performance of the behavior in question (e.g., behavior of peers, parents, employers, as well as individual competencies and skills). Finally, reinforcing factors sustain repeated performance of the target behavior (e.g., availability of resources, social approval, rules, or laws).

Once the problem has been mapped out in detail then intervention design can begin. In this stage health promoters need to consider what approach will be most effective. Should intervention take the form of a health education or social marketing campaign to change knowledge and attitudes, should it include individual or group skills development courses or perhaps lobbying policy makers? Answering these questions depends on the preceding analyses of the problem, including identification of political, regulatory, and organizational factors that may facilitate or hinder the development and implementation of any proposed intervention. Selection of intervention approaches, including appropriate behavior change techniques, must also be informed by an examination of peer-reviewed research to ascertain how effective particular types of intervention have been in the past when applied to similar problems. In addition, it is often prudent to test small-scale interventions and evaluate their effectiveness before investing in widespread dissemination. The PRECEDE-PROCEED framework also prescribes evaluation planning processes, which we will discuss below. Although evaluation comes after the implementation of health promotion initiatives it is critical to consider evaluation early in the planning process because, without evaluation, we cannot distinguish between effective and ineffective interventions.

The "intervention mapping" process (Bartholomew, Parcel, Kok, Gottlieb, & Fernández, 2011; Kok, Schaalma Ruiter, Brug, & van Empelen, 2004) incorporates many elements of the PRECEDE-PROCEED (PP) framework. IM provides a very useful project management guide in six stages that are depicted in Figure 4.3. These are as follows:

1. Needs assessment (as in phases 1–2 of PP).
2. Analysis of antecedents and determinants of the identified health or QoL problem (as in phase 3 of PP) followed by a detailed specification of the changes the intervention aims to induce, i.e., the performance and change objectives. Performance objectives are the specifications of the health-related behavior the intervention targets. Change objectives are broader including changes in the behavioral determinants that may be needed within the target group.
3. Selection of theory-based intervention methods, or change techniques (overlapping with phase 4 of PP) and practical applications, that is, materials and implementation procedures that allow one to apply change techniques in particular contexts).
4. Development and production of intervention components.
5. Anticipation of program adoption, implementation and sustainability (similar to phase 5 of PP).
6. Anticipation of process and outcome evaluations (as in phases 6–9 of PP).

Although intervention mapping is presented as a series of six steps, Bartholomew et al. (2011) emphasize that this is an iterative, rather than linear, process. Intervention planners move back and forth between the steps as they plan and develop the intervention. However, the process is also cumulative; each step is based on previous steps, and inattention to a particular step may lead to inadequate design and intervention failure.

An example of intervention mapping application is the development of the "Long Live Love" HIV-prevention program for Dutch adolescents, which has been widely adopted in schools in the Netherlands (Schaalma & Kok, 2006). In this case, the needs assessment clarified that many teenagers in schools are sexually active but not consistent condom users and, therefore, susceptible to sexually transmitted infections.

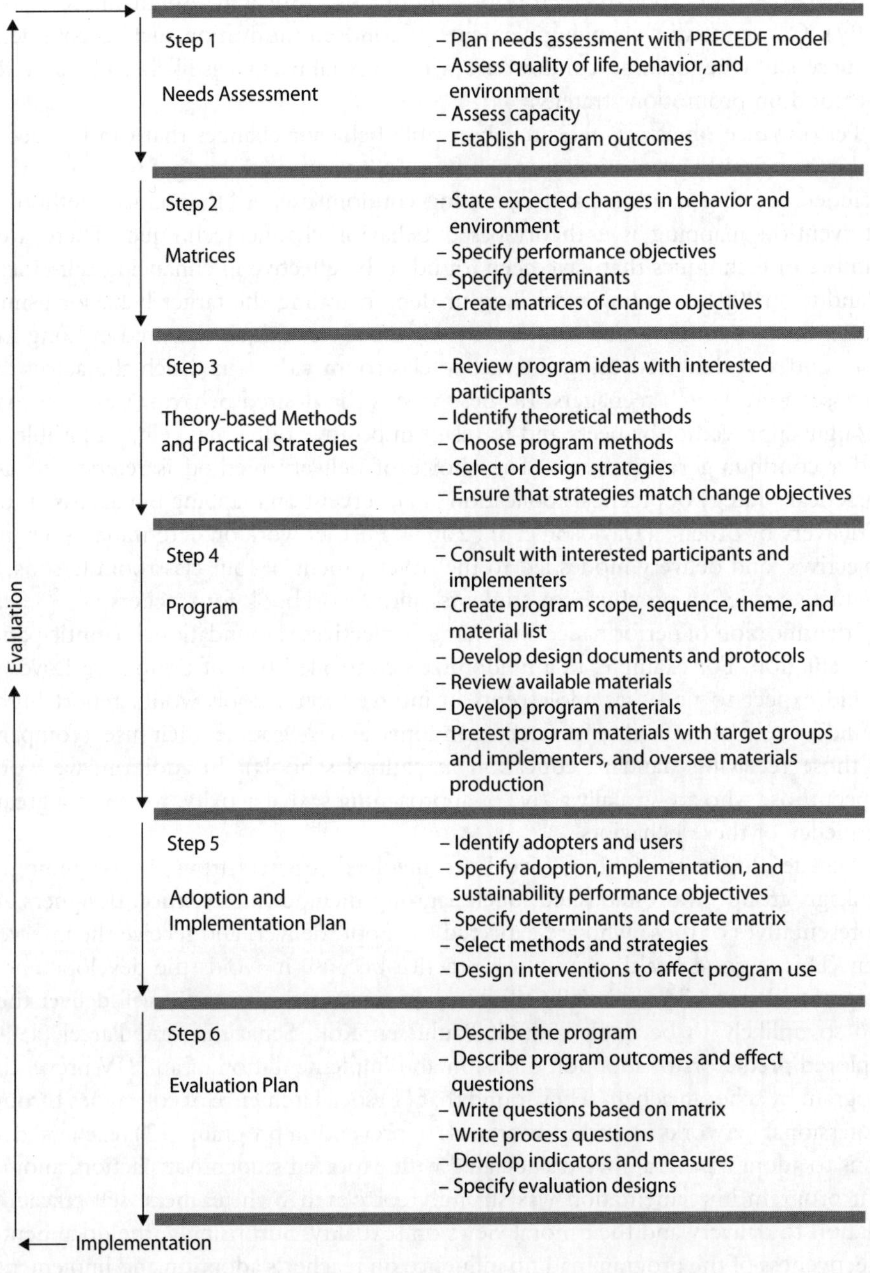

Figure 4.3. The intervention mapping process (Bartholomew et al., 2006)

Preliminary work also clarified that interventions might be especially effective if they focused on establishing condom use from first intercourse onwards, before unprotected sex had become habitual. Analysis of determinants indicated that a series of change targets including self-efficacy are important predictors of condom use. Key preparatory behaviors, such as carrying condoms and discussing condom use with one's partner, are good predictors of condom use (Sheeran, Abraham, & Orbell, 1999). Consequently, changing elements of condom motivation such as confidence in successfully negotiating condom use with a sexual partner is likely to be an effective condom promotion strategy.

Performance objectives refer to observable behavior changes that can be used to evaluate a health promotion intervention. In the case of Long Live Love, these included carrying condoms and discussing condom use. A "theoretical method" in intervention mapping is a theory-based behavior change technique. There are a number of techniques that have been found to be effective in enhancing self-efficacy (Bandura, 1999) including modelling or demonstrating the target behavior using a model that the target group can identify with. This technique was used in Long Live Love and was delivered using interactive classroom videos in which the actors and actresses were Dutch teenagers. In these videos the desired behavior was seen to be strongly approved of by peers and to result in positive outcomes (e.g., enjoyable sex and a continuing relationship). The choice of delivery method is referred to as a "practical strategy or practical application" in intervention mapping but also as "mode of delivery by others" (Davidson et al., 2003). Further work on determinants, change objectives, and delivery modes led to the development of four classroom lessons, an interactive video, a brochure for students, and a workbook for teachers.

Identification of performance and change objectives is foundational to anticipation of evaluation. For example, in a randomized controlled trial of Long Live Love, we would expect to find that adolescents in intervention schools would report higher confidence in their ability to carry condoms and negotiate their use (compared to those receiving standard education in control schools). In addition, we would expect those who are sexually active or approaching sexual activity, to report a greater frequency of these behaviors.

The development of Long Live Love involved teachers from the beginning. A "linkage group" was established. Such a group includes intervention designers and representatives of those who are expected to adopt, deliver, and receive the intervention. This is good health promotion practice because it avoids the development of programs that, while potentially effective, are unattractive to those will deliver them and so unlikely to be implemented. Paulussen Kok, Schaalma, and Parcel (1995) explored predictors of adoption diffusion and implementation of an HIV prevention program by schoolteachers. They found that (1) social influence of colleagues through professional networks predicted awareness of prevention programs, (2) teachers' decisions to adopt a program were associated with expected student satisfaction, and, (3) that program implementation was strongly correlated with teachers' self-efficacy in relation to delivery and their moral views on sexuality. Surprisingly, the documented effectiveness of the program had no influence on teacher's adoption and implementation decisions!

High-quality planning involves consideration of approaches have been effective in similar contexts. For example, Peters, Kok, Ten Dam, Buijs, and Paulussen (2009) conducted a systematic review of reviews examining the effectiveness of school-based health promotion interventions targeting sexual, substance abuse, and nutrition behaviors. They found strong evidence that effective school-based interventions across all three domains shared five characteristics, namely,

1. the use of theory in intervention design;
2. targeting social influences, especially social norms;
3. targeting cognitive and behavioral skills;
4. training those delivering the intervention; and
5. including multiple components.

The reviewers also found evidence for an association between effectiveness and parent involvement and effectiveness and inclusion of a greater number of intervention sessions, although this evidence for these characteristics was weaker than for the five characteristics listed above.

So does planning quality affect intervention effectiveness? Mullen, Green, and Persinger (1985) examined 70 patient education evaluation studies that were methodologically sound and assessed the effectiveness of intervention in terms of increased knowledge and adherence to medical advice in relation to a variety of conditions. The design of these interventions was evaluated using six quality criteria as follows.

1. Consonance: the degree of fit between the intervention design and the intervention objectives.
2. Relevance: the tailoring of the program to knowledge, beliefs, circumstances, and prior experiences of the group that the intervention targets, as assessed by prior research.
3. Individualization (or personal tailoring): the provision of opportunities for participants to have personal questions answered or instructions paced according to their individual progress.
4. Feedback: the provision of information for participants on the extent to which they are achieving planned change, for example, increasing knowledge or performing specified behaviors (including physiological feedback such as, e.g., fitness or blood pressure measurements).
5. Reinforcement: including components in the intervention that are designed to reward the target behaviors (other than feedback) after the behavior has been enacted (e.g., social approval).
6. Facilitation: the provision of means for the learner to take action to reduce barriers to action (e.g., subsidies or organized social support).

This study showed that the best predictor of intervention effectiveness was the planning quality score derived from characterizing intervention planning in terms of these six criteria. Thus good planning is prerequisite to effective health promotion.

Theoretical Framework for Health Promotion: Information, Motivation, and Behavioral Skills

Whether health promotion focuses on population community/organizational or individual changes, understanding and promoting behavior change is central to most health promotion initiatives. There are many theories that identify the psychological determinants of behavior (see Abraham, Sheeran, & Johnston 1998 for an overview

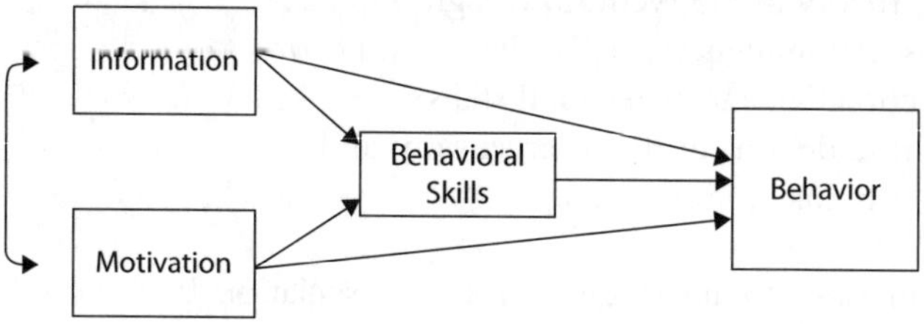

Figure 4.4. The Information-Motivation-Behavioral Skills model (Fisher & Fisher, 1992)

and see Michie et al. (2005) for a series of dimensions in term of which any behavior change initiative may be understood). Two theories combined provide an especially useful framework for health promotion. First, the Information-Motivation-Behavioral Skills model (IMB; Fisher & Fisher, 1992; Fisher, Fisher, Bryan, & Misovich, 2002; and see Figure 4.4.) and, second, an integrative theory of the components of motivation (Fishbein et al., 2001).

The IMB proposes that, having identified behaviors to be promoted amongst a specified target group, health promoters should initially ask themselves, "What is missing amongst the target population that explains why these behaviors are not already being performed?" Do they lack key information? Is there a general lack of motivation? Alternatively, is the problem a lack of the behavioral skills needed to translate well-informed motivation into action? In answering these questions it is critical to precisely define the target group. For example, having identified a low socioeconomic status group of teenagers as at risk of unwanted pregnancy and sexually transmitted infections (STIs)—are they unaware of the risks they face, or are key drivers of motivation such as attitudes and norms absent? Perhaps forgetfulness and low goal priority are key determinants of unprotected sex? Answering such questions and thereby identifying which determinants of action are missing is essential to intervention design and may necessitate preliminary pilot research, sometimes referred to as "elicitation research."

When information is readily accessible, easy to understand, directly relevant to the target audience, and refers to a behavior that is easy to change, then information provision alone can change health-related behavior. For example, media coverage of food scares such as Bovine Spongiform Encephalopathy can lead to widespread changes in behavior such as beef purchase (e.g., Tyler, 2001; Swientek, 2001). However, the presence of information does not guarantee relevance or accessibility. For example, packaged food and drinks include comprehensive nutritional information, but information relevant to the relationship between consumption and weight gain may be absent or incomprehensible to most consumers. For example, do you know how much exercise you need to take to consume the calories in a cup of coffee? A woman weighing 11 stone walking at 3 miles an hour would need approximately 45 minutes to burn off the 200 calories in a whole milk latte but slightly less than 30 minutes to burn off the 120 calories in a skimmed milk latte (see NHS Choices website, http://www.nhs.uk/Pages/HomePage.aspx). Imagine that all packaged foods and all restaurant meals were labeled with the number of minutes it would take the average adult to "walk off" the calories included in any food or drink product (e.g., 45 for a whole milk latte). Would this make a difference to food purchase and consumption decisions and so to eating patterns? Certainly, information is only likely to influence health-related behavior if it is relevant and easily accessible.

Even when good information is readily available, people may not be motivated to change their behavior. So what change targets are likely to boost motivation? In an integration of theories of motivation Fishbein et al. (2001) provided a useful checklist. This integrative framework includes insights from social cognitive theory (Bandura, 1999), the health belief model (Becker, Haefner, & Maiman, 1977), the theories of reasoned action and planned behavior (Ajzen, 1991; Fishbein & Ajzen, 1975). Three prerequisites of behavior are identified:

1. a strong *intention*,
2. the necessary *skills* to perform the behavior, and
3. an absence of *environmental constraints* that could prevent the behavior.

These prerequisites echo the IMB model because they specify motivation (that is, intention) and behavioral skills. The model extends IMB and endorses the PRECEDE-PROCEED framework by highlighting that, for many behaviors, the barriers to performance are not only a lack of information, motivation, or behavioral skills, but also the way in which the environment affects motivation and the feasibility of action. What exactly is relevant in the environment varies according to the target behavior. For example, the amount of money invested in advertising may be an important determinant of behavior. Consequently, advertising bans (e.g., on tobacco) can be an effective behavior change intervention. Alternatively, physical architecture may impede or facilitate health-related behaviors. For example, if people are to be encouraged to wash their hands then readily available, attractive hand-washing facilities and fast hand-drying options need to be provided. Consequently, behavior-specific elicitation research is required to examine carefully environmental prompts and barriers to the target behavior prior to intervention design.

The Fishbein et al. (2001) model also provides a useful list of cognitions that are likely to enhance and sustain motivation (or intention). Motivation is likely to be strengthened when a person

1. perceives the advantages (or benefits) of performing the behavior to outweigh the perceived disadvantages (or costs),
2. perceives the social (normative) to perform the behavior to be greater than that not to perform the behavior,
3. believes that the behavior is consistent with his or her self-image,
4. anticipates the emotional reaction to performing the behavior to be more positive than negative, and
5. has high levels of self-efficacy.

Each or all of these components may become primary targets for a health promotion intervention. For example, teenage norms regarding condom carrying and condom use may be important determinants of teenage STI transmission. Similarly, an intervention may aim to change the perceived benefits and costs of condom use or shift the consensual image of teenagers who consistently use condoms. As intervention mapping and IMB prescribe, motivational targets depend on an analysis clarifying which motivational components are already shared or missing amongst the target group.

Self-efficacy, that is, the belief that one can successfully perform a given behavior in a specified context, is an important determinant of motivation and action. People rarely persist with goals they do not feel they can achieve. Those who believe they can succeed set themselves more challenging goals. They exert more effort, use more flexible problem solving strategies and are more persistent *because* they believe they will eventually succeed. High self-efficacy also minimizes stress which, in turn, enhances skilled performance (Bandura 1999).

Bandura (1999) identifies four main change approaches (i.e., mastery experiences, vicarious experiences, verbal persuasion, and altering emotional arousal) likely to be effective in enhancing self-efficacy. First, experience of successfully performing the target behaviors gives people confidence because they know they have previously succeeded. This recommends setting graded tasks in which learners succeed before the difficulty threshold is raised. Second, modelling can be effective because observing others' success, especially others like ourselves, can increase self-efficacy. People can be persuaded by arguments demonstrating that others (like them) are successful in meeting challenges similar to their own (thereby changing descriptive norms), as well as by persuasion highlighting their own skills and past success. Finally, stress and anxiety during performance can undermine self- efficacy so that interventions designed to reduce anxiety and encourage reinterpretation of arousal (as normal) may enhance self-efficacy and facilitate skilled performance. This matching of psychological determinants to appropriate intervention approaches is a critical aspect of stage 3 of the intervention mapping process.

Behavior change may necessitate learning different types of behavioral skills. Self-regulatory skills are cognitive skills which, for example, help people consider longer-term consequences of current action, evaluate their current behavior, set new goals, prioritize goals in the face of other demands, plan action before and during goal-relevant experiences, and prompt exertion of appropriate effort when opportunities present themselves. When helping people to develop such skills, initial learning may involve conscious rehearsal of the skill followed by practice over time so that the self regulatory response becomes habitual or automatic. For example, implementation intention formation refers to the formation of if-then plans in which the "if" specifies a context or environmental prompt and the "then" specifies the targeted behavior (Sheeran, Milne, Webb, & Gollwitzer, 2005). Martin, Sheeran, Slade, Wright, and Dibble (2009) found that helping young women attending contraception clinics to make specific plans about how to overcome a series of obstacles that could derail their contraception intentions made it more likely that subsequent clinic visits involved requests for additional contraceptive supplies (indicating ongoing protection) rather then pregnancy testing or emergency contraception (suggesting a failure of protection). In this case, conscious planning facilitated effective contraception. Similarly, Schinke, and Gordon (1992) developed and evaluated an effective culture-specific intervention, including a self-completion book using comic strip characters and rap music verse to encourage effective safer sex regulation amongst black teenagers. The aim was to develop self-monitoring and planning skills as well as rehearsed scripts that could disrupt and control interaction patterns that might lead to unprotected sex.

Learning and practising motor skills may also be prerequisite to enactment of target health-related behaviors. For example, correct condom use depends upon a basic understanding of infection control as well as the manual skills involved in opening and using a condom correctly. Certain medication regimes require patients to learn to use devices such as inhalers or needles. Consequently, patients and health care workers may need special instruction in order to ensure good adherence and treatment effectiveness (Kools, Van de Wiel, Ruiter, & Kok, 2006). Moreover, even apparently simple skills such as hand washing which is crucial to infection control in hospitals may require instruction (Pittet et al., 2000).

Skills needed to seek and secure others' support for change are also important. For example, the skills required to negotiate condom use with a reluctant partner or the skills to refuse to eat traditional but unhealthy foods. The relevant social skills depend on the target behavior but assertiveness training (that is, being able to express one's own wants and needs in an honest and nonaggressive manner) and negotiation skills are often prerequisite to managing interactions that arise when individuals begin to change their behavior.

Applying the IMB theoretical framework involves identifying what is missing amongst the target group in terms of the determinants or antecedents of the target behavior. Providing information is unlikely to be effective if the target group is well informed. Similarly, attempting to enhance motivation amongst a group who, in general, already intend to change is unlikely to prompt behavior change. For example, most smokers want to quit but are not confident about their ability to do so. Hence, focusing on self-efficacy and skill development is likely to be more effective than attempting to enhance motivation to quit by emphasizing the negative health consequences of smoking. Thus, assessment of readiness to change through elicitation research is an important aspect of effective intervention planning and design and should guide the selection of behavior change techniques.

The Transtheoretical, or Stages of Change Model (Prochaska, DiClemente, & Norcross, 1992) provides a framework for assessing readiness to change and has been widely applied. Unfortunately, there is little evidence supporting distinctions between many of the stages defined by this model (Sutton, 2000; Littell & Girvin, 2002). Consequently, West (2005) suggested that this model provides a poor basis for intervention planning. Brug et al. (2005) conclude that only the major stage distinction between those who are and are not motivated to change is well supported. This mirrors the proposals of the IMB model, which recommends assessing pre-existing knowledge and providing information where needed, assessing motivation, and, where motivation is lacking, providing interventions to change determinants of motivation (see the Fishbein et al., 2001 model). Finally, amongst those who are already motivated, assessing a variety of behavioral skills, as well as self-efficacy, which, if absent, may undermine the translation of intentions into action or mean that a health behavior is not maintained over time.

Selecting Effective Behavior Change Techniques

Behavior change techniques (BCTs) are referred to as "theoretical methods" in intervention mapping because they are methods of bringing about a specified change amongst a particular target group based on a theoretical understanding of determinants underpinning that change. The Fishbein et al. (2001) model of motivation identifies five distinct change targets that may boost motivation. Thus, if motivation is low, intervention designers may consider BCTs that have the potential to change participants' perception of the advantages and costs of a specified action and/or their perception of what others are doing and approve of in relation to that action or BCTs capable of enhancing self-efficacy, and so forth. By exploring what information, elements of motivation, and behavioral skills are missing in the target group and setting clearly defined change objectives health promoters considerably narrow the range of BCTs relevant to the planned intervention.

A list of BCTS that have been reliably identified across a range of behavior change interventions was provided by Abraham and Michie (2008) who identified 26 distinct BCTs used in interventions described in 195 published papers. Table 4.1. is a development of that list. The table provides brief descriptions of 40 distinct BCTs grouped according to the change targets that may be identified during intervention planning. This list is not exhaustive and some of the listed BCTs are closely related. Nonetheless, this menu of BCTs illustrates how identification of psychological targets enables health promoters to focus on a group of corresponding BCTs. The list provides an easy to understand selection of previously-applied techniques that may be applied and combined to enhance the effectiveness of behavior change interventions.

Some standardized approaches to intervention design, such as relapse prevention (Marlatt & Donovan, 2005) and motivational interviewing (Rollnick & Miller, 1995) combine a series of BCTs. This is appropriate because intervention change targets such as stress reduction, improved time management, or improved communication skills may require application of a variety of BCTs. Health promotion interventions may also involve organizational change, community interventions, and legislation. When trying to influence environmental decision makers, individual-level BCTs may be applied in addition to political interventions such as: advocacy, empowerment and lobbying for legislative change (see Kok, Gottlieb, Commers, & Smerecnik, 2008).

The science of behavior change is not sufficiently advanced to allow specification of how effective each of the listed BCTs is in promoting particular behaviors. Nonetheless, three recent meta-analytic studies provides useful guidance on the potential effectiveness of particular BCTs. For example, in a systematic review of interventions designed to promote physical activity and/or healthy eating, Michie, Abraham, Whittington, McAteer, and Gupta (2009) found that different intervention designers had selected different BCTs even when targeting very similar behaviors amongst very similar target groups. Drawing upon the BCTs defined by Abraham and Michie (2008), and Carver and Scheier's (1998) control theory, Michie et al. (2009) found that prompting self monitoring combined with other BCTs designed to promote goal setting and enhance self regulatory skills (see Table 1), specifically,

Table 4.1. Illustrative Behavior Change Techniques Grouped by Change Targets

Techniques Designed to Change Cognitive and Affective Attitudes

Provide general information on behavior-health link
Information about the relationship between the behavior and health.

Provide information on material consequences
Information focusing on what will happen if the person performs the behavior, including the benefits and costs (or negative consequences) of action or inaction.

Provide information on affective consequences
Information concerning how the person may/will feel if (s)he performs or does not perform the behavior, including enjoyment and anticipation of regret.

Prompt self assessment of affective consequences
After attempts at performing target behaviors prompt the person to reflect on, assess and evaluate how they felt about performing the behavior.

Induce cognitive dissonance
Create a discrepancy in the person's thinking about their current or past behavior and a representation of themselves or their values. In resolving this discrepancy they may judge their current/past behavior more or less favourably—depending on the contrast created.

Techniques Designed to Change Risk Perception

Provide information about personal susceptibility to negative consequences
Personalized information about negative consequences for recipients, using pronouns such as "you" as in "you are at risk."

Prompting to assess own risk
Asking participants to assess their own susceptibility and severity, i.e., challenges participants to predict what is likely to happen to them if they engage in a risky behavior.

Techniques Designed to Change Normative Beliefs

Provide information about others' behavior
Information about what other people (including significant others such as friends) are doing, i.e., indicates that a particular action or sequence of actions is common or uncommon amongst a group.

Provide information about others' approval
Information about how other people/specific others judge/approve of the participant's behavior.

Provide opportunities for social comparison
Provides a setting in which social comparison occur, e.g., in group classes or case studies in text or video.

Plan or organize social support/social change
Providing or helping the participant to arrange interaction with others who can help them change their behavior, e.g., support groups and buddy systems.

Continued

Table 4.1. *Continued*

Techniques Designed to Change Identity

Prompt identification as role model/position advocate
Focusing on how the person may be an example to others and affect others' behavior, e.g., being a good example to children. Could include persuading others of the importance of adopting/changing the behavior (e.g., giving a talk).

Techniques Designed to Change Goal Setting and Motivation

Prompt intention/goal formation
Encouraging the person to set a general goal or make a behavioral resolution, e.g., "I will take more exercise next week."

Prompt specific planning/goal setting
Encouraging detailed planning of what the person will do including a very specific definition of the behavior, e.g., frequency (such as how many times a day/week), intensity (e.g., speed), duration (e.g., for how long) and context (e.g., where the behavior will be performed).

Prompt review of behavioral goals
Reconsideration of previously set goals/intentions, usually after an attempt to enact them.

Prompt barrier identification
Encourage participants to anticipate potential barriers and plan ways of overcoming them, e.g., competing goals or lack of resources.

Agree behavioral contract
Explicit written agreement of the participant's resolution witnessed by another (e.g., signing a contract).

Techniques Designed to Enhance Self-Efficacy and Self-Regulation

Provide instruction
Telling participants how to perform a behavior or preparatory behaviors, e.g., face-to-face instructions providing "tips."

Model/Demonstrate the behavior
Showing participants how a behavior is performed and that it can be rewarding or is reinforced, e.g., face-to-face in a group class or using video of others successfully performing the behavior.

Prompt mental rehearsal of successful performance
Guiding participants to imagine themselves performing the behavior successfully in relevant contexts. Could involve graded tasks.

Use argument to bolster self efficacy
Involves telling the person that they can successfully perform the behavior, arguing against self-doubts and asserting that they can and will succeed.

Reattribution
Helping person reinterpret (previous) failure in terms of either unstable and/or changeable attributions and previous successes in terms of stable, internal attributions.

Table 4.1. *Continued*

Set graded tasks
Set the person easy-to-perform tasks, making them increasingly difficult until target behavior is performed.

Prompt practice
Guiding participants in practicing the behavior in classes and/or as homework assignments.

Prompt self monitoring of behavior
Participants are asked to keep a record of specified behavior/s. This could, e.g., take the form of a diary or completing a questionnaire about their behavior.

Provide feedback on performance
Providing data about recorded behavior or commenting on how well or badly a person has performed an action.

Techniques Designed to Establish Behaviors Using Encouragement and Rewards

Provide general encouragement
Praising or rewarding participants for effort or performance without making this contingent on specific behavioral performance.

Provide contingent rewards
Praising or rewarding participants but only when they perform specified actions or actions.

Prompt self-reward
As above, but in this case the person provides their own reward for performing the behavior. The reward is not part of the intervention which focuses on self-reward skills.

Prompt self-talk
Encouraging participants to talk to themselves (aloud or silently) before and during planned behaviors to encourage and support action.

Prompting generalization
Once a behavior is performed in a particular situation, the person is encouraged or helped to try it in another situation.

Shaping
First rewarding participants for any approximation to the target behavior and then later only for progressively for more accurate or demanding tasks.

Techniques Designed to Establish Behaviors Using Self-Selected Environmental Prompts or Reminders from Others

Teach to use prompts/cues
Teaching participants to identify environmental prompts which can be used to remind them to perform the behavior.

Use of follow-up prompts
Sending letters, making telephone calls, visits, or follow-up meetings after the main intervention has been completed.

Continued

Table 4.1. *Continued*

Techniques Designed to Change Emotional States in Readiness for Action

Fear arousal
Involves presentation of risk and/or mortality information relevant to the behavior and highlighting negative outcomes (e.g., death or serious illness) using verbal communication of threats and/or emotive images.

Self-affirmation
Involves encouraging people to acknowledge their good and valued characteristics. For example, by writing down desirable characteristics before receiving a message highlighting personal risk and/or negative consequences.

Guided imagery to alter mood
Teach the person to use images of place, emotion, and achievement to enhance positive mood and confidence.

Illustrative Techniques Designed to Enhance Social Skills

Instruction on resisting social pressure
Involves the identification of social pressures to engage in risky behaviors and building skills and strategies that should be used in response.

Assertiveness training
Teaching people to honestly express their needs and desires in a nonaggressive but confident manner.

Negotiation skills training
Teaching people to understand others' perspectives and seek compromises that allow people with conflicting needs or desires to find solutions that optimize achieving what everyone wants.

(1) prompting intention formation (2) prompting specific planning, (3) prompting reviews of behavioral goals, and, (4) providing feedback on performance were associated with greater effectiveness. The average *d*[1] for interventions including these specified BCTs was .42 compared to .26 for interventions without self monitoring and one or more of the other four BCTs).

In another study assessing the impact of BCT inclusion on intervention effectiveness, Webb and Sheeran (2006) found that interventions including information provision, goal setting, modelling, and skill training yielded small-to-medium effects on behavior change (with *ds*[1] around 0.3). Interventions including use of contingent rewards and provision of social support were more effective (with *d*s between 0.5 and 0.6).

In a meta-analysis of 354 HIV-prevention interventions and 99 control groups, examining the relationship between intervention content and intervention effectiveness in relation to condom use promotion, Albarracín, Gillete, Earl, Glasman, and Durantini (2005) found that the most effective interventions provided (1) information, (2) arguments to promote positive attitudes towards condom use, (3) behavioral skills relevant to condom use, and (4) self-regulatory or skills training. In addition, provision of condoms and HIV counselling and HIV testing enhanced intervention effectiveness.

By contrast, inclusion of threat or fear appeals did not enhance the effectiveness of condom-promoting interventions. The approaches to behavior change considered by Albarracín et al. (2005) are more broadly defined than the BCTs in Table 1. Nonetheless, these findings can be easily related to the groups of BCTs in the table.

Albarracín et al. (2005) found some approaches to be effective with one target group but not another. Arguments targeting normative beliefs were found to enhance intervention effectiveness when the target audience was under 21 years of age but to reduce effectiveness amongst older recipients. Thus age moderates the relationship between inclusion of normative arguments and intervention effectiveness. Findings also confirmed that arguments and training designed to teach behavioral skills are successful at changing behavior for most recipients, but training in condom use skills enhanced the effectiveness of intervention for men but not interventions delivered to women. Thus gender moderated the relationship between condom use skills training and intervention effectiveness. These findings emphasize how important it is to evaluate the effectiveness of interventions for particular groups and to use the results of such evaluations to tailor future interventions to specific audiences.

Fear appeals have been widely used in health promotion. Consequently, there is substantial evidence on the effectiveness of this approach (De Hoog, Stroebe, & de Wit, 2007). Fear appeals can be effective and may be appropriate when the target group is unaware of, or underestimates, a serious threat. However, fear appeals may be ineffective (e.g., Albarracín et al., 2005) or even counterproductive if the target group lack the self-efficacy and skills required to perform the behavior (e.g., quitting smoking). A fear appeal should emphasize personal susceptibility to a threat and the negative consequences of ignoring the threat as well as the effectiveness of the recommended protection and self efficacy enhancement (Witte & Allen, 2000). Collectively, these techniques should prompt protective intentions. However, fear appeals require careful design and cautious use because, if people do not believe they can protect themselves (i.e., have low self-efficacy), they may protect themselves psychologically through defensive cognitive responses. When defensive processing (or "fear control") occurs, recipients may dismiss the message as untrustworthy—rejecting it altogether—or rejecting its relevance to them (Ruiter, Abraham, & Kok, 2001). De Hoog et al. (2007) also conclude that messages that are frightening are no more effective then those that simply state the negative consequences of inaction.

Intervention Evaluation

Many health promotion interventions are not evaluated. Moreover, even when evaluations are undertaken they may only assess whether the target audience noticed the intervention (e.g., whether or not they remembered a campaign) or whether they were satisfied with it (e.g., whether they thought a program was useful). Such evaluations fail to answer the central evaluation questions, namely (1) was the intervention effective in bringing about the change it was designed to induce and (2) how did it work?

Assessing whether an evaluation changed health or QoL may not be possible immediately after the intervention because the effects may take time to manifest themselves. For example, an intervention designed to change healthy eating and physical activity may be evaluated in terms of weight loss and fitness over a period of months (e.g., at 2 and 12 months follow-up). If the predicted effects on weight and fitness are to emerge then they will follow changes in the performance targets or targeted behaviors. Changes in eating and physical activity should be immediately evident in the weeks following the intervention. Consequently, many health promotion interventions can be evaluated immediately in terms of changed health behavior and later in terms of the impact of any health behavior change on improved health and QoL.

The most basic evaluation is a comparison (in terms of behavior or health) between participants assessed at baseline (i.e., before the intervention) and at follow-up (i.e., after they have received the intervention). If no change is observed then the intervention is unlikely to have been effective. However, such comparisons are not conclusive because they do not take account of natural changes occurring at the same time as the intervention. For example, in a situation in which health behavior is known to be deteriorating (e.g., amongst a group of teenagers who are developing less healthy eating habits) a no-change result could imply that an intervention has been effective in stalling ongoing deterioration. Hence evaluations need to involve a comparison group within which ongoing processes (apart from the intervention itself) can be observed. Matched control group designs allow this. For example, students at one school might receive an intervention while those at a comparable control school do not. While such designs are an advance on before–after comparisons they may leave relevant characteristics unbalanced between the intervention and control groups. For example, a school that volunteers to implement an intervention may be qualitatively different to one that does not and such differences may facilitate the operation of the intervention. Consequently, the ideal evaluation design is a randomized control trial in which participants are randomly allocated to the intervention and the (no intervention or standard care) control groups. In such a design we can be more confident that characteristics and processes that would facilitate the operation of the intervention have been evenly distributed amongst the intervention and control groups. Randomized control trials may operate at an individual level (e.g., when individual students in a class are randomly allocated), at a group level (e.g., when classes are allocated), or at an institutional level (e.g., when schools are allocated). In the latter designs multilevel modelling must be used to control for any pre-existing differences in the allocated groups or institutions.

Sometimes it is unethical to withhold an intervention from participants. For example, a new approach to sex and relationships education could not be tested by depriving children in a control school of such education. In these cases, the intervention may be compared to an existing intervention such as current education or routine care. Such designs (using "active controls") challenge the intervention not just to be effective but to be more effective than existing interventions.

A recent meta-analysis of 62 previous meta-analyses of health behavior change interventions (including 1,011 primary-level intervention evaluations) found that these interventions primarily targeted eating and physical activity, sexual behavior, addictive behaviors, stress management, screening for women, and use of health services (Johnson, Scott-Sheldon, & Carey, 2010). In general, these interventions were effective with small to medium-sized *d*s ranging from .08 to .45. Those targeting women and older participants were more effective. Thus age and gender tend to moderate the effectiveness of health promotion interventions. Interesting shorter interventions were also found to be more effective. Health promoters should not be discouraged by small effect sizes. Small changes across a population (for example, in fitness) can have a large effect on the prevalence illnesses such as coronary vascular disease and diabetes (Rose, 1992).

In addition to effect size, an important indicator of the value of an intervention is its cost-effectiveness. For example, if behavior change observed in the intervention group leads to fewer medical consultations and treatments compared to the control group this could result in considerable public health savings. The NICE (2007) guidance strongly recommends conducting cost-effectiveness evaluations of health promotion initiatives. This requires tracking the cost of intervention delivery so that an accurate cost per person can be calculated. It also requires longer-term outcome measures including use of medical services and QoL over time (as well as behavior change measures). Where such analyses are undertaken they tend to show that when health promotion interventions are effective in changing health-related behavior they are also cost-effective because medical consultations and treatments are very expensive (see Friedman, Sobel, Myers, Caudill, & Benson, 1995 for illustrations).

Anticipating the likely effect size of an intervention allows pre-evaluation power analysis, that is, calculating the number of participants needed to give the evaluation trial a good chance of detecting the effect. The smaller the anticipated effect, the larger the number of people required. Attrition—that is, people failing to complete an intervention or the follow-up measures—can create problems for evaluation studies. For example, if 50% of those in the intervention group drop out then, even if the intervention is very successful (amongst the remaining 50% compared to no-intervention controls) then the overall impact of this intervention will be limited. Attrition problems can be addressed by employing an intention-to-treat in which all randomized participants are included in the analyses, counting drop-outs as showing no change. This is important when attrition in the intervention group is high.

Validated measures of behavior are required to evaluate behavior change interventions but other outcomes should also be assessed. These include psychological determinants assumed to be involved in the change process upon which the design is based (e.g., measures of attitudes, normative beliefs, or the extent to which participants engaged in recommended planning). If expected changes in such determinants occur in a successful intervention then the inclusion of these measures allows *mediation analyses* to be conducted, thereby testing whether the assumed change mechanisms account for the success of the intervention. This helps clarify *how* the intervention worked. For example, if an intervention was designed to facilitate healthy eating and increases in physical activity by means of specific planning, then an evaluation should assess the impact on planning as well as behavior and health outcomes such as weight loss or improved fitness (see Luszczynska, Sobczyk, & Abraham, 2007 for an example of such mediation analyses).

When an intervention is not effective, it is important to know whether it failed because it was not capable of generating the predicted effects. Mediation analyses can help clarify this. For example, if an intervention designed to induce specific planning failed to do so then this provides an immediate explanation for its failure to change behavior or health. Alternatively, the intervention may have the potential to be effective but may not have been delivered as designed (e.g., classes were not taught as described in the manual or participants did not read or attend the intervention). To assess fidelity of delivery a process evaluation is required (see phase 6 of PP). This involves examining whether the intervention is being delivered as designed *during* delivery.

Even well-designed, effective, competently-evaluated interventions may have little impact on health if they are not adopted or do not reach the target audience for which they were designed. Glasgow, Bull, Gillette, Klesges, and Dzewaltowski (2002) and Green and Glasgow (2006) explain how health promoters can optimize the applied relevance of their interventions using the RE-AIM framework:

1. Reach,
2. Effectiveness,
3. Adoption,
4. Implementation, and
5. Maintenance.

"Reach" refers to how many of the target population were involved in an evaluation and how representative they were of that target population. For example, if an intervention was evaluated using economically advantaged participants, then questions would arise as to whether it would also be effective for economically less advantaged people.

"Effectiveness" relates to the range of effects an intervention might have. For example, even if it changed behavior, did it enhance QoL or have any unintended consequences (e.g., did participants find it onerous or upsetting)?

"Adoption" refers to whether the users (e.g., nurses, teachers, managers, members of the public) are persuaded of the utility of the intervention. This is likely to depend on how easily it is implemented, whether they or their clients/participants like it and whether it is compatible with their other main goals (Paulussen et al., 1995). Interventions are unlikely to be used if adopters cannot afford them. Understanding this adoption and diffusion process is critical to the overall impact of any intervention (Rogers, 2003). Establishing a linkage group at the outset of intervention design, as recommended by IM, makes it more likely that intervention designers will understand how adopters and participants will view the intervention.

"Implementation" refers to the ease and feasibility of faithful delivery. If an intervention is complex, expensive, or requires specialist training or teams of people to deliver it, then it is less likely to be sustainable in real-world settings.

Finally, "maintenance" refers to the longer-term sustainability of the intervention in real-world settings. For example, if an organization or community does not have the resources to deliver an intervention then, no matter how effective it is, it will be dropped over time. Similarly, if implementation problems are encountered, an intervention may be adapted and this may result in unintentional deletion of effective BCTs. These practical considerations are as important as observed d values, if health promotion efforts are to have an impact on health and policy.

Intervention planning should anticipate each of these elements of evaluation and appropriate evaluation measures and methods should be developed as the intervention develops through intervention mapping stages.

Conclusions

The view of health promotion outlined here corresponds closely to the guidance on behavior change offered by NICE (2007). Health promoters should view health and QoL needs within social contexts and, as the social ecological perspective suggests, intervene at all relevant levels from the individual to the political. Planning and careful intervention design are essential, as prescribed in the PRECEDE-PROCEED and intervention mapping models. In particular, identification of key determinants of relevant health-related behavior and relevant deficits amongst the target group are important, as defined by the Information-Motivation-Behavioral Skills model. Careful matching of behavior change techniques to outcome objectives and selection of techniques for which there is supporting evidence enhances the likelihood of intervention effectiveness. Effectiveness must be carefully assessed indicating the extent to which the intervention had psychological, behavioral, health, and QoL effects as well as whether the intervention worked as predicted. Cost-effectiveness is an important guide to the value of interventions and will influence adoption and diffusion which need to be planned for, from the outset.

Note

1 Cohen's *d* is an effect size measure, which is widely used to indicate the extent to which an intervention has been effective. It is calculated by subtracting the post-intervention mean scores (e.g., on a fitness measure) of the intervention and control group and dividing this by the average variation in this measure across both groups (i.e., the pooled standard deviation). For example, if the control group has an average post-intervention score of 1 on the outcome measure (such as fitness) at follow-up while the intervention group has an average post-intervention score of 2 then subtracting them gives a value of 1. If the overall variation (or standard deviation) in this measure across both groups was 0.5 then the *d* value for this trial would be 2.0. In other words the intervention had an average outcome that was two standard deviations higher than the control group. This would be a very large effect.

References

Abraham, C., & Graham-Rowe, E. (2009). Are worksite interventions effective in increasing physical activity? A systematic review and meta-analysis. *Health Psychology Review*, *3*, 108–144.

Abraham, C., & Michie, S. (2008). A taxonomy of behavior change techniques used in interventions. *Health Psychology*, *27*, 379–387.

Abraham, C., Sheeran, P., & Johnston, M. (1998). From health beliefs to self-regulation: Theoretical advances in the psychology of action control. *Psychology and Health*, *13*, 569–591.

Ajzen, I. (1991). The theory of planned behavior. *Organizational Behavior and Human Decision Processes, 50,* 179–211.

Albarracín, D., Gillete, J. C., Earl, A. N., Glasman, L. R., & Durantini, M. R. (2005). A test of major assumptions about behavior change: A comprehensive look at the effects of passive and active HIV-prevention interventions since the beginning of the epidemic. *Psychological Bulletin, 131,* 856–897.

Bandura, A. (1999). Health promotion from the perspective of social cognitive theory. *Psychology and Health, 13,* 623–650.

Bartholomew, L. K., Parcel, G. S., Kok, G., & Gottlieb, N. H. (2006). *Planning health promotion programs. An intervention mapping approach.* San Francisco, CA: Jossey-Bass.

Bartholomew, L. K., Parcel, G. S., Kok, G., Gottlieb, N. H., & Fernández, M. E. (2011). *Planning health promotion programs: an intervention mapping approach, 3rd edition.* San Francisco, CA: Jossey-Bass.

Becker, M. H., Haefner, D. P., & Maiman, L. A. (1977). The health belief model of prediction of dietary compliance: A field experiment. *Journal of Health and Social Behavior, 18,* 348–366.

Belloc, N. B., & Breslow, L. (1972). Relationship of physical health status and health practices. *Preventive Medicine, 9,* 469–421.

Brug, J., Conner, M., Harré, N., Kremers, S., McKellar, S., & Whitelaw, S., 2005. The Transtheoretical Model and stages of change: A critique. *Health Education Research, 20,* 244–258.

Cancer Research UK. (2009). Cancer Statistics. Retrieved from http://info.cancerresearchuk.org/cancerstats/incidence/#table

Carver, C. S., & Scheier, M., F. (1998). Control theory: A useful conceptual framework for personality-social, clinical and health psychology. *Psychological Bulletin, 92,* 111–135.

Davidson, K. W., Goldstein, M., Kaplan, R. M., Kaufmann, P. G., Knatterund, G. L., Orleans, C. T., … Whitlock, E. P. (2003). Evidence-based behavioral medicine: What is it and how do we achieve it? *Annals of Behavioral Medicine, 26,* 161–171.

De Hoog, N., Stroebe, W., & de Wit, J. B. F. (2007). The impact of vulnerability to and severity of a health risk on processing and acceptance of fear-arousing communications: A meta-analysis. *Review of General Psychology, 11,* 258–285.

Department of Health. (2008). Raising the profile of long term conditions care: A compendium of information. Leeds. Department of Health. Retrieved from www.dh.gov.uk/publication

Engbers, L. H., van Poppel, M. N. R., Chin A., Paw, M. J. M., & van Mechelen, V. (2005). Worksite health promotion programs with environmental changes: A Systematic Review. *American Journal of Preventive Medicine, 29,* 61–70.

Fishbein, M., & Ajzen, I. (1975). *Belief, attitude, intention theory and research.* Reading, MA: Addison-Wesley.

Fishbein, M., Triandis, H. C., Kanfer, F. H., Becker M., Middlestadt, S. E., & Eichler, A. (2001) Factors influencing behavior and behavior change. In A. Baum, T. A. Revenson & J. E. Singer (Eds.), *Handbook of Health Psychology* (pp. 3–17). Mahwah, NJ: Lawrence Erlbaum Associates.

Fisher, J. D., & Fisher. W. A. (1992). Changing AIDS-risk behavior. *Psychological Bulletin, 111,* 455–471.

Fisher, J. D., Fisher, W. A., Bryan, A. D., & Misovich, S. J. (2002). Information-motivation-behavioral skills model-based HIV risk behavior change intervention for inner-city high school youth. *Health Psychology, 21,* 177–186.

Friedman, R., Sobel, D., Myers, P., Caudill, M., & Benson, H. (1995). Behavioral medicine, clinical health psychology and cost offset. *Health Psychology, 14*, 509–518.

Glasgow, R. E., Bull, S. S., Gillette, C., Klesges, L. M., Dzewaltowski, D. M. (2002). Behavior change intervention research in healthcare settings: A review of recent reports with emphasis on external validity. *American Journal of Preventive Medicine, 23*, 62–69.

Gostin, L. O. (2004). Law and ethics in population health. *Australian and New Zealand Journal of Public Health, 28*, 7–12.

Green, L. W., & Glasgow, R. E. (2006). Evaluating the relevance, generalization, and applicability of research: Issues in external validation and translation methodology. *Evaluation and the Health Professions, 29*, 126–153.

Green, L. W., & Kreuter, M. W. (2005). *Health program planning: An educational and ecological approach* (4th ed.). St. Louis: McGraw-Hill.

Green, L. W., Kreuter, M. W., Deeds, S. G., & Partridge, K. B. (1980). *Health education planning: A diagnostic approach.* Palo Alto, CA: Mayfield.

Hingson, R. W., & Howland, J. (2002). Comprehensive community interventions to promote health: Implications for college-age drinking problems. *Journal of Alcohol Studies, Suppl. No. 14*, 226–240.

International Diabetes Federation. (2009). Facts & Figures. Did you know? Retrieved from www.idf.org/home/index.cfm?unode=3B96906B-C026-2FD3-87B73F80BC22682A

Johnson, B. T., Scott-Sheldon, L. A. J., & Carey, M. P. (2010). Synthesis of meta-analytic evidence of health behavior change. *American Journal of Public Health, 100*, 2193–2198.

Kaplan, R. M. (1990). Behavior as the central outcome in health care. *American Psychologist, 45*, 1211–1220.

Khaw, K., T., Wareham, N., Bingham, S., Welch, A., Luben. R., & Day, N. (2008). Combined impact of health behaviors and mortality in men and women: The EPIC-Norfolk prospective population study, *PLOS Medicine, 5*, (open access- doi:10.1371). Retrieved from http://medicine.plosjournals.org/perlserv/?request=get-document&doi=10.1371/journal.pmed.0050012

King, A. C., Carl, F., Birkel, L., & Haskell, W., L. (1988). Increasing exercise among blue-collar employees: The tailoring of worksite interventions to meet specific needs. *Preventive Medicine, 17*, 357–365.

Kok, G., Schaalma H. P., Ruiter R. A .C., Brug, J. & van Empelen, P. (2004). Intervention Mapping: A protocol for applying health psychology theory to prevention programmes. *Journal of Health Psychology, 9*, 85–98.

Kok, G., Gottlieb, N. H., Commers, M., & Smerecnik, C., (2008). The ecological approach in health promotion programs: A decade later. *American Journal of Health Promotion, 23*, 437–442.

Kools, M., Van de Wiel, M. W. J., Ruiter, R. A. C., & Kok, G. (2006). Pictures and text in instructions for medical devices: Effects on recall and actual performance. *Patient Education & Counseling, 64*, 104–111.

Littell, J. H., & Girvin, H. (2002). Stages of change. A critique. *Behavior Modification, 26*, 223–273.

Luszczynska, A., Sobczyk, A., & Abraham, C. (2007) Planning to lose weight: RCT of an implementation intention prompt to enhance weight reduction among overweight and obese women. *Health Psychology, 26*, 507–512.

Marlatt, G. A., & Donovan, D. M. (Eds.). (2005). *Relapse prevention: Maintenance strategies in the treatment of addictive behaviors.* New York: Guilford.

Martin, J., Sheeran, P., Slade, P., Wright, P., & Dibble, T. (in press). Implementation intention formation reduces consultations for emergency contraception and pregnancy testing among teenage women. *Health Psychology*, *28*, 762–769.

Michie, S., Johnston, M., Abraham, C., Lawton, R., Parker, D., & Walker, A. (2005). Making psychological theory useful for implementing evidence based practice: A consensus approach. *Quality and Safety in Health Care*, *14*, 26–33.

Michie, S., Abraham, C., Whittington, C., McAteer, J., & Gupta, S. (2009). Identifying Effective Techniques in Interventions: A meta-analysis and meta-regression. *Health Psychology*, *28*, 690–701.

Mokdad, A. H., Marks, J. S., Stroup, D. F., & Gerberding, J. L. (2004). Actual causes of death in the United States, 2000. *Journal of the American Medical Association*, *291*, 1238–1245.

Moskowitz, J. T., Epel, E. S., & Acree, M. (2008). Positive affect uniquely predicts lower risk of mortality in people with diabetes. *Health Psychology*, *27*, (Suppl.), S73–S82.

Mullen, P. D., Green, L. W., & Persinger, G. (1985). Clinical trials of patient education for chronic conditions: A comprehensive meta-analysis. *Preventive Medicine*, *14*, 75–81.

National Institute of Health and Clinical Excellence. (NICE). (2007). Behavior change at population, community and individual levels (Public Health Guidance 6). London, NICE. Retrieved from www.nice.org.uk/search/searchresults.jsp?keywords=behavior+change&searchType=all

Paulussen, T. G. W. M., Kok, G., Schaalma, H., & Parcel, G. (1995). Diffusion of AIDS curricula among Dutch secondary school teachers. *Health Education Quarterly*, *22*, 227–243.

Perdue, W. C., Mensah, G. A., Goodman, R. A., & Moulton, A. D. (2005). A legal framework for preventing cardiovascular diseases. *American Journal of Preventive Medicine*, *29*, 139–145.

Peters, L. H. W., Kok, G., Ten Dam, G. T. M., Buijs, G. J., & Paulussen, T. G. W. M., 2009. Effective elements of school health promotion across behavioral domains: A systematic review of reviews. *BMC Public Health*, *9*: 182, doi:10.1186/1471-2458-9-182.

Pittet, D. S., Hugonnet, S., Harbarth, P., Mourouga, V., Sauvan, S., Touveneau, & Perneger, T. V. (2000). Effectiveness of a hospital-wide programme to improve compliance with hand hygiene. *Lancet*, *356*, 1307–1312.

Prochaska, J. O., DiClemente, C. C., & Norcross, J. C. (1992). In search of how people change: Applications to addictive behaviors. *American Psychologist*, *47*, 1102–1114.

Rogers, E. M. (2003). *Diffusion of innovations* (5th ed.). New York: Free Press.

Rollnick, S., & Miller, W. R. (1995). What is motivational interviewing? *Behavioral and Cognitive Psychotherapy*, *23*, 325–334.

Rose, G. (1992). *The strategy of preventive medicine*. Oxford: Oxford University Press.

Ruiter, R. A. C., Abraham, C., & Kok, G. (2001). Scary warnings and rational precautions: A review of the psychology of fear appeals. *Psychology and Health*, *16*, 613–630.

Sacks, G., Swinburn, B., & Lawrence, M. (2008). Obesity Policy Action framework and analysis grids for a comprehensive policy approach to reducing obesity. *Obesity Reviews*, *10*, 76–86.

Sargent, R. P., Shepard, R. M., & Glantz, S. A. (2004). Reduced incidence of admissions for myocardial infarction associated with public smoking ban: Before and after study. *British Medical Journal*, *328*, 977–980.

Schaalma, H., & Kok, G. (2006). A school HIV-prevention program in the Netherlands. In L. K. Bartholomew, G. S. Parcel, G. Kok, & N. H. Gottlieb (Eds.), *Planning health promotion programs. An intervention mapping approach* (pp. 511–544). San Francisco, CA: Jossey-Bass.

Schinke, S. P., & Gordon, A. N. (1992) Innovative approaches to interpersonal skills training for minority adolescents. In R. J. DiClemente (Ed.), *Adolescents and AIDS; A generation in jeopardy* (pp. 181–193). Newbury Park, CA: Sage.

Sheeran, P., Abraham C., & Orbell, S. (1999). Psychosocial correlates of heterosexual condom use: A meta-analysis. *Psychological Bulletin, 125*, 90–132.

Sheeran, P., Milne, S., Webb, T. L., & Gollwitzer, P. M. (2005). Implementation intentions and health behaviours. In M. Conner & P. Norman (Eds.), *Predicting health behaviour: Research and practice with social cognition models* (2nd ed., pp. 276–323). Maidenhead: Open University Press.

Stirling, A., Lobstein, T., Millstone, E., & the PorGrow Research Team (2007). Methodology for obtaining stakeholders assessments of the obesity policies in the PorGrow project. *Obesity Reviews, 8* (Suppl. 2) 17–27.

Sutton, S. (2000). A critical review of the transtheoretical model applied to smoking cessation. In P. Norman, C. Abraham & M. Conner (Eds.), *Understanding and changing health behaviour: From health beliefs to self-regulation* (pp. 207–225). Reading, UK: Harwood Academic Press.

Swientek, B. (2001). Let them eat cake: Mad cow disease prevention in Europe. Retrieved from http://findarticles.com/p/articles/mi_m3289/is_1_170/ai_70204304

Tyler, R. (2001). *BSE/"mad cow disease" crisis spreads 'throughout Europe.* Retrieved from www.wsws.org/articles/2001/jan2001/bse-j23.shtml

Vartiainen, E., Paavola, M., McAlister, A., & Puska, P. (1998). Fifteen-year follow-up of smoking prevention effects in the North Karelia Youth Project. *American Journal of Public Health, 88*, 81–85.

Webb, T., L., & Sheeran, P. (2006). Does changing behavioral intentions engender behavior change? A meta-analysis of the experimental evidence. *Psychological Bulletin, 132*, 249–268.

West, R. (2005). Time for a change: Putting the Transtheoretical (Stages of Change) Model to rest. *Addiction, 100*, 1036–1039.

Wilkinson, R. G. (1996). *Unhealthy societies; The afflictions of inequality.* Routledge, London.

Witte, K., & Allen, M. (2000). A meta-analysis of fear appeals: Implications for effective public health campaigns. *Health Education & Behavior, 27*, 591–615.

World Health Organization. (1948). Preamble to the Constitution of the World Health Organization as adopted by the International Health Conference, New York, 19–22 June, 1946; signed on 22 July 1946 by the representatives of 61 States (*Official Records of the World Health Organization, 2*, 100) and entered into force on 7 April 1948.

5

Clinical Neuropsychology

Ronald Ruff and Christina Weyer Jamora

Clinical neuropsychology is a field of study focused on the relationship between brain and behavior (Crockett, Clark, & Klonoff, 1980). The purpose of this chapter is to place the discipline in its historical context, while providing an overview of both the cognitive and emotional domains that neuropsychologists examine. This chapter also seeks to highlight the differences between providing neuropsychological services in the inpatient and outpatient settings, and to identify future directions for the field.

A Brief History of Neuropsychology

Neuropsychology has its roots in the century-old quest to better understand the brain's role in human behavior. The initial models for understanding brain–behavior relationships were focused on localizing language deficits. Paul Broca (1861) was a pioneer in the field who posited that deficits of language expression could be traced to damage in the left frontal lobe. He supported this finding by evaluating an individual with a stroke who was able to understand verbal commands, but unable to speak fluently. A postmortem autopsy revealed damage to the third frontal gyrus in the left inferior frontal lobe. Today, this region of the brain is still referred to as Broca's region. Similarly, Karl Wernicke (1874) discovered that when a patient's ability to speak is preserved but comprehension is compromised, this is often caused by damage to the left superior temporal gyrus, which is referred to as Wernicke's region. These two discoveries provide an example of a double dissociation, an important method neuropsychologists use to investigate brain function (Teuber, 1955). That is, when damage to a particular brain region causes a specific behavioral deficit, this does not necessarily rule out the possibility that damage to other brain regions

---

IAAP Handbook of Applied Psychology, First Edition. Edited by Paul R. Martin, Fanny M. Cheung, Michael C. Knowles, Michael Kyrios, Lyn Littlefield, J. Bruce Overmier, and José M. Prieto.

causes the same deficit. Thus, an association of Behavior A with Brain Region 1 is merely a single association and is insufficient to offer a definitive conclusion. However, a more solid conclusion can be reached when a double dissociation demonstrates that Behavior A (e.g., Broca's aphasia) is associated with Brain Region 1 (the left inferior frontal lobe) while Behavior B (Wernicke's aphasia) is associated with Brain Region 2 (the left superior temporal lobe) and *the inverse is not true* (Weiskrantz, 1991).

In the following years, the view that complex behaviors could be localized in circumscribed cerebral regions was actively pursued and led to the labeling of regions as "centers" for "counting," "reading," "volitional action," and even "personal and social ego" (Kleist, 1934; Vogt, 1951). In response to this localization movement, an antilocalization movement emerged, claiming that it was naïve to identify innate "centers" in circumscribed regions. For example, Lashley (1929) argued that, while the primary cortical regions were functionally specific, the associated cortices were equally involved in complex higher functions. As is often the case in science, the two polarized viewpoints were eventually synthesized. In an excellent review of this rich history, Luria (1966) carefully examined the scientific merits of both viewpoints, and in a well-reasoned manner, juxtaposed the two orientations. Luria stated that "the brain is a highly differentiated system whose parts are responsible for different aspects of the unified whole" (p. 33). As to our understanding of the effects of localized brain lesions, Luria stated "a lesion of a single, circumscribed area of the cerebral cortex often leads to the development, not of an isolated symptom, but of a group of disturbances, apparently far removed from each other" (p. 83).

In the mid 20th century, three converging events provided the impetus for the discipline of neuropsychology to emerge. (1) Neurologists including Broca and Wernicke had since the mid 19th century chronicled their observation that associated certain cognitive deficits with specific brain regions. (2) In the early 20th century, psychologists had established the scientific methods for testing behavior. This gave the impetus to develop reliable and valid tests that allowed for the quantification of cognitive abilities like memory, intelligence, and attention. (3) By the mid 20th century, neurosurgical techniques for evacuating brain tumors were advancing, but localizing these tumors to an exact area of the brain remained challenging. Since neuropsychological tests were superior to clinical observations, various neurosurgeons solicited psychologists to assist in the localization. As the demand grew for localizing brain lesions on the basis of tests, the discipline of neuropsychology was born. The first generation of neuropsychologists included Luria in Russia, Milner in Canada, Hecaen in France, Zangwill in England, and Halstead, Teuber, and Benton in the United States. These pioneers ushered in the "Period of Neuropsychological Localization." From its inception, neuropsychology was, to a large extent, an applied discipline, because most neuropsychologists worked in medical centers examining patients to ascertain the location of brain lesions.

With the introduction of the computerized tomography scanners in the late 1970s, test-based localization was replaced by neuroimaging techniques and the practice of brain localization was forever changed. Neuropsychologists were phased out as front-line clinicians involved in brain localization. Indeed, today it would be considered substandard practice for a neurosurgeon to evaluate a tumor based on neuropsychological localization. However, the need for neuropsychological evaluations persisted simply because patients, family members, treating physicians, and employers wanted to know to what extent the patient's cognition was compromised by the brain damage. Thus, the clinical need for cognitive assessments was retained, but the focus shifted from localization to the quantitative assessment of cognitive declines caused by acquired brain damage. Thus, in 1980, the "Period of Neurocognitive Evaluations" was ushered in and has remained the dominant school of thought up to the present time.

It is important to note that in the 1970s another major shift in the field of psychology occurred that led the focus away from the school of behaviorism towards cognitive psychology. A new generation of psychologists advanced theories and research that led to a refinement of cognitive constructs, such as attention, memory, and verbal abilities. These advancements were pivotal for the discipline of neuropsychology, and this cognitive research was integrated into the discipline's understanding of brain–behavioral relationships. New neuropsychological tests were developed based on a more refined understanding of cognition. Both in hospital and outpatient settings, more and more neuropsychologists started to use tests that captured specific cognitive constructs like working memory, sustained visuospatial attention, and figural fluency. Neuropsychological journals began publishing articles on cognitive constructs like automatic processing versus controlled search, perceptual and conceptual priming, and semantic versus phonological fluency.

In recent years, clinical neuropsychologists have branched out. Instead of working primarily in departments of neurosurgery or neurology, many, if not most neuropsychologists now work in departments of psychiatry and rehabilitation. Neuropsychologists also work in outpatient settings, providing clinical and forensic assessments and psychotherapy to patients with a range of neurological disorders. In their examinations the following cognitive domains are assessed.

Cognitive Domains

It is commonly accepted that certain neuropsychological tests capture particular domains; however, most tests tap into multiple domains instead of just one (see Figure 5.1. for an overview of the cognitive functions). Therefore, it is overly simplistic to consider these domains in isolation. Instead, cognition should be understood as a dynamic interplay between various systems, with each test tapping into the multifactorial aspects of cognition even if one or a few areas are being targeted.

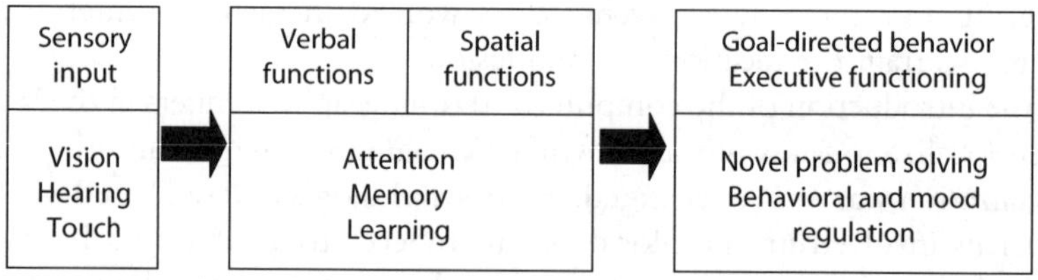

Figure 5.1. Cognitive functions

Moreover, some aspects of cognition are generically integral to many tests, such as comprehending the test instructions and paying attention during the testing.

Luria (1980) described the human brain as processing information in a hierarchical manner and according to a system of three "zones." The first or primary zone registers sensory input. The secondary zone facilitates perception by processing sensory input. In the third or tertiary zone, executive functioning initiates problem solving.

As to the neuropsychological application, the primary zone is evaluated in an individual after a brain injury by observing how alert the patient becomes when presented with sensory stimulation.

Establishing an individual's basic abilities to perceive, process, and store information in both the verbal and visuospatial modalities involves the secondary zone. Evaluating higher-level skills such as planning ahead, prioritizing, and problem solving allows for an assessment of the tertiary zone.

Sensory and motor skills

At the outset of a neuropsychological examination, one must explore the potential limitations of the patient's sensory modalities. Since most cognitive functions cannot be assessed without sensory input and motor output, it is particularly important to establish whether there are visual or auditory problems that require the examiner to modify the test procedures. Moreover, eye–hand coordination can compromise various test performances. Thus, to better understand motor speed and eye–hand coordination, tests such as the Finger Tapping Test (motor speed—Reitan & Davidson, 1974; Straus, Sherman, & Spreen, 2006), Grooved Pegboard Test (eye–hand coordination—Layfayette Instruments, 1989; Straus, Sherman, & Spreen, 2006), and Strength of Grip Test (motor strength—Reitan & Davidson, 1974; Straus, Sherman, & Spreen, 2006) are administered. Finally, olfactory tests are administered if the patient complains of a loss or reduction in smell.

The sensory systems for auditory and visual perception are localized in the temporal and occipital cortices, respectively. The motor strip is located in the posterior region of the frontal lobe, whereas the somatosensory strip is found in the anterior portion of the parietal lobe (Honey & Sporns, 2008; Prigatano, Johnson, & Gale, 2004).

Attention and concentration

Attention and concentration are vital parts of cognition that serve as a foundation for other neuropsychological domains. Based on a literature review, Niemann, Ruff, and Kramer (1996) posit that the construct of attention and concentration can be broadly divided into three categories: 1. arousal/alertness and sustained attention; 2. selective attention; and 3. energy-related attention, such as effort, resource allocation, and speed of information processing.

1. Arousal refers to an individual's state of general alertness. For example, when a stroke or brain trauma patient emerges from a coma, the patient's arousal and alertness can be diminished and interferes with the patient's ability to adequately process information in response to environmental demands. Sustained attention is

defined as the degree to which vigilance can be maintained over a long period of time (Davies, Jones, & Taylor, 1984; Cohen, Malloy, Jenkins, & Paul, 2006). For example, activities like reading a book, listening to a lecture, or driving a car require sustained attention. If the task is variable, there is less need for sustained attention; instead, it is monotonous tasks (e.g., driving for hours) that require effortful sustained attention. In terms of the brain regions involved, several studies have indicated that the right hemisphere is responsible for sustained visual attention (Dimond, 1979; Heilman & Van Den, 1980; Whitehead, 1991).

2. Selective attention can be defined as the ability to prioritize while processing information (Kornhuber, 1984). Moreover, this theory posits that the focus of our attention is influenced by the amount and type of distracting stimuli typically present in the environment. For example, if a brain-injured individual receives physical therapy in a gym where other patients are also treated, then the conversations between other patients and their therapist can be distracting. However, if these concurrent conversations were held in a foreign language that the patient does not understand, then the distraction would be less pronounced. The 2 and 7 Selective Reminding Test and Continuous Performance Test II are examples of measures that tap into selective and sustained attention (Ruff and Allen, 1996; Conners, 2000).

3. Energy-related domains, such as effort, resource allocation, and speed of processing are germane to information processing. Mental energy can vary from day to day, and factors such as medication and physical pain can contribute to low energy. Effort includes the ability to monitor the environment, incorporate feedback, and evaluate outcomes. Norman and Shallice (1986) have introduced the concept of the "supervisory attentional system," which allows information to be integrated and processed without being encoded into permanent memory (e.g., being able to say the alphabet backwards). When there are impairments in the supervisory attentional system, then novel tasks in particular become more difficult to complete.

Pain, fatigue, and medication effects often contribute to a patient's poor arousal. Multiple pain medications can negatively impact attention and concentration. To understand the confounding effects of these factors, clinicians often ask about pain intensity and medication type, dosage, and administration, before beginning a neuropsychological testing session. It is also advisable to have individuals rate their pain and energy levels at various points during the testing session.

Memory and learning

While there are many different types of memory, two broad categories of memory include: (1) remote memory (i.e., remembering information from one's past or before a neurological injury), and (2) recent memory (i.e., memory for recent events or recall of information since the onset of neurological injury). Recent memory impairments are far more common and are typically assessed in a standard neuropsychological battery. The term "short-term" memory refers to retention over short intervals (e.g., for up to 15 minutes) whereas "long-term" memory describes retention after 15 minutes (Sweet, Moberg, Suchy, 2000; Ruff & Schraa, 2008; Thorne & Page, 2009). Subsumed under long-term memory are two types of memories, namely declarative memory and procedural memory. Declarative memory captures one's ability to remember and "declare" information like one's city of birth or what one ate three days ago. Procedural memory refers to one's capacity to retain a learned skill such as tying shoe laces or riding a bicycle. Most often declarative memory is verbally mediated whereas procedural memory is a visual-motor skill (Ewert, Levin, & Watson, 1989; Squire, 1987). This distinction is particularly relevant in the rehabilitation setting, since many patients have very pronounced problems in declarative memory and for example are simply unable to recall what medications to take or who to call in case of an emergency. However, even if declarative memory is severely compromised, procedural memory most often remains functional even after a stroke or brain injury. Thus, even when a patient has declarative memory deficit, she or he can still learn new motor skills like using a wheelchair or eating with the non-dominant arm when the dominant arm is paralyzed. For a more in-depth discussion of the neuropsychology of memory, the reader is referred to Squire and Schacter (2003).

In terms of neuroanatomical location, damage to the temporal and frontal lobes often results in memory and learning deficits (Baldo, Delis, & Kramer, 2002; Crosson, Sartor, Jenny, Nabors, & Moberg, 1993). In right-hand dominant individuals, the left hemisphere is involved in memory and in learning verbal information (e.g., names) while the right hemisphere is involved in memory and in learning visuospatial information (e.g., faces). Thus, neuropsychologists as a rule administer both memory and learning tests that are processed in the verbal and visuospatial modes to better understand a patient's functioning in these areas and to inform treatment planning. Examples of memory and learning tests that are commonly used include the Wechsler Memory Scales (Wechsler, 2009), Rey Complex Figure Test (Meyers & Meyers, 1995), California Verbal Learning Test-II (Delis, Kramer, Kaplan, & Ober, 2000), and Ruff-Light Trial Learning Test (Ruff & Allen, 1999). For a more comprehensive list of neuropsychological tests see Lezak, Howieson, and Loring (2004).

Although clinicians often speak about memory and learning interchangeably, both the underlying cognitive processes and brain involvements are different. As a rule, neuropsychologists test memory functioning by providing information (e.g., reading the person a story) and then later asking the person to recall the information. This type of declarative memory assessment is more specific to temporal lobe functioning. The degree of neuronal loss in the hippocampus, mammillary bodies, and fornices (commonly thought of as crucial temporal lobe memory structures) has been related to memory loss, and directly impacts patients' rehabilitation outcomes (Hopkins, Tate, & Bigler, 2005). Learning, on the other hand, is usually assessed by giving a patient the same string of information multiple times (e.g., asking the patient to learn a list 15 words across 5 trials), which also taps into functions in the temporal lobe but relies in addition on the frontal lobe for structuring to facilitate the learning process (Salorio et al., 2005). Although, some patients' memories are severely compromised (e.g., they are unable to recall the story after hearing it one time), the learning of new information is less impaired (e.g., retention is only possible through multiple repetitions). The inverse can also occur when, for example, someone is able to recall a story, but lacks the ability to incorporate an appropriate strategy for learning a list of unrelated words.

Often, survivors of brain traumas are left with persistent memory and learning impairments. Thus, neuropsychologists can help patients and their caregivers understand which domains are preserved and which functions are compromised. Understanding the stage (i.e., encoding, storage, or retrieval) at which the memory mechanisms break down can also help to inform treatment strategies. For example, severely amnestic patients cannot recall information without some type of prompting. However, they can often select the correct answer when given cues in a multiple-choice format. These patients need assistance with retrieving information through means such as ample cueing. Conversely, those patients with attention problems will likely have difficulty encoding new information and will understandably have poor recall and recognition because the information was insufficiently consolidated at the outset. For these patients, strategies like reducing environmental distractions, repeating information out loud, and using written notes can be helpful. For individuals with memory storage problems, overlearning can be beneficial (i.e., learning something not only to mastery but repeating it for days and days until the information is more reliably recalled).

Language

During the clinical interview, the assessment of language dysfunction focuses on the patient's fluidity during conversational speech, the frequency of paraphasias (selecting an incorrect word or phoneme), and pronounced word-finding difficulties (dysnosmia). If language deficits are suspected, selected tests from the Boston Diagnostic Aphasia Exam (Goodglass, Kaplan, & Barresi, 2000), such as the cookie theft picture (conversational production), the Boston Naming Test (naming objects), the Complex Ideational Material Test (auditory language comprehension), and repetition (expressive speech) can be useful. For a more thorough review of language-related disorders, the reader is referred to Goodglass (2002) and Spreen and Risser (2002).

Most people have occasional word-finding difficulties, but patients who have experienced brain injuries often have particular difficulty with this area of language. To cope with pronounced word-finding difficulties, individuals may tend to circumlocute to express themselves, (i.e., substitute a descriptive paraphrase for a word that they are unable to retrieve, such as "the thing on the wall that controls the heat" for "the thermostat"). Thus, a conversation can, at times, appear to be tangential, if not bizarre. These circular descriptions are not due to a thought disorder *per se* but rather to a flaw in word retrieval.

Of all the various aspects of language, being able to understand what other people are saying is vital to the success of rehabilitation of language disorders in patients (Demir, Altinok, & Aydin, 2006). In particular, preserved auditory comprehension has been found to be an important factor in overall recovery (Demir et al., 2006).

Visual/spatial perceptional and construction skills

Spatial orientation can be compromised for personal and extrapersonal spatial processing. Personal spatial orientation ranges from reliably identifying one's right arm to finding one's way to the grocery store. However, when neuropsychologists assess visuospatial functions, they typically focus on extrapersonal spatial processing. Extrapersonal spatial processing allows a person, independent of where their body is positioned, to appreciate the relationship between objects. Thus, a patient in San Francisco can be tested on her ability to know what direction should be taken when traveling from Chicago to Philadelphia (extrapersonal spatial ability).

Constructional deficits, in which the patient has difficulty drawing various shapes and integrating spatial objects, are commonly assessed in neuropsychological test batteries. Tests that assess visuospatial ability include the Rey Osterreith Complex Figure-Copy (Meyers & Meyers, 1995), the Judgment of Line Orientation Test (Benton, Varney, & Hamsher, 1978), and the Wechsler Block Design, Visual Reproduction Copy, and Discrimination Subtests (Wechsler, 2009). However, both qualitative and quantitative aspects are important to take into account when rating a patient's performance. The patient's test scores may technically fall within the average range, but qualitatively, a copy of a figure can still look quite distorted. This would, of course, mean that the person's performance is not truly average. The quantitative test scoring procedure by itself would fail to capture this aspect of the patient's performance, and noting this discrepancy in the neuropsychological report would be important.

Executive functioning

Executive functioning refers to those cognitive processes involved in abstract reasoning, cognitive flexibility, and problem solving. More succinctly, executive systems decide how and whether a behavior occurs, as well as when and under what conditions it takes place (Lezak, Howieson, & Loring, 2004; Ruff, 2004). Frontal lobe systems also play a role in motor planning and in making decisions in a fluid and adaptive manner as to what information should be stored (e.g., working memory), as well as modulating arousal and the focus of attention. (Stuss & Knight, 2002).

Goldberg (2001), a student of Luria, provided a helpful analogy that compared the role of executive function to that of an orchestra conductor. Just as a conductor aims to achieve a certain interpretation and then directs individual musicians and sections of the orchestra accordingly, the executive system is responsible for formulating goals, coordinating various cognitive skills, and applying them in the correct order. According to Goldberg, executive functioning is more "metacognitive" than cognitive in that it provides the organizational architecture from which all functions are expressed.

Compromised executive functioning is usually associated with frontal lobe deficits; however, in reality, it is a functional system that relies on many areas of the brain. For example, subcortical structures serve to connect various frontal lobe functions. Thus, individuals with predominantly subcortical impairments (such as vascular dementia, and HIV-related cognitive impairment) have profound executive functioning impairments. Another aspect of executive functioning is visual–spatial problem solving. Individuals who take a piecemeal approach rather than an integrated approach when copying a geometric figure show deficits in visual–spatial reasoning. This is common with right frontal hemisphere impairments, where an individual cannot "see the forest for the trees." The intersection between executive functioning and visual–spatial reasoning is paramount for novel problem solving. As Goldberg (2001) and others have posited, the right hemisphere is more specialized in processing novel information as compared to the left hemisphere which is more adept in processing information that is practiced, routinized, and familiar.

Executive functioning is extremely difficult to assess for a number of reasons. Most significant is the frontal lobes' dependence on and interaction with subcortical and posterior cortical functions. Moreover, most structured neuropsychological testing is administered in the comfort of a quiet room with few distractions. Such testing does not capture novel problem solving in an unpredictable environment. Nonetheless, one test, the Wisconsin Card Sorting Test (Heaton, Chelune, Talley, Kay, & Curtiss, 1993), has long been considered the gold standard for evaluating executive functioning. In this test, the individual is asked to discover the rules by which to sort a deck of cards. This test requires intact working memory, since multiple potential sorting strategies must be kept in mind. Indeed, studies have shown that one's performance in this test is negatively influenced by deficits in working memory (Barcelo & Rubia, 1998; Fristoe, Salthouse, & Woodard, 1997; Monchi, Petrides, & Petre, 2001). Ríos, Periáñez, and Muñoz-Céspedes (2004) found the Wisconsin Card Sort (Heaton et al., 1993), Trail Making Test (Reitan & Davidson, 1974), and the Stroop Word Reading Test (Golden & Freshwater, 2002; Stroop, 1935) were all helpful in teasing out the various components of information processing speed, interference effects, and executive control.

Verbal and visual fluency tests also tap into executive functioning. These tests gauge a patient's ability to quickly reach a solution to a problem based on vague and minimal rules. The Controlled Oral Word Association Test (Benton, Hamsher, & Sivan, 1994) is designed to assess a person's ability to quickly generate words. The non-verbal correlate of this test is the Ruff Figural Fluency Test (Ruff, 1996), where the individual is asked to draw as many different designs as possible by connecting a series of dots. Both the verbal and figural tests are self-directed and timed. Functional imaging, EEG, and lesion studies have shown that the verbal fluency tests are correlated with left frontal lobe functioning, while figural fluency correlates with right hemisphere functioning (Ruff, Allen, Farrow, Niemann, & Wylie, 1994; Ruff, Light, & Parker, 1997; Warkentin, Risberg, & Nilsson, 1991).

Executive functioning obviously has real-world implications. Higher cortical abilities, such as reasoning and thinking flexibly, impact how individuals function in their social and professional lives (Lam, Priddy, & Johnson, 1991). Patients with moderate to severe deficits in cognitive flexibility can have dramatic difficulty coping with the world around them (Prigatano, 1992). Patients with deficits in social perception and problem-solving can lack the ability to connect with and understand others. Specifically, they have trouble recognizing and interpreting the emotional expressions of others, understanding sarcasm, recognizing a faux pas, and engaging in other areas of social reasoning (MacDonald & Flanagan, 2004; Milders, Fuchs, & Crawford, 2003).

Damage to different regions of the frontal lobe can lead to distinct behavioral changes. For example, damage to the dorsolateral region is associated with a combination of lethargy, apathy, inability to initiate behavior, slowed processing speed, and emotional blunting analogous to individuals who underwent frontal lobotomies. In contrast to the dorsolateral syndrome, the orbitofrontal syndrome is in many ways the opposite and results in emotional disinhibition, moods that oscillate between euphoria and rage, and poor or complete lack of impulse control. Both the dorsolateral and orbitofrontal syndromes result in marked personality changes that have detrimental effects on an individual's long-term social relationships (Snow, Douglas, & Ponsford, 1998). For a more detailed discussion of executive functioning, the reader is referred to Goldberg (2001) and Stuss and Knight (2002).

Intelligence

Assessing intelligence as part of a neuropsychological examination can provide an important framework from which to understand the nature of a person's impairments. Neuropsychologists should attempt to assess the patient's postmorbid profile of strengths and weaknesses relative to their premorbid intelligence. For example, a mild level of impairment on a verbal list-learning task should be interpreted very differently for an English literature professor with superior premorbid verbal intelligence than for a person who premorbidly had a childhood learning disability and completed only a few years of formal education. This viewpoint is supported by the research that has proposed the concept of a neuronal reserve. Research has documented that higher levels of education and intelligence are linked with an increased neuronal reserve (Kesler, Adams, Blasey, & Bigler, 2003). In turn, when the brain is damaged, the neuronal reserve is diminished (Kesler et al., 2003; Satz, 1993; Stern, 2002). Ropacki and Elias (2003) found that repeated traumatic brain injuries led to a cumulative reduction of the neuronal reserve with each successive traumatic brain injury, thus leading to progressively poorer outcomes. Note too that, as we age, our neuronal reserve gradually declines. This explains why a brain injury at age 25 has a lesser impact than a similar injury at age 75 (Vollmer et al., 1991).

For a more comprehensive review of neuropsychological tests that are available in any of the above domains, see Lezak, Howieson, and Loring (2004) and Strauss, Sherman, and Spreen (2006).

Emotional Functioning

Psychological disturbances in individuals with brain impairments may result from: (1) the person's adjustment reaction to his or her limitations; (2) damage to emotional centers in the brain; or (3) a combination of the above (Cullum, 1989). Catastrophic medical events often make individuals feel lonely, scared, frustrated, angry, and depressed when faced with their new limitations. These psychological adjustment difficulties are related to degrees of self-awareness, age at injury, severity of injury, and level of education before the onset of neurological illness or injury (Anson & Ponsford, 2006). Brain-based emotional impairments frequently result in lack of initiation, affective lability, overly intense emotional displays, disinhibition, or marked personality changes (Rödholm, Starmark, Ekholm, & von Essen, 2002; Wood & Williams, 2007).

Emerging literature suggests that certain psychiatric illnesses like major depression, obsessive compulsive disorder, and schizophrenia have cognitive components as well

(Favre et al., 2009; Feil, Razani, Boone, & Lesser, 2003; Kuelz, Hohagen, & Voderholzer, 2004; Martin, Huber, Reif, & Exner, 2008). Specifically, major depression has been associated with slowed processing speed, cognitive inflexibility, decreased word generation, and diminished abstract reasoning (Feil et al., 2008). On neuroimaging exams, individuals with obsessive compulsive disorder show abnormal functioning in the caudate nucleus and orbitofrontal cortical circuit (Saxena, Brody, Schwartz, & Baxter, 1998; Saxena & Rauch, 2000), and therefore show deficits in executive functioning and memory difficulties secondary to flawed organizational encoding strategies (Kuelz et al., 2004; Savage & Rauch, 2000). Individuals with schizophrenia, in turn, have been shown to have abnormalities in the dorsolateral prefrontal cortex (Weinberger, Berman, & Zec, 1986) with deficits in attention, executive functioning, and memory (Martin et al., 2008).

A variety of instruments are used to assess emotional functioning. Instruments commonly used to assess psychological distress include the Minnesota Multiphasic Personality Inventory-II (Butcher et al., 2001), the Millon Clinical Multiaxial Inventory-III (Millon, Millon, & Davis, 1997), the Ruff Neurobehavioral Inventory (Ruff & Hibbard, 2003), the Neurobehavioral Rating Scale-Revised (Vanier, Mazaux, Lambert, Dassa, & Levin, 2000), the Symptom Check List 90-Revised (Derogatis, 1977), the Katz Adjustment Scale-Revised (Baker, Schmidt, Heinemann, Langley, & Miranti, 1998; Katz & Lyerly, 1963), the Personality Assessment Inventory (Morey, 1991), and the Beck Depression-II and Anxiety Inventories (Beck, & Steer, 1993; Beck, Steer, & Brown, 1996); see chapter 13 for a more comprehensive description of psychological assessments and evaluations.

Premorbid personality

Neurological disorders occur in people with widely varying personalities and life experiences. Thus, it is important to obtain an accurate understanding of patients as integrated people before the onset of their neurological illnesses to provide a framework for understanding their current functioning. For example, a pre-existing history of psychiatric illness has been linked to poorer outcomes post brain injury. Thus, it is important to ascertain the nature, severity, and duration of any premorbid psychiatric illnesses (Stulemeijer, Vos, Bleijenberg, & van der Werf, 2007). It is also important to ascertain whether an individual had any premorbid personality vulnerabilities that may predispose them to negative adjustment reactions post brain injury. For example, an individual with controlling and perfectionist tendencies before their injury is likely to have difficulty adjusting to restrictions common in medical units, such as preset meal times, rigid medication administration schedules, and limits on the number of visitors (Prigatano, 1992; Ruff, Camenzuli, & Mueller, 1996).

Reasons for Neuropsychological Testing Referrals

The American Academy of Neurology (AAN, 1996) authored a position paper that specifies the following reasons for physicians to request a neuropsychological examination: (a) when mental status examination reveals mild or questionable cognitive deficits; (b) when either the recovery or decline of a brain disorder needs to be quantified; (c) when cognitive strengths and weakness are considered for a patient's prospective return to school, work, etc.; (d) when deciding to provide specific rehabilitation or other therapeutic services; (e) when a comprehensive profile buttressed with clinical, laboratory and imaging data may assist in diagnosis; (f) when considering epilepsy surgery; and (g) when litigation pertains to the patient's cognitive status.

Application of neuropsychology in the inpatient setting

Individuals with neurological injuries that have a sudden onset, such as a stroke or traumatic brain injury, are typically transitioned through an acute and postacute rehabilitative hospital stay. The breadth and depth of the neuropsychological assessment varies depending on a variety of factors, including severity of brain damage, reasons for referral, and healthcare setting. In the early stages of recovery, neuropsychologists can help assess when a patient's acute confusion resolves. Neuropsychologists can also provide education and psychological support for the patient and also for family members and friends. Once the person's level of impairment can be adequately determined, the neuropsychologist can facilitate understanding the interaction among the patient's physical, cognitive, and emotional symptoms. Additionally, neuropsychologists may be called upon to comment on issues of capacity, readiness for discharge, discharge needs, and appropriate placement. Prior to discharge, a prognostic estimate and the recommendations for post-discharge treatments are best achieved with the duel aim of identifying deficiencies as well as preserved competencies or relative strengths.

Neuropsychology in the outpatient setting

Most patients in the outpatient setting receive a comprehensive neuropsychological test battery. These batteries can comprise either a fixed set of tests such as the Halstead-Reitan (Reitan and Davidson, 1974), Luria-Nebraska Batteries (Golden, 1995), and Neuropsychological Assessment Battery (Stern and White, 2003) or a selected set of tests typically referred to as a flexible battery (Lezak, Howieson, & Loring, 2004). Over time the use of flexible neuropsychological test batteries, as opposed to a fixed battery approach, has become more common (Sweet, Moberg, and Suchy, 2000). This flexible approach includes administering a collection of tests tailored to the patient's presenting problems. Most flexible batteries assess each of the cognitive domains outlined above. Figure 5.2 depicts a schematic illustration of the flexible testing approach in the context of neuropsychological evaluation.

Using the same set of tests allows clinicians to track the patient's progress over time. Thus, using a flexible approach that includes a core battery (i.e., the same group of tests) can increase efficiency, allowing for a full exploration of specific questions or deficits, and the ability to modify the battery's length depending on the patient's severity and type of brain damage. Moreover, a mixed model approach avoids the potential pitfalls of a purely flexible approach, which has been criticized for encouraging circular hypothesis testing (i.e., finding only what one seeks). The flexible approach

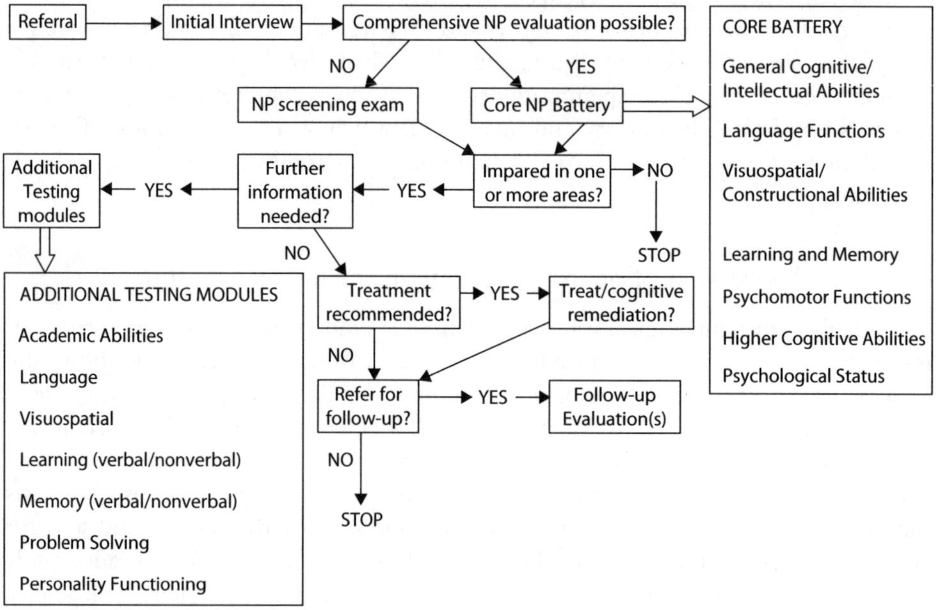

Figure 5.2. Decision making process for test selection

has also been criticized for multiplying Type I errors or arriving at significant findings because there are no overall, fixed-battery statistical controls. (Hom, 2003; Russell, Russell, & Hill, 2005). These criticisms can be avoided in large part by using a mixed model approach that juxtaposes a fixed core and flexibly adds further tests as are clinically indicated. Given that the aim of our discipline is to provide comprehensive neurocognitive description, a mixed model approach should, however, include all the main cognitive domains, such as motor and sensory functions, language and visuospatial skills, as well as intelligence, attention, memory, learning, and executive functioning. The length and difficulty of these test batteries, however, may be reduced on a case-by-case basis.

For outpatient cases, symptom validity tests must be included to evaluate effort, malingering and exaggeration (Bush et al, 2005; Rogers, 2008). If neuropsychologists engage in forensic evaluations, either in the civil or criminal context, specialization is required (Heilbronner, 2008; Kreutzer et al., 1990); see Chapter 14 for a description of Forensic Psychology.

Future Direction for Neuropsychology

An overview of the historical progression of the discipline of neuropsychology and its future direction is shown in Table 5.1. In the past, neuropsychologists were hired in medical centers to determine *where* brain lesions were localized, though eventually computerized neuroimaging rendered that function obsolete. Thereafter,

Table 5.1. Historical Progression of Neuropsychology as a Discipline

Where is a behavioral malady localized? Neurologists described specific dysfunctions as being associated to focal brain lesions (19th to mid-20th century)
How can we scientifically quantify behavior? Psychologists developed psychometrics and the dissociation paradigm (1940s inception of neuropsychology)
What discrete behaviors should be assessed? Cognitive psychology introduced measurable constructs of cognition that can be mapped to brain areas (1970s to present time)
When or in what context is a specific behavior most relevant? Ecologically valid tests capture (1) daily functioning *when* driving, cooking, working, etc.; (2) specific contexts *when* fatigued, medicated, depressed, in pain, etc.; and (3) cultural diversity *when* Asian-, African- or Mexican-American, etc. (1990s yet not mainstream)
Why are we ultimately interested in capturing brain–behavior relationships? To provide restorative and compensatory treatments (1980s with insufficient empirical validation)

neuropsychologists focused on *how* to best quantify cognitive deficits caused by neurological disorders. Cognitive science helped define *what* cognitive constructs are most pertinent for neuropsychological examinations. The future of neuropsychology will benefit from expanding in three further directions. First, advancements are needed to determine *when* cognitive deficits impact daily functioning. That is, additional research is needed to more fully understand the extent to which test results predict daily functions; i.e., when test results correspond with daily functioning then "ecological validity" is established. Second, to remain a viable discipline, the question as to *why* we provide neuropsychological examinations must be re-examined. To learn from history, the "Period of Neuropsychological Localization" ended with the emergence of computerized neuroimaging. Third, it is conceivable that computerized testing, and even computer-generated reports, could replace much of what clinical neuropsychologists perform today. Thus, it is important to explore additional ways in which the discipline of neuropsychology can adapt its services to best meet our patient's needs. This is best achieved if neuropsychologists explore ways to enable our assessments to be more ecologically valid, rehabilitate cognitive deficits, and advance our psychotherapeutic treatments for those with neuropsychologic issues. Specifically, our discipline must adapt psychotherapy and advance the efficacy of cognitive rehabilitation to benefit patients with neurological and neuropsychiatric disorders.

Ecological validity: Advancing the generalizability of neuropsychological testing

Establishing a bridge between test results and daily functioning is paramount for rendering an ecologically valid diagnosis and prognosis, and specifying pertinent recommendations (Sbordone & Long, 1996). Neuropsychological test results alone are often insufficient to determine if an individual is capable of returning to her or his former employment or educational pursuit. Testing alone cannot assess whether a patient has sufficient decisional capacity to parent three young children, drive safely, and cook alone. This type of evaluation requires a multimethod assessment approach that takes into account the person's daily functioning. In short, ecological validity encompasses *when* an individual is at risk for not functioning safely and adequately in her/his daily routines. In addition to test results, confounds, such as reduced energy, high stress levels, chronic pain, and types of medication must be taken into consideration. Finally, ecological assessments must incorporate the individual's socio-economic and cultural background and values.

To date, four approaches have been implemented for capturing ecological validity. The first approach relies on tests that mimic the demands of everyday functioning. For example, the Rivermead Behavioural Memory Test (Wilson, Cockburn, & Baddeley, 1985) assesses memory by simulating everyday tasks such as remembering what and how many medications to take at preset times. Although this approach captures relevant data, the tests are administered in a structured setting, and therefore, do not necessarily reflect the idiosyncratic distractions that are typically part of an individual's daily environment. The second method is based on standard neuropsychological tests, such as the Independent Living Scale (Loeb, 1996), which are correlated with everyday activities in school, work, and other daily activities. The third approach that is used clinically is to interview significant others as to the difficulties that the person encounters in his or her daily activities. Finally, questionnaires that pose questions to both the patient and their significant others regarding functional abilities can provide important information as well. Not only do these various techniques need to be further refined, but a combination of techniques, and altogether new techniques are needed (Chaytor & Schmitter-Edgecombe, 2003).

Neuropsychologists as primary caregivers for cognition

The brain controls the physical, emotional and cognitive functions. Physicians are the primary caregivers for diagnosing and treating the physical problems associated with brain disorders. Emotional maladjustments fall under the expertise of psychiatrists and clinical psychologists. The time has come for neuropsychologists to assert themselves as the primary caregivers for their patients' cognitive health (Ruff, 1999, 2003). To achieve this goal, the discipline of neuropsychology must expand beyond being a diagnostic discipline by advancing treatments for cognitive problems.

As with physical and emotional health, cognitive health is paramount for maintaining a high quality of life. Thus, individuals and society could benefit from neuropsychologists expanding the scope of their discipline to more vigorously focus on efficacious treatments of cognitive deficits. However, if after establishing a differential diagnosis, neuropsychologists have no efficacious treatments to offer, then the value of their contribution is obviously limited.

Cognitive rehabilitation can be defined as a systematic program targeting cognitive functions and possibly aberrant behaviors to help a person achieve the highest level of functioning and independence possible. Cognitive rehabilitation treatments typically take two forms: direct retraining of cognitive impairments, and teaching compensatory strategies to work around cognitive deficits. In the past, many neuropsychologists abstained from treating the person's cognitive deficits with cognitive remediation out of a perceived lack of evidence-based efficacy for such treatments.

However, in the last two decades, there has been a surge of research in cognitive rehabilitation resulting in almost 1,000 articles being written. Meta-analytic reviews by Cicerone et al. (2000, 2005) and Rohling, Faust, Beverly, and Demakis (2009), as well as a controlled study by Smith et al. (2009) with over 400 individuals, have found there is sufficient evidence to support the use of cognitive remediation following stroke or traumatic brain injury, as well as for the normal aging population. These studies found that impairments in attention and concentration, language, memory, and visuospatial neglect and scanning significantly improved after retraining. Overall, interventions tend to be more effective for individuals with milder injuries (Cicerone et al., 2005). More severely impaired individuals benefit more from external aids and adjustments in their environment; these interventions focused on working around their cognitive deficits. Also, with more severely injured individuals, pharmacological agents such as Bromocriptine and methylphenidate have been utilized to address symptoms such as apathy and lethargy. However, future research is warranted that combines cognitive rehabilitation with medications (i.e. cognotropic drugs) (Goldberg, 2001).

The primary goal in cognitive remediation is to transfer newly learned skills to enhance daily functioning. Thus, gains should not only be captured in the training materials, but these gains should translate to improvements in the patients' daily functioning. To achieve this, interventions must involve training of both the cognitive domains and functional skills (Gordon & Hibbard, 1991). These cognitive interventions should emphasize a balance between shoring up specific weaknesses, and enhancing strengths.

Adapting psychotherapy for individuals with neurological deficits

The training received as a clinical psychologist has only limited applications for persons with neurological illnesses. That is, examining childhood adjustment difficulties like attachment disorders or the genesis of defense mechanisms, has minimal utility for adults who are attempting to cope with a life-altering illness. Indeed, most often, a person's goal in seeking treatment is expressed as a desire to return to the person she/he was before the catastrophic illness. Thus, dynamic or analytical psychotherapy has limited application although cognitive-behavioral strategies can be applied to specific aspects of neurological deficits. Tragically, most serious neurological illnesses result in permanent physical, cognitive, and emotional symptoms, and, therefore, neuropsychologists must advance new psychotherapeutic interventions that specifically assist individuals with brain injuries to cope and accept the new challenges facing them.

Because most patients express a strong desire for symptom reduction, it is logical for therapists to focus on treating the many problems that have resulted from the neurological illness. However, we recommend that this approach be modified according to the following five steps.

1. It is most often beneficial to start by focusing on the individual's strengths and preserved resources. Although most people initially find this counterintuitive, a person's preserved resources can provide a realistic bridge for learning to cope and

deal with their new difficulties. Instances of preserved resources can include an appreciation for supportive family members. Moreover, social, financial, recreational, and spiritual resources should be explored. Thus, throughout the treatment, a balanced perspective should be maintained between preserved strengths and weaknesses. Ideally, if a balanced approach is continually provided, the overidentification of being a "brain-damaged" victim can be replaced with the self-perception of being a survivor who is managing his or her life with a serious illness. If the focus is primarily on the person's deficits, the therapist essentially colludes with him or her in accepting strengths as superfluous. This, in turn, can reinforce the person's tendency to ignore and underutilize his or her strengths.

2. In providing psychotherapy to individuals with neurological illnesses, it is important to recognize that the great majority of these patients have significantly reduced physical and mental energy. When the patient is exhausted, well-meaning therapeutic interventions often fail. Indeed, an overly intensive treatment schedule can present a burden rather than a relief. Before introducing elaborate treatment regiments, the patient and the therapist must both understand what level of energy is available. An individual with a traumatic brain injury said it best when he likened his injured body to a car, saying: "Just because my car was in a collision, does not mean that the gas tank got bigger and the engine gets more mileage." This prompted the patient and therapist to jointly develop a simple checklist that allowed the patient to record his daily energy levels. Monitoring over weeks and months provided insights into the daily fluctuations, and allowed the therapist and patient to identify activities that were especially draining. This tracking captured subtle gains that otherwise would have likely gone unrecognized. Moreover, patients should be encouraged to integrate exercise, balanced nutrition, restful sleep, and stress reduction into their daily lives. If adjustments in these areas result in increased energy, then the patient's motivation is enhanced to maintain his or her ongoing energy management.

3. The person's pre-injury expectations for the future must be identified and understood. Significant emotional pain and turmoil often results from future plans that have been irrevocably altered when, for example, a carpenter's stroke leads to a completely paralyzed right arm, or when a salesperson experiences pronounced word-finding difficulties. In this context, premorbid personality characteristics also need to be assessed, since these often influence future expectations. For example, a perfectionist who equates attaining goals with the purpose of life will likely be highly anxious if her or his post-injury future is perceived as hopelessly far removed from those goals.

Most of us have certain expectations for our future. Emotional pain and depression are often proportionate to the degree to which these expectations are no longer attainable. The source for this depression must be treated by first grieving the loss of the expected future. Thereafter, it is essential to explore a new and realistic future (Ruff, 2003). While psychologists are trained to treat potential issues from the clients' past, with individuals who have sustained a catastrophic illness it is often more imperative to first explore their future expectations. Indeed, the source of the depressive symptoms is frequently the loss of the expected future that is then further magnified by a hopeless and helpless attitude toward that future.

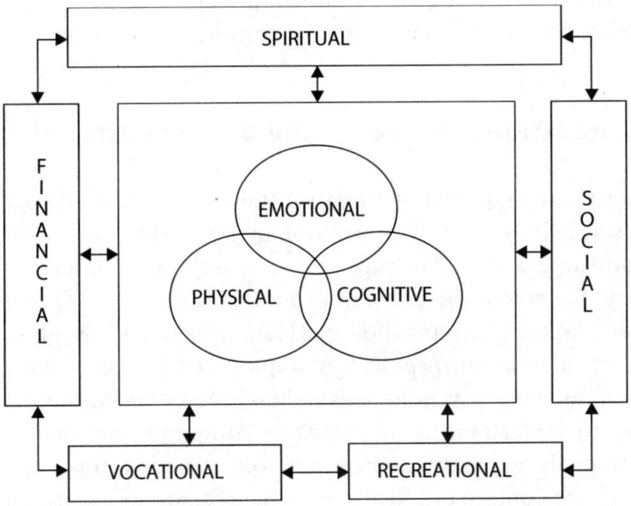

Figure 5.3. Patient-based model

4. It is only after the above three areas have been thoroughly addressed that the patient should detail the extent to which deficits interfere with daily routines. A patient-based model can be particularly helpful in understanding the interactions between various domains of a person's life (see Figure 5.3.). Self-report questionnaires that focus on pre- versus postmorbid comparison of these functions can be particularly useful (Ruff Neurobehavioral Inventory; Ruff & Hibbard, 2003). The patient and therapist should jointly identify realistic goals. It is essential that these goals are prioritized according to the newly created future expectations, while at the same time assuring that the patient's energy, strengths, and resources are sufficient to achieve these goals. Note that when a person loses her or his motivation for working toward goals, it is often because she or he perceives the goal as either insignificant or unattainable. Thus, goals should not be set in cement at the outset, but rather re-evaluated over the course of rehabilitation.

Throughout treatment, neuropsychologists are uniquely qualified to evaluate the impact of brain-based emotional alterations and the psychological struggles of coping with their cognitive residuals (Grant & Adams, 2009). Brain-based emotional problems can include difficulties in accurately perceiving emotion in someone's facial expression, vocal intonation, gestures or even speech content. Mood dysregulation can result in depression, mania, or both. Moreover, high levels of anxiety and irritability are common effects of brain damage. Indeed, even longstanding personality traits can be radically altered by neurological illnesses. For example, a shy introverted person can be transformed into an outspoken, disinhibited person. A highly energetic and organized person may become lethargic and lacking in initiative. Thus, psychotherapeutic interventions with neurological patients must take into account these brain-based emotional changes, while providing coping strategies for dealing with cognitive, physical, vocational, social, and recreational limitations.

Qualifications for Becoming a Neuropsychologist

It is preferable to complete a comprehensive training as a clinical psychologist prior to pursuing a specialization in neuropsychology (Hannay et al., 1998). Individuals interested in pursuing a career in clinical neuropsychology should become familiar with the Policy Statement of the Houston Conference on Specialty Education and Training in Clinical Neuropsychology (Hannay et al., 1998). Just as the clinical psychologist's training in *psychopathology* requires both classroom and internship training, so does the neuropsychologist's training require both theoretical and experiential training to understand *neuropathology*. Although most graduate schools in clinical psychology incorporate neuropsychology courses, this exposure alone is insufficient. In-depth coursework focusing on neuroanatomy, neuroscience, and neuroimaging techniques is required. Most importantly, clinical exposure to a range of neurological illnesses is essential, including dementia, traumatic brain injury, cerebrovascular disease, movement and demylinating disorders, epilepsy, and neurotoxicity. By evaluating a spectrum of individuals with neurological disorders, a practical knowledge base can be established for assessing the complexities of symptom constellations such as aphasia, agnosia, acalculia, dyslexia, anomia, neglect syndromes, amnesia, and anosmia (Heilman & Valenstein, 2003).

The cognitive residuals that are common in different psychiatric disorders should also be appreciated; since these issues often coexist. Training should also focus on understanding complex medical issues, and medical record and report writing skills. Indeed, report writing should incorporate detailed observations made during testing. Especially when there is a question of secondary gain, special attention should be given to motivational fluctuations, the effects of pain, exaggerations, poor effort, and the faking of deficits.

Summary and Conclusions

While basic science remains focused on localizing the various brain regions associated with specific cognitive functions, modern clinical neuropsychology is centered on quantifying an individual's cognitive strengths and weaknesses. Evaluating the patient's emotional status following a neurological illness is also central to clinical neuropsychology. The future of applied neuropsychology will benefit from predicting everyday functioning on the basis of test data and clinical observations. Similarly, more innovative methods must be developed for capturing executive function. Most importantly, efficacious treatments must be advanced in the future to ameliorate—at least in part—the cognitive declines associated with aging, neurological and neuropsychiatric disorders. Finally, our society at large will greatly benefit if neuropsychologists emerge as the primary health care providers for cognitive deficiencies and rehabilitation similar to the position physicians have earned in providing health care.

References

American Academy of Neurology. (1996). Assessment: Neuropsychological testing of adults. Considerations for neurologists. *Neurology, 47*, 592–599.

Anson, K., & Ponsford, J. (2006). Coping and emotional adjustment following traumatic brain injury. *Journal of Head Trauma Rehabilitation, 21*, 248–259.

Baker, K., Schmidt, M., Heinemann, A., Langley, M., & Miranti, S. (1998). The validity of the Katz Adjustment Scale among people with traumatic brain injury. *Rehabilitation Psychology, 43*, 30–40.

Baldo, J., Delis, D., & Kramer, J. (2002). Memory performance on the California Verbal Learning Test-II: Findings from patients with focal frontal lesions. *Journal of the International Neuropsychological Society, 8*, 539–546.

Barcelo, F., & Rubia, F. (1998). Non-frontal P3b-like activity evoked by the Wisconsin Card Sorting Test. *Neuroreport, 9*, 747–751.

Beck, A. T., & Steer, R. A. (1993). *Beck Anxiety Inventory manual.* San Antonio, TX: Psychological Corporation.

Beck, A. T., Steer, R. A., & Brown, G. K. (1996). *Beck Depression Inventory-II manual.* San Antonio, TX: Psychological Corporation.

Benton, A. L., Hamsher, K. de S., & Sivan, A. B. (1994). *Multilingual Aphasia Examination.* Iowa City, IA: AJA Associates.

Benton, A. L., Varney, N., & Hamsher, K. (1978).Visuospatial judgment: A clinical test. *Archives of Neurology, 35*, 364–367.

Broca, P. (1861). Nouvelle observation d'aphemie produite par une lesion de moitié posterieure des deuxième et troisième circonvolutions frontale. *Societe Anatomique de Paris, 6*, 398–407.

Bush, S. S., Ruff, R. M., Tröster, A. I., Barth, J. T., Koffler, S. P., & Pliskin, N. H., ... Silver, C. H. (2005). Symptom validity assessment: Practice issues and medical necessity. Position Paper by the NAN Policy & Planning Committee. *Archives of Clinical Neuropsychology, 20*, 419–426.

Butcher, J. N., Graham, J. R., Ben-Porath, Y. S., Tellegen, A., Dahlstrom, W. G., & Kaemmer, B. (2001). *Minnesota Multiphasic Personality Inventory-2 (MMPI-2): Manual for administration, scoring, and interpretation, revised edition.* Minneapolis, MN: University of Minnesota Press.

Chaytor, N., & Schmitter-Edgecombe, D. (2003). The ecological validity of neuropsychological tests: A review of the literature on everyday cognitive skills. *Neuropsychological Review, 13*, 181–197.

Cicerone, K. D., Dahlberg, C., Kalmar, K., Langenbahn, D. M., Malec, J. F., Bergquist, T. F., ... Morse, P. A. (2000). Evidence-based cognitive rehabilitation: Recommendations for clinical practice. *Archives of Physical Medicine and Rehabilitation, 81*, 1596–1615.

Cicerone, K. D., Dahlberg, C., Malec, J. F., Langenbahn, D. M., Felicetti, T., Kneipp, S., ... Catanese, J. (2005). Evidence-based cognitive rehabilitation: Updated review of the literature from 1998 through 2002. *Archives of Physical Medicine and Rehabilitation, 86*, 1681–1692.

Cohen, R., Malloy, P., Jenkins, M., & Paul, R. (2006). Disorders of attention. In P. Snyder, P. Nussbaum, & D. Robins (Eds.), *Clinical neuropsychology: A pocket handbook for assessment.* Washington, D.C.: American Psychological Association.

Conners, C. K. (2000). Conners' Continuous Performance Test II: Computer program for windows technical guide and software manual. North Tonwanda, NY: Multi-Health Systems.

Crockett, D., Clark, C., & Klonoff, H. (1980). Correlation and consistency of WISC IQ in sibling and nonsibling pairs. *Journal of Consulting and Clinical Psychology, 48*, 427–430.

Crosson, B., Sartor, K., Jenny, A., Nabors, N., & Moberg, P. (1993). Increased intrusions during verbal recall in traumatic and nontraumatic lesions of the temporal lobe. *Neuropsychology, 7*, 193–208.

Cullum, M. (1989). Cerebral imaging and emotional correlates. In E. Bigler, R. Yeo, & E. Turkheimer (Eds.), *New Neuropsychological function and brain imaging* (pp. 269–293). New York: Plenum Press.

Davies, D. R., Jones, D. M., & Taylor, A. (1984). Selective- and sustained-attention tasks: Individual and group differences. In R. Parasuraman & D. R. Davies (Eds.), *Varieties of attention* (pp. 395–447). Orlando: Academic Press.

Delis, D. C., Kramer, J. H., Kaplan, E., & Ober, B. A. (2000). *CVLT-II: California Verbal Learning Test, second edition, adult version manual.* San Antonio, TX: The Psychological Corporation.

Demir, S., Altinok, N., & Aydin, G. (2006). Functional and cognitive progress in aphasic patients with traumatic brain injury during post-acute phase. *Brain Injury, 20*, 383–1390.

Derogatis, L. (1977). *The SCL-90-R: Administration, scoring and procedures manual.* Baltimore: Clinical Psychometric Research.

Dimond, S. (1979). Performance by split-brain humans on lateralized vigilance tasks. *Cortex, 15*(1), 43–50.

Ewert, J., Levin, H., & Watson, M. (1989). Procedural memory during posttraumatic amnesia in survivors of severe closed head injury: Implications for rehabilitation. *Archives of Neurology, 46*, 911–916.

Favre, T., Hughes, C., Emslie, G., Stavinoha, P., Kennard, B., & Carmody, T. (2009). Executive functioning in children and adolescents with Major Depressive Disorder. *Child Neuropsychology, 15*(1), 85–98.

Feil, D., Razani, J., Boone, K., & Lesser, I. (2003). Apathy and cognitive performance in older adults with depression. *International Journal of Geriatric Psychiatry, 18*, 479–485.

Fristoe, N., Salthouse, T., & Woodard, J. (1997). Examination of age-related deficits on the Wisconsin Card Sorting Test. *Neuropsychology, 11*, 428–436.

Goldberg, E. (2001). *The executive brain: Frontal lobes and the civilized mind.* Oxford: Oxford University Press.

Golden, C. (1995). *The Luria Nebraska Neuropsychological Battery-Form III.* Los Angeles: Western Psychological Services.

Golden, C., & Freshwater, S. (2002). *Stroop Color and Word test.* Wood Dale, IL: Stoelting.

Goodglass, H. (2002). *Assessment and aphasia and related disorders* (3rd ed.). New York: Lea & Febiger.

Gordon, W., & Hibbard, M. (1991). The theory and practice of cognitive remediation. In J. Kreutzer, & P. Wehman (Eds.), *Cognitive rehabilitation for persons with traumatic brain injury: A functional approach* (pp. 13–22). Baltimore: Brookes.

Goodglass, H., Kaplan, E., & Barresi, B. (2000). *The Boston Diagnostic Aphasia Exam-3.* Lutz, FL: Psychological Assessment Resources.

Grant, I., & Adams, K. M. (2009). *Neuropsychological assessment of neuropsychiatric and neuromedical disorders* (3rd ed.). New York: Oxford University Press.

Hannay, H. J., Bieliauskas, L., Crosson, B., Hammeke, T. A., Hamsher, K. de S., & Koffler, S. P. (1998). Policy statement. Proceedings of the Houston Conference on Specialty Education and Training in Clinical Neuropsychology. *Archives of Clinical Neuropsychology, 13*, 160–166.

Heaton, R., Chelune, G., Talley, J., Kay, G., & Curtiss, G. (1993). *Wisconsin Card Sorting Test manual: Revised and expanded.* Odessa, Florida: Psychological Assessment Resources.

Heilbronner, R. L. (2008). *Neuropsychology in the courtroom.* New York: Guilford Press.

Heilman, K., & Van Den, A., (1980). Right hemisphere dominance for attention: The mechanism underlying hemispheric asymmetries of inattention (neglect). *Neurology, 30,* 327–330.

Heilman, K. M., & Valenstein, E. (2003). *Clinical neuropsychology* (4th ed.). New York: Oxford University Press.

Hom, J. (2003). Forensic neuropsychology: Are we there yet? *Archives of Clinical Neuropsychology, 18,* 827–845.

Honey, C., & Sporns, O. (2008). Dynamical consequences of lesions in cortical networks. *Human Brain Mapping, 29,* 802–809.

Hopkins, R., Tate, D., & Bigler, E. (2005) Anoxic versus traumatic brain injury: Amount of tissue loss, not etiology, alters cognitive and emotional function. *Neuropsychology, 19,* 233–242.

Katz, M., & Lyerly, S. (1963). Methods for measuring adjustment and social behavior in the community: I. rationale, description, discriminative validity and scale development. *Psychological Reports, 13,* 503–535.

Kesler, S., Adams, H., Blasey, C., & Bigler, E. (2003). Premorbid intellectual functioning, education, and brain size in traumatic brain injury: An investigation of the cognitive reserve hypothesis. *Applied Neuropsychology, 10*(3), 153–162.

Kleist, K. (1934). *Gehirnpathologie. Handbuch der ärztlichen Erfahrungen im Weltkriege.* Leipzig: Barth.

Kornhuber, H. (1984). Attention, readiness for action, and the stages of voluntary decision: Some electrophysiological correlates in man. In O. Creutzfeldt, R. Schmidt, & W. Willis (Eds.), *Sensory-motor integration in the nervous system: International symposium held on the occasion of the 80th birthday of Sir John Eccles* (pp. 420–429). New York: Springer-Verlag.

Kreutzer, J., Harris-Marwitz, J., & Myers, S. (1990). Neuropsychological issues in litigation following traumatic brain injury. *Neuropsychology, 4,* 249–259.

Kuelz, A., Hohagen, F., & Voderholzer, U. (2004). Neuropsychological performance in obsessive-compulsive disorder: A critical review. *Biological Psychology, 65*(3), 185–236.

Lafayette Instruments. (1989). *Instruction manual for the 32025 Grooved Pegboard Test.* Lafayette, IN: Lafayette Instruments.

Lam, C., Priddy, D., & Johnson, P. (1991). Neuropsychological indicators of employability following traumatic brain injury. *Rehabilitation Counseling Bulletin, 35,* 68–74.

Lashley, K. S. (1929). *Brain mechanisms and intelligence.* Chicago: University of Chicago Press.

Lezak, M., Howieson, D., & Loring, D. (2004). *Neuropsychological assessment* (4th ed.). New York: Oxford University Press.

Loeb, P. A. (1996). *Independent Living Scales manual.* San Antonio, TX: Psychological Corporation.

Luria, A. (1966). *Higher cortical functions in man* (2nd ed.). New York: Basic Books.

Luria, A. (1980). Neuropsychology in the local diagnosis of brain damage. *Clinical Neuropsychology, 2,* 1–7.

MacDonald, S., & Flanagan, S. (2004). Social perception deficits after traumatic brain injury: Interaction between emotion recognition, mentalizing ability, and social communication. *Neuropsychology, 18,* 572–579.

Martin, V., Huber, M., Rief, W., & Exner, C. (2008). Comparative cognitive profiles of obsessive-compulsive disorder and schizophrenia. *Archives of Clinical Neuropsychology, 23*, 487–500.

Meyers, J., & Meyers, K. (1995). *Rey Complex Figure Test and recognition trail professional manual.* Odessa, FL: Psychological Assessment Resources.

Milders, M., Fuchs, S., & Crawford, J. (2003). Neuropsychological impairments and changes in emotional and social behaviour following severe traumatic brain injury. *Journal of Clinical and Experimental Neuropsychology, 25*(2), 157–172.

Millon, T., Millon, C., & Davis, R. (1997). *Millon Clinical Inventory-III manual.* Minneapolis, MN: National Computer Systems.

Monchi, O., Petrides, M., & Petre, V. (2001). Wisconsin Card Sorting revisited: Distinct neural circuits participating in different stages of the task identified by event-related functional magnetic resonance imaging. *Journal of Neuroscience, 21*, 7733–7741.

Morey, L. C. (1991). *The Personality Assessment Inventory, professional manual.* Odessa, FL: Psychological Assessment Resources.

Niemann, H., Ruff, R., & Kramer, J. (1996). An attempt towards differentiating attentional deficits in traumatic brain injury. *Neuropsychology Review, 6*, 11–46.

Norman, D., & Shallice, T. (1986). *Attention to action: Willed and automatic control of behavior* (Technical Report No. 99). Center for Human Information Processing. Reprinted in revised form in Davidson, R., Schwartz, G., & Shapiro, D. (Eds.), *Consciousness and self-regulation* (Vol. 4). New York: Plenum Press.

Prigatano, G. (1992). Personality disturbances associated with traumatic brain injury. *Journal of Consulting and Clinical Psychology, 60*, 360–368.

Prigatano, G., Johnson, S., & Gale, S. (2004). Neuroimaging correlates of the Halstead Finger Tapping Test several years post-traumatic brain injury. *Brain Injury, 18*, 661–669.

Reitan, R., & Davidson, R. (1974). *Clinical neuropsychology: Current status and applications.* New York: Winston/Wiley.

Ríos, M., Periáñez, J., & Muñoz-Céspedes, J. (2004). Attentional control and slowness of information processing after severe traumatic brain injury. *Brain Injury, 18*, 257–272.

Rödholm, M., Starmark, J., Ekholm, S., & von Essen, C. (2002). Organic psychiatric disorders after aneurysmal SAH: Outcome and associations with age, bleeding severity, and arterial hypertension. *Acta Neurologica Scandinavica, 106*, 8–18.

Rogers, R. (2008). *Clinical assessment of malingering and deception* (3rd ed.). New York: Guilford Press.

Rohling, M., Faust, M., Beverly, B., & Demakis, G. (2009). Effectiveness of cognitive rehabilitation following acquired brain injury: A meta-analytic re-examination of Cicerone et al.'s (2000, 2005) systematic reviews. *Neuropsychology, 23*, 20–39.

Ropacki, M., & Elias, J. (2003). Preliminary examination of cognitive reserve theory in closed head injury. *Archives of Clinical Neuropsychology, 18*, 643–654.

Ruff, R. M. (1996). *Ruff Figural Fluency Test, professional manual.* Odessa, FL: Psychological Assessment Resources.

Ruff, R. M. (1999). Discipline specific approach vs. individual care. In: N. R. Varney and R. J. Roberts (Eds.). *Mild head injury: causes, evaluation and treatment* (pp. 99–113). Mahwah, New Jersey: L. Erlbaum.

Ruff, R. M. (2003). A friendly critique of neuropsychology: Facing the challenges of our future. *Archives of Clinical Neuropsychology, 18*, 847–864.

Ruff, R. M. (2004). Sequelae of traumatic brain injury. In H. Winn (Ed.). *Youman's neurological surgery* (5th ed., pp. 5181–5201). Philadelphia: Saunders.

Ruff, R. M., & Allen, C. (1996). *Ruff 2 & 7 Selective Attention Test, professional manual.* Odessa, FL: Psychological Assessment Resources, Inc.

Ruff, R. M., & Allen, C. (1999). *Ruff-Light Trail Learning Test, professional manual.* Odessa, FL: Psychological Assessment Resources, Inc.

Ruff, R. M., Allen, C. C., Farrow, C. E., Niemann, H. and Wylie, T. (1994). Figural fluency: Differential impairment in patients with left vs. right frontal lobe lesions. *Archives of Clinical Neuropsychology, 9*, 41–45.

Ruff, R. M., Camenzuli, L., & Mueller, J. (1996). Miserable minority: Emotional risk factors that influence the outcome of a mild traumatic brain injury. *Brain Injury, 10*, 551–565.

Ruff, R. M. & Hibbard, K. (2003). *Ruff Neurobehavioral Inventory, professional manual.* Odessa, FL: Psychological Assessment Resources.

Ruff, R. M., Light, R., & Parker, S. (1997). The psychological construct of word fluency. *Brain and Language, 57*, 394–405.

Ruff, R. M., & Schraa, J. (2008). Neuropsychological assessment. In B. Bolton and R. Parker (Eds.), *Handbook of measurement and evaluation in rehabilitation* (pp. 233–254). Austin, TX: Pro-ed.

Russell, E., Russell, S., & Hill, B. (2005). The fundamental psychometric status of neuropsychological batteries. *Archives of Clinical Neuropsychology, 20*, 785–794.

Salorio, C., Slomine, B., Grados, M., Vasa, R., Christensen, J., & Gerring, J. (2005). Neuroanatomic correlates of CVLT-C performance following pediatric traumatic brain injury. *Journal of the International Neuropsychological Society, 11*, 686–696.

Satz, P. (1993). Brain reserve capacity on symptom onset after brain injury: A formulation and review of evidence for threshold theory. *Neuropsychology*, 273–295.

Savage, C., & Rauch, S. (2000). Cognitive deficits in obsessive-compulsive disorder. *American Journal of Psychiatry, 157*, 1182.

Saxena, S., Brody, A., Schwartz, J., & Baxter, L. (1998). Neuroimaging and frontal-subcortical circuitry in obsessive-compulsive disorder. *British Journal of Psychiatry, 173*(35), 26–37.

Saxena, S., & Rauch, S. (2000). Functional neuroimaging and the neuroanatomy of obsessive-compulsive disorder. *Psychiatric Clinics of North America, 23*, 563–586.

Sbordone, R. J., & Long, C. J. (1996) *Ecological validity of neuropsychological assessment.* Delray Beach, FL: Lucie Press.

Smith, G., Housen, P., Yaffee, K., Ruff, R., Kennison, R., Mahncke, H., Zelinski, H. M. (2009). A cognitive training program based on principles of brain plasticity: Results from improvement in memory with plasticity-based adaptive cognitive training (IMPACT) study. *Journal of the American Geriatric Society, 1*, 1–10.

Snow, P., Douglas, J., & Ponsford, J. (1998). Conversational discourse abilities following severe traumatic brain injury: A follow-up study. *Brain Injury, 12*, 911–935.

Spreen, O., & Risser, A. (2002). *Assessment of aphasia* (2nd ed.). New York: Oxford University Press.

Squire, L. (1987). *Memory and brain.* New York: Oxford University Press.

Squire, L., & Schacter, D. (2003). *Neuropsychology of memory* (3rd ed.). New York: Guilford Press.

Stern, R. A., & White, T. (2003). *Neuropsychological Assessment Battery.* Lutz, FL: Psychological Assessment Resources.

Stern, Y. (2002). What is cognitive reserve? Theory and research application of the reserve concept. *Journal of the International Neuropsychological Society, 8*, 448–460.

Strauss, E., Sherman, E., & Spreen, O. (2006). *A compendium of neuropsychological tests: Administration, norms, and commentary* (3rd ed). Oxford: Oxford University Press.

Stroop, J. R. (1935). Studies of interference in serial verbal reactions. *Journal of Experimental Psychology, 18*, 643–662.

Stulemeijer, M., Vos, P., Bleijenberg, G., & van der Werf, S. (2007). Cognitive complaints after mild traumatic brain injury: Things are not always what they seem. *Journal of Psychosomatic Research*, *63*, 637–645.

Stuss, D., & Knight, R. (2002). *Principles of frontal lobe function*. New York: Oxford University Press.

Sweet, J., Moberg, P., & Suchy, Y. (2000). Ten-year follow-up survey of clinical neuropsychologists: Part II. private practice and economics. *The Clinical Neuropsychologist*, *14*, 479–495.

Teuber, H. L. (1955). Physiological psychology. *Annual Review of Psychology*, *6*, 267–296.

Thorne, A., & Page, M. (2009). Current issues in understanding interactions between short-term and long-term memory. In A. Thorne & M. Page (Eds.), *Interactions between short-term and long-term memory in the verbal domain* (pp. 1–15). New York: Psychology Press.

Weinberger, D., Berman, K., & Zec, R. (1986). Physiologic dysfunction of dorsolateral prefrontal cortex in schizophrenia: I. Regional cerebral blood flow evidence. *Archives of General Psychiatry*, *43*(2), 114–124.

Weiskrantz, L. (1991). Dissociations and associates in neuropsychology. In R. G. Lister & H. J. Weingartner (Eds.), *Perspectives on cognitive neurosciences* (pp. 847–864). New York: Oxford University Press.

Wood, R., & Williams, C. (2007). Neuropsychological correlates of organic alexithymia. *Journal of the International Neuropsychological Society*, *13*, 471–479.

Vanier M., Mazaux, J., Lambert, J., Dassa, C., & Levin, H. (2000). Assessment of neuropsychologic impairments after head injury: Interrater reliability and factorial and criterion validity of the Neurobehavioral Rating Scale—Revised. *Archives of Physical Medicine Rehabilitation*, *81*, 796–806.

Vogt, O. (1951). Die anatomische Vertiefung der menschlichen Hirnlokalisation. *Klinische Wissenshaft*, *78*.

Vollmer, D., Torner, J., Jane, J., Sadovnic, B., Charlebois, D., Eisenberg, H., ... Marshall, L. F. (1991). Age and outcome following traumatic coma: Why do older patients fare worse? *Journal of Neurosurgery*, *75*, S37–S49.

Warkentin, S., Risberg, J., & Nilsson, A. (1991). Cortical activity during speech production: A study of regional cerebral blood flow in normal subjects performing a word fluency task. *Neuropsychiatry, Neuropsychology, & Behavioral Neurology*, *4*(4), 305–316.

Wechsler, D. (2009). *Wechsler Adult Intelligence Scale—Fourth edition administration and scoring manual*. San Antonio, TX: The Psychological Corporation.

Wernicke, C. (1874). *Der aphasische Symptomenkomplex*. Berlin: Breslau, Cohn, & Weisgert.

Whitehead, R. (1991). Right hemisphere processing superiority during sustained visual attention. *Journal of Cognitive Neuroscience*, *3*, 329–334.

Wilson, B. A., Cockburn, J., & Baddeley, A. D. (1985). *The Rivermead Behavioural Test*. London: Pearson Assessment.

6

Counseling Psychology

Frederick T. L. Leong, Mark L. Savickas, and Mark M. Leach

In this chapter, we will provide an overview of the field of counseling psychology as one of the specialties within applied psychology. We begin with an historical survey, followed by an attempt at defining the field in relation to some similar and overlapping specialties. Next, we attend to the trends and key developments within the field, emphasizing an international perspective. We end the chapter with a discussion of the challenges and opportunities for this field as well as an articulation of the potential future developments in the field. We want to point out that there is a heavy focus on the field from the perspective of the United States, not because of that country's superiority but because the field has been most active there. For example, despite its long history, the International Association of Applied Psychology did not include a division on counseling psychology until 2002. Only recently has there been a growth of counseling psychology training programs and research activities outside of North America. In most countries around the world, psychological training and research related to mental health had been provided primarily by clinical and school psychology for the past several decades while counseling psychology has been strongly embedded and isolated in the mid-western part of the United States.

History

In their review of the history of counseling psychology in the United States, Leong and Leach (2008) suggested that significant changes have occurred since its beginnings, and these developments can be understood from a framework of the first and second halves of the 20th century. During the first half of the 20th century, counseling psychology was shaped by three interrelated areas, the vocational guidance

IAAP Handbook of Applied Psychology, First Edition. Edited by Paul R. Martin, Fanny M. Cheung, Michael C. Knowles, Michael Kyrios, Lyn Littlefield, J. Bruce Overmier, and José M. Prieto.

movement, the mental health movement, and the psychology of individual differences. First, the vocational guidance movement in the United States began with Frank Parsons in 1908 with his pioneering work at the Vocational Guidance Bureau in Boston. His classic book, *Choosing a Vocation*, (Parsons, 1909) outlined the fundamental beliefs of the Trait-and-Factor model for career counseling that provided the beginnings of an organized vocational guidance movement. Since counseling psychology grew in part from the vocational guidance movement, its history can be traced back to Parson's work, particularly in establishing the person–environment paradigm (Leong & Leach, 2008).

Second, the "mental health movement" gave rise to the development of the specialty of counseling psychology in the United States. This movement considered clients' mental illnesses as treatable and that treatment should be more compassionate than previously established in the US. Early mental health pioneers such as Dorothea Dix established mental hospitals and clinics that provided therapies focusing on client health and humane care. These agencies spawned the thousands of community mental health centers, counseling centers, and other mental health clinics that currently exist in the United States (Leong & Leach, 2008).

Finally, the field of individual differences and its tool of psychometrics in psychology were significant in developing the specialty of counseling psychology. As an early approach to the scientific study of human beings, some of the pioneering psychologists (e.g., Francis Galton, J. M. Cattell, Alfred Binet) recognized the significance of developing ways to evaluate and quantify psychological processes and behaviors. Their efforts to develop psychometric methods and tests to assess these processes and behaviors resulted in the field of differential psychology, also known as the psychology of individual differences. This field created the scientific study of areas quite common today such as individual variation in ability factors and personality traits. The accurate assessment and measurement of individual differences has become a centralized component of the discipline of psychology. These intersecting events resulted in a psychological assessment orientation that is a cornerstone for current clinical, school, and counseling psychology.

In fact, it is a psychometric contribution that is one of counseling psychology's major contributions, if not the major contribution, to psychology as a discipline (Pelling, 2004). Specifically, it is the measurement of vocational interests that has always been a cornerstone for the science and practice of counseling psychology. E. K. Strong published in 1927 the interest inventory that still bears his name and is widely used. The *Strong Interest Inventory* measures an individual's resemblance to individuals working in a wide variety of occupations. The closer the resemblance an individual scores to an occupation group, the more likely that occupation could be a good fit for the individual. In the middle of the 20th century, John Holland simplified the matching paradigm for interest measurement by formulating a typology of vocational personality types and work environments. The scores on his popular *Self-Directed Search* indicate the individual's degree of resemblance to the six prototypes. Given the profile of the six scores, the counselor can match clients with occupations comprised of people with similar profiles. Using interest inventories to provide career counseling continues to be a defining feature and core service of counseling psychology around the globe (Tien, 2007). Ironically, the field of psychometrics in psychology is under threat and a recent task force was established by the American Psychological Association to study how we can attract and recruit more psychology students to enter the field given its diminishing numbers.

World War II significantly altered and advanced the trajectory of counseling psychology in the United States, paving the way for changes during the second half of the 20th century. The end of World War II resulted in thousands of military personnel returning to civilian life. At the time, the mental health system was ill-equipped to handle the massive number of military personnel requiring services. Wanting to respond to the significant needs of not only the veterans but their families, the federal government created the Veterans' Administration (VA). Within the VA, hospitals and clinics were established to assist veterans and their families as they made a massive readjustment to civilian life.

After World War II, the transformation from vocational guidance to counseling psychology accelerated when guidance personnel assisted returning veterans by providing personal counseling (Leong & Leach, 2008). The Veterans' Administration prompted the switch from vocational guidance to personal counseling by asserting that returning soldiers who re-entered the labor market needed more than simply a match to a job. They needed additional personal counseling for mental problems and physical rehabilitation, especially counseling that dealt with emotions surrounding the war and their adjustment. With the emergence of research on psychotherapy by clinical psychologists, the methods of psychotherapy heralded by Carl Roger's non-directive counseling (in contrast to directive vocational guidance) would turn vocational psychologists with an interest in psychometrics into counseling psychologists with an interest in people, not problems (Super, 1957). Concurrently, vocational researchers revised their point of view on the relation of individuals to work as they shifted attention from studying occupational requirements, routines, and rewards to studying the characteristics of individuals and their careers. Based on the success of "counseling" with returning soldiers and attention to studying individual differences, counseling psychologists turned their attention to schools and colleges focusing on students' personal adjustment and personality.

Gelso and Fretz (2001) observed that the significant influx of counseling psychologists into the VA system created a key training ground for counseling psychology as an emerging specialty. They began working in the VA's Division of Medicine and Neurology under the newly created job title of counseling psychologist.

By the end of the 1940s counseling psychology began to detach from its roots in vocational guidance and mental health counseling, and the field began to grow. The Boulder conference of 1949 is still possibly the most influential conference on counseling psychology training models, as programs today continue to evolve based on the principles from this conference. Occurring just prior to the Northwestern Conference where training standards for counseling psychologists were developed in relation to the VA, the Boulder conference developed the scientist-practitioner model as the primary training model for clinical psychologists. This model stresses the interaction of psychological science and practice, meaning that science is the foundation for practice, and practice helps propel the science. Counseling psychologists also found the model beneficial. It was at the Greyston Conference in 1964, that counseling psychologists reaffirmed this model as their primary training model. In addition to highlighting the interaction between science and practice, this model is important for the field of counseling psychology inasmuch as it enabled the field to differentiate itself from its guidance roots. The emphasis on science, which was associated with the profession of psychology, separated counseling psychologists from counselors. Over 20 years later counseling psychologists again reaffirmed the scientist-practitioner model at the Georgia conference in 1987, and the 2001 Houston and 2008 Chicago conferences continued this principle. Today, though other models are available, very few counseling psychology programs do not directly espouse a scientist-practitioner model.

As counseling psychology developed, it was aided by several other significant events, such as the founding of the *Journal of Counseling Psychology* in the 1950s, now established as one of the most widely read, cited, and respected journals in the field. Divisional and related journals have emerged over time, most notably the *Counseling Psychologist*, the *Journal of Vocational Behavior*, and the *Journal of Career Assessment*. Additionally, various handbooks have undergone multiple editions such as the *Handbook of Counseling Psychology* and the *Handbook of Vocational Psychology*. A new *Review of Counseling Psychology* will be published biennially, which will include the latest developments in the field. In addition, the American Psychological Association has also signed a contract to produce a new *Handbook of Counseling Psychology* within its newly established handbook program.

The Society of Counseling Psychology within the American Psychological Association (APA) has almost 3,000 members, with multiple interest sections and groups. It is clearly a vibrant division within the APA, with many members holding APA executive and board positions. There are approximately 70 APA-accredited training programs in the country, a significant increase over the past few decades.

Outside of the United States, counseling psychology was also developing to meet the needs of various countries. Within Asia, it was the Association of Psychological and Educational Counselors of Asia (APECA-Asia), which was established in 1976, that was at the forefront of this movement. It was led by faculty members from Chinese University of Hong Kong with colleagues from the Philippines, Malaysia and Singapore. They held their 30th anniversary conference in 2006 <www.apeca-asia.com/> and have been publishing a regional journal, the *Asian Journal of Counseling* with Alvin Leung as Editor.

In mainland China, the Chinese Psychological Society has had a clinical and counseling psychology specialization division and in 2007 adopted a set of guidelines for professional registration and code of ethics. At least in China, clinical and counseling psychology are labeled together as the same specialization. This is still a fledgling profession and the training was very varied in the past. The new guidelines require postgraduate training in clinical/counseling psychology at masters or doctoral level, with specified curriculum and training duration. In Chinese, counseling and psychotherapy both refer to a form of psychological help to clients by talking to them and/or applying psychological principles, instead of using other forms of physical treatment. With reference to indigenous approaches in assessment and treatment that have been developed to address special cultural contexts, there has also been some significant development as illustrated by the scientific program of the recent World Congress of Psychotherapy in Beijing in October 2008 <www.wcp2008.org/sprogram.doc>.

Defining the Field

Counseling psychology employs a wide array of assessment and intervention strategies to help individuals, families, groups, and organizations with their educational, developmental, and adjustment concerns. Training programs are generalist in nature, though each program may have emphasis areas depending on the interests of the faculty. The combination of the breadth of the activities undertaken and the training structure have often resulted in counseling psychologists being referred to as the "general practitioners" of psychological specialties (Gelso & Fretz, 2001).

Within the United States, counseling psychology is one of four major applied specialties in professional psychology, the others being clinical psychology, school psychology, and industrial/organizational psychology. The first three are considered health service specialties while the latter is not. When compared with the other three applied specialties in psychology, counseling psychology is most similar to clinical psychology, and a few clinical and counseling training programs are either housed within the same university department or combined programs (Leong & Leach, 2008). Clinical psychology is the largest of all the applied specialties in the United States and comprises one of the largest divisions within the APA. The size of the division is expected given that over 200 APA-accredited clinical psychology programs are in existence compared with approximately 70 APA-accredited programs in counseling psychology. Though there is significant overlap between the two specialty areas when compared to other mental health professions, some important differences exist. One interesting note is that the majority (over 80%) of the counseling psychology programs are housed in colleges and schools of education rather than departments of psychology.

Given its history of emphasizing clients' strengths and assets instead of their deficits and pathology, counseling and clinical psychologists diverge along four primary interrelated dimensions. Counseling psychologists (a) generally intervene with people experiencing adjustment difficulties and moderate levels of psychological problems as opposed to severe psychopathology, (b) stress short-term interventions, (c) typically provide outpatient as opposed to inpatient services, and (d) are unique among applied psychologists in providing individual career counseling and educational interventions. Conversely, clinical psychologists highlight training in psychopathology and are more likely to include a broader range of assessment tools, including projective tests. Both counseling and clinical psychologist overlap significantly when providing individual, family, and group counseling and psychotherapy in that they use some of the same theories, models, and approaches (Leong & Leach, 2008).

It has been repeatedly observed that the two specialties appear to have moved closer together in recent years. Over twenty years ago Garfield (1985) noted that more and more clinical psychologists were beginning to work with less disturbed clients. A part of this trend can be attributed to the larger number of clinical training programs producing a significant number of clinicians, including the development of a growing number of professional psychology schools that tend to produce higher number of graduates. Given the increased numbers of clinical psychologists they have begun to move outside their historical areas of practice (i.e., hospitals, VA medical centers, community mental health centers). Clinical psychologists have now moved into university counseling centers, a domain previously reserved for counseling psychologists. Clinical psychology has also spearheaded the positive psychology movement that emphasizes the assets and strengths of clients, further blurring the boundaries between the two specialties. Finally, as mentioned above, there are growing numbers of APA-accredited programs that offer combined training in clinical-counseling-school psychology in the United States.

The applied specialty of school psychology also overlaps with counseling psychology, though to a lesser degree than clinical psychology. While counseling psychology tends to focus on adult populations, especially university and college students, school psychology focuses primarily on school children within the K-12 educational setting. There are counseling psychology programs that include child and adolescent components, but most focus on the clinical and research emphasis on adults. School psychologists highlight educational and psychological assessment, and intervention with K-12 students, and evaluations for special education and other placement decisions. They are also engaged in consultation with parents, school administrators, and teachers regarding students with special needs. Unlike counseling psychologists, they are more likely to be engaged in evaluation and consultation and less likely to be involved in individual counseling and psychotherapy with their clients (Leong & Leach, 2008).

Finally, counseling psychology overlaps with the applied specialty area of industrial/organizational (I/O) psychology. Industrial/organizational psychologists apply psychological theories and research to industrial-organizational settings, but it differs from the other applied specialties in that it is not a health service profession. Specifically, I/O psychologists are not trained to diagnose and treat individuals with mental health problems. Instead, I/O psychologists are involved in the assessment and enhancement of employee and managerial satisfaction, effectiveness, and performance in organizations. However, a major area of overlap between counseling and I/O psychology is that both specialties have interests in career and vocational development. They do differ slightly in that counseling psychology approaches career and vocational issues from the individual client's perspective and relies on counseling interventions. I/O psychologists, conversely, tend to use an organizational perspective and approach career and vocational problems in the workplace, due to the fact that they are primarily employed by organizations. Also, counseling psychology includes the career development and choices of children, adolescents, and young adults, whereas I/O psychologists concentrate on the career development of adults and are interested in concerns of career adjustment, job performance and satisfaction, and job tenure (low turnover) (Leong & Leach, 2008). Interestingly, despite its focus on career counseling, the majority of psychologists involved in the new field of executive coaching or life coaching are not counseling psychologists but instead come primarily from clinical and industrial/organizational backgrounds. At the same time, the vocational guidance that served as the historical roots of the field, has now been dominated by masters-level counselors rather than counseling psychologists.

Counseling psychology's primary focus on the individual, whether fitting workers to work or fitting work to workers, distinguishes it from organizational psychology's focus on work structures and from occupational sociology's focus on occupations.

As such, I/O psychology's main objective is to enhance organizational effectiveness even when dealing with individuals' career and vocational adjustment issues. In essence, I/O psychology's objectives are to implement its theories and interventions at a higher level of analysis (i.e., organizational or group level in contrast to the individual level) when compared to counseling psychology.

Roles

As indicated by Gelso and Fretz (2001), counseling psychology has three different but interrelated roles: the remedial, preventative, and developmental roles. Counseling psychologists acting in a remedial role intervene to assist clients with existing or emerging mental health problems. This type of work, especially for those in practice, constitutes the majority of their daily activities. There are a variety of mental health concerns presented by clients that are treated, such as anxiety and depression and marital concerns, among many others. Preventative approaches incorporate ways to avoid the occurrence of certain problems (primary prevention) or the reduction of the severity of problems that occur (secondary prevention). For example, counseling psychologists may offer a primary prevention program in which they offer substance abuse education presentations on campus to first-year students in order to prevent future abuse, while secondary prevention may include a support group for students concerned about their substance use behaviors. Finally, counseling psychologists acting in a developmental role seek to help clients with their normal developmental challenges and transitions such as vocational choices or marital adjustment or retirement planning. Counseling psychologists in their "general practitioner" role consider the whole lifespan and work with children, adolescents, and adults.

In carrying out these three roles, counseling psychology emphasizes four unique perspectives: focusing on strengths, growth and lifespan development, person–environment interaction, and cultural diversity (Gelso & Fretz, 2001). As mentioned above, emphasizing client strengths and assets rather than focusing primarily on deficits or pathology (the "medical model") has had a long tradition in the field. Similarly, highlighting growth and lifespan development means that counseling psychologists work with concerns associated with developmental tasks and transitions (e.g., moving from high school to university, job transitions), thus focusing less on severe psychopathology. Counseling psychologists do treat clients with severe mental illnesses such as schizophrenia, but are generally more likely to treat adjustment problems than severe mental disorders.

Finally, counseling psychology has focused considerably on cultural diversity in the provision of counseling services to its clients. Some have mentioned that counseling psychology has taken a leadership position within the field of psychology itself through the incorporation of cultural diversity into its training, science, and practice settings (Gelso & Fretz, 2001). From the pivotal position paper on cross-cultural counseling competencies (Sue et al., 1982) commissioned by the Division of Counseling Psychology in 1980 to the recent passage of the Multicultural Guidelines for Education, Training, and Practice in 2003, counseling psychologists have influenced psychology considerably by promoting greater attention and sensitivity to cultural issues in the American Psychological Association. This advocacy for a multicultural perspective in professional psychology has also led to the advancement in the development of theories, models and empirical studies on the topic (Leong & Leach, 2008). Due to its importance within counseling psychology, multiculturalism will be expounded upon below while discussing trends and key developments.

Trends and Key Developments

We have discussed above some of the historical changes that have occurred in counseling psychology in the US, including its beginnings with a focus on hygiology, vocational guidance, health, and prevention efforts. Many of these are still maintained to various degrees, yet other fields have also adopted them. However, as highlighted by Gelso and Fretz (2001), counseling psychology still values an emphasis on strengths, relatively brief interventions, prevention efforts, vocational issues, and multiculturalism at both the national and international levels. Recently the multicultural movement has increased its emphasis on the relationship to social justice, highlighting issues such as counseling advocacy and social activism (Toporek, Gerstein, Fouad, Roysircar, & Israel, 2005). In this section a very brief introduction of multiculturalism and social justice will be presented, followed by an analysis of counseling psychology topics found over the past five years in counseling and counseling psychology journals in Asia, Australia, North America, and the United Kingdom. The purpose of the analysis is to determine common and disparate features of counseling psychology research among geographic regions.

Multiculturalism

Multiculturalism as a value of counseling psychology began to emerge over the past few decades, resulting in the development of clinical cultural competency guidelines and an explosion of empirical and non-empirical research. Arredondo and Perez (2006) succinctly outlined the events that led to the recently developed multicultural competence guidelines for counseling psychologists (see Pope-Davis, Coleman, Liu, & Toporek, 2003). They began their overview with the 1964 Civil Rights Act and discussed the complementary efforts among the American Psychological Association, the American Counseling Association, and other organizations to bring about changes to their respective professions. In part because of social movements in the US, the 1970s saw the beginnings of increased numbers of publications that focused on the needs of ethnic minority groups, rather than simply maintaining the ethnocentric bias that what is good for one group works equally well for another.

The 1980s saw an increase in policy papers and publications on culture, including the first paper outlining 10 multicultural competencies (Sue et al., 1982). Other competency papers were constructed soon after and sections and divisions within a variety of psychological organizations developed. Multiple textbooks, professional articles, and culture-specific journals began to be published, and today multiculturalism is considered to be closely aligned with counseling psychology in the US. Due in part to counseling psychology's influence, multiculturalism has spread to many other fields both within and outside psychology, and it has become part of counseling psychology training and program accreditation at the national level.

As a natural extension of the U.S. multiculturalism movement, in the late 1980s *The Counseling Psychologist*, one of the top counseling psychology journals in the US, initiated an International Forum section. This section was responsible for developing an international focus to counseling psychology, and was one of the first, formal measures taken by the Society of Counseling Psychology to internationalize the field. There have been a number of empirical and nonempirical articles written about the influence of counseling psychology in various countries, and the roles that various psychological constructs play from international perspectives. For example, in just one issue, Leong and Blustein (2000) discussed a global vision for counseling psychology, various authors included articles about counseling psychology in China (Leung, Guo, & Lam, 2000) and Israel, (Barak & Golan, 2000), and constructs such as perfectionism in India (Slaney, Chadha, Mobley, & Kennedy, 2000) and family interactions in Samoa (Poasa, Mallinckrodt, & Suzuki, 2000) were presented. The International Forum has become a central resource for counseling psychologists interested in international issues.

Social justice

In many countries, as in the US, there are population shifts and sociopolitical movements that offer new opportunities and challenges not only to society itself, but to counseling psychologists. New and changing worldviews create both the need and prospects to review and evaluate our current research and training foci. Social justice is both a foundation and a natural outgrowth for counseling psychology, as it combines multicultural issues with strength-based models. It focuses on empowerment at the individual, social, and political levels.

Social justice applications and research have developed over the past decade. For example, increases in immigration have led to immigration summit meetings over the past decade that include the role of counseling psychology in assisting in the transition for immigrants. Sexual orientation advocacy has led to the advent of new research and interventions, led by counseling psychologists. Additionally, recent discussions of the role of religious and spiritual faith in treatment have gained momentum. Regardless of the group mentioned, there has been a significant increase in working toward social justice and equality.

The social justice movement in counseling psychology stemmed from a 2001 counseling psychology conference in Houston and has resulted in a plethora of publications and presentations. Many of the new multiculturally based texts now include sections on social justice, and a handbook has been developed that highlights research efforts, and training and intervention efforts that have been undertaken (Toporek et al., 2005). Given these and other values and emphasis areas described earlier (e.g., vocational, prevention) it is not difficult to make the transition from U.S. counseling psychology to international counseling psychology. In order to determine the values and emphases areas of counseling psychology on an international level, it would be beneficial to the field to evaluate the research using multiple international counseling-related journals. Unfortunately, little is formally known about the content of counseling psychology research internationally, though there have been recent articles discussing the field of counseling psychology from a global perspective (see the January 2007 special issue in *Applied Psychology: An International Review*). The following section will provide a glimpse of the counseling research areas conducted from multiple countries and published in counseling and counseling psychology journals from four geographic global regions. The purpose of this comparison is to both determine common research themes that have gained importance in these journals, as well as offer some conclusions as to their relationship to U.S. counseling psychology values in order to evaluate common themes internationally.

Journals evaluated

Examining journal content allows readers a glimpse of the important topics of interest to counseling psychology. Much of the literature is based in U.S. journals, though a review of this literature is limiting and possibly ethnocentric. In order to fully appreciate the robust field of counseling psychology, readers should understand and become familiar with the growing amount of literature found internationally. Approaches to counseling topics, emphasis areas, and other areas may or may not be consistent across countries and cultures. Thus, rather than focus exclusively on U.S.-based counseling psychology journals we have perused the literature over the past five years from seven journals that publish counseling and counseling psychology research, the *Asian Journal of Counselling (AJC)*, the *Australian Journal of Guidance and Counselling (AJGC)*, the *British Journal of Guidance and Counselling (BJGC)*, the *Canadian Journal of Counselling (CJC)*, *The Counseling Psychologist (CP)*, *Counseling Psychology Quarterly (CPQ)*, and the *Journal of Counseling Psychology (JCP)*. From these journals, four geographic regions are included (Asia, *AJC*; Australia, *AJGC*; North America, *CJC, JCP, TCP*; United Kingdom, *BJGC, CPQ*) though there can be much diversity even within regions. The structure of the journals should be briefly noted. All of the journals can include special issues or special sections specific to a particular topic, accounting for multiple articles on a particular topic. The APA Society of Counseling Psychology's *The Counseling Psychologist* is structured such that each issue is composed of a major contribution on a specific topic (e.g., heterosexism, vocational theories, methodological approaches to counseling psychology), which may have either one or a few closely related articles, followed by comment articles by experts in the field.

The purpose of this section is to determine common and uncommon topics of study across journals as they relate to traditional counseling psychology values and themes (e.g., the theme that counseling psychology has historically contributed to supervision research and development). Unfortunately, no evaluation has been conducted specifically examining counseling psychology values across countries, so we are initially limited by the values inherent in the country that formalized counseling psychology. It would be expected that counseling and counseling psychology would hold several consistent values regardless of country, though we also recognize cultural features and professional values unique to a particular country. It would also be expected that values and emphasis areas from other regions will emerge from the results.

For the past five years each journal article was evaluated for content areas. Of course, some articles covered multiple areas and could be included in multiple sections. For example, "the relationship between problem-solving efficacy and coping amongst Australian adolescents" (Frydenburg & Lewis, 2009) could fall under topics of coping, culture, and adolescents. The purpose of the evaluation was not to rank-order the most frequently studied topics (in part, due to one article covering multiple areas or a special issues on a topic that would artificially increase its numbers), but to determine general areas of study. Therefore, no cutoff score was used to determine a rank order. However, trends and important content areas can be determined. It should also be noted that because of the diversity of topics examined in psychology, there is greater within-group variation than between-group variation.

Common topics consistent with traditional counseling psychology values and themes

A review of the literature indicated similarities across the majority of journals that are consistent with the traditional values and themes inherent in U.S. counseling psychology (see Gelso & Fretz, 2001). The primary values and themes include multiculturalism, vocational issues, supervision, and prevention.

Multicultural issues. A topic with significant consistency across journals involved multiculturalism. All journals published a significant number of articles that included diversity themes, with the U.S. journals highlighting this area. The *Australian Journal of Guidance and Counselling* included articles on indigenous mental health, an issue of significant importance given the increased recognition and inclusion of aboriginal populations, mental health benefits, and indigenous practices. The *Canadian Journal of Counselling*, U.S. journals, and *Counselling Psychology Quarterly* published numerous articles on cultural competence. For example, *The Counseling Psychologist* recently published articles on "Multicultural competence and social justice training in Counseling Psychology and counselor education: A review and analysis of a sample of multicultural course syllabi" (Pieterse, Evans, Risner-Butner, Collins, & Mason, 2009) and "Development and psychometric evaluation of the Counseling Women Competencies Scale" (Ancis, Szymanski, & Ladany, 2008). Both capture very different components of cultural competence yet also attest to the continued exploding interest in this area. Other coverage of cultural areas includes *Counselling Psychology Quarterly* publishing a special issue on counseling psychology around the world, and internationalizing the curriculum. The *British Journal of Guidance and Counselling* included studies conducted in many different countries and cultures, including China, Israel, New Zealand, and South Africa, to name but a few.

As expected, the U.S. journals focused on a higher proportion of cultural groups within the US, and included few samples from outside the US, which was limiting. They also included more work utilizing within-group theoretical and practical multicultural approaches than found in other journals. Topics included sexual orientation, gender role strain, racism and discrimination, multicultural competence, acculturation, sexism, multiracial issues, internalized heterosexism, xenophobia, diversity and health, religious orientation, social justice training, and racial and ethnic identity with various U.S. cultural groups. Some of these topics can be found in other journals but not to the same extent. These topics were included significantly in *The Counseling Psychologist* and the *Journal of Counseling Psychology*, the latter of which included diverse participant samples appropriate for the topics listed above. For example, studies were included examining African Americans and counseling, intergenerational conflict among the Hmong, and acculturation issues among Asian Americans. A special section on the etiology of mental illness across cultures was also included. It was evident by examining the journals that U.S. counseling psychologists have developed and used more instruments designed to assess within-group variations of diverse groups, leading to more published articles in these areas.

Indirectly, practically all journals published articles on cultural issues such as international students, immigration, and acculturation. Given increases in international students and the emergence of increased immigration issues in North America, Europe, Asia, and Australia it is not difficult to see why counseling psychologists would be interested in studying these groups. Related to these issues is the recent emphasis in the US on social justice. Only the U.S. journals offered articles specifically on social justice. This would be expected given the relative youth and origins of the area. It is expected that counseling psychology journals in both the US and abroad will increase their inclusion of social justice issues as the field develops, just as they are focusing on other areas of multiculturalism.

In sum, while all journals published articles in multiculturalism, the U.S. journals appeared to include a greater proportion of them, and focused more exclusively on U.S. samples and within-group variables. Other journals tended to include more samples from a variety of countries, and focused less on within-group variations. Counseling psychology in the US has been historically ethnocentric on a global stage (e.g., Leong & Leach, 2007), and it would be beneficial to include more international studies in U.S. journals. Momentum in that area is underway. Three recent presidents of the Society of Counseling Psychology of the APA have included internationalization as their theme, and the 2008 counseling psychology conference in Chicago emphasized internationalism. Additionally, a special issue on counseling psychology internationally was published recently (see the 2007 issue of *Applied Psychology: An International Quarterly*). To be truly multicultural is to expand beyond borders. The same could be said of many other journals assessed for this chapter. The Asian journal included more countries proportionally than any other journal, though, of course, it was limited to the Asian region. The inclusion of multiple countries may not be the best indicator of multiculturalism, but it does offer some indication of the breadth of diversity.

Vocational research. Both U.S. journals, along with the *British Journal of Guidance and Counselling* and the *Canadian Journal of Counselling*, have emphasized vocational issues, including applications of vocational models with various samples, evidence-based practices in career development, and career selection among university students. For example, Dewe and Trenberth (2004) argued that the gap between coping research and practice has not diminished over the years given the vast amounts of work-stress research conducted. They discussed the disconnections between the measurements and strategies that coping researchers present, and their limitations in applied settings and multifaceted clinical issues. The authors presented their ideas to increase thinking in transactional-process approaches when considering stress and coping. As another example, Baudouin, and Hiebert (2007) published a special issue on evidence-based practice in career development in the *Canadian Journal of Counselling*. Special issues devoted to vocational counseling issues were found in the *British Journal of Guidance and Counselling* and the *Canadian Journal of Counselling*, and both the U.S. *Journal of Counseling Psychology* and *The Counseling Psychologist* frequently published articles on vocational psychology.

Supervision research. The *British Journal of Guidance and Counselling* and the *Canadian Journal of Counselling* published a noteworthy number of articles on counselor development and supervision, including a special issue by the *Canadian Journal of Counselling*. Supervision research in the US attained its zenith during the period from the mid-1980s to the turn of the century. Researchers are still actively engaged in this topic, though it appears that counseling journals representing other countries and organizations are publishing more articles and extending the supervision literature wider than those currently being published in the US.

Prevention research. Prevention, another historical value of counseling psychology, was the topic of multiple articles in the *Australian Journal of Guidance and Counselling*, especially with regard to children and adolescents, though other journals included articles in this area such as *The Counseling Psychologist* and the *Journal of Counseling Psychology*. For example, Runions (2008) provided a brief review of aggression literature among young children and presented a multisystemic approach to attending to aggression in earlier grade levels. In the same issue, Larmar (2008) highlighted a strength-based prevention and early intervention program that can be implemented in both home and school environments. The U.S. journals continue to include articles on prevention (e.g., Adams, 2007; Griffin & Miller, 2007; Pössel, Seemann, & Hautzinger, 2008), and the subject area is considered a foundation of counseling psychology research in the US.

Additional areas. As expected, the U.S. journals included a higher proportion of articles covering what are often viewed as traditional counseling psychology topics that have received significant attention over the past 20 years. For example, topics such as expectations about counseling, attachment theory, psychological distress, self-stigma, and identity issues can be found frequently in these journals. In sum, it appears that there is a moderate amount of overlap among countries and journals regarding research on values and themes consistent with counseling psychology. Now we turn to values and themes not specific to counseling psychology.

Common themes not specific to counseling psychology

Trauma. A few common themes were found in the journals that are not necessarily emphasized in the U.S. journals. Practically all of the journals, with the exception of the U.S. journals, published a large number of articles surrounding trauma-related issues, including vicarious trauma and posttraumatic growth. For example, in *Counseling Psychology Quarterly*, Sheikh (2008), a UK psychologist, highlighted the positive variables that contributed to posttraumatic growth based on Tedeschi and Calhoun's (1996) work, such as close relationships, greater appreciation of life, personal strength, hope, and spiritual changes. Sheikh extended the work to counseling psychology practice, addressing both the research involved in practice as well as therapeutic strategies and issues to consider. Recommendations were made based on counselor values and behaviors, and applied to individuals, groups, and families, including cross-cultural considerations. As another example, Kadambi and Truscott (2008), in the *Canadian Journal of Counselling* used a mixed-methods design to create a concept map of traumatizing events that counselors experience when working with survivors of sexual violence.

In a post-traumatic stress disorder (PTSD) and suicide study, Wright, Borrill, Teers, and Cassidy (2006) published an article in *Counselling Psychology Quarterly* about prison officers that examined the mental health consequences after an individual committed suicide while in custody. The study utilized hierarchical multiple regressions to create path models that offered predictions of the variables associated with the post-suicide PTSD. Over 63% of participants did not exhibit clinical levels of PTSD symptoms, largely due to mediators such as optimism, problem-solving style, locus of control, and social support. Optimism and certain problem solving types accounted for the greatest amount of variance with the non-PTSD group, while the PTSD group showed virtually no predictive relationships other than prior experience of dealing with a suicidal death.

Given global events like disasters, wars, and general social upheaval, along with personal traumatic events such as sexual and physical assaults, it is easy to understand the interest in the number of studies related to trauma. Interestingly, U.S. journals focused less on trauma even though recent events such as the World Trade Center attacks, Iraq and Afghanistan wars, hurricanes and other natural disasters, and school shootings, offer opportunities for such research. There have been many trauma-related studies in other journals by counseling psychologists, but trauma content in the two U.S. Counseling Psychology journals is noticeably less frequent than in the other journals examined.

Suicide. Both the UK journals and the *Canadian Journal of Counselling* included a higher proportion of articles on suicide than the other journals. For example, in the *British Journal of Guidance and Counselling*, Bostik and Everall (2007) conducted a qualitative study with 50 adolescents to assess the influence of relationship attachment in overcoming suicidal thoughts and feelings given no professional intervention. All respondents reported the existence of a secure attachment with at least one individual. These relationships offered four qualities that distinguished them from other relationships, and helped alter respondents' negative self-perceptions and provided hope. These relationship qualities included being (a) accepting, (b) permanent, (c) encouraging and supportive, and (d) close and intimate. These relationships allowed respondents to feel comfortable and express themselves more fully to the other individual, made them feel less isolated, and helped them to create new life meanings.

At-risk youth. The *Australian Journal of Guidance and Counselling* included more articles about at-risk youth, the need for increased mental health services, and bullying behaviors. In the *Australian Journal of Guidance and Counselling*, Eacott and Frydenberg (2008) used a mixed-methods design to implement a universal coping skills program for youth at risk of depression. Their results indicated that the program helped reduce the youths' reliance on non-productive coping strategies. This type of study has implications well beyond Australia's borders. Both the *Asian Journal of Counselling* and the *British Journal of Guidance and Counselling* included at-risk youth and/or bullying articles.

Also related to youth, the *Asian Journal of Counselling* published a special issue on school counseling in multiple countries, including Japan, South Korea, and Hong Kong. For example, Yagi (2008) discussed the influence of government agency policies on school counseling in Japan, the diverse needs found in and among schools, and the role of counseling within the schools. Overall, journals outside the US were more likely to publish articles on youth, youth services, interventions, and resources. For readers interested in the incorporation of youth issues in counseling psychology it would be beneficial to review the literature from a broad, international perspective.

Additional areas. Both the *Australian Journal of Guidance and Counselling* and *Counselling Psychology Quarterly* journals included greater numbers of articles related to depression, including coping with depression, than the other journals. The *Canadian Journal of Counselling* tended to include more articles on the "pathological" end of the spectrum, including body image and substance abuse, though it shared a number of articles on eating disorders with the *Journal of Counseling Psychology*. The *British Journal of Guidance and Counselling* also emphasized other areas such as grief and loss, counselor development, help-seeking behaviors, immigrants, refugees, and international students, and online services. Both the *Canadian Journal of Counselling* and the *British Journal of Guidance and Counselling* also included more articles utilizing qualitative designs than the other journals. Though qualitative designs have found favor among many counseling psychologists in the US (see Yeh & Inman, 2007), they are published less frequently in the U.S. journals examined than found in the other journals.

In sum, there are themes such as trauma, suicide, depression, childhood and adolescent risk issues that were not consistent with traditional counseling psychology, at least as it was originally conceived in the US. Most of the non-U.S. journals, especially the *British Journal of Guidance and Counselling* and the *Canadian Journal of Counselling*, included higher proportions of qualitatively-designed studies than the U.S. journals.

All journals included a wide array of research areas. For example, *Counselling Psychology Quarterly* emphasized a variety of areas including counseling psychology identity issues, cognitive behavior therapy, training and education, and coping. The *Asian Journal of Counselling* displayed the greatest proportional sample variability (smaller number of published articles per issue but greater national variability) in terms of content and research project country of origin. Though not all articles explicitly addressed culture-specific psychological constructs, the samples covered many Asian countries including China, Japan, Korea, and the Philippines. While the other journals included samples from a variety of countries, they were the exception rather than the rule.

Trends over time in the US

Since the early days of counseling psychology in the US, the field has emphasized research and intervention areas such as vocational development and prevention efforts. While these and other areas still remain the cornerstone of counseling psychology, a number of trends and areas have occurred that contrast with its history. Given the results of the analysis reported above, this section will address both continuations and contrasts of emphasis areas with the history of counseling psychology.

Vocational research. An origin of counseling psychology stemmed from vocational development, and the trend continues today, though it is manifested much differently than its beginnings. The inclusion of vocational work resulted from service men and women needing career directions and jobs after World War II. Counseling psychology helped fill the need by developing new instruments that assessed career interests and values, and by providing services to assist the returning soldiers. Over the next three decades the vocational psychology subfield flourished through the continued development of new theories, instruments, and interventions. Its popularity resulted in the development of new journals (*Career Development Quarterly, Journal of Vocational Behavior*) which allowed for even further theoretical and intervention development.

Since the 1980s there has been a gradual decrease in the importance placed on vocational development in many training programs, for at least two reasons. First, there has always been a gap between "regular" and "career" counseling, rather than a view of them as intertwined. Unfortunately, career counseling is often considered a stepchild of personal counseling, deemed less important because of the perceived increased complexity of personal counseling. Of course, a vocation is an important component of most people's lives, and is considered an important component of counseling. However, it often becomes a clinical issue only if client concerns are directly related to work. Additionally, many students and faculty have also often viewed them as separate issues. Individual courses in vocational psychology can indirectly lead to perceptions that they are separate from other counseling courses. Overall, there has never been the melding, wished for by vocational psychologists, that integrates vocational issues into the counseling session, regardless of the presenting concern, and career counseling has never attained the status to which it strives.

Second, there are a variety of subdisciplines and fields, and businesses outside psychology, that have increased their own focus on vocational issues and diminished the emphasis within counseling psychology's domain. For example, both clinical psychology and social work have begun to develop career interests and emphases. Additionally, companies have now specialized in vocational development, decreasing interventions once reserved for counseling psychologists. There has been significant vocational theory and instrument development over the years by counseling psychologists, but others such as industrial/organizational psychologists have utilized these theories and instruments in practice and business settings. Companies that utilize career-related services are often more likely to contact an I/O than a counseling psychologist. Though the majority of vocational research is still conducted by counseling psychologists, they are less likely than I/O psychologists to implement their knowledge in educational, business, and organizational settings.

Positive psychology. Though the field of "positive psychology" has fairly recently developed, counseling psychology can claim its roots in its philosophical foundations. Counseling psychology has traditionally emphasized strength-based approaches, viewing the client from empowered and positive frameworks. Individual components previously embedded in counseling psychology approaches are now also areas of study within the positive psychology domain such as hope, coping skills, authenticity, relationships, positive emotions, and well-being. Recently, the emerging area of positive psychology has advanced these underlying counseling psychology values with new research, associations, conferences, and professional journals and textbooks. There are counseling psychologists who conduct research and engage in positive psychology practices, and it is expected that strengths will continue to be a mainstay of counseling psychology. Though counseling psychology has maintained its strength-based focus it is clear that this area is more permeable than previously considered.

Multiculturalism. As mentioned previously, counseling psychology was instrumental in advancing multiculturalism in psychology, and other fields. It was positioned well to include cultural issues and respond to social movements based on its values of inclusion, social justice, and equality. The majority of the work in this area began in the mid-1980s, and its growth is clearly evident. The strength of, and emphases placed on, multiculturalism can easily be found today in counseling psychology journal articles and textbooks, training programs, and conferences. Through collaborations with other APA divisions (e.g., Division 35, Society for the Psychology of Women; Division 45, Society for the Psychological Study of Ethnic Minority Issues), many areas of psychology, not just counseling psychology, now include multiculturalism, and it appears that the work being conducted on culture will only increase over the next decade. The recent social justice movement grew from earlier works in multiculturalism and includes advocacy and social action.

Prevention. It is evident from the journal analysis that prevention continues to have a significant influence within the counseling psychology literature in the US. Many articles continue to be published in this area. Additionally, the social justice movement incorporates prevention, as social justice models often include efforts to prevent negative influences and emphasize empowerment within communities. An historical issue in the US is that it is often difficult to obtain funding for prevention efforts in psychology, as the outcomes can be defined differently and may be longer-term than intervention efforts. However, work in prevention continues to be an important component of counseling psychology.

Challenges

The first challenge facing counseling psychology in the international arena is the question of identity. Psychologists in different countries who identify themselves with counseling invest the specialty of counseling psychology with a wide variety of conceptual and operational definitions. The challenge for the future of counseling psychology and its internationalization is to elaborate some common understanding, a shared vision and mission, that promotes a unified association of counseling psychologists who share a coherent practice and research agenda. This mission must build on past accomplishments yet propel the group into the future. The establishment of Division 16 in the International Association of Applied Psychology (IAAP) certainly was a first step in this identity work in an international forum. The members of Division 16 are working as a multinational group to formulate a superordinate definition of the specialty and to articulate an identity broad enough to include counseling psychologists around the globe while at the same time distinct enough to keep clinical psychology from subsuming counseling psychology in major areas of the world.

Before establishing a home in IAAP, counseling psychologists around the globe seemed to be importing the North American view of the specialty and then adapting it to meet their local needs. This practice has resulted in the current situation in which counseling psychology, from an international perspective, is loosely defined and implicitly understood (Leong & Leach, 2007). We are reminded of the tautological definition of intelligence that defined intelligence as what intelligence tests measure. To some degree, around the globe, counseling psychology is implicitly understood to be whatever counseling psychologists do in that country. The loose definition includes a focus on fostering normal development and facilitating adjustment to life transitions and personal stress. It makes the specialty developmental rather than remedial as it concentrates on helping clients resolve problems in daily living rather than treating serious mental illness. In short, counseling psychologists seek to enhance functioning and improve well-being by helping people solve problems, make decisions, and pursue goals. Its practitioners often work in schools and universities rather than in clinics and hospitals. Its origins in most countries are rooted in providing educational and vocational guidance. The major theorist for counseling practice seems to be Carl Rogers, with some psychologists in various countries viewing counseling psychology as essentially a form of Rogerian psychotherapy. Because of their interest in providing vocational guidance to working-class youth and adults, many practitioners of counseling psychology have become deeply involved in feminist, multicultural, and social justice issues, particularly as these apply to the provision of counseling interventions.

The overarching vision of counseling psychology may be stated as providing interventions that concentrate on the daily life adjustment issues faced by reasonably well-adjusted people, particularly as they cope with career transitions and personal development. Young and Nicol (2007), in a succinct and elegant statement, generalized this overarching conception of counseling psychology as a specialty by emphasizing that counselors help individuals link their lives to the social context in which they live. This distinguishes counseling as a psychosocial intervention as opposed to clinical psychology and psychotherapy which concentrate on psychological issues, often devoid of true attention to context.

The definition formulated by Young and Nicol raises awareness that the complexity of postmodern life has increased the salience of culture issues for counseling psychology. Making and implementing choices is difficult enough for individuals who live in stable cultures and communities. They are required to fit themselves to predictable circumstances and travel well-worn paths. The adaptive difficulties increase for individuals who in live in less stable cultures and changing communities. They must construct and manage a self in a medium of transforming life trajectories and emerging career pathways. The Young and Nicol formulation provides a conceptual umbrella for counseling in both types of society and comprehensively includes its breadth of applications.

While breadth of application is an important asset to counseling psychology, it may also be its greatest weakness. In a sense, counseling psychologists are the generalists of applied psychology, much as family physicians are the generalists in medicine. This can make it difficult to draw strong boundaries and state what counseling psychology is not. Counseling psychologists present a diffuse identity because they engage in a wide range of activities with varied client groups across diverse life situations in different kinds of setting using a range of theories and techniques. Just a quick scan of the tables of contents in counseling psychology journals shows the diversity of research and practice. This ability to wear many hats may enhance the vitality and attractiveness of the discipline for its practitioners. Nevertheless, it also causes vagueness about what counseling psychologists share in common. Within counseling psychology, it is considered a strength to be a generalist, yet applied and professional psychologists in other subdisciplines strive to be specialists. Counseling psychologists need to balance the roles of generalist and specialist in promulgating a clear professional identity that makes its work distinctly recognizable to clients and colleagues yet does not constrain the innovation and creativity for which it is known.

Part of the breadth, as well as the definitional issues and identity diffusion, arises from the very designation "counseling" psychology. Many mental health specialists view counseling as a process used by clinical psychologists, organizational consultants, school psychologists, and social workers. Other professionals see counseling as synonymous with Rogerian psychotherapy. Claiming what other professionals consider a generic technique as an independent discipline has caused, and will continue to cause, confusion and difficulty. Actually, some counseling psychologists have thought the name a mistake starting with the President of the Counseling Psychology Division (17) in the American Psychological Association when the Division first took that name (Scott, 1980, p. 35).

Another reason that counseling psychology has definitional problems and identity issues is because it lacks a reasonably distinct evidence base. Counseling psychologists typically apply the empirical research and theoretical conceptualizations from other disciplines. It has incorporated as central to its work the psychology of individual differences and vocational psychology, then added developmental and preventative psychology, followed by social psychology and learning theory, and finally multicultural psychology. The core paradigm is not clear. If anything the core would be counseling process research and supervision of the process. With the expansion of applications, the core content domain in North America has moved away from its origins in vocational guidance and career development.

A consistent definition and a coherent professional identity for counseling psychology must pertain to the social realities and specific needs in diverse countries. To date, counseling psychology has been dominated by the West, especially North America, and particularly the United States. It is unlikely that empirical methods from North America can be easily adopted in cultures that prefer more intuitive and experiential practices. To flourish internationally, counseling psychology cannot be viewed primarily as a Western specialty rooted in logical positivism.

Future Developments

So where do the opportunities lie to meet these challenges and provide a service to communities? While not attempting to predict the future, we do clearly see several possibilities. The first concerns a return to the roots of counseling psychology, believing that as it begins so it will go on. People engage their culture through working. Counseling psychology began as vocational guidance to help newcomers to industrial cities match their abilities to factory jobs. After World War II, with the rise of corporate bureaucracies and a suburban middle class, vocational guidance developed into career counseling. In the American Psychological Association, the Division of Guidance and Counseling became the Division of Counseling Psychology. The early 1950s saw counseling psychologists formulate numerous theories of career development to link personal goals to economic activities in corporate cultures. Eventually, counseling psychology in North America reduced its commitment to career development activities and shifted its focus to the counseling process and supervision concerns and then feminist, multicultural, and social justice issues. With less concentration on career issues, counseling psychologists seemed to develop stronger overlap with psychologists who identify with the Society of Clinical Psychology, Society for the Psychology of Women, and Society for the Psychological Study of Ethnic Minority Issues.

Today, as we support the internationalization of counseling psychology, we find that in developing countries and industrial states, counseling psychologists concentrate on vocational guidance and career development concerns. This concentration provides them with a unique identity with which to make important and needed social contributions. While in North America counseling psychologists face many identity issues because of their diffuse interests and activities, the clear focus in European and Asian countries supports strong identity. So, one significant future development is formulation of indigenous vocational counseling models, methods, and materials. We see this already occurring, for example, in Australia (Pryor & Bright, 2009; Patton & McMahon, 2008) and South America (Stead & Watson, 2006). While the models are unique to each country, they share a vision of counseling psychology's mission as helping individuals prepare for and engage in productive work lives. Along with encouraging the construction of indigenous models, methods, and materials, counseling psychologists should support the expansion outside the West of training opportunities for new professionals. Many of the leaders of counseling psychology have been trained in the Euro-American tradition. If they were not actually trained in the West, their research and practice have been strongly influenced by colleagues from those regions. The production of indigenous theories and techniques must be accompanied by arranging opportunities for professionals to be trained in their use by the local experts who constructed them.

In information economies and knowledge societies there is also a need for new models, methods, and materials for career management. As the machine age and corporate culture of the 20th century recedes, these countries face a new social arrangement of work. Stable jobs with health benefits and pensions are fast disappearing. They are being replaced with temporary work positions called contingent, contract, and consulting. In the first decade of the 21st century, Western societies experienced a break with previous forms of the social organization of occupations and work. Rapid advances in information technology and the opening of world markets produced a globalization of economies. Globalization is the process by which cultures influence each other to become more alike through trade, immigration, and exchange of information and ideas. Globalization of the economy is changing jobs, healthcare, pensions, and home ownership. Once taken for granted, these things are no longer guaranteed. Old success formulas no longer work. The knowledge societies of the 21st century require new thinking about work life because things once taken for granted are at issue. The global economy poses new questions about work lives, especially the question of how individuals can negotiate a lifetime of job changes without losing their sense of self and social identity.

In response to this fundamental question of the second modernity, career theories and techniques must change to assist world workers adapt to their vocational situations. Career theories based on a social constructionist epistemology, for example, respond to the needs of today's mobile workers who may feel fragmented and confused as they encounter a restructuring of occupations, transformation of the labor force, world work, and multicultural imperatives. In an uncertain world, developing skills and talents remain important, yet there is no substitute for a grounded sense of self. Thus, these constructionist career theories concentrate on self-constructing through work and relationships. The work ethic of the romantic era of the 19th century agricultural economy involved a calling. The work ethic of the scientific era of the 20th-century industrial economy involved what you were called in that your job title established your social position. The work ethic for the postmodern era of the 21st-century information economy involves the individual calling out for what they seek. In short, the ethic has moved from being called (agricultural economy) to what you are called (industrial economy) to what you call for (global economy). Well-being in knowledge societies requires that individuals take possession of their lives by connecting who they are to what they do. To provide assistance to individuals that moves them from finding their life work to constructing how to make their lives work requires a science of intervention that deals with designing a life and planning how to use work in that life. To this end, career construction theories and life-design counseling concentrate on life-framing decisions.

The counseling practices of the second modernity rest on social constructionist epistemologies, narrative psychology, and qualitative research. New constructs such as biographicity replace the matching procedures of test and tell. In the information age, individuals must rely on autobiographical reasoning to provide a sense of agency and guidelines for decision making as they navigate the multiple transitions they will continue to face. No longer is there a standard life course as described by Super's (1957) meta-narrative of life stages with developmental tasks. Instead, postmodern life is fragmented and episodic. The modern narrative was linear. Super told a story of coherence and continuity—you graduate from school, leave home, stabilize in a job for life, form an intimate relationship, raise children, and retire. The postmodern narrative may be in any order and cyclical. You may leave home, get married, get a job, lose a job, move your family in with your parents, and return to school. This calls for individualization of the life course with concomitant counseling for life design, rather than translating a crystallized self-concept into a life-time occupation. These new methods acknowledge a period of life or life stage called "emerging adulthood" composed of non-standardized life trajectories. Fundamentally, the new counseling methods view work as a context for human development. Rather than focusing on decision making, they concentrate on the articulation of intentions and the narration of guidelines for living. Work is not assumed to be the core role. In information societies, many people are turning to family and friends as their most salient life roles, with work being what they do, not who they are.

In the first decade of the 21st century, counseling psychologists can lead the way in helping world workers and the global community adapt to the postmodern information era. In this regard, it may be possible to organize international networks of practitioners and researchers to collaborate in addressing issues raised by the global economy and the restructuring of the world's workforce along with the migration and change it continues to occasion. Counseling psychologists are using new information technologies to build practice research networks and international research collaboratories. For example, counseling psychologists from around the globe are networking to build a collaboratory to conduct research on career adaptability and a second collaboratory to craft methods and materials with which to implement the model of life-design interventions. Of course, there are other topics around which counseling psychologists could build virtual communities. This could include interest groups that concentrate on a particular topic of wide concern to the continued internationalization of counseling psychology. These virtual communities could concentrate on issues of social justice, multicultural counseling, migration, and careers in different contexts.

The information era propelled by technology also offers new opportunities to use technology in counseling. While computer-assisted vocational guidance is well established, there are new visions and possibilities for counseling over the internet. The model of life design counseling has opened the possibility of life coaching in which counseling psychologists contract with clients to provide consultation for specified periods. Occupational information has become available as never before. Hopefully, second life technology will soon provide realistic job previews.

So, many future developments in counseling psychology may lie in unification around the definition that counselors help individuals link their lives to the social context in which they live. This provides a coherent and unified identity as specialist in brief psychosocial interventions that foster life satisfaction and well-being. It also enables a conception of counseling psychology that moves beyond the current fragmentation of subspecialties focused on either career or relationships and quantitative methods or qualitative techniques. The new definition leads to a concentration on life-design that foster both/and thinking while concentrating on personal development through work and relationships. Life-design intervention models may provide the conceptual home for methods and materials that previously contested each other.

Rather than focusing on meaning modification and adjustment, life-design counseling may focus on meaning management and adaptability. Whether or not this is the direction counseling psychology takes as it internationalizes its practices, we know that there must be some new direction if the specialty is to remain relevant in the second modernity as it was during the first modernity.

References

Adams, E. (2007). Moving from contemplation to preparation: Is counseling psychology ready to embrace culturally responsive prevention? *The Counseling Psychologist, 35*, 840–849.

Ancis, J. R., Szymaski, D. M., & Ladany, N. (2008). Development and psychometric evaluation of the Counseling Women Competencies Scale. *The Counseling Psychologist, 36*, 719–744.

Arredondo, P., & Perez, P. (2006). Historical perspectives on the multicultural guidelines and contemporary applications. *Professional Psychology: Research and Practice, 37*, 1–5.

Barak, A., & Golan, G. (2000). Counseling psychology in Israel: Successful accomplishments of a nonexistent specialty. *The Counseling Psychologist, 28*, 100–116.

Baudouin, R., & Hiebert, B. (2007). Introduction to special issue on evidence-based practice in career development. *Canadian Journal of Counselling, 41*, 127–129.

Bostik, K. E., & Everall, R. D. (2007). Healing from suicide: Adolescent perceptions of attachment relationships. *British Journal of Guidance & Counselling, 35*, 79–96.

Dewe, P., & Trenberth, L. (2004). Work stress and coping: Drawing together research and practice. *British Journal of Guidance & Counselling, 32*, 143–156.

Eacott, C., & Frydenberg, E. (2008). At-risk students in a rural context: Benefits and gains from a coping skills program. *Australian Journal of Guidance and Counselling, 18*, 160–181.

Frydenberg, E., & Lewis, R. (2009). The relationship between problem-solving efficacy and coping amongst Australian adolescents. *British Journal of Guidance* & *Counselling, 37*, 51–64.

Garfield, S. L. (1985). Clinical psychology. In E. M. Altmaier and M. E. Meyer (Eds.), *Applied specialties in psychology* (pp. 19–44). New York: Crown Publishing Group/Random House.

Gelso, C. J., & Fretz, B. R. (2001). *Counseling psychology* (2nd ed.). Ft Worth, TX: Harcourt Brace Jovanovich, Inc.

Griffin, J.P., Jr., & Miller, E. (2007). A research practitioner's perspective on culturally relevant prevention: Scientific and practical considerations for community-based programs. *The Counseling Psychologist, 35*, 850–859.

Kadambi, M.A., & Truscott, D. (2008). Traumatizing aspects of providing counseling in community agencies to survivors of sexual violence: A concept map. *Canadian Journal of Counselling, 42*, 192–208.

Larmar, S. (2008). The Early Impact Program: Strengthening child competencies. *Australian Journal of Guidance and Counselling, 18*, 128–140.

Leong, F. T. L., & Blustein, D. L. (2000). Toward a global vision of counseling psychology. *The Counseling Psychologist, 28*, 5–9.

Leong, F. T. L., & Leach, M. M. (2007). SWOT analysis and global counseling psychology. *Applied Psychology: An International Review, 56*, 165–181.

Leong, F.T.L. & Leach, M. M. (2008). Introduction: Counseling Psychology. In F. T. L. Leong and M. M. Leach (Eds.), *Counseling psychology* (pp. xv–xxvi). Aldershot: Ashgate Publishing Limited.

Leung, S. A., Guo, L., & Lam, M. P. (2000). The development of counseling psychology in higher educational institutions in China: Present conditions and needs, future challenges, *The Counseling Psychologist, 28*, 81–99.

Poasa, K. H., Mallinckrodt, B., & Suzuki, L. A. (2000). Causal attributions for problematic family interactions: A qualitative, cultural comparison of Western Samoa, American Samoa, and the United States. *The Counseling Psychologist 28*, 32–60.

Parsons, F. (1909). *Choosing a vocation*. Boston: Houghton Mifflin.

Patton, W., & McMahon, M. (2008). *Career development and systems theory*. Rotterdam, The Netherlands: Sense Publishing.

Pelling, N. (2004). Counselling psychology: Diversity and commonalities across the Western world. *Counselling Psychology Quarterly, 17*, 239–245.

Pieterse, A. L., Evans, S. A., Risner-Butner, A., Collins, N. M., & Mason, L. B. (2009). Multicultural competence and social justice training in counseling psychology and counselor education: A review and analysis of a sample of multicultural course syllabi. *The Counseling Psychologist, 37*, 93–115.

Pope-Davis, D. B., Coleman, H. K., Liu, W. M., & Toporek, R. L. (2003). *Handbook of multicultural competencies in counseling and psychology*. Thousand Oaks, CA: Sage Publications.

Pössel, P., Seemann, S., & Hautzinger, M. (2008). Impact of comorbidity in prevention of adolescent depressive symptoms. *Journal of Counseling Psychology, 55*, 106–117.

Pryor, R. G. L., & Bright, J. E. H. (2009). Archetypal narratives in career counselling: A chaos theory application. *International Journal for Educational and Vocational Guidance, 8*, 71–82.

Runions, K. (2008). A multi-systemic school-based approach for addressing childhood aggression. *Australian Journal of Guidance and Counselling, 18*, 106–127.

Scott, C. W. (1980). History of the Division of Counseling Psychology. In J. M. Whitely (Ed.), *The history of counseling psychology* (pp. 25–40). Monterey, CA: Brooks/Cole.

Sheikh, A. I. (2008). Posttraumatic growth in trauma survivors: Implications for practice. *Counselling Psychology Quarterly, 21*, 85–97.

Slaney, R. B., Chadha, N., Mobley, M., & Kennedy, S., (2000). Perfectionsim in Asian Indians: Exploring the meaning of the construct in India. *The Counseling Psychologist, 28*, 10–31.

Stead, G. B., & Watson, M. B. (Eds.). (2006). *Career psychology in the South African context* (2nd ed.). Pretoria, South Africa: J. L. Van Schaik.

Strong, E. K., Jr. (1927). *Vocational Interest Blank*. Stanford, CA: Stanford University Press.

Sue, D. W., Bernier, J. E., Durran, A., Feinberg, L., Pedersen, P., Smith, E. J., & Vasquez-Nuttall, E. (1982). Position paper: Cross-cultural counseling competencies. *The Counseling Psychologist, 10*, 45–52.

Super, D. E. (1957). *The psychology of careers*. New York: Harper & Row.

Tedeschi, R., & Calhoun, L. G. (1996). The posttraumatic growth inventory: Measuring the positive legacy of trauma. *Journal of Traumatic Stress, 9*, 455–472.

Tien, H-L. S. (2007). Practice and research in career counseling and development—2006. *Career Development Quarterly, 56*, 98–140.

Toporek, R. L., Gerstein, L. H., Fouad, N. A., Roysircar, G., & Israel, T. (2006). *Handbook for social justice in counseling psychology*. Thousand, Oaks, CA: Sage Publications.

Wright, L., Borrill, J., Teers, R., & Cassidy, T. (2006). The mental health consequences of dealing with self-inflicted death in custody. *Counselling Psychology Quarterly*, *19*, 165–180.

Yagi, D. T. (2008). Current developments in school counseling in Japan. *Asian Journal of Counselling*, *15*, 141–155.

Yeh, C. J., & Inman, A. G. (2007). Qualitative data analysis and interpretation in counseling psychology: Strategies for best practices. *The Counseling Psychologist*, *35*, 369–403.

Young, R. A. & Nicol, J. J. (2007). Counselling psychology in Canada: Advancing psychology for all. *Applied Psychology: An International Review*, *56*, 20–32.

7

Autonomy in Learning and Instruction

Roots, Frames, and Concepts of a Basic Issue

Peter Nenniger

Discussions about the value, place, conditions, and effects of autonomous learning are part of a centennial tradition in educational, instructional, and psychological contexts. In recent decades, a widespread and heterogeneous corpus of theoretical concepts, as well as a large field of application areas, has been developed. Various fields of the educational sciences and of psychology are concerned with the respective phenomena in a wide variety of modes and perspectives. However, the majority of the more recent key concepts are included in theories about self-directed or self-regulated learning.

Even in our own day, however, there exists no simple and straightforward definition of autonomous learning (even in contrast to the heteronomous kind). It is rather an area that comprises a complex, superordinate set of functions located at the crossroads of several subdomains of psychology (e.g., cognition, problem solving, decision making, metacognition, conceptual change, motivation, volition, etc.) and education (didactics, instructional methods, learning environments, mediated instruction, explorative teaching, etc.). Equally, the actual state of research—even as regards central issues concerning self-regulation and self-direction in learning—is predominantly characterized by multiple, only partially coherent theories that mostly include selected parts of learning and emphasize different aspects of self-regulation or self-direction, accompanied by a multitude of studies about conditions and effects, by a lack of explanations of the underlying mechanisms, and finally, by a rather implicit consideration of the dynamics of learning (for overviews see Boekaerts, Pintrich, & Zeidner, 2000; Puustinen & Pulkkinen, 2001; Zimmerman & Schunk, 2001). For this reason, it is not surprising that claims for a more differentiated, but also more coherent understanding of this issue are increasingly put forward (cf. Nenniger, van den Brink, & Bissbort, 2009).

IAAP Handbook of Applied Psychology, First Edition. Edited by Paul R. Martin, Fanny M. Cheung, Michael C. Knowles, Michael Kyrios, Lyn Littlefield, J. Bruce Overmier, and José M. Prieto.

In order to respond at least partially to these claims, a systematic approach is attempted, inasmuch as an inventory of exemplar elements of self-direction and self-regulation will be arranged within the body of learning and instruction. After a sketch of the roots of autonomy in learning, frameworks of comprehensive theoretical concepts representing the basics of self-directed or self-regulated learning are shown. On this foundation a selection of representative models of self-directed and self-regulated learning are outlined in order to elaborate the state of the art in this field and to situate their position within educational and instructional contexts. Finally, an outlook will be attempted on aims and desiderata for further theoretical and related methodological developments and on areas for promising applications.

Roots of Independent or Autonomous Learning

Depending on culture and history, the idea of autonomy has been conceived in different ways and its meaning and importance have been appreciated differently.

In traditions of the eastern hemisphere aspects of autonomy are mostly rooted in Confucian attitudes to education and learning, embedded in a collectivist orientation, with strong sense of hierarchy and attribution of success as much to effort as to innate ability (cf. Wu, 1977; Ho & Crookall, 1995; Littlewood, 1999). Despite or sometimes in contrast to this cultural background and the respective experiences, Asian students develop a rich pattern of persuasive and subtle individual interpretations of their traditions (Barker, 1993) so that in the last decades autonomy in learning and studying have been positively appreciated and gave rise to changes in the respective learning styles (Kember & Gow, 1990; 1991; Biggs, 1994; 1996; Jin & Cortazzi, 1996; Marton, Dall'Alba, & Tse, 1996; Woodrow & Sham, 2001).

In the western hemisphere traditions, understanding of autonomy generally goes back to the Age of Enlightenment, in which reason was advocated as the primary source and legitimacy for authority and in which the capacity to live according to causes, motives, and aims that were considered as one's own was an attribute of reason. The Kantian tradition of moral philosophy (Kant 1785/1956) was determinant for an understanding of autonomy, referring to a person's capacity for self-determination, as the essence of human dignity and, consequently, entailing every person's obligation to demonstrate fundamental respect for others. Notwithstanding Comenius had already recognized in both his pansophia (Comenius, 1657a/1986) and in his didactics (Comenius 1657b) the individual's need for learning during his or her entire life, Kant's successor, Herbart, has to be considered as the founder of a systematic foundation for autonomous learning based on philosophy and psychology as well (cf. Anhalt, 1999). Herbart (1806, 1841) recognized in every child's individuality a unique potential ready to be fulfilled and transformed by education in a framework of moral and intellectual development (cf. Blyth, 1981). In consequence, the ultimate goal of education is the creation of character strength through educative instruction as a combination of objective knowledge and will. For this purpose, based on his psychological theory of apperception, Herbart (1824) formulated a didactic methodology of formal steps that assured that new ideas would be properly presented to the student so that he could associate them with his existing ideas and structure them as a system, the apperceptive mass. Dewey (1896, 1910), in his discussion with the Herbartians (cf. DeGarmo, 1916; Kliebard, 1981), recognized the high degree of similarity between Herbart's formal steps methodology and his thoughts on learning as problem solving by reflective thinking. However, he deemed its appropriate place to be in the planning phase of students' learning and distinguished between the logic of the formal steps and sequence in a course of learning. In consequence, the teachers' tasks do not consist in imprisoning learners in the succession of all steps but in following and assisting them flexibly in their own way. These ideas bore fruit in a large number of open didactical concepts fostering autonomous learning, such as Gaudig's (1925) approach of free brainwork at school (*freie geistige Schularbeit*) or Petersen's (1937/1971) doctrine of guidance in instruction (*Führungslehre des Unterrichts*) in Germany or different variations of the project method such as Kilpatrick's (1918, 1927) in the US or Frey's (1982) in Switzerland.

Although the more recent discussion of autonomous learning in the last decades has been dominated by theories of learning and instruction (e.g., with respect to self-esteem see Deci & Ryan, 1995), it is easier to distinguish a specific perspective rather than a clear distinction between self-directed or self-regulated learning. Most commonly, explanations in the educational domain refer to self-direction of the course of learning, while those in the psychological domain refer to self-regulation of the processes within learning. Thus, in research about self-directed learning an autonomous learner is typically described as a person who solves problems or develops new ideas with minimal external guidance in selected areas of endeavor (see Betts and Knapp, 1981), whereas descriptions of self-regulated learners mainly concentrate on how learners regulate their learning by deploying and giving emphasis to specific cognitive, emotional, motivational, volitional, and metacognitive processes (see Schiefele & Pekrun, 1996; Efklides, 2001).

Frames of Self-Directed and Self-Regulated Learning

The above sketch of the roots underlying autonomous learning leads to the assumption that both self-direction and self-regulation are situated within a number of more general conceptual frames that embody the main characteristics of the respective kind of learning. For this reason it seems advisable to specify frames that comprise a number of exemplar conceptualizations that typically substantiate self-direction and/or self-regulation in learning.

Frames of self-direction

With respect to self-direction the following conceptualizations may be considered as basic frames.

A first cognitively oriented frame for self-direction can be traced back to Herbart's (1841) view of the ideal course of learning as apperception in a process of relating new to already existing ideas and integrating them into a total, the apperceptive mass. The four steps include: (1) clearness, i.e., focusing attention on each single object of learning so that its properties become clear, (2) association, i.e., expanding thinking by reflection on how these objects might be associated with each other, (3) system, i.e., reaching more general ideas about the structure of the associated objects, and (4) method, i.e., achieving the ability to apply the structure of associated objects within new contexts and in generating new ideas. Further, to represent a learning sequence, the steps also represent a hierarchy that determines the quality of achieved learning as perception of the new ideas, as their reproduction within the existing ones, or as conceptual thinking and understanding. This psychologically founded concept anticipated conceptualizations like "cognitive structure" in Ausubel's theory of meaningful verbal learning (Ausubel, 1963; Ausubel, Novak, & Hanesian, 1978), in which conditions for a successful and lasting integration of new elements into the already existing cognitive structure were postulated as the necessary initial and basic state for any autonomy in learning and gave way to further descriptions of cognitive learning.

Taking account of Galperin's (1969) ideas, a second conceptual frame for self-direction can be attributed to Davydov's (1972) distinguishing of four stages along the course from lower to higher learning activity, characterized by an increasing importance of language and thought to the detriment of behavior: (1) Departing from an action-related ground, learning evolves via learning from (2) direct and (3) indirect perception of learning environments up to learning as (4) acquisition of symbolic knowledge. Elaborating Davydov's concept, Lompscher (1975, 1989) distinguished and specified inherent analytical and synthetic operations at each stage as operative skills (like concretizing, classifying, generalizing, differentiating, ordering, synthesizing, or analyzing) and placed them into a scheme of learning activity describing how operations specifically depend on each other. The insight into these structural properties within the scheme of operations made it possible to describe various forms of the course of learning activity (*Verlaufsformen des Lernens*) as deliberately chosen sequences in the use of specific operative skills—as, for example, a learning activity that typically started with ordering the characteristics of an issue and continued with synthesizing and classifying them in order to culminate in generalizing a new and broader notion). A methodical consequence relevant for self-direction in learning finally appears in Machmutow's (1972, 1975) didactic approach in which he formulates "critical trace back" of the course of achieving objectives as a necessary element in problem solving instruction that enables the learner to find out his or her own optimal path to goal achievement.

A third frame immediately referring to self-direction addresses the question of how elements of learning are arranged, or how to arrange them as a path or aggregate them into a higher order sequence as self-directed learning progresses. This concerns, on a more specific level, the deployment and use of appropriate learning strategies and, on a more general level, concepts to do with monitoring, controlling, and steering self-direction. With respect to the first level, such concepts may be mentioned as Weinstein & Mayer's (1986) description of learning strategies as characteristic goal-oriented semi-ordered structures of associated operative skills (like rehearsal, organization, elaboration, monitoring, metacognition) or Mandl & Friedrich's (1992) characterization of the differences in cognitive qualities and functions within the (e.g., problem-solving-oriented) course of learning. The second level is closely linked with concepts referring to consequences of metacognition like the serial organization of learning (Roberts & Erdös, 1993; including emotions: Efklides, 2006b) or conditions and effects of the use of self-monitoring or sequencing strategies in the course of learning or problem solving (Snyder, 1974; Schunk & Zimmerman, 1997). Completing the preceding, rather cognitively oriented concepts, Heckhausen & Kuhl's (Heckhausen, 1977; Heckhausen & Kuhl, 1985) Rubicon Model of Action Control can be regarded as an approach highlighting the motivational perspective in self-direction. Applying their model to learning, self-direction can be described through a sequence of motivational and volitional phases, depending in its course on the characteristics of the learning situation. However, self-direction can also be grasped as a sequence of decisions at critical states (denoted as pre-decisional, pre-actional, actional and post-actional) along the course of learning, which not only refer to the path along which but also to the extent to which learning took place.

Altogether, self-direction in learning is mainly explained within conceptual frames in which learning is conceived as the evolution of existing structured knowledge or skills based on different levels of learning. In addition, the different levels of learning are regarded as hierarchies or semi-ordered structures of mutually associated operative abilities and skills and as performed in qualitatively different forms of aggregation following immediate or strategic decisions based on individual perception, reflection, experience, motivation, and emotion along a sequence of critical states on the course of learning (Vermunt, 1996).

Frames of self-regulation

With respect to self-regulation in learning the following conceptualizations may be considered as basic frames.

As for processes regulating and sustaining the course of learning, we may detect the origins of another first frame in Herbart's psychology (1824). In this concept, three components, temper, affect, and cognitions, and the processes associated with them, constitute the conditions that influence and structure the associations of ideas and result in interests as combinations of unbiased knowledge and motivation. Regarding a person's mass of associations, processes of learning depend on individual willingness to accept new ideas and on the organization of already existing ideas. Hence, whatever a learner's open-mindedness, efficiency and sustainability in the acquisition of new ideas are a function of how they are associated with the student's whole circle of thinking as well as to what degree their association enables a student to make leaps of generalization to create more general ideas that had not been explicitly part of how the mind was previously organized, or to apply new ideas and/or new forms of mental organization in contexts different from those in which they were acquired.

An important part of a second frame has its origin in Bruner's (Bruner, 1966, 1977) concept of discovery learning. In this view, learning is based on the disposition of problem-solving skills that are acquired in autonomous acts of discovery including three simultaneous processes: (1) the acquisition of new knowledge and skills, (2) their transformation into new states and (3) the evaluation of the result of the transformation. In total, the processes are characterized by an independent and active treatment of information that provides for a generalizable organization of the cognitive structure, and for stable attitudes and motives promoting discovery and intrinsic motivation. Not unlike Herbart's ideas, the prerequisites for successful discovery are problems adequate to the learner's state of knowledge and skills, based on examples fully representing the structure of a discipline and submitted to the learners in a spiral curriculum that evolves on different levels of representation (enactive, iconic, symbolic). A further, partially similar as well as complementary facet of this frame has its origin in the foundations of Aebli's psychological didactics (Aebli 1983, 1987), originating from Piaget's ideas about the development of intellectual abilities (e.g., Piaget, 1961, 1967). In this view, efficient learning is based on two concepts: basic operative learning and higher learning. The degree and the quality of a learner's autonomy relies on the degree of availability and his or her disposal of basic operative skills, i.e., on appropriate tools of thinking at increasing but suitable levels of availability. Hereby, appropriateness depends on the achieved level of intellectual development at which the learning processes take place: at the level of pure actions, at the level of perceptions, or at the level of operations (even structurally assembled as notions). Availability refers to immediacy in the disposal of operative skills: disposing consciously, having symbolic (partially unconscious) access, or having automatized (mainly unconscious) access.

A third frame, mainly encompassing higher-level learning, refers to metacognition. On the one hand, it consists of acquired metacognitive knowledge about the disposal of cognitive processes relating to people's characteristics (i.e., general knowledge of human learning processes, as well as individual knowledge of one's own learning processes) and to tasks and strategies (i.e., knowledge about cognitive and metacognitive strategies, as well as conditional knowledge about their appropriate use; see Flavell, 1979, 1987). The respective regulatory processes are monitoring and control activities that ensure cognitive goal achievement. They not only plan and monitor activities, they also check the outcomes and consequences of such activities. Simultaneously they contribute to the selection and employment of learning-related regulatory strategies. On the other hand, metacognition also includes metacognitive experiences about the use of metacognitive strategies or metacognitive regulation (Brown, 1987), since, in addition to actual task-specific knowledge, metacognitive experiences also comprise feelings, judgments, or estimates that can trigger immediate nonconscious as well as conscious analytic control. For this reason metacognitive experiences simultaneously influence both affective and cognitive regulatory processes and therefore bridge cognitive and motivational components of self-regulation in learning (Efklides, 2002, 2004, 2006a; Fontini & Efklides, 2009).

Emphasizing the motivational perspective of self-regulation, a fourth frame has its origin in Yerkes and Dodson's (1908) studies of the relation between stimulus and affect strength. Expanded and specified in McClelland and Atkinson's expectancy x value model of achievement motivation (Atkinson, 1957, 1964, 1974; Atkinson & Feather, 1966) as well as in its modifications and extensions by Nuttin (Nuttin, 1980; Nuttin & Lens, 1985), and in particular by Heckhausen and his collaborators (Heckhausen, 1977; Heckhausen & Rheinberg, 1980; Heckhausen & Kuhl, 1985), the core of such concepts consists in the idea, that, depending on the characteristics of the person (motives) and the environment (e.g., importance and difficulty of a task), there exists an individual region of stimulation that optimally activates the start and maintenance of the process of learning. More specifically, role and relations between motivation and regulation are at the center of Kuhl's (1985) analysis. He considers regulation as a complementary aspect of motivation that influences (e.g., self-regulatory) processes with regard to the flow of action (and learning as part of it). The distinction between regulation and motivation, metacognition and volition, additionally offers an explanation of students' use of differential strategies for the regulation of their motivational and cognitive engagement and their achievement in learning in terms of their motivational (state vs. action) orientation. With an analogous idea Berlyne (1954, 1960) complemented the above rather quantitative views of learning and motivation in his research on stimulus quality and a person's exploration in so far as, instead of the stimulus strength of an environment, he considered the properties of the stimulus configuration (e.g., novelty, conflict, etc.). More precisely for the domain of learning and instruction, Lind (1976) focused his concept on the impact of characteristics in the presentation of content and the emergence of learner interest. A further step on this track beyond the presentation of content was Nenniger's (1987) consideration of the meaning and significance of content as motivating factors. In this concept the value component of the expectancy x value model was qualitatively elaborated as coherence or incoherence with an individual's value and belief system, both motivating learning, however, as the attraction or avoidance of the goal. Because of their broad influence on various models of self-regulated learning (cf. Schunk, 1989), Ryan & Deci's intrinsic motivation and self-determination theory (Deci & Ryan, 1985; Ryan & Deci, 2000) has to be considered as an approach that gives emphasis to the degree of a person's involvement in all aspects of activation and intention of the learning process. In their qualitative description they give a complementary view of the process characteristics just outlined (Deci & Ryan, 2002). The main focus is on activities initiated and maintained for their own sake as being interesting and satisfying, having their source in individuals' tendencies and psychic needs for self-motivation and personality integration as well as on conditions that promote the respective associated processes, such as seeking after novelty and challenges, exploring, extending, and exercising one's own capacities, and learning (Ryan, Kuhl, & Deci, 1997). Depending on the degree of such involvement, grades of motivation can be aligned along a hierarchical continuum from external (reward- or punishment-oriented), via introjected and identified (aware of own competence), up to integrated (internalized and autonomous) and associated with characteristic modes of regulation (Deci & Ryan, 1991; Ryan & Deci, 2000). In an additional approach, closely related to Ryan and Deci's concept, Krapp (2002, 2007) points to the role of interest with respect to the selectivity and persistence of behavior (cf. Prenzel, 1988; Renninger, Hidi, & Krapp, 1992). Distinguishing between individual and situational interest, he emphasizes the impact of conditions evoking or contributing to the emergence of long-lasting individual interests and demonstrates the consequences in the regulation of learning processes (Hidi, Renninger, & Krapp, 2004; Hidi & Renninger, 2006; Hidi & Ainley, 2008).

Finally, the fifth frame relates to a perspective that has more recently been developed by Pekrun. In his social-cognitive control-value theory of emotions, Pekrun (1992, 2000) pointed to the importance of emotions in students' self-regulated learning and achievement as far as they affect brain functions important for learning, memory, motivation, and development. Research on emotional intelligence in the context of academic learning and achievement shows that emotions have long-term memory effects in so far as they facilitate or impede the self-regulation of learning and performance, induce and sustain student interest in learning, direct attentional processes and the use of cognitive processes as well as triggering modes of information processing and problem solving (Pekrun, Götz, Titz, & Perry, 2002; Pekrun, 2009). In this context, recent research underlines the mediating role of moods and emotions on self-regulatory processes, opening fields for more systematic explanations (Pekrun, 2005; Götz, Frenzel, Pekrun, & Hall, 2005; Pekrun, Elliot, & Mayer 2006).

Altogether self-regulation in learning is mainly explained by conceptual frames in which the processes regulating and sustaining the course of learning include cognitive, metacognitive, motivational, and emotional components that are enlargements as well as transformations of diversely organized structures of knowledge and skills. The respective, diversely conceived processes include a variety of modes in their cognitive, motivational, and emotional functioning as well as in their dependence on internal and external conditions and in their mutual relations. Relatively common characteristics make up the distinctions between qualitatively different levels of cognitive processing, their dependence on diverse characteristics of the perceived learning environment (e.g., stimulating components, context, etc.) and of internal conditions (e.g., knowledge base, mood, motives, interest, etc.) as well as on their interactions. The main differences have to do with preferences of a quantitative (e.g., degree, threshold) or qualitative (e.g., organization, pattern, or other structural properties) character, the impact of the process-related conditions, and their immediate or strategic or pertinent regulative significance.

Although within most of the above frames the different conceptualizations concern various aspects of learning, they approach the nature of both self-directed and self-regulated learning when regarded as an active process in which learners independently establish the objectives guiding their learning and try to monitor, control, and regulate their behavior and learning (cognition, motivation, and emotion) in order to achieve their own goals. On the one hand, the respective conceptualizations take account of a complex conglomerate of different, learner-related (behavioral, cognitive, motivational, emotional) and environmental factors. Therefore, research domains like goal setting, cognitive structuring, learning strategies, metacognition, learning, motivation, and interest, as well as emotion all—to a different extent—form part of the respective concepts of self-direction and self-regulation in learning (see, e.g., Heikkilä & Lonka, 2006; Nicol & Macfarlane-Dick, 2006). On the other hand these conceptualizations have found constructivist principles (see, e.g., Paris & Byrnes, 1989) relating to learning as an active, situated, self-directed processus of interactions with objects of learning, which is regulated by the learner depending on his or her interest and intrinsic motivation including favorable emotions and mainly concerns the selection of learning objects, the amount of learning time, and the method of access.

Concepts of Self-Directed and Self-Regulated Learning

Based on a general idea of the autonomous individual, theoretical lines about the autonomous learner have first been systematically outlined in the foregoing paragraphs as roots and concepts from which various educational and psychological subdomains have grown. Then, they have been categorized within frames, relevant to both self-direction and self-regulation in learning. Against this background, the following section is dedicated to an overview of selected concepts and models of self-directed and self-regulated learning that represent central modes of theorizing about these issues and are apt to give rise to further elaborations and developments.

Concepts of self-directed learning (SDL)

In the following concepts a view of self-direction is elaborated that progresses from a rather outside-oriented look at the course of learning within institutional contexts towards a more inside-oriented look at the individual conditions of the person.

According to Candy (1991) self-directed learning is a comprehensive concept that can be described in two interacting domains: the amount of control within an institutional setting (total teacher control vs. total learner control) and learner control in situations outside the formal institutional setting ("autodidaxy" as the individual, noninstructional pursuit of learning opportunities in the natural societal setting). Furthermore, as a concept, self-direction encompasses the perspectives of process and product and refers to four distinct components: "autonomy" as a personal attribute, "self-management" as capacity and willingness to conduct one's own education independently, "learner-control" as a mode of organizing instruction in formal settings and "learner control" as the individual pursuit of learning opportunities in natural societal settings. The different modes of self-directed learning can be described as specific interactions of the above dimensions. However, the levels learners can achieve in the different dimensions may depend on how familiar they are with an issue or how similar the area may be to one they have experienced before.

In their Personal Responsibility Orientation Mode, Brockett & Hiemstra (1991) provide a rationale for two primary aspects of self-direction in learning: process orientation and goal orientation. The first aspect concerning the processus, emphasizes the learner's responsibility for planning, implementing, and evaluating a learning process. The second aspect, concerning the goal, is focused on the learner's assumption of responsibility for his or her own learning. In their model the components "process" and "personal responsibility" were combined and integrated the social context as a further component referring to the places that form the learning environment (Hiemstra, 2000).

Like Hiemstra's concept, Garrison's Three-Dimensional Model of self-directed learning also includes the perspectives of self-direction in learning as a personal attribute and as the learning process, but the focus lies on the use and disposal of resources, learning strategies, and motivation to learn (Garrison, 1992, 1997). The model integrates the following three dimensions that reflect basic issues of self-directed learning: self-management (as contextual control focused on goal setting, use of resources, and external support for learning), self-monitoring (as cognitive responsibility focused on monitoring one's own cognitive and metacognitive processes in planning and modifying one's own learning-task- and learning-goal-related thinking), and motivation (with two components as motivation to participate in a learning process and as task motivation as keeping the learner on track and persisting in the learning process).

In his Theory of Self-Directed Learning, Knowles (Knowles, 1975; Long & Associates, 1985) describes the surface of self-direction as a sequence of actions taking place along the course of learning in which the learner takes the initiative—with or without the help of others—in (1) diagnosing his or her own needs concerning learning, (2) establishing learning goals, (3) identifying the necessary human and material resources, (4) choosing and implementing appropriate learning strategies and (5) evaluating the learning outcomes. In extending and complementing the above model, Nenniger and Straka elaborated the two-shells model of motivated self-directed learning (cf. Straka & Nenniger, 1995; Straka, Nenniger, Spevacek, & Wosnitza 1996; Nenniger, 1999; Straka & Schaefer, 2002; Straka & Macke, 2004) already taking account of interactions between motivation and cognition along the course of learning. The course of self-directed learning is therefore described as a spiraled progression of learning based on expectations and appraisals toward and from learning experience. In analogy to Knowles model, self-directed learning starts by diagnosing needs with respect to its own contentual and procedural interest, and continues by progressively establishing goals and identifying the necessary resources, in interaction with choosing and implementing appropriate learning strategies and finally evaluating and attributing the learning outcomes. For this purpose self-directed learning is comprised within two (an exterior and an interior) shells. Regarding the course of learning and taking account of related cognitive and motivational processes, the model is defined as follows: The exterior shell of the model includes the motivational part of self-directed learning that influences the processes of the interior shell, including the volitional part where learners actively perform learning. As, however, the interior shell is embedded in the outer shell, experience of performed learning recursively affects the outer shell. Thus, the course of self-directed learning is not only thought of as a linear sequence but as an evolving spiral. In terms of theories of learning, motivation, and interest, the concept of the exterior shell as related to the initial phase of learning refers to an interest-based diagnosis of learning needs that determines whether a person starts learning or not, and, if so, enters the interior shell. As related to the terminal phase of a learning sequence, it refers to the evaluation of the ongoing learning experience and the attribution of the achieved result within a frame of causal ascriptions (cf. Weiner, 1986). In consequence, it is part of the feedback from the learning experiences of the interior shell that affects recursively students' further interest-based needs for future learning and studying and thus directs learning toward the next level of the spiral within the ongoing course of learning (or stops it from proceeding further). Whereas the outer shell refers to the course of learning, the concept of the inner shell takes account of the related processes and conceives ongoing learning as an interactive oscillation between progressive goal setting and identifying the necessary resources and the complementary choice and implementation of appropriate learning strategies.

In sum, the majority of the models of self-directed learning highlight learners' direction of their learning processes within a certain learning situation with the aim of achieving the settled goals. From a behavior-oriented perspective, while pursuing their course of learning, self-directed learners learn strategically by actively selecting, structuring, and creating learning environments that support their learning processes. From the metacognitive perspective they monitor the progress of their own learning by learning activities that mainly include extensive, autonomous planning, organizing, and evaluating. From a motivational point of view they act on an enhanced level of self-efficacy and intrinsic motivation. However, some authors (such as Brookfield, 1988) have already noted inconsistencies between the theoretical, practical, and methodological components of the different concepts, whereas particularly application-oriented authors in the fields of vocational, further, and adult education (e.g., Pressley, 1995; Beck & Krumm, 2001; Sembill, Wolf, Wuttke, & Schumacher, 2003) develop from more general approaches images of an ideal self-directed learner with high metacognitive consciousness, combining broad domain-specific knowledge with high abilities in reflection, planning, designing, and implementation within a specific project.

Concepts of self-regulated learning

In analogy to the foregoing view of concepts of self-directed learning a systematic outline has also been elaborated for the concepts of self-regulated learning. Starting from a model including most fundamental regulatory processes, it progresses to more complex concepts that consider an increased number of processes with their mutual relations at different stages and levels and take account of additional social and environmental conditions.

In their Two-Processes Model of Self-Regulated Learning, Corno & Mandinach (1983) and Corno (1986) emphasize cognitive functions of volitional elements (cf. Corno, 1989, 2001). They characterize self-regulation by two processes—information acquisition and information transformation—and five strategies—alerting, monitoring, selecting, connecting, and planning. Selecting, connecting, and planning strategies as components of the information transformation processes are situated at the center of self-regulated learning and specify ongoing learning. Information acquisition processes consist of alertness and monitoring strategies, have their place at the start and at the end of a learning phase and describe the quality of the cognitive engagement. The relationship between the two processes is not merely inclusive but to an important extent metacognitive and thus part of self-regulation.

In accord with the majority of conceptions of self-regulation in learning, Winne (Winne, 1995; Butler & Winne, 1995; Winne & Hadwin, 1998) regards the self-regulated learner as metacognitive, motivated for learning, and strategic. In his four-stage model the functions of self-regulation are described in the following four phases: (1) development of a task model, (2) creation of goals related to the model of the task and subsequent selection of appropriate cognitive operations, (3) engagement in the course of learning by applying the chosen tactics and strategies, and (4) construction of products as outcomes of each cognitive operation, included eventual revision, adjustment of the proper task model, and adaptation of the corresponding goals and strategies. The model reflects an integrating consideration of the main determinants of learning together with the cognitive processes involved. Each phase refers to metacognitive monitoring and control and, accordingly, the quality of self-regulation in learning is determined (1) by the accuracy of the task model and access to information supposed to be necessary, (2) by the quality of the learners' repertoire of effective study tactics and learning strategies, (3) by knowledge and access to standards for monitoring changes in the domain of learning, the fit of study tactics and learning strategies to the assigned tasks, and disposal of the cognitive operations inherent in study tactics and learning strategies, as well as (4) by active metacognitive skillfulness in monitoring and controlling the course of learning (Winne, 2001).

In her Three-Layered Model of Self-Regulated Learning Boekaerts (1996, 1997, 1999) extends the above view with regard to paths of regulation within motivation and cognition. She describes motivational and cognitive regulation as a complex, interactive process distinguishing three regulatory systems: (1) regulation of the self (i.e., choice of goals and resources), (2) regulation of the learning process (i.e., use of metacognitive knowledge and skills to direct one's learning) and (3) regulation of the modes of information processing (i.e., choice of information-processing strategies) including three levels of regulation: (1) goals, (2) strategies, and (3) domain-specific knowledge resulting in six components that represent a prior knowledge potentially available or currently accessible if self-regulated learning is to occur. As a result, the individual components show high mutual dependency so that, for example, deficits in knowledge can impede or exclude self-regulation in learning, while the three regulatory systems involved in self-regulated learning have to be considered as a valid representation of the processes and regulatory mechanisms of self-regulated learning. This may be one of the reasons that in later versions the strict subdivision of the individual components in the original six-component model has been replaced by a more general depiction of three layers in self-regulated learning (cf. Boekaerts, 1999).

In his model of self-regulation, Zimmerman (1989, 1995, 2000), on the one hand, describes self-regulated learning as a cyclic sequence with the components forethought (i.e., setting goals, selecting strategies and methods, assessing self-efficacy, assessing mastery or performance goal orientation and assessing interest), performance control (i.e., focusing attention, self-instruction, and the self-monitoring of the learning progress) as well as self-reflection (i.e., self-evaluation, attribution, and self-reactions, and adaptation) and including as processes planning, setting goals, organizing, self-monitoring, and self-evaluating, which may take place at various points of a learning sequence. On the other hand he characterizes self-regulated learners as people who are self-aware, knowledgeable, and decisive in their approach. They can be regarded as self-starters who are self-instructed and self-reinforced and display effort and persistence accompanied by great self-efficacy, strong positive self-attributions, and high intrinsic task interest. Furthermore, their learning typically shows self-selection, structuring, and the creation of optimal environments, calling on advice, information, and places suitable to gather new information (Zimmerman, 1990, pp. 4–5). Later on, Schunk and Zimmerman (1997) and Zimmerman (2000) recognized that the development of self-regulatory skills has to be conceived within the framework of a social-cognitive theory and extended their concept toward one of a cyclic socio-cognitive self-regulation of learning including self-regulatory and coregulatory components.

Pintrich's (Pintrich, 2000; Pintrich, 2004; Pintrich & DeGroot, 1990; Pintrich & Garcia, 1994) theoretical contribution serves rather as a comprehensive framework that outlines the conditions for successful promotion of self-regulated learning than as a model describing self-regulatory processes in learning themselves. Self-regulated learning is mainly conceived within the frame of achievement motivation as an active, constructive process, guided by individual goals and a contextual frame. In this process interactions between learner, context, and overall achievement are mediated and cognitive engagement as well as academic performance are regulated by the three motivational components: (1) expectancy, referring to expected success in performing a task, (2) value, referring to appreciation of and beliefs about the importance of the task and (3) affect, referring to emotional reactions to the task. Ideally, the regulatory processes associated can be described as a sequence of phases including planning, self-monitoring, control, and evaluation. But the phases do not necessarily constitute a linear or hierarchical progression. They may—also depending on students' prior experience—progress in partially simultaneous multiple dynamic interactions, which do not exclude parts of them from also referring to external regulation of some kind.

In sum, the above models of self-regulated learning typically situate motivational processes at the beginning or at the term of a learning episode or at a critical, decisive phase. Furthermore, self-regulated learning tends to take place over different stages in a rather non-linear, cyclic, or recursive sequence. Associated processes regulate the initiation, maintenance, or termination of learning or link evaluation and causal ascriptions with accompanying positive or negative emotions as well as expectations and beliefs in various ways. Regulation of cognitive processes relates to the progress of attention as well as cognitive functions and performance, in particular of learning strategies. Metacognitive regulation mainly refers, on the one hand, to processes of goal orientation and goal-oriented planning, monitoring, control, and evaluation and, on the other, to different sorts of adaptation. Finally, regulatory processes may depend on different traits of the person, such as skillfulness, interest, self-awareness, and so forth.

Actual State, Desiderata, and Future Prospects

Although in the majority of models self-regulation is attributed to the individual, to a significant extent extensions of models include more explicitly social processes with the argument that self-regulated learning is not necessarily individual because in many cases any kind of instructors and learners or groups of learners form a community that constructs knowledge, skills, and attitudes and develops social competencies via interpersonal relations that do not exclude coregulation. (Nichols, 1996; Raidal & Volet, 2009; Volet, Summers, & Thurman, 2009; Wosnitza & Volet, 2009).

In further complements note is taken of the differential influence of environmental conditions insofar as self-regulation is often performed in situated processes related to specific environments (Brown, Collins, & Duguid, 1989; Wosnitza & Nenniger, 2001) or to sociocultural environments that refer differentially to cultural values such as autonomy and independence (cf., e.g., McCaslin & Hickey, 2001).

Following critics that deplore the lack of consideration given to intention and content-related processes in the description of self-directed learning and its regulatory processes, recent conceptualizations (such as Nenniger, van den Brink, & Bissbort, 2009) include elements of phenomenographical descriptions of different (e.g., surface, intermediate, deep, strategic) approaches to learning (Marton & Säljö, 1976a, 1976b; Biggs 1979; Entwistle & Ramsden 1983; Kember 1996; Entwistle & Tait, 1990) as complementary components. Departing from the results of research (Wild, 1995; Van den Brink, 2006) that have already identified typical and substantial forms of co-action between self-direction in learning and different approaches to learning, they pledge themselves in their deliberations on a theory of "differential approaches to self-direction" to a broader understanding of (1) how students learn, (2) how they differ in their learning, and (3) how they make their choices among the whole variety of approaches to self-direction in learning by a simultaneous inclusion of intention and content orientation in metacognitive and motivational processes.

A further desideratum relating to the course of self-directed learning as well as its regulation aims at a more coherent explanation of their dynamics and the structural properties of the recursive course of learning (Nenniger, 1999, Nenniger, van den Brink, & Bissbort, 2009) or within the interactions of the regulatory systems (Boekaerts, 1997). For this purpose a functional description of the regulatory component in self-direction (i.e., a description of the functional properties of the ongoing regulatory processes, e.g., steadiness, parsimony, direction, linearity, etc.) is needed, so that, with a better coverage of alterations in cognitive structures over time (as when they are extended, shrunk, altered, stabilized, or becoming (in)coherent, etc., a factor already applied in structural biology; cf. Pugesek, Tomer, & von Eye, 2003), we can deepen the qualitative aspect of the dynamics.

With respect to issues needing further consideration, a continuation of the debate on didactic models regarding value, place, and the effects of autonomy versus heteronomy in learning and instruction is required, covering, for example, questions about the suitability of direct instruction or self-direction in view of the transfer of knowledge and skills to new contexts, to metacognitive reflection but also of the knowledge of subject matter. Also required is a complementary view to the predominantly achievement-oriented approaches to self-regulation, by means of which theories concerning interest, meaningfulness, and content could contribute to a much wider perspective.

However, further theoretical advancement requires developments (or adaptations) of a suitable methodology (cf. Nenniger, 2005). In the experimental design we need further elaborations of an "in vivo" online instrument to observe multiple modes of self-direction and self-regulation (as, e.g., Sembill, Wolf, Wuttke, & Schumacher, 2003, or Winne's traces methodology, cf. Nenniger, 2006; Perry & Winne, 2006). In data analysis what is needed are methods for functional descriptions of processes or pattern recognition of cause–effect relationships (as, e.g., Boekaerts & Cascallar, 2006).

In addition, we have to be aware that most of our empirical research only covers a restricted field of application: mostly experimental settings at universities (psychology!), education and didactics at school (Lemos, 1999; for an overview cf. Boekaerts & Corno, 2005) and university, and partially further education with adults (Brockett, 1985). Important areas like vocational education or the education of preschoolers (problem of development!) are rarely examined (cf. Nenniger, 2005).

Reconsidering the above roots, frames, and concepts in the perspective of a history of ideas, it seems that reflection and research have already reached a sound but widespread basis for a more general explanation of autonomous learning. Issues that deserve to be put forward have to do with a consolidation of the multiple approaches, so that, despite the wide variety of ideas about self-directed and self-regulated learning, including the phenomena associated with it, we will advance our recognition from a multi-faceted picture towards some more insightful patterns about autonomy.

References

Aebli, H. (1983). *Zwölf Grundformen des Lehrens. Eine allgemeine Didaktik auf psychologischer Grundlage [Twelve basic forms of instruction. General didactics on a psychological foundation*]. Stuttgart: Klett-Cotta.

Aebli, H. (1987). *Grundlagen des Lehrens* [Foundations of instruction]. Stuttgart: Klett-Cotta.

Anhalt, E. (1999). *Bildsamkeit und Selbstorganisation. Johann Friedrich Herbarts Konzept der Bildsamkeit als Grundlage für eine pädagogische Theorie der Selbstorganisation organismischer Aktivität* [Plasticity and self-organisation. Johann Friedrich Herbart's concept of plasticity as a foundation for a pedagogical theory of the self-organisation of organismic activity] (Dissertation). Weinheim: Deutscher Studien Verlag.

Ausubel, D. P. (1963). *The psychology of meaningful verbal learning*. New York: Grune & Stratton.

Ausubel, D., Novak, J., & Hanesian, H. (1978). *Educational psychology: A cognitive view* (2nd ed.). New York: Holt, Rinehart, & Winston.

Atkinson, J. W. (1957). Motivational determinants of risk-taking behavior. *Psychological Review*, *64*, 359–373.

Atkinson, J. W. (1964). *An introduction to motivation*. Princeton, NJ: Van Nostrand.

Atkinson, J. W., & Feather, N. T. (Eds.). (1966). *A theory of achievement motivation*. New York: Wiley.

Atkinson, J. W. (1974). Motivational determinants of intellectual performance and cumulative achievement. In J. W. Atkinson & J. O. Raynor (Eds.), *Motivation and achievement* (pp. 389–410). Washington, DC: Winston.

Barker, M. (1993). Perceptions of social rules in intercultural and intracultural encounters: A study of Australian and ethnic Chinese university students (Unpublished Ph.D thesis). University of Queensland, St Lucia, Queensland.

Beck, K., & Krumm, V. (Eds.). (2001). *Lehren und Lernen in der beruflichen Erstausbildung* [Instruction and learning in basic vocational training]. Opladen, Germany: Leske + Budrich Verlag.

Berlyne, D. E. (1954). A theory of human curiosity. *British Journal of Psychology*, *45*, 180–191.

Berlyne, D. E. (1960). *Conflict, arousal, and curiosity*. New York: McGraw Hill.

Betts, G. T., & Knapp, J. (1981). The autonomous learner model: A secondary model. In A. Arnold (Ed.), *Secondary programs for the gifted and talented*. Los Angeles, CA: National/State-Leadership Training Institute.

Biggs, J. B. (1979). Individual differences in study processes and the quality of learning outcomes. *Higher Education*, *8*, 381–394.

Biggs, J. B. (1994), Asian learners through western eyes: an astigmatic paradox. *Australian and New Zealand Journal of Vocational Research*, *2*(2), 40–63.

Biggs, J. B. (1996), Approaches to learning of Asian students: A multiple paradox, in Pandey, J. (Ed.), *Asian Contributions to Cross-Cultural Psychology* (pp.180–99). New Delhi: Sage.

Blyth, A. (1981). From individuality to character: the Herbartian sociology applied to education. *British Journal of Educational Studies, 29*(1), 69–79.

Boekaerts, M. (1996). Self-regulated learning at the junction of cognition and motivation. *European Psychologist, 1*(2), 100–112.

Boekaerts, M. (1997). Self-regulated learning: A new concept embraced by researchers, policy makers, educators, teachers, and students. *Learning and Instruction, 7*, 161–186.

Boekaerts, M. (1999). Self-regulated learning: Where are we today? *International Journal of Educational Research, 31*, 445–457.

Boekaerts, M., & Cascallar, E. (2006). How far have we moved toward the integration of theory and practice in self-regulation? *Educational Psychology Review, 18*(3), 199–210.

Boekaerts, M., & Corno, L. (2005). Self-regulation in the classroom: A perspective on assessment and intervention. *Applied Psychology, 54*(2), 199–231.

Boekaerts, M., Pintrich, P. R., & Zeidner, M. (Eds.). (2000). *Handbook of self-regulation.* San Diego, CA: Academic Press.

Brockett, R. G. (1985). The relationship between self-directed learning readiness and life satisfaction among older adults. *Adult Education Quarterly, 35*, 210–219.

Brockett, R. G., & Hiemstra, R. (1991). *Self direction in adult learning. Perspectives, on theory, research, and practice.* London: Routledge.

Brookfield, S. D. (1988). Conceptual, methodological and practical ambiguities in self-directed learning. In H. B. Long & Associates, *Self-directed learning: Application & theory* (pp. 11–38). Athens, GA: University of Georgia, Adult Education Department.

Brown, A. L. (1987). Metacognition, executive control, self-regulation, and other more mysterious mechanisms. In F. E. Weinert & R. H. Kluwe (Eds.), *Metacognition, motivation, and understanding* (pp. 65–116). Hillsdale, New Jersey: Lawrence Erlbaum Associates.

Brown, J. S., Collins, A., and Duguid, P. (1989). Situated cognition and the culture of learning. *Educational Researcher, 18*(1), 32–41.

Bruner, J. S. (1966). *Toward a theory of instruction.* Cambridge, MA: Harvard University Press.

Bruner, J. S. (1977) *The process of education* (2nd ed.). Cambridge, MA: Harvard University Press.

Bruner, J. S., & Postman, L. (1949). On the perception of incongruity: A paradigm. *Journal of Personality, 18*, 206–223.

Butler, D. L., & Winne, P. H. (1995). Feedback and self-regulated learning: A theoretical synthesis. *Review of Educational Research, 65*, 245–281.

Candy, P. C. (1991). *Self-direction for lifelong learning: A comprehensive guide to theory and practice.* San Francisco: Jossey-Bass.

Comenius, J. A. (1657a/1986). *Pampaedia* (facsimile). Dover: Buckland.

Comenius, J. A. (1657b). *Opera didactica omnia, ab anno 1627 da 1657 continuata.* Amsterdam.

Corno, L (1986). The metacognitive control components of self-regulated learning. *Contemporary Educational Psychology, 11*, 333–346.

Corno, L. (1989). Self-regulated learning: A volitional analysis. In B. J. Zimmerman & D. H. Schunk (Eds.), *Self-regulated learning and academic achievement: Theory, research, and practice* (pp. 111–142). New York: Springer-Verlag.

Corno, L. (2001). Volitional aspects of self-regulated learning. In B. J. Zimmerman & D. H. Schunk (Eds.), *Self-regulated learning and academic achievement: theoretical perspectives* (2nd ed., pp. 191–226). Mahwah, NJ: Erlbaum.

Corno, L., & Mandinach, E. (1983). The role of cognitive engagement in classroom learning and motivation. *Educational Psychology, 19*(2), 88–108.

Davydov, V. V. (1972). *Teorija razvivajuščego obučenija.* [Theory of developmental teaching.] Moscow: Intor.

Deci, E. L., & Ryan, R. M. (1985). *Intrinsic motivation and self-determination in human behavior*. New York: Plenum.

Deci, E. L., & Ryan, R. M. (1991). A motivational approach to self: Integration in personality. In R. Dienstbier (Ed.), *Nebraska Symposium on Motivation: Vol. 38. Perspectives on motivation* (pp. 237–288). Lincoln, NE: University of Nebraska Press.

Deci, E. L., & Ryan, R. M. (1995). Human autonomy: The basis for true self-esteem. In M. Kemis (Ed.), *Efficacy, agency, and self-esteem* (pp. 31–49). New York: Plenum.

Deci, E. L., & Ryan, R. M. (Eds.). (2002). *Handbook of self-determination research*. Rochester, NY: University of Rochester Press.

DeGarmo, C. (1916 [1895]). *Herbart and the Herbartians*. New York: Charles Scribner's Sons.

Dewey, J. (1896). *Interest in relation to training of the will*. Chicago: University of Chicago Press.

Dewey, J. (1910). *How we think*. Boston: Heath.

Efklides, A. (2001). Metacognitive experiences in problem solving: Metacognition, motivation, and self-regulation. In A. Efklides, J. Kuhl, & R. M. Sorrentino (Eds.), *Trends and prospects in motivation research* (pp. 297–323). Dordrecht, the Netherlands: Kluwer.

Efklides, A. (2002). The systemic nature of metacognitive experiences: Feelings, judgments, and their interrelations. In M. Izaute, P. Chambres, & P.-J. Marescaux (Eds.), *Metacognition: Process, function, and use* (pp. 19–34). Dordrecht, the Netherlands: Kluwer.

Efklides, A. (2004). The multiple role of metacognitive experiences in the learning process. In M. Wosnitza, A. Frey, & R. S. Jaeger (Eds.), *Lernprozess, Lernumgebung und Lerndiagnostik. Wissenschaftliche Beiträge zum Lernen im 21. Jahrhundert* (pp. 256–266). Landau, Germany: Verlag Empirische Paedagogik.

Efklides, A. (2006a). Metacognitive experiences: The missing link in the self-regulated learning process. A rejoinder to Ainley and Patrick. *Educational Psychology Review*, *18*, 287–291.

Efklides, A. (2006b). Metacognition and affect: What can metacognitive experiences tell us about the learning process? *Educational Research Review*, *1*, 3–4.

Entwistle, N., & Ramsden, P. (1983). *Understanding student learning*. London: Croom Helm.

Entwistle, N. J., & Tait, H. (1990). Approaches to learning, evaluations of teaching, and preferences for contrasting academic environments. *Higher Education*, *19*, 169–194.

Flavell, J. H. (1979). Metacognition and cognitive monitoring: A new area of cognitive-developmental inquiry. *American Psychologist*, *34*, 906–911.

Flavell, J. H. (1987). Speculations about the nature and development of metacognition. In F. E. Weinert & R. H. Kluwe (Eds.), *Metacognition, motivation and understanding* (pp. 21–29). Hillsdale, NJ: Lawrence Erlbaum Associates.

Fontini, D., & Efklides, A. (2009) Meta-cognitive experiences as the link between situational characteristics, motivation, and affect in self-regulated learning. In M. Wosnitza, S. A. Karabenick, A. Efklides, & P. Nenniger (Eds.), *Contemporary motivation research* (pp. 117–146). Göttingen: Hogrefe & Huber.

Frey, K. (1982). *Die Projektmethode* [The project-method]. Weinheim: Beltz.

Galperin, P. Y. (1969). Stages in the development of mental acts. In M. Cole & I. Maltzman (Eds.), *A handbook of contemporary Soviet psychology* (pp. 249–273). New York: Casic.

Garrison, D. R. (1992). Critical thinking and self-directed learning in adult education: An analysis of responsibilities and control issues. *Adult Education Quarterly*, *42*(3), 136–148.

Garrison, D. R. (1997). Self-directed learning: Toward a comprehensive model. *Adult Education Quarterly*, *48*(1), 18–33.

Gaudig, H. (1925). *Freie geistige Schularbeit in Theorie und Praxis* [Free brainwork at school in theory and practice]. Breslau: Hirt.

Götz, T., Frenzel, A. C., Pekrun, R., & Hall, N. (2005). Emotional intelligence in the context of learning and achievement. In R. Schulze & R. Roberts (Eds.), *Emotional intelligence: An international handbook* (pp. 233–253). Göttingen: Hogrefe & Huber Publishers.

Heckhausen, H. (1977). Achievement motivation and its constructs: A cognitive model. *Motivation and Emotion, 1*, 283–329.

Heckhausen, H., & Kuhl, J. (1985). From wishes to action: The dead ends and short cuts on the long way to action. In M. Frese & J. Sabini (Eds.), *Goal-directed behaviour: The concept of action in psychology* (pp. 134–159). Hillsdale, NJ: Erlbaum.

Heckhausen, H., & Rheinberg, F. (1980). Lernmotivation im Unterricht, erneut betrachtet [Learning motivation in classroom, revisited]. *Unterrichtswissenschaft, 8*, 7–47.

Herbart, J. F. (1806). *Allgemeine Pädagogik aus dem Zweck der Erziehung abgeleitet* [Inclusive pedagogy, derived from the purpose of education]. Göttingen: Röver.

Herbart, J. F. (1824). *Lehrbuch zur Psychologie* (2. überarbeitete Auflage) [Textbook of psychology (2nd rev. ed.)]. Königsberg: Unzer.

Herbart, J. F., (1841). *Umriss pädagogischer Vorlesungen* [Outline of pedagogical lectures]. Göttingen: Dieterich.

Heikkilä, A., & Lonka, K. (2006). Studying in higher education: Students' approaches to learning, self-regulation and cognitive strategies. *Studies in Higher Education, 31*, 99–117.

Hiemstra, R. (2000). Self-directed learning: The personal responsibility model. In G. A. Straka (Ed.), *Conceptions of self- directed learning* (pp. 93–108). Münster/New York: Waxmann.

Hidi, S., & Ainley, M. (2008). Interest and self-regulation: Relationships between two variables that influence learning. In B. J. Zimmerman & D. H. Schunk (Eds.), *Motivation and self-regulated learning: Theory, research, and applications* (pp. 77–109). Mahwah, NJ.: Erlbaum.

Hidi, S., & Renninger, K. A. (2006). The Four-Phase Model of interest development. *Educational Psychologist, 41*(2), 111–127.

Hidi, S., Renninger, K. A., & Krapp, A. (2004). Interest, a motivational construct that combines affective and cognitive functioning. In D. Y. Dai & R. J. Sternberg (Eds.), *Motivation, emotion and cognition: Integrative perspectives on intellectual functioning and development* (pp. 89–115). Mahwah, NJ: Erlbaum.

Ho, J., & Crookall, D. (1995). Breaking with Chinese cultural traditions: Learner autonomy in English language teaching. *System, 23*(2), 235–243.

Jin, L., & Cortazzi, M. (1996). This way is very different from Chinese ways. In M. Hewings & T. Dudley-Evans (Eds.). *Evaluation and course design in EAP* (pp. 205–216). Hemel Hempstead: Prentice Hall Macmillan.

Kant, I. (1785/1956) Grundlegung zur Metaphysik der Sitten [Foundations of the metaphysics of morals.]. In I. Kant, *Werke in sechs Bänden* (Bd. 4: *Schriften zur Ethik und Religionsphilosophie*). Darmstadt: Akademische Verlagsgesellschaft.

Kember, D. (1996), The intention to both memorise and understand: another approach to learning. *Higher Education, 31*, pp. 341–354.

Kember, D., & Gow, L. (1990), Cultural specificity of approaches to study. *British Journal of Educational Psychology, 60*, pp. 356–363.

Kember, D., & Gow, L. (1991), A challenge to the anecdotal stereotype of the Asian student. *Studies in Higher Education, 16*(2), pp. 117–128.

Kilpatrick, W. H. (1918). The project method. *Teachers College Record, 19*, 319–335.

Kilpatrick, W. H. (1927). School method from the project point of view. In M. B. Hillegas (Ed.), *The classroom teacher* (pp. 203–240). Chicago: Teacher Inc.

Kliebard, H. M. (1981). Dewey and the Herbartians: the genesis of a theory of curriculum. *Journal of Curriculum Theorizing*, *3*, 154–161.

Knowles, M. S. (1975). *Self-directed learning*. Chicago: Follett.

Krapp, A. (2002). An educational-psychological theory of interest and its relation to self-determination theory. In E. L. Deci & R. M. Ryan (Eds.), *The handbook of self-determination research* (pp. 405–427). Rochester: University of Rochester Press.

Krapp, A. (2007). An educational-psychological conceptualisation of interest. *International Journal of Educational and Vocational Guidance*, *7*(1), 5–21.

Kuhl, J. (1985). Volitional mediators of cognition–behavior consistency: Self-regulatory processes and action versus state orientation. In J. Kuhl & J. Beckmann (Eds.), *Action control: From cognition to behaviour* (pp. 101–128). Berlin: Springer.

Lemos, M. S. (1999). Students' goals and self-regulation in the classroom. *International Journal of Educational Research*, *31*, 471–485.

Lind, G. (1976). Micro-evaluation of subject-matter-directed motivation. *Studies in Educational Evaluation*, *2*, 103–120.

Littlewood, W. (1999). Defining and developing autonomy in East Asian contexts. *Applied Linguistics*, *20*(1), 71–94.

Lompscher, J. (Ed.). (1975). *Theoretische und experimentelle Untersuchungen zur Entwicklung geistiger Fähigkeiten* [Theoretical and experimental studies related to the development of mental skills]. Berlin: Volk und Wissen.

Lompscher, J. (1989). Formation of learning activity in pupils. In H. Mandl, E. de Corte, N. Bennett, & H. F. Friedrich (Eds.), *Learning and instruction. European research in an international context* (Vol. 2.2) (pp. 47–66). Oxford: Pergamon Press.

Long, H. B. & Associates (1985). *Self-directed learning: Application and theory*. Athens, Georgia: University of Georgia, Adult Education Department.

Machmutow, M. I. (1972). *Teorija I praktika problemiogo obučenjia*. [Theory and praxis of teaching problems.]. Kasan: Institute for research on Vocational Education.

Machmutow, M. I. (1975). *Problemnoje obučenjie*. [Problems of teaching.]. Moscow: Pedagogika.

Mandl, H., & Friedrich, H. F. (Eds.). (1992). *Lern- und Denkstrategien. Analyse und Intervention* [Strategies of learning and thinking. Analysis and intervention.]. Göttingen: Hogrefe.

Marton, F., Dall'Alba, G., & Tse, L. (1996), Memorising and understanding: the keys to the paradox? In D. A. Watkins & J. B. Biggs (Eds.), *The Chinese Learner* (pp. 69–83). University of Hong Kong, Comparative Education Research Centre/Australian Council for Educational Research, Hong Kong/Melbourne.

Marton, F., & Säljö, R. (1976a). On qualitative differences in learning: I. Outcome and process. *British Journal of Educational Psychology*, *46*, 4–11.

Marton, F., & Säljö, R. (1976b). On qualitative differences in learning: II. Outcome as a function of the learner's conception of the task. *British Journal of Educational Psychology*, *46*, 115–127.

McCaslin, M., & Hickey, D. T. (2001). Self-regulated learning and academic achievement: A Vygotskian view. In B. J. Zimmerman & D. Schunk (Eds.), *Self-regulated learning and academic achievement: Theoretical perspectives*. Mahwah, NJ: Erlbaum.

Nenniger, P. (1987). How stable is motivation by contents? In E. de Corte, H. Lodjwiks, R. Parmentier, & P. Span (Eds.), *Learning and Instruction: European research in an international context* (Vol. *1*, pp. 159–168). Oxford: Pergamon Press.

Nenniger, P. (1999). On the role of motivation in self-directed learning. The "Two Shells-Model of Motivated Self-directed Learning" as a structural explanatory concept. *European Journal of Psychology of Education*, *14*(1), 71–86.

Nenniger, P. (2005). Commentary on self-regulation in the classroom: A perspective on assessment and intervention. *Applied Psychology, 54*(2), 239–244.

Nenniger, P. (2006). Comment on Perry & Winne's "Learning from learning kits: gStudy traces of students' self-regulated engagements with computerized content". *Educational Psychology Review, 18*(3), 233–237.

Nenniger, P., van den Brink, K., & Bissbort, D. (2009). On a differential explanation of self-direction in motivating learning environments. In M. Wosnitza, S. A. Karabenick, A. Efklides, & P. Nenniger (Eds.), *Contemporary motivation research: From global to local perspectives* (pp. 147–166). New York: Hogrefe.

Nichols, J. D. (1996). Cooperative Learning: A motivational tool to enhance student persistence, self-regulation, and efforts to please teachers and parents. *Educational Research and Evaluation, 2*, 246–260.

Nicol, D. J., & Macfarlane-Dick, D. (2006). Formative assessment and self-regulated learning: A model and seven principles of good feedback practice. *Studies in Higher Education, 31*, 199–218.

Nuttin, J. B. (1980) *Théorie de la motivation humaine* [Theory of human motivation.]. Paris: PUF.

Nuttin, J. B., & Lens, W. M. (1985). *Future time perspective and motivation: Theory and research method.* Hillsdale, N.J.: Erlbaum.

Paris, S. G., & Byrnes, J. P. (1989). The constructivist approach to self-regulation and learning in the classroom. In B. J. Zimmerman & D. H. Schunk (Eds.), *Self-regulated learning and academic achievement: Theory, research, and practice* (pp. 169–200). New York: Springer-Verlag.

Pekrun, R. (1992). The impact of emotions on learning and achievement: Towards a theory of cognitive/motivational mediators. *Applied Psychology: An International Review, 41*(4), 359–376.

Pekrun, R. (2000). A social cognitive, control-value theory of achievement emotions. In J. Heckhausen (Ed.), *Motivational psychology of human development.* Oxford: Elsevier.

Pekrun, R. (2005). Progress and open problems in educational emotion research. *Learning and Instruction, 15*(5), 497–506.

Pekrun, R. (2009). Global and local perspectives on human affect: Implications of the control-value theory of achievement emotions. In M. Wosnitza, S. A. Karabenick, A. Efklides, & P. Nenniger (Eds.), *Contemporary motivation research* (pp. 97–116). Göttingen: Hogrefe & Huber.

Pekrun, R., Elliot, A. J., & Maier, M. A. (2006). Achievement goals and discrete achievement emotions: A theoretical model and prospective test. *Journal of Educational Psychology, 98*(3), 583–597.

Pekrun, R., Götz, T., Titz, W. & Perry, R. P. (2002). Academic emotions in students' self-regulated learning and achievement: A program of qualitative and quantitative research. *Educational Psychologist, 37*(2), 91–106.

Perry, N. E., & Winne, P. H. (2006). Learning from learning kits: gStudy traces of students' self-regulated engagements with computerized content. *Educational Psychology Review, 18*, 211–238.

Petersen, P. (1937/1971). *Führungslehre des Unterrichts* [The doctrine of guidance in instruction] (10th ed.). Weinheim: Beltz.

Piaget, J. (1961). *La psychologie de l'intelligence* [The psychology of intellegence]. Paris: Armand Colin.

Piaget, J. (1967). *Logique et connaissance scientifique* [Logic and scientific knowledge]. Paris: Gallimard.

Pintrich, P. R. (2000). Multiple goals, multiple pathways: The role of goal orientation in learning and achievement. *Journal of Educational Psychology*, *92*, 544–555.

Pintrich, P. R. (2004). A conceptual framework for assessing motivation and self-regulated learning in college students. *Educational Psychology Review*, *16*, 385–407.

Pintrich, P. R., & DeGroot, E. V. (1990). Motivational and self-regulated learning components of classroom academic performance. *Journal of Educational Psychology*, *82*, 33–40.

Pintrich, P. R., & Garcia, T. (1994). Self-regulated learning in college students: Knowledge, strategies and motivation. In P. R. Pintrich, D. R. Brown, & C. E. Weinstein (Eds.), *Student motivation, cognition, and learning: Essays in honor of Wilbert J. McKeachie* (pp. 113–134). Hillsdale, NJ: Erlbaum.

Prenzel, M. (1988). *Die Wirkungsweise von Interesse. Ein pädagogisch-psychologisches Erklärungsmodell.* [The functioning of interest. A pedagogical and psychological explicatory model]. Opladen: Westdeutscher Verlag.

Pressley, M. (1995). More about the development of self-regulation: Complex, long-term, and thoroughly social. *Educational Psychologist*, *30*, 201–212.

Pugesek, B. H., Tomer, A., & von Eye, A. (Eds.). (2003). *Structural equation modelling: applications in ecological and evolutionary biology.* Cambridge: Cambridge University Press.

Puustinen, M. & Pulkkinen, L. (2001). Models of self-regulated learning: a review. *Scandinavian Journal of Educational Research*, *45*(3), 269–286.

Raidal, S. & Volet, S. E. (2009). Preclinical students' predispositions towards social forms of instruction and self-directed learning: A challenge for the development of autonomous and collaborative learners. *Higher Education*, *57*(5), 577–596.

Renninger, K. A., Hidi, S. & Krapp, A. (Eds.). (1992). *The role of interest in learning and development.* Hillsdale, NJ: Erlbaum.

Roberts, M. J., & Erdos, G. (1993). Strategy selection and metacognition. *Educational Psychology*, *13*, 259–266.

Ryan, R. M., Kuhl, J., & Deci, E. L. (1997). Nature and autonomy: An organizational view of social and neurobiological aspects of self-regulation in behavior and development. *Development and Psychopathology*, *9*, 701–728.

Ryan, R. M., & Deci, E. L. (2000). Self-determination theory and the facilitation of intrinsic motivation, social development, and well-being. *American Psychologist*, *55*, 68–78.

Schiefele, U. & Pekrun, R. (1996). Psychologische Modelle des fremdgesteuerten und selbstgesteuerten Lernens [Psychological models of other- and self-regulated learning.]. In F. E. Weinert (Ed.), *Enzyklopädie der Psychologie. Pädagogische Psychologie.* (Vol. 2, pp. 249–278). Göttingen: Hogrefe.

Schunk, D. H. (1989). Social-cognitive theory and self-regulated learning. In D. H. Schunk & B. J. Zimmerman (Eds.), *Self-regulated learning and academic achievement: Theory, research and practice* (pp. 83–110), New York: Springer-Verlag.

Schunk, D. H., & Zimmerman, B. J. (1997). Social origins of self-regulatory competence. *Educational Psychologist*, *32*(4), 195–208.

Sembill, D., Wolf, K., Wuttke, E., & Schumacher, L. (2003). Self-organized learning in vocational education—Foundation, implementation, and evaluation. In K. Beck (Ed.), *Teaching-learning processes in vocational education* (pp. 267–295). Berlin: Lang.

Snyder, M. (1974). Self Monitoring of expressive behavior. *Journal of Personality and Social Psychology*, *30*, 526–537.

Straka, G. A., & Nenniger, P. (1995). A conceptual framework for self-directed-learning readiness. In H. B. Long & Associates (Eds.), *New dimensions in self-directed learning* (pp. 243–255). Oklahoma City: University of Oklahoma.

Straka, G. A., Nenniger, P., Spevacek, G., & Wosnitza, M. (1996). A model for motivated self-directed learning. *Education*, *53*, 19–30.

Straka, G. A. & Macke, G. (2004). The impact of experienced work conditions on dimensions of self-directed learning. In M. Wosnitza, A. Frey, & R. S. Jäger (Eds.), *Lernprozess, Lernumgebung und Lerndiagnostik. Wissenschaftliche Beiträge zum Lernen im 21. Jahrhundert* (pp. 17–125). Landau: Verlag Empirische Pädagogik.

Straka, G. A., & Schaefer, C. (2002). Validating a more-dimensional conception of self-directed learning. In T. M. Egan & S. A. Lynham (Eds.), *Conference proceedings of the Academy of Human Resource Development (AHRD)* (Vol. 1, pp. 239–246). Honolulu, HI: Academy of Human Resource Development.

Van den Brink, K. (2006). Conceptual relations between "self-regulated learning" and "approaches to learning" (Unpublished doctoral dissertation). Faculty of Psychology, University of Koblenz-Landau, Landau.

Vermunt, J. D. (1996). Metacognitive, cognitive and affective aspects of learning styles and strategies. A phenomenographic analysis. *Higher Education*, *31*, 25–50.

Volet, S. E., Summers, M., & Thurman, J. (2009). High-level co-regulation in collaborative learning: How does it emerge and how is it sustained? *Learning and Instruction*, *19*(2), 128–143.

Weiner, B. (1986). *An attributional theory of motivation and emotion*. New York: Springer.

Weinstein. C. E., & Mayer, R. E. (1986). The teaching of learning strategies. In M. C. Wittrock (Ed.), *Handbook of research on teaching* (3rd ed., pp. 315–327). New York: Macmillan.

Wild, K. P. (1995). *Beziehungen zwischen Belohnungsstrukturen der Hochschule, motivationalen Orientierungen der Studierenden und individuellen Lernstrategien beim Wissenserwerb* [Relations between reward structures at the university, motivational orientations of students and individual learning strategies in the acquisition of knowledge] (Arbeiten zur Empirischen Pädagogik und pädagogischen Psychologie, Nr. 34. Gelbe Reihe). Neubiberg, Germany: Universität der Bundeswehr München.

Winne, P. H. (1995). Inherent details in self-regulated learning. *Educational Psychologist*, *30*, 173–187.

Winne, P. H. (2001). Self-regulated learning viewed from models of information processing. In B. J. Zimmerman & D. H. Schunk (Eds.), *Self-regulated learning and academic achievement* (2nd ed., pp. 153–189). Mahwah, NJ: Erlbaum.

Winne, P. H., and Hadwin, A. F. (1998). Studying as self-regulated learning. In D. J. Hacker, J. Dunlosky, & A. C. Graesser (Eds.), *Metacognition in educational theory and practice* (pp. 277–304). Mahwah, NY: Erlbaum.

Woodrow, D., & Sham, S. (2001). Chinese pupils and their learning preferences. *Race, Ethnicity and Education*, *4*, 377–394.

Wosnitza, M. & Nenniger, P. (2001). Perceived learning environments and the individual learning process: the mediating role of motivation in learning. In S. Volet & S. Järvelä (Eds.), *Motivation in learning contexts: Theoretical advances and methodological implications* (pp. 171–187). London: Elsevier.

Wosnitza, M. & Volet, S. E. (2009). A framework for personal content goals in social learning contexts. In M. Wosnitza, S. A. Karabenick, A. Efklides, & P. Nenniger (Eds.), *Contemporary motivation research: From global to local perspectives* (pp. 49–67). Göttingen and New York: Hogrefe & Huber.

Wu, T.-Y. (1977) *The learning process in the East Asian tradition* (Tung Ya ch'uan t'ung ti chih hsüeh fang fa yü ching shen). Occasional paper series, no. 60. Singapore: Institute of Humanities and Social Sciences, College of Graduate Studies, Nanyang University.

Yerkes, R. M. & Dodson, J. D. (1908). The relation of strength of stimulus to rapidity of habit formation. *Journal of Comparative Neurology and Psychology, 18*, 459–482.

Zimmerman, B. J. (1989). Models of self-regulated learning and academic achievement. In B. J. Zimmerman & D. H. Schunk (Eds.), *Self-regulated learning and academic achievement: Theory, research and practice* (pp. 1–25). New York: Springer-Verlag.

Zimmerman, B. J. (1990). Self-regulated learning and academic achievement: An overview. *Educational Psychologist, 25*, 3–17.

Zimmerman, B. J. (1995). Self-regulation involves more than meta-cognition: A social cognitive perspective. *Educational Psychologist, 30*, 217–221.

Zimmerman, B. J. (2000). Self-efficacy: An essential motive to learn. *Contemporary Educational Psychology, 25*, 82–91.

Zimmerman, B. J., & Schunk, D. H. (Eds.). (2001). *Self-regulated learning and academic achievement: Theoretical perspectives.* Hillsdale, NJ: Erlbaum.

8

Vocational Psychology

David L. Blustein, Kerri A. Murphy, Maria T. N. Coutinho, Christine Catraio, and Faedra R. Backus

As the field of vocational psychology passes its centennial (with its origin typically denoted by the publication of Frank Parsons' 1909 classic entitled *Choosing a Vocation*), attention has been devoted to assessing its current status and future trajectory (e.g., Blustein, 2006; Savickas & Baker, 2005). According to some scholars, the rich body of work that has been produced in vocational psychology has made enormous contributions to the welfare of individuals and organizations (see Herr, Cramer, & Niles, 2004; Robitschek & Woodson, 2006). Yet, Savickas and Baker argued that "by most accounts, the field of vocational psychology is at low ebb. Its contributions go unnoticed by most psychologists and few recruits enter the field" (p. 15). In this chapter, we explore the question of the vitality of vocational psychology using a wide-angle lens to examine the current status and future potential of the field. We seek to respond to the assessment of Savickas and Baker by reviewing the state of the discipline with the intention of providing a roadmap for the reinvigoration of the field. As we argue throughout this chapter, an essential tool in evaluating the current status and future opportunities for vocational psychology is to expand its purview, encompassing an explicit international focus and embracing everyone who works or wants to work (Athanasou & Van Esbroeck, 2008; Blustein, 2006).

Definitional and Historical Perspectives

Vocational psychology is known as the specialty within applied psychology that "conducts research to advance knowledge about vocational behavior, improve career interventions, and inform social policy about work issues" (Savickas & Baker, 2005, p. 15). In contrast to the related fields of work and organizational psychology, the emphasis of vocational psychology is on work-related concerns, dilemmas, and adjustment challenges at an individual level (Blustein, 2008). Vocational psychology provides the

IAAP Handbook of Applied Psychology, First Edition. Edited by Paul R. Martin, Fanny M. Cheung, Michael C. Knowles, Michael Kyrios, Lyn Littlefield, J. Bruce Overmier, and José M. Prieto.

theoretical and empirical support for career counseling, career development education, and public policy initiatives pertaining to education, career development, and labor policy (Savickas & Baker, 2005). Vocational psychology scholars generally work on the construction of assessment tools, development of career choice and development theories, exploration of intrapersonal, interpersonal, and more distal barriers and resources that influence career development, facilitation of the career decision-making and exploration processes, exploration of the interaction of work roles with other social roles, and expansion of the impact and efficacy of career interventions.

In short, vocational psychology is the specialty within applied psychology that seeks to provide the theoretical and empirical framework for work-related counseling, career development programs in schools and organizations, and public policy interventions. Career counseling represents the application of vocational psychology to the design and delivery of services to client populations (Athanasou & Van Esbroeck, 2008). Another term that is often used within vocational psychology is career development, in which the focus is on the processes by which individuals crystallize, specify, implement, and adjust to career choices (Super, Savickas, & Super, 1996). In this chapter, we focus on vocational psychology as the "figure" with career counseling and career development representing aspects of the "ground."

Among the professionals working within vocational psychology are academic scholars who teach and conduct research in universities, generally in counseling programs and to a lesser extent in counseling centers and other service provision agencies. Furthermore, some vocational psychologists work for government agencies and test development organizations. Career counseling practitioners in North America generally have a minimum of a master's degree in counseling or a related field and work in schools, government agencies, non-profit organizations, colleges and universities, organizations, and in independent practices. Career practitioners from other regions, such as Europe and Asia, often have a bachelor's degree in career counseling or vocational guidance; these degrees are generally more focused in their training than the broader liberal arts programs of North American universities (and often are consistent with master's level practitioners in North America).

In this chapter, we use the term *career* to denote work that reflects a relatively strong degree of individual volition and that represents a hierarchical trajectory of related jobs and training experiences (Super, 1983). Following the life-span view of career, we review the pre-implementation process of selecting and making work-based decisions, managing work-based challenges and transitions, and balancing overlapping life roles. We also include a focus on working in this chapter, which Blustein (2006) defined as involving "effort, activity, and human energy in given tasks that contribute to the overall social and economic welfare of a given culture. This includes paid employment as well as work that one does in caring for others within one's family and community" (p. 3).

Trends and Key Developments in Vocational Psychology

As reflected in the contributions of Parsons and other pioneers in this field (e.g., Kitson, 1925), the major questions that have been posed relate to how individuals can maximize their satisfaction and manifest their values, interests, and abilities in the world of work (Holland, 1997; Lent, Brown, & Hackett, 2002; Savickas, 2005). In this section, we review the major theoretical perspectives that have been used to explicate the career choice, development, and adjustment processes.

Holland's theory of career choice

Person–environment fit (P–E fit) theories, and indeed many of the major theoretical models within vocational psychology, endorse a view that individuals seek out occupations that provide a good fit between their attributes and the characteristics of a given work environment. The major assumptions of the P–E fit model are as follows: (1) the individual is capable of making rational decisions; (2) people and work environments differ in reliable, meaningful, and consistent ways; (3) the greater the congruence between the individual and the work environment, the greater the likelihood of a successful match (Chartrand, 1991). The P–E relationship is seen as a dynamic process in which the person and environment are mutually influential.

Holland's theory (Holland, 1997; Spokane & Cruza-Guet, 2005) and the theory of work adjustment (TWA; Dawis & Lofquist, 1984; Dawis, 2005) represent contemporary hallmarks of P–E-fit theory. (To conserve space, we focus on Holland's theory, which has generated the most research and practice applications. We refer readers to Dawis, 2005 for an overview of TWA.) Holland developed a taxonomy that encompasses six different personality and work environment types, organized within a hexagonal framework. Each of these six types (realistic, investigative, artistic, social, enterprising, and conventional) represents a cluster of interests and reflects relatively coherent personality types, denoting different problem-solving approaches, as well as interpersonal orientations. Individuals and environments are characterized by more than one type; a profile consisting of the three most predominant types is generally used to describe the individual and work environment (Spokane & Cruza-Guet, 2005).

The empirical research generated from Holland's theory has spanned a wide array of issues, including the study of choice congruence, the development and validation of measures, and the assessment of the effectiveness of P–E-fit-based interventions (Holland, 1997; Spokane & Cruza-Guet, 2005; Spokane, Luchetta & Richwine, 2002). Spokane and Cruza-Guet concluded their review of empirical research by noting that "a surprising amount (though certainly not all) of this research has been supportive of the existence of a limited set of [personalty and occupational] types, the underlying circular (or hexagonal) structure of those types, the validity of the instruments to measure types, and to a lesser extent, the interactive proposition of the theory" (p. 38).

Despite the primarily supportive conclusions reached by Spokane and Cruza-Guet (2005), critiques of Holland's theory have been raised regarding its applicability in relation to gender differences. For example, women tend to score higher on social and conventional types and these types often lead to lower paying jobs (Fitzgerald, Fassinger, & Betz, 1995). Questions have arisen about the utility of Holland's theory with women, as it has been criticized for supporting the status quo and conforming with traditional gender-based norms of occupational roles. While innovative assessments have been developed to reduce the impact of cultural and gender biases, the reality of interest development is that it is strongly influenced by socialization; as such, the differences noted in research parallel the reality of differential access to opportunities.

Spokane and Cruza-Guet's (2005) review identified considerable research that has replicated the Holland hexagon in different regions of the globe. However, our review of this literature reveals that while much consistency exists in the fundamental structure of interests, many of the samples in these studies consisted of college students and workers with a relative degree of choice in their lives. Questions remain regarding the utility of a choice model with individuals who do not have many options in their educational and work-based opportunities.

Developmental perspectives

The developmental position views one's work life within a nexus of relational, familial, community, and leisure-based life contexts across the life span (Super et al., 1996). Two of the most influential developmental perspectives identified in career theory include Super's (1980; Super et al., 1996) life-span, life-space theory of career development and Savickas' (2002, 2005) career construction theory. The life-span, life-space theory of career development (Super, 1957; Super et al., 1996) was developed over the course of 60 years through empirical research and critiques from researchers and practitioners about the limitations of P–E fit theories.

Super's theory (Super et al., 1996) addresses two primary dimensions: the first is known as the life-space or latitudinal dimension that refers to the roles or social space that an individual occupies; the second is the longitudinal dimension that depicts life stages. Additionally, the life-span, life-space perspective introduced a contextual dimension situating the work role in relation to other complementary and competing social roles enacted by individuals across the course of their lives, including *student*, *homemaker*, and *leisurite*, among others. Super believed that life structures change over time as individuals adapt to both predictable and unexpected work-based challenges. Developmental stages (i.e., growth, exploration, establishment, maintenance, and disengagement) are currently understood to be flexible as individuals recycle through developmental stages and tasks throughout their lives based on their dynamic circumstances and the salience of various roles throughout their lives (Super et al., 1996).

Although few would argue that Super's work has made hallmark contributions to the field of vocational psychology, it has been critiqued for being "segmented" and noncohesive in nature (Brown, 1990). Additionally, concerns have been raised about the relative lack of attention to the needs of women, people of color, and to the full scope of cultural and contextual factors that affect career decisions. Furthermore, Super's original propositions and career theory emerged during a time when many men spent their work lives in a single company or organization while many women worked as homemakers or in sexually segregated occupations. Super (1990; Super et al., 1996) addressed some of these concerns in his later work by applying his theory to women's career development and to the role of gender in the everyday social lives of individuals.

As a means of extending Super's work into the 21st century, Savickas (2002, 2005) developed career construction theory, which has emerged as one of the most important recent theoretical contributions in vocational psychology. Career construction theory "asserts that individuals construct their careers by imposing meaning on their vocational behavior and occupational experiences" (p. 43). Career construction theory, similar to Super's life-span, life-space theory, sought to augment P–E-fit theories, not to replace them. Savickas has devoted considerable effort to embedding his theory into an explicit contextual framework that affirms cultural influences and historical trends. For example, the use of the story as a cohering aspect of career development necessarily attends to distinctions in the impact of culture in framing how individuals construct meaning in their lives.

Savickas asserted that careers are constructed in the environment and that career development is characterized by *adaptation* to the environment as opposed to individuals' internal maturation processes. In other words, individuals construct their own realities, and their subsequent careers, based upon a particular social and cultural context (Savickas, 2005). As such, career construction theory has the unique capacity to have global relevance given its flexibility and its avoidance of rigid statements about the nature and trajectory of career development. Savickas further proposed that career construction theory takes into account an individual's subjective experience, past experiences and future aspirations related to work. From an applied perspective, the use of narrative counseling is central in helping clients to identify themes of vocational personality, general life themes, and career adaptability.

In sum, the contributions of both Super and Savickas have been instrumental in underscoring that career choice and development occur in a context that has developmental, social, political, and relational dimensions. The initial contributions by Super furnished a clear trajectory of the ebbs and flows of work across the spectrum of human development. Savickas' contributions have thoughtfully advanced the constructivist scaffolding of Super's work. When considered collectively, the developmental perspectives have been central in expanding the vision of vocational psychologists beyond unitary choices about work and circumscribed adjustment challenges at work. One of the most salient growth edges for the developmental perspectives is to integrate recent advances in developmental theory, such as the contributions of Lerner (2002). Another challenge, which is endemic to existing perspectives in vocational psychology, is to expand theory development to include the work lives of individuals with less choice in their lives.

Social cognitive career theory

Social cognitive career theory (SCCT; Lent et al., 2002) emerged out of the cognitive revolution as an attempt to unify multiple career theories and to offer a recursive model of causality in the career decision and adjustment processes. Self-efficacy is one of the central components of SCCT and refers to the dynamic set of self-beliefs that are domain-specific and that interact complexly with other personal, behavioral and environmental factors (Lent et al.). People are thought to develop interests when they view themselves as competent in an activity and anticipate that performing that activity will produce valued outcomes.

In the original application of social cognitive theory to vocational psychology, Betz and Hackett (1981) provided compelling evidence that self-efficacy is a major factor in understanding the circumscribed aspirations of women, particularly in relation to occupations that have traditionally been dominated by men. This focus on gender issues has foreshadowed an emphasis on using social cognitive theory to delineate how contextual factors frame the career development process. While SCCT has clearly expanded the emphasis on context in career development, it has also been critiqued for not going far enough in transcending the individualistic focus of most career development theories (Blustein, McWhirter, & Perry, 2005; Chronister & McWhirter, 2003). More specifically, discrimination and oppression in the workforce are external factors, which are not easily overcome by strengthened self-efficacy in a particular domain for individuals of color, women, LGBT individuals, and those with disabling conditions (Blustein et al., 2005). While self-efficacy is inarguably a powerful factor in many aspects of career development processes, the factors that shape self-efficacy are not universally distributed and vary considerably based on individual differences and societal affordances (Blustein, 2006).

In addition to SCCT, Peterson, Lumsden, Sampson, Reardon, and Lenz (2002) have developed another important cognitive-based theory, known as Cognitive Information Processing (CIP). This theory utilizes thought and memory process research in addition to problem-solving research to inform career decision-making processes for individuals. While space limitations prohibit a more detailed examination of CIP, this theoretical contribution holds promise as a potentially rich framework to work with clients who experience some degree of choice in their working lives.

Social constructionist and contextual action theory

The social constructionist view, from which contextual action theory (Young & Valach, 2004) is based, asserts that knowledge is constructed through social processes and is not universal (Blustein, 2006). Social constructionist thought draws from a multidisciplinary base including sociology, literary studies, and postmodern approaches to epistemology (Young & Collin, 2004). According to this perspective, knowledge is situated within the context, and therefore is historically and culturally bound. Moreover, language is considered not as a reflection of reality but as "both a pre-condition for thought and a form of social action" (Young & Collin, 2004, p. 377). Social constructionist perspectives challenge logical positivist assumptions and question the status quo, allowing for voices of those who are often ignored to be included in the psychological discourse and for oppressive practices to be examined and challenged . Some fundamental strengths of this perspective, according to Young and Collin, are the opportunities to challenge fundamental assumptions and to examine the person and environment interaction and the role of context and culture in vocational theory and practice.

Richardson's (1993) contribution initially outlined a social constructionist agenda for vocational psychology, observing how the experience of working is co-constructed within relationships and, more broadly, within cultural and social contexts. More recently, Richardson and colleagues (Richardson, Constantine, & Washburn, 2005) have adopted a post-modern stance to the study of working. Her perspective of postmodernism encompasses a challenge to the notion that a universal reality exists in conjunction with an argument that theory be developed with the goal of being useful. An exemplar of this approach can be found in the Richardson et al. (2005) definition of vocational psychology as a "field [that] is comprised of theory, research, and intervention practices, that is committed to the importance of work and relationships in people's lives, to helping people live healthy and productive lives, to social justice, especially with respect to providing access to opportunity for those marginalized or disadvantaged due to social locations such as gender, race, and class" (p. 59). Following this definition, Richardson et al. argue that vocational psychological theory needs to explicate how people can live healthy lives professionally and personally, which she believes are two core aspects of the sociocultural context of most contemporary societies. The contribution of Richardson et al. (2009) on the role of intention in identity formation and expression holds particular promise in understanding the subtle processes by which individuals construct their beliefs and values about their work lives.

Young and Valach, also relying upon social constructionist assumptions, have advanced a contextual action theory, with a focus on goal-directed action (Valach & Young, 2004; Young & Valach, 2004). The contextual position, according to Young and Valach, seeks to explore the meaning that individuals construct in relation to preimplementation and postimplementation work-related behavior. As Young and Valach have argued, meaning arises amidst joint actions that entail individuals interacting with others in their lives (parents, friends, counselors, etc.).

Another important development in social constructionist thought has been advanced by Guichard (2005; Guichard & Dumora, 2008). Reflecting the rich philosophical tradition that has emerged from French intellectual life, Guichard has sought to explicate how self-construction functions for individuals seeking to find meaning in their work lives. Individuals' identities are described as dynamic psychological structures in which individuals construct their array of possible selves (Guichard, J., personal communication, 18 February, 2009). Like Young and Valach (2004), Guichard endorses the notion that subjective experience and evolving self-constructions need to be enacted in action plans. Moreover, Guichard argues cogently that self-construction occurs over the life span.

Major Research Initiatives in Vocational Psychology: An Illustrative Review

In the material that follows, we review several issues, which we believe capture the most important lines of inquiry in contemporary vocational psychology. The selection of these topics is based on our objective of defining the parameters of the discipline and of outlining a roadmap for the reinvigoration of the field.

Gender and vocational psychology

As an outgrowth of the feminist movement, a number of scholars (e.g., Betz & Hackett, 1981; Harmon, 1973; Richardson, 1974) have identified structural problems in the vocational psychology of the mid 20th century, primarily defined by its focus on men and its portrayal of issues regarding family and work as a "woman's concern." In Fassinger's (2008) summary, numerous disadvantages for women at work were detailed, including less pay for the same work, sexist practices in education, training, and the workplace, and sexual harassment. These practices, when considered collectively, result in a "chilly" work environment, underscoring sexist practices throughout many social systems around the globe.

In addition, Fassinger (2008) noted that girls and women continue to be underrepresented in the science, technology, engineering, and math (STEM) career pipeline in the United States and in many other nations. STEM skills have become increasingly important in providing individuals with the capacity to assume high technology positions in the workplace, which help to generate new jobs and improvements in productivity, thereby enhancing the wealth of communities and nations (National Science Foundation, 2004). From an individual perspective, improvements in the quality and quantity of individuals in the STEM pipeline can be instrumental in furnishing people with access to upward social mobility (National Science Foundation, 2004). As detailed in the educational and work-based literatures (e.g., Fassinger, 2008; Seymour & Hewitt, 1997), various factors function to reduce access to STEM courses, STEM-related career exploration, and STEM-based career plans. These factors include sexist attitudes in STEM courses by teachers and students, lower expectations for girls and women in STEM courses, and structural barriers in STEM careers, such as inadequate opportunities for balancing work and family (Ceci & Williams, 2007; Chapa & De La Rosa, 2006).

The next step in gender and work research is to explore the impact of gender role socialization on various aspects of work-related behavior with a focus on both women and men. According to Mahalik et al. (2005), "gender role norms ... provide guidance for women and men about how they are supposed to act, think, and feel, as well as constrain women and men from certain behaviors that are 'off limits' (Gilbert & Scher, 1999)" (p. 417). Mahalik and his colleagues have articulated a multidimensional construct to account for conformity to masculine and feminine gender norms (Mahalik et al., 2003, 2005). This body of work has been useful in explicating various aspects of psychological functioning that are gendered in complex and nuanced ways. We believe that the integration of new advances in a gendered psychology (e.g., Good & Brooks, 2005; Kimmel, 2007) can powerfully advance our understanding of vocational psychology.

Culture, race, and vocational psychology

The multicultural movement has profoundly influenced the direction of contemporary psychology across both applied and basic research domains (Berry, Poortinga, & Pandey, 1997; Ponterotto, Casas, Suzuki, & Alexander, 2001). Similarly, vocational psychology has been transformed as scholars have increasingly sought to understand how culture and race impact various aspects of vocational behavior (Helms & Piper, 1994; Stead, 2004, 2007). Consistent with Helms and Cook (1999), we define race as a phenotypic attribute of individuals that evokes a wide array of responses. Following Stead's (2004) analysis, culture refers to "the historical nature of a group of people, and reflects on their norms, beliefs, symbols, and traditions (Bauman, 1999). Culture is not a static phenomenon but alters and adjusts to increasing contact with people from other cultures" (p. 393).

When considered collectively, race and culture are thought to be social constructs that derive meaning within micro-level interpersonal interactions and within macro-level historical, social, and political contexts. Stead (2004) critiqued the dominant discourse based on logical positivism by observing that many of the major constructs in vocational psychology (self-concept, self-efficacy, interests, etc.) are relevant to circumscribed communities and are not endemic to vocational life around the globe. This observation is buttressed by a review of the chapters in the Athanasou and Van Esbroeck (2008) collection, which reveals considerable distinctions in theoretical formulations, assessment, and educational and career guidance practices around the globe.

Decision making, exploration, and vocational psychology

Following the seminal work of Super (1957, 1990), research on career decision making and exploration have been hallmarks of vocational psychology. In the decision-making realm, one of the most noteworthy initiatives has sought to conceptualize rational and nonrational approaches to making educational and work-based decisions. Rational approaches, which have emerged from Parsons' notions, are based on the use of a long-term view and systematic analysis of options; nonrational approaches are characterized by the reliance on one's intuition or emotional knowledge and/or the input and support of others in one's relational context.

The scholarship of Gati has perhaps best exemplified the rational perspective. Using cognitive models and computer-based analogs, Gati and Tal (2008) developed a prescriptive decisional model, which includes prescreening, in-depth exploration, and choice (PIC). This model uses scholarship from vocational psychology (e.g., Parsons, 1909; Holland, 1997), as well as decisional theory (e.g., Janis & Mann, 1977), in advancing a set of prescriptive recommendations that are thought to enhance one's decisional outcomes. Phillips and Jome (2005) noted that it is difficult to assess the utility of a prescriptive model such as the Gati and Tal contribution, noting that "not only did the available evidence refute the notion that a classical 'rational' model accurately reflects real-life decision-making processes, but also that there was little reason to even consider the classical model adaptive in the context of career decisions" (p. 138). Phillips and Jome then detailed the challenges to rational decision making, including the limitations of human information processing and the reality that a host of other factors likely influence the nature and outcomes of career-related decisions.

A further examination of the Phillips and Jome (2005) critique reveals another line of decision-making theory and research that merits attention in this chapter. Beginning with an empirical exploration of decision-making styles, Phillips and her colleagues concluded that rational decision making may not be as essential in the real-world of career choice and development (e.g., Phillips, 1997). Instead, Phillips has suggested that intuitive and relationally embedded approaches to decisional tasks may in fact be adaptive as these approaches provide a means for consultation with others as well as the inclusion of emotion and intuition, which are central in psychological functioning.

The career exploration area also has generated informative findings in recent scholarship. Career exploration entails activities, both internal and external to the person, which are designed to enhance self-knowledge and knowledge of one's educational and occupational contexts (Blustein, 1997). During the past few decades, scholars have identified several factors that promote exploration, including self-efficacy, some degree of immanence, and an internalized motivational orientation (Bartley & Robitschek, 2000; Blustein, 1997). As Bartley and Robitschek noted, analyses using the predictors identified thus far in the empirical literature only accounted for approximately one third of the variance in exploratory behavior. Given the modest variance that has been identified to date in the empirical research, we believe that further theory development is needed to advance scholarship in career exploration.

In this vein, the Flum and Blustein (2000) contribution used self-determination theory (Ryan & Deci, 2000) as one of the intellectual foundations for a renewed theoretical framework in career exploration. Flum and Blustein observed that exploration provides a means for individuals to author their own work-based narratives, thereby enhancing their sense of control and autonomy. Flum and Blustein also argued that exploration can facilitate the internalization of externally motivating factors that can ultimately be instrumental in promoting self-determination. Taken together, theory and research on career exploration underscore the need for more research, optimally based on theoretical formulations that are culturally embedded and expansive with respect to the diversity of people who work and who seek to work.

Work adjustment in adulthood: A selected review

While vocational psychology has typically focused on preimplementation issues, a considerable body of research and theory has been devoted to the individual's adjustment after the transition to the working world. We have selected a few illustrative issues that underscore the range and depth of issues facing adults as they grapple with work-related tasks.

Work–family interactions. Work–family conflict refers to the complications and challenges that can arise in balancing work and family responsibilities. Previous research has indicated that the work environment predicts work-family conflict (e.g., Barnett & Hyde, 2001; Carlson, 1999). More specifically, job satisfaction and low work–family conflict are associated with work environments in which employers are perceived to value their employee's life outside of work (Grandey, Cordeiro, & Michael, 2007; Haddock, Zimmerman, Ziemba, & Lyness, 2006).

Barnett and Hyde (2001) proposed an expansionist theory that argues that multiple roles are advantageous. Their perspective is primarily based on majority culture in the US (i.e., middle class, White, heterosexual) and the idea that "we do not presume to have proposed a timeless, universal theory" (p. 794). Barnett and Hyde challenge the conventional views that men and women have innate roles, that multiple roles are inherently stressful, and that traditional theories about gender and work do not reflect the current reality for both women and men.

Unemployment. Unemployment can be one of the most difficult challenges in life and serves as a direct threat to the survival of an individual and his/her family. Previous research has shown that unemployment is associated with poor health (McKee-Ryan, Song, Wanberg, & Kinicki, 2005) and negatively impacts psychological well-being (Thomas, Benzeval, & Stansfeld, 2005). One of the key roles for vocational psychologists is to conduct research and develop effective practices (both at the individual and systemic levels) to assist individuals struggling with adjustments in employment. Fouad and Bynner (2008) also suggested that psychologists can advocate for supportive policies, such as family leave, flexible employment policies, affordable child care, and the promotion of career readiness skills that goes beyond obtaining a job and also promotes an individual's ability to maintain employment. Fouad and Bynner further highlighted that government resources are important in supporting individuals through difficult and unpredictable transitions, such as unemployment, especially individuals living in poverty or struggling with the transition from school to work.

Challenges and Opportunities for Vocational Psychology

Our review thus far has highlighted the many ways in which vocational psychology has been able to conceptualize the personal and occupational dimensions of work and career for a wide variety of people. However, as Savickas and Baker (2005) observed, vocational psychology is not effectively expanding or reinforcing its ranks with younger scholars. Our view of this dilemma is based on a critical assessment of the limitations of current discourse in vocational psychology. We believe that traditional theories are constrained in their capacity to include the work needs and experiences of those with little or no volition in their work lives. We have developed an excellent scholarly foundation that can explicate the vocational lives of a small proportion of the globe's population. As an alternative, Blustein (2006) proposed the psychology-of-working perspective, which seeks to draw attention to the importance of work in all of our lives, including careful consideration of the contextual factors that influence one's work experiences.

Psychology of working: A new framework for vocational psychology

One of the core elements of the psychology of working is the explicit focus on including all working people (and those who are seeking to enter the workforce) under the intellectual "tent" of vocational psychology. In addition, the psychology-of-working perspective seeks to understand the connections among working and other life experiences, including relationships, citizenship, and caregiving roles (Blustein, 2006). A key element of the psychology of working is the identification of three primary potential functions that working can fulfill in one's life.

The first function of working is as a source of survival and power; simply put, paid employment furnishes the means by which individuals obtain food and shelter, as well as power and social status. Many people without the luxury of choosing a volitional and self-determined career path work primarily to provide for their families, with little to no status or power resulting from their employment.

The second function of working is as a means of social connection (Blustein, 2006). Optimally, working provides people with access to others, typically in a consistent and predictable fashion that can nurture our natural strivings for relational connections (Flum, 2001). In addition, working furnishes people with a means of contributing to the overall public welfare, which can enhance the connection that people experience to society in general.

The third function that working can fulfill is self-determination, which is derived from Deci and Ryan's motivational theory (1985; Ryan & Deci, 2000). Self-determination refers to the experience of pursuing activities because they are intrinsically interesting and/or fulfill objectives that are valued (Deci & Ryan, 1985). This role focuses on the connection between work and motivation, highlighting three contextual factors that can make work more relevant and meaningful in one's life: autonomy, relatedness, and competence. If these three conditions are present, even difficult and seemingly unrewarding work has the potential to become a source of self-worth and value in one's life.

Implicit in the above concepts, but warranting additional attention in the analysis of working, is the issue of social barriers and working. Vast and troubling inequalities in access to the world of work continue to plague most societies around the globe, with racism, classism, sexism, ableism, and heterosexism playing a pervasive role in access to work, compensation, and in the dignity afforded to people (Blustein, 2006, 2008; Helms & Cook, 1999; Richardson, 2000). Work clearly plays a very different role in one's life when it is unfair, unreliable, and low-paying as opposed to when it is fair, steady, and financially rewarding. With a few exceptions (e.g., Harmon & Farmer, 1983; Smith, 1983; Richardson, 1993), most of the discourse in vocational psychology has focused on middle-class, relatively privileged populations who have a modicum of volition in their education, training, and work-related decisions. We believe that an expanded agenda for vocational psychology can provide a powerful antidote to the malaise in the field that was described by Savickas and Baker (2005).

Globalization: A challenge and an opportunity

Globalization, characterized by important technological advances, open markets, and, subsequently, increased levels of interdependence and connection at the individual and national level, has had a tremendous impact on the world of work (Coutinho, Dam, & Blustein, 2008; Friedman, 2006; Paredes et al., 2008). There is a lack of consensus on the definition of globalization, and often discussions of this topic seem to favor definitions that emphasize the economic conceptualization of globalization (Paredes et al., 2008). In most analyses of globalization, an emphasis has been placed on the openness of economic markets, the interdependence of the world economy, and advances in transportation and communication technologies which allow for rapid and efficient exchange of goods and services across the world (Friedman, 2006; Paredes et al., 2008). In addition, with the greater accessibility of mobile telephones, televisions, and computers, a transformation is taking place in the ease and manner in which individuals communicate ideas, and the way cultural values and traditions coexist throughout the world (Friedman, 2006).

The changes wrought by globalization have serious implications in the world of work. A growing sense of job insecurity across work sectors is evident in that many workers are faced with often considerable changes in positions across their working lives, as well as greater competition for work and often less beneficial working conditions and pay (Coutinho et al., 2008; Paredes et al., 2008). In addition, the work structure has changed dramatically, with many people working flexible schedules, including part-time, temporary, and freelance positions as well as working from home and other remote locations.

Vocational psychologists are faced with the challenge of staying abreast of these changes so that our research and practices are consistent with the intense and shifting needs that clients face in managing their work lives. Workers without the guarantee of long-term employment are compelled to be flexible and to be able to identify skill sets that are marketable and employable (Paredes et al., 2008). Increasingly blurred boundaries between work and personal lives require that psychologists are prepared to intervene and develop plans that address issues in a broad array of life arenas (work, relationships, coping skills, etc). In addition, due to the increased mobility of the world population, vocational psychologists need to be ready to work with an increasingly diverse population in terms of race, culture, gender, sexual orientation, and religious affiliation (Blustein, 2006; Paredes et al., 2008).

Global poverty

An issue that has been on the periphery of the prevailing vocational psychological discourse is that of global poverty. We believe that one of the means of reinvigorating our specialty is to tackle some of the thorny work-based problems that have long plagued working people (and people who want to work). Recent analyses reveal that there are approximately 2.5 billion people (40% of the population) living in poverty throughout the world (Sachs, 2005). According to Sachs, a wide range of social, political, and environmental factors have contributed to economic growth and global standing, such as geographic location/natural resources, government policies and stability, economic growth or stagnation, and science and technology. Economic growth and the implementation of effective and focused social programs are critical to end poverty. Although sustained economic growth is associated with the reduction of poverty rates, some countries with growth have also experienced difficulties in reducing poverty.

The crisis of global poverty, at first glance, might seem too pervasive and pernicious for vocational psychologists to have any meaningful impact. However, one of the key ameliorative conditions to a strong economy is an educated population that is well trained to meet the economic challenges of the 21st century. In our view, the relationship between the expansion of the world of work and vocational guidance activities is recursive. Most scholars have viewed the industrial revolution as the major impetus to the development of career guidance (O'Brien, 2001; Savickas & Baker, 2005). However, we also believe that focused and effective work-based scholarship and systematic interventions can enhance the quality of a citizenry to assume increasingly diverse and productive work roles, thereby facilitating greater occupational attainment, and ideally greater wealth production for a given nation or community.

While the solutions are complex and will necessarily be multifaceted, we believe that vocational psychologists can play a significant role in the public policy teams that are seeking to ameliorate global poverty. One contribution that can be immediately helpful is an expansion of research on the connection between educational attainment and career development education. By ensuring that academic development is linked to the labor market needs and growth potential of a given region, vocational psychologists may be able to help a community focus limited resources on maximizing student performance and developing the most competitive workforce possible at a given point in time. From a more macro-level perspective, we believe that vocational psychology scholarship can document the importance of work in people's lives. Some of this has been detailed in recent vocational psychology (e.g., Blustein, 2006; Richardson, 1993; 2000) and in other social scientific literatures (e.g., Lamont, 2000; Wilson, 1996).

Another potential tool to tackle pervasive and structural poverty is the enhancement of career development interventions for individuals with less than adequate choices in education and work. Blustein, Kenna, Gill, and DeVoy (2008) described interventions that might be particularly useful in working with clients without much education and training. The recommendations included an explicit focus on skill building, empowerment, enhancing critical consciousness, and scaffolding toward greater volition (via social and political advocacy on the part of counselors and psychologists).

The aging population

Aging workers represent another population whose unique work-related contributions and challenges are often overlooked (Perry & Parlamis, 2006; Sterns & Miklos, 1995). For the most part, mandatory retirement ages are enforced at national, occupational, and company levels across the globe, forcing workers to step down from their jobs once they have reached a predetermined age. Often, governments and companies justify mandatory retirement with the argument that workers cannot optimally fulfill their job requirements once they experience the mental and physical changes that are assumed to come with age (Sterns & Miklos, 1995). However, this observation is not consistent with empirical research in aging, which has indicated that "there is no difference between job performance of older and younger workers" (Warr, 1994, p. 309). Perry and Parlamis concluded that the "lack of an *overall* [italics in original] relationship between age and job performance may be explained by the fact that although age is related to declines (e.g., response speed, working memory), these may be offset by other factors (e.g., experience) and they are likely to occur after the age at which people retire from the workforce (Greller & Simpson, 1999; Warr, 1994)" (p. 351).

Though aging workers often possess the power to make their own decisions about the timing of retirement, economic conditions have forced many older and aging workers to postpone retirement or to return to work after an initial retirement, with the primary cause of aging workers postponing retirement being lack of financial security (Sargeant, 2004). As economic conditions continue to change and members of the baby-boomer generation increasingly move into retirement, it will be necessary for vocational psychologists to recognize and respond to the unique needs of these workers. In addition, as Perry and Parlamis noted, the prevalence of age discrimination at the workplace requires extensive research and public policy advocacy.

Future Developments in the Field

Consistent with Savickas and Baker (2005), one can argue that vocational psychology, when examined via the lens of 20th-century theories and problems, is stagnating. However, as we push the boundaries of vocational psychology to embrace all workers and potential workers around the globe and to affirm diverse global perspectives, the challenges and the framework for intellectual rejuvenation are also evident. In this section, we identify several important new trajectories for vocational psychology that can help to create the framework for a more inclusive discipline that can respond to a broader and more challenging array of problems.

Localized knowledge and global knowledge

One of the key points of the social constructionist critique of traditional social scientific discourse is that knowledge is rarely, if at all, universal (Blustein, Schultheiss, & Flum, 2004). We believe that this is particularly pertinent in vocational psychology where cultural beliefs, economic factors, historical trends, and political realities have such a profound effect on the nature of education and work (Blustein, 2006; Stead, 2004). For the most part, the vocational psychology of the 20th century has sought to achieve a universal appeal, with broad, sweeping statements about the utility of P–E fit, the importance of autonomy in career decision making, and the value of individualistic achievement. We believe that a major growth edge exists in the development of localized theories, often derived from indigenous psychologies.

Using the South African context, Stead and Watson (2006) described the importance of indigenous psychologies by noting the limitations in importing psychological knowledge and practices from the US and other Western nations to countries that do not share many common cultural attributes with European–American cultures. The essence of indigenous psychologies is the valuing of aspects of knowledge and culture that are unique to a given setting. Just as many of the concepts in North America and Europe reflect inherent values of these cultures, vocational psychology emerging from other regions of the world should strive to integrate cultural artifacts and realities that are unique to a given community.

By affirming indigenous psychology, we are also providing a means for the creation of localized knowledge that can help to advance the work lives of individuals around the globe. Consistent with the position of Stead and Watson (2006), we advocate that localized theories and research, based on an explicit incorporation of cultural values, are necessary to advance the work lives of individuals across diverse communities. Building on the Stead and Watson framework, we believe that a reciprocal relationship exists between localized knowledge and universal knowledge. In this vein, localized knowledge may suggest some broader themes and issues among populations living in different cultural contexts; clearly, these observations and findings would need to be evaluated in different communities and regions of the world.

At the same time, tenets that form the essence of traditional vocational psychology theory should be evaluated for their efficacy in a given cultural context before being adopted for use in counseling practice and public policy. For example, the Western value of individuals selecting an occupation or field based on their own values, interests, and dreams may not be viable in communities where collectivist values reign and the needs of the community are viewed as more important than individual needs. We believe that vocational psychologists need to be aware of their values and how their values may influence their scholarship and practice.

The methodologies employed for localized research may vary, ranging from traditional positivistic theory-testing studies to exploratory narrative investigations (Stead & Watson, 2006). The important factor in developing localized theories is to derive meaningful constructs from the lived experience of individuals in a given culture. Given the need to develop theories from the ground up, it is likely that qualitative and narrative tools will be most useful. We also believe that localized theories will be particularly useful in developing the sort of vocational psychological practices and public policy input that can support movements to reduce and eradicate global poverty.

Vocational psychology and public policy

Another promising future direction for vocational psychology can be built upon recent efforts by scholars around the globe (e.g., Blustein, 2006; Herr, 2003; Santos & Ferreira, 1998; Watts, Law, Killeen, Kidd, & Hawthorn 1996) to generate public policy recommendations from vocational psychology research. One particularly compelling exemplar of this movement is found in the recommendations by the National Career Development Association of the US, which has advanced a legislative agenda to guide government policy. These recommendations (detailed in the following website: http://associationdatabase.com/aws/NCDA/pt/sd/news_article/5502/_self/layout_details/false) include proposals about worker training, the importance of creating individualized career plans in high school, and practitioner training.

An area that we believe is particularly ripe for public policy input is in creating and revising educational policy on the linkage between education and work (Blustein, 2006). Considerable public debate has taken place about the significant challenges that many nations face in preparing students for the 21st-century workforce (Reich, 2000; Wilson, 1996). Various initiatives around the globe (e.g., Heinz, 2002; Kenny et al., 2007) have provided strong rationales and programs that enhance the linkage between school and future work options. The basic assumption of these efforts is that students may not easily internalize the fact that academic skills can translate into a volitional and satisfying work life. Given the evidence that this sort of internalization is indeed adaptive for students (Kenny et al., 2007; Solberg, Howard, Blustein, & Close, 2002), we believe that scholarship devoted to enhancing our understanding of the school–work linkage is essential. Moreover, the findings from these studies have the potential to shape school reform efforts around the globe.

Internalizing the context

As we noted earlier in the discussion about gender and race, recent developments in these areas have focused less on biological distinctions and more on the social constructions of these human attributes. This literature has identified important insights into the way in which race (Helms & Cook, 1999), gender (Mahalik et al., 2005), and ethnicity (Phinney & Ong, 2007) are internalized into psychological structures and belief systems. Indeed, some of the most important research in psychology in recent years has been devoted to the complex ways in which individuals internalize their demographic attributes (Helms & Cook, 1999), their gender roles (Mahalik et al., 2005), their motivational orientations (Ryan & Deci, 2000), and their cultural contexts (Berry, Phinney, Sam, & Vedder, 2006). While we believe that vocational psychologists need to create scholarship that will compel more equitable policies, we are aware that a focus on individual psychology is both our heritage and our area of specialty. Moreover, by examining how social barriers are internalized, we can further document the pernicious impact of racism, sexism, heterosexism, and the like.

Two particularly compelling constructs that may be fruitful in subsequent vocational psychological scholarship are racial identity status and gender role conformity. Helms and Piper (1994) outlined the many ways the internalization of the social construction of race can affect individuals of color as well as majority populations in multiracial contexts. In regard to gender, the contributions of Mahalik and his colleagues have identified the multifaceted ways that conformity to gender role norms affects many aspects of psychological functioning, such as health behaviors (Mahalik, Burns, & Syzdek, 2007), attitudes toward gay and lesbian sexual orientations (Mahalik et al., 2003), and vocational personality types (Mahalik, Perry, Coonerty-Femiano, Catraio, & Land, 2006). We believe that further research on these constructs and other forms of internalization may be informative in the development of the next generation of theories and practices on working.

An expanded view of an adaptive work life

One of the major limitations of the 20th-century approach to vocational psychology has been the rather circumscribed focus on career choice satisfaction, job tenure, and congruence as viable work-related outcomes (Holland, 1997; Super et al., 1996). While we certainly advocate for the creation of social and economic structures to support increased opportunities so that more and more people can experience congruence and satisfaction, we do not believe that vocational psychologists should continue to ignore the vast majority of workers who do not have much access to the resources needed to create a volitional work life.

In this context, we recommend that vocational psychologists consider three interrelated dimensions of working as part of the array of adaptive outcomes for working people. One dimension is devoted to a dignified working life. Dignity at work is characterized by safe and healthy working conditions, work-based relationships that honor diversity, respect for human rights, occupational safety considerations, respectful supervisors, and access to humane policies on work-family conflicts (Lamont, 2000). Two other relevant dimensions are Savickas' (2005) notions of meaning and mattering. Savickas noted that "rather than choose among attractive options, some individuals may have to take the only job that is available to them, often a job that grinds on the human spirit because its tasks are difficult, tedious, and exhausting. Nevertheless, the work that they do can be meaningful to them and matter to their community" (p. 44).

Exploring these three dimensions, naturally, engenders some complications. First, they are very difficult to define operationally. Second, these attributes may inadvertently serve to reduce the focus on the injustices that exist that create privileged and less privileged working lives. (Privileged working lives generally reflect the manifestation of internal values, interests, and aspirations in the world of work. Less privileged working lives are characterized by the attainment of jobs that are often not consistent with one's hopes and dreams, primarily as a means of survival.) However, the advantage of exploring dignity encourages vocational psychologists to confront inequities at work that may result in abusive or discriminatory contexts. The focus on meaning and mattering may function to give voice to the full range of working people who have been neglected in vocational psychology. By encouraging all working people to share their experiences of meaning and mattering, we have an opportunity to gain expanded insight into the nature of working in the 21st century.

International, cross-cultural, and interdisciplinary collaboration

Given the challenges noted in this chapter, we believe that a core future direction that will enhance scholarship and practice is international and interdisciplinary collaboration. As globalization continues to diversify the workforce and create international organizations and scholarly communities, we must make a collaborative effort to understand the work lives of citizens of all countries and communities. One of the manifestations of globalization is the increasing linkage of intellectual ideas across national and geographic boundaries. While there are some exceptions (Fouad & Bynner, 2008; McMahon & Watson, 2007; Reitzle & Vondracek, 2000), much of the knowledge in vocational psychology has not benefited from cross-national and cross-cultural fertilization. The advent of multicultural career counseling, which has emerged from the multicultural movement within psychology, writ large (Helms & Cook, 1999), has provided a useful foundation for the development of a more inclusive and culturally affirming vocational psychology.

In addition, we believe that vocational psychologists need to develop interdisciplinary research teams to tackle the full scope of problems that working presents in the 21st century. A review of related fields such as occupational sociology (Vallas, Finlay, & Wharton, 2009; Wilson, 1996), management (Arthur, 1996; Hall, 1996), industrial/organizational psychology (Spector, 2006), and public policy (Friedman, 2006) reveals a wealth of knowledge about the massive shifts in the workplace, globalization, the impact of lack of work in the lives of people and communities, and a host of other pressing challenges.

Conclusion

While many of the overt indices of the health of a given discipline no doubt support many of the Savickas and Baker (2005) observations noted at the outset of this chapter, we believe that the seeds of rejuvenation are clearly evident. The sources of an expanded and intellectually compelling vocational psychology for the 21st century lie in the adoption of a wide-angle lens that also can view the depth and nuance of vocational behavior around the globe. Consistent with the psychology-of-working movement (Blustein, 2006; Richardson, 1993), we envision that vocational psychology will be transformed as it embraces the full gamut of workers and individuals who want to work. In addition, we anticipate that the massive shifts in the economy will force a parallel reappraisal of vocational psychology as the reality of working becomes increasingly unstable even for the relatively privileged workers who have been the focus of traditional vocational psychology research and practice. We hope that our contribution will facilitate the emergence of a vocational psychology that will help current and future generations of students and workers create work lives of dignity, meaning, and mattering, and, optimally, of self-determination.

References

Arthur, M. B. (1996). Career development and participation at work: Time for mating? *Human Resource Management*, *27*, 181–200.

Athanasou, J. A., & Van Esbroeck, R. (Eds.). (2008). *International handbook of career guidance.* London: Springer.

Barnett, R. C., & Hyde, J. S. (2001). Women, men, work, and family. *American Psychologist*, *56*, 781–796.

Bartley, D. F., & Robitschek, C. (2000). Career exploration: A multivariate analysis of predictors. *Journal of Vocational Behavior*, *56*, 63–81.

Bauman, Z. (1999). *Culture as praxis.* London: Sage.

Berry, J. W., Phinney, J. S., Sam, D. L., & Vedder, P. (Eds.). (2006). *Immigrant youth incultural transition: Acculturation, identity, and adaptation across national contexts.* Mahwah, NJ: Lawrence Erlbaum Associates Publishers.

Berry, J. W., Poortinga, Y. H., & Pandey, J. (Eds.). (1997). *Handbook of cross-cultural psychology* (2nd ed., Vols. 1–3). Boston: Allyn & Bacon.

Betz, N. E., & Hackett, G. (1981). The relationship of career-related self-efficacy expectations to perceived career options in college women and men. *Journal of Counseling Psychology*, *28*, 399–410.

Blustein, D. L. (1997). A context-rich perspective of career exploration across the life roles. *Career Development Quarterly*, *45*, 260–274.

Blustein, D. L. (2006). *The psychology of working: A new perspective for career development, counseling, and public policy.* Mahwah, NJ: Lawrence Erlbaum Associates.

Blustein, D. L. (2008). The role of work in psychological health and well-being: A conceptual, historical, and public policy perspective. *American Psychologist*, *63*, 228–240.

Blustein, D. L., Kenna, A. C., Gill, N., & DeVoy, J. E. (2008). The psychology of working: A new framework for counseling practice and public policy. *Career Development Quarterly*, *56*, 294–308.

Blustein, D. L., McWhirter, E. H., & Perry, J. C. (2005). An emancipatory communitarian approach to vocational development theory, research, and practice. *The Counseling Psychologist, 33*, 141–179.

Blustein, D. L., Schultheiss, D. E. P., Flum, H. (2004). Toward a relational perspective of the psychology of careers and working: A social constructionist analysis. *Journal of Vocational Behavior, 64*, 423–440.

Brown, D. (1990). Summary, comparison, and critique of the major theories. In D. Brown & L. Brooks (Eds.), *Career choice and development: Applying contemporary theories to practice* (2nd ed., pp. 338–363). San Francisco: Jossey-Bass.

Carlson, D. S. (1999). Personality and role variables as predictors of three forms of work-family conflict. *Journal of Vocational Behavior, 55*, 236–253.

Ceci, S. J. & Williams, W. M. (Eds.). (2007). *Why aren't more women in science? Top researchers debate the evidence. Washington*, DC: American Psychological Association.

Chapa, J., & De La Rosa, B. (2006). The problematic pipeline: Demographic trends and Latino participation in graduate science, technology, engineering, and mathematics programs. *Journal of Hispanic Higher Education, 5*, 203–221.

Chartrand, J. M. (1991). The evolution of trait-and-factor career counseling: A Person x Environment fit approach. *Journal of Counseling & Development, 69*, 518–524.

Chronister, K. M. & McWhirter, E. H. (2003). Applying social cognitive career theory to the empowerment of battered women. *Journal of Counseling & Development, 81*, 418–425.

Coutinho, M. T., Dam, U. C., & Blustein, D. L. (2008). Globalisation and psychology of working. *International Journal for Vocational and Educational Guidance, 8*, 5–18.

Dawis, R. V., & Lofquist, L. H. (1984). *A psychological theory of work adjustment.* Minneapolis: University of Minnesota Press.

Dawis, R. (2005). The Minnesota theory of work adjustment. In S. D. Brown & R.W. Lent (Eds.), *Career development and counseling: Putting theory and research to work* (pp. 3–23). Hoboken, NJ: John Wiley & Sons, Inc.

Deci, E. L., & Ryan, R. M. (1985). The general causality orientations scale: Self determination in personality. *Journal of Research in Personality, 19*, 109–134.

Fassinger, R. E. (2008). Workplace diversity and public policy: Challenges and opportunities for psychology. *American Psychologist, 63*, 252–268.

Fitzgerald, L. F., Fassinger, R. E., & Betz, N. E. (1995). Theoretical advances in the study of women's career development. In W. B. Walsh & S. H. Osipow (Eds.), *Handbook of vocational psychology* (2nd ed., pp 67–110). Mahwah, NJ: Erlbaum.

Flum, H. (2001). Relational dimensions in career development. *Journal of Vocational Behavior, 59*, 1–16.

Flum, H., & Blustein, D. L. (2000). Reinvigorating the study of vocational exploration: A framework for research. *Journal of Vocational Behavior, 56*, 380–404.

Fouad, N. A. & Bynner, J. (2008). Work transitions. *American Psychologist, 63*, 241–251.

Friedman, T. L. (2006). *The world is flat: A brief history of the twenty-first century updated and expanded.* New York: Farrar, Straus and Giroux.

Gati, I. & Tal, S. (2008). Decision-making models and career guidance. In J. A. Athanasou & R. Van Esbroeck (Eds.), *International handbook of career guidance* (pp. 157–185). London: Springer.

Gilbert, L. A., & Scher, M. (1999). *Gender and sex in counseling and psychotherapy.* Needham Heights, MA: Allyn & Bacon.

Good, G. E., & Brooks, G. R. (2005). *The new handbook of psychotherapy and counseling with men: A comprehensive guide to settings, problems, and treatment approaches* (Rev. & abridged ed.). San Francisco: Jossey-Bass.

Grandey, A. A., Cordeiro, B. L., & Michael, J. H. (2007). Work–family supportiveness organizational perceptions: Important for the well-being of male blue-collar hourly workers? *Journal of Vocational Behavior*, *71*, 460–478.

Greller, M. M., & Simpson, P. (1999). In search of late career: A review of contemporary social science research applicable to the understanding of late career. *Human Resource Management Review*, *9*, 309–347.

Guichard, J. (2005). Life-long self-construction. *International Journal for Educational and Vocational Guidance*, *5*, 111–124.

Guichard, J., & Dumora, B. (2008). A constructivist approach to ethically grounded vocational development interventions for young people. In J. A. Athanasou & R. Van Esbroeck (Eds.). *International Handbook of Career Guidance* (pp. 187–208). London: Springer.

Haddock, S. A., Zimmerman, T. S., Ziemba, S. J. & Lyness, K. P. (2006). Practices of dual earner couples successfully balancing work and family. *Journal of Family and Economic Issues*, *27*, 207–234.

Hall, D. T. (1996). *The career is dead—Long live the career: A relational approach to careers.* San Francisco: Jossey-Bass.

Harmon, L. W. (1973). Sexual bias in interest measurement. *Measurement & Evaluation in Guidance*, *5*, 496–501.

Harmon, L. W., & Farmer, H. S. (1983). Current theoretical issues in vocational psychology. In W. B. Walsh & S. H. Osipow (Eds.), *Handbook of vocational psychology* (Vol. 1, pp. 39–77). Hillsdale, NJ: Lawrence Erlbaum Associates.

Heinz, W. R. (2002). Transition discontinuities and the biographical shaping of early work careers. *Journal of Vocational Behavior*, *60*, 220–240.

Helms, J. E., & Cook, D. A. (1999). *Using race and culture in counseling and psychotherapy: Theory and process.* Needham Heights, MA: Allyn & Bacon.

Helms, J. E., & Piper, R. E. (1994). Implications of racial identity theory for vocational psychology. *Journal of Vocational Behavior*, *44*, 124–138.

Herr, E. L. (2003). The future of career counseling as an instrument of public policy. *Career Development Quarterly*, *52*, 8–17.

Herr, E. L., Cramer, S. H., & Niles, S. G. (2004). *Career guidance and counseling through the lifespan: Systemic approaches* (6th ed.). Needham Heights, MA: Allyn & Bacon.

Holland, J. L. (1997). *Making vocational choices: A theory of vocational personalities and work environments* (3rd ed.). Odessa, FL: PAR.

Janis, I. L., & Mann, L. (1977). *Decision making: A psychological analysis of conflict, choice, and commitment.* New York: Free Press.

Kenny, M. E., Gualdron, L., Scanlon, D., Sparks, E., Blustein, D. L., & Jernigan, M. (2007). Urban adolescents' constructions of supports and barriers to educational and career attainment. *Journal of Counseling Psychology*, *54*, 336–343.

Kimmel, M. (2007). *The gendered society* (3rd ed.). New York: Oxford University Press.

Kitson, H. D. (1925). *The psychology of vocational adjustment.* Oxford, England: Lippincott.

Lamont, M. (2000). *The dignity of working men: Morality and the boundaries of race, class, and immigration.* New York: Russell Sage Foundation.

Lent, R. W., Brown, S. D., & Hackett, G. (2002). Social cognitive career theory. In D. Brown (Ed.), *Career choice and development* (pp. 255–311). San Francisco: Jossey-Bass.

Lerner, R. (2002). *Concepts and theories of human development* (3rd ed.). Mahwah, NJ: Lawrence Erlbaum Associates.

Mahalik, J. R., Burns, S. M., & Syzdek, M. (2007). Masculinity and perceived normative health behaviors as predictors of men's health behaviors. *Social Science & Medicine*, *64*, 2201–2209.

Mahalik, J. R., Locke, B. D., Ludlow, L. H., Diemer, M. A., Scott, R. P. J., Gottfried, M., & Freitas, G. (2003). Development of the conformity to masculine norms inventory. *Psychology of Men & Masculinity, 4*, 3–25.

Mahalik, J. R., Morray, E. B., Coonerty-Femiano, A., Ludlow, L. H., Slattery, S. M., & Smiler, A. (2005). Development of the conformity to feminine norms inventory. *Sex Roles, 52*, 417–435.

Mahalik, J. R., Perry, J. C., Coonerty-Femiano, A., Catraio, C., & Land, L. N. (2006). Examining conformity to masculinity norms as a function of RIASEC vocational interests. *Journal of Career Assessment, 14*, 203–213.

McKee-Ryan, F., Song, Z., Wanberg, C. R., & Kinicki, A. J. (2005). Psychological and physical well-being during unemployment: A meta-analytic study. *Journal of Applied Psychology, 90*, 53–76.

McMahon, M., & Watson, M. (2007). An analytical framework for career research in the post-modern era. *International Journal for Educational and Vocational Guidance, 7*, 169–179.

National Science Foundation. (2004). *Women, minorities, and people with disabilities in science and engineering.* Arlington, VA (NSF 04-317).

O'Brien, K. M. (2001). The legacy of Parsons: Career counselors and vocational psychologists as agents of social change. *Career Development Quarterly, 50*, 66–76.

Paredes, D. M., Choi, K. M., Dipal, M., Edwards-Joseph, A. R. A. C., Ermakov, N., Gouveia, A. T., … Benshoff, J. M. (2008). Globalization: A brief primer for counselors. *International Journal for the Advancement of Counselling, 30*, 155–166.

Parsons, F. (1909). *Choosing a vocation.* Boston: Houghton-Mifflin.

Perry, E. L., & Parlamis, J. D. (2006). Age and ageism in organizations: A review and consideration of national culture. In A. M. Konrad, P. Prasad, & J. K. Pringle (Eds.), *Handbook of workplace diversity.* (pp. 345–370). Thousand Oaks, CA: Sage Publications, Inc.

Peterson, G. W., Lumsden, J. A., Sampson, J. P., Jr., Reardon, R. C., & Lenz, J. G. (2002). Using a cognitive information processing approach in career counseling with adults. In S. G. Niles (Ed.), *Adult career development: Concepts, issues and practices* (3rd ed., pp. 98–117). Columbus, OH: National Career Development Association.

Phillips, S. D. (1997). Toward an expanded definition of adaptive decision making. *Career Development Quarterly, 45*, 275–287.

Phillips, S. D., & Jome, L. M. (2005). Vocational choices: What do we know? What do we need to know? In W. B. Walsh, & M. L. Savickas (Eds.), *Handbook of vocational psychology: Theory, research, and practice* (3rd ed., pp. 127–153). Mahwah, NJ: Lawrence Erlbaum Associates Publishers.

Phinney, J. S., & Ong, A. D. (2007). Conceptualization and measurement of ethnic identity: Current status and future directions. *Journal of Counseling Psychology, 54*, 271–281.

Ponterotto, J. G., Casas, J. M., Suzuki, L. A., & Alexander, C. M. (Eds.), (2001). *Handbook of multicultural counseling* (2nd ed.). Thousand Oaks, CA: Sage Publications, Inc.

Reich, R. B. (2000). *The future of success: Working and living in the new economy.* New York: Alfred A. Knopf.

Reitzle, M., & Vondracek, F. W. (2000). Methodological avenues for the study of career pathways. *Journal of Vocational Behavior, 57*, 445–467.

Richardson, M. S. (1974). The dimensions of career and work orientation in college women. *Journal of Vocational Behavior, 5*, 161–172.

Richardson, M. S. (1993). Work in people's lives: A location for counseling psychologists. *Journal of Counseling Psychology, 40*, 425–433.

Richardson, M. S. (2000). A new perspective for counsellors: From career ideologies to empowerment through work and relationships practices. In A. Collin & R. A. Young (Eds.), *The future of career.* (pp. 197–211). New York: Cambridge University Press.

Richardson, M. S., Constantine, K., & Washburn, M. (2005). New directions for theory development in vocational psychology. In W. B. Walsh & M. L. Savickas (Eds.), *Handbook of vocational psychology: Theory, research, and practice* (3rd ed., pp. 51–83). Mahwah, NJ: Lawrence Erlbaum Associates Publishers.

Richardson, M. S., Meade, P., Rosbruch, N., Vescio, C., Price, L., & Cordero, A. (2009). Intentional and identity processes: A social constructionist investigation using student journals. *Journal of Vocational Behavior, 74*, 63–74.

Robitschek, C., & Woodson, S. J. (2006). Vocational psychology: Using one of counseling psychology's strengths to foster human strength. *The Counseling Psychologist, 34*, 260–275.

Ryan, R. M., & Deci, E. L. (2000). Self-determination theory and the facilitation of intrinsic motivation, social development, and well-being. *American Psychologist, 55*, 68–78.

Sachs, J. D. (2005). *The end of poverty.* New York: Penguin Press.

Santos, E. J. R., & Ferreira, A. (1998). Career counseling and vocational psychology in Portugal: A political perspective. *Journal of Vocational Behavior, 52*, 312–322.

Sargeant, M. (2004). Mandatory retirement age and age discrimination. *Employee Relations, 26*, 151–166.

Savickas, M. L. (2002). Career construction: A developmental theory of vocational behavior. In D. Brown (Ed.), *Career choice and development* (pp. 149–205). San Francisco: Jossey-Bass.

Savickas, M. L. (2005). The theory and practice of career construction. In S. D. Brown & R. W. Lent (Eds.), *Career development and counseling: Putting theory and reaserch to work* (pp. 42–70). Hoboken, NJ: John Wiley & Sons, Inc.

Savickas, M. L., & Baker, D. B. (2005). The history of vocational psychology: Antecedents, origin, and early development. In W. B. Walsh & M. L. Savickas (Eds.), *Handbook of vocational psychology: Theory, research, and practice* (3rd ed., pp. 15–50). Mahwah, NJ: Lawrence Erlbaum Associates Publishers.

Seymour, E., & Hewitt, N. M. (1997). *Talking about leaving: Why undergraduates leave the sciences.* Boulder, CO: Westview.

Smith, E. J. (1983). Issues in racial minorities' career behavior. In W. B. Walsh & S. H. Osipow (Eds.), *Handbook of vocational psychology: Vol. 1. Foundations* (pp. 161–222). Hillsdale, NJ: Lawrence Erlbaum Associates.

Solberg, V. S., Howard, K. A., Blustein, D. L., & Close, W. (2002). Career development in the schools: Connecting school-to-work-to-life. *The Counseling Psychologist, 30*, 705–725.

Spector, P. E. (2006). *Industrial and organizational psychology: Research and practice* (4th ed.). New York: John Wiley & Sons, Inc.

Spokane, A. R., & Cruza-Guet, M. C. (2005). Holland's theory of vocational personalities in work environments. In S. D. Brown & R. W. Lent (Eds.), *Career development and counseling: Putting theory and research to work* (pp. 24–41). Hoboken, NJ: John Wiley & Sons, Inc.

Spokane, A. R., Luchetta, E. J., & Richwine, M. H. (2002). Holland's theory of personalities in work environments. In D. Brown & Associates (Eds.), *Career choice and development* (4th ed., pp. 373–426). San Francisco: Jossey Bass.

Stead, G. B. (2004). Culture and career psychology: A social constructionist perspective. *Journal of Vocational Behavior, 64*, 389–406.

Stead, G. B. (2007). Cultural psychology as a transformative agent for vocational psychology. *International Journal for Educational and Vocational Guidance, 7*, 181–190.

Stead, G. B., & Watson, M. B. (Eds.). (2006). *Career psychology in the South African context* (2nd ed.). Pretoria, South Africa: J. L. Van Schaik.

Sterns, H. L., & Miklos, S. M. (1995). The aging worker in a changing environment: Organization and individual issues. *Journal of Vocational Behavior, 47*, 248–68.

Super, D. E. (1957). *The psychology of careers.* New York: Harper & Row.

Super, D. E. (1980). A life-span, life-space, approach to career development. *Journal of Vocational Behavior, 13*, 282–298.

Super, D. E. (1983). Assessment in career guidance: Toward truly developmental counseling. *Personnel and Guidance Journal, 61*, 551–562.

Super, D. E. (1990). A life-span, life-space approach to career development. In D. Brown & L. Brooks (Eds.), *Career choice and development: Applying contemporary theories to practice* (2nd ed., pp. 197–261). San Francisco: Jossey-Bass.

Super, D. E., Savickas, M. L., & Super, C. M. (1996). The life-span, life-space approach to careers. In D. Brown & L. Brown (Eds.), *Career choice and development* (3rd ed., pp. 121–178). San Francisco: Jossey-Bass.

Thomas, C., Benzeval, M., & Stansfeld, S. A. (2005). Employment transitions and mental health: An analysis from the British household panel survey. *Journal of Epidemiology & Community Health, 59*, 243–249.

Valach, L., & Young, R. A. (2004). Some cornerstones in the development of a contextual action theory of career and counseling. *International Journal for Educational and Vocational Guidance, 4*, 61–81.

Vallas, S. P., Finlay, W., & Wharton, A. S. (2009). *The sociology of work: Structures and inequalities.* New York: Oxford University Press.

Walsh, W. B., & Savickas, M. L. (2005). *Handbook of vocational psychology: Theory, research, and practice* (3rd ed.). Mahwah, NJ: Lawrence Erlbaum Associates Publishers.

Warr, P. (1994). Age and employment. In H. C. Triandis, M. D. Dunnette, & L. M. Hough (Eds.), *Handbook of industrial and organizational psychology, vol. 4* (2nd ed., pp. 485–550). Palo Alto, CA: Consulting Psychologists Press.

Watts, A. G., Law, B., Killeen, J., Kidd, J. M., & Hawthorn, R. (1996). *Rethinking careers education and guidance: Theory, policy and practice.* New York: Routledge.

Wilson, W. J. (1996). *When work disappears: The world of the new urban poor.* New York: Random House.

Young, R. A., & Collin, A. (2004). Introduction: Constructivism and social constructionism in the career field. *Journal of Vocational Behavior, 64*, 373–388.

Young, R. A., & Valach, L. (2004). The construction of career through goal-directed action. *Journal of Vocational Behavior, 64*, 499–514.

9

Work Psychology

Robert A. Roe

Work psychology was born over a century ago as part of applied psychology ("psychotechnics"; Münsterberg, 1914). It grew out of a need to understand and resolve human problems, mainly fatigue, errors, and accidents, associated with the use of new technologies such as the telegraph, electric streetcar, automobile, and printing machinery. The development of work psychology was largely driven by advances in transportation, production, communication, and computing technologies. It particularly flourished in sectors such as aviation, defense, energy, chemical production, and computing, where increasingly complex systems posed rising demands on human operators while making organizations more dependent on their performance. Over the years the scope of work psychology has broadened, including such topics as workload, mental models, and work strategies, but the emphasis on preventing malfunction and deterioration of performance has remained.

In the last few decades the field has expanded further, as firms in search of competitive advantage have become interested in psychological factors in competence, creative performance, and innovation. Public organizations became aware of the impact of work-related stress and illness, calling upon work psychology to help in resolving frictions between work and private life, and promoting the working population's well-being. As a result, work psychology no longer concentrates on "what can go wrong," but also addresses the positive side of human work related activity (Bakker & Schaufeli, 2008).

Work psychology does not only distinguish itself by the types of work-related problems it tries to understand and resolve, but also by its theoretical and methodological approach. Its dominant perspective, that of the workers as an "embedded agent", comes with theories about processes involved in task execution, their effects, and influencing conditions. Work psychology prefers experimental methods and

IAAP Handbook of Applied Psychology, First Edition. Edited by Paul R. Martin, Fanny M. Cheung, Michael C. Knowles, Michael Kyrios, Lyn Littlefield, J. Bruce Overmier, and José M. Prieto.

longitudinal designs, and it uses instruments and interventions that are geared to processes rather than individual differences. One might say that work psychology follows the logic of "general psychology" rather than that of "differential psychology." Both content and approach give work psychology a distinct character in the discipline of psychology, and—at least in some countries—as a profession.

What is Work Psychology?

In order to define work psychology it is necessary to first define work. Since work is a multifaceted phenomenon that is studied from many disciplinary angles, the term "work" carries many different meanings. From the viewpoint of psychology, work is a "socially embedded" activity with a "productive purpose." Work is embedded in social structures, known as organizations: it is done *with* other people and *for* other people. It emerges from a division of labor, vertical among superiors and subordinates, horizontal with near and remote colleagues (in teams and beyond), and it aims at people (clients or customers), who benefit from the activities performed, directly or indirectly. Work is productive in the sense that it creates something that did not exist or brings about change. It transforms the reality in a way that beneficiaries perceive as valuable. The transformation is achieved by means of goal-directed action using feedback about progress and outcomes. It is based on cognition and involves specific mechanisms such as perception, imagination, and memory. More often than not, equipment is used for preparing and executing actions and delivering outcomes. Actions are distributed over time, synchronized with actions of others (colleagues, clients, relatives and friends in private life) and woven into a common stream of activity. Although work is usually performed in an employment relationship and in exchange for a financial reward, these characteristics are not essential—from a psychological angle, housekeeping and volunteer activities are work as well. However, work has an element of obligation in the sense of a commitment to act and deliver, stemming from the value-for-others that may or may not be formalized and sanctioned in an organizational framework.

Work can also be seen as embedded in people's life-span and career. From this perspective it is something a person engages him/herself in for a certain period of time. By using personal resources, providing learning opportunities as well as exposure to stimulating and harmful conditions, work has an impact on the person in the shorter and the longer term.

A definition of work including these aspects is: "Work is the goal-directed transformation of objects, guided by cognition and executed with the help of tools, performed by a person in the context of a social relationship, aiming to produce benefits for others and having an impact on the person him/herself." Work psychology can now be defined as "a field of applied psychology dedicated to the study of work, its impact on the person, and the improvement of the effectiveness of work as well as the safety, health, and well-being of those involved." Work psychology is part of the broader field of work and organizational psychology (or industrial/organizational psychology), just like personnel psychology and organizational psychology.[1] The field of work psychology can be divided into three major subject areas:

1. *The performance of work tasks.*

The area covers productive and creative task performance and its outcomes. It aims to understand how goal-directed action functions, and how people succeed (or fail) to change the work environment in accordance to the task. The focus is on four subjects: (1) the task or work goal, how it is mentally represented, stored, recalled, and changed; (2) the actions by which task goals are executed, psychological resources addressed, and mechanisms involved in activity regulation over time; (3) the performance that arises from these actions, unfolding over time, and leading to cumulative task accomplishment; and (4) errors, failure to perform as expected. The theories relating to performance strongly emphasize cognitive processes, but also cover motivational and emotional processes. Much of the research has been devoted to the conditions under which people do not perform well—regulation failure (*Fehlregulation*, see Schönpflug & Dunne, 1989).

2. *The impact of work on the person.*

The second area addresses the opposite effect, that is, how people are affected by the activities they perform and by environments. The research examines workload and other facets of resource utilization, as well as their impact on the health, well-being, and competence of the working person. There are three main subjects: (1) psychological states associated with the utilization of resources, such as workload, work pressure, fatigue, stress, and burnout, and the regulatory processes and mechanisms involved in their emergence and control; (2) accidents and other events that have a reversible or permanent impact on the state and health condition of the person; and (3) learning processes during task performance and their effect on competence development.

3. *Human work in a system context.*

The third area concerns the dynamics of human action and interaction in man–machine systems and their impacts on those involved. Here the focus is on the role of the human operator in relation to: (1) particular physical and social environments, for example, in aircraft, control rooms, operating theaters, offices or virtual work systems; (2) man–machine systems and interfaces at different levels of automation; and (3) work teams and processes within and between them. The research typically relies on findings from the other two areas (task performance and worker impacts) and looks at factors that hinder or promote effective system functioning under steady state as well as unexpected conditions.

Theory and Research in Work Psychology

This section gives an idea of the kind of theories and models guiding research in work psychology, grouped by area. Most of what follows is not much contended. Work psychology is characterized by a tendency to build on earlier work and further develop existing theories.

Task performance

Performing tasks is typically seen as a forward propagating process that begins with defining a task and ends with its completion. However, the process is not linear. It involves *regulatory cycles* that steer the activity and control its speed in accordance with the requirements of the task. The so-called "action regulation theory" (Bergman & Richter, 1994; Hacker, 1994, 1998), the most comprehensive theory of performance, describes the process in the following way. The *tasks* that are given to people in an organizational context (tasks-as-given, or objective tasks) are interpreted and redefined by the person into task goals (tasks-as-taken, subjective tasks). This is a complex process that has cognitive (understanding) as well as motivational (willing) aspects. *Mental models* of the subjective task, the setting, and the tools are used in generating action plans that are executed under cognitive control. When action plans are executed, lower-order activities are generated in a forward-downward (sequential-hierarchical) manner. Execution follows self-regulation principles: the results of activities are compared to the task using various types of feedback, and corrected if necessary. The self-regulation process aims for closure but is also flexible. This enables the worker to circumvent hindrances and accommodate changing conditions. *Feedback* on outcomes of task performance influences learning (competence development) and motivation (self-efficacy and aspiration level) and thereby has an impact on subsequent performance.

Much research effort has been spent on the *resources* needed for action execution, including its regulation, and the mechanisms by which they are provided, utilized, and restored. The emphasis has been on information-processing resources, primarily attention, and on mechanisms belonging to the central and autonomous nervous system. Crucial for the understanding of human performance is that resources are limited, that they are depleted when used, and that they must be restored in order to allow further action. Regarding attention some important discoveries have been made. First, attentional demands depend on the familiarity with the task, resulting from earlier learning, and the *mode of operation* that follows from this. Three or more modes of operation (also referred to as "regulation levels") have been distinguished, differing in the degree of controlled vs. automatic processing: knowledge-based, rule-based, skill-based (Hacker, 1998; Rasmussen, 1986). Second, *attentional capacity* depends on the state of the person. It can be raised through a compensatory effort mechanism. Third, attentional capacity is multidimensional: research has shown that there is a central processing capacity, important for planning, steering, and controlling the action, next to capacities to handle perceptual and motor processes (determined by arousal and activation) and capacities to process information of different modalities (e.g., visual, auditory; Wickens & McCarley, 2008).

A prerequisite for good performance is an optimal *workload*, which means that required resources match available resources. If the workload becomes either too high or too low, performance may deteriorate, but this can be counteracted by compensatory effort. It has been found that compensatory effort often prevents performance from serious decline and thereby "protects" task execution (the notion is "graceful degradation"). However, this aggravates resource depletion and may undermine the person's future capacity to perform (Tattersall & Hockey, 2008).

Research has emphasized the *dynamic nature* of the whole system. Demands fluctuate as a result of the work flow in the organization, environmental changes, success or failure of the performance, and many other factors. Also, the state of the person fluctuates with the diurnal cycle, the alternating performance of work and nonwork tasks, experiences in social interaction, and so on. The use of resources during the work process leads to their depletion and calls for restoration before further work can be done. The depletion–recovery process has become a crucial part of the theory of task performance. It has been found that both the workload and the speed of resource depletion can to some degree be controlled, namely by the choice of *work strategy*. This means that the work strategy serves as a means to balance the requirements of the task against the available resources. Some strategies favor the task while others protect the person or seek an acceptable equilibrium. There is evidence of multiple work strategies associated with varying degrees of effort and distress (Tattersall & Hockey, 2008). The work strategy can only exercise a beneficial effect if the work place offers room to make a choice on the working method, the speed etc. This can explain why (room for) *control* is a major health-related factor at the workplace.

Some effects of task performance are *cumulative* and can be understood as trends that gradually change the work capacity of the working person. On the positive side there is a clear link between performance and competence development. The more a person performs a particular task, the higher the level of competence, and the lower the level of effort needed. On the negative side work capacity declines as a result of failing recovery and damage of the sensory and psychomotor apparatus, following from excessive workload and external influences.

Much interest has been given to the study of work capacity in relation to biological factors, such as diurnal and hormonal cycles, and aging. Research on *aging* has focused on the opposing effects of decline in basic cognitive functions and of increasing competence with experience (Warr, 2001), which explains why the age–performance relationship differs widely with the type of job.

The impact of work on the person

While certain impacts of work are inherent in the performance process (see above), work impacts as such, and particularly negative impacts, have attracted a great deal of research. The main topics addressed have been workload, work pressure, fatigue, stress, and burnout. Although researchers have sometimes used one-directional cause–effect models and differential methodologies to support these models, all these impacts are reversible. For work psychology it is important to understand how the effects emerge and vanish, and to unravel the mechanisms of recovery and control. This can help to reduce the negative impacts of work in everyday life. In an effort to integrate relevant theories and models Roe & Zijlstra (2000) give the following account of the major work impacts, the processes involved, and their interrelationships.

Following the logic of action regulation theory (ART), *work demands* inherent in the objective task have an indirect effect on the *workload*. The workload follows from the way in which the task is interpreted and put into action by the person, that is, from the subjective task. The time (duration, hours of the day) during which the demands operate also matters. This, and the fact that the workers differ in their resources, explains why the same objective demands can cause markedly different degrees of workload among people. Identical demands can also produce a varying workload due to changes in the person's state and the strategy chosen. As already mentioned, the strategy can be a means to control the workload, and therefore to reduce the necessity to expend compensatory *effort* and the likelihood of cumulative negative effects of performance over time.

When the strategy fails to sufficiently reduce workload, work pressure emerges. *Work pressure* is a feeling of tension produced by an anticipated volume for work in excess of the capacity to handle it. Here, dynamics matter: if the amount of work to be done accumulates faster than it can be processed, work pressure arises. Work pressure can be counteracted in various ways. Besides a change in work strategy, these include, for example, reduction of the task supply, improved planning, and mobilization of support. Work pressure can temporarily improve performance by expending extra effort, but for the same reason it will reduce effectiveness in the long term. It is often seen as a stressor that produces anxiety and hinders the regulation of the work activity.

After a certain amount of time, dependent on the amount of workload and effort, resources will be depleted to such a degree that *recovery* is needed (Meijman & Mulder, 1998). This is where the notion of rest comes into play. Resource depletion is normally accompanied by the experience of *fatigue*, which is characterized by an unwillingness to continue the activity. Research has differentiated between physical fatigue, which is unwillingness to engage in any action, and mental fatigue, which is unwillingness to engage in the same action (Van der Linden, Frese, & Meijman, 2003). Fatigue signals a need for recovery and typically invokes change of activity—either rest or another (e.g., distracting, or nondemanding) activity that allows the depleted resources to be restored.

Among the several ways in which recovery can be achieved (Sonnentag, Binnewies, & Mojza, 2008), sleep is a major mechanism. Much research has been done into the sleep process and its restorative power (e.g., Fletcher & Dawson, 2001). Next to sleep duration sleep quality has been found to be a major determinant of effective recovery.

When people face demands that they cannot effectively cope with, due to lack of resources, lack of control, inadequate strategies, and/or insufficient recovery, *stress* emerges. The volume of research on stress has been enormous, and much insight has been gained in factors that may produce stress (stressors), the physiological and mental effects (strain), ways of coping, and social support. Two models that have attracted a great deal of research on work stress, i.e. the Job-Demand-Control model (Karasek & Theorell, 1990), which predicts high stress in jobs with high demands and little control, and the Effort–Reward Imbalance model (Siegrist, 1996), which predicts high stress in case of large effort and low reward. Differential evidence has largely supported these predictions (e.g., Van Veghel, 2005). Although stress is known to be a nonspecific phenomenon that can have many different origins, recent research with the Demand Induced Strain Compensation Model has demonstrated the usefulness of identifying specific demands and resources and the degree to which they match (De Jonge & Dormann, 2006). Examples of demands are quantity, difficulty, intensity, emotiveness, responsibility, temporality, and multiplicity. Stress only has a chance to emerge when people lack the resources to deal with the demands.

There is conspicuous imbalance in stress research in the sense that we know much more about its emergence than about its disappearance. Yet, it is clear that stress is a phenomenon with a limited *lifetime* in most cases. Stress can be counteracted by, among other things, reinterpreting the situation (reappraisal), changing the situation (fight) or leaving the situation (flight). Research aims for a better understanding of effective coping, by the person and those in the social environment (e.g., Dewe, Cooper, Hodgkinson, & Ford, 2007) .

If work stress is not controlled well, a *chronic stress syndrome* will develop. It can be seen as an enduring state of emotional arousal and resource depletion, maintained by ineffective coping strategies (e.g., substance use). Chronic stress is particularly likely to emerge after exposure to extreme stressors that keep being recalled, triggering negative emotions. In recent years much attention has been given to a form of chronic stress known as *burnout* (Maslach, 1982). The term refers to exhaustion, a state of severe depletion of mental energy. It is usually associated with a particular type of task or work setting in which demands were high and initially effective performance broke down. Other symptoms are apathy, incompetence, and emotional instability. Burnout, like other forms of chronic stress, usually vanishes after some time but the ultimate effect may not always be positive. People may remain susceptible to relapse or may suffer from illness and other health conditions that take additional time to be cured. These findings underline the importance of early prevention of stress.

A critical factor in these processes is *time*. Which outcomes will occur depends how work and non-work are intertwined, how work periods are interrupted by rest breaks, how working hours relate to the standard day-night pattern, and so forth. Researchers have devoted much attention to the effects of such factors and the design of work time arrangements (Thierry & Jansen, 1998).

Research on the positive impacts of work has for long concentrated on job satisfaction and intrinsic motivation. Recently researchers have focused on *engagement* (Bakker, Schaufeli, Leiter, & Taris, 2008). Like many studies on stress this research has mainly used differential methods and looked for correlations with particular job and environmental features, and for moderating effects of personal characteristics. Some studies have used a person–job fit logic and looked for the effect of congruence between preferred and actual job characteristics. Warr (2007), summarizing the research, has drawn an analogy with vitamins and suggested that some (A-D) characteristics, such as control and opportunity for skill use, are harmful when they become too strong, whereas others (C-E), such as availability of money and physical security, simply have no additional effect. Another positive work outcome is *competence*. It is generally acknowledged that executing tasks while receiving feedback is accompanied by a learning process that results in self-efficacy and competence. Several work-related factors have been identified as enhancing competence development (Bartram & Roe, 2008). Due to the use of differential nonequivalent samples and between-subject methods of analysis, this research provides little information on within-person processes.

Human work in a systems context

This area is dedicated to the study of the effective and ineffective performance of a man–machine system in which the human being fulfils the role of operator. Topics mentioned earlier, relating to the performance process and the impacts on the person, are now studied in connection with the allocation of tasks to the person and the machine, whereby the machine can have different degrees of complexity and levels of automation. The main questions are: (1) Can the system *function reliably and effectively* given variability on the part of the operator, the machine, and the environment? and (2) What can be done to make the system *resilient*, that is, capable of overcoming malfunction and restoring performance within acceptable limits?

The research can be categorized by referring to the level of automation within the system and the role of the operator. Three basic levels of automation have been distinguished:

1. *manual control*

The machine performs some function and the operator controls its operation directly and manually (e.g., a dentist's drill).

2. *indirect control*

The machine performs some function with the help of a computer device controlled by the operator (e.g., a computer numerical control machine).

3. *supervisor control*

The machine performs some function under the control of a computer that is supervised by the human operator (e.g., the flight management system in an aircraft).

Human performance in a system with *manual control* resembles performance as described earlier. For the system to function well the operator needs a mental model of the work object, the task, the equipment, and possible states of the system. He/she must also have acquired sufficient skill (competence) to perform the task with the help of equipment, and be aware of the situation, including the transient state of the work object, as it changes during the action (situational awareness). In the case of *indirect control* the operator needs an additional mental model, i.e., that of the computer and its mediating role, as well as a wider range of mental models of system states. More training is required to attain competence in operating the system under various conditions. Situational awareness becomes more important and has to be expanded so as to comprise the unfolding situation and the functioning of the system, including the operation of the computer. If the computer fails, the operator may have to switch to the mode of operation that belongs to direct manual control, which implies another set of mental models and skills. In a system with *supervisory control* the demands on the operator are even higher. A larger set of mental models is required, comprising all major parts of the system, including the controlling computer and possible system states. Likewise situational awareness has to be more comprehensive and include a still wider range of system states, including possible malfunction of the computer. In case of malfunction the operator is expected to switch to indirect or manual control, which requires a notably different set of competences. The possibility to do so has been the subject of an extensive theoretical discussion about the *level of automation* and the optimal allocation of tasks between the computer and the operator. It has been argued that if human operators are taken out "of the loop" and their control tasks are given to a computer, they have no opportunity to develop and maintain the skills necessary to intervene in case of unexpected situations of computer breakdown (Bainbridge, 1987; Endsley & Kiris, 1995).

Research has identified many possible reasons why systems sometimes do *not* function as expected. First, work demands exceed people's perceptual, cognitive, or motor limitations and therefore cannot be handled adequately. Second, operators have not been trained properly and lack the necessary mental models and skills. Third, people make errors and act in ways that bring the system into unforeseen and perhaps uncontrollable states. Fourth, operators are distracted and lose situational awareness. Fifth, the impact of executing the work tasks alters the state of the person, for example causes fatigue or stress, which results in general performance degradation. When the system's malfunction is perceived quickly enough and the operator is properly trained and equipped, he/she may take corrective action and bring the system back into its normal operating range. When this is not the case, accidents may occur and dramatic effects may ensue, particularly with higher automation levels.

Research studies can be divided in two main categories. The first category is that of human error and safety. The term *human error* is used to refer to cases where people fail to perform as expected. Research has identified many sources of error, that is, shortcomings in the regulation processes underlying performance that lead to unexpected and undesired outcomes. Several error taxonomies have been proposed. For instance Arnold & Roe (1987) have categorized errors according to mental function (observation, identification, interpretation, task definition, procedure formation/execution) and level of regulation. Although errors are often linked to accidents, "human error" is neither a necessary nor a sufficient condition for the occurrence of accidents—defined as unexpected and undesirable events that bring damage or harm to the system and/or its environment. Errors can be detected and recovered and therefore do not necessarily have harmful effects. The work of Reason (1990, 1997) and others has demonstrated that systems can be designed in such a way that they have several defense layers. Unsafe acts resulting from human error may not lead to accidents if they are stopped at one of these layers. Accidents typically emerge when two or more unsafe acts happen in combination and when system defenses fail. This is more likely to occur in settings with a poor safety climate (Zohar & Luria, 2005). The relevance of defining *systems safety* as an organizational matter involving the creation and maintenance of defense layers has been shown in many accidents analyses (Chmiel, 2008; Wilpert & Fahlbruch, 2002). A paradoxical finding is that when people are encouraged to make errors—in learning situations—they become better at error detection and recovery, and therefore make fewer errors. This underlines the importance of safety culture and safety management (Heimbeck, Frese, Sonnentag, & Keith, 2003).

The second category is that of *human factors in systems design*. Work psychologists prefer to be involved in systems design at an early stage to guarantee that major design choices involve human factors considerations. While the initial focus was on "smaller" issues, related to tasks and interface ergonomics, "larger" issues such as defining systems functions and allocating these to machines and people, have increasingly been seen as more important (Salvendy, 2006). Many psychologists have adopted the principles of the sociotechnical systems approach which posits that system design only gives good results when the social and technical subsystems are optimized simultaneously and are well integrated. Following this approach in the design of the overall system creates room for successful task and interface design (Strohm, 2002; Van Eijnatten, 1998). Other approaches emphasizing the human factor have become known under labels such as soft systems design, human-oriented system design, and user-centered systems design (Mumford & Axtell, 2003).

Work psychologists posit that systems can only function effectively and reliably when the design accounts for human characteristics. *Functional characteristics* relate to human capabilities and limitations, that is, what people are able to perceive, remember, choose, and motorically execute. They are covered by guidelines for human-machine task allocation (known as Fitts-lists; Fitts, 1951). *Operational characteristics* relate to how people plan, initiate, direct, monitor, and carry out actions. They have been addressed by the so-called "action facilitation approach" (Arnold & Roe, 1989), which provides guidelines for optimal support of the operator's activity regulation, covering such aspects as orientation on the work situation, action preparation, action execution, flexibility, monitoring, rationalization, workload optimization, and individual differences.

The design literature covers a broad range of issues, from interface layout and human–computer interaction to mental models and situational awareness in distributed settings (Salvendy, 2006). At present systems are supposed to keep performing well under a wide range of dynamically changing conditions. Both nominal and non-nominal (exceptional, unpredicted) situations and variability in the state of the operator and the equipment must be accommodated. The new notion is *system resilience.* This casts a new light on the classical issue of level of automation. Automation at the highest possible level endangers system resilience. One would rather accept a lower level of automation to guarantee effective operator performance. An alternative is *adaptive automation* which implies a dynamically changing task allocation, for example, depending on the workload of the operator (Kaber, Riley, Tan, & Endsley, 2001). Given the importance of operator performance, much importance is nowadays assigned to extensive and repeated training in full-scale simulators and to cognitive flexibility, the ability to selectively switch between multiple representations, strategies, and tasks.

Professional Activities of Work Psychologists

The professional activities of work psychologists are all related to establishing, maintaining, and restoring safe and effective work. They can be categorized in several ways depending on the setting in which the activities are conducted and the way in which they are grouped into occupational roles. There are three main types of settings where work psychologists operate:

1. *Research and Development institutions.*

These are mostly specialized laboratories or organizational departments dedicated to human factors, engaged in basic research and the development of methods for system design. They are found in space, air, naval, rail, and road transportation, in process industries engaged in steel, conventional and nuclear energy, chemical, and food production, various branches of the military, and in universities. They are also present in industries manufacturing consumer products, such as computer software, mobile telephones, and office equipment, where research is related to product development.

2. *Centers of expertise in work hygiene and safety.*
These specialized centers operating at the national level or in particular sectors are dedicated to basic and applied research on a broad range of issues, from sleep research, to environmental noise reduction, and the promotion of safety.

3. *Work environment services.*
These services are found in all industries. They monitor working conditions and intervene so as to protect worker health and well-being, and to (re)integrate disabled workers. They also provide managers and workers with tools to avoid work problems.

Work psychologists typically work in multidisciplinary environments where they collaborate with engineers, physiologists, work hygienists, medical doctors, social workers, and … other psychologists. This reflects the fact that work is a multifaceted phenomenon and that its optimization calls for contributions from several disciplines.

The professional activities of work psychologists can be characterized as follows. First, work psychologists often do *research,* fundamental as well as applied. They study specific problems to gain a deeper understanding before searching for solutions. Second, they take part in *design,* that is, the creation of work arrangements and work environments. This is done in such a way that human capabilities and limitations are taken into consideration. Its aim is preventive: creating work and working conditions under which people can work well. Design activities can be subdivided into two main categories (i.e., macro-ergonomic design aiming at the design of complex production, information, or communication systems, and meso/micro-ergonomic design, aiming at the design of jobs, work stations, equipment, software, manuals, procedures, and so on). Third, they engage in *educating, training*, and *instructing* other professionals, managers, and workers with regard to workload, work methods, working hours, and the like. Training of workers normally aims at developing knowledge, skills, attitudes, and competences needed to perform tasks and roles effectively and safely. Fourth, they *conduct analyses* of work tasks and work environments, as well as performance, errors, and accidents to identify factors in need of improvement. This can take the form of monitoring large numbers of employees using surveys and health statistics, as well as individual examinations driven by complaints, symptoms, and accidents. Fifth, they develop and apply *interventions* aiming at improvements through changes in the work environment, work schedules, work strategies, methods of coping, or through additional training and task reallocation. Work psychologists participate in workplace improvements that involve redesign, but also in individually advising and counseling individuals experiencing work-related problems or returning to work after burnout or illness.

Work psychologists use a broad variety of diagnostic methods. There are many techniques for analyzing tasks and work activities (e.g., Dunckel, 1999; Hoffman & Militello, 2009), workload (e.g., Tattersall & Hockey, 2008), work performance

(Charlton & O'Brien, 2002) and errors and accidents (Strauch, 2004). There are also techniques to evaluate workplaces and generate recommendations for improvement (REBA, Pohlandt, Richter, Jordan, & Schulze, 1999; TBS-GA, Richter & Hacker, 2003). Moreover, there are numerous guidelines for the design of jobs, workplaces and work time arrangements (Karwowski, 2006; Thierry & Jansen, 1998).

New Developments in Work

The changing economic landscape and technological developments along with the emergence of new business strategies have brought—and continue to bring—dramatic changes in the nature of work (Andriessen & Vartiainen, 2006; Holman, Wall, Clegg, Sparrow, & Howard, 2003; Roe et al., 1995). Lean manufacturing, integrated manufacturing systems, supply-chain partnering, call centers, telework, e-business are just a few catchwords that designate such changes. What people do at work and how they do it, is becoming very different indeed. Most people now work in services, interacting with other customers either in a direct manner, or mediated by information and communication technology. Work in industry and transportation is changing due to the use of highly automated systems. A great deal of work has become virtual in the sense that people interact with remote computers, systems and people, which can neither be seen nor influenced directly (Hinds & Kiesler, 2002). The dispersion of work over time from the scale of the day to that of the year has changed as well.

Meanwhile populations of working people are also changing. Many countries witness shifts in proportions of women and men, older and younger people, people of different ethnic backgrounds and so on, which interact with generational changes in attitudes to work, preferences for types of activities, and career patterns. Growing numbers of working women imply a greater co-incidence of work roles with child-rearing and household roles. The workforce of most western countries is aging, which implies a greater incidence of decline in physical and cognitive resources. New generations of workers are demanding more self-determination, that is, more control at the workplace and more self-employment. Ethnic groups may also reveal different preferences for salaried employment vs. self-employment, as well as for particular work roles.

The major trends can be described as changes

- from manual to mental or knowledge work
- from face-to-face and hands-on to mediated work
- from work in a single location to work in multiple/mobile locations
- from synchronized to asynchronous work
- from persistent to temporary work
- from ongoing to fragmented work
- from fixed to flexible hours
- from work with stable content and demands to work with variable content and demands
- from routine to creative work
- from individual to team work

- from supervised with assigned goals to non-supervised work with self-set goals
- from supply to demand driven work
- from single-role to multirole work.

Researchers have proposed various labels to designate new types of work, such as mental information work (MIW), electronic work (eWork), distributed work (dWork), flexible work (flexWork), and knowledge work (Roe et al., 1995; Vartiainen et al., 2007). It must be acknowledged that these concepts grasp only a small part of the newly emerging reality of work, and that the trends are not homogeneous. Changes come in different combinations and give work different appearances in different contexts. To assess the potential implications of the various changes for the way in which people perform work tasks, how they are affected by this and how the system as a whole functions, if seems useful to distinguish between some prototypes:

1. *High-end complex systems.*
In complex systems using advanced technologies and higher-order supervisory control well-selected and trained human operators perform highly critical roles. Such systems are found in transportation, especially aircraft operations and air traffic management, military command and control, and process industries.
2. *Distributed organizations.*
In virtual environments stretching throughout geographically dispersed organizations, larger numbers of well-educated people conduct knowledge work, using a variety of electronic media. Examples can be found in software development, publishing, commerce, and project work.
3. *Call centers.*
Larger numbers of people, usually with limited skill, are concentrated in spaces equipped with standard computer and telephone facilities where they handle incoming and/or outgoing phone calls with remote customers on behalf of one or more corporate clients. Examples are call centers of airlines, internet providers, and banks.
4. *Single knowledge workers.*
Individual people, typically self-employed, work alone at home or in a private office using a computer connected to the internet, a scanner, a printer, a telephone, etc., conducting knowledge and creative work in a virtual environment that may comprise several remote people. Examples are self-employed text writers, translators, and consultants.

Of course, there are many other types of work in our age. In some professions people will work at multiple locations or during travel, carrying most of their electronic equipment with them. In automated production plants workers are engaged in low-end feeding or off-bearing work. Moreover, there remains a fair amount of manual and informational service work without significant educational demands.

It is obvious that the type of work done, the temporal regime, the spatial layout, the level of automation, and the degree of virtuality differ widely between all these situations. The demands to be met and the difficulties experienced by people fulfilling the work roles show great contrasts. For instance, operators in high-end systems will need to develop elaborate mental models and a wide portfolio of skills with regular training in high-fidelity simulators. They must meet very high demands on situational awareness and cognitive flexibility while dealing with great risks. Single knowledge workers are exposed to distractions and conflicting demands from the home environment. Demands and temporal constraints posed by clients and partners may cause large variations in workload, while possibilities for buffering and mobilizing support from others are small. In the absence of clear working hours their workday may get "blurred," or they may work too long and suffer from lack of sleep. They may need time management to reach deadlines while keeping workload under control.

Challenges for Work Psychology

These changes in work pose challenges to work psychology. Perhaps the greatest challenge is to *monitor* what really happens, that means, to do descriptive research documenting what work is currently like in various contexts. Such research should describe the "work itself" in terms of what, where, how, and when. It should distinguish between contexts and be sensitive to changes in environments, organizational forms, and types of products and services that affect the nature of the work activity. Given the ongoing nature of the change process and the uncertainties of global economic and technological changes, it is important that the research be continuing, and that the knowledge obtained be time-stamped, so that researchers become aware of the possibility that knowledge they generate may be of limited validity when seen from a long-term perspective.

Next, there is a need to understand the *psychological processes* implied in new forms of work. This might be seen as examining the validity of known theories and models in new contexts, and as complementing or revising them as needed. A critical issue is how to account for further change. If it is assumed that work will continue to change, the research should somehow be open to ongoing elaborations and revisions of theory, rather than developing models for say telework or dWork that would implicitly assume a (new) steady state. Finding the balance between retaining what is still valid and discovering what is new will not be easy. An interesting example is provided by Hacker (2009) in a recent book on the work psychology of service work: building on notions and models that were developed in earlier days when work was predominantly industrial, he extends ART to novel forms of service work in which other people are the work object, work goals are open, and the transformation is of a "dialogical-interactional" nature.

The challenges posed by the changes in work are affecting the research agenda of work psychologists in many respects. Below are a number of issues that are currently being investigated, grouped by the three content areas that were mentioned before: work performance, work impacts, and human work in a systems context. Some references are given to illustrate recent research.

Work performance

Work with non-material objects. Tasks involving the transformation of non-material work objects, although existing for centuries, have only recently become a popular research topic. They include, for example, writing, designing, advising, informing, and nursing, which imply different transformation processes that need to be studied in some detail. Research is beginning to explore different kinds of knowledge work, creative work, service work, that involve "open" and dynamic tasks where there is no predefined end state to be reached (Hacker, 2009).

Basic issues in eWork/dWork. The main question addressed by researchers is: "what makes work in an electronic or distributed environment different from traditional work?" Many issues that have been well explored in earlier decades are now investigated in new settings. The most important are: workload and effort management, use of tools and equipment, mobile work, working in different locations, attention and memory, time-sharing, and situational awareness. An example is research into new dimensions of situational awareness, such as of coworkers' location, availability, and current activity (Nieminen & Mannonen, 2007).

Virtual work. In electronic and distributed environments people imagine a virtual space in which they engage in mediated collaboration with clients and others. This is a quickly expanding field of research. Several researchers are studying intra- and inter-team cognition (Letsky, Warner, Fiore, & Smith, 2008), including shared mental models and shared situational awareness, team processes such as trust and conflict (Shin, 2005; Wilson, Straus, & McEvily, 2006), and collaboration in communities of practice (Verburg & Andriessen, 2006).

Time and work. People working at different locations and collaborating with different people on a variety of tasks face new demands in regulating their activities over time. Research is addressing the dynamics of performance, interruptions, and cognitive flexibility (Kapitsa & Blinnikova, 2003), activity flows during the workday (Vartiainen et al., 2007), deadlines and time management practices (Claessens, Roe, & Rutte, 2009), and synchronization in interactions with others (Ancona & Waller, 2007; Tschan et al., 2009).

Management of multiple duties and complexity. Regardless of whether they collaborate with others or work alone, and whether they are mobile or work at a steady place, people may be responsible for carrying out multiple duties. Although many studies have investigated how people manage single goals, research on multiple goal management has just begun (Kirchberg, Roe, & Van Eerde, 2009; Mitchell, Harman, Lee, & Lee, 2008). Aspects covered are higher order and multilevel self-regulation, dynamic aspects of motivation, management of workload, work pressure and stress. A related issue is how people handle complex task packages which imply demands on multiple levels of regulation (Vartiainen et al., 2007).

Work impact

Virtual and real work spaces. Working in multiple locations and during travel implies workscapes (including multi-location and mobile) and time arrangements that may invoke other behavior and exert other influences. Hence, research is exploring how physical, virtual, and social spaces define new workscapes (Vartiainen et al., 2007), how these workscapes influence people's workflow, workload, privacy, and security, and to what degree they produce work–home interferences. Research also looks at the use of software tools such as email and the problems involved (Nieminen & Mannonen, 2007).

Working hours. Research focuses on emerging work time patterns including the "blurred working day" (Vartiainen, 2007) in which activities intersperse in an unpredicted manner. As traditional fixed patterns vanish, classical issues like the compressed work week and long working hours (Beckers et al., 2008) are now studied again in new settings. The same is true for diurnal rhythms and time zones related to shifts (also virtual shifts) and travel.

Worker states in virtual work. As new stressors emerge, stress continues to be an important topic for researchers. With more variable demands, other states require attention as well—on the one hand time pressure and hurry, on the other hand boredom and satiation. With the growing significance of service work there is an interest in learning more about the emergence and effects of emotions and moods, and about the effects of controlling them as part of the work role (Zapf, Vogt, Seifert, Mertini, & Isic, 1999).

Managing impact. Important for this topic are research on new work strategies, particularly proactive strategies for dealing with work pressure, fatigue, and stress. The question is what people can do themselves to adjust work schedules, work flow, task allocation, and the division of work duties and home/family duties to prevent problems. Dealing with health and illness—for example, the question of whether people should stay home or go to work when sick is becoming a more salient topic as well (Hansen & Andersen, 2008).

Change. While change has long been considered as extraneous, it is clear that it is a constant factor in any work situation. So, research should not only study work during stable episodes that are broken by transitions but also address how change affects the work process and the work experience on an ongoing basis (Vartiainen et al., 2007). There are many change issues that could take on a different appearance if they were studied as an inherent part of work. Research could elucidate the effects of interruptions and changes in work activities due to changes in work tools (e.g., software upgrades), work procedures, or workplaces, as well as the impacts of role change and learning processes, and uncertainties about future work conditions and tasks. Research on the obsolescence of competences, unlearning and relearning is also important.

Delayed and remote impacts. Research on the long-term impact of work, for instance on the question of how work affects personality, has always been difficult, because of the complexities of research design. However, this remains an important research topic. There is a need to know more about the long-term effects of work-related stress, burnout, and illness, and how they differ with types of work, work environments, and career paths. There is some research about the effects of employment contracts over time (Kompier, Ybema, Janssen, & Taris, 2009).

Human work in a systems context

Systems design. With human–machine systems being increasingly interlinked and becoming more complex, the problems of human-centered systems design augment. There is a continuing interest among researchers in methods and techniques for systems design. A large part of the research remains devoted to the design of systems with advanced levels of automation with the human in and out of the loop. However, there is also research on collaborative systems for knowledge and creative work, and communities of practice, with a focus on software support, social dimensions, and effective management practices (Antunes & André, 2006).

Human roles. Ongoing system development and new (e.g., dynamic) approaches to task allocation have an impact on the role of human operators. This calls for research on what works well (performance) and what leads to failure (errors) in steady-state as well as unexpected and emerging situations. Increasingly important are dynamic aspects of operator behavior and possibilities to exercise control over them. Several studies try to gain a better understanding of collaborative work among knowledge and creative workers covering both the social and the individual aspects of it (Gao, Lee, & Zhang, 2006).

System functioning. There is a growing interest in coordinated action in relation to system resilience, a topic that is investigated with the help of high-fidelity simulators. To better understand collaboration in virtual environments several researchers have turned to macro-cognition, that is, cognitive processes involving multiple operators. This includes research on mental models (types, adequacy, development, sharedness) and situational awareness, but explicitly includes communication and coordination (Schraagen, Militello, Ormerod, & Lipshitz, 2008).

Several of the issues listed above are not totally new. For example workload and interruptions have been studied in earlier days when more traditional forms of still work prevailed (Zijlstra, Roe, Leonova, & Krediet, 1999). They are being investigated again in order to check the validity of previous findings, and to be explored further. Other issues, such as shared mental models and multiple goal management, are new and call for fresh research in novel settings (Letsky, Warner, Fiore, & Smith, 2008).

Research on the aforementioned topics comes with a range of methodological innovations. For instance, researchers study the interactions between people in distributed systems by analyzing emails and computer logs (Griffiths, Sharpies, & Wilson, 2006), and they study mobility by analyzing data on travel, presence in multiple locales and so forth. There is also an increasing use of computer- and PDA-based diary methods (Navarro, Arrieta, & Ballén, 2007). Video-recordings of team interactions are analyzed with software for automatic pattern recognition (Bischof et al., 2001).

The *professional activities* of work psychologists will undoubtedly profit from the new research and instrument development, but there seems no reason to expect great changes in the types of activities that work psychologists fulfill. What may change is the relative importance of the contributions that work psychologists deliver in the multidisciplinary setting in which they operate. As the complexity of man–machine systems keeps increasing, with multiple levels of computer control, the role left for the operators becomes more and more critical. This implies a greater need to understand the cognitive and behavioral processes involved in operators' actions. Likewise, with the ongoing spread of virtual work in distributed environments that keep expanding, a heavy emphasis is placed on human cognition and symbolic action. Work psychologists are in a unique position to elucidate these processes and to translate research evidence into practical measures. Although this may strengthen the role of work psychologists as experts in analysis and design, their educational role should not be overlooked. They may make an important contribution by educating ICT engineers, architects, management experts, HRM professionals and others in critical "human factors," and by training and consulting operators and virtual workers themselves. Perhaps work psychologists can also help to bridge the growing knowledge gap between the technical experts involved in systems development and the end users by establishing dialogues and supporting the communication between them.

Future Perspective

Work psychology started over a century ago in response to problems of work that could neither be diagnosed nor resolved with common sense or the methods from other sciences, medicine, engineering, and sociology. Since those days the field of applied psychology has flourished. Increasing differentiation in work roles, the progressive use of mechanical and information technologies, and rising demands on performance have enhanced the need to know what people do when they work, what determines the success and failure of their performance, how work can be designed and managed in such a way that its effects on people are beneficial rather than harmful, and how sociotechnical systems can be created that function safely and effectively. With changes in work continuing at a remarkably high rate, the need for knowledge about work keeps growing. Realizing that what is called work today is widely different from what was called work as recently as three decades ago, the "need to know more" is only increasing. The direction of the research can partially be predicted from the changes in organizational forms and technologies that were outlined in this chapter. Thus, we are likely to see research on new jobs (such as the drone pilot or business continuity manager), on virtual work in changing network configurations, collaboration under conditions of nonsynchronicity, and so on. However, the content of research will also depend on the direction that business, military, and government interests will take in the decades to come. Research may, as in the past, also be driven by major catastrophes such as aircraft crashes, accidents in nuclear plants, military disasters, or terrorist attacks. What will happen in this realm cannot be predicted—we can only hope that the drive towards preventive research is powerful enough to avoid tragic events that will call upon work psychology research afterwards.

I expect that to some degree future research will address topics that were relatively neglected in the past. The role of emotions, vitality and self-image in work performance and their unconscious as well as conscious regulation can be mentioned as examples. In addition we may expect that research will open some new avenues that shed more light on previously studied matters and produce new diagnostic and intervention tools. It is a great challenge to incorporate new findings in existing theories as well as to integrate theoretical models that were developed in isolation into a coherent theoretical framework. Self-regulation theory may offer a suitable framework to integrate performance and impact phenomena that have traditionally been studied under distinct headings (Kanfer, 2005; Roe, 1999).

A strong case can be made for a temporal approach to theory-building whereby performance, impacts, and system functioning are modeled in an explicitly dynamic way and regulatory processes are studied as they happen, that is, as recurrent cyclic patterns over time (Mitchell & James, 2001; Roe, 2008). Such an approach could, for example, improve our knowledge of environmental scanning or self-monitoring processes and thereby give a better understanding of situational awareness and self-awareness during the performance process. It could likewise enhance our insight into how people develop and share mental models. Compared to other domains of applied psychology that have been dominated by the differential paradigm and the use of questionnaires, work psychology has greater chances of advancement, since much of its theory is of a general rather than a differential nature.

The future might also bring a stronger focus on diagnosing and optimizing work in practice. Many of the techniques and instruments that have been developed in the past have been made for psychologists or other expert users. With the higher levels of education and greater emphasis on professional autonomy among system operators and knowledge workers, there is a need to develop more tools for self-diagnosis and self-management by nonexperts. New tools might, for instance, help people to monitor and control their own workload, emotional arousal, or level of fatigue. Independently operating knowledge professionals might also profit from new tools for dynamically managing multiple goals (Kirchberg, Roe, & Van Eerde, 2009). Another possibility to broaden the scope of application of work psychology is the development of information materials and guidelines on positive aspects of work (Bakker & Schaufeli, 2008). Such a development might counterbalance the rather strong emphasis on the negative side of work that has prevailed in the past.

Let me conclude by making a remark on the status of work psychology at the global stage. Work psychology as described in this chapter has its roots in European psychology and has mainly been developed in the western hemisphere. Therefore, it mainly reflects work as it has emerged and developed in that part of the world, particularly in the industrialized and computerized sectors of the economy. Although these types of work also exist in other parts of the world—particularly in aviation, power supply, and the military—we should be aware that there are other types of work, technically less advanced and including more manual and social activity. If we take a broader perspective, differences in standard of living, terms of employment, labor relations, and types of economic activity become apparent, and with them differences in work tasks, working conditions, performance requirements, and the resources that people can rely on. Work psychology should become more sensitive to such differences, make sure that they are accounted for in theories and models, and make efforts to develop tools for diagnosis and intervention that are suitable for local use in specific locales next to tools that can be used globally. A global work psychology would not only rely on western ideas and findings as presented in this chapter, but also incorporate theories and research from other parts of the world that may not have been published in English and have therefore remained unnoticed by western colleagues. This makes improved communication and information sharing among researchers and practitioners in work psychology a challenging objective.

Note

1 The term "work psychology" is sometimes used as a synonym of Work and Organizational Psychology, but it should be clear that in this chapter it is conceived in a more confined way. It is translated as "Arbeitspsychologie" (German), "psychologie du travail" (French), "psicologia del trabajo" (Spanish), "psicologia del lavoro" (Italian), to mention a few examples.

References

Ancona, D. G., & Waller, M. J. (2007). The dance of entrainment: Temporally navigating across multiple pacers. In R. Hodson & B. Rubin (Eds.), *Research in the sociology of work* (Vol. 17, pp. 115–146). Amsterdam: Elsevier.

Andriessen, J. H. E., & Vartiainen, M. (Eds.). (2006). *Mobile virtual work: A new paradigm?* Heidelberg: Springer.

Antunes, P., & André, P. (2006). A conceptual framework for the design of geo-collaborative systems. *Group Decision and Negotiation*, *15*(3), 273–295.

Arnold, A. G., & Roe, R. A. (1987). User errors in human–computer interaction. In M. Frese, E. Ulich & W. Dzida (Eds.), *Psychological issues in human-computer interaction in the workplace* (pp. 203–220). Amsterdam: Elsevier.

Arnold, A. G., & Roe, R. A. (1989). Action facilitation: A theoretical concept and its use in interface design. In M. J. Smith & G. Salvendy (Eds.), *Work with computers: Organizational, management, stress, and health aspects* (pp. 191–198). Amsterdam: Elsevier Science Publishers.

Bainbridge, L. (1987). Ironies of automation. In J. Rasmussen, K. Duncan & J. LePlat (Eds.), *New technology and human error* (pp. 271–283). Chichester: John Wiley.

Bakker, A. B., & Schaufeli, W. B. (2008). Positive organizational behavior: Engaged employees in flourishing organizations. *Journal of Organizational Behavior*, *29*(2), 147–154.

Bakker, A. B., Schaufeli, W. B., Leiter, M. P., & Taris, T. W. (2008). Work engagement: An emerging concept in occupational health psychology. *Work & Stress*, *22*(3), 187–200.

Bartram, D., & Roe, R. A. (2008). Individual and organisational factors in competence acquisition. In W. J. Nijhoff, R. J. Simons & A. F. Nieuwenhuis (Eds.), *The learning potential of the workplace*. Rotterdam: Sense Publishers.

Beckers, D. G. J., van der Linden, D., Smulders, P. G. W., Kompier, M. A. J., Taris, T. W., & Geurts, S. A. E. (2008). Voluntary or involuntary? Control over overtime and rewards for overtime in relation to fatigue and work satisfaction. *Work & Stress*, *22*(1), 33–50.

Bergman, B., & Richter, P. (1994). *Die Handlungsregulationstheorie. Von der Praxis einer Theorie*. Göttingen: Hogrefe.

Bischof, A., Stark, H., Blumenstein, R., Wagner, T., Brechmann, A., & Scheich, H. (2001). A semiautomatic method for adding behavioral data to videotape records in combination with the Noldus Observer system. *Behavior Research Methods, Instruments & Computers, 33*(4), 549–555.

Charlton, S. G., & O'Brien, T. G. (Eds.). (2002). *Handbook of human factors testing and evaluation.* Mahwah, NJ: Lawrence Erlbaum Associates Publishers.

Chmiel, N. (2008). Organizations, technology and safety. In N. Chmiel (Ed.), *Introduction to work and organizational psychology. A European perspective* (pp. 234–253). Oxford: Blackwell.

Claessens, B. J. C., Roe, R. A., & Rutte, C. G. (2009). Time management: Logic, effectiveness and challenges. In R. A. Roe, M. J. Waller, & S. Clegg (Eds.), *Time in organizational research* (pp. 23–41). London: Routledge.

De Jonge, J., & Dormann, C. (2006). Stressors, resources, and strain at work: A longitudinal test of the triple-match principle. *Journal of Applied Psychology, 91*(6), 1359–1374.

Dewe, P., Cooper, G. L., Hodgkinson, G. P., & Ford, J. K. (2007). Coping research and measurement in the context of work related stress. In *International Review of Industrial and Organizational Psychology 2007.* (Vol. 22, pp. 141–191). New York: John Wiley & Sons Ltd.

Dunckel, H. (Ed.). (1999). *Handbuch psychologischer Arbeitsanalyseverfahren* (Vol. 14). Zürich: VDF Hochschulverlag an der ETH Zürich.

Endsley, M. R., & Kiris, E. O. (1995). The out-of-the-loop performance problem and level of control in automation. *Human Factors, 37*(2), 381–394.

Fitts, P. M. (1951). *Human engineering for en effective air navigation and traffic control system.* Washington, D.C.: National Research Council.

Fletcher, A., & Dawson, D. (2001). A quantitative model of work-related fatigue: Empirical evaluations. *Ergonomics, 44*(5), 475–488.

Gao, J., Lee, J. D., & Zhang, Y. (2006). A dynamic model of interaction between reliance on automation and cooperation in multi-operator multi-automation situations. *International Journal of Industrial Ergonomics, 36*(5), 511–526.

Griffiths, G., Sharpies, S., & Wilson, J. R. (2006). Performance of new participants in virtual environments: The Nottingham tool for assessment of interaction in virtual environments (NAÃVE). *International Journal of Human-Computer Studies, 64*(3), 240–250.

Hacker, W. (1994). Action regulation theory and occupational psychology: Review of German empirical research since 1987. *German Journal of Psychology, 18*(2), 91–120.

Hacker, W. (1998). *Allgemeine Arbeitspsychologie. Psychische Regulation von Arbeitstätigkeiten.* Bern: Verlag Hans Huber.

Hacker, W. (2009). *Arbeitsgegenstand Mensch: Psychologie dialogisch-interaktiver Erwerbstätigkeit.* Lengerich: Pabst.

Hansen, C. D., & Andersen, J. H. (2008). Going ill to work: What personal circumstances, attitudes, and work-related factors are associated with sickness presenteeism? *Social Science & Medicine, 67*(6), 956–964.

Heimbeck, D., Frese, M., Sonnentag, S., & Keith, N. (2003). Integrating errors into the training process: The function of error management instructions and the role of goal orientation. *Personnel Psychology, 56*(2), 333–361.

Hinds, P. J., & Kiesler, S. (2002). *Distributed work.* Cambridge, MA: MIT Press.

Hoffman, R. R., & Militello, L. (2009). *Perspectives on cognitive task analysis: Historical origins and modern communities of practice.* New York: Psychology Press.

Holman, D., Wall, T. D., Clegg, C. W., Sparrow, P., & Howard, A. (Eds.). (2003). *The new workplace: A guide to the human impact of modern working practices.* Chichester: John Wiley.

Kaber, D. B., Riley, J. M., Tan, K. W., & Endsley, M. R. (2001). On the design of adaptive automation for complex systems. *International Journal of Cognitive Ergonomics*, *5*(1), 37–57.

Kanfer, R. (2005). Self-regulation research in work and I/O psychology. *Applied Psychology: An International Review*, *54*(2), 186–191.

Kapitsa, M. S., & Blinnikova, I. V. (2003). Task performance under the influence of interruptions. In G. R. J. Hockey, A. W. K. Gaillard, & O. Burov (Eds.), *Operator functional state* (pp. 323–329). Amsterdam: IOS Press.

Karasek, R., & Theorell, T. (1990). *Healthy work: stress, productivity, and the reconstruction of working life.* New York: Basic Books.

Karwowski, W. (2006). *Handbook of standards and guidelines in ergonomics and human factors.* Mahwah, NJ: Lawrence Erlbaum Associates Publishers.

Kirchberg, D. M., Roe, R. A., & Van Eerde, W. (2009). *Understanding how people manage multiple goals at work: A theoretical model and its implications.* Paper presented at the Academy of Management. Annual Meeting, Chicago, August 7–11, 2009.

Kompier, M., Ybema, J. F., Janssen, J., & Taris, T. (2009). Employment contracts: Cross-sectional and longitudinal relations with quality of working life, health, and well-being. *Journal of Occupational Health*, *51*, 193–203.

Letsky, M. P., Warner, N. W., Fiore, S. M., & Smith, C. A. P. (Eds.). (2008). *Macrocognition in teams: Theories and methodologies.* Aldershot: Ashgate.

Maslach, C. (1982). *Burnout. The cost of caring.* Englewood Cliffs, NJ: Prentice Hall.

Meijman, T. F., & Mulder, G. (1998). Psychological aspects of workload. In P. J. D. Drenth, H. Thierry, & C. J. De Wolff (Eds.), *Handbook of work and organizational psychology* (2nd ed.). Hove: Psychology Press.

Mitchell, T. R., Harman, W. S., Lee, T. W., & Lee, D. Y. (2008). Self-regulation and multiple deadline goals. In R. Kanfer, G. Chen, & R. D. Pritchard (Eds.), *Work motivation: Past, present, and future.* New York: Routledge.

Mitchell, T. R., & James, L. R. (2001). Building better theory: Time and the specification of when things happen. *Academy of Management Review*, *26*(4), 530–547.

Mumford, E., & Axtell, C. (2003). Tools and methods to support the design and implementation of new work systems. In D. Holman, T. D. Wall, C. W. Clegg, P. Sparrow, & A. Howard (Eds.), *The new workplace: A guide to the human impact of modern working practices* (pp. 331–346). Chichester: John Wiley.

Münsterberg, H. (1914). *Grundzüge der Psychotechnik.* Leipzig: Barth.

Navarro, J., Arrieta, C., & Ballén, C. (2007). An approach to the study of the dynamics of work motivation using the diary method. *Nonlinear Dynamics, Psychology, and Life Sciences*, *11*(4), 473–498.

Nieminen, M. P., & Mannonen, P. (2007). Technology in distributed and mobile work. In M. Vartiainen, M. Hakonen, S. Koivisto, P. Mannonen, M. P. Nieminen, V. Ruhomäki, & A. Vartola (Eds.), *Distributed and mobile work: Places, people and technology* (pp. 156–187). Helsinki: Otatieto.

Pohlandt, A., Richter, P., Jordan, P., & Schulze, F. (1999). Rechnergestütztes Dialogverfahren zur psychologischen Bewertung von Arbeitsinhalten (REBA). In H. Dunckel (Ed.), *Handbuch psychologischer Arbeitsanalyseverfahren* (pp. 341–363). Zürich: VDF.

Rasmussen, J. (1986). *Information processing and human-machine interaction.* Amsterdam: North-Holland.

Reason, J. (1990). *Human error.* Cambridge: Cambridge University Press.

Reason, J. (1997). *Managing the risks of organizational accidents.* Aldershot: Ashgate.

Richter, P., & Hacker, W. (2003). *Tätigkeitsbewertungssystem—Geistige Arbeit.* Zürich: VDF.

Roe, R. A. (1999). Work performance: A multiple regulation perspective. In C. L. Cooper & I. T. Robertson (Eds.), *International Review of Industrial and Organizational Psychology* (Vol. 14, pp. 231–335). Chichester: John Wiley & Sons.

Roe, R. A. (2008). Time in applied psychology: The study of "what happens" rather than "what is." *European Psychologist, 13*(1), 37–52.

Roe, R. A., Van den Berg, P. T., Zijlstra, F. R. H., Schalk, R. J. D., Taillieu, T. C. B., & Van der Wielen, J. M. M. (1995). New concepts for a new age: Information service organizations and mental information work. In *Work and organizational psychology: European contributions of the nineties* (pp. 249–262). Oxford: Erlbaum (UK), Taylor & Francis.

Roe, R. A., & Zijlstra, F. R. H. (2000). Work pressure. Results of a conceptual and empirical analysis. In M. Vartiainen, F. Avallone, & N. Anderson (Eds.), *Innovative theories, tools, and practices in work and organizational psychology* (pp. 29–45). Ashland, OH: Hogrefe & Huber Publishers.

Salvendy, G. (2006). *Handbook of human factors and ergonomics* (3rd ed.). Hoboken, NJ: John Wiley & Sons Inc.

Schönpflug, W., & Dunne, E. (1989). Behavioral regulation and "dysregulation": XIV. Effort, task assignment, and time limitation/Regulation und Fehlregulation im Verhalten. XIV: Anstrengung und ihre Auswirkungen auf die Leistung. *Psychologische Beitrage, 31*(3–4), *1989*, 1450–1471.

Schraagen, J. M., Militello, L. G., Ormerod, T., & Lipshitz, R. (Eds.). (2008). *Naturalisticdecision making and macrocognition.* Aldershot: Ashgate.

Shin, Y. (2005). Conflict resolution in virtual teams. *Organizational Dynamics, 34*(4), 331–345.

Siegrist, J. (1996). Adverse health effects of high-effort/low-reward conditions. *Journal of Occupational Health Psychology, 1*, 27–41.

Sonnentag, S., Binnewies, C., & Mojza, E. J. (2008). "Did you have a nice evening?" A day-level study on recovery experiences, sleep, and affect. *Journal of Applied Psychology, 93*(3), 674–684.

Strauch, B. (2004). *Investigating human error: Incidents, accidents and complex systems.* Aldershot: Ashgate.

Strohm, O. (2002). Organizational design and organizational development as a precondition for good job design and high job performance. In S. Sonnentag (Ed.), *Psychological management of individual performance* (pp. 95–111). Chichester: John Wiley.

Tattersall, A. J., & Hockey, G. R. J. (2008). Demanding work, technology and human performance. In N. Chmiel (Ed.), *An introduction to work and organizational psychology* (pp. 169–189). Oxford: Blackwell Publishing.

Thierry, H., & Jansen, B. (1998). Work schedules and behavior at work. In P. J. D. Drenth, H. Thierry, & C. J. De Wolff (Eds.), *Handbook of work and organizational psychology* (pp. 89–119). Hove: Psychology Press.

Tschan, F., McGrath, J. E., Semmer, N. K., Arametti, M., Bogenstätter, Y., & Marsch, S. U. (2009). Temporal aspects of processes in ad-hoc groups: A conceptual schema and some research examples. In R. A. Roe, M. J. Waller, & S. R. Clegg (Eds.), *Time in organizational research* (pp. 42–61). London: Routledge.

Van der Linden, D., Frese, M., & Meijman, T. F. (2003). Mental fatigue and the control of cognitive processes: Effects on perseveration and planning. *Acta Psychologica, 113*(1), 45–65.

Van Eijnatten, F. (1998). Developments in sociotechnical systems design. In P. J. D. Drenth, H. Thierry, & C. J. De Wolff (Eds.), *Handbook of work and organizational psychology.* Hove: Psychology Press.

Van Veghel, N. (2005). *Two models at work. A study of interactions and specificity in relation to the demand-Control Model and the Effort-Reward Imbalance Model.* Helmond: Drukkerij Van Stipthout.

Vartiainen, M. (2007). Distributed and mobile work places. In M. Vartiainen, M. Hakonen, S. Koivisto, P. Mannonen, M. P. Nieminen, V. Ruhomäki, & A. Vartola (Eds.), *Distributed and mobile work: Places, people and technology* (pp. 13–85). Helsinki: Otatieto.

Vartiainen, M., Hakonen, M., Koivisto, S., Mannonen, P., Nieminen, M. P., Ruhomäki, V., & A. Vartola (Eds.). (2007). *Distributed and mobile work: Places, people and technology.* Helsinki: Otatieto.

Verburg, R. M., & Andriessen, J. H. E. (2006). The assessment of communities of practice. *Knowledge & Process Management, 13*(1), 13–25.

Warr, P. (2001). Age and work behavior. In C. L. Cooper & I. T. Robertson (Eds.), *International Review of Industrial and Organizational Psychology* (Vol. 16, pp. 1–36). London: Wiley.

Warr, P. (2007). *Work, happiness and unhappiness.* Mahwah, NJ: Lawrence Erlbaum Associates.

Wickens, C. D., & McCarley, J. S. (2008). *Applied attention theory.* Boca Raton: CRC Press Taylor & Francis Group.

Wilpert, B., & Fahlbruch, B. (Eds.) (2002). *System safety: Challenges and pitfalls of intervention* Oxford: Elsevier Science.

Wilson, J. M., Straus, S. G., & McEvily, B. (2006). All in due time: The development of trust in computer-mediated and face-to-face teams. *Organizational Behavior and Human Decision Processes, 99*(1), 16–33.

Zapf, D., Vogt, C., Seifert, C., Mertini, H., & Isic, A. (1999). Emotion work as a source of stress: The concept and development of an instrument. *European Journal of Work and Organizational Psychology, 3*, 371–400.

Zijlstra, F. R. H., Roe, R. A., Leonova, A. B., & Krediet, I. (1999). Temporal factors in mental work: Effects of interrupted activities. *Journal of Occupational and Organizational Psychology, 72*(2), 163–185.

Zohar, D., & Luria, G. (2005). A multilevel model of safety climate: Cross-level relationships between organization and group-level climates. *Journal of Applied Psychology, 90*(4), 616–628.

10

Organizational Psychology

Robert E. Wood, Victoria Roberts, and Jennifer Whelan

The Purpose and Beginnings of Organizational Psychology

The psychological approach to the study of organizational phenomena has as its primary interest the description, prediction, and explanation of the behavior of individuals and teams in organizational settings in order to better understand, influence, and manage people, processes, and outcomes in organizations (e.g., Kreitner & Knicki, 2007). Psychology, which provides the focus of the topics and literature reviewed in this chapter, is only one of several basic disciplines that underpin the study of organizational phenomena. The two areas of basic psychology that have had the greatest impact on research in organizational psychology and resulting practice are individual differences and social psychology. The first has typically been focused on the study of traits, cognitive abilities, behavioral styles, and other stable individual differences. At the team level, the analyses of the structures and properties of teams equate to the individual traits. Approaches based on social psychology have studied cognitive, affective, and behavioral processes and their outputs, such as attitudes, beliefs, and evaluations at the individual and team levels. Recently, a more integrative approach has emerged in which the trait/structural and process approaches have begun to be combined in both individual (e.g., Minbashian, Wood, & Beckmann, 2010) and team studies (Stewart & Barrick, 2000).

The origins of modern organizational psychology (OP) are generally linked with the Hawthorne studies conducted during the 1930s and the writings of Elton Mayo (1933), who interpreted the results from a psychological perspective rather than the industrial engineering perspective that had guided the studies' original designs. Contemporaries of Mayo also began to introduce psychological constructs into their descriptions and explanations of organizational phenomena. Among the more

IAAP Handbook of Applied Psychology, First Edition. Edited by Paul R. Martin, Fanny M. Cheung, Michael C. Knowles, Michael Kyrios, Lyn Littlefield, J. Bruce Overmier, and José M. Prieto.

influential were ATT executive Chester Barnard (1938), whose book exerted a strong influence on the later work of Herbert Simon and James March (March & Simon, 1958), and Mary Parker Follet (Metcalf & Urwick, 1942), whose writings on topics such as power and conflict, negotiations and employee participation took into account the attitudes, beliefs, and needs of workers. These early management scholars, and others who followed, influenced the work of psychologists who laid the foundations for what has become the domain of OP.

Any reviewer unfamiliar with the OP field will be struck by the diversity of theories and related variables that are applied in the study of organizational phenomena. The diversity notwithstanding, there is considerable coherence in the accumulated knowledge from OP research and that knowledge is applied widely and to great benefit across a wide range of activities within organizations.

The theories and variables employed in OP research can be categorized into those that have been imported from psychology and used to explain a range of organizational phenomena and those that have been developed within the field to explain specific organizational phenomena. Examples of the first category are attribution theory (Weiner, 1980), identity theory (Tajfel & Turner, 1979) and the five-factor model of personality (Costa & McCrae, 1985). Examples of theories developed within OP include Goal Theory (Locke & Latham, 1990), Organizational Citizenship Behavior Theory (Organ, 1988), escalation theory (Ross & Staw, 1986) and many different leadership theories such as Path–Goal Theory (House, 1996).

The Domain of Organizational Psychology

The distinctiveness of OP arises from the organizational qualifier, which is what differentiates it from other applied fields of psychology, such as educational psychology and sports psychology. The organizational qualifier defines the domain of OP in two ways. First, the types of questions addressed in OP research are typically focused on phenomena that happen in and around organizations, and are focused on problems of interest to leaders and workers in organizations. Second, the organization in OP refers to a context in which behavior occurs including, for example, differentiated roles, hierarchies of goals, power and authority, systems and processes, contingent rewards, and emergent phenomena such as culture. Context is one of several basic constructs that underpin OP thinking and research.

Just like the organizations in which behavior is studied, OP is a constantly evolving discipline in which researchers seek to understand, predict, and explain behavior and to propose solutions to emerging organizational problems. New technologies, new structural forms, changing market conditions, emerging economies such as China and India, and phenomena such as sustainability, globalization, and intergenerational changes in the beliefs and values of population cohorts all shape the issues of interest and the contexts in which OP research is conducted. Researchers, consultants, and practitioners all address broad questions such as "What makes people and teams motivated, productive, and satisfied at work?" as well as many more specific questions about how to predict and manage organizational phenomena such as absenteeism, turnover, conflict, and leadership and team effectiveness. The rise in interest for specific research questions often occurs in response to emergent phenomena, but research may also shape practitioner interest. For example, the study of voluntary or extra-role behavior within organizations has paralleled the emergence of reduced bureaucracy and flatter organizational structures. This research, which is reviewed later, includes specific questions about the prediction and management of functional behaviors such as organizational citizenship and proactivity, dysfunctional behaviors such as deviance, harassment, and unethical conduct.

Another evolution in OP is the emergence of new psychological concepts and theories in basic psychological disciplines that are then used in the study of organizational phenomena. High-impact examples of these include Locus of Control (Rotter, 1956, 1966), judgment heuristics and Prospect Theory (Tversky & Kahneman, 1972), Attribution Theory (Weiner, 1986), self-efficacy theory (Bandura, 1986), conceptions of ability and goal orientation (Dweck, 1999) and Identity Theory (Haslam, 2004). The application of these theories from psychology is a source of innovation for OP research, however, there is also the risk that new concepts obtain a fashionable or fad status (Dunnette, 1976; Dunnette & Hough, 1991; Starbuck, 2009) and escape the rigorous early evaluations that are the norm for most OP research publishing. This is particularly the case when consultants and practitioners take up new concepts before they have been properly validated in research, a recent example of which is the construct of emotional intelligence (Goleman, 1995). While concepts such as emotional intelligence can be of great value to practitioners, the quick take-up of ideas within organizations sometimes outpaces what is known through rigorous research, leading to prescriptions and applications that go beyond what can be known with confidence about the concept. Research may catch up and contribute to practice, as is happening with emotional intelligence, or the concept may fall out of fashion with practitioners due to problems in application. Alongside the fads and fashions, however, there have been many enduring theories, such as goal setting, organizational citizenship, escalation theory, and the five-factor model of personality, that have produced an accumulated body of valid results, often across a diverse range of applications.

Another way to define the OP field is to categorize the phenomena studied based on levels of analyses, such as individual, interpersonal, and team, and to further discriminate between cognitive, affective, and behavioral processes and variables at each level. Such taxonomic efforts are useful for descriptive purposes and summaries of what is, and is not, known about a topic. However, they can oversimplify the true complexity of a topic, due to the multilevel and dynamic nature of many organizational phenomena. For example, leadership research is often placed in the interpersonal and team level of analysis, which is consistent with a definition of leadership as a process of engaging and influencing others. However, leadership has also been studied as individual-implicit theories, behaviors, and personal attributes, as well as an organizational-level phenomenon. Therefore, while acts of leadership impact on other people, the most robust and useful explanations of leadership are more likely to come through a multilevel analysis of those actions and the related psychological processes, and how they change over time and across contexts.

A Selective Review of Organizational Psychology Research

In the space available, a comprehensive review of the topics that fall within OP research would be too superficial to be useful and, therefore, this section presents a selective review of a limited set of research topics. The topics presented have been chosen for one of two reasons. First, we present a series of topics that represent the building blocks of the OP discipline, including organizational context, personal factors, performance, well-being and turnover, and the interactions between individual and organizational contexts. From a practitioner perspective, the usefulness of OP depends on how effectively it can predict, explain, and enhance the performance, well-being, and retention of individuals and teams in organizational settings. Second, we have chosen a set of topics that have been the focus of extensive research over the past five years, based on a count of publications in leading OP journals, and provide a reasonable cross-section of the specific research questions being studied in OP. This second set of topics includes leadership, teams, discretionary behavior, both positive and negative, justice, organizational change and culture.

The organizational context

Organizational context creates "situational opportunities and constraints that affect the occurrence and meaning of organizational behavior as well as the functional relationships between variables" (Johns, 2006, p. 386). Taking the context into account affects the questions, study designs, and analyses undertaken by OP researchers. According to Rousseau and Fried (2001), it is only through consideration of the organizational context that organizational psychologists can fully understand and accurately predict individual and team behaviors. Context may refer to the properties of the organization, a more immediate and more dynamic situation in which an individual or team is operating, and/or a specific task that is being performed.

Within OP, context is conceptualized and measured by one of three approaches that focus on either nominal features, structural properties, or psychological properties of the context. "Nominal features" (Mischel & Shoda, 1995, 1998) refers to the surface features of contexts that can be described independently of the individuals being studied. Examples include occupation, organizational level, location, team type, physical characteristics (lighting, space, etc), equipment, assigned targets, deadlines, and resources. The structural approach seeks to identify the latent or deep structure of the context, again independently of the individuals who may work in that context. Examples include norms, diversity, information networks, culture, team cohesion, and task complexity. The psychological properties of context are the individual encodings or perceptions of the nominal features and structural properties of situations filtered through the knowledge and motivations of the respondent. Examples include perceived novelty, task challenge, and justice.

Many contextual variables can be represented as having either nominal, structural, or psychological properties. For example, a budgeting and review system is a nominal property of an organizational context. However, it can also be represented as levels of accountability based on the frequency counts of reported and related actions, which is a structural property, or also as an individual employee's experience of perceived accountability, which is a psychological property. Other variables are more uniquely one or the other, such as type of team (virtual versus face to face, a nominal feature), team diversity (a structural property), and team morale (a psychological property).

While the study of the effects of context is a defining feature of OP, context remains unexplored and unexplained in many OP studies (Johns, 2006). This raises several potential problems for the application of knowledge from OP research. First is the extent of generalizability of conclusions from studies that do not measure and test the effects of context. Effects may vary in strength and direction across different contexts, thus making any prescription based on the results of a single study of questionable value for contexts that differ from the one in which the study was conducted. For example, Johns (2006, p. 389) cites a study of teams by Langford and Locke (2000) in which the correlations between social cohesion and group effectiveness varied across different contexts from +.28 in a social service agency to -.65 in a military context. Clearly prescriptions about group cohesion based on a study of either social service agencies or military teams would be incorrect for the other context.

Fortunately, OP researchers typically conduct multiple studies of related topics and meta-analyses of large sets of studies to enable context effects to be systematically examined, thus leading to more finely tuned conclusions about the effects of different variables. For example, meta-analyses have shown that the size of performance effects due to goals (Wood, Mento, & Locke, 1986), feedback (Kluger & Denisi, 1996), self-efficacy (Stajkovic & Luthans, 1998), and goal orientation (Utman, 1997) are all moderated by the complexity of the task being worked on. This effect had previously not been considered in the individual studies of goal effects, which treated the task and other contextual factors as fixed.

Personal factors

Much OP research assumes a model of the individual that includes their traits, beliefs, attitudes, values, self-regulatory and emotional processes and states, and their abilities and behaviors. These are described within one of two broad approaches: individual differences and psychological processes. These two approaches reflect differences in the underlying approaches to the personality and social psychology disciplines from which OP is derived (Cervone, 1997).

Within the individual differences tradition in OP, the individual is viewed as a distinct entity made up of fixed traits, dispositional beliefs, abilities, and behavioral styles whose content is defined independently of context, situations, and tasks. Examples of this approach include the five-factor model of personality (FFM; McCrae & Costa, 1999), dispositional beliefs such as implicit theories (Dweck, 1999), and self-esteem (Brockner, 1988; Brockner et al., 2001) cognitive abilities (Bertua, Anderson, & Salgado, 2005) and behavioral styles such as motivational traits (Kanfer & Ackerman, 2005; Kanfer & Heggestad, 1997). These concepts and others like them describe stable differences between individuals and consistency in individual beliefs, attitudes, abilities, emotional responses, and behaviors across settings and over time.

The individual differences approach to personal factors has seen a resurgence over the past two decades, a development that can be largely attributed to the conceptualization of personality in terms of the five-factor model (FFM; McCrae & Costa, 1987, 1989). The factors of the FFM are predominantly viewed as decontextualized traits that remain relatively stable over the life span and this is reflected both in the research questions it has generated and the research designs and methodologies that have been employed to study personality at work.

Differences between people in personal factors are related to differences in performance (e.g., Barrick & Mount, 1991) and well-being outcomes (e.g., Judge, Heller, & Mount, 2002), as well as critical behaviors such as leadership (e.g., Judge, Bono, Ilies, & Gerhardt, 2002). There is strong evidence that cognitive ability, in particular general mental ability ("g"; Spearman, 1904), is a predictor of task performance (Bertua et al., 2005) that can be replicated across different cultures (Salgado, 2003). Specific cognitive abilities such as verbal, numerical, perceptual, and spatial abilities are also strong predictors of job performance (Bertua et al., 2005). Job experience, declarative and procedural knowledge moderated by job complexity, (Dye, Reek, & McDaniel, 1993) and job experience contingent on job complexity, have also been found to predict performance (Sturman, 2003). For personality traits proposed by the FFM (Digman, 1990; McCrae & Costa, 1989) there is consistent and strong evidence that conscientiousness (i.e., degree of being orderly, self-disciplined, achievement-orientated, reliable, and perseverant) is a predictor of task proficiency (Barrick & Mount, 1991). Weaker evidence suggests that other individual difference factors such as self-esteem, generalized self-efficacy, locus of control, and emotional stability, also influence task performance (Judge & Bono, 2001).

Theories within the psychological processes approach in OP describe dynamic within-person processes that determine responses to contextual influences, which may be highly variable across settings and over time. Originating from social psychology, this perspective focuses on person–situation dynamics, and addresses factors such as personal and social identification processes, interpersonal and intergroup behavior, leadership, and decision making. The aim is to explain variability in individual responses across situations and over time as a result of changes in cognitive and affective responses to contexts, particularly situations and tasks, such as self-set goals (e.g., Locke & Latham, 1990) and self-efficacy (Bandura, 1997). To the degree that variability in responses across situations is systematic, this variability may serve as the basis of units of personality that capture the dynamic aspects of individuals (Mischel & Shoda, 1995, 1998). Consistent with this view, a more dynamic approach has started to emerge within the general personality literature that highlights the importance of integrating person-situation contingency units into the study of personality (e.g., Fleeson, 2001; Fournier, Moskowitz, & Zuroff, 2008). A growing body of work in social psychology (e.g., Fleeson, 2007; Fournier et al., 2008) has established situation–response contingencies as meaningful personal factors that can be used to predict individual responses in different contexts. Furthermore, these situation–response contingencies are treated as an expression of a stable underlying personality system of the individual, which is described as a set of mediating processes whose interactions result in predictable responses across different settings (e.g., Mischel & Peake, 1982; Shoda, Mischel, & Wright, 1994; Wright & Mischel, 1987).

Organizational researchers are beginning to adopt this new approach to personal factors (e.g., Minbashian, et al., in press), which offers the potential for new areas of research in OP.

Performance

Performance is the most common outcome measure in organizational psychology research (Campbell, McCloy, Oppler, & Sager, 1993; Sonnentag & Frese, 2002) and one that is of particular interest to consultants and practitioners who utilize OP knowledge. Questions such as "What works?" or "How effective is a particular practice?" are most likely to be raised in relation to a performance criterion. There is general consensus within organizational psychology that job performance is a multidimensional concept and that each dimension is itself multidimensional (e.g., Campbell et al., 1993; Motowidlo, Borman, & Schmit, 1997; Organ, 1997; Pulakos, Arad, Donovan, & Plamondon, 2000; Rotundo & Sackett, 2002; Sonnentag, Volmer, & Spychala, 2008; Viswesvaran & Ones, 2000).

The structure of job performance broadly distinguishes between either performance processes (i.e., behaviors; actions) or outcomes (i.e., the results of a behavior) (Borman and Motowidlo, 1993; Campbell et al., 1993; Roe, 1999). Performance processes are organized into three distinct categories: task or in-role performance, contextual or extra-role performance, and adaptive performance (Borman & Motowidlo, 1997; Smith, Organ, & Near, 1983).

Performance processes (i.e., behaviors) (Campbell, 1990, Campbell, et al., 1993; Roe, 1999), refers to what the person or teams do when working on a task. Only those behaviors that are considered relevant for achieving the task and organizational goals are considered performance. Furthermore, the definition of performance when referring to behaviors is relative to some standard of execution of the behavior and only includes behaviors that can be empirically measured (Motowidlo et al., 1997; Campbell, et al., 1993). This has led to the development of a range of observation and rating scales (e.g., Behaviorally Anchored Rating Scales: Smith & Kendal, 1963; Cain-Smith & Kendall, 1973; Behavioral Observation Scales: Latham & Wexley, 1977), and other forms of appraisal.

Performance outcomes refer to the products of individual or team efforts and may be counted, as in sales revenue, units produced, errors, or observed and rated by an assessor relative to a standard, such as the grading of a report or quality assessments. Performance outcomes will typically be influenced by more than the behaviors of the individual or team executing the task, and will include the effects of technology, resources, and other forms of support. As with behavioral performance processes, outcomes are typically judged relative to a standard, which may be past levels of outcomes, expectations, or norms. Performance outcomes, however, are separate from performance effectiveness, which refers to the evaluations of the results of performance (i.e. the financial value of the sales) and productivity, which refers to the ratio between effectiveness and the cost of attaining the outcomes (Campbell et al., 1993; Pritchard, 1992).

The distinction between task performance and contextual performance has been the focus of considerable attention in OP research (Borman & Motowidlo, 1997;

Motowidlo & Schmit, 1999). Task performance refers to in-role behaviors that are recognized in formal reward systems and job descriptions as contributing to organizational performance as it relates to the production of goods and services (Motowidlo, Dunnette, & Carter, 1990; Williams & Karau, 1991). Various taxonomies have been developed for categorizing the behaviors that contribute to task performance and many organizations have lists of competencies and other forms of appraisal criteria that describe the required task performance behaviors for roles and job families (e.g., Campbell, 1990; Borman & Brush, 1993).

Contextual performance refers to extra-role tasks that are often performed without formal compensation. By facilitating task performance, contextual performance supports the social and psychological environment in an organization, and indirectly contributes to its functioning. Subfactors of contextual performance include: (a) "stabilizing" behaviors such as OCB (Organizational Citizenship Behavior; Organ, 1988) and prosocial organizational behaviors (Le Pine & Van Dyne, 2002), and (b) "proactive" behaviors (Sonnentag and Frese, 2002) which include personal initiative, (Frese, Kring, Soose, & Zempel, 1996; Crant, 1995; Parker, Williams, & Turner, 2006) and taking charge (Morrison & Phelps, 1999). The latter group of behaviors is closer to the adaptive behaviors category, which is emerging as a separate category in the performance taxonomy (e.g., Chen, Thomas, & Wallace, 2005).

The discretionary nature of contextual performance typically means that it is not part of the employee's formal contract with the organization and therefore not enforceable, but it may be part of the psychological contract that an individual has with the organization (Rousseau, 1996). Recent studies propose that certain forms of contextual performance, such as OCB, should be incorporated into task performance. This is a reflection of the competency frameworks of organizations, many of which include definitions of competencies that are very similar to those used to describe OCB's, proactive behaviors, and adaptive performance by OP researchers. Korsgaard, Meglino, Lester, and Jeong (2010) also note that the definition of OCB has evolved from describing behavior that is not monitored or rewarded to including behaviors that are observed and rewarded within the formal reward system. The merging of contextual and task performance, as in the case of OCB, is an example of how the OP field has evolved in response to changes in organizations, and it has implications for explaining and predicting the particular form of "contextual" performance when the prosocial behavior shifts from unmonitored and unrewarded to expected and rewarded, and therefore more tightly linked to self-interested motivational mechanisms such as impression management (Bolino, 1999).

Task and contextual performance are also of interest because they are determined by different factors, some of which have implications for the selection and development activities of organizations. For example, general mental ability ("g"), which is a strong predictor of performance across a very wide range of tasks, jobs and roles (Schmidt & Hunter, 1998), does not predict contextual performance (Chan & Schmitt, 2002; Hattrup, O'Connell, & Wingate, 1998; Le Pine & Van Dyne, 2001; Van Scotter & Motowidlo, 1996). Meta-analytic results also indicate that the narrow dimensions of trait conscientiousness, such as dependability and achievement, incrementally predict extra-role behaviors such as job dedication, counterproductive work behaviors, and interpersonal facilitation above and beyond global conscientiousness

(Dudley, Orvis, Lebiecke, & Cortina, 2006). Differences in positive and negative affect influence contextual performance such as OCB (Kaplan, Bradley, Luchman, & Haynes, 2009). Job autonomy predicts control orientation and self-efficacy, which in turn predicts proactive behavior through control orientation and self-efficacy (Ohly, Sonnentag, & Pluntke, 2006; Parker et al., 2006; Speier & Frese, 1997). Furthermore, job knowledge (i.e., declarative knowledge) mediates between individual dispositions (e.g., cognitive ability and personality) and contextual performance, in particular, proactive and adaptive performance (Parker, Wall, & Jackson, 1997; Fay & Frese, 2001; Chen et al., 2005).

Personal well-being

After performance, the personal well-being or mental health of individual employees within organizations is the second most common criterion used in OP studies. Well-being has been operationalized in a variety of ways but the most common measures are of job satisfaction and stress. Job satisfaction is a "pleasurable or positive emotional state resulting from one's job or job experience" (Locke, 1976). The sources of satisfaction with one's job have been categorized in various ways but the most enduring typology has been that of Smith, Kendall, and Hulin (1969) who identified the work performed, rewards (particularly pay), growth opportunities, supervision (or leadership), and coworkers as key sources of job satisfaction.

Of central importance to OP has been the question of how job satisfaction is related to performance. The scholarly forerunners of OP such as Mayo (1933) and early writers such as Herzberg (1959, 1987) and Maslow (1943) believed that the satisfaction of human needs at work, the origins of job satisfaction, were a major determinant of work performance. The belief that a happy (i.e. satisfied) worker is a more productive worker is still a widely held belief. Studies of the relationship between job satisfaction and performance have been the subject of several reviews including a comprehensive meta-analytic review by Judge, Thoresen, Bono, & Patton (2001) which suggested only a moderate positive relationship between job satisfaction and productivity. This study also found that the relationship between performance and job satisfaction was not a straightforward one. For example, there was a significantly stronger positive relationship between job satisfaction and performance for more complex jobs, compared to less complex jobs. Thus it is likely that a combination of psychological and organizational contextual factors moderate the relationship between job satisfaction and performance.

In contrast to job satisfaction, the second component of well-being, stress, deals with the more negative and extreme emotional, cognitive, behavioral, and physical reactions to work. The measurable stress reactions most frequently assessed in OP include smoking, heart rate, and burnout. Stress is a multidisciplinary topic that is researched in medicine, clinical psychology, health psychology, and engineering psychology, as well as OP. Stress is of particular interest to OP researchers because organizational contexts are the source of many of the determinants of stress, such as workload and other task demands, interpersonal conflict, personal control, segmentation of work and home demands, and social support. Additionally, stress imposes a heavy cost on organizations through health-related claims and disruption of personal lives, turnover, and performance. Job stress is related to job performance both directly and indirectly through job satisfaction and turnover, such that individuals who are stressed perform less effectively and are more likely to leave the organization (Fried, Shirom, Gilboa, & Cooper, 2008).

Not all individuals have the same stress reactions to stressors in the organizational context. Personal factors that influence reactions to stressors in the organizational context include the person's desire for control, level of commitment, perceived efficacy to cope with the stressors, and actual coping skills. In many contexts, coping efficacy and coping skills are the products of political skill and job experience (Zellars, Perrewé, Rossi, Tepper , & Ferris, 2007).

Voluntary turnover

The loss and replacement of employees can be a costly and disruptive process, which is why voluntary turnover is of interest to OP researchers and practitioners. As would be expected, turnover is a product of attitudes and intentions that relate to the organizational context, personal factors, and alternative opportunities. An extensive meta-analysis by Griffeth, Hom, and Gaertner (2000) showed that proximal factors that predicted actual voluntary turnover included lower levels of job satisfaction and organizational commitment, perceived procedural injustice, higher levels of job-searching behaviors, quitting cognitions, and quitting intentions. The more distal predictors of these factors included both organizational contextual factors such as high levels of workplace stress, poor workgroup cohesion, lack of autonomy and poor leadership; external factors included the presence of alternatives, and increased range of search methods. Finally, Griffeth et al. (2000) also found that behaviors such as lateness, absenteeism, and poor performance were antecedents of quitting.

Other studies have identified nominal properties of organizational contexts that influence turnover, including unionization, internal promotion practices (versus external recruitment), alternative dispute resolution practices, and human resource systems that facilitate staff involvement (Guthrie, 2001). One important and consistent finding in the study of voluntary turnover is that effects of different predictors are mediated through conscious intentions to leave the organization (Tett & Meyer, 1993). Additionally, research has found that turnover can be viewed as a process that begins with general job dissatisfaction, which gives rise to considerations of alternatives, job-searching behavior and preparations for quitting (Blau, 1993; Sager, Griffeth, & Hom, 1998). The practical implication of these findings is that managers should be alert to the intentions of key employees and act before they convert their intentions into a resignation.

Interactions of individuals and organizations

The relationship between individuals and teams and the organizational contexts in which they work is at the core of many models and theories within OP. The most general framework for the study of this relationship is the Person–Environment (P–E) fit theory, which "refers to the congruence, match, or similarity between the person and environment (Edwards, 2008). In P–E theory, matching or congruence is described in terms of rewards and demands of the environment and their "fit" with the preferences or capabilities of the person. The achieved fit has been described as either supplementary or complementary (Muchinsky & Monahan, 1987). Supplementary fit describes the person's relationship with other people in their environment and occurs when the person "supplements, embellishes, or possesses characteristics that are similar to other individuals in their environment" (Kristof, 1996). Complementary fit occurs when "a person's characteristics 'make whole' the environment or add what is missing" (Muchinsky & Monahan, 1987) and refers to two types of matching. The first type of matching is demand–abilities fit, which refers to the matching of a person's capabilities with the demands of the environment, such as time, effort, commitment, knowledge, and abilities. Fit occurs when the person's contributions match the demands of the environment. The second form of complementary fit is needs–supply fit, which refers to the match between the environmental supplies of psychological, social, technological, financial, and other resources, to the needs of the individual, which may relate to immediate task needs or longer term growth needs.

In P–E fit conceptualizations, the individual and the situation are conceptualized as separate entities but are described and measured on common dimensions to allow for a consideration of matching. Thus, for example, individual capabilities and environment demands may be defined in terms of "expertise" and "knowledge requirements," respectively. P–E fit has been used as an explanatory variable for a range of outcomes, including job satisfaction (Locke, 1976), selection (Sekiguchi, 2004), culture (Chatman, 1989), stress (Edwards, 1996), vocational success (Holland, 1997), attraction-selection-retention (Schneider, 1987; Schneider, Smith, & Paul, 2001), and goal alignment (Vancouver & Schmitt, 1991).

Leadership

Leadership research has produced a large body of OP knowledge and resulted in many prescriptions for the practice of leadership in organizations. While there is general agreement that leadership includes acts that "engage and influence other people toward some goal" the study of leadership has been conducted within a range of frameworks, models, and theories. These include trait-based, behavioral, competence-based, contingency-focused, and relationship-based approaches to leadership. In general terms, these approaches respectively describe what leaders do, when leaders are effective, the characteristics of leaders, and the interactions between leaders and followers.

Behavioral theories provide a good example of how leadership researchers have evolved their approaches in response to the challenges of leadership in organizations. Following World War II, research groups at the University of Michigan and Ohio State University each developed models that described leadership in terms of task- or performance-oriented behaviors, and people or team maintenance behaviors (Yukl, 2007). These early models provided functional descriptions of leadership behaviors for small teams and were very influential in the development of leadership training for mid- and lower-level managers. Other behavioral approaches include studies of the language of leaders (House, 1996) and entrepreneurial leadership (Nicholson, 1998).

The most comprehensive study of leadership behaviors is the international study conducted by the GLOBE team, led by House (1996). GLOBE is an example of how leadership research builds cumulatively on prior findings and is progressive in responding to the changing needs of managers in organizations with the growth of multi-national corporations (MNCs) and the globalization of business. House and his colleagues have taken the US-based behavioral models of leadership and extended them in the cross-cultural comparisons of leadership styles. This comprehensive study of leadership was conducted across 62 countries and collected data from 17,300 middle managers in 951 organizations. One of the many useful outputs of the GLOBE program has been a set of valid measurement instruments assessing six culturally universal leadership dimensions; charismatic/value-based, participative, team-oriented, self-protective, humane-oriented, and autonomous.

Over the last three decades, interest in leadership at senior executive levels, where engaging and influencing actions are targeted at a range of stakeholders with many of whom the leader has no direct contact, has led to the emergence of behavioral descriptions of leadership as either transformational or transactional (Burns, 1978; Bass, 1985). Transformational leadership describes behaviors for leading change within organizations such as creating, communicating, and modeling a vision, and inspiring employees to strive towards challenging goals. As well as providing the guidance, clarity of expectations, and support spelt out in early behavioral leadership theories, the transformational leader engages and influences followers by appealing to their values and aspirations (Burns, 2003). By way of contrast, transactional leadership describes a style that engages and influences followers toward the efficient achievement of organizational objectives through transactions such as linking job performance to valued rewards, and ensuring employees have adequate resources (Burns, 2003). Critics of transformational leadership note that the model does not allow for the effects of situational factors. For example, transformational leadership may be effective when organizational change is necessary, but not during a period of stability.

Contingency models of leadership describe differences in the impacts of leadership styles (e.g., transformational or transactional leadership) for different types of employees, and in different organizational contexts (Fiedler, 1967; Vecchio, Justin, & Pearce, 2008). Situational determinants of leadership include top management team heterogeneity (functional, educational specialty, educational level, and skill categories), and industry environmental dynamism, which describes the rate of unpredicted change in a number of industry employees, industry revenue, industry research, and in development intensity. These situational factors determine the kind of leadership required for a particular task. According to contingency models of leadership, there is no ideal leader or style of leadership, but rather leadership is more effective if it fits the requirements of the situation. For example, task-oriented leaders have been found to be more effective in extremely favorable or unfavorable situations, whereas relationship-oriented leaders perform best in situations with moderate favorability.

The competence approach to leadership emphasizes the personality characteristics, self-concept, leadership motivation, knowledge, cognitive flexibility, and emotional intelligence of a leader (Judge & Piccolo, 2004). The most prominent example of a competence approach is the study of charismatic leadership, which focuses on the personal dispositions or relational quality of the leader that are argued to provide referent power over followers (Fanelli & Misangyi, 2006). Charisma is a disposition that describes the compelling attractiveness or charm that a leader is able to use as a tool to engage and influence the behavior of followers.

Approaches that focus on the properties of relationships between leaders and followers date back to the earlier exchange theories of power and influence (Blau, 1964; Emerson, 1962). More recent relationship approaches include analyses of the impact that followers' implicit theories of leadership (leadership prototypes) and expectations have on the leader's engagement and influence attempts (Epitropaki & Martin, 2004; Iles, Filmer, Spitzmuller, & Johnson, 2006). Other relationship approaches include shared leadership and servant leadership. Shared leadership describes a type of leadership that is broadly distributed among team members and is characterized by informal behaviors, enthusiasm, and shared knowledge to engage and influences followers (Raelin, 2005). Servant-style leadership is where leaders engage and influence followers through service in the role of coach, steward, or facilitator of follower performance (Greenleaf, 2002).

The most extensive body of research from the relationship approach to leadership is that on Leader-Member exchange (LMX), which focuses on the quality of the relationship between a superior and subordinate, leader and follower (Graen & Uhl-Bien, 1995). LMX describes how much employees trust and respect their leader and how willing they are to follow his or her guidance through three phases of interaction (Gerstner & Day, 1997). The first phase of role taking entails the assessment of new team members' competencies. This is followed by a negotiation between a team member and their leader on the role to be taken, and the tasks and expectations associated with it. Finally, during the routinization phase, patterns of ongoing exchange are established and embedded (Liden, Sparrowe, & Wayne, 1997).

The concept of LMX has been applied to a range of interpersonal relationships, including interactions between team members, employees and customers, an employee and spouse, mentor and mentee, trustor and trustee, and between parties in a negotiation (Graen & Uhl-Bien, 1995). LMX predicts both leaders' assessments and objective measures of follower performance. However, the strength of the relationships between LMX and performance is influenced by organizational context, in particular, this relationship is stronger in organizational contexts where there is greater feedback and empowerment (Chen, Lam, & Zhong, 2007). Other properties of organizational context that moderate the LMX–performance relationship include advisor and team member support, task autonomy, and organizational culture. Followers who perform better as result of stronger LMX include those with better political skills and internal locus of control.

Prescriptions based on leadership research have produced many beneficial outcomes for organizations. Across all approaches, leadership has consistently been demonstrated to make a difference to the performance and well-being of followers and teams. While the specific indicators of performance and well-being vary from approach to approach, and from study to study, there is general support for the conclusion that leadership does make a difference. For example, Kuoppala, Lamminpää, Liira, and Vaino (2008) reviewed research showing that effective leadership predicts greater self-reported well-being, including lower rates of sick leave in subordinates. In addition, good leadership is also related to higher job satisfaction and organizational commitment, greater work safety, in particular the prevention of injury or disability, more OCB, and less dysfunctional or deviant workplace behavior.

Teams

In OP, teams are viewed as complex, adaptive, dynamic systems that are embedded within organizational contexts (Ilgen, 1999; Ilgen, Hollenbeck, Johnson, & Jundt, 2005). A team is a unit of two or more individuals who interact interdependently to achieve a common objective (Baker & Salas, 1997; Bell, 2007). The defining characteristic of any real team, as distinct from a group, is the level of interdependence of its members (Cordery, 2003; Hackman, 2002; Levi, 2001). Teams have become a basic building block in organizations because they allow for the completion of tasks that require more than one individual, are suited to solving complex problems in a dynamic and challenging environment, and have a synergistic effect as team members work collaboratively to achieve common goals (Cohen & Bailey, 1997; Pfeffer, 1997).

The conceptualization of teams within OP parallels that of individuals in that it includes both the structural properties of teams and the dynamic cognitive, affective, and behavioral processes through which their outcomes are achieved (McGrath, 1964; Kozlowski & Ilgen, 2006; Ilgen et al., 2005). For example, the functional similarities in motivational processes across the individual and team levels of analysis can be observed through the examination of the antecedents and outcomes of individual and team motivation (Ilgen et al., 2005).

Based on well-established social psychological research on group processes (Tuckman, 1965), a three-way temporal classification of teams was suggested by Ilgen and colleagues (2005) to illustrate the progression of a team from its formation to its general functioning, and finally to its finishing phase, where the team completes one episode in the developmental cycle and begins a new cycle. According to Ilgen, during the forming phase team members develop interpersonal trust, and are engaged in team planning and structuring (Stout, Cannon-Bowers, Salas, & Milanovich, 1999), and developing shared mental models (Austin, 2003). Perceptions of collective efficacy and psychological safety have been shown to positively impact team performance and effectiveness (Beal, Cohen, Burke, & McLendon, 2003; Edmondson, 1999). There is strong evidence that cooperation (Wagner, 1995), as well as information sharing amongst team members (LePine & Van Dyne, 2001) is related to more effective team performance during this phase.

During the functioning stage, team bonding has been shown to have a positive influence on high performing teams (Beal et al., 2003), and that managing diversity and conflict is necessary during this phase (Lavery, Franz, Winquist, & Larson, 1999; Littlepage, Robison, & Reddington, 1997). Recent empirical evidence suggests that teams with a learning orientation tend to perform better, although in the case of high performing teams, this effect is particularly evident in the earlier stages of the team's life-cycle (Bunderson & Sutcliffe, 2003). Additionally, effective processes for managing task and relationship conflict minimizes the impact of conflict on group functioning and team member satisfaction (Montoya-Weiss, Massey, & Song, 2001).

Team research has been extensive in OP, and in psychology more generally, and has contributed greatly to the development of knowledge of the design, leadership, and functioning of teams within organizations (e.g., Kozslowski & Ilgen, 2008). Among the structural properties of teams, composition is one that has been researched extensively and which has produced many prescriptions for the design and formation of teams. Team composition is studied in terms of both average levels of skills and knowledge across team members, and the degree of diversity of skills, knowledge, and personality traits of team members (Chao & Moon, 2005; Harrison & Klein, 2008).

More recently, OP researchers have examined questions of alignment, or fit, between individuals, teams, and contexts using multilevel analytical techniques (Kozlowski & Klein, 2000), including the alignment of team role structures (functional versus divisional) with properties of the broader organizational context (Hollenbeck, Moon, Ellis, West, & Ilgen, 2002). These approaches allow consideration of the complexity, meaningfulness, valance, and autonomy of the task (Cohen & Bailey, 1997; Gladstein, 1984; Hackman, 1987; Tannenbaum, Beard, & Salas, 1992), as well as levels of interdependence amongst team members (Campion, Medsker, & Higgs, 1993; Stewart & Barrick, 2000; Wageman, 1995) as antecedents of team performance indices such as productivity, efficiency, team flexibility, goal attainment, well-being, and satisfaction.

Positive discretionary behavior

Organizational citizenship behavior (OCB*)* is discretionary prosocial behavior that has a positive effect on the psychological, social, and organizational context of work. Citizenship behaviors contribute to the "maintenance and enhancement of the social and psychological context that supports task performance" (Organ, 1997, p. 91). OCBs are extra-role and discretionary in the sense that they go beyond the strict definition of the job description and do not lay claim to any contractual recompense expected from the formal reward system (Organ, Podsakoff, & MacKenzie, 2006). Since the first empirical studies on OCB conducted by Bateman & Organ (1983) linking quantitative measures of output to more subtle qualitative aspects of work, OCB research has identified many different forms of citizenship behaviors including altruism, courtesy, sportsmanship, conscientiousness, civic virtue, interpersonal facilitation, job dedication, helping coworkers, loyalty, obedience, participation, personal industry, and individual initiative. OCB can be differentiated into behavior directed at coworkers and other people, called OCB-I, and behavior directed more generally toward the organization, called OCB-O. Examples of OCB-I include helping coworkers and interpersonal facilitations, while OCB-O examples include loyalty, job dedication, and civic virtue (Williams & Anderson, 1991).

Individual propensities to perform citizenship behaviors are influenced by several personal factors, particularly the Five Factor Model (McCrae & Costa, 1989) personality traits of agreeableness and conscientiousness. Individuals who are high in agreeableness are more likely to help others (OCB-I), whereas those high in conscientiousness are more likely to focus their citizenship efforts on the organization (OCB-O) (Ilies, Scott, & Judge, 2006; Organ & Ryan, 1995). Other personality traits such as prosocial personality (Penner, Dovidion, Piliavin, & Schroeder, 2005), empathy, helpfulness, and perspective taking (Kamdar, McAlister, & Turban, (2006) also influence individual propensities to engage in citizenship behaviors. Organizational contextual factors such as job satisfaction and organizational commitment are also predictors of OCB (Podsakoff, MacKenzie, Paine, & Bachrach 2000), in addition to psychological perceptions of organizational context including perceptions of interpersonal and procedural justice, which predict OCB-I and OCB-O, respectively (Colquitt, Conlon, Wesson, Porter, & Ng, 2001).

Other properties of the organizational context that have a more direct impact on the level of citizenship behaviors include characteristics of tasks and social relationships, which create an environment that can either encourage or discourage citizenship behavior (Bowler & Brass, 2006; Spitzmuller et al., 2008). Among interpersonal relationships, those with leaders, supervisors, and coworkers are important determinants of citizenship, particularly OCB-I (Ilies, Nahrgang, & Morgeson, 2007). Interpersonal citizenship behaviors tend to be targeted at specific individuals within an employee's social context, for example, employees tend to reciprocate high-quality LMX relationships with OCB-I directed specifically at their leader (Kamdar & Van Dyne, 2007), and they reciprocate high-quality relationships with coworkers by providing more interpersonal citizenship behavior directed at those coworkers (Anderson & Williams, 1996; Kamdar & Van Dyne, 2007).

As discussed earlier, while OCB and other forms of contextual performance are important in their own right and for their contributions to organizational culture and capability, the more direct relationships between OCB and performance outcomes are also of interest. Across 168 independent samples that have examined the performance effects of OCB, the evidence indicates that OCBs do contribute to a number of individual-level and organizational-level outcomes (Podsakoff, Whiting, & Podsakoff, 2009). Individual-level outcomes of citizenship behaviors include higher managerial ratings of employee performance and reward allocations, and lower levels of turnover and absenteeism. Those who perform OCB also benefit through more positive self-evaluations and higher levels of well-being, including better physical and mental health and personal development (Penner et al., 2005; Spitzmuller et al., 2008). Organizational-level outcomes that are related to citizenship behaviors include productivity, efficiency, reduced costs, customer satisfaction, and unit-level turnover (Podsakoff et al., 2009). At the team level, there is a significant body of evidence that performance is positively related to the levels of OCB by team members (Nielsen, Hrivnak, & Shaw, 2009).

Negative discretionary behavior

While discretionary behaviors such as OCB are of interest for their potential positive contributions to contextual and task performance, dysfunctional discretionary behaviors such as deviance, theft, aggression, and sexual harassment are of interest because of their negative impact on individual, team and organizational well-being and performance. Discretionary dysfunctional behaviors include "workplace deviance behavior" (Robinson & Bennett, 1995), "counterproductive work behavior" (Sackett & Devore, 2001), "organizational misbehavior" (Vartia, 1996), and "antisocial behavior" (Giacaloni & Greenberg, 1997). Specific examples include workplace bullying, aggression, and violence (Neuman & Baron, 1998; O'Leary-Kelly, Griffin, & Glew, 1996). As with OCB, dysfunctional organizational behavior can be categorized into that which is directed at other people (e.g., verbal threats, criticism, ostracization, ridicule, etc) and that which is directed toward the organization (e.g., theft, sabotage, etc).

Dysfunctional behaviors, particularly those focused on other individuals (ODB-I), are further differentiated based on the magnitude of their impact, the form of the action, and legal definitions. For example, bullying is defined as "a repeated and prolonged pattern of exposure to negative acts by an individual or group" (Einarsen, 2000; Rayner, Hoel, & Cooper., 2002), in order to differentiate it from similar, but more isolated acts. Sexual harassment is an example of an ODB-I that has a both a legal definition and an OP definition. In law, sexual harassment is defined as "unwelcome sexual advances, request for sexual favors, and other verbal or physical conduct of a sexual nature [that] constitute sexual harassment when this conduct explicitly or implicitly affects an individual's employment, unreasonably interferes with an individual's work performance, or creates an intimidating, hostile, or offensive work environment" (Equal Employment Opportunity Commission, 1980). Within OP sexual harassment is defined as "unwanted sex-related behavior at work that is appraised by the recipient as offensive, exceeding her resources, or threatening her well-being" (Fitzgerald, Drasgow, Hulin, Gelfand, & Magley, 1997). While consistent with the legal definition, this OP definition focuses more directly on the specific behaviors and the victim's psychological encoding of his or her experience of those behaviors.

Why does dysfunctional behavior occur in the workplace? Personality correlates of dysfunctional behavior include low conscientiousness (Salgado & Rumbo, 2002), a lack of integrity (Sackett & Wanek, 1996), trait anger (Lee & Allen, 2002), state hostility and satisfaction (Judge, Scott, & Illes, 2006), agreeableness (Colbert, Mount, Harter, Witt, & Barrick, 2004), self-esteem, locus of control (Fox & Spector, 1999), and responsibility and risk-taking (Ashton, 1998). Attitudes that lead to aggressive or violent behavior include revenge (Douglas & Martinko, 2001) and job dissatisfaction (Hershcovis et al., 2007).

Organizational contexts that undermine an individual's autonomy and sense of control can trigger dysfunctional behavior (Lawrence & Robinson, 2007) as can environments in which prolonged interpersonal conflict and incivility occur (Penny & Spector, 2005). Contextual factors that are more likely to lead to more extreme forms of dysfunctional behavior, such as aggression and violence, include those that encourage high risk (Harvey & Keashly, 2003), and are characterized by interpersonal conflict (Hershcovis et al., 2007), low surveillance (Greenberg & Barling, 1999), low interactional justice (Inness, Barling, & Turner, 2005), and aggressive supervision (Hershcovis et al., 2007). Hershcovis and colleagues (2007) found that from three possible interpersonal sources of aggression—supervisors, coworkers and outsiders—supervisor aggression has the strongest adverse effects on attitudes (i.e., job satisfaction, affective commitment, and turnover intent), and the strongest positive effects on dysfunctional behavior (i.e., interpersonal deviance, organizational deviance, and lower work performance).

The interactions between personal and situational factors that lead to harmful behavior in the work place have also been studied. Colbert and his colleagues (2004) found that personality factors such as conscientiousness, stability, and agreeableness reduce the likelihood of dysfunctional behavior in response to negative perceptions of the work environment. Penny and Spector (2005) found that negative affect increases the likelihood of harmful behavior when the work environment contains stressors. Other contextual factors can alter the relationship between personal factors and dysfunctional workplace behavior including the perception of interpersonal injustice (Judge et al., 2006), procedural injustice, perceived organizational sanctions against aggression, and a lack of organizational support (Colbert et al., 2004).

ODB-I has been found to have a range of negative effects on the psychological and physical health of targets, including general health and symptoms of depression, general stress, and anxiety, posttraumatic stress disorder, and impaired psychological well-being (Cortina & Berdahl, 2008). The effects of sexual harassment on targets include job dissatisfaction (Lapierre, Spector, & Leck, 2005) and increased levels of withdrawal behaviors such as absenteeism, tardiness, work neglect, and turnover, as well as decrements in the employee's organizational commitment, performance, and productivity (Cortina & Berdahl, 2008). The negative effects of sexual harassment are not limited to the targets of the behavior but also extend to members of the victim's team, including impaired team relationships, increased team conflicts, distractions from the team task, lowered justice perceptions, imbalanced performance demands, and lowered team performance (Parker & Griffin, 2002).

Justice in organizations

Justice refers to the individual or organizational quality of being morally just or righteous, adhering to the principle of just dealing, and the exhibition of these qualities in action (Cohen-Carash & Spector, 2001). Organizational justice refers to people's perceptions of fairness in the workplace. Justice in organizations is of interest to OP practitioners and researchers who believe that justice in organizations should be consistent with principles of justice in society. Additionally, this is an important aspect of OP research and practice for those who recognize that justice in organizations influences many performance and well-being outcomes (i.e., Colbert et al., 2004). As already noted, a sense of justice increases the likelihood that discretionary behaviors will be positive and not negative.

Different types of justice that are identified and studied in OP research include distributive, procedural, and interactional justice (Cohen-Carash & Spector, 2001). Distributive justice refers to the perceived fairness of outcome allocations, typically judged by comparing outcomes or rewards to inputs or investments (Adams, 1965; Homans, 1961; Leventhal, 1976). Procedural justice refers to the perceived fairness in the method, practice, process, and conduct of decision making and resource allocation (Thibaut & Walker, 1975). Procedural justice also takes consideration of justice beyond the psychological properties of the organizational context, and treats it as an analytical property of the organization context. Leventhal (1980), for example, described the properties of procedural justice in terms of a set of process control rules for resource allocation systems, including consistency across people and time, bias suppression, accuracy of information, correctability, representativeness, and ethicality. Interactional justice refers to the perceived fairness of interpersonal communication and is closely related to interpersonal justice, that is, respect and propriety in dealing with others, and informational justice, which includes justification and truthfulness in communications (Bies & Moag, 1986).

Perceptions of organizational justice are influenced by the values of individuals, including their cultural values (Cole, Bernerth, Walter, & Holt, 2009). For example, Brockner et al., (2001) found that perceptions of poor procedural justice had a greater negative impact on organizational commitment in individualistic societies, where personal self-concepts are more salient, compared to societies that are more like collectivities, such as those in East Asia. Other personal factors that influence individual justice perceptions and reactions include the employee's affective state, implicit theories of their leader/supervisor, social information, and personal or social identity. When an outcome violates a central aspect of an employee's personal or social identity, objectively fair procedures will not improve perceptions of procedural and distributive justice (Alge, 2009).

The effects of justice perceptions include increased OCB (Fassina, Jones, & Uggerslev, 2008), plus greater organizational commitment, job satisfaction, and trust (Brockner et al., 2001). In a meta-analysis of the effects of perceptions of organizational justice, Colquitt et al., (2001) confirmed that distributive, procedural, interpersonal, and informational justice were positively related to several organizational outcomes, including job satisfaction, organizational commitment, organizational citizenship behavior, and performance.

Organizational culture

Organizational culture is a complex and multi-level concept (Ott, 1989; Schein, 1985) that describes the characteristics of the organization that are captured in common and widely shared understandings and expectations of the organizational context, behavior, and events. The shared understandings, expectations, and interpretations include values and assumptions of members, norms that invoke sanctions when broken by members, standards of behavior that members are expected to display, and goals that members pursue while at work. Shared interpretations include members' perceptions of work practices in areas such as innovation and risk-taking, level of precision and attention to detail, performance expectations, consideration for coworkers, collaboration and teamwork, stability versus growth, and the level of aggressive and competitive behaviors (O'Reilly, Chatman, & Caldwell, 1991). While organizational culture is based on shared intra-personal factors and behaviors, it is often manifested and transmitted through stories and legends, systems and processes, rituals and ceremonies, language, and the physical structures and symbols of the organization. The strength of an organization's culture will be influenced by the alignment of the content of values, norms, beliefs and behaviors, and alignment across the different levels, such as the alignment of appraisal and reward systems and processes with values such as merit, equity and transparency.

Culture serves several different functions within organizations, including behavioral control, providing members with sense of organizational identity, agreement about what the organization stands for, stability within the workplace, and the creation of cohesion (Schein, 2004). Evidence suggests a modest positive relationship between strength of organizational culture and performance, employee well-being, and organizational commitment, and this relationship is dependent on the alignment of salient values with the external environment and the people within the organization, the level of organizational agility necessary to adapt to changes in the external environment, and the emergence of new values within the organization over time. Research has shown that strong cultures with unanimity of purpose and high levels of commitment to shared values lessen employees' propensity to leave the organization (Vandenberghe, 1999).

Personal (P–E) fit with culture is largely achieved through the systems and processes that are used to attract, select, and retain people whose values and personality characteristics are consistent with the organization's values and characteristics (Schneider, 1987; Schneider, Smith, Taylor, & Fleenor, 1998; Giberson, Resick, & Dickson, 2005). Socialization processes during the attraction and selection processes for new employees can be used to accelerate the learning of, and adjustment to, organizational values, expected behaviors, and the social knowledge necessary to assume their roles in the organization, thus increasing the P–E fit with culture, newcomer adjustment, and embeddedness in the organization (Allen, 2006; Saks, Uggerslev, & Fassena, 2007; Cooper-Thomas & Anderson, 2005). Better P–E cultural fit has also been found to reduce turnover (Allen et al., 2006).

Organizational culture becomes particularly salient when one organization acquires or merges with another organization, and strategies to merge and align divergent organizational cultures are required in order to ensure successful subsequent performance. Merging strategies include the assimilation of the acquiring organization's culture, deculturation of the acquired organization, integration of two or more cultures into a new composite culture, or, alternatively, the preservation of distinct entities with minimal exchange of culture or organizational practice (Malekazedeh & Nahavandi, 1990; McShane, Olekalns, & Travaglione, 2010). Many mergers and acquisitions fail to realize the value promised in the business case due to a failure to create an effective culture in the new entity (Haspeslagh & Jemison, 1991).

Professional Activities of Organizational Psychologists

The professional activities of organizational psychologists encompass a wide range of roles in universities, consulting firms, and organizations in the public, private, and not-for-profit sectors. The primary functions of those in organizational psychology roles include research and the development of knowledge, teaching, consulting, and advising on specialized OP issues within organizations. Organizational psychologists, because of their deep knowledge of people, teams and organizations, often get promoted into senior leadership roles within organizations. Briefly, the aims, rewards, and social networks for the different types of roles performed by organizational psychologists are as follows.

Research functions include a mixture of applied and basic research aimed at addressing questions of "What activities or interventions produce the best performance and/or well-being outcomes?" and "Why or how do activities or interventions produce different outcomes?" Organizational psychologists located within university schools of psychology and management conduct most, but not all OP research. Organizational psychologists working within consulting firms also conduct applied research, particularly as it relates to the development, validation, and application of assessment tests and surveys. University-based organizational psychologists strive to publish their research findings in peer-reviewed journals in order to contribute to the general body of knowledge in the domain, gain the recognition of their peers in professional societies, and to obtain promotion. This is less common among organizational psychologists working within consulting firms, who maintain greater confidentiality around their results in order to protect intellectual property and the resulting revenues from the copyright of assessment tests and surveys. As a result, some of the largest databases on individuals and teams are not available for research that can be published and integrated into the body of OP knowledge. OP research is primarily published in psychology and management journals.

Teaching and dissemination of OP knowledge occurs in different modes across a range of settings. OP knowledge is disseminated through university-based degree courses and executive programs, coaching programs, industry training courses, and company-based training programs. Written forms of dissemination include textbooks, popular management books, and, increasingly, internet blogs and magazine articles that discuss and promote findings from OP research published in academic journals. Consultants, academics, trainers, practitioners, professional writers, and bloggers all contribute to the dissemination of OP knowledge. Many of those communicating OP knowledge, either through training programs or publications, do not have any formal training in OP, which can lead to problems of quality control in relation to the validity and content of what is being communicated. However, many trainers, coaches, and consultants belong to professional psychological associations and industry training associations that include certification requirements and other forms of quality assurance.

Consulting and advising services are provided to individuals and organizations by organizational psychologists working in consulting firms and by university-based OP academics who combine consulting activities with their research and teaching duties. The functions of consulting and advice services includes helping practitioners to define and solve problems, personal guidance on problems, development and career advice, design and evaluations of systems and interventions, and expert testimonies.

Practice includes all the application of OP knowledge and training in the performance of work roles within organizations. These include specialized OP roles in areas such as change management, selection, and training, as well as the application of OP knowledge in management and other roles. In particular, OP knowledge in the areas of leadership and teams are key contributors to the successful performance of many roles within modern organizations.

Challenges, Opportunities, and Future Directions for Organizational Psychology

At the beginning of this chapter, we noted that OP research has evolved in response to changes in organizations and the issues that confront people who work in them. Many of these changes were a result of broader forces in the societies and environments in which organizations operate. That will continue to be true in the future. With that in mind, we review some of the forces or trends that are influencing organizations and impacting on the issues that will be of interest to OP researchers, consultants and practitioners. These include:

Globalization. Globalization has already presented a number of challenges to organizations, and OP research is examining its consequences as organizations adapt to changing international requirements. Cross-cultural researchers have already developed extensive bodies of knowledge that provide guidance to OP researchers and practitioners (e.g., Smith, Peterson, & Thomas, 2008). Within that context, two particular issues are of current interest. First, a shift in production facilities and staff to developing nations, particularly China, India, and the Middle East has resulted in the emergence of localization programs (Fryxell, Butler, & Choi, 2004). As organizations establish facilities in other countries, often as a way to reduce costs, localization, which is the replacing of expatriate managers with local staff, is increasing. In many countries, localization is included as part of foreign investment rules as a part of knowledge transfer and national development strategies. From the global organizations' perspective, localization reduces many of the problems associated with expatriate staff and can enhance the development and implementation of regional strategies. However, it is reliant upon programs that support the development of skills and competencies in local populations. Forstlechner (2010) conducted research into localization programs in the United Arab Emirates, or "Emiritization" and highlights the importance of the development and support of processes upon which successful localization is based, particularly with respect to recruitment, human resource development, and staff retention. This work also suggests that the phenomenon of localization is currently underresearched in OP and likely to become a key focus in the coming years as greater numbers of organizations attempt to develop the infrastructure, skills, and competencies required by an international organization in local populations.

A second challenge presented by increasing globalization pertains to the need for, and consequences of, greater workforce mobility. While mobile phone and internet technologies have enabled greater effectiveness of employees who travel across multiple locations, there remain a number of challenges to organizations managing remotely located or highly mobile employees. Educating employees on regional and national diversity in policies and practices, cultural and language obstacles, balancing the health and family concerns of employees who travel frequently, and maintaining the organizational commitment of highly mobile employees are ongoing concerns in organizations with highly mobile workforces. These must be weighed against the market expansion opportunities presented by globalization (Marchal & Kegels, 2003).

Technology. While there is considerable OP research being conducted on the effects of technology, such as virtual teams (Jarvenpaa, Knoll, & Leidner, 1998) and use of the internet at work (Wellman, Haase, Witte, & Hampton, 2001) for example, the continuing development of new information and communication technologies is further changing the way people in the workplace interact with each other, solve problems, and relate to their organizations. Internet use, online social networking, working from home, and video and phone conferencing have changed the way in which many organizations manage their human resources. While face-to-face communication is still the most preferred option, email and social media site use are becoming more popular, with the use of social media sites increasing by 62% in the USA last year. Over 70% of employees report using social media tools for business purposes (Fleishman Hillard Inc., 2009). However, an increasing number of organizations are attempting to constrain the use of social media in the workplace because of its impacts on productivity. This has resulted in greater monitoring of behavior by staff leading to the potential for greater control and invasions of privacy. The complexities associated with the array of impacts now being discussed in relation to the use of the internet represents an important opportunity for OP research to examine the ways in which new technologies are utilized in the workplace, and the conditions under which they deliver benefits or represent problems in the organizational setting.

Environment and sustainability. Again, while OP researchers have worked on questions of sustainability, environmental concerns are increasing and there is a lot more that OP can offer to the shaping of human behaviors that contribute to environmental issues and the changes that are required for effective sustainability. Increasing environmental pressure may require solutions to problems at all levels of organizations to manage issues of ethics and sustainability. This is not a new concern. As far back as 1992, 67% of managers believed environmental issues were important for their organization (Andersson & Bateman, 2000). However, environmental issues are considered by many to be too complex or too economically unviable to be readily understood and responded to in organizations (Shrivastava, 1995). At the same time, it is widely recognized that environmental disasters, such as the Exxon Valdez oil spill and the Chernobyl nuclear reactor plant meltdown, are the product of human behavior in organizations and that the causes lie in the cultures, systems and processes that are the subject of OP research. Furthermore, organizations can reap many benefits from embracing and managing environmental and sustainability concerns. Perez, Amichai-Hamburger, & Shterental (2009) found that organizations with environmental management systems (EMSs) enjoyed more positive perceptions of their environmental commitment, both outside of and within their organization. Additionally, such organizations recorded greater levels of OCBs by employees. Thus, we expect the understanding and management of environmental issues to become more widely spread within organizations as societal debates, such as those around global warming, touch more lives. OP researchers should be in the vanguard of research to better understand, predict, and manage environmental problem-solving throughout organizations.

Conclusion

OP researchers are applied scientists whose work is ultimately used to better understand, influence and manage people, processes, and outcomes in organizations (e.g., Kreitner & Knicki, 2007). True to this mission, the field of OP has developed comprehensive bodies of knowledge across many different areas that are of practical benefit to organizations and those who work in them. We are confident that the field will continue to evolve in response to the forces and trends identified in the previous section and will remain relevant to consultants and practitioners.

In concluding, we would like to make an appeal to the consultants and practitioners who use the knowledge produced by OP research. The integration of research and practice is very much a product of the samples and data that OP researchers have access to for addressing research questions. Organizational survey firms like Hewett and ISR own many of the largest and best longitudinal databases, with the most diverse and most representative samples. These databases and others like them that are collected within large organizations are generally not available to OP researchers outside the organizations who collect the data. Therefore, while there may be commercial reasons for not making the data available for publication, the potential for their adding useful practical knowledge to OP is not realized. Additionally, the practitioners and consultants who own these databases typically word their measures to capture the issues of direct interest to practitioners in specific organizational contexts and do not concern themselves with the construct validity of the measure. For example, when asking about job satisfaction a question such as "Are you satisfied with your job?" may provide a manager with all the information that he or she needs, however, it provides an inadequate link to the general construct of job satisfaction as it is operationalized in OP research, and therefore is of questionable value in analyses to examine the relationships of the variable with others (Schwab, 1980). The lack of collaboration between scholarly researchers, practitioners, and consultants on the conduct of large-scale research projects is a great opportunity missed. Examples like the GLOBE studies discussed earlier illustrate the mutual benefits that can emerge from collaborations around such projects.

References

Adams, J. S. (1965). Inequity in social exchange. In L. Berkowitz, (Ed.), *Advances in experimental social psychology* (pp. 267–299). New York: Academic Press.

Alge, B. J. (2001). Effects of computer surveillance on perceptions of privacy and procedural justice. *Journal of Applied Psychology, 86*(4), 797–804.

Allen, D. G. (2006). Do organizational socialization tactics influence newcomer embeddedness and turnover? *Journal of Management, 32*(2), 237–256.

Anderson, S. E., & Williams, L. J. (1996). Interpersonal, job, and individual factors related to helping processes at work. *Journal of Applied Psychology, 81*(3), 282–296.

Andersson, L., & Bateman, T. (2000). Individual environmental initiative: Championing natural environmental issues in U.S. business organizations. *Academy of Management Journal, 43*, 548–570.

Ashton, M. C. (1998). Personality and job performance: The importance of narrow traits. *Journal of Organizational Behavior, 19*, 289–303.

Austin, J. R. (2003). Transactive memory in organizational groups: The effects of content, consensus, specialization, and accuracy on group performance. *Journal of Applied Psychology, 88*, 866–878.

Baker, D. P., & Salas, E. (1997). Principles for measuring teamwork: A summary and a look toward the future. In M. T. Brannick, E. Salas, & C. Prince (Eds.), *Team performance and measurement* (pp. 331–355). Mahwah, NJ: Erlbaum.

Bandura, A. (1997). *Self-efficacy: The exercise of control.* New York: Freeman.

Barnard, C. (1938). *Functions of the executive.* Cambridge, MA: Harvard University Press.

Barrick, M. R., & Mount, M. K. (1991). The big five personality dimensions and job performance: A meta-analysis. *Personnel Psychology, 44*, 1–26.

Bass, B. M. (1985). *Leadership and performance.* New York: Free Press.

Bateman, T. S., & Organ, D. W. (1983). Job satisfaction and the good soldier: the relationship between affect and employee "citizenship." *Academy of Management Journal, 26*, 587–595.

Beal, D. J., Cohen, R. R., Burke, M. J., & McLendon, C. L. (2003). Cohesion and performance in groups: A meta-analytic clarification of construct relations. *Journal of Applied Psychology, 88*(6), 989–1004.

Bell, S. T. (2007). Deep-level composition variables as predictors of team performance: A meta-analysis. *Journal of Applied Psychology, 92*(3), 595–615.

Bertua, C., Anderson, N., & Salgado, S. R. (2005). The predictive validity of cognitive ability tests: A UK meta-analysis. *Journal of Occupational and Organizational Psychology, 78*, 387–409.

Bies, R. J., & Moag, J. F. (1986). Interactional justice: Communication criteria of fairness. In R. J. Lewicki, B. H. Sheppard, & M. H. Bazerman (Eds.), *Research on negotiations in organizations* (pp. 43–55). Greenwich, CT: JAI Press.

Bolino, M. C. (1999). Citizenship and impression management: good soldiers or good actors? *Academy of Management Review, 24*, 82–98.

Borman, W. C., & Motowidlo, S. J. (1993). Expanding the criterion domain to include elements of contextual performance. In N. Schmitt & W. C. Borman (Eds.), *Personnel selection in organizations* (pp. 71–98). New York: Jossey-Bass.

Borman, W. C., & Motowidlo, S. J. (1997). Introduction: Organizational citizenship behavior and contextual performance. Special issue of *Human Performance*, Borman, W. C., & Motowidlo, S. J. (Eds.). *Human Performance, 10*, 67–69.

Borman, W. C., & Brush, D. H. (1993). More progress toward a taxonomy of managerial performance requirements. *Human Performance, 6*, 1, 1–21.

Bowler, W. M., & Brass, D. J. (2006). Relational correlates of interpersonal citizenship behavior. A social network perspective. *Journal of Applied Psychology, 91*, 1, 70–82.

Blau, P. M. (1964). *Exchange and power in social life.* New York: John Wiley & Sons.

Brockner, J. (1988). *Self-esteem at work: Research, theory and practice.* Lexington, MA: Lexington Books.

Brockner, J., Ackerman, G., Greenberg, J., Gelfand, M. J., Francesco, A. M., Chen, Z. X., ... Shapiro, D. (2001). Culture and procedural justice: The influence of power distance on reactions to voice. *Journal of Experimental Social Psychology, 37*(4), 300–315.

Bunderson J. S., & Sutcliffe, K. A. (2003). Management team learning orientation and business unit performance. *Journal of Applied Psychology. 88*, 552–560.

Burns, J. M. (1978) *Leadership.* New York: Harper & Row.

Burns, J. M. (2003). *Transforming Leadership: 8.* New York: Atlantic Monthly Press.

Cain-Smith, P., & Kendall, L.M. (1973). Retranslation of expectations: An approach to the construction of unambiguous anchors for rating scales. *Journal of Applied Psychology, 47*, 149–155.

Campbell, J. P. (1990). Modeling the performance prediction problem in industrial and organizational psychology. In M. D. Dunnette & L. M. Hough (Eds.), *Handbook of industrial and organizational psychology* (pp. 687–732). Palo Alto, CA: Consulting Psychologists Press, Inc.

Campbell, J. P., McCloy, R. A., Oppler, S. H., & Sager, C. E. (1993). A theory of performance. In N. Schmitt & W. C. Borman (Eds.), *Personnel selection in organizations* (pp. 35–70). San Francisco: Jossey-Bass.

Campion, M. A., Medsker, G. J., & Higgs, A. C. (1993). Relations between work group characteristics and effectiveness: Implications for designing effective work groups. *Personnel Psychology, 46*, 823–843.

Cervone, D. (1997). Social-cognitive mechanisms and personality coherence: Self-knowledge, situational beliefs, and cross-situational coherence in perceived self-efficacy. *Psychological Science, 8*, 43–50.

Chan, D., & Schmitt, N. (2002). Situational judgment and job performance. *Human Performance, 15*, 233–253.

Chao, G., & Moon, H. (2005). A cultural mosaic: Defining the complexity of culture. *Journal of Applied Psychology, 90*, 1128–1140.

Chatman, J. A. (1989). Improving interactional research: A model of person–organization fit. *Academy of Management Review, 14*(3), 333–349.

Chen, G., Thomas, B., & Wallace, J. C. (2005). A multilevel examination of the relationships among training outcomes, mediating regulatory processes, and adaptive performance. *Journal of Applied Psychology, 90*, 827–841.

Chen, Z., Lam, W., & Zhong, J. A. (2007). Leader–member exchange and member performance: A new look at individual-level negative feedback-seeking behavior and team-level empowerment climate. *Journal of Applied Psychology, 92*(1), 202–212.

Cohen, S. G., & Bailey, D. E. (1997). What makes teams work: Group effectiveness research from the shop floor to the executive suite. *Journal of Management, 23*, 3, 239–290.

Cohen-Carash, Y. & Spector, P. E. (2001). The role of justice in organizations: A meta-analysis. *Organizational Behavior and Human Decision Processes, 86*, 278–324.

Colbert, A. E., Mount, M. K., Harter, J. K., Witt, L. A., & Barrick, M. R. (2004). Interactive effects of personality and perceptions of the work situation on workplace deviance. *Journal of Applied Psychology, 89*, 599–609.

Cole, M. S., Bernerth, J. B., Walter, F., & Holt, D. T. (2009). Organizational justice and individuals' withdrawal: unlocking the influence of emotional exhaustion. *Journal of Management Studies, 47*(3), 367–390.

Colquitt, J. A., Conlon, D. E., Wesson, M. J., Porter, C. O., & Ng, Y. K. (2001). Justice at the millennium: A meta-analytic review of 25 years of organizational justice research, *Journal of Applied Psychology*, 425–445.

Cooper-Thomas, H. D., & Anderson, N. (2005). Organizational socialization: A field study into socialization success and rate. *International Journal of Selection and Assessment, 13*, 2, 116–128.

Cordery, J. (2003). Teamwork. In D. Holman, T. D. Wall, C. W. Clegg, P. Sparrow, & A. Howard (Eds.), *The new workplace: A guide to the human impact of modern working practices* (pp. 95–114). Hoboken, NJ: Wiley.

Cortina, L., & Berdahl, J. L. (2010). Sexual harassment in organizations: A decade of research in review. In C. L. Cooper & J. Barling (Eds.), *Handbook of organizational behavior*. Thousand Oaks, CA: Sage.

Costa, P. T., Jr., & McCrae, R. R. (1985). *The NEO personality inventory manual.* Odessa, FL: Psychological Assessment Resources.

Crant, J. M. (1995). The proactive personality scale and objective job performance among real estate agents. *Journal of Applied Psychology, 80*, 532–537.

Digman, J. M. (1990). Personality structure: Emergence of the five-factor model. *Annual Review of Psychology, 41*, 417–440.

Douglas, S. C., & Martinko, M. J. (2001). Exploring the role of individual differences in the prediction of workplace aggression. *Journal of Applied Psychology, 86*, 547–559.

Dudley, N. M., Orvis, K. A., Lebiecke, J. E., & Cortina, J. M. (2006). A meta-analytic investigation of conscientiousness in the prediction of job performance: Examining the intercorrelations and incremental validity of narrow traits. *Journal of Applied Psychology, 91*, 40–57.

Dunnette, M. D. (Ed.). (1976). *Handbook of industrial and organizational psychology.* Chicago: Rand McNally.

Dunnette, M. D., & Hough, L. M. (Eds.). (1991). *Handbook of industrial and organizational psychology (4 vols.).* Palo Alto, CA: Consulting Psychologists Press.

Dweck, C. S. (1999). *Self-theories: Their role in motivation, personality and development.* Philadelphia: The Psychology Press.

Dye, D. A., Reek, M., & McDaniel, M. (1993). The validity of job knowledge measures. *International Journal of Selection and Assessment, 1*, 153–162.

Edmondson, A. (1999). Psychological safety and learning behavior in work teams. *Administrative Science Quarterly, 44*(2), 350–383.

Edwards, J. R. (1996). An examination of competing versions of the person–environment fit approach to stress. *Academy of Management Journal, 39*(2), 292–339.

Edwards, J. R. (2008). To prosper, organizational psychology should ... overcome methodological barriers to progress. *Journal of Organizational Behavior, 29*, 469–491.

Einarsen, S. (2000). Harassment and bullying at work: A review of the Scandinavian approach. *Aggression and Violent Behavior, 5*, 379–401.

Emerson, R. (1976). Social exchange theory. In A. Inkeles, J. Colemen, & N. Smelser (Eds.). *Annual review of sociology.* Palo Alto, CA: Annual Reviews.

Epitropaki, O., & Martin, R. (2004). Implicit leadership theories in applied settings: Factor structure, generalizability, and stability over time. *Journal of Applied Psychology, 89*, 293–310.

Equal Employment Opportunity Commission (1980). Guidelines on discrimination because of sex (Sect. 1604.11) *Federal Register, 45*, 74676–74677.

Fanelli, A., & Misangyi, V. (2006). Bringing out charisma: CEO charisma and external stakeholders. *Academy of Management Review, 31*(4), 1049–1061.

Fassina, N. E., Jones, D. A., & Uggerslev, K. L. (2008). Meta-analytic tests of relationships between organizational justice and citizenship behavior: Testing agent-system and shared-variance models. *Journal of Organizational Behavior, 29*(6), 805–828.

Fay, D., & Frese, M. (2001). The concepts of personal initiative (PI): An overview of validity studies. *Human Performance, 14*, 97–124.

Fiedler, F. E. (1967). *A Theory of Leadership Effectiveness*, New York: McGraw-Hill.

Fitzgerald, L. F., Drasgow, F., Hulin, C. L., Gelfand, M. J., & Magley, V. J. (1997). Antecedents and consequences of sexual harassment in organizations: A test of an integrated model. *Journal of Applied Psychology, 82*(4), 578–589.

Fleeson, W. (2001). Towards a structure- and process-integrated view of personality: Traits as density distributions of states. *Journal of Personality and Social Psychology, 80*, 1011–1027.

Fleeson, W. (2007). Situation-based contingencies underlying trait-content manifestation in behavior. *Journal of Personality, 75*, 825–861.

Fleishman Hillard, Inc. (2009). *How to use every social media tool in the box to engage employees.* Paper presented at the IABC Social Media Conference, New York, USA.

Forstenlechner, I. (2010). Workforce localization in emerging Gulf economies: The need to fine-tune HRM. *Personnel Review, 39*(1), 135–152.

Fournier, M. A., Moskowitz, D. S., & Zuroff D. C. (2008). Integrating dispositions, signatures, and the interpersonal domain. *Journal of Personality and Social Psychology, 94*(3), 531–545.

Fox, S., & Spector, P. E. (1999). A model of work frustration-aggression. *Journal of Organizational Behavior, 20*, 915–31.

Frese, M., Kring, W., Soose, A., & Zempel, J. (1996). Personal initiative at work: Differences between East and West Germany. *Academy of Management Journal, 39*, 37–63.

Fried, Y., Shirom, A., Gilboa, S., & Cooper, C. L. (2008). The mediating effects of job satisfaction and propensity to leave on role stress-job performance relationships: Combining meta-analysis and structural equation modeling. *International Journal of Stress Management, 15*(4), 305–328.

Fryxell, G., Butler, J., & Choi, A. (2004). Successful localization programs in China: an important element in strategy implementation. *Journal of World Business, 39*, 268–282.

Gerstner, C. R. and Day, D. V. (1997). Meta-analytic review of leader-member exchange theory: Correlates and construct issues. *Journal of Applied Psychology, 82* 6, 827–844.

Giacalone, R. A., & Greenberg, J. (Eds.). (1997). *Antisocial behavior in organizations.* Thousand Oaks, CA: Sage.

Giberson, T. R., Resick, C. J., & Dickson, M. W. (2005). Embedding leader characteristics: An examination of homogeneity of personality and values in organizations. *Journal of Applied Psychology, 90*(5), 1002–1010.

Gladstein, D. L. (1984). Groups in context: A model of task group effectiveness. *Administrative Science Quarterly, 29*, 499–517.

Goleman, D. P. (1995). *Emotional intelligence: Why it can matter more than IQ for character, health and lifelong achievement.* New York: Bantam Books.

Graen, G. B., & Uhl-Bien, M. (1991). The transformation of work group professionals into self-managing and partially self-designing contributors: Toward a theory of leadership-making. *Journal of Management Systems, 3*(3), 33–48.

Greenberg, L., & Barling, J. (1999). Predicting employee aggression against co-workers, subordinates and supervisors: The roles of person behaviors and perceived workplace factors. *Journal of Organizational Behavior, 20*, 897–913.

Greenleaf, R. K. (2002). *Servant leadership: A journey into the nature of legitimate power and greatness (25th anniversary ed.).* New York: Paulist Press.

Griffeth, R. W., Hom, P. W., & Gaertner, S. (2000). A meta-analysis of antecedents and correlates of employee turnover: Update, moderator tests, and research implications for the next millennium. *Journal of Management. 26*(3), 463–488.

Guthrie, J. P. (2001). High-involvement work practices, turnover, and productivity: Evidence from New Zealand. *Academy of Management Journal, 44*(1), 180–190.

Hackman J. R. (1987). The design of work teams. In J. W. Lorsch (Ed.), *Handbook of organizational behavior* (pp. 315–42). Englewood Cliffs, NJ: Prentice-Hall.

Hackman, J. R. (2002). *Leading teams: Setting the stage for great performances.* Boston, MA: Harvard Business School Press.

Harrison, D. A., & Klein, K. J. (2007). What's the difference? Diversity constructs as separation, variety or disparity in organizations. *Academy of Management Review, 32*, 1199–1228.

Harvey, S., & Keashly, L. (2003). Predicting the risk for aggression in the workplace: Risk-factors, self-esteem and time at work. *Social Behavior and Personality*, *31*, 807–814.
Haslam, S. A. (2004). *Psychology in organizations: The social identity approach* (2nd ed.). Thousand Oaks, CA: Sage Publications.
Haspeslagh, P. C., & Jemison, D. B. (1991). *Managing acquisitions: Creating value through corporate renewal.* New York: The Free Press.
Hattrup, K., O'Connell, M. S., & Wingate, P. H. (1998). Prediction of multi-dimension criteria: Distinguishing task and contextual performance. *Human Performance*, *11*, 305–319.
Hepworth, W., & Towler, A. (2004). The effects of individual differences and charismatic leadership on workplace aggression. *Journal of Occupational Health Psychology*, *9*, 176–185.
Herbert, S., & March, J. G. (1958). *Organizations.* New York: Wiley.
Hershcovis, M. S., Turner, N., Barling, J., Arnold, K. A., Dupre, K. E., Inness, M., LeBlanc, M. M., & Sivanathan, N. (2007). Predicting workplace aggression: A meta-analysis. *Journal of Applied Psychology*, *92*(1), 228–238.
Herzberg, F. (1959). *The Motivation to work*, New York: John Wiley and Sons.
Herzberg, F. I. (1987). One more time: How do you motivate employees? *Harvard Business Review*, *65* (5), 109–120.
Holland, J. L. (1997). *Making vocational choices: A theory of vocational personalities and work environments.* Odessa, FL: Psychological Assessment Resources.
Hollenbeck, J. R., Moon, H., Ellis, A. P. J., West, B. J., & Ilgen, D. R. (2002). Structural contingency theory and individual differences: examination of external and internal person-team fit. *Journal of Applied Psychology*, *87*, 599–606.
Homans, G. C. (1961). *Social behavior: Its elementary forms.* London: Routledge and Kegan Paul.
House, R. J. (1996). Path-goal theory of leadership: Lessons, legacy, and a reformulated theory. *Leadership Quarterly*, *7*(3), 323–352.
Ilgen, D. R. (1999). Teams in organizations: Some implications. *American Psychologist*, *54*, 129–139.
Ilgen, D. R., Hollenbeck, J. R., Johnson, M., & Jundt, D. (2005). Teams in organizations: From input-process-output models to IMOI models. *Annual Review of Psychology*, *56*, 517–543.
Ilies, R., Filmer, I. S., Spitzmuller, M., & Johnson, M. (2006). *Personality and citizenship behavior: The role of affect and satisfaction.* Paper presented at the 66th Annual Meeting of the Academy of Management in Atlanta, Georgia.
Ilies, R., Nahrgang, J., & Morgeson, F. P. (2007). Leader–member exchange and citizenship behaviors: A meta-analysis. *Journal of Applied Psychology*, *92*(1), 269–277.
Ilies, R., Scott, B. A., & Judge, T. A. (2006). The interactive effects of personal traits and experience states on intraindividual patterns of citizenship behavior. *Academy of Management Journal*, *49*(3), 561–575.
Inness, M., Barling, J., & Turner, N. (2005). Understanding supervisor-targeted aggression: A within-person between jobs design. *Journal of Applied Psychology*, *90*, 731–739.
Jarvenpaa, S. L., Knoll K., & Leidner, D. E. (1998). Is anybody out there?: Antecedents of trust in global virtual teams Source. *Journal of Management Information Systems*, *14*(4), 29–64.
Johns, G. (2006). Constraints on the adoption of psychology-based personnel practices: Lessons from organizational innovation. *Personnel Psychology*, *46*(3), 569–592.
Judge, T. A., & Bono, J. E. (2001). Relationship of core self-evaluation traits—self-esteem, generalized self-efficacy, locus of control, and emotional stability—with job satisfaction and job performance: A meta-analysis. *Journal of Applied Psychology*, *86*, 80–92.

Judge, T. A., Bono, J. E., Ilies, R., & Gerhardt, M. W. (2002). Personality and leadership: A qualitative and quantitative review. *Journal of Applied Psychology, 87*(4), 765–780.

Judge, T. A., Heller, D., & Mount, M. K. (2002). Five-factor model of personality and job satisfaction: A meta-analysis. *Journal of Applied Psychology, 87*(3), 530–541.

Judge, T. A., & Piccolo, R. F. (2004). Transformational and transactional leadership and their effects on creativity in groups. *Creative Research Journal, 13*, 185–195.

Judge, T. A., Scott, B. A., & Illes, R. (2006). Hostility job attitudes and workplace deviance: Test of a multilevel model. *Journal of Applied Psychology, 91*, 126–138.

Judge, T. A., Thoresen, C. J., Bono, J. E., & Patton, G. K. (2001). The job satisfaction–job performance relationship: A qualitative and quantitative review. *Psychological Bulletin, 127*, 376–407.

Kamdar, D., McAlister, D. J., & Turban, D. B. (2006). All in a day's work: How follower individual differences and justice perceptions predict OCB role definitions and behavior. *Journal of Applied Psychology, 91*(4), 841–855.

Kamdar, D., & Van Dyne, L., (2007). The joint effects of personality and workplace social exchange relationships in predicting task performance and citizenship performance. *Journal of Applied Psychology, 92*(5), 1286–1298.

Kanfer, R., & Ackerman, P. L. (2005). Work competence: A person-orientated perspective. In A. J. Eliott & C. S. Dweck (Eds.), *Handbook of competence and motivation* (pp. 336–353). New York: Guilford Publications.

Kanfer, R., & Heggestad, E. (1997). Motivational traits and skills: A person-centered approach to work motivation. In L. L. Cummings and B. M. Staw (Eds.), *Research in organizational behavior*, 19, (pp. 1–57). Greenwich, CT: JAI Press.

Kaplan, S., Bradley, J. C., Luchman, J. N., & Haynes, D. (2009). On the role of positive and negative affectivity in job performance: A meta-analytic investigation. *Journal of Applied Psychology, 94*(1), 162–176.

Kreitner, R., & Knicki, A. (2007). *Organizational behavior* (7th ed.). Boston: McGraw-Hill.

Korsgaard, M. A., Meglino, B. M., Lester, S., & Jeong, S. S. (2010). Paying you forward or me back: Understanding rewarded and unrewarded organizational citizenship behavior. Provisional acceptance. *Journal of Applied Psychology, 95*(2), 277–290.

Kozlowski, S. W. J., & Ilgen, D. R. (2006). Enhancing the effectiveness of work groups and teams. *Psychological Science in the Public Interest, 7*(3), 77–124.

Kozlowski, S. W. J., & Ilgen, D. R. (2008). The Science of Team Success. *Scientific American*, June/July, 54–61.

Kozlowski, S. W., & Klein, K. J. (2000). A multilevel approach to theory and research in organizations: Contextual, temporal, and emergent processes. In K. J. Klein & S. W. Kozlowski (Eds.), *Multilevel theory, research, and methods in organizations: Foundations, extensions, and new directions* (pp. 3–90). San Francisco: Jossey-Bass.

Kluger, A. N., & DeNisi, A. (1996). Effects of feedback intervention on performance: A historical review, a meta-analysis, and a preliminary feedback intervention theory. *Psychological Bulletin, 119*(2), 254–284.

Kristof, A. L. (1996). Person-organization fit: an integrative review of its conceptualizations, measurement, and implications. *Personnel Psychology, 49*, 1–49.

Kuoppala, J., Lamminpää, A., Liira, J., & Vaino, H. (2008). Leadership, job well-being, and health effects—A systematic review and a meta-analysis. *Journal of Occupational and Environmental Medicine, 50*, 904–915.

Langford, S. R., & Locke A. (2000). A successful transfer of lessons learned in aviation psychology and flight safety to health care: the MedTeams system. *Proceedings of Patient Safety Initiative 2000: Spotlighting Strategies, Sharing Solutions* (pp. 45–49). October 4–6, 2000. Chicago: National Patient Safety Foundation.

Latham, G. P., & Wexley, K. N. (1977). Behavioral observation scales for performance appraisal purposes. *Personnel Psychology, 30*, 255–268.

Lapierre, L. M., Spector, P. E., & Leck, J. D. (2005). Sexual versus nonsexual workplace aggression and victims' overall job satisfaction: A meta-analysis, *Journal of Occupational Health Psychology, 10*(2), 155–169.

Lavery, T. A., Franz, T. M., Winquist, J. R., & Larson, J. R. (1999). The role of information exchange in predicting group accuracy on a multiple judgment task. *Basic Applied Social Psychology, 21*, 281–289.

Lawrence, T., & Robinson, S. L. (2007). Workplace deviance as organizational resistance. *Journal of Management, 33*, 378–394.

Lee, K., & Allen, N. J. (2002). Organizational citizenship behavior and workplace deviance: The role of affect and cognitions. *Journal of Applied Psychology, 87*, 131–142.

LePine, J. A., & van Dyne, L. (2001). Voice and cooperative behavior as contrasting forms of contextual performance: Evidence of differential relationships with big five personality characteristics and cognitive ability. *Journal of Applied Psychology, 86*, 326–336.

Leventhal, G. S. (1976). The distribution of rewards and resources in groups and organizations. In L. Berkowitz & W. Walster (Eds.), *Advances in experimental social psychology* (pp. 91–131). New York: Academic Press.

Leventhal, G. S. (1980). What should be done with equity theory? New approaches to the study of fairness in social relationships. In K. Gergen, M. Greenberg & R. Willis (Eds.), *Social exchange: Advance in theory and research* (pp. 27–55). New York: Plenum Press.

Levi, D. (2001). *Group dynamics for teams.* Thousand Oaks, CA: Sage.

Liden, R. C., Sparrowe, R. T., & Wayne, S. J. (1997). Leader–member exchange theory: The past and potential for the future. *Research in Personnel and Human Resources Management, 15*, 47–119.

Littlepage, G., Robison, W., & Reddington, K. (1997). Effects of task experience and group experience on group performance, member ability, and recognition of expertise. *Organizational Behavior and Human Decision Processes, 69*, 133–147.

Locke, E. A. (1976). The nature and consequences of job satisfaction. In M. D. Dunnette (Ed.), *Handbook of industrial and organizational psychology* (pp. 1297–1349). Chicago: Rand-McNally.

Locke, E. A., & Latham, G. P. (1990). *A theory of goal setting and task performance.* Englewood Cliffs, NJ: Prentice Hall.

Malekazedeh, A. R., & Nahavandi, A. (1990). Making mergers work by managing cultures. *Journal of Business Strategy*, May–June, 55–57.

Marchal, B., & Kegels, G. (2003). Health workforce imbalances in times of globalization: brain drain or professional mobility? *International Journal of Health Planning and Management, 18*(1), 89–101.

Maslow, A. H. (1943). A Theory of Human Motivation. *Psychological Review, 50*, 4, 370–396.

Mayo, E. (1933). *The human problems of an industrial civilization.* New York: Macmillan.

McCrae, R. R., & Costa, P. T., Jr. (1989). The structure of interpersonal traits: Wiggin's circumplex and the five-factor model. *Journal of Personality and Social Psychology, 56*, 586–595.

McCrae, R. R., & Costa, P. T., Jr. (1987). Validation of the five-factor model of personality across instruments and observers. *Journal of Personality and Social Psychology, 52*, 81–90.

McGrath, J. E. (1964). *Social psychology: A brief introduction.* New York: Holt, Rinehart and Winston.

McShane, S., Olekalns, M., & Travaglione, T. (2010), *Organisational behaviour on the Pacific Rim* (3rd ed.). North Ryde, Australia: McGraw Hill.

Metcalf, H. C., & Urwick, L. (Eds.) (1942). *Dynamic administration: The collected papers of Mary Parker Follett.* New York: Harper & Bros.

Mischel, W., & Peake, P. K. (1982). In search of consistency: measure for measure. In M. P. Zanna, E. T. Higgins, & C. P. Herman (Eds.), *Consistency in social behavior: The Ontario symposium* (pp.187–207). Hillsdale, NJ: Erlbaum.

Minbashian, A., Wood, R. E., & Beckmann, N. (in press). Task-contingent conscientiousness as a unit of personality at work. *Journal of Applied Psychology*, doi: 10.1037/a0020016.

Mischel, W., & Shoda, Y. (1995). A cognitive-affective system theory of personality: Reconceptualizing situations, dispositions, dynamics, and invariance in personality structure. *Psychological Review, 102*, 246–268.

Mischel, W., & Shoda, Y. (1998). Reconciling processing dynamics and personality dispositions. In *Annual Review of Psychology, 49* (pp. 229–258). Palo Alto, CA: Annual Reviews Inc.

Montoya-Weiss, M. M., Massey, A. P., Song, M. (2001). Getting it together: temporal coordination and conflict management in global virtual teams. *Academy of Management Journal, 44*, 1251–1262.

Morrison, E. W., & Phelps, C. C. (1999). Taking charge at work: Extra-role efforts to initiate workplace change. *Academy of Management Journal, 42*, 403–419.

Motowidlo, S. J., Borman, W. C., & Schmit, M. J. (1997). A theory of individual differences in task and contextual performance. *Human Performance, 10*, 71–83.

Motowidlo, S. J., Dunnette, M. D., & Carter, G. W. (1990). An alternative selection procedures: The low fidelity simulation. *Journal of Applied Psychology, 75*, 640–647.

Motowidlo, S. J., & Schmit, M. J. (1999). Performance assessment in unique jobs. In D. R. Ilgen & E. D. Pulakos (Eds.), *The changing nature of job performance: Implications for staffing, motivation and development* (pp. 56–86). San Francisco, CA: Jossey-Bass.

Muchinsky, P. M., & Monahan, C. J. (1987). What is person-environment congruence? Supplementary versus complementary models of fit. *Journal of Vocational Behavior, 31*(3), 268–277.

Neuman, J. H., & Baron, R. A. (1998). Workplace violence and workplace aggression: Evidence concerning specific forms, potential causes, and preferred targets. *Journal of Management, 24*, 391–419.

Nicholson, N. (1998). Personality and entrepreneurial leadership: A study of the heads of the UK's most successful independent companies. *European Management Journal, 16*(5), 529–539.

Nielsen, T. M., Hrivnak, G. A., & Shaw, M. (2009). Organizational citizenship behavior and performance: A meta-analysis of group-level research. *Small Group Research, 40*(5), 555–577.

Ohly, S., Sonnentag, S., & Pluntke, F. (2006). Routinization, work characteristics and their relationships with creative and proactive behaviors. *Journal of Organizational Behavior, 27*, 257–279.

O'Leary-Kelly, A. M., Griffin, R. W., & Glew, D. J. (1996). Organization-motivated aggression: A research framework. *Academy of Management Review, 21*, 225–253.

O'Reilly, C. A., Chatman, J., & Caldwell, D. F. (1991). People and organizational culture: A profile comparison approach to assessing person-organization fit. *Academy of Management Journal, 34*, 487–516.

Organ, D. W. (1988). *Organizational citizenship behavior: The good soldier syndrome.* Lexington, MA: Lexington Books.

Organ, D. W. (1997). Organizational citizenship behavior: It's construct clean-up time. *Human Performance, 10*(2), 87–97.

Organ, D. W., Podsakoff, P. M., & MacKenzie, S. B. (2006). *Organizational citizenship behavior: Its nature, antecedents and consequences.* Thousand Oaks, CA: Sage Publications.

Organ, D. W., & Ryan, K. (1995). A meta-analytic review of attitudinal and dispositional predictors of organizational citizenship behavior. *Personnel Psychology, 48*(4), 755–802.

Ott, J. S. (1989). *The organizational culture perspective.* Pacific Grove, CA: Brooks/Cole.

Parker, S. K., Wall, T. D., & Jackson, P. R. (1997). "That's not my job": Developing flexible employee work orientations. *Academy of Management Journal, 40*, 899–929.

Parker, S. K., Williams, H. M., & Turner, N. (2006). Modeling the antecedents of proactive behavior at work. *Journal of Applied Psychology, 91*, 636–652.

Parker, S. K., & Griffin, M. A. (2002). What is so bad about a little name-calling? Negative consequences of gender harassment, over performance demands, and psychological distress. *Journal of Occupational Health Psychology, 7*, 195–210.

Penner, L. A., Dovidion, J. F., Piliavin, J. A., & Schroeder, D. A. (2005). Prosocial behavior: Multilevel perspectives. *Annual Review of Psychology, 56*, 365–392.

Penny, L. M., & Spector, P. E. (2005). Job stress, incivility, and counterproductive workplace behavior: The moderating role of negative affectivity. *Journal of Organizational Behavior, 26*, 777–798.

Perez, O., Amichai-Hamburger, Y., & Shterental, T. (2009). The dynamic of corporate self-regulation: ISO 14001, environmental commitment, and organizational citizenship behavior. *Law & Society Review, 43*, 593–630.

Pfeffer, J. (1997). *New Directions for Organization Theory: Problems and Prospects.* Oxford University Press USA.

Podsakoff, P. M., MacKenzie, S. B., Paine, J. B., & Bachrach, D. G. (2000). Organizational citizenship behaviors: A critical review of the theoretical and empirical literature and suggestions for future research. *Journal of Management, 26*(3), 513–563.

Podsakoff, N. P., Whiting, S. W., & Podsakoff, P. M. (2009). Individual and organizational level consequences of organizational citizenship behaviors: A meta-analysis. *Journal of Applied Psychology, 94*(1), 122–141.

Pritchard, R. D. (1992). *Organizational productivity, in industrial and organizational psychology* (2nd ed.). Palto Alto, CA: Consulting Psychologists Press.

Pulakos, E. D., Arad, S., Donovan, M. A., & Plamondon, K. E. (2000). Adaptability in the workplace: Development of a taxonomy of adaptive performance. *Journal of Applied Psychology, 85*, 612–624.

Raelin, J. A. (2005). We the leaders: In order to form a leaderful organization. *Journal of Leadership and Organizational Studies, 12*(2), 18–29.

Rayner, C., Hoel, H., & Cooper, C. L. (2002). *Workplace bullying: What we know, who is to blame and what can we do?* London: Taylor and Francis.

Robinson, S. L., & Bennet, R. J. (1995). A typology of deviant workplace behaviors: a multidimensional scaling study, *Academy of Management Journal, 38*, 555–572.

Roe, R. A. (1999). Work performance: A multiple regulation perspective. In C. L. Cooper & I. T. Robertson (Eds.), *International review of industrial and organizational psychology* (pp. 231–335). Chichester: Wiley.

Ross, J., & Staw, B. M. (1986). Expo86: An escalation prototype. *Administrative Science Quarterly, 31*(2), 274–297.

Rotter, J. B. (1954). *Social learning and clinical psychology.* New York: Prentice-Hall.

Rotter, J. B. (1966). Generalized expectancies of internal versus external control of reinforcements. *Psychological Monographs, 80*, 1–28.

Rotundo, M., & Sackett, P. (2002). The relative importance of task, citizenship, and counterproductive performance to global ratings of job performance: A policy capturing approach. *Journal of Applied Psychology*, *87*(1), 66–80.

Rousseau, D. M. (1996). *Psychological contracts in organizations: Understanding written and unwritten agreements.* Newbury Park, CA: Sage.

Rousseau, D. M., & Fried, Y. (2001). Location, location, location: Contextualizing organizational research. *Journal of Organizational Behavior*, *22*, 1–13.

Sackett, P. R., & Devore, C. J. (2001). Counterproductive behaviours at work. In N. Anderson, D. Ones, H. Sinangil, & C. Viswesvaran (Eds.), *Handbook of industrial, work, and organizational psychology* (pp. 145–164). London: Sage.

Sackett, P. R., & Wanek, J. E. (1996). New developments in the use of measures in honesty, integrity, conscientiousness, dependability, trustworthiness and reliability for personnel selection. *Personnel Psychology*, *49*, 787–830.

Sager, J. K., Griffeth, R. W., & Hom, P. W. (1998). A comparison of structural models representing turnover cognitions. *Journal of Vocational Behavior*, *53*, 254–273.

Saks, A. M., Uggerslev, K. L., & Fassina, N. E., (2007). Socialization tactics and newcomer adjustment: A meta-analytic review and test of a model. *Journal of Vocational Behavior*, *70*(3), 413–446.

Salgado, J. F. (2002). The big five personality dimensions and counterproductive workplace behavior. *International Journal of Selection and Assessment*, *10*, 17–125.

Salgado, J. F. (2003), Predicting job performance using FFM and non-FFM personality measures, *Journal of Occupational and Organizational Psychology*, *76*(3), 323–346.

Salgado, J. F., & Rumbo, A. (2002). Personality and job performance in financial services managers. *International Journal of Selection and Assessment*, *5*(2), 91–100.

Schein, E. H. (1985). *Organizational culture and leadership; A dynamic perspective.* San Francisco: Jossey-Bass.

Schein, E. H. (2004). *Organizational culture and leadership* (3rd ed.). Jossey-Bass. San Francisco, CA.

Schmidt, F. L., & Hunter, J. E. (1998). The validity and utility of selection methods in personnel psychology: practical and theoretical implications of 85 years of research finding. *Psychological Bulletin*, *124*, 262–274.

Schneider, B. (1987). The people make the place. *Personnel Psychology*, *40*, 437–453.

Schneider, B., Smith, D. B., & Paul, M. C. (2001). P–E fit and the attraction–selection–attrition model of organizational functioning: introduction and overview. In M. Erez & U. Kleinbeck (Eds.), *Work Motivation in the Context of a Globalizing Economy* (pp. 231–246). Mahwah, NJ: Erlbaum.

Schneider, B., Smith, D. B., Taylor, S., & Fleenor, J. (1998). Personality and organizations: A test of the homogeneity of personality hypothesis. *Journal of Applied Psychology*, *83*, 462–470.

Schwab, D. P. (1980). Construct validity in organizational behavior. In L. L. Cummings & B. Staw (Eds.), *Research in Organization Behavior* (pp. 3–43). Greenwich, CT: JAI Press.

Sekiguchi, T. (2004). Person-organization fit and person-job fit in employee selection: A review of the literature, *Osaka Keidai Ronshu*, *54*, 179–196.

Shoda,Y., Mischel, W., & Wright, J. C. (1994). Intraindividual stability in the organization and patterning of behavior: incorporating psychological situations into the idiographic analysis of personality. *Journal of Personality and Social Psychology*, *67*(4), 674–687.

Shrivastava, P. (1995). Ecocentric management for a risk society. *Academy of Management Review*, *20*, 118–137.

Smith, P. C., & Kendall, L. M. (1963). Retranslation of expectations—An approach to the construction of unambiguous anchors for rating-scales, *47*(2), 149–155.

Smith, C. A., Organ, D. W., & Near, J. P. (1983). Organizational citizenship behavior: Its nature and antecedents. *Journal of Applied Psychology*, *68*, 653–663.

Smith, P. C., Kendall, L. M., & Hulin, C. L. (1969). The measurement of satisfaction. In *Work and retirement: A strategy for the study of attitudes.* Chicago: Rand McNally.

Smith, P., Peterson, M., & Thomas, D. (Eds.). (2008). *Handbook of cross-cultural management research.* Oxford: Sage.

Sonnentag, S., & Frese, M. (2002). Performance concepts and performance theory. In S. Sonnentag (Ed.), *Psychological management of individual performance* (pp. 249–289). Chichester: Wiley.

Sonnentag, S., & Frese, M. (2002). Performance concepts and performance theory. In S. Sonnentag (Ed.), *Psychological management of individual performance* (pp. 3–25). Chichester: Wiley.

Sonnentag, S., Volmer, J., & Spychala, A. (2008). Job performance. In C.L. Copper & J. Barling (Eds.), *The Sage handbook of organizational behavior* (pp. 427–447). London: Sage Publications.

Spearman, C. (1904). General intelligence, objectively determined and measured, *American Journal of Applied Psychology*, *15*, 201–293.

Speier, C., & Frese, M. (1997). Generalized self-efficacy as a mediator and moderator between control and complexity at work and personal initiative: A longitudinal study in East Germany. *Human Performance*, *10*(2), 171–192.

Spitzmüller, C., Neumann, E., Spitzmüller, M., Rubino, C., Keeton, K. E., Sutton, M. T., & Manzey, D. (2008). Assessing the influence of psychosocial and career mentoring on organizational attractiveness. *International Journal of Selection and Assessment. 16*(4), 403–415.

Stajkovic, A., & Luthans, F. (1998). Self-efficacy and work-related performance: A meta-analysis. *Psychological Bulletin*, *124*, 240–261.

Starbuck, W. H. (2009). The constant causes of never-ending faddishness in the behavioral and social sciences. *Scandinavian Journal of Management*, *25*, 108–116.

Stewart, G. L., & Barrick, M. R. (2000). Team structure and performance: assessing the mediating role of intra-team processes and the moderating role of task type. *Academy of Management Journal*, *43*, 2, 135–148.

Stout, R., Cannon-Bowers, A., Salas, E., & Milanovich, D. M. (1999). Planning. shared mental models, and coordinated performance: An empirical link is established. *Human Factors*, *1*, 61–71.

Sturman, M. C. (2003). Searching for the inverted u-shaped relationship between time and performance: Meta-analyses of the experience/performance, tenure/performance, and age/performance relationships. *Journal of Management*, *29*, 609–640.

Tajfel, H., & Turner, J. (1979). An integrative theory of intergroup conflict. In W. G. Austin & S. Worschel (Eds.), *The social psychology of intergroup relations* (pp. 94–109). Monterey, CA: Brooks-Cole.

Tannenbaum, S. I., Beard, R. L., & Salas, E. (1992). Team building and its influence on team effectiveness: An examination of conceptual and empirical developments. In K. Kelley (Ed.), *Organization development and change* (pp. 117–153). Amsterdam:lsevier.

Tett, R. P., & Meyers, J. P. (1993). Job satisfaction, organizational commitment, turnover intention, and turnover: Path-analyses based on meta-analytic findings. *Personnel Psychology*, *46*, 259–293.

Thibaut, J., & Walker, L. (1975). *Procedural justice: A psychological analysis.* Hillsdale, NJ: Erlbaum.

Tuckman, B. W. (1965). Developmental sequence in small groups. *Psychological Bulletin*. *63*(6), 384–399.

Tversky, A., and Kahneman, D. (1979). Prospect theory: An analysis of decision making under risk. *Econometrica*, *47*(2), 263–292.

Utman, C. H. (1997). Performance effects of motivational state: A meta-analysis. *Personality and Social Psychology Review*, *1*, 170–182.

Vancouver, J. B., & Schmitt, N. (1991). An exploratory examination of person-organization fit: Organizational goal congruence. *Personnel Psychology*, *44*, 333–352.

Vandenberghe, C. (1999). Organizational culture, person-culture fit, and turnover: A replication in the health care industry. *Journal of Organizational Behavior*, *20*(2), 175–184.

Van Scotter, J. R., & Motowidlo, S. J. (1996). Interpersonal facilitation and job dedication as separate facets of contextual performance. *Journal of Applied Psychology*, *81*, 525–531.

Vartia, M. (1996). The sources of bullying: Psychological work environment and organizational climate. *European Journal of Work and Organizational Psychology*, *5*, 203–214.

Vecchio, R. P., Justin, J. E., & Pearce, C. L., (2008). The utility of transactional and transformational leadership for predicting performance and satisfaction within a path–goal theory framework. *Journal of Occupational and Organizational Psychology*, *81*(1), 71–82.

Viswesvaran C., & Ones, D. S. (2000). Measurement error in "Big Five factors" personality assessment: Reliability generalization across studies and measures. *Educational and Psychological Measurement*, *60*, 224–235.

Wageman, R. (1995). Interdependence and group effectiveness. *Administrative Science Quarterly*, *40*, 145–180.

Wagner, J. A., III. (1995). Studies of individualism-collectivism: Effects on cooperation in groups. *Academy of Management Journal*, *38*, 152–172.

Weiner, B. (1980). *Human motivation*. Hillsdale, NJ: Lawrence Erlbaum.

Wellman, B., Haase, A. Q., Witte, J., & Hampton, K. (2001). Does the Internet increase, decrease, or supplement social capital? *American Behavioral Scientist*, *45*(3), 436–455.

Williams, L. J., & Anderson, S. E. (1991). Job satisfaction and organizational commitment as predictors of organizational citizenship and in-role behaviors. *Journal of Management*, *17*, 601–617.

Wood, R. E., Mento, A. J., & Locke, E. A. (1987). Task complexity as a moderator of goal effects: A meta analysis. *Journal of Applied Psychology*, *72*, 416–425.

Williams, K. D., & Karau, S. J. (1991). Social loafing and social compensation: The effects of expectations of co-worker performance. *Journal of Personality and Social Psychology*, *61*, 570–581.

Wright, J. C., & Mischel,W. (1987). A conditional approach to dispositional constructs: The local predictability of social behavior. *Journal of Personality and Social Psychology*, *53*(6), 1159–1177.

Yukl, G. A., (2007). *Leadership in Organizations* (7th ed.). Upper Saddle River, NJ: Pearson Education.

Zellars, K. L., Perrewé, P. L., Rossi, A. M., Tepper, B. J., & Ferris, G. R. (2007). Moderating effects of political skill, perceived control, and job-related self-efficacy on the relationship between negative affectivity and physiological strain. *Journal of Organizational Behavior*, *29*, 549–571.

11

Personnel/Human Resource Psychology

Cynthia D. Fisher

This chapter is about the industrial side of Industrial/Organizational Psychology, usually associated with research and practice in personnel or human resource management in organizations. The field is described in different ways in different countries. For example, in the United States *industrial psychology* has been concerned with enhancing individual job performance through appropriate selection, training, and appraisal of staff. The overriding concern is with improving performance outcomes for management, largely through empirical research (Zickar & Gibby, 2007). In the United Kingdom, *occupational psychology* is the preferred term, reflecting a broader focus on selection and other personnel/human resource management practices to improve performance as well as a long-standing concern with employee well-being and vocational choice. In Germany the preferred term is *work psychology* (Warr, 2007).

This chapter begins with a brief overview of the history of industrial psychology and then highlights major contributions and recent developments in the areas of job analysis, selection, training and development, and performance appraisal. It ends with a discussion of the science–practice gap and the future of the field. A chapter of this length can only hit the high points of such a broad applied psychology discipline. More detailed treatments of current knowledge in industrial psychology are compiled in a series of recent handbooks by Anderson, Ones, Sinangil, and Viswesvaran (2002), Kozlowski (in press), and Rogelberg (2007).

Efforts to apply the fledgling science of psychology to the world of work began shortly before World War I. The rise of large-scale industrialization created a need for improved employee selection and placement, scientific work design, and development of effective incentive systems. The concurrent development of the first tests of physical and mental abilities provided the tools to begin scientific selection. The *Journal of Applied Psychology* commenced publication in 1917. The development of

IAAP Handbook of Applied Psychology, First Edition. Edited by Paul R. Martin, Fanny M. Cheung, Michael C. Knowles, Michael Kyrios, Lyn Littlefield, J. Bruce Overmier, and José M. Prieto.

the field was accelerated by World War I, with the US, UK, and Germany all allocating considerable resources to the development of means of testing and placing recruits into suitable military roles. In the US, the development and deployment of the Army Alpha and Beta mental ability tests showed that large-scale group testing was feasible and productive. In the UK an additional wartime concern involved studying and improving the health, safety, and well-being of munitions plant workers who suffered from fatigue and extremely long working hours. The successes of wartime industrial psychology were transferred to industry during the postwar boom. About the same time universities began training industrial psychologists in greater numbers and the field began to be recognized as a discipline. World War II brought another boost as industrial psychologists again turned their attention to military staffing issues with the development of the Army General Classification Test and the first assessment centers (Campbell, 2007; Salas, deRouin, & Gade, 2007). The field has continued to develop since that time, focusing on the core issues of job analysis, selection, training, and appraisal. A more detailed history of industrial psychology is available in Koppes (2007).

Job Analysis

Job analysis has been an integral part of the practice of industrial psychology since the very first test validation efforts shortly before World War I. Job analysis is simply describing the content of a job, usually in terms of important duties or tasks and/or the human behaviors and knowledge, skills, and abilities required to execute those duties (see Brannick, Levine, & Morgeson, 2007 for more on job analysis). It is essential to understand the job thoroughly in order to choose selection practices likely to be valid, develop appraisal criteria with which to measure job performance, design training, set pay, develop career ladders, and so on.

The last few years have seen discussions of whether job analysis is still relevant in a changing world. Traditional job analysis is past-oriented, focusing on describing a job as it is currently performed rather than as it might come to be performed in the future. Yet job content may be less stable over time as organizations become more agile and flexible, making time-consuming and expensive job analysis studies unattractive and likely to be quickly outdated. Further, responsibility for accomplishing duties increasingly is located at team rather than job level, and job analysis has historically concentrated on individual jobs (Singh, 2008).

At the same time, a competing approach to traditional job analysis, *competency modeling*, has gained widespread acceptance with practitioners and is now employed to describe managerial jobs in a substantial majority of large organizations. Competency models usually contain a limited number of generic worker-oriented attributes that are felt to characterize, to varying degrees, high performance in a wide range of jobs. They are chosen to emphasize and communicate strategically important behaviors and cultural values, such as customer service and innovation, throughout the organization—a function completely lacking in traditional job analysis. Competencies are used to tie together human resource practices, especially in training and appraisal. Competency modeling has been criticized as less rigorous and much less detailed than traditional job analysis, as using less psychometrically sound means of development and data collection, and as lacking the specific detail needed to guide employee selection efforts (Shippmann et al., 2000). However, it does have a more strategic orientation than traditional job analysis. Some experts feel that competency modeling and job analysis serve different purposes, and that both can contribute to the effective management of people in organizations (Sanchez & Levine, 2009).

Job analysis, like research on it, is alive and well. The past two decades have seen research on the accuracy and reliability of job data collected, as it may be impacted by rater expertise, training, and information processing errors (Morgeson & Campion, 1997). A significant advance in the field has been provided by a major project of the U.S. Department of Labor, the Occupational Information Network (O*NET). This web-based resource was developed as the successor to the Dictionary of Occupational Titles. O*NET provides "multiple windows on the world of work" by using both job specific and generic descriptors of work performed and worker attributes (Peterson et al., 2001). The generic taxonomies provided by O*NET have been adapted in innovative ways to meet the job analysis needs of specific organizations (see Reiter-Palmon, Brown, Sandall, Buboltz, & Nimps, 2006 for an example).

Selection

Improving employee selection was one of the first and has long been one of the most central concerns for industrial psychologists. The standard paradigm involves measuring relevant individual differences in job candidates (predictors) and using them to predict individual performance after hire (the criterion). Before predictors can be used, however, they must be proven to be valid in significantly predicting post-hire performance on the criterion measure. The basic model for *criterion-related validation* has been in place since about 1920 (Vinchur, 2007). It includes:

1. Conduct a thorough job analysis to identify the knowledge, skills, and abilities (KSAs) likely to be required to complete job tasks;
2. Develop a criterion measure of job performance;
3. Design or choose one or more selection devices to measure KSAs that appear to be important for job performance;
4. Administer selection devices and criterion measures to employees and empirically determine the relationship between them;
5. Determine a decision rule for using scores on the selection devices for hiring.

An alternate model for validation, *content validation*, involves developing predictors that demonstrably tap the same content as is required on the job (as in a work sample test or interview) rather than a construct such as manual dexterity or cognitive ability. A thorough job analysis and a content evaluation panel of subject matter experts are used to document the overlap between the job and the predictors (Lawshe, 1975). For example, a written test of knowledge of building codes could be developed as part of the selection process for building inspectors.

As scientists, industrial psychologists have always felt that validation was essential before selection devices were put into use. However, the passage of the Civil Rights Act of 1964 in the United States, together with subsequent laws and landmark court cases, made careful validation even more essential. Unvalidated selection devices that produce adverse impact on protected classes of job applicants (e.g., women, minorities) are likely to attract costly litigation. Legislation banning discrimination is common in many countries, and a survey of its effects on the practice of employee selection in 22 countries is presented by Myors et al. (2008).

Until the late 1970s, the validity of selection devices was considered to be "situation-specific," because the same test often produced quite different validity coefficients across studies conducted in different organizations or on slightly different jobs. Thus, local validation studies were thought to be required in all cases. All this changed when Schmidt and Hunter (1977) developed a statistical means to combine validity coefficients across studies and to adjust for the effects of sample size, differential unreliability in criterion measurement, and restriction in range to produce estimated population correlations between predictors and criteria. Their research strongly suggested that validity coefficients were not as situation-specific as previously assumed, and that much of the observed variation between studies could be explained by errors and statistical artifacts. This opened the door to *validity generalization*, or using meta-analytic estimates of the validity of a class of predictors for predicting performance in a class of jobs rather than relying entirely on local validation studies. Validity generalization is undoubtedly the biggest advance in the field in the past 50 years. Its basic concepts and core findings have gained wide acceptance, though there is plenty of quibbling about how statistical corrections are made and how best to apply meta-analytic findings in practice (Murphy, 2003). Legal issues have somewhat slowed the adoption of conclusions from validity generalization studies in the United States, primarily because tests of general mental ability, which validly predict performance across jobs, consistently produce adverse impact on some minority groups.

Meta-analyses have been conducted on validity coefficients for a wide range of individual difference traits (e.g., general mental ability (GMA), conscientiousness) that may be measured in selection as well as for some selection methods (e.g., structured interviews, assessment centers) with less specific content. One of the most robust findings of validity generalization research is that GMA is a significant predictor of performance on a very wide range of jobs, with validity coefficients being especially strong on more complex jobs (Hunter & Hunter, 2004; Salgado et al., 2003) and when predicting training performance. The importance of GMA in predicting job performance across jobs has been replicated in meta-analyses on European data as well (Bertua, Anderson, & Salgado, 2005; Hülsheger, Maier, & Stumpp, 2007; Salgado, et al., 2003). There has been a debate on whether the measurement of more specific abilities in addition to GMA is useful, with some concluding that specific abilities account for relatively little variance beyond GMA (Ree, Earles, & Teachout, 1994) and other suggesting that specific abilities are still useful for placement/classification decisions (Zeidner & Johnson, 1994).

Schmidt and Hunter (1998) report meta-analytic estimated validities for a number of commonly used predictors, as well as the incremental validity that might be expected when combining each predictor with a test of general mental ability (GMA). Consistently strong predictors include GMA, work sample tests, structured interviews, job knowledge tests, and integrity tests. Biographical data and assessment centers are also generally valid, with slightly lower average coefficients. The most useful combinations are GMA plus a work sample test, integrity test, or structured interview.

Meta-analyses have also shed some light on the processes by which individual differences influence job performance. For instance, the effects of general mental ability and of work experience on performance are largely mediated by job knowledge (Hunter, 1986; Schmidt, Hunter, & Outerbridge, 1986). It seems likely that the effects of personality on job performance will prove to be mediated by motivation (Barrick, Stewart, & Piotrowski, 2002; Judge & Ilies, 2002).

One of the persistent issues in validation research involves the criterion of job performance. Criteria, especially when they consist of performance ratings from a single source, are often considered to be worrisomely unreliable. Correcting for unreliability in the criterion is one reason that meta-analytic estimates of validity are higher than observed validities. In addition to unreliability, criteria may also be deficient. Traditionally, criterion measures have focused on the performance of core job tasks. Recently there have been calls to expand the criterion domain to include measures of organizational citizenship behavior, counterproductive work behavior, adaptive performance, and teamwork performance (Cascio & Aguinis, 2008a; Van Iddekinge & Ployhart, 2008). Whether these measures should stand alone or be aggregated into a single measure of overall performance has also been debated. Various aspects of performance are often found to be correlated, with evidence that a large general factor underlies well over half of the variance in performance ratings even after accounting for halo error (Viswesvaran, Schmidt, & Ones, 2005). On the other hand, distinct aspects of performance may be best predicted by different predictors, such as citizenship behavior being predicted by conscientiousness while core task performance is predicted by GMA (Murphy & Shiarella, 1997).

Some scholars have also noted a mismatch between criterion measures and predictors in most validation studies. Criterion measures usually assess *typical performance* on the job over a long period of time, whereas the predictors are often measures of ***maximum performance*** under high motivation to do well (e.g., ability tests). Typical performance depends on both ability and motivation, with motivation being especially important when jobs are autonomous such that incumbents have choices about what to do, how intensely to do it, and how persistently to do it. Cascio and Aguinis (2008a) have suggested that predictors be broadened to assess typical performance so that both motivation and ability can be displayed. Longer and more realistic work samples such as internships and contract work are suggestions for such predictors. Cascio and Aguinis (2008a) also note that performance takes place in a social and strategic milieu, what they call *in situ*, and that validity is likely to be maximized if selection measures are collected in similar circumstances. In essence, they are suggesting that some situational specificity in test validity exists. The sections to follow explore findings and recent research on specific selection devices.

Selection devices

Psychologists have developed, studied, and applied a wide range of measures of individual characteristics for the purpose of predicting job performance. A review of many of them is available in Thomas (2004) *The Comprehensive Handbook of Psychological Assessment, Volume 4 Industrial and Organizational Assessment* (see also Farr & Tippins, 2010, for current views). In the paragraphs that follow, some of the "success stories" for predicting performance will be highlighted, consensus findings will be summarized, and current research issues or controversies will be described.

Ability tests for selection. Standardized ability tests are among the most effective predictors of later job performance. Measures of general mental ability, whether collected directly from single tests of intelligence or created from a battery of specific ability tests (verbal, mathematical, reasoning, etc.), validly predict overall job performance on all jobs, and more strongly so for more complex jobs (Schmidt & Hunter 1998; 2004; Sackett, Borneman, & Connelly, 2008; see also a special issue of *Human Performance* in 2002 for 12 articles on this topic). Somewhat surprisingly, GMA has also been shown to negatively predict counterproductive work behavior such as abuse of others or misuse of property (Dilchert, Ones, David, & Rostow, 2007). Dilchert et al. suggest that more intelligent individuals may have the foresight to anticipate the consequences of deviant behavior and thus inhibit themselves from displaying it. Taken together, this evidence would seem to strongly support the use of testing for GMA in most selection programs. However, some firms are skittish due to likely adverse impact or concern about applicant reactions. They may use education requirements as a proxy for GMA, which is less contentious but also considerably less effective (Berry, Gruys, & Sackett, 2006).

A relatively recent development in ability testing is the use of unproctored online testing of job applicants. Concerns have been raised about reduced standardization of testing conditions, loss of security of test items, practice effects for repeated test takers, and cheating (Tippins, 2009). Advantages to organizations are very much quicker and less expensive screening of large and geographically dispersed applicant pools before smaller numbers of successful candidates are assessed in person.

Some scholars have criticized overreliance on general intelligence and suggest that there are multiple intelligences which are not perfectly correlated, can add unique variance to the prediction of job performance, and have not been sufficiently researched or applied in selection. *Practical* and *emotional* intelligence are the other dimensions most often mentioned, and both have stimulated research and intense debate over the past few years.

Practical intelligence has been conceptualized in several ways. One is as job-specific tacit knowledge acquired through experience. This procedural knowledge allows good judgments to be made when encountering specific real world problems within the domain of the person's expertise. In the work setting, it is most often measured by job specific situational judgment tests (SJTs) in which applicants choose the best and worse responses to a series of realistic scenarios (McDaniel & Whetzel, 2005). There has been an explosion of research and popularity of SJTs in the past 15 years. There is evidence that SJTs add to the prediction of job performance beyond GMA and personality (Weekley & Ployhart, 2006). Other forms of context-specific ability tests constructed to mirror the content and judgments required for successful performance on specific jobs include *job knowledge* and *work sample tests*. These have long been regarded as quite useful and highly valid when selecting candidates who are already expected to have relevant job skills (Hunter & Hunter, 1984), though Roth, Bobko, and McFarland (2005) have recently suggested that validity may be less than originally estimated.

The other approach to practical intelligence regards it as a stable individual difference that is not context-specific (Sternberg & Hedlund, 2002) and may involve the ability to learn readily from experience in almost any domain. It has been described as "street smarts" or "common sense." Practical intelligence is still quite a new concept, with considerable debate about its existence, measurement, utility, and relationship to GMA (Gottfredson, 2003). *Adaptability* is a related new ability concept that also may become more useful in the future (Pulakos, Arad, Donovan, & Plamondon, 2000; Pulakos et al., 2002).

Situational judgment/tacit knowledge tests often contain a considerable proportion of scenarios requiring decisions about how best to proceed in a sensitive or complex social situation. As such, they may tap yet another ability, *emotional intelligence*, that has received a great deal of attention in the past few years. Emotional intelligence is also a relatively new concept, sometimes defined and measured as a skill, and sometimes viewed as closer to a personality trait. Claims for the importance of emotional intelligence have outstripped convincing evidence (Murphy, 2006) and many industrial psychologists have been wary of the hype surrounding the concept at this early stage of development. A recent meta-analytic review by Joseph and Newman (2010) has offered support for the predictive validity of mixed measures of emotional intelligence, though validity may be situation-specific. It appears that emotional intelligence is most important on jobs requiring teamwork, leadership, working under stress, and when emotional labor demands are high.

Personality tests for selection. One of the most contentious and active areas of research for the past 15 years has surrounded the issue of personality testing for selection purposes. Personality testing became popular after World War II but fell into disrepute after a review by Guion and Gottier (1965) concluded that personality did not consistently predict job performance. Personality testing has made a huge comeback after a meta-analysis by Barrick and Mount (1991). They used the "Big Five" typology to organize the many personality scales used in previous validation studies and concluded that the personality trait of conscientiousness had a nonzero relationship to job performance across jobs. This article spawned a number of further meta-analyses (see Ones, Dilchert, Viswesvaran, & Judge, 2007 and Barrick, Mount, & Judge, 2001 for summaries) and a considerable amount of debate about the level of validity and wisdom of use of personality measures for employee selection (Morgeson et al., 2007a; 2007b; Ones et al., 2007; Tett & Christiansen, 2007).

Most meta-analyses show quite small uncorrected correlations between single personality traits and overall job performance, from about zero to .15 (Moregeson et al., 2007b). When corrections are applied, the correlations increase but are still quite modest, and are most consistently present for the trait of conscientiousness.

Personality traits appear to be somewhat stronger (but still modest) predictors of organizational citizenship behavior and counterproductive work behavior than of core task performance, and are also useful in predicting leadership. When all the Big Five measures are combined in a multiple regression equation, the prediction of outcomes is improved.

Advocates of personality for selection point out that validities are quite respectable when personality measures are contextualized (ask about how one feels and behaves at work rather than in general), when personality traits are selected based on a thorough job analysis and logical rationale about which traits might support performance in that job, when jobs are high in autonomy (and thus the situation is "weak"), and when criteria to be predicted are discretionary behaviors such as citizenship rather than those dominated by ability like objective core task performance (Hogan, 2005; Hough & Oswald, 2008). Personality is largely uncorrelated with ability, so can add incremental validity when used with cognitive ability tests. Further, personality tests produce much less or no adverse impact on minority groups compared to cognitive ability tests.

The issues remaining in personality testing for selection are many and vigorously debated. One is whether, if validities really are low, personality testing should be used in high stakes situations like selection at all (Morgeson et al., 2007b). Others argue that validities are reasonable in the right circumstances, though the validity of personality tests is more situation-specific than the validities of many ability constructs (Hough & Oswald, 2008; Tett & Burnett, 2003; Tett & Christiansen, 2007). Or alternatively, that it is necessary to consider a configuration of traits rather than single traits to best predict performance (Judge & Erez, 2007). Another issue in personality testing involves concerns about applicants being motivated to "fake good" in a selection context, and the effect that this may have on predictive validity. The conclusion seems to be that applicants often do try to present themselves positively but that effects on validity are inconsequential (Hogan, Barrett, & Hogan, 2007).

A third issue is the level of specificity at which personality traits should be measured for selection purposes. Most of the meta-analyses have been at the level of fairly broad traits as represented by the Big Five typology. It has been argued that this is an appropriate level at which to measure traits for selection, because overall job performance is a broad criterion and prediction is maximized when measures are congruent in specificity (Ones & Viswesvaran, 1996). Another alternative is to assess at the narrower level of subtraits that comprise each of the Big Five, and it has been shown that subtraits of conscientiousness (e.g., achievement and dependability) can add value in predicting some specific aspects of performance beyond the effects of global conscientiousness (Dudley, Orvis, Lebiecki, & Cortina, 2006). A third alternative is to measure personality even more broadly than the Big Five, in the form of compound traits such as integrity or customer service orientation. Integrity testing is a possible "success story" for industrial psychology, as explained in more detail below.

Integrity tests have been developed to predict employee theft but have also been found to predict overall job performance, counterproductive work behavior, and absenteeism. Two types of integrity tests exist. One is the *overt integrity test,* which asks about actual past theft, attitudes toward theft, estimates of others' dishonest behavior, and so on. These are usually empirically keyed by comparing groups who have committed dishonest behavior with those who have not. This approach, while successful, has led to overt integrity tests being criticized for lacking construct validity. While overt tests appear to be transparent, they are in fact surprisingly valid.

The other kind of integrity test is *personality-based*, assessing dependability, thrill seeking, conformity, rejection of authority, and so on. Personality-based integrity tests have been described as *compound* trait measures that are related to the Big Five dimensions of conscientiousness, agreeableness, and neuroticism, as well as the "Big Sixth" personality factor of honesty/humility (Marcus, Lee, & Ashton, 2007). Validities of the two types of tests are similar for predicting overall job performance (rho .41) and both types are also useful for predicting counterproductive work behaviors (Ones, Viswesvaran, & Schmidt, 1993). Actual theft, a low base-rate phenomenon, is somewhat more difficult to both measure and predict. Personality-based integrity tests have also been shown to predict absenteeism (Ones, Viswesvaran, & Schmidt, 2003). See Berry, Sackett, and Wiemann (2007) for a review of recent advances and issues in integrity testing for selection. Integrity tests, however, are not without their critics. There are concerns about faking, both false positive and false negative predictions, and applicant reactions to instruments that may appear invasive (Karren & Zacharias, 2007).

Interviews. Interviews are among the most commonly used selection procedures. One of the clearest findings in our literature is that interviews that are structured in terms of both questions asked and scoring procedures do a better job of predicting job performance than unstructured interviews (Huffcutt & Arthur, 1994). Interviews are usually well accepted by applicants, produce less adverse impact than ability tests, and contribute incrementally to the prediction of performance beyond GMA and personality. A structured interview is a method not a construct, and interview questions may be used to assess a variety of attributes including personality, mental ability, job knowledge, and specific skills (Huffcutt, Roth, Conway, & Stone, 2001). It has been suggested that interviews often capture motivational variables, and so may be especially effective in predicting typical performance (Klehe & Latham, 2006).

Structured interviews may be seen as a major success story for industrial psychologists in terms of influencing practice. Two particular forms, the situational interview ("what would you do if ..."; Latham, Saari, Pursell, & Campion, 1980) and the behavior description interview ("tell me about a time you ..."; (Janz, Hellervik, & Gilmore, 1986) are very effective and have been widely accepted in organizations. Evidence suggests that behavior description interviews are more valid than situational interviews for complex jobs (Huffcutt, Roth, Conway, & Klehe, 2004).

Assessment centers and individual assessment. Assessment centers are another success story for industrial psychology. An assessment center is a content-valid half-day to three-day series of simulations of work tasks, most often designed for supervisory or managerial roles. Exercises usually include an in-basket test, a leaderless group discussion, role plays, and other problem-solving activities. Psychological tests, public speaking tasks, and interviews may be included as well. Assessors rate candidates on multiple skill dimensions (e.g., leadership, planning, persuasiveness) after each exercise, and again at the end of all exercises.

Assessment centers are most often used for selection, with either internal or external candidates, and also provide useful information regarding the development needs of candidates. The overall assessment ratings produced at the end of assessment centers are predictively valid for job performance, promotions, and salary advancement. Assessment center performance is correlated with GMA and personality, and there are mixed findings on the extent to which assessment center ratings have incremental validity beyond these predictors (Meriac, Hoffman, Woehr, & Fleisher, 2008; Schmidt & Hunter, 1998). See Thornton and Rupp (2006) for a comprehensive treatment of assessment center issues.

There has been a long-standing paradox regarding the construct validity of assessment center ratings. Ratings of the same dimension do not show the expected convergent validity across exercises, and ratings of different dimensions show low discriminant validity within exercises. Lance (2008) believes that this should not be viewed as a problem with the construct validity of assessment centers, but rather as reflecting valid exercise-specific variance in performance. Assessment centers would then be viewed as a collection of independent work samples, each requiring somewhat different behaviors from assessees, analogous to tests in a test battery (Thornton & Gibbons, 2009). Regardless of the structure of assessment center ratings, the fact remains that a carefully constructed set of exercises, closely tied to a job analysis or competency model for the job, assessed by trained and qualified raters, is likely to validly predict job performance.

Some psychologists, including those with industrial or clinical backgrounds, conduct *individual assessments* for selection purposes. The assessment may consist of a variety of tests as well as an in-depth interview, and culminates in a written description of the strengths and weaknesses of a candidate for a particular upper management position. Development needs may also be specified (Prien, Schippmann, & Prien, 2003; Jeanneret & Silzer, 1998). Hollenbeck (2009) suggests that executive selection will increase in importance given the recent spectacular failures of some CEOs. He also suggests that the traditional validation paradigm employed by industrial psychologists does not fit the executive selection context due to sample size problems, the likelihood that GMA is uniformly high among executive candidates, and the importance of "character" rather than specific behaviors to success in extremely complex and responsible jobs.

Conclusions about selection. Despite selection being the most studied area in industrial psychology, critics point out that industrial psychologists haven't gotten much better at predicting job performance over the past decades, just better at massaging their data with increasingly complex corrections that increase estimates of true validity (Cascio and Aguinis, 2008a). Nevertheless, there are some outstanding success stories in the selection domain. Validity generalization, assessment centers, situational judgment tests, and behavioral interviews are among the best of these.

Training and Development

Industrial psychologists have long been interested in the training of job-related skills. Collectively, organizations spend many billions of dollars training their employees each year. Fortunately, recent meta-analyses and other reviews have established that training is effective and produces sizable improvements in performance at individual and organizational levels (Aguinis & Kraiger 2009; Arthur, Bennett, Edens, & Bell, 2003; Collins & Holton, 2004; Tharenou, Saks, & Moore, 2007). The past two decades have seen an explosion of research and theorizing on training in organizations. Kozlowski and Salas (2009) have produced an edited book summarizing current theory and future research needs.

Much of the early research and practice in training and development was guided by the instructional systems design model (ISD, Goldstein, 1986). This model specifies that training efforts should begin with a thorough needs assessment to determine who needs to be trained, in what content, and to verify that the proposed training fits the organizational context. Following needs assessment, training should be designed using learning principles, delivered, and evaluated. Part of evaluation often includes examining the extent to which the training transfers to the job and is actually used by trainees. Recent research has expanded our understanding of all aspects of the training process from pretraining factors to training delivery to posttraining evaluation to transfer.

The ISD model has been supplemented with a strong focus on the social and organizational contexts surrounding training, with the conclusion that pre- and posttraining factors may be as important to training effectiveness and transfer as is the design of the training program itself (Salas & Cannon-Bowers, 2001; Saks & Belcourt, 2006). Greater attention has been paid to the trainee and his or her perceptions and motivation before, during, and after training (Beier & Kanfer, 2009; Colquitt, LePine, & Noe, 2000). Pretraining employee factors that contribute to improved trainee motivation to learn and training outcomes include self-efficacy, learning goal orientation, internal locus of control, achievement motivation, (low) anxiety, job involvement, and organizational commitment. After training, transfer of training to the job is critical. Trainee level variables such as posttraining self-efficacy, motivation to transfer, employee reactions/evaluations of the training program, and complexity of mental models developed predict transfer. The organizational context is also important in the form of climate for transfer, peer and supervisor support for using new skills, rewards for transfer, and early and frequent opportunities to apply newly learned skills on the job (Baldwin, Ford, & Blume, 2009).

Advances have also been made in understanding processes and design issues during training. Technology-delivered training (e-learning, web-based instruction) has exploded over the past few years. Organizations find it convenient and cost-effective, and there is evidence that it is generally at least as effective as traditional classroom instruction (Sitzmann, Kraiger, Stewart, & Wisher, 2006). Researchers have developed guidelines for how to design technology-delivered instruction that suits human information processing limitations (Mayer, 2009). Many technology-delivered training programs greatly increase the amount of *learner control*, with some systems allowing learners to choose the pace, sequence, content, method of presentation, and difficulty of material. Learner control, however, does not automatically guarantee improved outcomes (Kraiger & Jerden, 2007; deRouin, Fritzsche & Salas, 2005). Individual differences in trainee motivation and meta-cognitive/self-regulatory skills may moderate the effects of learner control on learning outcomes, and supplying adaptive guidance helps trainees make wise choices in using their control (Bell & Kozlowski, 2002).

Traditional approaches to training focus on the teaching of specific knowledge and procedures to relatively passive trainees who are expected to avoid errors during training and faithfully replicate what they have been taught once on the job. As work environments become more dynamic and complex, trainees need to learn to learn continuously after formal training events, and to generalize and apply their knowledge in adaptive ways to novel situations encountered on the job. Recent research has advanced knowledge of how to design training interventions to best stimulate *adaptive transfer*, often using the flexibility and learner control possible in technology-delivered training. *Active learning*, in which trainees experiment to discover and construct mental models of the task, appears to be effective in producing adaptive transfer. Active learning generally proceeds more successfully when trainees adopt a learning goal orientation, are encourage to make and learn from errors (*error management training*), and engage in metacognitive monitoring and control of their learning and emotions (Bell & Kozlowski, 2008; Keith & Frese, 2008). Learning during training may be slower as trainees experiment and learn from mistakes, but this process creates more sophisticated mental models and facilitates adaptive transfer to novel situations after training. However, there may be some aptitude by treatment interactions, with active learning and error management training being more effective for those high on cognitive ability and learning goal orientation. The science of designing training to optimally stimulate adaptive learning and transfer is still in the early stages of development but shows great promise (Bell & Kozlowski, 2009).

The training of supervisors, manager, and leaders accounts for the lion's share of training expenditures in most organizations, yet relatively little is known about how leaders learn to lead. Recently there has been progress made in theorizing about leader development over the life course, with agreement emerging that goal orientation, leader identity, and leader efficacy are important in explaining leader development trajectories (Avolio & Hannah, 2008; Day, Harrison, & Halpin, 2009). A fairly recent but now widespread tool in leader development is one-to-one executive coaching (Kilburg, 2000). Some executive coaches are industrial psychologists, though a number come from other disciplines such as consulting or clinical psychology, or from specialties outside of psychology. Practice is far ahead of research on the topic of executive coaching, and rigorous evaluations of coaching effectiveness are rare (Bono, Purvanova, Towler, & Peterson, 2009; Feldman & Lankau, 2005).

In sum, recent developments in the training literature draw on knowledge of cognitive psychology, motivation, personality, and social processes in organizations. The importance of the environment surrounding training events and of individual differences in trainees beyond cognitive ability have been recognized. Trainee actions in the form of exploration, self-assessment, and self-regulation strategies are increasingly seen as essential to deep learning and effective adaptive transfer.

Performance Appraisal and Performance Management

Performance appraisal has always been of interest to industrial psychologists. From the very earliest days, performance measures were needed as criteria against which to validate selection tests. For the first half of our history, the overriding concern in performance appraisal was the accuracy of measurement of performance. The dominant metaphor for appraisal was the "test," with hopes for the high reliability and construct validity expected of a good test (Folger, Konovsky, & Cropanzano, 1992). Considerable research attention was given to the development of improved rating formats to increase interrater agreement and reduce errors such as leniency, severity, and halo. An example is the *behaviorally anchored rating scale*.

In 1980, Landy and Farr called for an end to research on appraisal formats, as only minor improvements in accuracy could be attributed to format. Research subsequently focused on the rater side of the equation, exploring how raters recognize, categorize, recall, and integrate performance information, and the characteristic problems accompanying such human information processing (DeNisi, 1996). Much of this research was conducted in the laboratory and added relatively little to the practice of performance appraisal in organizations. The 1980s also saw progress on rater training, with *frame of reference training* showing the most promise. Accuracy and error were still salient concerns, though some pointed out that training raters to reduce distributional and halo errors sometimes harmed rather than enhanced accuracy (Hedge & Kavanagh, 1988).

While some research continues on issues of measurement, criterion validity, and the definition of performance (see Bennett, Lance, & Woehr, 2006), attention also has turned to the social and organizational context surrounding appraisal. Farr and Jacobs (2006) suggest that performance appraisal now belongs as much to the "organizational" side of I/O psychology as to the "industrial" side, because trust in the system and in the rater are critical to the success of appraisal and feedback systems. Folger et al. (1992) proposed a "due process" metaphor for appraisal. Others have pointed out that appraisal is "a formal accountability system nested within a complex social, emotional, cognitive, political, and relationship context" (Ferris, Munyon, Basik, & Buckley, 2008, p. 146). Levy and Williams (2004) note the importance of user reactions (both rater and ratee) to appraisal systems, and suggest that appraisal effectiveness may be influenced by purpose of appraisal, feedback culture, rater–ratee relationships, affect, impression management, participation, and rater motivation as well as structural aspects of the appraisal system.

Another change in focus for performance appraisal research has been towards the understanding of performance feedback and related processes to improve performance in organizations. Performance appraisal has historically been seen as a discrete, usually annual event in which employees are judged by their immediate supervisor. The purpose of the judgment may include administrative reasons such as test validation, training evaluation, or the determination of merit pay. Alternatively or in addition, the purpose may include planning for future skills development, career progression, and/or motivation and performance improvement via the setting of annual goals. Now appraisal is increasingly seen as part of a more continuous process of *performance management* that involves goal setting, feedback, coaching and development, evaluation of performance, and reward for performance (Smither, in press; Smither & London, 2009).

New means of assessing performance have also gained popularity. In particular, *360 degree* or *multisource feedback* has become widely used, with several studies exploring its impact on ratees. Smither, London, & Reilly (2005) summarized this work and concluded that improvements following receipt of multisource feedback are generally modest, with gains most likely to occur when "feedback indicates that change is necessary, recipients have a positive feedback orientation, perceive a need to change their behavior, react positively to the feedback, believe change is feasible, set appropriate goals to regulate their behavior, and take actions that lead to skill and performance improvement" (p. 33).

A contentious trend in appraisal is the use of forced distribution systems to categorize each employee's overall performance into one of three to five categories such as "A," "B," or "C." Typically no more than 15–20% of employees in a group are allowed to be rated in the top performer "A" category. The majority must be placed in the B category, and the worst 5–10% must be categorized C. A's may be heavily rewarded, whereas C's may be encouraged or required to leave. When C's are discharged, the system has been called *rank and yank*. Proponents claim that this approach creates a performance-oriented culture, motivates employees, promotes truth in appraisal, raises average workforce performance level, and attracts high ability employees (Grote, 2005). Opponents are concerned about damage to trust, culture, and cooperation, as well as issues of unfairness, legal challenge, political game playing, and the questionable assumption that all groups have the same distribution of true performance (Dominick, 2009). Further, there is the danger that eventually the bottom few percent who are forced out will be better employees than those who can be brought in to replace them. Scullen, Bergey, & Aiman-Smith (2005) cleverly simulated the effects of rank and yank systems on average workforce performance under conditions of varying selection ratio and validity of selection processes used to replace those fired, percent fired per year, and accuracy of employee performance categorization. The best results were obtained when employee categorization was accurate, 10% were fired, the selection ratio was low, and the validity of the selection process was high. Larger gains were seen in the first few years of the simulation when departing C performers were most likely to be replaced by better hires, with workforce performance stabilizing after 3–5 years in many scenarios.

The Research–Practice Gap in Industrial Psychology

There have long been complaints of a research–practice gap in industrial psychology, reflecting the two major employment options in the field. In the US, 60% of SIOP members are employed as practitioners (Silzer, Cober, Erickson, & Robinson, 2008). They may be sole practitioners/consultants, employed in consulting firms, or employed by private businesses and governments. The remaining 40% are employed as academics, split equally between business schools and psychology departments.

The research–practice gap ostensibly involves academics pursuing esoteric and irrelevant research topics in excruciating detail, versus practitioners who are either ignorant of cutting-edge research or unable or unwilling to apply scientific findings in their organizations.

There is evidence that a gap does indeed exist. Rynes, Colbert, and Brown (2002) showed that HR practitioners (many of whom were not industrial psychologists) held a number of misconceptions about the validity of employee selection devices (see also Anderson, 2005). Highhouse (2008) laments practitioner beliefs that intuition, honed by experience, produces selection decisions superior to those based on validated tests and empirical decision rules. Rynes, Giluk, and Brown (2007) attribute some of the gap to lack of coverage, and/or inaccurate coverage, of key research findings in practitioner journals. Deadrick and Gibson (2009) suggest there is also a long-standing "interest gap," with HR practitioners finding different topics most useful. They compared article topics in two academic industrial psychology journals (*Personnel Psychology* and *Journal of Applied Psychology*) and two practitioner publications (*Human Resource Management* and *HR Magazine*) over 30 years, and found persistent and sizeable difference in the appearance, and presumably importance, of topics in these two types of outlets. Specifically, HR practitioners were much more interested in compensation and rewards than were academics, with very few publications on those topics appearing in the academic literature.

There is little evidence that the research–practice gap is closing, despite continued efforts by SIOP and journal editors (e.g., Burke, Drasgow, & Edwards, 2004; Rynes et al., 2007; and the Scientist-Practitioner Forum and its predecessor in *Personnel Psychology* since 1994). In fact, a previous bridge between the two camps, the practioner-researcher, formerly embodied in the personnel research units within large companies, seems to be dying out compared to the situation several decades ago, with practitioners much less frequently engaging in active research themselves (Silzer, et al., 2008). Cascio and Aguinis (2008b) analysed the author affiliations of all publications in the *Journal of Applied Psychology* and *Personnel Psychology* between 1963 and 2007, and found that the number of articles by practitioners declined considerably over time. A number of useful suggestions for closing the gap have been put forward (see Anderson, 2007; Gelade, 2006; Hyatt, et al., 1996; Rynes, 2007).

In conclusion, industrial psychology is alive and well in universities and in organizations, even though the links between the two venues may be imperfect. Industrial psychology has had a number of success stories over the years, and vital new developments are now occurring in many areas. However, there are possible changes on the horizon, as discussed below.

Industrial and/or Organizational Psychology?

It seems fitting to end this chapter with a consideration of the future of industrial psychology in relation to organizational psychology. I/O scholars trained in psychology departments usually develop some expertise and appreciation for both the industrial and the organizational sides of the discipline. However, I/O psychologists are increasing employed in business schools, where they often produce doctoral graduates whose expertise and interests are exclusively in organizational behavior. Doctoral students who specialize in personnel/HR in business schools acquire additional knowledge of business strategy and industrial relations, but may lack the rigorous foundation in measurement and psychometrics provided in industrial psychology degrees. This raises some concerns about the future supply of well-trained industrial psychology researchers—the kind of people needed to carry on the work reviewed in this chapter.

In 2009–2010 SIOP again considered changing its name. Alternatives included Applied Organizational Psychology, Business Psychology, Organizational and Work Psychology, and the front runner Organizational Psychology. Some members felt that the word "Industrial" was archaic and limiting, and noted that the term is not commonly used to describe the profession elsewhere in the world. Additional arguments in favour of a name change include the current name being too long, tending to polarize those specializing in personnel/individual difference psychology from those specializing in areas derived from social psychology, and lacking clarity to clients and others outside the profession. Other members saw "Industrial" in the name of the Society as essential to their identity and worried about losing the unique focus on the topics reviewed in this chapter should a name change be approved (SIOP Exchange, 2009). Ultimately, after a close ballot, the name SIOP was retained.

Regardless of what the Society or the profession is called, there seems to be a trend toward organizational aspects being understood as important contingencies governing the success of industrial/HR innovations and applications. Context is important, employee motivation is important, perceptions are important. The increased appreciation of the effects of "O" on the practice of "I" has appeared in most sections of this chapter. For instance, discussions of situation-specificity in personality test validity and using typical performance measures to predict *in situ* performance assert that organizational contexts vary and impact predictor performance. Training effectiveness is now known to depend critically upon the pre and post training social, cultural, and task environments in which trainees are embedded. And as Farr and Jacobs (2006) concluded in a book entitled *Performance Measurement*, it is impossible to understand performance appraisal without understanding trust. While we continue to need rigorous research on the industrial side of I/O psychology, effective application also relies on developing practices that fit into profoundly human organizational systems. Industrial/organizational psychologists are well placed to meet this challenge.

References

Aguinis, H., & Kraiger, K. (2009). Benefits of training and development for individuals and teams, organizations, and society. *Annual Review of Psychology*, *60*, 451–474.

Anderson, N. (2005). Relationship between practice and research in personnel selection: Does the left hand know what the right is doing? In A. Evers, N. Anderson, & O. Voskuijl (Eds.), *The Blackwell handbook of personnel selection* (pp. 1–24). Malden, MA: Blackwell Publishing.

Anderson, N. (2007). The practitioner–researcher divide revisited: Strategic-level bridges and the roles of IWO psychologists. *Journal of Occupational & Organizational Psychology*, *80*, 175–183.

Anderson, N., Ones, D. S., Sinangil, H. K., & Viswesvaran, C. (Eds.). (2002). *Handbook of industrial, work and organizational psychology, Volume 1: Personnel psychology.* Thousand Oaks, CA: Sage.

Arthur W., Jr., Bennett W., Jr., Edens, P. S., & Bell, S. T. (2003). Effectiveness of training in organizations: A meta-analysis of design and evaluation features. *Journal of Applied Psychology, 88*, 234–245.

Avolio, B. J., & Hannah. S. T. (2008). Developmental readiness: Accelerating leader development. *Consulting Psychology Journal: Practice and Research, 60*, 331–347.

Baldwin, T. T., Ford, J. K., & Blume, B. D. (2009). Transfer of training 1988–2008: An updated review and agenda for future research. In G. P. Hodgkinson & J. K. Ford (Eds.), *International Review of Industrial and Organizational Psychology, 24*, 41–70.

Barrick, M. R., & Mount, M. K. (1991). The Big Five personality dimensions and job performance: A meta-analysis. *Personnel Psychology, 44*, 1–26.

Barrick, M. R., Mount, M. K., & Judge, T. A. (2001). Personality and performance at the beginning of the new millennium: What do we know and where do we go next? *International Journal of Selection and Assessment, 9*, 9–30.

Barrick, M. R., Stewart, G. L., & Piotrowski, M. (2002). Personality and job performance: Test of the mediating effects of motivation among sales representatives. *Journal of Applied Psychology, 87*, 43–51.

Beier, M. E., & Kanfer, R. (2009). Motivation in training and development: A phase perspective. In S. W. J. Kozlowski & E. Salas (Eds.), *Learning, training, and development in organizations* (pp. 65–97). New York: Psychology Press.

Bell, B. S., & Kozlowski, S. W. J. (2002). Adaptive guidance: Enhancing self-regulation, knowledge, and performance in technology-based training. *Personnel Psychology, 55*, 267–306.

Bell, B. S., & Kozlowski, S. W. J. (2008). Active learning: Effects of core training design elements on self-regulatory processes, learning, and adaptability. *Journal of Applied Psychology, 93*, 296–316.

Bell, B. S., & Kozlowski, S. W. J. (2009). Toward a theory of learner-centered training design. An integrative framework of active learning. In S. W. J. Kozlowski & E. Salas (Eds.), *Learning, training, and development in organizations* (SIOP Frontiers Series; pp. 261–298). New York: Routledge Academic.

Bennett, W., Jr., Lance, C. E., & Woehr, D. J. (Eds.). (2006). *Performance measurement: Current perspectives and future challenges.* Mahwah, NJ: Lawrence Erlbaum.

Berry, C. M., Gruys, M. L., & Sackett, P. R. (2006). Educational attainment as a proxy for cognitive ability in selection: Effects on levels of cognitive ability and adverse impact. *Journal of Applied Psychology, 91*, 696–705.

Berry, C. M., Sackett, P. R., & Wiemann, S. (2007). A review of recent developments in integrity test research. *Personnel Psychology, 60*, 271–301.

Bertua, C., Anderson, N., & Salgado, J. F. (2005). The predictive validity of cognitive ability tests: A UK meta-analysis. *Journal of Occupational & Organizational Psychology, 78*, 387–409.

Bono, J. E., Purvanova, R. K., Towler, A. J., & Peterson, D. B. (2009) A survey of executive coaching practices. *Personnel Psychology, 62*, 361–404.

Brannick, M. T., Levine, E. L., & Morgeson, F. P. (2007). *Job and work analysis: Methods, research, and applications for human resource management.* Thousand Oaks, CA: Sage Publications, Inc.

Burke, C. S., Pierce, L. G., & Salas, E. (Eds.). (2006). *Understanding adaptability: A prerequisite for effective performance within complex environments.* Amsterdam, Netherlands: Elsevier.

Burke, M. J., Drasgow, F., & Edwards, J. E. (2004). Closing science-practice knowledge gaps: Contributions of psychological research to human resource management. *Human Resource Management*, *43*, 299–304.

Campbell, J. P. (2007). Profiting from history. In L. L. Koppes (Ed.), *Historical perspectives in industrial and organizational psychology* (pp. 441–457). Mahwah, NJ: Lawrence Erlbaum.

Cascio, W. F., & Aguinis, H. (2008a). Chapter 3: Staffing twenty-first-century organizations. *The Academy of Management Annals*, *2*, 133–165.

Cascio, W. F., & Aguinis, H. (2008b). Research in industrial and organizational psychology from 1963 to 2007: Changes, choices, and trends. *Journal of Applied Psychology*, *93*, 1062–1081.

Collins, D. B., & Holton, E. F. (2004). The effectiveness of managerial leadership development programs: A meta-analysis of studies from 1982 to 2001. *Human Resource Development Quarterly*, *15*, 217–248.

Colquitt, J. A., LePine, J. A., & Noe, R. A. (2000). Toward an integrative theory of training motivation: A meta-analytic path analysis of 20 years of research. *Journal of Applied Psychology*, *85*, 678–707.

Day, D. V., Harrison, M. M., & Halpin, S. M. (2009). *An integrative approach to leader development: Connecting adult development, identity, and expertise*. New York: Routledge.

Deadrick, D. L., & Gibson, P. A. (2009). Revisiting the research–practice gap in HR: A longitudinal analysis. *Human Resource Management Review*, *19*, 144–153.

DeNisi, A. S. (1996). *A cognitive approach to performance appraisal: A program of research*. London: Routledge.

deRouin, R. E., Fritzsche, B. A., & Salas, E. (2005). Learner control and workplace e-learning: Design, person, and organizational issues. *Research in Personnel and Human Resource Management*, *24*, 181–214.

Dilchert, S., Ones, D. S., Davis, R. D., & Rostow, C. D. (2007). Cognitive ability predicts objectively measured counterproductive work behaviors. *Journal of Applied Psychology*, *92*, 616–627.

Dominick, P.G. (2009). Forced rankings: Pros, cons, and practices. In J. W. Smither & M. London (Eds.), *Performance management: Putting research into practice.* (pp. 411–443). San Francisco: Jossey-Bass.

Dudley, N. M., Orvis, K. A., Lebiecki, J. E., & Cortina, J. M. (2006). A meta-analytic investigation of conscientiousness in the prediction of job performance: Examining the intercorrelations and the incremental validity of narrow traits. *Journal of Applied Psychology*, *91*, 40–57.

Farr, J. L., & Jacobs, R. (2006). Trust us: New perspectives on performance appraisal. In W. Bennett, Jr., C. E. Lance, & D. J. Woehr (Eds.), *Performance measurement: Current perspectives and future challenges* (pp. 321–337). Mahwah, NJ: Lawrence Erlbaum.

Farr, J. L., & Tippins, N. T. (Eds.). (2010). *Handbook of employee selection*. London: Routledge Academic.

Feldman, D. C., & Lankau, M. J. (2005). Executive coaching: A review and agenda for future research. *Journal of Management*, *31*, 829–848.

Ferris, G. R., Munyon, T. P., Basik, K., & Buckley, M. R. (2008). The performance evaluation context: Social, emotional, cognitive, political, and relationship components. *Human Resource Management Review*, *18*, 146–163.

Folger, R., Konovsky, M. A., & Cropanzano, R. (1992). A due process metaphor for performance appraisal. *Research in Organizational Behavior*, *14*, 129–177.

Gelade, G. A. (2006). But what does it mean in practice? *The Journal of Occupational and Organizational Psychology* from a practitioner perspective. *Journal of Occupational & Organizational Psychology, 79*, 153–160.

Goldstein, I. L. (1986). *Training in organizations: Needs assessment, development, and evaluation* (2nd ed.). Monterey, CA: Brooks/Cole.

Gottfredson, L. S. (2003). Dissecting practical intelligence theory: Its claims and evidence. *Intelligence, 31*, 343–397.

Grote, D. (2005). *Forced ranking: Making performance management work.* Harvard Business School Press.

Guion, R. M., & Gottier, R. F. (1965). Validity of personality measures in personnel selection. *Personnel Psychology, 18*, 135–164.

Hedge, J. W., & Kavanagh, M. J. (1988). Improving the accuracy of performance evaluations: Comparison of three methods of performance appraiser training. *Journal of Applied Psychology, 73*, 68–73.

Highhouse, S. (2008). Stubborn reliance on intuition and subjectivity in employee selection. *Industrial and Organizational Psychology, 1*, 333–342.

Hogan, R. (2005). In defense of personality measurement: New wine for old whiners. *Human Performance, 18*, 331-341.

Hogan, J., Barrett, P., & Hogan, R. (2007). Personality measurement, faking, and employment selection. *Journal of Applied Psychology, 92*, 1270–1285.

Hollenbeck, G. P. (2009). Executive selection—What's right … and what's wrong. *Industrial and Organizational Psychology, 2*, 130–143.

Hough, L. M., & Oswald, F. L. (2008). Personality testing and industrial-organizational psychology: Reflections, progress, and prospects. *Industrial and Organizational Psychology, 1*, 272–290.

Huffcutt, A. I., & Arthur, W., Jr., (1994). Hunter and Hunter (1984) revisited: Interview validity for entry-level jobs. *Journal of Applied Psychology, 79*, 184–190.

Huffcutt, A. I., Roth, P. L., Conway, J. M., Klehe, U. (2004). The impact of job complexity and study design on situational and behavior description interview validity. *International Journal of Selection & Assessment, 12*, 262–273.

Huffcutt, A. I., Roth, P. L., Conway, J. M., & Stone, N. J. (2001). Identification and meta-analytic assessment of psychological constructs measured in employment interviews. *Journal of Applied Psychology, 86*, 897–913.

Hülsheger, U. R., Maier, G. W., & Stumpp, T. (2007). Validity of general mental ability for the prediction of job performance and training success in Germany: A meta-analysis. *International Journal of Selection & Assessment, 15*, 3–18

Hunter, J. E. (1986). Cognitive ability, cognitive aptitudes, job knowledge, and job performance. *Journal of Vocational Behavior, 29*, 340–362.

Hunter, J. E., & Hunter, R. F. (1984). Validity and utility of alternative predictors of job performance. *Psychological Bulletin, 96*, 72–98.

Hyatt, D., Cropanzano, R., Finder, L.A., Levy, P., Ruddy, T. M., Vandaveer, V., & Walker, S. (1996). Bridging the gap between academics and practice: Suggestions from the field. *The Industrial-Organizational Psychologist, 35*, 29–32.

Janz, T., Hellervik, J., & Gilmore, D. C. (1986). *Behavior description interviewing.* Boston: Allyn and Bacon.

Jeanneret, R., & Silzer, R. (1998). *Individual psychological assessment: Predicting behavior in organizational settings.* San Francisco: Jossey-Bass.

Joseph, D. L., & Newman, D. A. (2010). Emotional intelligence: An integrative meta-analysis and cascading model. *Journal of Applied Psychology, 95*, 54–78.

Judge, T. A., & Erez, A. (2007). Interaction and intersection: The constellation of emotional stability and extraversion in predicting performance. *Personnel Psychology, 60*, 573–596.

Judge, T. A., & Ilies, R. (2002). Relationship of personality to performance motivation: A meta-analytic review. *Journal of Applied Psychology, 87*, 797–807.

Karren, R. J., & Zacharias, L. (2007). Integrity tests: Critical issues. *Human Resource Management Review, 17*, 221–234.

Keith, N., & Frese, M. (2008). Effectiveness of error management training: A meta-analysis. *Journal of Applied Psychology, 93*, 59–69.

Kilburg, R. R. (2000). *Executive coaching: Developing managerial wisdom in a world of chaos.* Washington: American Psychological Association.

Klehe, U., & Latham, G. (2006). What would you do—really or ideally? Constructs underlying the behavior description interview and the situational interview in predicting typical versus maximum performance. *Human Performance, 19*, 357–382.

Koppes, L. L. (Ed.) *Historical perspectives in industrial and organizational psychology.* Mahwah, NJ: Lawrence Erlbaum.

Kozlowski, S. W. J. (Ed.). (in press). *The Oxford handbook of industrial and organizational psychology.* Oxford: Oxford University Press.

Kozlowski, S. W. J., & Salas, E. (Eds.) (2009). *Learning, training, and development in organizations (SIOP Frontiers Series).* New York, NY: Routledge Academic.

Kraiger, K., & Jerden, E. (2007). A meta-analytic investigation of learner control: Old findings and new directions. In S. M. Fiore and E. Salas (Eds.) *Toward a science of distributed learning* (pp. 65–90). Washington DC: APA Books.

Lance C. (2008). Why assessment centers do not work the way they are supposed to. *Industrial and Organizational Psychology: Perspectives on Science and Practice,1*, 84–97.

Landy, F. J., & Farr, J. L. (1980). Performance rating. *Psychological Bulletin, 87*, 72–107.

Latham, G. P., Saari, L. M., Pursell, E. D., & Campion, M. A. (1980). The situational interview. *Journal of Applied Psychology, 65*, 422–427.

Lawshe, C. (1975). A quantitative approach to content validity. *Personnel Psychology, 28*, 563–575.

Levy, P. E., & Williams, J. R. (2004). The social context of performance appraisal: A review and framework for the future. *Journal of Management, 30*, 881–905.

Marcus, B., Lee, K., & Ashton, M. C. (2007). Personality dimensions explaining relationships between integrity tests and counterproductive behavior: Big Five, or one in addition? *Personnel Psychology, 60*, 1–34.

Mayer, R. E. (2009). Research-based solutions to three problems in web-based training. In S. W. J. Kozlowski & E. Salas (Eds.), *Learning, training, and development in organizations* (SIOP Frontiers Series; pp. 203–227). New York, NY: Routledge Academic.

McDaniel, M. A., & Whetzel, D. L. (2005). Situational judgment test research: Informing the debate on practical intelligence theory. *Intelligence, 33*, 515–525.

Meriac, J. P., Hoffman, B. J., Woehr, D. J., & Fleisher, M. S. (2008). Further evidence for the validity of assessment center dimensions: A meta-analysis of the incremental criterion-related validity of dimension ratings. *Journal of Applied Psychology, 93*, 1042–1052.

Morgeson, F. P., & Campion, M. A. (1997). Social and cognitive sources of potential inaccuracy in job analysis. *Journal of Applied Psychology, 82*, 627–655.

Morgeson, F. P., Campion, M. A., Dipboye, R. L., Hollenbeck, J. R., Murphy, K., & Schmitt, N. (2007a). Are we getting fooled again? Coming to terms with limitations in the use of personality tests for personnel selection. *Personnel Psychology, 60*, 1029–1049.

Morgeson, F. P., Campion, M. A., Dipboye, R. L., Hollenbeck, J. R., Murphy, K., & Schmitt, N. (2007b). Reconsidering the use of personality tests in personnel selection contexts. *Personnel Psychology, 60*, 683–729.

Murphy, K. R. (Ed.). (2003). *Validity generalization: A critical review*. Mahwah, NJ: Lawrence Erlbaum.

Murphy, K. R. (Ed.). (2006). *A critique of emotional intelligence: What are the problems and how can they be fixed?* Mahwah, NJ: Erlbaum.

Murphy, K. R., & Shiarella, A. H. (1997). Implications of the multidimensional nature of job performance for the validity of selection tests: Multivariate frameworks for studying test validity. *Personnel Psychology, 50*, 823–854.

Myors, B., Lievens, F., Schollaert, E., Van Hoye, G., Cronshaw, S.F., Mladinic, A., ... Sackett, P. R. (2008). International perspectives on the legal environment for selection. *Industrial and Organizational Psychology, 1*, 206–246.

Ones, D. S., Dilchert, S., Viswesvaran, C., & Judge, T. A. (2007). In support of personality assessment in organizational settings. *Personnel Psychology, 60*, 995–1027.

Ones, D. S., & Viswesvaran, C. (1996). Bandwidth-fidelity dilemma in personality measurement for personnel selection. *Journal of Organizational Behavior, 17*, 609–626.

Ones, D. S., Viswesvaran, C., & Schmidt, F. L. (1993). Comprehensive meta-analysis of integrity test validities: Findings and implications for personnel selection and theories of job performance. *Journal of Applied Psychology, 78*, 679–703.

Ones, D. S., Viswesvaran, C., & Schmidt, F. L. (2003). Personality and absenteeism: A meta-analysis of integrity tests. *European Journal of Personality, Supplement 1, 17*, S19–S38.

Peterson, N. G., Mumford, M. D., Borman, W. C., Jeanneret, P. R., Fleishman, E. A., Levin, K. Y., ... Dye, D. M. (2001). Understanding work using the occupational information network (O*NET): Implications for practice and research. *Personnel Psychology, 54*, 451–492.

Prien, E. P., Schippmann, J. S., & Prien, K. O. (2003). *Individual assessment: As practiced in industry and consulting*. Mahwah, NJ: Lawrence Erlbaum.

Pulakos, E. D., Arad, S., Donovan, M. A., & Plamondon, K. E. (2000). Adaptability in the workplace: Development of a taxonomy of adaptive performance. *Journal of Applied Psychology, 85*, 612–624.

Pulakos, E. D., Schmitt, N., Dorsey, D. W., Arad, S., Borman, W. C., & Hedge, J. W. (2002). Predicting adaptive performance: Further tests of a model of adaptability. *Human Performance, 15*, 299–323.

Ree, M. J., Earles, J. A., & Teachout, M. S. (1994). Predicting job performance: Not much more than g. *Journal of Applied Psychology, 79*, 518–524.

Reiter-Palmon, R., Brown, M., Sandall, D. L., Buboltz, C. B., & Nimps, T. (2006). Development of an O*NET web-based job analysis and its implementation in the U. S. Navy: Lessons learned. *Human Resource Management Review, 16*, 294–309.

Rogelberg, S. G. (Ed.) (2007). *Encyclopedia of industrial and organizational psychology, Vol 1–2*. Thousand Oaks, CA: Sage.

Roth, P. L., Bobko, P., & McFarland, L. A. (2005). A meta-analysis of work sample test validity: Updating and integrating some classic literature. *Personnel Psychology, 58*, 1009–1037.

Rynes, S. L. (2007) Let's create a tipping point: What academics and practitioners can do, alone and together. *Academy of Management Journal, 50*, 1046–1054.

Rynes, S. L., Colbert, A. E., & Brown, K. G. (2002). HR Professionals' beliefs about effective human resource practices: Correspondence between research and practice. *Human Resource Management, 41*, 149–174.

Rynes, S. L., Giluk, T. L. & Brown, K. G. (2007). The very separate worlds of academic and practitioner periodicals in human resource management: Implications for evidence-based management. *Academy of Management Journal, 50*, 987–1008.

Sackett, P. R., Borneman, M. J., & Connelly, B. S. (2008). High stakes testing in higher education and employment: Appraising the evidence for validity and fairness. *American Psychologist, 63*, 215–227.

Saks, A. M., & Belcourt, M. (2006). An investigation of training activities and transfer of training in organizations. *Human Resource Management, 45*, 629–648

Salas, E., & Cannon-Bowers, J. A. (2001). The science of training: A decade of progress. *Annual Review of Psychology, 52*, 471–499.

Salas, E., deRouin, R. E., & Gade, P. A. (2007). The military's contribution to our science and practice: People, places, and findings. In L. L. Koppes (Ed.) *Historical perspectives in industrial and organizational psychology* (pp. 169–189). Mahwah, NJ: Lawrence Erlbaum.

Salgado, J. F., Anderson, N., Moscoso, S., Bertua, C., de Fruyt, F., & Rolland, J. P. (2003). A meta-analytic study of general mental ability validity for different occupations in the European community. *Journal of Applied Psychology, 88*, 1068–1081.

Sanchez, J. I., & Levine, E. L. (2009). What is (or should be) the difference between competency modeling and traditional job analysis? *Human Resource Management Review, 19*, 53–63.

Schmidt, F. L., & Hunter, J. E. (1977). Development of a general solution to the problem of validity generalization. *Journal of Applied Psychology, 62*, 529–540.

Schmidt, F. L., & Hunter, J. E. (1998). The validity and utility of selection methods in personnel psychology: Practical and theoretical implications of 85 years of research findings. *Psychological Bulletin, 124*, 262–274.

Schmidt, F. L., Hunter, J. (2004). General mental ability in the world of work: Occupational attainment and job performance. *Journal of Personality and Social Psychology, 86*, 162–173.

Schmidt, F. L., Hunter, J. E., & Outerbridge, A. N. (1986). Impact of job experience and ability on job knowledge, work sample performance, and supervisory ratings of job performance. *Journal of Applied Psychology, 71*(3), 432–439.

Scullen, S. E., Bergey, P. K., & Aiman-Smith, L. (2005). Forced distribution rating systems and the improvement of workforce potential: A baseline simulation. *Personnel Psychology, 58*, 1–31.

Shippmann, J. S., Ash, R. A., Battista, M., Carr, L., Eyde, L. D., Hesketh, B., Kehoe, J., Pearlman, K., Prien, E. P., & Sanchez, J. I. (2000). The practice of competency modeling. *Personnel Psychology, 53*, 703–740.

Silzer, R., Cober, R., Erickson, A., & Robinson, G. (2008). SIOP practitioner needs survey final survey report. Retrieved May 19, 2009 from www.siop.org/Practitioner%20Needs%20Survey.pdf

Singh, P. (2008). Job analysis for a changing workplace. *Human Resource Management Review, 18*, 87–99.

SIOP Exchange. (2009). Last chance to comment on possible SIOP name change! Retrieved July 6, 2009 from http://siopexchange.typepad.com/the_siop_exchange/2009/07/last-chance-to-comment-on-possible-siop-name-change.html

Sitzmann, T., Kraiger, K., Stewart, D., & Wisher, R. (2006). The comparative effectiveness of web-based and classroom instruction: A meta-analysis. *Personnel Psychology,59*, 623–664.

Smither, J. W. (in press). Performance management. In Kozlowski, S. W. J. (Ed.) *The Oxford handbook of industrial and organizational psychology*. Oxford: Oxford University Press.

Smither, J. W. & London, M. (Eds.). (2009). *Performance management: Putting research into practice.* San Francisco: Jossey-Bass.

Smither, J. W., London, M., & Reilly, R. R. (2005). Does performance improve following multisource feedback? A theoretical model, meta-analysis, and review of empirical findings. *Personnel Psychology, 58*, 33–66.

Sternberg, R. J., & Hedlund, J. (2002). Practical intelligence, g, and work psychology. *Human Performance, 15*, 143–160.

Tett, R. P., & Burnett, D. D. (2003). A personality trait-based interactionist model of job performance. *Journal of Applied Psychology, 88*, 500–517.

Tett, R. P., & Christiansen, N. D. (2007). Personality tests at the crossroads: A response to Morgeson, Campion, Dipboye, Hollenbeck, Murphy, and Schmitt (2007). *Personnel Psychology, 60*, 967–993.

Tharenou, P., Saks, A. M., & Moore, C. (2007). A review and critique of research on training and organizational-level outcomes. *Human Resource Management Review, 17*, 251–273.

Thomas, J. C. (Ed.) (2004). *Comprehensive handbook of psychological assessment, Vol. 4: Industrial and organizational assessment.* Hoboken, NJ: John Wiley & Sons.

Thornton, G. C., III, & Gibbons, A. M. (2009). Validity of assessment centers for personnel selection. *Human Resource Management Review, 19*, 169–187.

Thornton, G. C., III, & Rupp D. E. (2006). *Assessment centers in human resource management.* Mahwah, NJ: Erlbaum.

Tippins, N. T. (2009). Internet alternative to traditional proctored testing: Where are we now? *Industrial and Organizational Psychology, 2*, 2–10.

Van Iddekinge, C. H., & Ployhart, R. E. (2008). Developments in the criterion-related validation of selection procedures: A critical review and recommendations for practice. *Personnel Psychology, 61*, 871–925.

Vinchur, A. J. (2007). A history of psychology applied to employee selection. In Koppes, L. L. (Ed.), *Historical perspectives in industrial and organizational psychology* (pp. 193–218). Mahwah, NJ: Lawrence Erlbaum.

Viswesvaran, C., Schmidt, F. L., & Ones, D. S. (2005). Is there a general factor in ratings of job performance? A meta-analytic framework for disentangling substantive and error influences. *Journal of Applied Psychology, 90*, 108–131.

Warr, P. (2007). Some historical developments in I-O psychology outside the United States. In L. L. Koppes (Ed.), *Historical perspectives in industrial and organizational psychology* (pp. 81–107). Mahwah, NJ: Lawrence Erlbaum.

Weekley, J. A., & Ployhart, R. E. (Eds.). (2006). *Situational judgment tests: Theory, measurement, and application.* Mahwah, NJ: Lawrence Erlbaum.

Zeidner, J., & Johnson, C. D. (1994). Is personnel classification a concept whose time has passed? In M. Rumsey, C. Walker, & J. Harris (Eds.) *Personnel selection and classification* (pp. 377–410). Hillsdale, NJ: Erlbaum.

Zickar, M. J., & Gibby, R. E. (2007). Four persistent themes throughout the history of I-O psychology in the United States. In L. L. Koppes (Ed.) *Historical perspectives in industrial and organizational psychology* (pp. 61–80). Mahwah, NJ: Lawrence Erlbaum.

12

Occupational Health Psychology

José M. Peiró and Lois Tetrick

Psychology, since the beginning of the 20th century, has helped to make workplaces more human and productive. Work and organizational psychology, as well as other subdisciplines in psychology, has made contributions to improving health and safety at work and to enhancing work's positive consequences. Public health, occupational health and safety, medicine, management and ergonomics have also contributed to the same aims. During the last few decades occupational health psychology (OHP) has progressively been established as a discipline. During this period several definitions have been offered emphasizing OHP's different facets and functions. The National Institute for Occupational Safety and Health (NIOSH) defines OHP as "the application of psychology to improving the quality of work life, and to protecting and promoting the safety, health and well-being of workers" (see www.cdc.gov/niosh/topics/stress/ohp/ohp.html). The European Academy of Occupational Health Psychology defined the discipline as "the contribution of the principles and practices of applied psychology to occupational health issues. It is the study of psychological, social and organizational aspects of the dynamic relation between work and health" (Houmondt, Leka, & Bulger, 2008, p. 150). Both definitions emphasize the application of scientific knowledge to health at work. Other definitions emphasize its scientific nature. As Quick (1999, p. 83) states

> OHP is an emerging specialty in the science, practice and profession of psychology. So, the scope of the discipline needs to cover scientific research to provide and test theoretical models and offer scientific evidence that contributes to the understanding of processes and relations between antecedents and health outcomes in the work and organizational context. This knowledge and the development of intervention models, methods, and tools have to support professional interventions to assess the risks and

IAAP Handbook of Applied Psychology, First Edition. Edited by Paul R. Martin, Fanny M. Cheung, Michael C. Knowles, Michael Kyrios, Lyn Littlefield, J. Bruce Overmier, and José M. Prieto.

other indicators relevant for safety and health and also the individual and contextual factors that will influence them.

Interestingly enough, a number of authors have recently suggested different extensions of the discipline. First, OHP should not only be limited to preventing illness and accidents among workers or restoring health but should also deal with the promotion of health, well-being and flourishing (Macik-Frey, Quick, & Nelson, 2007; Schaufeli, 2004). Second, it should explicitly consider and promote healthy workplaces as contexts where people may use their talents and gifts to "achieve high performance, high satisfaction, and well-being" (Quick, 1999, p. 82). Third, an individual approach has to be complemented by the collective one, paying attention to promoting healthy organizations and analyzing cross-level interactions (Murphy, 1999; Peiró, 2008). Fourth, time perspective needs to be considered in a more comprehensive manner combining short- vs. long-term goals and outcomes (Hofmann & Tetrick, 2003); a proactive and anticipatory approach is needed to enhance prevention (Peiró, 2008). Also close consideration of the dynamics of risk prevention and health promotion is required. Fifth, there is need for explicit attention to work phenomena outside the work place (such as unemployment, work–family issues, cultural context, etc.) and finally, the broader societal context including legislation, policies, juridical issues, and the role of social agents deserves attention (Brotherton, 2003).

OHP is changing its emphasis from preventing illness and injuries to creating healthy people and organizations, consistent with positive psychology. Formerly, based on a disease model, the main focus was on finding the causes and aetiology of diseases and on identifying and preventing work factors that deteriorate workers' health and contribute to morbidity and mortality. Now, a positive approach provides additional models: the wellness model (including "well-being, higher level functioning and a positive or optimistic view of the future") and the environmental one (that adds the "criterion of effective performance of tasks and roles demanded by the external environment"; see Hofmann & Tetrick, 2003, 6-7). Positive OHP views health as a set of experiences that encompasses several components such as autonomy, personal growth, mastery of the environment, positive relationships with others, purpose in life, and self-acceptance (Ryff, Singher & Love, 2004). Luthans and Avolio (2009) have incorporated the concept of psychological capital that includes as core components efficacy, hope, optimism, and resiliency. Psychological capital is an interesting metaphor because, starting from the "abundance" idea, where there are more resources than needed, they can be invested to generate more wealth and promote thriving and flourishing. These experiences in turn provide reserves to cope with potential difficulties. Warr (2007), pursuing the perspective that work may promote happiness, pointed out the need to broaden the environmental characteristics of work as well as the person-centerd approaches relevant to understanding how people assess their happiness and unhappiness (social comparison, cultural and demographic differences). In sum, positive occupational health psychology should extend previous contributions of the discipline by focusing on human strengths and positive institutions and on their development.

Scope of the Field

OHP has a long past, rooted in a number of disciplines, yet has a relatively short history as a newly emerged discipline. The definition of OHP has differed somewhat in Europe and the USA, especially in its multidisciplinary character. In Europe OHP is basically limited to the disciplines of psychology, while in the USA OHP encompasses other disciplines (occupational health and safety, public health, medicine, etc.). In this context, it is still difficult to set clear boundaries for the discipline and precisely identify its contents. However, several attempts have been made to identify the research topics (Kang, Staniford, Dollard, & Koompiert, 2008; Macik-Frey, et al., 2007), the contents of the curricula (Barnes-Farrell, 2006; Houdmont, Leka, & Bulger, 2008; Tetrick & Ellis, 2002) and the fields of professional practice (Sinclair, Hammer, Oeldorf-Hirsch, & Brubaker, 2006). In order to integrate these contributions we formulate a scheme that takes into account several axes (see Table 12.1). First, we consider the type of science according to the distinction formulated by Simon (1969) between natural (explanatory) and artificial (intervention or design) sciences. Second, we take into account the focus of the processes: knowledge vs. skills. Third, we distinguish different contents following a multilevel structure. Fourth, we will also consider the competencies required for professional practice.

Types of science. Explanatory science aims to understand existing reality while design (artificial) science aims at changing reality. OHP has components of both because it deals with a reality that is by its very nature created and modified by

Table 12.1. A Model to Describe the Current Scope of OHP (Based on ENOP Reference Model, Roe Coetsier, Levy Léboyer, Peiró, and Wilpert, 1994)

Type of science	*Focus*	*Individual*	*Job context*	*Groups and work units*	*Organization*	*Work-Non-work interface*	*Societal*
Explanatory	Knowledge Skills	1	3	5	7	9	11
Intervention	Knowledge Skills	2	4	6	8	10	
Research		Research competencies (scientist-practitioner model). Support for evidence-based practice.					
Professional practice competency-based.		Blocks professional competencies (to be developed by supervised practice) 1. Goal definition 2. Assessment (also: Diagnosis) 3. Development (also: Design) 4. Intervention (and implementation) 5. Evaluation 6. Information 7. Enabling competences.					

man. This distinction should not be confused with that between fundamental and applied research. Both explanatory and design sciences have their fundamental research, and both can be applied by practitioners to singular individual or organizational problems.

Focus. The model differentiates knowledge (emphasis on theory and empirical evidence) vs. skills or "know-how." In the *explanatory-knowledge cells:* we consider theories and models useful to understand, explain, predict, and interpret phenomena at every level considered. In the *explanatory-skills cells*: we consider skills to use different methods and tools to obtain empirical evidence and explanatory knowledge (assessment, interview, observation skills, etc.) in the same domains. In the *intervention-knowledge cells*: we include theories about change and relevant principles to design interventions aiming to improve the phenomena considered in every cell. In the *intervention-skills cells:* we include know-how knowledge and the expertise to implement the professional interventions.

Mapping the domains. As OHP deals with multilevel and layered phenomena we propose to organize the contents of the discipline according to the following areas: Individual, job context, group and work units, organization, work and non-work interface and societal issues. There is already a certain tradition to organize the topics following a multilevel rationale. Different contents of OHP can be organized in a matrix where type of science and focus is combined with the content areas. Thus we obtain a matrix that provides a comprehensive organization of the scope of the discipline. In each cell methodological issues are included as well as topics coming from emerging approaches. However, the cells should not be considered "closed" but interrelated. In many instances the most relevant issues are cross-level and thus the same topic needs to be considered at different levels, and dealt with in different cells. For the sake of clarity we will only point out some of the topics in every cell not aiming to offer an exhaustive list. Following this scheme the research topics, contents of the curricula, and to a certain extent the areas of professional practice can be mapped. Nevertheless, an alternative rationale (more process- than topic-oriented) may be useful for professional practice. In what follows we provide a classification of those topics according to the cells of the model:

1. *Individual: explanatory (knowledge and skills).* Demographics: Gender, aging, immigrant and migrant workers. Positive organizational behavior. Attendance, motivation. Values, beliefs and cognitions. Employee commitment and work engagement. Mood and emotions. Well-being and happiness at work. Problematic work behavior. Accidents, safety behaviors and attitudes. Psychological contract. Job stress theory. Coping. Physical, psychophysiological and psychological implications of stressful work. Recovery, workaholism and burnout. Health and well-being. Job insecurity, substance abuse. Musculoskeletal disorders. Common mental health problems (anxiety, depression, stress). Measuring tools of individual variables. Vulnerable or handicapped workers. Resilience, adaptability and hardiness, type A behavior pattern, self-efficacy; controllability awareness, self-monitoring. Self-reliance. Sense of coherence. Protean career attitudes.

2. *Individual: intervention (knowledge and skills).* Monitoring and management of sickness absence and return to work. Rehabilitation and managing presenteeism. Behavioral and attitude change and persuasion. Risk perception and communication. Design of the work environment. Health promotion. Stress interventions centered in the person. Training programs to prevent occupational risks and promote health at work. Cognitive behavior therapy based stress management. Training. Primary, secondary, and tertiary stress prevention techniques. Health and safety training interventions.

3. *Job content and context: explanatory (knowledge and skills).* Risk factors for occupational stress. Safety in the workplace. Virtual work. Technology. Workload. Identification of emerging risks. Nonstandard workplaces (flexiwork, telework, etc.). Time and work schedules. Task attributes (complexity, autonomy, physical and psychosocial demands, etc.). Worker's role. Job and work content measuring tools. Emotional labor. Adaptation to vulnerable groups and to handicapped workers. Workload and work pace. Working hours. Shiftwork, overtime work. New forms of work: Boundaryless job. Decision latitude and control. Work arrangements.

4. *Job content and context: intervention (knowledge and skills).* Work and job design. Environment design. Personal protective equipment. Stress interventions centered in job content and working conditions. Ergonomics. Improving work practices. Task and technical interventions. Improving working conditions (ergonomics, time and workload). Improving role clarity. Evaluation of interventions at the workplace. Designing nonstandard workplaces (flexiwork, telework) and time and work schedules.

5. *Social, groups and work units: explanatory (knowledge and skills).* Social support, Relationships at work. Aggression, violence and harassment. Interpersonal conflicts. Work unit safety climate. Leadership. Virtual teams. Teamwork. Evaluation of work units. Identification of emerging risks; psychosocial work environment. Collaborative technology. Teamwork and safety processes.

6. *Social, groups and work units: intervention (knowledge and skills).* Team building and development. Combating psychosocial risks in groups. Promoting social support. Participatory interventions for risk prevention and health promotion. Improving social relationships. Management development. Interventions in interpersonal and intergroup conflicts. Managers' training in coaching. Group and normative influences for safety improvement. Evaluation of work unit interventions.

7. *Organization: explanatory (knowledge and skills).* Organizational safety climate and culture. Job insecurity climate. Organizational justice. Psychological contract. Accidents. Technology. Education and training. Workers' compensation. Identification of emerging risks. Organizational structure. Management practices and production methods (e.g., high-performance work systems). Human resources and employment policies and practices. Career development. Performance. Lean production. Service systems.

8. *Organization: intervention (knowledge and skills):* Organizational interventions for the reduction of work-related stress. Preparation for retirement. Evaluation of organizational interventions. Change management and organizational development. Managing the interaction with unions' representatives and safety and health committee in the organization. Employee assistance programs. Wellness programs.

Survey feedback strategies to improve safety climate. Organizational restructuring, mergers, privatization, etc. Participatory action research in stress interventions. Safety programs. Behavioral risk management. Healthy culture planning. Safety climate interventions. High-performance management to promote safety.

9. *Work/nonwork interface: explanatory (knowledge and skills).* Work–family issues. Work–life balance. Employment issues. Job loss and unemployment. Identification of emerging risks. Sleep and work. Retirement. Labor market conditions.

10. *Work/nonwork interface: intervention (knowledge and skills).* Conciliation programs. Design of family supportive work environments. Promoting employment programs.

11. *Societal level (general).* Legislation on safety and health. Compliance with occupational safety laws and regulations. The use of governmental guidance on the management of work-related stress and health promotion. Information on new legislation. Economic, social, and technological factors at a national and international level. Changing demographics and labor supply. Government policies. Globalization and other macro level changes. Cultural and cross-cultural issues relevant for OHP.

Competency models for research and professional practice. Fullagar and Hatfield (2005, p. 155) described the practitioner's job of occupational health psychologists as being to "review, evaluate, and analyze work environments and design programs and procedures to promote worker health and reduce occupational stress caused by psychological, organizational, and social factors. To apply principles of psychology to occupational health problems." These authors describe the main activities to be policy planning, employee screening, training and development, and organizational development and analysis. Often OHP practitioners work with management to reorganize the work setting with the aim of improving worker health. These activities require mastering a number of competencies that are encompassed in the Europsy model for the European Certificate of Psychology (Europsy Team, 2009). The blocks of competencies considered in that model are:

1. Goal definition: Interacting with the client for the purposes of defining the goals of the service that will be provided.
2. Assessment (also, Diagnosis): Establishing relevant characteristics of individuals, groups, organizations, and situations by means of appropriate methods.
3. Development (also, Design): Developing services or products on the basis of psychological theory and methods for use by clients or psychologists.
4. Intervention (and implementation): Identifying, preparing, and carrying out interventions that are appropriate for reaching the set goals, using the results of assessment and development activities.
5. Evaluation: Establishing the adequacy of interventions in terms of adherence to the intervention plan and the achievement of set goals.
6. Information: Providing information to clients in a way that is adequate to fulfil the clients' needs and expectations.
7. Enabling competencies: Professional strategy, continuing professional development, professional relations, marketing and sales, accountability, practice

management and quality assurance. Finally, research and development is considered an enabling competency, because professional practice is conceived to be based on the scientist-practitioner model and based on empirical evidence.

Achievements and Challenges in Relevant Areas

As is apparent from the above description of OHP, the field is broad. Therefore, in this section, we review some of the core topics where considerable progress has been made and the implications of these findings for practice. In addition we offer some thoughts on important gaps in the literature which need to be addressed. Admittedly, we cannot cover all possible topics nor can we give exhaustive reviews of the literature relevant to the topics we do discuss.

Organizational level

Employees work in organizations that are social environments. The link between environmental factors and health is a key focus of OHP and considerable research has demonstrated a clear link between the work context and health. In this section we cover three aspects of the work context: the employee–employer relationship, work systems and design, and opportunities for growth and development.

Employer–employee relationships. Social exchange theory has been applied to enhance our understanding of the employee–employer relationship. According to it, employers and employees exchange resources with the expectations that the obligations of one party will be reciprocated by the other party. In the work environment, these mutual obligations have been conceptualized as a psychological contract (Rousseau, 1995). Relational psychological contracts, as opposed to transactional contracts, are based on social exchange and engender trust and a sense of fairness (Gracia, Silla, Peiró, & Fortes-Ferreira, 2007). When an employee senses that his/her employer has not fulfilled their obligations to him/her, psychological contract breach occurs, which may result in lack of trust, if not mistrust, and a sense of injustice. A similar phenomenon is described by the effort–reward imbalance model of job stress (Siegrist, 1998; see later section on stress).

The research literature has demonstrated that injustice is related to ill health in both cross-sectional and longitudinal studies as reflected by self-report indicators of ill health and physiological measures of ill health. Spell and Arnold (2007) found evidence for group-level justice climate based on the perceptions of the members of the groups studied, and this group-level justice climate moderated individuals' perceptions of justice and ill health as reflected by depression and anxiety. Head et al. (2007), based on the Whitehall II study, found that low relational justice (fairness of interpersonal relations at work) and effort–reward imbalance were related to increased risk of long episodes of sickness absences. Xie, Schaubroeck, and Lam (2008) also found that distributive justice (fairness of outcomes) was related to emotional exhaustion, chronic upper respiratory infection (UR), acute UR, and Immunoglobulin A (IgA) reflecting immune function over a 3-year period. These relations were moderated by the value placed on traditionality. Further, this study found that distributive justice may actually moderate the relation between job stressors and the physiological measures of health. However, Inoue et al. (2009) found that organizational injustice, specifically interactional justice, was related to oxidative DNA damage, which is associated with coronary heart disease, but the components of Effort–Reward Imbalance (ERI) and the components of the job demands–control model of job stress were not related to this marker for coronary heart disease.

The research findings to date clearly implicate injustice as a source of ill health from several theoretical perspectives. The actual mechanisms may differ depending on what aspect of ill health one considers and these differences may have practical implications for preventing ill health. However, the question still remains whether and how justice may promote positive health. There are numerous studies that demonstrate that justice is positively related to job satisfaction (Colquitt, Conlon, Wesson, Porter, & Ng, 2001) but we know much less about other aspects of the relation of justice and fairness to positive health.

Improving work systems and job design. The organization of work has been a focus of study and practice for decades (Parker & Wall, 1998). Much of this work has looked at the motivational aspects of job characteristics (e.g., Hackman & Oldham, 1980) or for safety. However, recent conceptualizations of the organization of work take a more holistic approach to designing work systems to include job and task characteristics, group-level factors and organizational-level factors. This section will focus on the motivational characteristics of the job and task and some aspects of the social characteristics.

Perhaps the most frequently studied motivational characteristics of jobs are those contained in the job characteristics model of motivation (Hackman & Oldham, 1980): skill variety, task identity, task significance, feedback from the job itself, and autonomy. These five job characteristics have been shown to be positively related to performance and satisfaction but have been less studied with respect to health and well-being (Humphrey, Nahrgang, & Morgeson, 2007). In a recent meta-analysis Humphrey et al. augmented these five motivational job characteristics with information processing, job complexity, specialization, and problem solving. They found that absenteeism, which was not restricted to sickness absenteeism, was negatively related to autonomy, task identity, and feedback from the job, and stress also was negatively related to autonomy, task identity, and feedback from the job. However, the results were somewhat different for burnout/exhaustion, which was negatively related to autonomy, task identity, and task significance but not to feedback from the job, and anxiety, which was only negatively related to autonomy and feedback from the job. None of the aspects of well-being included in this meta-analysis were related to job complexity and there were not enough studies to examine the relations between well-being and information processing demands of the job. Thus, aspects of well-being included in this meta-analysis were generally negatively related to motivational job characteristics but there were slightly different patterns for each aspect of well-being.

Humphrey et al. (2007) also included several social characteristics of jobs in their meta-analysis. These included interdependence, feedback from others, and social support. Stress was found to be negatively related to all three of these social characteristics, and burnout/exhaustion was found to be negatively related to feedback from others and social support (there were not enough studies to examine the relation between interdependence and burnout). Absenteeism was negatively related to social support, but not related to interdependence, and anxiety was negatively related to social support (there were not enough studies to examine the relations of anxiety with interdependence and feedback from others).

As might be expected from these results, Humphrey et al. (2007) found that the motivational characteristics explained approximately 15% of the variance in the well-being outcomes (only 6% in absenteeism) with the social characteristics explaining another 6% of the variance (only 2% for absenteeism). The lower explained variance for absenteeism may very well reflect that a distinction was not made between sickness absenteeism and absenteeism for other reasons. There were not enough studies to examine the predictive power of work context for absenteeism but the predictive power of work context in predicting stress and burnout/exhaustion yielded interesting results. Work context explained an additional 16% of the variance in stress beyond the motivational and social characteristics and an additional 2% of the variance in burnout/exhaustion.

This recent meta-analysis thus supports the importance of work systems in employee well-being. However, as Humphrey et al. (2007) point out, the studies tended to be cross-sectional and employed primarily self-report measures of well-being. Brand, Warren, Carayon, and Hoonakker (2007) also addressed the relation of job characteristics to employee health outcomes based on data from the Wisconsin Longitudinal Study. Health outcomes were based on self-report data of psychological distress, cardiovascular health, and musculoskeletal health outcomes. After controlling for education, earnings, and health-related behaviors, Brand et al. found that physical job characteristics were positively related to (ill)health, cognitive job characteristics were not related to health outcomes, and job control was related (negatively) to depression. Although these studies differ in approach and measures, the literature does support the negative impact of poor work systems. However, as was the case with organizational justice, the literature does not provide a clear picture of the effects of positive work characteristics on positive health beyond the positive relations between work characteristics and job satisfaction. One might predict that the social context at work is a major factor in promoting positive health, which is supported by our subsequent discussion of leadership, support, and coping.

Opportunities for growth. One aspect of the work environment that was not mentioned above is the opportunity for learning and growth. Hacker (1993) proposed that one of the principles of job design is to ensure that employees have opportunities for personal development. One might argue that this aspect is incorporated in the job characteristics model (Hackman & Oldham, 1980) in that the core psychological states include meaningfulness based on the use of multiple skills and feedback. Recently, Coyle-Shapiro and Conway (2005), in their examination of the elements of psychological contracts, found that employees perceived opportunities for training and development as part of what their employers were under an obligation to provide. However, studies of the organization of work have not addressed the relation between opportunities for growth and employee health until recently.

Rau (2006) is one of the few studies to do so. In this study prior theorizing about the opportunities for learning and growth were integrated with the process of recovery to examine the relation of learning opportunities on the job with nocturnal recovery of cardiovascular activity after workload, sleep disturbances, mental health, life satisfaction, and vocational success. Learning opportunities were "objectively" assessed with the help of experts and included procedural degrees of freedom, temporal degrees of freedom, decision authority, responsibility, information about results, and feedback in addition to incumbents' self-reports of their decision latitude and job demands. The results supported the relation between learning opportunities on the job and objectively assessed health as reflected by nocturnal recovery of heart rate and blood pressure but not for the subjective health parameters of sleep disturbances and ability to relax.

Research to date provides strong evidence for the design of jobs that include opportunities for training and development. This appears to be a relatively common promise that employees believe that their organizations have made to them and is part of their psychological contracts. Failure to provide these opportunities may result in ill health based either on psychological contract theory, organizational justice theory, or recovery theory. Further, provision of learning and development opportunities on the job may have direct effects on employees' ability to recover from the demands of their work as well as providing a mechanism for developing positive health.

Group level

Social support and organizational climate influence on health and well-being. Humans are social beings; interacting with each other and living together are essential elements of their life. Affiliation is a basic need and social ties are important assets. Social exchange and reciprocity contribute to building groups and communities. At work, interactions are frequent with colleagues, supervisors, bosses, clients, and other people and they are, in many instances, needed to get the work done effectively. But, in addition to the instrumental function of interaction, there are other functions of social activities at work: developing affiliation, identity, a sense of belonging, and giving and receiving support. These social functions not only influence productivity and effectiveness but also influence well-being and health. When interpersonal relations deteriorate, the situation becomes really stressful and harmful for individuals. Mobbing, harassment and aggression are forms of interaction that deteriorate health and well-being at work and produce burnout and mental health problems.

In this context social support has been considered a central construct to understand occupational health and well-being at work. Within the organizational context, sources of social support are co-workers, subordinates and other colleagues (Beehr, Jex, Stacy, & Murray, 2000), supervisors and/or managers (Kickul & Posig, 2001), family members (Poelmans, O'Driscoll, & Beham, 2005) and organizations themselves (Wallace, Edwards, Arnold, Frazier, & Finch, 2009). Support also has been differentiated by types according to the basic function it fulfils: instrumental (providing resources to cope), emotional (providing care, love, and sympathy), informational (providing useful information to help with coping), and appraisal (providing feedback that enhances self-esteem) (House, 1981).

The positive effects of social relations on health have been pointed out by several theoretical models. The vitamin model formulated by Warr (2007) includes contact with others as one of the principal work environment characteristics that influence health and well-being in terms of quantity and quality. Empirical evidence shows that social support of different types is negatively related to ill health, including depression (Beehr, et al. 2000; Totterdell, Wood, & Wall, 2006) and emotional exhaustion (Lee & Ashford, 1996). It is interesting to note that these relations are not always linear. De Jonge, Dormann, & van den Tooren, (2008) observed nonlinear significant associations between social support and job-related emotional exhaustion and context-free depression. They pointed out that less happiness appeared at low levels of support and an "additional decrement" at very high levels of support.

There is also evidence of a negative relation between different types of social support and a number of stress experiences, suggesting that its effect on health may be mediated through support's reduction of experienced stress. Moreover, several theoretical models have considered social support as a buffer between stress and strain or health. The Michigan model assumes that it is a relevant part of the social environment that moderates the relation between stressors and their outcomes. Additionally, the Demand–Control Model formulated by Karasek (1979) and extended by Johnson, Hall, and Theorell (1989) identifies stressful jobs as those with high demand and low control and low support. This moderating effect has been supported relative to cardiovascular risk (Winnubst & Schabracq, 1996) and the other negative effects of stressors on health (Viswesvaran, Sanchez, & Fisher, 1999). Support has also been conceptualized as a resource which can be part of an individual's coping repertory (Greenglass, 1993). As Wills (1990) concluded in his functional support model, close relationships help a person to cope with stress because in such a situation he or she can disclose and discuss problems and concerns with supportive others and receive advice tailored to his or her needs.

Wills' (1990) finding leads to another interesting issue: the process of seeking support and its effectiveness. Carver, Scheier, and Weintraub (1989) analyzed the relations of seeking support with other types of coping. They found that seeking social support was associated not only with active coping and with planning, but also with focus on and venting of emotions, which in turn is linked to such strategies as denial and disengagement. The authors interpreted these results to suggest "the tendency to seek out social support may have both good and bad overtones and whether it is primarily good or bad may depend on what other coping processes are occurring along with it" (p. 274).

Organizational and supervisory support have received special attention in studies dealing with occupational health and well-being. Perceived Organizational Support (POS) is the degree to which employees believe the organization is committed to them as individuals rewarding their work effort and providing tangible benefits and socio-emotional resources (Eisenberger, Aselage, Sucharski, & Jones, 2004). In a meta-analysis, Rhoades and Eisenberger (2002) found consistent relations with the antecedents and consequences of POS. Relevant antecedents are fairness of treatment, support from organizational representatives, and human resources practices. Relevant outcomes of POS were enhanced felt obligations towards the organization and affective commitment, and reduced strain in stressful situations. In fact the negative relation between POS and psychosomatic and mental complains and other problems such as fatigue, burnout, anxiety, and headaches have been repeatedly found.

The closest face of the company for employees is the supervisor leading many to conclude that supervisory support is exceedingly relevant for employees' health and well being. It has been found that perceptions of supervisors' support (PSS) has a strong influence on subordinates' POS (Eisenberger, Stinglhamber, Vandenberghe, Sucharski, & Rhoades, 2002). Interestingly, Rhoades and Eisenberger (2006) found that supervisors' POS was positively related to their subordinates' PSS. Subordinates' PSS, in turn, was positively associated with their POS, in-role and extra-role performance. Moreover, subordinates' PSS mediated the positive relation of supervisors' POS with subordinates' POS. This raises the issue of whether there is a climate for support within organizations based on employees' shared perceptions. The study of the support climate in work units and in organizations has been carried out with the Focus questionnaire (Van Muijen et al., 1999). Starting from the competing values model, four facets of organizational climate are measured: support, goals, rules, and innovation. The support measure includes both formal (organizational) and informal support (from colleagues). This measure of organizational climate has proved to be a significant antecedent of different health and performance indicators (Gonzalez-Romá, Fortes-Ferreira, & Peiró, 2008; Gonzalez-Romá, Peiró, & Tordera, 2002).

Leadership and occupational health. Leadership is an important concept for understanding occupational health and risk prevention at work. "Formal leadership" has often been linked to management and to the hierarchical line in organizations. Managers, especially when they fulfil a leadership function, play a pivotal role and may influence the behaviors and health of organizations as well as the healthy behaviors of their members (Britt, Davison, Bliese, & Castro, 2004). However, they may also be significant sources of stress. Tepper (2000) pointed out that employees who perceive their supervisors to be abusive, experience low levels of job and life satisfaction, lower levels of affective commitment and higher psychological distress. In more severe situations, when managers and supervisors display mobbing behaviors (Hoel, Cooper, & Faragher, 2001) they become hard stressors for the victims. Additionally, with poor, autocratic and authoritarian leadership, managerial mobbing behaviors may facilitate mobbing episodes from others.

Lack of supervisory support negatively relates to well-being at work (e.g., Schaufeli, González-Romá, Peiró, Geurts, & Tomás, 2005). Further, supervisory social support was found to be significantly and negatively correlated to the three dimensions of burnout, lack of personal accomplishment, emotional exhaustion, and depersonalization (Gil-Monte & Peiró, 2000). Other leadership behaviors such as communication and feedback play a role in the contribution of supervisors to stress and well-being of their subordinates. In this way Cartwright and Cooper (1994) pointed out that poor supervisor–subordinate relationships characterized by low supervisory supportiveness, low quality of communication, and lack of feedback reduce individual well-being and contribute substantially to feelings and experiences of stress.

Studies grounded on theoretical models of leadership also have analyzed the relation between leadership and followers' well-being. Basing their study on the Ohio

State Model of leadership, Seltzer and Numerof (1986) found that individuals who rated their supervisors high on consideration also reported low levels of burnout and a similar relation was found with initiating structure. According to Leader Member Exchange (LMX) theory, the quality of the leader–member interaction may vary from one vertical dyad to another. Tordera, Peiró, González-Romá, Fortes-Ferreira, and Mañas, (2006) found that the quality of LMX had an impact on psychological well-being both concurrently and with a 12-month lag. LMX was related to enthusiastic–depressed, full of energy–tired and anxious–relaxed variables. In sum, from different leadership perspectives the relation between leaders' behaviors and followers' strain is well established. However, leadership may contribute in other ways to their subordinates' well-being.

Leaders may influence other stressors, which in turn will reduce employees' strain and enhance their well-being (Kelloway, Sivanathan, Francis, & Barling, 2004). In fact, leaders may create and contribute to stressful working conditions such as increasing role stress by putting excessive or ambiguous demands on their subordinates or may produce injustice perceptions because of their performance assessment or reward allocation practices. However, if leaders are competent they may improve the work environment, work arrangements, and social context. For example, Peiró, González-Romá, Ripoll, and Garcia (2001) found that leaders' initiating structure behavior and leaders' influence on decision making had significant positive relation to role clarity, although the relation to role conflict was not statistically significant. Yet, in another study, both initiating structure and consideration behavior showed significant correlations with role clarity and work team climate dimensions. Similarly, research based on LMX theory supports a negative relation of LMX quality to role conflict and role ambiguity (Gerstner & Day, 1997). Recently Harris and Kacmar (2006) found that the relationship between LMX and stress is best characterized as curvilinear with individuals who enjoy high-quality LMX relationships with their supervisors experiencing more stress than do their counterparts in moderate-quality LMX relationships. This could be the result of the extra pressure that subordinates in high-quality LMX relationships feel to reduce their feelings of obligation and meet the expectations of their bosses.

In recent years a more positive approach to stress has been emerging. Leaders may play an important role in creating the conditions for positive experiences and in sense making within the work environment. Transformational leaders go beyond exchange relationships through idealized influence, inspirational motivation, intellectual stimulation, and individualized consideration (Bass & Riggio, 2006). Several studies have shown that transformational leadership contributes to the well-being of employees by putting in action additional resources. Arnold, Turner, Barling, Kelloway, and McKee (2007) reported that transformational leadership by supervisors exerted a positive influence on the psychological well-being of workers mediated by the meaningful perceptions of work. The evidence reviewed shows that transformational leadership generates new resources and/or improves existing resources to enhance employees' well-being. Leadership also influences followers' beliefs and interpretations of the meaning of work in a way that enhances well-being. In this context, charismatic and transformational leadership may represent an important resource to promote proactive coping and opportunities for growth.

Nevertheless, not everything about transformational leadership is good news. Several authors have pointed out that the strategies used by charismatic and transformational leaders could be manipulative and used for self-serving purposes. Thus, research has turned to differentiating authentic transformational leaders from their self-serving counterparts. Authentic transformational leaders strive to do what is right and fair for all stakeholders of the organization and may willingly sacrifice self-interests for the collective good of their work unit or organization (Michie & Gooty, 2005).

Individual level

Stress at work. Stress is one of the core topics in OHP and most probably the one with the longest tradition within the discipline. Several issues have attracted researchers' interests, including the nature of work stressors and taxonomies of stressors; the objective–subjective nature of stress and appraisal processes; the emotional, cognitive, and behavioral responses to stress; coping styles and behaviors such as the consequences of stress experiences for individuals (physical, psychological, psychosocial, etc.) and organizations (costs, loss of productivity, absenteeism, etc.). A number of individual characteristics (personality traits, demographics, etc.) and environmental ones (social support, cultural context, etc.) have been considered.

"Stressors" have been conceptualized in different ways. Some authors consider them in terms of frequency of occurrence, intensity, duration, and predictability (Pratt & Barling, 1988). The combination of these dimensions produces several categories of stressor such as acute, chronic, daily, and catastrophic stressors or disasters. Other taxonomies, based on the contents, have also been proposed. Peiró (1999) categorized the main stressors in the literature into the following eight groups: (1) stressors related to physical environment, environmental hazards, and working conditions (noise, temperature, space available, etc.); (2) work arrangements (shifts, workload, etc.); (3) job contents such as control, complexity, skill use opportunities, variety, task identity, meaning of the tasks, feedback from the task, etc.; (4) role stressors (role conflict, role ambiguity, role overload, etc.); (5) stressors derived from social relations and social interactions (relationships with supervisors, co-workers, subordinates, customers, etc.); (6) stressors related to developmental aspects of work such as job mobility, promotions, career development, and career transitions; (7) stressors derived from organizational features such as the technology used, the structure and the social climate in the organization; and (8) stressors relating to the interface between work and other life spheres (work–family and family–work conflicts, etc.), unemployment, and the like.

Some theoretical models focus not only on the content of stressors but the process by which a certain environmental (external) or personal (internal) feature becomes stressful for an individual. Karasek & Theorell's (1990) model suggests that the source of stress arises from the misfit between the existing demands and the control (decision latitude) to cope with those demands. A similar model, extending the notion of control to the broader one of "resource", has been formulated by Demerouti, Bakker, Nachreiner, and Schaufeli (2001), where resources are not only considered at the job level but also at the group and organizational level. Interestingly, Hobfoll

(2001) posited that individuals strive to develop resource surpluses to offset the possibility of future losses and, when confronted with stressful stimuli, try to minimize their net loss of resources.

Alternatively, Warr's (2007) Vitamin Model differentiates nine types of stressors: no opportunity for control, no opportunity for skill use, externally generated goals, lack of variety, environmental uncertainty, low availability of money, lack of physical security, lack of opportunity for interpersonal contact, and poorly valued social position. These stressors are grouped in two categories: those similar to vitamins BC, which produce stress in low quantities while large quantities have no negative effects, and those similar to vitamins AD which produce negative effects both if they are insufficient or if they exceed certain thresholds.

Although the concept of person–environment fit is important to understand work stress, it is not comprehensive enough to encompass the emergent stress types at work. Issues such as the intricate dynamics of exchange between the parts involved in the work situation deserve attention. So, it is important to understand the balance in the exchange between the employees and the company (e.g., Effort–Reward Imbalance; Siegrist, 1998) or between different actors in the work setting. In understanding this balance several social mechanisms and processes become relevant, such as social comparison (Carmona, Buunk, Peiró, Rodríguez, & Bravo, 2006), and fairness and reciprocity (Shore et al., 2004). Justice models considering distributive, procedural, interactional, and informational justice and their interactions provide an interesting theoretical framework for approaching the study of work stress and both positive and negative outcomes stemming from such experiences (Moliner, Martínez-Tur, Peiró, & Ramos, 2005).

During the last decade, De Jonge and Dormann (2003) developed the Demand-Induced Strain Compensation (DISC) model that aims to overcome the limitations of the Demand–Control and the Effort–Reward Imbalance models. It is built on four principles. First is the need to recognize the multidimensionality of the job demands, resources, and strain concepts. Each of those concepts contains physical, cognitive, and emotional components. Second is the Triple Match Principle stating that the strongest interactive relations between demands and resources and strains occur when they are based in qualitatively identical components. For instance, the relations between emotional demands from customers and emotional exhaustion of employees will be optimally mitigated by emotional support from supervisors and coworkers. Third, the compensation principle states that the negative effects produced by demands can be compensated through the activation of resources, and this effect will be optimal when job resources are activated, which come from the same domain as the demands. Fourth, the principle of balance posits the optimal conditions for active learning and growth exist when a balance of high job demands and correspondingly high job resources occurs. Some empirical evidence has accrued for this model (De Jonge et al., 2008).

This brings us to recent developments on positive stress that broaden the focus of research, drawing attention to the conditions in which stressful situations may lead to the promotion of well-being and growth. Nelson and Simmons (2003) have defined eustress as "a positive psychological response to a stressor, as indicated by the presence of positive psychological states" (p. 104). However, it can also be defined as a stimulus, analyzing the characteristics of stressors that prompt a positive and growing stress experience. Cavanaugh, Boswell, Roehling, and Boudreau (2000) have differentiated two categories of stressors: challenge stressors and hindrance stressors (see also Wallace et al., 2009). In our view, distress and eustress can occur simultaneously in response to the same demand, but they will result from different appraisal processes as a challenge or as a hindrance (McGowan, Gardner, & Fletcher, 2006). These processes produce different emotions, positive, negative, or mixed. In fact, both types of emotions may co-occur throughout the stress process and that is why more emphasis has been placed recently in the study of positive emotions in the stress process and in the role of coping in generating these emotions (Folkman & Moskowitz, 2004). Proactive coping may lead individuals to cumulate a reserve of resources to better cope with new demands. This reserve increases the probability of individuals appraising the demands as opportunities rather than as threats and this may increase the probabilities of growth, development, and flow. Under circumstances where high demands are met with adequate resources and the challenge is converted in an experience of success (Grebner, Elfering, & Semmer, 2008) "savoring" emerges. It is an enjoyable experience in response to the opportunity for development produced by eustress in a parallel way as coping is the response to stressors perceived as taxing or threatening.

Finally, we point out recent developments considering work stress from a multilevel perspective (Bliese & Jex, 2002; Peiró, 2008). This approach emphasizes an interest in the stress of collective units such as teams or organizations. The collective approach questions the individualized, decontextualized consideration of stress and the emphasis on an agentic perspective in which the ability to manage and control stress is seen as only resting with the individual. Considering collective stress phenomena implies paying attention to how shared stress appraisal emerges. Socialization processes, organizational culture, reward systems, leadership, interaction among members and contagion processes may play a role in the emergence of a stressful climate in the organization. Once produced, a climate of stress will have a contextual influence on individual stress perceptions. It will contribute to the emergence of shared emotions and affective responses. Thus, multilevel research on stress is extended to the understanding of collective emotions and affect. Several authors have examined these phenomena (George, 1996; González Romá, Peiró, Subirats, & Mañas, 2000).

Similarly, the study of coping is being extended to coactive and collective coping, in addition to the individual kind. Individual coping, especially when problem-focused, is often ineffective or even counterproductive in work organizations, because the control of the sources of stress are not close to the individuals. Coactive coping occurs when individuals in a group or work unit use similar individual ways of coping because the members of the unit learn the effectiveness or utility of those strategies from each other (maybe by vicarious learning). For instance, a culture of absenteeism could emerge in an organization through a process of coactive coping. If somebody finds that absence on account of sickness is an effective way of coping by "flying away" from work stress, and others also find this strategy helpful, then this "coactive" coping contributes to the emergence of an absenteeism culture. On other occasions, collective coping may take place. This occurs when a group faced with a common perceived threat or noxious situation collectively initiates actions to prevent, eliminate, or reduce the stressful situation, to interpret the situation in a more positive way or to alleviate its negative consequences. The study of coactive and collective coping has shown new relevant processes in organizations (Länsisalmi, Peiró, & Kivimäki, 2000; Torkelson, Muhonen, & Peiró, 2007).

Interfaces and conciliation between work and other spheres of life. The focus on the work environment in the work and organizational psychology literature has reflected an artificial boundary between employees' work-life and other aspects of their lives. With the increased participation of women in the labor force in the late 1970s and 80s, the need to consider multiple domains of employees' lives became apparent. In the ensuing decades, there has been a growing literature on the relation between work and family life, not only for women but also for men, although there still is not a lot of empirical literature on other life domains.

Much of the earlier work examining the work–family interface focused on organizational policies and practices that facilitated individuals' juggling their family responsibilities and their work responsibilities (Kossek & Ozeki, 1998, 1999; Poelmans & Beham, 2008). Although this work did enhance our understanding of the adoption of family-friendly policies, it also became clear that the relation of the existence of these policies, as well as their actual availability and use, were much more complex (Lapierre et al., 2008; Poelmans & Beham, 2008). Therefore, the current literature seeks to understand at a psychological level managers' allowance of the use of family-friendly policies and practices, organizational adoption of family-friendly policies and practices, and employees' perceptions of the availability and consequences of their use of family-friendly policies.

Early work on the work–family interface focused on work family conflict (WFC). This approach assumed that the relation between work and family was negative and unidimensional; later, Frone (2003) differentiated family interfering with work (FIW) and work interfering with family (WIF) and the need to consider both directions of interference. He suggested that factors in the work environment predict WIF and factors in the family environment predict FIW (Frone, 2003). This domain specificity seems to hold for work factors predicting WIF, but the support is not as strong for family factors predicting FIW. Several recent meta-analyses have been conducted examining the antecedents and consequences of WFC. Byron (2005) focused on antecedents. She found that for the most part work-related factors of job involvement, hours spent at work, and job stress were positively related to WIF, and work support and scheduled flexibility were negatively related to WIF. Somewhat unexpectedly, based on the domain-specificity hypothesis, job involvement and job stress were also positively related to FIW, and work support and scheduled flexibility were negatively related to FIW. Hours of nonwork activities and family stress were positively related to FIW and family support was negatively related to FIW. Family stress also was positively related to WIF. Ford, Heinen, and Langkamer (2008) subsequently addressed the issue of domain-specificity using meta-analytic structural equations modeling, and found that WIF was not a complete mediator of the effects of job factors on family satisfaction although FIW was a complete mediator of the effects of family factors on job satisfaction. These results suggest that there are additional dynamics in the work–family interference models that we have thus far identified.

One potential explanation for this failure to find domain-specificity is that prior meta-analyses have not included the positive effects of work on family and family on work. Consistent with our increased attention on positive psychology, it has been recognized that work and family can have positive effects on each other; these positive effects have been labelled positive spillover (Hanson, Hammer, & Colton, 2006) or work–family facilitation (Wayne, Grzywacz, Carlson & Kacmar, 2007). Positive spillover and work–family facilitation reflect positive effects of enacting one's family role and one's work role. Although the two concepts have some nuances of difference, the literature has presumed the same bidirectional relations as has been the case with WFC, and it has generally been considered that positive spillover and work–family facilitation have positive effects on job attitudes, family attitudes, and health. In one of the few longitudinal studies, Hammer, Cullen, Neal, Sinclair, and Shafiro (2005) did not find work–family facilitation, in either direction, to be related to depression one year later. However, there has been some support for positive aspects of work to be related to work–family facilitation and positive aspects of family life to be related to family–work facilitation (Grzywacz, Carlson, Kacmar, & Wayne, 2007). This literature is still emerging and to our knowledge no meta-analyses have been conducted to examine whether they have different correlates.

Final Comments

Before we close this chapter we would like to highlight three issues that are especially important for future developments. First, OHP needs to develop a global perspective. Second, OHP needs to incorporate, and perhaps place more emphasis on, positive health. Last, OHP needs to expand the discipline on the basis of social needs.

In relation to the first issue, currently the mainstream of research and interventions of OHP considers work mainly in the developed regions of the world. However, it is important to approach these and other issues in the developing countries. The contributions of researchers and professionals from all regions, especially the developing countries themselves, should be better supported and taken into consideration.

Relative to an increased emphasis on positive occupational psychology, attention needs to be paid not only to primary, secondary, and tertiary prevention but also to "countervailing interventions." These countervailing interventions are a set of strategies not directly aimed at preventing risks and health problems but at enhancing development and promoting growth and positive experiences. Kelloway, Hurrell, and Day (2008) define countervailing interventions as those aiming to "increase the positive experience of work rather than decreasing the negative aspects" (p. 433). Hope, optimism, trust, and self-efficacy are basic elements of well-being and may be enhanced at work. Thus, in relation to health promotion, work should not necessarily be considered as the problem. In fact, there are jobs that may be better considered as the solution. The challenge would be to design and implement jobs promoting these positive effects.

Finally, the discipline should be expanded to make stronger contributions to the program of decent work developing appropriate multilevel interventions. Few studies have been published which have been carried out in developing countries and on issues and problems of inhuman, exploitative, and alienating work performed in very poor working conditions, even though this is affecting a large number of workers all over the world, including millions of children. It is important to raise awareness among psychologists about the limits of the published work on OHP and to draw more attention to this broader reality, not only to raise cooperation between OHP practitioners from different parts of the world, but also to better understand and improve this situation. OHP has as its mission to promote more humane work as an important way of constructing the world humans inhabit and of promoting the growth of human beings themselves.

References

Arnold, K. A., Turner, N., Barling, J., Kelloway E. K., & McKee, M. C. (2007) Transformational leadership and psychological well-being: The mediating role of meaningful work. *Journal of Occupational Health Psychology*, *12*(3), 193–203.

Barnes-Farrell, J. (2006). History of OHP and education of OHP professionals in the United States. In S. McIntyre & J. Houdmont (Eds.), *Occupational health psychology: Key papers of the European Academy of Occupational Health Psychology* (Vol. 7, pp. 425–426). Maia, Portugal: ISMAI Publishers.

Bass, B. M., & Riggio, R. E. (2006). *Transformational leadership* (2nd ed.). Mahwah, NJ: Erlbaum.

Beehr, T. A., Jex, S. M., Stacy, B. A., & Murray, M. A. (2000) Work stressors and coworker support as predictors of individual strain and job performance. *Journal of Organizational Behavior*, *21*, 391–405.

Bliese, P. D., & Jex, S. M. (2002). Incorporating a multilevel perspective into occupational stress research: Theoretical, methodological, and practical implications. *Journal of Occupational Health Psychology*, *7*, 265–276.

Brand, J. E., Warren, J. R., Carayon, P., & Hoonakker, P. (2007). Do job characteristics mediate the relationship between SES and health? Evidence from sibling models. *Social Science Research*, *36*, 222–253.

Britt, T. W., Davison, J., Bliese, P. D., & Castro, C. A. (2004). How leaders can influence the impact that stressors have on soldiers. *Military Medecine*, *169*(7), 541–545.

Brotherton, C. (2003). The role of external policies in shaping organizational health and safety. In D. A. Hofmann & L. E Tetrick (eds.), *Health and safety in organizations* (pp. 372–396). San Francisco: Jossey-Bass.

Byron, K. (2005). A meta-analytic review of work–family conflict and its antecedents. *Journal of Vocational Behavior*, *67*, 169–198.

Carmona, C., Buunk, B. P., Peiró J. M., Rodríguez, I., & Bravo, M. J. (2006). Do social comparison and coping styles play a role in the development of burnout? Cross-sectional and longitudinal findings. *Journal of Occupational and Organizational Psychology*, *79*, 85–99.

Cartwright, S., & Cooper, C. L. (1994). *No hassle: Taking the stress out of work*. London: Century Books.

Carver, C. S, Scheier, M. F. & Weintraub, J. K. (1989). Assessing coping strategies. A theoretically based approach. *Journal of Personality and Social Psychology*, *56*, 267–283.

Cavanaugh, M. A., Boswell, W. R., Roehling, M. V., & Boudreau, J. W. (2000). An empirical examination of self-reported work stress among U.S. managers. *Journal of Applied Psychology*, *85*, 65–74.

Colquitt, J. A., Conlon, D. E., Wesson, M. J., Porter, C. O. L. H., & Ng, K. Y. (2001). Justice at the millennium: A meta-analytic review of 25 years of organizational justice research. *Journal of Applied Psychology*, *86*, 425–445.

Coyle-Shapiro, J., & Conway, N. (2005). Exchange relationships: Examining psychological contracts and perceived organizational support. *Journal of Applied Psychology*, *90*, 774–781.

De Jonge, J., & Dormann, C. (2003). The DISC model: Demand-induced strain compensation mechanisms in job stress. In M. F. Dollard, H. R. Winefield, & A. H. Winefield (Eds.), *Occupational stress in the service professions* (pp. 43–74). London: Taylor & Francis.

De Jonge, J., Dormann, C., & van den Tooren, M. (2008): The demand-induced strain compensation model. Renewed theoretical considerations and empirical evidence. In K. Näswall, J. Hellregen, & M. Sverke (Eds.), *The individual in the changing working life*. (pp. 67–87). Cambridge: Cambridge University Press.

Demerouti, E., Bakker, A. B., Nachreiner, F., & Schaufeli, W. B. (2001). The job demands-resources model of burnout. *Journal of Applied Psychology*, *86*, 499–512.

Eisenberger, R. Aselage, J., Sucharski, I. L., & Jones, J. R. (2004). Perceived organizational support. In J. Coyle-Shapiro, L. Shore, S. Taylor, & L. Tetrick (Eds.), *The employment relationship: Examining psychological and contextual perspectives* (pp. 207–205). Oxford: Oxford University Press.

Eisenberger, R., Stinglhamber, F., Vandenberghe, C., Sucharski, I. L., & Rhoades, L. (2002). Perceived supervisor support: Contributions to perceived organizational support and employee retention. *Journal of Applied Psychology*, *87*, 565–573.

Europsy Team. (2009): *EuroPsy European Certificate in Psychology regulations revised*. Brussels: Mimeo, EFPA.

Folkman, S., & Moskowitz, J.T. (2004), Coping: Pitfalls and promise. *Annual Review of Psychology*, *55*, 745–774.

Ford, M. T., Heinen, B. A., & Langkamer, K. L. (2007). Work and family satisfaction and conflict: A meta-analysis of cross domain relations. *Journal of Applied Psychology*, *92*, 57–80.

Frone, M. R. (2003). Work–family balance. In J. C. Quick & L. E. Tetrick (Eds.), *Handbook of occupational health psychology* (pp. 143–162). Washington, DC: American Psychological Association.

Fullagar, C., & Hatfield, J. (2005). *Occupational health psychology. Charting the field*. Paper presented at the 20th annual SIOP conference, April 15–17, Los Angeles, CA.

George, J. M. (1996). Group affective tone. In M. A. West (Ed.), *Handbook of work group Psychology* (pp. 77–94). Chichester: John Wiley & Sons.

Gerstner, C. R., & Day, D. V. (1997). Meta-analytic review of leader–member exchange theory: Correlates and construct issues. *Journal of Applied Psychology*, *82*(6), 827– 844.

Gil-Monte, P., & Peiró, J.M. (2000). Un estudio comparativo sobre criterios normativos y diferenciales para el diagnóstico del síndrome de quemarse por el trabajo (burnout) según el MBI-HSS en España. *Revista de Psicología del Trabajo y de las Organizaciones*, *16*(2), 135–149.

González-Romá, V., Fortes-Ferreira, L. & Peiró, J. M. (2008) Team climate, climate strength and team performance. A longitudinal study. *Journal of Occupational and Organizational Psychology*, *82*, 511–536.

Gonzalez-Romá, V., Peiró, J. M., Subirats, M., & Mañas, M. A. (2000). The validity of affective work team climates. In M. Vartiainen, F. Avallone, & N. Anderson (Eds.), *Innovative theories, tools, and practices in work and organizational psychology* (pp. 97–109). Göttingen: Hogrefe and Huber Publishers.

González-Romá, V., Peiró, J. M. & Tordera, N. (2002). An examination of the antecedents and moderator influences of climate strength. *Journal of Applied Psychology, 87*, 465–473.

Gracia, F. J., Silla, I., Peiró, J. M., & Fortes-Ferreira, L. (2007). The state of the psychological contract and its relation to employees' psychological health. *Psychology in Spain, 11*, 33–41.

Grebner, S., Elfering, A., & Semmer, N. (2008). Subjective occupational success. A resource in the stress process. In J. Houdmont & S. Leka (Eds.), *Occupational health psychology: European perspectives in research, education and practice.* (pp. 89–110) Nottingham: Nottingham University Press.

Greenglass, E. R (1993). The contribution of social support to coping strategies. *Applied Psychology. An International Review, 42*, 323–340.

Grzywacz, J. G., Carlson, D. S., Kacman, K. M., & Wayne, J. H. (2007). A multi-level perspective on the synergies between work and family. *Journal of Occupational and Organizational Psychology, 80*, 559–574.

Hacker, W. (1993). Objective work environment: Analysis and evaluation of objective work characteristics. In L. Levi & J. L. Petters (Eds.), *A healthier work environment: Basic concepts and methods of measurement* (pp. 42–57). Copenhagen, Denmark: WHO Regional Office for Europe.

Hackman, J. R., & Oldham, G. R. (1980). *Work design*. Reading, MA: Addison Wesley.

Hammer, L. B., Cullen, J. C., Neal, M. B., Sinclair, R. R., & Shafiro, M. V. (2005). The longitudinal effects of work–family conflict and positive spillover on depressive symptoms among dual-earner couples. *Journal of Occupational Health Psychology, 10*, 138–154.

Hanson, G. C., Hammer, L. B., & Colton, C. L. (2006). Development and validation of a multidimensional scale of perceived work-family positive spillover. *Journal of Occupational Health Psychology, 11*, 249–265.

Harris, K. J., & Kacmar, K. M. (2006): Too much of a good thing: the curvilinear effect of leader–member exchange on stress. *The Journal of Social Psychology, 146*, 65–84.

Head, J., Kivimäki, M., Siegrist, J., Ferrie, J. E., Vahtera, J., Shipley, M. J., & Marmot, M. G. (2007). Effort–reward imbalance and relational injustice at work predict sickness absence: The Whitehall II study. *Journal of Psychosomatic Research, 63*, 433–440.

Hobfoll, S. E. (2001): The influence of culture, community and the nested-self in the stress process: Advancing conservation of resources theory. *Applied Psychology. An International Review, 50*(3), 337–369.

Hoel, H., Cooper, C. L., & Faragher, B. (2001) The experience of bullying in Great Britain. The impact of organizational status. *European Journal of Work and Organizational Psychology, 10*, 443–465.

Hofmann, D. A., & Tetrick, L. E. (2003): The etiology of the concept of Health. Implications for "organizing" individual and organizational health. In D. A. Hofmann & L. E Tetrick (Eds.) *Health and safety in organizations* (pp. 1–28). San Francisco CA: Jossey-Bass.

Houdmont, J., Leka, S. & Bulger, C. A. (2008): The definition of curriculum areas in occupational health psychology. In J. Houdmont & S. Leka (Eds.), *Occupational health psychology: European perspectives in research, education and practice* (pp. 145–170). Nottingham: Nottingham University Press.

House, J. S. (1981) *Work, stress and social support.* Reading, MA: Addison Wesley.

Humphrey, S. E., Nahrgang, J. D., & Morgeson, F. P. (2007). Integrating motivational, social and contextual work design features: A meta-analytic summary and theoretical extension of the work design literature. *Journal of Applied Psychology*, *92*, 1332–1356.

Inoue, A., Kawakami, N., Ishizaki, M., Tabata, M., Tsuchiya, M., Akiyama, M., ... Shimazu, A. (2009). Three job stress models/concepts and oxidative DNA damage in a sample of workers in Japan. *Journal of Psychosomatic Research*, *66*, 329–334.

Johnson, J. V., Hall, E. M., & Theorell, T. (1989). Combined effects of job strain and social isolation on cardiovascular disease morbidity and mortality in a random sample of the Swedish male working population. *Scandinavian Journal of Work, Evironment, and Health 15*, 271–79.

Kang, S. Y., Staniford, A. K., Dollard, M. F., & Kompier, M. (2008) Knowledge development and content in occupational health psychology. A systematic analysis of the Journal of Occupational Health Psychology and Work & Stress, 1996–2006. In J. Houdmont & S. Leka (Eds.), *Occupational health psychology: European perspectives in research, education and practice* (pp. 27–62). Nottingham: Nottingham University Press.

Karasek, R. A. (1979). Job demands, job decision latitude and mental strain: implications for job redesign. *Administrative Science Quarterly*, *24*, 285–308.

Karasek, R. A., & Theorell, T. (1990). *Healthy work: Stress, productivity and the reconstruction of working life*. New York: Basic Books.

Kelloway, E.K, Hurrell, J. J., Jr., & Day, A. (2008) Workplace interventions for occupational stress. In K. Näswall, J. Hellgren, & M. Sverke (Eds.) *The individual in the changing working life* (pp. 419–441). Cambridge: Cambridge University Press.

Kelloway, E. K., Sivanathan, N., Francis, L., & Barling, J. (2004). Poor leadership. In J. Barling, E. K. Kelloway, & M. R. Frone (Eds.), *Handbook of work stress* (pp. 89–112). Thousand Oaks, CA: Sage.

Kickul, J., & Posig, M. (2001) Supervisory emotional support and burnout: An explanation of reverse buffering effects. *Journal of Managerial Issues*, *13*, 328–344.

Kossek, E. E., & Ozeki, C. (1998). Work–family conflict, policies, and the job–life satisfaction relationship: A review and directions for organizational behavior-human resources research. *Journal of Applied Psychology*, *82*, 139–149.

Kossek, E. E., & Ozeki, C. (1999). Bridging the work–family policy and productivity gap: A literature review. *Community, Work & Family*, *2*, 7–32.

Länsisalmi, H., Peiró, J. M., & Kivimäki, M. (2000). Collective stress and coping in the context of organizational culture. *European Journal of Work and Organizational Psychology*, *9*, 527–559

Lapierre, L. M., Spector, P. E., Allen, T. D., Poelmans, S., Cooper, C. L., O'Driscoll, M. P., ... Kinnunen, U. (2008). Family-supportive organization perceptions, multiple dimensions of work-family conflict, and employee satisfaction: A test of model across five samples. *Journal of Vocational Behavior*, *73*, 92–106.

Lee, R. T., & Ashford, B. E. (1996). A meta-analytic examination of the correlates of the three dimensions of job burnout. *Journal of Applied Psychology*, *81*, 123–133.

Luthans, F., & Avolio, B. J. (2009). The "point" of positive organizational behavior. *Journal of Organizational Behavior*, *30*, 291–307.

McGowan, J., Gardner, D., & Fletcher, R. (2006) Positive and negative affective outcomes of Occupational Stress. *New Zealand Journal of Psychology*, *35*, 92–98.

Macik-Frey, M., Quick, J. C., & Nelson, D. L. (2007) Advances in occupational health: From a stressful beginning to a positive future. *Journal of Management*, *33*, 809–840.

Michie, S., & Gooty, J. (2005). Values, emotions and authenticity: Will the real leader please stand up? *The Leadership Quarterly*, *16*, 441–457.

Moliner, C., Martínez-Tur, V., Peiró, J. M., & Ramos, J. (2005). Linking organizational justice to burnout: Are men and women different? *Psychological Reports*, *96*, 805–816.

Murphy, L. (1999): Healthy work organizations: A research agenda. *Revista de Psicología del Trabajo y de las Organizaciones, 15,* 223–236.

Nelson, D. L., & Simmons, B. L. (2003). Health psychology and work stress: A more positive approach. In J. C. Quick & L. Tetrick (Eds.), *Handbook of occupational health psychology* (pp. 97–119). Washington, DC: American Psychological Association

Parker, S. K., & Wall, T. D. (1998). *Job and work design: Organization work to promote well-being and effectiveness.* Thousand Oaks, CA: Sage.

Peiró, J. M. (1999): *Desencadenantes del estrés laboral* [Stressors at work]. Madrid: Pirámide.

Peiró, J. M. (2008): Stress and coping at work: new research trends and their implications for practice. In K. Näswall, J. Hellgren, & M. Sverke (Eds.) *The individual in the changing working life* (pp. 284–310). Cambridge: Cambridge University Press.

Peiró, J. M., González-Romá, V., Ripoll, P., & Gracia, F. (2001). Role stress and work team variables in Primary Health Care Teams: A structural equations model. In J. de Jonge, P. Vlerick, A. Büssing, & W.B. Schaufeli (Eds.), *Organizational psychology and health care at the start of a new millennium* (pp. 105–122). Munich, Rainer Hampp Verlag.

Poelmans, S., & Beham, B. (2008). The moment of truth: Conceptualizing managerial work–life policy allowance decisions. *Journal of Occupational and Organizational Psychology, 81,* 393–410.

Poelmans, S., O'Driscoll, M., & Beham, B. (2005) An overview of international research on the work–family interface. In S. Poelmans (Ed.), *Work and family. An international research perspective.* (pp. 3–46). Mahwah, N.J.: Lawrence Erlbaum.

Pratt, L. L., & Barling, J. (1988). Differentiating between daily events, acute and chronic stressors. A framework and its implications. In J. J. Hurrel, Jr., L. R. Murphy, S. L. Sauter & C. L. Cooper (Eds.), *Occupational stress: Issues and development in research* (pp. 41–53). London: Taylor & Francis.

Quick, J. C. (1999) Occupational health psychology: Historical roots and future directions. *Health Psychology, 18,* 82–88.

Rau, R., (2006). Learning opportunities at work as predictor for recovery and health. *European Journal of Work and Organizational Psychology, 15,* 158–180.

Rhoades, L., & Eisenberger, R. (2002). Perceived organizational support: A review of the literature. *Journal of Applied Psychology, 87,* 698–714.

Rhoades, L., & Eisenberger, R. (2006) When supervisors feel supported: Relationships with subordinates, perceived supervisor support, perceived organizational support, and performance. *Journal of Applied Psychology 91,* 689–695.

Roe, R. A., Coetsier, P., Levy Léboyer, C., Peiró, J. M., & Wilpert, B. (1994). The teaching of work and organizational psychology in Europe. Towards the development of a reference model. *The European Work & Organizational Psychologist, 4*(4), 355–365.

Rousseau, D. M. (1995). *Psychological contracts in organizations: Understanding written and unwritten agreements.* Thousand Oaks, CA: Sage.

Ryff, C. D., Singer, B. H., & Love, G. D. (2004). Positive health: Connecting well-being with biology. *Philosophical Transactions of the Royal Society of London, 359,* 1383–1394.

Schaufeli, W. B. (2004): The future of occupational health psychology. *Applied Psychology. An International Review, 53,* 502–517.

Schaufeli, W., González-Romá, V., Peiró, J. M., Geurts, S., & Tomás, I. (2005). Withdrawal and burnout in health care: On the mediating role of lack of reciprocity. In C. Korunka & P. Hoffmann. (Eds.), *Change and Quality in Human Service Work, Volume 4* (pp. 205–226). München, Germany: Hampp Publishers.

Seltzer, J., & Numerof, R. E. (1986). Supervisory leadership and subordinate burnout. *Academy of Management Journal, 31,* 439–446.

Shore, L. M., Tetrick, L. E., Taylor, M. S., Shapiro, J. A., Liden, R. C., Parks, J. M., ... Van Dyne, L. (2004) The employee–organization relationship: A timely concept in a period of transition. In J. Martocchio and G. Ferris (Eds.), *Research in personnel and human resources management* (Vol. 23, pp. 291–370). Oxford: Elsevier.

Siegrist, J. (1998). Adverse health effects of effort-reward imbalance at work: Theory, empirical support, and implications for prevention. In C. L. Cooper (Ed.), *Theories of organizational stress* (pp. 190–204). Oxford: Oxford University Press.

Simon, H. (1969). *The sciences of the artificial.* Cambridge, MA: MIT Press.

Sinclair, R. R., Hammer, L. B., Oeldorf-Hirsch, A., & Brubaker, T. (2006, March). Do academics and practitioners agree on occupational health psychology priorities? *Paper presented at Work, Stress, and Health 2006: Making a Difference in the Workplace*, Miami, FL.

Spell, C. S., & Arnold, T. J. (2007). A multi-level analysis of organizational justice Climate, structure, and employee mental health. *Journal of Management, 33*, 724–751.

Tepper, B. J. (2000). Consequences of abusive supervision. *Academy of Management Journal, 43*(2), 178–190.

Tetrick, L. E., & Ellis, B. (2002): Developing an OHP curriculum that addresses the needs of organizations and labor unions in the USA. In C. Weikert, E. Torkelson & J. Pryce (Eds.), *Occupational health psychology: Empowerment, participation and health at work.* Nottingham: I-WHO Publications.

Tordera, N., Peiró, J. M., González-Romá, V., Fortes-Ferreira, L., & Mañas, M. A. (2006). *Leaders as health enhancers: A longitudinal analysis of the impact of leadership in team members' well-being.* Paper presented at the 26th International Congress of Applied Psychology, July 16–21, Athens, Greece.

Torkelson, E., Muhonen, T., & Peiró, J. M. (2007) Constructions of work stress and coping in a female- and a male-dominated department. *Scandinavian Journal of Psychology. 48*, 261–270.

Totterdell, P., Wood, S., & Wall, T. (2006) An intra-individual test of the demands-control model: a weekly diary study of psychological strain in portfolio workers. *Journal of Occupational and Organizational Psychology, 79*, 63–84.

Van Muijen, J. J., Kopman, P., De Witte, K., De Cock, G., Susanj, Z., Lemoine, F., ... Turnipseed, D (1999). Organizational culture: The FOCUS questionnaire. *European Journal of Work and Organizational Psychology, 8*, 551–568.

Viswesvaran, C., Sánchez, J. I., & Fisher, J. (1999). The role of social support in the process of work stress: A meta-analysis. *Journal of Vocational Behavior, 54*, 314–334.

Wallace, J. C., Edwards, B. D., Arnold, T., Frazier, M. L., & Finch, D. M. (2009). Work stressors, role-based performance, and the moderating influence of organizational support. *Journal of Applied Psychology, 94*, 254–262.

Wayne, J. H., Grzywacz, J. G., Carlson, D. S., & Kacmar, K. M. (2007). Work–family facilitation: A theoretical explanation and model of primary antecedents and consequences. *Human Resource Management Review, 17*, 63–76.

Warr, P. (2007). *Work, happiness and unhappiness.* New York: Lawrence Erlbaum Associates.

Wills, T. A. (1990). Social support and interpersonal relationships. In M. S. Clark (Ed.), *Review of personality and social psychology*, (Vol. 12, pp. 265–289). Newbury Park, CA: Sage.

Winnubst, J. A. M., & Schabracq, M. J. (1996). Social support, stress and organization: Towards optimal matching. In M. J. Schabracq, J. A. Winnubst, & C. L. Cooper (Eds.), *Handbook of work and health psychology* (pp. 87–102). Chichester: Wiley.

Xie, J. L., Schaubroeck, J., & Lam, S. S. K. (2008). Theories of job stress and the role of traditional values: A longitudinal study in China. *Journal of Applied Psychology, 93*, 831–848.

13

Human Factors and Ergonomics

José J. Cañas, Boris B. Velichkovsky,
and Boris M. Velichkovsky

Definition

In its triennial report, the International Ergonomics Association (IEA, 2000) defined ergonomics as the scientific discipline that deals with understanding the interaction between humans and other elements of a sociotechnical system. In this definition, ergonomics is the profession that applies theory, principles, data, and design methods to optimize human well-being and the overall performance of a system. It is in particular responsible for the design and evaluation of tasks, jobs, products, environments, and systems to make them compatible with the abilities, needs, and limitations of people.

The word "ergonomics" comes from the Greek "ergon" meaning work and "nomos," which means law. Therefore, etymologically, this is the science of work. The term has been used historically in the European tradition. In the American tradition the term "human factor engineering" is used to refer to the same issues, so both terms can be now considered as synonyms and are used interchangeably. The latter is evidenced by the fact that the "Human Factor Society," founded in Tulsa (Oklahoma) in 1957, is now called the "Human Factor and Ergonomics Society" (HFES). Another term which is often used in the same context is "Engineering psychology" (Wickens & Hollands, 2000).

The early precursors of the new discipline could be set around the time of World War I. They had their background in the pioneering studies of Frederic Bartlett (1886–1969), Hugo Münsterberg (1863–1916) and Frederick Winslow Taylor (1856–1915) on applied psychology and industrial management. The design of new machines (e.g. the first cars or tanks) revealed the importance of taking into account the characteristics of the people who should operate them. It was found that many

IAAP Handbook of Applied Psychology, First Edition. Edited by Paul R. Martin, Fanny M. Cheung, Michael C. Knowles, Michael Kyrios, Lyn Littlefield, J. Bruce Overmier, and José M. Prieto.

people had difficulties in operating more complex machines, especially warplanes. This led the army to recruit psychologists, who were assigned the task of developing and administering tests to select soldiers and to assign them to different tasks. These applied psychologists set up the first human factors laboratories, which continued their work after the war ended. But it was World War II that provided the final impetus for the establishment of ergonomics as a discipline with industrial and academic recognition. Moreover, this war involved an enormous amount of people and artifacts, many of them newly created, such as radar, which made the idea of selecting a few special individuals to use previously designed artifacts unworkable. The idea that emerged, and has had an enormous impact on the development of the discipline, was that the devices should be designed taking into account the characteristics of the human beings who will use them, and not adapted to people once they are designed.

In Europe, the focus of ergonomics is to be found in industry, and it has been linked to an interest in improving worker performance and satisfaction. The discipline began with an emphasis on the design of equipment and workplaces, although, in principle, it dealt with biological, rather than psychological aspects. In this way, studies began on anthropometry, work medicine, architecture, lighting, and so on. Back in the 1980s, European ergonomists began to worry largely about advanced psychological aspects and the "European Association of Cognitive Ergonomics" (EACE) emerged, leading to a confluence of interests with human factors and cognitive science professionals on the other side of the Atlantic.

The definition of ergonomics is extended today to all human activities in which artifacts are utilized. Ergonomists (with many applied psychologists among them) are involved in a permanent search for comprehensive approaches in which the physical, cognitive, social, and environmental aspects of human activities can be considered. Although ergonomists often work on different economic sectors or particular tasks, these application domains are constantly evolving, creating new ones and changing the perspective of the old ones. Accordingly, one can recognize today four main domains of expertise crucial for investigating interaction between humans and sociotechnical systems.

- *Physical ergonomics* deals with the anatomical, anthropometric, physiological, and biomechanical parameters in static and dynamic physical work. Among the main topics are the physical postures that people adopt when they are working, fatigue, and other problems associated with handling physical and musculoskeletal tasks associated with physical efforts.
- *Cognitive ergonomics* is a subdiscipline of ergonomics that studies the cognitive processes at work with an emphasis on an understanding of the situation and on supporting reliable, effective, and satisfactory performance. This approach addresses problems such as attention distribution, decision making, formation of learning skills, usability of human–computer systems, the cognitive aspects of mental load, stress, and human errors at work.
- *Neuroergonomics* is a relatively new development that involves the application of more in-depth neurophysiological methods such as brain imaging techniques. This advanced methodology can be used for evaluating the customers' preferences

for one or another design of human–computer interface or for a particular version of industrial products (this latter task is sometimes related to the field of "neuromarketing").
- *Social or organizational ergonomics* deals with the optimization of sociotechnical work systems, including their structures, policies, and organizational processes. Thus, ergonomists are often involved in the social design of communication systems, interaction routines within the working groups, times and shifts schedules in a company, and other related issues.

By its very definition ergonomics is a multidisciplinary endeavor. Scientists and practitioners from many disciplines have been interested in designing or changing different aspects of sociotechnical systems. Therefore, they all might be called "ergonomists" in a sense, with further specifications depending on particular emphasis—from the physical and neurophysiological to the mental and socio-organizational aspects—of the interest at hand.

Areas of Application

In this chapter, the primary emphasis will be on ergonomic issues related to applied psychology. Its interest in complex behaviors, mental activities, and the resources of human information processing puts cognitive ergonomics in the focus of present analysis. Even with such constraints, however, it is difficult to make a straightforward classification of domains of application because ergonomists work in all areas of life in which there is a cognitive design problem. A simple classification based on two criteria is elaborated below.

Industrial areas

Human–computer interaction. For many years, the computer has been the most sophisticated artifact in our lives, visibly present both within and outside the workplace. Due to the overwhelming importance of information technologies, the term cognitive ergonomics is often replaced by Human Computer Interaction (HCI or, from a more technical perspective, CHI). However, in most cases, computers are only parts serving the functioning of larger technical systems, so our interaction with them is not as explicit as when a personal computer is in use. For example, there are computing devices in the engines of modern cars but drivers interact with the car and not with these "invisible computers." For this reason, one should talk rather about the cognitive ergonomics of human-machine interaction and rethink interaction with computers as interaction with everyday computerized artifacts (Sellen, Rogers, Harper, & Rodden, 2009).

Transportation. Some of the most important artifacts in our lives are used to support human mobility. Cars, buses, trains, boats, planes, etc. have to be designed to enable their users to have effective, efficient, and safe transportation. Although some of these artifacts are used by only one person, an analysis of dynamic transportation situations indicates that cognitive ergonomists must take a more global viewpoint that includes considering many persons who interact with each other through a large number of artifacts under conditions of severe time constraints and deadly hazards. Therefore, although ergonomics has been involved in the design of the cockpit of airplanes and cars (e.g., being recently involved in designing assistant systems for helping car drivers to drive safely), experts in this profession have also begun to be interested in the development of the whole sociotechnical system that has to be considered in air traffic or railway transportation. This is the area where most of specialized cognitive technical systems that support human activity have been developed and some of the crucial problems of interaction with artifacts were initially detected (see, in particular, the sections "Situation awareness and attention" and "Mental models," below).

Control processes. The area known as "process control" has a long tradition of research and practice in ergonomics. The term "process" refers here to that kind of industry known as "processing industry." A processing industry is one where energy and matter interact and transform one into another (Woods, O'Brien, & Hanes, 1987). A typical example of such an industry is nuclear power plants. But the paper production and the milk pasteurization industries also belong to this category. There is one ergonomically relevant characteristic that distinguishes among examples of processing industries. One can say that the various process industries differ in their degree of dependence on the artifacts that play a mediating role between the operators and the physical processes that they control. In the extreme case such as a nuclear power plant, all control must be done through artifacts. In many other cases, there may be a relatively direct relationship between human control operations (observations and/or actions) and the physical process.

Therefore, in general terms, in the process control domain one or more persons work to control a physical system using one or more artifacts. These individuals interact directly with the mediating artifacts, but not with the physical system that they are controlling. Unlike what happens in the interaction of a person with a computer when she or he is writing a text, in process control there is an external world, which is the physical industrial system that the person—or persons—perceive and control through the mediating artifact, which, of course, can be a computer (Ken'ichi, Kunihide, & Seiichi, 1997).

Intervention areas

Design. Design is at the heart of the ergonomist's profession (Dowell & Long, 1998). The design of a new system is the process that happens from the conceptualization of the artifact until when it is used by the people for whom it is intended. From the point of view of cognitive ergonomists, there are two aspects of interest in system design (Carroll, 1991). On the one hand, they are interested in "the process" of design itself. That is, cognitive ergonomists want to understand how people devise a new system, and what are the individual and group factors involved in making decisions that lead to certain solutions defining the system. Furthermore, cognitive ergonomists would like to know whether the solutions adopted suit the needs and characteristics of users. Their main role in this sense is to describe the human being at all levels of functional organization appropriate for the system being designed (Velichkovsky, 2005; Wickens & Hollands, 2000). Therefore, cognitive ergonomists are interested in both the human being who designs and the human being interacting with the system that has been or has to be designed.

The work of cognitive ergonomists in the design process has undergone serious changes over the last decades. In the early days of human factor engineering, they were called on to explain why a particular design had not worked. Later on, they were called on to intervene directly in the design process (Wickens & Hollands, 2000). Today, the process of innovation requires that ergonomists "proactively" supply ideas and empirical data for the design of future artifacts improving human performance and public acceptance of new technologies (Akoumianakis & Stephanidis, 2003; Kohler, Pannasch, & Velichkovsky, 2008).

Technological innovation. The concept of "user-centered design" was developed during the 1980s in the design of technologies (Norman, 1986). Until then, system design issues were driven mainly by technological innovations. User-centered design aims at describing the human being who interacts with the system from the viewpoint of cognitive science. Then, based on those characteristics cognitive ergonomists provided engineers with a set of principles to be considered in the design. This paradigm has led to the establishment of usability research that has contributed greatly to the effectiveness, efficiency, and satisfaction of users in their interaction with the technologies and to a better interaction between users through technology (Holzinger, 2005).

However, one can at present witness a paradigm shift in the interaction that requires a change in how to understand and to evaluate usability. The change is motivated by the design of new applications and services under the influence of increasingly fast convergence of nano-, bio- and information technologies with cognitive science (see, e.g., *NBIC-Report*, 2006). This new development has several features that force cognitive ergonomists to rethink the concept of interaction. Those features are, first of all, that applications are designed to be used in intelligent and mobile environments. Secondly, they can be based on a wide spectrum of new materials, such as bidirectional organic glasses (transparent organic light emitting diodes, TOLEDs) and reactive polymers, making new forms of multimodal interaction with digital environments as well as ubiquitous computing possible. Last but not least, new applications, especially in time-demanding military and transportation domains, are supposed to be adaptable to the current intention, state of knowledge, and emotion of the user. The concept of "user-centred design" is becoming too nonspecific as obviously the same user may be in different cognitive-affective states and may have changed intentions at different moments of time.

Safety and accident investigation. Historically, there have been three approaches to the study of human error. The first was taken from the field of engineering and led to the development of a range of techniques, generically called the "human reliability analysis" (HRA). These techniques are based on the assumption that the actions of a person in a workplace can be considered from the same point of view as the operations of a machine. The objective is to predict the likelihood of human error and evaluate how the entire work system is degraded as a result of this error alone or in connection with the operation of the machines, the characteristics of the task, the system design, and the characteristics of individuals (Swain & Guttmann, 1983). This approach has led to a considerable progress in the efforts to predict the occurrence of human error. However, it has been criticized as insufficient. Reason (1992) particularly notes that the main difficulty is the estimation of error probability. In designing new systems, there are no prior data on the error probabilities. One can count on data from simple components, such as errors that are committed reading a piece of data from a dial or entering it into a keyboard, but not the errors that may be committed by interacting with the system.

The second approach was adopted from cognitive psychology. In this, ergonomics seek to know the mental processes responsible for committing an error (Norman 1981; Reason, 1992). They assume that errors are not caused by irresponsible behavior or defective mental functioning. They may be rather the consequence of not having taken into account how a person perceives, attends, remembers, makes decisions, communicates, and acts in a particularly designed work system. This standpoint suggests investigating the causes of human errors by analyzing the characteristics of human information processing. Here, the first step has been the classification of errors according to the level of processing involved in the behavior that led to the error. Although there are more elaborate classifications today, it is possible to make a synthesis based on the classical scheme proposed by Jens Rasmussen (1983). He distinguishes three types of errors depending on the level and degree of cognitive control involved in the erroneous behavior. The three types of errors can be largely attributed to the familiarity that the person has with the system:

- *Errors based on skills:* When a person is very familiar with the task, her or his actions are overlearned as a low-level pre-programmed sequence of operations that do not require and often are not under conscious control. If one of these actions is poorly performed or the sequence is applied in an unusual order, a skill-based error occurs.
- *Errors based on rules:* The selection of actions in a situation often depends on the implementation of a set of rules of the type IF (condition) THEN (action). The activation of the right rules depends on the interpretation of the situational conditions. If a situation is misinterpreted the retrieved rule will be inappropriate as well. In other words, an error based on rules will occur.
- *Errors based on knowledge:* When we encounter a new problem situation, so that existing skills and learned rules are of little help, it is necessary to plan a novel action sequence to its resolution. This is a higher-order cognitive activity demanding a lot of conscious control. If the actions are not planned correctly, a knowledge-based error will occur.

Cognitive ergonomists took those classifications for granted in their attempts to find explanations of action slips and errors based on the cognitive models. However, the explanations have been criticized for being insufficient to facilitate the prediction and prevention of errors. Indeed, it was difficult to predict errors from explanations based only on the hypotheses about human cognitive system. Therefore, a third approach has been developed recently to combine the reliability analysis developed by engineers with cognitive modelling. This approach starts from the basic assumption that the behavior of a person is determined by the context in which it occurs. The work system creates dynamic, ever-changing situations. It is therefore necessary to take into account the context and all levels of organization that contribute to system safety: the system's technology, the individual, the group, the organizational management, and cultural factors. In other words, it is not sufficient to estimate errors only from the perspective of human information processing (Wilpert, 2001).

According to this new approach, the person and her or his working environment should be considered as a highly interactive joint cognitive system (Hollnagel and Woods, 2007). The interaction between the two components is of a crucial importance for any ergonomic analysis. Based on these assumptions, several authors have proposed a methodology for estimating the probability of human errors depending on specific situation in which human–machine interaction occurs. The methodology presupposes two steps of analysis: (1) to identify the types of errors that are possible for a specific task in a given scenario of event development; (2) to classify these types of errors by their ranges of probability to identify which are the most probable and which are the least probable within the given joint cognitive system (Hollnagel, 1998; Cacciabue, 2004).

Theories and Models

In their everyday practical work ergonomists may well be more interested in improving what people do rather than what people know or feel. However an enduring improvement in performance seems to be possible only if the underlying cognitive representations as well as attitudes and competences of participating persons are known. This is why the Chomskian distinction between competence and performance becomes very important for cognitive ergonomists (Amalberti, 2001). In addition to this theoretical distinction, influential concepts are being borrowed, on the one hand, from ecological psychology and activity theory (Gibson, 1979; Leontiev, 1978) and, on the other hand, from the rapidly growing field of cognitive neuroscience (Hancock & Parasuraman, 2003).

Conceptual developments

With reference to Herbert Simon (1969), cognitive ergonomics sometimes is called "cognitive engineering." Simon's book "The sciences of the artificial" had an enormous influence on the development of the discipline in the early 1970s. In this book and in a number of follow-up publications, he thoroughly argued that cognitive science must have its own area of application, i.e., the design of artifacts. To that end, he proposed the establishment of a "science of the artificial" related to cognitive science in the same sense as in the traditionally understood relationship between applied—engineering—disciplines and basic sciences.

Cognitive engineering deals with the problems of designing an effective mental work and the tools with which this work is done (Hollnagel & Woods, 1983). Therefore, the object of cognitive ergonomics is formulated around the concepts of "mental work" and the "cognitive tool (artifact)." Mental work is performed by cognitive systems that use knowledge to produce changes in the environment or domains of work. An artifact is any item manufactured by a human being with the purpose of improving any aspect of human behavior or mental operation. It can be a physical object (a computer mouse) or an abstract entity (a computer program) or an object representing a physical object (a drawing of a factory). The artifacts have been created to act on the environment, to modify any aspect of it, and to obtain information that allows us to know its characteristics and how it changed our actions.

Donald Norman (1986) was one who also argued for a combination of knowledge from cognitive science and engineering to solve design problems. According to him, the objectives of such a strategy would be twofold: (1) to understand the fundamental principles of human actions that are relevant to the development of principles of engineering design; and (2) to build systems that are pleasant to use. The first goal suggests a slight change in accents with respect to the original proposal of Simon. In fact, it put the discipline in line with the vision of some advanced experts in engineering (Vincenti, 1990): the establishment of cognitive engineering as a discipline of human action independent from, albeit related to, cognitive science from which it could borrow knowledge about cognitive processes. However, this proposal remained unattended for a decade, and ergonomics evolved according to Simon's idea of understanding the cognitive engineering as an applied *pendant* to cognitive science. An example of this view can be found in some textbooks on human factors engineering (see, e.g., Wickens & Hollands, 2000), which are organized according to topics of human information processing. In this way, the list of chapters is the same as the list of chapters that can be found in any textbook of cognitive psychology.

A better acceptance of Norman's ideas occurred when it became apparent how difficult it is to directly implement the results of cognitive psychology to explain the problems of design. These difficulties are currently causing a paradigm shift that will have repercussions beyond cognitive ergonomics itself, forcing a rethink of many fundamental issues that emerged from the cognitive revolution of the middle of the 20th century.

In the classical conceptualization, the artifact and the human being were considered independent from the context where the interaction between them took place. Thereafter, the aim of ergonomists was to study the characteristics of human information processing and provide designers with these data whenever they needed those characteristics to make decisions about the design of the artifact. This conceptualization has been called into question. First of all, due to technological progress, artifacts are designed today with a level of automation that enables them to be considered as (nearly) intelligent systems, almost at the same level as some (absentminded) human beings. Even if the last thesis can be disputed, contemporary artifacts often have a dynamic that is independent of the control actions that humans may impose on them. The difference, of course, is that artifacts are designed for human beings, while the human beings have evolved and been modified by evolution, development, and learning. Secondly, it is believed that human behavior is shaped by the sociotechnical context in which it occurs and not only by the internal peculiarities of human information processing.

These considerations have been laid down in the paradigm of the joint cognitive systems (Dowell & Long, 1998; Hollnagel & Woods, 2007). The main message of the proponents of this approach is a broad interactionism: for a solution of cognitive design problems human behavior must be modelled as activity, in its interaction with the environment and with the other cognitive systems—both human and artificial—that there are in the environment. Therefore, in this new conceptualization of cognitive engineering the meaning of cognition itself is being reformulated in more dynamic and situational terms.

The meaning of cognition in cognitive ergonomics

In the traditional understanding, "cognition" refers to the acquisition, maintenance, and use of knowledge as examples of operations within the realm of human information processing. However, within dissident conceptions such as the joint cognitive paradigm, cognition should be understood in a broader sense, exceeding the limits of the individual's brain or body. An example is the Gibsonian notion of "affordance," which refers to all aspects of the environment supporting specific actions of individuals (Gibson, 1979). This notion is of obvious significance for cognitive engineering, to such a degree that some authors declare the design of affordances to be the main goal of human factors engineering (Vicente, 1999). In a similar vein, Norman (1986) stresses the importance of "external memory." Under influence of these ideas, the meaning of cognition in cognitive ergonomics now refer to highly organized distributed systems ("distributed cognition"), such as the military, air traffic control, aircraft cabins, or navigation systems for large ships. Both people and artifacts are jointly regarded as agents within such a system. The focus is placed on the transfer and processing of information within and between agents. In this framework, cognition is viewed as a phenomenon that emerges from the work of the system as a whole (Hutchins, 1995).

One consequence of this redefinition has been the incorporation of theories that have been developed outside the mainstream cognitive research. This is the explanation for a discovery of activity theory (see Leontiev, 1978), which has its roots in European romanticism and Marxist philosophy. Activity theory, with its focus on the sociocultural origins of human thought and action, is now considered as a promising starting point for research in cognitive ergonomics (Nardi, 1996). Accordingly, there are no sharp distinctions between consciousness and behavior, and thus between external actions and internal thoughts, a distinction that is common for traditional cognitive science and ergonomics. Thoughts without external actions are considered as internalized social actions, similar to corresponding external actions (Vygotsky, 1978). As soon as the sociocultural context is considered, the scope of analysis becomes broader than in cognitive science. These contexts include communicating with others as well as the context in which the person is growing. The cultural context also includes the history of the artifacts, actions, and people.

The incorporation of new approaches and theories of cognition into ergonomics led to a discussion on the relative merits of macro- and microtheories whereby the dominating view stressed the importance of the overarching explanations. For instance, Klein and colleagues (2003) proposed that cognitive ergonomists should create macrotheories that incorporate all the complexity of interaction within a socio-technical system. Simultaneously to this holistic trend, one can testify to the growing influence of concepts borrowed from the field of cognitive neuroscience. Being closely related to the progress in methods of brain and behavioral research, the second trend recently led to the development of neuroergonomics (Parasuraman & Wilson, 2008; Velichkovsky & Hansen, 1996). This tendency is especially evident, in the analysis of several traditional topics of human factors studies which are discussed below.

Conceptual topics

Situation awareness and attention. In performing complex tasks such as flying an airplane, it is necessary to process huge amounts of data on what is happening in the cabin, where there may be more members of the crew, in the air outside the plane, and even at the airport and the control tower. This information must be attentively handled, retained, interpreted, and used to make necessary decisions for the airplane to fly properly and land safely. The processes of conscious perception and understanding of the situation are generically called "situation awareness." In many application domains, ergonomists need this concept to describe cognitive processes that are responsible for the acquisition, storage, and use of information available to the person doing the work. Although there are several ways to define what situation awareness is, the model proposed by Endsley (1995) is widely accepted today. According to this author, situation awareness is the perception of elements in the environment within a volume of time and space, the comprehension of their meaning and projection of their status in the near future. Therefore, it includes three levels of information processing: (1) perception of the elements of the environment; (2) understanding the current situation; and (3) predicting (projecting) the situation's future development.

One of the reasons for this rapidly growing interest in situation awareness is the instability of human performance related to the automation of work processes. The problems—or "ironies"—of automation were first noted by Lisanne Bainbridge in a seminal paper (Bainbridge, 1983). With a high degree of automation, the human operator is out of loop of controlling processes. As a result, operators are less well practiced in their abilities to take over the process when an automatic unit fails. This deterioration results from the fact that the manual and cognitive skills decline due to the absence of active participation in the process. Furthermore, it becomes more difficult with progressing automation to gain access to knowledge about system behavior. Many authors see the solution to such problems in adaptive automation, which could take the current state of knowledge of human operator into account and, in this way, support a better division of labor between humans and machines. However, the solution presupposes reliable and timely feedback information about human understanding of the situation. This is the area where neuroergonomics seems to have serious chances of success (Parasuraman & Wilson, 2008). In particular, neurocognitive studies of attention build the main source of knowledge about mechanisms of situation awareness. These studies have elucidated three different attentional networks in the human brain (Posner, Rueda, & Kanske, 2007) and up to six levels of cognitive organization (Velichkovsky, 2005). Changing the balance of these networks can explain fluctuation in the level of human performance over time, as in the case of driver's behavior in hazardous situations (see Velichkovsky, Rothert, Kopf, Dornhoefer, & Joos 2002).

There seems to be a new understanding in ergonomics that some degree of attention and situation awareness is always required to control the performance of any task, no matter how seemingly simple and safe it is. Today this is a topic of vital importance in many areas of ergonomics from military applications, industry, and transportation to the work of medical professionals. For example, a recent WHO-funded study has shown that the rate of postoperative mortality in a number of hospitals across the world could be reduced by nearly 40% if before the surgery medical personnel had answered questions from a simple checklist of situation awareness: "Are we at the right place here?", "Is that our patient?", "What organ [are] we going to operate on?" (Haynes et al., 2009).

Mental models. When interacting with a system, people normally have some knowledge of its structure and functioning. This small-scale subjective representation of system's structure and functioning is called a mental model (see Johnson-Laird, 1983). Taking into account the peculiarities of users' mental models in the design of artifacts is considered to be crucial for an efficient interaction. Therefore, the investigation of mental models is one of the central themes in cognitive ergonomics (Cañas, Antolí , & Quesada, 2001; Ken'ichi et al., 1997).

Mental models have been studied in applied psychology and ergonomics from several different perspectives. First of all, it is normally expected that having a relatively exact mental model facilitates the acquisition of manual skills for dealing with a physical system. More recently, interest has been extended to the supervision of automatically controlled systems, where the skills that come into play are cognitive operations of detection, diagnosis, and compensation for failures that the system may have. Computational analysis of mental models complexity has been widely used to predict the understanding of instructions that describe how to deal with a technical system. Finally, in the area of HCI, researchers have consistently proven that when a person interacts with the computer she or he acquires knowledge about its structure and operation. Interestingly, this acquisition may be less efficient with relatively easy-to-use graphical user interfaces than with old-fashioned command line interfaces. Other research has shown that the acquisition of an adequate mental model of the computer facilitates learning a programming language (Cañas, Bajo, & Gonzalvo, 1994; Kieras & Bovair, 1984; Navarro & Cañas, 2001).

Learning with and about artifacts. The topic of learning is so important in ergonomics that it cannot be ignored in any attempt to establish a conceptual framework for this discipline. However, one has to distinguish between several related subtopics and address them separately. First of all, there is the basic issue of the variety of learning. As in the case of attention, discussed above, there seem to be at least three neurocognitive systems participating in different forms of skill and knowledge acquisition. Norman (1986) describes three forms of learning in the following terms: (1) *accretion*, that is, an accumulation of factual knowledge such as usually takes place during classical academic education; (2) *tuning*, a gradual adaptation in the parameters of our actions, leading to a steady—albeit not necessarily monotonic—improvement in performance; and (3) *restructuring*, which is a form of higher-order learning by discovery of new conceptual relationships. It should be noted that the last form of learning is directly related to the issue of conceptual change that is of paramount importance both in science education and in learning to work with new technological tools (Chi & Roscoe, 2002).

On a more practical level, after designing a new artifact users must learn to interact with it. This fact has become a crucial issue in modern industry due to two factors. First, new artifacts are increasingly more complex requiring the development of more complex cognitive abilities. Second, technological progress is so fast that nobody can expect to learn to interact with an artifact and continue using it for long time. For example, a couple of decades ago we were writing with typewriters, and now we do that with computers and text editing programs that have changed during these years in a radical way. Thus, in a conceptual scheme of the joint cognitive system, the topic of learning is as important as the topic of design itself. In this sense, much work of cognitive ergonomists has been and will remain focused on the acquisition of the mental models of artifacts, which we discussed previously.

Another major issue of learning is the designing of teaching aids. The people responsible for education have always used educational tools—from the blackboard and chalk to modern "intelligent tutoring systems"—to do their work (Scaife & Rogers, 2005). Educational institutions and companies have followed a classic approach until recently, that is, training in classes with students and teachers in the same space at the same time, with face-to-face communication. In the global economy, computer-mediated communication and distributed work environments are becoming increasingly important. In particular, large enterprises maintain widespread operations and large numbers of employees working on the same project and with similar tools, although they are geographically separated. This has now made feasible the programs of distance learning that are based on the computer imitation of a presence in the same spatial environment (as virtual or mixed reality) as an important option (Kohler, Pannasch, & Velichkovsky, 2008). Simultaneously, universities are trying to find proper technological tools of bringing educational training to all places where there might be a student or an employee who requires it (Salas & Cannon-Bowers, 2001).

Decision making. One of the most active areas of human factors engineering from the beginning has been what is known as the "control of critical incidents." This category includes subtopics such as fire control, medical emergencies, control centers and civil emergencies, military operations, stock market crises, the rescue of victims of kidnappings, and so forth. In dealing with these issues, ergonomists have been using several terms that could be considered at least partial synonyms: "command and control," "dynamic decision-making," "distributed decision-making," "natural decision-making," and "decision science" (Artman, 1998; Brehmer, 1992; Zsambok & Klein, 1997). In all these cases there is a common feature, which is that the persons who have to control these incidents should make decisions under time pressure and with little information to prevent (often) catastrophic consequences. Therefore, although control of critical incidents involves a number of complex psychological processes, decision making is considered to be the most important of them.

Several interrelated trends are characteristic for contemporary decision-making studies in ergonomics. Mainly, their authors turned away from tasks borrowed from formal logics to more naturalistic situations. As noted by Beach and Lipshitz (1993), psychologists have been traditionally focused on the endpoint of decision making: the choice between alternatives that are already given by the task conditions. They have usually investigated inexperienced subjects and assessed the quality of decisions according to "rational" criteria from context-free models. There are reasons to doubt the applicability of results found in these studies to real-world situations (Hutchins, 1995). Indeed, if the conditions are changing, as in the control of critical incidents, the findings may be of marginal value. In natural situations, people are highly experienced and have to generate new alternatives under time pressure. Moreover, the training of professionals, which is based on formal algorithms of decision making, can be rather misleading as the need to take a quick and obvious decision leaves no time to contrast it with other theoretically possible moves (Salas, Cannon-Bowers, & Johnston, 1997). The combination of time pressure and the highly significant outcomes explains the interest that decision science demonstrates in "hot," (i.e., affectively loaded), rather than to "cold" cognition (see e.g. Kahneman, 2003).

Organizational processes. Decision making in a group and its relations with the leadership and related matters (see, e.g., Heller, 1992) is the central topic of organizational psychology, which is discussed in one of the chapters of this handbook. Contemporary ergonomics has taken a slightly different stance, by concentrating efforts on analysis and optimization of the role that knowledge has on the productive activities of human groups. To this end, the term "knowledge management," which refers to the process of generation, storage, and retrieval of knowledge within a social-technical system, is often used. This topic is of increasing importance for cognitive ergonomics since knowledge management requires the use of high-tech artifacts. While it is true that large machinery began to be manufactured in the industrial revolution in the 19th century, and products that were manufactured by human beings were physical objects, today everybody recognizes that knowledge is also generated by human activity. Recognition of this fact is now so general that it is easy to hear that a lot of socioeconomic activity aims to produce knowledge. Furthermore, an obvious fact is also recognized: in the production of objects, organizations generate knowledge of these objects and of the processes of manufacturing and distribution.

The role that knowledge plays can be analyzed from many perspectives, but from the point of view of cognitive ergonomics one has to consider three of them. Firstly, there are many human activities where knowledge is explicitly generated in the development of products. Secondly, there is valuable knowledge that is generated implicitly as people are continuously involved in their activities. This is true of most productive activities at all levels and in all sectors. For example, in a factory where there are certain objects with which workers gain personal experience in a production process, that experience is not acquired in the training courses given by the company, or in the manuals of the machines' producers. That knowledge is often lost when a worker is removed from a job due to retirement, illness, or relocation. Finally, there are countless activities where knowledge must be shared among members of a real or virtual organization. This is the case, for example, in a civil emergency in which members of a professional group must put their knowledge together, communicate, and coordinate their actions to achieve a common goal in order to provide the service required by society.

Mental workload and stress. All work requires human effort. Whenever a person is faced with a task, she or he must implement cognitive resources leading to a variety of functional states that are known in ergonomics by the terms "mental workload," "fatigue," "stress," and the like. Ergonomists have always had an interest in this topic since it was recognized that every time a person has to perform some task that requires more resources than those that she or he has available, that person will be overloaded, and that can affect work performance and, in a long run, her or his mental and physical health. Even if the development of specialized human–computer interfaces has been intended to reduce the demands for cognitive resources, sometimes tools developed to assist people impose additional burdens on them leading to excessive stress and loss of situation awareness with disastrous consequences. There are, of course, ample cases of bitter ironies known from the history of many half-automated systems in transportation and elsewhere.

The concept of mental workload was proposed in the 1970s to explain how cognitive resources are allocated and coordinated to perform several tasks simultaneously. After all these years, the concept has proven to be an important but somewhat vague instrument in the work of ergonomists. It would be important to have an exact and measurable definition of human cognitive limitations during engineering of new systems allowing designers to predict which implementation will maximize the effectiveness and still leave the user a residual capacity to cope with unexpected demands (Yeh & Wickens, 1988). In addition, the labor legislation of industrialized countries recognizes that mental workload affects mental and physical health. Therefore, the law requires companies to evaluate the mental workload to which workers and employers are exposed.

One finds references to mental load in the research areas that have traditionally been identified as "dual task performance," "task execution time-sharing," "task switching," and "working memory." The last notion is used because it combines the idea of a fixed amount of cognitive resources with active operations on them. For example, it has been argued that many of the mistakes made when interacting with a computer are caused by an excessive load of working memory (Olson & Olson, 1990; Gevins et al., 1998). The field of study has been recently extended to increasingly complex multitasking situations that share characteristics with dual tasks, but also possess other features that require high-level coordination during the information processing.

However, there are some persistent problems with the notion of mental workload. First, this is an overtly mentalist concept. Second, the nature of cognitive resources and their relations to structural and operational constrains of processing remain unknown. Numerous hypotheses, models, and theories have been proposed to clarify these issues (Meyer & Kieras, 1997). One of the widely accepted ones is the model of multiple resources by Christopher Wickens (1984). According to it, there is more than one kind of resource, such as those enabling verbal and nonverbal processing. If tasks share the same resources and are performed concurrently, increasing the difficulty of one of them will lead to decline in their performance. If each task addresses different pools of resources, manipulation of the difficulty of one of them would not affect performance. Thus, the combination of resources within and between cognitive dimensions determines the level of mental load. However, the exact nomenclature of cognitive resources is also unclear. The hopes for progress in understanding limitations of human information processing are currently related to functional brain imaging studies (Hancock & Parasuraman, 2003).

Any limitation in performance should also be considered from the perspective of a variety of human functional states such as fatigue, monotony, and stress (Leonova, 1998). Stress is increasingly the major concern in the life of industrialized nations. Time shortage, available skills, and the subjective significance of the task are the main factors causing subjective feelings of acute stress. Both the conceptual basis of contemporary stress research and its methodology—ranging from subjective questionnaires to biochemical analysis of "stress hormones" and genomic studies—seem to demonstrate a positive contrast to many other areas of empirical investigations in ergonomics and human factors engineering. Within this interdisciplinary context, a consistent interest in individual differences opens the way to an understanding of the mechanisms of human stress resilience and its prediction in borderline conditions.

Methodologies

The methods used in ergonomics aim to explain and predict the consequences of taking certain decisions during the design of a sociotechnical system (i.e., the introduction of a new artifact). In this sense, the methodology does not differ in general terms from those used in cognitive psychology and other human factors disciplines such as anthropology and sociology. However, it is necessary to clarify that for ergonomists any explanation has to be followed by prediction. An important aspect of ergonomic methods is that they can be applied before or after the introduction of a change in the system. When they are applied before the introduction of the change, the aim is to explain and predict the consequences of change. When they are applied after the change, the goal is usually to explain and evaluate those consequences in terms of the effectiveness of this change in improving the interaction between system components.

Ethnographic method and field studies

The ethnographic method is applied when ergonomists have to analyze a completely unknown situation (Garfinkel, 1967). Being initially used in anthropology and sociology, it represents a kind of immersion of the researcher in the environment to describe and explain the observed phenomena. The emphasis is on observation relatively free of theory and on a "qualitative" rather than "quantitative" description of what is observed. This approach emerged to replace methods based on structural interviews and questionnaires. It is argued that interviews and questionnaires lose an important aspect of the task, which is the implicit knowledge closely tied to the routines, trials, and intuitive personal adaptations. Since this knowledge is unconscious and is behind rapid responses in real tasks, people are simply too overloaded to make it explicit when answering questionnaires and interviews. In addition, questionnaires and interviews seem to be not truly helpful when trying to analyze the interrelationships between several persons.

Researchers using the "ethnomethodology" often argue that their observations are not driven by any assumptions. However, it is difficult to believe that ergonomists would be able to shed all their prior knowledge to observe a situation without bias (Shapiro, 1994). Without going into details of a methodological discussion that is raging in the philosophy of science, many ergonomists prefer to use a well-established method, called field study, in which as in the ethnographic method, one observes and describes a situation without seriously interfering with it, but the observations are guided by assumptions that are explicitly established from the outset.

Standards and evaluation testing

In many cases, a task can be easily categorized as belonging to one or another standard situation. For example, when introducing a new software application within the common platform of a graphical user interface, one has to consult the corresponding guidelines on designing dialogs and the overall requirements for human–computer interaction (Karwowski, 2005). The International Standardization Organization (ISO) is the highest instance in the hierarchy of industrial, national, and international bodies involved in regulation of human interaction and work with artifacts. In specific situations, one should consult standards developed by other institutions, such as the Commission Internationale de l'Éclairage (CIE) which is the authority on light, illumination, color, and color spaces.

Even if the application of standards is not immediately possible, the theoretical and empirical development of human factors and ergonomics allows analysis of artifacts by use of known principles and data without carrying out experimental research. For example, there is sufficient documented knowledge about human sensory and motor systems to make it unnecessary to conduct a new experiment every time there is a need to design a new display or a mouse (Boff, 1986). In addition, there are a large number of reference sources that respond to the growing need for specific instruments and methods for testing the usability of human–system interfaces (Charlton & O'Brien, 2002; Holzinger, 2005). All indications are that the emerging market for information on these tools and standardized techniques will continue to grow at a fast pace in the 21st century.

Experiment

When a system is being designed or evaluated, it is possible to propose several design alternatives. These alternatives can be considered experimental hypotheses and tested by conducting a controlled experiment as is usually done in psychology and in most of natural sciences. In a multivariable laboratory experiment, one can easily change the color and the number of the menu items in a word processor to see their main effects and their interaction on the time that a group of users needs to select an option. The big problem with the experimental method is a trade-off relationship between ecological validity and necessary control of independent variables. As a high degree of ecological validity is of primary importance for ergonomic research, ergonomists often have difficulties in applying experimental methods. For example, when designing a new interface to be used by air traffic controllers, ergonomists are faced with the following characteristics that make it difficult to run experiments: (1) The subjects are experts in implementing the tasks to be analyzed and they depend on their existing skill and knowledge; (2) The tasks are complex and cannot be divided into linearly ordered components; (3) It is impossible to perform a long series of similar trials and preserve the subject's state of attention and motivation; (4) The behavior is complex and cannot be decomposed, so that simple imposed answers do not interfere with higher-order, cognitive components of behavior; (5) Implementation of the tasks to be studied depends on the overall situation that cannot always be repeated; and (7) The tasks are distributed among several people, each one with her or his own role, so that the complexity of experimental design and data analysis is additionally multiplied.

Still, there seems to be no method—in the immediate and middle-term perspective—that could better fulfil the task of investigating scientifically based human factors and ergonomic research than experiment. Paradoxically, one can achieve a higher applicability of experimental data by more in-depth laboratory research. For example, the promises of neuroergonomics are related to establishing the brain mechanisms of different forms of attention (Posner, Rueda, & Kanske, 2007). The success of direct diagnostics of their state of activation and the emerging techniques of brain–computer interfaces depends on the progress made in cognitive science. In the longer run, one can hope to replace most real experimental work by running computational experiments with virtual artifacts and users.

Simulation

Simulation of the situation. One way to conduct experimental research and to avoid the problem of ecological validity is by simulating real-world situations. This is what researchers are currently doing in complex situations such as air traffic control and nuclear plant control. Although simulators are used primarily to train people who work in these situations they can also be used to perform experiments with them. Simulators are a powerful tool for experimental research of complex behaviors in the laboratory. With the development of computer graphics and the technology of virtual reality, it is possible to simulate real situations with sufficient psychological validity. Furthermore, since the computers themselves are becoming increasingly present in the actual situation, to work with them is relatively easy. For example, in the control room of a nuclear power plant, controllers work primarily with computers operating keyboards, mouse, and so on. Therefore, to build a simulator of a control room to study these processes, it is only necessary to create computer programs that simulate the events that occur in the plant. The fundamental problem with simulators is that it is not easy to reproduce the emotional stress of real situations.

One can distinguish three types of simulators that can be used in experimental research: entertainment simulators (video games), training simulators, and those explicitly designed for experimental research. The last are often the most appropriate because they have components that the researchers can use to change parameters of the situation that are of interest ot them. These simulators are also designed to reflect how accurate the responses of subjects are and to measure other dependent variables such as reaction time.

Simulation of the human being. Ergonomists study complex behaviors that are difficult to dissect (Klein et al., 2003). They are also interested in a broad range of phenomena to predict human behavior and functional states under sometimes hazardous conditions. In addition, many industrial artifacts nowadays are first produced in a fast-prototype manner, as a virtual mock-up suitable for some forms of usability testing. An ideal counterpart of this partially virtual world would be, of course, a virtual human dummy that implements some of the essential characteristics of potential users. The contemporary efforts along these lines concentrate on the biomechanical and optical features of human beings (Duffy, 2008).

It is obviously more difficult to create computer simulations of the human mind, so that cognitive ergonomists could make predictions about other forms of observable behavior only on the basis of computational experiments. There are two main areas of methodical progress in view of the simulation of cognitive processes and representations. The first area is that of methods of psychosemantics and knowledge engineering (Kendal & Creen, 2007). They are used to elucidate semantic representations an individual or a group have about some domain of activity. The methods can be applied as an early step in building expert systems. Work done within the second area envisages the modeling of human cognitive processing as a whole. These computational simulations usually belong to one of the following global cognitive architectures: ACT-R (Anderson et al., 2004), SOAR (Newell, 1990), CCT (Kieras & Polson, 1985) and EPIC (Meyer & Kieras, 1997). A relatively recent requirement for these models is that they are also involved in neurocognitive testing, delineating a road to a neuromorphic modeling of the user's mind.

Conclusion and Future Issues

Today ergonomics is an established discipline where professionals with interdisciplinary backgrounds work together in designing sociotechnical systems with the common goal of fitting them to human needs and well-being. The work is embedded in the activities of international scientific associations such as the IEA, HFES, and EACE as well as the International Association of Applied Psychology (IAAP). The reports on ergonomic research and applications can be found in a number of well-cited journals—*Ergonomics*, *Human Factors*, *Le Travail Humain*, *Human Technology*, and *Cognition, Technology and Work*, to name but a few. Most of the leading universities around the world offer undergraduate and graduate programs in which students are trained to become human factors and ergonomics professionals. The Professional Standards and Education Committee of the IEA certifies ergonomists, maintains a directory of ergonomics educational programs and provides guidance on the quality of professional education.

The future agenda of human factors research and applications is set up by how technology will be developed and used in society. At the high end of technological development, there will be many options to meet the human factors challenges as they were carefully listed on eve of the new millennium (Nickerson, 1992). It will inevitably come to a further convergence of the basic technologies with the resulting enhancement of human performance (*NBIC Report*, 2006). One can expect that usability evaluation will be soon evolved to a more scientifically based and predictive endeavor. Another expectation is that of a proliferation of completely new forms of interface. Some of them may have nano-dimensions fulfilling their roles within the molecular machinery of human cognitive–affective processes. With a high probability, neuroergonomics will not long have the status of the youngest "science of the artificial" perhaps being combined with something like computational ergonomics. Due to the uneven pace of these processes, there will, however, be regions and domains, where people will still have to perform hard, dirty, unpleasant physical tasks around the clock without proper gratification. Here human factors experts and ergonomists, along with politicians and social workers, should seek to improve the work environment of such individuals by more traditional means (Hancock & Parasuraman, 2003).

All these processes, whether they are directly responding to people's needs or are driven by some inherent logic of development in science and technology, have a tremendous influence on our life. Their future influence on the cultural and political transformation of human society will be comparable with the impact the introduction of the internet and mobile communication have had during the last two decades. By continuing their service to society, experts in human factors and ergonomics will obviously have a particularly attentive look at the human side of our interaction with machines, computers, and other increasingly sophisticated artifacts. It remains to be hoped that their professional efforts will lead to a better fulfilment of human needs and values in the years to come.

Acknowledgment

We would like to thank José Maria Prieto for his expert commentary and editing of this chapter. Our work was facilitated by grants from the European Commission (Network of Excellence COGAIN 511598 and NEST-Pathfinder PERCEPT 043261), the European Social Foundation (Junior Research Group CogITo), the Russian Foundation for Basic Research (08-06-00284a, 09-06-00293a and 09-06-12003obr_M) and the Russian Foundation for Humanities (08-06-00342a and 09-06-01035a).

References

Akoumianakis, D., & Stephanidis, C. (2003). Blending scenarios of use and informal argumentation to facilitate universal access. *Behavior and Information Technology, 22*, 227–244.

Amalberti, R. (2001). *La conduite de systèmes à risques*. Paris: Presses Universitaires de France.

Anderson, J. R., Bothell, D., Byrne, M. D., Douglass, S., Lebiere, C., & Qin, Y. (2004). An integrated theory of the mind. *Psychological Review, 111*(4), 1036–1060.

Artman, H. (1998). Co-operation and situation awareness within and between time-scales in dynamic decision making. In Y. Waern (Ed.) *Cooperative process management* (pp. 117–130). London: Taylor & Francis.

Bainbridge, L. (1983). Ironies of automation. *Automatica, 19*(6), 775–779.

Beach, L. R., & Lipshitz, R. (1993). Why classical theory is an inappropriate standard for evaluating and aiding most human decision making. In G. A. Klein, J. Orasanu, R. Calderwood, & C. E. Zsambok (Eds.), *Decision making in action* (pp. 21–35). Norwood, NJ: Ablex.

Boff, K. R. (Ed.). (1986). *Handbook of perception and human performance*. New York: Wiley.

Brehmer, B. (1992). Dynamic decision making: Human control of complex systems. *Acta Psychologica, 81*, 211–241.

Cacciabue, P. C. (2004). *Guide to applying human factors methods*. London: Springer-Verlag.

Cañas, J. J., Antolí, A., & Quesada, J. F. (2001). The role of working memory in measuring mental models of physical systems. *Psicologica, 22*, 25–42.

Cañas, J. J., Bajo, M. T., & Gonzalvo, P. (1994). Mental models and computer programming. *International Journal of Human-Computer Studies, 40*, 795–811.

Carroll, J. M. (1991). *Designing interactions*. New York: Cambridge University Press.

Charlton, S. G., & O'Brien, T. (Eds.). (2002). *Handbook of human factors testing and evaluation* (2nd ed.). Mahwah, NJ: Lawrence Erlbaum Associates.

Chi, M. T. H., & Roscoe, R. D. (2002). The processes and challenges of conceptual change. In M. Limon & L. Mason (Eds.), *Reconsidering conceptual change*. Dodrecht: Kluwer.

Dowell, J., & Long, J. B. (1998). Conception of the cognitive engineering design problem. *Ergonomics, 41*, 126–139.

Duffy, V. G. (Ed.). (2008). *Handbook of digital human modeling*. Boca Raton, FL: CRC Press.

Endsley, M. (1995). Toward a theory of situation awareness in dynamic systems. *Human Factors, 37*, 32–64.

Garfinkel, H. (1967). *Studies in ethnomethodology*. Englewood, NJ: Prentice-Hall.

Gevins, A., Smith, M. E., Leong, H., McEvoy, L., Whitfield, S., Du, R., & Rush, G. (1998). Monitoring working memory load during computer-based tasks with EEG pattern recognition methods. *Human Factors, 40*, 79–91.

Gibson, J. J. (1979). *An ecological approach to visual perception*. Boston: Houghton Mifflin.

Hancock, P. A., & Parasuraman, R. (2003). Human factors and ergonomics. In L. Nadel (Ed.), *Handbook of cognitive science* (Vol. 2, pp. 410–418). London: Nature Publishing.

Haynes, A. B., Weiser, T. G., Berry, W. R., Lipsitz, S. R., Breizat, A. S., Dellinger, E. P., Herbosa, … Gawande, A. (2009). A surgical safety checklist to reduce morbidity and mortality in a global population. *New England Journal of Medicine, 360*, 491–499.

Heller, F. A. (Ed.). (1992). *Decision-making and leadership*. Cambridge, UK: Cambridge University Press.

Hollnagel, E. (1998). *Cognitive Reliability and Error Analysis Method: CREAM*. Kidlington, Oxford: Elsevier Science.

Hollnagel, E., & Woods, D. D. (1983). Cognitive systems engineering: New wine in new bottles. *International Journal of Man–Machine Studies, 18*, 583–600.

Hollnagel, E., & Woods, D. D. (2007). *Joint cognitive systems: Foundations of cognitive systems engineering*. New York: Taylor & Francis.

Holzinger, A. (2005). Usability engineering methods for software developers. *Communications of the ACM, 48*, 71–74.

Hutchins, E. (1995). *Cognition in the wild.* Cambridge, MA: MIT Press.

IEA. (2000). *International Ergonomics Association: Triennial report.* Santa Monica, CA: IEA Press.

Johnson-Laird, P. N. (1983). *Mental models.* Cambridge, UK: Cambridge University Press.

Kahneman, D. (2003). Maps of bounded rationality. *The American Economic Review, 93*(5), 1449–1475.

Karwowski, W. (Ed.). (2005). *Handbook of standards and guidelines in ergonomics and human factors.* Boca Raton, FL: CRC Press.

Kendal, S., & Creen, M. (2007). *An introduction to knowledge engineering.* London: Springer-Verlag.

Ken'ichi, T., Kunihide, S., & Seiichi, Y. (1997). Structure of operator's mental models in coping with anomalies occurring in nuclear power plants. *International Journal of Human–Computer Studies, 47*, 767–789.

Kieras, D. E., & Bovair, S. (1984). The role of a mental model in learning to operate a device. *Cognitive Science, 8*, 255–273.

Kieras, D. E., & Polson, P. G. (1985). An approach to the formal analysis of user complexity. *International Journal of Man–Machine Studies, 22*, 365–394.

Klein, G., Ross, K. G., Moon, B. M., Klein, D. E, Hoffman, R. R., & Hollnagel, E. (2003). *IEEE Intelligent Systems, 18*, 81–85.

Kohler, P., Pannasch, S., & Velichkovsky, B. M. (2008). Enhancing mutual awareness, productivity and feeling: Cognitive science approach to design of groupware systems. In P. Saariluoma & H. Isomäki (Eds.), *Future interaction design* (Vol. 2, pp. 31–54). London: Springer-Verlag.

Leonova A. B. (1998). Basic issues in occupational stress research. In J. G. Adair, D. B. Belanger, & K. L. Dion (Eds.), *Advances in psychological sciences.* (Vol. 1, pp. 307–332). Hove, UK: Psychology Press.

Leontiev, A. N. (1978). *Activity, consciousness, personality.* Englewood Cliffs, NJ: Prentice Hall.

Meyer, D., & Kieras, D. (1997). A computational theory of executive cognitive processes and multiple-task performance. *Psychological Review, 104*, 3–65.

Nardi, B. (1996). *Context and consciousness: Activity theory and human–computer interaction.* Cambridge, MA: MIT Press.

Navarro, R., & Cañas, J. J. (2001). Are visual programming languages better? The role of imagery in program comprehension. *International Journal of Human-Computer Studies, 54*, 799–829.

NBIC-Report: Converging technologies for improving human performance. (2006). Washington, DC: NSF and U.S. Department of Commerce.

Newell, A. (1990). *Unified theories of cognition.* Cambridge, MA: Harvard University Press.

Nickerson, R.S. (1992). *Looking ahead: Human factors challenges in a changing world.* Hillsdale, NJ: Lawrence Erlbaum Associates.

Norman, D. A. (1981). Categorization of action slips. *Psychological Review, 88*, 1–15.

Norman, D. A. (1986). Cognitive engineering. In D. A. Norman & S. W. Draper (Eds.), *User-centred system design.* Hillsdale, NJ: Lawrence Erlbaum Associates.

Olson, J. R., & Olson, G. M. (1990). The growth of cognitive modelling in human-computer interaction since GOMS. *Human-Computer Interaction, 5*, 221–265.

Parasuraman, R., & Wilson, G. F. (2008). Putting the brain to work: Neuroergonomics past, present, and future. *Human factors, 50*(3), 468–74.

Posner, M. I., Rueda, M. R., & Kanske, P. (2007). Probing the mechanisms of attention. In J. T. Cacioppo, L. G., Tassinary, & G. G. Berntson (Eds.), *Handbook of psychophysiology* (pp. 410–432). New York: Cambridge University Press.

Rasmussen, J. (1983). Skills, rules, knowledge: signals, signs and symbols and other distinctions in human performance models. *IEEE Transactions: Systems, Man and Cybernetics, 13*, 257–267.

Reason, J. (1992). *Human error*. New York: Cambridge University Press.

Salas, E., & Cannon-Bowers, J. A. (2001). The science of training: A decade of progress. *Annual Review of Psychology, 52*, 471–499.

Salas, E., Cannon-Bowers, J. A. & Johnston, J. H. (1997). How can you turn a team of experts into an expert team? In C. E. Zsambok & G. Klein (Eds.), *Naturalistic decision making* (pp. 359–370). Mahwah, NJ: Lawrence Erlbaum Associates.

Scaife, M., & Rogers, Y. (2005). External cognition, innovative technologies, and effective learning. In P. Gardenfors & P. Johansson (Eds.), *Cognition, education, and communication technology* (pp. 181–201). Mahwah, NJ: Lawrence Erlbaum Associates.

Sellen, A., Rogers, Y., Harper, R., & Rodden, T. (2009). Reflecting human values in the digital age. *Communications of the ACM, 52*, 58–66.

Shapiro, D. (1994). The limits of ethnography. In R. Furuta & C. Neuwirth (Eds.), *Proceedings of the conference on Computer Supported Cooperative Work*. Chapel Hill, NC: ACM Press.

Simon, H. (1969). *The science of the artificial*. Cambridge, MA: MIT Press.

Swain, A. D., & Guttmann, H. E. (1983). *Handbook of human reliability analysis with emphasis on nuclear power plant applications*. Albuquerque, NM: Sandia National Laboratories.

Velichkovsky, B. M. (2005). Modularity of cognitive organization: Why it is so appealing and why it is wrong? In W. Callebaut & D. Rasskin-Gutman (Eds.), *Modularity: Understanding the development and evolution of natural complex systems* (pp. 335–356). Cambridge, MA: MIT Press.

Velichkovsky, B. M., & Hansen, J. P. (1996). New technological windows into mind. In *CHI-96: Human factors in computing systems* (pp. 496–503), New York: ACM Press.

Velichkovsky, B. M., Rothert, A., Kopf, M., Dornhoefer, S. M. & Joos, M. (2002). Towards an express diagnostics for level of processing and hazard perception. *Transportation Research, Part F. 5*(2), 145–156.

Vicente, K. (1999). *Cognitive work analysis*. Mahwah, NJ: Lawrence Erlbaum Associates.

Vincenti, W. G. (1990). *What engineers know and how they know it*. Baltimore: Johns Hopkins University Press.

Vygotsky, L. S. (1978). *Mind in society*. Cambridge, MA: Harvard University Press.

Wickens, C. D. (1984). Processing resources in attention. In D. Parasuraman (Ed.), *Varieties of attention* (pp. 63–101). London: Academic Press.

Wickens, C. D., & Hollands, J. G. (2000). *Engineering psychology and human performance* (3rd ed.). Upper Saddle River, NJ: Prentice-Hall.

Wilpert, B. (2001). The relevance of safety culture for nuclear power operations. In B. Wilpert & N. Itoigawa (Eds.), *Safety culture in nuclear power operations* (pp. 6–14). Boca Raton, FL: CRC Press.

Woods, D. P., O'Brien, J. F., & Hanes, L. F., 1987. Human factors challenges in process control. In G. Salvendy (Ed.), *Handbook of human factors* (pp. 1724–1770). New York: Wiley.

Yeh, Y., & Wickens, C.D. (1988). Dissociation of performance and subjective measures of workload. *Human Factors, 30*, 111–120.

Zsambok, C. E., & G. Klein (1997). *Naturalistic decision making*. Mahwah, NJ: Lawrence Erlbaum Associates.

14

Technical Advances and Guidelines for Improving Testing Practices

Ronald K. Hambleton, David Bartram, and Thomas Oakland

The number of educational and psychological tests administered each year around the world continues to grow. Educational reform in many countries has resulted in a major expansion of state and national testing programs—for example, in the United States today, every student from the 3rd to the 8th grade (ages 8 to 13 years) and at one grade in high school must be administered mathematics and reading tests, and at several of these grade levels, science tests too. The result is the administration of nearly eighty million achievement tests each year in the 50 state testing programs in the US. Add to this number several times 80 million tests to account for all of the diagnostic tests that are being given in the US to support the assessment of student progress and it is clear that just in the US, the growth of educational testing in the public schools has been substantial.

More than 50 countries are participating in Trends in International Mathematics and Science Studies (TIMSS) with assessments of 9 and 13 year olds, more than 60 countries are participating in the Organization for Economic Cooperation and Development's (OECD's) Programme for International Student Assessment (PISA) with assessments of 15 year olds in mathematics, science, and reading, and more than 40 countries are participating in Progress in International Reading Literacy (PIRLS). These testing programs too, while not requiring large numbers of participating students, are focused on providing important information to governments to facilitate their own educational reform initiatives, and the findings from international assessments are often the basis for curriculum reform and increasing the amount of testing in each participating country.

We do not know just how well these achievement tests, and tests used in clinical work and industrial testing, are being constructed, adapted from one language and culture to others, administered and scored, and how well the test score information

IAAP Handbook of Applied Psychology, First Edition. Edited by Paul R. Martin, Fanny M. Cheung, Michael C. Knowles, Michael Kyrios, Lyn Littlefield, J. Bruce Overmier, and José M. Prieto.

is actually being used to make effective decisions about individuals and programs. What is clear, on the other hand, is that the testing methodology to support these individual and programmatic decisions is very much on the increase and more statistically sophisticated than in the past: We have seen the transition from classical measurement models and methods to modern measurement models and methods (often called "item response theory"; Hambleton, Swaminathan, & Rogers, 1991) to better construct, equate, and evaluate tests; we have seen the increased use of generalizability theory to better understand the size and importance of various sources of error in testing such as errors due to rater leniency and stringency (Brennan, 2001); structural equation modeling has replaced factor analysis as a framework for studying the factorial structure of tests, groups of tests, and validation (Byrne, 1998, 2001, 2006); we have seen the transition from paper and pencil testing to computer-based testing to facilitate new test designs such as those that can shorten testing times (e.g., adaptive tests) and to support immediate test scoring and score reporting (Bartram & Hambleton, 2006); and we have seen the introduction of new types of items such as those capable of measuring higher-level thinking skills and providing diagnostic information to help improve learning (e.g., Leighton & Gierl, 2008; Zenisky & Sireci, 2002).

It would be tempting to write about all of these emerging advances and provide technical details, but space in this chapter is limited, and others have already written books on many of these same subjects (see, e.g., Bartram & Hambleton, 2006; Brennan, 2006; Downing & Haladyna, 2006; Leighton & Gierl, 2008; Lord, 1980). What we will do instead, is provide overviews of those testing topics that seem especially pertinent or consequential to an international audience of readers.

A brief review of types of tests and test uses around the world is provided in the next section of the chapter. Then, we will touch on several psychometric topics that are having consequences for developers and users of tests around the world—item response theory (IRT), computer-based testing, detection of potentially biased test items (sometimes called "differential item functioning"), test adaptation methodology, and global norming.

IRT has international consequences because all of the major international comparative studies of achievement are using IRT in test development, equating, and scoring, and test developers in many countries are gradually switching their testing practices to include IRT modeling of their test data.

In 10 to 20 years, computers may be the primary mode for administering tests in many countries around the world. Differential item functioning is a general approach for detecting assessment material that may be unfair to specific subgroups of persons such as minorities, females, or the elderly. Unfairness in testing is a major threat to test score validity and so it remains a concern wherever testing is being done. Unfairness is an especially important problem when tests are being translated and adapted for use in many countries. Many of our popular educational and psychological tests are being modified and used in many languages and cultures. Appropriate psychometric strategies are needed and must be used if these adapted tests are to remain valid in all of these different contexts. The topic of constructing global norms for some popular tests remains an important challenge too. Finally, recent International Test Commission (ITC) and European Federation of Psychologists'

Associations (EFPA) initiatives to develop guidelines for informing testing practices, surely one of the important ways for improving testing practices around the world, will be considered.

Brief History of Test Use

Test development and test use constitute one of the most important contributions from the behavioral sciences and may be the most important technical contribution from the discipline of psychology. Lubinski and Dawis (1995), for example, wrote, "The psychological test stands as the most important invention that psychological science has bequeathed to society."

Test development and use began more than 3000 years ago (Wang, 1993) when China developed tests for use in the selection of civil servants. Foundations for modern testing practices were laid during the late 19th and early 20th centuries, given the pioneering work by Fechner in Leipzig Germany, Wundt in London, and Binet in Paris, among others, in response to the needs for tests.

At first, tests were used primarily in Western Europe and the United States to assist research efforts and to identify children with special needs. Today, test use is universal. Most countries use some forms of tests from the "cradle to the grave." Group and individually administered tests are used by a wide range of professionals (e.g., educators, educational policy-makers, researchers, counselors, management specialists, medical specialists, occupational therapists, physical therapists, psychologists, social workers, speech pathologists) to assess aptitudes, achievement, adaptive behavior, intelligence, language, motor, perception, personality, and other personal qualities. The uses have become pervasive, given society's reliance on them to assist in: describing current behaviors and other personal qualities; estimating future behaviors; assisting guidance and counseling services; establishing intervention methods; evaluating personal progress; screening for special needs; diagnosing disabling disorders; assessing vocational aptitudes; helping place persons in jobs or programs; assisting in determining whether persons should be credentialed, admitted/employed, retained, or promoted; and assisting in research as well as various administrative, planning, and evaluation purposes. As seen later in this chapter, test development and use have benefitted from technical advancements in measurement theory and methods (e.g., psychometric methods) as well as professional standards and guidelines that inform both the public and professionals as to proper test uses (Grigorenko, 2009; Oakland, 2004, 2009; Mpofu & Oakland, 2010).

Use of standardized tests with children may be most common: popular constructs for assessment with children include measures of achievement, intelligence, and personality. Measures of perceptual-motor abilities, vocational interests and aptitudes, school readiness, and social development are used, albeit less commonly (Hu & Oakland, 1991; Oakland & Hu, 1991, 1992, 1993). The ubiquitous teacher-constructed achievement tests, ones almost everyone took in school, do not qualify as standardized tests because they are not constructed for use beyond a teacher's classroom and do not have the test administration controls, and other qualities, that are normally associated with standardized tests. At the same time, classroom assessments probably are the most frequently administered tests to children and surely can be counted in the billions each year.

Test use with adults also is common and near universal. Tertiary educational institutions use them commonly to make entrance, retention, and graduation decisions. State and national boards use them to certify and license vocations and professions. Professionals use them to evaluate medical, social, and psychological problems. The business community uses them to assist in selecting, training, retaining, and promoting employees as well as certifying attainment of critical abilities and skills of persons at entry and mid-management levels and above (Bartram & Coyne, 1998a; DiMilia, Smith, & Brown, 1994; Gowing & Slivinski, 1994; Muniz, Prieto, Almeida, & Bartram, 1996; Schuler, Frier, & Kauffmann, 1993; Shackleton & Newell, 1994; Sireci et al., 2008).

Although universal, test use differs considerably among the more than 220 countries. Some conditions external to the psychological and other behavioral sciences impact test development and use. These conditions include a well-established and universally attended public education system that serves children who do and do not have special education needs, perceived national need for a broad range of tests, organizations (e.g., universities, test development companies) that have sufficient professional and financial resources and a willingness to utilize their resources by providing leadership for test development and distribution, the presence of a relatively large and stable marketplace for tests, public attitudes that favor meritocracy over equalitarianism, that emphasize individualism over collectivism, and that value science and technology, as well as holding a positive attitude toward test use. Tests must be seen as reliable, valid, legal, ethical, cost-effective, humane, and helping address important personal and social needs. The positive qualities that impact test development and use commonly are found in Australia, Canada, Western Europe, the United States, and a few other countries. Thus, they have a well-established testing infrastructure.

Some conditions internal to psychology impact test development and use. These include a sufficiently mature discipline of psychology that relies more heavily on science than theory, recognizes the importance of individual differences and the need to differentiate among these differences, has developed specialists in psychometric methods, and has a strong professional association that assumes leadership for developing professional and ethical standards for test development and use. Additionally, a country must have a sufficiently large and motivated number of licensed psychologists, who see value in using tests, purchase them, restrict their use to properly prepared practitioners, and respect copyright by not photocopying test materials without permission.

Conditions external to psychology are less favorable in countries that have or had strong ties to communism or socialism or strongly value collectivism (e.g., People's Republic of China, countries that formed the Soviet Union, as well as Mexico and those in Central and South America). Test development and use generally are lowest among the 22 Arab countries and 55 African countries (Hu & Oakland, 1991; Oakland & Hu, 1991, 1992, 1993). Although South Africa has well-developed testing resources, their use is still somewhat restricted.

An estimated 80% or more of the world's population resides in countries in which locally developed standardized tests are either somewhat uncommon or rare (Oakland 2009). Countries that have few locally developed tests tend to rely on the use of tests developed elsewhere. The practices of translating and adapting these foreign-developed tests into the local language and not acquiring national norms or not examining the test's reliability and validity were and remain common. Additionally, few countries have the strong national association of psychology needed to establish and enforce standards for test development and use (Leach & Oakland, 2007). Lacking these internal resources, the leadership of international associations, including the International Test Commission (ITC), is needed to provide guidance as to the proper ways to develop, adapt, and use tests.

Technical Advances in Testing

The professional journals such as the *International Journal of Testing*, *British Journal of Mathematical and Statistical Psychology*, *Applied Psychological Measurement*, and the *Journal of Educational Measurement* are filled with contributions advancing the field of educational and psychological testing—from highly technical topics such as those introducing new IRT model parameter estimation methods, approaches for assessing IRT model fit, and the development of complex software for item response theory and structural equation modeling, to applied topics such as those associated with methods for detecting biased items in a test, building norms tables, and choosing scales for score reporting. But several topics seem to be especially relevant for measurement specialists and psychologists working in international contexts and they will be briefly considered next.

Modern test theory and practices

The field of test development and analysis has been carried out within the framework of classical test theory since the early part of the last century (see, e.g., Gulliksen, 1950). Many good tests have been constructed, and the fields of education and psychology have been greatly enhanced by the knowledge gained from the test data collected. At the same time, there are several prominent shortcomings of the classical test model. First, classical test models focus on test scores, but test scores are totally dependent on the choice of items in a test—give easy items to candidates and they score highly; give them harder items and they score lower. Descriptions of candidates (often called "trait scores") using item-dependent scores restricts the uses of those scores. For example, candidates taking different sets of items in a test measuring the same construct cannot easily be compared. What is needed is a descriptor of candidate traits that is free from the particular choice of test items that are administered. This would make it possible, for example, to compare candidates to one another, to norms, or to performance standards, even though the candidates may not only have seen different test items measuring the construct, but sets of test items that may differ substantially in their difficulty.

Second, a similar problem arises with item statistics such as item difficulty levels (e.g., p values) and discrimination indices (e.g., point biserial correlations). These very useful item statistics in test development are "examinee sample dependent" and so they cannot be used with any accuracy to build tests when the sample of examinees used to obtain the item statistics does not closely match the characteristics of the population for whom the final version of the test is intended. Sample-dependent-item statistics have limited usefulness in test development unless field test samples match the population for whom tests are being constructed. Obtaining item statistics that are independent of the particular sample of examinees in which they are estimated, has been a long-time goal of specialists in the testing field. The use of item statistics independent of the sample of examinees in which they were estimated would make the functioning of tests in practice to be much more predictable, and lend extra value to item banks used in test development.

But "item-dependent test scores" and "examinee-dependent item statistics" are not the only shortcomings of the classical approach to building tests and using scores. The standard classical test model (with no strong assumptions about error) provides a single estimate of error for interpreting all scores on a test (i.e., the standard error of measurement) but it is well known that errors of measurement are not equal for all examinees, and it would be desirable if individual estimates of error were available. This would add precision to scores for many test score uses. Classical modeling too is hampered by the fact that the modeling is done at the test score level (that is, test score is assumed to be equal to true score plus error score), and this hampers its utility in contexts when item-level modeling is needed to provide greater flexibility in test design. For more information on the shortcomings of classical test theory and classical person and item statistics, readers are referred to Hambleton, Swaminathan, and Rogers (1991) and Lord (1980).

Modern test theory, more commonly known as "item response theory," can overcome the shortcomings described above. Item response theory is a statistical framework that connects, through probabilistic models, the items in a test to the trait or traits that the test is measuring. By modeling the data at the item level, rather than the test level, as is done in classical test theory, the test developer gains increased flexibility. Many specific psychometric models within the IRT framework have been proposed: The Rasch model, the three-parameter logistic model, and the graded response model are three of the most popular, and there are another 100 or so other models that have been developed (see, e.g., van der Linden & Hambleton, 1997). There are now IRT models available to handle just about every type of educational and psychological data including less common nominal response data and continuous response data (van der Linden & Hambleton, 1997).

When an IRT model can be shown to fit the item level data, many advantages are available to the test developer: Item statistics are not dependent on the particular examinee sample used in item calibration, examinee trait scores (sometimes called "ability" or "proficiency") are independent of the particular choice of test items from the domain of items measuring the construct of interest that were administered, and an estimate of the error in each examinee's score becomes available.

Additional advantages include the reporting of items and examinees on a common scale which creates the possibility for optimal test designs (e.g., adaptive testing), and enhanced score reporting (see, for example, Hambleton & Zenisky, 2008). Also, the contribution of each item to measuring trait scores across the trait score continuum (known as the "item information function") is available—a unique feature that is a great aid in test development.

All of these special model features create important advances in testing practices. Item banking is more feasible, test design to meet specific needs becomes possible (e.g., tests can easily be designed to maximize the decision-making potential of a test), optimal test designs can be used to shorten testing time or simply to improve measurement precision, and equating of scores on test forms is easily handled and IRT models may improve test score equating, especially at the tails of the score distribution.

Psychologists need to have a working knowledge today of item response theory models because they are being used in the construction of many educational and psychological tests and large-scale international assessments such as TIMSS and PISA. For example, all 50 states of the US are using IRT models with some aspects of their state-wide testing programs. These uses include test development, the identification of biased test items, test score equating, and score reporting. Many commercially available educational and psychological tests too are using IRT modeling (e.g., the Woodcock-Johnson Psycho-Educational Test Battery, and all of the major national standardized achievement tests in the United States). Finally, technical manuals for tests will not be completely readable by psychologists without a working knowledge of item response theory. Item statistics, field testing, the reporting of reliability, test construction, and test evaluation, are all going to be addressed within an IRT framework in the coming years for many standardized tests.

Computer-based testing

Administering tests at a computer or over the internet is becoming very popular in education and psychology (see Bartram & Hambleton, 2006). In fact, we would predict that the biggest change in testing in the next 20 years may very well be the uses of computers in testing. There are four features of computer-based testing: (1) tests are administered and scored by computer, and candidates have considerable flexibility in when they take the tests, (2) test designs for computer-administered tests might vary from fixed forms (i.e., every candidate sees the same test items, or one of several available parallel forms), to candidates seeing blocks of items (prepackaged to cover the appropriate test content, pitched to a desired level of difficulty and with each one chosen to match a candidate's actual performance during the test) to a fully adaptable test with items chosen to reflect the candidate performance during the test (this is sometimes called "adaptive testing"), (3) the test items may be based in new item formats not available with paper and pencil administered tests (such as test items that may involve audio and/or visual stimuli), and (4) the tests are IRT-based (that is item response theory is used in item selection, and test scoring).

Perhaps a few words about each feature would be appropriate next. As for the first, this is proving to be a huge advantage in high-stakes credentialing, aptitude, and admissions testing. Here, when candidates feel they are ready, they can schedule to take the test they need with the testing authorities. A testing site is selected, the candidate shows up at the appropriate place and time, and the test is administered via a computer. Also, in principle, candidates can receive their scores when they have finished the test. The same advantage applies to psychological tests and other low-stakes assessments. (Note, that psychological tests too might on occasion be "high-stakes" and then the same concerns for test security can be raised.) Later, we will consider several modes in which these tests might be administered.

The second feature has to do with available computer-based test designs. The least suitable in many situations would be the administration of a single form of a test to all candidates. Since candidates would normally take the test on different days, test security would be a major problem with this design. This single-form design would be fine with many psychological tests when test item security is not an issue. Since many tests administered at a computer are high-stakes, it would be much more common to use a test design in which the computer selects items at random for candidates from a bank of available items (subject to content and difficulty constraints), and then adjust the scores for nonequivalence after the administration. It would be easy to control for content during the item selection process. This design is often called "linear on the fly" and has the advantage of test security since the overlap of items administered across candidates can be kept low with a sufficiently large item bank.

Another very popular test design is called "adaptive testing," and here the choice of items depends on how a candidate is performing during the test administration. Candidates doing well are given harder test items; candidates doing poorly are given easier test items. Testing is discontinued when some specified level of score precision is reached for the candidate or a maximum number of test items has been administered. These adaptive test designs often result in a 50% reduction in testing time without any loss in measurement precision. A variation of item-level adaptive testing is to assign blocks of test items (perhaps 10 to 20 items) and these blocks are chosen to be easier or harder based upon a candidate's performance during the test. The special advantage of a block of items design (called "multistage testing") is that candidates have a chance to skip items or change answers to items within the block prior to moving onto the next assigned block of items in the test (Jodoin, Zenisky, & Hambleton, 2006). Skipping test items and allowing candidates to change answers are two features of testing that candidates indicate they value when taking tests and so the multistage test design has become popular with some testing programs (see, for example, the Graduate Record Exam and the credentialing exam for accountants in the US). Again, one of the advantages of all of these adaptive test designs is that tests can be shortened with no loss in measurement precision (see, for example, several chapters in Mills, Potenza, Fremer, & Ward, 2002, and Bartram & Hambleton, 2006).

The least well-developed feature of computer-based testing at the present time, but a feature nonetheless, is the use of new item formats to capitalize on the power of computer-administered tests. It is expected that the power of the computer might permit the assessment of higher-level thinking skills and skills that cannot usually be measured with paper and pencil tests (such as skills that require a candidate to work through a series of steps to complete a problem), as well as enhance the fidelity of testing for candidates. Visual and audio features become readily available as do test items that might require candidates to rank-order choices, provide short answers (that can be computer scored), provide numerical answers, and so forth. For a comprehensive set of possibilities, see Zenisky and Sireci (2002).

Many credentialing exams such as those used in medicine, accounting, and architecture today capitalize on the possibility for new item formats with computer-based tests. More new item formats are being introduced all the time.

The fourth feature is that nearly all computer-based testing applications are IRT-based. Item response models are not only valuable in item selection because candidates and items are being reported on a common scale (and so optimal item selections can be made), but also item response models can be used to equate scores when candidates are not being administered tests of the same difficulty. Computer-adaptive testing with candidates in principle seeing unique sets of items, and sets of items that can vary substantially in difficulty, could not be done easily without the aid of item response modeling for item selection, and test score equating.

There seems little doubt that eventually all, or nearly all, educational and psychological tests will be administered at a computer terminal or over the internet. The particulars of the administration will vary by application. Perhaps the biggest problem to overcome will be associated with test security in high-stakes tests such as those used in selection and credentialing. Constructing large item banks, controlling the frequency of use of particular items in a test, scrambling the order of items and answer choices, and implementing strategies for the early detection of exposed items, are just four of the approaches that are currently being studied for their effectiveness. Without test security, the advantages of computer-based testing will be lost. Fortunately, considerable progress has already been made to address the problem (see, Wild & Ramaswamy, 2008 and Tippins, 2009, and the related commentaries in the same journal issue).

Detecting potentially biased test items

Detecting items in a test that may be unfair to subgroups of candidates such as females, members of ethnic groups (such as Blacks, Hispanics, and Asians), candidates taking the test in a second language, older persons, and candidates with physical handicaps has always been a concern to test developers. Because of the high stakes that are now so often associated with test results, the study of items for potential biases has become about as common as item analysis in the test development process. In fact, item analyses today have been broadened with achievement tests to include item bias analyses considering at least gender and ethnicity.

Today, a whole new set of statistical procedures has evolved for detecting potentially biased test items and they can be applied to items that are binary or polytomously scored (Camilli & Shepard, 1993; Holland & Wainer, 1993). First, it is necessary to identify the two groups of interest—sometimes they are called in the testing literature the "majority" and "minority" groups or other times the "reference" and "focal" groups. Both classical and modern procedures are available too for handling more than two groups simultaneously but they will not be considered here.

In principle, all of these currently popular procedures are "conditional" in that the members of the majority and minority groups must be "matched" first on the trait measured by the test. Often this is done using the total score on the test in which the item of interest is located. Less frequently, candidates in the two groups of interest may be matched on scores on a criterion that is separate from the test in which the item of interest is located (but correlated with it). In the first instance, it is said that an internal criterion is used; in the latter situation, it is said that an external criterion is used. But the use of an external criterion is not common in practice because it is usually more time-consuming to locate external criteria. (The advantage of an external criterion is that it avoids the confounding of the item score and the test score, since the item score is included in the test score. This confounding can be eliminated, but then it is more time-consuming to remove the test item to run the analysis and this must be repeated for each test item.) Quite simply, the test score is convenient, and often suffices, as long as there are not more than a few biased items in the full test.

Basically, after candidates in the two groups of interest are "matched" on the trait measured by the test (e.g., have the same score of 10 on the test), the performances of the two groups on the test item are compared. Since the candidates are matched on the construct measured by the test, the performance of the two groups on the test item should be approximately the same (except for sampling errors). When performances are substantially different, a question is raised about the fairness of the item in the two groups. But these comparisons are not just made at a single test score point, they are made at all the intervals along the test score scale (at each test score with large samples, and at intervals along the test score scale, e.g., 0 to 4, 5 to 8, 9 to 12, etc., when only smaller samples are available). Some type of aggregation of these comparisons of majority and minority group performance across the score scale is made (i.e., summing the group differences at each score point or in each score interval), and then a decision is made about the fairness of the test item in the two groups. Much study has been made of the aggregation of the differences along the test score scale and this has produced a wide array of statistical procedures that have become popular for the detection of potentially flawed test items (e.g., the Mantel-Haenszel procedure, logistic regression, standardization, area procedure, and many more). Sometimes the aggregation is carried out over only the interval of the score scale where the minority group is located; other times the frequency distributions of the majority and minority groups are considered in the aggregation; other times again, curves are fit to the performance data for each group and then compared. There are no end of procedures available in the technical literature (see, e.g., Camilli & Shepard, 1994).

Of course, too, the procedure, whichever one it is, is repeated for each of the available test items. Finally, each item that is identified through the procedure must be studied so that the potential cause or causes for the differences can be hypothesized. Sometimes the differences might be explained in terms of the language used in the test item—it may be less familiar to one group than the other. Another possibility is that the situation depicted in the test item is more familiar to persons in one culture or age group than another. A test item about baseball would be an example. The final disposition of each test item (to include or not include the item in the test) will depend on the reason or reasons that are identified for the observed differences.

These so-called "differential item functioning" or "Dif" studies are now a central part of test development and are usually done during the field testing stage of test development. Failure to identify items that are unfair to minority groups will reduce the validity of any tests in which the problematic items are used. One of the biggest problems with these studies is obtaining a large enough sample of candidates in the minority group of interest. With only a small sample, statistical tests have only limited power to detect problematic items. In these instances, judgmental methods for detecting potentially flawed items become especially important.

Clearly, psychologists need to become familiar with these statistical approaches for detecting potentially biased test items. Historically, the view has been that judgmental review applied to the test items is sufficient, regardless of the available sample sizes, for detecting potentially biased test items, but they are not, because often the causes of the problems in items are subtle and may go undetected with only judgmental reviews. It would take an empirical study to identify these problematic items and so psychologists are encouraged to include both judgmental and statistical approaches for detecting potentially biased test items in their test development work.

Methods of test adaptation

Ype Poortinga from the University of Tilburg in the Netherlands stated that he thought that 80% of the cross-cultural research findings prior to 1990 were flawed because of a failure to adequately translate or adapt the instruments used in cross-cultural research. By extension, Professor Poortinga, one of the leaders in the field of cross-cultural psychology, was also criticizing some of the early international comparative studies of achievement. He was also very concerned about many of the psychological tests that were being used in countries without proper translations and without validation studies to insure their utility. Our own review of this cross-cultural literature and international comparative studies of achievement literature came to the same conclusion. This is why the International Test Commission prepared the *Guidelines for Adapting Tests* (Hambleton, 1994) which are described in more detail in a later part of this chapter.

Test adaptation methodology has advanced tremendously in the last 20 years (see, for a current review of the topic, Hambleton, Merenda, & Spielberger, 2005). No more is it sufficient to use a nonprofessional translator or two to translate a test from one language and culture to another and then back-translate for the purpose of validating the translation—strategies that have been widely used in many countries. No more is it sufficient to expect to validate a test in a second language and culture via the use of a small empirical study using bilinguals. The standards today are much higher.

Today, the cross-cultural testing and research fields benefit from the International Test Commission Guidelines for Test Adaptation with the focus on a two-pronged methodology—the first part incorporates the use of multiple translators in a variety of possible designs including those described as forward and backward designs, and the second part incorporates the use of a variety of statistical procedures for thoroughly compiling empirical evidence to investigate the validity of the test adaptation (Hambleton, Merenda, & Spielberger, 2005). Empirical evidence comes in the form of investigations of (1) the construct equivalence of tests across language and cultural groups (here the structural equation methodology is prominent), (2) method biases such as any biases in the testing procedure due to time, item format, directions, and so forth (these approaches tend to be judgmental), and (3) item level biases (like those described in the last section) due to inappropriate language and concepts. Today, psychologists need to be able to use many new judgmental designs and statistical methods to properly translate and adapt their research instruments for use in other languages and cultures. More about the guidelines themselves will be provided later in the chapter.

Global norms[1]

It is still standard practice to prepare norms for tests using national samples—generally with some acknowledgment to ethnic mix demographics but often with no analysis of the size of effects associated with cultural demographics. However, the notion of "national culture" and the identification, in testing, of norms with nationally defined standardization samples or, more commonly, aggregations of user norms, is highly problematic. T*he unit of analysis* and the level of aggregation of data should not be defined in terms of some arbitrary political construct (like a nation) unless it can be shown that this corresponds to a single culture or homogeneous group.

Definition of the unit of analysis should be tied to the operational definition of culture and the basic notion of relative homogeneity within and heterogeneity between groups. Culture only matters for assessment purposes when it is related to some effect or impact on scores that is a group level effect and which is large enough to result in misinterpretation of individual level scores. Next the topic of global norms will be considered.

Aggregation of Norm Groups Across and Within Countries, Cultures and Languages

The key question to answer in choosing a norm reference group was clearly stated (Cronbach 1990) as "Does the norm group consist of the sort of persons with whom [the candidate] should be compared?" (p. 127). Cronbach made clear that this does not even entail comparing people to others from their own demographic group. In answering Cronbach's question, the test user also needs to consider whether the focus should be on a broad or a narrow comparison. The broader the comparison group, the greater the degree of aggregation required across situational, temporal, endogenous, or exogenous population variables. A norm group could be narrowly defined, for example as sampling 20-year-old white English-speaking males who are graduates in science subjects and who were born between 1980 and 1982, or broadly defined, for example as sampling adult working people tested between 1950 and the present day and working in Europe. More commonly, norms represent aggregations of specific populations.

But what is the use of aggregation across countries? Such aggregation has three features:

1. it has the potential benefit of reducing the problem of country-related sample biases where these are present;
2. it does not conceal effects of cultural differences, which are hidden by using culture-specific norm groups;
3. but it has the potential negative effect, where there are real language biases, of treating apparent country differences as "real" rather than being due to translation bias.

There is not sufficient space in this chapter to go into details of procedures for aggregation, but some guidelines have been suggested by Bartram (2008a). These guidelines describe the formation of norm groups by the aggregation of suitably weighted populations or user norms for a specific purpose. Key to this process is checking that the constructs measured by the test are invariant across samples. It makes no sense to aggregate data from two scales which happen to have the same name but actually measure different things. For complex multi-dimensional instruments, construct equivalence can be checked by seeing if scale variances and scale inter-correlations are invariant across samples (see for example, recent work with structural equation modeling—e.g., Byrne, 1998, 2001, 2006).

Recommended practice

Where more than one language has been used in questionnaire administration or where a single language of administration has been used but the candidates are from different linguistic and cultural backgrounds, this should be taken into account during the interpretation process. This can be achieved through working with local experts who are familiar with the culture. Without this it is very easy to misinterpret behavior or fail to appreciate underlying potential because the person is conforming to unfamiliar business or social practices.

Comparing all candidates' scores to the same (multinational, multicultural or multilingual) norm will accentuate the differences due to the cultural behavior patterns of their background—even though these may be moderated by experience of the different environment. Because the scores are influenced by these arbitrary cultural differences in behavior, the measurement of the level of the underlying trait will suffer. On the other hand using only the individual language norms for each candidate will reflect the underlying trait levels without relating to any differences between cultural norms that may be relevant.

In international contexts, inferences from scores should take into account both factors. In interpreting the score it is important to know whether it shows, say, a moderate or extreme tendency to behave in a particular manner in general (relative to the "home" country norm) and how this would seem in a different context (multinational norm).

Comparison of each of the local language norms with an aggregated multinational norm will show where the average profiles diverge. This information should be available to the interpreter, either through the norm information for the different groups, or through qualitative data on where a particular pair of countries or norms differs.

In summary, for international assessments it is recommended that both local, national, and relevant multinational aggregations of national norms are used and that areas where these give rise to differences in scale scores (such as sten or stanine scores or some other variation of derived scores), should be highlighted and considered by users in the light of what is known about possible sample, translation or cultural effects.

International Guidelines for Testing

Why do we need international guidelines?

In the relatively recent past, it was possible to think of individual countries as "closed systems." Changes could be made in terms of best practice, procedures, and laws affecting the use of tests in one country without there being any real impact on practice or law in other countries. People tended to confine their practice of assessment to one country and test suppliers tended to operate within local markets—adapting prices and supply conditions to the local professional and commercial environment. This situation has changed substantially today. Individual countries are no longer "closed" systems. Educational and psychological testing is an international business. Many test publishers are international organizations, selling their tests in a large number of countries. Many of the organizations using tests for selection and assessment at work are multinational companies. In each country test suppliers and test users are likely to find differences in practices related to access, user qualifications, legal constraints on test use, and more.

Not only are organizations becoming more global in their outlook, so too are individuals. The increased mobility of people and the opening of access to information provided by the internet have radically changed the nature of the environment in which testing is carried out across the world.

Despite globalization, there remain large variations between countries in the standards they adopt and the provision they make for training in test use. There are differences in the regulation of access to test materials and the statutory controls and powers of local psychological associations, test commissions, and other professional bodies (Bartram & Coyne, 1998a, 1998b; Muniz et al., 1999; Muniz et al., 2001). There is a clear need to establish international agreement on what constitutes good practice and what the criteria should be for qualifying people as test users.

There are three key issues in test practice. First, one has to ensure that the tests available meet minimum technical quality standards. Second, one needs to know that the people using them are competent to do so. Third, one needs to know that the assessment process follows good practice. Standards for testing can, therefore, be compared to a three-legged stool: One needs standards relating to the quality of the instruments used; the competences of the people using them, and the processes and procedures followed in their use. If any one of the "legs" is missing, the stool will fall over. Addressing all three issues satisfactorily is the key to using tests successfully in practice.

The International Test Commission (ITC) guidelines

The International Test Commission (ITC) is an association of national psychological associations, test commissions, publishers and other testing organizations, and individuals, committed to the promotion of effective testing and assessment policies and to the proper development, evaluation and uses of educational and psychological instruments. The ITC is responsible for the *International Journal of Testing* and publishes a regular newsletter, *Testing International* (available from the ITC website: www.intestcom.org). Three ITC projects bear directly on the need for international guidelines: The *ITC Guidelines on Adapting Tests*, the *ITC Guidelines on Test Use* and the *ITC Guidelines on Computer-Based Testing and Testing on the Internet.* All these guidelines can be obtained from the ITC website. What follows is a brief description of each of the sets of guidelines.

ITC guidelines on adapting tests

As previously noted, these guidelines focus on the qualities required of tests adapted for use across language and cultural groups. They were developed by a 13-person committee representing a number of international organizations (see Hambleton, 2005; van de Vijver & Hambleton, 1996). The objective was to produce a detailed set of guidelines for adapting psychological and educational tests for use in various different language and cultural contexts. This is an area of major importance as tests become used in more countries, and as tests developed in one country get used in others. Several of the more popular intelligence and personality tests are now available in more than 100 languages (e.g., the Wechsler Intelligence Scales and the Minnesota Multiphasic Personality Test).

Adaptation needs to consider the whole cultural context within which a test is to be used. Indeed, the adaptation guidelines apply whenever tests are moved from one cultural setting to another—regardless of whether there is even a need for translation. Hambleton (1994) described the project in detail and outlined the 22 guidelines that have emerged from it. In the first edition of the guidelines they were divided into four main categories: Those concerned with the cultural context, those concerned with the technicalities of instrument development and adaptation, those concerned with test administration, and those concerned with documentation and interpretation. Over the past several years work has been ongoing on the first major update and revision to these guidelines (see, Hambleton et al., 2010).

ITC guidelines on test use

The focus of these guidelines is on two of the legs of the three-legged standards stool addressed earlier in the chapter: Competence of the test user and good practice in the process of educational and psychological testing. The work carried out by the ITC to promote good practice in test adaptations was an important step towards assuring uniformity in the quality of tests adapted for use across different cultures and languages. The test use guidelines focus on the competences required of the person doing the testing.

The test use guidelines project was started in 1995 (for details, see Bartram, 2001, 2006). The aim was to provide a common international framework from which specific national standards, codes of practice, qualifications, user registration criteria, and so on could be developed to meet local needs. The intention was not to "invent" new guidelines, but to draw together the common threads that run through existing guidelines, codes of practice, standards, and other relevant documents, and to create a coherent structure within which the guidelines could be understood and used.

The competencies defined by the guidelines were to be specified in terms of assessable performance criteria, with general outline specifications of the evidence that people would need for documentation of competence as test users. According to the guidelines, these competences needed to cover such issues as:

- professional and ethical standards in testing,
- rights of the candidate and other parties involved in the testing process,
- choice and evaluation of alternative tests,
- test administration, scoring and interpretation, and
- report writing and feedback.

The ITC Guidelines on Test Use project received backing from national psychological associations around the world and from international bodies such as the European Association of Psychological Assessment (EAPA) and the European Federation of Psychologists' Associations (EFPA). The Guidelines were also endorsed by many European and US test publishers. Copies of the full Guidelines were published in the first issue of the ITC's *International Journal of Testing* (ITC, 2001) and are now available in 14 different languages at the ITC website (www.intestcom.org).

ITC guidelines on computer-based testing and testing on the internet

The advent of the internet has had a major impact on how tests are designed and delivered. For many years, computer-based testing had been waiting for a medium within which to flourish. Just as the invention of moveable type made wide-scale publishing of books possible, so the advent of the World Wide Web made it possible to distribute computer-based testing on a global scale (Bartram, 2008b).

In 2001, the ITC Council initiated a project on developing guidelines on good practice for computer-based and internet-based testing (for details of the development, see, Coyne & Bartram, 2006). As for the ITC Guidelines on Test Use, the aim was not to "invent" new guidelines but to draw together common themes that ran through existing guidelines, codes of practice, standards, research papers, and other sources, and to create a coherent structure within which these guidelines could be used and understood. Furthermore, the aim was to focus on the development of guidelines specific to computer-based and internet-based testing, not to reiterate good practice issues in testing in general. Clearly, any form of testing and assessment should conform to good practice issues regardless of the method of presentation.

These guidelines were intended to complement the existing ITC Guidelines on Test Use and on Test Adaptation, with a specific focus on computer-based and internet-delivered testing.

Contributions to the guidelines were made by educational and psychological testing specialists, including test designers, test developers, test publishers, and test users drawn from a number of countries. Many of these contributions came through the ITC Conference held in Winchester, UK in 2002 (subsequently published in Bartram & Hambleton, 2006). The Guidelines were completed in 2005 (ITC, 2006). They incorporated material from the report of the APA Task Force on Testing on the Internet (Naglieri et al., 2004) as well as building on other relevant guidelines, such as the ATP Guidelines on Computer-based Testing (Association of Test Publishers, 2002).

The ITC guidelines addressed four main issues:

1. Technology—ensuring that the technical aspects of CBT/Internet testing were considered, especially in relation to the hardware and software required to carry out the testing.
2. Quality—ensuring and assuring the quality of testing and test materials and ensuring good practice throughout the testing process.
3. Control—controlling the delivery of tests, test-taker authentication, and prior practice.
4. Security—security of the testing materials, privacy, data protection, and confidentiality.

Each of these is considered from three perspectives in terms of the responsibilities of:

1. The test developer
2. The test publisher
3. The test user.

In addition, a guide for test takers was prepared.

A key feature of the Guidelines is the differentiation of four different modes of test administration:

1. Open mode—Where there is no direct human supervision of the assessment session. Internet-based tests without any requirement for registration can be considered an example of this mode of administration.
2. Controlled mode—Remote administration where the test is made available only to known test-takers. In internet tests, such tests require test-takers to obtain a logon username and password. These often are designed to operate on a one-time-only basis.
3. Supervised (Proctored) mode—Where there is a level of direct human supervision over test-taking conditions. For internet testing this requires an administrator to log in a candidate and confirm that the test has been properly administered and completed.

4. Managed mode—Where there is a high level of human supervision and control over the test-taking environment. In CBT, this is normally achieved by the use of dedicated testing centers, where there is a high level of control over access, security, the qualification of test administration staff, and the quality and technical specifications of the test equipment.

The main impact of the computer or internet on testing practice within the work and organizational sphere has been on the adoption of "controlled" mode for large-scale assessment in employment testing. This has introduced a whole range of new challenges for test designers around ensuring security of test content, protection against cheating, and methods of candidate authentication (Bartram, 2008b). In the educational context, three of the modes of administration are found: With low-stakes testing such as the rapidly expanding area of diagnostic testing, the controlled mode is used. For many of the high-stakes tests administered to students in the public schools, the supervised mode is being used. For high-stakes tests such as those used for credentialing or licensure, or for tests used in admissions testing, managed mode is the norm. For the high-stakes uses of tests in education, test security is the biggest threat to test validity (Wild & Ramaswamy, 2008).

National and European guidelines

The various surveys carried out by the ITC and EFPA have all shown that the Standards for Educational and Psychological Testing (AERA, APA, & NCME, 1999) have been widely adopted as the authoritative definition of technical test standards. While the US has provided a clear lead in this area, the issue of test user qualifications has not been addressed in the US to the same degree as it has been in Europe. The APA Task Force on Test User Qualifications (TFTUQ) developed guidelines that inform test users and the general public of the qualifications that the APA considers important for the competent and responsible use of psychological tests (DeMers et al., 2000). However, the word "qualification" was used to indicate competence rather than the award of some certificate or license or the outcome of a credentialing process. These guidelines described two areas of test user competence: Generic competences that serve as a basis for most of the typical uses of tests, and specific competences for the optimal use of tests in particular settings or for specific purposes.

Practitioners in the field want to insure that their practices conform to internationally recognized standards of good practice. However, it is not sufficient just to set standards. Having formulated standards, there is a need for independent examination to see whether in daily practice those standards are met. In several countries, initiatives to set up independent quality audit procedures have been started.

The EFPA standards

As noted earlier, standards and guidelines need to cover tests, the people who use tests, and the testing process. The EFPA have addressed the first two of these through the development of test review criteria and test user standards.

The EFPA Test Review Criteria were developed by combining the best features of the British, Dutch, and Spanish procedures in a single document. This and the detailed test review criteria were adopted by EFPA in 2001. The EFPA Test Review Criteria and supporting documentation are available from the EFPA website: www.efpa.eu. The British Psychological Society and Norway have both adopted these standards as the basis for all their reviews and other countries (including Sweden, Denmark, and Russia) are planning to follow suit. The British reviews are available online at www.psychtesting.org.uk.

EFPA in conjunction with the European Association of Work and Organizational Psychologists (EAWOP) has also developed a European set of standards defining test user competence. The ITC Guidelines on Test Use were used as the framework for these standards. The EFPA standards are now being used as the basis for a major review in the UK of the British Psychological Society (BPS) standards for test use and also form the basis for work in Sweden, Norway, Spain, the Netherlands, and Denmark on the development of competence-based test user certification procedures. Plans are now under way to establish a European system for the accreditation of national test user certification schemes that meet the EFPA standards.

Guidelines and standards for the assessment process

The third leg of the three-legged test standards stool is that of good practice in how testing is carried out. While much of this is covered in the standards and guidelines for test users, a focus on good practice in the delivery of tests has been addressed as an issue on its own. The European Association of Psychological Assessment (EAPA) set up a Task Force under the direction of Professor Rocio Fernandez-Ballesteros to develop Guidelines for the Assessment Process (GAP: Fernandez-Ballesteros, 1997; Fernandez-Ballesteros et al., 2001). The results of this work are a set of guidelines that look broadly at assessment as a process, particularly as a clinical intervention, rather than just focusing on tests and testing.

In Germany, work was also focused on looking at assessment as a process. The focus there was rather narrower than the GAP project, concentrating on assessment for selection and recruitment. Ackerschott (2000) reported that 80% to 90% of work-related psychological assessment services in Germany, as in most other countries, are provided by nonpsychologists with a wide range of different backgrounds in terms of skill and experience. He noted that there is currently no control or regulation regarding the quality of the services they provide. The test commission of the Federation of German Psychologists Associations (BDP) initiated the DIN 33430 project by applying to the German Association of Standardization (DIN) for a standard covering assessment in work and organizational settings. Subsequently this became the starting point in 2007 for an International Organization for Standardization (ISO) project. This project has been contributed to by most of those involved in the developments of the various national and international standards and guidelines reviewed above. The outcome of this work, ISO 10667, is due for publication by 2011.

Summary regarding international testing guidelines

A great deal of progress has been made in the development and dissemination of standards and guidelines to help improve testing and test use. The three sets of ITC Guidelines have rapidly become accepted as defining the international framework within which local test standards should fit, and onto which they should be mapped. Countries have explored and are exploring different ways of delivering quality, through test reviewing and registration, test user training, accreditation of service delivery procedures, and the establishment of test institutes. The ITC and EFPA will continue to work together to pick up on these national and regional developments and take forward their roles of providing internationally agreed frameworks within which local diversity can be accommodated.

Conclusions

Several trends in testing seem clear and these were the ones we emphasized in this chapter. First, the amount of testing is very much on the increase across the world—this increase is seen in educational testing especially, but also in psychological testing. At the same time, technological advances are changing the nature of that increased testing. New testing models associated with item response theory are influencing many of the technical advances—see, for example, approaches for test development and evaluation, score equating, the detection of biased test items, test scoring, and test score reporting.

Perhaps even more influential in the future will be the applications of computers and computer technology to testing. With access to computers and the internet for test administrations, new test designs such as adaptive testing are being introduced. New computer technology is changing the way we are going to be building (e.g., automated test construction) and scoring tests (e.g., automated scoring of constructed response items), and is influencing what it is we can measure (e.g., higher-order thinking skills, problem-solving skills, etc.). For a much more comprehensive review of the field of testing and where developments are moving, readers are encouraged to read Brennan (2006) and Downing and Haladyna (2006).

We were also pleased to report the availability of a wide array of guidelines for testing—for adapting tests, for test use, and for the testing process itself. The field is well served by guidelines from the AERA, APA, and NCME in the US, the three sets of ITC guidelines, as well as guidelines from the BPS, EFPA, and the EAPA. At the same time, with many changes coming in the testing field, and with many complaints already about the relatively poor training of psychologists in some countries in the area of assessment theory and practices, the time has certainly arrived to do something to increase the level of assessment competence. Perhaps this is one of the areas in which international organizations such as the International Association of Applied Psychology (IAAP), EFPA, EAPA, and the ITC can take leadership by (1) imposing higher expectations on all of those people involved in producing tests and using assessments, (2) designing and implementing training programs and other activities to increase the level of technical training in the assessment field, and (3) supporting the wider use of guidelines already available for improving testing practices.

Note

1 This section is an update of material that appeared in a paper by Byrne et al. (2009).

References

Ackerschott, H. (2000). *Standards in testing and assessment: DIN 33430.* Paper presented at the Second International Congress on Licensure, Certification and Credentialing of Psychologists, Oslo, Norway.

American Educational Research Association, American Psychological Association, & National Council on Measurement in Education. (1999). *Standards for educational and psychological testing.* Washington DC: American Educational Research Association.

Association of Test Publishers. (2002). Guidelines for computer-based testing. Retrieved from the Association of Test Publishers' website: www.testpublishers.org/documents.htm

Bartram, D. (1996). Test qualifications and test use in the UK: The competence approach. *European Journal of Psychological Assessment, 12*, 62–71.

Bartram, D. (2001). The development of international guidelines on test use: The International Test Commission Project. *International Journal of Testing, 1*, 33–53.

Bartram, D. (2008a). Global norms: Towards some guidelines for aggregating personality norms across countries. *International Journal of Testing, 8*, 315–333.

Bartram, D. (2008b). The advantages and disadvantages of online testing. In S. Cartwright & C. L. Cooper (Eds.), *The Oxford handbook of personnel psychology* (pp. 234–260). Oxford: Oxford University Press.

Bartram, D., & Coyne, I. (1998a). Variations in national patterns for testing and test use: The ITC/EFPPA international survey. *European Journal of Psychological Assessment, 4*, 249–260.

Bartram, D., & Coyne, I. (1998b). The ITC/EFPPA survey of testing and test use within Europe. In *Proceedings of the British Psychological Society's Occupational Psychology Conference* (pp. 197–201). Leicester, UK: British Psychological Society.

Bartram, D., & Hambleton, R. K. (Eds.). (2006). *Computer-based testing and the Internet.* Chichester, UK: John Wiley & Sons.

Brennan, R. L. (2001). *Generalizability theory.* New York: Springer-Verlag.

Brennan, R. L. (Ed.). (2006). *Educational measurement* (4th ed.). Westport, CT: Greenwood Publishing Group.

Byrne, B. M. (1998). *Structural equation modeling with LISREL, PRELIS, and SIMPLIS: Basic concepts, applications, and programming.* Mahwah, NJ: Erlbaum.

Byrne, B. M. (2001). *Structural equation modeling with AMOS: Basic concepts, applications, and programming.* Mahwah, NJ: Erlbaum.

Byrne, B. M. (2006). *Structural equation modeling with EQS: Basic concepts, applications, and programming.* Mahwah, NJ: Erlbaum.

Byrne, B. M., Oakland, T., Leong, F. T. L., van de Vijver, F. J. R., Hambleton, R. K., Cheung, F. M., & Bartram, D. (2009). A critical analysis of cross-cultural research and testing practices: Implications for improved education and training in psychology. *Training and Education in Professional Psychology, 3*, 94–105.

Camilli, G., & Shepard, L. (1994). *Methods for identifying biased test items.* Thousand Oaks, CA: Sage Publications.

Coyne, I., & Bartram, D. (2006). Design and development of the ITC Guidelines on Computer-Based and Internet-Delivered Testing. *International Journal of Testing, 6,* 133–142.

Cronbach, L. J. (1990). *Essentials of psychological testing* (5th ed.). New York: Harper and Row.

DeMers, S. Y., Turner, S. M., Andberg, M., Foote, W., Hough, L., Ivnik, R., … Rey-Casserly, C. M. (2000). *Report of the Task Force on Test User Qualifications.* Washington, D.C.: Practice and Science Directorates, American Psychological Association.

DiMilia, L., Smith, P. A., & Brown, D. F. (1994). Management selection in Australia: A comparison with British and French findings. *International Journal of Selection and Assessment, 2,* 80–90.

Downing, S., & Haladyna, T. (Eds.). (2006). *Handbook of test development.* Mahwah, NJ: Erlbaum.

Fernandez-Ballesteros, R. (1997). Task force for the development of guidelines for the assessment process (GAP). *The International Test Commission Newsletter, 7,* 16–20.

Fernandez-Ballesteros, R., De Bruyn, E. E. J., Godoy, A., Hornke, L. F., Ter Laak, J., Vizcarro, C., … Zaccagnini, J. L. (2001). Guidelines for the assessment process (GAP). *European Journal of Psychological Assessment, 17,* 187–200.

Gowing, M. K., & Slivinski, L. W. (1994). A review of North American selection procedures: Canada and the USA. *International Journal of Selection and Assessment, 2,* 102–114.

Grigorenko, E. (Ed.). (2009). *Multicultural psychoeducational assessment.* New York: Springer.

Gulliksen, H. (1950). *Theory of mental tests.* New York: Wiley.

Hambleton, R. K. (1994). Guidelines for adapting educational and psychological tests: A progress report. *European Journal of Psychological Assessment, 10,* 229–244.

Hambleton, R. K. (2005). Issues, designs and technical guidelines for adapting tests in multiple languages and cultures. In R. K. Hambleton, P. Merenda, & C. Spielberger (Eds), *Adapting educational and psychological tests for cross-cultural assessment* (pp. 3–38). Mahwah, NJ: Erlbaum.

Hambleton, R. K., Bartram, D., Berberoglue, G., Gregoire, J., Muniz, J., & van de Vijver, F. (2010). *International Test Commission Guidelines for Test Adaptation* (2nd ed.). A presentation at the 7th Congress of the International Test Commission (see also, www.intestcom.org).

Hambleton, R. K., Merenda, P., & Spielberger, C. (Eds). (2005). *Adapting educational and psychological tests for cross-cultural assessment.* Mahwah, NJ: Erlbaum.

Hambleton, R. K., Swaminathan, H., & Rogers, H. J. (1991). *Fundamentals of item response theory.* Thousand Oaks, CA: Sage Publications.

Hambleton, R. K., & Zenisky, A. (2008, July). *A key for valid uses of tests: Making test score reports more understandable and user-friendly.* An invited presentation at the 6th Congress of the International Test Commission, Liverpool, England.

Holland, P. W., & Wainer, H. (Eds.). (1993). *Differential item functioning.* Mahwah, NJ: Erlbaum.

Hu, S., & Oakland, T. (1991). Global and regional perspectives on testing children and youth: An international survey. *International Journal of Psychology, 26*(3), 329-344.

ITC. (2001). International Guidelines on Test Use. *International Journal of Testing, 1,* 95–114.

ITC. (2006). International Guidelines on Computer-Based and Internet-Delivered Testing. *International Journal of Testing, 6,* 143–171.

Jodoin, M., Zenisky, A., & Hambleton, R. K. (2006). Comparison of the psychometric properties of several computer based test designs for credentialing exams with multiple purposes. *Applied Measurement in Education, 19*(3), 203–220.

Leach, M. M., & Oakland, T. (2007). Ethics standards impacting test development and use: A review of 31 ethics codes impacting practices in 35 countries. *International Journal of Testing, 7*, 71–88.

Leighton, J. P., & Gierl, M. J. (Eds.). (2008). *Cognitive diagnostic assessment for education: Theory and applications.* New York: Cambridge University Press.

Lord, F. M. (1980). *Applications of item response theory to practical testing problems.* Mahwah, NJ: Erlbaum.

Lubinski, D., & Dawis, R. V. (Eds.). (1995). *Assessing individual differences in human behavior.* Palo Alto, CA: Davies-Black.

Mills, C. N., Potenza, M., Fremer, J., & Ward, W. C. (Eds.). (2002). *Computer-based testing: Building the foundation for future assessments.* Mahwah, NJ: Erlbaum.

Mpofu, E., & Oakland, T. (Eds.). (2010). *Assessment in rehabilitation and health.* Boston, MA: Pearson, Allyn, & Bacon.

Muñiz, J., Bartram, D., Evers, A., Boben, D., Matesic, K., Glabeke, K., ... Zaal, J. N. (2001). Testing practices in European countries. *European Journal of Psychological Assessment, 17*, 201–211.

Muñiz, J., Prieto, G., Almeida, L., & Bartram, D. (1999). Test use in Spain, Portugal, and Latin American countries. *European Journal of Psychological Assessment, 15*, 151–157.

Naglieri, J. A., Drasgow, F., Schmit, M., Handler, L., Prifitera, A., Margolis, A., & Velasquez, R. (2004). Psychological testing on the Internet: New problems, old issues. *American Psychologist, 59*, 152–162.

Oakland, T. (2004). Use of educational and psychological tests internationally. *Applied Psychology: International Review, 53*, 157–172.

Oakland, T. (2009). How universal are test development and use? In E. Grigorenko (Ed.), *Multicultural psychoeducational assessment.* New York: Springer.

Oakland, T., & Hu, S. (1991). Professionals who administer tests with children and youth: An international survey. *Journal of Psychoeducational Assessment, 9*(2), 108–120.

Oakland, T., & Hu, S. (1992). The top ten tests used with children and youth worldwide. *Bulletin of the International Test Commission, 19*, 99–120.

Oakland, T. & Hu, S. (1993). International perspectives on tests used with children and youth. *Journal of School Psychology, 31*, 501–517.

Schuler, H., Frier, D., & Kauffmann, M. (1993). *Personalauswahl im europaischen Vergleich.* Göttingen: Verlag fur Angewandte Psychologie.

Shackleton, V., & Newell, S. (1994). European management selection methods: A comparison of five countries. *International Journal of Selection and Assessment, 2*, 91–102.

Sireci, S. G., Baldwin, P., Martone, A., Zenisky, A. L., Kaira, L., Lam, W., ... Hambleton, R. K. (2008). *Massachusetts adult proficiency test technical manual: Version 2.* Amherst, MA: University of Massachusetts, Center for Educational Assessment.

Tippins, N. T. (2009). Internet alternatives to traditional proctored testing: Where are we now? *Industrial and Organizational Psychology: Perspectives on Science and Practice, 2*(1), 2–10.

van der Linden, W. J., & Hambleton, R. K. (Eds.) (1997). *Handbook of modern item response theory.* New York: Springer.

van de Vijver, F., & Hambleton, R. K. (1996). Translating tests: Some practical guidelines. *European Psychologist, 1*, 89–99.

Wang, Z. M. (1993). Psychology in China: A review. *Annual Review of Psychology, 44*, 87–116.

Wild, C. L., & Ramaswamy, R. (Eds.). (2008). *Improving testing: Applying process tools and techniques to assure quality.* Mahwah, NJ: Erlbaum.

Zenisky, A. L., & Sireci, S. G. (2002). Technological innovations in large-scale assessment. *Applied Measurement in Education, 15*(4), 337–362.

Important websites

The International Test Commission: www.intestcom.org
The International Organization for Standardization: www.iso.org
The European Federation of Psychologists Associations: www.efpa.eu
The American Psychological Association: www.apa.org
The British Psychological Society's Psychological Testing Centre: www.psychtesting.org.uk

15

A Century of Psychology and Law

Successes, Challenges, and Future Opportunities

James R. P. Ogloff

> My only purpose is to turn the attention of serious men to an absurdly neglected field [psychology and law] which demands the full attention of the social community. (Munsterberg, 1908, p. 12)
>
> The development of the synthesis of law and psychology will be a long and perhaps a tedious process; but it is a process, however much patience it may require, which for the law will yield a fruitful harvest. (Cairns, 1935, p. 219)

While it is difficult to mark the true beginning of the field of psychology and law or "legal psychology," a conventional marker is Munsterberg's seminal work, *On the Witness Stand: Essays on Psychology and Crime* (1908). The existence of the contemporary field of psychology and law has therefore now passed the first century mark. Given that milestone, it is appropriate and fitting to reflect on the development of the field. Having spent more than 25 years in it, this is a particularly exciting opportunity for me. It is my view that by considering the development and progress of the field, we may be able to identify some successes, challenges, and, ultimately, future opportunities.

To begin, I will consider the early development of the field. Many will be surprised to learn of the rather inauspicious beginnings that essentially led to its demise by World War II. The modern rise of psychology and law really began in the 1960s and has continued ever since. Two areas of research that have led to successes in practice and policy development will be briefly reviewed. The first is an area in which I have worked for many years, the prediction of risk for violence. This area comes from the area of clinical forensic psychology. To demonstrate an example from experimental psychology, I will also briefly note that considerable advances that have been made in the police lineup literature that is derived from the eyewitness testimony literature. Despite the successes, many challenges exist and will be discussed. Finally, the chapter

IAAP Handbook of Applied Psychology, First Edition. Edited by Paul R. Martin, Fanny M. Cheung, Michael C. Knowles, Michael Kyrios, Lyn Littlefield, J. Bruce Overmier, and José M. Prieto.

concludes with a review of some of the factors that I believe are necessary to realize future opportunities for the field.

From a Humble Beginning[1]

As noted at the outset, conventional wisdom suggests that the beginning of the field of psychology and law is marked by Munsterberg's book, *On the Witness Stand.* Although Freud suggested in a 1906 speech to Austrian judges that psychology has important applications for their field (Brigham, 1999), he did not elaborate his views in print. Munsterberg's book was a bold attempt to argue that the emerging field of psychology had much to offer the law. Munsterberg, who is seen as the founder of applied psychology (Boring, 1950; Moskowitz, 1977), came out of the Wundt school of German experimental psychology and spent his career in the psychology department at Harvard University focusing on applying psychology to "real-world" applications including, for example, organizational psychology. In *On the Witness Stand*, he traversed areas of experimental psychology (e.g., memory) and gave examples of how results from those areas could be applied to the law.

The book was met with criticism, particularly in the law where it was seen as pretentious and not grounded in science. In 1909 the renowned legal evidence scholar, John H. Wigmore (1909), criticized Munsterberg's work in a satire published in the *Illinois Law Review*. Wigmore's criticism, reflecting the sentiment of many other legal scholars, was that Munsterberg's claims were exaggerated, and that psychology had not ascertained the data necessary to support Munsterberg's criticisms of the law. In his satire, Wigmore subjected Munsterberg's work to the scrutiny of cross-examination in a mock libel trial in which Munsterberg was accused of claiming more than his science could support or offer. Not surprisingly, Munsterberg was found guilty of exaggerating his claims (Ogloff, Tomkins, & Bersoff, 1996).

Not only did *On the Witness Stand* receive criticism from those in the law, it was not well received in psychology or other social sciences. It was not embraced in any publication. Munsterberg's ideas—particularly the notion about developing a field of applied psychology—were criticized by none other than the early psychology luminary Professor Titchener (see Cairns, 1935). Titchener held firmly, as was the prevailing sense at the time, that psychology should remain pure and scientific, and should not be concerned with the application of its findings. Even Cairns, in his book, *Law and the Social Sciences*, argued for the advancement of social science, including psychology, in the law. There, he referred to Munsterberg's book as a "rash and presumptuous little book" (Cairns, 1935, p. 169). Only those who have attempted to trace back the roots of this field have signified the foresight that Munsterberg had (e.g., Loh, 1981; Ogloff, 2000, 2001).

Interestingly, while Wigmore's (1909) criticism of Munsterberg (1908) is widely known and cited, the fact is that in his article Professor Wigmore pointed out that while psychology had little to offer the law at that time, the law would pay attention to relevant psychological findings when they became available. Ironically, then, the ideological concerns of Titchener and those who shared his sentiments likely did as much to hold back the application of psychology to the law as did the law's own reticence to open its arms to psychology. Despite its age, the following quotation by Cairns remains apropos:

> When a court lays down a rule of conduct which has a purely psychological content, it is no perversion of the method of science for the psychologist to determine whether or not the rule is psychologically valid. But the belief on the part of psychologists that it does constitute a perversion of scientific method, has been a real obstacle in the path of a synthesis of law and psychology at the points where they overlap. (Cairns, 1935, p. 172)

Despite its tenuous beginnings, psychology and law has developed rather dramatically in the 100 years since Munsterberg's book was published (Ogloff, 2000). In particular, too, developments have been made in the field of clinical forensic psychology—the application of clinical psychology to the legal system (e.g., pretrial assessments, presentence assessments, medico-legal evaluations, offender and forensic patient rehabilitation). This chapter will now turn to issues regarding the definition of legal psychology.

Defining the Field

As a number of terms have been used, often interchangeably, to refer to the interface of psychology and the law, it is important to begin with a discussion of the definition of the field. While this might seem like a minor matter, it has been a vexed and sometimes contentious one (Brigham, 1999). Some of the terms that have been used include: forensic psychology, psychology and law, law and psychology, legal psychology, and psycholegal studies. Conventionally, the field has been referred to as "psychology and law" or "law and psychology" in North America and continental Europe while "forensic psychology" has been more commonly employed in the United Kingdom, Australia, and New Zealand. Elsewhere I have noted that these terms are problematic because they imply that the field is merely some combination of law and psychology (Ogloff, 2000). This is becoming increasing less true since, as the field has developed, it has evolved into a specialist area of both psychology and law that borrows from those disciplines but has evolved a unique epistemology, expertise, and even empirical techniques (Small, 1993).

Another complication is what to call those who work in the field. Within psychology there are any number of specializations, virtually all of which are known by the subject matter followed by the term "psychology" (e.g., child psychology, health psychology, sport psychology, organizational psychology). Those who work in the specialty are similarly known by the term for the subject matter followed by "psychologist" (e.g., child psychologist, health psychologist, sport psychologist, organizational psychologist). Terms that have been employed, like "forensic psychologist," "criminal psychologist," or "correctional psychologist" have come to be commonly associated with the criminal justice field (Otto, Heilbrun, & Grisso, 1990), which is problematic since the terms are too narrow to capture the breadth and diversity of the field. Moreover, with the popularization of all things forensic, particularly forensic science, those of us in the field are forever having to explaining what "forensic" means in the context of forensic psychology.

A term I favor, which is broad enough to cover all areas of law to which psychology can be applied, is "legal psychology" (Ogloff, 2000). This term is not new and is not my own. Rather, books and articles published as far back as the 1920s used this term to describe the field (Brown, 1926; Burtt, 1931; Hutchins & Slesinger, 1929). The term also appears later in influential works such as *Legal and Criminal Psychology* (Toch, 1961). For want of a better term, then, it would be appropriate to label this field as "legal psychology." As I have argued elsewhere, legal psychology has a number of advantages over other names (Ogloff, 2000). It is sufficiently broad to capture all of the applied and experimental work undertaken by those in the field. It recognizes that the field is more than some combination of psychology and of law. It is thankfully free of unhelpful connotations. The term legal psychology parallels terms employed to describe other fields of psychology (e.g., biological psychology, clinical psychology, cognitive psychology, developmental psychology). Finally, those working in the field would have a common identity since they would be referred to as "legal psychologists."

While legal psychology could be used as the umbrella term for the field, areas of focus within the field could be referred to more specifically. For example, those who work clinically with offenders and/or forensic psychiatric patients could be called "clinical forensic psychologists" (or, I would prefer "clinical legal psychologists" but given the convention, forensic psychologist is probably more realistic). Those who work in the area of research could be known as "experimental legal psychologists" and so on.

Just as there is no universally accepted term for our field, nor is there a consensus regarding its definition. While every psychology textbook—and those of most disciplines—commences with a definition of the field, this has not been the case with legal psychology. This might reflect the lack of consensus, and possible confusion, which exist. For present purposes, it is necessary to have a broad definition to encompass the range and diversity of activities in which those who work in the field engage. The definition I shall adopt here is as follows:

> Legal psychology is the scientific study of the effect of law on people; and the effect people have on the law. Legal psychology also includes the application of the study and practice of psychology to legal institutions and people who come into contact with the law. (Ogloff, 2000, p. 458)

The definition provided adequately covers the breadth of the field. All laws are designed to regulate human behavior. Psychology is the scientific study of behavior and mental processes. Therefore, legal psychology is the field that evaluates the assumptions that the law must make about human behavior, as well as studying the way in which the law responds to the changes in society that require changes in law. Moreover, those who work in the clinical or applied domains assess or treat individuals who come into contact with the law.

While it is particularly ambitious, if we could adopt a uniform name for the field as well as a uniform definition, some of the confusion that surrounds the field could be overcome. Having wrestled with the definition of the field and those who work in it, I turn to a brief overview of the rise of legal psychology over the past century.

The Rise(s) of the Field of Legal Psychology

Strictly speaking, it is incorrect to say that there has been a single legal psychology movement, though many commentators have written so. Conventionally, it is generally believed that the psychology and law or legal psychology movement began in the mid 1960s. Certainly, the field has commenced and evolved to very different extents—and in very different forms—across countries. Even in the United States, where the field has perhaps been most secure, there have really been two legal psychology movements over the past century (Ogloff, 2000). The first movement occurred from the turn of the 20th century until approximately 1940 and the second began in the late 1960s and exists to the present.

In brief, the first of the legal psychology movements was born from developments at the end of the 19th century in American academic law and jurisprudence that moved away from "black letter" or "formalist" law to law that makes reference to, and incorporates the consideration of, social movements and individuals (Holmes, 1881). Reflecting this view, Holmes wrote that:

> The life of the law has not been logic: it has been experience. The felt necessities of the time, the prevalent moral and political theories, intuitions of public policy, avowed or unconscious, even the prejudices which judges share with their fellow-men, have had a good deal more to do than the syllogism in determining the rules by which men should be governed. (p. 1)

This quotation, and the movement it reflected, opened the door (if only slightly) to information obtained from the social sciences, including psychology. Debates in legal academe and jurisprudence to this day reflect the divide between those legal academics and jurists who adhere to "strict interpretation" of laws and those who believe it is proper and necessary for the law to consider and take into account the experiences and realities of people and society.

The arguments noted above were played out in the United States most recently in the Senate confirmation hearings for Justice Sonia Sotomayor, who was the first Hispanic justice on the United States Supreme Court. During her confirmation hearings, conservative members of the Senate Judiciary Committee asked questions about Justice Sotomayor's views regarding her approach to the interpretation of the constitution. Despite President Obama, who nominated her, praising her by saying she would bring an element of empathy to the Court, during the hearings, Justice Sotomayor stated that she "saw a judge's duty as applying the law, not making it" (Editorial, 2009, p. A20). This is despite the fact that she was previously quoted as having said that "a 'wise Latina' judge could decide cases better than a white man" (p. A20). The Senate confirmed the nomination on August 6, 2009.

The belief that developed in the late 19th century among legal scholars, which insisted that to fully understand the law we must examine and understand the social contexts from which the law was derived and that ultimately are influenced by the law (Friedman, 1985; Purcell, 1973), came to be known as sociological jurisprudence (White, 1976). It was no longer enough to "know the law" by studying judicial opinions, the method that had become the cornerstone of legal systems in North America that were based on English common law. Indeed, Oliver Wendell Holmes (1897) wrote that "for the rational study of law ... the black-letter man may be the man of the present, but the man of the future is the man of statistics and the master of economics" (p. 469).

A number of related movements emerged over time that essentially challenged the law to be aware of social and legal "realities" in coming to decisions and in developing jurisprudence (see Schlegel, 1980; Tomkins & Oursland, 1991; White, 1972). Perhaps the best known and most influential of these groups was the legal realists (Schlegel, 1980).

Notwithstanding Munsterberg's "trial," movements such as sociological jurisprudence and legal realism led to the integration of social science, including psychology, into the law school curriculum. At the same time, too, the importance of social realities were beginning to be recognized by the courts, including the United States Supreme Court in a pivotal case, *Muller v. Oregon* (1908). In this case, which involved a laundry owner who was found to have violated a statute that restricted the workday of women to 10 hours, the lawyer representing the State of Oregon, Louis Brandeis, presented information to the United States Supreme Court in the form of a brief that contained mostly nonlegal materials. Although the material would be considered paternalistic now, the brief included empirical studies and other information bearing on the topic of the effects of excessive work, especially on women. Relying in part on the brief, the Supreme Court upheld the constitutionality of the statute. The term "Brandeis brief" soon became used to describe any collection of nonlegal materials submitted in a court case, and the term remains in use in the United States today.

The legal realism view which emerged in the late 1920s and early 1930s has had a deep and lasting impact on the law, although legal realism had ceased to be a force by the 1950s. Many of the ideas from legal realism have, nonetheless, been incorporated into contemporary legal thinking. From the 1920s until the 1940s, several eminent American law schools included social science material into their law courses. Even more surprising, perhaps, is that psychologists and other social scientists were hired as faculty members in law schools beginning in the late 1920s—despite not having law degrees (Kalman, 1986; Loh, 1981; Schlegel, 1980; Stevens, 1983). As alluded to previously, it is interesting that in the 1920s and 1930s two books were published on the topic of "legal psychology" (Brown, 1926; Burtt, 1931), a phenomenon not seen again until the 1990s. While this pattern was most clearly seen in the United States, similar developments were also made in Canada (Ogloff, 1990).

Despite its promising beginning, the early legal psychology movement did not succeed (Ogloff, 2000, 2001). It is the case that psychologists were working in areas of the criminal justice system and legal system more broadly; however, much of that work consisted of simply applying general psychology practice to people in the legal system. This is quite different from what we now see with specially trained and experienced people working at the interface of the legal system and psychology. The

1960s, however, saw a rebirth of the legal psychology movement, *per se*, which has now grown larger and stronger than was the case in the past (Ogloff et al., 1996; Tapp, 1976). There are now many textbooks on legal psychology, including forensic psychology, correctional psychology, and psychology and law. Legal textbooks typically include relevant psychological information and research. Some law schools now have social scientists on faculty—once again including those who do not have a law degree (Melton, Monahan, & Saks, 1987; Wexler, 1990). There are a range of post-graduate programs in legal psychology areas (e.g., forensic, experimental) in many countries around the world. One cannot keep pace with the plethora of journals, books, and psychological tests that now constantly spring up. National and transnational professional societies have been established and they continue to grow (i.e., American Psychology-Law Society/Division 41 of the American Psychological Association, the European Association of Psychology and Law). There have now been three international meetings of psychology and law societies (the first two included the American Psychology-Law Society and the European Association of Psychology and Law and the third included the Australian and New Zealand Association of Psychiatry, Psychology, and Law). As this chapter was being written, a fourth joint meeting was being planned.

Despite its long history, though, the legal psychology movement has had a relatively limited impact on law, and, until recently, it was focused primarily in North America, the UK, and some European countries. Developments in other countries, like Australia, have come somewhat later (1970s and 1980s). The field is developing internationally. Moreover, the field is still very much the study of areas in psychology that are relevant to law, rather than an integrated study of law and psychology. This is most apparent in the area of clinical forensic psychology, where it is still the case that psychologists are generally trained in areas of clinical and applied psychology which can then be applied in legal settings.

The influence of the legal psychology movement from within law has been less significant. Unfortunately, for example, relatively few lawyers belong to the so-called psychology and law societies. This is in contrast to the beginning of the American Psychology-Law Society, founded some 35 years ago, when lawyers constituted almost half of members. Now, by contrast, there are very few lawyer members who do not also hold a post-graduate degree in psychology. One notable exception—a professional society with a relatively large proportion of lawyers—is the Australian Association of Psychiatry, Psychology, and Law with approximately 20% lawyer members.

Under the legal psychology umbrella, the clinical forensic psychology movement is doubtless the area that has grown most quickly. While forensic psychiatry was established early in the 20th century, forensic psychology did not become established until the 1960s. Its development closely paralleled the clinical psychology movement more generally. Initially those clinical psychologists who worked in the forensic field performed many of the same roles as clinical psychologists working in hospitals and other settings. Accordingly, their work consisted of conducting psychological assessments and treatment of people in the forensic mental health and criminal justice systems. Specialist forensic psychology roles were recognized by the 1970s and 1980s when psychologists, working independently, were able to provide expert evidence in courts. Similarly, the rise of correctional psychology began in the 1980s with countries like Canada and New Zealand, with national correctional services, having hundreds of specialist correctional/forensic psychologists in the employ of the forensic services (Otto et al., 1990).

Having provided an overview of the field and a brief review of its development, I turn now to a discussion of two areas within legal psychology that have realized some degree of tangible success. The examples are in the area of violence risk assessment and police lineup procedures. The former is an example of developments in clinical forensic psychology and the latter in the area of experimental psychology and law. A discussion of successes in these areas is important since it shows, convincingly, that a concerted effort—usually including relevant empirical research—can and does shape the policy and practice of the law. Perhaps valuable lessons can be learned from these examples.

Two Examples of Some Success

The development of violence risk assessment

As the example which follows shows, only 30 years ago very little was known about valid violence risk assessments. There was discordance between the law's expectations—that psychologists and psychiatrists could predict risk accurately—and the reality of the research. This discordance was illuminated in the infamous case of *Barefoot v. Estelle* (1983). Thomas Barefoot was convicted in Texas of murdering a police officer to prevent himself from being arrested under suspicion of raping a three-year-old child. Barefoot had an extensive criminal history, comprising offenses ranging from theft to aggravated assault. Under the Texas legislation, the jury had to decide that if he was not executed he would go on to seriously harm or kill another person. A psychiatrist gave expert evidence at the sentencing hearing suggesting that Barefoot would kill again if not executed. Exactly how the psychiatrist arrived at that conclusion was unknown—particularly since he did not have the benefit of examining Barefoot. The case was appealed to the United States Supreme Court with the petitioner arguing that the application of the law was unconstitutional. The American Psychiatric Association submitted an *amicus curiae* (friend of the court) brief arguing that psychiatrists could not predict risk for violence with any reasonable degree of accuracy and, as such, the law requiring such evidence was unworkable. Relying on logic only a Supreme Court could muster, White, J. wrote in his opinion for the Court that "neither petitioner nor the [American Psychiatric] Association suggests that psychiatrists are always wrong with respect to future dangerousness, only most of the time" (p. 896).

The Court noted further that, despite the poor research findings at the time, "it makes little sense, if any, to suggest that psychiatrists, out of the entire universe of persons who might have an opinion on this issue, would know so little about the subject that they should not be permitted to testify" (pp. 896–897). Thus, based in part on the logic represented in the above quotations, the death penalty was upheld and Mr. Barefoot was executed on the 29th of November in 1984.

As the Barefoot case exemplifies, the law often turns to psychiatrists or psychologists to help it determine what level of risk a person presents. The determination of one's level of risk, though, is a question that is complex and difficult to answer with an acceptable degree of accuracy. As recently as the 1970s, violence predictions were compared to "flipping coins in the courtroom" (Ennis & Litwack, 1974, p. 693). In the intervening decades, the situation has improved considerably, though there is still a great distance to go.

The field of violence risk assessment involves at least three "generations" of development, which demonstrate how empirical research, leading to modification of clinical practice, can help bridge the schism that existed between the expectations of the law and the clinical realities, at the time of Barefoot's case in the early 1980s. Each of these generations will be briefly outlined below.

First generation of violence risk assessment. The first generation of violence risk assessment is known as "unstructured clinical judgement" (Heilbrun, Ogloff, & Picarello, 1999). It was characterized by clinicians using implicit judgment to determine whether an individual was "dangerous." Clinicians were responsible for determining which pieces of information are relevant to the individual case and for synthesising and combining the information to come to a conclusion. Studies conducted to investigate the validity of unstructured clinical judgments showed that this approach was subject to high degrees of error, and that such an approach was not valid (Ogloff & Davis, 2005).

A landmark study by Cocozza and Steadman (1976) referred explicitly to clinical predictions of violence. The researchers followed 257 indicted defendants in the state of New York who had been found incompetent to stand trial during the years 1971 and 1972. Two psychiatrists had assessed each defendant for dangerousness; 60% of them were considered dangerous. Of those released into the community, 49% of the "dangerous" group and 54% of the "not-dangerous" group were rearrested for an offense over a three-year period. Perhaps more relevant to the topic of violence was the finding that only 14% of the dangerous group and 16% of the not-dangerous group were subsequently rearrested for *violent* offences. Cocozza and Steadman concluded that there was "clear and convincing evidence" (p. 1084) of mental health professionals' inability to accurately forecast violence.

The view that predicting dangerousness was a seemingly futile practice was also advanced by the mental health professions. An American Psychiatric Association (1974) task force argued that "the state of the art regarding predictions of violence is very unsatisfactory. The ability of psychiatrists or any other professionals to reliably predict future violence is unproved" (p. 30). This was followed four years later by an American Psychological Association (1978) task force, which similarly stated that " psychologists are not professionally competent to make such judgments" (p. 1110). Nevertheless, mental health professionals continued to be seen as the only people even remotely qualified to assess violence risk.

From his analysis of the fledgling literature, Monahan (1981) identified several errors that were routine in clinical predictions of violence, including a lack of specificity in defining the outcome that was being predicted, ignoring statistical base rates of violence, relying upon illusory correlations (i.e., variables that actually had little or no relationship with violence), and failing to incorporate environmental or contextual information into assessments of risk. To remedy these errors, Monahan (1981) made two specific recommendations: "an increased emphasis on using statistical concepts in clinical prediction, and a heightened sensitivity to environmental and contextual variables" (p. 63). The former recommendation has since been followed with considerable enthusiasm in the literature and characterizes the second generation of violence risk assessment.

The second generation of violence risk assessment. The so-called "second generation" of risk assessment focused upon the identification of appropriate variables for the prediction of violence and culminated in the development of "actuarial" risk assessment tools. In contrast to unstructured clinical opinion, actuarial decision making "involves a formal, algorithmic, objective procedure (e.g., equation) to reach the decision" (Grove & Meehl, 1996, pp. 293–294). Actuarial tools were developed based solely on the statistical relationship between a range of predictive variables ("risk factors") and the likelihood of violence. To accomplish this task, researchers coded a wealth of possible risk factors (e.g., demographic factors, criminal and violence history, psychiatric history, substance abuse history) from correctional and psychiatric files. They subsequently obtained the criminal records of those released and identified who had recidivated violently. Statistical analyses were used to identify those factors that, when combined, most reliably related to violence. Scores on actuarial instruments are related to a probability estimate. This indicates how many people in the development sample, at each particular score or category, were violent during a defined follow-up period. This can be compared to the base rate of reoffending. Aside from the clinical judgment needed to obtain the information for each predictor, the final assessment of risk is purely mechanical when using an actuarial approach (Quinsey, Harris, Rice, & Cormier, 2006).

Actuarial approaches have been found to perform the task of violence risk assessment better than the *unstructured* judgment of the clinician and to do so with adequate levels of accuracy (Quinsey et al., 2006). This holds for several different forms of violence prediction tasks. For example, Hanson and Bussière (1998) analysed 61 studies of sexual offenders and found that actuarial predictions of offending were superior to clinical judgment for sexual recidivism (r = .46 versus r = .10), violent recidivism (r = .46 versus r = .06), and general recidivism (r = .42 versus r = .14). Similarly, Bonta, Law, and Hanson (1998) conducted a meta-analysis of 64 samples of mentally disordered offenders. They found that correlations favored the actuarial predictions over clinical judgment for both general recidivism (Zr = .39 versus Zr = .11) and violent recidivism (Zr = .27 versus Zr = .16).

It can be seen that the second generation of violence risk assessment, based on actuarial prediction, led to more accurate assessments than had been obtained previously. The superiority of actuarial predictions is presumed to be due to two reasons: (1) clinicians seem to experience difficulty identifying relevant risk factors and (2) even when the clinician *can* identify pertinent predictors of violence, they cannot combine and weight them as efficiently as the actuary. There is little doubt that actuarial methods promote predictive validity and reliability, as the task of identifying and combining the predictors is specific and transparent. Regardless of the eventual outcome, the decision-making strategy is plain to see. This contrasts with the use of unstructured clinical judgment, where it is often difficult to determine retrospectively what the clinician was basing his or her decision on. Belfrage (1998) illustrated this difficulty by examining three years of legislatively mandated risk predictions by forensic psychiatrists in Sweden. It was found that 90% of the 640 offenders sentenced to forensic psychiatric treatment were identified as posing a "risk of severe criminality" (p. 59). Considering that the base rate for violent recidivism in this population was approximately 50%, there was a significant overidentification of high-risk offenders. Nevertheless, Belfrage examined the details of offenses, psychiatric morbidity, criminal records, history of violence, substance abuse, and gender, but could find no differentiation between those considered by the clinicians to pose a risk and those who did not. Therefore, the decision-making processes of the clinicians involved could not be determined, even by reference to seemingly common risk factors.

One further advantage of actuarial methods is that the algorithmic procedure ensures that important risk factors are adhered to, with no chance of considering illusory correlations (one of the errors identified by Monahan, 1981). While actuarial methods have strengths over unstructured clinical judgment, some have noted that actuarial instruments developed on one sample can lead to problems with generalizability when applying them to different populations (Davis & Ogloff, 2008; Douglas & Ogloff, 2003; Douglas, Ogloff, & Hart, 2003; Mullen & Ogloff, 2009). The instruments also do not allow for the consideration of rare, but clearly important aspects of the individual case (e.g., individuals with low risk who make realistic threats to kill or seriously injure others). Actuarial measures are generally comprised of relatively static risk factors which are in effect historical markers that cannot be changed (e.g., criminal history, age at first offense). As such, the actuarial measures cannot be used to measure change over time.

The final limitation of actuarial measures is that they are comprised of risk factors that are risk markers, which are not necessarily causally related to risk outcome (e.g., age; Mullen & Ogloff, 2009). Therefore, the measures do not enable an assessor to identify areas that require intervention to subsequently reduce the risk of future violence. This is, of course, not a problem when the task is purely one of predicting violence. However, the goal of risk assessment in the field is not one of accurate prediction *per se*, but of violence prevention and management (Mullen & Ogloff, 2009). If an instrument is comprised solely of static risk factors an individual's level of risk cannot change. Thus, risk management cannot be based upon the variables in the instrument and must rely upon clinical judgment, with all of its previously described biases. These problems of rigidity and neglect of risk management were addressed by the third generation of violence risk assessment.

The third generation of violence risk assessment. The third generation of violence risk assessment saw the conceptual transition from the notion of predicting dangerousness to assessing and managing risk. This necessitated moving beyond measuring risk markers to identifying risk factors that could be targeted for intervention to reduce an individual's level of risk for violence. Dangerousness was previously construed, or at the very least appeared to be construed, as a stable characteristic of the individual (Heilbrun et al., 1999; McNiel et al., 2002; Mullen, 2000). Conversely, risk assessment and management involves the disaggregation of dangerousness into three parts: risk factors (predictor variables), harm (i.e., seriousness and type of aggression), and risk level (the probability of harm occurring). Furthermore, the level of risk was no longer a dichotomous construct (dangerous versus not dangerous) but was thought of in terms of probabilities that could fluctuate over time and under different circumstances (Monahan & Steadman, 1994; Mullen & Ogloff, 2009).

The first attempt toward addressing the fluctuating nature of risk and incorporating some of the advantages of clinical judgment (e.g., flexibility, case-specific focus) into a formal process was a hybrid approach known as *adjusted actuarial prediction* (Hanson, 1998; Ogloff, 1994). In this approach, the assessing clinician obtains a specific probability estimate from the use of an actuarial tool, but subsequently cautiously adjusts the estimate based upon important idiosyncratic considerations. This approach soon developed into what has come to be known as the structured professional judgment (SPJ) approach to violence risk assessment. While this approach has a similar focus to adjusted actuarial prediction, SPJ is not merely a combination of clinical and actuarial methods. Rather, it attempts to incorporate the strengths of both approaches into a single decision-making strategy.

The SPJ approach consists of tools that are professional guidelines for clinical assessment (for example, the Historical-Clinical-Risk Management-20 (HCR-20; Douglas, Webster, Hart, Eaves, & Ogloff, 2002; Webster, Douglas, Eaves, & Hart, 1997), which includes 10 static and 10 dynamic risk factors. Instruments like the HCR-20 include a number of risk factors, both static and dynamic, that are derived rationally from consideration of the violence risk prediction literature. The evaluator must carefully score each of these risk factors from an administration manual. While a total "score" can be calculated, it has no substantive meaning in terms of a probability estimate, other than the fact that a higher score means that more risk factors are present. Thus, assessing clinicians are advised not to sum the items in an actuarial fashion. Rather, after carefully coding each risk factor they make what is considered to be a structured clinical opinion of low, moderate, or high risk. The term "structured" indicates that these opinions are not mechanical, but are nevertheless distinct from unstructured clinical opinion. There is no specified method for making the structured rating (Boer, Hart, Kropp, & Webster, 1997; Douglas & Ogloff, 2003; Webster et al., 1997), which reflects the view that interactions between risk factors are likely to be nonlinear and idiographic (Hart, Kropp, & Laws, 2003). Unlike actuarial prediction, SPJ allows for the consideration of case-specific risk factors that the clinician feels are relevant to the individual (de Vogel, de Ruiter, van Beek, & Mead, 2004). One further development in a recently published SPJ scheme is that of identifying "risk scenarios" (Hart et al., 2003). This draws upon assessment methods that carefully consider an individual's previous pattern of violence, in consideration of known violence risk factors, and is heavily focused upon risk management.

Scores on SPJ measures can be totalled to arrive at an overall risk level score. Using this approach, research evaluating several SPJ instruments has indicated comparable predictive validity to actuarial tools (Douglas, Ogloff, Nicholls, & Grant, 1999). Simply totalling scores on the SPJ risk measures, though, is not how the instruments were designed to be employed. Rather, the clinician is meant to use the risk factors as guidelines to enable structured decision making. SPJ measures also explicitly provide guidance to clinicians for considering low base-rate or other idiosyncratic factors in their consideration of an individual's level of risk for violence. This is very different than the actuarial approach which characterized the second generation of violence risk prediction.

To assess whether the SPJ approach could increase the predictive validity of violence risk judgments, Douglas, Ogloff, and Hart (2003) compared the predictive validity of the HCR-20 violence risk instrument completed in one of two ways. The first approach consisted of totalling the 20 risk factors on the HCR-20 and in the second approach, the HCR-20 was totalled, but raters were able to modify the overall level of risk using their clinical judgment after considering all of the information available. Results of this novel study showed that using the SPJ approach to structure clinical judgment regarding risk for violence produced a significantly greater degree of predictive accuracy than using the HCR-20 scores alone.

These results were striking, since 60 years of psychological literature regarding the prediction of *any* outcome has routinely found that actuarial approaches outperform subjective clinical judgment (Grove & Meehl, 1996; Meehl, 1954, 1986; Sarbin, 1943, 1944). The difference is that the SPJ approach requires clinicians to comprehensively and systematically review valid violence risk factors in consideration of idiographic factors. Subsequent studies have also found that the SPJ instruments are more accurate when used as guides to making a structured "clinical" rating (de Vogel & de Ruiter, 2005; de Vogel et al., 2004; Kropp & Hart, 2000).

The above findings show that a structured approach to clinical decision making can be as accurate, and in some cases more so, than a purely actuarial approach. Previous descriptions of clinical judgment as impressionistic and subjective (Grove & Meehl, 1996) do not appear as relevant to SPJ. Furthermore, using a structured instrument appears to avoid many of the clinical biases identified by Monahan (1981). SPJ schemes encourage specification of the criterion, minimize the deleterious effects of making illusory correlations, and, in some cases, encourage consideration of contextual features.

Perhaps the greater strength of the SPJ approach, other than its predictive validity, is the fact that it can be used to guide and track risk management efforts over time. For example, the HCR-20 (Webster et al., 1997), includes 10 static and 10 dynamic (or changeable) risk factors. Belfrage and Douglas (2002) found that scores on the dynamic items lowered over the course of hospitalization. To this end, a risk management companion manual has been published that details management strategies for each of the 10 dynamic items (Douglas et al., 2002).

Predictive validity of formal violence risk assessment schemes

From the commencement of research attention to the challenges associated with violence risk prediction, the challenge has been to develop risk assessment measures and approaches that can satisfy the need within different areas of the law to determine, with an acceptable degree of accuracy, which individuals present increased levels of risk for violence. Fortunately, some 30 years later, the concomitant increase in research activity regarding violence risk assessment has resulted in greatly increased predictive power. Unlike the "one-in-three" accuracy rate reported by Monahan (1981), the effect size for violence risk assessment is now superior to that of many other health-care activities. This was illustrated by Douglas, Cox, and Webster (1999) a decade ago when they compared the standardized effect sizes of a variety of health-care practices. The effect size for violence risk assessment—at that time—was strong across various studies. This was greater than the effect of chemotherapy on breast cancer which had small effect sizes, or psychotherapy in general, bypass surgery on angina pain, and electroconvulsive therapy on depression—all of which have moderate effect sizes. This certainly does not mean that violence risk assessment is infallible (Mullen & Ogloff, 2009). Nonetheless, it does indicate that the field has clearly advanced over the past three decades to where such assessments can be made with at least a modicum of accuracy. As important, within the law, the assumption that psychiatrists and psychologists can predict risk for violence with a degree of accuracy that can have probative value for legal decision makers has generally been satisfied (e.g., R. v. Peta, 2007).

Documentation of lineup biases and the development and validation of new identification procedures

The example regarding the development of the violence risk assessment field arose from the applied psychology, and particularly the clinical psychology, area. Useful examples of the success of the field of law and psychology may also be drawn from the experimental psychology domain. Arguably the area that has seen the greatest success is research and policy development in the area of the police lineup. Although a narrower area than violence risk assessment, this work has had significant implications, given the countless police lineups that occur annually. Police lineups have been used to assist witnesses in the identification of perpetrators; however, research revealed that a range of errors in police lineups likely led to wrongful convictions. As this section will show, there have been many parallels between research and practice developments in the research areas pertaining to police lineups and violence risk assessment.

Lindsay, Brigham, Brimacombe, and Wells (2002) identified five factors that are important for the successes identified in the eyewitness research area, which includes police lineup research, as follows:

1. The research questions are suitable for examination using the experimental method. This has enabled the illumination of the cause-effect relationships of important variables.
2. There is an established history of research in memory in psychology which has provided a foundation for research in the eyewitness area.
3. Interestingly, they note the criterion variables (i.e., accuracy of recall or identification) are well defined and measurable.
4. Those who work in the eyewitness research area broadly have published their work in high-impact journals in psychology. This has led to the work being well regarded and respected by mainstream experimental psychologists.

5. The work of the researchers has identified an area of law which has experienced serious problems (i.e., mistaken identifications and wrongful convictions).

Two of the above points (1, 2) are unique to legal psychology topics in experimental psychology. The fourth point is virtually always possible in experimental topics as compared to clinical or applied ones where it has been easier for researchers to publish their work in mainstream rigorous journals. Points 3 and 5 above overlap, though, with successful areas of research in applied legal psychology, including as one can see above, the assessment of risk for violence area. These points are important for the success of the field and I shall return to them in the final section of this chapter. Now I turn to a brief discussion of the successes of the lineup research area.

As noted at the outset of this section, police lineups are used frequently and are a routine part of police work. Unfortunately, though, research beginning in the 1970s showed that the identification procedures being used by many police forces led to a high degree of false positives in witness identification using lineups (e.g., Lindsay & Wells, 1980; Malpass & Lindsay, 1999). These findings are remarkably similar to those from the violence risk prediction field, which also found high rates of false positives—but of course in the area of risk prediction. In the case of lineups, there were false identifications, and some of them resulted in false convictions.

As with the risk assessment field, having identified errors in lineup procedures that were being employed, researchers began to undertake studies to investigate the causes of the errors and, eventually, new methodologies were developed and evaluated to increase the accuracy of the lineup practices and procedures that were employed. As summarized by Lindsay and his colleagues (2002), the research identified a number of procedural errors used by police that led to the errors in identification, as follows:

> These procedural biases include structural lineup bias (e.g., the suspect fits the eyewitness' description of the culprit whereas the others in the lineup do not) as well as instructional bias (e.g., failing to warn eyewitnesses that the actual culprit might not be in the lineup) and administration bias (such as cues from the lineup administrator as to which person is the suspect; e.g., having only the suspect wearing clothing similar to that worn by the criminal during the crime). (pp. 204–205)

As a result of the above research, defence lawyers were able to successfully challenge the identification results of many lineups. Further research found that even unbiased lineups resulted in high rates of false positive identifications (Lindsay et al., 2002). Police forces began to carefully evaluate their procedures and researchers turned their attention to investigations of valid lineup procedures. Two significant enhancements that were implemented were found to reduce the false positive identifications and to reduce the false conviction rates. The first modification resulted in the introduction of a "blank lineup." The witness is shown a lineup in which the suspect is not present and is only subsequently shown a lineup with an actual suspect if the witness does not wrongly identify someone from the blank lineup. Another modification that has been successful in reducing false positive identifications has been the introduction of the sequential lineup. Using this technique, police shows the eyewitness only one person at a time, rather than being shown all suspects at once (Lindsay & Wells, 1985).

Based on the above research, and more general research on eyewitness testimony, significant policy developments have been made. In particular, governments have incorporated the research findings into national reports that have led to major reforms in countries around the world. Rarely have developments in psychological research, regardless of the field, had such a direct impact on public policy (Lindsay et al., 2002).

Some Challenges and Opportunities

Despite the example of success in the area of violence risk assessment, there remain a great many challenges for the field and those who work in it. In this section of the chapter, I shall highlight some of those challenges. As the two examples presented above show, considerable success in both research and legal policy has been realized through solid and progressive research endeavors. By now, from an academic and research perspective, there is no doubt that the field of legal psychology is flourishing internationally. There are now more than 10 well-recognized journals in the field, there are literally dozens of textbooks, and there are postgraduate training programs available across North America, many countries in Europe, Australia, New Zealand, and a smattering of countries on other continents (e.g., Asia, South America, and Africa).

In law and policy, though, the rationality of empirical outcomes does not always result in rational policy development. In my own scholarly work, two examples that have emerged pertain to subjects that evoke strong public opinion: the death penalty (e.g., Ogloff, 1987; Honeyman & Ogloff, 1996; Ogloff & Chopra, 2004) and legal attempts to manage sex offenders (e.g., Doyle & Ogloff, 2009; Ogloff & Doyle, 2009; Mercado & Ogloff, 2007; Wood & Ogloff, 2006). In both cases, the empirical evidence raises serious questions about the assumptions underlying the policies that have been developed, yet in both areas the empirical evidence is often overlooked. With respect to the death penalty, a review of the research literature shows that many "common sense" assumptions that underlie the death penalty are not grounded in the empirical reality. For example, there is no good evidence that jurisdictions with the death penalty have lower rates of serious offending than those jurisdictions that have abolished the death penalty. Similarly, the evidence does not suggest that there is any appreciable change in the level of serious violence or homicide in jurisdictions over time as they introduce, abolish, or reintroduce the death penalty (Ogloff & Chopra, 2004). Nonetheless, several jurisdictions, particularly in the United States, retain the death penalty and policy debate is essentially devoid of empirical evidence. The same holds true for most jurisdictions that have abolished the death penalty. Despite the research base in the area of capital punishment that can squarely address the assumptions that underlie the operation and effect of the death penalty, policy decisions are generally made on moral grounds—whether the decision is to retain or abolish capital punishment.

It is the case now that most developed democracies, except notably the United States, do not execute offenders. However, there is a movement towards the post-sentence detention or ongoing supervision of sexual offenders in the United States, Australia, and New Zealand (Mercado & Ogloff, 2007; Wood & Ogloff, 2006). Recent analyses of the assumptions that underlie these legislative attempts—higher rate of recidivism among sex offenders, ability to predict exactly which sex offenders will re-offend—has shown that they are not supported by the literature (Doyle & Ogloff, 2009; Ogloff & Doyle, 2009).

While it is not my view that policy decisions should reflect an Aristotelian approach where knowledge, rationality, and logic always prevail, I believe that in a modern democracy relevant empirical knowledge should be considered when fashioning policy. So, why have policymakers, lawmakers, and the judiciary generally placed so little emphasis on relevant empirical research from psychology? Loh (1981) is quoted as having written, perhaps facetiously, that "the law uses psychology like a drunk uses a lamp post—more for support than illumination." The cleverness of the quotation should not make one underestimate its veracity—it is often the case that the information that supports the positions undertaken by the policymaker, lawmaker, or judiciary is usually rather selectively extracted from the literature. By contrast, contradictory information is sometimes ignored.

I began this chapter by noting the seminal contributions of Munsterberg in his book *On the Witness Stand*. With prescience, he wrote that

> The lawyer alone is obdurate. The lawyer and the judge and the juryman are sure that they do not need the experimental psychologist. They do not wish to see that in this field pre-eminently applied experimental psychology has made strong strides … They go on thinking that their legal instinct and their common sense supplies them with all that is needed and sometimes more. (p. 11)

Although written a century ago, for the most part the quotation could apply to the contemporary situation. Previously (Ogloff, 2000), I suggested that there are two reasons that the law does not incorporate relevant psychological findings into the decisions made. The first, being generous, was that legal policymakers and decision makers may simply be unaware of the work that exists. Second, while being aware of the work in the field and the findings, decision makers choose not to incorporate them into their decision making. In this case, they either question the validity of the findings or show deliberate indifference to the findings. While we cannot force decision makers and policy makers to make law and decisions in accordance with our findings, it behoves us to ensure that relevant findings from psychological research make their way into the public area. This requires more than publishing our findings in so-called "high-impact" journals that might be quite obscure sources for the legal decision maker.

Drawing from the successes in risk assessment and police lineups discussed previously, there are mechanisms that can be employed to help ensure that research findings are considered by decision makers and policymakers. For example, in addition to publishing applied research findings in peer-reviewed scholarly journals with high-impact factors, researchers should take the opportunity to publish summaries of applied work in outlets that are accessible to those who can use them in developing policy or making decisions. Examples include law association or bar association magazines and interdisciplinary journals. Moreover, opportunities should be taken to address lawyers and decision makers at conferences and related fora to apprise them of relevant research findings. Opportunities exist as well for individual experts (researchers and clinicians) to provide expert testimony in cases in which judges and jurors are educated about relevant findings. This process is typically slow going, since individual decisions typically carry very little weight. Finally, interdisciplinary societies that engage members from law, psychology, and related disciplines can serve as an ideal mechanism to exchange information and knowledge. For example, the Australian and New Zealand Association of Psychiatry, Psychology and Law (ANZAPPL) was founded 30 years ago to provide an opportunity for lawyers, psychiatrists, and psychologists to convene to discuss matters of shared interest. In practice this consists across the Australian States and New Zealand in having presentations. There is an annual transnational conference and some states host annual weekend retreats on some relevant topic. ANZAPPL publishes a successful scholarly journal, *Psychiatry, Psychology, and Law*. Although the current membership has more psychologists than lawyers or psychiatrists, there is healthy representation from all three disciplines. In addition, professionals from other relevant disciplines may join the society and often attend meetings and conferences.

The future of our discipline is uncertain; however, it is by now safe to say that it will in all likelihood continue to grow and develop. Much of the development now is expanding beyond North America and the UK, where it has traditionally been strongest. In particular, clinical forensic psychology has gone from strength to strength such that in many countries roles that were once reserved for psychiatrists—such as conducting assessments to determine whether a patient is criminally responsible—are now routinely fulfilled by psychologists. Only recently, however, have those in the area of legal psychology more broadly really begun to develop an integrated approach to the study of the law and legal systems. To a large extent, the success and impact of the legal psychology movement depends on the quality and diversity of our scholarship, and our ability to apply that knowledge to the legal system.

Although the number of psychologists working in areas relevant to the law has grown, the areas in which people work remain relatively narrow, both within clinical forensic psychology and experimental psychology and law. A review of manuscripts that were submitted to *Law and Human Behavior*, a leading journal in legal psychology, shows that topics remain quite restricted to the following areas, in order, of frequency of submission: jury decision making, eyewitness identification, scientific commentary, psychological assessment in forensic psychology, legal attitudes, corrections, legal commentary, violence risk prediction, technical evidence, police, expert witnesses, and psychological interventions in forensic settings (Wiener et al., 2002).

To take full advantage of future opportunities, it will be important to work across broader areas of law where psychology is relevant. The range is really almost limitless within the law since all areas of law make assumptions about human behavior in order for the law to be effective. For example, many jurisdictions, following the so-called "law and order" movement have been enacting legislation to set sentencing lengths in an attempt to reduce judicial discretion. All of this is done, however, based on the assumption that increasing sentence duration will lead to a reduction in offending. However, very little research has been done to determine whether in fact increasing sentencing length actually reduces offending.

Conclusion

Legal psychology is at an exciting crossroads in its development. Unlike the initial movement that began more than 100 years ago—only to disappear a couple of decades later—the past 50 years has seen steady growth in the field. It is particularly appropriate, given the international forum for this chapter and the presentation upon which it was based, to note that while legal psychology may have had its contemporary birth in the United States, it has begun to develop and mature in a great many countries. For the field to remain viable and thrive, such acceptance and advances are necessary.

Given the diversity of names that have been used to characterize the field, it is important that we agree upon a uniform name for the field. I have suggested legal psychology. It is broad enough to capture all of the work that is done within the interface of psychology and the law—including work from experimental psychology and law as well as clinical forensic psychology. It is also consistent with the form that other areas of specialization within psychology take (e.g., child psychology, sport psychology, clinical psychology, health psychology).

As the examples provided in this chapter regarding the assessment of risk for violence and police lineup procedures show, the areas have advanced from both a research perspective and with respect to legal policy. By expending concerted research effort, with appropriate methodology, we are able to influence laws and legal policy in a way that reflects the research outcomes. As noted, however, it is simply not the case that the law, and those involved in development of law and policy, accept our research findings *holus-bolus* and use them where appropriate to support or refute legal policy development. Brief examples from empirical work regarding the death penalty and the post sentence detention of sexual offenders were provided to make this point. The need to ensure that our findings are made available to decision makers was discussed and mechanisms for increasing their visibility were noted. In particular, it was suggested that we publish our work beyond narrow journals that only those in psychology or related disciplines will read. Interacting individually and in professional groups with those who influence the development of law will be important.

Beyond taking explicit steps to ensure that our research findings are known to decision makers, it is my view that we must continue to broaden the topics of our work. As the law affects the lives of people almost infinitely—regulating myriad activities—it makes assumptions about people and how they will behave. As such, those who work in legal psychology can evaluate the assumptions in order to determine the efficacy, or lack thereof, of the law. Therefore, to remain effective and to take advantage of future opportunities, researchers and clinicians alike will need to ensure that they seize upon opportunities that can benefit from the application of psychological knowledge and analysis. Only then, can continued success over the next 100 years be assured.

Acknowledgment

I am grateful to many colleagues who have influenced my thinking in areas related to the content of this chapter. In particular, I would like to thank Gary Melton, Michael Davis, Kevin Douglas, and Sonia Chopra—all of whom have contributed to and influenced my thinking in these areas.

Note

1 These sections of the chapter are based on my previous work (Ogloff, 2000, 2001).

References

American Psychiatric Association. (1974). *Clinical aspects of the violent individual.* Washington, DC: Author.

American Psychological Association. (1978). Report of the task force on the role of psychology in the criminal justice system. *American Psychologist*, *33*, 1099–1113.

Barefoot v. Estelle, 463 U.S. 880 (1983).

Belfrage, H. (1998). Making risk predictions without an instrument: Three years' experience of the new Swedish law on mentally disordered offenders. *International Journal of Law and Psychiatry*, *21*, 59–64.

Belfrage, H., & Douglas, K. (2002). Treatment effects on forensic psychiatric patients measured with the HCR-20 violence risk assessment scheme. *International Journal of Forensic Mental Health*, *1*, 25–36.

Boer, D., Hart, S., Kropp, P., & Webster, C. (1997). *Sexual violence risk-20: Professional guidelines for assessing risk of sexual violence.* Vancouver, British Columbia: British Columbia Institute on Family Violence and Mental Health, Law, and Policy Institute, Simon Fraser University.

Bonta, J., Law, M., & Hanson, K. (1998). The prediction of criminal and violent recidivism among mentally disordered offenders: A meta-analysis. *Psychological Bulletin*, *123*, 123–142.

Boring, E. G. (1950). *A history of experimental psychology* (2nd ed.). New York: Appleton-Century-Crofts.

Brigham, J. (1999). What is forensic psychology anyway? *Law and Human Behavior*, *23*, 273–298.

Brown, M. (1926). *Legal psychology: Psychology applied to the trial of cases, to crime and its treatment, and to mental states and processes.* Indianapolis, IN: The Bobbs-Merrill Co.

Burtt, H. (1931). *Legal psychology.* New York: Prentice-Hall.

Cairns, H. (1935). *Law and the social sciences.* London: Kegan Paul, Trench Trubner and Co.

Cocozza, J., & Steadman, H. (1976). The failure of psychiatric predictions of dangerousness: Clear and convincing evidence. *Rutgers Law Review*, *29*, 1084–1101.

Davis, M., & Ogloff, J. R. P. (2008) Key considerations and problems in assessing risk for violence. In D. Canter & R. Zukauskiene (Eds.), *Psychology and law: Bridging the gap* (pp. 56–81). Aldershot, UK: Ashgate.

de Vogel, V., de Ruiter, C., van Beek, D., & Mead, G. (2004). Predictive validity of the SVR-20 and Static-99 in a Dutch sample of treated sex offenders. *Law and Human Behavior*, *28*, 235–251.

de Vogel, V., & de Ruiter, C., (2005). The HCR-20 in personality disordered female offenders: A comparison with a matched sample of males. *Clinical Psychology and Psychotherapy*, *12*, 226–240.

Douglas, K., Cox, D., & Webster, C. (1999). Violence risk assessment: Science and practice. *Legal and Criminological Psychology*, *4*, 149–184.

Douglas, K., & Ogloff, J. (2003). Multiple facets of risk for violence: The impact of judgmental specificity on structured decisions about violence risk. *International Journal of Forensic Mental Health*, *2*, 19–34.

Douglas, K., Ogloff, J. R. P., & Hart, S. (2003). Evaluation of a model of violence risk assessment among forensic psychiatric patients. *Psychiatric Services*, *54*, 1372-1379.

Douglas, K., Ogloff, J., Nicholls, T., & Grant, I. (1999). Assessing risk for violence among psychiatric patients: The HCR-20 violence risk assessment scheme and the Psychopathy Checklist: Screening Version. *Journal of Consulting and Clinical Psychology*, *67*, 917–930.

Douglas, K., Webster, C., Hart, S., Eaves, D., & Ogloff, J. (Eds.). (2002). *HCR-20 violence risk management companion guide*. Burnaby, BC: Mental Health Law and Policy Institute, Simon Fraser University.

Doyle, D. J., & Ogloff, J. R. P. (2009). Calling the tune without the music: A psycho-legal analysis of Australia's post-sentence legislation. *The Australian and New Zealand Journal of Criminology*, *42*, 179–203.

Editorial. (21 July 2009). *New York Times*, p. A20.

Ennis, B., & Litwack, T. (1974). Psychiatry and the presumption of expertise: Flipping coins in the courtroom. *California Law Review*, *62*, 693–752.

Friedman, L. M. (1985). *A history of American law* (2nd ed.). New York: Simon & Schuster.

Grove, W., & Meehl, P. (1996). Comparative efficiency of informal (subjective, impressionistic) and formal (mechanical, algorithmic) prediction procedures: The clinical-statistical controversy. *Psychology, Public Policy, and Law*, *2*, 293–323.

Hanson, R. (1998). What do we know about sex offender risk assessment? *Psychology, Public Policy, and Law*, *4*, 50–72.

Hanson, R., & Bussière, M. (1998). Predicting relapse: A meta-analysis of sexual offender recidivism studies. *Journal of Consulting and Clinical Psychology*, *66*, 348–362.

Hart, S., Kropp, P., & Laws, D. (2003). *The risk for sexual violence protocol (RSVP): Structured professional guidelines for assessing risk of sexual violence*. Vancouver, British Columbia: Mental Health, Law, and Policy Institute, Simon Fraser University and British Columbia Institute on Family Violence.

Heilbrun, K., Ogloff, J. R. P., & Picarello, K. (1999). Dangerous offender statutes: Implications for risk assessment. *International Journal of Psychiatry and Law*, *22*, 393–415.

Holmes, O. W. (1881). *The common law* (new ed., edited by M. DeWolfe Howe, 1963). Cambridge, MA: Harvard University Press.

Holmes, O. W. (1897). The path of the law. *Harvard Law Review*, *10*, 457–478.

Honeyman, J., & Ogloff, J. R. P. (1996). Capital punishment: Arguments for life and death. *Canadian Journal of Behavioral Science*, *28*, 1–20.

Hutchins, R. M., & Slesinger, D. (1929). Legal Psychology. *Psychological Review*, *36*, 13–26.

Kalman, L. (1986). *Legal realism at Yale, 1927–1960*. Chapel Hill, NC: University of North Carolina Press.

Kropp, P., & Hart, S. (2000). The Spousal Assault Risk Assessment (SARA) Guide: Reliability and validity in adult male offenders. *Law and Human Behavior, 24*, 101–118.

Lindsay, R., & Wells, G. (1980). What price justice? Exploring the relationship of lineup fairness to identification accuracy. *Law and Human Behavior, 4*, 303–313.

Lindsay, R., & Wells, G. (1985). Improving eyewitness identification from lineups: Simultaneous versus sequential lineup presentation. *Journal of Applied Psychology, 70*, 556–564.

Lindsay, R., Brigham, J., Brimacombe, C., & Wells, G. (2002). Eyewitness research. In J. R. P. Ogloff (Ed.), *Taking psychology and law into the twenty-first century* (pp. 200–224). New York: Kluwer Academic/Plenum Publishers.

Loh, W. D. (1981). Perspectives on psychology and law. *Journal of Applied Social Psychology, 11*, 314–355.

Malpass, R., & Lindsay, R. (1999). Measuring lineup fairness. *Applied Cognitive Psychology, 13*, S1–S7.

McNiel, D., Borum, R., Douglas, K., Hart, S., Lyon, D., Sullivan, L., & Hemphill, J. (2002). Risk assessment. In J. R. P. Ogloff (Ed.), *Taking psychology and law into the twenty-first century* (pp. 147–170). NY: Kluwer Academic/Plenum Publishers.

Melton, G. B., Monahan, J., & Saks, M. J. (1987). Psychologists as law professors. *American Psychologist, 42*, 502–509.

Meehl, P. (1954). *Clinical versus statistical prediction: A theoretical analysis and a review of the evidence.* Minneapolis: University of Minnesota Press.

Meehl, P. (1986). Causes and effects of my disturbing little book. *Journal of Personality Assessment, 50*, 370–375.

Mercado, C., & Ogloff, J. R. P. (2007). Risk and the preventive detention of sex offenders in Australia and the United States. *International Journal of Law and Psychiatry, 30*, 49–59.

Monahan, J. (1981). *Predicting violent behavior: An assessment of clinical techniques.* Beverly Hills, CA: Sage.

Monahan, J., & Steadman, H. J. (Eds.) (1994). *Violence and mental disorder: Developments in risk assessment.* Chicago: University of Chicago Press.

Moskowitz, M. (1977). Hugo Munsterberg: A study in the history of applied psychology. *American Psychologist, 32*, 824–842.

Mullen, P. E. (2000). Dangerousness, risk, and the prediction of probability. In M. G. Gelder, J. J. Lopez-Ibor, & N, Andreasen (Eds.), *New Oxford textbook of psychiatry, Volume 2* (pp. 2066–2078). Oxford: Oxford University Press.

Mullen, P. E., & Ogloff, J. R. P. (2009) Assessing and managing the risk of violence towards others. In M. Gelder, J. Lopez-Ibor, N. Andreasen, & J. Geddes (Ed.), *New Oxford textbook of psychiatry* (2nd ed., pp. 1991–2002). Oxford: Oxford University Press.

Muller v. Oregon., 208 U.S. 412 (1908).

Munsterberg, H. (1908). *On the witness stand: Essays on psychology and crime.* New York: Doubleday, Page.

Ogloff, J. R. P. (1987). The juvenile death penalty: A frustrated society's attempt for control. *Behavioral Sciences and the Law, 5*, 447–455.

Ogloff, J. R. P. (1990). Law and psychology in Canada: The need for training and research. *Canadian Psychology, 31*, 61–73.

Ogloff, J. R. P. (1994). Dangerousness and risk assessment. In Correctional Service of Canada (Ed.), *Psychology assessment project: Policy and practice guidelines* (Chapter 18). Ottawa: Correctional Services of Canada.

Ogloff, J. R. P. (2000). Two steps forward and one step backward: The law and psychology movement(s) in the 20th century. *Law and Human Behavior, 24*, 457–483.

Ogloff, J. R. P. (2001). Jingoism, dogmatism and other evils in legal psychology: Lessons learned in the 20th century. In R. Roesch, R. Corrado, & R. Dempster (Eds.), *Psychology in the courts: International advances in knowledge* (pp. 1–20). Amsterdam: Harwood Academic.

Ogloff, J. R. P., & Chopra, S. (2004). Stuck in the dark ages: Supreme Court decision-making and legal developments in capital punishment. *Psychology, Public Policy and Law, 10*, 379–416.

Ogloff, J. R. P., & Davis, M. R. (2005). Assessing Risk for Violence in the Australian Context. In D. Chappell & P. Wilson (Eds.), *Issues in Australian Crime and Criminal Justice* (pp. 301–338), Chatswood: Lexis Nexis Butterworths.

Ogloff, J. R. P., & Doyle, D. J. (2009) A clarion call: Caution and humility must be the theme when assessing risk for sexual violence under post-sentence laws. *Sexual Abuse in Australia and New Zealand, 1*, 59–69.

Ogloff, J. R. P., Tomkins, A. J., & Bersoff, D. N. (1996). Education and training in psychology and law/criminal justice: Historical foundations, present structures, and future developments. *Criminal Justice and Behavior, 23*, 200–235.

Otto, R. K., Heilbrun, K., & Grisso, T. (1990). Training and credentialing in forensic psychology. *Behavioral Sciences and the Law, 8*, 217–232.

Purcell, E. (1973). *The crisis of democratic theory: Scientific naturalism and the problem of value.* Louisville, KY: University Press of Kentucky.

Quinsey, V., Rice, M., Harris, G., & Cormier, C. (2006). *Violent offenders: Appraising and managing risk* (2nd ed.). Washington, DC: American Psychological Association.

R. v. Peta, CA 48/06 [2007] NZCA 28.

Sarbin, T. (1943). A contribution to the study of actuarial and individual methods of prediction. *American Journal of Sociology, 48*, 593–602.

Sarbin, T. (1944). The logic of prediction in psychology. *Psychological Review, 51*, 210–228.

Schlegel, J. H. (1980). American legal realism and empirical social science: The singular case of Underhill Moore. *Buffalo Law Review, 29*, 195–323.

Small, M. A. (1993). Legal psychology and therapeutic jurisprudence. *Saint Louis University Law Journal, 37*, 675–713.

Stevens, R. (1983). *Law school: Legal education in America from the 1850s to the 1890s.* Chapel Hill, NC: University of North Carolina Press.

Tapp, J. L. (1976). Psychology and the law: An overview. *Annual Review of Psychology, 27*, 359–404.

Toch, H. (1961). *Legal and criminological psychology.* New York: Holt, Rinehart, & Winston.

Tomkins, A., & Oursland, K. (1991). Social and social scientific perspectives in judicial interpretations of the Constitution: A historical view and an overview. *Law and Human Behavior, 15*, 101–120.

Webster, C., Douglas, K., Eaves, D., & Hart, S. (1997). *HCR-20: Assessing risk for violence (version 2).* Burnaby, BC: Mental Health, Law, and Policy Institute, Simon Fraser University.

Wexler, D. B. (1990). Training in law and behavioral sciences: Issues from a legal educator's perspective. *Behavioral Sciences and the Law, 8*, 197–204.

White, G. (1972). From sociological jurisprudence to realism: Jurisprudence and social change in early twentieth-century America. *Virginia Law Review, 58*, 999–1028.

White, G. (1976). *The American judicial tradition: Profiles of leading American judges.* New York: Oxford University Press.

Wiener, R., Winter, R., Rogers, M., Seib, H., Rauch, S., Kadela, K., ... Warren, L. (2002). Evaluating published research in psychology and law. In J. R. P. Ogloff (Ed.), *Taking psychology and law into the twenty-first century* (pp. 371–405). New York: Kluwer Academic/Plenum Publishers.

Wigmore, J. H. (1909). Professor Munsterberg and the psychology of testimony: Being a report of the case of Cokestone v. Munsterberg. *Illinois Law Review*, *3*, 399–445.

Wood, M., & Ogloff, J. R. P. (2006). Victoria's Serious Sex Offenders Monitoring Act: Implications for the accuracy of sex offender risk assessment. *Psychiatry, Psychology and the Law*, *13*(2), 182–198.

16

Applied Sport Psychology

Beware the Sun, Icarus

Peter C. Terry

> You have power over your mind—not outside events. Realize this, and you will find strength. (Marcus Aurelius, AD 121–180)

Most athletes, especially those at the highest levels of competition, recognize that their performances are influenced by psychological variables. Tiger Woods, Cristiano Ronaldo, Michael Phelps, Maria Sharapova, and Rafael Nadal have all used sport psychology techniques to enhance their own impressive performance levels. Applied sport psychology, however, is not necessarily about developing sporting titans or even about performance at all. It is, in the broadest sense, about using psychological principles, knowledge, strategies, and techniques to address *any* issue in sport.

There are, of course, many different approaches taken by applied practitioners. Some do see their principal role as promoting enhanced athletic performance via the application of psychological techniques, an approach often referred to as psychological skills training or simply as mental training. Other practitioners tend to emphasize the psychological well-being of sport participants and the avoidance of harm brought about by involvement in sport. Some, depending on their training in psychology, are oriented toward the prevention or treatment of pathogenic behaviors, such as disordered eating or compulsive exercising. Alternatively, practitioners may take a holistic approach toward their clients, implementing interventions to promote happiness, quality of life, and enhanced self-esteem, in the knowledge that such personal development may also provide benefits to athletic performance.

The field of applied sport psychology also varies in scope as well as approach. In many parts of the world, applied sport psychology is seen to encompass the exercise domain, whereas in other countries, such as Australia, the sport psychology community has, until very recently, been reluctant to broaden the focus of its field in this

IAAP Handbook of Applied Psychology, First Edition. Edited by Paul R. Martin, Fanny M. Cheung, Michael C. Knowles, Michael Kyrios, Lyn Littlefield, J. Bruce Overmier, and José M. Prieto.

way. It is increasingly common for sport psychologists to apply their knowledge and skills to other areas of performance, such as business, performing arts, medicine, law, aviation, or the military (e.g., Ievleva & Terry, 2008). Some international organizations incorporate cognate disciplines such as motor development and motor control, but typically, in the modern era, these areas of neuroscience have asserted their independence and no longer fall under the banner of sport psychology.

Sport psychology is a hybrid profession, born out of an uneasy alliance between physical education and psychology. It has brought together individuals from clinical, counseling, organizational, developmental, educational, and health psychology, all with an interest in sport, who have joined forces with those from a physical education, or latterly a sport sciences, background. In essence, it is a melting pot where theoretical perspectives, research paradigms, and applied strategies have been exchanged, initially with mutual suspicion, but more recently with a growing enthusiasm. Although early practitioners were often psychotherapists and psychiatrists with an emphasis on repair of weakness or prevention of pathogenic behavior, sport psychologists have typically come from backgrounds where interventions focused on enhancing existing strengths, fulfilling potential, and empowering athletes and their coaches. In other words, the positive psychology movement started in sport well before it was popularized elsewhere in the psychology world (see Seligman & Csikszentmihalyi, 2000).

Applied sport psychologists tend to work either in academia, teaching into sport psychology programs and supervising the next generation of practitioners; or in private practice, consulting with individuals and/or teams of athletes; or they are employed by organizations responsible for helping to develop and prepare athletes for high-level competition, such as at the Australian Institute of Sport (AIS). In some countries, applied sport psychology is a relatively mature specialization with its own literature, methods, professional practices, and national organizations, where neophyte practitioners progress from specialist postgraduate university programs into an identifiable career path. In other parts of the world, however, applied sport psychology remains in a developmental stage, struggling to establish its identity, demonstrate its worth and create the academic pathways that will allow the field to flourish.

Historical Overview of Applied Sport Psychology

Although applied sport psychology is perceived by many as a relatively new discipline, its historical roots can be traced back to the 19th century and beyond. "Control the controllables" may be a ubiquitous catchcry of contemporary sport psychologists, but it is certainly not a new principle. As the opening quote from Marcus Aurelius demonstrates, the challenge of distinguishing controllable internal influences on physical performance from uncontrollable external forces was understood even in ancient times. Similarly, Smith and Si (2005) have identified that many of the principles espoused by sport psychologists existed in traditional Chinese culture, especially those related to "skill formation, physical competition, competitive tactics, and mental training" (p. 397). It is also freely acknowledged that several techniques taught by applied practitioners to assist physical and emotional control, such as meditation and centering (a refocusing technique using diaphragmatic breathing), have their origins in ancient eastern philosophies.

The birthplace of applied sport psychology is somewhat clouded by historical uncertainty, although its recorded origins lie in Europe. Not only did a publication by Carl Friedrich Koch on the psychology of callisthenics appear in Germany as early as 1830, but experimentation in sport psychology was known to have been carried out in Wilhelm Wundt's first ever psychology laboratory, established at the University of Leipzig in 1879. Many sources give credit to Norman Triplett of Indiana University for having produced the first journal publication in sport psychology in 1898, based on his research into psychological factors in cycle racing. His conclusion that the presence of another contestant participating simultaneously in the races "served to liberate latent energy not ordinarily available" also represents a landmark in the development of social facilitation theory and in social psychology more generally. There were, however, earlier publications addressing the reaction times of fencers (Scripture, 1894) and athletes (Fitz, 1895) originating from Yale and Harvard Universities, respectively. Other landmarks in the infancy of sport psychology included Rieger's case study of the effects of hypnosis on muscular endurance in 1884 and Patrick's 1903 study of the psychology of gridiron football (see Table 16.1.)

In 1908, American researchers Robert Yerkes and John Dodson published their classic paper on the relationship between stimulus strength and rapidity of habit formation. Their experiments involved teaching mice to correctly choose which passageways to enter under conditions of increasing task difficulty, using electric shocks of varying intensities as a disincentive for choosing incorrectly. They concluded that "an easily acquired habit, ... which does not demand difficult sense discriminations or complex associations, may readily be formed under strong stimulation, whereas a difficult habit may be acquired readily only under relatively weak stimulation" (Yerkes & Dodson, 1908, p. 482). This has historically been extrapolated by the sport psychology community as demonstrating an inverted-U relationship between physiological arousal and athletic performance that is moderated by skill complexity. Although the extent of this extrapolation appears rather excessive, the Yerkes-Dodson inverted-U hypothesis has appeared in almost every sport psychology textbook of the past 50 years.

Kornspan (2007) has discussed the influential role in the development of sport psychology played by Pierre du Coubertin, the French aristocrat best known for organizing the first modern Olympic Games in 1896. Not least was his publication of the article *La Psychologie du Sport* (Coubertin, 1900) significant in particular because, according to Kornspan, it may have been the first time that the term sport psychology was used. Coubertin continued to publish on psychological aspects of sport throughout his prolific writing career until his death in 1937.

The world's first laboratory dedicated to investigating psychological aspects of sport was established in Germany in 1920 by Carl Diem, a sports administrator, former athlete, and fervent admirer of Pierre de Coubertin. A similar laboratory was set up by A. Z. Puni at the Institute of Physical Culture in Leningrad, Russia in 1925. Another, more widely celebrated pioneer of sport psychology, the University of Illinois psychologist Coleman Griffith, established the first sport psychology laboratory in America in 1925. He also published two seminal books on sport psychology,

Table 16.1. Selected Historical Developments in the Early Years of Sport Psychology

Date	*Author*	*Development*
1830	Koch	Paper published in Germany on psychology of callisthenics
1884	Rieger	Case study published on hypnosis and muscular endurance
1894	Scripture	Paper published on reaction time of fencers
1895	Fitz	Paper published on reaction time of athletes
1898	Triplett	Paper published on social facilitation in cycling
1900	De Coubertin	*La Psychologie du Sport* published
1903	Patrick	Paper published on psychology and American football
1908	Yerkes and Dodson	Paper published on relationship between stimulus strength and rapidity of habit formation
1920	Diem	Sport psychology laboratory established in Berlin, Germany
1925	Puni	Sport psychology laboratory established in St. Petersburg, Russia
1925	Griffith	Sport psychology laboratory established at the University of Illinois, USA
1926	Ma	Paper published in China on psychological benefits of sport
1926	Griffith	*Psychology of Coaching* textbook published
1928	Griffith	*Psychology of Athletics* textbook published

the *Psychology of Coaching* in 1926—acknowledged as the first ever sport psychology textbook—and *Psychology and Athletes* in 1928. Developments in Asia also started to occur around this time. The first known paper on sport psychology to be published in that part of the world was produced in China by John Ma, in 1926. The paper, titled "Transfer value of sports" in translation, addressed the character-building and personality-development qualities of sport participation, a theme that had been commonly subscribed to by educationalists during the Victorian era in England.

The period of development in sport psychology from 1920–1940 has been labeled the Griffith era (Gould & Pick, 1995). Griffith is commonly acknowledged as America's first sport psychologist, having devoted most of his professional career to the field, whereas the earlier pioneers had tended to engage in sport psychology research as something of a tangent to their primary areas of interest. According to Gould and Pick, "prior to 1925, sport psychology was more of a hobby than a field" (p. 394), but in that year Griffith established the Research in Athletics Laboratory at the University of Illinois where the field of applied sport psychology gained academic respectability.

Griffith was a strong advocate of the principle of learning about the psychology of sport from the best coaches and athletes of the time. In a memorable interview with a prominent American football player of the era, Harold "Red" Grange, Griffith sought to understand the degree of conscious processing that occurred during exceptional performances (see Gould & Pick, 1995, pp. 396–397). Interviewed about his stellar performance during the 1924 Illinois–Michigan game, in which he scored four touchdowns in the first 12 minutes, the only detail that Grange could remember was that a Michigan player had a hole in his sock. This was interpreted as evidence of the automaticity of peak performance that remains a principle of applied sport psychology to the present day. Griffith also became an early scientist-practitioner in the field when he was engaged by the Chicago Cubs baseball team in 1938 to investigate the psychological factors influencing performance among all the players at the club.

The period from 1950–1980 saw sport psychology continue to take forward strides. In particular, Franklin Henry at the University of California at Berkeley played a central role in helping to move the psychological study of sport and physical activity out of the domain of physical education and into a field that embraced a more scientific approach to its investigation. Henry established a graduate training program in the psychology of physical activity that produced some of the field's most influential researchers and practitioners. Similar programs were established at the Universities of Illinois, Maryland, Indiana and Oregon.

Other landmarks for the field during this period included publication of *Psychology of Coaching* by John Lawther in 1951, *Problem Athletes and How to Handle Them* by clinical psychologists Bruce Olgilvie and Thomas Tutko in 1966, and *Psychology of Physical Activity* by Bryant Cratty of UCLA in 1967. This era also saw sport psychology diverge from the discipline of motor learning, with the former focusing on how psychological factors such as personality and anxiety influenced athletic performance, and the latter concerning itself more with how motor skills were developed.

Trends and Key Developments in Applied Sport Psychology

A recent book, *Essential Readings in Sport and Exercise Psychology*, edited by Dan Smith and Michael Bar-Eli in 2007, brings together many of the most influential publications in the field. The book traces the evolution of sport psychology over the past 100 years by reproducing abridged versions of 50 key articles, from Norman

Triplett's early research publication in 1898 through to the modern classics of applied practice. Along the way, some of the central controversies in sport psychology are addressed, such as whether psychological traits predict athletic excellence (the so-called "credulous-skeptical debate") and whether sport builds character or simply reveals it. The text also chronicles the development of sport-oriented measures to assess variables such as competition anxiety, imagery ability, attentional and interpersonal style, group cohesion, and leadership behavior. As the content becomes more contemporaneous, the coverage becomes progressively more applied, including seminal papers on the integration of theory, research, and practice; ethical beliefs and behaviors; and certification in applied sport psychology.

There is no doubt that sport psychology has gained considerable global momentum over recent decades. I have selected a few prominent examples of publications, research programs, and applied work that have laid the foundations for today's practitioners. The first example is Rainer Martens' landmark 1979 paper, intriguingly-titled "About smocks and jocks," in which he made critical comments regarding the application of traditional reductionist paradigms to investigate real world issues in sport. He called for researchers (the *smocks*) to get out of their laboratory coats and into the environment of the athletes (the *jocks*) in order to conduct better field research that properly contextualized research questions before attempting to answer them. Many researchers have since risen to this challenge, which has helped to shape contemporary applied research efforts. Martens has been a highly influential figure in the development of sport psychology through his research into the relationship between anxiety and performance, his methodological commentaries and, not least, through the establishment of Human Kinetics publishers, which has led the way in bringing sport psychology literature to a global audience.

A second example is the use of idiographic techniques for explaining relationships between emotions and sport performance developed over the past 30 years by sport psychology researcher and practitioner Yuri Hanin, a Russian by birth, who has been working at the Research Institute for Olympic Sports in Jyväskylä, Finland since 1991. Hanin's approach, referred to as Individualized Zones of Optimal Functioning (IZOF), provides a theoretical underpinning and a mechanism for identifying the emotions most closely associated with good and poor performances on an individual basis by tracking the emotion–performance link over time (see Hanin, 1997). The IZOF approach emphasizes that the content, form, and intensity of emotional experiences are linked to performance in idiosyncratic ways and that, crucially, there are zones of emotional states that are optimal for performance rather than prescribed levels of particular emotions. This approach has proven efficacious in Hanin's applied work with athletes and has gained widespread acceptance as an important methodological advance.

Another very influential group of researchers in the field of applied sport psychology over several decades has been the Canadian triumvirate of Bert Carron, Neil Widmeyer, and Larry Brawley (see, e.g., Carron, Widmeyer, & Brawley, 1985). Their work on the conceptualization, measurement, development and benefits of group cohesion among sports teams represents an exemplar for the profession. Although they are primarily theoreticians and researchers, Carron, Widmeyer, and Brawley have provided a very solid body of evidence to inform the efforts of applied practitioners responsible for assessing and influencing group dynamics among groups of athletes.

Advances in applied sport psychology in Eastern Europe also warrant mention. At the height of their powers in the 1970s and 1980s, Soviet Bloc countries were a dominant force in world sport. This success was attributed in no small measure to an army of sport scientists and sport psychologists whose innovative research and applied work gave their athletes a competitive edge. This innovation included advanced use of psychological techniques that were applied to sport having earlier been developed as part of the Soviet space program. Dissemination of the details of this applied work in English-language journals was extremely limited under the restrictive Soviet regime although Williams and Straub (2006) include details of its nature, such as the application of self-regulation training to "voluntarily control such bodily functions as heart rate, temperature, and muscle tension, as well as emotional reactions to stressful situations" (p. 9).

These techniques were applied systematically to athletes throughout the Soviet Union in the form of autogenic training, visualization, and self-hypnosis, as part of a state-controlled and -funded program to demonstrate the superiority of the Soviet system via international success in sport. During this period, Eastern European practitioners perhaps led the world in the application of sport psychology, an advantage eroded by the disintegration of the Soviet Union in 1989 and the demise of widespread, systematic use of sport psychology.

From the 1980s, Olympic teams regularly included sport psychologists among their on-site support staff. The Soviet Union was a pioneer in this respect at the 1980 Olympic Games in Moscow, with Australia following suit by appointing its first team psychologist to the 1984 Olympics in Los Angeles. The United States Olympic Committee established a sport psychology advisory board in 1980 and appointed its first full-time sport psychologist in 1985. By 1996 more than 20 sport psychologists were working with the U.S. athletes in preparation for the Atlanta Olympics.

Throughout its development, sport psychology has experienced skepticism from some prominent athletes and coaches, which has served to stigmatize the field in the eyes of others in the sport community. A highly publicized boost for the acceptance of applied sport psychology occurred after tennis player Pat Cash won the Wimbledon singles title in 1987 and famously climbed through the crowd to hug his support team. His sport psychologist, Australian Jeffrey Bond, received one of the first hugs and subsequent glowing acknowledgment from the new champion of Bond's significant role in the victory. The resulting photograph and story were beamed around the world, creating a more positive image for the applied sport psychology profession.

The globalization of sport psychology

Applied sport psychology has been organized on a global scale since 1965 when the International Society of Sport Psychology (ISSP: www.issponline.org) was formed during the 1st International Congress of Sports Psychology in Rome with Ferruccio Antonelli, an Italian psychiatrist, as its first President. Salmela (1992) provided fascinating insights into the academic posturing and political wrangling that accompanied the formation of the fledgling ISSP, in particular the autocratic way in which the European-dominated society was founded, a managing council appointed, and a constitution adopted all in the space of less than 30 minutes. Salmela also pays tribute to Antonelli's subsequent publication of the 1,296-page conference proceedings in Italian, English, French, and German, described as "a landmark both in scholarship and globalism for the newly developed field of sport psychology" (Salmela, 1992, p. 4).

Antonelli also, reportedly single-handedly, launched the *International Journal of Sport Psychology* (IJSP) in 1970 as the first journal dedicated solely to sport psychology. The first published article was produced by the American author William P. Morgan, subsequently one of the most influential researchers in the field, entitled "Pre-match anxiety in a group of college wrestlers". The IJSP has endured a chequered history in terms of the quality of some published articles but it remains alive and well today and is one of very few journals to have promoted a truly global perspective on the field, including contributions in languages other than English and abstracts translated at various times in its history into French, Spanish, and German.

Since the inception of the ISSP, other international associations to coordinate and promote applied sport psychology activities have spread across almost every continent (see Table 16.2). The North American Society for the Psychology of Sport and Physical Activity (NASPSPA: www.naspspa.org) was formed in 1966 under the stewardship of Arthur Slater-Hammel from Indiana University and held its first conference

Table 16.2. Development of International Organizations in Sport Psychology

Organization	*Formed*	*Congress frequency*	*Number of congresses*
African Association of Sport Psychology	Planned	Not applicable	Not applicable
Asian South Pacific Association of Sport Psychology	1989	Every 4 years	6 to 2011
Association of Applied Sport Psychology	1986	Annually	24 to 2010
European Federation of Sport Psychology	1969	Every 4 years	13 to 2011
International Association of Applied Psychology Division 12	1992	Every 4 years	5 to 2010
International Society of Sport Psychology	1965	Every 4 years	12 to 2009
North American Society for the Psychology of Sport and Physical Activity	1966	Annually	44 to 2010
South American Society of Sport Psychology	1986	Every 4 years	11 to 2008

a year later. Around the same time in Europe, the Fédération Européenne de Psychologie des Sports et des Activités Corporelles (FEPSAC: www.fepsac.com) led by Miroslav Vanek from Charles University in Prague, was established in 1969 to allow the Francophile and Eastern Bloc countries to assert their independence from the umbrella ISSP organization.

International organizations in other parts of the world followed these developments. The South American Federation of Sport Psychology (SOSUPE) consolidated its membership in 1986 under the presidency of Benno Becker, Jr., from Brazil, although its progress has been somewhat variable since then. The countries of Asia and the South Pacific region (including Australasia), some of which had established their own national organizations from the 1970s onwards, came together to form the Asian-South Pacific Association of Sport Psychology (ASPASP: www.aspasp.org) in 1989 under the leadership of Atsushi Fujita of Japan. There have been calls for an African Association of Sport Psychology to be established (Abrahamson, 2001) but, at the time of writing, such an initiative has not yet come to fruition.

The tendency for some sport psychology organizations to laud researchers and theoreticians with little apparent capacity to bridge the theory–practice divide over applied practitioners who operate daily at the coalface, has created sufficient frustration in the applied ranks to prompt the formation of new organizations. In 1986, the Association for Applied Sport Psychology (AASP, formerly AAASP: www.appliedsportpsych.org) was formed to provide leadership in the applied practice area because many founding members perceived NASPSPA to be too oriented toward theoretical and research perspectives.

Other psychology organizations of international renown have embraced sport psychology as a legitimate subdiscipline. The American Psychological Association created Division 47 for Exercise and Sport Psychology in 1986 with William P. Morgan as its inaugural President and more than 1,000 members and student affiliates. Division 12 of the International Association of Applied Psychology (IAAP) was founded in 1992 during the 23rd International Congress of Applied Psychology in Madrid, Spain as an initiative of Glyn Roberts, from the Norwegian University of Sport Science in Oslo, who became the inaugural President.

It is very difficult to estimate the total number of applied sport psychologists worldwide. According to information provided in the three editions of *The World Sport Psychology Sourcebook* (Lidor, Morris, Bardaxoglou, & Becker, 2001; Salmela, 1981, 1992) the profession enjoyed rapid growth in many parts of the world during the period 1981–2001 (see Figure 16.1.). Growth was particularly striking in Europe, Asia, and North America. A word of caution is warranted, however, because the methods used to estimate numbers in 1981, 1992, and 2001 varied somewhat. Different country lists were used at the three time points, and individuals at various stages of training were included, with some countries reporting only those who were fully trained and accredited whereas others included postgraduate students in their estimates. Hence, although the growth trend is probably a fair reflection of the field, the raw figures are an overestimate of the true number of qualified practitioners.

The most recent edition of *The World Sport Psychology Sourcebook* (Lidor et al., 2001) provided detailed reports on activities in 48 countries spread over six geographical regions. This overview demonstrates the vitality and enthusiasm for the

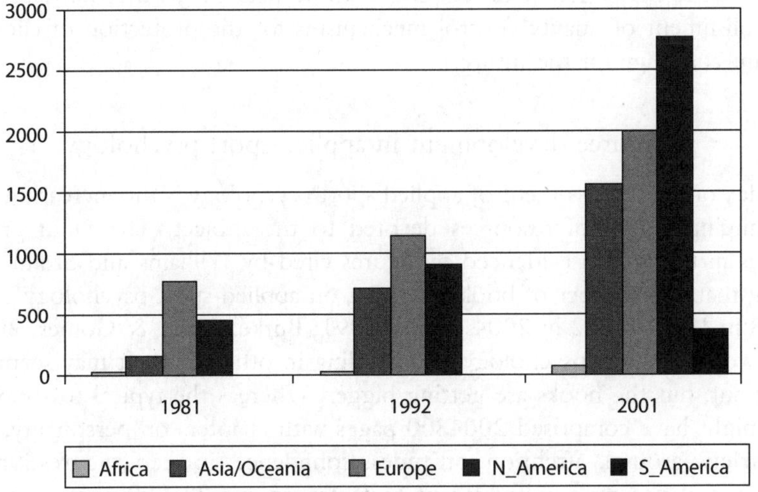

Figure 16.1. Estimated global growth of sport psychology 1981–2001 (based on Lidor et al., 2001; Salmela, 1981, 1992)

field in 23 countries of Europe, 11 in Asia, 7 in South America, 3 in Africa, and 2 each in North America and Oceania. Of the 48 countries reviewed, 44 (91.6%) had established academic programs in sport psychology at undergraduate level, postgraduate level, or both, although only 12 of the 48 countries (25%) had a formal accreditation process in sport psychology.

Practitioner training and accreditation

An important trend in applied sport psychology relates to the processes by which practitioners are trained and accredited. Morris, Alfermann, Lintunen, and Hall (2003) have conducted an international review of these processes, on behalf of the ISSP. Their paper, which is highly recommended to those readers interested in knowing more about the subject, contains detailed information about how sport psychology is organized, administered and accredited in many countries around the world.

Essentially, there are two routes to becoming an applied sport psychologist. The first is to complete a degree program in psychology, followed by specialist postgraduate training in sport psychology that includes experience of working with clients under supervision. The second is to complete a degree program in sport sciences or a closely allied subject that includes some sport psychology, followed by postgraduate training in psychology, again including experience of working with clients under supervision. In the modern era, these can be considered to be the minimum standards for the training of sport psychologists.

A fundamental influence upon how applied sport psychology develops in a country concerns the legislation regarding use of the term psychologist. In Scandinavia, North America, and Australia, for example, the term psychologist is protected by law and all practitioners who present themselves as applied sport psychologists must be licensed psychologists. In the developing world few such legislative barriers exist and the establishment of quality control mechanisms for the protection of clients is an important challenge for the future.

Resource development in applied sport psychology

One index of the development of applied sport psychology is the increasing number and changing nature of resources devoted to the subject. The rapid growth of resources in the area is evidenced by figures cited by Williams and Straub (2006), showing that the number of books focusing on applied sport psychology expanded from 48 in 1991 to 282 in 2004 (Sachs, 1991; Burke, Sachs, & Gomer, 2004).

The world of sport psychology is expanding in other ways. It may seem trite to point it out, but the books are getting bigger. Whereas the typical textbook in the 1980s might have comprised 200–300 pages with chapters on personality, motivation, anxiety, arousal, attention, attitudes, confidence, imagery, aggression, group dynamics, and not much else, recent texts are often 700–800 pages with 30–40 chapters on topics as diverse as biofeedback applications (Blumenstein & Bar-Eli, 2005), spirituality in sport psychology (Nesti, 2009), passion in sport (Vallerand, Donahue, & Lafrenière, in press), or use of music interventions (Karageorghis & Terry, 2009). It seems that those writing in the area of applied sport psychology not only have more to say than formerly, but have begun to open many new avenues of investigation.

Three recent textbooks are illustrative of the direction in which the field of applied sport psychology is moving. The first, *The Sport Psychologist's Handbook* (Dosil, 2006), is a 700-page resource offering sport-specific performance enhancement techniques for more than 20 different sports. The second, *Applied Sport Psychology–A Case-Based Approach* (Hemmings & Holder, 2009), similarly provides situation-specific coverage of 11 different sports. The increased specificity of interventions is a welcome feature, befitting a discipline reaching maturity, which is likely to continue further into the future. The third example, the *Routledge Handbook of Applied Sport Psychology* (Hanrahan & Andersen, 2010), has redefined the range of topics covered in textbooks. New features in this text include chapters on working with athlete survivors of sexual victimization, athletes with physical, sensory, or intellectual disabilities, athletes who have experienced the death of a teammate, and providing services via telephone or email.

A perennial frustration for new professionals coming into the field of applied sport psychology is how to get a feel for the reality of applied practice. What do experienced practitioners actually DO with athletes and coaches? What works, what doesn't, and why? Resources that address these questions candidly are rare. Neophyte practitioners have produced detailed reflections on their early applied experiences (e.g., Tonn & Harmison, 2004; Woodcock, Richards, & Mugford, 2008) one of which, entitled *Thrown to the Wolves*, aptly summed up the feeling of being ill-equipped for the challenge. Typically though, experienced practitioners, if and when they write about their applied work, produce rather sanitized or idealized versions of what the world of applied practice is like. Very few have been prepared to pen a "warts and all" account of strategies that didn't work juxtaposed with those that were effective. Simons and

Andersen (1995) produced one of the first articles that attempted to get to the core of professional practice by reporting on their interviews with 11 experienced sport psychology practitioners. The interviews provide a vivid educational journey through the unpredictable world of consulting with athletes, raising many issues commonly faced by sport psychologists and offering valuable insight into strategies for dealing with them. Although most of the practitioners interviewed identified a consistent approach that guided their applied work, all acknowledged that there are many different ways to be effective.

Andersen continued his attempt to capture the realities of the applied field in his 2005 text entitled *Sport Psychology in Practice*, which provides thorough coverage of previously overlooked or glossed over areas of applied sport psychology such as alcohol abuse, erotic transference and counter-transference, and issues specific to gay and lesbian athletes. An excellent paper by Fifer, Henschen, Gould, and Ravizza (2008) has provided insightful accounts of the approaches that succeed with athletes and, by implication, those that do not.

A series of DVDs produced by Virtual Brands, showing experienced practitioners in action, also provides fly-on-the-wall glimpses into the world of applied sport psychology. Topics covered in the series include a basic *Introduction to Teaching Mental Skills for Sport* (Gould, 2001), *Brief Contact Interventions in Sport Psychology* (Zaichowsky, Van Raalte, Giges, & Ravizza, 2002), and *Keys to Effective Sport Psychology Consulting* (Ravizza, 2008). Other DVDs in the series focus on specific populations, such as *Mental Skills for Young Athletes* (Gould, 2005) or on specific sports, such as *Mental Skills for Equestrian Athletes* (Schuijers, 2008).

The trend toward previously under-represented areas has continued with the publication in 2009 of *Cultural Sport Psychology*, edited by Robert Schinke and Stephanie Hanrahan, the first text to focus exclusively on cultural aspects of applied sport psychology. A wide range of contributors offer first-hand experiences of working with athletes in countries as diverse as Brazil, England, Ghana, Israel, Japan, Kuwait, Nigeria, Russia, Singapore, Sweden, and the US, and also with specific minority groups, including Indigenous athletes in Canada and Aboriginal athletes in Australia.

As the field of applied sport psychology has expanded, several books have been produced that focus on a single area of interest. The focus of such texts has included competitive anxiety (Martens, Vealey, & Burton, 1990), concentration (Moran, 1996), emotions (Hanin, 2000), flow (Jackson & Czikszentmihalyi, 1999), imagery (Morris, Spittle, & Watt, 2005), mood (Lane, 2007), and self-efficacy (Feltz, Short, & Sullivan, 2008). Other books have been written that address specifically the psychological aspects of potential problems faced by athletes that are common across many different sports. Such problems include injury (Pargman, 1993), overtraining (Richardson, Andersen, & Morris, 2008), burnout (Raedeke & Smith, 2009), under-recovery (Kellmann, 2002), and the challenges of retirement from sport (Gordon & Lavallee, in press).

In addition to the range of resources produced for the academic market, there are several excellent publications aimed at the general population of athletes, coaches, and anyone seeking personal improvement in sport. Classics in this genre include Timothy Gallwey's *Inner Game* series covering tennis, golf, skiing, and the crossover between sport and business (Gallwey, 1974, 1977, 1981, 2000). Another popular text has been Terry Orlick's *In Pursuit of Excellence*, first published in 1980 and recently into its fourth edition (Orlick, 2008). An influential pioneer of applied sport psychology for more than 30 years, Orlick has spawned a global excellence movement that has helped to cross-fertilize applied psychology techniques across a wide range of performance environments. In 1998, Orlick established *The Journal of Excellence* as the first journal that had performance excellence as its sole focus. While about half of the articles featured in the journal since its inception have focused on the psychology of sport performance, other performance domains featured include medicine, opera, music, acting, television presenting, education, space exploration, Mount Everest expeditions, and a growing number of articles dedicated to excellence in business.

In terms of psychological testing, there are more than 300 tests developed specifically for use in sport and exercise psychology (Ostrow, 1996) in addition to the broad range of general psychology tests that an applied practitioner might have cause to use. As a barometer of the significant growth of sport psychology in recent years, the number of published tests developed specifically for use in the area increased by approximately 80% during the period 1990–1996. The areas of motivation, attitudes, confidence, and anxiety have attracted the most interest from test developers, with no fewer than 170 different scales to assess various aspects of these constructs alone.

It should be noted, however, that many of these discipline-specific tests have not been subjected to rigorous psychometric scrutiny. Even those tests whose psychometric properties have been subjected to peer review would tend not to meet the exacting standards of psychological tests used in, for example, the medico-legal field, such as the Minnesota Multiphasic Personality Inventory-2 (MMPI-2; Butcher et al., 2001). The relatively weak standard of psychological testing in applied sport psychology is an area that the field should address as it evolves further. Of course, many applied sport psychologists eschew the use of psychology tests altogether in favour of more qualitative approaches.

Journal content in applied sport psychology

Another way to chronicle developmental trends in applied sport psychology is to trace the content of publications in the most important journals in the field. Articles on applied sport psychology can be found in many well-established journals, including the *International Journal of Sport Psychology, Journal of Sport & Exercise Psychology, International Journal of Sport and Exercise Psychology, Psychology of Sport and Exercise, Research Quarterly for Exercise and Sport,* and the *Journal of Sports Sciences.* There are, however, two journals, *The Sport Psychologist* (established in 1987) and the *Journal of Applied Sport Psychology* (established in 1989), that promote applied aspects of sport and exercise psychology as their *raison d'être.*

A content analysis of all papers published in these two journals since their inception, was conducted recently (Terry, Curran, & Mecozzi, in preparation). Results showed the American domination of these two applied journals to have diminished over time and the influence of authors from other parts of the world, the UK in particular, to have grown. Notably, the percentage of papers first authored by males

Table 16.3. Author Characteristics of Journal Articles in Applied Sport Psychology, 1987–2009 (n = 1,017)

Characteristic	*1987–1992 (n = 220)*	*1993–1998 (n = 268)*	*1999–2004 (n = 261)*	*2005–2009 (n = 268)*
First Author Sex (%)				
Male	80	71	67	60
Female	20	29	33	40
First Author Country (%)				
USA	76	57	49	34
Canada	11	18	16	15
Australia	5	9	5	6
UK	3	9	20	30
Other	5	7	11	15

Note: Journals represented are *The Sport Psychologist* (TSP) and *Journal of Applied Sport Psychology*. TSP data for the period 1987–1992 were taken from Vealey (1994).

has fallen from 80% during the period 1987–1992 to 60% during the 2005–2009 period (see Table 16.3).

Clinical issues in applied sport psychology

Another feature of the contemporary literature in applied sport psychology is the increased recognition of the incidence of mental health issues among athletes and the impact of clinical factors on both athletic performance and athlete well-being. There has been a spate of very public acknowledgments by several icons of the sporting world regarding their chronic battles against a range of clinical issues. Kelly Holmes, Britain's dual gold medalist from the 2004 Athens Olympic Games, is one high-profile athlete who has talked openly about her long-term struggle against clinical depression. Another is Marcus Trescothick, the England cricketer who resigned suddenly from international cricket in 2006 during a tour to India. He wrote insightfully and at length about his battle with the "black wings of depression" in his autobiography *Coming Back To Me* (Trescothick, 2008). In an article on depression in sport, published in *The Lancet*, the suggestion was made that "athletes may be more predisposed than the general population to depression, because of the physical and psychological demands placed upon them by the sporting environment" (Mummery, 2005, p. S36). It is possible that the alleged increased risk of depression caused by factors in the sport environment may be more than offset by the demonstrated psychological benefits of physical activity. If, however, Mummery's suggestion proved to be accurate, then the numbers of athletes suffering, often in silence, from depression worldwide would be enormous.

Eating disorders are another category of clinical issue that frequently afflict athletes, male as well as female. Many successful athletes have documented their battles with eating disorders, including Romanian gymnast Nadia Comaneci, American tennis player Zina Garrison, Irish jockey Richard Dunwoody, and Austrian ski-jumper Christian Moser. The incidence of subclinical disordered eating and clinical eating disorders among athletes is uncertain; with reported prevalence rates varying widely in different studies (see Petrie & Greenleaf, 2007 for a review). A meta-analysis of the extant literature has indicated that athletes have a higher incidence of clinical eating disorders than nonathletes (Hausenblas & Carron, 1999). Furthermore, a recent randomized, controlled study involving 186 elite, female athletes in Norway (Torstveit, Rosenvinge, & Sundgot-Borgen, 2008) found that an alarming 46.7% of those participating in "leanness" sports (e.g., distance running, figure skating, gymnastics, diving) met the criteria for a clinical eating disorder. Hence, it appears likely that sport psychologists will, in the course of consulting with athletes, deal with some who are at risk of, or will develop, a clinical eating disorder.

Successful athletes have similarly acknowledged other mental health issues. In Australia, tennis star Scott Draper wrote candidly about his battle to overcome obsessive-compulsive disorder (Draper, Petkovski, & Fox, 2007). Rugby league legend Andrew Johns shocked the nation with his revelations, broadcast on live television in 2008, about the chronic drug habit that he endured throughout much of his playing career. International rugby union player Enrique (Topo) Rodrigues, who played for both Argentina and Australia, has not only spoken and written openly about his own bipolar disorder but, in 2007, established the Topo Foundation for Education (TF4E), to educate high school students, sporting clubs and other community group members about mental health issues.

In previous eras, public admission of mental health issues by athletes, especially males, was rare perhaps because it did not sit well with the stereotypical view of the heroic, superhuman performer. The scientific literature has also reflected, and perhaps influenced, changing societal attitudes toward mental health among athletes with the publication of the textbook *Clinical Sport Psychology* (Gardner & Moore, 2006), which includes various assessment tools and a range of evidence-based intervention practices for addressing clinical issues. This publication was followed in 2007 by the launch of the *Journal of Clinical Sport Psychology*, which promotes the integration of clinical, counseling and sport psychology.

Challenges and Opportunities for Applied Sport Psychology

Two enduring challenges for applied sport psychology are (a) to educate the sporting community and the general public about what sport psychology can and cannot achieve, and (b) to ensure that claimed benefits are pitched at the right level and are supported by compelling evidence. Just as, in Greek mythology, Icarus flew too close to the sun, melted the wax that held his wings together, and fell to his death, so the profession of applied sport psychology risks losing its credibility if practitioners overpromise on what can realistically be achieved (metaphorically flying too close to the sun) and then fail to deliver on their promises. Gould and Pick (1995, p. 403) warned of practitioners who "oversell their research and consulting services and make unrealistic claims of their effectiveness" and even Coleman Griffith (1925, p. 193) alluded to this danger, with his words "A great many people have the idea that the psychologist is a sort of magician who is ready, for a price, to sell his services to one individual or to one group of men." Equally, if applied sport psychologists downplay the performance gains and the other benefits that their profession can deliver (perhaps the equivalent of Icarus remaining with his feet firmly on the ground) then the sports world will look elsewhere for specialist assistance.

Public understanding of the role of an applied sport psychologist remains incomplete at best, with practitioners often characterized in the media as people brought in to "motivate" teams or to deal with "problem" athletes (perceptions originally encouraged by the title of Ogilvie and Tutko's textbook in 1966). Nevertheless, the profession has made sufficient inroads into the culture of elite sport to be seen in many countries as a valuable, even essential, part of a support team, and has received enough public accolades from grateful athletes and coaches for the profession as a whole to have demonstrated its worth.

Some countries routinely include one or more psychologists as part of their delegations at major international events, such as the Olympic Games. Australia, for example, included 12 psychologists in its team for the 2000 Olympic Summer Games in Sydney. Perhaps this represented the zenith of the profession's influence in that country, however. At the Beijing Olympic Games of 2008, the number of psychologists in the Australian team had shrunk to five and former champion athletes were being invited to fill some of the advisory and motivational roles previously the responsibility of the psychologists. Moreover, the number of specialist postgraduate programs in sport psychology in Australia had halved during the same period, as universities became less willing to sustain niche areas of study, and membership of the Australian Psychology Society's (APS) College of Sport Psychologists had fallen.

There are several possible explanations for these trends in Australia. They may reflect the additional resources allocated to support services in the lead-up to hosting the 2000 Olympics that subsequently waned as part of a natural cycle of events. Alternatively, the trends may reflect an exodus on the part of some of the best practitioners away from the relatively poorly paid arena of sport, transferring their skills in performance psychology into the richer pickings of the corporate world.

These trends may, however, reflect disillusionment within the world of elite sport about what applied sport psychology can truly deliver. Regardless of the orientation that a practitioner may choose, the primary interest of the elite sport community is, and always will be, performance enhancement and competition results. Despite the occasional public protestation to the contrary, athlete happiness and well-being is considered to be of secondary importance, and even then as something that may assist performance rather than as a duty of care. In short, the elite sport environment, which is the main consumer of sport psychology services (Biddle, 1995, p. xvi), is a hard-nosed, results-driven world. This does not always sit well with the personal philosophy of the practitioner nor dovetail perfectly with their professional code of ethics. It is a world that expects, or even requires, sport psychologists to report back to coaches and others on athletes' mindsets, to expose drug cheats rather than provide them with psychological support, and to disclose performance-related information to other sports medicine professionals.

Whether such a cycle of the profession growing, peaking, and apparently subsiding is being replicated in other countries is very difficult to determine but it is certainly a possibility. Of course, in many countries the profession is still forging its identity

Table 16.4. Developmental Stage of Sport Psychology Organizations in ASPASP in 2009

Highly developed	*Developing*	*Recently established*	*Individuals only*
Australia	India	IR Iran	Iraq
PR China	Indonesia	Malaysia	Macau China
Japan	Hong Kong China	Singapore	Philippines
New Zealand	Thailand		Vietnam
South Korea			
Chinese Taipei			

and growing its influence. Perhaps the Australian experience will provide a salutary lesson for those systems still in a developmental phase.

From a geographical perspective, applied sport psychology has traditionally had a strong North American, European, and Australasian orientation, with most research and resource material originating from those areas. There have, however, been concomitant developments in other regions of the world. In Asia, applied sport psychology has a longstanding tradition in Japan, Korea, and China, but in other parts of that continent the profession still resembles the illegitimate offspring of uncaring parent disciplines that show precious little interest in its future development. One opportunity for the global community of applied sport psychologists, therefore, is to encourage development in regions where the field is still struggling to gain credence.

The President of ASPASP, Tony Morris, recently reported to the Olympic Council of Asia on the development of sport psychology in the region (Morris, 2009). He identified that only 25% of eligible countries in Asia were members of ASPASP and, of those, few had well-established sport psychology organizations (see Table 16.4). Therefore, as many of the countries of Asia develop their sporting and public health systems there is an opportunity for the international sport psychology community to play a role in helping to shape this development.

A recent increase in the number of applied practitioners in China has paralleled that country's rise to dominance in the world of international sport. From 2007, the Sport Psychology Association (part of the Chinese Psychological Association) and the Sport Psychology Society (part of the China Society of Sport Sciences) have collaborated to accredit practitioners and to integrate applied sport psychologists within national teams. A total of 33 sport psychologists delivered mental training programs in the lead-up to the 2008 Beijing Olympic Games, where 45 of the 51 gold medals won by Chinese athletes came from teams that had received sport psychology support.

The opportunity for the international sport psychology community to influence development is even more acute in Africa where, with the exception of South Africa and a handful of other countries, the field is still largely in its infancy. Promisingly, the four-yearly *World Congress of Sport Psychology* was held on African soil for the first time in 2009, in Marrakesh, organized by the Moroccan Association of Sport Psychology under the auspices of the ISSP and, as a mark of the significance of the event, with royal patronage from HRH Prince Moulay Rachid.

Broadening the influence of applied sport psychology in society as a whole also represents a huge opportunity for the profession. This would involve strengthening the nexus between sport psychology techniques and daily life. Given that sport psychologists routinely help athletes to handle pressure, to become more resilient, to enhance self-esteem, and to fulfil potential, there is a huge opportunity for such processes to be applied to life challenges that lie outside of sport or exercise. By stretching the concept of performance to include daily functioning at work, interpersonal relationships, or leisure pursuits, sport psychologists have the capacity to influence the psychological well-being of a much wider spectrum of society.

Future Directions in Applied Sport Psychology

Sport psychology has a strong tradition of striving to establish a solid evidence base for the interventions it espouses. Compared to some other areas of psychology, sport psychology can claim that the evidence base is already fairly strong—it is after all more straightforward to demonstrate improved performance against the clock in sport than, say, show that an organization is functioning more harmoniously or that a person is happier in a relationship. Additionally, there have been many attempts to summarize objectively the effectiveness of interventions commonly applied with athletes and exercisers, using meta-analytic techniques. Table 16.5. shows the results of several meta-analyses that have summarized the effects of various psychological variables or the efficacy of interventions. The weighted mean effects reflect the importance of the variable or the benefit of the intervention across a wide range of outcome variables, not just enhanced performance. Findings show that interventions provide significant benefits, mostly in the small-to-moderate range but in some instances, such as the effects of exercise on depression, in the moderate-to-large category.

It should be noted that the findings included in these meta-analyses have been underpinned by research methods that, in some cases, have fallen short of the highest standards. There are almost no double blind, placebo-controlled tests (generally regarded as the gold standard of scientific evidence) of the efficacy of interventions used in applied sport psychology. Although it is true that such designs do not lend themselves to tests of the effectiveness of, for example, mental imagery, it seems inevitable that researchers in the area will move toward progressively more rigorous evaluations of the techniques and strategies that they prescribe to athletes and coaches.

An inevitable future development for the applied sport psychology field will be to optimize strategies for utilizing the internet for research and dissemination of knowledge in the area and, ultimately, for providing effective web-based interventions. As with other areas of applied psychology, sport has embraced the vast potential of the internet. Web-based research in applied sport psychology is now fairly commonplace and online journals have been established. For example, www.athleticinsight.com was launched in 1999 as the online journal for sport psychology, offering free access to research findings and professional practice techniques via a quarterly online publication. Another internet resource for applied practitioners is the multidisciplinary *Journal of Sports Science and Medicine* (www.jssm.org), which provides no-cost articles on sport psychology, available in 11 languages via TranslateGoogle™. There is

Table 16.5. Summary of Meta-Analyses Conducted in Applied Sport Psychology

Effect	*Meta-analysis*	*Mean effect size*
Anxiety on performance	Woodman and Hardy (2003)	−0.10
Cohesion on performance	Carron, Colman, Wheeler and Stevens (2002)	0.66
Exercise on affect	Reed and Ones (2006)	0.47
Exercise on anxiety	Wipfli, Bradley, Rethorst and Landers (2008)	0.48
Exercise on body image	Hausenblas and Fallon (2006)	0.24
Exercise on cognitive functioning	Etnier et al. (1997)	0.25
Exercise on depression	Craft and Landers (1998)	0.72
Exercise on mood	Terry and Mizzi (in preparation)	0.36
Exercise on self-concept	Huang and Guo (2008)	0.37
Goal-setting on performance	Terry and van der Wijngaart (in preparation)	0.54
Imagery on performance	Curran and Terry (2010)	0.53
Mood on performance	Beedie, Terry, & Lane (2000)	0.31
Music on performance	Terry, Karageorghis, Curran, Lim, and Mecozzi (in preparation)	0.28
Self-confidence on performance	Woodman and Hardy (2003)	0.24

Note: Where more than one meta-analysis has been conducted in an area, the most recent one is listed.

also a burgeoning number of websites offering online services in applied sport psychology that include downloadable mp3 files and podcasts in addition to the usual array of multimedia educational resources. Quality control is clearly a central issue in the largely unregulated world of the internet services, although some sites are offered by highly qualified practitioners.

One of the biggest challenges facing web-based delivery of applied sport psychology is to demonstrate its efficacy with compelling evidence. Scientific evaluations of online interventions in sport psychology are still quite rare, although some have been published. Doumas and Haustveit (2008) reported the effectiveness of a web-based personalized feedback program for reducing binge drinking among intercollegiate athletes. This is acknowledged as a significant social problem in the United States, where over 30% of college students meet the Diagnostic and Statistical Manual of Mental Disorders (DSM-IV: American Psychiatric Association, 1994) criteria for alcohol abuse (Knight et al., 2002), and where student athletes have been shown to drink more heavily and more frequently than nonathletes (e.g., Doumas, Turrisi, Coll, & Haralson, 2007). On a much larger scale, Mummery and his colleagues (e.g., Mummery, Schofield, Hinchliffe, Joyner, & Brown, 2006) have reported on the challenges of implementing a whole-of-community, web-based intervention for increasing physical activity. The researchers provided evidence of the effectiveness of the *10,000 Steps* initiative, a walking program that uses a pedometer and a daily log to monitor physical activity via a website full of exercise tips (see www.10000steps.org.au).

It seems highly likely that applied practitioners will have the option to incorporate more technology into their professional practice in the future. Biofeedback technology involving electroencephalography (EEG) is becoming progressively more portable, user-friendly, and affordable, opening up potential uses in the field that were previously impossible, such as assessing brain activity associated with optimum performance wirelessly in sports such as archery or shooting. Similarly, the ever-expanding capacity of cell phones offers a range of future applications, including remote delivery by practitioners of individualized interventions for athletes or exercisers combining music, video clips, and personalized instructions. Virtual reality technology similarly offers potential for more sophisticated use of simulation training, allowing athletes to "practice" in venues they have not yet visited, in environmental conditions they have not yet experienced, and against competitors they have not yet faced.

Another future development for the field is to ensure that ethically grey areas of professional practice are clarified for practitioners in black and white. When working "on the road" with a team of athletes, the consulting office is replaced by a hotel room, a corner of the gym floor, a seat on the bus, or a table in the coffee shop. Similarly, the well-planned, progressive intervention is usurped out of necessity by brief, sometimes impromptu encounters to address the pressing issues of the day. Thankfully, the literature supports the efficacy of these typically solution-focused, strengths-based "teachable moments" to address aspects of athlete performance or mindset (see Giges & Petitpas, 2000). Similarly, the DSM-IV manual is sometimes eclipsed by a seat-of-the-pants approach to often unique issues that can severely test the professional skills of the applied practitioner. The one-hour consulting session becomes a distant memory as the interventions are interspersed with the demands of 24-hour journeys across multiple time zones (Terry, 2010). In fact, with the travel schedules of many of today's athletes, consultations increasingly occur via email or telephone. The equivalence of such forms of consultation compared to traditional face-to-face methods is uncertain but this is clearly an issue that the profession of applied sport psychology will need to address.

In sum, the reality of applied sport psychology bears little resemblance to textbook or classroom models. To be effective, it requires an extensive bag of tricks in the form of a wide range of highly developed intervention skills, the ability to intervene at a moment's notice, the capacity to withstand skepticism, challenge, and occasional open hostility, and the tenacity to maintain a consistent therapeutic approach when it appears to be having no beneficial outcomes.

Athletes are often taught by sport psychologists to "learn to love adversity" (e.g., Loehr, 1986). This principle may apply even more to the psychologists themselves, who will certainly need to learn to take the rough with the smooth, and to accept the challenge of making a real difference to the lives and performances of athletes and coaches without overpromising and underdelivering. Unlike Icarus, they must learn to spread their wings and fly but avoid melting in the heat of the sun. Sport psychologists who travel with teams will need to resign themselves to the fact that working conditions will not be ideal, to understand that stamina, resilience, and a sense of humor are key professional attributes, and to learn to treat those twin impostors—triumph and disaster—just the same because they are rarely a true reflection of the quality of the service provided. The field of applied sport psychology has certainly come a very long way since its origins more than 100 years ago, but as its practitioners would doubtless prescribe, it must strive to set new goals, develop new techniques and identify new directions as it moves through the 21st century.

References

Abrahamson, E. (2001). Africa. In R. Lidor, T. Morris, N. Bardaxoglou, & B. Becker, Jr. (Eds.), *The world sport psychology sourcebook* (3rd ed., pp. 20–22). Morgantown, WV: Fitness Information Technology.

American Psychiatric Association. (1994). *Diagnostic and statistical manual of mental disorders* (4th ed.). Washington, DC: Author.

Andersen, M. B. (Ed.). (2005). *Sport psychology in practice.* Champaign, IL: Human Kinetics.

Beedie, C. J., Terry, P. C., & Lane, A. M. (2000). The profile of mood states and athletic performance: Two meta-analyses. *Journal of Applied Sport Psychology, 12*, 49–68.

Biddle, S. J. H. (Ed.). (1995). *European perspectives on exercise and sport psychology.* Champaign, IL: Human Kinetics.

Blumenstein, B., & Bar-Eli, M. (2005). Biofeedback applications in sport. In D. Hackfort, J. L. Duda, & R. Lidor (Eds.), *Handbook of research in applied sport and exercise psychology: International perspectives* (pp. 185–198). Morgantown, WV: Fitness Information Technology.

Burke, K. L., Sachs, M. L., & Gomer, S. (Eds.). (2004). *Directory of graduate programs in applied sport psychology* (7th ed.). Morgantown, WV: Fitness Information Technology.

Butcher, J. N., Graham, J. R., Ben-Porath, Y. S., Tellegen, A., Dahlstrom, W. G., & Kaemmer, B. (2001). *Minnesota Multiphasic Personality Inventory-2 revised edition.* Minneapolis, MN: University of Minnesota Press.

Carron, A. V., Colman, M. M., Wheeler, J., & Stevens, D. (2002). Cohesion and performance in sport: A meta-analysis. *Journal of Sport & Exercise Psychology, 24*, 168–188.

Carron, A. V., Widmeyer, W. N., & Brawley, L. R. (1985). The development of an instrument to assess cohesion in sports teams: The Group Environment Questionnaire. *Journal of Sport Psychology, 7*, 244–266.

Coubertin, P. de (1900). La psychologie du sport. *La Revues Des Deux Mondes, 70*, 161–179.

Craft, L. L., & Landers, D. M. (1998). The effect of exercise on clinical depression and depression resulting from mental illness: A meta-analysis. *Journal of Sport & Exercise Psychology, 20*, 339–357.

Curran, M., & Terry, P. C. (2010). What you see is what you get: A meta-analytic review of the effects of imagery in sport and exercise domains. In V. Mrowinski, M. Kyrios, & N. Vouderis (Eds.), *Proceedings of the 27th International Congress of Applied Psychology* (p. 314). Melbourne, VIC: Australian Psychological Society.

Dosil, J. (Ed.). (2006). *The sport psychologist's handbook.* Chichester, England: John Wiley.

Doumas, D. M., & Haustveit, T. (2008). Reducing heavy drinking in intercollegiate athletes: Evaluation of a web-based personalized feedback program. *The Sport Psychologist, 22*, 212–228.

Doumas, D. M., Turrisi, R., Coll, K. M., & Haralson, K. (2007). High risk drinking in college athletes and nonathletes across the academic year. *Journal of College Counseling*, *10*, 163–174.

Draper, S., Petkovski, S., & Fox, M. (2007). *Too good: The Scott Draper story*. Sydney: Random House.

Etnier, J. L., Salazar, W., Landers, D. M., Petruzello, S. J., Han, M., & Nowell, P. (1997). The influence of physical fitness and exercise upon cognitive functioning: A meta-analysis. *Journal of Sport & Exercise Psychology*, *19*, 249–277.

Feltz, D. L., Short, S., & Sullivan, P. (2008). *Self-efficacy in sport: Research and strategies for working with athletes, teams, and coaches*. Champaign, IL: Human Kinetics.

Fifer, A. M., Henschen, K., Gould, D., & Ravizza, K. (2008). What works when working with athletes. *The Sport Psychologist*, *22*, 356–377.

Fitz, G. W. (1895). A location reaction apparatus. *Psychological Review*, *2*, 37–42.

Gallwey, W. T. (1974). *The inner game of tennis*. New York: Random House.

Gallwey, W. T. (1977). *Inner skiing*. New York: Random House.

Gallwey, W. T. (1981). *The inner game of golf*. New York: Random House.

Gallwey, W. T. (2000). *The inner game of work*. New York: Random House.

Gardner, F., & Moore, Z. (2006). *Clinical sport psychology*. Champaign, IL: Human Kinetics.

Giges, B., & Petitpas, A. (2000). Brief contact interventions in sport psychology. *The Sport Psychologist*, *14*, 176–187.

Gordon, S., & Lavallee, D. (in press). Career transitions in competitive sport. In T. Morris & P. C. Terry (Eds.), *The new sport and exercise psychology companion*. Morgantown, WV: Fitness Information Technology.

Gould, D. (2001). *Teaching mental skills for sport*. Wilbraham, MA: Virtual Brands.

Gould, D. (2005). *Mental skills for young athletes*. Wilbraham, MA: Virtual Brands.

Gould, D., & Pick, S. (1995). Sport psychology: The Griffith era, 1920–1940. *The Sport Psychologist*, *9*, 391–405.

Griffith, C. R. (1925). Psychology and its relation to athletic competition. *American Physical Education Review*, *30*, 193–199.

Hanin, Y. (1997). Emotions and athletic performance: Individual zones of optimal functioning model. *European Yearbook of Sport Psychology*, *1*, 29–72.

Hanin, Y. (Ed.). (2000). *Emotions in sport*. Champaign, IL: Human Kinetics.

Hanrahan, S. J., & Andersen, M. B. (Eds.). (2010). *Routledge handbook of applied sport psychology: A comprehensive guide for students and practitioners*. Milton Park, England: Routledge.

Hausenblas, H. A., & Carron, A. V. (1999). Eating disorder indices and athletes: An integration. *Journal of Sport & Exercise Psychology*, *21*, 230–258.

Hausenblas, H. A., & Fallon, E. A. (2006). Exercise and body image: A meta-analysis. *Psychology & Health*, *21*, 33–47.

Hemmings, B., & Holder, T. (Eds.). (2009). *Applied sport psychology—A case-based approach*. London: Wiley-Blackwell.

Huang, Z. J., & Guo, Z. P. (2008). Meta-analysis concerning relationship between physical exercise and self-concept. *Journal of Wuhan Institute of Physical Education*, *42*, 57–60.

Ievleva, L. & Terry, P. C. (2008). Applying sport psychology to business. *International Coaching Psychology Review*, *3*, 8–18.

Jackson, S., & Czikszentmihalyi, M. (1999). *Flow in sports*. Champaign, IL: Human Kinetics.

Karageorghis, C. I., & Terry, P. C. (2009). The psychological, psychophysical, and ergogenic effects of music in sport: A review and synthesis. In A. J. Bateman & J. R. Bale (Eds.), *Sporting sounds: Relationships between sport and music* (pp. 13–36). London: Routledge.

Kellmann, M. (2002). *Enhancing recovery: Preventing underperformance in athletes.* Champaign, IL: Human Kinetics.

Knight, J. R., Wechsler, H., Kuo, M., Seibring, M., Weitzman, E. R., & Schuckit, M. (2002). Alcohol abuse and dependence among U.S. college students. *Journal of Studies on Alcohol, 63*, 263–270.

Koch, C. F. (1830). *Die Gymnastik aus dem Gesichtspunkte der Diätetik und Psychologie* [Callisthenics from the viewpoint of dietetics and psychology]. Magdeburg, Germany: Creutz.

Kornspan, A. S. (2007). The early years of sport psychology: The work and influence of Pierre de Coubertin. *Journal of Sport Behavior, 30*, 77–94.

Lane, A. M. (Ed.). (2007). *Mood and human performance: Conceptual, measurement and applied issues.* Hauppauge, NY: Nova Science.

Lidor, R., Morris, T., Bardaxoglou, N., & Becker, B., Jr. (Eds.) (2001). *The world sport psychology sourcebook* (3rd ed.). Morgantown, WV: Fitness Information Technology.

Loehr, J. (1986). *Mental toughness training for sports: Achieving athletic excellence.* Brattleboro, VT: Stephen Greene Press.

Martens, R. (1979). About smocks and jocks. *Journal of Sport Psychology, 1*, 94–99.

Martens, R., Vealey, R. S., & Burton, D. (1990). *Competitive anxiety in sport.* Champaign, IL: Human Kinetics.

Moran, A. P. (1996). *The psychology of concentration in sport performers: A cognitive analysis.* Hove, England: Psychology Press.

Morris, T. (March, 2009). Sport psychology in Asia. In *Proceedings of the 1st Olympic Council of Asia Congress*, Kuwait City, Kuwait.

Morris, T., Alferman, D., Lintunen, T., & Hall, H. (2003). Education and accreditation of sport psychologists: A global review. *International Journal of Sport and Exercise Psychology, 1*, 139–154.

Morris, T., Spittle, M., & Watt, A. P. (2005). *Imagery in sport.* Champaign, IL: Human Kinetics.

Mummery, K. (2005). Depression in sport. *The Lancet, 366*, S36–S37.

Mummery, W. K., Schofield, G., Hinchliffe, A., Joyner, K., & Brown, W. (2006). Dissemination of a community-based physical activity project: The case of 10,000 Steps. *Journal of Science and Medicine in Sport, 9*, 424–430.

Nesti, M. (2009). *Sport and spirituality: An introduction.* London: T & F Books.

Ogilvie, B. C., & Tutko, T. A. (1966). *Problem athletes and how to handle them.* London: Pelham.

Orlick, T. (2008). *In pursuit of excellence* (4th ed.). Champaign, IL: Human Kinetics.

Ostrow, A. C. (1996). *Directory of psychological tests in the sport and exercise sciences* (2nd ed.). Morgantown, WV: Fitness Information Technology.

Pargman, D. (Ed.) (1993). *Psychological bases of sport injuries.* Morgantown, WV: Fitness Information Technology.

Petrie, T. A., & Greenleaf, C. A. (2007). Eating disorders in sport: From theory to research to intervention. In G. Tenenbaum & R. C. Eklund (Eds.), *Handbook of sport psychology* (3rd ed., pp. 352–378). Hoboken, NJ: Wiley.

Raedeke, T. D., & Smith, A. L. (2009). *The Athlete Burnout Questionnaire manual.* Morgantown, WV: Fitness Information Technology.

Ravizza, K. (2008). *Keys to effective sport psychology consulting* [DVD]. Wilbraham, MA: Virtual Brands.

Reed, J., & Ones, D. S. (2006). The effect of acute aerobic exercise on positively activated affect: A meta-analysis. *Psychology of Sport and Exercise, 7*, 477–514.

Richardson, S. O., Andersen, M., & Morris, T. (2008). *Overtraining athletes: Personal journeys in sport.* Champaign, IL: Human Kinetics.

Sachs, M. L. (1991). Reading list in applied sport psychology: Psychological skills training. *The Sport Psychologist, 5,* 88–91.

Salmela, J. (1981). *The world sport psychology sourcebook* (1st ed.). Ithaca, NY: Mouvement.

Salmela, J. (1992). *The world sport psychology sourcebook* (2nd ed.). Champaign, IL: Human Kinetics.

Schinke, R. J., & Hanrahan, S. J. (Eds.). (2009). *Cultural sport psychology.* Champaign, IL: Human Kinetics.

Schuijers, R. (2008). *Mental skills for equestrian athletes [DVD].* Wilbraham, MA: Virtual Brands.

Scripture, E. W. (1894). Tests of mental ability as exhibited in fencing. *Studies from the Yale Psychology Laboratory, 2,* 122–124.

Seligman, M., & Csikszentmihalyi, M. (2000). Positive psychology: An introduction. *American Psychologist, 55,* 5–14.

Simons, J. P., & Andersen, M. B. (1995). The development of consulting practice in applied sport psychology: Some personal perspectives. *The Sport Psychologist, 9,* 449–468.

Smith, D. E., & Bar-Eli, M. (Eds.). (2007). *Essential readings in sport and exercise psychology.* Champaign, IL: Human Kinetics.

Smith, D. E., & Si, G. (2005). Educational programs for sport psychologists in Asia. In D. Hackfort, J. L. Duda, & R. Lidor (Eds.), *Handbook of research in applied sport and exercise psychology: International perspectives* (pp. 397–409). Champaign, IL: Human Kinetics.

Terry, P. C. (2010). It's nice to go travelling, BUT ... In S. J. Hanrahan & M. Andersen (Eds.) *Routledge handbook of applied sport psychology: A comprehensive guide for students and practitioners* (pp. 345–354). Milton Park, England: Routledge.

Terry, P. C., Curran, M., & Mecozzi, A. (in preparation). *Trends in applied sport psychology: Content analysis of journal publications 1992–2009.*

Terry, P. C., Karageorghis, C. I., Curran, M. L., Lim, J. T. N. & Mecozzi, A. (in preparation). *Effects of music in sport and exercise: A meta-analysis.*

Terry, P. C., & Mizzi, L. (in preparation). *Benefits of exercise on mood: A meta-analysis.*

Terry, P. C., & van der Wijngaart, S. (in preparation). *Goal-setting in sport and exercise: A meta-analysis.*

Tonn, E., & Harmison, R. J. (2004). Thrown to the wolves: A student's account of her practicum experience. *The Sport Psychologist, 18,* 324–340.

Torstveit, M. K., Rosenvinge, J. H., & Sundgot-Borgen, J. (2008). Prevalence of eating disorders and the predictive power of risk models in female elite athletes: A controlled study. *Scandinavian Journal of Medicine & Science in Sports, 18,* 108–118.

Trescothick, M. (2008). *Coming back to me: The autobiography.* London: Harper Collins.

Triplett, N. (1898). The dynamogenic factors in pacemaking and competition. *American Journal of Psychology, 9,* 507–533.

Vallerand, R. J., Donahue, E. G., & Lafrenière, M-A. K. (in press). Passion in sport: A look at athletes, coaches, and fans. In T. Morris & P. C. Terry (Eds.), *The new sport and exercise psychology companion.* Morgantown, WV: Fitness Information Technology.

Vealey, R. S. (1994). Knowledge development and implementation in sport psychology: A review of *The Sport Psychologist,* 1987–1992. *The Sport Psychologist, 8,* 331–348.

Williams, J. M., & Straub, W. F. (2006). Sport psychology: Past, present, future. In J. M. Williams (Ed.), *Applied sport psychology: Personal growth to peak performance* (5th ed., pp. 1–14). New York: McGraw Hill.

Wipfli, B. M., Rethorst, C. D., & Landers, D. M. (2008). The anxiolytic effects of exercise: A meta-analysis of randomized trials and dose-response analysis. *Journal of Sport & Exercise Psychology*, *30*, 392–410.

Woodcock, C., Richards, H., & Mugford, A. (2008). Quality counts: Critical features for neophyte professional development. *The Sport Psychologist*, *22*, 491–506.

Woodman, T., & Hardy, L. (2003). The relative impact of cognitive anxiety and self-confidence upon sports performance: A meta-analysis. *Journal of Sports Sciences*, *21*, 443–457.

Yerkes, R. M., & Dodson, J. D. (1908). The relation of strength of stimulus to rapidity of habit-formation. *Journal of Comparative Neurology and Psychology*, *18*, 459–482.

Zaichowsky, L. D., Van Raalte, J. L., Giges, B., & Ravizza, K. (2002). *Brief contact interventions in sport psychology* [DVD]. Wilbraham, MA: Virtual Brands.

Part II

Substantive Areas of Applied Psychology

17

Applied Geropsychology

Rocío Fernández-Ballesteros and Martin Pinquart

With increasing life expectancy and at the same time, decreasing fertility, the world is experiencing "population aging" (United Nations, 2001, 2002, 2005), that is, an increase in the proportion of older people in comparison with younger people (Glass & Eversley, 1965). Moreover, over the next 50 years, population aging is expected to continue. The increase in life expectancy and in the proportion of older adults in the total population is paralleled by an increase in research in basic and applied geropsychology.

As has been emphasized by Schroots (1995), there are three models in geropsychology or psychogerontology: age, aging, and the aged. The psychology of age is devoted to age differences; it compares groups of people of various ages. The psychology of aging deals with the changes in average functioning of individuals across their life span. The psychology of the aged is concerned with the thematic study of the issues facing diverse groups among the elderly. Because this chapter is devoted to "applied geropsychology," it can be stated that geropsychology is devoted to the aged, based on the knowledge developed from the psychology of age differences and the psychology of aging.

The applied psychology of the aged is *the study of the problematic and nonproblematic elderly from a psychological perspective* (Schroots, 1995, p. 48). It is important to emphasize that applied geropsychology cannot be reduced to just the problematic aged. Biomedical studies of aging generate a negative view of old age because from a biological point of view aging is a continuous process of loss of functionality (reinforcing the existing stereotypes of the aged). However, from a psychological point of view, psychosocial functioning cannot be understood with the same principles that govern biological processes (Gould, 1981). Although there is an increasing risk of decline and a decreasing potential for growth across the adult life span, the nature

IAAP Handbook of Applied Psychology, First Edition. Edited by Paul R. Martin, Fanny M. Cheung, Michael C. Knowles, Michael Kyrios, Lyn Littlefield, J. Bruce Overmier, and José M. Prieto.

of adult development has to be understood as multidimensional in which gains and losses can coexist (Heckhausen, Dixon, & Baltes, 1989).

Several theoretical concepts about life-span development are relevant for applied geropsychology (e.g., Baltes, Lindenberger, & Staudinger, 2006). Psychological development is a lifelong process. There is large interindividual variability in age-associated changes, and variability increases at least up to the seventh decade of life. In recognition of the heterogeneity of aging, authors agree on three different forms of aging: usual or normal, pathological, and optimal or successful (Baltes & Baltes, 1990; Fries, 1989; Rowe & Khan, 1997, 1998). Normal aging refers to growing old, even when some manifest illness occurs; the individual continues being independent. Optimal aging is the aging that would be possible under optimal personal and environmental conditions with high physical, psychological, and social functioning. Finally, pathological aging refers to changes due to physical and/or mental illness inducing disability and dependency in the older individual.

In addition to interindividual variability, there is also much within-person variability in psychological development (plasticity; Fernández-Ballesteros, Zamarrón, & Tarraga, 2005). Thus, individuals have a dynamic capacity for change across the life-span, and effective interventions are needed to promote positive change, maintain functioning, reverse negative changes (if possible), or at least delay age-associated negative changes to foster well-being across old age

But, applied geropsychology cannot be reduced to clinical geropsychology that characterizes older adults' functioning as pathological nor is that the only area in which psychologists can apply their knowledge. Because old age can be classified according to several levels of functioning (usual, pathological and successful; e.g., Baltes & Baltes, 1990; Fries, 1989), geropsychology has to deal within these three types of functioning. In summary, psychologists can contribute to the extension of healthy life through the promotion of active aging, health maintenance, and the prevention of disability through the development of healthy habits and lifestyles (Fernández-Ballesteros, 2008; Fries, 1989; Rowe & Kahn, 1997, 1998). These topics are important recommendations in the II International Plan of Action on Aging (United Nations, 2002) and the World Health Organization (WHO, 2001, 2002).

Key Issues in Applied Geropsychology

Sterns and Camp (1998) have suggested that being an applied geropsychologist or applied gerontologist is to be an "interventionist" professional. In fact, a main goal of applied geropsychology is to increase older adults' well-being and quality of life, but applied geropsychology cannot be reduced to interventions in a narrow sense. More broadly, applied geropsychology can be defined as geropsychological research and practice designed to produce and apply knowledge that will address practical goals associated with the aging process and older adults. Several main topics of applied geropsychology have been identified, including (a) clinical geropsychology (psychological assessment, counseling, psychotherapy, rehabilitation, interventions for caregivers of ill older adults), (b) cognitive aging (e.g., consequences of cognitive decline for medication use and risk for traffic accidents, training of cognitive abilities), (c)

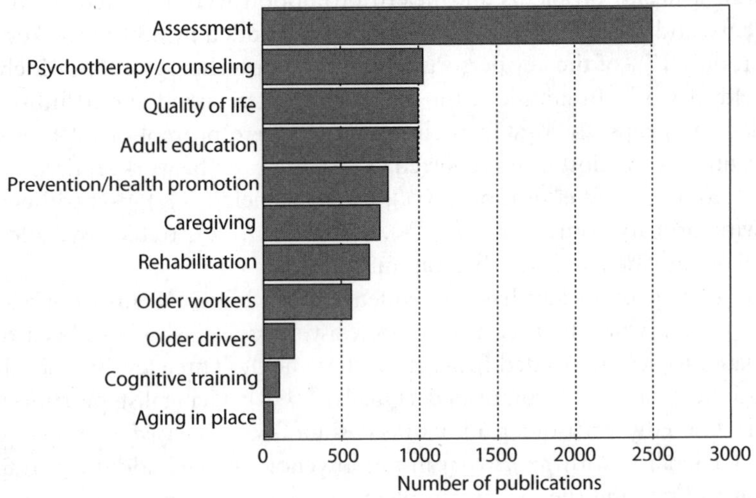

Figure 17.1. Number of papers on selected applied geropsychological topics in the PsycINFO data base

aging and work (e.g., designing a work place that supports older workers in their efforts to remain contributory, age-sensitive trainings), (d) promotion of lifelong learning in general, (e) improving quality of life (e.g., psychological well-being, personal competence), and (f) ensuring enabling and supportive environments such as assisted devices that reduce functional limitations from physical, sensory, and cognitive impairment (for overview, see Fernández-Ballesteros, 2006; Sterns & Camp, 1998).

For identifying the most prominent topics of applied geropsychology, we searched the abstracts in the PsycINFO data base for applied geropsychological topics. The results of this search are presented in Figure 17.1.

In a study with experts from the field of geropsychology from 30 European countries, key persons were asked to identify the three most important fields of application of geropsychology in their country (Pinquart, Fernández-Ballesteros, & Torpdahl, 2007). Geropsychology was most often applied in the clinical field (70% of the countries under investigation). Specialists in the field of clinical psychology provide assessment, consultation, and intervention services related to psychological adaptations in later life (e.g., adapting to age-related changes, bereavement), psychopathology (e.g., affective disorders, dementias), behavioral problems (e.g., wandering, aggressive behavior), problems in daily living (e.g., marital and family problems, coping with acute and chronic stressors), medical and legal decision-making capacity (e.g., legal guardianship), independent living arrangements, and behavioral competencies (e.g., driving, management of medications, self-care skills, financial management). About 60% of the key persons reported the social field as one of the three most important applications of geropsychology in their country (e.g., psychological assessment, competency determinations, help with dealing with age-associated developmental tasks, and staff development in long-term care settings). Applying geropsychology in the prevention of health problems and health promotion were reported by 40% of the respondents, and the field of adult education was included by 33% of the key persons. However, only 17% of the key persons reported geropsychology being widely applied in the field of work. In addition, the key persons were asked about future fields of application in geropsychology in their countries. Here promotion of healthy aging and prevention were most often reported (33%), followed by work/retirement (27%), life-long learning/adult education (20%), the social field (20%), psychotherapy (7%), liaison with primary somatic units (7%), caregiving (7%), traffic psychology (3%), successful aging (3%), and health economics (3%).

As the graying of society has consequences for different fields of application of psychology (e.g., work, leisure, health care), psychologists who have been trained in aging-related topics are needed for each of these fields. Three levels of specialization of practitioners can be distinguished (Qualls, 1998): Generalist practitioners who work very limitedly with older adults need some *basic knowledge* of age-associated changes. Generalists with *proficiency* in geropsychology need additional training for evaluating and treating the unique problems of aging in a variety of settings. Finally, specialists who will operate at the *expertise* levels of practice need advanced skills in geropsychology for providing advanced practice skills, generating new knowledge, setting standards for practice, and providing training at the specialty and proficiency levels. Amongst others, training in applied geropsychology at the proficiency level is offered in clinical psychology and aging doctoral programs (for overview, see DeVries, 2005), programs in industrial geropsychology (e.g., Sterns & Camp, 1998), and as part of broad master programs in gerontology (see, for example, the European Master Programme in Gerontology; Heijke, 2004). But none of these programs are yet common offerings across all universities.

This chapter presents some of the relevant work on selected topics of applied geropsychology: assessment, behavioral interventions, promotion of successful aging, and caregiving.

Assessment

As shown in Figure 17.1., "Assessment" is the topic with highest number of references in PsycINFO and has been reported as an important field in geropsychology research and in training in European countries (Pinquart et al. 2007).

Ethical and conceptual prerequisite

Let us emphasize that—beyond national ethical principles—applied geropsychologists should take into consideration a set of general principles, norms, or guidelines for psychological practice with older adults. The American Psychological Association (2000) published a set of guidelines whose main objective was to "develop criteria to define the expertise necessary for working with older adults and their families and for evaluating competencies at both the generalist and specialist levels" (p. 238). We are trying to introduce some of these guidelines related to assessment as well as other applied settings.

First of all, given that professionals usually hold nihilistic attitudes regarding older adults, Fernández-Ballesteros, Reig, and Zamarrón (2008) emphasize four essential considerations: (1) Geropsychologists must have stamped into their knowledge systems that, even if age is an important biological factor, *per se* it cannot explain psychological functioning. Across the life span and into old age, the human being is an agent acting in an active and interventive world (e.g., Bandura, 1986). (2) Historical and situational factors should be taken into consideration in the assessment as well as strength and weaknesses in behavioral competences. (3) Social and environmental resources (within the family, the community, etc.) which could optimize and/or compensate behavioral components should be carefully assessed (Baltes & Baltes, 1990). (4) From a conceptual point of view, the idea that plasticity (modifiability) is always present across the life span—even in people who are frail and very old—must be kept in mind throughout the process of psychological assessment (Smith & Baltes, 1999; Fernandez-Ballesteros et al., 2003; Fernández-Ballesteros, Zamarron, & Tarraga, 2005).

Geropsychological assessment characteristics

Older adults have a set of common characteristics associated with age; therefore, psychological assessments have a set of characteristics. These include:

1. *Comprehensive multidimensional and multilevel assessment.* It is commonly claimed by experts that a geropsychological assessment should be comprehensive and multidimensional, taking into consideration several dimensions of the individual assessed (e.g., Kane & Kane, 1981; Fernández-Ballesteros et al., 2008; Wahl & Lehr, 2003) as well as the different levels of functioning of the individual and his/her context.

Table 17.1. shows several multilevel dimensions from physical functioning and health to environmental contexts, and quality of life. This Table shows also a set of selected instruments and describes the contents assessed and some psychometric properties of the instruments. Most of the instruments included in Table 17.2. were developed for older populations.

Finally, it should be emphasized that good practice in psychological assessment involves the utilization of multidimensional, multilevel, and multimethod assessment.

2. *Idiographic and nomothetic assessment.* In some cases, psychological assessment consists of an idiographic functional analysis of the individual; other cases require a normative analysis of a set of psychological characteristics in order to make comparisons between the individual assessed and a normative sample. In both cases, most of the available instruments are developed for young adults. As stipulated by APA Guideline 10, "Psychologists strive to be familiar with the theory, research, and practice of various methods of assessment with older adults, and knowledgeable of assessment instruments that are psychometrically suitable for use with [them]"; and by Guideline 11, "Psychologists strive to understand the problems of using assessment instruments created for younger individuals when assessing older adults and to

Table 17.1. Multiple Dimensions Assessed by Selected Instruments in Geropsychological Assessment

Assessed dimension	*Selected instruments*	*Content and psychometric information*
Functional and physical competence and health	Katz Index of Activities of Daily Living (Katz, Ford, Moskowitz, Jackson, & Jaffe, 1963)	Includes bathing, dressing, toileting, transfer, continence, and feeding. Assess assistance received. Higher interrater reliability in three- than in four- or five-point scales.
	ADL/IADL (Lawton & Brody, 1969)	Assess basic and instrumental activities for daily living. Internal consistency in each subscales are higher than .70.
	Balance	Assess competence for standing on only one foot. Predictive power for fall. Concurrent validity with ADL.
	SF-36 (Ware, 2001)	A multipurpose, short-form health survey with 36 questions. It yields an 8-scale profile of functional health and well-being scores. High subscales internal consistency (.93-.68) and test–retest reliability.
Cognitive functioning	Wechsler Adult Intelligence Scale (WAIS and WAIS-III) (Wechsler, 1958, 1998)	Widely used in clinical setting. Reduced versions (Verbal subtests: vocabulary and comprehension; performance subtests: blocks and object assembly). High internal consistency in all subscales (>.70), predictive and discriminant validity. Norms until more than 85 years old. Norms are provided.
	AVLT-Learning Potential (Fernández-Ballesteros et al., 2003; Fernández-Ballesteros 2006)	A list of 15 words (Rey, 1964) are taught through 7 trials (the last one a delayed trial). Posttest scores and gains scores correctly (89%) classified health elders, mild cognitive impaired (MCI) individuals, and Alzheimer disease patients.
	Mini Mental State Examination (MMSE; (Folstein, Folstein, & McHugh, 1995)	30 items assessing orientation, memory, naming, understanding, viso-motor coordination. Cut-off score by education for cognitive impairment. 87% sensitivity.
	The Rivermead Behavioral Memory Test (Wilson, Cockburn, & Baddeley, 1991)	12 tasks with high ecological validity are administered assessing memory for names and objects, design recognition, orientation, faces, appointments, routes, messages, dates, stories. High interrater reliability (100% agreement), parallel-form reliability run .67 to .84, test–retest reliability coefficient was .78. Neurological patients significantly lower scores than the control groups; high correlations with other memory tests and everyday observations of memory lapses.

Affect, control and coping	Positive and Negative Affect Schedule (PANAS; Watson, Clark, & Tellegen, 1988)	A list with 10 positive and 10 negative adjectives. Construct validity very high (two-factor solution), internal consistency of both scales high.
	Philadelphia Geriatric Morale Scale (PGCMS; Lawton, 1972)	22 items (reduced to 15) questionnaire, response format YES/NO. Two-half reliability .79, internal consistency .81, test–retest reliability .80. Concurrent validity with instruments assessing well-being (correlations. .47 to .80).
	Geriatric Depression Scale (GDS; Yesevage, Brink, Rose et al., 1983)	30 items questionnaire, response format Yes/No. A cut-off 11 sensitivity 84% (classified correctly depressive elders) and a 95% specificity.
	Perceived Control (Pearlin & Schooler, 1978)	13 items (7 EC, 6 IC) rating scale (4); results come from the EXCELSA-P Study (Fernández-Ballesteros, Zamarrón, Rudinger, et al., 2004). It is very sensitive to age, Alpha coefficient run from .82 to .53. High test–retest reliability. Internal control subscale predicts competence.
	Ways of Coping Checklist (Short form) Folkman & Lazarus, 1996).	Checklist scales, individuals respond to each item on a four-point Likert scale, indicating the frequency with which each strategy is used classified in the following: confrontive, distancing, self-controlling, seeking social support, accepting responsibility, escape–avoidance, planful problem solving, positive reappraisal. Reliability across subscale scores ranged from .60 to .75. Factors related to this variability were age and format of administration.
Social Relationships	Lubben Social Networks (Lubben, 1988)	27- item scales, assessing family, friend networks and confidence, caregiving and general intimacy. High test–retest reliability (.78), subscales internal consistency and predictive power of competence (Fernández-Ballesteros, Zamarrón, Rudinger, et al., 2004).
	Convoys of social relationships (Antonucci & Akiyama, 1995)	An open instrument collecting those social networks individuals place in a close-distance dimension. Convergent validity between respondents and significant others.

Continued

Table 17.1. *Continued*

Assessed dimension	*Selected instruments*	*Content and psychometric information*
Environmental resources	The Housing Enabler (Iwarsson, 1999)	This instrument is a reliable assessment tool of the accessibility of the housing environment and the immediate outdoor environment. Interrater reliability. Kappas for the different domains assessed run .68 to .87.
	The Multiphasic Environment Assessment Procedure (MEAP; Moos & Lemke, 1996)	Assessed residential setting through five subscales (physical and environmental features, policy and organizational characteristics, residents and personnel characteristics, social climate dimensions, and rating scales). Fernández-Ballesteros (1996) added three more dimensions (residential satisfaction, needs, environment–behavior interactions). Internal consistency of the subscales runs from .99 through .47. Interrater reliability runs from .99 to .69. Norms for USA and Spain residential facilities (respectively by Moos and Lemke, 1996, and Fernández-Ballesteros , 1996.)
	Checklist for Evaluating Residential Factors (Morese & Wisocki, 1991)	A simple instrument that contains three domains: Physical environment (9 items), social environment (5 items), and mobility (3 items). No psychometric data are provided.
Quality of life	World Health Organization Quality of Life Scales (WHOQOL, 1993)	The World Health Organization has produced a generic quality of life questionnaire (WHOQOL-100), together with an abbreviated version of 26 items (WHOQOL-BREF) assessing five domains: Physical and mental health, social relations, and environmental conditions. Preliminary data suggest that the WHOQOL-BREF provides a valid and reliable alternative providing data about its sensitivity to change.
	Quality of Life Inventory (QOLI; Firsch, 1994)	QOLI is a questionnaire assessing subjectively 15 domains: Health, self-esteem, goals and values, money, work, play, learning, creativity, helping, love, friends, children, relatives, home, neighborhood, and community. Domain internal consistency runs from .62 to .79. Concurrent validity with measures of several personality traits and well-being.
	Schedule for Evaluation of Individual Quality of Life (SEIQoL; Browne et al., 1994)	SEIQoL is an idiographic instrument which allows the individual to nominate and weight those domains of greater relevance for his/her quality of life. Several samples arrive to different domains.
	Cuestionario Breve de Calidad de Vida (CUBRECAVI; Fernandez-Ballesteros & Zamarrón, 1996a, 2007)	A screening questionnaire assessing the following nine domains of QoL: physical and mental health (subjectively and objectively), functional abilities, social integration (social network, and social satisfaction), activity and leisure, environmental quality, life satisfaction, social and health services (use and satisfaction), education, and income. There are questions to allow the individual to weight all these domains. The manual provides data about internal consistency (.92 to .47), construct validity, and sensitivity to intervention programs and norms for Spanish elders as well as for other elders from Latin America. Also, there are data about the influence of impression management.

develop skill in tailoring assessments to accommodate older adults' specific characteristics and contexts."

Thus, an important aspect of assessment in old age is that it should contain both idiographic examination of some of the individual psychological functioning and, also, nomothetic assessment for making comparisons between the subjects and a normative sample of older adults. In both cases, geropsychologists have to examine carefully the quality of the adaptation of the materials and norms to older adults. Table 17.1. also provides data on which instruments have norms and which are idiographic instruments. It is also important to emphasize that some standard instruments do not have norms but are criterion-based. For example, as is shown in Table 17.1., the MMSE has a cut-off for screening mental impairment; because mental status is strongly related to education, this cut-off is at least partially education-based.

In summary, geropsychological assessment can be idiographically or nomothetically based but the assessor should always take into consideration the appropriateness of the instrument for the older adult assessed.

3. *Interaction of assessor-assessed.* Behind any geropsychological assessment (as any other type of assessment) is the interaction between the assessor and the assessed. This interaction is governed by at least two conditions: (a) the stereotypes and wrong beliefs the assessor has about the aged, and (b) the specific historical and concurrent conditions in the assessed individual.

As stated in APA Guideline 2, "Psychologists are encouraged to recognize how their attitudes and beliefs about aging and about older individuals may be relevant to their assessment and treatment of older adults, and to seek consultation or further education about these issues when indicated." Several studies have pointed out that negative appraisal of age, aging, or the aged acts on the individual as a threat (e.g., Schooll & Sabat, 2008), but negative stereotyping also has an effect on the assessor who can make wrong inferences by attributing dysfunctions to age rather than to (modifiable) environmental factors (e.g., Fernández-Ballesteros, Bustillos, Huici, & Caprara, 2006).

Also, since there is usually a cohort distance between the assessor and the client, some of the clients' historical characteristics may be neglected by the assessor. For example, the assessor needs to be aware that the older client could have low primary education, or be less habituated to a psychological consultation, and unaccustomed to being assessed. Also, the assessor has to take into consideration physical conditions (such as a need for help with hearing or vision) before starting the assessment sessions.

The process of assessment, intervention, and evaluation

As has been pointed out by the European Association of Psychological Assessment (EAPA) Guidelines for the Assessment Process (GAP; Fernández-Ballesteros et al., 2001), psychological assessment is a long process of decision making and solving problems starting when a given person/institution (client) asks a certified psychologist a question about a subject/single case. This question can involve operations such as description, classification (or diagnosis), prediction, or intervention.

Although some authors use "assessment" and "evaluation" as interchangeable terms, Cronbach (1990) has emphasized that assessment refers to an individual (or group of individuals), whereas, by contrast, evaluation is concerned with treatments or interventions. In the common evaluation literature, there are general recommendations about how to select sensitive, efficient, reliable, and valid targets for evaluating change (dependent variables) and which are the most suitable designs (e.g., Nezu & Nezu, 2008). Here, three main recommendations regarding treatment evaluation in old age are emphasized: (1) The use of multiple measures and multiple informants. Usually older adults are assessed through rating scales filled out by professionals in clinical settings without taking into consideration observations made by relatives in natural settings or self-reports by the older adult. In order to neutralize the variance due to method, multiple measures from multiple informants (including the older person) must be taken. (2) "Maturation" is an important threat for treatment validity in older adults. As Campbell and Stanley (1966) pointed out, "maturation" (in our case it could be "involution") is one of the internal validity threats defined as changes in participants due to time (age) and confounded with treatment. The intervention and change process may take a long time; additionally, positive changes expected in older adults after a given treatment can be attenuated by time (due to age-associated or illness-associated declines), which may lead to the erroneous conclusion that treatment has had no effects. (3) In common practice, use of a multiple-baseline design can help target multiple measures coming from multiple informants assessed across time.

Key issues in assessment

Wahl and Lehr (2004) thoroughly described a number of factors that must be taken into consideration when older persons are assessed. Also Fernández-Ballesteros, Reig, and Zamarrón (2008) described some problematic issues. Let us summarize those that are most important:

1. The use of multidimensional, multilevel, multimethod instruments is a necessary strategy in geropsychological assessment;
2. Older adults have less experience with testing than younger adults such that more time needs to be allowed. Also, instruments not prepared for older population should be avoided, particularly when age norms are necessary but are not provided;
3. Performance tests which require (speeded) motor behavior or other strongly age-related conditions should be avoided (when they are not the target for assessment);
4. When a very old adult cannot fill out a questionnaire, it never should be filled out by their relatives; rather, the information can be collected by interviewing the older adult. (Data about the nonequivalence of protocols administered through self-report and through interview are provided by EXCELSA results; Fernández-Ballesteros, Zamarrón, Rudinger et al., 2004);

5. A response format using Likert-type scales should be simplified as much as possible; reliability is increased when no more than 3–4 point rating scales are provided;
6. Fatigue and motivational and emotional aspects should be carefully taken into consideration throughout the assessment process; the elderly tire quickly and their attention may drift;
7. Assessors must consider that social desirability or impression management are response biases of high frequency in older populations (Fernández-Ballesteros & Zamarrón, 1996); and
8. A major theoretical-methodological challenge in psychological assessment is construct equivalence; for example, depression or quality of life may be not the same at different ages. Idiographic assessment may be preferable in some cases.

Behavioral Interventions

Only a few studies have analyzed the overall prevalence of psychiatric morbidity in the elderly, and the prevalence varies depending on the assessed age groups and the methods of assessment. Overall psychiatric morbidity, usually implying the need for professional help, affects about 20 to 25% of persons aged 65 and older. For example, in a study of people aged over 70 years, Wernicke, Linden, Gilberg, and Helmchen (2000) found that 18.8% of the older adults suffered from insomnia, 13.8% were affected by dementia, 4.8% by major depression, 4.2% by anxiety disorders, and 2% by dysthymia. Other psychiatric diagnoses, such as schizophrenia, were less common. We will focus on psychological interventions for the four most prevalent psychiatric disorders and summarize their effects with the help of meta-analyses.

Nonorganic sleep disorders

Between 9% and 19% of older adults report sleep difficulties on a persistent basis (Wernicke et al., 2000), and the prevalence of insomnia increases with age. Insomnia may take the form of poor sleep quality or lack of restful sleep, reduced duration of sleep, problems falling asleep, or waking repeatedly through the night. Chronic sleep disturbance may lead to disturbances in mood, energy, and performance during the day, and it is associated with declines in quality of life and health functioning such as increased risk for cardiovascular disease.

A meta-analysis by Irwin, Cole, and Nicassio (2006) of 23 randomized controlled studies supports the effectiveness of behavioral interventions for the treatment of insomnia. The strategies used in behavioral treatments were heterogeneous, including relaxation practice, stimulus control that renews the association of bed and bedtime stimuli with sleep rather than sleep-competing activities, sleep restriction by limiting the time spent in bed, cognitive-behavioral therapy that changes dysfunctional beliefs about sleep that lead to emotional distress and further sleep problems, and instruction on "sleep hygiene" about the impact of lifestyle habits on sleep. The meta-analysis found moderate to large effects of behavioral treatments on sleep quality (improvement of $d = .76$ standard deviation units), sleep latency ($d = -.50$), and wakening after sleep onset (d = −.64). Different types of intervention (cognitive-behavioral treatment, relaxation, behavioral interventions only) revealed similar effects. Similar improvements in the outcome measures were shown in adults and older adults 55 years of age and older. Thus, the authors concluded that behavioral interventions constitute an important part of the arsenal of efficacious interventions for patients with chronic insomnia.

Cognitive decline/dementia

It has been estimated that nearly one quarter of all Americans over age 65 may suffer from memory loss and mild cognitive impairment, with increases of about 10 additional percent for every 10 years of age after age 65 (Unverzagt et al., 2001). Many older adults with cognitive decline will develop Alzheimer's disease and other forms of dementia. For example, in Western Europe, rates of dementia increase from 0.9% in 60–64-year-olds to 24.8% in those aged 85 years and older (Ferri et al., 2005; ILCE-Merk, 2006).

Cognitive training and cognitive rehabilitation are methods that aim to help people with mild cognitive impairment and early-stage dementia make the most of their memory and residual cognitive capacity. Training programs are guided by the assumption that practice has the potential to improve, or at least maintain, cognitive functioning in a given domain. They involve guided practice on sets of tasks that reflect particular cognitive functions, such as memory, attention, or problem solving, which can be done in a variety of settings and formats. However, a meta-analysis of nine randomized studies on the effects of cognitive training with patients with early stages of Alzheimer's disease or vascular dementia found, on average, no significant positive effects of cognitive training (Clare & Woods, 2008). There were also no significant negative effects, such as frustration or depression of the trained older adult. It remains open whether insufficient practice (frequency, intensity, and duration) may explain the lack of significant effects or whether some gains resulting from intervention may not be captured adequately by standardized outcome measures. Because only nine studies could be included in the meta-analysis, more research is needed for testing whether positive training results may be found under specific conditions.

Reality Orientation (RO) is a psychological intervention aimed at reducing confusion and inappropriate behaviors in people with dementia. It operates through the presentation of orientation information (e.g., time-, place-, and person-related), and it is usually applied in residential or inpatient settings. The level of cognitive demands of RO can be adapted to the cognitive abilities of the participants. Reality orientation has been divided into (a) a 24-hour informal format and (b) a classroom or group format. The informal format depends on continuously available environmental cues and memory aids such as clocks, calendars, newspapers, door labels, and incidental conversations that support orientation. The classroom format involves groups of about 6 people with similar levels of cognitive function, meeting for 30–60 minutes, 3–5 times weekly, with one or two facilitators focusing on specific orientating tasks. A meta-analysis of 6 controlled randomized studies showed that classroom RO used for older people with dementia has a moderate statistically significant beneficial effect on measures of basic cognitive abilities (d = .59) and reducing behavior problems (*d* = .64; Spector, Davies, Woods, & Orrell, 2000). Unfortunately, there are still insufficient data on whether improvement is sustained over longer time intervals.

Recent advances in the development of interventions for people with mild to moderate levels of dementia combine aspects of reality orientation and cognitive stimulation into Cognitive Stimulation Therapy (CST) which involves 14 sessions of themed activities, typically run twice a week over a 7-week period. CST has shown significant benefits in cognition and participant-rated quality of life when compared against a no-treatment control group. However, the initial cognitive improvements following CST were only sustained at 4-months follow-up when the initial CST was followed by a program of maintenance CST sessions (Spector, Woods, & Orrell, 2008).

Available data indicate that demanding cognitive trainings are more adequate for reducing age-associated cognitive decline in healthy older adults than in adults with dementia. Cognitive trainings with healthy older adults have shown small to moderate improvements even at 5-year follow-ups, although training-related gains were specific to the trained abilities (Willis et al., 2006). Less cognitively demanding interventions, such as RO and CST, have positive short-term effects on cognitive functioning of dementia patients, but, given the progressive cognitive decline in dementias and Alzheimer's disease, training effects may be difficult to sustain over longer periods.

Depression

Depression is one of the most common mental disorders in advanced age. Estimates of the point prevalence of major depression in community-dwelling older adults range from 1.5 to 5%. In addition, minor depression and dysthymia are present in about 10% of older adults (Hendrie, Callaham, & Levitt, 1993; Lyness, Caide, King, Cox, & Yeodino, 1999). Depressive conditions contribute to medical illness and disability in later life, increase risk of institutionalization, and amplify risk for all-cause mortality and suicide (for an overview, see Blazer, 2002).

A recent meta-analysis of 57 controlled psychological intervention studies with clinically depressed older adults (60 + years; *n* = 1,956 treated patients) showed that after controlling for nonspecific change in control group members, self-rated depression improved by *d* = .84 and clinician-rated depression improved by *d* = .93 (Pinquart, Duberstein, & Lyness, 2007). Effect sizes were large for cognitive and behavioral therapy (CBT; *d* = 1.06) and reminiscence (*d* = 1.00), and medium for psychodynamic therapy (*d* = .76), psychoeducational interventions (*d* = .70), and supportive interventions (*d* = .57). However, interpersonal therapy had only very small and nonsignificant effects on depression in older adults. Interestingly, age differences in treatment effects were not observed. Weaker effects were found in samples of physically ill or cognitively impaired patients and in patients with major depression as compared to less severe forms of depression. The data indicate that major depression might be relatively more difficult to treat with psychotherapy than other forms of depression, perhaps due to the presence of more chronic or severe symptoms (Pinquart, et al., 2007).

A comparison of psychotherapy and pharmacotherapy showed similar efficacy in studies that included only patients with major depression (clinician-rated depression: *d* = .96 and *d* = .79). The effects of psychotherapy on clinician-rated depression were even stronger than pharmacotherapy in studies that included patients with minor depression or dysthymic disorder (*d* = 1.18 vs. *d* = .66; Pinquart, Duberstein, & Lyness, 2006).

Anxiety disorders

Although anxiety disorders are less common in the elderly than in younger adults, estimates of the point prevalence in community-dwelling older adults range from 1% to 19% (US Department of Health and Human Services, 1999). General Anxiety Disorder (GAD) is the most common anxiety disorder in older adults, with prevalence rates of about 5% (Flint, 2005). Other anxiety disorders, such as phobic disorders (.7 to 7%) and panic disorder (0.1 to 1%), are less common (Flint, 1994). Anxiety disorders have been related to disability (DeBeurs et al., 1999) and steeper declines in memory performance (DeLuca et al., 2005). In addition, there is considerable comorbidity of geriatric depression and anxiety disorders.

A comparative meta-analysis of 32 studies of treatments focused on anxiety disorders in older adults (*n* = 2,484) receiving psychotherapeutic/behavioral interventions or pharmacotherapy showed similar levels of reduction in anxiety symptoms in both behavioral interventions and pharmacotherapy, when controlling for nonspecific change in the control group (*d* = .80 and *d* = .83; Pinquart & Duberstein, 2007). However, when analyzing absolute levels of improvement, greater reductions of anxiety symptoms are found in pharmacotherapy than in behavioral interventions (*d* = 1.76 vs. *d* = .81). Intriguingly, in the control groups, greater reduction in anxiety was found in pill-placebo control groups (used in pharmacological interventions) than in waiting-list control groups (used in psychotherapeutic studies)—perhaps reflecting biased expectations for forms of treatment. Treatment effects did not differ between CBT and other behavioral interventions. Positive treatment effects of pharmacological and behavioral interventions were maintained at the follow-up. Contrary to the belief that older patients would benefit less from treatments than younger patients, the observed effect sizes of pharmacological and behavioral interventions were similar, or even larger, than those reported in meta-analyses of studies conducted on younger patients.

In summary, the meta-analyses provided clear evidence that psychotherapeutic and other behavioral interventions are efficacious in reducing insomnia, depressive symptoms, and anxiety symptoms in older adults. Cognitive interventions have been found to improve the trained cognitive abilities in healthy older adults, but there is not enough evidence from high-quality studies for a benefit from cognitive training for patients with early stages of dementia. The present findings suggest that for minor clinical depression not meeting the criteria for major depression, psychotherapy should be preferred over pharmacotherapy. Because psychotherapeutic and pharmacological treatments were similarly effective for major depression, treatment choice should be based on contraindications, availability of psychotherapy in the community, and treatment preferences of the older adults or their guardians. As long as there are no medical contraindications and contradicting patient preferences, pharmacotherapy might be recommended over behavioral interventions for the treatment of anxiety disorders in old age, although behavioral interventions are a satisfactory alternative in most circumstances. We conclude that old age is no contra indication against using effective psychotherapeutic treatment; intervention effects do not wane with increasing age, at least in the age range of 60 to 80 years.

Prevention and Promotion

As pointed out earlier, broad variability can be found in the ways people age; usually, they are classified as "usual," "pathological," and "successful" aging by authors. The balance between both positive and negative changes across life span leads to the diversity of forms of aging; if we keep in mind a standard distribution shape, "usual" (or normal) age could be defined as the average functioning of the older individual at physical, psychological, and social levels, "pathological" and "successful" (or optimal) aging would be located at the two sides of this distribution. But what percentages of older adults may be assigned to these three categories?

Successful aging is defined through a set of bio-psycho-social criteria: good health and physical conditions, high cognitive and emotional functioning, and social participation and involvement (Rowe & Kahn, 1989; Fernández-Ballesteros, 2008). Nevertheless, not all researchers have defined successful aging with similar indicators. Peel, McClure, and Bartlett (2005) reviewed those cross-sectional and longitudinal empirical studies on successful aging that identified percentages of successful aging. Although the proportion of people aging successfully will depend on the definition of successful aging used in a particular study, an average of 25% (range 49% to 12.7%) of individuals can be identify as "successfully aging"; that is, about one fourth of the participants of empirical studies on successful aging are aging well (for a review see Fernández-Ballesteros, 2008).

Pathological aging has been defined as poor health, and/or physical disability, and/or deficit in the activities of daily living (both basic and instrumental), all with a need for care. If data about dependency in the elderly are examined, about 25% of adults older than 65 suffer from such disabilities (see, e.g., Manton & Gu, 2001). Obviously, prevalence depends on individual differences in age, education, SES as well as national differences in socio-economic trends (education, health protection system, etc.).

If, as noted in the preceding paragraphs, 25% can be classed as "successfully aging" and 25% classed as "pathologically aging", it can be estimated that about 50% of older individuals can be placed in the "usual" category, defined as people who rate their health, and physical and psychosocial functioning as average by several bio-psycho-social indicators. Finally, these proportions of successful, usual, and pathological aging are in agreement with the distribution of older people reporting "very good or fairly good," "average," and "fairly poor or poor" health (see, e.g., Ferrucci, Heikinnen, Waters, & Baroni, 1995).

Any policy on aging must increase the proportion of successful agers by reducing the prevalence of dependency in old age. At population level, the objective of any healthy or active aging promotion program must be evaluated through population indicators, looking for increasing healthy life expectancy and disability-free life expectancy, and reducing disability rate and disability-phase life expectancy (Jaegger,

Table 17.2. Negative Conditions Associated with Aging, Medical Problems and Illnesses, and Behavioral Preventive or Protective Factors

Negative psychological conditions	*Examples of behavioral preventive or protective factors*	*Medical problems and illnesses*	*Examples of behavioral preventive or protective factors*
Low physical fitness	Aerobic exercise, weight control, not smoking	Blood pressure, CVD, peripheral diseases	Exercise, diet, stress control, not smoking
Low mobility, flexibility, balance	Stretching, flexibility & balance exercise	Osteoarticular diseases	Exercise, diet, weight control
Low reaction time, speed	Training	Dementia	Lifelong education, cognitive, sociocultural activities Aerobic exercise
Decline in intelligence and memory	Lifelong education, cognitive activities Cognitive & memory training Aerobic exercises	Depression and anxiety	Social skills training Pleasant activities Cognitions
Low control, negative self-stereotypes	Improving control and self-efficacy for aging	Inmuno- neuro-psychological system regulation	Stress control and coping Positive emotions
Social isolation, anxiety, and sadness	Social skills training Promoting pro-social behaviors, Social networks Pleasant event and coping trainings	Cancer	Diet, not smoking

Source: Fernández-Ballesteros, 2008, based on Fries, 1989

Matthews, Matthews, Robinson, & Robine, 2007). In fact, Marin and Zaidi (2007) collected a series of indicators to assess the Second International Plan of Action on Aging (United Nations, 2002).

WHO has developed a set of policy guidelines that formalize action recommendations on the life-style and behavioral factors we have noted in the text and in Table 17.2.

Promoting healthy aging and preventing dependency

As has been pointed out by WHO (2002), from a life course perspective, the process of aging well starts from birth and continues throughout infancy, adolescence, and adulthood. Health, physical and functional capacity, cognitive capacity, and emotional and social relationships increase in childhood and peak in early adulthood; on average, these peaks are followed by a slow decline. The rate of decline, however, is dependent upon factors related to lifestyles, schooling, selected profession, intellectual and cultural activities, coping with stressful situations, social participation, etc. All of these factors provided by the environment (from a physical, cultural, and political point of view) and selected by the individual, can contribute to health and a good life throughout the aging process. If individuals do not optimize their development across their life span, they are at higher risk for disability in old age caused by different types of morbidity (stroke, diabetes, dementia, and/or social isolation, etc.).

Life-long health promotion programs have to be complemented with other programs during adulthood and old age. Thus, several *prevention programs* have been developed and implemented to improve medical and geriatric care in institutional health services based on: (1) the prevalence of most common diseases in old age and their repercussion in mortality (life expectancy) and disability (disability life expectancy), and (2) the risk of or protective factors for those more prevalent diseases and negative conditions. Several health promotion programs have been implemented to promote health behaviors and prevent prevalent diseases. Up to now, almost no integrative meta-analyses are available on the effects of such prevention and behavioral health promotion programs in old age. Meta-analysis of the effects of exercise interventions on functional status outcomes yielded modest but statistically significant effect sizes for functional performance and physical performance but not for activities of daily living (Gu & Conn, 2008).

Although there are evaluation studies looking at the efficacy, effectiveness, and efficiency of health promotion and illness prevention programs (such as "Community Healthy Activities Model Program for Seniors" or "Multiple Risk Factor Intervention programs," e.g., Clark, Nigg, Greene, Riebe, & Saunders, 2002; Li, Zhang, He, & Zhang, 2001; Moe et al., 2002; Toobert, Strycker, Glasgow, Barrera, & Bagdale, 2002), there are not yet any clear conclusions about their effectiveness and long-term effects on health and quality of life. Regarding health promotion and illness prevention programs, usually called "psychosocial interventions"—based on the relationships between healthy habits and disease—Syme has noted that "to develop more effective prevention programs, we will have to train a new generation of active aging experts who can not only provide people with risk information but also work with them as partners in achieving mutually agreed upon goals" (Syme, 2003, p. 400). Geropsychologists should participate as experts in the task of developing and evaluating new health promotions and illness preventions programs; in fact they *are* experts both in changing behaviors and in evaluating change.

Promoting active and productive aging

Positive or successful aging does not mean only long and healthy life, but also active and productive life; as Glass (2003, p. 282) said: "It refers to the capacity to function across many domains, including cognitive, social and emotional ... envisioning exceptional functioning as possible."

As has been mentioned, healthy and active aging implies a life-long process. Baltes and Baltes (1990) formulated a psychological theory and definition of successful aging defining it as the process of selective optimization with compensation (SOC).

The SOC theory predicts that, across one's life span, a positive developmental trajectory might maximize growth (gains) minimizing decline (losses). Selection, optimization, and compensation are processes behind the promotion of human growth, development, and successful aging; for example, through selecting physical activities the individual optimizes his or her sensory-motor repertoires, through reading and writing the individual reaches the highest level of linguistic skills, involvement in social contexts usually increases social skills and high participation. Also, when losses occur, as expected in old age, they can be compensated through new training or new strategies for solving difficult problems and situations (see Freund & Baltes, 2007).

Since WHO (2002) published the booklet *Active ageing*, several programs entitled "active ageing" have been implemented at community level, for example, the "California Active Aging Project" (Hooker et al. 2005; Hooker & Cirill, 2006), "Active For Life" (AFL), "Active Ageing South Australia," and the "Active Ageing European Union Policy." Also, several electronic information and self-help books are available on the internet or published (e.g., Bond et al., 1995; Fernández-Ballesteros, 2002; Fries, 1989; Rowe & Kahn, 1998); other multimedia programs such as "Vital Ageing" have been developed (for a review, see Fernández-Ballesteros, 2005, 2008).

After a review of these programs, it can be concluded that most of them consist of the promotion of physical exercise and its consequences on social relationships and participation; only one program (the European Union "Policy on Active Ageing") refers to workplace/employment, and only one ("Vital Ageing") takes into consideration several domains for promoting successful aging, including the cognitive. Finally, very few of these programs have been evaluated. It is concluded that much more evaluative research must be conducted. Geropsychologists need to be involved in the development, implementation, and evaluation of much more comprehensive multidimensional programs to promote active aging and prevent disability during old age.

Caregiving

The increase in life expectancy has led to a growing number of older adults being in need of help and personal care. The majority of this support is provided by informal caregivers, who are in most cases spouses and adult children. Almost everyone is involved in caregiving at one time or another, and over half are likely to provide 20 hours or more care per week at some point in their lives (Hirst, 2002).

Providing care for a frail older adult is a stressful experience that may erode the psychological well-being and physical health of caregivers. In a meta-analysis, caregivers reported higher levels of symptoms of distress (d = .43 standard deviation units) and of depressive symptoms (d = .37), lower levels of positive psychological well-being (d = .19), and slightly lower levels of physical health (d = .09) than noncaregivers (Pinquart & Sörensen, 2003a). Providing care to demented adults is especially stressful; larger differences were found between caregivers of dementia clients and noncaregivers than between caregivers of physically impaired adults and noncaregivers (Pinquart & Sörensen, 2003a). In has been reported that 20–50% of dementia caregivers themselves suffer from clinical depression (Zarit & Femia, 2008).

Care recipients' behavior problems show stronger associations with caregiver outcomes than other stressors. In addition, higher levels of care provision and greater physical impairments of the care recipient are associated with higher levels of caregiver sense of burden and depression (Pinquart & Sörensen, 2003b). Furthermore, experiencing the suffering of a chronically ill family member may have an independent effect on the psychological health of other family members, even if they do not provide care (Schulz et al., 2008).

Given the high levels of psychological distress in informal caregivers, several forms of intervention have been developed and evaluated. Psychologists are actively involved in the development and application of most of these forms of interventions, and the following paragraphs will focus on these programs.

Interventions most often focus on (a) reduction of the level of objective stressors (e.g., reducing symptoms in the care recipient or the amount of support provided), (b) reduction of psychological distress (e.g., caregiver burden and depression), (c) increasing the resources of the caregiver (e.g., coping abilities, self-efficacy, availability of social support), and (d) delay of institutionalization. Some interventions have also included other goals, such as improving the quality of family ties or promoting the positive health-related behaviors of caregivers.

A meta-analysis on the effects of 127 controlled intervention studies with informal dementia caregivers has been published (Pinquart & Sörensen, 2006).

This chapter reports a number of updates based on 154 studies with 15,519 caregivers in the intervention condition and 14,136 caregivers in the control condition. The effect sizes in these updates, reported below, control for non-specific change in the control group.

1. Cognitive-behavioral therapy (CBT) with caregivers focuses on identifying and modifying caregiving-related beliefs, developing a new behavioral repertoire to deal with caregiving demands, and fostering activities that may promote the subjective well-being of the caregiver. CBT has the strongest effect on caregiver depression ($d = -.91$ standard deviation units) and caregiver burden ($d = -.46$).
2. Psychoeducational interventions are the most often applied interventions for caregivers. They focus on the structured presentation of information about the illness of the care recipient and caregiving-related issues, and they may or may not include active participation of participants (e.g., role playing, applying new knowledge to individual problems). These interventions have the strongest effect on caregiver knowledge and perceived abilities ($d = .72$). However, only the active—but not the passive—psychoeducational interventions reduce caregiver burden ($d = -.16$) and depression ($d = -.39$).
3. Interventions targeted at reduction of symptoms (e.g., behavior problems) and at increasing the competence of the care recipient (e.g., training of cognitive abilities) were expected to have an indirect effect on psychological distress of caregivers. Although they did have a small significant effect on symptoms of the care recipient ($d = -.36$), the hoped-for effect on caregiver depression and burden could not be shown.
4. Compared to the other forms of intervention already discussed, supportive interventions are less structured. For example, they may be organized as a

professionally led support group or as a self-help group. In this kind of intervention, caregivers learn that other caregivers have similar problems and how others deal with their problems. A meta-analysis showed that these interventions do not have significant effects on any outcome variables (Pinquart & Sörensen, 2006). Although the empirical base for the present analysis is small, supportive interventions cannot be recommended as an intervention of choice.

5. Finally, multicomponent interventions combine the above components, but also add nonpsychological aspects (e.g., a center-based day-care program that offers congregate care for a certain number of weekly hours). Only multicomponent interventions were found to reduce the risk for institutionalization (Risk ratio *RR* .51), but effects on other outcomes were less clear.

6. As a tool for evaluating the practical effects of the interventions, we compared the elevated levels of distress and depression of caregivers in comparison to noncaregivers to the observed intervention effects. For example, the difference between levels of depressive symptoms of dementia caregivers and noncaregivers is about $d = .65$ standard deviation units (Pinquart & Sörensen, 2003a). As cognitive-behavioral therapy resulted in a decline of depressive symptoms of $d = -.91$, we can conclude that this form of intervention reduced the level of depressive symptoms of caregivers below the level that could be expected in noncaregivers. Results were less positive for symptoms of distress (elevated symptoms: $d = .85$; reduction of symptoms: $d = -.46$), but these numbers are difficult to compare because most intervention studies used caregiving-specific measures of symptoms of distress whereas nonspecific measures had to be used when comparing caregivers to noncaregivers. Nonetheless, despite practically meaningful effects, psychological interventions are not able to eliminate all caregiving-specific stressors so that very large declines in caregiver burden are unlikely to be found.

Fewer applied psychological studies have focused on formal caregivers. Behavioral observation studies by Margaret Baltes (1996) found that formal caregivers of older adults actually reward dependent behavior on the part of care recipients and most often ignore—or even punish—independent behavior. Thus, dependency among elderly care recipients is often learned.

An intervention program aimed at changing the behavior of formal caregivers was developed and evaluated. Caregivers learned how to promote independent self-care behaviors. Note that the intervention has been applied to older adults whose dependent behavior could not be explained by physical illnesses or dementia. Intervention research showed that the training of the formal caregiver increased independence–supportive behavior. In addition, changes in caregiver behavior were associated with an increase in independent self-care behavior of the older adults, although they could not completely eliminate dependent behavior (Baltes, 1996).

In summary, interventions targeted at reducing the psychological distress of caregivers, improving competence in coping with caregiving demands, and reducing symptoms and promoting competence of care recipients are an important concern within applied geropsychology. Future work with informal caregivers should provide flexible interventions that screen for needs and preferences of the caregivers and match the offered components to their needs. For example, because the majority of caregivers are not clinically depressed, many caregivers will not need cognitive-behavioral interventions that are based on the principles of depression therapy, but they may need other interventions, such as respite.

Concluding Remarks

The rapid increase in the absolute numbers and proportions of older adults creates a growing need for applied geropsychology. This has several implications.

First, geropsychology should become a regular topic in training at Bachelor level in the field of psychology. In addition, courses at Master level should include information on aging-related topics in applied fields (e.g., psychological assessment and evidence-based interventions with older adults in programs of clinical psychology; age-associated change in performance and motivation of older workers in programs of industrial and organizational psychology). Recommendations for the integration of aging-related topics into teaching undergraduates in different fields of psychology (Whitbourne & Cavanaugh, 2003) and in clinical geropsychology in particular (Hinrichsen & Zweig, 2005) have been published.

Second, as assessment and intervention research has shown that applied geropsychology provides significant contributions of practical value for the physical and mental health, cognitive abilities, emotional motivational and psychosocial functioning, physical competence, and quality of life of older adults in general. Interventions shown as effective should be made available to all older adults in need. Adaptations may be needed according to the cultural conditions of each country. Given the fact that controlled randomized studies often find stronger intervention effects than in ordinary practice (e.g., due to restricted inclusion criteria and highly motivated therapists), we need research on the effectiveness of interventions with older adults in their daily routine.

Third, whereas the effects of several kinds of interventions have been well demonstrated in some areas (e.g., cognitive-behavioral interventions with depressed older adults, anxious older adults, and caregivers), more efforts are needed in developing and evaluating effective behavioral interventions in the fields of cognitive impairment, prevention, and health promotion. Evaluations have to include the assessment of long-term effects.

Fourth, an analysis of the training for and application of geropsychology in Europe showed a large degree of heterogeneity between countries. Whereas applied geropsychology was well established in some countries, few if any psychologists were trained for working with older adults in others (Pinquart et al., 2007). The heterogeneity would probably be much larger if other continents were included. Thus, efforts are needed to decrease this gap by establishing applied geropsychology as an important field of applied psychology in all countries across the globe.

Fifth and finally, guidelines for defining the expertise necessary for working with older adults and their families and for evaluating competencies at both the generalist and specialist levels, should be developed and approved at an international level.

References

American Psychological Association. (2000). *Training guidelines for practice in clinical geropsychology.* Washington DC: APA Division 12, Section II (Clinical Psychology).

Antonucci, T., & Akiyama, H. (1995). Convoys of social relationships: Family and friendships within a little span context. In R. Blieszner & V. Bedford (Eds.), *Handbook of aging and the family* (pp. 355–371). Westport, CT: Greenwood Press.

Baltes, M. (1996). *The many faces of dependency in old age.* Cambridge: Cambridge University Press.

Baltes, P. B., & Baltes, M. (1990). Psychological perspectives on successful aging: The model of selective optimization with compensation. In P. B. Baltes & M. M. Baltes, (Eds.), *Successful aging: perspectives from the behavioral sciences* (pp. 1–35) Cambridge, UK: Cambridge University Press.

Baltes, P. B., Lindenberger, U., & Staudinger, U. M. (2006). Life span theory in developmental psychology. In R. Lerner (Ed.), *Handbook of child psychology* (6th ed., Vol. 1, pp. 569–664). Hoboken, NJ: Wiley.

Bandura, A. (1986). *Social foundation of thoughts and actions.* Englewood Cliffs, CA: Prentice Hall.

Blazer, D. (2002). *Depression in later life.* New York: Springer.

Bond, L., Culter, S., & Grams, A. (Eds.). (1995). *Promoting successful and productive aging.* Newbury Park, CA: Sage Publication.

Browne, J. P., O'Boyle, H. M., McGee, H. M., Joyce, C. R. B., McDonald, N. J., O'Malley, K., & Hiltbrunner, B. (1994). Individual quality of life in the healthy elderly. *Quality of Life Research, 3,* 235–244.

Campbell, D. T., & Stanley, J. C. (1966). *Experimental and quasi-experimental designs for research.* Chicago, IL: Rand McNally & Company.

Clare, L., & Woods, B. (2008). Cognitive rehabilitation and cognitive training for early-stage Alzheimer's disease and vascular dementia. *Cochrane Database of Systematic Reviews, 4,* 1–41.

Clark, P. G., Nigg, C. R., Greene, G., Riebe, D., & Saunders, S. D. (2002). The study of exercise and nutrition in older Rhode Islanders (SENIOR): Translating theory into research. *Health Education Research, 17,* 552–561.

Cronbach, J. L. (1990). *Psychological testing* (5th ed.). New York: Harper & Row.

DeBeurs, E., Beekman, A. T., van Balkom, A. J., Deeg, D. J., van Dyck, R., & van Tilburg, T. (1999). Consequences of anxiety in older persons: Its effect on disability, well-being, and use of health services. *Psychological Medicine, 29,* 583–593.

DeLuca, A. K., Lenze, E. J., Mulsant, B. H., Butters, M. A., Karp, J. F., Dew, M. A., & Reynolds, C. F. (2005). Comorbid anxiety disorder in late life depression: Association with memory decline over four years. *International Journal of Geriatric Psychiatry, 20,* 848–854.

DeVries, H. M. (2005). Clinical geropsychology training in generalist doctoral programs. *Gerontology & Geriatrics Education, 25*(4), 5–20.

Ferri, C. L., Prince, M., Brayne, C., Brodaty, H., Fratiglioni, L., Ganguli, M., … Alzheimer's Disease International. (2005). Global prevalence of dementia: a Delphi consensus study, *The Lancet, 366,* 2112–2117.

Fernández-Ballesteros, R. (Ed.). (1996). *Sistema de Evaluación de Residencias de Ancianos. SERA.* Madrid: INSERSO.

Fernández-Ballesteros, R. (2002). *Vivir con Vitalidad* (5 Vols.). Madrid: Pirámide.

Fernández-Ballesteros, R. (2005). Evaluation of "VITAL AGEING-M": A psychosocial programme for promoting optimal ageing. *European Psychologists. 10*, 146–156.

Fernández-Ballesteros, R. (2006). Geropsychology: An applied field for the 21st century. *European Psychologist, 11*, 312–323.

Fernández-Ballesteros, R. (2008). *Active aging. The contribution of psychology.* Göttingen: Hogrefe & Huber.

Fernández-Ballesteros, R., Bustillos, A., Huici, C., & Caprara, M. G. (2006). *The role of self-perception of ageing in memory performance of explicit stereotype threat: Preliminary report.* Madrid: IMSERSO Institute.

Fernández-Ballesteros, R., De Bruyn, E. E. E., Godoy, A., Hornke, L. F., Ter Laak, J., Vizcarro, C., ... Zacchagnini, J. L. (2001). Guideliness for the Assessment Process (GAP): A proposal for discussion. *European Journal of Psychological Assessment, 17*, 187–200.

Fernández-Ballesteros, R., Reig, A., & Zamarrón, M.D. (2008). Evaluación en psicogerontología. In R. Fermández-Ballesteros (Ed.), *Psicología de la vejez. Una psicogerontología aplicada.* (pp. 35–96). Madrid: Pirámide.

Fernandez-Ballesteros, R., & Zamarrón, M. D. (1996a). *Calidad de vida en la vejez en distintos contextos en la Vejez. CUBRECAVI.* Madrid: INSERSO.

Fernández-Ballesteros, R., & Zamarrón, M.D. (1996b). New findings on social desirability and faking. *Psychological Reports, 78*, 1–3.

Fernandez-Ballesteros, R., & Zamarrón, M. D. (2007). *Cuestionario breve de calidad de vida en la vejez.* Madrid: TEA.

Fernández-Ballesteros, R., Zamarrón, M. D., Rudinger, G., Schroots, J., Drusini, A., Heikinnen, E., ... Rosenmayr, L. (2004). Assessing competence. The European Survey on Ageing Protocol. *Gerontology, 50*, 330–347.

Fernández-Ballesteros, R., Zamarrón, M. D., & Tárraga, L. (2005). Learning potential, a new method for assessing cognitive impairment. *International Psychogeriatrics, 17*, 119–128.

Fernández-Ballesteros, R., Zamarrón, M. D., Tárraga, L., Moya, R., & Iñiguez, J. (2003). Cognitive plasticity in healthy, mild cognitive impairment individuals and Alzheimer's patients. *European Psychologist, 8*, 148–159.

Ferrucci, L., Heikinnen, E., Waters, E., & Baroni, A. (1995). *Pendulum health and quality of life in older Europeans.* Florence: INRCA & WHO.

Firsch, R. (1994) *QOLI Quality of Life Inventory. Manual and treatment manual.* Minneapolis, MN: National Computer System.

Flint, A. (1994). Epidemiology and comorbidity of anxiety disorders in the elderly. *American Journal of Psychiatry, 151*, 640–649.

Flint, A. (2005). Generalized anxiety disorder in elderly patients: Epidemiology, diagnosis, and treatment options. *Drugs & Aging, 22*, 101–114.

Folkman, A., & Lazarus, R. S. (1991). *Stress and coping.* New York: Columbia University Press.

Folstein, M. F., Folstein, S. E., & McHugh, P. R. (1975). Mini mental state examination. A practical method for grading the cognitive state of the patients for the clinician. *Journal of Psychiatric Research, 12*, 189–198.

Freund, A. M., & Baltes, P. B. (2007). Toward a theory of successful aging: Section, optimization and compensation. In R. Fernández-Ballesteros (Ed.), *GeroPsychology. A European perspective for an aging world.* (pp 239–244). Göttingen: Hogrefe & Huber.

Fries, J. F. (1989). *Aging well.* Reading, MA: Addison-Wesley.

Glass, D. V., & Eversley, D. E. C. (1965). *Population in history.* London: Edward Arnold.

Glass, T. A. (2003). Assessing the success of successful aging. *Annals of Internal Medicine, 139*, 282–283.

Gould, R. L. (1981). *The mismeasure of man.* New York: Norton.

Gu, M. O., & Conn, V. S. (2008) Meta-analysis of the effects of exercise interventions on functional status in older adults. *Research in Nursing & Health*, *31*, 594–603.

Heckhausen, J., Dixon, R. A., & Baltes, P. B. (1989). Gains and losses in development throughout adulthood as perceived by different age groups. *Developmental Psychology*, *25*, 109–121.

Heijke, L. (2004). The European master's programme in gerontology. *European Journal of Aging*, *1*, 106–108.

Hendrie, H. C., Callaham, C. M., & Levitt, E. E. (1995). Prevalence rates of major depressive disorders: The effects of varying diagnostic criteria in an older primary care population. *American Journal of Geriatric Psychiatry*, *3*, 119–131.

Hinrichsen, G. A., & Zweig, R. A. (2005). Models of training in clinical geropsychology. *Gerontology & Geriatrics Education*, *25*(4), 1–4.

Hirst, M. (2002). Transitions to informal care in Great Britain during the 1990s. *Journal of Epidemiology and Community Health*, *56*, 579–587.

Hooker, S. P., & Cirill, L. A. (2006). Evaluation of community coalition's ability to create safe, effective exercise classes for older adults. *Evaluation and Program Planning*, *29*, 242–250.

Hooker, S. P., Seavey, W. Weismed, C. E., Harvey, D. J., Stewart, A. L. Gillis, D. E., Nicholl, K. L., & King, A. C. (2005). California Active Aging Community Grant Program: Translating science into practice to promote physical activity in older adults. *Annals of Behavioral Medicine*, *29*, 155–165.

ILC-Merk. (2006). *The state of ageing and health in Europe*. London: The Merk Company Foundation.

Irwin, M. R., Cole, J. C., & Nicassio, P. M. (2006). Comparative meta-analysis of behavioral interventions for insomnia and their efficacy in middle-aged adults and in older adults 55+ years of age. *Health Psychology*, *25*, 3–14.

Iwarsson, S. (1999). The housing enabler: An objective tool for assessing accessibility. *British Journal of Occupational Therapy*, *62*, 491–497.

Jaegger, C., Matthews, R., Matthews, F., Robinson, T., & Robine, J.-M. (2007). The burden of disease on disability-free life expectancy in later life. *Journal of Gerontology*, *62A:* 408–414.

Kane, R. A., & Kane, R. L. (1981). *Assessing the elderly. A practical guide to measurement.* Lexington, MA: Lexington Book.

Katz, S., Ford, A. B., Moskowitz, R. W., Jackson, B. A., & Jaffe, M.W. (1963). Studies of illness in the aged: The Index of ADL. *Journal of the American Medical Association*, *185*, 914–919.

Lawton, M. P. (1975). The Philadelphia Geriatric Centre Moral Scale (PGCMS). *Journal of Gerontology*, *30*, 85–89.

Lawton, M. P., & Brody, E. M. (1969). Assessment of older people. *The Gerontologist*, *9*, 179–186.

Li, C., Zhang, M., He, Y., & Zhang, K. (2001). Impact of healthy behavior on successful aging: A 5-year follow-up study among community elderly. *Chinese Mental Health Journal*, *51*, 325–326.

Lubben, N. (1988). Assessing social networks among elderly populations. *Family and Community Health*, *11*, 42–52.

Lyness, J. M., Caine, E. D., King, D. A., Cox, C., & Yoediono, Z. (1999). Psychiatric disorders in older primary care patients. *Journal of General Internal Medicine*, *14*, 249–254.

Manton, K. G., & Gu X., (2001). Changes in the prevalence of chronic disability in the United States black and non-black population above age 65 from 1982 to 1999. *Proceedings of the National Academy of Sciences of the United States of America*, *98*, 6354–6359.

Marin, B., & Zaidi, A. (Eds.). (2007). *Mainstreaming ageing*. Aldershot: Ashgate.

Moe, E. L., Elliot, D. L., Goldberg, L., Kuehl, K. S., Stevens, V. J., Breger, R. K. R., ... Dolen, S. (2002). Promoting healthy lifestyles: Alternative models' effects (PHLAME). *Health Education Research*, *17*, 586–596.

Moos, R., & Lemke, S. (1996). *The Multiphasic Environment Assessment Procedure (MEAP)*. Palo Alto, CA: Sage.

Morese, C., & Wisocki, P. A. (1991). Residential factors in behavioral programming for the elderly. The checklist for evaluating residential factors. In P. A. Wisoki (Ed.), *Handbook of clinical behavior therapy with the elderly client*. New York: Plenum.

Nezu, A. M., & Nezu, C. M. (2008). *Evidence-based outcomes research. A practical guide to conducting reandomized controlled trials for psychological interventions*. New York: Oxford University Press.

Pearlin L. I., & Schooler, C. (1978). The structure of coping. *Journal of Health and Social Behaviour*, *19*, 2–21.

Peel, N. M., McClure, R. J., & Bartlett, H. P. (2005). Behavioral determinants of health aging. *American Journal of Preventive Medicine*, *28*, 298–304.

Pinquart, M., & Duberstein, P. (2007). Treatment of anxiety disorders in older adults—A meta-analytic comparison of behavioral and pharmacological interventions. *American Journal of Geriatric Psychiatry*, *15*, 639–651.

Pinquart, M., Duberstein, P., & Lyness, J. M. (2006). Treatments for later life depressive conditions: A meta-analytic comparison of pharmacotherapy and psychotherapy. *American Journal of Psychiatry*, *163*, 1493–1501.

Pinquart, M., Duberstein, P., & Lynness, J. M. (2007). Effects of psychotherapy and other behavioral interventions on clinically depressed older adults: A meta-analysis. *Aging and Mental Health*, *11*, 645–657.

Pinquart, M., Fernández-Ballesteros, R., & Torpdahl, P. (2007). Teaching, research, and application of geropsychology in Europe—Report from the Task Force of the European Federation of Psychologists' Associations on Geropsychology. *European Psychologist*, *12*, 229–233.

Pinquart, M., & Sörensen, S. (2003a). Differences between caregivers and noncaregivers in psychological health and physical health: A meta-analysis. *Psychology and Aging*, *18*, 250–267.

Pinquart, M., & Sörensen, S. (2003b). Predictors of caregiver burden and depressive mood: A meta-analysis. *Journal of Gerontology, Psychological Sciences*, *58*, 112–128.

Pinquart, M., & Sörensen, S. (2006). Helping caregivers of persons with dementia: Which interventions work and how large are their effects? *International Psychogeriatrics*, *18*, 577–595.

Qualls, S. H. (1998). Training in geropsychology: Preparing to meet the demand. *Professional Psychology: Research and Practice*, *29*, 23–28.

Rowe, J. W., & Kahn, R. L. (1997). Successful aging. *The Gerontologist*, *37*, 433–440.

Rowe, J. W., & Kahn, R. L. (1998). *Successful aging*. New York: Random House.

Schooll, J. N., & Sabat, S. T. (2008). Stereotypes, stereotype threat and ageing: Implications for the understanding and treatment of people with Alzheimer's disease. *Ageing & Society*, *28*, 103–130.

Schroots, J. J. F. (1995). Psychological models of aging. *Canadian Journal of Aging*, *14*, 44–67.

Schulz, R., McGinnis, K. A., Zhang, S., Martire, L. M., Hebert, R. S., Beach, S. R., ... Belle, S. H. (2008). Dementia patient suffering and caregiver depression. *Alzheimer Disease & Associated Disorders*, *22*, 170–176.

Smith, J., & Baltes, P. B. (1999). Trends and profiles of psychological functioning in the very old. In P. B. Baltes & K. U. Mayer (Eds.), *The Berlin aging study. Aging from 70 to 100* (pp 197–226). Cambridge: Cambridge University Press.

Spector, A., Davies, S., Woods, B., & Orrell, M. (2000). Reality orientation for dementia: a systematic review of the evidence of effectiveness from randomized controlled trials. *The Gerontologist*, *40*, 202–212.

Spector, A., Woods, B., & Orrell, M. (2008). Cognitive stimulation for the treatment of Alzheimer's disease. *Expert Reviews in Neurotherapy*, *8*, 751–757.

Sterns, H., & Camp, C. J. (1998). Applied gerontology. *Applied Psychology: An International Review*, *47*, 175–198.

Syme, S. L. (2003). Psychosocial Interventions to improve successful aging. *Annals Internal Medicine*, *139*, 400–402.

Toobert, D. J., Strycker, L. A., Glasgow, R. E., Barrera, M., & Bagdale, J. D. (2002). Enhancing support for health behavior change among women at risk for heart disease. The Mediterranean Lifestyle Trial. *Health Education Research*, *17*, 574–585.

United Nations. (2001). *World population aging*. New York: United Nations.

United Nations. (2002*). II International Plan of Action on Aging*. New York: United Nations.

United Nations. (2005). *2005 world population data sheet*. New York: The Population Reference Bureau.

Unverzagt, F. W., Gao, S., Baiyewu, O., Ogunniyi, A. O., Gureje, O., Perkins, A. … Hendrie, H. C. (2001). Prevalence of cognitive impairment: Data from the Indianapolis Study of Health and Aging. *Neurology*, *57*, 1655–1662.

US Department of Health and Human Services. (1999). *Mental health: A report of the Surgeon General*. Rockville: Author.

Wahl, H.-W., & Lehr, U. (2003) Applied fields: gerontology. In. R. Fermández-Ballesteros (Ed.), *Encyclopedia of psychological assessment* (Vol. 1, pp. 63–69). London: Sage.

Ware, J. E. (2001). *User's manual for the SF-36v2 health survey*. Lincoln, RI: Quality Metric.

Watson, D., Clark, L. A., & Tellegen, A. (1988). Development and validation of brief measures of positive and negative affect: The PANAS Scales. *Journal of Personality and Social Psychology*, *54*, 1063–1070.

Wechsler, D. (1958). *The measurement and appraisal of adult intelligence*. Baltimore: Williams & Witkin.

Wechsler, D. (1998). *The Wechsler Adult Intelligence Scales* (3rd ed.). San Antonio, CA: The Psychological Corporation.

Wernicke, T. F., Linden, M., Gilberg, R., & Helmchen, H. (2000). Ranges of psychiatric morbidity in the old and the very old: Results from the Berlin Aging Study (BASE). *European Archives of Psychiatry and Clinical Neuroscience*, *250*, 111–119.

Whitbourne, S. K., & Cavanaugh, J. C. (2003). *Integrating aging topics into psychology: A practical guide for teaching*. Washington, DC: American Psychological Association

WHO. (2001). *Health and ageing. A discussion paper*. Geneva: World Health Organization.

WHO. (2002). *Active ageing. A policy framework*, Geneva: World Health Organization.

WHOQOL. (1993). Study protocol for the World Health Organization project to develop a Quality of Life assessment instrument (WHOQOL). *Quality of Life Research*, *2*, 153–159.

Willis, S. L., Tennstedt, S. L., Marsiske, M., Ball, K., Elias, J., Koepke, K. M. et al. (2006). Long-term effects of cognitive training on everyday functional outcomes in older adults. *JAMA*, *296*, 2805–2814.

Wilson, R., Cockburn, S., & Baddeley, A. (1985). *Rivermead Behavioural Memory Test*. Titchfield: Thames Valley Test Company.

Yesevage, J. A., Brink, T. L., Rose, T. L., Lum, O., Huang, V., Adey, M. D., Leirer, M. D. (1983). Development and validation of a geriatric depression screening scale. *Journal of Psychiatric Research*, *17*, 37–49.

Zarit, S. H., & Femia, E. E. (2008). A future for family care and dementia intervention research? Challenges and strategies. *Aging and Mental Health*, *12*, 5–13.

18

Environmental Psychology

Robert Gifford, Linda Steg, and Joseph P. Reser

Environmental psychology is the study of transactions between individuals and their physical settings (Gifford, 2007a). In these transactions, individuals change their environments, and their behavior and experiences are changed by their environments. It includes theory, research, and practice aimed at making the built environment more humane and improving human relations with the natural environment. Considering the enormous investment society makes in the physical environment (including buildings, parks, streets, the atmosphere, and water) and the huge cost of misusing nature and natural resources, environmental psychology is a key component of both human and environmental welfare.

Environmental psychologists work at three levels of analysis: (a) fundamental psychological processes like perception of the environment, spatial cognition, and personality as they filter and structure human experience and behavior, (b) the management of social space: personal space, territoriality, crowding, and privacy, and the physical setting aspects of complex everyday behaviors, such as working, learning, living in a residence and community, and (c) human interactions with nature and the role of psychology in climate change (e.g., Gifford, 2008a).

The history of environmental psychology has been reviewed elsewhere (see Bechtel & Churchman, 2002; Bell, Greene, Fisher, & Baum, 2001; and Gifford, 2007a). But, for perspective, we note that early 20th-century psychologists studied the effect of noise (United States) and heat (England) on work performance, while scholars in Germany and Japan explored concepts and moral philosophy related to environmental psychology. By mid-century, environmental psychology was a clearly established discipline with work on topics such as sensory isolation, personal space, and building design. Journals devoted to the field were established; the most prominent of these are the *Journal of Environmental Psychology* and *Environment and Behavior*.

IAAP Handbook of Applied Psychology, First Edition. Edited by Paul R. Martin, Fanny M. Cheung, Michael C. Knowles, Michael Kyrios, Lyn Littlefield, J. Bruce Overmier, and José M. Prieto.

While recognizing the value of theory and research, many environmental psychologists nevertheless prefer to *apply* knowledge. Instead of working in a research setting, many enter into consultancy or public service to make good use of research findings for developing policy or solving local problems. Some are geared to improving the built environment (e.g., Preiser, Vischer, & White, 1991), while others are dedicated to overcoming sustainability problems in the natural and global ecosystems (e.g., Gifford, 2007b; Nickerson, 2003).

The Distinctiveness of Environmental Psychology

Most psychologists examine the relations between environmental stimuli and human responses in one way or another. However, what sets environmental psychology apart is its commitment to research and practice that subscribe to these goals and principles: (a) Improve the built environment and stewardship of natural resources, (b) Study everyday settings (or close simulations of them), (c) Consider person and setting as a holistic entity, (d) Recognize that individuals actively cope with and shape environments; they do not passively respond to environmental forces, and (e) Work in conjunction with other disciplines. Figure 18.1 broadly depicts the scope of environmental psychology.

Theoretical Bases

Seven major theoretical approaches guide environmental psychologists, although many focused theories deal with specific issues. First, *stimulation theories* conceptualize the physical environment as a crucial source of sensory information (e.g., Wohlwill, 1966). The adaptation-level approach begins with the assumption that people adapt

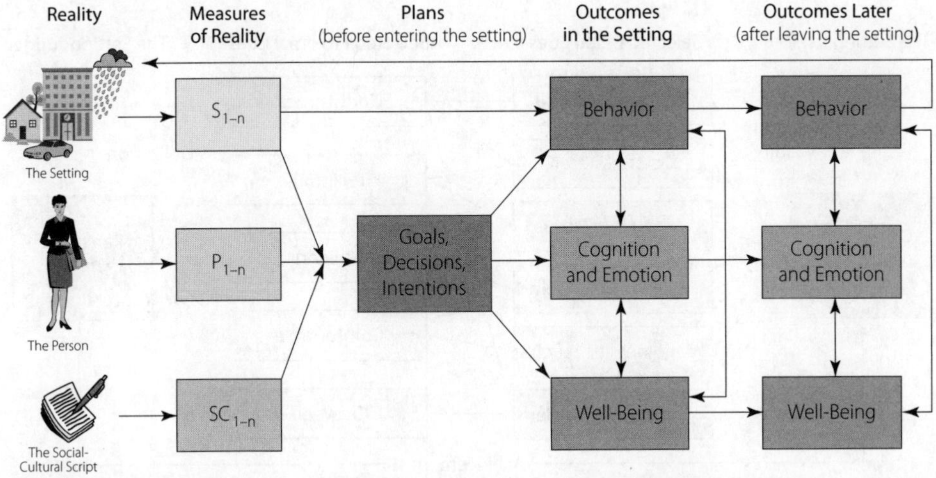

Figure 18.1. An overview of environmental psychology's scope (Gifford, 2007a)

to a certain level of environmental stimulation (e.g., Helson, 1964). Too much or too little stimulation is the focus of arousal, overload (e.g., Cohen, 1978), restricted environmental stimulation (Suedfeld, 1980), and stress theories (e.g., Evans, 1982). Second, *control* theories emphasize the importance of an individual's real, perceived, or desired control over stimulation (e.g., Barnes, 1981), and boundary regulation theories (e.g., Altman, 1975). Third, *ecological psychology* asserts the importance of behavior settings, naturally occurring small-scale social-physical units consisting of regular patterns of person–environment behavior (Barker, 1968). Fourth, *integral approaches* such as interactionism, transactionalism, and organismic theory attempt to describe the full, complex interrelationship of persons and setting (Stokols & Shumaker, 1981; Altman & Rogoff, 1987). Fifth, *operant approaches* downplay abstract principles, instead adopting a direct problem-solving approach that employs behavior modification techniques (e.g., Geller, 1987). Sixth, *environment-centered* theories such as the spiritual–instrumental model and ecopsychology raise the issue of the environment's own welfare and its ability to support our own well-being (e.g., Clayton & Brook, 2005). Seventh, *social psychology-based* theories explain which factors affect proenvironmental behaviour and how they can be encouraged.

Environmental Perception and Spatial Cognition

Environmental psychologists emphasize understanding how individuals respond to complex everyday scenes (e.g., Ittelson, 1978). A person's level of awareness, degree of adaptation, and necessary selectiveness in attending to environmental cues within complex real scenes mean that people sometimes miss important elements of a scene resulting in negative consequences for health or safety (e.g., Stamps, 2005). Environmental perception varies importantly with personal and cultural differences; people often see and interpret the same scene differently. Brunswik's (1956) probabilistic functionalism (see Figure 18.2.), Gibson's (1976) theory of affordances, Berlyne's

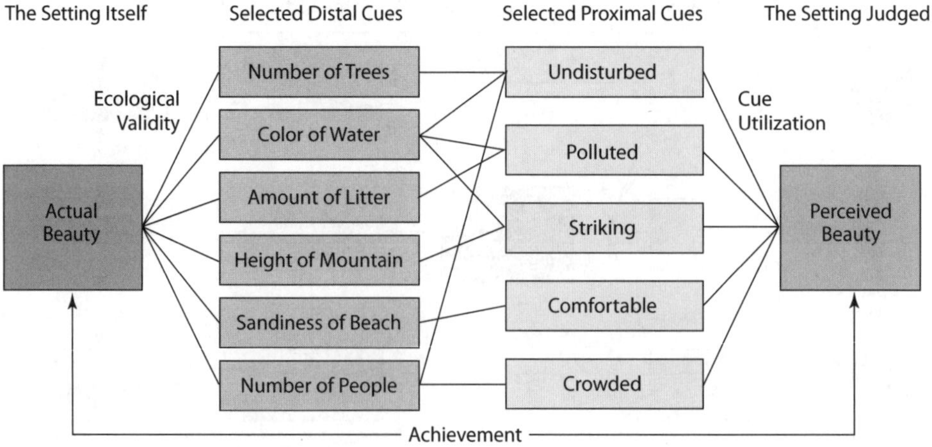

Figure 18.2. Brunswik's lens model, adapted for environmental perception (Gifford, 2007a)

(1974) collative properties, and the phenomenologist's approach (e.g., Seamon, 1982) all represent valuable ways to understand how people "read" their world.

Spatial cognition researchers have shown that human information processing does not resemble mechanical information processing (e.g., Lynch & Rivkin, 1959), yet is generally effective. However, spatial cognition heuristics that ordinarily work sometimes lead to errors (e.g., Montello, 1991). Theories of spatial cognition begin from different points of departure: the setting itself (e.g., Lynch, 1960), cognitive development (e.g., Moore, 1979), and brain physiology (e.g., O'Keefe & Nadel, 1978). Some of the most useful practical research has resulted in better signs for wayfinding in buildings and transit (Levine, 1982), and for helping people afflicted with Alzheimer's to navigate more easily (Passini, Pigot, Rainville, & Tetreault, 2000).

Managing Social Space

People use the physical space among them according to complex rules and strong preferences. Although these rules and preferences are not always conscious, their importance suddenly becomes clear when they are compromised. Personal space, territoriality, and crowding are the main dimensions of social space.

Personal space

Personal space is the dynamic distance and orientation component of interpersonal relations (Gifford, 2007a). It has been studied longer and more than almost any other aspect of environmental psychology (e.g., Sommer, 1959).

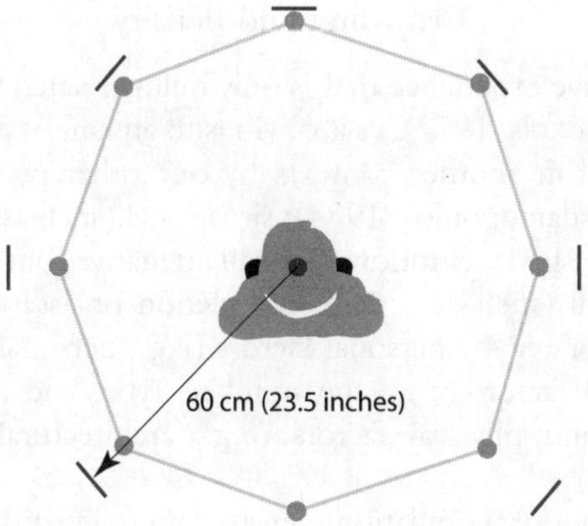

Figure 18.3. The average dimensions of personal space for North American university students approached from different directions; these distances will vary with culture and situation (from Gifford, 2007a)

Inferences about others are often drawn on the basis of the interpersonal distance they choose (e.g., Patterson & Sechrest, 1970). Many personal and situational influences interact with preferences for particular interpersonal distances. For example, males have larger personal spaces. Attraction and cooperation generally lead to smaller interpersonal distance, whereas less positive contexts such as stigma and unequal status lead to larger distances. When the physical setting is less spacious, larger interpersonal distances are selected. Cultural differences in interpersonal distance exist (e.g., Hall, 1966), but other factors often alter cultural preferences.

Territoriality

Territoriality in humans is a pattern of behavior and experience related to the control, usually by nonviolent means such as occupation, law, custom, and personalization, of physical space, objects, and ideas. Seven forms of territory (primary, secondary, public, objects, ideas, interactional, and body) have been distinguished (Altman, 1975); defense strategies (prevention, reaction, and social boundaries) are employed in response to infringements (invasion, violation, and contamination). Males are often more territorial than females. Careful arrangements of dwelling exteriors and street plans (defensible space) enhances residents' territoriality and reduces crime (e.g., Newman, 1972).

Personalization, marking, and status are used much more often than physical aggression to control space and ideas. Theories of territoriality stress its organizing function and evolution more than its relation to aggression (Edney, 1976). Architects can and should incorporate knowledge about territoriality to allow building users as much control as they are capable of responsibly exercising and as the organizational context allows; territory holders then benefit from a greater sense of self-determination, identity, and even safety.

Crowding and density

Crowding is a subjective experience that is only mildly related to the objective index, population density (Stokols, 1972), as is obvious to anyone at a good party or anyone who has felt crowded in another contexts by one other person. It exists in three modes (Montano & Adamopoulos, 1984): situational (such as feeling constrained or having expectations dashed), emotional (usually negative, but positive emotions can occur), and behavioral (such as activity completion or assertiveness). Crowding is accentuated or ameliorated by personal factors (e.g., personality, expectations, attitudes, gender), social factors (e.g., the number, type, and actions of others, and attitude similarity), and physical factors (e.g., architectural features and spatial arrangements).

Prolonged high indoor population density often impairs mental and physical health, task performance, child development, and social interaction (e.g., Evans & Saegert, 2000). Individuals in some cultures seem to cope with high density better, but sensory overload and lack of personal control lead to many negative outcomes. Short-term high density may have positive outcomes when social and physical conditions are positive. High outdoor density, as in large cities, certainly can provide an enjoyable variety of social and cultural experiences. In general, high density tends to magnify pre-existing social conditions (Freedman, 1975). To reduce the negative effects of high density through environmental design, more space is not always needed. Rather, careful environmental design (such as partitioning and behavioral zoning) can ease crowding within a limited space.

Encouraging Proenvironmental Behavior

Many environmental problems are rooted in human behavior, and can thus be managed by promoting proenvironmental behavior (Gardner & Stern, 2002). Attempts to improve environmental quality via behavior changes will be more effective when one (1) selects behavior that significantly affects environmental quality, (2) examines which factors cause those behaviors, and (3) applies and evaluates interventions that change these antecedents and the behavior (Geller, 2002; Steg & Vlek, 2009). This section provides a brief overview of how environmental psychologists have addressed the last two issues.

Factors that influence behaviors with environmental impact

In order to decide which factors should be targeted to encourage proenvironmental actions, one needs to understand which factors promote or inhibit proenvironmental behavior. Below, we discuss two types of individual motivations to engage in environmental behavior: perceived cost and benefits, and normative concerns. We indicate how these perspectives may be integrated into a coherent framework. Next, we elaborate on contextual factors and habits.

Motivational factors: Cost-benefit deliberations, and normative concerns. The theory of planned behavior (TPB; Ajzen, 1991) assumes that individuals choose alternatives with highest benefits against lowest costs (e.g., in terms of money, effort, and/or social approval). The TPB proposes that behavior follows from an individual's intention. Intentions depend on attitudes towards the behavior (the degree to which engagement in behavior is positively valued), social norms (social pressure from important others to engage in a particular behavior), and perceived behavioral control (beliefs on whether one is capable of performing the behavior). The TPB was successful in explaining various types of environmental behavior, including travel mode choice, household recycling, waste composting, water use, meat consumption, and general proenvironmental behavior (e.g., Harland, Staats, & Wilke, 1999; Heath & Gifford, 2002).

Acting proenvironmentally is often associated with higher costs. Therefore, moral and normative concerns are believed to play an important role in environmental behavior. Indeed, people are more likely to engage in proenvironmental actions when they subscribe to values beyond their immediate own interests, that is, self-transcendent, altruistic, or biospheric values, while egoistic or self-enhancement values are negatively related to environmental behavior (e.g., De Groot & Steg, 2007; 2008). Also, stronger environmental concern is associated with acting more proenvironmentally, although relationships are generally weak. Environmental concern is less predictive of behavior-specific beliefs than are values, probably because values reflect a wider range of motivations (Steg, De Groot, Dreijerink, Abrahamse, & Siero, 2011).

The norm-activation model (NAM; Schwartz, 1977) and the value-belief-norm theory (VBN theory; Stern, 2000) assume that people act proenvironmentally when they feel a moral obligation to do so, which depends on the extent to which people are aware of the problems caused by their behavior, and feel responsible for these problems and their solution. VBN theory further proposes that problem awareness is rooted in environmental concern and values. The NAM and VBN theories are reasonably successful in explaining low-cost environmental behavior and "good intentions" such as willingness to change behavior, political behavior, environmental citizenship, or policy acceptability (e.g., Gärling, Fujii, Gärling, & Jakobsson, 2003; Nordlund & Garvill, 2003; Steg, Dreijerink, & Abrahamse, 2005). However, in situations characterized by high behavioral costs or strong constraints on behavior, such as reducing car use, their explanatory power is generally low (e.g., Bamberg & Schmidt, 2003). In such settings, the TPB appears to be more powerful in explaining behavior, probably because the TPB also considers non-environmental motivations and perceived behavioral control (see Steg & Vlek, 2009).

Cialdini, Kallgren, and Reno (1991) distinguish two types of social norms: injunctive norms (the extent to which behavior is supposed to be commonly approved or disapproved) and descriptive norms (the extent to which behavior is perceived as common practice). The most salient norm influences behavior most. Indeed, people are more likely to violate a particular norm when others do so as well (Cialdini et al., 1991). Moreover, norm violations spread, that is, when people see that a particular norm is being violated, they are more likely to violate other norms as well, suggesting that perceptions of norm violations reduce the likelihood of normative behavior in general (Keizer, Lindenberg, & Steg, 2008).

Various scholars have integrated concepts and variables from different theoretical frameworks, showing that behavior results from multiple motivations. Goal-framing theory (Lindenberg & Steg, 2007) explicitly acknowledges that behavior results from multiple motivations. This theory distinguishes three goals that "frame" the way people process information and act upon it: a hedonic goal-frame "to feel better right now," a gain goal-frame "to guard and improve one's resources," and a normative goal-frame "to act appropriately." In a given situation, one of these goals is presumed to be focal (it is the goal-frame), while other goals are in the background and increase or decrease the strength of the focal goal.

Contextual factors. Many contextual factors may facilitate or constrain environmental behavior and influence individual motivations, such as the availability of recycling facilities, or the quality of public transport (e.g., Ölander & Thøgersen, 1995). Only a few scholars in this field have included contextual factors in their studies (e.g., Guagnano, Stern & Dietz, 1995; Black, Stern, & Elworth, 1985), and surprisingly, contextual factors are not typically included in theories to explain environmental behavior. When environmental psychology aims to study transactions between humans and their environments, effects of contextual factors on behavior should be studied more extensively. This may reveal whether important barriers for proenvironmental action should be removed.

Habit. The theoretical frameworks discussed above generally imply that individuals make reasoned choices. However, in many cases, environmental behavior (e.g., car use) is habitual and guided by automated cognitive processes (e.g., Aarts, Verplanken, & Van Knippenberg, 1998). Temporarily forcing car drivers to use alternative travel modes appeared to induce long-term reductions in car use, especially among habitual car drivers (Fujii & Gärling, 2003). This suggests that habitual drivers have inaccurate and modifiable perceptions of the pros and cons of different transport modes.

Interventions

Various strategies for behavior change have been identified, each focusing on a different set of behavioral determinants. A distinction can be made between informational strategies that aim to change prevalent motivations, perceptions, cognitions and norms, and structural strategies that aim to change the context in which behavioral choices are made (Messick & Brewer, 1983). Informational and structural strategies are described next, but their effectiveness in promoting different types of environmental behavior in detail is not, because this has been extensively reviewed elsewhere (e.g., Abrahamse, Steg, Vlek, & Rothengatter, 2005; Dwyer, Leeming, Cobern, Porter & Jackson, 1993).

Informational strategies. Informational strategies target motivational factors, without actually changing the external context in which choices are made. First, informational strategies can be aimed to increase actors' awareness of environmental problems and of the environmental impacts of their behavior, and/or to increase their knowledge of behavioral alternatives and their pros and cons. Information campaigns hardly result in behavior changes (see Abrahamse et al., 2005, for a review).

Second, persuasion strategies may be employed, for example, to influence actors' attitudes, strengthen their altruistic and ecological values, and/or strengthen their commitment to act proenvironmentally. Commitment strategies appeared to be successful in encouraging proenvironmental behavior (see Abrahamse et al., 2005). Eliciting implementation intentions in which people not only indicate that they intend to change their behaviour, but also how they plan to do so, appeared to be effective as well (e.g., Bamberg, 2002). Furthermore, promising results have been found with individualized social marketing approaches, in which information is tailored to the needs, wants and perceived barriers of individual segments of the population (e.g., Abrahamse et al., 2007).

Third, social support and role models can be provided to strengthen social norms, and to inform individuals about the perceptions, efficacy, and behavior of others.

Modeling and providing information about the behavior of others appeared to be successful in supporting proenvironmental behavior. However, comparative feedback can be counterproductive when people take the behavior of others as a reference point for which to strive. This boomerang effect can be neutralized by adding injunctive norm information, which conveys social approval (Schultz, Nolan, Cialdini, Goldstein, & Griskevicius, 2007).

Informational strategies in themselves are especially effective when the proenvironmental behavior is not very costly, and when individuals do not face severe external constraints on behavior. Furthermore, they are an important element in the implementation of structural strategies that force individuals to change their behavior.

Structural strategies. When acting proenvironmentally is rather costly or difficult because of external barriers to proenvironmental actions, the circumstances under which behavioral choices are made need to be changed so as to make proenvironmental actions more attractive, and to reduce the attractiveness of environmental harmful actions. First, the availability and quality of products and services may be altered via changes in physical, technical, and/or organizational systems (e.g., provision of recycling bins). Second, legal regulations can be implemented (e.g., prohibiting the use of harmful propellants in spray cans). Third, prices of different behavior options may be changed (e.g., road pricing, CO_2 taxes).

Structural strategies either aim to reward approved behavior, or punish disapproved behavior. When rewards and penalties are strong, people can attribute their behavior change to the incentive and not to their personal convictions. As a result, attitudes may not change and behavior changes will only last for as long as the incentive is in place. Rewards will be not be effective if they fail to make proenvironmental behavior more attractive than environmentally harmful options, to activate goals to change behavior, and to facilitate the implementation of such goals (Gärling & Schuitema, 2007).

Evaluating the effectiveness of interventions. Studies aimed at evaluating an intervention's effectiveness should follow experimental research designs that reveal the effectiveness of single as well as combinations of interventions for one or more "treatment" groups and a comparable control group. Because an intervention may have only short-lived effects, whether it has lasting long-term effects needs study (Abrahamse et al., 2005). First, it is important to monitor (changes in) behavioral determinants in order to understand why intervention programs were successful or not. This also allows change agents to adapt interventions to increase its effectiveness. Second, changes in environmental impact should be monitored, because this is the ultimate goal of behavioral interventions in the environmental domain. Based on this, feedback can be provided to the target population so as to inform members about the effects of their efforts on environmental quality. This may strengthen their commitment to change behavior, and to maintain the changes realized. Third, one also would need to know about changes in people's quality of life, which is an important component of the more general notion of sustainable development (Steg & Gifford, 2005).

Besides studying the actual effects of interventions, environmental psychologists have studied the perceived effectiveness and acceptability of environmental policies before such policies are implemented, particularly in the travel domain (see Steg & Schuitema, 2007, for a review). These studies reveal, among other things, that policies are more acceptable when they are believed to be more fair, when they are effective in reducing relevant problems, and when they do not seriously affect individual freedom. Moreover, policies are more acceptable to people who have strong environmental values, who are highly aware of the problem, and who feel a strong moral obligation to reduce the problems. Policies that increase the attractiveness of proenvironmental behavior are evaluated as more effective and acceptable than policies aimed at decreasing the attractiveness of environmentally harmful behavior, and people prefer policies aimed at promoting the adoption of energy-efficient equipment to policies aimed at reducing the use of existing equipment (e.g., Poortinga, Steg, Vlek & Wiersma, 2003; Steg, Dreijerink & Abrahamse, 2006).

Conclusions

Environmental psychologists have an important role to play in the management of environmental problems through the promotion of behavior change. Behavioral interventions are generally more effective when they are systematically planned, implemented, and evaluated. Individuals can contribute significantly to achieving long-term environmental sustainability by adopting proenvironmental behavior patterns. The challenge for environmental psychologists is to understand the individual and structural factors and processes that threaten environmental sustainability, so that proenvironmental behaviors can be facilitated worldwide.

The Psychology of Resource Management

Energy conservation, recycling, fresh water, and pollution are instances of everyday commons dilemmas. The choices people make—sometimes to take (as in fishing) and sometimes to give (as in greenhouse gases) influence the fate of many desirable resources. People in commons dilemmas must decide whether to try to serve their own interest quickly, which risks total failure for self, others, and the resource, or, through restraint, to benefit all participants more moderately, with the crucial consequence that the resource is preserved for the future (Hardin, 1968). Many characteristics of the resource, individuals, and proximate constraints that influence these choices have been identified (see Figure 18.4).

For example, conservation often (but not always) improves when the resource becomes scarce. Uncertainty about the resource almost always leads to overharvesting. Narcissistic or egocentric harvesters take more than others (e.g., Biel & Garling, 1995). When more harvesters have access to a resource, each tends to take more, but if they have a sense of community, cooperation is greater (e.g., Dawes & Messick, 2000). Regulations do not govern harvesting absolutely, but of course they have an influence. For example, when harvests are publicly known, cooperation is greater and when the resources are partitioned into zones that each harvester controls, the commons is managed more sustainably.

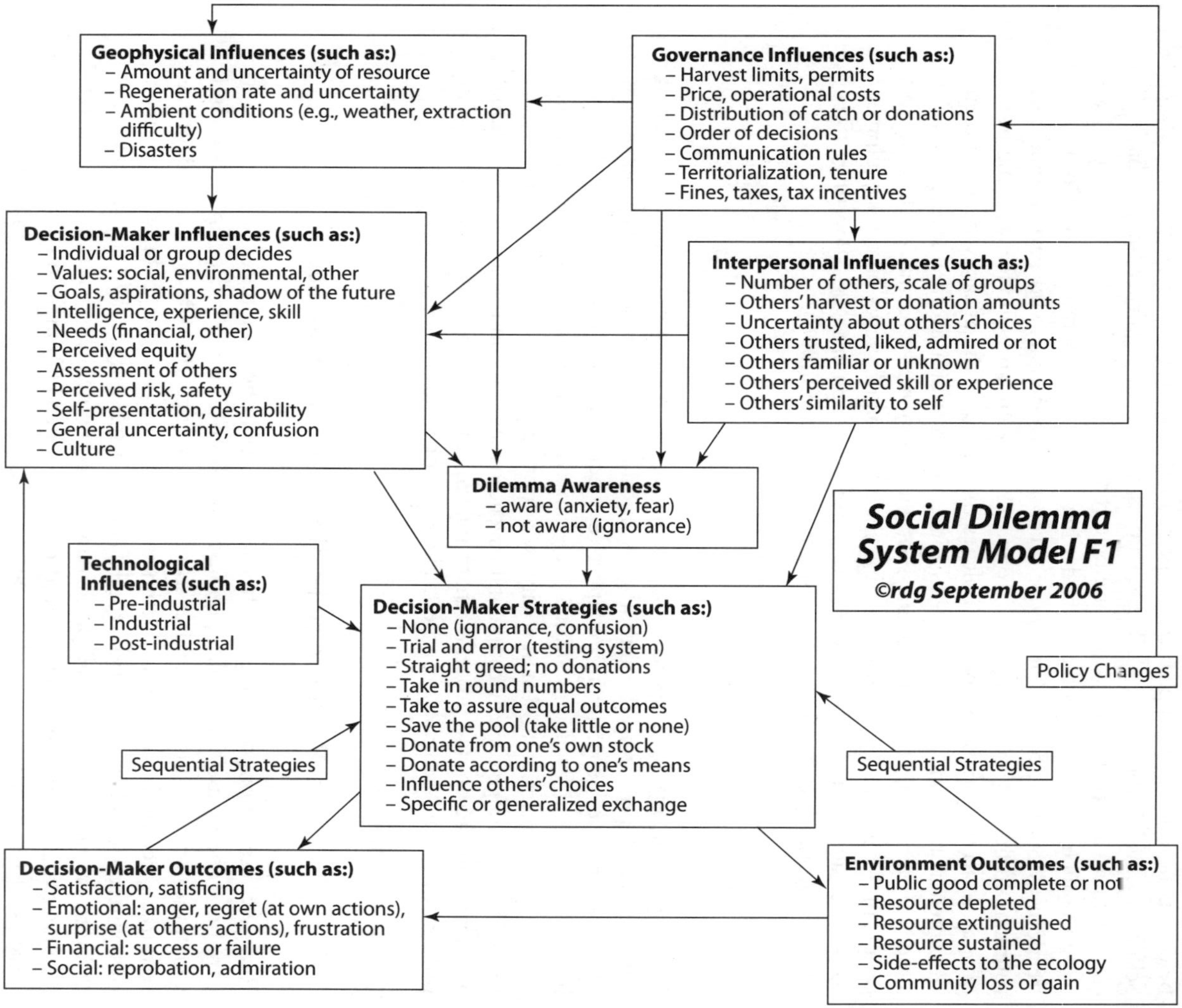

Figure 18.4. Many of the factors that influence decision making in a commons dilemma (Gifford, 2008b)

Residential Environmental Psychology

Home is the most important physical setting for most people. Environmental psychologists distinguish the physical structure (house, apartment) from its meaning structure (home). Individuals normally called homeless might more properly be called houseless, although if their last residence loses its meaning, they truly are homeless. Residential satisfaction depends on many determinants, including stage of life, socioeconomic status, personality and values, hopes for the future, norms for one's peers, and relationships with neighbors. Of course, physical features of the residence—such as its form (Michelson, 1977), architectural style (Nasar, 1989), floor plan, colors, outdoor areas around the residence, as well as cultural background affect residential preferences, choices, and satisfaction. Poor-quality housing affects the socioemotional health of children and adults (Evans, Wells, Chan, & Saltzman, 2000; Gifford, 2007c; Gifford & Lacombe, 2006).

People arrange their residential interiors in fairly predictable patterns that are related to lifestyle, social class, and culture (e.g., Bonnes, Giuliani, Amoni, & Bernard, 1987). Adapting to new residences can be stressful, depending on whether a person has some choice in doing so, prefers to explore new settings in general (Stokols & Shumaker, 1982), or whether the change represents a downgrading.

In relation to the amount of time people spend in their residences, and their psychological importance, this aspect of environmental psychology is under-researched. This is partly because conducting research in residences usually is, understandably, seen as an intrusion of privacy.

The Environmental Psychology of Neighborhoods and Cities

A vast global movement to the city is underway. What happens once nearly everyone lives so close together? Environmental psychologists explore person–environment relations in cities, public places, the neighborhood, the community, and on the streets. A general model for this is presented in Figure 18.5.

Residents' personal factors and the physical aspects of the city (stressors and amenities) are presumed to influence the way residents think about their cities and neighborhoods (whether they are satisfied or not, fearful or not, attached to them or not, mentally healthy or mentally unhealthy). The physical aspects of the city, personal factors, and these cognitions are presumed to affect residents' actual behavior in urban public places such as streets, parks, and stores. These behaviors may be pro-social, anti-social, or neither; they include everyday behaviors, such as how fast people walk, kids playing in parks, or where people choose to sit in public areas. They also include behavior in retail settings such as shoppers' reactions to store music and displays. The model further states that these behaviors, in turn, are presumed to influence cognitions (just as cognitions influence behaviors) and the urban planning and design process. The design process, to complete the cycle, influences the physical shape of the city as zoning and other bylaws govern what sort of buildings, streets, and parks

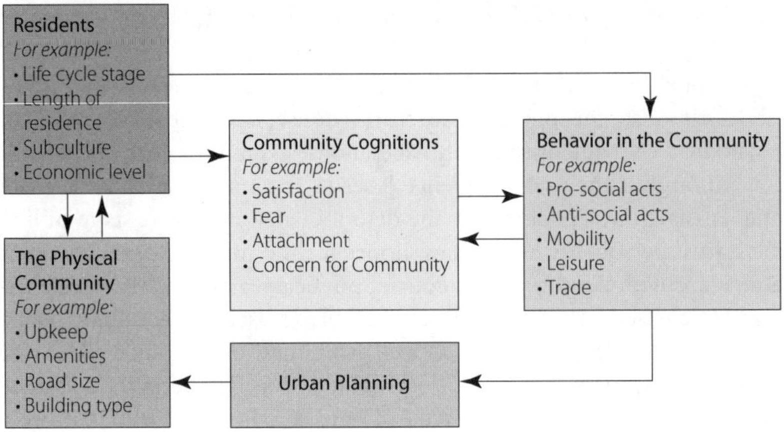

Figure 18.5. The environmental psychology of public life (Gifford, 2007a)

get built. The cycle then continues. Environmental psychologists have studied all phases of the model in Figure 18.5.

Cities can be very stressful: noise, traffic, density, and pollution usually are much greater than in rural places. We humans have only lived in such large agglomerations for a tiny fraction of the time we have been a species; it is reasonable to say that cities are unnatural. Personal safety is a very important urban problem. Some danger is caused by poverty and social breakdown, but defensible space principles combined with a take-back-the-streets community attitude can significantly reduce crime. Other physical forces facilitate urban aggressiveness: temperatures up to 85°F/29°C degrees appear to increase the risk of violence (Baron & Ransberger, 1978). A less obvious aggression-causing problem may be air pollution; in addition to being a health risk, it may also trigger violence in some individuals (Rotton, Frey, Barry, Milligan, & Fitzpatrick, 1979).

On the other hand, cities obviously are attractive. William Whyte, a champion of the city's possibilities, argued that people gravitate toward high density and thrive on it. According to Whyte, the vendors, performers, and eccentrics make cities exciting. Clearly, cities have benefits; besides the interesting street life, these include more cultural, educational, medical, leisure, social, and shopping resources, not to mention greater opportunity for jobs. Environmental psychology has contributed scientific evidence on both the psychological benefits and costs of urban living.

Neighborhoods and retail stores: The building blocks of cities

Neighborhoods are psychological (Guest & Lee, 1984). Generally, a neighborhood's physical qualities are more important than its social qualities (Fried, 1984), unless (on the positive side) residents have special bonds with each other or (on the negative side) residents are at war, or nearly so. However, a pleasant, green, natural, residential-only area is not everyone's favorite place; more important is whether the community fills one's needs and whether one is adapted to its pattern of stimulation (Michelson, 1977).

Place attachment is psychologically important. It cannot be instantly attained; residents need to spend time in a place, to hear stories, to be part of a spiritual quest centered there (Hay, 1998). Many people eventually lose the places to which they have become attached, with the attendant experiences of loss and grief (Norris-Baker & Scheidt, 1990).

People do much on local and urban streets that seems close to nothing, perhaps because they do most of it automatically, without reflecting. However, upon closer examination, this "nothing" turns out to be a fascinating mixture of thoughts and activities. We monitor our progress through the city in responsive, operational, or inferential modes (Appleyard, 1976). We walk at a speed that reflects the pulse (or at least the size) of the city (Gifford, Ward, & Dahm, 1977). Our walks follow planned patterns even when we are unaware of our plans. We carefully avoid interaction with most people we meet on the street, but we try to maximize social order (Lofland, 1973). Surprisingly, perhaps, elderly men hang out in malls more than teens (Brown, Sijpkes, & MacLean, 1986). We "know" some people in public places that we do not really know—familiar strangers (Milgram, 1977).

The physical environment is not widely studied as a factor in retail behavior, but awareness of and research on its influence is growing (e.g., Ng, 2003). Well-known effects include location and store size. However, at the interior level, the way that shelves, aisles, displays, and odors affect the emotions and behavior of consumers is gradually becoming clear (Hawkins, Best, & Coney, 1983).

Educational Environmental Psychology

The physical features of schools and other learning settings as a whole affect student and teacher outcomes. For example, many learning experiences are affected by school size (e.g., Barker & Gump, 1964). Students in larger schools have an edge in the variety of things they can learn about. Yet, partly because time at school is limited, students in large schools do not actually participate in more activities than students in small schools. Students in large schools more often learn and enjoy as spectators; students in small schools more often learn and enjoy as participants. In most areas of learning, students in small schools achieve more because they develop competence through direct involvement in activities.

Interior school design has a variety of influences on students and teachers (e.g., Ahrentzen, 1981). Temporary or low walls increase distractibility. Acquisition, maintenance, and dynamic walls can be strategically used to match students' normal viewing patterns with current versus background educational information (Creekmore, 1987). When students learn in a given setting, that material is better recalled in the same setting—or when a vivid memory of that setting is evoked (e.g., Smith, 1979).

Evidence strongly suggests that noise interferes with learning both while it occurs and, if the learner is subjected to noise for long periods, even after the noise is gone (Cohen & Weinstein, 1982). To combat noise, instructors have changed their methods—sometimes sacrificing a good pedagogical technique for a quiet one—and successfully employed behavior modification techniques such as sound-activated electrical relays that control reinforcers such as music and extra recess time (e.g., Strang & George, 1975).

Incandescent lighting is preferred by many, but it is more expensive than fluorescent lighting, which has not been shown to have dramatic negative effects on the performance or health of most students. Despite the inadequate methodology in some studies, and the lack of significant differences in others, it appears that light does affect some kinds of performance, such as basic cognitive and motor activities (Munson & Ferguson, 1985). Short exposures to the different kinds of light in many studies may have led to incorrect conclusions that light has no effects. As with noise, the important effects may be on specific subgroups of individuals; when studies of whole classes or schools are done, large effects on a few learners may be obscured by the absence of effects on most learners.

Few simple, direct relations exist between indoor climate and educational behavior. Perhaps the best-supported conclusion is that performance is best in slightly cool but not humid classrooms (Ahrentzen, Jue, Skorpanich, & Evans, 1982).

The amount, arrangement, and design of space in educational settings is very important for classroom performance and related behaviors. High density may affect learning when the activity involves physical movement around the classroom, when learning depends on some classroom resource that is not increasing as fast as the number of learners, when a particular situation seems crowded to a learner, and when the concept to be learned is complex (e.g., Rohe & Patterson, 1974). Among preschoolers, high density alters the child's choice of activities and time spent on off-task activities (e.g., Kantrowitz & Evans, 2004). Numerous classroom arrangement features have been linked to educational performance (e.g., Weinstein, 1977; Koneya, 1976). All such findings depend in part on grade level, type of tasks, and teaching style.

High density may affect learning (e.g., Weinstein, 1979). Space in classrooms affects student and teacher feelings. Most students and teachers prefer lower-density classrooms, because lower densities usually feel less crowded. Providing satisfying physical arrangements within schools is best accomplished by furnishing a variety of layouts. Softer, more home-like classrooms appear to improve student learning (e.g., Wollin & Montagne, 1981), but will not become common until the attitudes of authorities, teachers, and students change. In terms of social behavior, increased social density leads to increased aggression and withdrawal when other resources, architectural features, and teaching style do not counteract it (Weinstein, 1979).

Environmental competence involves learning about the environment (Steele, 1980). Three kinds of it include (1) personal style, attitudes and awareness of physical setting; (2) knowledge of physical settings, including technical knowledge, how to unearth new information, knowledge about how social systems control space, knowledge of person–environment relations; and (3) practical environmental skills such as scouting, matching, personalization, and creative custodianship. Programs in and out of school teach many different facets of environmental competence, from basic environmental ethics to campfire starting to architectural design. Although some subareas of environmental competence have received attention, the concept as a whole so far has not received as much as it deserves.

Workplace Environmental Psychology

Working can provide some of the best and some of the worst experiences in life. Many factors determine a person's productivity, stress, and satisfaction at work but, for decades, psychologists have realized that the physical environment is an important influence on employee productivity and satisfaction.

Environmental psychologists conduct research on the relations between the physical environment and (a) getting to work, (b) performance, feelings, social behavior, health, and stress at work, and (c) trying to enjoy life after work (by traveling). Throughout, the tempting but simplistic notion that changes in the physical setting will directly determine employee behavior must be rejected.

Getting to work

Most research on getting to work has been broadly concerned with encouraging people to choose less energy-intensive means of commuting as part of the general drive towards sustainability. Environmental psychologists have created demographic profiles of car and urban transit riders (e.g., Hartgen, 1974), devised models of commuter preference (Levin & Louviere, 1981), provided positive information about urban transit and evaluated existing transit systems (Stern, 1982), offered reduced fares (Studenmund & Connor, 1982), and promoted car sharing (Bonsall, Spencer, & Tang, 1983). Commuting often is stressful, but the majority still drive, suggesting that the description of it as an addiction (Reser, 1980) is not far wrong. However, the more promising approaches are being sorted out from the less promising ones, and progress must be made, because the worldwide growth in cars and driving is not sustainable, and certainly has very mixed effects on the quality of life (e.g., Gifford & Steg, 2007).

At work

Noise has many effects on work activities and feelings. In industrial settings, it can cause serious hearing loss. Loud noise is particularly dangerous when employees do not realize that deafness comes slowly and almost imperceptibly. Despite the common supposition that noise affects performance, research in natural settings shows (a) how complex the issue is and (b) that performance decrements depend on the task, the person, and the type of noise (e.g., Baker & Holding, 1993). Noise harms performance when certain combinations of employee, task, and type of noise co-occur, but not under some other circumstances. For certain tasks, noise may even arouse an employee enough to improve performance (e.g., Miller, 1974). Noise is a serious problem in modern open-plan offices. Employees find sound a problem both coming and going: sound entering their workspace is annoying, and when their own words escape over partitions too easily their privacy is compromised (Hedge, 1982). Office noise may even affect important interpersonal behavior, from mere impressions of others to important judgments regarding them (Sauser, Arauz, & Chambers, 1978). Some research suggests that long-term exposure to loud sounds has serious

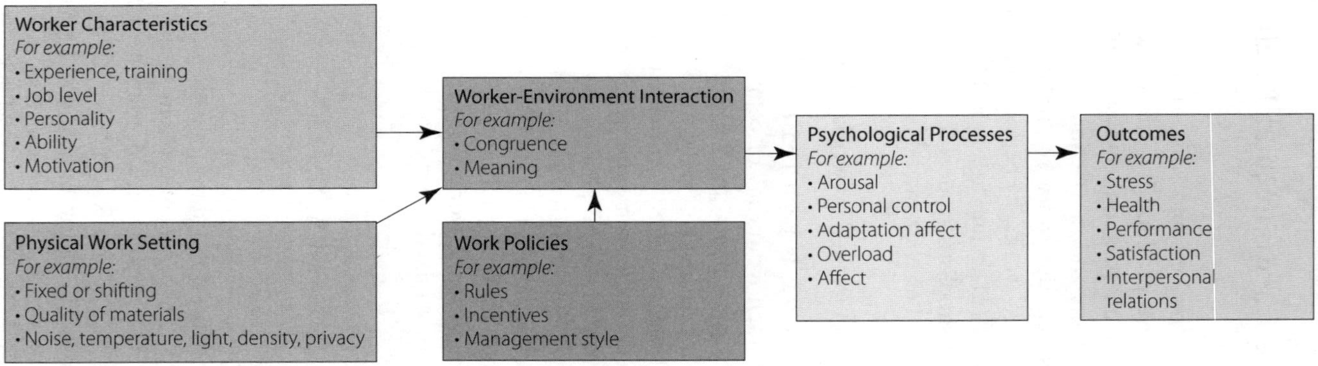

Figure 18.6. A model of the influences of the physical work setting on workers (Gifford, 2007a)

physiological effects beyond hearing loss, such as increased cardiovascular problems (Welch, 1979).

Indoor climate is measured by effective temperature, which includes humidity and air movement as well as temperature. Relatively extreme effective temperatures do not affect many work behaviors unless core body temperature is altered. The effects of temperature are also usually damped by access to heavier or lighter clothing. The amazing variety of temperature effects reported are partly the result of these measurement and clothing factors, as well as many others including degree of acclimatization, knowledge of coping strategies, motivation, and type of work (Gifford, 2007a, p. 385). Engineers have outlined well-described comfort envelopes, but environmental psychologists have discovered that comfort depends on perception as well as actual effective temperature and that optimal performance may be found outside the comfort envelope (Nelson, Nilsson, & Hopkins, 1987). Temperature stress occurs when individuals are initially subjected to temperatures far outside the comfort zone, but many people can adapt to these more extreme temperatures after longer-term exposure to them.

Several components of air—including carbon monoxide, air ions, and bad odors—may affect performance, but the effects are not striking under normal conditions (National Academy of Sciences, 1977). When air carries chemical impurities or disease-causing organisms, it can seriously impair health. Lack of control over noticeably bad air may affect persistence at work and, in some circumstances, foster negative feelings among employees.

Light affects work behavior primarily when it is quite insufficient (leading to low productivity and accidents) or improperly placed (leading to glare and eyestrain). A meta-analysis showed that within the normal range, increased illumination improves performance (Gifford, Hine, & Veitch, 1997). Many employees dislike fluorescent and other newer forms of lighting, some of which distort color (Megaw & Bellamy, 1983). Carefully placed local lighting could resolve some of these problems. Access to natural light and views is psychologically important.

Naturally occurring spatial arrangements have few documented effects on performance, but employees are very sensitive to space, and unhappy with many existing arrangements (Ng & Gifford, 1984). Many open-plan arrangements reduce desirable communication and increase undesirable communication (Zalesny & Farace, 1987). Office arrangements lead visitors to form impressions of the office-holder's character and status (Morrow & McElroy, 1981). Many organizations restrict the degree to which employees may arrange or personalize their offices and fail to adequately consult employees when offices are planned.

Environmental psychologists have been involved in the design of many work settings, from basic noise and light consultations to complete office designing. Better office designs are not only a basic right of employees, but they also save money for organizations. A comprehensive study found that improved layout and enclosure in offices would lead to productivity increases of 15% for managers and professional-technical employees, and 17.5% for clerical workers (Brill, Margulis, & Konar, 1984). Similar studies report 10 to 50% increases with better workplace designs (Gifford, 1992).

After work

The environmental psychology of travel is a new but growing area. Travelers affect destinations and are affected by them. Anticipation, travel, and recollection of travel involve environmental perception and cognition (Iso-Ahola, 1983). Recreational travel is an environmental trade-off, but as society is able to provide employees with more disposable income and time, it is a trade-off many are pursuing. Destination selection, acquisition of knowledge about destination, and behavior along the road are a few areas of developing research. Some destinations bring relief from anxiety; others throw travelers into environment shock (Pearce, 1981). Travelers ruin some physical settings and enhance almost none; romantic tourism is an undesirable luxury because it degrades natural settings (Walter, 1982). More careful planning of destination sites might spread the impact of visitors, offer more authentic experiences, and educate travelers while offering them solace from the working world.

Natural Environmental Psychology

The natural environment has been approached within environmental psychology in a variety of ways, with some appreciation of the fact that the natural environment was and remains the encompassing environment of which humans are an integral and adaptive part, notwithstanding some 30,000 years of extensive human alteration. The natural environment has been seen (a) as a complex stimulus environment for which we have hard-wired and functional sensitivities, preferences, and aversions (Ornstein & Ehrlich, 2000), (b) as the source of aesthetic appreciation and creative and spiritual inspiration (Williams & Harvey, 2001), (c) as part of fondly remembered and formative childhoods for many (Chawla, 1994; Ittelson, Proshansky, Rivlin, & Winkel, 1974), (d) as the basis of our planet's and our species' life support systems and the critical object of conservation initiatives (Schmuck & Schultz, 2002), (e) as a restorative and therapeutic venue and refuge from the overload and stresses of modern life (Hartig & Staats, 2003; Kaplan, 1995), (f) as an important design and planning criterion and set of principles for creating beautiful, comfortable, and life-enhancing human structures and settings (Thompson, 2000), and (g) as moral compass and existential and aesthetic touchstone (e.g., Berleant & Carlson, 2004).

Nature has both awesome power to disrupt lives or to act as a restorative agent. People have always believed that nature is restorative. The various ways in which it is restorative include facilitating cognitive freedom, ecosystem connectedness, escape, challenge, growth, guidance, a renewed social life, and health (Gifford, 2007a). Being in nature (e.g., Sullivan, Kuo, & DePooter, 2004), and even merely viewing nature (e.g., Ulrich, 1984), have restorative effects, although some researchers maintain that the same effects might be gained by features of nature that also may be found in civilization (Scopelliti & Giuliani, 2004). The two main mechanisms by which nature restores us are through refreshing attentional capacity (Kaplan, 1995) and improving mood.

The natural environment continues to be a very diverse domain of applied environmental psychological work, both in the context of designing 'nature' into human settings (Kaplan, Kaplan & Ryan, 1998) and in the context of designing with nature in mind (McHarg, 1991). The importance of acknowledging and incorporating the natural environment in planning and design is particularly salient in the context of health, well-being, and restoration benefit, with an extensive evidence base spanning three decades and myriad institutional and urban applications and settings (Hartig & Staats, 2003; Maller, Townsend, Prior, Brown, & St. Leger, 2006). These restoration benefits and indeed more fundamental psychological needs and processes have also been more widely acknowledged and embraced in clinical and counselling practice.

The Social Construction of Nature, the Environment, and Environmental Problems

"The environment," "nature," and other constructs used for referring to places, landscapes, homelands, and human settings are simultaneously constructions and idealized places as well as objective environments (e.g., Grauman & Kruse, 1990; Macnaghten & Urry, 1998). However, environmental psychologists have mainly focused on physical environments as the objectified research setting, with less consideration given to perceptual, cognitive, affective, social, cultural, and symbolic processes that are integrally involved in how we experience, understand, respond to, and transact with "objective" and "meaning-full" environments. Rich literatures exist on place meaning and attachment (Altman & Low, 1992), phenomenological ecology and environmental psychology (Seamon & Mugerauer, 1995), the conceptual and symbolic domain of place and placelessness, landscape and meaning (e.g., Berleant, 1997), and the status and implications of constructed spaces, places, and worlds (e.g., Robertson et al., 1996), but this important work is not well reflected in current urban and regional planning and environmental impact assessment, where dramatic changes to important places continue to exact appreciable human distress and costs (Van den Berg, Hartig, & Staats, 2007). Individual and sociocultural constructions of place and environment pose multiple challenges when issues related to risk, beauty, place meaning, environmental values, concerns, and behavioural intentions are involved. This is because the way we think about environmental risks, problems, and environmental quality profoundly influences the decisions we make, the environments we design and build, the intervention strategies and solutions we initiate in the face of perceived threats, and how we experience, respond, and adapt to our objectively 'real' natural and built environments.

Environmental Psychology and Architectural Design

Some buildings are human disasters; others are merely persistent nuisances to those who use them. Social design (Sommer, 1983) is a way of creating buildings that fit occupants and users better by involving them in the planning process. Social design is a remedy for the malady in which architects see themselves primarily as artists, ignoring the basic needs and activities of occupants. This is now widely recognized, yet many buildings are still constructed without significant user involvement.

Social design has numerous goals, problems and advantages. It aims to match settings to their occupants, to satisfy a variety of principal players' needs, to promote personal control in the building, and to encourage social support (Gifford, 2007a). Under some circumstances, other goals may be to increase productivity or to change behavior. The problems include a frequent lack of communication between those who pay for a building and those who use or occupy it, resistance to the extra effort of involving users and occupants, unrealistic expectations that socially designed buildings will directly cure various evils, conflict among principal players, and the false beliefs that some designers hold about those who will use a building (e.g., Heimsath, 1977). Social design usually means serving the needs of building occupants first, but it also offers benefits to architects and paying clients.

The design process includes programming, design, construction, use and adaptation, and postoccupancy evaluation (Zeisel, 1981). Programming consists of three phases: understanding the needs of building users, involving them in the possibilities of design, and translating their needs into design guidelines. Turning these guidelines into plans and reality is the job of architects and construction companies. The environmental psychologist returns later to conduct a postoccupancy evaluation, which examines the effectiveness of the program and design (e.g., Preiser, Vischer, & White, 1991).

Information and Communication Technologies and Environments

Perhaps the most profound global environmental change that has taken place during the emergence and development of environmental psychology has been the revolution in information technology. These profound changes have been commented upon by many (Hassan, 2008; McLuhan, 1964), but perspectives from psychologists are particularly helpful with respect to what these changes might portend for psychology, environmental psychology and environmental sustainability (Stokols & Montero, 2002; Subrahmanyam & Greenfield, 2009).

These convergent technologies are most compelling because they are transforming not only our technological extensions (Hall, 1976) and information environments (Norman, 2008), but the very nature of our transactions with, and understandings of, our natural and social environments. These technologies also pose challenges to optimal human functioning, human settings, and sustainable human–natural environment transactions (Stokols, Misra, Runnerstrom, & Hipp, 2009). Research on restoration, environmental stress, and virtual environment design suggest that this distancing of experience through mediated transactions and encounters with natural and actual environments fundamentally changes our connections with our world and how we view these connections, ourselves, and our world (Levi & Kocher, 1999; Reser, under review). Transactional approaches have always addressed the nature and quality of the information and feedback provided during environmental transactions (e.g., Altman, 1990; Reser, & Scherl, 1988), but the profound information technology transformations taking place as we enter this brave new world of screen culture, cyberspace, and virtual interactive experience requires a considered and perhaps radically different understanding of environmental transactions, and a re-examination of prevailing assumptions about direct perception and the nature of representation (e.g., Heft, 2001).

Conclusion—Changing Contexts, Horizons, and Challenges

Environmental psychology has been from its inception a moving target and enterprise, with reviews and characterizations often out of step with current involvements and applications, and ongoing changes. Of the many myriad strands to this, a number of transitions and challenges appear to be particularly noteworthy:

- Dramatically changing information technologies and information environments are fundamentally altering our transactions with the larger world—and with each other (Stokols et al., 2009; Subrahmanyam & Greenfield, 2009).
- Ecological psychology continues to challenge environmental psychology with respect to the nature and status of direct perception and experience (Heft, 2001; Reser, 2007), particularly in a world increasingly characterized by indirect and virtual experience and mediated "realities".
- Environmental psychology's increasing interest in the challenges and paradoxes of the local and global (Gifford et al., 2009; Uzzell, 2000) finds itself in a quandary, where thinking globally, acting locally, and responding personally are prerequisite for a sustainable existence, but are compromised by a convergent set of perceptual, media coverage, and information and communication technology biases.
- Problems related to distinctions between the physical and social environment have never been adequately resolved (Heft, 1998; Kaplan & Kaplan, 2009), but the changing nature of human settings and virtual "physical" and "social environments," and the intertwined nature of the biophysical and psychosocial underscores the fundamental importance of adequately conceptualizing "environmental" contexts to understanding human behaviour. Some believe that we need to reconsider alternative ways of understanding people-environment transactions (Reser & Bentrupperbäumer, 2008; Stokols et al., 2009).

These challenges are necessarily changing the face of environmental psychology, but perhaps no changes are more profound and consequential than the cascading impacts of climate change. Its mitigation and adaptation present an enormously consequential litmus test for the applicability and relevance of many areas of behavioral science, but particularly for environmental psychology (Gifford, 2008a; Reser & Swim, in press; Swim et al., 2009; Steg & Vlek, 2008; Uzzell & Räthzel, 2009). These challenges include increasingly fragile life support systems, the continuous threat and stress of media representations and risk communications, mitigation measures themselves, and the global human costs of socioeconomic and socio-political instability and disruption around the world. Although considerable emphasis has been placed on targeting environmentally significant behaviors, for cogent and compelling reasons, in the service of reducing greenhouse gases and climate change mitigation (e.g., Steg & Vlek, 2008; Gardner & Stern, 2002, 2008), equally persuasive and strategic arguments can be made for simultaneously focusing on other people–environment interfaces where the nature and outcomes of these transactions mediate both proenvironmental behaviors and the concurrent psychosocial impacts of perceived environmental changes. Each of these interfaces presents recurrent patterns of opportunities where targeted applied psychology interventions might make a substantive difference, ultimately in terms of *environmentally significant behaviours* (ESBs), but more immediately in terms of *psychologically significant responses* (Swim et al., 2009). Such an approach requires a rethinking of people–environment transactions, both directly in immediate 'real' environments, and indirectly with respect to virtual information environments.

Scientific psychology began in the 19th century, but not until the end of the 1950s was psychology's range extended in any serious way to the physical environment. From the vantage point of the early 21st century, the outmoded vision of a psychology that attempted to understand persons in a virtually empty physical context seems woefully inadequate. Environmental psychology not only fills in the background, but also the foreground and the built and natural settings within which all of life operates. Thus, environmental psychology is not only essential to a complete theoretical understanding of people, but also for every application of psychology to the understanding and improvement of everyday life and the environments in which it occurs.

References

Aarts, H., Verplanken, B., & Van Knippenberg, A. (1998). Predicting behaviour from actions in the past: Repeated decision making or a matter of habit? *Journal of Applied Social Psychology*, *28*, 1355–1374.

Abrahamse, W., Steg, L., Vlek, C., Rothengatter, J. A. (2005). A review of intervention studies aimed at household energy conservation. *Journal of Environmental Psychology*, *25*, 273–291.

Abrahamse, W., Steg, L., Vlek, C., & Rothengatter, J. A. (2007). The effect of tailored information, goal setting and feedback on household energy use, energy-related behaviors and behavioral determinants. *Journal of Environmental Psychology*, *27*, 265–276.

Ahrentzen, S. (1981). The environmental and social context of distraction in the classroom. In A. E. Osterberg, C. P. Tiernan, & R. A. Findlay (Eds.), *Design research interactions* (pp. 241–250). Ames, IA: Environmental Design Research Association.

Ahrentzen, S., Jue, G. M., Skorpanich, M. A., & Evans, G. W. (1982). School environments and stress. In G. W. Evans (Ed.), *Environmental stress* (pp. 224–255). New York: Cambridge University Press.

Ajzen, I. (1991). The theory of planned behavior. *Organizational Behavior and Human Decision Processes*, *50*, 179–211.

Altman, I. (1975). *The environment and social behavior: Privacy, personal space, territoriality, and crowding*. Monterey, CA: Brooks/Cole.

Altman, I. (1990) Toward a transactional perspective: A personal journey. In I. Altman & K. Christensen (Eds.), *Environment and behavior studies: Emergence of intellectual traditions* (pp 226–256). New York: Plenum.

Altman, I., & Low, S. M. (Eds.). (1992). *Human behavior and environment: Place attachment.* New York: Plenum.

Altman, I., & Rogoff, B. (1987). World views in psychology and environmental psychology: Trait, interactional, organismic and transactional perspectives. In I. Altman & D. Stokols (Eds.), *Handbook of environmental psychology* (pp. 245–281). New York: Wiley.

Appleyard, D. (1976). *Planning a pluralist city.* Cambridge, MA: MIT Press.

Bamberg, S. (2002). Effects of implementation intentions on the actual performance of new environmentally friendly behaviours – Results of two field experiments. *Journal of Environmental Psychology, 22*, 399–411.

Bamberg, S., & Schmidt, S. (2003). Incentives, morality or habit? Predicting students' car use for university routes with the models of Ajzen, Schwartz and Triandis. *Environment and Behavior, 35*, 264–285.

Baker, M. A., & Holding, D. H. (1993). The effects of noise and speech on cognitive task performance. *Journal of General Psychology, 120*, 339–355.

Barker, R. G. (1968). *Ecological psychology: Concepts and methods for studying the environment of human behavior.* Stanford, CA: Stanford University Press.

Barker, R. G., & Gump, P. V. (Eds.). *Big school, small school: High school size and student behavior.* Stanford, CA: Stanford University Press.

Barnes, R. D. (1981). Perceived freedom and control in the built environment. In J. H. Harvey (Ed.), *Cognition, social behavior, and the environment* (pp. 409–422). Hillsdale, NJ: Erlbaum.

Baron, R. A., & Ransberger, V. M. (1978). Ambient temperature and the occurrence of collective violence: The long hot summer revisited. *Journal of Personality and Social Psychology, 36*, 351–360.

Bechtel, R. B., & Churchman, A. (Eds.). (2002). *Handbook of environmental psychology.* New York: Wiley.

Bell, P. A., Greene, T. C., Fisher, J. D. & Baum, A. (2001) *Environmental psychology.* (5th ed.), New York: Harcourt College Publishers.

Berleant, A. (1997) *Living in the landscape: Toward an aesthetics of environment.* Lawrence, KA: University Press of Kansas.

Berleant, A., & Carlson, A. (Eds.). (2004) *The aesthetics of natural environments.* Peterborough, Ontario: Broadview Press.

Berlyne, D. E. (Ed.). (1974). *Studies in the new experimental aesthetics: Steps toward an objective psychology of aesthetic appreciation.* New York: Halsted Press.

Biel, A., & Garling, T. (1995). The role of uncertainty on resource dilemmas. *Journal of Environmental Psychology, 15*, 221–233.

Black, J. S., Stern, P. C., & Elworth, J. T. (1985). Personal and contextual influences on household energy adaptations. *Journal of Applied Psychology, 70*, 3–21.

Bonnes, M., Giuliani, M. V., Amoni, F., & Bernard, Y. (1987). Cross-cultural rules for the optimization of the living room. *Environment and Behavior, 19*, 204–227.

Bonsall, P., Spencer, A., & Tang, W. (1983). Ridesharing in Great Britain: Performance and impact of the Yorkshire schemes. *Transportation Research, 17*, 169–181.

Brill, M., Margulis, S. T., & Konar, E. (1984). *Using office design to increase productivity.* Buffalo, NY: Buffalo Organization for Social and Technological Innovation.

Brown, D., Sijpkes, P., & MacLean, M. (1986). The community role of public indoor space. *Journal of Architecture and Planning Research, 3*, 161–172.

Brunswik, E. (1956). *Perception and the representative design of psychological experiments.* Berkeley: University of California Press.

Chawla, L. (1994). *In the first country of places.* New York: State University of New York Press.

Cialdini, R. B., Kallgren, C. A., & Reno, R. R. (1991). A focus theory of normative conduct: A theoretical refinement and re-evaluation of the role of norms in human behavior. *Advances in Experimental Social Psychology, 24*, 201–234.

Clayton, S., & Brook, A. (2005). Can psychology help save the world? A model for conservation psychology. *Analyses of Social Issues and Public Policy*, *5*, 87–102.

Cohen, S. (1978). Environmental load and the allocation of attention. In A. Baum, J. E. Singer, & S. Valins (Eds.), *Advances in environmental psychology* (Vol. 1). Hillsdale, NJ: Erlbaum.

Cohen, S., & Weinstein, N. (1982). Nonauditory effects of noise on behavior and health. In G. W. Evans (Ed.), *Environmental stress.* New York: Cambridge University Press.

Creekmore, W. N. (1987). Effective use of classroom walls. *Academic Therapy*, *22*, 341–348.

Dawes, R. M., & Messick, D. M. (2000). Social dilemmas. *International Journal of Psychology*, *35*, 111-116.

De Groot, J. I. M., & Steg, L. (2007). Value orientations and environmental beliefs in five countries: Validity of an instrument to measure egoistic, altruistic and biospheric value orientations. *Journal of Cross-Cultural Psychology*, *38*, 318–332.

De Groot, J., & Steg, L. (2008). Value orientations to explain beliefs related to environmental significant behavior: How to measure egoistic, altruistic, and biospheric value orientations. *Environment and Behavior*, *40*(3), 330–354.

Dwyer, W. O., Leeming, F. C., Cobern, M. K., Porter, B. E., & Jackson, J. M. (1993). Critical review of behavioral interventions to preserve the environment. Research since 1980. *Environment and Behavior*, *25*, 275–21.

Edney, J. J. (1976). The psychological role of property rights in human behavior. *Environment and Planning: A*, *8*, 811–822.

Evans, G. W. (1982). (Ed.). *Environmental stress.* New York: Cambridge University Press.

Evans, G. W., & Saegert S. (2000). Residential crowding in the context of inner city poverty. In S. Wapner, J. Demick, C. T. Yamamoto, & H. Minami (Eds.), *Theoretical perspectives in environment-behavior research: Underlying assumptions, research problems , and methodologies* (pp. 247–267). New York: Kluwer Academic/Plenum Publishers.

Evans, G. W., & Stecker, R. (2003). Motivational consequences of environmental stress. *Journal of Environmental Psychology*, *24*, 143–165.

Evans, G. W., Wells, N. M., Chan, H. Y. E., & Saltzman, H. (2000). Housing quality and mental health. *Journal of Consulting and Clinical Psychology*, *68*, 526–530.

Freedman, J. L. (1975). *Crowding and behavior.* San Francisco: Freeman.

Fried, M. (1984). The structure and significance of community satisfaction. *Population & Environment: Behavioral and Social Issues*, *7*, 61–86.

Fujii, S., & Gärling, T. (2003). *Development* of script-based travel mode choice after forced change. *Transportation Research F*, *6*, 117–124.

Gardner, G. T., & Stern, P. C. (2002). *Environmental problems and human behavior* (2nd edition). Boston, MA: Pearson Custom Publishing.

Gardner, G. T., & Stern, P. C. (2008) The short list: The most effective actions U.S. households can take to curb climate change. *Environment*, *50*, 12-24.

Gärling, T., Fujii, S., Gärling, A., & Jakobsson, C. (2003). Moderating effects of social value orientation on determinants of proenvironmental intention. *Journal of Environmental Psychology*, *23*, 1–9.

Gärling, T., & Schuitema, G. (2007). Travel demand management targeting reduced private car use: Effectiveness, public acceptability and political feasibility. *Journal of Social Issues*, *63*(1), 139–153.

Geller, E. S. (1987). Environmental psychology and applied behavior analysis: From strange bedfellows to a productive marriage. In D. Stokols & I. Altman (Eds.), *Handbook of environmental psychology.* New York: Wiley.

Geller, E. S. (2002). The challenge of increasing proenvironmental behavior. In R. B. Bechtel & A. Churchman, *Handbook of environmental psychology* (pp. 525–540). New York: Wiley.

Gibson, J. J. (1976). *The theory of affordances and the design of the environment.* Paper presented at the annual meeting of the American Society for Aesthetics, Toronto.

Gifford, R. (1992). *Performance and related outcomes of inadequate offices: An annotated bibliography.* Report to the British Columbia Buildings Corporation.

Gifford, R. (2007a). *Environmental psychology: Principles and practice* (4th ed.). Colville, WA: Optimal Books.

Gifford, R. (2007b). Environmental psychology and sustainable development: Expansion, maturation, and challenges. *Journal of Social Issues, 63*, 199–212.

Gifford, R. (2007c). The consequences of living in high-rise buildings. *Architectural Science Review, 50*, 2–17.

Gifford, R. (2008a). Psychology's essential role in climate change. *Canadian Psychology/Psychologie Canadienne, 49*, 273–280.

Gifford, R. (2008b). Toward a comprehensive model of social dilemmas. In A. Biel, D. Eek, T. Gärling, & M. Gustafsson (Eds.). *New issues and paradigms in research on social dilemmas.* Springer.

Gifford, R., Hine, D. W., & Veitch, J. A. (1997). Meta-analysis for environment–behavior research, illuminated with a study of lighting level effects on office task performance. In G. T. Moore & R. W. Marans (Eds.), *Advances in environment, behavior, and design* (pp. 223–253). New York: Plenum.

Gifford, R., & Lacombe, C. (2006). Housing quality and children's socioemotional health. *Journal of Housing and the Built Environment, 21*, 177–189.

Gifford, R., Scannell, L., Kormos, C., Smolova, L., Biel, A., Boncu, S., ... Uzzell, D. (2009). Temporal pessimism and spatial optimism in environmental assessments: An 18-nation study. *Journal of Environmental Psychology, 29*, 1–12.

Gifford, R., & Steg, L. (2007). The impact of automobile traffic on quality of life. In T. Garling & L. Steg (Eds.), *Threats from car traffic to the quality of urban life: Problems, causes, and solutions* (pp. 33–51). Amsterdam: Elsevier.

Gifford, R., Ward, J., & Dahm, W. (1977). Pedestrian velocities: A multivariate study of social and environmental effects. *Journal of Human Movement Studies, 3*, 66–68.

Grauman, C. F., & Kruse, L. (1990) The environment: Social construction and psychological problems. In H. T. Himmelweit (Ed.), *Societal psychology* (pp. 212–229). London: Sage.

Guagnano, G. A., Stern, P. C., & Dietz, T. (1995). Influences on attitude-behavior relationships: A natural experiment with curbside recycling. *Environment and Behavior, 27*, 699–718.

Guest, A. M., & Lee, B. A. (1984). How urbanites define their neighborhoods. *Population & Environment: Behavioral & Social Issues, 7*, 32-56.

Hall, E. T. (1966). *The hidden dimension.* Garden City, NY: Doubleday.

Hall, E. T. (1976) *Beyond culture.* Garden City, NY: Doubleday & Company.

Hardin, G. (1968). The tragedy of the commons. *Science, 162*, 1234–1248.

Harland, P., & Staats, H., & Wilke, H. (1999). Explaining proenvironmental behavior by personal norms and the theory of planned behavior. *Journal of Applied Social Psychology, 29*, 2505–2528.

Hartgen, D. T. (1974). Attitudinal and situational variables influencing urban mode choice: Some empirical findings. *Transportation, 3*, 377–392.

Hartig, T., & Staats, H. (Eds.). (2003). Restorative environments. *Journal of Environmental Psychology, 23*, 103–198. Special issue focus [Restoration].

Hassan, R. (2008) *The information society: Cyber dreams and digital nightmares.* New York: Wiley.

Hawkins, D. I., Best, R. J., & Coney, K. A. (1983). *Consumer behavior: Implications for marketing strategy.* Plano, TX: Business Publications.

Hay, R. (1998). Sense of place in developmental context. *Journal of Environmental Psychology, 18*, 5–29.

Heath, Y., & Gifford, R. (2002). Extending the theory of planned behaviour: Predicting the use of public transportation. *Journal of Applied Social Psychology, 32*, 2154–2185.

Hedge, A. (1982). The open-plan office: A systematic investigation of employee reactions to their work environment. *Environment and Behavior, 14*, 519–542.

Heimsath, C. (1977). *Behavioral architecture: Toward an accountable design process.* New York: McGraw-Hill.

Heft, H. R. (1998). Essay review: The elusive environment in environmental psychology. *British Journal of Psychology*, 519–523.

Heft, H. R. (2001). *Ecological psychology in context: James Gibson, Roger Barker, and the legacy of William James's radical empiricism.* Mahwah, N.J.: Lawrence Erlbaum.

Helson, H. (1964). *Adaptation-level theory.* New York: Harper and Row.

Iso-Ahola, S. E. (1983). Towards a social psychology of recreational travel. *Leisure Studies, 2*, 45–56.

Ittelson, W. H. (1978). Environmental perception and urban experience. *Environment and Behavior, 10*, 193–213.

Ittelson, W. H., Proshansky, H. M., Rivlin, L. G., & Winkel, G. H. (1974). *An introduction to environmental psychology.* New York: Holt, Rinehart, Winston.

Kantrowitz, E. J., & Evans, G. W. (2004). The relation between the ratio of children per activity area and off-task behavior and type of play in day care centers. *Environment and Behavior, 36*, 541–557.

Kaplan, R., Kaplan, S. & Ryan, R. L. (1998) *With people in mind: Design and management of everyday nature.* Washington, DC: Island Press.

Kaplan, S. (1995). The restorative benefits of nature: Towards an integrative framework. *Journal of Environmental Psychology, 15*, 169–182.

Kaplan, S., & Kaplan, R. (2009). Creating a larger role for environmental psychology: The reasonable person model as an integrative framework. *Journal of Environmental Psychology, 29*(3), 387–389.

Keizer, K., Lindenberg, S., & Steg, L. (2008). The spreading of disorder. *Science, 322*, 1681–1685.

Koneya, M. (1976). Location and interaction in row and column seating arrangements. *Environment and Behavior, 8*, 265–282.

Levi, D., & Kocher, S. (1999) Virtual nature: The future effects of information technology on our relationship to nature. *Environment and Behavior, 31*, 203–226.

Levin, I., & Louviere, J. (1981). Psychological contributions to travel demand modeling. In I. Altman, J. F. Wohlwill, & P. B. Everett (Eds.), *Transportation and behaviour* (pp. 29–61). New York: Plenum.

Levine, M. (1982). You-are-here maps: Psychological considerations. *Environment and Behavior, 14*, 221–237.

Lindenberg, S., & Steg, L. (2007). Normative, gain and hedonic goal-frames guiding environmental behavior. *Journal of Social Issues, 63*(1), 117–137.

Lofland, L. (1973). *A world of strangers.* New York: Basic Books.

Lynch, K. (1960). *The image of the city.* Cambridge, MA: MIT Press.

Lynch, K., & Rivkin, M. (1959). A walk around the block. *Landscape, 8*, 24-34.

MacNaghten, P., & Urry, J. (1998) *Contested natures.* London: Sage.

Maller, C. J., Townsend, M., Prior, A., Brown, P. & St. Leger, L. (2006) Healthy nature healthy people: "Contact with nature as an upstream promotion intervention for populations." *Health Promotion International*, *21*, 45–54.

McHarg, I. L. (1971). *Design with nature*. Garden City, NY: Doubleday/Natural History Press.

McLuhan, M. (1964). *Understanding media: The extensions of man*. London: Routledge & Kegan Paul.

Megaw, E. D., & Bellamy, L. J. (1983). Illumination at work. In D. J. Oborne & M. M. Gruneberg (Eds.), *The physical environment at work*. New York: Wiley.

Messick, D. M., & Brewer, M. B. (1983). Solving social dilemmas: a review. In L. Wheeler & O. Shaver (Eds.), *Review of Personality and Social Psychology* (Vol. 4, pp. 11–44). Beverly Hills, CA: Sage.

Michelson, W. (1977). *Environmental choice, human behavior and residential satisfaction*. New York: Oxford University Press.

Milgram, S. (1977). *The individual in a social world: Essays and experiments*. Reading, MA: Addison-Wesley.

Miller, J. D. (1974). Effects of noise on people. *Journal of the Acoustical Society of America*, *56*, 729–764.

Montano, D., & Adamopoulos, J. (1984). The perception of crowding in interpersonal situations: Affective and behavioral responses. *Environment and Behavior*, *16*, 643–666.

Montello, D. R. (1991). Spatial orientation and the angularity of urban routes: A field study. *Environment and Behavior*, *23*, 47–69.

Moore, G. T. (1979). Knowing about environmental knowing: The current state of theory and research on environmental cognition. *Environment and Behavior*, *11*, 33–70.

Morrow, P. C., & McElroy, J. C. (1981). Interior office design and visitor response: A constructive replication. *Journal of Applied Psychology*, *66*, 646–650.

Munson, P., & Ferguson, R. (1985). *The extra-visual effects of fluorescent illumination on the behavior of school children*. Unpublished manuscript, University of Victoria.

Nasar, J. L. (1989). Symbolic meanings of house styles. *Environment and Behavior*, *21*, 235–257.

National Academy of Sciences. (1977). *Medical and biological effects of environmental pollutants*. Washington, DC: National Academy of Sciences.

Nelson, T. M., Nilsson, T. H., & Hopkins, G. W. (1987). Thermal comfort: Advantages and deviations. *Ashrae Transactions*, *93*(1), 1039–1047.

Newman, O. (1972). *Defensible space*. New York: Macmillan.

Ng, C. F. (2003). Satisfying shoppers' psychological needs: From public market to cyber-mall. *Journal of Environmental Psychology*, *23*, 427–237.

Ng, C. F., & Gifford, R. (1984). *Speech communication in the office: The effects of background sound level and conversational privacy*. Unpublished manuscript, University of Victoria.

Nickerson, R. S. (2003). *Psychology and environmental change*. Mahwah, NJ: Erlbaum.

Nordlund, A. M., & Garvill, J. (2003). Effects of values, problem awareness, and personal norm on willingness to reduce personal car use. *Journal of Environmental Psychology*, *23*, 339–347.

Norman, K. L. (2008) *Cyberpsychology: An introduction to human-computer interaction*. New York: Cambridge University Press.

Norris-Baker, C., & Scheidt, R. J. (1990). Place attachment among older residents of a "ghost Town": A transactional approach. *Proceedings of the 21st annual conference of the Environmental Design Research Association*, *21*, 333–340.

O'Keefe, J., & Nadel, L. (1978). *The hippocampus as a cognitive map*. Oxford: Clarendon Press.

Ölander, F., & Thøgersen, J. (1995). Understanding of consumer behaviour as a prerequisite for environmental protection. *Journal of Consumer Policy, 18*, 345–385.

Ornstein, R., & Ehrlich, P. (2000). *New world, new mind.* Malor Books.

Passini, R., Pigot, H., Rainville, C., & Tetreault, M. H. (2000). Wayfinding in a nursing home for advanced dementia of the Alzheimer's type. *Environment and Behavior, 32*, 684–710.

Patterson, M. L., & Sechrest, L. B. (1970). Interpersonal distance and impression formation. *Journal of Personality, 38*, 161–166.

Pearce, P. L. (1981). Environment shock: A study of tourists' reactions to two tropical islands. *Journal of Applied Social Psychology, 11*, 268–280.

Poortinga, W., Steg, L., Vlek, C., & Wiersma, G. (2003). Household preferences for energy-saving measures. A conjoint analysis. *Journal of Economic Psychology, 24*, 49–64.

Preiser, W. F. E., Vischer, J. C., & White, E. T. (Eds.). (1991). *Design intervention: Toward a more humane architecture.* New York: Van Nostrand Reinhold.

Reser, J. P. (1980). Automobile addiction: Real or imagined? *Man-Environment Systems, 10*, 279–287.

Reser, J. P. (2007). Ecological psychology in context: Revisiting Gibson, Barker, and James' radical empiricism—and rethinking environment and environmental experience. *Journal of Environmental Psychology, 27*, 1–13.

Reser, J. P. (under review). Public understandings of climate change: Reflections and reframings. *Risk Analysis.*

Reser, J. P., & Bentrupperbäumer, J. M. (2008). Framing and researching the impacts of visitation and use in protected areas. In N. Stork & S. Turton (Eds.), *Living in a dynamic tropical forest landscape: Lessons from Australia* (pp. 420–429). Oxford: Blackwell.

Reser, J. P., & Scherl, L. M. (1988). Clear and unambiguous feedback: A transactional and motivational analysis of environmental challenge and self encounter. *Journal of Environmental Psychology, 8*, 269–286.

Reser, J. P., & Swim, J. (in press). Adapting to and coping with the threat and impacts of climate change. *American Psychologist.*

Robertson, G., Mash, M., Tickner, L., Bird, J., Curtis, B. & Putnam, T. (Eds.). 1996. *FutureNatural: Nature/science/culture.* London: Routledge.

Rohe, W., & Patterson, A. H. (1974). The effects of varied levels of resources and density on behavior in a day care center. In D. Carson (Ed.), *Man–environment interactions: Evaluations and applications.* Stroudsberg, PA: Dowden, Hutchinson and Ross.

Rotton, J., Frey, J., Barry, T., Milligan, M., & Fitzpatrick, M. (1979). The air pollution experience and physical aggression. *Journal of Applied Social Psychology, 9*, 397–412.

Sauser, W. I., Jr., Arauz, C. G., & Chambers, R. M. (1978). Exploring the relationship between level of office noise and salary recommendations: A preliminary research note. *Journal of Management, 4*, 57–63.

Schmuck, P., & Schultz, P. W. (Eds.) (2002) *Psychology of sustainable development* (pp. 61–78). Boston: Kluwer.

Schultz, P. W., Nolan, J., Cialdini, R., Goldstein, N., & Griskevicius, V. (2007). The constructive, destructive, and reconstructive power of social norms. *Psychological Science, 18*, 429–434.

Schwartz, S. H. (1977). Normative influences on altruism. In L. Berkowitz (Ed.), *Advances in experimental social psychology, 10* (pp. 221–279). New York: Academic Press.

Scopelliti, M., & Giuliani, M. V. (2004). Choosing restorative environments across the lifespan: A matter of place experience. *Journal of Environmental Psychology, 24*, 423–437.

Seamon, D. (1982). The phenomenological contribution to environmental psychology. *Journal of Environmental Psychology, 2*, 119–140.

Seamon, D., & Mugerauer, R. (Eds.). 1995. *Dwelling, place and environment: Towards a phenomenology of person and world.* Dordrecht: Martinus Nijhoff Publishers.

Smith, S. M. (1979). Remembering in and out of context. *Journal of Experimental Psychology, 5*, 460–471.

Sommer, R. (1959). Studies in personal space. *Sociometry, 22*, 247–260.

Sommer, R. (1983). *Social design.* Englewood Cliffs, NJ: Prentice-Hall.

Stamps, A. E. (2005). Enclosure and safety in urbanscapes. *Environment and Behavior, 37*, 102–133.

Steele, F. (1980). Defining and developing environmental competence. In C. P. Alderfer & C. L. Cooper (Eds.), *Advances in experiential social processes, 2*, 225–244.

Steg, L., De Groot, J. I. M., Dreijerink, L., Abrahamse, W., & Siero, F. (2011). General antecedents of personal norms, policy acceptability, and intentions: The role of values, worldviews, and environmental concern. *Society and Natural Resources.*

Steg, L., Dreijerink, L., & Abrahamse, W. (2005). Factors influencing the acceptability of energy policies: testing VBN theory. *Journal of Environmental Psychology, 25*, 415–425.

Steg, L., Dreijerink, L., & Abrahamse, W. (2006). Why are energy policies acceptable and effective? *Environment and Behavior, 38*(1), 92–11.

Steg, L., & Gifford, R. (2005). Sustainable transport and quality of life. *Journal of Transport Geography, 13*, 59–69.

Steg, L., & Schuitema, G. (2007). Behavioural responses to transport pricing: a theoretical analysis. In T. Gärling & L. Steg (Eds.), *Threats to the quality of urban life from car traffic: problems, causes, and solutions* (pp. 347–366). Amsterdam: Elsevier.

Steg, L., & Vlek, C. (2009). Encouraging proenvironmental behaviour: An integrative review and research agenda. *Journal of Environmental Psychology, 29*, 309–317.

Stern, E. (1982). Bus services in rural areas. *Environment and Behavior, 14*, 94–112.

Stern, P. C. (2000). Toward a coherent theory of environmentally significant behavior. *Journal of Social Issues, 56*(3), 407–424.

Stokols, D. (1972). On the distinction between density and crowding: Some implications for further research. *Psychological Review, 79*, 275–278.

Stokols, D., Misra, S., Runnerstrom, M. G. & Hipp, J. A. (2009). Psychology in an age of ecological crisis: From personal angst to collective action. *American Psychologist, 64*, 181–193.

Stokols, D., & Montero, M. (2002) Toward an environmental psychology of the internet. In R. B. Bechtel & A. Churchman (Eds.), *Handbook of environmental psychology* (pp. 661–675). New York: Wiley.

Stokols, D., & Shumaker, S. A. (1981). People in places: A transactional view of settings. In J. H. Harvey (Ed.), *Cognition, social behavior and the environment.* Hillsdale, NJ: Erlbaum.

Stokols, D., & Shumaker, S. A. (1982). The psychological context of residential mobility and well-being. *Journal of Social Issues, 38*(3), 149–171.

Strang, H. R., & George, J. R. (1975). Clowning around to stop clowning around: A brief report on an automated approach to monitor, record, and control classroom noise. *Journal of Applied Behavior Analysis, 8*, 471–474.

Studenmund, A. H., & Connor, D. (1982). The free-fare transit experiments. *Transportation Research, 16*, 261–269.

Subrahmanyam, K., & Greenfield, P. M. (Eds.). (2009). Social networking on the internet—Developmental implications. *Journal of Applied Developmental Psychology, 29*, whole issue, 415–471.

Suedfeld, P. (1980). *Restricted environmental stimulation: Research and clinical applications.* New York: Wiley.

Sullivan, W. C., Kuo, F. E., & DePooter, S. F. (2004). The fruit of urban nature: Vital neighborhood spaces. *Environment and Behavior*, *36*, 678–700.

Swim, J., Clayton, S., Doherty, T., Gifford, R., Howard, G., Reser, J.P., Stern, P. & Weber, E. (2009). *Psychology and global climate change: Addressing a multi-faceted phenomenon and set of challenges.* Washington, DC: American Psychological Association.

Thompson, I. H. (2000). *Ecology, community, and delight: Sources of values in landscape architecture.* London: E. & F. N. Spon.

Ulrich, R. S. (1984). View through a window may influence recovery from surgery. *Science*, *224*, 420–421.

Uzzell, D. (2000) The psycho-spatial dimension to global environmental problems. *Journal of Environmental Psychology*, *20*(4) 307–318.

Uzzell, D., & Räthzel, N. (2009) Transforming environmental psychology. *Journal of Environmental Psychology*, *29*(3), 340–350.

Van den Berg, A. E., Hartig, T., & Staats, H. (2007). Preference for nature in urbanized societies: Stress, restoration, and the pursuit of sustainability. *Journal of Social Issues*, *63*, 79–96.

Walter, J. A. (1982). Social limits to tourism. *Leisure Studies*, *1*, 295–304.

Weinstein, C. S. (1977). Modifying student behavior in an open classroom through changes in the physical design. *American Education Research Journal*, *14*, 249–262.

Weinstein, C. S. (1979). The physical environment of the school: A review of the research. *Review of Educational Research*, *49*, 577–610.

Welch, B. L. (1979). *Extra-auditory health effects of industrial noise: Survey of foreign literature.* Aerospace Medical Research Laboratory, Aerospace Medical Division, Air Force Systems Command, Wright-Patterson AFB, June 1979.

Williams, K., & Harvey, D. (2001). Transcendent experience in forest environments. *Journal of Environmental Psychology*, *21*(3) 249–260.

Wohlwill, J. F. (1966). The physical environment: A problem for a psychology of stimulation. *Journal of Social Issues*, *22*(4), 29–38.

Wollin, D. D., & Montagne, M. (1981). College classroom environment: Effects of sterility versus amiability on student and teacher performance. *Environment and Behavior*, *13*, 707–716.

Zalesny, M. D., & Farace, R. V. (1987). Traditional versus open offices: A comparison of sociotechnical, social relations, and symbolic meaning perspectives. *Academy of Management Journal*, *30*, 240–259.

Zeisel, J. (1981). *Inquiry by design: Tools for environment–behavior research.* Monterey, CA: Brooks/Cole.

19

Community Psychology

Carolyn Kagan, Karen Duggan, Michael Richards, and Asiya Siddiquee

Community psychology (CP) as a field of applied psychology can be performed in interrelated but different ways:

- As a distinct psychological paradigm, a form of psychological praxis, integrating theory with practice and delineating a distinct ontology, epistemology, methodology, ethics, and politics.
- As a perspective that can inform and be integrated with other forms of applied psychology (as in community clinical psychology, community educational psychology, community organizational psychology, community environmental psychology, and so on)
- As a practice that is disguised in other community practices not called community psychology *per se*, such as community development, community mental health, social work, or social development via NGOs.

Seedat, Duncan, and Lazarus (2001, p. 4) draw a distinction between the CP of the Northern hemisphere and that of the South:

> CP in the northern hemisphere has tended to assume an accommodationist position seeking greater influence within the mainstream fraternity without necessarily challenging the restrictions and outcomes imposed by exploitative economic arrangements and dominant systems of knowledge production.... In contrast, in the southern hemisphere (for example in South Africa and Latin America), community psychology came to be associated with broad democratic movements seeking to dismantle oppressive state structures and ideological state apparatuses, which were also embodied in the disciplinary practices of the social and medical sciences during the previous colonial and apartheid eras.

IAAP Handbook of Applied Psychology, First Edition. Edited by Paul R. Martin, Fanny M. Cheung, Michael C. Knowles, Michael Kyrios, Lyn Littlefield, J. Bruce Overmier, and José M. Prieto.

The turn to a critical community psychology in many parts of the North (e.g. Nelson and Prilleltensky, 2005) and the limited development of a transformative CP practice in some parts of the South (e.g., Bhatia & Sethi, 2007; Cheng & Mak, 2007) make these distinctions difficult to uphold quite so clearly, however.

In this chapter we will try and capture the essence of community psychological praxis, whether in a distinct, integrated, or disguised form. From the outset it is important to situate ourselves as authors of the chapter. We are all linked to Manchester Metropolitan University's (MMU) community psychology group, which is characterized by an emphasis on soft systems thinking, critical action research (Burns, 2007), action learning, collaboration and interdisciplinarity (Kagan, Lawthom, Siddiquee, Duckett, & Knowles, 2007). Of the authors, MR is currently a CP practitioner and studying for a Masters in CP. KD works as a development project manager in the University and is studying for a PhD in CP. AS has a PhD in CP and lecturers in psychology at MMU. CK initiated CP at MMU and is the first (full or titular) Professor of Community Social Psychology in the UK. Thus we are all viewing CP through the MMU prism bringing a range of experience and positionalities with us.

What is Community Psychology?

CP has emerged in different ways in different parts of the world (Reich, Reimer, Prilleltensky, & Montero, 2007). Different sociopolitical contexts have aided or hindered the growth of CP, and have shaped its development. Whilst there are regional and local differences in emphasis, there is an emerging consensus about the nature of CP that has come about through:

- Personal and institutional connections as a result of overseas scholar training, national, regional, and international conferences, and sabbatical visits;
- The dominance of textbooks and journals, published in English, emanating from the USA. This is due in part to the size of the U.S. psychology industry and in part to the critical mass of CP practitioners;
- The influence of Latin American CP, via publications in Spanish but with increasing availability of key ideas made available in English.

The spread of ideas in CP is similar to that of other types of psychology (e.g. Brock, 2006; Lubek et al., 2006) and of processes of colonization of thought (Hardt & Negri, 2000), but practices are tailored to local issues and conditions with their own local historical, political, and ideological contexts for CP praxis. We will try and present CP in its complexity and not fall into the trap of assuming CP is USA-CP.

A well-used definition of CP is offered by Dalton, Elias, and Wandersman from the US (2001, p. 5):

> Community psychology concerns the relationships of the individual to communities and society. Through collaborative research and action, community psychologists seek to understand and to enhance quality of life for individual, communities and society.

A rather different view comes from Latin America:

> A dynamic and complex notion of community as CP's object and active subject of research and action is at the basis of understanding of the field in Latin America.... CP has as one of its bases the active conception of the people integrating the communities; ... CP is made with them, not just for them, or carried out in a community environment. ... [A]wareness of the need to work on de-ideologizing and strengthening, or empowering, community groups, movements and stakeholders in order to foster social change [is] one of the main tasks for CP in Latin America. ... Transformations are then decided with the community as well as influenced by the political character of the processes leading to them. (Montero & Varas Diaz, 2007, p. 62)

Our summary of CP and the boundaries of its interests can be summarized thus:

> Community psychology offers a framework for working with those marginalised by the social system that leads to self-aware social change with an emphasis on value based, participatory work and the forging of alliances. It is a way of working that is pragmatic and reflexive, whilst not wedded to any particular orthodoxy of method. ... It is *community* psychology because it emphasises a level of analysis and intervention other than the individual and their immediate interpersonal context. It is community *psychology* because it is nevertheless concerned with how people feel, think, experience and act as they work together, resisting oppression and struggling to create a better world. (Burton, Boyle, Harris & Kagan, 2007, p. 219: emphasis in original)

The kinds of problems that CP addresses have deep historical roots, and are characterized by "journeys ... of pain and suffering, dislocation and colonization, oppression and marginalization" (Nelson & Prilleltensky, 2005, p. 24). CP has, then, an explicit political purpose—the redistribution of social and personal power through processes of social change and transformation.

CP Paradigm: The Integration of Theory, Research, and Action

CP is an action science that attempts to link the goals of understanding and action, theory and practice, through research. Nelson and Prilleltensky (2005) outline three paradigms for community research relevant to CP. The post-positivist paradigm emphasizes empirical analytical knowledge; the constructivist paradigm emphasizes meaning and experiential knowledge; and the critical paradigm emphasizes critical, emancipatory knowledge. They argue that all three paradigms are relevant to CP. We, however, stress the need for an epistemological break with other applied psychologies, and reject the assumptions implicit in a post-positivist paradigm, namely that there is an external reality that can be understood through the reduction of social phenomena to component parts that are causally related (Kagan & Burton, 2001; Kagan, Duckett, Lawthom, & Burton, 2005). Despite the post-positivist paradigm retaining some hold over CP, we would argue with Montero that the CP paradigm belongs to a construction and critical transformation paradigm. Montero (1998, p. 67) argues for an epistemological base that assumes that

> society is a collective construction effected by persons who consider that their life circumstances must be transformed, and about which they have developed a critical perspective. This standpoint differs from hard constructivist conceptions for which "reality" is a construction of cognizant individuals.

Both hard constructivist and post-positivist approaches to social problems and social change look very much like an applied social psychology rather than CP.

The extent to which theory, research, and action are linked varies. Hegemonic CP, evolving as it did in the USA, Canada, and Australia, for example, was a firmly pragmatic discipline, with intervention and prevention (of ill health, psychological distress, community breakdown) at its core. Theory integrated with practice characterizes Latin American CP and some suggest that this integration, into a CP praxis, is one of the main characteristics of CP (Burton & Kagan, 2002; Nelson & Prilleltensky, 2005) and distinguishes it from both activism (practice without theory) and critical deconstruction of psychology (theory without action). CP praxis has action research at its core, which can lead, as we will see below, to work that focuses on understanding and/or action and/or evaluation and/or critical reflection—or any combination of these things.

The focus of the practice and the methods used vary in place and time: the concerns of postapartheid South Africa, for example, differ markedly from those in postindustrial Britain, or those experienced within a fragmenting Scandinavian social welfare system, or those in parts of Latin America where the popular majorities are active in the construction of society. Oppression, liberation, resistance, social transformation are key concepts in CP, unlikely to be much in evidence in other applied psychologies.

Whilst there is wide variation in practice, Kagan, Duckett et al. (2005, p. 285) suggest there is, perhaps, consensus on the following:

- Vision: a commitment to improving the collective human condition;
- Values: a recognition that CP practice cannot be value-free and an explicit articulation of the personal and collective values that underpin practice;
- Context: a focus which places people within their historical, cultural, environmental, and political contexts, thereby countering the individualistic bias and victim-blaming ideology of mainstream psychology;
- Multi-level and reflexive practice: an emphasis on long term projects and collaboration, working with the complexity of people's natural environments with reflection at the core.

Social Change

If CP is concerned with social change, it is necessary to outline what this might look like. Most CP practitioners will agree that it is important to have a vision of the kind of society towards which we are working: a more just society. This is not so much an end point, some kind of utopian ideal society, but more of a direction for movement.

> Enhanced well-being, social inclusion, and empowerment of nondominant groups who are marginalized by social systems are components of a vision for a more just society. A community psychological perspective would encourage us, and the people we work with, to have such a vision to guide our actions and frame our reflections. This vision unleashes our creativity and criticality, enmeshes our hopes and desires and engages our political values in our work. (Kagan, Duckett et al., 2005, p. 285)

Such a vision of a just society is underpinned by ideas of what should be, rather than what is, and is helped by the articulation of values. Nelson and Prilleltensky (2005, p. 32) argue that in its attempts to be recognized as an (objective) science, applied psychology has ignored the ethical and value dimensions to its work, and thereby by default upholding the societal status quo, reproducing and maintaining oppressive and exploitative social relations. Whilst CP recognizes the importance of values, and their importance in guiding not just the vision for change, but CP practice itself, the ways they are articulated varies.

We suggest three metavalues, under which most other values articulated by community psychologists (CPs) can be placed: *justice*; *stewardship*; and *community*. A concern for *justice* leads to human rights, including the right to have a more equal and equitable distribution of resources; the right to live in peace and in freedom from constraints; the right to equality and fair treatment; and the right to self-determination and collective gains. *Stewardship* contributes to duties and responsibilities including a duty to look after our world and the people in it; a duty to enable people to make a contribution and gain a sense of belonging; a duty not to waste things, people's lives, or time; and a duty to think long-term, make things last longer than us, and to do things as right as we can. A concern for *community* reflects people's hopes and desires including hope for companionship, love, acceptance, and tolerance; hope to be included and for diversity to be welcomed and celebrated; and hope that our individual and collective flaws will not hide our potential and that we will be accepted for who we are. In one sense, these values are not particularly helpful—who could argue against them? On the other hand, though, as a guide for CP praxis they are useful to articulate and revisit in relation to any specific piece of CP work, particularly in terms of their implications for practice moving in the general direction of a more just society. Table 19.1. outlines the implications for CP praxis which flow from the aforementioned rights, duties and hopes of these values.

There is a clear link between values and principles of practice. Kagan and Burton (2001) note that a clear vision of greater social justice and explicitly stated values could lead us to develop an academic critique of psychology and go no further. However, along with Lather (1986) we think it important that CP pushes for the possibilities of an alternative science with emancipatory goals and does not just settle for arguments against the possibilities of an objective science. In so doing, CP has begun to form an "epistemological break" with mainstream psychology (Hesse, 1980). Again, whilst there are some differences, there are also some similarities in the core characteristics of CP.

Table 19.1. Core Values and their Implications for Community Psychological Praxis

Justice	*Stewardship*	*Community*
This means we: work with people who are oppressed or marginalized by the social system, enabling them to affect change; work to enhance the possibility that people can more actively control their own lives in ways that are culturally appropriate; are concerned with collective control or agency as well as with social influence, political power, and legal rights; might, for example, in a UK context, highlight inequities in how human services operate, work with people to secure access to the necessary supports, or work with services on a change agenda so that they work in a more inclusive and nondiscriminatory way.	This means we: work as efficiently as we can, maximizing both human and material resources; involve other people as fully as possible, emphasizing their strengths and potential with a focus on the context of their lives; endeavor to work in ways that will lead to long-lasting change and not just short-term fixes, building on indigenous ways of conducting social relations; work as facilitators of others and are open to learning from others; are committed to innovation, and to the harnessing of people's creativity, whilst recognizing that some existing ways of working with people are at best ineffective and at worst make things worse for them.	This means we: attempt to strengthen people's sense of belonging and commitment to each other; value diversity and recognize and respect differences, based on, for example, class, beliefs, culture, gender, sexual orientation, and ability; work to understand antidiscriminatory practice, and are able to mediate in conflict situations; have a commitment to continual learning from practice, appreciate it is never possible to know everything, but that it is possible to be open to learning and sharing with others so that they too can learn; engage in reflective practice and emphasize evaluation of our work and of the projects with which we are connected.
Linked values:	*Linked values*:	*Linked values*:
Individual wellness	Citizen participation	Sense of community
Respect for human diversity	Collaboration and community strengths	Health
Self-determination, participation and social justice	Holism	Caring, compassion, and support for community structures
Commitment and accountability to oppressed groups	Respect for diversity, autonomy, organization, work, cooperation, and commitment (practical and social)	Democracy
Liberty	Social consciousness	Community and social solidarity
Conscience		Citizenship and social responsibility
Achievement		
Power and autonomy		

Characteristics of CP

Ecological metaphor

One of the epistemological breaks achieved by CP is to look beyond the individual for explanations of social experience and for solutions to social issues, whilst at the same time viewing people as agentic and purposeful with the potential to influence and change their situations. The person-in-context (where context is multilevel) is often the unit of analysis and change. An ecological perspective also offers up possibilities for understanding and action at levels beyond the individual, for example in the wider eco-system in which human experience is located.

Nelson and Prilleltensky (2005, p. 33) claim the value of the ecological metaphor for CP

> lies in its ability to contextualize the issues and problems that face disadvantaged people over time and across multiple levels of analysis and to embrace holism over reductionism. The ecological metaphor views human problems and competencies within the context of characteristics of the individual, ... micro analysis ... meso-level analysis ... and macro-level analysis.

Ecological thinking underpins many CP methods and strategies for change. However, whilst progressive insights may follow from ecological thinking, the same metaphor underpins conservative, reactionary, and reductionist thinking in psychology. Evolutionary psychology, for example, using the same metaphor, stresses "survival of the fittest" and the maintenance of "homeostatic equilibrium" as both social goals and social explicators. As Kagan and Burton (2001, p. 6) warn, these are concepts that are underpinned by the illusion of positivist science and not values that explicitly move us in the direction of a more just society.

Whole-systems perspectives

The ecological metaphor implies a focus on systems thinking, both as a catalyst to understanding and as a guide to action. Systems interventions are rooted in an ecological perspective on change. Human (or soft) systems are best conceptualized as complex social environments that can be both oppressive and supportive and that change over time. Any particular part of a social system can be, at the same time, oppressive and supportive. For example, families, public or private health and welfare agencies, hospitals, neighborhood regeneration and renewal policies and institutions, schools, social development work including NGOs all provide support to enable people to maintain identity, secure material resources, and at times resist the consequences of oppression. However, as Leonard (1975, p. 56) reminds us:

> [they] carry to greater or lesser degree the marks of economic exploitation and the cultural hegemony of the ruling class.

The bureaucratic and dehumanizing effects of health and welfare processes, the socialization of children for the demands of the labor market, the apathy following the failures in local decision making, for example, are all features of oppression (see, e.g., Cooke & Kothari, 2002). Both the presence and absence of particular social institutions provide sites for mobilization and change. Systems perspectives enable unintended consequences of actions to be examined at different levels and for action to take place between different parts of a system in which people are embedded.

Once again, there is nothing inherently progressive about systems perspectives and other applied psychologies also adopt systems thinking. Indeed, it is worth reminding ourselves that many systems approaches are founded on conservative, consensus-orientated (rather than change-oriented) ideologies with a concern for maintaining the status quo. CP, so long as it recognizes the contradictions inherent in systems perspectives, has the potential for enhancing the supportive features of some (elements) of the systems in the interests of the people (Midgley, 2000). Seidman (1988) suggests it is the dialectical relationship between people and systems that offers CP its unique position in applied psychology.

This view echoes that of Freire (1972) and reflects recent approaches to the connections between human agency and social structure (e.g., Bhaskar, 1987).

> It is as transforming and creative beings that men, in their permanent relations with reality, produce not only material goods—tangible objects- but also social institutions, ideas and concepts. Through their continuing praxis, men simultaneously create history and become historical-social beings. (Freire, 1972, p. 73)

It also challenges Western views of the contained individual, rather than seeing the inherent interconnections between people, reflected in indigenous ontologies (Bame Nsamenang, Nkwnti Fru, & Asma Browne, 2007; Sampson, 1988).

Interdisciplinarity

A focus on whole systems invites work with different parts of the system, with the interconnections between different parts of the system or with the system as a whole, and this in turn will require a further epistemological break with mainstream psychological knowledge. Interdisciplinarity helps CP address these different level complexities. Not only does CP draw on, and work at the boundary of other disciplines, such as anthropology, sociology, economics, and history, for example, it draws on other professional practices, such as environmental, management, operational research, organizational change and development, and social development fields.

CP praxis seeks interdisciplinary understanding about how oppression is caused and maintained, and uses this understanding as a guide to appropriate action. An interdisciplinary position in and of itself does not lead to social change. CP expertise is only one source of understanding of any social issue and most would agree that this needs to be combined with lay or popular knowledge for a full understanding to be obtained. Thus, interdisciplinarity is combined with humility about the limits of formal expert knowledge in CP practice.

Diversity, inclusion, and assets perspectives

CP has always tried to resist the marginalization of people and groups of people through difference, and to celebrate diversity (Kagan, Duckett et al., 2005; Trickett, Watts, & Birman, 1994). CP has challenged the ideological homogeneity of mainstream psychology by embracing the challenges offered by ethnic psychologies, feminist and women's psychology, gay and lesbian psychology, disability studies and postcolonial studies. Each of these critiques of the mainstream views difference positively and seeks to build on assets not to remove deficits. A commitment to diversity, inclusion and assets leads CPs to work across boundaries, to work with others on social problems, and to recognize that it is not necessary to have a background in psychology to work community psychologically. As Kagan, Duckett et al (2005, p. 287) put it:

> Through engaging with a power analysis of diversity, community psychologists seek to facilitate the empowerment of economically and politically non-dominant groups through inclusive individual, group and collective action. Resources and capacities are restored, developed or improved through the organisation and maintenance of networks for the interchange of knowledge, goods and services and psychological resources.

Collaboration, participation, and action research

CP stresses the importance of collaborative and participative approaches to both research and action, and various versions of action research, including participative and prefigurative action research, dominate the field in many parts of the world (Constanzo, 2007; Kagan & Burton, 2000; Montero, 2000;). Action research is a process for exploring the progress and limitations of change. Kagan, Burton and Siddiquee (2007) remind us that action research predates CP and has its roots in indigenous approaches to knowledge and invention and certainly predates most Anglo-American histories of the approach.

Not all CP work follows the whole process of action research (of problem definition, planning for change, implementing change, reflection and evaluating change). Much CP work addresses in the main one part of the process. Thus, some work sets out to establish the current situation in order to aid understanding and point to priorities for change (e.g., Albanesi, Cicognani, & Zani, 2004). Other work focuses on evaluation of interventions or social processes and how they influence and are influenced by the social actors involved (e.g., Estrada, Ibarra, & Sarmiento, 2007; Suarez, Springett, & Kagan, 2009). Other studies focus on the processes of change (e.g., Schrader, Macmillan, & Burton, 2009).

Action research does not imply any particular method and CP praxis includes many different ways of collecting information and making sense of it, where possible working collaboratively with those affected by an issue or by change. This collaboration implies a specific kind of relationship between CP practitioner and those we work with. Through processes of collaborative working, "ordinary" or common knowledge, transmitted through traditions and everyday life contributed by community members, is combined with the "expert" scientific knowledge of the CPs, derived from their learning and experience. Montero (1998) suggests that this process of negotiation and sharing of different forms of expertise is guided by two principles: the reality and possibilities principles. The reality principle underpins explorations of how circumstances are perceived and experienced at any moment in time; and the possibilities principles underpins the assessment of what kinds of changes are needed and the goals to be sought.

> "Reality" without "possibilities" leads to helplessness and passivity. "Possibilities" without "reality" lead to confusion and loss of perspective, therefore inducing failure and helplessness. (Montero, 1998, p. 66)

It should be clear, then, that it is important for CP praxis to be immersed in the lived experiences of people who are marginalized, oppressed and dispossessed.

The key elements of CP praxis are then:

- Movement towards a more just society and its underpinning values
- The use of the ecological metaphor
- A whole-systems perspective
- Interdisciplinarity
- Diversity, inclusion and an assets perspective
- Undertaking action research with collaboration and participation.

Table 19.2. summarizes these key characteristics and their implications for community psychological praxis.

Strategies for change

Given the key characteristics outlined above, it may now be possible to identify strategies of CP practice that further social change and transformation towards a more just society. We will firstly summarize these strategies, then give some examples of their implementation from our own work. Following this we will outline some other key CP strategies used in different parts of the world. Our four key strategies, summarized in Table 19.3., include:

1. Furtherance of critical consciousness;
2. Creation of new forms of social relations (or new social settings);
3. Development of alliances and counter systems; and
4. Giving away psychology.

What follows are some case studies from our own work (presented using first person narratives; author initials indicate which author is linked with which case study), illustrating the first three strategies and incorporating the fourth, giving psychology away throughout. In relation to each case example, we highlight some of the tensions and dilemmas experienced in practice. Each strategy illustrates in different ways different stages of the action research cycle, which includes the following: *plan* which refers to the planning stage, *act* referring to the stage during which action is taken,

Table 19.2. Key Characteristics of CP and Their Implications for Community Psychological Praxis

Key characteristic	*Implication for community psychological praxis*
Movement towards a more just society and its underpinning values	A just society is one that is underpinned by explicit, progressive values and these same values should underpin our CP practice
The use of the ecological metaphor	CP looks outside the individual for explanations of social experience and sometimes for solutions, whilst at the same time viewing people as agentic and purposeful, creating and created by social structures
A whole-systems perspective	CP, so long as it recognizes the contradictions inherent in systems perspectives, has the potential for harnessing natural resources in order to enhance supportive features of complex social systems in the interests of the people and for identifying causes of oppression
Interdisciplinarity	CP praxis must seek interdisciplinary and interprofessional understanding about how oppression is caused and maintained and use this understanding as a guide to appropriate action in collaboration with others
Diversity, inclusion, and an assets perspective	CP praxis must seek to be inclusive and build on people's creative energies, whilst being open to challenging (and being challenged about) assumptions about the status quo and the use of power, both as it relates to the issue in question and to CP practice itself
Undertaking action research with collaboration and participation	Action research in pursuit of social change, with action and transformation at its core, underpins work that seeks understanding as well as change processes. CP works as near to the people as possible and in participation with them, combining expert and popular knowledge in order to challenge the status quo and achieve change

evaluate during which evaluation occurs, and *reflect* which is the stage involving reflection. These stages are underpinned by self-awareness and Figure 19.1. illustrates the cyclical relationship between the different stages.

Change Strategy 1: Furtherance of critical consciousness (planning and action)

I (MR) work with young men (13–25 years old) on identity, sex, sexuality, and relationships in some of the most deprived, workless parts of Northwest England. One of the most serious social issues affecting young people in the United Kingdom today is the teenage pregnancy rate. At the moment, the UK has the highest teenage birth and abortion rates in Western Europe (United Nations Statistic Division,

Table 19.3. Strategies for Change and CP Praxis

Change strategy	*CP praxis*	*Key concepts*
Furtherance of critical consciousness	We can work to develop dialogical relationships which enable group conscientization and possibilities for change. We must be prepared to share our "expert voice" and remain open to learning	Radical change can only come from consciousness developed as a result of exchange rather than imposition (Leonard, 1975, p. 59). Problematization, conscientization deideologization, de-naturalization and conversion are key steps in the development of critical consciousness and social action (Montero, 2004) Critical reflection is key to critical praxis (Freire, 1972)
Creation of new forms of social relations (or new social settings)	We can facilitate the bringing together of people with common interests in new ways, and their allies and help them connect with the interests of others for greater power to change	Group conscientization is a more powerful force for change than individual (Leonard, 1975) The creation of new social settings is a long-standing CP strategy (Sarason, 1972), these can be physical or relationship spaces New methods, such as storytelling, arts activities, sport, for example, can provide new ways for people to relate to each other for change (Kelly, 2000)
Development of alliances and countersystems	We can work to develop alliances that will challenge the status quo, build a countersystem and form part of wider emancipatory social movements	Empowerment can be understood as a social practice through the development of strategic alliances (Burton & Kagan, 1996) The creation of the ecological "edge" is a way of working that maximizes natural resources and sustainable change (Kagan, 2007) The development of a critical mass for change, through the harnessing of diverse interests and the strengthening of networks requires high levels of skill (Gilchrist, 2004)

Table 19.3. *Continued*

Change strategy	*CP praxis*	*Key concepts*
Giving away psychology	We have opportunities to use psychological knowledge and expertise in liberatory ways, to make concepts and practices accessible and to develop participatory working relationships	The demystification of psychological processes alongside the use of expert knowledge is necessary for collaborative work (Kagan & Burton, 2001) It is essential that we take the time to get to know the lived experiences of those with whom we are working and use our intersubjectivity positively (Edge, Kagan, & Stewart, 2004; Montero, 2004) Methodological pluralism and creativity are the hallmarks of CP work but we need the humility to work with and through others, retain a stance of critical reflection and openness to learning ourselves as well as commitment to training others (Francescato, Arcidiancono, Albanesi & Mannarini, 2007))

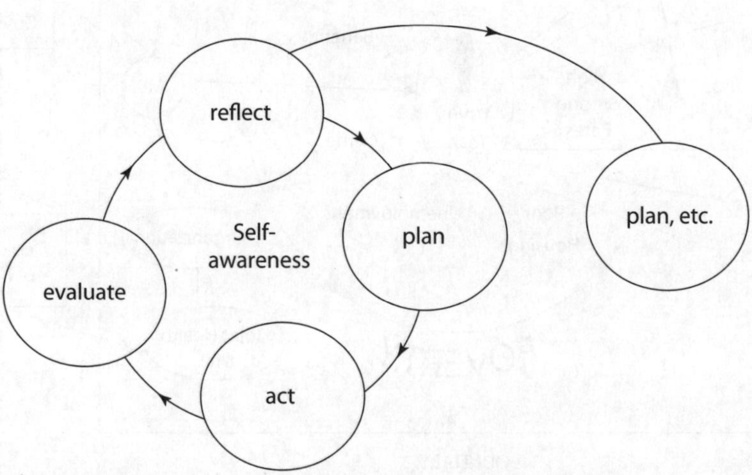

Figure 19.1. Action research cycle and CP

2008), and Manchester, where I work, has the third highest rate in the UK. This can be attributed to many things including poverty, incomplete education, and peer pressure. My brief is to ensure those young men and boys have an adequate sex education and thereby reduce teenage pregnancies. My work is mainly concentrated in Wythenshawe, one of the largest social housing areas in Europe. It is an area of little ethnic diversity and contains some of the most deprived areas in Manchester, which, itself, remains one of the most deprived districts in England (Talukder & Frost, 2008). Educational attainment is low and work prospects are bleak: white working-class young men are the most persistent low educational achievers compared to other ethnic groups and women (Cassen & Kingdon, 2007). The projects on which I work create a place for young men to leave their macho image behind and say what they really think, believe, and feel: they enable young men to develop critical consciousness about themselves in a wider social context. The system in which I work is illustrated in Figure 19.2. in the form of a rich picture. A rich picture is a graphical technique used to represent a situation, problem, or concept (Checkland & Scholes, 1999).

I work with the men in groups, creating spaces for dialogue that combine my expertise with the tacit knowledge brought by them. I developed the themes and facilitation methods for the sessions in consultation with other stakeholders, such as

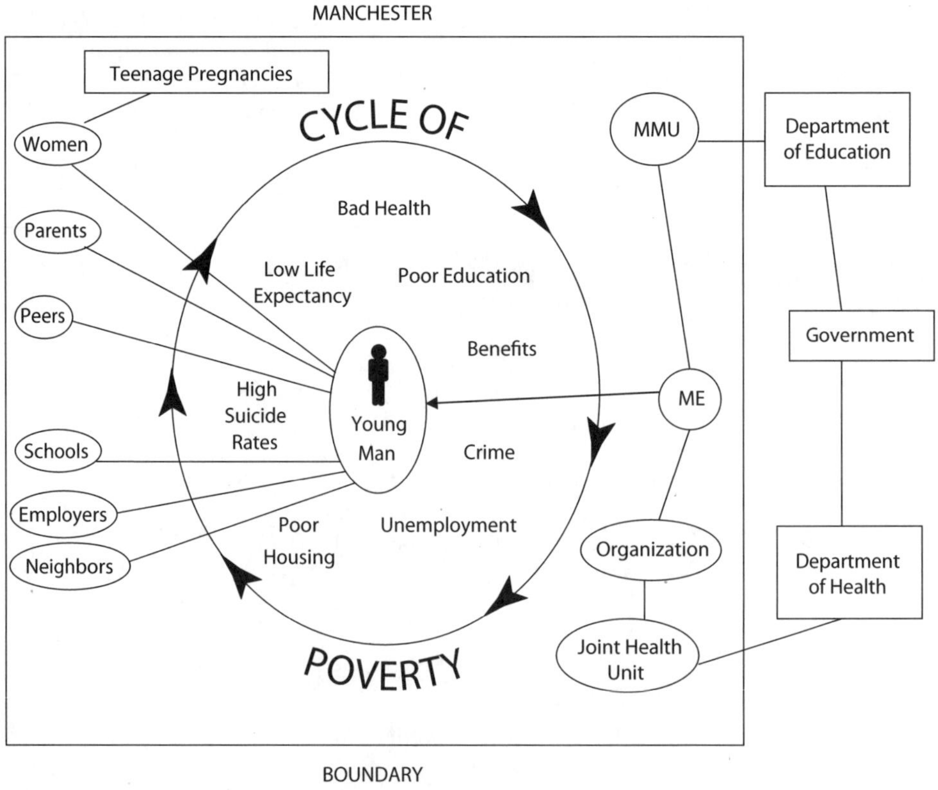

Figure 19.2. Furtherance of critical consciousness—rich picture

youth workers and community workers, and young men are invited to join the sessions via various young people's agencies in Manchester. The sessions focus explicitly on relationships and sexual behavior, and implicitly on the men's feelings about themselves and their place in the world.

Through the groups I am aiming to enable the men to find new ways of thinking about themselves and acting in society: moving beyond their internalized expectations of excluded youth to becoming agentic, positive, and active community participants. I aim to establish dialogical relationships through which the processes of deideologization and conscientization could occur (Freire & Faundez, 1989; Montero, 2004). My approach is that learning is best achieved through dialogue between people. Through sharing our feelings, emotions and thoughts the dialogic process can take place: we are thereby enabled to become aware of the possibilities for positive change (Freire & Faundez, 1989).

We start by considering "women", including their portrayal in the mass media. The important overarching theme to this session is equal opportunities, and I challenge the prevailing sexist attitudes towards women. The issues explored in this session are vital in the context of teenage pregnancy and high levels of sexually transmitted diseases. The men begin to build the foundations of respectful relationships with women through understanding their feelings, and their differences and similarities with men. For the first time the young men begin to see sex as part of relationships, with pregnancy having long-term consequences.

Next, we consider "fatherhood." We take part in creative and expressive activities to evoke thoughts and feelings on fatherhood. We consider the importance of fatherhood and the effects a good and bad father might have on children. There are different responses to this session. Some young men tell me they felt uncomfortable talking about the negative experiences of fatherhood, whilst others seemed to use it as a chance to cathartically express their positive and negative experiences. It was particularly poignant in some sessions when some young men expressed their feelings following their partners' miscarriage or abortion. The group listened attentively and showed support. For me these were special moments because these young men are often labeled as "troublemakers" or "hooligans."

After this we consider the dynamics of a "relationship," both in heterosexual and homosexual relationships. We also consider transgender and bisexuality. The young men with whom I work struggle, to the point of hatred, to come to terms with respecting other sexualities. We explore the concept of "love" and having a successful relationship using activities that have ranged from scenario-based work to crosswords. These activities are tools that help develop skills in debate and critical thinking for the young men: they help to problematize the issue (Montero, 2004). The activities are simple, but effective.

Finally we focus on the different types of contraception and their potential positive and negative implications. We discuss and explore different types of sexually transmitted diseases and how to access services that can help and advise. This session varies: for example, in one final session, I took a group to a sexual health clinic to show them how to access help and advice; on another occasion we all went for dinner, which gave the group an opportunity to relax and express themselves in a different, safe environment.

I am a mid-20's young man brought up and living in the same area as the men with whom I work. As a CPs I use psychological knowledge to enhance accessibility and participatory working relationships (Leonard, 1975), to elicit ideas and feelings, and to stimulate thoughts and attitudes. Despite my work being ameliorative, by providing a "safe space" environment for the young men, they develop critical awareness, which can be the springboard to achieve change. Through sharing psychological knowledge, and continuous reflection on my involvement, I am abdicating my "expert" position in order to share knowledge and strengthen the dialogical process.

The way my work is organized militates against the development of long-term relationships with the young men and I am unable to form the longer-term relationships that would deepen critical awareness. In my work I am caught between working as a CP practitioner and as a youth worker, each with its own value base and ideology. "Youth work" can be defined as activities that seek to impact *upon* young people and is increasingly being commodifed (Smith, 2003). The focus of CP is on working *with* people in their social contexts with power and empowerment being central themes. This paradox between youth work and CP has started to change my relationship with my manager: I am managed as if I were a youth worker. The challenge for me is to try to ensure that the values and methods of CP continue to play a role in developing the young men in their personal development and relationship building and develop positive attitudes that form the basis for healthy, productive change in sexual practices and attitudes. As to the reduction in teenage pregnancies? This complex phenomenon will need a more complex solution than informal education with young men.

Change Strategy 2: Creation of new forms of social relations (or new social settings) (evaluation)

The creation of a new social setting (in which refugee women came together in an electronic women's village hall to learn internet skills) was used as a strategy for change. I (AS) carried out an evaluation of the success of the new social setting in collaboration with the host organization. The Community Internet Project (CIP) was developed and hosted by the Manchester Women's Electronic Village Hall (WEVH). The WEVH was established in 1992 as a center run by women for women, providing Information Communication Technology (ICT) training and resources. Its ethos is rooted in the needs of women and consequently the courses they deliver are organized around school hours and vacations, and as part of the training women are offered personal development, counseling, and career guidance.

Refugee women in the UK are marginalized in multiple ways (Goodkind & Deacon, 2004) and are subjected to a number of disempowering experiences that threaten their identity. As refugees they experience greater levels of dependency on their husbands (in some cases propagated by an asylum status dependent on their husband's application); a loss of social support networks; increased loneliness and isolation; and increased childcare concerns and responsibilities (Bloch, Galvin, & Harrell-Bond, 2000). In comparison to male counterparts, women suffer greater language and communication barriers (due to past cultural restraints on education); increased levels of fear from abuse within their locality; and due to multiracial, mixed-sex accommodation, fear and abuse within their housing (Dumper, 2002). The boundaries of past identities are skewed in new sociocultural settings, and women often take the role of maintaining cultural identity, the challenge of finding employment, or the possibility of unemployment (Bloch et al., 2000). Training opportunities are rarely pursued by refugee women due to a preoccupation with other more pressing concerns (such as housing and family); caring responsibilities; lack of literacy (both native and English-language); opposition from men; and cultural barriers (Feeney, 2000).

As a strategy of change and empowerment, the CIP offered a minimum of 25 hours of training during which the women were taught basic computer skills with a particular emphasis on how to use the internet. Transport costs were paid for and crèche facilities were provided. All the women had an Indefinite Leave to Remain asylum status (i.e., permanent residency); and prior to the CIP had little or no internet-related technical competency. The evaluation included semi-structured interviews with all the women and the course tutor (see Siddiquee & Kagan, 2006). Figure 19.3. presents a rich picture (Checkland & Scholes, 1999) of the connections between different stakeholders involved in the system I was evaluating.

The "evaluator" and the "WEVH" are on the fringe of the system. The WEVH acted as a "gatekeeper" providing access to the setting and participants for the evaluation, whilst I, the evaluator, provide an evaluation of the service which the WEVH

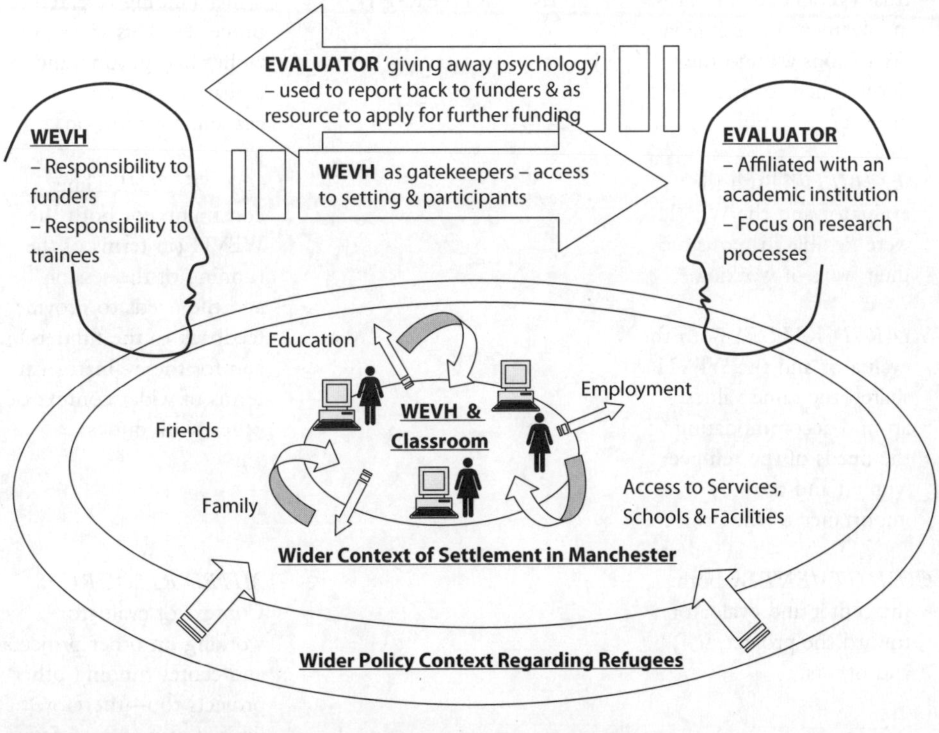

Figure 19.3. Creation of new social settings—rich picture

can use to report back to funders and used to obtain additional funding . Central to the evaluation was the WEVH classroom setting in which the refugee women met and learnt ICT skills. Also, through a process of dialogue (or sharing narratives) the women were able to develop critical consciousness and used the internet in empowering ways to counteract their marginalized status (e.g., access to services such as housing, search for employment, and education opportunities). Their interactions and use of the internet is embedded within the wider context of their settlement in Manchester.

Whilst the rich picture summarizes the relationship between me, the evaluator, and the WEVH (in terms of the WEVH as gatekeeper and me in the role of "giving away psychology") Table 19.4. summarizes some of the additional factors that were facilitators or barriers to effectively working in collaboration and partnership within the WEVH. These are presented in the form of a force-field analysis (Lewin, 1951):

Table 19.4. Force-field Analysis Illustrating Facilitators and Barriers to Effective Working in Collaboration and Partnership with the WEVH

Facilitators		*Barriers*
TRUST The evaluator was able to build a good working relationship with the WEVH and established trust (generated through involvement in preliminary discussions around the development of the project).	EFFECTIVELY WORKING IN COLLABORATION AND WORKING IN PARTNERSHIP	*POWER* The evaluator was established as having a position of authority as "owning psychology" and understanding research processes. This was due to her background and affiliation with an academic institution.
FLEXIBILITY Both the evaluator and the WEVH were flexible in terms of their ways of working.		*LACK OF TIME* Time constraints for both the WEVH (in terms of the running of the session and the needs to provide feedback to the funders) and for the evaluator (in terms of wider context of other work duties).
SHARED VALUES Both the evaluator and the WEVH shared the same values around accommodating the needs of the refugee women and the importance of the project.		
COMMITMENT By both the center and evaluator toward the project, self, and others.		*LIMITED RESOURCES* Context of evaluator working on other projects and center running other projects too—therefore limited resources to focus fully on the CIP.

Evaluation can be a useful tactic for sharing expertise. In this instance, I brought my "expertise" in the form of research methods and analysis to collect, analyze, and interpret data and provide a written report for the WEVH, validating the work they did and the achievements of the women. The evaluation was successful overall, as a strong participatory working relationship was developed and collaborative working with the WEVH was achieved. This success may in part be due to the fact that I was not employed by the WEVH and thus was autonomous in terms of the working relationship. I used my skills to generate trust with the women and my ethnic status as a member of an ethnic minority may have facilitated this process.

Critically reflecting on the evaluation, however, I accept that my commitment to the organization was not strong: once the evaluation was complete the relationship with the women and the center did not continue. This illustrates the sometimes rather mercenary and utilitarian aspect of evaluation—where the needs of the evaluation commissioners and my academic employers do not necessarily coincide with those of the project. Indeed, often the values and needs of the academic world can be in direct conflict with those of CPs working in particular settings.

The CIP was successful in creating a safe, new social setting, within which the women were able to share experiences related to their settlement and the evaluation revealed evidence of critical consciousness—whereby the women were reflecting on their marginalized status and ways of counteracting this. The setting provided women with an opportunity for dialogical communication and resulted in increased social capital, networking and empowerment (Siddiquee & Kagan, 2006). However, this setting was not open to all and its penetrability was limited to those who could speak English. Other exclusionary criteria include men and women who were either working full-time or with full-time caring responsibilities who would be unable to attend (this is in part reflected in the numbers of women who did not complete the sessions). The penetrability, inclusion, and exclusion of new social settings is key to their success as a change strategy.

Change Strategy 3: Development of alliances and countersystems (planning, action, and evaluation)

The forming of alliances and coalitions is a tool for empowerment and for sustainable change (Alinsky, 1971; Burton & Kagan, 1996; Roberts, 2004). The work reported here was work I (KD) was involved with that sought to engage young people in order to raise educational and life aspirations and thereby life opportunities (Duggan, 2007). The Labour Government that came into office in the UK in 1997 had proposed raising entry to higher education (HE) to 50% by 2010, moving from levels of about 15%. An integrated Aimhigher program was introduced to underpin what became known as a strategy for widening participation (in higher education). "Raising Achievement and Aspirations through Football" was one of nine Aimhigher national projects that was awarded funding from July 2004 until March 2006. My role in the project was that of Project Manager, working from a higher-education base. I had a key responsibility to develop alliances by bringing the identified stakeholders and partners together to work toward an innovative model of social inclusion, using football (i.e., soccer) as a vehicle to widen participation. The major stakeholders, and

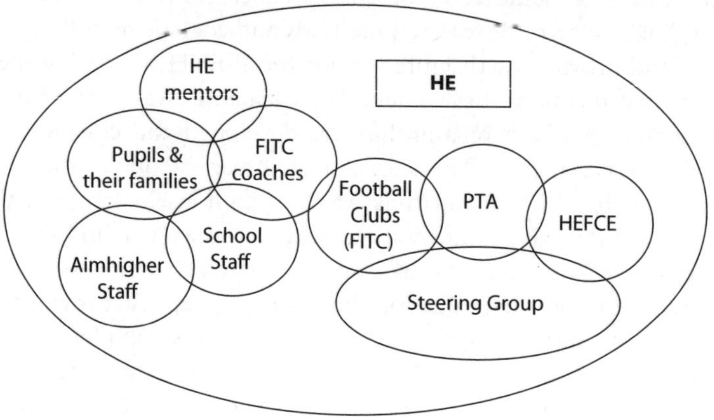

Figure 19.4. Alliances, collaborations, and organizational "edges"

their interlinkages are shown in Figure 19.4. My professional position is that of an applied CPs. During the work I sought to engage in a praxis that entailed an action research process, informed throughout by a theoretical understanding of collaborations and alliances, stakeholder interests, resistance to change, and boundary thinking.

In collaboration with staff from schools and football clubs, homework clubs were set up in 60 schools across nine previously identified Aimhigher regions across England. The purpose of the homework clubs were to encourage selected boys and girls from Years 9, 10, and 11 (n = 1500) from disadvantaged areas who had the potential to perform well academically, but who were underachieving, to obtain better scores in national tests. Linked to each school was one of 27 professional football clubs geographically positioned as local to the school and these formed "clusters." The incentive for those who attended the homework club was to be given the opportunity to engage with professional football coaches who offered the young people football skills and coaching qualifications.

Parents were encouraged to get involved in the scheme and were also offered the opportunity to gain coaching qualifications from the football clubs. Parents also received information, advice, and guidance as how best to support their son/daughter in raising levels of attainment provided by school staff involved in the project. Higher-education student ambassadors/mentors were employed to support homework club school staff, who assisted Aimhigher co-ordinators and Football in the Community (FITC) staff in raising awareness of higher education and raising the aspirations of the young people by acting as role models.

Through my role as project manager I followed an action research process, seeking to capture information about the utility of "homework clubs" and the impact of additional "football coaching," as well as trying to respond to the professional perspectives of the different groups of staff who support young learners. Upon reflection, my action research approach was perceived as different, and the combination of project manager and action researcher created a number of tensions. Not only was I acting as a steward, negotiating at the interfaces of different coalitions, and forging new alliances, I was also trying to produce research of academic integrity.

The original intention was to identify football clubs that wanted to participate and then approach the Aimhigher Steering Groups (ASGs) in those areas to negotiate with their schools and Aimhigher borough coordinators, culminating in the selection by them of the target schools. In the end, due to the timing of the start of the project, this was not possible and schools were recruited directly and linked with local football clubs in clusters, which antagonized the Aimhigher coordinators and steering groups. I was appointed after the funding was approved and when clusters of schools and clubs had been identified. Projects had started to operate but only approximately 40% were up and running. The exclusion of the Aimhigher coordinators from the selection process created tensions in some regions, and I was met with hostility in these places, but with enthusiasm in others. This illustrates the importance of boundary judgements: who is in and who is out of particular stages of decision making (Kagan, Caton, Amin, & Choudry, 2005). My challenge was to overcome the resistance I encountered.

Through the action research process it was important to collect information so that all involved could see how their part in the overall project was contributing to a national movement for change. I used multiple methods of data collection and analysis, informing both the processes of project implementation and its impact. This approach relied on different project partners collecting local information and it was sometimes difficult to gain commitment to doing this. It was not always clear to them—or to my manager—why as a project manager I should want to be collecting data. In the end I used the tactic of preparing project publicity to provide a rationale for obtaining and presenting data. For example, I persuaded project partners that the project would gain a great deal from being featured in the programs of key football matches, and for this I would need case study material, including photographs and quotes from different partners. The kinds of data I collected included:

- Case study profiles of school and football club activity;
- Attitude questionnaires completed by pupils (complete before-and-after data sets were difficult to obtain);
- Attendance monitoring by school coordinators of pupils/homework clubs;
- Comparisons of predicted vs. actual attainment scores;
- End-of-project evaluation from pupils, school staff and football coordinators (little data collected due to management pressure not to focus on research).

Key decision makers valued some aspects of the data collection and not others, and I was actively discouraged from completing data collection (as project manager, not researcher). My concerns were disregarded by those with more power than me and I sometimes felt I was "tricking" partners into giving information (such as in providing a template for "publicity").

Auto-ethnographic accounts (Freeman, 1993) allow us to write about self as a subject of larger social or cultural enquiry and place the "self" in context. As a project manager and an action researcher, I felt a little exposed as I grappled with the tensions that emerged from my roles and responsibilities to the project and to myself.

The dilemmas for me centered round a way of working that was very different from what was expected of me as a project manager alone.

Some rich alliances were formed within this project and three years on, the schools continue to work with football clubs that they were affiliated to as a result of it. Comparing predicted against actual test scores provided evidence that the young people at risk of underachieving academically performed better than expected after becoming engaged with the project. Through the formation of alliances, we developed a collective responsibility to raise achievement and aspirations of young people through football. As a result, the practitioners from both the sport and education sectors engaged in an exciting knowledge exchange partnership which required professionals to rethink professional identity boundaries for long-lasting change.

Roles and Skills of CP

From the case examples we can see that the CPs might play a range of different roles and that these will often change over time. In addition, a range of different skills are needed to enact the roles. As Figure 19.5. illustrates, at the heart of both skills and roles is critical self-awareness and sensitivity to the particular context, including environmental, social, policy, and cultural contexts. We can see that CP is a reflexive praxis.

The strategies for CP praxis we have outlined above are general strategies, illustrated in a local context. These include facilitation, education, representation, and technical roles and a range of skills. The case examples are all taken from an urban context in a rich, postwelfare country with centralized and bureaucratic public services. In this context we find a lot of our work is at the interface of different public and third sector organizations. In other places, specific foci and methods of CP practice have emerged (see examples not only in the CP journals, but also other compendia such as Bokszczanin 2007; Constanzo, Ossandón, Frade, Salazar, & Arenas, 2007; Martín González, 1998; Nelson and Prilleltensky, 2005; Riech, Reimer, Prilleltensky, & Montero, 2007; Rappaport and Seidman, 2000; Sanchez Vidal, Zambrano Constanzo, and Palacín Lois, 2004; Seedat et al., 2001; Thomas and Veno, 1992). Some of the more distinctive issues include:

- Population decline
- Migration and population churn
- Indigenous and minority communities: indigenous epistemologies; models and research practices
- Social policy analysis and development
- Policing and community safety
- Injury control and safety in complex environments
- Post conflict and disaster reconstruction
- Collective social justice and reconciliation
- Rural and remote communities
- Work–life issues and employment

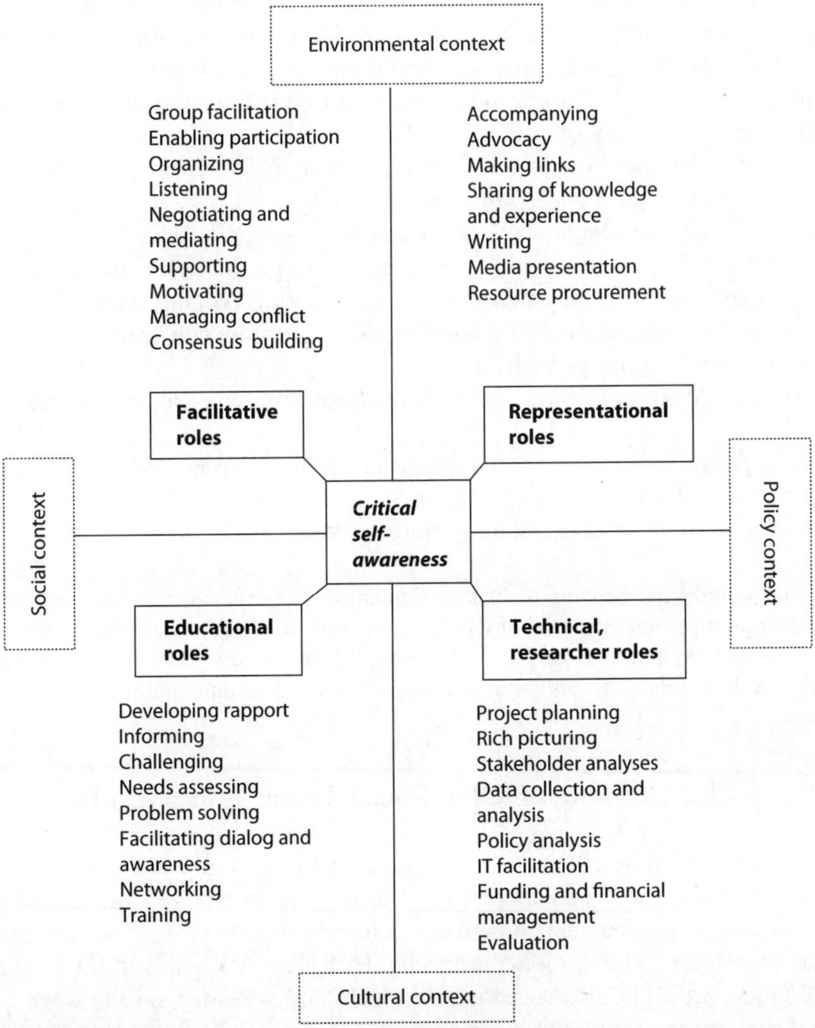

Figure 19.5. Roles and skills of community psychologists with critical self-awareness at the core and in particular social, cultural, policy, and environmental contexts

- Forced labor and modern slavery
- Waste management
- Community sanitation.

CPs have focused on all parts of the life course and different life stages and have addressed urban and rural issues. We have outlined some of our CP strategies, organized around systems thinking (Foster-Fishman & Behrens, 2007) and action research processes. Other specific techniques, outlined in the above compendia, include:

From Australia: Development of iterative-generative reflective practice.
From the USA: Measurement of psychological sense of community; techniques for ecological analyses; the application of empowerment frameworks.
From Canada: Social network intervention and mutual aid; community economic development; theory of cognitive CP.
From Latin America: Participatory action research; liberation psychology; community participation and community networks.
From Germany: Socioecological perspectives.
From Italy: Community profiling and networking; multidimensional organizational analysis; affective education and empowering training strategies.
From Norway: Mediation and reconciliation community conferencing.
From Portugal: Anthropoanalytic perspective.
From South Africa and from Ireland: Consciousness-raising groups (Moane, 2009).

There is a promise of a different CP praxis emerging in some areas of the majority world that is relatively new to CP. Bame Nsamenang et al. (2007, p. 403), predict a movement away from contemporary (mostly Western) CP:

> We are positing the impetus to look at Cameroon and other African nations from a different perspective in the field of CP—to come with an abandonment, so to speak, of Western methodologies in exchange for the discovery of new methods, new ways of understanding, new concepts about development and community efforts.

The Context of CP—Social Issues and Trends

The challenges faced by CP are local, regional, and global, and these frame not only our praxis but also the lived experiences of those with whom we work. Some of the old, deep societal schisms remain between rich and poor, North and South, men and women, minorities and majorities, and so on. However, as Kagan and Burton (2001) suggest, there are additional social trends which have a bearing on the work we do.

Neoliberalism has tightened its grip worldwide. From a neoliberal perspective the world is treated as one large and many smaller markets: everything is costed and commodified, including time, commitment, natural resources, and human relations themselves. Electronic communication has rendered talk between people a commodity and social networking internet sites have done the same for personal relationships. These relationships can be bought, stored, and retrieved. The worldwide financial crisis that exists at the time of writing presents hitherto unknown possibilities for reconstructing a new social order built on social solidarity.

Population movements have increased as more and more people are displaced through conflict and war, through internal and external economic migration, through searches for the means to survive as the degeneration of natural resources drives them from their homes, through escape from starvation as people can no longer feed themselves, and natural disasters (often through human activity). At the same time a new harshness towards minorities has developed, and people are increasingly being treated as group entities (such as illegal migrants, refugees, offenders, etc.) to be processed and dealt with as such, forced to live away from the rest of us (Fals Borda, 1998). The social injustices, indignities, and abuses that follow such repression are individualized, kept private, and hidden from view.

In many places there has been what Habermas (1989) has identified as the colonization of the lifeworld (or erosion of the public sphere leading to a decline in public debate). Political debate and understanding comes from a highly edited media; places for public congregation are restricted as public and community space is privatized and rules for association become ever more restrictive; protest is suppressed and participation in civic life has contracted.

Finally, and perhaps of the greatest importance and urgency is the environmental, ecological, and planetary challenge. The threats to a sustainable environment and the social mechanisms that contribute to this are well known in the economically dominant world and there can be no excuse for the slow action being taken. Not everyone, however, has access to information with which they can take action to resist the destruction. Enforced powerlessness needs to be overcome and an awakening to the effects of environmental destruction must be stimulated.

We are living in a time of unprecedented intersecting crises across the world that threaten the human condition and progress toward a more just society, with those most vulnerable and marginalized at greatest risk. The climate, financial, energy, economic, population, and food crises together increase the vulnerabilities of communities and those within them, presenting new challenges for international community psychology. We need new understanding about how *communities* can become more resilient, protect themselves from further systemic shock, and provide the foundation for a socially just world. Communities are made of people and we must learn from effective individual, group, and collective processes to work for social change that will stem planetary destruction and move beyond individual and national self-interests. We know what the challenge is. Now we must combine our meagre CP resources with, for example, those of social movements, environmentalists, economists, politicians, and historians and bring to bear all those analytic and practical tools that have been developed as part of CP praxis.

References

Albanesi, C., Cicognani, E., & Zani, B. (2004). Adolescents' sense of community: Which measures for which communities? In A. Sanchez Vidal, A. Zambrano Constanzo & M. Palacín Lois (Eds.), *Psicología comunitaria Europa: Communidad, poder, ética y valores* [European Community Psychology: Community, ethics, & values] (pp. 288–293). Barcelona: Publicacions Universitat de Barcelona.

Alinsky, S. (1971). *Rules for radicals.* New York: Random House.

Bame Nsamenang, A., Nkwenti Fru, F., & Asma Browne, M. (2007). The roots of community psychology in Cameroon. In S. Reich, M. Reimer, I. Prilleltensky, & M. Montero (Eds.), *International community psychology: History & theories* (pp. 392–406). New York: Springer.

Bhatia, S., & Sethi, N. (2007). History & theory of community psychology in India: An international perspective. In S. Reich, M. Reimer, I. Prilleltensky, & M. Montero, (Eds.), *International community psychology: History & theories* (pp. 180–199). New York: Springer.

Bhaskar, R.A. (1987). *Scientific realism and human emancipation*. London: Verso.

Bloch, A., Galvin, T., & Harrell-Bond, B. (2000). Refugee women in Europe: Some aspects of the legal and policy dimensions. *International Migration*, *38*(2), 169–190.

Bokszczanin, A. (Ed.). (2007). *Community psychology; Social change in solidarity*. Opole, Poland: University of Opole Press.

Brock, A. C. (Ed.). (2006). *Internationalizing the history of psychology*. New York: New York University Press.

Burns, D. (2007). *Systemic action research. A strategy for whole-systems change*. Bristol: Policy Press.

Burton, M., & Kagan, C. (1996). Rethinking empowerment: Shared action against powerlessness. In I. Parker & R. Spears (Eds.), *Psychology and society: Radical theory and practice* (pp. 197–209). London: Pluto Press.

Burton, M., & Kagan, C. (2002). Community psychology: Why this gap in Britain? *History and Philosophy of Psychology*, *4*(2), 10–23.

Burton, M., Boyle, S., Harris, C., & Kagan, C. (2007). Community psychology in Britain. In S. Reich, M. Reimer, I. Prilleltensky, & M. Montero, (Eds.), *International community psychology: History and theories* (pp. 219–237). New York: Springer.

Cassen, R., & Kingdon, G. (2007). *Tackling low educational achievement*. York: Joseph Rowntree Foundation.

Checkland, P., & Scholes, J. (1999). *Soft systems methodology in action*. Chichester: John Wiley.

Cheng, S.-T., & Mak, W. S. (2007). Community psychology in a borrowed place with borrowed time: The case of Hong Kong. In S. Reich, M. Reimer, I. Prilleltensky, & M. Montero, M. (Eds.), *International community psychology: History & theories* (pp. 200-216). New York: Springer.

Constanzo, A. Z. (2007). Participacíon y empoderamiento comunitario: Rl de las metodologías implicativas. In A. Z. Constanzo, G. R. Ossandón, I. M. Frade, D. A. Salazar, & R. P.-L. Arenas (2007). *Psicología comunitaria en Chile: Evolución, perspectivas, y proyecciones*. Santiago: RIL Editores.

Constanzo, A. Z., Ossandón, G. R., Frade, I. M., Salazar, D. A., & Arenas, R. P.-L. (2007). *Psicología comunitaria en Chile: Evolución, perspectivas y proyecciones*. Santiago: RIL Editores.

Cooke, B., & Kothari, U. (Eds.). (2001). *Participation. The new tyranny?* London: Zed Books.

Dalton, J. H., Elias, M. J. & Wandersman, A. (2001). *Community psychology: Linking individuals and communities*. Belmont, CA: Wadsworth.

Dumper, H. (2002). *Is it safe here? Refugee women's experiences in the UK*. London: Refugee Action.

Duggan, K. (2007). Shifting the widening participation goalposts. Raising achievement and aspirations through football. In FACE (Ed.), *Transformation, progression and hope: Whatever happened to life long learning?* (p. 16). London: UEL/FACE.

Edge, I., Kagan, C., & Stewart, A. (2004). Living poverty: Surviving on the edge. *Clinical Psychology, Issue 38*, 28–31.

Estrada, A. M., Ibarra, C. & Sarmiento, E. (2007). Regulation and control of subjectivity and private life in the context of armed conflict in Colombia. *Community, Work, and Family*, *10*(3), 257–281.

Fals Borda, O. (1998). *People's participation: Challenges ahead*. London: Intermediate Technology Publications.

Feeney, A. (2000). Refugee employment. *Local Economy*, *15*(4), 343–349.

Foster-Fishman, P., & Behrens, T. R. (2007). Systems change reborn: Rethinking our theories, methods, and efforts in human services reform and community-based change. *American Journal of Community Psychology, 39*(3–4), 191–196.

Francescato, D., Arcidiacono, C., Albanesi, C., & Mannarini, T. (2007). Community psychology in Italy: Past developments and future perspectives. In S. Reich, M. Reimer, I. Prilleltensky, & M. Montero, (Eds.), *International community psychology: History and theories* (pp. 263–281). New York: Springer.

Freeman, M. (1993). *Rewriting the self.* London: Routledge

Freire, P. (1972). *Pedagogy of the oppressed.* Harmondsworth: Penguin.

Freire, P., & Faundez, A. (1989). *Learning to question: A pedagogy of liberation.* Geneva, World Council Churches.

Gilchrist, A. (2004). *The well-connected community: A networking approach to community development.* Bristol: Policy Press.

Goodkind, J. R., & Deacon, Z. (2004). Methodological issues in conducting research with refugee women: Principles for recognizing and recentering the multiply marginalized. *Journal of Community Psychology, 32*(6), 721–739.

Habermas, J. (1989). *The structural transformation of the public sphere.* Cambridge, MA: Massachusetts Institute of Technology Press.

Hardt, M., & Negri, A. (2000). *Empire.* Cambridge, MA: Harvard University Press.

Hesse, M (1980). *Revolution & reconstruction in the philosophy of science.* Bloomington: Indiana University Press.

Kagan, C. (2007). Working at the edge: Making use of psychological resources through collaboration. *The Psychologist, 20*(4), 224–227.

Kagan, C., & Burton, M. (2000). Prefigurative action research: an alternative basis for critical psychology? *Annual review of Critical Psychology, 2*, 73–88

Kagan, C., & Burton, M. (2001). *Critical community psychological practice for the 21st century.* Manchester: IOD Research Group.

Kagan, C., Burton, M., & Siddiquee, A. (2008). Action research. In C. Willig & W. Stainton-Rogers (Eds.), *Handbook of qualitative methods in psychology.* London: Sage.

Kagan, C., Caton, S., Amin, A., & Choudry, A. (2005). *Boundary critique, community psychology, and citizen participation.* Paper delivered to the European Community Psychology Conference, Berlin, September 2004. Retrieved March 19, 2009 from www.compsy.org

Kagan, C., Duckett, P., Lawthom, R., & Burton, M., (2005). Community psychology and disabled people. In D. Goodley & R. Lawthom (Eds.), *Disability and psychology: Critical introductions and reflections* (pp. 170-186). London: Palgrave.

Kagan, C., Lawthom, R., Siddiquee, A., Duckett, P., & Knowles, K. (2007). Community psychology through community action learning. In A. Bokszczanin (Ed.), *Community psychology; Social change in solidarity.* Opole, Poland: University of Opole Press.

Kelly, K. (2000). Action research, performance & critical hermeneutics. *Annual Review of Critical Psychology, 2*, 89–108.

Lather, P. (1986). Research as praxis. *Harvard Educational Review 56*(3), 247–277.

Leonard, P. (1975). Towards a paradigm for radical practice. In M. Bailey & M. Brake (Eds.), *Radical social work* (pp. 46–62). London, Edward Arnold.

Lewin, K. (1951). *Field theory in social science.* New York: Harper & Row.

Lubek, I., Innis, N. K., Kroger, R. O., McGuire, G. R., Stam, H. J., & Herrmann, T. (2006). Faculty genealogies in five Canadian universities: Historic-graphical and pedagogical concerns. *Journal of the History of the Behavioral Sciences, 31*(1), 52–72.

Martín Gonzalez, A. (Ed.). (1998). *Psicología comunitaria: Fundamentos y aplicaciones.* Madrid: Editorial Síntesis, S.A.

Midgley, G. (2000). *Systemic intervention: Philosophy, methodology and practice.* New York: Kluwer Academic/Plenum Press.

Moane, G. (2009). Reflection on liberation psychology in action in an Irish context. In M. Montero, & C. Sonn (Eds.), *Psychology of liberation: Theory & applications* (pp. 135–154). New York, Springer.

Montero, M. (1998). Psychosocial community work and transformation of society. *Community Work and Family, 1*(1), 65–78.

Montero, M. (2000). Participation in participatory action research. *Annual Review of Critical Psychology, 2*, 131–143.

Montero, M. (2004). *Introducción a la Psicología Communitaria: Desarollo, conceptos y procesos.* Buenos Aires: Editorial Paidós SAICF.

Montero, M., & Varas Diaz, N. (2007). Latin American community psychology: Development, implications and challenges within a social change agenda. In S. Reich, M. Reimer, I. Prilleltensky, & M. Montero (Eds.), *International community psychology: History and theories* (pp 63–98). New York: Springer.

Nelson, G., & Prilleltensky, I. (Eds.). (2005). *Community psychology: In pursuit of liberation and well-being.* Basingstoke: Palgrave Macmillan.

Rappaport, J., & Seidman, E. (Eds.). (2000). *Handbook of community psychology.* New York: Kluwer Academic/Plenum Publishers.

Reich, S., Reimer, M., Prilleltensky, I., & Montero, M. (Eds.). (2007). *International community psychology: History and theories.* New York: Springer.

Roberts, J. M. (2004). *Alliances, coalitions & partnerships: Building collaborative organisations.* Gabriola Island, BC: New Society Publishers.

Sampson, E. E. (1988). The debate on individualism: Indigenous psychologies of the individual and their role in personal and societal functioning. *American Psychologist, 43*(10), 15–22.

Sanchez Vidal, A., Zambrano Constanzo, A., & Palacín Lois, M. (Eds.). (2004). *Psicología comunitaria Europa: Communidad, poder, ética y valores* [European community psychology: Community, ethics, & values]. Barcelona: Publicacions Universitat de Barcelona.

Sarason, S. (1972). *The creation of settings and the future societies.* San Francisco: Jossey-Bass.

Schrader McMillan, A., & Burton, M. (2009). From parent education to collective action: Childrearing with love in post-war Guatemala. *Journal of Community & Applied Social Psychology, 19*(3), 198–211.

Seedat, M., Duncan, N., & Lazarus, S. (2001). *Community psychology: Theory, method and practice. South African and other perspectives.* Cape Town: Oxford University Press.

Seidman, E. (1988). Back to the future, community psychology: Unfolding a theory of intervention. *American Journal of Community Psychology, 16*(1), 3–24.

Siddiquee, A., & Kagan, C. (2006). The impact of the internet on refugee women: Examining a community internet project, *Journal of Community and Applied Social Psychology, 16*(3), 189–206.

Smith, M. K. (2003). From youth work to youth development. The new government framework for English youth services. *Youth & Policy 79*, retrieved from www.infed.org/archives/jeffs_and_smith/smith_youth_work_to_youth_development.htm

Suarez, J.-C., Springett, J., & Kagan, C. (2009). Critical connections between participatory evaluation, organizational learning, and intentional change in pluralistic organizations. *Evaluation: The International Journal of Theory, Research, and Practice, 15*(3), 321–342.

Talukder, R., & Frost, L. (2008). *Manchester City Council: Index of Multiple deprivation 2007.* Manchester: Manchester City Council, Economic development Unit. Retrieved March 3, 2009 from www.manchester.gov.uk/downloads/F1_IMD2007.pdf

Thomas, D. R., & Veno, A. (Eds.). (1992). *Psychology and social change: Creating an international agenda*. Palmerston North, NZ: Dunmore Press.

Trickett, E.J., Watts, R., & Birman, D. (Eds.). (1994). *Human diversity: Perspectives on people in context*. San Francisco: Jossey Bass.

United Nations Statistics Division. (2008). *Statistics and Indicators on Men & Women: Table 2b, indicators on childbearing*. Retrieved March 3, 2009 from http://unstats.un.org/unsd/Demographic/Products/indwm/indwm2.htm

20

Behavioral Economics Applied

Suggestions for Policy Making

Gerrit Antonides

The works of Herbert Simon on "satisficing" (1982) and "bounded rationality" (1959) in decision making and those of George Katona (1975) on the role of "consumer expectations" in the spending of their budgets founded the ever burgeoning field of "behavioral economics." Since then, Kahneman, Slovic, and Tversky (1982) have been expanding the field with their research on heuristics and biases in decision making, and on decision making under risk (Kahneman & Tversky, 1979; Tversky & Kahneman, 1992). All of this work took place on the interface of economics and psychology and has cast serious doubt on the standard neoclassical economic model, which is based on strong assumptions concerning rationality, preferences, and choice processes.

Gradually, behavioral economics became accepted as a more realistic way of doing economics (McFadden, 1999; Rabin, 1998; Thaler, 1980), and publications in the field were cited more often (Laibson & Zeckhauser, 1998). Recently, even authors of economic textbooks have started to include chapters on behavioral economics (e.g., Frank, 2008; Varian, 2006). Since the 1970s, several academic societies and journals were founded in this interdisciplinary field: the American-based Society for the Advancement of Behavioral Economics (associated with the *Journal of Socio-Economics*), the Institute of Behavioral Finance (*Journal of Behavioral Finance*), and the European-based International Association for Research in Economic Psychology (*Journal of Economic Psychology*).

Most of the work in behavioral economics has been conducted in the laboratory or used surveys to develop new theory. Gradually, the theory has been applied in different fields, including marketing, finance, law, and social policy areas. The theory and research findings have been described extensively in a number of published volumes (Altman, 2006; Camerer, Loewenstein, & Rabin, 2004; Kahneman, Slovic,

IAAP Handbook of Applied Psychology, First Edition. Edited by Paul R. Martin, Fanny M. Cheung, Michael C. Knowles, Michael Kyrios, Lyn Littlefield, J. Bruce Overmier, and José M. Prieto.

& Tversky, 1982; Kahneman & Tversky, 2000; Lewis, 2008). Here we will focus on possible applications of behavioral economics in the policy of governments, consumer interest groups, and companies.

I shall start the chapter with an introduction to behavioral economics, then continue with the issue of applying behavioral economic findings to policy, describe a number of possible applications, and finally reflect on the potential of behavioral economics for policy applications.

What is Behavioral Economics?

Mullainathan and Thaler (2000) have defined behavioral economics as "the combination of psychology and economics that investigates what happens in markets in which some of the agents display human limitations and complications" (p. 1094). In doing so, behavioral economics studies the ways in which behavior differs from the standard economic model to improve the explanation of economic behavior. Important differences are recognitions of bounded rationality in decision processes, bounded willpower, bounded selfishness, and esteem needs in the human motivation to reach particular objectives.

An account of bounded rationality has been given by Kahneman (2003a, 2003b), who distinguished between two types of thinking (see also Stanovich & West, 2000): (1) an intuitive, automatic, associationist, and unconscious type (called System I) and (2) an analytic, controlled, rule-based, and conscious type (called System II). System II-type thinking is the most similar to the decision processes assumed in the standard economic model, taking into account all available information, weighing pros and cons of multiple alternatives, considering a portfolio of decisions in making one particular decision, and using a long-term perspective. In contrast, System I-type thinking implies using short-cuts and heuristics in decision making, taking single decisions one at a time, and using a myopic perspective. Which system dominates is a matter of debate: Kahneman (2003b) assumes that System I is the default system, and only when one becomes aware that this does not lead to satisfactory solutions may System II be used. Economists adopting the standard model usually assume that System II is the default system, although they may allow for System I-type thinking if the stakes are not high or if the decision-making resources are low due to limited time or limited decision-making capacities (Ratchford, 2001; Shugan, 1980; Stigler, 1961).

It should be mentioned that the use of System I does not always lead to worse outcomes than using System II. Dijksterhuis, Bos, Nordgren, and Van Baaren (2006) have found that unconscious thought may even help in making better decisions, once decision makers have considered the available information, than conscious thought alone. Wilson and Schooler (1991) found that conscious thought under some conditions may even lead to worse choices than no conscious thought. An interesting question is whether System I and System II are two poles of one decision-making dimension or are two separately operating systems. The discipline of neuropsychology eventually may provide answers in this respect (see, e.g., McClure, Laibson, Loewenstein, & Cohen, 2004).

A number of System I phenomena have been studied in behavioral economics. One is the human sensitivity to outcome changes rather than to final outcomes. Whereas the standard economic model assumes the maximization of utility by increasing total outcomes, behavioral economics has found that people dislike negative changes much more than they like commensurate positive changes with respect to a certain reference point (Kahneman & Tversky, 1979). This phenomenon is called "loss aversion." Furthermore, persistence of a change may lead to adaptation to the new situation and a consequent change in the reference point (Kahneman, Knetsch, & Thaler, 1991; Van Praag & Freijters, 1999). Repeated adaptation to positive changes in welfare may lead to the so-called hedonic treadmill according to which people never become satisfied with the outcomes that are realized (Kahneman, 1999). A related phenomenon is people's preference for happy endings and increasing sequences of outcomes rather than happy beginnings or decreasing outcome sequences, the latter of which should be preferred according to the standard economic model (Kahneman, 1999).

Sensitivity to changes—and especially loss—can explain several other effects, including the "endowment effect," the "status quo effect," the "sunk cost fallacy effect," the "mental accounting effect," and the "framing effect." The so-called endowment effect refers to the fact that people value the loss of an item more negatively than they value the gain of such an item positively (Kahneman, Knetsch, & Thaler, 1990; Thaler, 1980). Also, sensitivity to changes explains a preference for the status quo because a deviation from the status quo is usually considered a negative change (Samuelson & Zeckhauser, 1988). Deviating from the status quo may be considered painful for different reasons: (1) decision makers might believe that defaults are suggestions by the policy maker or marketer; (2) deviating may require effort, whereas accepting the default is effortless; (3) deviating is considered as a loss which generally looms larger than a commensurable gain; and (4) commission may lead to more regret than omission in case of bad results (Johnson, Bellman, & Lohse, 2002). The sunk cost fallacy is another instance of loss aversion, which captures the idea that spent money still hurts, even when it cannot be retrieved (Thaler, 1980). The sunk cost fallacy may lead to the investment trap, an example of which was the development of the Concorde airplane (Staw, 1976). The theory of mental accounting is based on the evaluation of gains and losses as either separate or integrated events, resulting in different evaluations of attractiveness (Thaler, 1980, 1985, 1999).

By stating the same decision problem in different words, the problem itself may be perceived as different. The "Asian disease problem," presented to a number of physicians, is a famous example of this framing effect (Kahneman & Tversky, 1979). In the "Asian disease problem" 600 people are expected to die and two different programs are developed to combat the disease. In one version, program A will save 200 people, whereas program B will save 600 people with a probability of 1/3. In another version, program C will result in 400 people dying, whereas program D will result in 600 people dying with a probability of 2/3. Although all expected outcomes in the two versions are the same, the framing in terms of lives saved and people dying differs, resulting in 72% of the physicians presented with the first version preferring the safe program A, and 78% presented with the second version preferring risky program D. Except for showing the effect of framing, the "Asian disease" experiment shows risk-averse preferences for positive outcomes (lives saved), and risk-seeking preferences for negative outcomes (people dying).

In addition to decision processes deviating from the standard economic model, behavioral economics has studied various motivations, including impatience, altruism, esteem needs, and fairness.

High impatience indicates bounded willpower because it frequently prevents people from reaching long-term objectives that they actually prefer, for example, savings or good health. High impatience may result from highly discounted future outcomes, for example future energy savings from current purchase of energy-efficient equipment (Antonides & Wunderink, 2001; Gately, 1980; Hausman, 1979). It has been found that the discount rate is especially high in the near future, rather than in the distant future (Thaler, 1981), which is called hyperbolic discounting (Laibson, 1997). Such discounting may result from an empathy gap, that is, the belief that current preferences will be the same in the future (Loewenstein, O'Donoghue, & Rabin, 2003). For example, projection bias may induce people to consume too much food in the present while regretting this behavior in the future, indicating lack of foresight of the preference change. Indeed, when asked whether they would like a healthy or unhealthy snack in one week, most people choose the healthy snack. However, when asked a week later, they tend to choose the unhealthy snack (Read & Van Leeuwen, 1998). This phenomenon also reflects "impulsiveness" and lack of "self-control" as studied in other areas of psychology (Logue, 1988, 2000).

Several human preferences indicate bounded selfishness, including altruism and fairness. Altruistic preferences show up in all kinds of gift giving, helping, and donating behavior (Khalil, 2004). Ethical investing is another example (Cullis, Jones, & Lewis, 2006). Preferences for fairness show up in division of money by an allocator, whether in dictator games or ultimatum games (Camerer & Thaler, 1995), in tipping behavior (Lynn, 2006), opinions about pricing mechanisms (Kahneman, Knetsch, & Thaler, 1991) and fairness judgments within households (Antonides & Kroft, 2005).

Esteem needs show up in unrealistically positive views of the self (Babcock & Loewenstein, 1997; Messick, Bloom, Boldizar, & Samuelson 1985), unrealistic optimism or irrational exuberance (Shiller, 2000), illusion of control (Langer 1975; Wohl & Enzle, 2002), self-serving attributions (Mezulis, Abramson, Hyde, & Hankin, 2004), counterfactual thinking (Sherman & McConnell, 1996), and overconfidence (Barber & Odean, 2001). Another indication of esteem needs is procedural utility, that is, a preference for fair procedures in reaching outcomes (Frey, Benz & Stutzer, 2004). Procedural utility may be increased by treating individuals with respect and giving them "voice," thus increasing their sense of self-worth and self-determination.

The mental processes considered here also have been studied in neuroeconomics. For example, Smith, Dickhaut, McCabe, and Pardo (2002) showed that the gain–loss feature was more related to different brain activity in risky choice tasks than in other choice tasks. An overview of neuroeconomic research is provided in Camerer, Loewenstein, and Prelec (2005).

Most research in behavioral economics has been conducted to develop new theories, frequently in the lab. However, possible applications of behavioral economic research in policy, marketing, law, finance, and health are also evident from field studies and surveys, and will be considered next.

Applying Behavioral Economics to Policy

Behavioral economics has found many instances in which people reach suboptimal solutions or act against reaching their objectives. As Loewenstein states it (2007), "people often don't know what's best for themselves (and when they do, often have trouble getting themselves to do it)." There are several routes to helping people to reach better solutions, which may be applied in the policy of the government, consumer interest groups, and companies: teaching, learning, communication, and changing the context of the choice situation. In addition, rules and laws may be applied with the goal of demotivating undesirable behavior.

Teaching implies educating people in decision-making skills. Teaching can take place in formal education, in upbringing, or in special courses. Indeed, computation, language, and search skills may help people to find information, and to weigh the benefits and disadvantages of choice alternatives. In fact, such skills are already assumed within the standard economic model. Peters et al. (2006) found that people who responded better to a numeracy scale also did better on probability judgment tasks. However, as is evident from behavioral economic research, people still make systematic errors in decision problems. One approach for improvement, propagated by Bazerman and Moore (2009), is to make people aware of possible heuristics, biases, and motivational factors influencing their decision making. This might be accomplished by offering warnings about possible biases and showing their direction, providing feedback, and an extensive program of training (Fischhoff, 1982). In the first stage, experiencing the effect of biases in decision making is meant to unfreeze habitual decision-making processes. In the second stage, decision-making deficiencies should be clarified, their roots should be explained, and decision makers should be reassured that such deficiencies should not threaten one's self-esteem. These conditions should provide for a change in their thinking. In the third stage, the new type of decision making should be practiced, and feedback should be continued in order to reinforce the new type of decision making. Several techniques are considered helpful in this respect: analogical reasoning, taking an outsider's view, using linear models and other statistical decision aids, and understanding biases in others (Bazerman & Moore, 2009). Finally, counseling may prove effective in helping people solve decision problems and overcome biases. One drawback of this approach is that it requires motivation from the participants themselves (which in itself is prone to bias). Furthermore, it might work in the wrong direction in cases where unconscious thought would provide better solutions.

Learning desired behavior may be useful in helping people obtain their long-term objectives. From psychology it is well known that different types of learning may be effective in changing people's behavior, for example, classical and operant conditioning, social learning, and insight learning (e.g., Bandura, 1986; Mowrer & Klein, 2001). In the case of economic behavior, the pricing mechanism, including taxes and subsidies, is often used to provide (dis)incentives for certain types of behavior, for example, not smoking (Hursh, 1991; Gallet & List, 2003). Learning provides conditions for correcting one's mistakes and should lead to utility maximization according to the standard economic model, for example, arbitrage in financial markets. However, arbitrage appears to be unsuccessful in changing investors' behavior, as is evident from the existence of many anomalies in stock markets (see, e.g., Nofsinger, 2008). Furthermore, in many economic decisions, opportunities for learning are either absent (e.g., in the case of pensioning) or very costly (e.g., choosing an education) (Mullainathan & Thaler 2000). Also, learning may result in suboptimal outcomes if the wrong type of feedback is provided, for example, short-term feedback (reward) instead of long-term feedback, or total results instead of marginal results (Antonides & Maital, 2002; Herrnstein, 1991). Finally, providing financial incentives may crowd out the intrinsic motivation for desired behavior, such as volunteer work (Frey, 1992).

Another way that learning may take place is via communication. Communication may be effective to some extent in changing people's behavior, conditional on requirements of motivation and ability (Petty & Cacioppo, 1986). However, the effect of advertising on sales is considered low (Vakratsas & Ambler, 1999). The effect of communication may be due to changing the cognitive or affective determinants of purchasing behavior. In addition, it may lead to focusing on the target behavior, thus making it more likely for the actor to pay attention to the behavior involved. Thaler and Sunstein (2008) mention several examples of combining social effects with communication (i.e., telling taxpayers that 90% of all taxpayers have already complied in full, and telling college students that most of them have four or fewer alcoholic drinks each week). These communications were effective in reducing undesirable behavior.

Rules and laws may be designed by governments to direct the behavior of citizens and other agencies in society. For example, a law prohibiting smoking in public spaces will be aimed at less tobacco consumption and at reduction of the external effects of smoking (i.e., reducing the effect on nonsmokers). Rules and laws generally are considered paternalistic ways of regulation. The ban on smoking in public spaces restricts the freedom of smokers to smoke, and the freedom of nonsmokers to be in the company of smokers. On the other hand, the law protects people who do not want to be in the company of smokers. This law is quite paternalistic in the sense that it denies the responsibility of smokers to care for nonsmokers, and limits the freedom of nonsmokers who willingly put themselves at risk in the company of smokers. It also denies the responsibility of smokers to care for themselves.

Teaching in formal education and upbringing is also paternalistic by definition. Special courses are not paternalistic to the extent that they are voluntary. Changing the incentives in economic environments, such as taxes, is considered paternalistic because they cannot be avoided by the users of the taxed goods and services. In contrast, communication is much less paternalistic because it can easily be avoided by people who gather information themselves or who willingly neglect the communication.

Recently, behavioral economic policy applications have been proposed as examples of liberal paternalism or light paternalism (Camerer, Issacharoff, Loewenstein, O'Donoghue, & Rabin, 2003; Thaler & Sunstein, 2003; Loewenstein & Haisley,

2008). Such measures do not affect rational decision makers, who are not influenced by particular biases as described above. Instead of overcoming the biases studied in behavioral economics as a way to improve decision making, the context of choice situations may be changed such that the biases actually work to the advantage of the decision maker.[1] This approach is advocated in Camerer et al. (2003) and Thaler and Sunstein (2008). In effect, such an approach may be considered as a countervailing power against marketing efforts that induce people to consume products and services on the market, regardless of their own desired objectives. For example, a common marketing promotion instrument is offering the possibility of delayed payment if consumers decide to buy in the present, thus exploiting consumer impatience. Below, opportunities for employing the discounting mechanism to the advantage of the consumer will be considered. It is not always the case that the context works to the advantage of either the consumer or the market (Camerer et al., 2003). In some cases the interests of both parties may be aligned, as in the case of health insurance, drug adherence, and stock market investments (all beneficial to consumers and profitable for the market).

Next, we are ready to provide an overview of policy applications that have been or may be derived from behavioral economic theory.

Behavioral-Economic Policy Applications

In this section, I provide a number of examples that have been or may be applied in policy measures by the government, consumer protection bodies and market agencies.

Because behavioral economic biases are considered "irrational" from the standard economic point of view, using such biases in policy measures is called asymmetric paternalistic. Rational decision makers are assumed to be unaffected by the use of such biases, whereas others may be aided in reaching their objectives better.

Providing information

To the extent that consumers are unable to do calculations by themselves, providing ready-to-use information may help consumers in making better decisions. Examples are information on product price per unit, and information on effective annual percentage rate in the case of loans. To the extent that consumers are unable to judge the quality of goods or the effects of consumption, labels and warnings may be provided. For example, energy efficiency labels, eco-labels, safety-approving labels, "smoking causes death," "past results are no guarantee of future performance," labels, and so on. To limit the detrimental effects of nonprofessional services, licenses may be granted to qualified professionals, for example, physicians, psychologists, or taxi drivers.

A relatively new type of information is customer reviews, usually placed on the internet, for example, for books, hotels, and even for private buyers and sellers of second-hand goods. Customer reviews are quite informative for so-called experience goods, whose quality only becomes evident after the purchase. Another recent and related development is brand comparison websites, which rank-order brands given several criteria, for example, interest charged on loans and mortgages or prices of television sets. Brand comparison may lead to different consumer evaluations than single product evaluations (Hsee, 1996, 1998), especially if the brands contain hard-to-evaluate attributes, such as energy efficiency of electronic equipment or speaker power consumption in stereo sound equipment.

Changing the status quo

Changing the status quo situation of decision makers has proven a very effective measure to change their preferences and behavior. Several examples of status quo differences have been documented:

Organ donations. These are essential in current medical practice. Lack of organ supply may lead to waiting lists for transplantation and untimely death for those at the bottom of the waiting list. No doubt, organ donation is effective in reaching higher well-being of patients, and expected well-being of nonpatients (because they all run the risk of becoming a patient). Johnson and Goldstein (2003) studied different consent regimes concerning organ donations in different countries in the European Union. In Denmark, the Netherlands, the UK and Germany, the status quo is no organ donation after one's death. However, one can make up a donor codicil in which one agrees with organ donation in such cases. In Austria, Belgium, France, Hungary, Poland, Portugal, and Sweden, the status quo is to donate organs, unless one makes a formal objection. In the former countries, organ donation consent varies between 4 and 28%, whereas in the latter countries consent exceeds 85%.

Retirement saving. This is quite beneficial to keep one's current welfare level after retirement. However, many people who rely on voluntary saving do not save enough to reach this objective. Madrian and Shea (2001) describe the results of a change from a voluntary 401(k) saving plan requiring explicit opt-in election to a default of enrollment in a saving plan from which participants could opt out if they did not wish to participate. Overall participation increased from 49% (opt-in) to 86% (opt-out). The difference was even higher for blacks (from 22% to 81%), the lowest age groups (25% to 74%) and the lowest pay groups (from 13% to 80%). The influence of a status quo was also evident in a change from a freely chosen contribution rate (old system) to a default rate of 3% (new system). Whereas only 12% chose a contribution of as high as 3% under the old system, 76% chose this default rate of 3% under the new system. Contributions for most employees could be allocated to nine different funds, including a money market fund, bond fund, stable value fund, and various stock funds. Under the old system, participants had to allocate their contributions, whereas, under the new system, the default allocation was in the money market fund (the default allocation could be changed freely, however). Less than 20% of the participants in the old system invested in the money market fund and only 6% invested all contributions in this fund, whereas 90% of participants in the new system invested in the money market fund, and 75% invested all their money in this fund. These results show the strong influence of default options, indicating status quo bias, on participation rates, contribution rates, and choice of funds.

Marketing examples. In marketing, the status quo bias may be used in presenting a brand as the status quo alternative that consumers obviously should buy. Drivers' preferences for car insurances were investigated in a natural quasi-experiment (Johnson, Hershey, Meszaros & Kunreuther, 1993). In New Jersey, the default option of car insurance is coverage, excluding the right to sue, which may be purchase additionally. In Pennsylvania, the default option is coverage, including the right to sue, which may be redeemed. In New Jersey, 20% acquired the full right to sue, whereas in Pennsylvania, 75% retained the full right to sue. Thus, the economic impact of the status quo alternative for consumers may be considerable. Obviously, in Pennsylvania consumers on average spent more on the car insurance than in New Jersey. This result can be generalized to other choices. Park, Sung, and Macinnis (2000) found that consumers spent more in the purchase of a car if they were presented with a fully loaded product, and were asked to delete options they did not want (scaling down) than if they were presented with a base model, and were asked to add options they did want (scaling up). Levin, Schreiber, Lauriola, and Gaeth (2002) found similar results for scaling up or scaling down a pizza. Levin, Prosansky, Heller, and Brunick (2001), using a job applicant screening task, found that more applicants were considered if applicants had to be excluded from further consideration than when applicants had to be included for further consideration.

Brand switching. Status quo bias would also prevent consumers from switching from one supplier to another supplier of goods or services. In a study by Hartman, Doane, and Woo (1991), consumers were split into several groups according to the number of electricity outages they had experienced per year. Each group was shown several alternatives, including different frequencies of electricity outages associated with different bills, higher (lower) bills were associated with less (more) outages. In the group, characterized by 3 outages per year, 60.2% preferred the status quo to the alternative combinations; in the group, characterized by 15 outages per year, 58.3% preferred the status quo. Although the reliability of electric current was quite different in the two groups, both preferred the situation they were accustomed to. Hence, the status quo may also be indicated as an adaptation effect. Once adaptation has occurred, it becomes unlikely for consumers to deviate from their adaptation level.

Everyday-life decisions. Other examples of the status quo bias resulting from adaptation in everyday life are decisions to keep or fire personnel, decisions to move into another dwelling, and decisions to stay in their marriage or have a divorce. In the area of consumer behaviour, one may think of decisions to cancel one's automatically continued subscription to a magazine or journal, decisions to give up one's membership of a club or union, and decisions to give up one's current provider of telecommunication or internet services. In many instances, transaction costs cannot fully explain the decision to stick to the status quo. In the consumer behaviour examples, a change from automatic continuation into automatic discontinuation is likely to be effective in changing consumer decisions from keeping-on into switching.

Decision format. Status quo effects may easily be induced by slight changes in decision format order. Johnson, Bellman, and Lohse (2002) studied the effects of negative framing and opt-in versus opt-out formats in questions frequently asked on the internet. The question "Notify me about more health surveys," to be answered by marking an open tick box, yielded 48% compliance in an experiment conducted in an online-panel. A similar question in which the tick box was already marked yielded 74% compliance. Obviously, the status quo in the first format implies no notification of health surveys, whereas in the second format the status quo is notification. Negative wording of the question "Do NOT notify me about more health surveys" yielded 96% compliance (with an open tick box), showing higher compliance in the opt-out than in the opt-in case.

Presentation order. The order of information presentation may also induce the status quo bias. Joachims, Granka, Pan, Hembrooke, and Gay (2005) reported on an experiment studying the effect of the presentation order of Google search results. The first hit was clicked in 42% of the cases, whereas the second hit was clicked in only 8% of the cases. Since clicking the first hit might be caused by excellent ranking on the part of the search engine, in another condition in the experiment the first two hits were swapped unnoticed. Although clicks on the first hit were a bit lower, the first hit still obtained 34% of the clicks, the second hit obtained 12%. Although the participants paid some attention to the quality of the hits, the order of presentation was far more likely to influence clicking on the hits.

Framing

The specific context created by the wording of a decision problem constitutes a decision frame. Different descriptions of the same decision problem may lead to different evaluations of the decision alternatives, hence to different decisions (Levin, Schneider, & Gaeth, 1998). Relating to behavioral economic phenomena, framing may alter the reference point with respect to which the outcomes of decisions are evaluated (either as gains or losses, in many instances).

Attractiveness. Levin and Gaeth (1988) studied consumer judgments of meat that was described either as 75% "lean" or 25% "fat." Although the two meat qualifications imply the same type of meat, the "lean" meat was evaluated as more lean, of higher quality, less greasy, and more tasty than "fat" meat. This study shows that attractive descriptions are evaluated more favorably than unattractive descriptions.

Fairness. Kimes and Wirtz (2001) studied fairness considerations concerning dinner prices for hotel guests of Cornell University's Statler Hotel. They found that guests considered weekend dinner prices announced as higher than weekday prices to be more unfair than weekday prices announced as lower than weekend prices. The same was found for price surcharges for eating between 6 and 8 p.m. versus discounts for eating before or after that time period, and for price surcharges for window seats versus price discounts for regular seats. The framing of price differences in terms of gains to the individual (discounts) was generally considered as fairer than framing in terms of losses to the individual (surcharges). See also Kahneman, Knetsch, and Thaler (1986).

Train delay. For the past couple of years, the Dutch railways have no longer been announcing train delays. Instead, they announce that the train will depart in 10 minutes (in the case of a 10-minute delay). Although the message gives the same information, a delay will be perceived as a loss, whereas departure in 10 minutes will be perceived as more neutral. The latter message should be evaluated as more pleasant than the former, presumably leading to higher customer satisfaction.

Income as bonus or rebate. Epley, Mak, and Idson (2006) studied whether income that was described as a bonus (perceived as a gain) would be more readily spent than income described as a rebate (perceived as a reduced loss). In one of their studies, they gave Harvard undergraduate students $50, as either a bonus or a tuition rebate. One week later, the bonus students reported spending $22 and saving $28, whereas rebate students reported spending $10 and saving $40. Even more striking results were found when students could spend $25 either framed as "bonus money" or "rebate money." The former group spent $11.16, whereas the latter spent $2.43. The results might explain why President George W. Bush's $38 billion "tax rebate" in 2001 was not spent as expected. The implications of this kind of research should be clear in times of economic recession in which low consumer spending is problematic.

Zero cost. Shampanier, Mazar, and Ariely (2007) showed the power of offering goods for free as compared with a price reduction of the same goods. When people could choose between a Hershey's chocolate costing 1¢ and a Lindt truffle costing 15¢ (or choose no chocolate at all), 14% chose the Hershey's. However, when the Hershey's were offered for free, and the price of Lindt was 14¢, 42% chose the Hershey's. The authors considered the power of the "free" frame so strong that they advise companies and policy makers to drive prices of additional services, such as shipping costs, to zero to boost demand of consumers and citizens dramatically. The same policy could be applied to "zero calories," "zero cost of medical checkups," "zero registration and inspection costs" for electric cars, etc. (Ariely, 2008).

Underannuitization. Another policy-relevant framing issue is related to what is called the underannuitization puzzle, referring to the fact that few individuals purchase life annuities. Not purchasing life annuity may result in longevity risk (i.e., limited consumption beyond one's expected lifetime). Brown, Kling, Mullainathan, and Wrobel (2008) found evidence for framing effects leading to different preferences for purchasing annuity. One of their consumption frames was: "Mr. Red can spend $650 each month for as long as he lives in addition to social security. When he dies, there will be no more payments." The corresponding investment frame was: "Mr. Red invests $100,000 in an account which earns $650 each month for as long as he lives. He can only withdraw the earnings he receives, not the invested money. When he dies, the earnings will stop and his investment will be worth nothing." Comparable alternatives for savings accounts were constructed for each of the two frames. If the choice between life annuity and a savings account was presented in a consumption frame, 72% of their respondents preferred life annuity. However, if the same choice was presented in an investment format, only 21% preferred life annuity. Because the investment frame prevails on the insurance market, the results might explain underannuitization, and suggest ways to change this behavior.

Mental accounting. A related type of framing is mental accounting (i.e., the mental coding of gains and losses according to the value function in prospect theory: Kahneman & Tversky, 1979). Because of the concave value function for gains (marginally decreasing with larger gains), Thaler (1985) has argued that separation should be evaluated as more attractive than integration of gains. For example, he found that winning money in two different lotteries ($50 and $25) was evaluated as more pleasurable than winning the same amount in one lottery ($75). Conversely, because of the convex shape of the value function for losses (marginally increasing with smaller losses), integration of losses should be preferred to separation. For example, one tax payment of $150 was considered as less upsetting than two separate tax payments of $100 and $50. Moreover, it was found that separating small gains from a relatively large loss was preferred to integration ("silver lining," as in the case of rebates), and integrating losses with relatively large gains was preferred to separation (as in the case of normal purchases, where payment is integrated with receipt of the good). Mental accounting rules may be applied in marketing and government policy. For example, tax withholding is aimed at integrating gains (income) and losses (taxes), credit cards function so as to integrate losses (payments) into one bill. In this respect, recent market liberalization of utility services in Europe has one adverse effect. Whereas in former days, consumers received one bill from the government, many services have been split, resulting in separate billing for different services, thus separating one loss into many smaller losses.

Setting budgets. The idea of mental accounting is based on the mental separation of events. One instance of such behavior is setting budgets for categories of expenses, possibly resulting in underconsumption (Heath & Soll, 1996). Setting budgets seems to be mostly applied by consumers at low income and wealth levels and by those who have difficulties making ends meet. In these circumstances, setting budgets facilitates keeping track of one's expenses (Antonides, De Groot, & Van Raaij, in press). Setting budgets appears to be an attractive technique which may be advocated by family economic advisers.

Contrast, compromise, and format effects

It has been found that adding inferior alternatives to a choice set may increase people's preferences for the original choice options (Huber, Payne, & Puto, 1982). Likewise, preference for a choice alternative is generally higher when the alternative has mediocre qualities than extreme (high or low) qualities compared to other choice alternatives (Kivetz, Netzer, & Srinivasan, 2004). Also, changing the format of a decision problem, by placing a choice alternative within a series of choice options, or by varying the number of choice options may lead to increased preference for the original choice alternatives.

Attractiveness. It is well known that other people's physical attractiveness as well as one's own ratings of attractiveness may be influenced by contrasting physical appearances (Geiselman, Haight, & Kimata, 1984; Smeesters & Mandel, 2006; Thornton & Moore, 1993). This knowledge is widely applied in advertising. In general, contrast effects tend to increase the attractiveness of a choice option by comparing it with an inferior alternative. Although the inferior alternative is unlikely to be selected, the attractiveness of the other choice alternatives may increase (Simonson, 1999). Similar findings have been reported by Tversky and Griffin (1991). For example, people who spent some time in an extremely pleasant (unpleasant) room rated their own housing situation as relatively unpleasurable (pleasurable) after this event. The effect was not found for events unrelated to the housing situation (e.g., pleasant or unpleasant weather). Possible applications may be presenting an audience with two related messages, extremely varying in attractiveness. The attractive message is probably favored more than when it is presented in isolation.

Compromising. Compromise effects tend to increase the attractiveness of options in between superior and inferior alternatives. In other words, if the preference order is A>B>C>D, B would be favored more in the triplet A, B, C than in the triplet B, C, D. This result has been observed in several experiments, for example, regarding consumer choice of cameras (Simonson & Tversky, 1992), paper towels (Simonson 1989), and investment options (Benartzi & Thaler, 2002). However, sometimes a taste for extreme options has been found, for example, in the case of ice cream and insurance options (Simonson, 1989). Simonson (1999) explains the different pattern of findings by assuming that the marginal utility of increasing attribute values is sometimes decreasing (e.g., computers with more memory) and sometimes increasing (ice cream with exceptional taste). Kelman, Rottenstreich, and Tversky (2000) presented one group of participants in an experiment with a criminal story, which could be classified either as murder or manslaughter. In another group, a third classification, murder with special circumstances was possible. In the first group 47% classified the case as manslaughter, in the second group only 19% chose manslaughter. The compromise alternative, murder with special circumstances, became the most popular alternative, selected by 42% of the second group. Further research seems to be needed in this area. Kivetz, Netzer and Srinivasan (2004) developed several models to explain the findings. Depending on the type of marginal utility (decreasing or increasing), these effects may be put to use in product offerings, messages, proposals, or experiences.

Presentation order. Different experiences may be presented in different order, subsequently affecting people's evaluations of such experiences. In general, for single outcomes, such as having a French dinner in one month or in two months, people favor the sooner event, indicating impatience. However, in a series of dinners, they prefer having the French dinner after a (less preferred) Greek dinner (Loewenstein & Prelec, 1991), indicating patience. Hence, for series of outcomes, people display different preferences than for single outcomes.

In the case of income streams, such preferences clearly result in objectively inferior outcomes (Loewenstein & Sicherman, 1991). Hsee (1996) found that the salary series \$23,000 in year 1, \$24,000 in year 2, \$25,000 in year 3, and \$26,000 in year 4 was preferred to the salary series \$27,000 in year 1, \$25,000 in year 2, \$25,000 in year 3, and \$24,000 in year 4 if the series were presented to different groups. This result is clearly due to the increasing versus decreasing salaries in the two series. However, if people could compare the two series, they preferred the second series because now they noticed that it was $1,000 higher in each year.

Series of events. In series evaluations, people tend to value the most extreme outcome and the final outcome, also called the "peak and end" rule (Kahneman, 1994). Ross and Simonson (1991) presented participants with both an attractive and a less interesting computer game. The order of the games was varied in two conditions. Those who played the games in the order less interesting → more attractive later evaluated the computer diskette containing the games more highly, and showed higher willingness to pay for the diskette than did the group that experienced the two games in the reverse order. This is in agreement with the above-mentioned findings. These ideas may be applied to the presentation of series of experiences, for example, in fun parks, movies, television commercials, and call-center conversations (Verhoef, Antonides, & De Hoog, 2004).

Investing. The "1/n heuristic" applies to the influence of the number of choice options on decision making. Benartzi and Thaler (2001) have found a systematic tendency to spread investments more or less equally over the number of available investment options, regardless of risk preferences and regardless of the type of choice alternatives. Although the 1/n heuristic may only occur with a small number of investment options (Huberman & Jiang, 2004), it still has practical implications because most investors consider only three to four different investment funds.

Probability effects

Several other issues may also be used in policy applications, including effects concerning small probabilities and a preference for certainty.

Small probabilities. People tend to neglect small probabilities and instead focus on the magnitude of the outcome (Kahneman & Tversky, 1979), which may explain why they frequently play the lotteries and overvalue the risk of terrorism (Sunstein, 2003). Furthermore, neglecting small probabilities may lead to underinsurance against high-outcome low-probability events and to not wearing seat belts. Hence, Slovic, Fischhoff, and Lichtenstein (1978) have argued to change the driver's perspective from a single-trip perception of risk into life-time risk of not wearing seat belts. Although nowadays in many countries wearing seat belts is enforced by law, the advice may still be useful for other types of risky behavior. Jolls and Sunstein (2006) have advocated making the total cumulative risk more available to the actor's mind in such cases, possibly increasing the likelihood of proper action to minimize the risk. The effect of small probabilities is also evident in unethical or criminal behavior. For example, small probabilities of being caught also tend to decrease deterrence in tax evasion, traffic, etc. Mazar and Ariely (2006) stress the importance of pushing the probability of being caught to 100% if possible.

Certainty. The preference for certainty (Kahneman & Tversky, 1979) implies that a change from 99% into 100% for an attractive event (from 1% into 0% for unattractive events) is valued more highly than a change from, say, 49% into 50%. This kind of preference has implications for the offering of insurance policies, because complete coverage insurance is disproportionally favored to incomplete insurance. For example, an insurance policy that fully covers fire but not flood will be preferred to an insurance offering a reduction of the overall probability of loss for the two events (Slovic, Fischhoff, & Lichtenstein, 1982).

Motivational effects

Impatience. Impatience generally results in the advancement of consumption, sometimes followed by immediate regret after the purchase. Hence, "cooling-off" devices have been implemented in law and regulation that either allow for undoing the purchase act (e.g., in the case of internet purchases or door-to-door sales) or delay action until after the cooling-off period (e.g., having an abortion or euthanasia). Impatience may be stimulated by "buy now, pay later" promotions of retailers, thus advancing the benefits and delaying the cost of purchase. Impatience may be discouraged by, for example, taxes on goods for which people are impatient, for example, snacks (also called "sin taxes," see O'Donoghue & Rabin, 2003).

High impatience implies that people discount future outcomes heavily. Read and Van Leeuwen (1998) and Gattig (2002) have found that the rate of subjective discounting is generally higher for hedonic goods or "want" items (e.g., snacks) than for utilitarian goods or "should" items (e.g., healthy products). This process may explain why advance orders at DVD rental services contain relatively many "should" movies such as documentaries and art films, whereas people tend to watch relatively many "want" movies such as comedies and action movies once they have arrived (Milkman, Rogers, & Bazerman, 2007). Likewise, consumers tend to order more "should" items (such as vegetables) when ordering in advance at an online grocery store than "want" items (such as ice cream) (Rogers, Milkman, & Bazerman, 2007) while at the store the opposite is true. Also, Rogers and Bazerman (2008) found that more people may agree with a gas tax to be implemented in the future than with one that is implemented immediately.

A related idea is a new saving schema in which employees were offered the opportunity to save from their future income *increases*, rather than from their current income (Thaler & Benartzi, 2004). In the first place, the saving action was delayed, which made it easier to become accepted; in the second place, saving from an income increase was acceptable because it was considered a forgone gain, rather than a loss of income. Finally, those who enrolled in the saving schema were likely to stay with the schema because this schema had become the status quo. As a result, employees in the so-called "Save More Tomorrow Program" saved 10% more of their income after the fourth pay raise, than before joining the program.

The "Save More Tomorrow Program" is an example of a self-imposed self-control strategy, of which Thaler and Sunstein (2009) mention several other examples, for example, Christmas saving clubs, people putting themselves on a list of people who are banned from casinos, and people depositing money with a third party, which is saved if they reach a particular goal but is lost otherwise.

Heat of passion. Strong motivational effects may occur in the heat of passion. Ariely and Loewenstein (2006) show that sexually aroused men rated a number of sexual activities as much more attractive, and rated the likelihood of engaging in immoral behaviors like date rape higher than non-sexually aroused men. Similar mechanisms would play a part in such activities as safe sex or safe driving (Ariely, 2008). Generally, offering people self-control devices as indicated above would help overcome these motivational biases. For example, voluntarily equipping one's car with an alcohol lock could be such a self-control device.

Altruism and fairness. People frequently show concern for others and for fair treatment of themselves and others. For example, people tend to prefer an outcome distribution of $500 for themselves and $500 for another person over $600 for themselves and $800 for the other person (Loewenstein, Thompson, & Bazerman, 1989). People even provide costly punishments to others whom they observe behaving unfairly (Fehr & Fischbacher, 2003), even as outside observers (Fehr & Fischbacher, 2004). Altruism and fairness seem to be anchored in social norms, and fairness violations may even harm larger group performance. For example, correlations have been found between pay equity and the quality of company products (Cowherd & Levine, 1992) and pay equity and performance of a major league baseball team (Depken, 2000).

Kahneman, Knetsch, and Thaler (1986) have discovered several circumstances influencing fairness judgments. Firstly, forgone gains (e.g., cutting a bonus) are perceived as more fair than straight losses (e.g., cutting wages). Secondly, it is considered unfair to exploit shifts in demand (e.g., to raise prices in the case of shortage). Thirdly, it is considered more fair to keep revenues in case of increased efficiency of production than in case of reduced costs. These results may be taken into account in government policies, and the wage and pricing policies of firms. For example, a manager's bonus for increasing a firm's productivity generally would be considered as fair, except in the case of lay-offs (causing a loss to fired personnel).

Esteem needs. In general, people tend to keep up a positive image of themselves. Hence, they keep up positive illusions that may lead to higher well-being (Taylor & Brown, 1988), believe that they are less likely to experience negative events (Weinstein, 1980), hold more positive expectations for their personal financial situation than for the general economy, make self-serving attributions concerning the causes of success and failure (Weiner, 1985), and minimize the opportunity for regret, for example by playing in a postal code lottery (Zeelenberg & Pieters, 2004). Such motivations and their subsequent actions may be harmful in that they may lead to lower objective outcomes, for example, losing money (by gambling) or getting a disease (by assuming their invulnerability and not taking vaccinations).

An important factor in the satisfaction of esteem needs is procedural fairness (Lind & Tyler, 1988), which is more likely achieved in more democratic institutions (Frey & Stutzer, 2000), in independent jobs such as self-employment (Benz & Frey, 2004), and by treating taxpayers with dignity and respect rather than as "subjects" who have to be forced to pay their dues (Feld & Frey, 2002).

Another issue related to esteem needs is honesty. Mazar, Amir, and Ariely (2008) have studied the conditions for cheating on one's performance in a quiz or math test.

Cheating was made possible by letting the participants (after their test) complete a scoring sheet on which the correct answers were shown. They were then paid, sometimes in money, sometimes in tokens that could be cashed in for money. They found that some cheating occurred, although far less than was possible. In one of their experiments, the participants in the control condition (no cheating possible) scored 3.5 out of 20 possible correct answers, those in the cheating condition who were paid money scored 6.2. No cheating occurred in conditions in which the participants had to recall the Ten Commandments or had to sign an honor code statement. The latter effect shows that honesty reminders tend to reduce dishonest behavior. Participants in the cheating condition who were paid in tokens scored 9.4. Apparently, when the payment was not immediately related to money the most cheating occurred. Ariely (2008) found further evidence for the latter effect by observing students' behavior after putting either six-packs of Coke or six one-dollar bills in their communal fridges when they were away from their dormitories. The Coke was consumed within 72 hours, whereas the money remained untouched for 72 hours. These findings indicate that payments or rewards made in another medium than money tend to induce more dishonesty than payments in real money. Ariely (2008) suggests that more dishonesty can be expected because payments in real money are gradually being replaced by credit or debit cards.

Conclusion

In this chapter, I have provided a brief overview of the main issues studied in behavioral economics and tried to show how the results may be applied in the policy making of the government, consumer interest groups, and firms. Interest in policy applications has increased in the recent past, as is evident from a number of field studies. Frey and Stutzer (2007) even state that "experimental economics has dissociated itself from the rest of economics and has less influence than it otherwise could" (p. 6). It appears that now is the time to take behavioral economics out of the laboratory into the field and to fruitfully apply it to help solving real problems of society.

We have argued that policy making might well be based on five mechanisms: teaching, learning, rules and laws, changing the context of choice, and playing on motivations (see Table 20.1.). Behavioral economics has yielded some new insights in these mechanisms and their effects, which may be applied in actual practice.

Earlier, policy making based on economics frequently used the pricing and taxing mechanisms to pursue policy aims. Policy making based on psychology frequently relied on social marketing and communication techniques. Both types of policy making can benefit from using insights from the interdisciplinary area of behavioral economics and economic psychology. In addition to providing the benchmark policy based on rational actor's behavior, interdisciplinary research may provide further insights of how to improve the benchmark policy. For example, if the benchmark policy would be to increase consumer spending by giving consumers more income, a new policy could include ways in which consumer spending is optimized, for example, by giving the income to consumers as bonus money in their current accounts rather than as reduced taxes.

Table 20.1. Summary of Mechanisms Applied in Policy Making, Their Effects and Drawbacks

Mechanism	*Policy*	*Effects*	*Drawbacks*
Teaching	Providing information Education Courses Counseling	Increased knowledge Increased skills Less vulnerability to biases	Requires motivation
Behavioral change	Providing incentives Communication	Extrinsic motivation to change attitudes or behavior	Crowding out intrinsic motivation Limited opportunities for learning Sometimes leading to suboptimal behavior
Rules and laws	Enforcing desired behavior Enabling participation	Limiting undesired behavior Procedural utility	Maintenance cost Paternalism
Changing context of choice	Status quo changes Framing outcomes and probabilities Contrast, compromise, formatting	Switching behavior Changing attractiveness	
Playing on motivations	Commitment to future behavior Altruism and fairness Respecting esteem needs	Limiting impulsivity Limiting greed Increasing self-worth Limiting dishonesty	

In sum, economics was considered the basic discipline describing economic behavior in market environments. Behavioral economics has shown that standard economic analysis is insufficient to realistically describe and understand market actors' behavior. Hence, policy applications could benefit from including behavioral economic insights, thus aiming for a higher degree of success.

Note

1 The latter claim has been questioned by Rizzo and Whitman (2008).

References

Altman, M. (Ed.). (2006). *Handbook of contemporary behavioral economics.* Armonk, NY: M. E. Sharpe.

Antonides, G., De Groot, I. M., & Van Raaij, W. F. (in press). Mental budgeting and the management of household finance. *Journal of Economic Psychology.*

Antonides, G., & Kroft, M. (2005). Fairness judgments in household decision making. *Journal of Economic Psychology, 26,* 902–913.

Antonides, G., & Maital, S. (2002). Effects of feedback and educational training on maximization in choice tasks: Experimental-game evidence. *Journal of Socio-Economics, 31*(2), 155–165.

Antonides, G., & Wunderink, S. R. (2001). Subjective time preference and willingness to pay for an energy-saving durable good. *Zeitschrift für Sozialpsychologie, 32*(3), 133–141.

Ariely, D. (2008). *Predictably irrational. The hidden forces that shape our decisions.* London: HarperCollins.

Ariely, D., & Loewenstein, G. (2006). The heat of the moment: The effect of sexual arousal on sexual decision making. *Journal of Behavioral Decision Making, 19,* 87–98.

Babcock, L., & Loewenstein, G. (1997). Explaining bargaining impasse: The role of self-serving biases. *Journal of Economic Perspectives, 11,* 109–126.

Bandura, A. (1986). *Social foundations of thought and action: A social cognitive theory.* Englewood Cliffs, NJ: Prentice-Hall.

Barber, B., & Odean, T. (2001). Gender, overconfidence, and common stock investment. *Quarterly Journal of Economics, 116,* 261–292.

Bazerman, M., & Moore, D. (2009). *Judgment in managerial decision making.* New York: John Wiley.

Benartzi, S., & Thaler, R. H. (2001). Naive diversification strategies in retirement saving plans. *American Economic Review, 91*(1), 79–98.

Benartzi, S., & Thaler, R. H. (2002). How much is investor autonomy worth? *Journal of Finance, 57*(4), 1593–1616.

Benz, M., & Frey, B. S. (2004). Being independent raises happiness at work. *Swedish Economic Policy Review, 11*(2), 95–134.

Brown, J. R., Kling, J. R., Mullainathan, S., & Wrobel, M. V. (2008). Why don't people insure late life consumption? A framing explanation of the under-annuitization puzzle. Cambridge, MA: National Bureau of Economic Research Working paper 13748.

Camerer, C. F., Issacharoff, S., Loewenstein, G., O'Donoghue, T., & Rabin, M. (2003). Regulation for conservatives: Behavioral economics and the case for "asymmetric paternalism." *University of Pennsylvania Law Review, 151,* 1211–1254.

Camerer, C. F., Loewenstein, G., & Prelec, D. (2005). Neuroeconomics: How neuroscience can inform economics. *Journal of Economic Literature, 43,* 9–64.

Camerer, C. F., Loewenstein, G. & Rabin, M. (Eds.). (2004). *Advances in behavioral economics.* Princeton: Princeton University Press.

Camerer, C. F, & Thaler, R. H. (1995). More dictator and ultimatum games. *Journal of Economic Perspectives, 9*(2), 209–219.

Cowherd, D. M., & Levine, D. I. (1992). Product quality and pay equity between lower-level employees and top management: An investigation of distributive justice theory. *Administrative Science Quarterly, 37*(2), 302–320.

Cullis, J., Jones, P., & Lewis, A. (2006). Ethical investing. Where are we now? In M. Altman (Ed.), *Handbook of contemporary behavioral economics* (pp. 602–625). Armonk, NY: M. E. Sharpe.

Depken, C.A. (2000). Wage disparity and team productivity: Evidence from major league baseball. *Economic Letters*, *67*, 87–92.

Dijksterhuis, A., Bos, M. W., Nordgren, L. F., & Van Baaren, R. B. (2006). On making the right choice: The deliberation-without-attention effect. *Science*, *311*, 1005–1007.

Epley, N., Mak, D., & Idson, L.C. (2006). Rebate or bonus? The impact of income framing on spending and saving. *Journal of Behavioral Decision Making*, *19*(4), 213–227.

Fehr, E., & Fischbacher, U. (2003). The nature of human altruism. *Nature*, *425*, 785–791.

Fehr, E., & Fischbacher, U. (2004). Third-party punishment and social norms. *Evolution and Human Behavior*, *25*, 63–87.

Feld, L. P., & Frey, B. S. (2002). Trust breeds trust: How taxpayers are treated. *Economics of Governance*, *3*, 87–99.

Fischhoff, B. (1982). Debiasing. In D. Kahneman, P. Slovic, & A. Tversky (Eds.), *Judgment under uncertainty: Heuristics and biases* (pp. 422–444). Cambridge, MA: Cambridge University Press.

Frank, R. H. (2008). *Microeconomics and behavior*. New York: McGraw-Hill.

Frey, B. S. (1992). Tertium datur: Pricing, regulating and intrinsic motivation. *Kyklos*, *45*(2), 161–184.

Frey, B. S., Benz, M., & Stutzer, A. (2004). Introducing procedural utility: Not only what, but also how matters. *Journal of Institutional and Theoretical Economics*, *160*(3), 377–401.

Frey, B. S., & Stutzer, A. (2000). Happiness, economy and institutions. *The Economic Journal*, *110*, 918–938.

Frey, B. S., & Stutzer, A. (2007). *Economics and psychology: A promising new cross-disciplinary field*. Cambridge, MA: MIT Press

Gallet, C. A., & List, J. A. (2003). Cigarette demand: a meta-analysis of elasticities. *Health Economics*, *12*(10), 821–835.

Gately, D. (1980). Individual discount rates and the purchase and utilization of energy-using durables: Comment. *Bell Journal of Economics*, *11*(1), 373–374.

Gattig, A. (2002). *Intertemporal decision making*. Groningen: Interuniversity Center for Social Science Theory and Methodology.

Geiselman, R. E., Haight, N. A., & Kimata, L. G. (1984). Context effects on the perceived physical attractiveness of faces. *Journal of Experimental Social Psychology*, *20*, 409–424.

Hartman, R. S., Doane, M. J., & Woo, C.-K. (1991). Consumer rationality and the status quo. *Quarterly Journal of Economics*, *106*, 141–162.

Hausman, J. A. (1979). Individual discount rates and the purchase and utilization of energy-using durables. *Bell Journal of Economics*, *10*(1), 33–54.

Heath, C., & Soll, J. B. (1996). Mental accounting and consumer decisions. *Journal of Consumer Research*, *23*, 40–52.

Herrnstein, R. J. (1991). Experiments on stable suboptimality in individual behavior. *American Economic Review*, *81*, 360–364.

Hsee, C. K. (1996). The evaluability hypothesis: An explanation for preference reversals between joint and separate evaluations of alternatives. *Organizational Behaviour and Human Decision Processes*, *67*(3), 247–257.

Hsee, C. K. (1998). Less is better: When low-value options are valued more highly than high-value options. *Journal of Behavioural Decision Making*, *11*(2), 107–121.

Huber, J., Payne, J. W., & Puto, C. (1982). Adding asymmetrically dominated alternatives: Violations of regularity and the similarity hypothesis. *Journal of Consumer Research*, *9*(1), 90–98.

Huberman, G., & Jiang, W. (2004). Offering versus choice in 401(k) plans: Equity exposure and number of funds. *Journal of Finance*, *61*(2), 763–801.

Hursh, S. R. (1991). Behavioral economics of drug self-administration and drug abuse policy. *Journal of the Experimental Analysis of Behavior*, *56*. 377–393.

Joachims, T., Granka, L., Pan, B., Hembrooke, H., & Gay, G. (2005). Accurately interpreting clickthrough data as implicit feedback. *Proceedings of the Conference on Research and Development in Information Retrieval* (SIGIR).

Johnson, E. J., Bellman, S., & Lose, G. L. (2002). Defaults, framing and privacy: Why opting in–opting out. *Marketing Letters*, *13*(1), 5–15.

Johnson, E. J., & Goldstein, D. G. (2003). Do defaults save lives? *Science*, *302*, 1338–1339.

Johnson, E. J., Hershey, J., Meszaros, J., & Kunreuther, H. (1993). Framing, probability distortions, and insurance decisions. *Journal of Risk and Uncertainty*, *7*, 35–51.

Jolls, C., & Sunstein, C. R. (2006). Debiasing through law. *Journal of Legal Studies*, *35*, 199–241.

Kahneman, D. (1994). New challenges to the rationality assumption. *Journal of Institutional and Theoretical Economics*, *150*, 18–36.

Kahneman, D. (1999). Objective happiness. In D. Kahneman, E. Diener, & N. Schwarz (Eds.), *Well-being: The foundations of hedonic psychology* (pp. 3–25). New York: Russell Sage.

Kahneman, D. (2003a). A psychological perspective on economics. *American Economic Review*, *93*, 162–168.

Kahneman, D. (2003b). Maps of bounded rationality: Psychology for behavioral economics. *American Economic Review*, *93*, 1449–1475.

Kahneman, D., Knetsch, J. L., & Thaler, R. H. (1986). Fairness as a constraint on profit seeking: entitlements in the market. *American Economic Review*, *76*(4) 728–741.

Kahneman, D., Knetsch, J. L., & Thaler, R. H. (1990). Experimental tests of the endowment effect and the Coase theorem. *Journal of Political Economy*, *98*(6), 1325–1347.

Kahneman, D., Knetsch, J. L., & Thaler, R. H. (1991). The endowment effect, loss aversion, and the status quo bias. *Journal of Economic Perspectives*, *5*, 193–206.

Kahneman, D., Slovic, P. & Tversky, A. (1982). *Judgment under uncertainty: Heuristics and biases.* Cambridge: Cambridge University Press.

Kahneman, D., & Tversky, A. (1979). Prospect theory: An analysis of decision under risk. *Econometrica*, *47*, 263–291.

Kahneman, D., & Tversky, A. (Eds.) (2000). *Choices, values, and frames.* Cambridge, UK: Cambridge University Press.

Katona, G. (1975). *Psychological economics.* New York: Elsevier.

Kelman, M., Rottenstreich, Y., & Tversky, A. (2000). Context-dependence in legal decision making. In C. R. Sunstein (Ed.), *Behavioral law and economics* (pp. 61–94). Cambridge, UK: Cambridge University Press.

Khalil, E. L. (2004). What is altruism? *Journal of Economic Psychology*, *25*, 97–123.

Kimes, S. E., & Wirtz, J. (2002). Perceived fairness of demand-based pricing for restaurants. *Cornell Hotel and Restaurant Administration Quarterly*, *43*, 31–37.

Kivets, R., Netzer, O., & Srinivasan, V. (2004). Alternative models for capturing the compromise effect. *Journal of Marketing Research*, *41*, 237–257.

Laibson, D. (1997). Golden eggs and hyperbolic discounting. *Quarterly Journal of Economics*, *112*(2), 443–477.

Laibson, D., & Zeckhauser, R. (1998). Amos Tversky and the ascent of behavioral economics. *Journal of Risk and Uncertainty*, *16*, 7–47.

Langer, E. J. (1975). The illusion of control. *Journal of Personality and Social Psychology*, *32* (2), 311–328.

Levin, I. P., & Gaeth, G. J. (1988). How consumers are affected by the framing of attribute information before and after consuming the product. *Journal of Consumer Research*, *15*, 374–378.

Levin, I. P., Prosansky, C. M., Heller, D., & Brunick, B. M. (2001). Prescreening of choice options in "positive" and "negative" decision making tasks. *Journal of Behavioral Decision Making, 14*, 279–293.

Levin, I. P., Schneider, S. L., & Gaeth, G. J. (1998). All frames are not created equal: A typology and critical analysis of framing effects. *Organizational Behavior and Human Decision Processes, 76*, 149–188.

Levin, I. P., Schreiber, J., Lauriola, M., & Gaeth, G. J. (2002). A tale of two pizzas: Building up from a basis product versus scaling down from a fully-loaded product. *Marketing Letters, 13*(4), 335–344.

Lewis, A. (2008). *Psychology and economic behavior.* Cambridge, UK: Cambridge University Press.

Lind, E. A., & Tyler, T. R. (1988). *The social psychology of procedural justice.* New York: Plenum Press.

Loewenstein, G. (2007). The economist as therapist: Behavioural economics and "light" paternalism. Retrieved January 30, 2009 from http://videolectures.net/iarep07_loewenstein_etb/

Loewenstein, G., & Haisley, E. (2008). The economist as therapist: Methodological ramifications of "light" paternalism. In A. Caplin & A. Schotter (Eds.), *The foundations of positive and normative economics: A handbook* (pp. 210–245). New York: Oxford University Press.

Loewenstein, G., O'Donoghue, T. & Rabin, M. (2003). Projection bias in predicting future utility. *Quarterly Journal of Economics, 118*(4), 1209–1248.

Loewenstein, G., & Prelec, D. (1992). Anomalies in intertemporal choice: Evidence and an interpretation. *Quarterly Journal of Economics, 107*, 573–597.

Loewenstein, G., & Sicherman, N. (1991). Do workers prefer increasing wage profiles? *Journal of Labor Economics, 9*, 67–84.

Loewenstein, G., Thompson, L., & Bazerman, M. (1989). Social utility and decision making in interpersonal contexts. *Journal of Personality and Social Psychology, 57*, 426–441.

Logue, A. W. (1988). Self-control. In W. T. O'Donohue (Ed.), *Learning and behavior therapy* (pp. 252–273). Needhan Heights, MA: Allyn & Bacon.

Logue, A. W. (2000) Self-control and health behavior. In W. K. Bickel & R. E. Vuchinich (Eds.), *Reframing health behavior change with behavioral economics* (pp. 167–192). Mahwah, NJ: Lawrence Erlbaum Associates.

Lynn, M. (2006). Tipping in restaurants and around the globe. In M. Altman (Ed.), *Handbook of contemporary behavioral economics* (pp. 626–643). Armonk, NY: M.E. Sharpe.

Madrian, B. C., & Shea, D. F. (2001). The power of suggestion: Inertia in 401(k) participation and savings behavior. *Quarterly Journal of Economics, 116*(4), 1149–1187.

Mazar, N., Amir, O., & Ariely, D. (2008). The dishonesty of honest people: A theory of self-concept maintenance. *Journal of Marketing Research, 45*(6), 633–644.

Mazar, N. & Ariely, D. (2006). Dishonesty in everyday life and its policy implications. *Journal of Public Policy and Marketing, 25*(1), 117–126.

McFadden, D. (1999). Rationality for economists? *Journal of Risk and Uncertainty, 19*, 73–105.

McLure, S. M., Laibson, D., Loewenstein, G., & Cohen, J. D. (2004). Separate neural systems value immediate and delayed monetary rewards. *Science, 306*(5695), 503–507.

Messick, D. M., Bloom, S., Boldizar, J. P., & Samuelson, C. D. (1985). Why we are fairer than others? *Journal of Experimental Social Psychology, 21*, 480–500.

Mezulis, A. H., Abramson, L. Y., Hyde, J. S., & Hankin, B. L. (2004). Is there a universal positivity bias in attributions? A meta-analytic review of individual, developmental, and cultural differences in the self-serving attributional bias. *Psychological Bulletin, 130*(5), 711–747.

Milkman, K. L., Rogers, T. & Bazerman, M. (2009). Highbrow films gather dust: Time-inconsistent preferences and online DVD rentals. *Management Science, 55*, 1047–1059.
Mowrer, R. R., & Klein, S. B. (2001). *Handbook of contemporary learning theories.* Mahwah, NJ: Lawrence Erlbaum.
Mullainathan, S., & Thaler, R. H. (2000). Behavioral economics. In N. J. Smelser & P. B. Baltes (Eds.), *International encyclopedia of the social and behavioral sciences* (pp. 1094–1100). Amsterdam: Elsevier.
Nofsinger, J. R. (2008). *The psychology of investing.* Upper Saddle River, NJ: Pearson, Prentice Hall.
O'Donoghue, T., & Rabin, M. (2003). Studying optimal paternalism, illustrated by a model of sin taxes. *American Economic Review, 93*(2), 186–191.
Park, C. W., Sung, Y. J., & Macinnis, D. J. (2000). Choosing what I want versus rejecting what I do not want: An application of decision framing to product option choice decisions. *Journal of Marketing Research, 37*, 187–202.
Peters, E., Vastfjall, D., Slovic, P., Mertz, C. K., Mazzocco, K., & Dickert, S. (2006). Numeracy and decision making. *Psychological Science, 17*, 407–413.
Petty, R. E., & Cacioppo, J. T. (1986). The elaboration likelihood model of persuasion. In L. Berkowitz (Ed.), *Advances in experimental social psychology* (Vol. 19, pp. 123–205). New York: Academic Press.
Rabin, M. (1998). Psychology and economics. *Journal of Economic Literature, 36*, 11–46.
Ratchford, B. T. (2001). The economics of consumer knowledge. *Journal of Consumer Research, 27*, 397–411.
Read, D., & Van Leeuwen, B. (1998). Predicting hunger: The effects of appetite and delay on choice. *Organizational Behavior and Human Decision Processes, 76*, 189–205.
Rizzo, M. J., & Whitman, G. (2008). The knowledge problem of new paternalism. New York University: Law & Economics Working Paper 08-60.
Rogers, T., & Bazerman, M. (2008). Future lock-in: Future implementation increases selection of "should" choices. *Organizational Behavioral and Human Decision Processes, 106*(1), 1–20.
Rogers, T., Milkman, K. L., & Bazerman, M. (2007). *I'll have the ice cream soon and the vegetables later: Decreasing impatience over time in online grocery stores.* Boston: HBS working paper.
Ross, W. T., & Simonson, I. (1991). Evaluations of pairs of experiences: A preference for happy endings. *Journal of Behavioural Decision Making, 4*, 273–282.
Samuelson, W., & Zeckhauser, R. (1988). Status quo bias in decision making. *Journal of Risk and Uncertainty, 1*, 7–59.
Shampanier, K., Mazar, N. & Ariely, D. (2007). Zero as a special price: The true value of free products. *Marketing Science, 26*(6), 742–757.
Sherman, S. J., & McConnell, A. R. (1996). The role of counterfactual thinking in reasoning. *Applied Cognitive Psychology, 10*, 113–124.
Shiller, R. J. (2000). *Irrational exuberance.* Princeton: Princeton University Press.
Shugan, S. M. (1980). The cost of thinking. *Journal of Consumer Research, 7*, 99–111.
Simon, H. A. (1959). Theories of decision-making in economics and behavioral science. *American Economic Review, 49*, 253–283.
Simon, H. A. (1982). *Models of bounded rationality.* MIT Press: Cambridge, MA.
Simonson, I. (1989). Choice based on reasons: The case of attraction and compromise effects. *Journal of Consumer Research, 16* (September), 158–74.
Simonson, I. (1999). The effect of product assortment on buyer preferences. *Journal of Retailing, 75*(3), 347–370.

Simonson, I., & Tversky, A. (1992). Choice in context: Tradeoff contrast and extremeness aversion. *Journal of Marketing Research, 29*, 281–295.

Slovic, P., Fishhoff, B., & Lichtenstein, S. (1978). Accident probabilities and seat belt usage: A psychological perspective. *Accident Analysis and Prevention, 10*(2), 281–285.

Slovic, P., Fishhoff, B., & Lichtenstein, S. (1982). Response mode framing and information processing effects in risk assessment. In R. M. Hogarth (Ed.), *New directions for methodology and social and behavioral science: The framing of questions and the consistency of response* (pp. 21–36). San Francisco: Jossey–Bass.

Smeesters, D., & Mandel, N. (2006). Positive and negative media image effects on the self. *Journal of Consumer Research, 32*, 576–582.

Smith, K., Dickhaut, J, McCabe, K., & Pardo, J. V. (2002). Neuronal substrates for choice under ambiguity, risk, gains, and losses. *Management Science, 48*(6), 711–718.

Stanovich, K. E., & West, R. F. (2000). Individual differences in reasoning: Implications for the rationality debate? *Behavioural and Brain Sciences, 23*(5), 645–665.

Staw, B. M. (1976). Knee-deep in the big muddy: A study of escalating commitment to a chosen course of action. *Organizational Behavior and Human Performance, 16*, 27–44.

Stigler, G. J. (1961). The economics of information. *Journal of Political Economy, 69*(3), 213–225.

Sunstein, C. R. (2003). Terrorism and probability neglect. *Journal of Risk and Uncertainty, 26* (2/3), 121–136.

Taylor, S. E., & Brown, J. D. (1988). Illusion and well-being: A social psychological perspective on mental health. *Psychological Bulletin, 103*(2), 193–210.

Thaler, R. H. (1980). Toward a positive theory of consumer choice. *Journal of Economic Behaviour and Organization, 1*, 39–60.

Thaler, R. H. (1981). Some empirical evidence of dynamic inconsistency. *Economic Letters, 81*, 201–207,

Thaler, R. H. (1985). Mental accounting and consumer choice. M*arketing Science, 4*, 199–214.

Thaler, R. H. (1999). Mental accounting matters. *Journal of Behavioural Decision Making, 12*, 183–206.

Thaler, R. H., & Benartzi, S. (2004). Save more tomorrow: Using behavioral economics to increase employee saving. J*ournal of Political Economy, 112*(1), S164–S187.

Thaler, R. H., & Sunstein, C. R. (2003). Libertarian paternalism. *American Economic Review, 93*(2), 175–179.

Thaler, R. H., & Sunstein, C. R. (2008). *Nudge. Improving decisions about health, wealth and happiness.* London: Penguin Books.

Thornton, B., & Moore, S. (1993). Physical attractiveness contrast effect: Implications for self-esteem and evaluations of the social self. *Personality and Social Psychology Bulletin, 19*, 474–480.

Tversky, A., & Griffin, D. (1991). Endowment and contrast in judgments of well-being. In R. J. Zeckhauser (Ed.), *Strategy and choice* (pp. 297–318). Cambridge, MA: MIT Press.

Tversky, A., & Kahneman, D. (1992). Advances in prospect theory: Cumulative representation of uncertainty. *Journal of Risk and Uncertainty, 5*, 297–323.

Vakratsas, D., & Ambler, T. (1999). How advertising works: What do we really know? *Journal of Marketing, 63*(1), 26–43.

Van Praag, B. M. S., & Frijters, P. (1999). The measurement of welfare and well-being: The Leyden approach. In D. Kahneman, E. Diener, & N. Schwarz (Eds.), *Well-being: The foundations of hedonic psychology* (pp. 413–433). New York: Russell Sage Foundation.

Varian, H. R. (2006). *Intermediate microeconomics: A modern approach.* London: W. W. Norton & Company.

Verhoef, P. C., Antonides, G., & De Hoog, A. N. (2004). Service encounters as a sequence of events: The importance of peak experiences. *Journal of Service Research*, *7*, 53–64.

Weiner, B. (1985). An attributional theory of achievement motivation and emotion. *Psychological Review*, *92*, 548–573.

Weinstein, N. D. (1980). Unrealistic optimism about future life events. *Journal of personality and Social Psychology*, *39*(5), 806–820.

Wilson, T. D., & Schooler, J. W. (1991). Thinking too much: Introspection can reduce the quality of preferences and decisions. *Journal of Personality and Social Psychology*, *60*, 181–192.

Wohl, M. J. A., & Enzle, M. E. (2002). The deployment of personal luck: Illusory control in games of pure chance. *Personality and Social Psychology Bulletin*, *28*, 1388–1397.

Zeelenberg, M., & Pieters, R. (2004). Consequences of regret aversion in real life: The case of the Dutch postcode lottery. *Organizational Behavior and Human Decision Processes*, *93*(2), 155–168.

21

Cross-Cultural Psychology in Applied Settings

Passages to Differences

Kaiping Peng and Susannah B. F. Paletz

During the past 30 years there has been a surge of interest in culture and cultural differences among psychologists, including applied psychologists. From our perspective, the cross-cultural psychology movement started with a desire to reclaim "culture" from its most popular working definitions in terms of "country" or "racial grouping" (Peng, Ames, & Knowles, 2001; Nisbett, Peng, Choi, & Norenzayan, 2001; Norenzayan, Choi, & Peng, 2007). Any nonmental facts such as geographical location or even the biological dispositions of members of the community can be meaningful only because they bear on mental events. Nationality or race may be psychologically relevant because they are enmeshed in a mental world of belief, value, attitude, and human actions, resulting in and being influenced by varying institutions, social structures, artifacts, and tools. In fact, psychological mental activities, such as desire, choice, judgment, decision making, communication, conflict resolution, competition, and cooperation are what really make important social science concepts—nationality, race, ethnicity, class, gender, sexual orientation—meaningful to individuals. Thus, cross-cultural psychology is the study of the way the human mind can be transformed, given shape and definition, and made functional in a number of different ways that are not uniformly distributed across cultural communities around the world (Schweder & Bourne, 1994).

Cross-cultural psychology has also emerged as an important field of applied psychological research as more and more studies have found that theories of psychology developed in the West and thought to be universal do not generalize well to other cultures. Grounded in a conception that mind and culture are mutually constituted, research in this field strives both to identify the effects of culture on the mind and

IAAP Handbook of Applied Psychology, First Edition. Edited by Paul R. Martin, Fanny M. Cheung, Michael C. Knowles, Michael Kyrios, Lyn Littlefield, J. Bruce Overmier, and José M. Prieto.

the effects of the mind on culture. It includes theories and debates about the forms of cultures themselves (e.g., individualism–collectivism) and how different cultures create differences in how we judge cause (e.g., attributions to forces internal vs. external to the individual), conceive of ourselves (e.g., independent of vs. interdependent with others), reason (analytic vs. holistic reasoning) and even perceive the world (e.g., what one attends to and remembers from a scene). Thus far, the most common comparisons have been between East Asian (Korean, Japanese, and Chinese) and European–American participants, from which researchers have discovered profound cultural differences in many seemingly basic social psychology findings. This is not to say East–West differences are the only ones examined: There has been research on other cultures, ethnicities, and nationalities, both subcultures within Eastern and Western countries (e.g., African Americans) as well as on members of cultures within Africa and Latin America (e.g., Morelli, Rogoff, & Angelillo, 2003, see also Smith, Bond, & Kağitçibaşi, 2006). For this review, however, we will focus on East–West differences. Much of this research has implications for how people from different cultures will behave in their everyday social contexts. As countries become more multicultural and trade and communication between nations becomes more common, the interaction between different cultural norms and psychological orientations will become more and more important.

In the field of cross-cultural psychology, there are two theoretical approaches that generate much of the debates and empirical studies. One is the notion of individualism–collectivism and the other is the holistic versus analytic cognitive orientations. Both approaches have specific predictions about possible behavioral differences between people of Eastern and Western cultural traditions and therefore indicate road maps of possible differences in cross-cultural applied settings such as business, law, politics, and international relations. Since we believe that cross-cultural psychology is not merely a content area of applied psychology but a unique approach, we are going to discuss the possible points of entry where cross-cultural contexts may be important to applied research. Hence, this article is not a review of all cross-cultural work in different applied settings, but a theoretical discussion of possible differences across all settings, particularly between cultures of the West (North America and Western Europe) and cultures of the East (East Asia).

Foundational Theories of Cross-Cultural Psychology

One of the most influential applied psychological studies examining cultural differences was Hofstede's (1980, second edition in 2003) massive study across IBM. Hofstede kept the organization under constant review and surveyed individuals in similar occupations across 50 countries between 1967 and 1978. By aggregating across nations, Hofstede determined four culture-level attributes. As behavior on the job is tightly constrained by occupational culture and technology, this was an effective method of teasing out national culture. Hofstede's (1980, 1983) four dimensions were individualism–collectivism, power distance, uncertainty avoidance, and masculinity–femininity.

Individualism–collectivism

Individualism–collectivism has since been conceptualized as two possibly compatible separate dimensions (Triandis, 1990, 1995). Furthermore, they may exist within the same person at different times or within cultures where one dominates (see Li & Aksoy, 2007). Individualism includes a focus on individual autonomy, self-determination, and efficacy; collectivism entails a focus on one's place within a social context and duty toward others, particularly in groups. A further iteration of individualism and collectivism incorporates the dimension of power distance to distinguish between horizontal and vertical individualism and collectivism (Li & Aksoy, 2007; Triandis & Gelfand, 1998). Horizontal individualism focuses on uniqueness and self-reliance, whereas vertical individualism emphasizes competition; horizontal collectivism is focused on pride and cooperation with peers, whereas vertical collectivism emphasizes duties toward those higher in the hierarchy (i.e., parents).

One of the most widely accepted interpretations explaining East–West differences is contrasting cultural conceptions of the person and that person's interdependence versus independence from the social context (Triandis, 1989; Markus & Kitayama, 1991). Markus and Kitayama (1991, similarly to Triandis, 1989) suggest that more individualistic cultures lead individuals to develop a more independent conception of the self, whereas collectivistic cultures lead individuals to develop a more *inter*dependent (connected with others, overlapping with others) conception of the self. For instance, while Americans on average assume that individual character is fixed and the social world is fluid, the Chinese on average assume individual character is fluid and the social world is fixed. Thus, in general, Asians have a stronger sense of collective autonomy, rather than the individual autonomy that governs American social thinking. Because Americans believe in individual autonomy and that individual character is fixed, they will be more likely to perceive the individual as a consistent explanation for behavior, rather than the situation. This tendency—to blame the behavior of strangers, particularly negative behavior, on individual character—has been previously termed the fundamental attribution error because it was so consistently shown. Morris and Peng (1994) found that this fundamental attribution error is particularly prevalent among Caucasian Americans, the participants in those earlier studies, and less prevalent among East Asians.

These cultural conceptions were probably influenced by the sociological and religious history of the cultures. Individualism in American culture is possibly rooted in the Judeo-Christian notion of the individual soul, and collectivism in Chinese culture is possibly rooted in Confucian precepts about the primacy of social relations and the virtue of role-appropriate behavior. While there has been some debate as to whether there is truly any empirical evidence to support the interdependent/independent self model (Matsumoto, 1999), this tradition and model remains quite influential in psychology today (Smith, Bond, & Kağitçibaşi, 2006).

Empirical evidence has substantiated this difference in perception of agency. For example, studies have shown that Asians may be just as susceptible to the fundamental attribution error when asked to examine a group entity rather than an individual. Even more interestingly, this aspect of attribution has been tested with nontransparent methods, or methods that participants do not consciously associate with social or cultural topics, such as perceptions of animal behavior. Morris and Peng's (1994) study featured designed animations of fish in which an individual fish swam in a different path from a group of fish. In explaining this behavior, Chinese participants attributed it less to the internal disposition of the fish and more to the group factors than did American participants. In fact, when asked "how does the individual fish feel?" neither group had trouble responding (e.g., lonely). However, when asked "how does the group of fish feel?" Chinese had no trouble responding (e.g., arrogant), but Americans had great difficulty in answering the question, showing confusion. Some subjects even asked, "What do you mean? Do you mean that blue fish there, or that pink fish?" pointing to an individual fish in the group, indicating an individual-centered perception.

Holistic and analytic orientations

In the past few years, research has delved into Eastern and Western cultural approaches to human thinking and cognition (Nisbett et al., 2001; Peng et al., 2001). The intellectual histories of East Asia and Europe are consistent with some differences in the two cultures' cognitive orientations. Western educational principles, assumptions about the mind, and philosophy originated with the ancient Greeks. The relevant parts of this perspective, which flourished during the Enlightenment, held an *analytic* stance, focusing on categorizing an object with reference to its attributes and explaining its behavior using rules about its category memberships. Ancient Chinese philosophy had a *holistic* stance, in which it examined the field in which the object was found and explained its behavior in terms of its relationship with the field. These differing intellectual approaches were manifested in differences in ancient Greek and Chinese science and mathematics. Ancient Greek scientists tended to see the behavior of objects as being exclusively due to the attributes of the object, as in Aristotelian physics. Thus, an ancient Greek would say that a stone drops in water because it has the property of gravity, whereas a piece of wood floats on water because it has the property of levity. Ancient Chinese physics was more similar to Galilean physics, which recognized that the behavior of objects is the result of an interaction between the object and the environment. Thus, whether a stone sinks or wood floats is not explainable by the objects' innate characteristics, but rather by their interactions with water.

Holistic thought is an orientation to the context or field as a whole, including attention to relationships between a focal object and the field and a preference for explaining and predicting events on the basis of such relationships. Holistic approaches are dialectical, meaning that there is an emphasis on change, a recognition of contradiction and the need for multiple perspectives, and a search for the "middle way" between opposing propositions (Peng & Nisbett, 1999). Eastern dialectical thinking accepts contradictory positions within the same person or situation. This stems from the belief that the world is in constant flux, and that the part cannot be understood except in relation to the whole. This cultural tendency helps explain why East Asians demonstrate less fundamental attribution error, because they perceive a person as operating in a larger context or field, and will try to understand his actions within that context.

This difference in thinking is demonstrated in research on the two cultures' attitudes towards psychological contradiction: people from East Asian cultures are more comfortable with contradictions than are Americans, reflected in examples of Chinese folk wisdom such as "beware of your friends, not your enemies" and "too humble is half proud." This difference in thinking has particular salience in the legal field when it is applied to social contradictions, or conditions in which two parties or two aspects of a social system are in conflict with each other. In one study, Peng and Nisbett (1999, 2000) demonstrated how different ways of thinking naturally suggest different forms of conflict resolution. The study presented two everyday-life scenarios to American and Chinese participants, one involving a mother–daughter conflict. Participants were asked to write down what they thought about these conflicts, explain their origin, and offer a resolution. Dialectical responses generally do not find exclusive fault with one side or the other. Chinese participants were much more likely to give dialectical responses, which attributed the cause of the problem to both sides and attempted to reconcile the contradiction. Seventy-two percent of the responses given by Chinese participants were dialectical, such as "both the mothers and daughters have failed to understand each other," whereas only 26% of the American responses were dialectical. Seventy-four percent of the responses given by Americans were non-dialectical, such as "mothers have to recognize daughters' rights to their own values."

The "holistic" and "analytic" modes of thought have also been shown to affect preferred modes of reasoning, in particular preferences for logical and intuitive reasoning. In a series of studies that pitted formal logic against intuitive reasoning, Ara Norenzayan and colleagues (Norenzayan et al., 2002) found that when an intuitive response based on experience and context was at odds with a logical or rule-based response, Koreans preferred the intuitive responses. However, when given purely abstract logic problems, there was no difference between the abilities of Korean and American students. Koreans were more "thrown off" by implausible conclusions of correct logical arguments than Americans and were more likely to say that logically valid arguments were ***invalid*** when the conclusion was implausible. They were also more likely to find valid arguments to be more convincing if they involved typical examples of categories.

Practical Implications of the Differences

The basic questions facing human beings are justice (what is right or wrong), nature (cause and effect of everything), and other people (how to deal with them), as well as the way we deal with them, such as judgment, choice, and actions. Foundational questions for applied psychology are actually about these basic questions almost all societies face.

Practical question 1: How to judge right and wrong?

Shweder and colleagues have proposed that there are at least three "codes of ethics" that coexist at different levels of emphasis in different communities. The *ethic of autonomy*, probably the most common among American academics and the basis of American law, stresses justice and individual freedom from interference: Harming or infringing upon the rights of other individuals is seen as the marker of immorality and injustice, and may induce feelings of anger. Another common ethic is the *ethic of community*, which stresses individual obligations to fulfill certain roles and duties; failure to fulfill interpersonal obligations is seen as immoral, and induces feelings of contempt. A third ethic is the *ethic of divinity*. This ethic responds to a sense or belief that there is a "natural order of things" that is sacred; actions that cause impurity or degradation of oneself or others, or disrespect to transcendental authority(/ies), are seen as immoral, and induce feelings of disgust.

Past moral development research in the US primarily focused on an abstract *ethic of autonomy* as the pinnacle of moral development, but cultural psychological research has shown that abstract moral principles based on the other ethics are more important in other cultures. For example, research comparing Hindu Indians and European Americans showed that interpersonal obligations, even to strangers, were seen in much stronger moral terms by Indians than by Americans, and were even seen as legitimately *regulated* actions. Moreover, when interpersonal obligations (e.g., getting to a friend's wedding) and justice violations (e.g., having to steal a train ticket to get there) were placed in opposition, Indians found the interpersonal obligations to have much greater moral weight than did Americans. Importantly, researchers have found cultural differences *among* Americans when justifying their views on politically charged issues such as suicide or divorce. For example, members of fundamentalist Baptist sects prefer arguments based on the ethic of divinity, whereas members of progressive sects were more likely to use an ethic of autonomy principles to defend their more liberal views. When laws and public conceptions of morality are different, the viability of the legal system may be undermined. The coexistence of these sometimes conflicting moral codes in different communities offers insight into current political debates, and promises to continue to affect inter- and intra-national debates on laws in the future. For example, the debate over same-sex marriage may be seen as a conflict between a specific ethic of divinity and the ethic of autonomy (or even the ethic of community).

Haidt and colleagues (1993) found universal affective reactions to harmless immoral behaviors, such as lying to dying mothers and disrespecting cultural icons. Interestingly, Haidt's data also showed that collectivistic South Americans are more likely to use moral judgments whereas individualist Americans are more likely to use neutral matter of fact judgments in evaluating such behaviors. Miller (1994) found that Asian moral judgments are based on relational factors or duty rather than on individual rights or harm to others. Haidt and Miller's findings seem to suggest that, because collectivist people will likely focus on the relational experience of a contractual interaction, moral codes governing relational conduct will be provoked in contract understanding among collectivistic people.

Cross-cultural psychologists have also examined conceptions of justice and fairness. Tyler, Lind and their colleagues suggest that Asian views of justice are more relational and Americans are more procedural. In the same tradition, Triandis (1995) and Leung and Bond (1984) argue that collectivist societies emphasize equality in fairness distributions whereas individualist societies emphasize equity in the allocation of justice. Licht, Goldschmidt, and Schwartz (2007) applied a cultural model to examine the interaction between corporate governance and value categories, and found that they are related in significant ways. Levinson and Peng (2003) examined the cultural psychological differences underlying tort law's causation inquiry, highlighting how laypeople's culturally variant causal attributions and fairness judgments often do not match American law's inquiry. Despite this progress, the nature and differences of justice and fairness in different cultures is still poorly understood.

Practical question 2: How to judge cause and responsibility?

There is much evidence that causal attributions between the East Asians and North American are different in fundamental ways. Morris and Peng (1994) and Lee, Hallahan, and Herzog (1996) have showed that Americans explain murders and sports events respectively by invoking presumed dispositions of the individual, whereas Chinese and Hong Kong citizens explain the same events with reference to contextual factors. Correspondingly, Peng and Knowles (2003) found that Chinese students are more likely to explain physical events on the basis of factors external to the object than Americans. In some of their experiments, Chinese students with no formal physical training were more likely to perceive causality to originate externally to the target object (e.g., gravity, medium, friction, field), whereas Americans referred to causes internal to the object (e.g., shape, weight, inertia).

Norenzayan, Choi and Nisbett (2002) found that Korean participants were more responsive to contextual factors when making predictions about how people in general would be expected to behave in a given situation and, much more than American participants, made use of their beliefs about situational power when making predictions about the behavior of a particular individual. Importantly, Norenzayan et al. (2002) found that Koreans and Americans endorsed beliefs about the causes of behavior that accorded with their explanations and predictions. Koreans placed more credence in situational theories than did Americans. Choi and Nisbett (1998) found similar results when they examined circumstances in which both Americans and Koreans mistakenly attributed behavior to the dispositions of a target actor. Koreans were much more willing to revise their mistaken inferences about dispositions than Americans.

Sensitivity to the role of contextual factors, and attention to the field, may have their drawbacks. In a series of experiments, Choi and Nisbett (2000) found that Koreans were more susceptible to the *hindsight bias*, that is, the tendency to believe that one could have predicted some outcome that in fact one could not have predicted. Choi and Nisbett argued that the Asians' greater susceptibility to this bias might be due to a tendency to attend more to contextual factors and to a tendency to causally model events less explicitly.

Through the course of hundreds of years of practice, the American law of contracts has attempted to come up with a fair, predictable way to deal with contractual interactions, particularly with respect to contract formation. These laws often rely on citizens as jury members to determine whether the parties entered into a contract in the first place. But do we, as laypeople, understand contracts and contract formation in ways consistent with these laws? Psychological research on responsibility attribution

(Piaget, 1932/1965; Heider, 1958), moral judgment (Haidt et al., 1993; Miller et al., 1994) and culturally influenced cognitions (Peng, Ames, & Knowles, 2001; Nisbett et al., 2001) leads us to examine empirically people's judgments of intent, morality, responsibility, and character as we strive to understand the psychological processes underlying perceptions of contractual behavior. It even allows us to examine how much morality, intent, and other factors affect laypeople's contract judgments across cultures. After all, contract law—contract formation in particular—relies on culture (Mautner, 2002).

Beyond the legal domain, these different conceptions of responsibility and justice may have implications for the workplace. Different conceptions of fairness and responsibility may lead to different assumptions regarding reward allocation, depending on both individualism–collectivism and power distance dimensions (Erez, 1997). Extrinsic rewards are a fundamental part of the working domain. If salary, benefits, and bonuses are assigned by equity versus equality when the other is expected, people may feel unfairly rewarded. This is something that multinational companies and people working abroad need to keep in mind.

Practical question 3: How to judge others' intents and responsibilities?

Closely related to questions of causality are judgments of intent and responsibility. This reliance on intentionality has clear psychological roots. Intentionality has been the cornerstone of "theory of mind" research in developmental psychology (Leslie, 1995; Gopnik & Meltzoff, 1997, Wellman, 1990) and is increasingly becoming an important part of attribution theory (e.g., Malle, 1994, 1999; Morris et al., 2001). Notions of intentionality in psychology can even be traced back to Heider's early assertion that intention is the central factor in personal causality (Heider, 1958). Children seem to understand mental states (beliefs, desires, and intents) of other people from a strikingly early age, possibly from birth (e.g., Astington, Harris, and Olson, 1988; Gopnik & Meltzoff, 1997; Perner, 1991; Wellman, 1990). As a result, the function of intentionality judgments has been generally assumed to be universal. However, the process by which people make intentionality judgments, particularly the factors that contribute to people's understanding of intentionality, has not been empirically examined, nor have intentionality judgments been examined empirically across cultures.

A related psychological process is the judgment of responsibility. Piaget (1932/1965) was the first to propose two distinctive criteria in judgments of responsibility. He argued that young children's judgments of responsibility are a function of the amount of harm done to other people, which he labeled as the "objective responsibility rule". Over the course of individual development, people learn to incorporate mental state information into responsibility judgments, coming to hold people responsible only for the outcomes they intended, which he labeled as "subjective responsibility." Heider (1958) proposed five levels of responsibility attribution: association, causality, foreseeability, intention and justification (Hamilton & Sanders, 1992), by which people display different levels of "sophistication" in responsibility judgments. Both Piaget and Heider seem to suggest that internal mental state judgments (e.g., of intention) are more important than pure association judgments or judgments regarding consequences in responsibility attributions. These studies suggest that the standard of judging intentions may be psychologically related to the overall notion of contracts—that someone should be held responsible for complying with their bargains.

However, cross-cultural studies on lay conceptions of justice may challenge the views of Piaget and Heider. In their expansive study of culture and moral judgment, Hamilton and Sanders (1992) found that Japanese judgments of responsibility and punishment were less sensitive to intention information than were American judgments. They attributed this diminishing role of intention in responsibility judgments to the greater impact of "relational" factors among Japanese, including the role of relationships, hierarchical distinctions, and solidarity between perpetrators and victims. This cultural explanation fits nicely into existing scholarship in cultural psychology indicating that Japanese culture tends to be more relational, collective, and interdependent, while American culture tends to be more individualistic and independent (Triandis, 1995; Markus & Kitayama, 1991). These studies on the importance of relational factors in Asian cultures indicate that a collectivist understanding of contracts may focus more on the relationship between contracting parties and less on the parties' individual intents in contract formation.

Practical question 4: How to deal with uncertainty and predict the future?

Estimates of probability and perceptions of the future have implications not only for economic judgments (e.g., stock assessments), but also for business decisions by managers. In 1977, Phillips and Wright (1977, also Wright & Phillips, 1980) carried out an interesting cross-cultural comparison between Chinese and British participants on probability judgment, such as questions like "Which river is longer: the Yangtze River or the Mississippi River?" They found that British people had a greater tendency to view the world in terms of uncertainty than did Hong Kong Chinese. British people were more likely to ascribe different degrees of uncertainty to events, and could then express the uncertainty as a numerical probability in response to general knowledge questions. The Chinese, on the other hand, were more likely to make extreme probability estimations (e.g., "100%" or "no chance"). These findings have been confirmed by more recent experiments undertaken with students in the United States, Japan, China, and many other Asian countries and regions by Yates and his colleagues (Yates et al., 1989; Yates, Lee, & Shinotsuka, 1996). This finding has implications for assessment and testing: If an American or British-derived exam involving probability assumes certain kinds of answers are the norm, then people from different cultures may be penalized for following a different norm regarding probability statements.

Phillips and Wright (1977) suggested that an individual's world view of causality influences his or her tendency to adopt probabilistic thinking. They distinguished a Laplacean worldview and a fatalistic worldview, and suggested that British people are more familiar with the Laplacean view that events do not just happen through the action of mysterious forces, but are caused by previous events acting according to natural laws that can be discovered by systematic investigation and inquiry. On the other hand, most of the Hong Kong Chinese tended to accept a fatalistic view. The British (Laplacean) probabilistic worldview, it was argued, tends to cultivate probabilistic thinkers, while the Hong Kong Chinese fatalistic worldview, in contrast, tends to foster nonprobabilistic thinkers. Holding this worldview, Hong Kong Chinese are more likely to accept uncertainty even at the risk of contradiction, but not to make fine differentiation between uncertainties.

Yates and his colleagues (1996) proposed an alternative explanation for the overconfidence phenomenon in probability judgments among Chinese on general knowledge questions. They suggested that the problem with Chinese participants' overconfidence in judgments about probability is that they usually generate fewer counterarguments for their judgments. According to the "argument recruitment model" described by Yates, Lee, & Shinotsuka (1996), when a person is confronted with a general knowledge question, the person first tries to bring to mind (or "recruit") arguments for and against each of the possibilities being considered, and then evaluates the relative strengths of the arguments. If the arguments generally favor one particular option, that alternative is selected as the correct one. The more heavily the arguments favor that option, the greater is the probability that the given alternative is correct. The Asian overconfidence may arise from the fact few counterarguments are generated for the questions (or propositions in general). Such a culture-specific characteristic may have roots in Chinese educational practices. In Chinese classrooms, teachers do not encourage questions or criticisms of textbooks and lectures, whereas the development of critical thinking is central to the ideology of American education (Yates, Lee, & Shinotsuka, 1996; Lee, Yates, Shinotsuka, Singh, Onglatco, Yen, Gupta, & Bhatnagar, 1995).

In a series of studies, Ji, Nisbett, & Su (2001) examined how beliefs about stability and change among North Americans and Asians affect their prediction of future events. They described various current states and asked whether participants thought the state would continue or change. For example, participants were told about a man who grew up in a poor family, and they were asked to predict whether he would remain poor in adulthood or grow rich one day. For each of four events, Chinese were more likely than Americans to think that the future would be different from the past. Ji and colleagues also presented participants with alleged recent trends in world events that participants were unlikely to have direct knowledge of, for example, participants were told that the world's economy has been growing in the last decade, and were asked to predict whether this trend would go up, go down, or remain the same. Chinese participants were more likely to predict that the next step would halt or reverse the direction of change, whereas Americans were more likely to predict that the trend would continue in a linear fashion. In one study, Chinese participants were more likely to predict reversals of trends in all but 1 of 12 cases (Ji et al, 2001).

Practical question 5: How to avoid dangers?

Related to assessments of the future and uncertainty, the current worldwide economic recession illustrates an important practical question: how to control risk? Risk perception is a specific form of probability judgments. In a series of studies, Weber and Hsee (1999; Hsee & Weber, 1999; Weber, Hsee, & Sokolowska, 1998) have examined American and Chinese cultural differences in risk preference (e.g., choosing between a smaller sure gain option versus a larger risky option). Contrary to the predictions of American and Chinese participants and popular stereotypes, Weber and Hsee found that Chinese were more risk-seeking and Americans were more risk-averse in their financial decisions. However, this difference was specific to the financial domain. In the social domain, the pattern was reversed, with Chinese being less risk-seeking. Congruent cultural differences also emerged when the authors analyzed the risk-seeking (or risk-avoiding) advice implied in Chinese and American proverbs.

Hsee and Weber (1999) propose a "cushion hypothesis," according to which people living in a collectivistic society (such as China) are more likely to receive financial help when in need than people living in an individualistic society (such as America). In a sense, a collectivist social order provides a "mutual insurance" or "cushion" against financial losses. As a result, Chinese perceive the same financial situation as being less risky than Americans. However, the same collectivist cushion that protects the Chinese from financial loss cautions them from taking social risks, as interpersonal harmony is of paramount importance in a collectivist society. In further support of this hypothesis, Hsee and Weber found that the cultural difference in risk preference in the financial domain was mediated by the larger size and better quality of the Chinese participants' social networks. The cultural difference was also found to result from different perceptions of the riskiness of the options, not from different risk–value tradeoffs (Hsee & Weber, 1999).

Practical question 6: How important are choices and autonomy?

It is a fundamental notion in Western psychology that people make choices every day and that these choices make up the narrative history of a person. Choice and autonomy are particularly important in the context of work. A growing body of cross-cultural research, however, suggests that strong desires for choice or control are not necessarily equally important to all. Choice or control does not necessarily increase performance or well being among people of different cultures.

In an experiment performed by Ji, Peng, and Nisbett (2000), Asian and Euro-Americans were given a series of covariation tests and the Rod-and-Frame test. They found, in general, that East Asians do worse on those tests than Euro-Americans when they have many choices, and reported less confidence in their self-evaluation of their own performances.

Iyengar and Lepper (1999) performed an experiment where Asian-American and Euro-American children played a computer game in which they had to solve arithmetic problems to send an animated rocket into outer space. In one condition, students could choose most of the game's optional settings, like the color of the space ship, the name of the astronaut and so forth. In another condition, the students were told that their mothers had been contacted and had configured the settings in a way they thought best for them. In the condition where their mothers chose the settings, Asian Americans' performance was better than in the personal choice condition, while European Americans did worse. Having control over peripheral "aesthetic" features of the situation improved the performance of European Americans but diminished that of Asian-American children. In another study, the researchers gave American, Chinese, and Japanese children anagrams to solve. In one condition the children got to decide for themselves which type to solve; in another, their mothers chose the type to solve. Again, American children did better when they chose for themselves, while Asian children did better when their mothers made the choice. Iyengar, when she began researching attitudes of Japanese and Chinese factory workers compared to Anglo-Americans in the US, found it difficult to have a conversation about choice with East Asians, and equally difficult to have a conversation with Americans about the need for group harmony. When asked to catalogue the number of choices made during the day, Americans reported 50% more than East Asians. And when asked to enumerate occasions when they would wish never to have a choice, 30% of Americans said that they could not imagine such a situation, while none of the Asians felt that way. There are within cultures ethnic differences as well. Iyengar found, in her ongoing research at Citigroup, that having the ability to choose when to take work breaks and how to perform one's job predicts employee satisfaction and enhanced performance among Anglo-Americans and African-Americans, but has no such relevance to Asian-American and Latin American employees. She also found that Americans performed better and were more satisfied with work activities they chose to do, while Asians tended to be more satisfied and performed better on tasks that trusted others, like well-regarded managers, have chosen for them.

Briley, Morris, and Simonson (2000) asked participants to choose among three consumer products that bore the following relation to one another: product A was superior to products B and C on one dimension and product C was superior to products A and B on a second dimension. In a control condition, Chinese and American participants were equally likely to choose product B, which was intermediate on both dimensions. In an experimental condition, participants had to justify their choices. This prompted the Americans to go for one of the more extreme choices, either A or C, which could be justified by the invocation of a single principle. In contrast, it caused the Chinese to be more inclined to choose the intermediate object, which they justified by saying that both dimensions were important.

Practical question 7: How to resolve conflicts and differences?

There is a long tradition for Chinese not to engage in debates and formal argumentation about absolute truth and conflict (e.g., Becker, 1986; Nakamura, 1964/1985). When Peng presented two types of arguments—logical linear and dialectical compromising—to Chinese and American students, the Chinese preferred the compromising arguments to the linear arguments. The two logical arguments were much superior in terms of sophistication, including Galileo's famous discussion concerning the falsity of Aristotle's assumption that a heavier object falls to the ground first, and David Hume's argument for the existence of God (adapted from Fisher, 1988). Two parallel dialectical arguments were generated to argue the same positions but applying the principle of holism. The participants were instructed to read these two types of arguments, A and B, for each topic, then to answer the following two questions:

(1) "Which argument is more persuasive (convincing) to you personally, A or B?" and (2) "Which argument do you like more, A or B?"

The results indicated that the Chinese participants preferred dialectical arguments more than did Americans, and found them generally more persuasive and likable. This cultural difference may explain the famous "Needham's paradox" in the history of physical science (Capra, 1975; Needham, 1962; Zukav, 1979). Needham's paradox is the question as to why the Chinese did not develop the modern physics of electromagnetism or quantum physics despite their rich concepts concerning "field" and "force over distance." One possibility is that naive dialectical thinking restricts any reductive, analytic, logical, or personal quests for a discrete true understanding of nature and the world. The finding is also consistent with the Chinese practice of polytheism (whereas Americans embrace monotheism) and the lack of religious wars like the Crusades or Jihads in Chinese history.

Cross-cultural comparisons of indigenous preferences for conflict resolution methods have also shown strong cultural variations with Asians typically favoring harmony-seeking procedures (Leung, 1987; Leung & Lind, 1986; Ohbuchi & Takahashi, 1994). Peng and Nisbett (1999) found that most of the American participants' resolutions of contradictions in everyday life were noncompromising, blaming one side for the problems, demanding changes from one side to attain a solution, and offering no compromise in dealing with interpersonal conflicts. In contrast, most of the Chinese responses were much more dialectical, usually blaming both sides and preferring a compromise approach to resolve the contradictions.

As Peng and Nisbett point out, both ways of thinking have their own flaws. For example, dialectical thinking tends to accept too much at face value, fail to generate counterarguments for a statement, and try to reconcile opposing views even when one viewpoint is inferior in terms of the evidence supporting it. They conclude that both ways of thinking have their strengths in different areas. The logical ways of dealing with contradiction demonstrated in Western thinking may be optimal for scientific exploration and the search for facts because of their aggressive, linear, and argumentative style. In fact, in Westerners, naive dialectical thinking seems to hurt problem finding, a type of creativity, particularly in low-contradiction problems (Paletz & Peng, 2009). However, "dialectical reasoning may be preferable for negotiating intelligently in complex social interactions" (Peng & Nisbett, 1999, p. 751). These complex social interactions are precisely the content of legal disputes. If Eastern holistic thinking is a more effective approach to understanding social behavior, then this supports the use of mediation, because mediation attempts to find a consensus between contradictory positions.

It is not surprising to learn that Asian cultures have a history of using mediation as the preferable form of dispute resolution. Mediation is the cornerstone of dispute resolution in China. The philosophy ruling China's dispute resolution is "first decide, then try." Approximately 70% of all cases in China are settled by mediation rather than legal judgments. Recently, Singapore formally reformed its judicial system to emphasize mediation, and lawyers touted it as "one of the best reforms" in Singapore's legal history. Asian cultures also prefer mediation because it "saves face," since both parties can be winners or share the burden of the loss together. "Nobody wants to lose or be seen to have lost." Because mediation focuses on restoring the relationship between the two parties, reflecting a holistic approach to the conflict, the opportunities for satisfaction on both sides is much greater. Because a mediated settlement is the result of the voluntary agreement of each party, it can only come about if each party believes he has gained something from it.

Other types of cultural norms may have an impact on non-legal conflict situations. Merritt (2000) mostly replicated Hofstede's (1980) four dimensions in a sample of over 9,000 pilots. Individualism–collectivism, power distance, masculinity–femininity, and uncertainty avoidance (particularly individualism–collectivism and power distance) were replicated above and beyond the strong norms of aviation. The implications of this finding revolve specifically around disagreements within the cockpit between pilots of different ranks. Crew (or cockpit) resource management (CRM), a specific pilot training module geared toward increasing the assertiveness of junior pilots in raising problems to senior pilots (who then should heed their juniors), was not as well received outside the United States as expected (Helmreich, Merritt, & Wilhelm, 1999). This is typically considered to be because of national differences in power distance, where CRM is more counternormative in some cultures than others (Helmreich et al., 1999). In some cultures, power distance makes it more difficult for a junior pilot to question the senior pilot, and more likely for a senior pilot to perceive pointed questions as threats. As a response, some airlines have incorporated culture training in their CRM training (Helmreich & Merritt, 1998). Some researchers have recommended that the framing of CRM should be around error management, with error as seen as a universal problem for pilots of any level of hierarchy to avoid, prevent, and mitigate (Helmreich et al., 1999).

Practical question 8: How to work with others?

Successful and appropriate leadership, whether in the cockpit or on the shop floor, is complex, difficult, and vital in all applied settings. Most organizations also require their members to work in teams. Although the antecedents and correlates of successful leadership and teamwork will not be dealt with in detail here, it is important to note that several cross-cultural studies have examined the effect of culture on both concepts.

Culture can have an impact on teamwork and team decision making in both multinational teams (e.g., Ilgen, LePine, & Hollenbeck, 1997) and in differences in teamwork across cultures (e.g., the success of quality circles in Japan and their relative failure in the United States, Erez, 1997). Taking the theme of individualism–collectivism, Earley (1993) found that individualism completely mediated country differences in social loafing. Social loafing, like the fundamental attribution error, is a commonly found effect in the United States. In social loafing, individuals work less hard when they think they are part of a team than when they think they are being evaluated individually. He found it was more prevalent in the United States than in Israel, and more prevalent in Israel than in China, but that the relationship between nationality and social loafing was almost entirely mediated by individualism scores. This is just one of many possible culturally influenced differences in teamwork across nations (Smith, Bond, & Kağitçibaşi, 2006).

In terms of leadership, the GLOBE (Global Leadership and Organizational Behaviour Effectiveness) project has surveyed over 17,000 managers across 62 nations (House et al., 2004). The participants were asked to select traits that they perceived to be associated with effective leaders. The findings were complex: some general patterns were found, as well as differences at the national and organizational level. Some of these differences were in line with Hofstede's dimensions of collectivism and power distance. For example, in-group collectivism at the level of the organization and nation was associated with a preference for charismatic leadership (and at the level of just the organization, a preference for team-oriented leaders), whereas high power-distance organizations and nations had a preference for self-protective leadership styles. A smaller but still impressive study by Smith and colleagues (2002, 2006) asked 7,000 managers in over 40 nations how much they relied on eight different sources for guidance in handling a set of specific work events. Hofstede's dimensions once again were relevant: relying on one's own experience was considered effective in lower power distance nations, whereas reliance on one's peers was considered more effective in collectivistic nations.

Concluding Remarks

This chapter has examined many findings in cross-cultural research and made suggestions about the possible implications for applied psychology. Much of the literature reviewed here focused on cultural differences, but this is not to deny that there are basic, universal, developmental processes. These similar psychological processes, however, must be tested cross-culturally. Possible similarities cannot be assumed and do not preclude the impact of culture on mental processes.

Human psychology takes places in specific cultural contexts. Cultural differences and differences that are created over time tend to be heightened in the applied settings compared to conventional psychological research laboratories. For most of its history, psychology proceeded as if studies and experiments were unrelated to the cultural environment in which the mind developed and functioned. This picture has been changing with the growth of cross-cultural research that investigates the ways by which cultural experiences are implicated in human psychology. Applied settings provide cultural environments to study psychology in real contexts by which inferences can be made about human universals as well as about culture-specific differences. For applied psychology, the cross-cultural psychology research paradigm promises to provide a firmer scientific grounding while encompassing the world's cultural diversity. As a result, cross-cultural psychology and applied psychology make a perfect research couple whose marriage is enhanced by complementarity rather than similarity.

References

Astington, J., Harris, P., & Olson, D. (1988). *Developing theories of mind.* Cambridge University Press.

Becker, C. B. (1986). Reasons for the lack of argumentation and debate in the Far East. *International Journal of Intercultural Relations, 10*, 75–92.

Briley, D., Morris, M., & Simonson, I. (2000). Reasons as carriers of culture: Dynamic versus dispositional models of cultural influence on decision making. *Journal of Consumer Research, 27*(2), 157–178.

Capra, F. (1975) *The Tao of Physics.* New York: Bantam.

Choi, I., & Nisbett, R. E. (1998). Situational salience and cultural differences in the correspondence bias and in the actor–observer bias. *Personality and Social Psychology Bulletin, 24*, 949–960.

Choi, I., & Nisbett, R. (2000). Cultural psychology of surprise: Holistic theories and recognition of contradiction. *Journal of Personality and Social Psychology, 79*(6), 890.

Earley, P. C. (1993). East meets West meets Mideast: Further explorations of collectivistic versus individualistic work groups. *Academy of Management Journal, 36*, 319–348.

Erez, M. (1997). A culture-based model of work motivation. In P. C. Earley & M. Erez (Eds.), *New perspectives on international industrial/organizational psychology* (pp. 193–242). San Francisco, CA: The New Lexington Press.

Fisher, A. (1988). *The logic of real arguments.* Cambridge: Cambridge University Press.

Gopnik, A., & Meltzoff, A. (1997). *Words, thoughts, and theories.* Cambridge, MA: The MIT Press.

Haidt, J., Koller, S., & Dias, M. (1993). Affect, culture, and morality, or is it wrong to eat your dog? *Journal of Personality and Social Psychology, 65*, 613–628.

Hamilton, V. L., & Sanders J. (1992). *Everyday justice*, New Haven, CT: Yale University Press.

Heider, F. (1958). *The Psychology of Interpersonal Relations.* New York: John Wiley and Sons.

Helmreich, R. L., & Merritt, A. C. (1998). *Culture at work in aviation and medicine: National, organizational, and professional influences.* Aldershot, England: Ashgate.

Helmreich, R. L., Merritt, A. C., & Wilhelm, J. A. (1999). The evolution of crew resource management training in commercial aviation. *International Journal of Aviation Psychology, 9*, 19–31.

Hofstede, G. (1980). *Culture's consequences: International differences in work-related values.* Beverly Hills, CA: Sage.

Hofstede, G. (1983). The cultural relativity of organizational practices and theories. *Journal of International Business Studies, 14*, 75–89.

House, R. J., Hanges, P. J., Javidan, M., Dorfman, P.W., Gupta, V., & GLOBE associates (2004). *Leadership, culture, and organizations: The GLOBE study of 62 nations.* Thousand Oaks, CA: Sage.

Hsee, C., & Weber, E. (1999). Cross-national differences in risk preference and lay predictions. *Journal of Behavioral Decision Making, 12*(2), 165–179.

Ilgen, D. R., LePine, J. A., & Hollenbeck, J. R. (1997). Effective decision making in multinational teams. In P. C. Earley & M. Erez (Eds.), *New perspectives on international industrial/organizational psychology* (pp. 377–409). San Francisco, CA: The New Lexington Press.

Iyengar, S., & Lepper, M. (1999). Rethinking the value of choice: A cultural perspective on intrinsic motivation. *Journal of Personality and Social Psychology, 76*, 349–366.

Ji, L., Nisbett, R., & Su, Y. (2001). Culture, change, and prediction. *Psychological Science, 12*(6), 450.

Ji, L., Peng, K., & Nisbett, R. (2000). Culture, control and perception of relations in environment. *Journal of Personality and Social Psychology, 78*, 943–955.

Lee, F., Hallahan, M., & Herzog, T. (1996). Explaining real-life events: How culture and domain shape attributions. *Personality and Social Psychology Bulletin, 22*, 732–741.

Lee, J., Yates, J., Shinotsuka, H., Singh, R., Onglatco, M., Yen, N., et al. (1995). Cross-national differences in overconfidence. *Asian Journal of Psychology, 1*(2), 63–69.

Leslie, A. M. (1995). A theory of agency. In D. Sperber, D. Premack, & A. J. Premack (Eds.), *Causal cognition: A multidisciplinary debate* (pp. 121–141). Oxford: Clarendon Press.

Leung, K., & Bond, M. (1984). The impact of cultural collectivism on reward allocation. *Journal of Personality and Social Psychology, 47*(4), 793–804.

Levinson, J. D., & Peng, K. (2003). Different torts for different cohorts: A cultural psychological critique of tort law's actual cause and foreseeability inquiries. *Southern California Interdisciplinary Law Journal, 13*, 195–226.

Li, F., & Aksoy, L. (2007). Dimensionality of individualism–collectivism and measurement equivalence of Triandis and Gelfand's scale. *Journal of Business and Psychology, 21*, 313–329.

Licht, A. N., Goldschmidt, C., & Schwartz, S. H. (2007). Culture rules: The foundations of the rule of law and other norms of governance. *Journal of Comparative Economics, 35*(4) 659–688.

Malle, B. F. (1994). *Intentionality and explanation: A study in the folk theory of behavior.* Unpublished doctoral dissertation, Stanford University, Stanford, CA.

Malle, B. (1999). How people explain behavior: A new theoretical framework. *Personality and Social Psychology Review, 3*(1), 23.

Markus, H. R., & Kitayama, S. (1991). Culture and the self: Implications for cognition, emotion, and motivation. *Psychological Review, 98*, 224–253.

Matsumoto, D. (1999). Culture and self: An empirical assessment of Markus and Kitayama's theory of independent and interdependent self-construal. *Asian Journal of Social Psychology, 2*, 289–310.

Mautner, M. (2002). Contract, Culture, Compulsion, or: What Is So Problematic in the Application of Objective Standards in Contract Law? *Theoretical Inquiries in Law, 3*(2), 545–575.

Merritt, A. C. (2000). Culture in the cockpit: Do Hofstede's dimensions replicate? *Journal of Cross-Cultural Psychology, 31*, 283–301.

Miller, J. (1994). Cultural diversity in the morality of caring: Individually oriented versus duty-based interpersonal moral codes. *Cross-Cultural Research, 28*(1), 3.

Morelli, G. A., Rogoff, B., & Angelillo, C. (2003). Cultural variation in young children's access to work or involvement in specialized child-focused activities. *International Journal of Behavioral Development, 27*, 264–274.

Morris, M. W., Menon, T., & Ames, D. R. (2001). Culturally conferred conceptions of agency: A key to social perception of persons, groups, and other actors. *Personality and Social Psychology Review, 5*, 169–182

Morris, M., & Peng, K. (1994). Culture and cause: American and Chinese attribution of physical and social events. *Journal of Personality and Social Psychology, 67*, 949–971.

Nakamura, H. (1964/1985). *Ways of thinking of Eastern peoples: India, China, Tibet, Japan.* Honolulu: East-West Center Press.

Needham, J. (1962) *Science and civilisation in China (Volume IV. Physics and physical technology).* Cambridge: Cambridge University Press.

Needham, R. (1972). *Belief, language, and experience.* Chicago: University of Chicago Press.

Nisbett, R. E., Peng, K., Choi, I., & Norenzayan, A. (2001). Culture and systems of thought: Holistic versus analytic cognition. *Psychological Review, 108*, 291–310.

Norenzayan, A., Choi, I., & Nisbett, R. (2002). Cultural similarities and differences in social inference: Evidence from behavioral predictions and lay theories of behavior. *Personality and Social Psychology Bulletin, 28*(1), 109.

Norenzayan, A., Choi, I., & Peng, K. (2007). Cognition and perception. In S. Kitayama & D. Cohen (Eds.), *Handbook of Cultural Psychology* (pp. 569–594). New York: Guilford Publications.

Ohbuchi, K., & Takahashi, Y. (1994). Cultural styles of conflict management in Japanese and Americans: Passivity, covertness, and effectiveness of strategies. *Journal of Applied Social Psychology, 24*(15), 1345–1366.

Paletz, S. B. F., & Peng, K. (2009). Problem finding and contradiction: Examining the relationship between naïve dialectical thinking, ethnicity, and creativity. *Creativity Research Journal, 21*, 139–151.

Peng, K., Ames, D., & Knowles, E. (2001). Culture and human inference. In D. Matsumoto (Ed.) *Handbook of culture and psychology: Perspectives from three traditions.* (pp. 245–264) New York: Oxford University Press.

Peng, K. & Knowles, E. (2003). Culture, education, and the attribution of physical causality. *Personality and Social Psychology Bulletin, 29*, 1272–1284

Peng, K., & Nisbett, R. E. (1999). Culture, dialectics, and reasoning about contradiction. *American Psychologist, 54*, 741–754.

Peng, K., & Nisbett, R. E. (2000). Dialectical responses to questions about dialectical thinking *The American Psychologist, 55*(9), 1067.

Perner, J. (1991). *Understanding the Representational Mind.* Cambridge, MA: MIT Press.

Phillips, L. D., & Wright, G. N. (1977). *Cultural differences in viewing uncertainty and assessing probabilities.* In H. Jungermann & G. de Zeeuw (Eds.), *Decision-making and change in human affairs* (pp. 507–519). Dordrecht: D. Reidel.

Piaget, J. (1932/1965). *The Moral Judgment of the Child.* (M. Gabain, Trans.) New York: Free Press. (Originally published 1932.)

Shweder, R. A., & Bourne, L. (1984). Does the concept of the person vary cross-culturally? In R. A. Shweder & R. A. Levine (Eds.), *Culture theory: Essays on mind, self, and emotion* (pp. 158–199). New York: Cambridge University Press.

Smith, P. B., Bond, M. H., & Kağitçibaşi, Ç. (2006). *Understanding social psychology across cultures: Living and working in a changing world.* London: Sage.

Smith, P. B., Peterson, M. F., & Schwartz, S. H. (2002). Cultural values, sources of guidance and their relevance to managerial behavior: A 47-nation study. *Journal of Cross-Cultural Psychology, 33*, 188–208.

Triandis, H. C. (1989). The self and social behavior in differing cultural contexts. *Psychological Review, 96*, 506–520.

Triandis, H. C. (1990). Cross-cultural studies of individualism and collectivism. In J. J. Berman (Ed.), *Nebraska Symposium on motivation, 1989: Cross-cultural perspectives* (Vol. 37, pp. 41–133). Lincoln, NE: University of Nebraska Press.

Triandis, H. C. (1995). *Individualism and collectivism.* Boulder, CO: Westview Press.

Triandis, H. C., & Gelfand, M. J. (1998). Converging measurement of horizontal and vertical individualism and collectivism. *Journal of Personality & Social Psychology, 74*, 118–128.

Weber, E., & Hsee, C. (1999). Models and mosaics: Investigating cross-cultural differences in risk perception and risk preference. *Psychonomic Bulletin and Review, 6*(4).

Weber, E., & Hsee, C. (1998). What folklore tells us about risk and risk taking: Cross-cultural comparisons of American, German, and Chinese proverbs. *Organizational Behavior and Human Decision Processes, 75*(2).

Wellman, H. (1990). *The child's theory of mind.* Cambridge, MA: MIT Press.

Wright, G. N., & Phillips, L. D. (1980). Cultural variation in probabilistic thinking: alternative ways of dealing with uncertainty. *International Journal of Psychology, 15*, 239–257.

Yates, J. F., Lee, J. W., Shinotsuka, H. (1996). Beliefs about overconfidence, including its cross-national variation. *Organizational Behavior & Human Decision Processes, 65*, 138–147.

Yates, J. F., Zhu, Y., Ronis, D. L., Wang, D. F., Shinotsuka, H., & Toda, M. (1989). Probability judgment accuracy: China, Japan, and the United States. *Organizational Behavior & Human Decision Processes, 43*, 145–171.

Zukav, G. (1979). *The dancing wu li masters: An overview of the new physics.* New York: Morrow.

Part III

Special Topics in Applied Psychology

22

Traffic Psychology
A State-of-the-Art Review

A. Ian Glendon

Extent of the Review

This chapter reviews a sample of refereed journal papers and book chapters on traffic psychology topics published during the years 1998–2008. The start date was the year that the journal *Transportation Research Part F: Traffic Psychology and Behaviour* (*TRF*) was initiated by IAAP's Division 13 inaugural president, Talib Rothengatter who, with other like-minded traffic psychology researchers, desired to see a specialist journal in this field. Talib Rothengatter edited *TRF* until his untimely death early in 2009.

In this chapter "traffic psychology" includes a range of behavioral and statistical approaches, but excludes engineering and environmental orientations. It is primarily concerned with cognitive, social, and behavioral relationships between people and vehicles. I reviewed 1472 empirical articles and chapters with a predominantly psychological or human factors/ergonomics approach. Nearly half (n = 727) were published in *Accident Analysis and Prevention* (*AAP*). Two other journals published large numbers of traffic psychology papers—*TRF* (247) and the *Journal of Safety Research* (*JSR*) (166). Three further journals—*Human Factors* (*HF*) (61), *Ergonomics* (56), and *Safety Science* (*SS*) (37) were also well represented. Fewer papers appeared in *Applied Ergonomics* (9), *Personality and Individual Differences* (9), *Work and Stress* (2), and the *Journal of Environmental Psychology* (2). While every attempt was made to review all empirical papers on traffic psychology published in these sources during the target years, papers on relevant topics that were not included have appeared, inter alia, in journals of experimental psychology, neuroimaging, alcohol and other drug use, and marketing. Only papers published in English-language journals and books were included, introducing a sampling bias.

IAAP Handbook of Applied Psychology, First Edition. Edited by Paul R. Martin, Fanny M. Cheung, Michael C. Knowles, Michael Kyrios, Lyn Littlefield, J. Bruce Overmier, and José M. Prieto.

Book chapters were from volumes devoted to traffic psychology topics with empirical content broadly comparable with refereed journals. Chapters published in the two *Traffic and Transport Psychology* volumes ($n = 82$) (Rothengatter & Huguenin, 2004; Underwood, 2005) were based respectively on papers delivered at the 2000 and 2004 International Conferences on Traffic and Transport Psychology (ICTTP). Chapters (64) in the three *Driver Behaviour and Training* volumes (Dorn, 2003, 2005, 2008) were based on papers presented at contemporaneous eponymous conferences. Hennessey and Wiesenthal (2005) comprised commissioned chapters (10) from traffic psychology researchers. Other chapters on traffic psychology topics published during the target years, reports and other publications in traffic psychology were not reviewed, many of which might differ in their methodology and focus from most journal papers and book chapters. No attempt was made to chart changes over the time period encompassed by this review on the grounds that it is too short to obtain meaningful results.

In the years 1998–2001, there were fewer than 100 traffic psychology publications per year. Between 2002 and 2007, 100–200 publications per annum appeared, while in 2008 there were almost 300 publications. While there is a clear upward trend in published traffic psychology research, it is instructive to examine the literature in disaggregated form in order to understand better how the field is structured and how research is undertaken.

Patterns of Authorship

The mean number of authors per paper was three (range 1–11; mode 2), with well over 4,000 authors represented, not all of whom would acknowledge the label of "traffic psychologist." Many researchers authored multiple papers. As just over 10% of papers in the sample were written by researchers from more than one country, this raises the question of the extent to which this is a truly international field. Of papers coauthored by researchers from more than one country, US researchers tended to coauthor papers with researchers based either in Canada or in a few developing countries. European-based researchers who coauthored papers across countries tended to do so with researchers from other countries in the broad European region—from the Scandinavian countries in the north to Spain, Greece, and Italy in the south, and from the UK and Ireland in the west to Turkey in the east. North American researchers published mainly in *AAP, HF* and *JSR*. European traffic psychologists tended to publish in *TRF, SS* and the books based upon conference papers.

To determine relative contributions of researchers from different countries, one point was allocated to each publication to be shared among all the authors in respect of country of affiliation indicated on the paper and converting these into percentages of the total number of publications. In the few cases where authors reported multiple affiliations, fractions were distributed pro rata. This exercise revealed that researchers from 52 countries published traffic psychology papers during the 11-year period. That these 52 countries are home to 68% of the world's population might suggest that traffic psychology research is an international phenomenon. However, of those occupying the first 20 places on this "league table" only Taiwan and Turkey were not OECD members, suggesting that traffic psychology researchers are overwhelmingly concentrated in relatively developed nations. One perspective on the disparity between countries' relative contributions may be gleaned from the fact that the first three countries on this list (United States, United Kingdom, Australia) contributed 53.74% of publications during the sampled period. The US alone accounted for just over one third of the total. At the other end of the table, the last 14 places were occupied by countries whose contributions were based upon the equivalent of one sole-authored publication or less. Over 100 nations, containing almost one third of the world's population, had no representation at all. These extremes are a reminder of the considerable imbalance between resources available for research between countries. Wealthy nations acting as a magnet for researchers can further increase disparities between developed and developing nations' relative research contributions. However, it also allows the possibility of researchers from developing countries sharing resources with those from wealthier nations to undertake comparative studies, including gathering data from their own countries. There is some evidence that this occurs to a limited extent in traffic psychology.

Taking countries' relative populations into account—in this case by dividing each country's relative contribution to the traffic psychology literature by its percent of the world population, a different pattern emerges. Without implying any political intent in distributing such resources, this might be considered to be a proxy for resources devoted to traffic psychology research as a ratio of population at risk. Half a dozen countries scored particularly highly on this index, with New Zealand, Sweden, Finland, Israel, Australia, and Norway occupying the top six positions—well ahead of the rest of the field. Newcomers to this "top 20" included Bahrain (rank 7), Hong Kong (15), Singapore (16), Qatar (17), and Kuwait (18). Taking population size into account tends to favor relatively smaller countries, which require only a few publications to make the upper reaches of this league table. It also provides a pointer as to where traffic psychology is an emerging field (e.g., some Gulf States). Larger countries tend to score poorly on this measure as they require a much larger proportion of publications to achieve a high ranking. Large developing countries score particularly poorly on this index, perhaps indicating where there is considerable scope for developing traffic psychology (e.g., China, India, Indonesia).

Other ways of indexing a country's performance in a field of scientific endeavor include taking account of per capita income, which could be considered a proxy measure of a country's wealth attributed to research in traffic psychology. With per capita income as the indexing criterion, in this case by dividing the percent of traffic psychology publications by per capita income for each country, the first four rankings revert to their "raw" state, with the list headed again by the United States, United Kingdom, Australia, and Sweden, followed by New Zealand, Canada, and Israel, and the overall pattern very much resembling the raw data ranks.

Given that an ultimate objective of research in this field is to reduce road casualties, it seems appropriate to use at least one road casualty measure. The author data can be indexed by reference to road deaths per 100,000 of population, which could be considered as a proxy measure of the extent to which a country devotes resources to research in traffic psychology in relation to its road death toll—the higher the index the greater the willingness to devote resources to this field of study compared with the "magnitude" of the problem. Obtaining accurate and reliable road casualty data across countries can be problematic, particularly where different reporting and recording systems exist and where a variety of statistical bases are employed to derive published figures. This, together with the small number of publications from many of the countries in the sample, means that only data for OECD countries were considered. Again the rank order, particularly at the top of this table, bears a strong resemblance to the raw figures, reflecting wealthy countries' ability to devote greater resources to both road safety interventions and traffic research. However, it also revealed that even wealthy countries differ considerably in their willingness or ability to fund research in this domain, although it is quite possible that in some countries resources devoted to road safety issues are directed through channels not reflected in publications sampled here. The English-language sampling bias also meant that countries where traffic psychology researchers publish mainly or extensively in non-English-language journals and books were underrepresented in these calculations.

Theoretical Orientations

Theories or models developed specifically to describe driving behavior include Näätänen and Summala's (1976) classic work on zero risk (also Summala & Näätänen, 1988), Heino's (1996) risk perspective exposition, various descriptions of risk homeostasis (also known as "risk compensation" or "target risk" and more generically as "behavioral adaptation"), first introduced into the driving domain by Wilde (1982, 2001), Lajunen's (1997) approach from personality and driving style, Groeger's (2000) cognitive approach, the driver stress model (Matthews, 2001), and task- or threat-oriented approaches (Fuller, 1984, 2005, 2008). However, only a handful of the empirical papers reviewed used any of these models as a conceptual basis. Of the reviewed papers around 15% adopted some recognizable theoretical framework or model as the conceptual basis for their study, while the remaining 85% were driven by data exploration, correlational designs or statistical modeling.

Of the 224 papers that adopted a recognizable conceptual framework around 10% were based on a model originating within traffic psychology (e.g., those listed above)—22 such theories or models were identified. A further 13 theoretical models were derived from other fields and modified for a driving or other road user context. For example, the transactional stress model has been adopted for driving applications. These 35 driving specific and derivative models reflected a broad range of conceptual frameworks for considering driving behavior, incorporating cognitive, visual, behavioral, social, individual, emotional, and human factors approaches, either singly or in some combination. Clearly driving and other road user behavior can be represented across and within multiple conceptual modalities.

A much larger number of papers among those adopting a conceptual basis for their empirical research applied an existing model from the literature to a driving context with little or no modification. These conceptual models took a variety of forms. Those that were essentially cognitive ($n = 28$) included such features as perception, appraisal, attention, memory, processing speed, or decision making. The largest category of theories or models ($n = 67$) were extended cognitive models, for example incorporating additional emotional, attributional, social, human factors, or behavioral components. Other models were derived from the broad social domain (n = 22), including personality/individual differences, developmental and cultural approaches as well as from social psychology. Fourteen models were developed from behavioral, learning or organizational approaches, while eight papers were based upon a miscellany of conceptual approaches.

In summary 174 theories, conceptual frameworks, or models that had some identifiable psychological component or origin were identified. Some two dozen of these frameworks were developed specifically to account for various aspects of driving or road use more generally. About half that number were derived from other psychological domains and applied to driving. Of models or conceptual frameworks that were applied from areas of psychology external to driving or road use, the largest number had a cognitive basis, either exclusively or in augmented form, for example to include social, behavioral or human factors aspects. Some form of augmented cognitive framework represented the largest category of applied conceptual model in the studies reviewed. Within this category the theory of planned behavior (TPB)—including its predecessor, theory of reasoned action (TRA)—and TPB variants was the most frequently adopted conceptual framework. While most of the conceptual frameworks identified appeared in only a single publication, the TPB was identified as the conceptual basis in 33 studies and the TRA in a further five studies.

Conceptual frameworks encompassing social, personality, cultural, and developmental approaches were fairly popular, while those based upon behavioral, learning, or organizational frameworks were also in evidence. Together these conceptual frameworks indicate both the richness and complexity of the subject material of driving and road use more generally, as well as the variety of theoretical and disciplinary backgrounds of those who choose to study this important field within applied psychology.

Methodology and Data

Study designs and data collection methods

The variety of methods available for studying driving behavior and road use more widely was described by Glendon (2007). Study designs and data collection methods described in the 1,472 sampled publications revealed four multiple measure designs—laboratory experiments, field experiments, quasi-experimental and cohort/epidemiological designs, each with a number of variants. However, single-measure cross-sectional designs were the most commonly adopted design for the widely-used questionnaire/survey data collection method. Only 28 studies were classified as either intervention or evaluation studies—less than 2% of publications sampled.

Nine distinct data gathering methods were identified, involving varying levels of participant involvement. At one extreme, mining existing databases (e.g., crash/collision data) required no active "participant" involvement. At the other end of the scale, taking neurological or neurophysiological measures requires a high level of participant agreement. Between these extremes were: indirect and direct observation methods, self-completion instruments, interviews, experimental tasks, simulations, and physical or physiological measures. Each basic method had two or more variants, reflecting the rich diversity of data gathering techniques available to traffic psychologists, as well as their variety of disciplinary backgrounds. There was a strong bias towards quantitative data, with only 27 studies—less than 2% of the sample—using qualitative data gathering as the only or main approach.

Participants

In traffic psychology research, participants can "cooperate" either actively or passively. Active participants agree to be surveyed, tested, or experimented upon, while passive participants' involvement does not require their personal agreement as data are gathered from such sources as anonymous roadside observations, archive data modeling —as in crash statistics—or analyzing data from other secondary sources. In the sampled period, the researchers studied some 875,000 active participants and accessed data on well over 50 million passive participants. Many of the latter were almost certain to have been included in multiple samples, while the real total is considerably larger than this figure, which was compiled only from studies reporting sample sizes—many did not do so. US researchers in particular can access extensive databases from which large samples may be drawn for statistical analysis, such access favoring data-driven modeling or exploratory approaches.

Unsurprisingly, the most commonly studied active road user participants were vehicle drivers or two-wheeled vehicle riders. Participants included 19 categories of car drivers (e.g., commuters, crash-involved, convicted, experienced, inexperienced, alcohol/drug users), 14 varieties of specialist drivers (e.g., bus/coach, commercial, police, taxi), five rider types (e.g., cyclists, motorcyclists), 22 categories of non-drivers—participants recruited for something other than their driving ability, and eight grouped samples (e.g., couples, family dyads, matched samples).

As part of triangulating data in a number of studies, driving-related data were collected or calculated concurrently and analyzed as part of the research study. The 32 categories of concurrent data identified were grouped under six main headings—moving traffic (e.g., traffic flows, driving speeds), geometric/environmental measures (e.g., road width, road curvature), vehicle characteristics (e.g., speed, distance travelled), historical records (e.g., medical), driver characteristics (e.g., mobile/cellular phone use), and crash data (e.g., on-site investigations).

Of the sampled studies, 146 identified secondary data sources used to analyze or model patterns or trends. Nearly half of these used some form of database (e.g., census, vehicle registration data), while the other two main categories were various types of legal and crash databases. In addition to secondary sources of passive participants, 87 studies used information from other sources as research variables. Economic, traffic data and legal indicators headed the list of secondary data sources.

Tests and other instruments used

To collect data on a vast range of variables, 542 tests, questionnaires, and other measures were used in these studies. There were 152 driving-specific measures—the remainder being generic measures. Driving-specific measures could be grouped at three levels. The first level comprised instruments measuring a single entity, such as behavior—either by direct observation (35) or self-reported driving/riding behaviors (7). The greatest variety and depth of measures was at the second level in the cognitive domain (78), in which measures could be classified as assessing knowledge (11), attributions (5), perception (5), attention (4), skills and abilities (4), and attitudes (3). Cognitive measures were also combined with self-reported behavior (3) and observed behavior (1) measures. Where separate cognitive measures were combined with behavioral measures at the third level, the largest number was classified as cognitive/attitudinal along with reported behavior (34)—many driving questionnaires were of this type.

Most of the 13 driving personality measures had an emotion orientation (e.g., driving anger, aggression). Other aspects of driving included self-reported behaviors (8), ergonomic (6), clinical (2), health (1), medical (1), and physical (1).

There was great variety among the 390 nondriving measures. Cognitive measures accounted for 120 of these, distributed among 34 varieties. The most frequently encountered were skills and abilities tests (18), perception measures (11), measures of attention (10) and measures of attitudes and self-reported behaviors (10). The next largest broad category was personality tests (67), many of these addressing emotional aspects (23). This was followed by various measures of vision (48), clinical/diagnostic assessments (38), physiological measures (23), health assessments (21), and organizational measures (11). There were also auditory assessments (7), social measures (7), ergonomic assessments (6), physical measures (6), behaviors that were observed (6) and self-reported (5), medical assessments (5), neurological measures (5), measures of emotions (4), motor skills measures (3), and biographical items (2), plus six unclassified measures.

Data analysis techniques

The rich variety of participant origins, data collection methods, and instruments employed was matched by considerable diversity in data analysis techniques. An initial listing of over 440 techniques identified in the sampled papers was grouped into 19 types, with a residual unclassified category. The main data analysis approaches identified, with numbers of variants and examples of each were: assumption tests (6, e.g., Bartlett's test), data classification (20, e.g., cluster analysis), data reduction (9, e.g., factor analysis), derivative tests (20, e.g., post hoc tests), descriptive (23, e.g., percentages, rates), effect size (12, e.g., odds ratios), event/survival analysis (9, e.g., Cox model), general techniques (26, e.g., sign test, *z*-test), generalized linear modeling—comprising non-GLM regression-based models (82, e.g., binary probit modeling, ordered logit modeling), general linear modeling (GLM) (53, e.g., ANOVA, multivariable regression), non-parametric GLM (12, e.g., Mann-Whitney *U* test), structural equation modeling (GLM) (2, e.g., path analysis), panel generalized linear modeling (9, e.g., multi-level modeling), panel GLM (15, e.g., generalized estimating equations), qualitative (20, e.g., inductive analysis, content analysis), reliability analysis (9, e.g., Cronbach's alpha), spatial analysis (9, e.g., social area analysis), time series analysis (8, e.g., autoregressive integrated moving average models), validity checks (9, e.g., sensitivity analysis—for predictive validity), not otherwise classified (87, e.g., Bayes analysis, Rasch analysis).

Traffic Psychologists' Affiliations

Unlike national-level organizations that represent applied psychologists in many other fields, few national psychology or ergonomics/human factors societies have specialist divisions for traffic psychologists. The prime organization for traffic psychologists is the International Association of Applied Psychology's Division 13—Traffic and Transportation Psychology. Where they belong to national-level bodies, traffic psychologists tend to join specialist organizations, the great majority of whose members represent road safety practitioner and professional groups including engineers, police, driving instructors, government officials at various levels, and human factors specialists. Opportunities exist in these forums for exchanging expertise and jointly conceptualising road safety problems, for example through national conferences and journals.

Further Evidence on Future Directions for Traffic Psychology

Delegates to the fourth International Conference on Traffic and Transport Psychology (Washington, DC, September 2008) provided some information on traffic psychology's immediate future. A conference questionnaire item invited respondents to indicate the direction that research within this field would develop within the next five years. Seventy-five delegates provided 127 interpretable responses, which were coded under six major headings.

The greatest number of responses concerned "Methodology" (33% of responses). The seven subheadings (N responses) were:

- *naturalistic research/observation* (9); studying "naturalistic driving" particularly prominent
- *brain activity* (8); neuroimaging was mentioned most frequently, plus cognitive factors associated with driving
- *interventions* (7); generic and specific intervention examples mentioned
- *greater focus on safety* (7); including addressing organizational aspects of safety related to driving
- *applications (e.g., simulation)* (6); emphasising the importance of applying theoretical and empirical work
- *measurement* (3); including improving existing techniques and developing new measures
- *qualitative* (2); pleas for more qualitative research.

The next category was "Road user groups" (21% of responses), divided into five subcategories:

- *older/less mobile drivers/road users* (12); including general and specific examples
- *younger drivers* (6); including parental involvement
- *commercial vehicle drivers* (4); including reference to rules, training, monitoring, and feedback
- *motorcyclists* (3); training figured prominently here
- *vulnerable road users* (2); generalized responses.

The third heading, "Environmental influences" (18% of responses), had four sub-headings:

- *internal* (8); included role of emotion, alcohol/other drugs, fatigue, and distraction
- *training/education* (8); included evaluation, graduated licensing and customization
- *external* (3); included community influence, external environment, and information presentation
- *testing* (3); included reference to field operational tests, hazard perception tests, and psychological tests generally.

The fourth heading included "Technology/automation" items (14% of responses) relating to driving and road use generally. The diverse responses (n = 18) included such topics as increased automated enforcement, in-vehicle assessment of driver impairment and investigation of possible hazards, and potential benefits of further automating driving tasks. The fifth heading, "Behavior change/transport mode" (7% of responses), comprised responses (n = 9) referring to changing behavior either in respect of driving or effecting change between transport modes (e.g., to more sustainable forms of transport). The sixth heading was "Theory" (5% of responses) with responses (n = 6) requesting a more robust theoretical approach in developing models of driving and other road user behavior. The seventh heading (3 responses) included two pleas for some/any developments in the field, one suggesting that extant efforts were too "scattered," while the final plea was for greater research emphasis in developing countries. Responses generally reflected a wide spectrum of interests and approaches within traffic psychology and were broadly consistent with the analyses of published work described above.

Conclusions and Future Challenges for Traffic Psychology

From this overview of recently published English-language empirical research, a strong researcher base within a number of countries emerges. A few thousand traffic psychologists and researchers in related fields, such as human factors/ergonomics, contributed to the scientific literature over the 11-year period. Notwithstanding the current healthy state of this disciplinary domain, some future challenges emerged from reviewing this sample of published work.

Internationalization

While many countries are represented in the traffic psychology research literature, the overwhelming bias is towards research being undertaken in the most developed countries, with no representation at all from many nations and minimal representation from some others. Generalization from studies undertaken in one culture to jurisdictions with different driving styles, road rules, and enforcement practices is problematic. A challenge for traffic psychology researchers is to obtain the necessary resources and collaborative partners to undertake research in traffic psychology and related issues in developing nations, where, given the generally much higher crash and fatality rates, there is the greatest potential to develop this subject domain to influence policy and practice. Future cross-national research cooperation can build upon existing collaborative networks to develop more comparative aspects in this field of study and inform both theoretical and applied components of traffic psychology. Cultural factors have been little studied within the traffic psychology literature, which could also be remedied by more comparative research.

Theory and conceptual models

Published research in traffic psychology is primarily characterized by an atheoretical approach—some 85% of papers reviewed had no discernable theoretical or conceptual basis for data collection and analysis. The array of conceptual models adopted in the remaining 15% of papers was highly fragmented. A small proportion of papers adopted models or theories developed specifically within the field of driving and other road user behavior, while the most frequently adopted model was from psychology's sociocognitive domain. This plethora of conceptual frameworks reflects the complexity and diversity of this field as well as the multidisciplinary backgrounds of those who study it. However, the absence of a coherent body of theory—or a few competing theories—that could underpin future research, may lead to further conceptual fragmentation on the one hand and continuing eschewing of theory altogether on the other. A comprehensive theory within traffic psychology would almost certainly need to be broadly based so as to encompass not only sociocognitive aspects, but also emotional, individual differences (e.g., personality), human factors and cultural components—and where appropriate, organizational elements—for example as predictors of behavioral outcomes. A major challenge for traffic psychologists is to develop a coherent body of driver/road user testable theory that can both guide research and be relevant to road safety applications.

Bridging the researcher–practitioner divide

The researcher–practitioner divide phenomenon is common to several areas of applied psychology—for a review of the debate within organizational psychology see Glendon, Myors, and Thompson (2007). The scientific literature is dominated by researchers based in universities and research institutes, while practitioners who publish articles on traffic-related topics overwhelmingly do so in professional journals. The challenge here is to locate and develop appropriate relationships with collaborative practitioner partners, particularly to develop evaluation and intervention field studies, which are currently represented in a small minority of research publications.

Methodological orientation

Independently of practitioner collaboration, another major challenge is to obtain resources for more intervention and evaluation studies. While the range of study designs, data collection techniques, participants and analysis techniques represents considerable research diversity, the most powerful tools in our scientific armoury—for example, field study interventions with comprehensive evaluation—have been very sparingly applied to many road transport problems involving human behavior and cognitions, particularly with safety outcomes. Longitudinal studies to evaluate intervention effects on vehicle and other road user crash/collision rates and injury reduction require considerable resources, which can be difficult to obtain in straitened economic circumstances. Opportunities to effect and to measure such reductions might be more available in developing countries where crash rates are highest and where the potential impact on safety could be maximized.

Extending the range and nature of variables studied and analyzed

The impressive range of data collection methods adopted within the sample of studies investigated belies the strong bias towards driver/other road user attitudes and perceptions, particularly gathered via questionnaire and other survey techniques. Attitude–behavior relationships have an extended history within psychology and criteria for establishing credible links have been known for more than 30 years (Ajzen & Fishbein, 1977). While behavioral field observations—using either external or in-vehicle methodologies—may be more costly and time-consuming than attitude surveys, they can provide a valuable validity check on less direct data gathering techniques. Greater adoption of triangulated methodologies could also be valuable in extending our knowledge—for example collating measures of attitudes and behavior, cognitions and skills, perceptions and motives. Decisions about variables to be included within a research study may be driven by short-term pressures to produce scientific publications rather than to make demonstrable road safety improvements.

Quantitative research dominates the empirical literature and a larger number of rigorously conducted qualitative studies could assist not only in theory development but also in a more grounded understanding of psychological components of driver/other road user behavior and cognitions—for example, motives, emotions, peer and other social pressure, substance use, and skill acquisition/maintenance. Grounded research could help traffic psychologists develop more user-defined variables, rather than adhering to those deemed appropriate by previous generations of researchers or pursuing content-free statistical modeling. Theoretical advances could also be made via this route.

Increasing opportunities exist to investigate neural processes associated with driving and other road user behaviors. While equipment and techniques currently available impose limitations on data that can be collected during naturalistic driving there would be opportunities to collect neural processing data in the course of driving simulations and experimental tasks relevant to driving (e.g., Calhoun, Pekar, & Pearlson, 2004).

Driving data are naturally hierarchical. Driving occurs within jurisdictions (nations, states, regions, etc.), on different road types (motorway, highway, suburban, rural, etc.) in a variety of vehicle types (passenger, work, private, etc.) driven by people with a range of individual characteristics (attitudes, perceptions, motives, etc.). Opportunities exist for multilevel modeling to represent these various features, estimated either as variable parameters or as fixed components within hierarchical models. Within the sampled literature, despite the considerable range and variety of statistical techniques applied, only a tiny number adopted a hierarchical modeling approach. If appropriate data can be collected there is considerable scope for examining the level at which variables significantly influence outcomes. This approach could also enhance theory building within traffic psychology.

Training

Few training programs for traffic psychologists exist; most researchers transfer from or straddle other psychological sub-disciplines (e.g., cognitive, social, organizational) or operate from cognate fields (e.g., ergonomics/human factors). Many traffic psychologists work in research units in which opportunities exist for new researchers to learn requisite competencies. Others may acquire relevant skills and techniques through mentoring by more experienced researchers. Training programs in traffic psychology might include a broad theoretical base—incorporating many of the theoretical approaches outlined in this chapter—introduce researchers to a range of direct and indirect measures of road user behaviors, cognitions, and emotions, and teach appreciation of the range of statistical techniques that can be applied to quantitative data. Special attention should be paid to designing and evaluating intervention studies focused on safety outcomes and on grounded qualitative approaches to data gathering and analysis. For graduate psychologists specialist masters programs could provide a springboard for traffic psychology careers, while undergraduate programs could provide greater depth. A desirable development would see aspiring traffic researchers from developing countries benefit from study programs in research centers in developed nations. A worthwhile initiative would be an international accreditation body for traffic psychology educational programs.

Extending traffic psychology to other transportation domains and beyond

While other transport modes were outside the sampling frame for this study, much may be learned by traffic psychologists exploring other transportation domains, for example through cross-modal work, to determine the extent to which theories, methodologies, and data collection/analysis may be either commonly or uniquely applied. Traffic psychology researchers whose interests extend to other fields of transportation psychology include Peter Hancock's human factors work in aviation psychology (e.g., Andre & Hancock, 1995), John Groeger's interests anchored within cognitive psychology, including how this might impact upon rail human factors (e.g., Groeger, Clegg, & O'Shea, 2005), and Ray Fuller, who in addition to developing theory within the field of traffic psychology, has maintained a longstanding involvement in aviation psychology human factors (e.g., McDonald, Fuller, & White, 1991). My personal interests in transport psychology extend to rail (e.g., Glendon & Evans, 2007) and civil aviation sectors (e.g., Evans, Glendon, & Creed, 2007).

To what extent are theories and applications within traffic psychology relevant across transportation modes—for example, civil aviation, rail, marine, space, military, transport on closed sites such as agriculture, construction, or mining, and transport involving animals? One potentially fruitful approach to cross-modal transport study may be through concepts and methodologies developed within cognitive ergonomics at the person–machine interface. Broader social and environmental factors are also known to have an impact, for example upon transport mode selection and individual commitment to environmental issues. The future may well witness further developments along all or some of the lines suggested here.

Acknowledgments

For their expertise and assistance in preparing this chapter special thanks to Stephen Cox, Michele Dunbar, Cassandra Gordon, Tashaal Green, and Peter Macqueen. For helpful comments on an earlier draft I thank Bryan Porter, José Prieto, and Joe Reser.

References

Ajzen, I., & Fishbein, M. (1977). Attitude–behavior relations: A theoretical analysis and review of empirical research. *Psychological Bulletin*, *84*, 888–918.

Andre, A. D., & Hancock, P. A. (1995). Special issue on pilot workload: Editorial. *International Journal of Aviation Psychology*, *5*, 1–4.

Calhoun, V. D., Pekar, J. J., & Pearlson, G. D. (2004). Alcohol intoxication effects on simulated driving: Exploring alcohol-dose effects on brain activation using functional MRI. *Neuropsychopharmacology*, *29*, 2097–2107.

Dorn, L. (Ed.). (2003). *Driver behaviour and training*. Aldershot, UK: Ashgate.

Dorn, L. (Ed.). (2005). *Driver behaviour and training: Volume II*. Aldershot, UK: Ashgate.

Dorn, L. (Ed.). (2008). *Driver behaviour and training: Volume III*. Aldershot, UK: Ashgate.

Evans, B., Glendon, A. I., & Creed, P. A. (2007). Development and initial validation of an aviation safety climate scale. *Journal of Safety Research*, *38*, 675–682.

Fuller, R. (1984). A conceptualization of driving behaviour as threat avoidance. *Ergonomics*, *27*, 1139–1155.

Fuller, R. (2005). Towards a general theory of driver behaviour. *Accident Analysis and Prevention*, *37*, 461–472.

Fuller, R. (2008, August–September). *Recent developments in driver control theory: From task difficulty homeostasis to risk allostasis*. Paper presented at the Fourth International Conference on Traffic Psychology, Washington, DC.

Glendon, A. I. (2007). Driving violations observed: An Australian study. *Ergonomics*, *50*, 1159–1182.

Glendon, A. I., & Evans, B. (2007). Safety climate in Australian railways. In J. R. Wilson, B. Norris, T. Clarke, & A. Mills (Eds.), *People and rail systems: Human factors at the heart of the railway* (pp. 409–417). Aldershot, UK: Ashgate.

Glendon, A. I., Myors, B., & Thompson, B. M. (2007). A perspective on the current state of organisational psychology. In A. I. Glendon, B. M. Thompson, & B. Myors (Eds.), *Advances in organisational psychology* (pp. 3–10). Brisbane: Australian Academic Press.

Groeger, J. A. (2000). *Understanding driving: Applying cognitive psychology to a complex everyday task.* Hove, UK: Psychology Press.

Groeger, J. A., Clegg, B. A., & O'Shea, G. (2005). Conjunction searching of simulated railway signals: A cautionary note. *Applied Cognitive Psychology, 19*, 973–984.

Heino, A. (1996). *Risk taking in car driving: Perceptions, individual differences and effects of safety incentives.* Zutphen, the Netherlands: Walburg Druk.

Hennessey, D. A., & Wiesenthal, D. L. (Eds.) (2005). *Contemporary issues in road user behavior and traffic safety.* New York: Nova Science.

Lajunen, T. (1997). *Personality factors, driving style and traffic safety.* Helsinki, Finland: Traffic Research Unit, University of Helsinki.

Matthews, G. (2001). A transactional model of driver stress. In P. A. Hancock & P. A. Desmond (Eds.), *Stress, workload, and fatigue* (pp. 133–163). Mahwah, NJ: Erlbaum.

McDonald, N., Fuller, R., & White, G. (1991). Fatigue and accidents: A comparison across modes of transport. In E. Farmer (Ed.), *Stress and error in aviation* (Proceedings of the 17th WEAAP conference, Vol 2, pp. 125–133). Avebury, UK: Avebury Technical.

Näätänen, R., & Summala, H. (1976). *Road user behaviour and traffic accidents.* North Holland: Oxford.

Rothengatter, T., & Huguenin, R. D. (Eds.) (2004). *Traffic and transport psychology: Theory and application.* Amsterdam: Elsevier.

Summala, H., & Näätänen, R. (1988). The zero-risk theory and overtaking decisions. In T. Rothengatter & R. de Bruin (Eds.), *Road user behaviour: Theory and research* (pp. 82–92). Assen/Maastricht, Netherlands: Van Gorcum.

Underwood, G. (Ed.). (2005). *Traffic and transport psychology: Theory and application.* Amsterdam: Elsevier.

Wilde, G. J. S. (1982). The theory of risk homeostasis: Implications for safety and health. *Risk Analysis, 2*, 209–225.

Wilde, G. J. S. (2001). *Target risk* (3rd ed.). Toronto: PDE Publications.

23

Applied Cognitive Psychology

Alice F. Healy and Lyle E. Bourne, Jr.

Definition and Scope of Applied Cognitive Psychology

Cognitive psychology is a branch of experimental psychology that focuses on the things that people do in their heads, that is, on mental processes. These include assimilating incoming information from the environment, acquiring and retaining new information, and carrying out more complex activities involving language, mathematical thinking, and decision making. As a branch of experimental psychology, the study of cognition is conducted in the laboratory using relatively artificial tasks and highly structured and controlled experimental designs. Most of this experimental work employs human adult subjects, although some laboratory investigations with children and animals are also relevant. The research is generally aimed to test theories and models of cognitive processes.

Like all basic scientific research, laboratory studies of cognitive psychology often have important practical implications. Thus, a relatively recent field of applied cognitive psychology has begun to emerge to examine these implications and show how laboratory results might serve to solve real-world problems. Indeed a journal called *Applied Cognitive Psychology* has been founded for this purpose, and a review of applications of basic cognitive research has recently appeared (Klatzky, 2009). The present chapter is written as a summary of the current status of this field, providing examples of effective applications of findings from basic research.

Contemporary Trends in Applied Cognitive Psychology

Contemporary trends in applied cognitive psychology fall into three major categories, depending on both the order and complexity of the processing involved. The first category focuses on perceptual input and the formulation of one or more ways of

IAAP Handbook of Applied Psychology, First Edition. Edited by Paul R. Martin, Fanny M. Cheung, Michael C. Knowles, Michael Kyrios, Lyn Littlefield, J. Bruce Overmier, and José M. Prieto.

responding to that information. The second category involves the learning and remembering of new facts and skills that might be required to respond to input information. Finally, the third category encompasses a variety of more elaborate mental activities that provide the foundation for deciding how to respond. Recent research in applied cognitive psychology falling under each of these categories has provided some valuable insights into how to use the empirically based principles and theories of cognitive psychology to understand better and to cope with everyday problems.

Input, output, and information processing

The first category includes a wide range of cognitive processes of which we have chosen to focus on three major topics that span the category: (a) attention and inattention-blindness, (b) stimulus-response compatibility, and (c) multitasking.

Attention and inattention-blindness. The major modality for processing environmental input by human beings is vision. There is a near infinite amount of information available in the visual field at any given time. Although all this information might be registered on the retinas of our eyes, it is unlikely that we are aware of all of it. Rather, we tend to focus our attention on those aspects of the visual field that are most salient or the most central to our given concerns at the moment. Thus, we neglect a large amount of information available to vision but left unattended. For example, in a restaurant, we might notice the waitperson when he or she arrives but neglect to register all of his or her distinguishing features. Later we might not be able to discriminate between our waitperson and others serving in the restaurant. Indeed, a different waitperson might show up at our table with our drinks or meals and we might fail to notice the difference. This is an example of what has been called in cognitive psychology *inattention-blindness*, where we fail to process something that occurs right before our eyes, thus illustrating a general cognitive limitation on information processing. Simons and Chabris (1999) provide a striking experimental example of this phenomenon. Subjects were shown a video of a basketball game and were asked to keep track of the number of times a player on one team passed the ball to a teammate. During the game, a strange thing happened. Someone dressed in a gorilla suit walked across the basketball court. At the end of the video, the subjects reported the number of passes and then were asked whether anything unusual happened during the game. Almost half of the subjects (46%) said that nothing unusual happened and failed to notice the gorilla incident. In fact, many expressed amazement when they subsequently learned that a gorilla walked through the court during the game. Apparently, the subjects' attention was so riveted on the game and the task of counting passes that they completely neglected an unusual and salient event in the scenario that they witnessed. The subjects' failure in this case is not attributable to their visual system but rather to their lack of attention.

A major everyday practical example of the potential applicability of research on inattention-blindness is the use of cell phones while driving a car. Drivers who are talking on the cell phone might miss important aspects of the road conditions and ongoing traffic that are clearly visible to them because their attention is diverted to the conversation. In other words, trying to carry on a cell phone conversation interferes with the more important task of operating the automobile in traffic. In effect, the drivers become "blind" to important traffic conditions because their attention is focused elsewhere. Strayer and Drews (2007) studied this possibility in a driving simulator with experimental subjects using a hands-free cell phone. When given a recognition test for important road signs or objects along the roadway in the driving scene, the experimental subjects performed significantly worse than did control subjects who did not use a cell phone. In fact, other related studies (Strayer, 2007) showed that performance of inattentive drivers was at least as poor as that of drivers who were intoxicated. Additional studies showed worse performance for drivers who used a cell phone relative to those who instead carried on a conversation with a passenger inside the car. In that case, perhaps the inattention of the driver could be compensated by the attention of the passenger. On the basis of this research, it is reasonable to consider legislation against cell phone use while driving, which could have the salutary effect of reducing serious accidents. Thus, research on inattention-blindness has potentially profound applications outside the laboratory, not only for cell-phone usage while operating vehicles or other machinery but in any situation where people might be distracted from perceiving threatening events in their environment (e.g., Hatfield & Murphy, 2007).

Stimulus–response compatibility. The design of interfaces between users and electronic devices requires a consideration of the compatibility between the stimulus display and the responses required of the users. The relationship between the presented stimuli and the prescribed responses needs to be compatible, or consistent, for optimal performance. Thus, if the user is presented with a stimulus appearing on the right or left side of a display, the required response should be made with the matching right or left hand, respectively. If the stimulus and response locations do not match, then there is an incompatibility and performance suffers. In fact, even when stimulus location is not relevant to the user's decision (e.g., the decision is based on the color of the stimulus rather than on its location), compatibility between the stimulus and response locations still strongly influences performance, following what has been called the *Simon effect.* There is much research documenting the adverse effect of stimulus–response incompatibility (see Proctor & Vu, 2006, for a summary of the evidence).

Yamaguchi and Proctor (2006) addressed this issue in a flight task environment. They used a spatial stimulus–response compatibility task in which subjects monitored instrument displays like that found in the glass cockpit of a commercial aircraft. Subjects' responses enabled them to control the actions of a simulated aircraft. The display made use of the typical "inside-out" format, simulating the pilot's view from inside the aircraft. Thus, the symbol denoting the aircraft in the display was stationary whereas the artificial horizon shown on the display tilted as the plane banked to the left or right, just as pilots would see it through their window. Every so often a visual signal, either red or green, appeared at the top of the display either on the right or the left side. A green signal indicated that subjects should make a compatible response by moving a yoke in the direction of the signal. In contrast a red signal indicated that subjects should make an incompatible response, moving the yoke in the opposite direction, away from the signal. They found a strong stimulus–response compatibility effect under these circumstances (i.e., faster responses with green than with red signals). The same stimulus–response compatibility effect was also observed when they used a less conventional "outside-in" display format, in which the artificial horizon was stationary and the aircraft symbol was tilted. The results demonstrate a major cognitive psychological phenomenon in the context of a complex, real-life situation. Thus, in this kind of dangerous environment, where human lives could be at stake, it is important that controls be designed so as to conform to compatibility and avoid incompatible arrangements between stimuli presented and responses to be made. In fact, following the Simon effect, incompatible stimulus–response locations should be avoided even when location is irrelevant to the task.

Multitasking. In everyday life, we are often required to do more than one task at a time. Multitasking is a skill, and it can be learned with effort and deliberate practice. An important demonstration of this learning phenomenon was reported by Spelke, Hirst, and Neisser (1976), who trained two students to perform two relatively difficult verbal tasks simultaneously. One task required the subjects to read short stories for comprehension in order to be prepared to answer questions about them. The other task required the subjects to write words that were dictated to them and search for relationships among those words. The subjects practiced these tasks concurrently for 85 1-hour sessions, and their performance on the two tasks was measured periodically during each session. In the early sessions, subjects found the combination of tasks quite difficult, resulting in slow reading rates and many errors. However, with practice their performance improved, and at the end they could do both tasks simultaneously roughly as well as either task alone. Spelke et al. concluded that subjects can learn skills that enable them to divide their attention between two specific tasks trained together at essentially no cost to either task and with no apparent limit.

One possibility is that with practice subjects were able to integrate the two separate tasks used by Spelke et al. (1976) into a single, functional task. Support for a functional task interpretation of these findings comes from a study by Healy, Wohldmann, Parker, and Bourne (2005), who examined practice effects in simultaneous time production and alphabet counting tasks. Accuracy on the primary task of time production suffered from the requirement of concurrent alphabet counting, but with practice performance improved. After extensive practice on the two tasks, time production at test was in fact more accurate when it was done in combination with the alphabet task than when it was done alone. The authors concluded that subjects had learned to integrate the two tasks (i.e., use the alphabet counting requirement to keep track of time), so that when the alphabet-counting requirement was removed, accuracy of time production actually decreased. The implication of these studies is that multitasking is based on skills that can be acquired with sufficient practice so that performing two routine tasks can in some circumstances be done as effectively as performing a single task. Note that this conclusion might seem inconsistent with the earlier described studies on the use of cell phones while driving. An important difference is that the multitasking experiments examined relatively routine tasks where unexpected events do not occur. The problem that cell-phone usage incurs with driving is evident when unexpected stimuli or events occur.

Learning and memory

Instruction and tutoring. A common assumption in education is that learning should be made as simple and easy as possible. But some educators have suggested that students need to be challenged in order to promote the most effective learning (Bjork, 1994). There is evidence that students learn the most when the material to be learned lies somewhat beyond what they already know, being neither too close nor too far away in difficulty (Wolfe et al., 1998). Thus, it might be necessary not to teach in the simplest way but rather to introduce moderately challenging difficulties into the learning situation. There are various ways to make the learning process difficult, but not all of them are equally desirable. McDaniel and Einstein (2005) have defined a set of criteria for determining desirable difficulties for comprehending and learning from textual material. Specifically, they argue that introducing difficulty is advantageous only if it requires the reader to engage in relevant cognitive processes that would not otherwise be undertaken. For example, McDaniel and Einstein showed that it was beneficial for comprehension to introduce difficulties that required students to engage in ways to organize the material that were not inherent in the material itself. Another example is McDaniel and Einstein's demonstration that encouraging students to elaborate on individual items of information in a text helps memory for the material, but only when the texts do not suggest that elaboration themselves. Some texts, because of the way they are written, invite elaboration whereas others do not. Thus, difficulty interacts with the type of text so that certain difficulties improve recall on some texts but not on others. Finally, McDaniel and Einstein showed that the benefit of desirable difficulties depends not only on the nature of the text but also on individual differences among learners. Coherent text (which is logically consistent and harmonious) is often thought to be needed for comprehension. However, the benefits of text coherence depend on the readers' prior domain knowledge (McNamara & Kintsch, 1996). Readers with low knowledge learn more effectively with high-coherence text, whereas, counter to intuition, readers with high knowledge benefit from a low-coherence text (which is more difficult to read) at least by measures reflecting the conceptual understanding of the text. Thus, it is important for educators to determine not only which difficulties to introduce but also to understand, for each type of text, which students are most likely to benefit from the introduction of these difficulties.

Studying and testing. Most people assume that learning takes place during study and that testing is merely an assessment of what has been learned. However, recent experiments have shown that testing can have benefits above and beyond its use as an assessment technique. Carpenter, Pashler, Wixted, and Vul (2008) demonstrated that a test can strengthen a person's knowledge of material as much as, or possibly even more than, further study can. These researchers asked people first to learn a set of obscure facts (e.g., *Greyhounds have the best eyesight of any dog*). Following this learning phase, the facts were divided into two equal groups, one of which was tested with feedback and the other merely studied once again for the same amount of time. Subjects were tested again on multiple occasions, ranging from 5 minutes to 42 days later. Those facts that were originally tested, as opposed to restudied, were remembered better at all retention intervals, and the rate of forgetting was generally less steep for the initially tested, as opposed to the initially restudied, facts. A strong testing effect has been found by other investigators as well, using a variety of materials and testing conditions. This result has implications for educational practice in that testing can be used to enhance both the learning process and the durability of what has been learned. One specific classroom application is the "clicker" technique, which is growing in popularity among educators. With this technique, each student is given a hand-held response device called a *clicker*, which is used to respond to periodic multiple-choice probe questions asked by the instructor about material recently presented in a lecture. At least anecdotal evidence strongly implies that not only do students enjoy the opportunity to demonstrate their knowledge on repeated tests with this technique, but also that this technique enhances their comprehension and memory for the material presented in the classroom. When the clicker technique is coupled with appropriate class discussions of their answers, students gain even more than from the use of clickers alone (Smith et al., 2009).

Training and skill acquisition. There is a distinction to be made between general education, as occurs in the classroom, which has been the focus of the preceding sections, and specific training, which typically addresses a well-defined task, such as those required in particular jobs. General education primarily involves learning facts, or *declarative* information, whereas specific training primarily involves learning skills, or *procedural* information. However, any specific task that requires training (e.g., air traffic control) will have both declarative (e.g., facts about each of several aircraft) and procedural (e.g., instructing pilots as to routes to take) components. In considering the training of such tasks, three criteria need to be considered: First is the speed or efficiency of learning. Second is the durability or retention of what has been learned. Third is the flexibility of the learning or its transferability to new situations. These criteria are useful in clarifying the differences between fact and skill learning. Facts are usually learned rapidly but are quickly forgotten. Skills, in contrast, are usually acquired slowly but are durable in time. Illustrating the difference in durability between fact and skill learning, people might not remember a name that they were given 30 seconds earlier if they are interrupted before they have a chance to use it, but they might remember how to drive a car years after learning how to do so even with no intervening practice. Although fact learning is less durable than skill learning, fact learning is more flexible than skill learning. Illustrating the difference in flexibility of fact and skill learning, people can use a name (i.e., a fact) that they have acquired in many different situations, including the learning of new facts, but people from the US might find it initially difficult to drive a car (i.e., a skill) in England, where driving on the left side of the road is required and the controls are on the right side of the car, so the reverse operations must be performed.

Healy, Bourne, and their collaborators (e.g., Healy, in press; Healy & Bourne, 1995) have proposed a number of principles for optimizing training in terms of the three criteria listed above (speed, durability, and flexibility). These training principles take into account the differences just described between fact and skill learning. One important principle is *procedural reinstatement.* According to this principle, training will be durable to the extent that the procedures required during training are also required by a retention test. However, by this principle, even small changes in the procedures from training to test will reduce performance. Thus, as noted above, skills are more durable but less flexible than facts. The procedural reinstatement principle has received empirical support from a number of laboratory studies. Showing the remarkable durability but limited transferability of skill learning is a study in which subjects learned to use a computer mouse to move a screen cursor from a central location to various target locations along the screen periphery (Healy, Wohldmann, Sutton, & Bourne, 2006). This study revealed that when the relationship between the mouse and the cursor movements was altered (e.g., both horizontal and vertical movements were reversed), subjects learned this new skill and retained it well over a 1-week delay but could not transfer it to a different situation when the relationship between the mouse and cursor movements was changed (e.g., horizontal movements were reversed but normal vertical movements were kept intact). In contrast, demonstrating the remarkable flexibility of fact learning, and also supporting a second training principle called *strategic use of knowledge*, is a study in which subjects learned a large number of new facts about unfamiliar people or foreign countries (Kole & Healy, 2007). This study showed that subjects could learn and retain more than twice as many facts if they associated the name of each unfamiliar person or country with the name of a familiar friend or relative (for whom they presumably know many facts) than if they formed no such associations. Developing strategies based on the use of existing declarative knowledge could facilitate both the efficiency and flexibility of training for specific jobs in many practical situations including those in the military or industry (e.g., when learning the parts of a piece of equipment).

Skill acquisition normally results from prolonged, deliberate practice of the movements required by the skill. For example, piano playing requires hours of daily practice at the keyboard before and after achieving proficiency (Ericsson, Krampe, & Tesch-Römer, 1993). Practicing a given piece enhances the learner's memory for the execution of specific finger movements required by that piece as well as the more general piano playing skill. Can a person profitably practice when no piano is available? Such an exercise would require mental practice, and the question arises whether mental practice is effective at all and, if so, whether it can be as effective as actual physical practice. Recent studies by Wohldmann, Healy, and Bourne (2007, 2008) tested these questions using a data entry task, in which subjects typed four-digit numbers presented on a computer monitor using a computer keyboard. They rehearsed the same set of numbers multiple times using either physical or mental practice. They were then tested on the practiced (old) numbers as well as on unpracticed (new) numbers. Subjects benefited from both mental and physical practice; that is, they were faster at typing numbers after practice than before. Both types of practice enhanced the ability to type the specific old numbers (like the specifically practiced songs of the piano player) and the ability to type new numbers, reflecting the acquisition of a more general skill. In fact, there were some circumstances in which mental practice was superior to physical practice. These findings imply that mental practice can be used to acquire and retain specific action sequences and to improve the more general skill involving those and related actions, supporting another, *mental practice*, principle of training. It is possible to practice a skill, such as piano playing, effectively even when the physical instruments or equipment required for that skill are not available. In fact, this technique has been used successfully in the training of Olympic athletes (Epstein, 1999)

Eyewitness identification and testimony. Research on memory has implications for a wide variety of everyday activities. Almost everything we do is dependent to some extent on our memory for past experiences. We assume that usually our memory is accurate although incomplete, but on occasion everyone has had the experience of "remembering" something that actually never occurred. Thus, there are false as well as true memories. False memories have been studied in various ways in the laboratory. One popular method involves the induction of a false memory of the occurrence of a word by requiring the subjects to study a list of related words. This original experimental paradigm was developed by Deese (1959), but subsequently expanded by Roediger and McDermott (1995). For example, subjects in one experiment heard a list of 12 words to remember, all of which were associated with the target word *chair*, which was not itself included in the list (e.g., *table, sit, sofa, desk, legs*). Immediately after hearing the list, subjects were to write down all of the words they could remember. Subjects wrote down the target word 40% of the time even though that word was never heard; this rate of recall was comparable to that found for words that actually occurred in the middle of the list. Following recall of six lists of this type, subjects were given a recognition test including both previously heard words and foil words not previously presented, including the target words. Subjects "recognized" the targets more than half the time and their confidence in this recognition was nearly as high as that for words actually presented on the list.

Demonstrating false memory in the laboratory has important practical applications to situations outside the laboratory. A classic example is eyewitness testimony about an accident or a crime given to police officers or in a courtroom. Is eyewitness testimony based on memory subject to the same influences seen in the laboratory? Eyewitness testimony has often been the basis for criminal convictions in the justice system, and some of these convictions have been recently overturned by subsequently examined DNA evidence. These findings suggest that the eyewitness testimony in these cases must have been based on false memory or inaccurate identification. Loftus and her colleagues (e.g., Loftus & Bernstein, 2005) have demonstrated the unreliability of eyewitness testimony based on memory in a variety of everyday situations and its strong dependence on the interrogation procedures employed. The implication is that people in general, and specifically law enforcement personnel, judges, courtroom lawyers, and jurors, need to be aware of the fallibility of human memory and the possible biases introduced by questioning procedures, and they should take those factors into account in deciding on guilt and innocence.

Higher mental processes

Language comprehension. Language is a uniquely human cognitive system for communicating both in written and in oral form. Language provides a way to represent knowledge about the world, so that it can be transmitted from one person to another. Language, and possibly also mathematics, requires the highest and most complex mental processes that human beings are capable of. Comprehending either text or spoken messages has been described by van Dijk and Kintsch (1983) in terms of a hierarchy of cognitive activities. In their view, a text or discourse consists of three levels of representation: the surface level (which depends on the actual words and word order), the textbase (which is a propositional structure that reflects the ideas contained in those words), and the situation model (which is an integration of the text propositions with the reader's or listener's prior world knowledge). Wade-Stein and Kintsch (2004) have used this theory as the foundation for educational software called *Summary Street*, developed to teach writing and improve text comprehension among middle-school children. The software also employs a computer-based method, known as Latent Semantic Analysis (LSA; Landauer & Dumais, 1997), to characterize the meaning of textual material. This method uses statistics about the co-occurrence of individual words and word combinations in existing texts. Two texts are said to be similar in meaning to the extent that these word statistics match. By comparing a text that has been read with a summary of that text that has been written by a student, LSA provides a measure of how well the student has comprehended the text. The students can then receive feedback informing them about inaccuracies and omissions in their summaries. With repeated attempts at summarizing the same text, the students can improve both their writing and their comprehension, often without any teacher intervention. LSA has also been used to grade answers given by students on essay examinations. Automatic computer grading by LSA has been shown to compare favorably with grades assigned by experienced teachers to the same essays. These innovations, which are based on basic research and theory in cognitive psychology coupled with advances in computer technology, point the way in which the person-power requirements of routine educational practices can be reduced, thereby lessening the burden on teachers who can then devote more time and attention to individual students where needed.

Mathematical cognition. The higher mental processes of human beings span quantitative (e.g., mathematics), as well as qualitative (e.g., language), domains. Quantitative thinking is required by many common activities, such as balancing a checkbook or filling out a tax form, although people often report having difficulty with the required calculations. Memory provides a foundation for many quantitative operations. In particular, working memory, which is our capacity to keep in mind a certain limited amount of information while we are engaged in cognitive processes (see, e.g., Baddeley, 1986), is importantly involved in these operations. Even in simple addition, we often have to carry over a digit or digits from one column to another, keeping the carry-over digit(s) in working memory.

Arithmetic and higher-order mathematics are taught throughout elementary, middle, and high school. Students differ in their mathematical abilities, and some of that difference is attributable to fear or anxiety about their competence to deal with numbers. Ashcraft and Krause (2007) demonstrated the important role of working memory both in making quantitative calculations and in the effect of anxiety on mathematical performance. They showed that imposing an irrelevant secondary task (i.e., letter recall) interfered with students' performance on solving two-column addition problems in their heads. The adverse effect of the secondary task was attributed to the need to use some of working memory's limited capacity for letter recall, thereby reducing the capacity available for the addition problems. They further found that students with high math anxiety were particularly susceptible to interference from a secondary task when solving arithmetic problems. Ashcraft and Krause interpret this effect by proposing that the working memory of high anxious subjects is already occupied by worries and concerns about their ability to perform these calculations. Are there ways to alleviate the load on working memory attributable to worries and concerns about doing well? In addition or alternatively, are there ways to alleviate the load on working memory attributable to calculations required by a problem? If so, the results of these studies have important practical implications for mathematics education. A simple possibility is to provide more physical support for the calculations themselves (e.g., scrap paper and pencil), which would relieve the burden on working memory but still provide for practice in calculation. There might be other possibilities as well, but the general rule would be to reduce demands on working memory, especially for students who exhibit high math anxiety.

Decision making. In an ideal world, people would always make rational decisions or judgments. However, one thing that cognitive psychology has demonstrated is that people are not always rational. More often than not, people rely on shortcuts or guesses when making choices. This phenomenon has been incorporated into a theoretical account of decision making by Tversky and Kahneman (1973; see also Kahneman, 2003). By this theory, the decisions that people make in any domain, ranging from economic to interpersonal, are based on simplified, intuitive processes falling in between automatic perception and deliberate reasoning. These intuitive processes are called *heuristics*. Three primary heuristics identified by Tversky and Kahneman are *anchoring*, *representativeness*, and *availability*. According to anchoring, an early event or object serves to control judgments concerning all subsequent events or objects. When making intuitive judgments or assessments about a person, the decision maker might depend on the first thing learned about that person (e.g., an instructor might rely on the fact that a student earns a very high grade on the first examination in the course). That first fact then serves as an anchor and, thus, changes the impact of later things learned (e.g., it might bias the instructor's judgments about subsequent course performance). According to representativeness, intuitive judgments rely heavily on prior knowledge or concepts regarding the object being judged. Suppose a theft has been committed and the police cordon off the crime area in an attempt to capture the culprit. One person stopped by the police is a little, old, gray-haired lady whom they immediately decide to release because that lady is not representative of thieves in general. The police have used a simplifying heuristic based on prior knowledge, but that heuristic might lead them to the wrong decision (should that lady turn out to be the actual thief). According to availability, judgments are influenced by how readily certain thoughts come to mind in a judgment situation. Suppose a person is asked whether there are more words with the letter *k* in the first position or with the letter *k* in the third position. The most common answer given by people is that there are more words beginning with *k* than those with *k* in the third position. In fact, just the opposite is true. People apparently base their decision on how readily they can think of words of each type, and it is much easier to generate words beginning with a given letter than to generate words with the same letter in the third position. It should be understood that heuristics, although not strictly rational, do not always lead to erroneous or faulty judgments. Most of the time, such simplifications are helpful and result in rapid and accurate decisions. But, being non-rational, sometimes they result in bad choices. Daniel Kahneman has shown how these heuristics apply to real-life economic decisions, such as stock purchases or gambles, which often go wrong. His basic cognitive psychology research documenting these effects earned him the 2002 Nobel Prize in Economics.

Challenges for the Future

There are many examples of applied cognitive psychology that have not been covered here because of space limitations. There are also a lot of questions that still remain unanswered about the applicability of basic research in cognitive psychology. One important set of questions concerns stress (e.g., from sleep deprivation, fatigue, noise, and time pressure) and how stress interacts with cognition. This is a critical set of questions because outside the laboratory stress is a common occurrence and may change task performance. For example, Beilock and Carr (2001) have demonstrated that stress often causes a highly skilled performer, such as a golf pro, to rely less on automated procedures and revert to conscious thought to control the actions (i.e., to switch from procedural to declarative knowledge). This change often results in a deterioration of performance and sometimes even causes the performer to choke (Staal, Bolton, Yaroush, & Bourne, 2008). Indeed, expanding on the classic Yerkes-Dodson law (see, e.g., Anderson, Revelle, & Lynch, 1989), Staal et al. have described various stress states that produce different types or levels of behavior. At low levels, stress can be facilitative of performance; at intermediate levels, stress can yield optimal performance; but at high levels, extreme stress can produce choking or panic when performance completely breaks down.

Another set of questions concerns the relationship between the brain and cognition, an area referred to as *cognitive neuroscience*. This is an area of burgeoning interest to cognitive psychologists, but we are not able to cover it fully in this chapter. An example of contemporary research on this topic that is likely to have important applications is work studying amnesic patients whose memory appears to be deficient for declarative information but relatively intact for procedural information, in contrast to Parkinson's patients who show the opposite pattern (e.g., Knowlton, Mangels, & Squire, 1996). Because different areas of the brain are damaged in these two types of patients, it is suggested that different areas of the brain are likely to mediate memory for procedural and declarative information. Understanding the neural mechanisms related to memory and other forms of cognition has important practical implications for treatment and early diagnosis of brain disorders. Questions like how to cope with stress and how to manage the cognitive effects of brain damage remain to be answered in the future by applied cognitive psychologists.

In conclusion, we have provided examples of how knowledge of cognitive processes can guide efforts to maximize human performance and to minimize human error in real-life situations. There are two challenges that face applied cognitive psychology in the future. First, some of the findings that have strong potential implications started as somewhat esoteric, theoretically based research with no clear applications evident. Basic research in cognition needs to be continued even if the immediate implications are not clear. Second, findings from cognitive psychology that do have clear implications for everyday life often have important policy implications. These findings need to be brought to the attention of the public and lawmakers with the goal of protecting or aiding individuals in the classroom, the workplace, and elsewhere.

Acknowledgment

Preparation of this chapter was supported in part by Army Research Office Grant W911NF-05-1-0153 to the University of Colorado.

References

Anderson, K. J., Revelle, W., & Lynch, M. J. (1989). Caffeine, impulsivity, and memory scanning: A comparison of two explanations for the Yerkes-Dodson Effect. *Motivation and Emotion*, *13*, 1–20.

Ashcraft, M. H., & Krause, J. A. (2007). Working memory, math performance, and math anxiety. *Psychonomic Bulletin & Review*, *14*, 243–248.

Baddeley, A. (1986). *Working memory.* Oxford: Oxford University Press.

Beilock, S. L., & Carr, T. H. (2001). On the fragility of skilled performance: What governs choking under pressure? *Journal of Experimental Psychology: General*, *130*, 701–725.

Bjork, R. A. (1994). Memory and metamemory considerations in the training of human beings. In J. Metcalfe and A. Shimamura (Eds.), *Metacognition: Knowing about knowing* (pp. 185–205). Cambridge, MA: MIT Press.

Carpenter, S. K., Pashler, H., Wixted, J. T., & Vul, E. (2008). The effects of tests on learning and forgetting. *Memory & Cognition*, *36*, 438–448.

Deese, J. (1959). On the prediction of occurrence of particular verbal intrusions in immediate recall. *Journal of Experimental Psychology*, *58*, 17–22.

Epstein, R. (1999). Helping athletes go for the gold. *Psychology Today*, *May/June,* Article 474. Retrieved December 11, 2008 from www.psychologytoday.com/articles/pto-19990501-000018.html

Ericsson, K. A., Krampe, R. T., & Tesch-Römer, C. (1993). The role of deliberate practice in the acquisition of expert performance. *Psychological Review*, *100*, 363–406.

Hatfield, J., & Murphy, S. (2007). The effects of mobile phone use on pedestrian crossing behaviour at signalised and unsignalised intersections. *Accident Analysis & Prevention*, *39*, 197–205.

Healy, A. F. (in press). Skill learning, enhancement of. In H. Pashler (Ed.), *Encyclopedia of the mind.* Thousand Oaks, CA: Sage.

Healy, A. F., & Bourne, L. E., Jr. (Eds.). (1995). *Learning and memory of knowledge and skills: Durability and specificity.* Thousand Oaks, CA: Sage.

Healy, A. F., Wohldmann, E. L., Parker, J. T., & Bourne, L. E., Jr. (2005). Skill training, retention, and transfer: The effects of a concurrent secondary task. *Memory & Cognition*, *33*, 1457–1471.

Healy, A. F., Wohldmann, E. L., Sutton, E. M., & Bourne, L. E., Jr. (2006). Specificity effects in training and transfer of speeded responses. *Journal of Experimental Psychology: Learning, Memory, and Cognition*, *32*, 534–546.

Kahneman, D. (2003). A perspective on judgment and choice: Mapping bounded rationality. *American Psychologist*, *58*, 697–720.

Klatzky, R. L. (2009). Giving psychological science away: The role of applications courses. *Perspectives on Psychological Science*, *4*, 522–530.

Knowlton, B. J., Mangels, J. A., & Squire, L. R. (1996). A neostriatal habit learning system in humans. *Science*, *273*, 1399–1402.

Kole, J. A., & Healy, A. F. (2007). Using prior knowledge to minimize interference when learning large amounts of information. *Memory & Cognition*, *35*, 124–137.

Landauer, T. K., & Dumais, S. T. (1997). A solution to Plato's problem: The latent semantic analysis theory of the acquisition, induction, and representation of knowledge. *Psychological Review*, *104*, 211–240.

Loftus, E. F., & Bernstein, D. M. (2005). Rich false memories: The royal road to success. In A. F. Healy (Ed.), *Experimental cognitive psychology and its applications* (pp. 101–113). Washington, DC: American Psychological Association.

McDaniel, M. A., & Einstein, G. O. (2005). Material appropriate difficulty: A framework for determining when difficulty is desirable for improving learning. In A. F. Healy (Ed.), *Experimental cognitive psychology and its applications* (pp. 73–86). Washington, DC: American Psychological Association.

McNamara, D. S., & Kintsch, W. (1996). Learning from texts: Effects of prior knowledge and text coherence. *Discourse Processes*, *22*, 247–288.

Proctor, R. W., & Vu, K.-P. L. (2006). *Stimulus–response compatibility principles: Data, theory and application*. Boca Raton, FL: CRC Press.

Roediger, H. L., III, & McDermott, K. B. (1995). Creating false memories: Remembering words not presented in lists. *Journal of Experimental Psychology: Learning, Memory, and Cognition*, *21*, 803–814.

Simons, D. J., & Chabris, C. F. (1999). Gorillas in our midst: Sustained inattentional blindness for dynamic events. *Perception*, *28*, 1059–1074.

Smith, M. K., Wood, W. B., Adams, W. K., Wieman, C., Knight, J. K., Guild, N., & Su, T. T. (2009). Why peer discussion improves student performance on in-class concept questions. *Science*, *323*, 122–124.

Spelke, E., Hirst, W., & Neisser, U. (1976). Skills of divided attention. *Cognition*, *4*, 215–230.

Staal, M. A., Bolton, A. E., Yaroush, R. A., & Bourne, L. E., Jr. (2008). Cognitive performance and resilience to stress. In B. J. Lukey & V. Tepe (Eds.), *Behavioral resilience to stress* (pp. 259–300). Boca Raton, FL: CRC Press.

Strayer, D. L. (2007, April). Multitasking on the information super highway: Why using a cell phone can make you drive like you're drunk. Invited Battig Memorial Lecture presented at the Seventy-seventh Annual Convention of the Rocky Mountain Psychological Association, Denver, CO.

Strayer, D. L., & Drews, F. A. (2007). Cell-phone-induced driver distraction. *Current Directions in Psychological Science*, *16*, 128–131.

Tversky, A., & Kahneman, D. (1973). Availability: A heuristic for judging frequency and probability. *Cognitive Psychology*, *5*, 207–232.

van Dijk, T. A., & Kinstch, W. (1983). *Strategies of discourse comprehension*. New York: Academic Press.

Wade-Stein, D., & Kintsch, E. (2004). Summary Street: Interactive computer support for writing. *Cognition and Instruction*, *22*, 333–362.

Wohldmann, E. L., Healy, A. F., & Bourne, L. E., Jr. (2007). Pushing the limits of imagination: Mental practice for learning sequences. *Journal of Experimental Psychology: Learning, Memory, and Cognition*, *33*, 254–261.

Wohldmann, E. L., Healy, A. F., & Bourne, L. E., Jr. (2008). A mental practice superiority effect: Less retroactive interference and more transfer than physical practice. *Journal of Experimental Psychology: Learning, Memory and Cognition*, *34*, 823–833.

Wolfe, M. B. W., Schreiner, M. E., Rehder, B., Laham, D., Foltz, P. W., Kintsch, W. & Landauer, T. K. (1998). Learning from text: Matching readers and text by latent semantic analysis. *Discourse Processes*, *25*, 309–336.

Yamaguchi, M., & Proctor, R. W. (2006). Stimulus-response compatibility with pure and mixed mappings in a flight task environment. *Journal of Experimental Psychology: Applied*, *12*, 207–222.

24

Rehabilitation Psychology

William Stiers, Kathryn Nicholson Perry, Paul Kennedy, and Marcia J. Scherer

Rehabilitation psychology practice is a specialty within the domain of professional health-service psychology that applies psychological knowledge and skills on behalf of individuals with physical and cognitive impairments and chronic health conditions; the purpose is to maximize their health and welfare, independence and choice, functional abilities, and social role participation and to minimize secondary health complications. Because chronic health conditions place the greatest demand on health-care services and the percentage of persons with chronic conditions is increasing (Hoffman, Rice, & Sung, 1996), rehabilitation psychology is increasingly relevant to many of today's important health care issues.

Rehabilitation psychology is based upon a distinctive body of theory and research (Shontz & Wright, 1980). It has existed as a formally organized specialty for over 50 years in the United States, although it is developing or not yet developed in other countries. In Europe and Australia, rehabilitation psychology is not generally recognized as a specialty by that name, and many psychologists working with persons with disabilities are called clinical psychologists, health psychologists, or neuropsychologists, even though they do specialized work that would be called rehabilitation psychology in the US. Stevens and Wedding (2004) describe that in India, Japan, Iran, Turkey, and Israel there are areas of psychology practice called rehabilitation psychology which are similar in focus to the US and Canada. In Russia, China, Egypt, and Pakistan activities related to what is called "rehabilitation psychology" have to do with prisoners, but may also include substance abuse rehabilitation, as in Poland, Indonesia, and the Philippines. In some cases, the word "rehabilitation" is used in regard to persons with primary mental health problems.

IAAP Handbook of Applied Psychology, First Edition. Edited by Paul R. Martin, Fanny M. Cheung, Michael C. Knowles, Michael Kyrios, Lyn Littlefield, J. Bruce Overmier, and José M. Prieto.

Historical Overview

Although the roots of psychological study can be traced back almost to the beginning of recorded history, in the Western world during the 1800s there began to be developed specialized areas of inquiry, such as social psychology, personality, and abnormal psychology, as well as psychological practice. Psychology practice was broadly thought of as clinical psychology in the early 1900s, although psychologists began working with specialized populations and problems, and began developing specialized techniques to do so.

In the 1940s, surrounding the time of World War II, health professionals in the US developed specialized concepts and practices to optimize the application of their professions to various traumatic injuries sustained as part of the conflicts. Physicians developed the concepts and practices of rehabilitation medicine, psychologists developed the concepts and practices of rehabilitation psychology, and nurses developed the concepts and practices of rehabilitation nursing. As rehabilitation psychologists worked alongside the emerging fields of rehabilitation medicine and nursing, early theorists and practitioners studied persons with physical and cognitive impairments, and conducted the early research on individual, interpersonal, and social reactions to persons' appearance and functional capacity, as well as the social psychology of stereotyping and prejudice related to disability (e.g., Barker, Wright, & Gonick, 1946; Barker & Wright, 1952; Dembo, Levitron, & Wright, 1956).

Definition and Scope of the Field

Rehabilitation psychologists provide services to individuals with traumatic, chronic, or congenital injuries or illnesses, as well as to their families, and to rehabilitation teams and programs. Rehabilitation psychologists help individuals with a wide variety of physical, sensory, cognitive, emotional, or developmental impairments improve, cope with, compensate for, and adjust to these conditions, so that they may maximize affective, cognitive, and behavioral functioning, as well as social, educational, vocational, and recreational participation. Such impairments and chronic health conditions may include spinal cord injury, brain injury, stroke, amputations, burns, work-related injuries, chronic pain, cancer, heart disease, multiple sclerosis, neuromuscular disorders, developmental disorders, and other conditions. Disability is a function of a person–task–environment interaction, so consideration is given to the network of biological, psychological, social, cultural, physical, and political environments in which the individual exists, and to the means of addressing barriers in each of these areas.

Rehabilitation psychologists work in hospitals and clinics, inpatient and outpatient rehabilitation centers, assisted living and long-term care facilities, and community agencies. Rehabilitation psychologists may also teach and conduct research at universities or colleges, consult to business and industry, and perform administrative or legal evaluations,. They may work for private or government programs. The broad field of rehabilitation psychology also includes development and management of

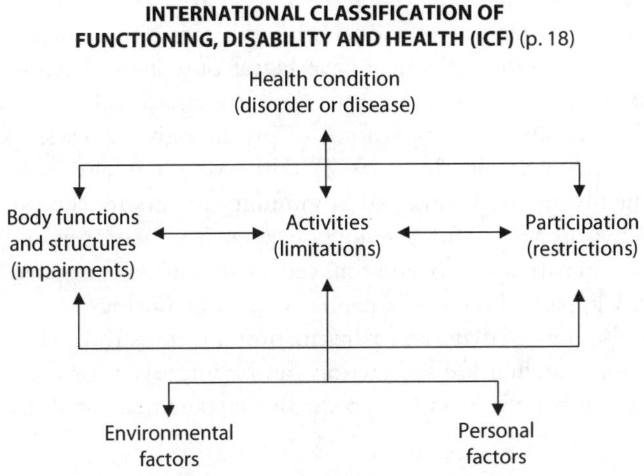

Figure 24.1. Concepts of disability

rehabilitation programs, policy development and public education related to injury prevention and health promotion, and advocacy for persons with disabilities and chronic health conditions.

Key Research Findings and Applications

Useful concepts

The concepts with which psychologists work define the approaches they take to particular issues. In rehabilitation psychology, there are a number of important concepts which lead to useful approaches to working with persons experiencing disability. The World Health Organization's International Classification of Functioning, Disability, and Health describes a model of disability as shown in Figure 24.1. (WHO, 2001).

This model replaces older terminology with newer terminology that reflects new concepts, and these new concepts have practical applications. Rather than the older terms *impairment*, *disability*, and *handicap*, the concepts of *body function and structure*, *activity*, and *participation* reflect new ways of thinking. *Disability* is a person–task–environment interaction, rather than something inherent in an individual, and it arises from the individual's condition, the task in which they are engaged, and the environment in which they engage with the task. For example, wheelchair users are less disabled in communication tasks than in mobility tasks, less disabled in physical environments with paved sidewalks and ramps than in physical environments without, and less disabled in social environments with acceptance of variations in body functions and structures than in social environments without.

Research supporting these concepts shows practical applications for reducing disability and secondary health conditions. Identical types of impairments may result in widely different levels of activity and participation. For example, an individual with pre-existing depression and poor coping skills may have low activity and participation following an injury, while an individual with the same injury who has significant optimism and good coping skills may have better outcomes. Therefore, even if the body functions/structures cannot be improved, it is still possible to improve activity and participation through the application of psychological knowledge and skills in working with individuals (Radloff, 1977). However, it is also true that systemic interventions involving the family and community to modify the physical environment, social environment, and public policy environment can also significantly increase activity and participation, and thus reduce disability (Farmer & Muhlenbruck, 2000; Farmer, Clippard, Luehr-Wiemann, Wright, & Owings, 1996; Rosenthal & Young, 1988). Because activity and participation are the strongest factors affecting quality of life, fundamental life satisfaction can be improved for the individual, and the community can benefit from the productive engagement of all its members.

Practical interventions

Changes in physical functioning, task functioning, and social functioning disrupt previously established personal, family, and community equilibriums. Changes in physical functioning often result in changes in body image, self-perceived attractiveness and value, and self-concept. Changes in task functioning and activity often result in changes in self-control, autonomy and privacy, and personal choice. Changes in social functioning and participation often result in disruption of established intrapersonal and interpersonal systems, including psychological, family, social, and vocational role sets. Norms, obligations, and responsibilities shift. Social status related to role functioning from which individuals derive self-esteem may be disrupted. In addition, individuals with disabilities and chronic health conditions may face negative stereotypes and prejudice from others.

At the individual level, persons experiencing disability can benefit from psychotherapy focused on shifting their emotional, cognitive, and behavioral emphasis from impaired sources of self-esteem to unimpaired sources, such as less reliance on physical abilities and more reliance on cognitive abilities and personality characteristics (Keany & Glueckauf, 1993; Wright, 1983). At the family and community level, such emotional, cognitive, and behavioral shifts in emphasis can also significantly reduce disability by helping develop accommodations in the physical and social environments.

There are substantial data showing that activity and participation behaviors are controlled through the well-known principles of classical and operant conditioning, and that behavioral approaches which increase task and social engagement, reduce the maintenance of disabling behaviors, and reduce psychophysiological symptoms can significantly improve function (Fordyce, 1976; Ince, 1980). The use of quota systems for quantifiable and observable behaviors, with baseline measurement and then gradual increases to build capacity and tolerance, are especially helpful in improving activity and participation, even when impairment does not change (Patterson & Ford, 2000).

Such processes are also helpful in rehabilitation of occupational injuries. For example, it has been shown that delivering health and rehabilitation services to injured workers in the workplace environment instead of in community care settings results in significantly fewer days away from work and reduced Worker's Compensation costs (Wegener, Kuhlemeier & Mitchell, 2002). The process of getting up, getting dressed, and going to the work site to participate in an on-site rehabilitation therapy clinic reduces length of time of disability.

In disability and chronic illness, coping and problem-solving behaviors are associated with better outcomes (Elliott, Godshall, Herrick, Witty, & Spruell, 1991; Elliott, Witty, Herrick, & Hoffman, 1991), both because these behaviors are associated with hope and empowerment, and because these behaviors can lead to mastery and enhancement of personal control (Gonzalez, Goeppinger & Lorig, 1990: McLaughin & Zeeberg, 1993). The focus on positive psychology, including post-traumatic growth has found that people experiencing acute onset of disability, such as spinal cord injury, report greater appreciation of family relationships, meaningful engagement, and appreciation of life (Chun & Lee, 2008), and often describe that their experience of disability has resulted in some positive changes in their life.

Developments in coping effectiveness training with persons with spinal cord injury (Kennedy, Duff, Evans, & Beedie, 2003; King & Kennedy, 1999; Mohr, Hart, & Vella, 2007) have shown that cognitive behavioral therapy techniques significantly reduce depression and anxiety by increasing the perceived manageability of SCI and decatastrophizing appraisals about SCI, and also increase adaptive coping through shared discussion and problem solving about living meaningful and satisfying lives. Positive emotions, cognitions, and behaviors are associated with increased activity and participation, and increased quality of life.

One specific aspect of coping effectiveness is that of sexuality. Sexuality is a normal part of peoples' lives, including persons experiencing disability. There has been significant attention to assessing sexuality with persons experiencing disability and to assisting them to express their sexuality as do people without disabilities, although with activity and environmental modifications as necessary (Richards, Lloyd, James, & Brown, 1992).

Self-management

In addition to direct work with individuals and caregivers, important work has been done to develop disease self-management strategies to improve disease-specific control and decrease secondary health complications (Lorig et al., 2008; Marks, Allegrante, & Lorig, 2005a; Marks, Allegrante, & Lorig, 2005b). These interventions have been shown to decrease symptoms, improve health behaviors, self-efficacy, and satisfaction with the health care system, and reduce health care utilization. There have been effective models that involve internet-based educational materials to deliver services to geographically distributed populations who are distant from medical facilities and providers. In addition, the use of peer educators can extend the effect of disease self-management strategies, and the use of internet-based matching can help patients locate near-by peers with similar health conditions. Educational interventions and peer networking can also be used to increase disease-management expertise in care-givers and to increase care giver self-care.

Cognitive rehabilitation

Rehabilitation psychology has developed specialized psychological and neuropsychological assessment instruments and procedures for persons experiencing physical disabilities that do not allow standardized test procedures (Caplan & Shechter, 1995; Dowler et al., 1997; Richards et al., 1988). These involve tests of intellectual and cognitive function that do not require usual motor or speech abilities and that are standardized for populations with physical impairments.

Rehabilitation psychologists have also developed many of the principles and practices of cognitive rehabilitation (Ben-Yishay & Diller, 1993; Cicerone et al., 2008). For example, it has been shown that comprehensive rehabilitation involving integrated treatment of cognitive, interpersonal, and functional skills within a therapeutic environment resulted in greater improvements in self-regulation of cognitive and emotional processes, community integration, employment, and quality of life compared with standard discipline-specific neurorehabilitation treatment. Community-based transitional living programs and community teams are especially effective in improving long-term social integration of persons with brain injury (Malec & Ponsford, 2000).

Meta-analyses has shown that some types of cognitive deficits respond better to restorative efforts to improve the underlying function, while other types of cognitive deficits respond better to compensatory efforts to accommodate the problem (Cicerone et al., 2000; Cicerone et al., 2005). There can be substantial benefit from cognitive-linguistic therapies for people with aphasia after left hemisphere stroke and substantial benefit from visual-spatial therapies for people with impaired visual awareness after right hemisphere stroke. It appears that these underlying abilities can be substantially improved through rehabilitation. However, more generalized problems with attention and memory do not respond well to therapies focused on remediation. Although there may be improvement in attentional or memory tasks with training, these improvements are often limited to the training tasks and do not generalize well to other, even similar, activities. However, strategy training to compensate for the underlying ability problems using cognitive orthoses appears to work better.

Cognitive orthoses can be considered in three categories. Internal orthoses include the use of contextual self-cueing to initiate behavior, mnemonics to organize behavior, associative memory to link behavioral steps, and repetition to develop procedural learning. Environmental orthoses include the use of visual flags to direct and engage attention, written labels to identify objects and locations, pill boxes to organize medications, and written instructions to guide task functioning. External orthoses include the use of timer alarms to cue behavioral initiation or cessation, calendars to organize and cue activities, and memory books to record and retrieve important information. One technological improvement in external prompting and guidance is the use of text messages delivered by cell phones or pagers at predetermined times. This can be done internally within some cell phones or personal digital assistants or by internet computer services which send specified messages at specified times.

Physical rehabilitation

Injury and disuse can lead to learned nonuse, where, for example, individuals immediately following stroke learn that they are paralyzed on one side of their body, and that they must use the less impaired side to accomplish activities. This then becomes a habit, and this nonuse can continue even after there has been some recovery, and they could begin to use both sides of their body. Constraint-induced therapy, where the more functional limb is restrained, and individuals are forced to use their less functional limb, can result in dramatic increases in function, even years after initial injury (Taub & Uswatte, 2000), by generating use-dependent cortical reorganization, where uninjured areas of the cerebral cortex develop new connections to take over control of important functions from injured areas (Celnik & Cohen, 2004).

Rehabilitation teams

Rehabilitation psychologists have also developed specialized knowledge and practices in regard to working with rehabilitation teams and programs (Malec & Ponsford, 2000; Farmer et al., 1996; Frank, 2001; Rohe, 1998), and the concept of team has been broadened to include family caregivers, as well as community, school, and work interactions (Farmer, Marien, Clark, Sherman, & Selva, 2004; Farmer, Clark, & Sherman, 2003; Farmer & Muhlenbruck, 2000). Family members who provide care are at risk for numerous physical, mental, emotional, social, and financial problems. Angry outbursts and incontinence are the most difficult problems for caregivers to deal with, and helping caregivers obtain and utilize social supports, and educating them about the causes of the negative behaviors is helpful in maintaining caregiver health and well-being (Elliott & Pezent, 2008; Grant, Elliott, Weaver, Bartolucci, & Giger, 2002; Lim & Zebrack, 2004). Addressing caregivers' needs improves the care given to the person experiencing chronic illness or disability, and, thus, improves outcomes (Holicky, 1996).

Ethics and disability

There is a tendency in the general population to assume that persons experiencing disability cannot have meaningful quality of life. However, many persons experiencing disability do have satisfactory quality of life, and they may even find positive personal growth through the experience of disability (Chun & Lee, 2008). There is also a tendency in the general population to equate disability of any type with diminished decision-making capacity. This is often a misconception, but even when decision-making capacity is reduced, it is important to recognize that decision-making capacity is context-dependent. Rehabilitation psychologists have developed specific ethical principles related to persons with disability and chronic health conditions, including persons with diminished decision-making capacity (Hanson, Guenther, Kerkhoff, & Liss, 2000; Kerkhoff, Hanson, Guenther, Ashkanazi, 1997), which acknowledges their independence and choice, and does not impose biased and inaccurate assumptions by persons who are outsiders to the disability experience.

Assistive technology

Assistive technology (AT) refers to anything that is used to maintain or increase functional capabilities. AT can include (a) mobility devices such as walkers and wheelchairs, (b) self-care devices such as extended reachers/grabbers, (c) dressing aids such as sock donners, button hooks, or holding clamps, (d) environmental control devices to operate lights, doors, and telephones, (e) reminder and alarm systems for eating, taking medication, and other daily activities, and (f) computer hardware, software, and peripherals that assist in use of computer-based products. More recent assistive technology includes direct auditory and optic cortex stimulation, computer-controlled muscle activation, and even computer-detected cortical activity to trigger muscle activation.

However, although there are numerous types of assistive technology, matching a person with an assistive device is complex. Person–technology mismatches can waste resources, frustrate and disappoint users and providers, and continue functional limitations, all of which can be addressed through psychological science (Scherer, Sax, Vanbiervliet, Cushman, & Scherer, 2005). The best match of consumer and device is based upon understanding users' physical, sensory, and cognitive abilities, as well as their needs, expectations, preferences, motivation, and reactions to technologies (Scherer et al., 2005). Consumer education about the device and its proper use is also critical, as are the perceptions and attitudes of others—attitudinal and cultural factors are a key component of a technology user's perspective (Scherer & Cushman, 2002).

Rehabilitation psychologists study perceptions and attitudes of users and others toward particular technologies, how technologies fit within their activities and contribute to their abilities to perform particular activities in daily life, and users' judgments of whether and how much particular technologies benefit them. Individuals are more likely to use AT when (a) the device meets their personal preferences and expectations, (b) they were involved in the selection, (c) they have realistic expectations, (d) the device provides perceived value and benefit, and (e) there is informed caregiver support. Given the uniqueness of the disability experience for any given individual, it is crucial that rehabilitation psychologists be included on the AT selection team.

Future Developments, Challenges, Opportunities

The biggest challenge in reducing disability for persons with physical and/or cognitive impairments is to change the social environment that restricts participation, that is, to increase the acceptance of variations in body functions and structures, and reduce negative stereotypes and prejudice. There is a need for additional research on how to effectively provide systemic interventions involving the family and community that can lead to modifications of the physical, social, and public policy environments to increase activity and participation and reduce disability. Further research on the assessment and treatment of caregivers is important in reducing health care costs.

There is also a need for additional research focused on shifting individuals' emotional, cognitive, and behavioral emphasis from impaired sources of self-esteem to unimpaired sources. Part of this may be through the use of classical and operant conditioning, where improved behavioral approaches could increase task and social engagement, and reduce disabling behaviors. However, further research on the most effective interventions to achieve this shift is needed.

It is clear that delivering health and rehabilitation services in normal community environments, including workplaces and other naturally occurring sites, can help reduce disability, and lessen the artificial distinction between "able-bodied" or "well" and "disabled" or "sick." Disability is a normal part of the human experience, whether due to injury or illness, or because of normal aging. Further research is needed to understand the best way in which to incorporate health care and rehabilitation into normal daily environments, instead of segregating it as if these were abnormal in some manner. Community-based transitional living programs and community teams are an important part of this research and development.

Additional research could help illuminate the way in which adversity can lead to post-traumatic growth, and how coping and problem solving behaviors can be developed, enhanced, and supported. Cognitive behavioral therapy and coping effectiveness training can assist with this, but the specific manner in which these are most effective has not yet been determined. Further development is also needed in ways to generate use-dependent cortical reorganization, and to develop cognitive orthoses that can best enhance daily functioning.

In rehabilitation psychology, as in all areas of professional health-service psychology, issues of education and training are fundamental to the conceptualization and development of the specialty. However, to date there has been a lack of consistency among programs, and a lack of coherence within some programs, in regard to the structure and process of rehabilitation psychology practitioner training. Research about training practices and outcomes is needed.

Public Policy Implications

It is estimated that 10% of the world's population, or approximately 650 million people, experience some form of disability, and this number is growing as a result of population growth, aging, a rise in chronic diseases, a rise in car crashes and violence, and medical advances that sustain life (WHO, n.d. a, n.d. b):

- It is estimated that each year there are 160 million work-related injuries worldwide (WHO, n.d. c);
- Global war injuries are estimated to be over 2 million per year (Peden, McGee, & Krug, 2002; WHO, n.d. d), and many of these injuries involve long-term disabilities such as limb injuries or loss, brain injuries, and spinal cord injuries (Henigsberg, Lagerkvist, Matek, & Kostovic, 1997). In some conflicts, mutilation in the form of cutting off limbs has been systematically used to demoralize opposing forces (Krug, Dahlberg, Mercy, Zwi, & Lozano, 2002);

- Landmines are also a major contributor to disability. Many mines remain from World War II; in addition, since the 1960s as many as 110 million mines have been spread throughout the world into an estimated 70 countries. An estimated 15,000–25,000 people a year are maimed or killed by landmines. Victims may have injuries to lower extremities, genitals, arms, chest, face and eyes, as well as suffering the psychological trauma of the incident and their injuries (Krug et al., 2002). Perhaps only a quarter of the persons with amputation due to landmines receive appropriate rehabilitative care (Walsh & Walsh, 2003);
- Earthquakes result in large numbers of individuals with amputations and spinal cord injuries (Rathore, Farooq, & Muzammil, 2008). Given that earthquakes also disrupt transportation and basic government and private services, this makes it especially challenging to help large numbers of people with newly acquired disabilities. In addition, it is difficult to discharge such patients to their home communities when these communities may be partially destroyed;
- Worldwide, the number of people killed in road traffic crashes each year is estimated at almost 1.2 million, while the number injured could be as high as 50 million. The total number of road traffic injuries worldwide is forecast to rise by 65% between 2000 and 2020, and road traffic crashes are the ninth leading contributor to the burden of disability worldwide (Peden et al., 2001).

In many countries, medical care and rehabilitation services for people with disabilities are less than optimal or simply do not exist (WHO, n.d. e). Rehabilitation teams from countries with greater medical specialization and infrastructure can assist by helping develop educational curricula for health professionals, helping develop rehabilitation teams, identifying local technological capacity which can be used to make sustainable prosthetics and orthotics (Meier & Smith, 2002), integrating the concept of rehabilitation into the general population (Raissi, 2007), and promoting rehabilitation psychology services.

It is also important to recognize that children and adults with disabilities are more likely to be victims of sexual and physical abuse than are individuals without disability (Grossman & Lundy, 2008; Sanghera, 2007; Oliván Gonzalvo, 2005; Smith & Strauser, 2008). The rate of abuse may be from 3 to 10 times more than in the general population (Kvam, 2000; Waldman, Swerdloff, & Perlman, 1999). They are more likely to be abused by family members, attendants, and health care providers, are more likely to suffer injury, and are more likely to experience repeated abuse. Higher levels of disability are associated with increased risk of sexual abuse, and less likelihood of disclosing the abuse (Hershkowitz, Lamb, & Horowitz, 2007; Kvam, 2000). Clearly public policies need to be implemented to protect persons experiencing disability.

Disability is the common outcome of many chronic health conditions, and disability is closely related to increased health care costs, which makes it important to maximize self-care for persons with disabilities and chronic health conditions, prevent secondary complications, and enhance caregiver functioning. Rehabilitation psychologists have developed models of assessment and treatment to address these issues (e.g., Crewe, 1991; Elliott and Shewchuk, 2003; Hill-Briggs, 2003). The work of rehabilitation psychologists to improve adjustment, increase function, develop adaptive and compensatory techniques, employ assistive technology and personal assistance, modify the physical environment, reduce social stigma, increase social integration and participation, and advocate for disability rights and consumer participation is important in reducing disability and enhancing quality of life for individuals, families, and communities.

References

Barker, R. G., Wright, B. A., & Gonick, M. R. (Eds.). (1946). *Adjustment to physical handicap and illness: A survey of the social psychology of physique and disability.* New York: Social Science Research Council.

Barker, R. G., & Wright, B. A. (1952). The social psychology of adjustment to physical disability. Preview. In J. Garrett (Ed.) *Psychological aspects of physical disability.* (Office of Vocational Rehabilitation, Rehabilitation Service Serial No. 210; pp. 18–32). Oxford, England: U.S. Government Printing Office.

Ben-Yishay, Y., & Diller, L. (1993). Cognitive remediation in traumatic brain injury: update and issues. *Archives of Physical Medicine and Rehabilitation, 74*(2), 204–213.

Caplan, B., & Shechter, J. (1995). The role of nonstandard neuropsychological assessment in rehabilitation: History, rationale, and examples. In L. Cushman and M. Scherer (Eds.). *Psychological assessment in medical rehabilitation.* (pp. 359–392). Washington, DC: American Psychological Association.

Celnik, P., & Cohen L. (2004). Modulation of motor function and cortical plasticity in health and disease. *Restorative Neurology and Neuroscience, 22*(3–5), 261–268.

Chun, S., & Lee, Y. (2008). The experience of posttraumatic growth for people with spinal cord injury. *Qualitative Health Research, 18*(7), 877–890.

Cicerone, K., Mott, T., Azulay, J., Sharlow-Galella, M., Ellmo, W., & Paradise, S. (2008). A randomized controlled trial of holistic neuropsychologic rehabilitation after traumatic brain injury. *Archives of Physical Medicine and Rehabilitation, 89*(12), 2239–2249.

Cicerone, K., Dahlberg, C., Kalmar, K., Langenbahn, D., Malec, J., Bergquist, T., ... Morse, P. (2000). Evidence-based cognitive rehabilitation: Recommendations for clinical practice. *Archives of Physical Medicine and Rehabilitation, 81*, 1596–1615.

Cicerone, K., Dahlberg, C., Malec, J., Langenbahn, D., Felicetti, T., Kneipp, S., ... Catanese, J. (2005). Evidence-based cognitive rehabilitation: Updated review of the literature from 1998 through 2002. *Archives of Physical Medicine and Rehabilitation, 86*(8), 1681–1692.

Crewe, N. (1991). Ageing and severe physical disability: Patterns of change and implications for services. *International Disability Studies, 13*(4), 158–161.

Dembo, T., Leviton, G., & Wright, B. (1956) Adjustment to misfortune: A problem of social-psychological rehabilitation. *Artificial Limbs, 3*(2), 4–62.

Dowler, R., Herrington, D., Haaland, K., Swanda, R., Fee, F., & Fiedler, K. (1997). Profiles of cognitive functioning and chronic spinal cord injury and the role of moderating variables. *Journal of the International Neuropsychological Society, 3*, 464–472.

Elliott, T., Godshall, F., Herrick, S., Witty, T., & Spruell, M. (1991). Problem-solving appraisal and psychological adjustment following spinal cord injury. *Cognitive Therapy Research, 15*, 387–398.

Elliott, T., & Pezent, G. (2008). Family caregivers of older persons in rehabilitation. *NeuroRehabilitation, 23*(5), 439–446.

Elliott, T., & Shewchuk, R. (2003). Social problem-solving abilities and distress among family members assuming a caregiving role. *British Journal of Health Psychology*, *8*(pt 2), 149–163.

Elliott, T., Witty, T., Herrick, S., & Hoffman, J. (1991). Negotiating reality after physical loss: Hope, depression, and disability. *Journal of Personality and Social Psychology*, *61*, 608–613.

Farmer, J., Clark, M., & Sherman, A. (2003). Rural versus urban social support seeking as a moderating variable in traumatic brain injury outcome. *Journal of Head Trauma Rehabilitation*, *18*(2):116–127.

Farmer, J., Clippard, D., Luehr-Wiemann, Y., Wright, E., & Owings S. (1996). Assessing children following traumatic brain injury: Promoting school and community reentry. *Journal of Learning Disabilities*, *29*, 532–548.

Farmer, J., Marien, W., Clark, M., Sherman, A., & Selva T. (2004). Primary care supports for children with chronic health conditions: Identifying and predicting unmet family needs. *Journal of Pediatric Psychology*, *29*(5), 355–367.

Farmer, D., & Muhlenbruck, L. (2000). Pediatric neuropsychology. In R. Frank & T. Elliott (Eds.), *Handbook of rehabilitation psychology* (pp. 377–397). Washington, DC: American Psychological Association.

Fordyce, W. (1976). *Behavioral methods for chronic pain and illness*. St. Louis: Mosby.

Frank, R. (2001). Rehabilitation. In A. Baum, T. Revenson, & J. Singer (Eds.), *Handbook of health psychology* (pp. 581–590). Mahwah, NJ: Lawrence Erlbaum Associates.

Gonzalez, V., Goeppinger, J., & Lorig K. (1990). Four psychosocial theories and their application to patient education and clinical practice. *Arthritis Care and Research*, *3*, 132–143.

Grant, J., Elliott, T., Weaver, M., Bartolucci, A., & Giger, J. (2002). Telephone intervention with family caregivers of stroke survivors after rehabilitation. *Stroke*, *33*, 2060–2065.

Grossman, S. F., & Lundy, M. (2008). Double jeopardy: A comparison of persons with and without disabilities who were victims of sexual abuse and/or sexual assault. *Journal of Social Work in Disability and Rehabilitation*, *7*(1), 19–46.

Hanson, S., Guenther, R., Kerkhoff, T., & Liss, M. (2000). Ethics: Historical foundations, basic principles, and contemporary issues. In R. Frank & T. Elliott (Eds.), *Handbook of rehabilitation psychology* (pp. 629–643). Washington, DC: American Psychological Association.

Henigsberg, N., Lagerkvist, B., Matek, Z., & Kostovic, I. (1997). War victims in need of physical rehabilitation in Croatia. *Scandinavian Journal of Social Medicine*, *25*(3), 202–206.

Hershkowitz, I., Lamb, M. E., & Horowitz, D. (2007). Victimization of children with disabilities. *American Journal of Orthopsychiatry*, *77*(4), 629–635.

Hill-Briggs, F. (2003). Problem solving in diabetes self-management: A model of chronic illness self-management behavior. *Annals of Behavioral Medicine*, *25*(3), 182–193.

Hoffman, C., Rice, D., & Sung, H. (1996). Persons with chronic conditions: Their prevalence and costs. *Journal of the American Medical Association*, *266*, 1473–1479.

Holicky, R. (1996). Caring for the caregivers: The hidden victims of illness and disability. *Rehabilitation Nursing*, *21*(5), 247–252

Ince, L. (1980). *Behavioral psychology in rehabilitation medicine*. Baltimore: Williams and Wilkins.

Keaney, K., & Glueckauf, R. (1993). Disability and value change: An overview and reanalysis of acceptance of loss theory. *Rehabilitation Psychology*, *38*, 199–210.

Kennedy, P., Duff, J., Evans, M., & Beedie, A. (2003). Coping effectiveness training reduces depression and anxiety following traumatic spinal cord injuries. *British Journal of Clinical Psychology*, *42*(pt 1), 41–52

Kerkhoff, T., Hanson, S., Guenther, R., & Ashkanazi, G. (1997). The foundation and application of ethical principles in rehabilitation psychology. *Rehabilitation Psychology*, *42*(1), 17–30.

King, C., & Kennedy, P. (1999). Coping effectiveness training for people with spinal cord injury: Preliminary results of a controlled trial. *British Journal of Clinical Psychology*, *38*(pt 1), 5–14.

Krug, E., Dahlberg, L., Mercy, J., Zwi, A., & Lozano, R. (2002). *World report on violence and health.* Geneva: World Health Organization.

Kvam, M. (2000). Is sexual abuse of children with disabilities disclosed? A retrospective analysis of child disability and the likelihood of sexual abuse among those attending Norwegian hospitals. *Child Abuse & Neglect*, *24*(8), 1073–1084.

Lim, J., & Zebrack B. (2004). Caring for family members with chronic physical illness: a critical review of caregiver literature. *Health and Quality of Life Outcomes*,*17*(2), 50.

Lorig, K., Ritter, P., Dost, A., Plant, K., Laurent, D., & McNeil, I. (2008). The expert patients programme online, a 1-year study of an Internet-based self-management programme for people with long-term conditions. *Chronic Illness*, *4*(4), 247–256.

Malec, J., & Ponsford, J. (2000). Postacute brain injury. In R. Frank and T. Elliott (Eds.), *Handbook of Rehabilitation Psychology* (pp. 417–439). Washington, DC: American Psychological Association.

Marks, R., Allegrante, J., & Lorig, K. (2005a). A review and synthesis of research evidence for self-efficacy-enhancing interventions for reducing chronic disability: Implications for health education practice (part I). *Health Promotion Practice*, *6*(1), 37–43.

Marks, R., Allegrante, J., & Lorig, K. (2005b). A review and synthesis of research evidence for self-efficacy-enhancing interventions for reducing chronic disability: Implications for health education practice (part II). *Health Promotion Practice*, *6*(2), 148–155.

McLaughin, J., & Zeeberg, I. (1993). Self-care and multiple sclerosis: A view from two cultures. *Social Science and Medicine*, *3*, 315–329.

Meier, R., III, & Smith, W. (2002). Landmine injuries and rehabilitation for landmine survivors. *Physical Medicine and Rehabilitation Clinics of North America*, *13*(1), 175–187.

Mohr, D., Hart, S., & Vella, L. (2007) Reduction in disability in a randomized controlled trial of telephone-administered cognitive-behavioral therapy. *Health Psychology*, *26*(5), 554–563.

Oliván Gonzalvo, G. (2005). What can be done to prevent violence and abuse of children with disabilities? *Annals of Pediatrics (Barcelona)*, *62*(2), 153–157.

Patterson, D., & Ford, G. (2000). Burn injuries. In R. Frank & T. Elliott (Eds.), *Handbook of rehabilitation psychology* (pp. 145–162). Washington, DC: American Psychological Association.

Peden, M., Krug, E., Mohan, D., Hyder, A. Norton, R., Mackay, M., & Dora, C. (2001) *Five-year WHO strategy on road traffic injury prevention.* Geneva: World Health Organization. Retrieved March 15, 2009 from http://whqlibdoc.who.int/hq/2001/WHO_NMH_VIP_01.03.pdf

Peden, M., McGee, K., & Krug, E. (Eds.). (2000). *Injury: A leading cause of the global burden of disease, 2000.* Geneva: World Health Organization. Retrieved March 15, 2009 from www.who.int/violence_injury_prevention/publications/other_injury/injury/en/index.html

Radloff, L. (1977) The CES-D scale: A self-report of depression scale for research in the general population. *Applied Psychological Measurement*, *1*, 385–401.

Raissi, G. (2007) Earthquakes and rehabilitation needs: experiences from Bam, Iran. *Journal of Spinal Cord Medicine*, *30*(4), 369–372.

Rathore, F., Farooq, F., Muzammil, S., New, P., Ahmad, N., & Haig, A. (2008). Spinal cord injury management and rehabilitation: Highlights and shortcomings from the 2005 earthquake in Pakistan. *Archives of Physical Medicine and Rehabilitation, 89*(3), 579–585.

Richards, J., Brown, L., Hagglund, K., Bua, G., & Reeder, K. (1988). Spinal cord injury and concomitant traumatic brain injury: Results of a longitudinal investigation. *American Journal of Physical Medicine and Rehabilitation, 67*, 211–216.

Richards, J., Lloyd, L., James, J., & Brown, J. (1992). Treatment of erectile dysfunction secondary to spinal cord injury: Sexual and psychosocial impact on couples. *Rehabilitation Psychology, 37*, 205–213.

Rohe, D. (1998). Psychological aspects of rehabilitation. In J. DeLisa & B. Gans (Eds.), *Rehabilitation medicine: Principles and practice* (3rd ed., pp. 189–212). Philadelphia: Lippencott-Raven.

Rosenthal, M., & Young, T. (1988). Effective family intervention after traumatic brain injury. *Journal of Head Trauma Rehabilitation, 3*(4), 42–50.

Sanghera, P. (2007). Abuse of children with disabilities in hospital: Issues and implications *Paediatric Nursing, 19*(6), 29–32.

Scherer, M., & Cushman, L. (2002). Determining the content for an interactive training programme and interpretive guidelines for the Assistive Technology Device Predisposition Assessment. *Disability Rehabilitation, 24*(1–3), 126–130.

Scherer, M., Sax, C., Vanbiervliet, A., Cushman, L., & Scherer, J. (2005). Predictors of assistive technology use: The importance of personal and psychosocial factors. *Disability Rehabilitation, 27*(21), 1321–1331.

Shontz, F., & Wright, B. (1980). The distinctiveness of rehabilitation psychology. *Professional Psychology, 11*(6), 919–924.

Smith, D., & Strauser, D. (2008). Examining the impact of physical and sexual abuse on the employment of women with disabilities in the United States: An exploratory analysis. *Disability Rehabilitation, 30*(14), 1039–46.

Stevens, M., & Wedding, D. (Eds.). (2004). *Handbook of international psychology*. Hove: Taylor and Francis Books.

Taub, E., & Uswatte, G. (2000). Constraint-induced movement therapy based on behavioral neuroscience. In R. Frank & T. Elliott (Eds.), *Handbook of rehabilitation psychology*. Washington, DC: American Psychological Association

Waldman, H., Swerdloff, M., & Perlman S. (1999). A "dirty secret": The abuse of children with disabilities. *ASDC Journal of Dentistry for Children, 66*(3), 197–202.

Walsh, N., & Walsh, W. (2003). Rehabilitation of landmine victims: The ultimate challenge. *Bulletin of the World Health Organization. 81*(9), 665–70. Epub 2003 Nov 14.

Wegener, S., Kuhlemeier, K., & Mitchell, C. (2002). Principles and practices of onsite rehabilitation. In Implementation and outcomes, symposium presented at the annual conference of the American College of Occupational and Environmental Medicine. 2002, Chicago, IL.

World Health Organization. (2001). *International classification of functioning, disability, and health*. Geneva: World Health Organization.

World Health Organization. (n.d. a). *World report on disability and rehabilitation*. Geneva: World Health Organization. Retrieved March 15, 2009 from www.who.int/disabilities/Concept%20NOTE%20General%202008.pdf

World Health Organization. (n.d. b). *Disability, including prevention, management and rehabilitation*. Geneva: World Health Organization. Retrieved March 15, 2009 from www.who.int/nmh/a5817/en/

World Health Organization. (n.d. c). *Occupational health and safety in the African region: Situation analysis and perspectives.* Geneva: World Health Organization. Retrieved March 15, 2009 from www.afro.who.int/des/phe/publications/occ_health_situation.pdf

World Health Organization. (n.d. d). *Collective violence.* Geneva: World Health Organization. Retrieved March 15, 2009 from www.who.int/violence_injury_prevention/violence/world_report/factsheets/en/collectiveviolfacts.pdf

World Health Organization. (n.d. e). *Capacity building.* Geneva: World Health Organization. Retrieved March 15, 2009 from www.who.int/disabilities/capacity_building/en/

Wright, B. (1983) *Physical disability: A psychological approach.* New York: Harper and Row.

25

Psychology and Societal Development

Girishwar Misra and Janak Pandey

> Psychology has meaning to the extent it can contribute to enhancing the quality of life of people
>
> Rama. C. Tripathi (2003, p. 236).

Notwithstanding the fact that disparities in the level of socioeconomic development across as well as within nations have a long history, this fact escaped the attention of psychologists for a long time and has still not occupied center stage. Caused by a variety of factors such as race- and caste-based discrimination, feudal structure, unjust distribution of resources, and colonization, these disparities demanded multidisciplinary perspectives. Psychology's preoccupation with covert mental processes in a decontextualized manner and its commitment to individualism drastically undermined its engagement with macro-level societal problems. As Jahoda (1973) has indicated, psychological data and theories, being products of specific cultural milieux, function inadequately in non-Western cultures. However, several developments in the post-World War II period, including the sociopolitical changes in African and Asian countries, realization of the relevance and historicity of social and psychological knowledge, exploration of alternative epistemologies, and increasing interaction with sister disciplines paved the way for the emergence of socially situated psychological perspectives (Oskamp, 1984; Sacks & Kidd, 1980; D. Sinha, 1983).

The interface with local realities made it increasingly clear that the psychological knowledge and practice imported from the West have limitations. The search for alternatives has brought into focus the importance of culture in many guises of psychology such as *cross-cultural*, *cultural*, *ethnic*, *societal*, and *indigenous*. To illustrate psychology's engagement with societal development and culture this chapter critically explores the case of India, and briefly examines the main trends in the development of indigenous psychology. It shows how the local stories of psychology unfold in partly shared and partly unshared intellectual spaces. It is observed that the question

IAAP Handbook of Applied Psychology, First Edition. Edited by Paul R. Martin, Fanny M. Cheung, Michael C. Knowles, Michael Kyrios, Lyn Littlefield, J. Bruce Overmier, and José M. Prieto.

of societal development and psychology's participation in it is structured by certain metatheoretical orientations. In conclusion, reflections on some of the challenges and possibilities in this academic and professional domain are presented.

Psychology's Involvement with Societal Development

Awareness of psychology's potential to contribute to national development was indicated by some senior psychologists in the 1950s (Klineberg, 1956; Murphy, 1953), and it was in the 1960s that a call was made to make psychology socially relevant to developing countries. This led to changes so that people were studied within their sociocultural contexts employing appropriate methods and concepts. In 1966 D. Sinha made a plea for entering the arena of social change to study the dynamics of change: facilitators, inhibitors, and consequences. In 1967 at Ibadan in Nigeria eminent psychologists tried to consolidate their concerns about the problems of national development (Hefner & DeLamater, 1968). The American Psychological Association (APA) published a volume on the problems of society (Korten, Cook, & Lacey, 1970). In 1978 the International Association of Applied Psychology (IAAP) took a major initiative to establish a division of psychology and national development, which was recently renamed as societal development. Soon after, the International Union of Psychological Science (IUPsyS) initiative set up a network with D. Sinha as its convener and subsequently published a special issue of *International Journal of Psychology* (IJP) on this theme (D. Sinha & Holtzman, 1984). On the occasion of the 50th anniversary of the United Nations, the APA organized a symposium on "Social Development and Human Security: A United Nations–Psychologists' Dialogue" (Tyler, 1995). Further, special issues of IJP on the role of psychology in different parts of the world (Adair & Kağitçibaşi, 1995) and of *Applied Psychology: An International Review* (Kim, 2002) provide assessment of the disciplinary developments and issues of national development. The third World Summit on Social Development held at Copenhagen during 5–12 March 1995 made it explicit that economic development is a tool, and the ultimate goal is providing for at least a minimally acceptable quality of life for everyone.

The call for the application of psychology in developing countries has been expressed by a number of social scientists across the globe (e.g., Akin-Ogundeji, 1991; Ayman, 1985; Ahmed & Gielen, 1998; Carr, & Schumaker, 1996; Enriquiz, 1992; Eze, 1991; Kamwendo, 1985; MacLachlan & Carr, 1994; Misra, 1990; Moghaddam & Taylor, 1986; D. Sinha & Kao, 1988; Wober, 1975). It is against this backdrop that psychologists in India and other developing countries started recognizing the role of psychology in societal development and using the psychological knowledge embedded in disparate cultural traditions.

Inspired by the activities of the Division of Psychological and Societal Development of the IAAP, research activities accelerated leading to the launching of several journals such as *Psychology and Developing Societies*, *Society and Natural Resources*, *International Journal of Rural Management*, and *Journal of Social Action*. In the recent past, psychologists have been increasingly engaged in critiquing as well as reconstructing the notion of development, identifying its indicators, designing social institutions and relationships, planning strategies for societal development, and conducting programs and policy evaluation.

Conceptualizing Societal Development: Changing Perspectives

Early concerns: Primacy of economic factors

In a general sense societal development was understood as progress, especially in material terms, and materialistic/economic development was used as the sole criterion of development. The challenge of catching up with the developed countries involved "temporal compression and cacophonic change" (Myrdal, 1968). As a result, the developing countries started experiencing massive industrial, urban, national, and democratic transformations simultaneously. The resulting instability caused social disorganization characterized by increasing incidence of violence, crime, delinquency, alienation, and change in the nature of work (Cherns, 1984).

The above framework of modernization, however, did not go well with the ethos of traditional cultures and they were judged to be lacking in the necessary readiness to develop and progress. This framework was born in Europe in the 19th century as a response to the urban and industrial revolution. It held modernization as the answer for all problems. It was, therefore, not surprising to find McClelland's (1961) special emphasis (see also Triandis, 1984) on the primacy of values of industrial society such as individuality and competitiveness (see also Franke, Hofstede, & Bond, 1991; Hufton, Elliot, & Illushin, 2002).

Need to go beyond economic development

The experience of equating economic growth with development, however, was found inappropriate, and modernization did not prove to be the solution to all problems. Therefore, endogenous development was advanced that respected the social and cultural characteristics of the people (Dube, 1988). Since the 1970s an integration of the social and economic aspects of development has come to the fore. Propounded by UNESCO (Huynh, 1979), this view emphasizes development based on the perceived needs and aspirations of the people, their traditional values, culture, and specific characteristics of the society in relation to existing and potential resources. This implies that any monolithic model of development cannot ensure societal development (Alechina, 1982; Alexander, 1993; J. B. P. Sinha, 1990). Gradually, development thinking moved toward "human development" (UNDP, 1990), which recognizes peoples' choices in terms of purchasing power, quality of education, and standard of health. The availability of opportunities, however, varies across cultures (Moghaddam, Bianchi, Daniels, Apter, & Harre, 1999). The Western model, therefore, may not necessarily be the only developmental trajectory and universally good for every culture. In an important sense human development (e.g., life expectancy, literacy, and gender discrimination) means supplementation of economic indicators.

In this context an important shift in thinking came through the notion of "sustainable development" which promises to meet the needs of the present without compromising the ability of future generations to meet their own needs.

The introduction of social capital has added another dimension to the discourse on development (Putnam, 1993). It is characterized by interpersonal trust, norms of reciprocity, and membership of civic society which act as resources for individuals and facilitate collective action for mutual benefit through networks and resource mobilization. However, interventions for development had largely ignored the community context of human welfare (Prilleltensky & Nelson, 2000; Shinn & Toohey, 2003).

In 2000, the UN identified a set of Millennium Development Goals aiming at concerted efforts to reduce poverty, child mortality, and disease prevalence while improving education, health, gender equity, environmental sustainability, and partnership. In particular Amartya Sen (1999, 2009) and Mahbub ul-Haq (1999) emphasized that development should include not only an increase in gross national product (GNP), but also enhancement of human capabilities. A shift toward a collective and process-oriented sociocultural approach to sustainable societal development through participatory development process is discernible.

Ideally, development should aim at *Sarvodaya* (the welfare of all) as propounded by Mahama Gandhi. It reflects a concern for inclusive development centered on a relational reality consisting of man and his society and environment (nature). Gandhi believed in a symbiotic way of life which maintained harmony across man, society and Nature. Gandhi propagated concepts like truth, self-control, women's emancipation, village uplift, *Swadeshi* (indigenous and national), justice with equality of opportunities and national integration.

The realization of the limits of development ideology with respect to its functionality and capacity to conserve environment and ecology seems to be a return to the dream of Mahatma Gandhi (1945). He argued in favor of constructive voluntarism for human development and emphasized cultural and social regeneration (Sheth & Sethi, 1998). Some of Gandhi's followers led social movements of voluntarism like the donation of surplus land (e.g., Vinoba Bhave's and Jai Prakash Narayan's land donation movement) and rendered selfless service to society .

Societal development stands for the process as well as the product pertaining to realization of the full potential of a society. As such it implies effective collective arrangements for the fulfillment of the entire spectrum of human needs—from the physical, to the psychological, and to the social and cultural. The goal of social welfare dominates the notion of societal development, which is achieved through effective interaction between the state and people (Mehta, 1998). In functional terms development implies creation of a sense of power in collectivities and individuals for solving their problems. With the recognition of role and place of institutions in societal development the emphasis has shifted from exclusive reliance on individuals to greater attention on collaborative efforts.

Today's development discourse is dominated by concerns for well-being, quality of life, social change and enlarging people's options, opportunities, choices and justice. This change assigns a critical role to psychologists in building capacity, inculcating positive self-image through participation, promoting collective values, building confidence to conduct group activities and taking collective action, and facilitating empowerment.

Strategies for Societal Development: The Indian Experience

During India's freedom struggle the leaders of anticolonial nationalism highlighted two concerns—denial of democracy and lack of development. Therefore, after the attainment of freedom, these two became cherished goals of the government. During the last six decades India and other similar nations have made interventions in planning and policy making so as to change and improve the quality of life of the deprived and marginalized, particularly the rural and tribal population, and particularly the womenfolk (see for details Dalal, 2010; Singhal & Tiwari, 2009). These sections of the population have a long history of subjugation, atrocities, discrimination, and disparities. In India, where 72.22% (according to the 2001 census) of the population still lives in rural areas, any consideration of societal development will remain unfinished without discussing the problem of rural development (RD). Being illiterate, having meager income and limited access to civic facilities, the rural as well as slum dwellers in cities are more vulnerable. The approach to RD has changed from a top-down to the bottom-up approach. The bottom-up approach envisages that decisions and power should be close to the bottom and should not be imposed from the outside. The government of India has initiated diverse programs since 1952. These programs address the people's needs in regard to poverty alleviation, infrastructure development, overcoming natural calamities, tribal welfare, common property resources, employment generation, livelihood, and so forth. The emphasis in RD has progressively shifted from growth to welfare and then from a responsive to an integrated approach. A strategic pro-poor policy is being adopted and agriculture is projected as the main component of development strategy. The approach to RD is moving beyond income generation to multifunctional development (Majumdar, 2002).

Some of the key programs include the Panchayati Raj (village government) Institution (PRI), Integrated Child Development Program, Watershed Development Program, Rural Women's Development and Empowerment Project, Joint Forest Management, Integrated Rural Development Program, and implementation of the Sustainable Livelihood and National Rural Employment Guarantee Act. For want of space we shall limit ourselves to one of these initiatives, namely PRI (see for the analysis of various programs, Bahuguna & Upadhyay, 2002; Gadgil & Guha, 1995; Singhal, 1995; Singhal & Tiwari, 2009; H. Sinha & Suar, 2003).

The PRI aims at governance through village council (*Gram Sabha*). It has been created through constitutional provision to strengthen the poor and harness social energy for development and social justice through active participation. The citizens of villages constitute the village council, which then becomes the basic unit of democracy. The council is made responsible for the implementation of developmental activities such as creating infrastructure (e.g., roads, schools, drinking water, drainage, health services, seed farms, etc.), and social organization and resource mobilization to achieve poverty alleviation and people's empowerment. It assigns a greater role to the vulnerable sections of the society in decision making through self-confidence and provision of effective participation as well as making administrative and financial powers available. A reservation in village councils up to 33.33% participation by women has been introduced. Further, to accelerate the process of development, capacity building, public confidence, and collective action are facilitated through training programs. The evidence lends support to positive effects of PRIs on village life (Jain, Buch, & Chaudhary, 1999; Mathew, 2003; Sastry & Vithal, 1988; Suar & Prasad, 1995). It has been found that social identity, group-based pride, and respect were critical in determining participation and development of institutional governance (H. Sinha & Suar, 2003). The entry of international funding agencies and the involvement of the NGO sector have changed the scenario. However, the unrealistic expectations, lack of coordination, and low motivation of the participants made the programs less successful (Jain, 1985). The questions of poverty, unemployment and inequality, provision for health and education could not be tackled according to the expectations (Dalal, Kumar, & Gokhale, 1999; Mehta, 1998).

Psychologists have shown a great deal of interest in developing psychological interventions for the eradication of poverty. Research programs by Rath (1982), Pareek (1968), D. Sinha (1969, 1990), Pandey and Singh (1985) and Misra and L. B. Tripathi (1980) stimulated considerable research on the cognitive, motivational, and social consequences of poverty and deprivation. Pareek (1994) has argued that, since the expectancy of reward through hard work and personal initiative has been low for centuries, the capacity to take initiative has declined. D. Sinha (1990) has concluded that the detrimental effects of poverty are accentuated by unfavorable proximal environment. Misra (2000) has noted that interventions should be planned to create in people a sense of empowerment to effect change in their environment. Mehta (1994) advocated for empowerment of the poor so that they can assert collectively to influence and change their living conditions (see also Misra & K. N. Tripathi, 2004). These micro-level findings, however, are often ignored and not taken into consideration in the course of macro-level planning. Recently Huston and Bentley (2009) have found that relative poverty and poverty as a heterogeneous condition has yet not been fully examined in the developmental context. For instance, in a study (Skevington 2009) of Quality of Life (QOL) in poverty settings in low-income countries, social status, concern for relationship, family life, and an egalitarian perception of political institutions were found to form important dimensions of QOL.

The spirit of voluntarism

Dalal (2010) has drawn attention to the role of voluntarism or selfless service for others' good (see also Kothari, 1998; Krishnan, 2005). The notion of *Loka Samgraha* (endeavour for the uplift of the common man) clearly emphasized the value of positive social action meant to facilitate social welfare. The relational notion of selfhood furnishes space for service to others, sacrifice, and renunciation. Traditionally a householder is supposed to take care of others as he is in debt to them.

After India's political independence, the country adopted a socialistic pattern of development. The main strategies were promotion of a mixed economy and development through centralized planning. With the change in government policies and increasing availability of funding, a large number of non-government organizations (NGOs) are directly involved in development projects. For instance *Swadhyaya* is a sociospiritual movement for self-development and social transformation (Giri, 1998). It upholds the equality and dignity of all human beings, sharing of resources, concern for the well-being of everyone in society and endeavors to bring about the growth and development of the community (Shah, Sheth, & Visaria, 1998).

The success of community development projects often depends on community participation and not merely on monetary and material resources. The human factors such as commitment and involvement of the people, compatibility of the program with attitude and motivation, and perception of its fairness and justice facilitate development initiatives. In contrast, lack of trust, disempowerment of local communities, and undermining of the native knowledge impede these efforts (Dalal, 2010).

Indigenous Psychology

Recent analyses of the developments in teaching, research, and professional growth indicate considerable gaps and disparities in the levels of attainment in training, domains of application, and theoretical contribution in different parts of the world (David & Buchanan, 2003; Stevens & Gielen, 2007). In general, the trends show the dominance of scientific imperialism in which Euro-American practices of knowledge creation and application are central and indigenous approaches remain peripheral (Brocks, 2006). The resistances to the dominant trend, however, have been building up and a critical stance is emerging in disciplinary discourses (Henriques, 1984; Holdstock, 2000; Kumar, 2008; Nicholas, 1993; Painter, Terre Blanche, & Henderson, 2006). There is a visible shift in favor of the cultural grounding of psychological understanding (Brocks, 2006; Escobar, 1995; Martin-Baro, 1996; Pickren, 2007; Rose, 1998; D. Sinha, 1997; J. B. P. Sinha, 1984, 1997; Smith, 1999). Indigenous approaches take many forms with reference to the content and methods of psychology. Its spirit is best captured in a recent appraisal by Danziger (2006). He views it as "a self-conscious attempt to develop variants of modern professional psychology that are more attuned to conditions in developing nations than the psychology taught at Western academic institutions" (p. 215).

The engagement of psychology with human functioning has predominantly been located in the cultural imperative of individualism. Within this framework freedom and independence are valued constituents of self. This makes individuation and separation from the group and society highly prized goals. Under the positivist spirit, the discipline was preoccupied with culturally bound and culturally blind practices. This perspective, however, does not transfer well to other cultural contexts that endorse less individuated models of personhood (Doi, 1986; Enriquez, 1992; Heelas & Locke, 1981; Hsu, 1985; Misra, 2003; Shweder & Sullivan, 1993; Triandis, 1989). In the last few decades a turn toward culturally informed perspective has taken place (e.g., Berry, Poortinga, Segall, & Dasen, 2002; Cole, 1998; Gergen, Gulerce, Lock, & Misra, 1996; Kakar, 1997; Marsella, 1998; Matsumoto, 2002; Misra & Gergen, 1993; Nisbett, 2003; Valsiner & Rosa, 2007). Also, culture is being treated more like a chronic situation or set of situations which determine attributes, life ways, and social practices (Kitayama & Cohen, 2007). Cultures are intersubjective, shared, and socially established systems of meanings and practices useful for navigating in the intentional worlds of everyday life. As meanings and concepts are shaped by culture, the enterprise of psychology is likely to benefit and become universal if it goes culture-inclusive and opens to the ideas from non-Western traditions.

The evolution of indigenous psychology as a field of research is a relatively recent phenomenon. Its emergence has been stimulated by psychologists from different parts of the world. D. Sinha (1965, 1997) from India and Virgilio Enriquez from the Philippines (Enriquiz, 1992) voiced concerns about the transplantation of Western psychological concepts, theories, and methods to other cultures and its consequences for knowledge generation and application. The movement was joined by other scholars from many places (Misra, 2003, 2006). The publication of *Indigenous Psychologies: Research and Experience in Cultural Context,* a comprehensive book edited by Kim and Berry (1993) crystallized the perspectives on indigenous psychologies. Indigenous psychologies deal with local understanding and culturally rooted conceptualizations. Subsequent publications (e.g., Adair & Diaz Loving, 1999; Allwood & Berry, 2005; Kim, 2001; Kim & Park, 2004; Misra & Mohanty, 2002; Paranjpe, 1998; Rao, Paranjpe, & Dalal, 2008; Sham & Hwang, 2005; D. Sinha, 1997; J. B. P. Sinha, 2002; Yang & Hwang, 2000) indicate that the scope and application of indigenous psychology is increasing. Indigenous psychology recognizes the importance of adopting culture as a vantage point for the content and context of psychological processes. Kim, Yang and Hwang (2006) have recently published *Indigenous and Cultural Psychology* which showcases the developments in indigenous psychology in a comprehensive manner. Indigenous psychology and indigenization of psychology are intellectually exciting, emancipatory and applied in nature and have potential to make psychology more inclusive and vital to human future.

Concluding Comments

The development of indigenous psychology is a significant departure from the Euro-American programmed functioning of the discipline of psychology. In a recent analysis Liu, Ng, Gastardo, Ma, and Wong (2008) noted that "as (a) whole, psychology is an industry produced of, by, and for citizens in wealthy and developed countries, who export their ways of thinking to developing societies in a way that can exacerbate inequalities … The future would demand parallel, distributed and pluralistic awareness of interconnectedness" (p. 1163). They note that Asia and to a lesser extent South America, as independent power blocks, need suitable psychologies. The future well-being of humanity depends on interdependence of different countries. Globalization has shown the possibility of the flow of influence from both directions. The increase in immigration, globalization, capital and labor flow, and assertion of identity demand intercultural communication and intercultural competence. It is important that more opportunities are created for university–community interaction, where academic departments take up social-developmental projects.

Technology has become an important player in societal development. As Wang, Chien, and Kao (2007) provide evidence from Southeast Asian countries, technology plays a critical role in enhancing national competitiveness. The revolutions in information, transportation, communication, and robotics are transforming the experience of time and space and consequently the habits of mind, motivations, and patterns of social interaction. The electronic media have made simultaneous presence of happenings across the globe. The structure of the life-world in terms of its content, form, and flow is fast changing. Humans are at the juncture of multiple pathways and are required to exercise their options.

At a macro level, the goal of human development consists of building just and inclusive societies. Thus, a comprehensive analysis of societal development in developing countries would require recognition of structural power and the dynamics of oppression and privilege. Methodologically transformative ways should be adopted for a broader and inclusive approach that demands multi- and cross-disciplinary perspectives. Developing countries like India are engaged in developing and nurturing this approach. Attention has been drawn towards the way sociocultural dynamics influence culturally appropriate psychology and indigenous perspectives (Pandey, 2004; Pandey & Singh, 2005). It is quite clear that the goals of national or societal development cannot be achieved through imposed categories of understanding. Also, these notions cannot be reduced to economic development.

It must be noted that the experience of development has not been a story of complete success. The emancipatory potential of nationalism was mostly used by the elites of most of the postcolonial nations to their own advantage as they were more conversant with the functioning of institutions of modern nation-states. In this process, a large section of these societies, especially the poor belonging to lower castes and classes and to tribal groups were denied the benefits of development (Bose & Jalal, 1997). As a result, many groups could not develop a sense of affiliation with the nation and a new trend of identity politics along the lines of caste, class, community, and ethnicity emerged. Communal riots, violence, demand for more autonomy within the framework of constitution, and secessionism are some of the reflections of the failure of state-sponsored developmentalism. Development programs initiated by the government and some international organizations often fail to address the grievances of masses.

The increasing interdependence among countries and increasing significance of global events make one realize that the question of societal development needs to be understood in local as well as global contexts. Many countries in different parts of the world are continuously subjected to political instability, corruption, military action, terrorism, and religious fundamentalism. Such a situation interferes with development processes (Escobar, 1995).

In an important sense societal development involves extended or inclusive identities that allow the coexistence of diverse and separate identities that are bound together by some form of overarching bond. This makes spirituality relevant. In terms of transpersonal and shared existence, spirituality motivates and allows one to lose one's ego and furnishes grounds for collaboration and collective participation. Non-Western cultures like India situate human affairs not only in the context of other humans but also in the context of transcendental or spiritual reality. Such a mode of thinking has still to receive adequate attention (Cross & Gore, 2005).

It is amply clear that the meaning and conditions of societal development is a subject of many disciplines. While some amount of progress has been achieved much is still desired; it needs to be contextualized in the local and specific eco-cultural contexts with a broad vision of holistic development. Psychology, in its received view, has adopted a micro, abstract, and artificial approach in appreciating social reality. As a consequence it has not been very successful in understanding how humans conduct themselves. Preoccupied with specializations, its perspective has become narrower. We need to listen and communicate continuously with the various players who are involved in this process. Academic perspectives need to be complemented by outside perspectives. This will allow us to attend to new fields and audiences and make the discipline more authentic and relevant for societal and national development.

References

Adair, J. G., & Diaz Loving, R. (Eds.). (1999). Indigenous psychologies: The meaning of the concepts and its assessment. *Applied Psychology: An International Review*, *48*(4), Special Issue.

Adair, J. G., & Kağitçibaşi, Ç. (Eds.). (1995). National development of psychology: Factors facilitating and impeding progress in developing countries. *International Journal of Psychology*, *30*(6), Special issue.

Ahmed, R. A., & Gielen, U. P. (Eds.). (1998). *Psychology in the Arab countries.* Menoufia, Egypt: Menoufia University Press.

Akin-Ogundeji, O. (1991). Asserting psychology in Africa. *The Psychologist*, *4*(1), 2–4.

Alechina, I. (1982). The contribution of the United Nations system to formulating development concepts. In UNESCO (Ed.), *Different theories and practices of development* (pp. 9–68). Paris: UNESCO.

Alexander, K. C. (1993). Dimensions and indicators of development. *Journal of Rural Development*, *12*(3), 257–267.

Allwood, C. M., & Berry, J. W. (2005). Origins and development of indigenous psychologies: An international analysis. *International Journal of Psychology*, *41*, 243–268.

Ayman, I. (1985). Academic and professional development of behavioral scientists for and in developing countries. In R. Diaz-Guerrero (Ed.), *Cross-cultural and national studies in social psychology* (pp. 421–429). North Holland: Elsevier Science Publishers.

Bahuguna, V. K., & Upadhyay, A. (2002). Forest fires in India: Policy initiatives for community participation. *International Forestry Review*, *2*, 122–128.

Berry, J. W., Poortinga, Y. H., Segall, M. H., & Dasen, P. R. (2002). *Cross-cultural psychology: Research and applications* (2nd ed.). Cambridge: Cambridge University Press.

Bose, S., & Jalal, A. (1997). Nationalism, democracy, and development. In S. Bose, & A. Jalal (Eds.), *Nationalism, democracy and development: State and politics in India* (pp. 1–9). New Delhi: Oxford University Press.

Brocks, A. C. (Ed.). (2006). *Internationalizing the history of psychology.* New York: New York University Press.

Carr, S. C. & Schumaker, J. F. (Eds.). (1996). *Psychology and the developing world.* Westport, CT: Praeger.

Cherns, A. B. (1984). Contribution of social psychology to the nature and function of work and its relevance to societies of the Third World. *International Journal of Psychology*, *19*, 97–112.

Cole, M. (1998). *Cultural psychology: A once and future discipline.* Cambridge, MA: Harvard University Press.

Cross, S. E., & Gore, J. S. (2005). Cultural models of self. In M. R. Leary & J. P. Tangney (Eds.), *Handbook of self and identity* (pp. 536–566). New York: Guilford Press.

Dalal, A. K. (2010). Psychological interventions for community development. In G. Misra (Ed.) *Psychology in India, vol. 3. Clinical and health psychology* (pp. 363–400). New Delhi: Pearson.

Dalal, A. K., Kumar, S., & Gokhale, D. (2000). *Participatory evaluation of community based rehabilitation.* Project report, Department of Psychology, University of Allahabad, Allahabad.

Danziger, K. (2006). Universalism and indigenization in the history of modern psychology. In A. C. Brock (Ed.), *Internationalizing the history of psychology* (pp. 208–225). New York: New York University Press.

David, H. P., & Buchanan, J. (2003). International psychology. In D. K. Freedheim (Ed.), *Handbook of psychology: History of psychology. 1.* (pp. 509–533). New York: Wiley.

Doi, T. (1986). *The anatomy of self: The individual versus society.* Tokyo: Kodansha.

Dube, S. C. (1988). Cultural dimensions of development. *International Social Sciences Journal, 40*, 505–511.

Enriquiz, V. G. (1992). *From colonial to liberation psychology: The Philippine experience.* Manila: De La Selle University Press.

Escobar, A. (1995). *Encountering development: The making and unmaking of the Third World.* Princeton, NJ: Princeton University Press.

Eze, N. (1991). The progress and status of psychology in Africa. *Journal of Psychology in Africa, 1*(4), 27–37.

Franke, R. H., Hofstede, G., & Bond, M. H. (1991). Cultural roots of economic performance: A research note. *Strategic Management Journal, 12*, 165–173.

Gadgil, M., & Guha, R. (1995). *Ecology and equity: The use and abuse of nature in contemporary India.* New Delhi: Penguin.

Gandhi, M. K. (1945). *Constructive programme: Its meaning and place.* Ahmedabad: The Navjivan Trust.

Gergen, K. J., Gulerce, A., Lock, A., & Misra. G. (1996). Psychological science in cultural context. *American Psychologist, 51*, 496–503.

Giri, A. K. (1998). *Global transformation: Post modernity and beyond.* Jaipur: Rawat Publications.

Heelas, P., & Lock, A. (Eds.). (1981). *Indigenous psychologies: The anthropology of the self.* London: Academic Press.

Hefner, E., & DeLamater, J. (1968). National development from a social psychological perspective. *Journal of Social Issues, 24*, 1–5.

Henriques, J. (1984). Social psychology and the politics of racism. In J. Henriques, W. Hollway, C. Venn, V. Walkerdine, & C. Urwin (Eds.), *Changing the subject: Psychology, social regulation and subjectivity* (pp. 11–25). London: Methuen.

Holdstock, T. L. (2000). *Re-examining psychology: Critical perspectives and African insights.* London: Routledge.

Hsu, F. L. K. (1985). The self in cross-cultural perspective. In A. J. Marsella, G. DeVos, & F. L. K. Hsu, (Eds.), *Culture and self: Asian and Western perspectives* (pp. 14–55). London: Tavistock.

Hufton, V., Elliot, J. G., & Illushin, L. (2002). Achievement motivation across cultures: Some puzzles and their implications for future research. *New Directions for Child and Adolescent Development, 96*, 65–85.

Huston, A. C., & Bentley, A. C. (2009). Human development in societal context. *Annual Review of Psychology, 61*, 411–437.

Huynh, C. T. (1979). *The concept of endogenous development centered on man.* Paris: UNESCO, SS-79/COF.601/COL.20.

Jahoda, G. (1973). Psychology and the developing country: Do they need each other? *International Social Science Journal, 25,* 461–475.

Jain, L. C. (1985). *Grass without roots: Rural development under government auspices.* New Delhi: Sage.

Jain, U., Buch, N., & Chaudhary, S. N. (1999). *Women in Panchayati Raj in Madhya Pradesh.* Unpublished project report, Mahila Chetna Manch, Bhopal.

Kakar, S. (1997). *The Indian psyche.* New Delhi: Oxford University Press.

Kamwendo, A. R. (1985). Developmental psychology research in Malawi. *Journal of Social Science, 12*(3), 133–152.

Kim, U. (2001). Culture, science and indigenous psychologies: An integrated analysis. In D. Matsumoto (Ed.), *Handbook of culture and psychology* (pp. 51–76). Oxford: Oxford University Press.

Kim, U. (2002). Introduction to the special section on factors influencing national development and transformation. *Applied Psychology: An International Review, 51*(2), 266–268.

Kim, U., & Berry, J. W. (Eds.). (1993). *Indigenous psychologies: Research and experience in cultural context.* Newbury Park, CA: Sage.

Kim, U., Yang, K.-S., & Hwang, K. K., (Eds.). (2006). *Indigenous and cultural psychology: Understanding people in context.* New York: Springer.

Kim, U., & Park, Y. S. (2004). Psychological analysis of human potential, creativity, and action: Indigenous, cultural, and comparative perspectives. State of the art lecture provided at the International Congress of Psychology, Beijing. August 8–13.

Kitayama, S., & Cohen, D. (Eds.). (2007). *Handbook of cultural psychology.* New York: Guilford Press.

Klineberg, O. (1956). The role of psychologists in international affairs. *The Journal of Social Issues, 9,* 1–18.

Korten, F. F., Cook, S. W., & Lacey, J. L. (Eds.). (1970). *Psychology and the problems of society.* Washington DC: American Psychological Association.

Kothari, R. (1998). The future of voluntarism. In M. L. Dantawala, H. Sethi, & P. Visaria (Eds.), *Social change through voluntary action* (pp. 182–189). New Delhi: Sage.

Krishnan, L. (2005). Concepts of social behavior in India: *Daan* and distributive justice. *Psychological Studies, 50* (1), 21–31.

Kumar, M. (2008). Practice of psychology in India: A critical overview. *The Social Engineer, 11,* 90–106.

Liu, J. H., Ng, S.-H., Gastardo-Conaco, C., & Wong, D. S. W. (2008). Action research: A missing comment in the emergence of social and cross-cultural psychology as a fully international and global enterprise. *Social and Personality Compass, 2/3,* 1162–1181.

MacLachlan, M., & Carr, S.C. (1994). Pathways to a psychology for development, reconstituting, restating, refuting, and realizing. *Psychology and Developing Societies, 6*(1), 21–28.

Majumdar, N. A. (2002). Rural development: New perceptions. *Economic and Political Weekly, 37*(39), 3983–3987.

Marsella, A. J. (1998). Toward a global community psychology: Meeting the needs of changing world. *American Psychologist, 53*(12), 1282–1291.

Martin-Baro, I. (1996). *Writings for a liberation psychology.* Cambridge, MA: Harvard University Press.

Mathew, G. (2003). Panchayati Raj institutions and human rights in India. *Economic and Political Weekly, 38*(2), 155–162.

Matsumoto, D. (Ed.). (2002). *The handbook of culture and psychology.* New York: Oxford University Press.

McClelland, D. C. (1961). *The achieving society.* Princeton: Van Nostrand.
Mehta, P. (1994). Empowering the people for social development. In R.N. Kanungo & M. Mendonca (Eds.), *Work motivation models for developing countries* (pp. 161–183). New Delhi: Sage.
Mehta, P. (1998). *Psychological strategy for alternative human development: India's performance since independence.* New Delhi: Sage.
Misra, G. (Ed.). (1990). *Applied social psychology in India.* New Delhi: Sage.
Misra, G. (2003). Implications of culture for psychological knowledge. In J. W. Berry, R. C. Misra & R. C. Tripathi (Eds.), *Psychology in human and social development* (pp. 118–215). New Delhi: Sage.
Misra, G. (2006). *Psychology and societal development: Paradigmatic and social concerns.* New Delhi: Concept.
Misra, G., & Gergen, K. G. (1993). On the place of culture in psychological science. *International Journal of Psychology, 28*, 225–243.
Misra, G., & Mohanty, A. K. (Eds.). (2002). *Perspectives on indigenous psychology.* New Delhi: Concept.
Misra G., & Tripathi K. N. (2004). Psychological dimensions of poverty and deprivation. In J. Pandey (Ed.), *Psychology in India revisited: Applied social and organizational psychology* (pp. 118–215). New Delhi: Sage.
Misra, G. & Tripathi, L. B. (1980). *Psychological consequences of prolonged deprivation.* Agra: National Psychological Corporation.
Moghaddam, F. M., & Taylor, D. M. (1986). What constitutes an "appropriate psychology" for the developing world? *International Journal of Psychology, 21*, 253–267.
Moghaddam, F. M., Bianchi, C., Daniels, K., Apter, M. J., & Harre, R. (1999). Psychology and national development. *Psychology and Developing Societies, 11*(2), 119–141.
Murphy, G. (1953). *In the minds of men.* New York: Basic Books.
Myrdal, G. (1968). *Asian drama: An enquiry into the poverty of nations* (Vol. 1). New York: Penguin Books.
Nicholas, L. J. (Ed.). (1993). *Psychology and oppression: critiques and proposals.* Johannesburg: Skotaville.
Nisbett, R. E. (2003). *The geography of thought.* New York: Free Press.
Oskamp, S. (1984). *Applied social psychology.* Englewood Cliffs, NJ: Prentice Hall.
Painter, D., Terre Blanche, M., & Henderson, J. (2006). Critical psychology in South Africa: Histories, themes and prospects. *Annual Review of Critical Psychology, 5*, 212–235
Pandey, J. (2004). Psychology in India enters the twenty-first century: Movement toward an indigenous discipline. In J. Pandey (Ed.), *Psychology in India revisited: Applied social and organizational psychology* (pp. 342–370). New Delhi: Sage.
Pandey, J., & Singh, A. K. (1985). Social psychological responses to perceived and objective indicators of poverty in India. In I. R. Lagunes & Y. H. Poortinga (Eds.), *From different perspectives: Studies of behavior across cultures* (pp. 148–156). Lisse: Swets and Zeitlinger.
Pandey, J., & Singh, P. (2005). Social psychology in India: Social roots and development. *International Journal of Psychology, 40*, 239–253.
Paranjpe, A. C. (1998). *Self and identity in modern psychology and Indian thought.* New York: Plenum Press.
Pareek, U. (1968). Motivational pattern and planned social change. *International Social Science Journal, 20*(3), 464–473.
Pareek, U. (1994). Interventions to deal with poverty. In U. Pareek (Ed.), *Beyond management* (pp. 118–128). New Delhi: Oxford and IBH.
Pickren, W.E. (2007). Tension and opportunity in post-World War II American psychology. *History of Psychology, 10*, 279–299.

Prilleltensky, I., & Nelson, G. (2000). Promoting child and family wellness: Priorities for psychological and social intervention. *Journal of Community and Applied Social Psychology, 10*, 85–105.

Putnam, R. (1993). The prosperous community: Social capital and public life. *American Prospect, 4*(13), 35–42.

Rao, K. R., Paranjpe, A. C., & Dalal, A. K. (Eds.) (2008). *Handbook of Indian psychology.* New Delhi: Cambridge University Press.

Rath, R. (1982). Problems of integration of disadvantaged to the mainstream. In D. Sinha, R.C. Tripathi, & G. Misra (Eds.), *Deprivation: Its social roots and psychological consequences* (pp. 151–175). New Delhi: Concept.

Rose, N. (1998). *Inventing our selves: Psychology, power, and personhood.* Cambridge: Cambridge University Press.

Sacks, M. & Kidd, R. (Eds.). (1980). *Advances in applied social psychology.* Hillsdale, NJ: Lawrence Erlbaum Associates.

Sastry, K. R., & Vithal, C. P. (1988). Participatory dimension in rural development: The case of Panchayati Raj. *Journal of Rural Development, 7*(6), 689–700.

Sen, A. (1999). *Development as freedom.* Oxford: Oxford University Press.

Sen, A. (2009). *The idea of justice.* London: Allen Lane.

Shah, V. P., Seth, N. R., & Visaria, P. (1998). Swadhyaya: Social change through spirituality. In M. L. Dantawala, H. Sethi, & P. Visaria (Eds.), *Social change through voluntary action* (pp. 57–73). New Delhi: Sage.

Sham, M., & Hwang, K. K. (2005). Responses to epistemological challenges to indigenous psychologies. *Asian Journal of Social Psychology, 8*(1), Special Issue.

Sheth, D. L., & Sethi, H. (1998). The NGO sector in India: Historical context and current discourse. *Voluntas 2*, 51.

Shweder, R. A., & Sullivan, M. (1993). Cultural psychology: Who needs it? *Annual Review of Psychology, 44*, 497–523.

Shinn, M., & Toohey, S. M. (2003). Community context of human welfare. *Annual Review of Psychology, 54*, 427–459.

Singhal, R. (1995). *Behavioural factors in institutional effectiveness.* JFM Study Series. Bhopal: Indian Institute of Forest Management.

Singhal, R., & Tiwari, P. S. N. (2009). Psychology and societal development. In Girishwar Misra (Ed.) *Psychology in India, vol. 2. Social and organizational processes* (pp. 407–452). New Delhi: Pearson.

Sinha, D. (1965). The integration of modern psychology with Indian thought. *Journal of Humanistic Psychology, 5*, 6–17.

Sinha, D. (1966). On the arena of social change. Presidential address at 33rd section of Psychology of Educational Sciences: Indian Science Congress, Chandigarh.

Sinha, D. (1969) *Indian villages in transition: A motivational analysis.* New Delhi: Associated Publishing House.

Sinha, D. (1983). Applied social psychology and problems of national development. In F. Blackler (Ed.), *Social psychology and developing countries* (pp. 7–20). New York: John Wiley.

Sinha, D. (1986). *Psychology in a third world country: The Indian experience.* New Delhi: Sage.

Sinha, D. (1990). Intervention for development out of poverty. In R. W. Brislin (Ed.), *Applied cross-cultural psychology* (pp. 77–97). Newbury Park: Sage.

Sinha, D. (1997). Indigenizing psychology. In J. W. Berry, Y. Poortinga & J. Pandey (Eds.), *Handbook of cross-cultural psychology: Theoretical and methodological perspectives* (Vol. 1, pp. 129–169). Boston: Allyn & Bacon.

Sinha, D., & Holtzman, W. H. (Eds.). (1984). The impact of psychology on third world development. *International Journal of Psychology, 19* (Special Issues nos. 1–2.)

Sinha, D., & Kao, H. S .R. (Eds.). (1988). *Social values and development: Asian perspectives.* New Delhi: Sage.

Sinha, H., & Suar, D. (2003). Forest and people: Understanding the institutional governance, social identity and peoples participation in Indian forest management. *Journal of Rural Development, 22*(4), 425–454.

Sinha, J. B. P. (1984). Toward partnership for relevant research in the third world. *International Journal of Psychology, 19*, 169–178.

Sinha, J. B. P. (1990). Role of psychology in national development. In G. Misra (Ed.), *Applied social Psychology in India* (pp. 171–199). New Delhi: Sage.

Sinha, J. B. P. (1997). In search of my Brahman. In M. H. Bond (Ed.), *Working at the interface of cultures: Eighteen lives in social sciences* (pp. 77–84). New York: Routledge.

Sinha, J. B. P. (2002). Towards indigenization of psychology in India. In G. Misra & A. K. Mohanty (Eds.) *Perspectives on indigenous psychology* (pp. 440–457). New Delhi: Concept.

Skevington, S. M. (2009). Conceptualizing dimensions of quality of life in poverty. *Journal of Community and Applied Social Psychology, 19*, 33–50.

Smith, L. T. (1999). *Decolonizing methodologies: Research and indigenous peoples.* London: Zed Books.

Stevens, M. J., & Gielen, U. P. (Eds.). (2007). *Toward a global psychology: Theory, research, intervention, and pedagogy.* Mahwah, NJ: Lawrence Erlbaum Associates.

Suar, D., & Prasad, S. K. (1995). The vital role of NGOs in Panchayat Raj. *Social Welfare, 41*(10), 16–17.

Triandis, H. C. (1984). Toward a psychological theory of economic growth. *International Journal of Psychology, 19*, 79–96.

Triandis, H. C. (1989). The self and social behavior in differing cultural contexts. *Psychological Review, 96*, 506–520.

Tripathi, R. C. (2003). Culture as a factor in community interventions. In J. W. Berry, R. C. Mishra, & R. C. Tripathi (Eds.), *Psychology in human and social development: Lessons from diverse cultures* (pp. 235–293). New Delhi: Sage.

Tyler, F. B. (August, 1995). UN psychology dialogue on world summit for development. In H. Naimark (Chair), *Social development and human security: A United Nations-psychologists dialogue.* Symposium organized at the meeting of the American Psychological Association, New York.

ul-Haq, M. (1999). *Reflections on human development.* New Delhi: Oxford University Press.

UNDP. (1990). *Human development report.* Oxford: Oxford University Press.

Valsiner, J., & Rosa, A. (Eds.). (2007). *The Cambridge handbook of sociocultural psychology.* New York: Cambridge University Press.

Wang , T.-Y., Chien, S.-C., & Kao, C. (2007). The role of technology development in national competitiveness: Evidence from Southeast Asian countries. *Technological Forecasting & Social Change, 74*, 1357–1373.

Wober, M. (1975). *Psychology in Africa.* Plymouth: Clarke, Doble and Brendon Ltd.

Yang, C. F., & Hwang, K. K. (2000). Indigenous, cultural, and cross-cultural psychologies. *Asian Journal of Social Psychology, 3*(3), Special Issue.

26

The Psychology of Religion and Religious Experience

David Fontana

Historical Background

The reasons for the relative neglect in the 20th century of the psychology of religion within mainstream psychology are open to debate (see Wulff, 1998 for a valuable extended discussion), but prominent among them is the desire by psychologists to identify psychology with the physical and biological sciences, which would exclude anything associated with religion, a subject seen by many as difficult to explore under laboratory conditions and as representing beliefs and practices explicable in terms of self-delusion, primitive conditioning, magical thinking, father fixation, and the like. An example of this attitude comes from Malony's finding (1972) that only 14 (1.1%) of a random sample of 1,111 members of the American Psychological Association reported an interest in religion—a vanishingly small number.

The Current Position

This relative neglect of religion has impoverished psychology. Whether one believes in the truth of religion or not, religious beliefs and practices are a continuing and significant influence upon human behavior. Paloutzian and Park (2005) describe them in fact as "the greatest force for good and evil in the history of the world," and the fact that religion has flourished for thousands of years and in virtually all cultures is ample evidence of its importance to individuals and society. Human motivation, morals, values, self-concepts, legal structures, relationships, philosophical systems, education, altruistic behaviors, hospital care, and attitudes to death and dying have all been intimately influenced by religious theory and practice. In addition,

IAAP Handbook of Applied Psychology, First Edition. Edited by Paul R. Martin, Fanny M. Cheung, Michael C. Knowles, Michael Kyrios, Lyn Littlefield, J. Bruce Overmier, and José M. Prieto.

life-changing religious experiences have been reported from all cultures and in all centuries (see, e.g., Hay, 1987 for recent examples). And religious differences, though often of minor significance in themselves, have proved a potent excuse for conflict between cultures and nations.

If belatedly, these facts are now becoming more recognized within psychology. The foundation of the *Journal for the Scientific Study of Religion* in 1961 and of the Psychology of Religion Division within the American Psychological Association in 1976 have been instrumental in furthering this recognition, and research papers on the psychology of religion are increasingly appearing in refereed journals. Something of the quantity and quality of these publications is evident in Emmons and Paloutzian (2003) and in a classic text by Wulff (1997). The fact that human behavior is no longer seen solely as a set of conditioned responses to the environment but as a consequence of the ability to perform intentional acts congruent with sets of beliefs has also helped to draw attention to the subject. However, much work remains to be done. Religion and spirituality are elusive concepts, and the tendency of many psychologists of religion is to focus upon what is measurable by appropriate scales, rather than upon narrative and other approaches that enable individuals to articulate their inner religious experience. Andresen (2001) emphasizes the time is right for developing cognitive approaches to the study of religion, yet to date these approaches are more apparent in the work of anthropologists, philosophers, sociologists, and specialists in comparative religion than in that of psychologists. The reason many psychologists are reluctant to adopt a subjectively oriented approach is that, from the scientific perspective, there is no way of investigating consciousness directly. However, it is within the field of consciousness that the individual experiences his or her religious life. The suggestion by Emmons and Paloutzian (2003) that psychology should adopt a multilevel interdisciplinary paradigm drawing upon many levels of analysis (some of which take account of consciousness) is thus particularly relevant for the psychologist of religion.

Wallace (2000), an expert on the introspective Buddhist approach to the study of mind, takes a similar view, arguing that a major impact of scientific materialism in the West is that it "alienates us from our firsthand experience of our own minds, which it equates with 'common sense' or 'folk psychology'" in the belief that subjective experience "is often, if not always misleading." And this despite the fact that discoveries by neuroscientists of the brain's influences upon mental processes draw extensively upon subjects' first-hand accounts of these processes. The time is right for the psychology of religion to insist it has a warrant to show the same reliance.

Religion as Social Phenomenon

Some acceptance of the role of first-hand accounts is becoming apparent in the increasing importance attached by psychologists of religion to attitude-based research. Donahue and Nielsen (2005) recognize that investigation of the degree to which attitudes and behavior are consistent with each other is now a core approach in social psychology, and within the psychology of religion this approach is beginning to make use of cognitive dissonance theory, social identity, secularization theory, and value systems. The research question involved is the extent to which religious beliefs and behavior are influenced by forces in the outside world, which, in turn, is related to broader questions on the origins of religious belief. To what extent is this belief a response to external forces and to what extent a response to private reflection and/or a sense of inner spiritual realities?

Watts (2002) distinguishes between social constructionism that emphasizes the role of the social context and perennialism that stresses the unmediated nature of religious experience as evidenced by the common core of religious experience across cultures. We return to perennialism when we discuss inner experiences more extensively, but social constructionism is clearly correct in maintaining that many religious beliefs are influenced by cultural factors. To this we can add that religious beliefs and experience also influence culture. Donahue and Nielsen (2005) in fact conclude their survey of religion and social behavior by observing that the investigation of religion's impact on social life is "the most vigorous area of study in the psychology of religion." Their survey shows the diversity of this impact, which ranges from the promotion of "prejudice, intolerance, and war" to the furthering of "understanding, tolerance, and peace." The problem is to discover the reasons for this diversity, and the degree to which it is influenced by other belief systems such as those associated with politics or nationalism. This is particularly so when religious teachings are open to conflicting interpretations. The question for research then arises, why do individuals favour one interpretation over another? What factors are in play when choices are made? McIntosh (1995) argues that religious meaning systems are a lens through which individuals perceive and interpret reality, which prompts us to ask to what extent do nonreligious belief systems influence these systems and perhaps cloud the lens? An authoritarian political system may influence adherents to favour religious interpretations that divide men and women into the righteous who deserve reward and the sinful who merit punishment, which then justifies persecution on the grounds that the destruction of dissenting groups and nations is obedience to the will of God.

Silberman makes clear in several publications that religious meaning systems have a marked ability to integrate social groups, and that once integration takes place groups adhere to their systems in the conviction that they constitute unquestionable truths (e.g., Silberman, 2005a, 2005b). This is particularly true of systems associated with charismatic leaders who convince through force of personality rather than through spiritual qualities. The result can lead to sects that further bind their members together by insisting independence is surrendered through the forfeit of money and personal property and an embargo upon leaving the group or marrying without the permission of the group leader. In long-established monastic traditions the rights of the individual are protected by canon law, but sect leaders typically are responsible only to themselves, and the potential damage of their behavior, reinforced by indoctrination and the promotion of guilt, is all too obvious.

Religion and Individual Psychology

Research summarized by Koenig, McCullough, and Larsen in their excellent *Handbook of Religion and Health* (2001) shows that regular churchgoing and religious belief convey significant health benefits. For example, one 21-year longitudinal study in the USA found that church attendance once a week or more is associated with a 25 to 33% reduction in mortality when compared with non-churchgoers, even when the benefits of belonging to organized social groups, of not smoking, and of leading a relatively healthy lifestyle are taken into account. An 18-year longitudinal study of 21,204 adults in the USA produced similar findings, and showed the average age at death of regular church-goers to be 81.9 years as against 75.3 years for non-church-goers. Some degree of health benefits exists even for those non-churchgoers with religious beliefs who follow practices such as meditation, prayer, or Bible study. Research also shows that churchgoers and those with religious beliefs adapt significantly better to illness than nonbelievers, seemingly because they accept that illness carries meaning and is associated with God's purpose. Some studies even reveal a 14% better survival rate for churchgoers than nonbelievers when faced by life-threatening conditions, particularly if the religious beliefs of the former are intrinsic rather than extrinsic on the I–E religious orientation scale discussed later. Whether this is an example of the mind–body connection or of spiritual healing, it suggests that religion is not just a set of dogmas but a matter of life-enhancing conviction. Research also shows that regular churchgoing and religious coping (see Pargament, Ano, and Wachholtz, 2005) are also helpful for psychological problems such as anxiety and depression (see also Koenig et al., 1993), for parents coping with bereavement (Maton, 1989), and even for dealing with the stress of kidney transplant surgery (Tix and Frazier, 1998).

Religion as Inner Experience

Can psychology probe more deeply into subjective experience to determine why religion can be life-enhancing? Psychologists' suspicion of subjectivity leads many to doubt that it can. Scharf (2000) comments that all research attempts into inner religious experience are "destined to remain well-meaning squirms that get us nowhere." In his view it is "ill-conceived to construe the object of the study of religion to be the inner experience of religious practitioners" because "any assertion to the effect that someone else's inner experience bears some significance for *my* construal of reality is situated, by its very nature, in the public realm of contested meanings." Scharf is correct in that someone else's inner experience may be very different from mine, even though the two experiences are described in similar language, but this is also true for the study of behavior—two sets of behavior may appear the same, yet the motivation behind each set may be quite different. In any case, the sharing of experience through language is part of the commerce of social life and indeed of psychotherapy and psychological counseling. If psychology ignores this fact, it forfeits any claim to being inclusive. And even though inner experience is not susceptible to empirical verification this does not necessarily disqualify it from exploration by reliable research. Such research can, for example, seek comparisons between the reported inner experiences arising from spiritual practices such as meditation, an approach encouraged in transpersonal psychology (now a Section of the British Psychological Society). Results reveal a striking similarity of higher stages of spiritual development between advanced meditators across individuals and cultures irrespective of the traditions to which they belong (Wilber, 1998). Recently so-called "Mindfulness Based Stress Reduction" (MBSR), a technique that seeks to make ancient meditation practices more broadly available, has shown that even brief training enhances stress-reduction, relaxation, pain management, and locus of control (e.g., Shapiro, Schwartz, and Bonner, 1998; also see Goldin 2001 for a survey), in addition to producing effects on left-sided brain activation and immune function (Davidson et al., 2003). It is possible to debate whether a religious practice such as meditation loses its spiritual connotations if taught in a secular context, or whether, irrespective of context, it retains spiritual as well as psychological effects, but it is pertinent to remember that all major meditation practices originated within religious traditions. However, embedding the practice in an overtly religious context does seem to enhance benefits. A comparison between mantra meditation using a spiritual mantra ("God loves me") with that using a secular mantra ("I am loved") showed the former to be associated with greater anxiety reduction, spiritual health and resistance to pain (Wachholtz and Pargament, 2005). Sceptics might argue that the former mantra is more successful because it is more personal and self-suggestive and thus constitutes a more positive affirmation, but those using it might disagree.

Further attempts to explore the influence of inner spiritual experience investigate its influence upon consequent behavior. For example, Ring's findings (1984) indicate that those reporting Near Death Experiences (which typically involve subjective impressions of spiritual realities and survival of physical death) subsequently show positive long-term changes in value systems, life goals, career orientation, social relationships, and spiritual inclinations. For present purposes it is unnecessary to debate whether or not Near Death Experiences (NDEs) really inform us about survival of clinical death (see, e.g., Fenwick and Fenwick, 1995 for a discussion of the relevant medical factors); the point is that individuals who report these experiences declare themselves convinced of their spiritual nature.

Studies yielding information on the relationship between spiritual experiences and changes in observable behavior are potentially reliable ways of assessing the comparative psychological importance of these experiences and their intellectual and emotional impact. Sudden conversion experiences provide further examples of spiritual transformations that prompt long-term changes in behavior. The literature on saints in all traditions provides numerous instances of how these experiences lead to profound reorientations of career and life goals, of personal relationships, and of concepts of reality and ultimate meaning. Furthermore, research suggests such experiences are not exclusive to saints, and that mid-level personality functions such as purposes, attitudes and values may also change among lay people, together with global-level aspects of personality such as self-definition and identity (Paloutzian, Richardson, & Rambo, 1999). However, core personality traits such as the Big Five seem unaffected (though perhaps this was not so for saints such as Saint Augustine, St. Francis, and St. Paul), though they may be expressed and directed in new ways.

Many attempts to explain the genesis of conversion experiences have been made by reference to psychological factors such as the impulse towards socialization, the search for meaning, the resolution of inner conflicts, and the satisfaction of needs for power and for self-transcendence (Paloutzian, 1996; Rambo, 1993; Levenson,

Jennings, Aldwin, & Shiraishi, 2005). Valuable as these attempts are, they do not shed much light on how conversion experiences actually seem to those who have them. The closest we have come to knowing more about these experiences is through the autobiographies of saints and through the accounts of first-hand religious experiences amassed by research centres such as the Princeton University Center for the Study of Religion in the USA and the Religious Experience Research Centre in the UK. Such accounts allow identification of the context in which religious experiences most frequently occur, and this context appears in fact to be similar in the USA and the UK. Contrary to sociological interpretations of religious experiences, the great majority of these experiences take place in solitude or silence rather than in religious gatherings. Approximately half occur in times of distress, while around a third happen spontaneously and for no obvious reason (e.g., Hay 1987, 2006). Again, contrary to attempts to associate spiritual experiences with the superstitious and unlettered, the findings show they appear most common among the well-educated and the middle classes. The natural world and spiritual practices such as meditation and prayer seem associated with religious experience, and the experience seems most frequently to take the form of a sense of presence (usually of God though sometimes of deceased loved ones or of an unnamed power). In the great majority of cases the experience is interpreted positively, and is seen as confirming religious belief.

Mystical Experience

Mystical experiences are at face value the most profound of all religious experiences, and consequently have attracted research attention. One problem is the definition of mystical experience, and it is disappointing that psychologists have made little use of the vast literature on mysticism presenting the reported experiences of Western mystics such as St. Teresa of Avila, Mother Julian of Norwich, St. John of the Cross, Jacob Boehm, and John Ruysbroeck, or of Eastern mystics such as Sri Ramakrishna, Swami Vivekananda, Sri Ramana Marshi, and Paramahansa Yogananda. Cox (1983), following on from Stace (1960), in a wide-ranging survey of Western mystical experience, considers that all contain an awareness of God that carries with it the "unitive acquisition of knowledge inaccessible to rational understanding," while despite the fact that Eastern mystics typically use terms such as "absolute reality," "emptiness," or "essential nature" in place of the word God, their experiences remain essentially similar to those in the West. In both Western and Eastern mysticism these experiences take two identifiable forms: transcendent mysticism in which God/absolute reality is perceived as being outside oneself, and immanent mysticism in which this reality is sensed as pervading and unifying all things. In the Hindu literature these two forms are described respectively as *savikalpa samadhi* and *nirvikalpa samadhi*, that is, as becoming one with the divine or as contemplating the divine ("becoming the sugar" or "tasting the sugar," in Sri Ramakrishna's words; see Fontana, 2003).

Factor analytic studies by Hood of mystical experiences have essentially confirmed these two forms, and augmented them with an *interpretive* factor that identifies differences between theistic and nontheistic attempts to put mystical experience into words (Hood, 2002). However, other psychologists of religion have tended to use the term "mysticism" for less exalted states than the core experiences of immanence or transcendence. Greeley (1975) considers that feelings of profound peace, the certainty that all is well, the conviction that love is central to all things, the assurance of personal survival, and the sense that everything has life are also mystical experiences, while Hardy (1987) lists in addition visions, bright lights, voices, transformation of the surroundings, and feelings of awe and reverence. Drawing upon sources such as these, Hood (1995) developed a 32-item scale to measure the incidence of less exalted mystical experience in appropriate samples of the population, and some subsequent studies put this incidence as high as one third, with positive responses most apparent in subjects whose religion emerges as intrinsic on the I–E scale described below.

This broadening of the meaning of mysticism risks blurring the distinction between less transcendent states and the profound experiences reported by the great mystics of West and East. This matters only if we are interested in what it is about religion that can produce the extraordinary "turning around in the deepest seat of consciousness" of which mystics speak, and if we are interested in what is meant in psychological terms by the states of "enlightenment," "samadhi," and "satori," associated with mystical experiences in the Eastern traditions. It is said that spiritual teachers who are themselves "enlightened" can recognize these states in their pupils when they occur, and major questions remain as to what guides this recognition, since the answers might provide searching insights into the essential core of mystical experience.

Assessing Individual Differences in Religious Orientation

The empirical study of religion by psychologists has made use of interviews and scales/questionnaires such as that of Hood (1995), mentioned above. Despite their obvious limitations (Do they ask the right questions? Can we place reliance upon the replies?) scales and questionnaires facilitate large-sample research and help focus the minds of respondents upon the areas of interest to researchers. One of the most widely used scales and one that has proved effective in identifying dimensions relevant to the individual's religiosity and to the concerns of psychologists is the I–E (Intrinsic–Extrinsic) religious orientation scale first assembled by Gordon six decades ago and further developed by Gorsuch and McPherson (1989). Hill and Hood (1999) review 11 attempts to design similar scales aimed at measuring qualitative differences in religious motivation, and, in spite of criticism by Kirkpatrick and Hood (1990) that the I–E concept is "theoretically impoverished and has really taught us little about the psychology of religion," it has helped throw light upon the relationship between religious orientation and such things as physical health, transcendent experiences, psychological health, coping ability, tolerance, and socially appropriate behavior (Donahue 1985, Donahue and Nielsen 2005).

An additional scale often used alongside the I–E dimensions seeks to measure "Q", a dimension of "Quest" or "Seeking," thought to represent the strength of an individual's religious seeking and development (Batson, Schoentade, & Ventis, 1993), and there is no shortage of additional measures (Hill, 2005 lists no fewer than 46 such scales) specifically designed to measure aspects of the psychology of religion and spirituality. However, valuable as these scales are, they tend to treat scores on the variables concerned as if they are analogous to static traits, whereas religious belief and experience can be labile, and in some cases more akin to state-based than to trait-based qualities. Much of this lability can be due to transitory disappointment at one's own behavior and at one's sense of spiritual adequacy, and to doubts over one's relationship with God. Religion relates not only to the spirit and the intellect but to the emotions and the senses, and short-term emotional and sensory variations can influence the strength of religious feelings. Furthermore, the religious impulse can lie fallow for a period before abruptly finding renewed energy. In addition, rating scales still do not provide access to what it really means to the individual to be religious. Ideally, we need to identify the concepts (or experiences) of God that underlie religious orientation. One person's intrinsic orientation may be toward a God of peace and love while that of another may be towards a God of anger and conquest. The first orientation may lead to sainthood, the second to terrorism. Part of the answer may be to allow religious people to speak for themselves through more in-depth interviews and autobiographical writings. Unfortunately, such work is time-intensive, which is why, as in other areas of psychology, religious research is predominantly nomothetic rather than idiographic, and thus reflects the researcher's perspective rather than that of the subject.

What of the Future?

The advances made in the psychology of religion over the last three decades are encouraging for all those interested in the subject. Researchers responsible for these advances have made various suggestions as to the direction in which the subject can go, and these are fully discussed in Wulff, 1997 and Paloutzian and Park, 2005. However, two somewhat neglected areas also warrant emphasis. The first is the way in which religion is practiced. The form of this practice varies widely in response to the individual's beliefs, to the religious and cultural tradition to which he or she belongs, and to personal cognitive and affective variables. Research is needed to identify the psychological consequence of these different practices. The most enduring—and potentially helpful—way of categorizing these practices dates back to early Hindu scriptures such as the Bhagavad Gita (5th Century BCE/1st Century CE). Essentially, it offers five different mutually supportive paths through which the devotee approaches God or the Absolute. These five paths, known as yogas (see Aurobindo, 1957 and Ghose, 1970), are known respectively as *hatha, karma, bhakti, gnana,* and *raja*. Hatha reflects the belief that through aesthetic practices and physical self-denial one can turn away from the material world and transmute physical energies into spiritual; karma that in serving others one is serving the Divine and surrendering the self; bhakti that through devotion and the immersion of the self in love and worship of the Divine one draws closer to the source; gnana that prayer and sacred studies facilitate the development of intuitive spiritual wisdom; and raja that meditation and the stilling of mental distractions enable the devotee to see into the true nature of the self and recognize its unity with the Divine (see Fontana, 2003, for more detail).

All five of these yogas include practices that can be either esoteric or exoteric, the former representing hidden and complex teachings and the latter those more accessible and readily understood. Collectively, the yogas demonstrate the recognition that religion is a tension in unity between doctrine, liturgy, and mysticism, and that the choices made as to practice are partly determined by the individual's cognitive and affective variables, as well as cultural conditioning and personal religious experience. If psychologists of religion wish to understand how individuals view and experience their religion, and to learn more about the many factors that influence their beliefs and behavior, it is important to recognize that although all traditions share a common core, religion cannot be treated for psychological purposes as a unitary phenomenon. Furthermore, it cannot be studied solely from the outside, in the way of many other social psychological phenomena. For a proper understanding the processes involved must also be studied if possible from the inside so that the researcher can assess how religion determines the way the individual lives life and views the nature of self and others.

The second rather neglected area concerns what believers in different traditions mean when they speak of the Divine. For example, the Hindu, although accepting many manifestations of the Divine, regards the Absolute (Brahman) as ineffable, and approachable only through the realization that the Atman, the indwelling spirit in man, is one with Brahman and returns to Brahman after many lifetimes. The various schools of Buddhism make no mention of a Divine Creator, and regard the Absolute, or Nirvana, as a state into which the enlightened being passes after death rather than as a being to be worshiped. Christianity worships a personal God, symbolized as a Heavenly Father, who knows and is known to worshipers. Among the many consequences of these different concepts is the Eastern view that all created things are one, and the Western view that all things have their individual relationship with God. In the East, individuality is therefore something to be transcended, while in the West it is something to be purified and sanctified. The psychological and cultural implications of these different views are too obvious to need emphasizing. Yet the psychology of religion has not fully engaged with them and acknowledged that even within each religious tradition there is a range of concepts of the Divine. Many years ago I carried out research into student teachers' concepts of God and was surprised to find an almost complete lack of any consensus, even though all sample members were Westerners and most professed a belief in God. Equal cause for surprise is that, many years later, the otherwise excellent *Handbook of the Psychology of Religion and Spirituality* (Paloutzian & Park, 2005) includes no reference to God in the index. Unless we know how people see God or their gods, we cannot expect to make real sense of their religion.

Equally surprisingly, the *Handbook* has no entry for the afterlife. Yet unless we have some knowledge of how religious believers conceptualize a possible life after death, we cannot fully understand how they conceptualize the present lifetime. Eastern religions and many New Age spiritual groups teach the existence of rebirth/reincarnation, which the Christian church ruled against at the Council of Constantinople (553 CE), and which Judaism has never accepted as part of orthodox belief. Obviously, the notion that we are reborn on earth lifetime after lifetime until we reach enlightenment and leave the cycle of birth and death produces a different attitude to earthly life from the belief we have only one lifetime, and that our conduct during it determines our destiny in the afterlife. The two beliefs can lead to divergent attitudes toward ourselves and toward others, since reincarnation can imply everyone is responsible for personal misfortunes in the present life. Reincarnation also indicates that the consequences of each lifetime are carried into the next, and that the present life is largely determined by past incarnations rather than by current endeavors and opportunities.

There are other important areas of the psychology of religion that merit more extensive future attention. These include the influence of prayer and the study of sacred literature, the presence of intimations of immortality, the influence of religious art and architecture, and that of pilgrimage and sacred rituals such as initiation, baptism, the Eucharist, and ordination. The different forms of liturgy also deserve attention. For example, in Christianity corporate worship is very different for the Roman Catholic and for the Quaker, and we need to know why some individuals are drawn to the one and some to the other (Prince Vladimir of Kiev is said to have favoured Orthodoxy in preference to Roman Catholicism for the Russian state church because of his preference for the music and ceremonies of the former). And there are major differences in doctrine within each tradition that are also worthy of study. The various schools of Buddhism and of Hinduism are so diverse that they could almost be regarded as different faiths. Within Christianity the doctrinal divergences between for example Anglicans and Unitarians are such that it is sometimes difficult to identify their common ground. Even within Christian denominations there are important differences—High Anglicans versus Evangelical Anglicans, Methodists versus Primitive Methodists, Strict Baptists versus Free Church Baptists, and so on.

Finally, there is also a need for increased focus on non-Christian religions such as Islam, Judaism, and Hinduism. What, for example, is the influence of the great religious festivals upon the Hindu, of Ramadan upon the spiritual life of the Moslem, of lengthy solitary retreats upon the Buddhist? What is the consequence for the Jew of the strict observance of the Sabbath? What is the consequence of the direct wordless transmission of spiritual realities said in Hinduism and Buddhism to take place between teacher and pupil? Overall it is important to emphasize that the consequences of religious beliefs and experience in all traditions for human behavior, motivation, and attitudes are very much part of the domain not only of the psychology of religion but of psychology generally. Only when this is fully recognized will the psychology of religion take its rightful place as a leading force within 21st-century scholarship.

References

Andresen, J. (2001). Towards a cognitive science of religion. Introduction to J. Andresen (Ed.) *Religion in mind: Cognitive perspectives on religious belief, ritual and experience.* New York: Cambridge University Press.

Aurobindo, Sri (1957). *The synthesis of yoga* (2nd ed.). Pondicherry: Sri Aurobindo Ashram.

Batson, C. D., Schoenrade, P., & Ventis, W. L. (1993). *Religion and the individual: A social-psychological perspective.* New York: Oxford University Press.

Cox, M. (1983). *Mysticism: The direct experience of God.* Wellingborough Northants: The Aquarian Press.

Davidson, R. J., Kabat-Zinn, J., Schumacher, J., Ronsenkranz, M., Muller, D., Santorelli, S. F., ... Sheridan, J. F. (2003). Alteration in brain and immune function by mindfulness meditation. *Psychosomatic Medicine 65*, 564–570.

Donahue, M. J. (1985). Intrinsic and extrinsic religiousness: Review and meta- analysis. *Journal of Personality and Social Psychology 48*, 400–419.

Donahue, M. J., & Nielsen, M. E. (2005). Religion, attitudes and social behavior. In R. F. Paloutzian & C. L. Park (Eds.), *Handbook of the psychology of religion and spirituality* (pp. 274–291). New York: The Guilford Press.

Emmons, R. A., & Paloutzian, R. F. (2003). The psychology of religion. *Annual Review of Psychology 54*, 377–402.

Fenwick, P., & Fenwick, E. (1995). *The truth in the light.* London and New York: HodderHeadline.

Fontana, D. (2003). *Psychology, religion and spirituality.* Oxford: Blackwell.

Ghose, C. K. (1970). *Yoga and the spiritual life.* New York: Tower Books.

Goldin, P. (2001). Mindfulness meditation research findings. Retrieved 31 October, 2010 from www-psych.stanford.edu/~pgoldin/Buddhism/MindfulnessMeditationSummary.doc

Gorsuch, R. L., & McPherson, S. E. (1989). Intrinsic/extrinsic measurement: I/E revised and single-item scales. *Journal for the Scientific Study of Religion, 28*, 348–354.

Greeley, A. M. (1975). *The sociology of the paranormal.* London: Sage.

Hardy, J. (1987). *A psychology with a soul.* London: Routledge & Kegan Paul.

Hay, D. (1987). *Exploring inner space* (Rev. ed.). Oxford: Mowbray.

Hay, D. (2006). *Something there: The biology of the human spirit.* London: Dartman, Longman, and Todd.

Hill, P. C. (2005). Measurement in the psychology of religion and spirituality. In R. F. Paloutzian and C. L. Park (Eds.), *Handbook of the psychology of religion and spirituality* (pp. 43–61). New York: The Guilford Press.

Hill, P. C. & Hood, R. W., Jr. (1999). *Measures of religiosity.* Birmingham, AL: Religious Education Press.

Hood, R. W., Jr. (1995). The facilitation of religious experience. In R. W. Hood, Jr. (Ed.), *The handbook of religious experience.* Birmingham, AL: Religious Education Press.

Hood, R. W., Jr. (2002). *Dimensions of mystical experience: Empirical studies and psychological links.* Amsterdam: Rhodopi.

Kirkpatrick L. A., & Hood, R. W., Jr. (1990). Intrinsic–extrinsic religious orientation: The boon or bane of contemporary psychology of religion. *Journal for the Scientific Study of Religion, 29*, 442–462.

Koenig, H. G., McCullough, M. E., & Larson, D. B. (2001). *Handbook of religion and health.* Oxford: Oxford University Press.

Koenig, H. G., Ford, S. M., George, L. K., Blazer, D. G., & Meador, K. G. (1993). Religion and anxiety disorder: an examination and comparison of associations in young, middle-aged, and elderly adults. *Journal of Anxiety Disorders, 7*, 321–342.

Levenson, M. R., Jennings, P. A., Aldwin, C. M., & Shiraishi, R. W. (2005). Self-transcendence: Conceptualization and measurement. *International Journal of Aging and Human Development, 60*, 127–143.

Malony, H. N. (1972). The Psychologist-Christian. *Journal of the American Scientific Affiliation, 24*, 135–144. Retrieved October 31, 2010 from www.asa3.org/ASA/PSCF/1972/JASA12-72Malony.html

Maton, K. I. (1989). The stress-buffering role of spiritual support: Cross-sectional and prospective investigations. *Journal for the Scientific Study of Religion. 28*, 310–323.

McIntosh, D. N. (1995). Religion as a schema, with implications for the relation between religion and coping. *The International Journal for the Psychology of Religion 5*, 1–16.

Paloutzian, R. F. (1996). *Invitation to the psychology of religion*. Needham Heights, MA: Allyn & Bacon.

Paloutzian, R. F., Richardson, J. T., & Rambo L. R. (1999). Religious conversion and personality change. *Journal of Personality 67*, 1047–1079.

Paloutzian, R. F., & Park C. L. (2005). Integrative themes in the current science of the psychology of religion. In R. F. Paloutzian & C. L. Park (Eds.), *Handbook of the psychology of religion and spirituality* (pp. 3–20). New York: The Guilford Press.

Pargament, K. I., Ano, G. G., & Wachholtz, A. B. (2005). The religious dimension of coping. In R. F. Paloutzian & C. L. Park (Eds.), *Handbook of the psychology of religion and spirituality* (pp. 479–495). New York: The Guilford Press.

Rambo, L. R. (1993). *Understanding religious conversions* (2nd ed.). New Haven, CT: Yale University Press.

Ring, K. (1984). *Heading towards omega*. New York: William Morrow.

Scharf, R. H. (2000). The rhetoric of experience and the study of religion. *Journal of Consciousness Studies, 7*(11–12), 267–287.

Shapiro, S. L., Schwartz, G. E., & Bonner, G. (1998). Effects of mindfulness-based stress reduction on medical and premedical students. *Journal of Behavioral Medicine, 21*, 581–599.

Silberman, I. (2005a). Religion as a meaning-system: Implications for the new millennium. *Journal of Social Issues, 61*(4), (special issue).

Silberman, I. (2005b) (Ed.). Religion as a meaning-system. *Journal of Social Issues, 61*, 4 (special issue).

Stace, W. T. (1960). *The teachings of the mystics*. New York: New American Library.

Tix, A. P., & Frazier, P. A. (1998). The use of religious coping during stressful life events: main effects, moderation, and mediation. *Journal of Consulting and Clinical Psychology, 66*, 411–422.

Wachholtz, A. B., & Pargament, K. I. (2005). Is spirituality a critical ingredient of meditation? Comparing the effects of spiritual meditation, secular meditation and relaxation, on spiritual, cardiac and pain outcomes. *Journal of Behavioral Medicine, 28*(4), 369–384.

Wallace, B. A. (2000). *The taboo of subjectivity: Towards a new science of consciousness*. Oxford: Oxford University Press.

Watts, F. (2002). *Theology and psychology*. Aldershot, UK: Ashgate.

Wilber, K. (1998). *The marriage of sense and soul*. Dublin: Newleaf.

Wulff, D. M. (1997). *Psychology of religion: Classic and contemporary* (2nd ed.). New York: Wiley.

Wulff, D. M. (1998). Rethinking the rise and fall of the psychology of religion. In A. L. M. Molendijk & P. Els (Eds.), *Religion in the making: The emergence of the science of religion* (pp. 181–202). Boston: Brill.

27

Media and Consumer Psychology

Frank R. Kardes, Perilou Goddard, Xiaoqi Han, and Bruce E. Pfeiffer

Enormous resources are spent on predicting, understanding, and influencing consumer behavior. In many industries, success depends on convincing consumers to use our products and services rather than competitors' offerings. Toward this end, consumers are inundated by marketing communications appearing in the traditional media (e.g., television, radio, and print advertising), the new media (e.g., the internet), and in retail stores (e.g., packaging, point-of-purchase displays). However, effective marketing communications require an in-depth understanding of the variables that capture the attention and interest of consumers; that influence how consumers acquire, retain, and revise product knowledge; and that influence how product knowledge is used as a basis for judgment and choice.

Consumer Attention and Interest

Because consumers are limited information processors that typically consider fewer than seven brands when making a purchase decision (consistent with Miller's [1956] magic number seven), capturing consumer attention and interest is critically important (Kardes, 1994; Wyer, 2005, 2008). A given product or service is valued more heavily when it is goal-relevant (the valuation effect) and valued less heavily when it is goal-irrelevant (the devaluation effect; Brendl, Markman, & Messner, 2003). Ironically, even money is devalued when hunger, thirst, or some other need is highly salient, even though money can be used, albeit indirectly, to satiate that need. Furthermore, the devaluation effect is typically much larger than the valuation effect (Markman & Brendl, 2005).

IAAP Handbook of Applied Psychology, First Edition. Edited by Paul R. Martin, Fanny M. Cheung, Michael C. Knowles, Michael Kyrios, Lyn Littlefield, J. Bruce Overmier, and José M. Prieto.

Salient and vivid stimuli capture attention automatically regardless of consumers' goals (Fiske & Taylor, 1991; Nisbett & Ross, 1980). Salience is determined by a difference-in-a-background (contextually novel, unexpected, complex, or moving stimuli stick out), and vividness is determined by concreteness, emotional interest, and psychological proximity. Surprising ads, such as mystery ads that hide the identity of the product until the end of the ad (Fazio, Herr, & Powell, 1992), ads that use multiple variations on a theme (Schumann, Petty, & Clemons, 1990), and ads that use upward camera angles (Meyers-Levy & Peracchio, 1992) are contextually salient and attention-drawing. Similarly, unusual packages, such as cylinders for Pringle's potato chips, plastic eggs for L'eggs panty hose, and 15-packs for Strohs beer, are salient and attention drawing. Salience effects are reduced when involvement or accuracy motivation is high (Howard-Pitney, Borgida, & Omoto, 1986).

Product Knowledge Acquisition

According to selective hypothesis testing theory, judgment involves generating and testing tentatively held hypotheses, or beliefs, interpretations, expectations, evaluations, or possibilities (Sanbonmatsu, Posavac, Kardes, & Mantel, 1998). Because the information available for judgment is often complex and available at different times in different formats by different sources, consumers often simplify the judgment formation and evaluation process by focusing on a single hypothesis at a time and by focusing selectively on hypothesis-consistent evidence while neglecting hypothesis-inconsistent evidence. Selective attention, selective retrieval, and the selective interpretation of ambiguous evidence occurs even when consumers are motivated to form an accurate judgment, although selective processes are amplified when consumers are motivated to find support for a preferred conclusion. When the evidence for a focal hypothesis meets a minimum confirmation threshold, the hypothesis is accepted prematurely and information processing ceases. When the evidence fails to meet the minimum confirmation threshold, the focal hypothesis is rejected and the alternative hypothesis is accepted even if the degree of support is weak for both.

More formally, the subjective probability that hypothesis A is true rather than alternative hypothesis B, is $P(A, B) = s(A)$, or the strength of the evidence supporting A, if $s(A)$ is greater or equal to confidence threshold t. Otherwise, $P(A, B)$ approaches zero regardless of the perceived strength of the evidence favoring B. Consequently, A tends to be accepted prematurely. Selective hypothesis testing theory suggests that subjective probability judgments are often non-relative (contrary to the implications of support theory; Tversky & Koehler, 1994), because the strength of the evidence favoring A is often considered in isolation, and the strength of the evidence favoring B tends to be ignored. When the strength of the evidence favoring A fails to meet confidence threshold t, A is rejected even when the strength of the evidence favoring B is weak, and B tends to be accepted prematurely.

Selective hypothesis testing can explain a wide range of judgmental phenomena—including probability estimation and prediction (e.g., anchoring, hindsight bias, probability overestimation, overconfidence, explanation and imagination effects), covariation perception (e.g., illusory correlation, theory-based covariation estimation, blocking), causal explanation (overestimation of causality, the fundamental attribution error), trait inference, rule discovery, and evaluation (e.g., attitude polarization, contingent valuation, preference reversal; Sanbonmatsu et al., 1998). For example, when asked to evaluate one hotel chain randomly selected from a set of four hotel chains, the focal brand was evaluated highly favorably regardless of which brand was selected (Posavac, Sanbonmatsu, Kardes, & Fitzsimons, 2004). In other words, all brands were rated as better than average even though this is impossible for a closed set, and even though a random selection process should reduce demand effects and other types of motivational biases. This brand positivity effect was mediated by the selective processing of information favorable to the focal brand (while neglecting information unfavorable to the focal brand) and moderated by the likelihood of comparative (vs. singular) processing.

Most consumers assume that price and quality are highly correlated, and this assumption leads consumers to focus on information that is consistent with this hypothesis (Cronley, Posavac, Meyer, Kardes, & Kellaris, 2005; Kardes, Cronley, Kellaris, & Posavac, 2004). Consequently, recognition and recall performance is better for high-price/high-quality brands and low-price/low-quality brands than for brands in the off-diagonal, and this leads to overestimation of the strength of the relation between price and quality. This overestimation increases the willingness of consumers to spend. Overestimation is reduced only when selective processing is discouraged due to low cognitive load, random information presentation, or a low need for cognitive closure. The need for cognitive closure refers to a preference for a definite answer to a judgmental problem, any answer rather than ambiguity, inconsistency, or confusion (Kruglanski & Webster, 1996). Selective processing, anchoring, priming, primacy, heuristic reasoning, and stereotyping effects decrease as the need for cognitive closure decreases.

Selective hypothesis testing can also induce product attribute information distortion (Russo, Carlson, & Meloy, 2006; Russo, Carlson, Meloy, & Yong, 2008; Russo, Meloy, & Medvec, 1998). When consumers begin to prefer tentatively one alternative over others, the attributes of the focal alternative are rated as more important or as more favorable, relative to attribute ratings assessed in a pretest or a control group. Information distortion can amplify the pioneering brand advantage (Carlson, Meloy, & Russo, 2006) or increase preference for an inferior alternative when attribute information is presented in a manner that leads to an early preference advantage for that alternative (Russo et al., 2006). Information distortion also mediates the Shafir (1993) preference reversal: A choose frame leads consumers to focus on positive attributes, whereas a reject frame leads consumers to focus on negative attributes (Meloy & Russo, 2004). This can lead consumers to choose and reject the same brand.

Product Knowledge Retention

Selective processing also influences how information is stored in memory. Advertising can change the manner in which products are experienced when ads precede product consumption (Ha & Hoch, 1989; Hoch & Ha, 1986) or follow product consumption (Braun, 1999). When an ad states that a particular brand of wine or coffee tastes well balanced, consumers frequently test this hypothesis by searching for hypothesis-consistent information, and this leads to premature hypothesis confirmation. Selective search can occur for stimulus information or for information stored in memory, depending on the timing of the ad and the consumption experience.

Most retail settings offer only a limited set of brands, and the brands that are offered often determine which brands are included in consumers' consideration sets, or the group of brands that are considered for purchase by consumers. Kardes, Sanbonmatsu, Cronley, and Houghton (2002) presented one of two sets of cameras (i.e., Olympus, Nikon, Konica or Minolta, Canon, Pentax) and asked consumers to estimate the likelihood that the best brand was included in the set they received. Likelihoods were overestimated in both sets, leading to an average total likelihood rating of 145.88%. In a follow-up study, consumers received a set of VCR brands offered by one store (singular judgment task) or by two stores (comparative judgment task). Choice deferral, or the reluctance to choose any brand (Dhar, 1997), was greater when consumers low in the need for cognitive closure received information for two stores, relative to the remaining conditions. Hence, consumers are more likely to focus on immediately available brands and neglect unmentioned brands in singular judgment task conditions and in comparative judgment task conditions when the need for cognitive closure is high.

The neglect of unmentioned brands increases as the number of brands presented increases due to part-list cuing induced inhibition (Alba & Chattopadhyay, 1985, 1986). Advertising reduces the ability of consumers to recall attribute information pertaining to competing brands due to proactive and retroactive associative interference, depending on the timing of target and nontarget ad exposure (Burke & Srull, 1988). Inhibition of nonfocal brands also occurs when focal brands are physically present (as in grocery stores) rather than mentioned by name only (Kardes, Cronley, & Kim, 2006). When no brands are mentioned by name, consumers are forced to generate their own consideration sets via memory search, and this leads to a strong advantage to brands enjoying strong brand-category associations in memory (Posavac, Sanbonmatsu, & Fazio, 1997; Posavac, Sanbonmatsu, & Ho, 2002). Associative strength depends on frequency, recency, and intensity of activation.

Product Knowledge Activation

Availability refers to the presence of information in memory, and accessibility refers to the "activation potential" of available information (Förster & Liberman, 2007). The level of accessibility of information stored in memory is determined by the strength of the association between stored knowledge and situational cues, the recency with which information has been acquired or last activated, the frequency of prior activation, and the amount of processing at the time of information acquisition (Wyer, 2008). Once accessed, information from memory influences how consumers interpret and evaluate products, services, and experiences.

Priming

The basic priming paradigm consists of two phases. In the first phase, participants are exposed to a stimulus that increases the accessibility of the primed construct. In the second phase, they perform a seemingly unrelated task and their judgments or behaviors are measured. When the applicability of a prime relative to a target is high, the prime influences subsequent judgments and behaviors concerning the target (Wyer, 2004, 2008). A wide variety of marketing communications have been shown to serve as priming stimuli (e.g., ads, internet messages, salesperson interactions, retail environments, consumer magazines). For example, people overestimate the occurrence of occupations (e.g., doctors, lawyers), objects (e.g., luxury cars, swimming pools), and behaviors (e.g., having wine with dinner, incidence of crime) shown frequently on television. This is particularly the case for heavy viewers, despite the fact that most people do not consider television to be a realistic representation of reality (O'Guinn & Shrum, 1997; Shrum, Wyer, & O'Guinn, 1998).

Priming effects have been demonstrated in a variety of domains and have been shown to influence perceptions, impressions, judgments, and behaviors. For instance, Herr (1986) demonstrated that exposure to exemplars of famous people influenced perceptions of an ambiguous description of a target's behavior. Yeung and Wyer (2004) found that induced affective states influenced participants' initial impressions of hedonic products. Kay, Wheeler, Bargh, and Ross (2004) demonstrated that the presence of situationally relevant objects (e.g., briefcases, portfolios, boardroom tables) can increase competitive behavior. Chartrand, Huber, Shiv, and Tanner (2008) used supraliminal and subliminal primes to automatically activate goals (e.g., prestige vs. thrift) and influence consumer choice outside of conscious awareness. Maimaran and Wheeler (2008) found that priming participants with novel, simple arrays of geometric shapes in different configurations influences variety seeking and uniqueness seeking in real choice situations. Yi (1990, 1993) found that large automobiles were evaluated more favorably when safety was primed than when fuel efficiency was primed. He also found that PCs with many features were evaluated more favorably when functionality was primed than when ease of use was primed. Fitzsimons, Chartrand, and Fitzsimons (2008) investigated the priming effects of brand logos. Subliminally priming brands (e.g., Apple, Disney) led participants to behave in a manner consistent with the brands' image (e.g., creativity, honesty). Labroo, Dhar, and Schwarz (2008) investigated the effects of semantic priming and perceptual fluency in product evaluations. They primed participants with an irrelevant visual identifier (e.g., a frog), and later adding this identifier to a product package increased perceptual fluency and product evaluations.

Further, several important moderators of the priming effect have been investigated, such as prior knowledge (Bettman & Sujan, 1987; Herr, 1989; Yi, 1993) and current goals (Strahan, Spencer, & Zanna, 2002). Subliminally priming a goal-relevant cognition (thirst) enhanced the persuasiveness of a goal-related ad (Super-Quencher ad), but only when participants were already thirsty. DeMarree, Wheeler, and Petty (2005) found that trait priming effects depend on individual differences in self-monitoring. Trait priming effects were found to be stronger for low (vs. high) self-monitors. Furthermore, choice depends on different shopping associations (possibility-driven vs. purpose-driven) and personality traits (introverts vs. extroverts), even when the prime is held constant (Wheeler & Berger, 2007).

Assimilation, contrast, and anchoring

A product can seem good or bad, large or small, heavy or light, or high or low on any dimension of judgment depending on what consumers compare it to. Assimilation refers to a shift in judgment toward a comparison or reference point, and contrast refers to a shift in judgment away from a reference point. Reference points are influenced by primes, attitudes, expectations, and contextually relevant stimuli. When target–reference point similarity is high, consumers engage in similarity testing and focus selectively on similarities between the target and the reference point; when target–reference point similarity is low, consumers engage in dissimilarity testing and focus selectively on dissimilarities between the target and the reference point (Mussweiler, 2003). Similarity testing and global processing (Förster, Liberman, & Kuschel, 2008) encourage consumers to include targets and reference points in the same category, and this leads to assimilation or a shift in judgments of the target towards the reference point (Schwarz & Bless, 1992). Dissimilarity testing and local processing encourage consumers to exclude targets from reference point categories, and this leads to contrast or a shift in judgments of the target away from the reference point.

Selective processing can also influence anchoring, or forming an initial judgment (or anchor or first impression) and then updating (or adjusting or fine-tuning) this judgment based on subsequent evidence (Tversky & Kahneman, 1974). Typically, adjustment is insufficient and final judgments tend to be too close to initial judgments. For example, thinking about large numbers often leads to large judgments, and thinking about small numbers often leads to small judgments. Numerical anchoring influences pricing decisions, probability estimates, gambles, predictions, and negotiations (Strack & Mussweiler, 2003).

The selective accessibility model suggests that anchors are tentatively held hypotheses that encourage consumers to focus on anchor-consistent information (Strack & Mussweiler, 2003). The standard anchoring paradigm consists of two tasks: a comparative judgment task followed by an absolute judgment task. In the comparative judgment task, participants are provided with an anchor and asked to make a judgment relative to the anchor. In the absolute judgment task, participants are asked to give an absolute estimate. The comparison task leads to the selective activation of knowledge consistent with the anchor and this knowledge influences subsequent absolute judgments.

Anchoring influences behavior as well as judgment. Consumers often intend to buy only one unit of a product when they shop (e.g., one container of milk), and one is a relatively low anchor. However, merely mentioning larger numbers can encourage consumers to consider higher anchors (Wansink, Kent, & Hoch, 1998). For example, multiple-unit pricing (e.g., 3 for $1.99, or 12 for the price of 10) encourages consumers to buy more than one unit for two reasons: (1) they want to obtain a volume discount, and (2) multiple units suggest an anchor value that is higher than one. Ironically, purchase quantity limits (e.g., a limit of 10 per customer) can also encourage consumers to use higher anchors and buy more than one unit even if they do not come close to purchasing the amount implied by the limit. Suggestive selling (e.g., grab 6 for studying, buy 8 and save a trip, buy 12 for your freezer) and expansion anchors (e.g., 101 uses around the house) also encourage consumers to consider larger anchors and to purchase more units.

Product Knowledge Utilization

Multiattribute judgment

According to multiattribute judgment models, such as information integration theory (Lynch 1985) and the theory of reasoned action (Sheppard, Hartwick, & Warshaw, 1988), evaluations of specific attributes are combined quantitatively to form overall evaluations or attitudes. Information integration theory is a decompositional model, meaning that overall attitudes (*A*) and attribute ratings (*si* for each attribute *i*) are measured and attribute importance weights (*wi*) are statistically estimated. The theory of reasoned action is a compositional model, meaning that attribute ratings (*ei*) and attribute weights (*bi* or beliefs about the likelihood with which an attitude object possesses each attribute *i*) are measured and *A* is estimated. More formally, the information integration model implies that $A = \Sigma wi\ si$, where *wi* sums to one. The theory of reasoned action implies that $A = \Sigma bi\ ei$. These equations suggest that attribute ratings are averaged according to information integration theory, and added according to the theory of reasoned action. Averaging implies that providing information about additional favorable attributes improves attitudes only when these attributes improve the overall average. Adding implies that providing information about additional favorable attitudes always improves attitudes. Empirically, amount of information or set size effects occur only when consumers are sensitive to the absence of relevant attribute information (Sanbonmatsu, Kardes, & Herr, 1992).

Dual-process models

Many dual-process models suggest that effortful multiattribute judgment processes occur only when the motivation and the ability to process information carefully are high, otherwise less effortful heuristic-based, category-based, schema-based, or implicit theory-based judgment processes are more likely (Chaiken & Trope, 1999; Wyer, 2004). In addition, attribute-based (or stimulus-based or data-driven) judgment processes occur only when information is analyzed or broken down into discrete units and when the implications of these units are construed independently (Wyer, 2004). This is likely when no prior judgment of the target is available from memory (e.g., the product is really new), information is of different types or is difficult to integrate (e.g., visual and verbal information in an ad), information is provided by different sources (e.g., a sales representative and a consumer magazine article), or information pertains to different objects (e.g., multiple brands).

Because of these constraints, consumers are often more likely to use prior knowledge and experience rather than specific attributes as a basis for judgment. When involvement or the motivation to process attribute information carefully is low, category-based judgment is likely (Brewer, 1988). Category knowledge contains information about a category's typical properties and characteristics, and identifying a brand as a member of the category permits consumers to infer that the brand possesses all of the properties and characteristics that are typical of the category. Of course, involvement is not the only determinant of category-based judgment. As the degree to which the features of a brand match or overlap with the features of a given category increases, or as category knowledge increases, the likelihood of category-based judgment also increases (Fiske & Neuberg, 1990; Sujan, 1985). Relevant categories include brands (e.g., all Sonys are good; Keller, 2008), products (e.g., all 35 mm cameras are good; Sujan, 1985), and countries of origin (e.g., all products made in Japan are good; Li & Wyer, 1994).

According to the theory of reasoned action, attitudes always influence behavior via an effortful intention–formation process. The MODE model emphasizes that this effortful intention–formation process occurs only when the motivation and the opportunity to deliberate are high (Fazio & Towles-Schwen, 1999). Otherwise, attitudes influence behavior without intention or awareness. Instead, when a relevant attitude is activated from memory, it influences perceptions of the attitude object via a selective perception process. Favorable (unfavorable) attitudes accentuate favorable (unfavorable) aspects of an attitude object. Favorable perceptions of an attitude object encourage approach behaviors (e.g., buy, use), and unfavorable perceptions encourage avoid behaviors (e.g., don't buy, don't use). Favorable global attitudes influence retail outlet selection when motivation or opportunity is low, and discrete attributes influence retail outlet selection when motivation and opportunity are high.

Dual-process models of persuasion suggest that when the motivation and the ability to process information carefully are high, consumers follow the high-effort central route (the elaboration likelihood model; Petty & Wegener, 1999) or systematic route (the heuristic/systematic model; Chen & Chaiken, 1999) to persuasion. This involves focusing on the strength of the arguments for or against a given attitudinal position. When motivation or ability is low, consumers follow the low-effort peripheral route or heuristic route to persuasion. This involves focusing on affective responses and feelings, and on persuasion heuristics, such as the length-implies-strength heuristic (long messages are better than short messages), the liking–agreement heuristic (likable sources and spokespersons can be trusted), and the consensus-implies-correctness heuristic (the majority opinion is usually valid). The elaboration likelihood model suggests that consumers follow either the central or the peripheral route. The heuristic/systematic model suggests that consumers can follow both routes simultaneously and that the systematic route overrides the heuristic route when the heuristic route fails to result in the formation of an attitude held with sufficient confidence.

The motivation to process information carefully can be influenced by many variables, including involvement, accountability, and the need for cognition (or the dispositional preference for effortful cognitive activities). The ability to process information carefully can also be influenced by many variables, such as time pressure, repetition, distraction, arousal, and recipients' characteristics (e.g., knowledge, intelligence, self-esteem). Recipients' characteristics influence reception, or the ability to attend to and comprehend persuasive messages, and yielding, or the tendency to agree with a persuasive message, in opposite ways (McGuire, 1972; Wyer, 1974). For example, as intelligence increases, reception increases and yielding decreases. Consequently, moderately intelligent recipients are most susceptible to persuasion. More formally, $A = R(1 - CA)$, or attitudes are a function of reception multiplied by yielding or 1 minus the likelihood and extent of counterargumentation. For complex messages, R is weighted more heavily than CA because consumers are likely to lack the cognitive resources needed to generate counterarguments. For simple messages, CA is weighted more heavily than R because consumers are likely to have abundant resources for generating counterarguments.

Process matching

Another important determinant of persuasion is the extent to which a message matches the processes consumers are likely to use to attend, comprehend, interpret, and respond to the message. Matching persuasive messages to consumers' self-schemas (Wheeler, Petty, & Bizer, 2005), the functional bases of consumers' attitudes (Petty & Wegener, 1998), the affective/cognitive bases of consumers' attitudes (Fabrigar & Petty, 1999; Venkatraman, Marlino, Kardes, & Sklar, 1990), or to specific emotions (DeSteno, Petty, Rucker, Wegener, & Braverman, 2004) facilitates message processing and increases persuasion when arguments are strong. However, mismatching is more effective when arguments are weak or when counterargumentation is likely. Because comparative advertising increases counterargumentation, comparative ads that encourage abstract comparisons ("best in class" claims) are more effective when the message context encourages concrete reasoning (small product categories, near future decisions), whereas comparative ads that encourage concrete comparisons ("better than the leading brand" claims) are more effective when the message context encourages abstract reasoning (large product categories, distant future decisions; Yang, Jain, Lindsey, & Kardes, 2009).

Availability–valence model

Memory-based judgments of products are influenced by the information that is most readily retrievable from memory and by the evaluative implications of this information (Kisielius & Sternthal, 1986). Availability, or more accurately, accessibility, depends on the recency, frequency, and intensity with which information is activated from memory. As intensity increases, elaborative processing increases and the number of concepts associated with a target concept in memory increases. As the number of associated concepts increases, the number of cues that can be used to reconstruct the target concept increases, and memory performance is enhanced (Mantonakis, Whittlesea, & Yoon, 2008). The availability-valence model can explain a wide range of judgmental phenomena, including the vividness effect (Kisielius & Sternthal, 1986), the sleeper effect (Hannah & Sternthal, 1984), the overjustification effect (Tybout & Scott, 1983), multiple-request compliance effects (Tybout, Sternthal, & Calder, 1983), and associative interference (Tybout, Calder, & Sternthal, 1981).

Concrete information is more attention drawing and memorable than abstract information, and, consequently, concrete information has a greater impact on judgment. The sleeper effect occurs when a credible message is delivered by a non-credible source. Initially, little persuasion occurs because the untrustworthy source leads consumers to discount the message. Over time, however, persuasion increases because memory for the source decreases at a faster rate than memory for the message. The overjustification effect occurs when multiple reasons for buying a product are accessible from memory. The perceived importance of any given reason is discounted as the total number of reasons for buying increases. Compliance increases when a small request is followed by a large target request (the foot-in-the-door effect) or when a large request is followed by a small target request (the door-in-the-face effect). The former effect increases as the magnitude and the accessibility of the initial request increases, provided that consumers comply with the initial request. The latter effect increases as the time interval between the initial and target request decreases because this increases the accessibility of the contrast between the initial and target requests. The accessibility of marketplace rumors can be reduced via associative interference produced by increasing the accessibility of multiple alternative associations.

Accessibility–diagnosticity model

Memory-based judgments of products are influenced by accessibility (or the most readily retrievable information), valence (or the evaluative implications of this information), and diagnosticity (or the perceived relevance of this information; Feldman & Lynch, 1988; Lynch, Marmorstein, & Weigold, 1988). This model can explain many important judgmental phenomena, including self-generated validity (or measurement-induced judgments constructed while responding to survey questions; Feldman & Lynch, 1988), the relative influence of global evaluations versus discrete attributes in choice (Lynch et al., 1988), and the vividness effect, the perseverance effect, and the negativity effect (Herr, Kardes, & Kim, 1991).

Studying judgments requires asking questions about judgments. Sometimes consumers retrieve previously formed judgments while responding to survey questions, and sometimes consumers construct new judgments while responding to survey questions (Feldman & Lynch, 1988). Consequently, mere measurement can lead to the formation of judgments that would not have been formed otherwise, and mere measurement can artificially increase the magnitude of correlations among attitudes, beliefs, intentions, and behaviors (Fitzsimons & Moore, 2008). One way to avoid erroneous research conclusions based on artificial, measurement-induced judgments is to adopt research procedures that assess the formation of spontaneously formed judgments and inferences (Kardes, Posavac, Cronley, & Herr, 2008).

Lynch et al. (1988) used interpolated tasks to assess the spontaneous use of global attitudes versus discrete attributes in memory-based choice. In experiment 1, the accessibility of discrete attribute information about a target brand was manipulated via associative interference (e.g., the presence or absence of instructions to memorize attribute information for four distractor brands). Next, participants were asked to perform one of several interpolated tasks: a choice task, a memory task, or an unrelated task. Finally, after a two-day delay, participants were asked to recall the attributes of the target brand and their evaluation of the target brand. When the attributes of the target brand were accessible due to low associative interference, target brand attribute recall during the final session was as high in choice task as in memory task conditions and higher than in unrelated task conditions. This pattern suggests that participants spontaneously used discrete attributes during choice even though they were not explicitly asked to do so. By contrast, when target brand attributes were inaccessible due to high associative interference, memory performance was greater in memory interpolated task conditions (due to a retrieval practice effect called hypermnesia) than in the remaining conditions. Hence, these participants did not even attempt to retrieve attribute information during the interpolated choice task. In a follow-up experiment, participants spontaneously used global attitudes as a basis for choice only when these attitudes were diagnostic (i.e., when attitudes considering price and attitudes not considering price were consistent rather than inconsistent).

Consistent with the implications of the accessibility–diagnosticity model, vivid word-of-mouth communications are more persuasive than pallid written communications even when these communications provide identical information (Herr et al., 1991). Moreover, the vividness effect is reduced or eliminated when other more diagnostic inputs for judgment are available. Specifically, when prior impressions of the target brand were perceived as highly diagnostic, a perseverance effect was observed instead of a vividness effect. Further, when negative attribute information was perceived as highly diagnostic, a negativity effect was observed instead of a vividness effect. In both cases, perceived diagnosticity was assessed in terms of Bayesian likelihood ratios computed from judgments of the extent to which a given piece of information discriminates between high- and low-quality brands. Prior impressions and negative attributes that strongly imply one focal hypothesis over other possibilities are weighed heavily in judgment, regardless of whether alternative possibilities are improbable or are simply overlooked.

Omission detection and inference formation

Omission neglect refers to insensitivity to missing or unknown information (e.g., attributes, features, properties, qualities, alternatives, options, cues, stimuli, or possibilities; Kardes et al., 2004, 2008). In everyday judgment, consumers must frequently rely on limited or incomplete information about products and services. The information may come from different sources (e.g., advertising, promotions, salespeople, reporters, word-of-mouth). These sources often provide information about some product attributes and benefits, but others are not mentioned due to situational constraints (e.g., limited time or space) or due to poor product performance. Insensitivity to missing information can lead to purchase decisions that consumers later regret. For example, hidden fees are often overlooked initially, when a purchase decision is made, but not later when the bill arrives. Similarly, some attributes that are overlooked when a purchase decision is made cannot be overlooked later when the product is actually consumed.

Research has demonstrated that detecting omissions is surprisingly difficult, and the failure to detect omissions often results in inappropriately extreme and confidently held judgments (Sanbonmatsu, Kardes, & Sansone, 1991; Sanbonmatsu et al., 1992; Sanbonmatsu, Posavac, & Stasney, 1997). Highly favorable (or unfavorable) evaluations are formed on the basis of moderately favorable (or unfavorable) evidence, and these evaluations are held with a high degree of confidence. Although more extreme judgments should be formed as the amount of diagnostic information presented increases, failure to notice that relevant information is missing encourages consumers to form extreme judgments regardless of how little is actually known. This occurs because consumers overestimate the importance of the presented information and underestimate the importance of missing information (Sanbonmatsu, Kardes, Houghton, Ho, & Posavac, 2003).

In a representative study, half of the participants received favorable information on four attributes of a target camera, and the remaining half received favorable information on eight attributes (Sanbonmatsu et al., 1992). Consumers who were either unknowledgeable or moderately knowledgeable about the product category formed extremely favorable evaluations of the target camera across set-size conditions. Only consumers who were highly knowledgeable about the product category formed more favorable product evaluations when the product was described on eight attributes than when the product was described on only four attributes.

The biasing effects of omission neglect have been found at all stages of information processing, including perception, learning, evaluation, persuasion, and choice. Although consumers typically neglect omissions, sensitivity to them can be enhanced by several contextual variables, including warnings, high prior knowledge, direction of comparison, nonalignable differences, criteria consideration, temporal construal, and positive affect (Bechkoff et al., 2009; Kardes et al., 2008).

Omission detection is one of the most important determinants of inference formation, or going beyond the given information by imputing values to missing attributes (Kardes et al., 2004, 2008). Consumers must first notice that important information is missing before they can form inferences to fill knowledge gaps. Pfeiffer and Kardes (2009) investigated two mechanisms for forming inferences about missing information. When an important omission is detected, consumers either anchor on the implications of the presented information and then adjust their judgments based on the implications of the missing information, or they discount the presented information. Consumers low in the need for cognitive closure (Kruglanski & Webster, 1996), low self-monitors (Snyder & Gangestad, 1986), and high maximizers (Schwartz et al., 2002) are more likely to use an anchoring-and-adjustment process, rather than a simple discounting process.

Inference formation often relies on a variety of implicit theories or prior beliefs about relations among people, objects, and events. Implicit theories aid in the generation of if–then linkages that form associations between information (e.g., cues, heuristics, arguments, knowledge) and inferential conclusions (Kardes et al., 2004, 2008; Kruglanski & Webster, 1996). A wide variety of implicit theories are used by consumers, including theories or assumptions about the relations among price, quality, warranty, packaging, reliability, durability, physical appearance, retail outlet, and so on. Consumers tend to believe that price and quality are highly correlated and use price as an indicator of quality (Cronley et al., 2005; Kardes et al., 2004). Implicit theories about quality and warranties, advertising, country of origin, and brand name are also commonly used (Kardes et al., 2004).

Awareness of one's own cognitive processes (metacognition) also plays an important role in inference formation and relies on implicit theories related to experiences of accessibility or fluency. Accessibility experiences refer to the subjective ease or difficulty with which stored knowledge comes to mind or the fluency with which information is processed (Schwarz, 2004). People use the ease or difficulty of the experience as important input in judgment tasks. If information is difficult to recall, people may infer that information is limited, scarce, of poor quality, or insufficient to form an attitude, support an argument, or make a decision. For example, Wänke, Bohner, and Jurkowitsch (1997) found that generating a single reason for choosing a BMW is easier, resulting in more favorable evaluations of the BMW, than generating 10 reasons. Not only is experiential ease an important input, it often dominates content (or the number of reasons actually generated) when the accessibility experience is perceived as diagnostic. The effects of accessibility experiences have been demonstrated in a number of domains, including self-perception, memory, interest, aesthetics, liking, truth, persuasion, confidence, prediction, diagnosis, temporal biases, and choice (Hirt, Kardes, & Markman, 2004; Novemsky, Dhar, Schwarz, & Simonson, 2007; Schwarz, 2004).

Public Policy Implications: The Case of Marketing Alcohol to Youth

Industry efforts to market alcoholic beverages illustrate the full range of persuasion efforts studied by consumer researchers, from traditional television and print advertising, to point-of-sale promotions and event sponsorship, to new marketing (e.g., branding, new product development, product placement, and viral marketing). In most countries, alcohol marketing aimed at adults is not controversial, particularly in light of recent evidence of health benefits associated with moderate drinking (Ryder, Walker, & Salmon, 2006). However, public health authorities worldwide are alarmed by the increasingly global and sophisticated alcohol marketing aimed toward young people. Relative to their numbers, 12- to 20-year-olds account for a disproportionate share of the world's alcohol-related problems, including premature deaths, disability, school failure, and crime (Jernigan & Mosher, 2005). In the US alone, drinking by those under age 21 accounts for 30% of the costs of alcohol use and abuse ($53 billion U.S.; Foster, Vaughan, Foster, & Califano, 2003). Current regulations are ineffective in deterring early drinking. For example, the legal drinking age in the US is 21, but over 50% of 12-year-olds and 80% of 18-year-olds have tried alcohol, 50% of 18-year-olds are current drinkers (Ellickson, Collins, Hambarsoomians, & McCaffrey, 2005), and 30% report binge drinking in the past month (Foster et al., 2003). The alcohol industry is often in conflict with public health advocates, who assert that mass-media depictions of drinking normalize alcohol consumption and create positive expectations for drinking (Connolly, Casswell, Zhang, & Silva, 1994).

Industry groups cite econometric studies to assert that advertising does not increase demand for their products; such studies usually focus on the relationship between aggregate-level advertising expenditure and sales (consumption) variables (Hastings, Anderson, Cooke, & Gordon, 2005). Most econometric studies show little or no effect of advertising on total consumption. However, such studies focus only on measured (traditional) advertising and do not capture the effects of broader marketing efforts such as viral marketing campaigns and point-of-purchase displays. Econometric studies also minimize the impact of advertising on young drinkers by aggregating them with older, established drinkers (Hastings et al., 2005). Moreover, econometric studies cannot show advertising's impact on alcohol consumption by underage drinkers because sales to them are illegal and cannot be isolated in econometric research protocols (Kelly & Edwards, 1998).

Public health researchers typically rely on consumer studies, in which the individual is the unit of analysis, to examine how alcohol advertising interacts with alcohol knowledge, attitudes, and motives (Hastings et al., 2005). Interestingly, these are the same type of studies used by the advertising industry to measure the effectiveness of its own campaigns. Consumer studies consistently show links between alcohol marketing in a variety of forms and youth drinking or intentions to drink.

Many early studies of alcohol marketing effects used cross-sectional designs. For example, Grube and Wallack (1994) showed that greater awareness of televised beer ads among 10- to 13-year-olds was associated with more positive beliefs about drinking and intentions to drink more frequently in adulthood. Snyder, Milici, Slater, Sun, and Strizhakova's (2006) review of cross-sectional studies revealed a significant mean correlation of 0.19 between self-reported exposure to alcohol ads and alcohol consumption. However, cross-sectional designs, even those in which possible confounding variables are controlled statistically, are still vulnerable to alternative interpretations, particularly those involving reverse causality. That is, a correlation between ad awareness and drinking may exist because drinkers are more likely to watch and remember ads, rather than because ads cause drinking (Ellickson et al., 2005). Only longitudinal designs can fully address this problem.

Results of longitudinal studies of youth conducted in the US and other western nations consistently show a relationship between marketing and alcohol consumption. Earlier studies (e.g., Connolly et al., 1994) relied on self-reported exposure to alcohol ads, while later studies (e.g., Stacy, Zogg, Unger, & Dent, 2004) used broader measures of exposure, such as self-reported behaviors associated with increased exposure to alcohol ads (e.g., time spent watching televised sports). Snyder et al. (2006) improved further on the methodology of previous longitudinal studies by measuring both ad recall and exposure to alcohol ads via per capita alcohol ad expenditures; the expenditure measure eliminates self-report bias as a source of contamination. In all cases, regardless of how exposure to alcohol marketing was measured, the pattern of results was the same: The more awareness of, familiarity with, and appreciation for alcohol marketing young people have, the more likely they are to drink now and in the future.

Ellickson et al. (2005) extended the examination of alcohol advertising beyond television and magazines to include point-of-purchase displays in stores and concession stands at sporting and music events. Of the students who had not consumed alcohol at age 11 or 12, 48% had started drinking by age 15 or 16. Among participants who were not drinking at age 11 or 12, exposure to in-store displays predicted drinking at age 15 or 16; Ellickson et al. hypothesized that such displays are pervasive, hard to ignore, and serve to normalize alcohol use. Among students who were already drinking at age 11 or 12, exposure to alcohol ads in magazines and beer concession stands at sports and music events predicted drinking frequency at ages 15–16; the researchers speculated that these types of alcohol marketing are more salient to youth who are already drinking.

Traditional forms of alcohol marketing (e.g., TV, radio, print, and outdoor ads) are rapidly giving way to more global and sophisticated "new marketing," including price-based promotions, viral marketing campaigns, product placement, branding, and new product development (Jernigan & Mosher, 2005). Public health research focused on new marketing lags far behind research on traditional marketing, in part because there are no agreed-upon techniques for measuring new marketing's impact (Jernigan, 2009). However, studies have shown that price promotions (e.g., happy hours, two-for-one drink specials) have a particular influence on young people, who tend to be price-sensitive (Casswell, 2009). Viral marketing takes advantage of young people's comfort with technology and social networking to promote brand affiliations, persuading them to pass on marketing messages (such as brand-affiliated parties or contests) to their friends, leading to the exponential spread of one-to-one marketing (Casswell & Maxwell, 2005; Jernigan & Mosher, 2005). One award-winning viral marketing campaign was New Zealand's "Smirnoff Half Day Off" (Casswell, 2009). Young people were encouraged via web banners, posters in bars and clubs, and announcements on youth radio to take the afternoon off on a specific date to join their friends at participating bars to drink Smirnoff beverages. Young people registered at a website to win $25 bar tabs and were asked to give contact information for three friends, thus propagating the marketing message virally.

New product development efforts targeted toward young people are most clearly illustrated by "alcopops," sweet-tasting beverages that mask the taste of alcohol and serve as a "starter" beverage, bridging the gap between soft drinks and traditional alcohol beverages (Mosher, 2009). Although they are similar in alcohol content to beer, such beverages often carry the brand names of distilled liquor (e.g., Smirnoff Ice, Bacardi Breezer), helping create brand loyalty for the more potent products. The industry admits that alcopops are targeted toward new or entry-level drinkers, but research shows that the drinks appeal disproportionately to young teens, especially girls (Mosher & Johnsson, 2005). Americans ages 12 to 20 are exposed to 92% more magazine ads for alcopops than are adult drinkers (Jernigan, Ostroff, & Ross, 2005). An Australian study (Gates, Copeland, Stevenson, & Dillon, 2007) demonstrated that both adult drinkers and children as young as 12 agreed that the Bacardi Breezer bottle and label were designed specifically to appeal to younger people.

Another new product targeting youth is the alcohol energy drink (Simon & Mosher, 2007). Such beverages are often priced lower than the comparable non-alcoholic energy drink, and packaging is so similar that store clerks, parents, and police often cannot tell them apart. These drinks are promoted via new marketing strategies such as sponsorship of youth-oriented extreme sporting events and with ad slogans designed specifically to appeal to young drinkers (e.g., "You can go home early when you're married," and "You can sleep when you're 30"). The biggest danger associated with alcohol energy drinks is that their high levels of caffeine may mask intoxication and lead to risky behaviors. O'Brien, McCoy, Rhodes, Wagoner, and Wolfson (2008) found that 24% of 4271 surveyed American college students reported drinking alcohol mixed with energy drinks in the past 30 days. Consumption of such drinks was associated with roughly twice the risk of a variety of negative alcohol-related consequences, including being taken advantage of sexually, taking advantage of someone else sexually, riding with an intoxicated driver, being physically injured, and requiring medical treatment.

There are several factors that may make young people especially vulnerable to persuasion attempts in general (Krosnick & Alwin, 1989) and to the influence of alcohol marketing in particular. Specific patterns of alcohol consumption help identify informal group membership and can even shape identity before drinking begins (McCreanor, Greenaway, Barnes, Borell, & Gregory, 2005). For example, preteens may share their appreciation for humorous and "edgy" alcohol promotions with one another, fostering an atmosphere supportive of drinking even though none of them has consumed alcohol yet. According to Casswell and Maxwell (2005), identity formation in adolescence increasingly involves specific brand affiliations; such affiliations may be especially important for youth in developing countries, where alcohol brand affiliation may be taken as a sign of affluence and Western identity (Jernigan & Mosher, 2005). Finally, pro-alcohol attitudes may cause selective hypothesis testing (Sanbonmatsu et al., 1998), leading young people to focus primarily on information that confirms their hypotheses ("drinking is cool") and discounting hypothesis-inconsistent information ("drinking is risky").

The alcohol industry often claims that advertising itself only affects brand choice, rather than stimulating demand (Saffer & Dave, 2002); however, converging evidence from consumer studies of tobacco, fast food, and alcohol shows that marketing measurably influences young people's consumption and adds weight to the public health field's concerns (Hastings et al., 2005). The alcohol industry denies targeting underage drinkers (Foster, Vaughan, Foster, & Califano, 2006). Garfield, Chung, and Rathouz (2003), however, found that as adolescent magazine readership increased, alcohol advertising frequency increased exponentially; Jernigan et al. (2005) found that American youth aged 12–20 were exposed to 24% more TV alcohol ads than were adults. The industry's claims to oppose underage drinking also ring hollow when research reveals that at least 17.5% of total consumer alcohol expenditures in the US comes from drinkers below the legal drinking age of 21. From a business standpoint, youth drinking is a good investment, in that it accounts for a substantial amount of current sales and helps ensure a steady stream of future customers, given that most adult heavy drinkers began drinking long before they were legally able to do so (Foster et al., 2006). Thus, the alcohol industry has a clear conflict of interest with regard to the regulation of youth-oriented marketing.

A lax regulatory environment aids the alcohol industry. According to the World Health Organization, about 15% of countries use industry self-regulation as the primary means of controlling exposure to alcohol marketing and 28–57% of countries have no restrictions whatsoever on alcohol adverting (Jernigan et al., 2005). The alcohol industry learned from the mistakes of the tobacco industry and often appears to cooperate with regulatory agencies while simultaneously working to reduce regulations to keep its marketing efforts unimpeded (Casswell, 2009). In the US, the Federal Trade Commission is charged with balancing the interests of the public with those of business; however, after many years of conservative political domination, the regulatory climate has become more favorable to business and less favorable to public health interests, and there has been less political will to regulate alcohol sales via higher taxes (Mosher, 2009). A further complication in the US is the Constitution's First Amendment protection of free speech, which has been interpreted by the courts to apply to most forms of commercial speech as well.

Several countries have taken action to effectively regulate some alcohol marketing; for example, Germany, Switzerland, France, Ireland, and the United Kingdom raised the taxes on alcopops and sales have subsequently plummeted (Mosher & Johnsson, 2005). In 2003, the Australian alcohol industry was threatened with new government regulations if marketing efforts did not conform swiftly to new standards, including changes in internet advertising and inclusion of public health experts on complaint adjudication panels (Australian Department of Health and Ageing, 2003). France's Loi Evin contains some of the world's strictest regulations on ad content (extending to a total ban on depictions of people) and has withstood several legal challenges, including at the European Court (Casswell & Maxwell, 2005).

Noted New Zealand researcher Sally Casswell (2009) asserts that the alcohol industry should be subject to the same sorts of public health and government intervention applied to the tobacco industry. However, alcohol advertising bans have been reduced or lifted in New Zealand, as well as Canada, Finland, and Denmark, sometimes in response to falling consumption and commercial broadcasters' need for advertising revenue. Moreover, one of the main reasons for the repeal of Prohibition in the US in the 1930s was the need for legal sources of employment during the Great Depression. Perhaps the current worldwide recession will bring similar pressures to bear on those seeking to regulate the expanding global alcohol market.

Summary

Consumer judgment and decision making is influenced by a large and complex set of variables that capture the attention and interest of consumers; influence how consumers acquire, retain, and revise product knowledge; and influence how product knowledge is used. Consistent with the implications of the selective hypothesis testing model, selective attention, selective encoding, and selective retrieval processes determine what information is likely to be used. The mass media prime a wide variety of concepts that influence the interpretation, evaluation, and choice of products and services. Dual-process models emphasize that effortful information processing occurs only when consumers are sufficiently motivated and able to do so; otherwise, a wide variety of simplifying processes are likely to be used. Rather than using all relevant information and knowledge, consumers typically rely on the subset of information and knowledge that is most readily accessible from memory, provided that this subset is perceived as relevant or diagnostic. Missing information is often neglected, even when this information is diagnostic, and accessibility experiences can override other more diagnostic pieces of information. Considered together, these psychological processes have important implications for understanding how consumers make judgments and decisions, and for how policymakers can help consumers make better judgments and decisions.

References

Alba, J. W., & Chattopadhyay, A. (1985). Effects of context and part-category cues on recall of competing brands. *Journal of Marketing Research, 22*, 340–349.

Alba, J. W., & Chattopadhyay, A. (1986). Salience effects in brand recall. *Journal of Marketing Research, 23*, 363–369.

Australian Department of Health and Ageing. (2003, August). Media releases: Governments introduce new alcohol advertising requirements. Retrieved February 24, 2009 from www.health.gov.au/internet/main/publishing.nsf/Content/health-mediarel-yr2003-tw-tw03034.htm

Bechkoff, J., Krishnan, V., Niculescu, M., Kohne, M. L., Palmatier, R. W., & Kardes, F. R. (2009). The role of omission neglect in responses to non-gains and non-losses in gasoline price fluctuations. *Journal of Applied Social Psychology, 39*, 1191–1200.

Bettman, J. R., & Sujan, M. (1987). Effects of framing on evaluation of comparable and noncomparable alternatives by experts and novice consumers. *Journal of Consumer Research, 14*, 141–154.

Braun, K. A. (1999). Postexperience advertising effects on consumer memory. *Journal of Consumer Research, 25*, 319–334.

Brendl, C. M., Markman, A. B., & Messner, C. (2003). The devaluation effect: Activating a need devalues unrelated objects. *Journal of Consumer Research, 29*, 463–473.

Brewer, M. (1988). A dual process model of impression formation. In R. S. Wyer & T. K. Srull (Eds.), *Advances in social cognition* (Vol. 1, pp. 1–36). Hillsdale, NJ: Erlbaum.

Burke, R. R., & Srull, T. K. (1988). Competitive interference and consumer memory for advertising. *Journal of Consumer Research, 15*, 55–68.

Carlson, K. A., Meloy, M. G., & Russo, J. E. (2006). Leader-driven primacy: Using attribute order to affect consumer choice. *Journal of Consumer Research, 32*, 513–518.

Casswell, S. (2009). Editorial: Alcohol industry and alcohol power—the challenge ahead. *Addiction, 104 (Supplement 1),* 3–5.

Casswell, S., & Maxwell, A. (2005). Regulation of alcohol marketing: A global view. *Journal of Public Health Policy, 26*, 343–358.

Chaiken, S., & Trope, Y. (Eds.). (1999). *Dual-process theories in social psychology*. New York: Guilford.

Chartrand, T. L., Huber, J., Shiv, B., & Tanner, R. J. (2008), Nonconscious goals and consumer choice. *Journal of Consumer Research, 25*, 189–201.

Chen, S., & Chaiken, S. (1999). The heuristic-systematic model in its broader context. In S. Chaiken & Y. Trope (Eds.), *Dual-process theories in social psychology* (pp. 73–96). New York: Guilford.

Connolly, G. M., Casswell, S., Zhang, J., & Silva, P. A. (1994). Alcohol in the mass media and drinking by adolescents: A longitudinal study. *Addiction, 89*, 1255–1263.

Cronley, M. L., Posavac, S. S., Meyer, T., Kardes, F. R., & Kellaris, J. J. (2005). A selective hypothesis testing perspective on price-quality inference and inference-based choice. *Journal of Consumer Psychology, 15*, 159–169.

DeMarree, K. G., Wheeler S. C., & Petty R. E. (2005). Priming a new identity: Self-monitoring moderates the effects of nonself primes on self-judgments and behavior. *Journal of Personality and Social Psychology, 89*, 657–671.

DeSteno, D., Petty, R. E., Rucker, D. D., Wegener, D. T., & Braverman, J. (2004). Discrete emotions and persuasion: The role of emotion-induced expectancies. *Journal of Personality and Social Psychology, 86*, 43–56.

Dhar, R. (1997). Consumer preference for a no-choice option. *Journal of Consumer Research, 24*, 215–231.

Dijksterhuis, A., Spears, R., Postmes, T., Stapel, D. A., Koomen, W., Van Knippenberg, A., & Scheepers, D. (1998). Seeing one thing and doing another: Contrast effects in automatic behavior. *Journal of Personality and Social Psychology, 75*, 862–871.

Ellickson, P. L., Collins, R. L., Hambarsoomians, K., & McCaffrey, D. F. (2005). Does alcohol advertising promote adolescent drinking? Results from a longitudinal assessment. *Addiction, 100*, 235–246.

Fabrigar, L. R., & Petty, R. E. (1999). The role of the affective and cognitive bases of attitudes in susceptibility to affectively and cognitively based persuasion. *Personality and Social Psychology Bulletin, 25*, 363–381.

Fazio, R. H., Herr, P. M., & Powell, M. C. (1992). On the development and strength of category-based associations in memory: The case of mystery ads. *Journal of Consumer Psychology, 1*, 1–14.

Fazio, R. H., & Towles-Schwen, T. (1999). The MODE model of attitude-behavior processes. In S. Chaiken & Y. Trope (Eds.), *Dual-Process Theories in Social Psychology* (pp. 97–116). New York: Guilford.

Feldman, J. M., & Lynch, J. G. (1988). Self-generated validity and other effects of measurement on belief, attitude, intention, and behavior. *Journal of Applied Psychology, 73*, 421–435.

Fiske, S. T., & Neuberg, S. L. (1990). A continuum of impression formation from category-based to individuating processes: Influences of information and motivation on attention and interpretation. In M. P. Zanna (Ed.), *Advances in experimental social psychology* (Vol. 23, pp. 1–74). New York: Academic Press.

Fiske, S. T., & Taylor, S. E. (1991). *Social cognition.* New York: McGraw-Hill.

Fitzsimons, G. J., & Moore, S. G. (2008). Should we ask our children about sex, drugs and rock & roll? Potentially harmful effects of asking questions about risky behaviors. *Journal of Consumer Psychology, 18*, 82–95.

Fitzsimons, G. M., Chartrand, T. L., & Fitzsimons, G. J. (2008). Automatic effects of brand exposure on motivated behavior: How Apple makes you "think different." *Journal of Consumer Research, 35*, 21–35.

Förster, J., & Liberman, N. (2007). Knowledge activation. In A. W. Kruglanski, & E. T. Higgins (Eds.), *Handbook of basic principles* (2nd ed., pp. 201–231). New York: Guilford.

Förster, J., Liberman, N., & Kuschel, S. (2008). The effect of global versus local processing styles on assimilation versus contrast in social judgment. *Journal of Personality and Social Psychology, 94*(4), 579.

Foster, S. E., Vaughan, R. D., Foster, W. H., & Califano, J. A. (2003). Alcohol consumption and expenditures for underage drinking and adult excessive drinking. *Journal of the American Medical Association, 289*, 989–995.

Foster, S. E., Vaughan, R. D., Foster, W. H., & Califano, J. A. (2006). Estimate of the commercial value of underage drinking and adult abusive and dependent drinking to the alcohol industry. *Archives of Pediatrics and Adolescent Medicine, 160*, 473–478.

Garfield, C. F., Chung, P. J., & Rathouz, P. J. (2003). Alcohol advertising in magazines and adolescent readership. *Journal of the American Medical Association, 289*, 2424–2429.

Gates, P., Copeland, J., Stevenson, R. J., & Dillon, P. (2007). The influence of product packaging on young people's palatability rating for RTDs and other alcoholic beverages. *Alcohol and Alcoholism, 42*, 138–142.

Grube, J. W., & Wallack, L. (1994). Television beer advertising and drinking knowledge, beliefs, and intentions among schoolchildren. *American Journal of Public Health, 84*, 254–259.

Ha, Y., & Hoch, S. J. (1989). Ambiguity, processing strategy, and advertising–evidence interactions. *Journal of Consumer Research, 16*, 354–360.

Hannah, D., & Sternthal, B. (1984). Detecting and explaining the sleeper effect. *Journal of Consumer Research, 11*, 632–642.

Hastings, G., Anderson, S., Cooke, E., & Gordon, R. (2005). Alcohol marketing and young people's drinking: A review of the research. *Journal of Public Health Policy, 26*, 296–311.

Herr, P. M. (1986). Consequences of priming: Judgment and behavior. *Journal of Personality and Social Psychology, 51*, 1106–1115.

Herr, P. M. (1989). Priming price: Prior knowledge and context effects. *Journal of Consumer Research, 16*, 67–75.

Herr, P. M., Kardes, F. R., & Kim, J. (1991). Effects of word-of-mouth and product-attribute information on persuasion: An accessibility-diagnosticity perspective. *Journal of Consumer Research, 17*, 454–462.

Hirt, E., Kardes, F. R., & Markman, K. D. (2004). Activating a mental simulation mind-set through generation of alternatives: Implications for debiasing in related and unrelated domains. *Journal of Experimental Social Psychology, 40*(3), 374.

Hoch, S. J., & Ha, Y. (1986). Consumer learning: Advertising and the ambiguity of product experience. *Journal of Consumer Research, 13*, 221–233.

Howard-Pitney, B., Borgida, E., & Omoto, A. M. (1986). Personal involvement: An examination of processing differences. *Social Cognition, 4*, 39–57.

Jernigan, D. H. (2009). The global alcohol industry: An overview. *Addiction, 104 (Supplement 1)*, 6–12.

Jernigan, D. H., & Mosher, J. F. (2005). Editors' introduction: Alcohol marketing and youth—Public health perspectives. *Journal of Public Health Policy, 26*, 287–291.

Jernigan, D. H., Ostroff, J., & Ross, C. (2005). Alcohol advertising and youth: A measured approach. *Journal of Public Health Policy, 26*, 312–325.

Kardes, F. R. (1994). Consumer judgment and decision processes. In R. S. Wyer & T. K. Srull (Eds.), *Handbook of Social Cognition* (Vol. 2, pp. 399–466). Hillsdale, NJ: Erlbaum.

Kardes, F. R., Cronley, M. L., Kellaris, J. J., & Posavac, S. S. (2004). The role of selective information processing in price-quality inference. *Journal of Consumer Research, 31*, 368–374.

Kardes, F. R., Cronley, M. L., & Kim, J. (2006). Construal-level effects on preference stability, preference-behavior correspondence, and the suppression of competing brands. *Journal of Consumer Psychology, 16*, 135–144.

Kardes, F. R., Posavac, S. S., Cronley, M. L., & Herr, P. M. (2008). Consumer inference. In C. P. Haugtvedt, P. M. Herr, & F. R. Kardes (Eds.), *Handbook of consumer psychology* (pp. 165–191). New York: Psychology Press.

Kardes, F. R., Sanbonmatsu, D. M., Cronley, M. L., & Houghton, D. C. (2002). Consideration set overvaluation: When impossibly favorable ratings of a set of brands are observed. *Journal of Consumer Psychology, 12*, 353–361.

Kay, A. C., Wheeler, S. C., Bargh, J. A., & Ross, L. (2004). Material priming: The influence of mundane physical objects on situational construal and competitive behavior choice. *Organizational Behavior and Human Decision Processes, 95*, 83–96.

Keller, K. L. (2008). *Strategic brand management.* Upper Saddle River, NJ: Prentice-Hall.

Kelly, K. J., & Edwards, R. W. (1998). Image advertisements for alcohol products: Is their appeal associated with adolescents' intention to consume alcohol? *Adolescence, 33*, 47–60.

Kisielius, J., & Sternthal, B. (1986). Examining the vividness controversy: An availability–valence interpretation. *Journal of Consumer Research*, *12*, 418–431.

Krosnick, J. A., & Alwin, D. F. (1989). Aging and susceptibility to attitude change. *Journal of Personality and Social Psychology*, *57*, 416–425.

Kruglanski, A. W., & Webster, D. M. (1996). Motivated closing of the mind: "Seizing" and "freezing." *Psychological Review*, *103*, 263–283.

Labroo, A. A., Dhar, R., & Schwarz, N. (2008). Of frog wines and frowning watches: Semantic priming, perceptual fluency, and brand evaluation. *Journal of Consumer Research*, *34*, 819–831.

Li, W. K., & Wyer, R. S. (1994). The role of country of origin in product evaluations: Informational and standard-of-comparison effects. *Journal of Consumer Psychology*, *3*, 187–212.

Lynch, J. G. (1985). Uniqueness issues in the decompositional modeling of multiattribute overall evaluations: An information integration perspective. *Journal of Marketing Research*, *22*, 1–19.

Lynch, J. G., Marmorstein, H., & Weigold, M. F. (1988). Choices from sets including remembered brands: Use of recalled attributes and prior overall evaluations. *Journal of Consumer Research*, *15*, 169–184.

Maimaran, M., & Wheeler, S. C. (2008). Circles, squares, and choice: The effect of shape arrays on uniqueness and variety seeking. *Journal of Marketing Research*, *45*, 731–740.

Mantonakis, A., Whittlesea, B. W. A., & Yoon, C. (2008). Consumer memory, fluency, and familiarity. In C. P. Haugtvedt, P. M. Herr, & F. R. Kardes (Eds.), *Handbook of consumer psychology* (pp. 77–102). New York: Psychology Press.

Markman, A. B., & Brendl, C. M. (2005). Goals, policies, preferences, and actions. In F. R. Kardes, P. M. Herr, & J. Nantel (Eds.), *Applying social cognition to consumer-focused strategy* (pp. 183–199). Mahwah, NJ: Erlbaum.

McCreanor, T., Greenaway, A., Barnes, H. M., Borell, S., & Gregory, A. (2005). Youth identity formation and contemporary alcohol marketing. *Critical Public Health*, *15*, 251–262.

McGuire, W. J. (1972). Attitude change: An information processing paradigm. In C. G. McClintock (Ed.), *Experimental social psychology* (pp. 108–141). New York: Holt, Rinehart, and Winston.

Meloy, M. G., & Russo, J. E. (2004). Binary choice under instructions to select versus reject. *Organizational Behavior and Human Decision Processes*, *93*, 114–128.

Meyers-Levy, J., & Peracchio, L. A. (1992). Getting an angle in advertising: The effects of camera angle on product evaluations. *Journal of Marketing Research*, *29*, 454–461.

Miller, G. A. (1956). The magical number seven, plus or minus two: Some limits on our capacity for information processing. *Psychological Review*, *63*, 81–97.

Mosher, J. F. (2009). Litigation and alcohol policy: Lessons from the U.S. tobacco wars. *Addiction*, *104 (Supplement 1)*, 27–33.

Mosher, J. F., & Johnsson, D. (2005). Flavored alcoholic beverages: An international marketing campaign that targets youth. *Journal of Public Health Policy*, *26*, 326–342.

Mussweiler, T. (2003). Comparison processes in social judgment: mechanisms and consequences. *Psychological Review*, *1*, 472–489.

Nisbett, R. E., & Ross, L. (1980). *Human inference: Strategies and shortcomings of social judgment.* Englewood Cliffs, NJ: Prentice-Hall.

Novemsky, N., Dhar, R., Schwarz, N., & Simonson, I. (2007). Preference Fluency in Choice. *Journal of Marketing Research*, *44*(3), 347–356.

O'Brien, M. C., McCoy, T. P., Rhodes, S. D., Wagoner, A., & Wolfson, M. (2008). Caffeinated cocktails: Energy drink consumption, high-risk drinking, and alcohol-related consequences among college students. *Academic Emergency Medicine*, *15*, 453–460.

O'Guinn, T. C., & Shrum, L. J. (1997). The role of television in the construction of consumer reality. *Journal of Consumer Research*, *23*, 278–294.

Petty, R. E., & Wegener, D. T. (1998). Matching versus mismatching attitude functions: Implications for scrutiny of persuasive messages. *Personality and Social Psychology Bulletin*, *24*, 227–240.

Petty, R. E., & Wegener, D. T. (1999). The elaboration likelihood model: Current status and controversies. In S. Chaiken & Y. Trope (Eds.), *Dual-process theories in social psychology* (pp. 41–72). New York: Guilford.

Pfeiffer, B. E. & Kardes, F. R. (2009). *Omission neglect and inferential adjustment.* Working paper, University of New Hampshire.

Posavac, S. S., Sanbonmatsu, D. M., & Fazio, R. H. (1997). Considering the best choice: Effects of the salience and accessibility of alternatives on attitude-decision consistency. *Journal of Personality and Social Psychology*, *72*, 253–261.

Posavac, S. S., Sanbonmatsu, D. M., & Ho, E. A. (2002). The effects of the selective consideration of alternatives on consumer choice and attitude-decision consistency. *Journal of Consumer Psychology*, *12*, 203–213.

Posavac, S. S., Sanbonmatsu, D. M., Kardes, F. R., & Fitzsimons, G. J. (2004). The brand positivity effect: When evaluation confers preference. *Journal of Consumer Research*, *31*, 643–651.

Russo, J. E., Carlson, K. A., & Meloy, M. G. (2006). Choosing an inferior option. *Psychological Science*, *17*, 899–904.

Russo, J. E., Carlson, K. A., Meloy, M. G., & Yong, K. (2008). The goal of consistency as a cause of information distortion. *Journal of Experimental Psychology: General*, *137*, 456–470.

Russo, J. E., Meloy, M. G., & Medvec, V. H. (1998). Predecisional distortion of product information. *Journal of Marketing Research*, *35*, 438–452.

Ryder, D., Walker, N., & Salmon, A. (2006). *Drug use and drug-related harm* (2nd ed.). Melbourne, Australia: IP Communications.

Saffer, H., & Dave, D. (2002). Alcohol consumption and alcohol advertising bans. *Applied Economics*, *34*, 1325–1334.

Sanbonmatsu, D. M., Kardes, F. R., & Herr, P. M. (1992). The role of prior knowledge and missing information in multiattribute evaluation. *Organizational Behavior & Human Decision Processes*, *51*, 76–91.

Sanbonmatsu, D. M., Kardes, F. R., & Sansone, C. (1991). Remembering less and inferring more: Effects of time of judgment on inferences about unknown attributes. *Journal of Personality & Social Psychology*, *61*, 546–554.

Sanbonmatsu, D. M., Posavac, S. S., Kardes, F. R., & Mantel, S. P. (1998). Selective hypothesis testing. *Psychonomic Bulletin & Review*, *5*, 197–220.

Sanbonmatsu, D. M., Posavac, S. S., & Stasney, R. (1997). The subjective beliefs underlying numerical probability overestimation. *Journal of Experimental Social Psychology*, *33*, 276–295.

Sanbonmatsu, D. M., Kardes, F. R., Houghton, D. C., Ho, E. A., & Posavac, S. S. (2003). Overestimating the importance of the given information in multiattribute consumer judgment. *Journal of Consumer Psychology*, *13*, 289–300.

Schumann, D. W., Petty, R. E., & Clemons, D. S. (1990). Predicting the effectiveness of different strategies of advertising variation: A test of the repetition-variation hypothesis. *Journal of Consumer Research*, *17*, 192–202.

Schwartz, B., Ward, A., Monterosso, J., Lyubomirsky, S., White, K., & Lehman, D. R. (2002). Maximizing versus satisficing: Happiness is a matter of choice. *Journal of Personality and Social Psychology*, *83*, 1178–1197.

Schwarz, N. (2004). Metacognitive experiences in consumer judgment and decision making. *Journal of Consumer Psychology*, *14*, 332–348.

Schwarz, N., & Bless, H. (1992). Constructing reality and its alternatives: An inclusion/exclusion model of assimilation and contrast effects in social judgment. In L. L. Martin, & A. Tesser (Eds.), *The construction of social judgments* (pp. 217–245). Hillsdale, NJ: Erlbaum.

Shafir, E. (1993). Choosing versus rejecting: Why some options are both better and worse than others. *Memory & Cognition*, *21*, 546–556.

Sheppard, B. H., Hartwick, J., & Warshaw, P. R. (1988). The theory of reasoned action: A meta-analysis of past research with recommendations for modifications and future research. *Journal of Consumer Research*, *15*, 325–343.

Shrum, L. J., Wyer, R. S., and O'Guinn, T. C. (1998). The effects of television consumption on social perceptions: The use of priming procedures to investigate psychological processes. *Journal of Consumer Research*, *24*, 447–458.

Simon, M., & Mosher, J. (2007). Alcohol, energy drinks, and youth: A dangerous mix. Retrieved February 16, 2009 from www.marininstitute.org/site/index.php?option=com_content&view=category&layout=blog&id=7&Itemid=28

Snyder, M., & Gangestad, S. (1986). On the nature of self-monitoring: Matters of assessment, matters of validity. *Journal of Personality and Social Psychology*, *51*, 125–139.

Snyder, L. B., Milici, F. F., Slater, M., Sun, H., & Strizhakova, Y. (2006). Effects of alcohol advertising exposure on drinking among youth. *Archives of Pediatric Adolescent Medicine*, *160*, 18–24.

Stacy, A. W., Zogg, J. B., Unger, J. B., & Dent, C. W. (2004). Exposure to televised alcohol use ads and subsequent adolescent alcohol use. *American Journal of Health Behavior*, *28*, 498–509.

Strack, F., & Mussweiler, T. (2003). Heuristic strategies for estimation under uncertainty: The enigmatic case of anchoring. In G. V. Bodenhausen and A. J. Lambert (Eds.), *Foundations of social cognition: A festschrift in honor of Robert S. Wyer, Jr.* (Vol. 10, pp. 79–95). Mahwah, NJ: Erlbaum.

Strahan, E. J., Spencer S. J., and Zanna, M. P. (2002). Subliminal priming and persuasion: Striking while the iron is hot. *Journal of Experimental Social Psychology*, *38*, 556–568.

Sujan, M. (1985). Consumer knowledge: Effects on evaluation strategies mediating consumer judgments. *Journal of Consumer Research*, *12*, 31–46.

Tversky, A., & Kahneman, D. (1974). Judgment under uncertainty: Heuristics and biases. *Science*, *185*, 1124–1130.

Tversky, A. and Koehler, D. J. (1994). Support theory: A nonextensional representation of subjective probability, *Psychological Review*, *101*, 547–567.

Tybout, A. M., Calder, B. J., & Sternthal, B. (1981). Using information processing theory to design marketing strategies. *Journal of Marketing Research*, *18*, 73–79.

Tybout, A. M., & Scott, C. A. (1983). Availability of well-defined internal knowledge and the attitude formation process: Information aggregation versus self-perception. *Journal of Personality and Social Psychology*, *44*, 474–491.

Tybout, A. M., Sternthal, B., & Calder, B. J. (1983). Information availability as a determinant of multiple request effectiveness. *Journal of Marketing Research*, *20*, 280–290.

Venkatraman, M. P., Marlino, D. Kardes, F. R., & Sklar, K. B. (1990). The interactive effects of message appeal and individual differences on information processing and persuasion. *Psychology & Marketing*, *7*, 85–96.

Wänke, M., Bohner, G., & Jurkowitsch, A. (1997). There are many reasons to drive a BMW: Does imagined ease of argument generation influence attitudes? *Journal of Consumer Research, 24*, 170–177.

Wansink, B., Kent, R. J., & Hoch, S. J. (1998). An anchoring and adjustment model of purchase quantity decisions. *Journal of Marketing Research, 35*(1), 71–81.

Wheeler, S. C. and Berger J. (2007). When the same prime leads to different effects. *Journal of Consumer Research, 34*, 357–368.

Wheeler, S. C., Petty, R. E., & Bizer, G. Y. (2005). Self-schema matching and attitude change: Situational and dispositional determinants of message elaboration. *Journal of Consumer Research, 31*, 787–797.

Wyer, R. S. (1974). *Cognitive organization and change: An information-processing approach.* Hillsdale, NJ: Erlbaum.

Wyer, R. S. (2004). *Social comprehension and judgment: The role of situation models, narratives, and implicit theories.* Mahwah, NJ: Erlbaum.

Wyer, R. S. (2005). The role of information processing in single-alternative and multiple-alternative judgments and decisions. In F. R. Kardes, P. M. Herr, & J. Nantel (Eds.), *Applying social cognition to consumer-focused strategy* (pp. 3–36). Mahwah, NJ: Erlbaum.

Wyer, R. S. (2008). The role of knowledge accessibility in cognition and behavior: Implications for consumer information processing. In C. Haugtvedt, P. M. Herr, & F. R. Kardes (Eds.), *Handbook of consumer psychology* (pp. 31–76). New York: Psychology Press.

Yang, X., Jain, S., Lindsey, C. D., & Kardes, F. R. (2010). *Effects of matching and mismatching construal levels on resistance to persuasion in comparative advertising.* Manuscript submitted for publication.

Yeung, C. W. M., & Wyer, R. S. (2004). Affect, appraisal and consumer judgment. *Journal of Consumer Research, 31*, 412–424.

Yi, Y. (1990). The effects of contextual priming in print advertisements. *Journal of Consumer Research, 17*, 215–222.

Yi, Y. (1993). Contextual priming effects in print advertisements: The moderating role of prior knowledge. *Journal of Advertising, 22*, 1–10.

28

Psychology Applied to Poverty

Stuart C. Carr and Chiwoza R. Bandawe

Psychology can be applied to poverty: (1) as a lens for scrutinizing its psychological features; and (2) as a means for contributing to poverty *reduction*. Reviews (e.g., Lever, 2007; Marsella, 1998; Sloan, 2003) suggest we have done better at the first than the second. Studies emphasize covariates of poverty like lowered self-esteem, depression, and impaired well-being (Lever, Piñol, & Uralde, 2005). Themes in the literature include "cultures of poverty" (Lewis, 1959), especially well-being deficits (for a critique, see Moreira, 2007), "personal attributes" in volunteer work and local enterprise development, (1960s–present), and public or lay "attributions" about poverty's causes (1970s–present). Lenses can magnify or distort, and the 1980s nurtured wariness about a potential for "psychologizing" poverty to reify, colonize, and even perpetuate poverty (Sinha & Holtzman, 1984). In the 1990s, optimism flickered that psychology could be more closely connected to health, education, and work, and through these conduits, contribute to the longer-term goal of poverty reduction itself (Carr & MacLachlan, 1998). That flicker has continued into the new millennium (Mohanty & Misra, 2000). However progress has not been rapid enough for psychology to be taken seriously, either by policy makers (Berry, Reichman, & Schein, 2008) or in-country groups (Carr, 2007).

Professional training in any discipline—psychology included—can leave the expert out of touch with clients' everyday needs (Nickerson, 1999). According to Nickerson, professionals easily become advocates for what they can *supply*, rather than what clients themselves need, and are prepared to use (*demand*). International aid and aid professionals have been subject to this very same criticism (for cogent examples, see Porter, Allen & Thompson, 1991; Easterly, 2006). Applied psychology too has been criticized for stressing supply before demand, in poverty reduction work (Carr et al., 2008). That has arguably left its science and practice appearing alien and irrelevant

IAAP Handbook of Applied Psychology, First Edition. Edited by Paul R. Martin, Fanny M. Cheung, Michael C. Knowles, Michael Kyrios, Lyn Littlefield, J. Bruce Overmier, and José M. Prieto.

to potential end-users and policy-makers (Akin-Ogundeji, 1991; Nsamenang, 2006). To help "give psychology away" (Miller, 1969), we distinguish clearly between demand and supply, and we use the former to delineate the latter not vice-versa.

Demand for poverty reduction services is arguably at an all-time high, providing a convenient and timely yardstick for reassessing psychology's supply. Yet supply and demand themselves can be differentiated. A familiar example is (a) content versus (b) process (Latham, 2006). How one implements training in practice, in response to genuine demand, can be as important as the technique or principle itself. Research with international emergency relief workers in the Pacific, for example, has shown that process skills (e.g., learning to suspend judgements about cultural practices), makes a difference to the efficacy of the aid itself (MacLachlan & McAuliffe, 2003). In sub-Saharan Africa, where poverty is closely linked to health, psychology can arguably go beyond merely describing the psychological content of well-being, working more alongside the producers of health—households (Bandawe, 2000; 2005). It is households that make decisions regarding health, and compliance with healthy regimens (Lewin, 1947). Hence applying psychology to poverty reduction is about both (i) content and (ii) process.

The Content of Demand

Demand for income

The best-known statistics are the World Bank's $1.25/2.50-a-day "development indicators." These denote respectively extreme poverty and "moderate" poverty.[1] The world contains around six billion people; about one-third being children. Of the 6 billion, 1.4 billion live in extreme poverty (<US$1.25 per day), while 3 billion live on <US$2.50 per day. More than 80% live in countries where income gaps are widening. The world's richest 20% command 75% of world income. China apart, global poverty has fallen only 10% since 1981. Much poverty today is in landlocked economies in sub-Saharan Africa, South Asia, and island nations like Oceania. Economically poorer communities suffer most from disasters like climate change and economic crisis (www.oecd.org/document/38/0,3343,en_2649_33731_31081126_1_1_1_1,00.html).

Demand for access

Poverty is not just about income or income inequality (Iceland, 2005). In education, 72 million primary school children are not in school, most of them girls. One billion people entered the new millennium unable to read a book or write their name. Child mortality from poverty is estimated at 30,000—daily. Between 27 and 28% of children in poorer countries are either underweight or stunted in growth, mainly in sub-Saharan Africa and South Asia. About 1.8 million children die annually from preventable diarrhoea; 2.2 million children die annually through not being immunized and 15 million children are orphaned by HIV/AIDS. Forty million people globally are HIV positive. Malaria infects 250–500 million people annually, killing one million. Ninety percent of deaths are in Africa; 80% are children. Around 2.6 billion people globally lack access to basic sanitation, 1.1 billion to water, 1.6 billion to electricity. These statistics are facets of poverty and cry out for its reduction. Poverty is multidimensional, so its reduction must be too (Kakwani & Silber, 2007).

Demand for freedom

A prominent multidimensional concept in poverty reduction is "Basic Capability" (Sen, 1999). In Laureate Sen's *capabilities model*, poverty is and stems (a) from restricted opportunity in society and education, (b) from poor health, and (c) from health care insecurity. The frustration that results is captured in *Voices of the Poor*, a landmark study whose participants were >60,000 people from 60 countries (Narayan, Patel, Schafft, Rademacher, & Koch-Schulte, 2000; Narayan, Chambers, Shah, & Petesch 2000; Narayan, & Petesch, 2002). Exemplars include: "Poverty is humiliation, the sense of being dependent on them, and of being forced to accept rudeness, insults, and indifference when we seek help" (Latvian woman); and from a woman in Egypt: "We face a calamity when my husband falls ill: Our life comes to a halt until he recovers and goes back to work" (World Bank, 2000, p. 4). These voices are frustrated but agentic. They reflect a sea-change in how cultures of poverty have been framed since Lewis (1959). Poverty is not reduced by "fixing" the individual, but by enabling the context.

Demand for enablement

In 2000, the member states of the United Nations articulated a plan for enabling the context (Annan, 2000). The "Millennium Development Goals" (Table 28.1.) are a succinct, influential summary of poverty-related demand up to their 2015 deadline (United Nations, 2006). They echo *Voices of the Poor*, and accord with Sen's model. The primary goal is poverty reduction (Millennium Development Goal 1). This is supported by a set of interlocking necessary conditions for enabling human freedom (Goals 2–8). The goals include, but are not confined to, international aid (Accra Agenda for Action, 2008). They reflect human needs, but they also situate them in applied behavioral context. From Table 28.1., the contexts include schools, communities, the environment, and workplaces—along with the people in each.

The Millennium Development Goals are no panacea for poverty elimination. There have been underwhelming "grand plans" before (Easterly, 2006). Predecessors reflected development thought-frames at the time (World Bank, 2000). They alternated from emphasizing infrastructure (1940s), community development (1950s), and technical assistance (1960s), to health/education (1970s), to market reform (1980s), and to governance (1990s). What *differentiates* the Millennium Development Goals is aspiration to integrate; they *encompass* infrastructure projects like schools, community clinics, development partnership via technical assistance in health and education, greater market access, and governance. Sweeping goals can be "too top-down," and later backfire (Locke & Latham, 2002). However, as in all strategic planning, the United Nations goals can be translated into smaller-scale interventions that are *s*pecific, *m*easurable, *a*ttainable, *r*ealistic, and *t*imely, to which we apply the

Table 28.1. The Millennium Development Goals

1. Eradicate extreme poverty and hunger (specifically, halve the proportion of people living on less than $US1 a day, and halve the proportion of people who go hungry)
2. Ensure that all boys and girls complete primary schooling
3. Promote gender equality and empower women, at all levels of education
4. Reduce under-five child mortality by two-thirds
5. Improve maternal health by reducing the maternal mortality ratio by three-quarters
6. Halt and begin to reverse the spread of HIV/AIDS, malaria, and other major diseases
7. Ensure environmental sustainability (integrate into country policies, reverse loss of environmental resources, halve proportion of people without access to potable water, improve the lives of 100 million slum dwellers)
8. Develop a global partnership for development (raise official development assistance, expand market access, enhance governance, manage national debt, increase access to affordable medicines, work with the private sector to harness new technology)

Source: Abridged from World Bank (2003) and from www.un.org/millenniumgoals/goals.html

acronym "s.m.a.r.t." (Sachs, 2005), because they represent a smart approach. Some of these s.m.a.r.t. actions, such as deworming people with bilharzia, are less obviously "psychological" than are others like assisting entrepreneurs to grow their business (www.unmillenniumproject.org/reports/).

Processes in Demand

Systems understanding

Identifying "what" contexts matter is not the same as identifying "how" they matter. Figure 28.1. portrays a poverty reduction *system*. The model reflects Table 28.1., for example the enterprising *employee* who becomes an *employer*, so gaining from Table 28.1. "market access" under Millennium Development Goal 8. In Figure 28.1., resources for development derive from three main sources—citizen, client, and consumer—none of whom is exclusively located in either richer or poorer countries, and each of whom can contribute respectively, for example via taxes, donations, or shares & investments. There is a continual interdependence between aid, community, and business groups. These include national and international aid agencies, global non-profits like World Vision, and corporations. These groups link in turn to the civil service (governments), local NGOs (non-government organizations), and local firms. Many millions of people work in these organizations worldwide, as civil servants, aid workers, and employee/rs. Their role in these organizational "front-line" positions, from Figure 28.1., is to serve the relatively needy citizen, client, and consumer.

The Paris Declaration on Aid Effectiveness

From Figure 28.1., poverty reduction entails multiple, cross-group *relationships* (Riddell, 2007). To make these manageable, policy principles have been developed.

POORER					**DEMAND**
CITIZEN		CLIENT		CONSUMER	*Poverty Reduction Strategy Papers*
⇩		⇩		⇩	
CIVIL SERVANT	⇔	AID WORKER	⇔	EMPLOYEE/R	*Capacity/Mobility*
⇕		⇕		⇕	
GOVERNMENTS		LOCAL NGOs	⇔	LOCAL FIRMS	*Budget vs. Project*
⇧	⇗	⇧	⇖	⇧	
AID AGENCIES	⇔	NON PROFITS	⇔	CORPORATIONS	*Social Responsibility*
⇧		⇧		⇧	
TAXES		DONATIONS		SHARES & INVESTMENTS	*Mediation*
⇧		⇧		⇧	
CITIZEN		CLIENT		CONSUMER	*Inter-disciplinarity*
RICHER					**SUPPLY**

Figure 28.1. A systems overview of poverty reduction[3]

Based on in-country workshops is the Paris Declaration on Aid Effectiveness (www.aidharmonization.org/secondary-pages/Paris2005). This lays out principles for implementing the Millennium Development Goals. For example, since international aid began, there has been "fragmentation" between aid agencies, projects and budgets, undermining coordination and increasing overheads (Easterly & Pfutze, 2008, p. 30). As a countermeasure, the principle of "harmonization" entails working collaboratively to decrease competition, duplication, inefficiencies, organizational crowding during disasters, and the like. Development assistance has also been driven by donors' wishes rather than the needs of the poor (Porter et al, 1991). To counteract this, "alignment" means that "donors base their overall support on countries' national development strategies, institutions, and procedures" (Accra Agenda for Action, 2008, p. 3). Alignment involves governments, local NGOs, and local firms. Hence local demand drives supply, not vice-versa.

Harmonization and alignment are not just about international aid (United Nations, 2008). They have arguably become watchwords for poverty reduction in general; a kind of meta-policy (Accra Agenda for Action, 2008). These tenets have created an unprecedented demand for expertise in "how" to implement the Millennium Development Goals in everyday poverty reduction work. For instance, a key role is envisaged for behavior *incentives*: "Donors and partner countries jointly commit to … strengthen incentives—including for recruitment, appraisal and training—for management and staff to work towards harmonization, alignment and results" (Paris Declaration, 2005, p. 6). These demands are familiar to applied psychologists. They clearly suggest tangible, s.m.a.r.t. contexts, like organizations and workplaces for example, where psychology can usefully be applied (OECD, 2003, p. 30).[2]

What Can We Supply?

Poverty Reduction Strategy Papers

In theory, Poverty Reduction Strategy Papers are designed as an exercise in participative planning, involving citizens, clients, and consumers from within the local community. In policy parlance, they should reflect alignment. Poverty Reduction Strategy Papers are supposed to articulate the Millennium Development Goals at an in-country level. They function something like a participant-planned application for funding. In practice, of course, Poverty Reduction Strategy Papers will privilege some groups and underrepresent others (Fakuda-Parr, 2008): For example, they may privilege the "social" sector (investments in education and health; Millennium Development Goals 2–6) over hunger and nutrition, the environment, and decent work (Millennium Development Goals 1, 7, & 8, respectively). What this means in practice then is that decent work requires *advocacy*, to move legitimate interests into the Poverty Reduction Strategy Papers and then secure some backing.

Under the auspices of the International Labor Organization (ILO), a behavioral training package has been developed to promote a "Decent Work Agenda" (Yiu & Saner, 2005). The handbook's end-users are International Labor Organization "constituents" (Ministries of Labor, employers' associations, Trade Unions, civil society groups and, from Figure 28.1., the average citizen). As Yiu and Saner point out, tackling unemployment (Fryer & Fagan, 2003), and fostering Decent Work, including decent pay, is an integral component of Millennium Development Goal 1. It can always come under threat from economic downturn (Yiu & Saner, 2005, p. 2: 4). The handbook itself is interdisciplinary and includes context-sensitive psychology. It features organizational change, persuasive communication, negotiating and bargaining, conflict resolution, political skill and networking, competency modeling, and group decision making. The manual is an outstanding example not only of how and where psychology can be useful. It also indicates what *kinds* of psychology might, usefully, play a role.

Those roles are not restricted to rights in labour. Issues in health too can be addressed, for example with community-based research and methods. Schistosomiasis (or bilharzia) is a water-borne infection that can cause serious damage to children's health (Table 28.1., Millennium Development Goal 6). Based on health promotion theory, cultural values, and consultation with the local community, a range of different interventions, from deworming to bilharzia clubs, can be implemented (Bandawe, 2000). Bandawe's methodology was quantitative and qualitative, participative and aligned. It tested what reduced high-risk behavior and actual infections. Both medical *and* social processes played a part in maximizing health. Such community-aligned, Millennium Development Goal-focused research has a potential to bring evidence-based practice into Poverty Reduction Strategy Papers and into the wider ethos of social equity in health and other sectors (Basu, 2007).

Community participation is a domain led by applied psychology in Latin America (Sánchez, Cronick, & Wiesenfeld, 2003). Influenced by the liberation pedagogy of Paulo Freire (1972), community social psychology is inherently interdisciplinary, inclusive, harmonized, and aligned. In terms of content rather than process, community social psychology's s.m.a.r.t. goals might entail, for example, setting up a housing loan scheme for low-income families or building a self-sustaining water supply system (Sánchez et al, 2003). Other disciplines contributing to s.m.a.r.t. goals could be architecture, engineering, geography, and economics. The process model is that researchers work with the community to hone its perspective on the poverty-related issue (problematization). Stakeholders formulate ways forward, pull together to implement a preferred solution, and collectively monitor and evaluate the process. Being iterative, proactive, participatory, and problem-focused, community social psychology is a form of "action research" widely found across Latin America (Scisleski, Maraschin, & Tittoni, 2006).

Processes aside, the frequent *outcome*, according to Sánchez et al.'s (2003) integrative review, is community empowerment and collective self-efficacy that enables poverty reduction. Community social psychology applies theories and techniques from community psychology and from social psychology, enabling people to break *out* of cultures of poverty into social action, empowerment, and well-being (Prilleltensky, 2003). As such, community social psychology has presaged the fostering of basic capabilities and has been a precursor to the Millennium Development Goals. Community social psychology has much to offer the wider community (Ardila, 2004).

Capacity and mobility

In Figure 28.1., applying psychology to assist with developing a Poverty Reduction Strategy Paper can help to build capacity for improving decent work, health, housing, and water. Capacity building—sometimes known as capacity development—plays a huge part in policy thinking (Manning, 2006). From Figure 28.1., development work entails collaboration between civil servant, aid worker, and employee/r. For example, a mine company might work with community services (government), and a non-profit organization (local NGO), to build a crèche for the children of workers (in local firms), which provides children's day-care and pre-school education (Table 28.1., Millennium Development Goals 1-3 & 8). The basic idea in any such processes is logical enough: Capacity can be developed—mutually—by combining task with relationship (Eyben, 2005).

"Capacity" has a different definition depending on the disciplinary lens through which it is viewed. Psychologists have favored individuals rather than, say, accounting or legal systems. An early key initiative was assisting the United States' Peace Corps to select international volunteers (Ward, Bochner, & Furnham, 2001). Through the 1960s, clinical ratings of the character structure of volunteers were used, albeit with low predictive validity, to guide volunteer screening, selection, and placement (Harris, 1973). Although the programme eventually failed, it nonetheless stimulated practice in cross-cultural *training*, not only within the Peace Corps itself (Barnes, 1985), but also across international education and business (Carr, 2007). Often overlooked, training must be provided for (aligned with) *local* workers (Pastor, 1997). Legacies from the literature today include theories of "culture shock," and extensive training with "culture assimilators" (Furnham & Bochner, 1986). These have stimulated a great deal of cross-cultural psychology (Smith, 2006). An abiding point in both literatures—cross-cultural and aid-focused—is that task does seem to depend on relationship.

Ironically, as psychologists' attention turned away from selection toward training, research with volunteers found that assessments of behavioral dispositions, such as other-centeredness and interest in local culture, *can* predict cultural adjustment, assignment completion, work performance, and outcomes of capacity development (Kealey, 1989). Job analysis and specification can pay in poverty reduction work. For example, critical incidents can be used to identify crucial intersections of knowledge, skills, and abilities. These have been identified in emergency aid and disaster relief incidents (MacLachlan & McAuliffe, 2003; www.hku.hk/psychology/ompg/). Performance-enhancing knowledge, skills, and ability sets are often relationship-based forms of cultural competence, which include skills in listening and tolerance (MacLachlan & McAuliffe, 2003, p. 279). Emerging interests include development workers' occupational health and well-being, not only that of the expatriate but also, crucially, that of the host nationals (Musa & Hamid, 2008; McFarlane, 2004; Wigley, 2005).

Cultural competence is crucial whenever diversity is sociocultural. Yet often overlooked is that much of the diversity in development work is also socio*economic*. A salient example is expatriate–local pay "dispersion" (Bloom, 1999). It is not uncommon for expatriate to local salary ratios to reach double figures, depending on which aid agencies are paying the particular, co-located expatriates' salaries. Because different agencies pay different expatriates differing amounts, often for the same type of work or job, even the differences between expatriates themselves are fragmentary. Hence remuneration differences are neither harmonized nor aligned economically. They can reproduce the very power differentials the organizations aim to reduce. Wide expatriate to local ratios are also sometimes found in the private sector within joint ventures, and within multinational firms operating in low-income settings.

Work justice theory (Colquitt, Conlon, Wesson, Porter, and Ng, 2001; Greenberg, 2008) predicts that comparatively well-paid expatriates may experience a degree of awkwardness about the remuneration gap. Working harder to justify the gap is one possible solution predicted by theory, but this is not sustainable because nobody can work ten times harder than a counterpart at the same job without burning out. A more viable alternative, again predicted by theory and research on work justice, is that over time and surreptitiously, the more highly remunerated workers will develop compensatory self-*perceptions* of inflated input, for example "If I am paid so much more, I must be worth the money." Cognitions like that would not be conducive to maximized effort, and to that extent may result over time in demotivation. From a local perspective meanwhile, as Peter Drucker observed, "Very high salaries at the top … disrupt the team. They make people in the company see their own top management as adversaries rather than as colleagues. … And that quenches any willingness to say 'we' and to exert oneself except in one's own immediate self-interest" (1986, p. 14). Local workers can therefore reasonably be expected to disengage from the relationship ("you earn the higher salary, you solve the problem!"). This could exacerbate expatriates' culture shock levels, and any self-delusion ("I must be better, I do all the work!"). Hence vicious circles of escalating, mutual disengagement could follow.

An organizational survey of local and expatriate aid lecturers in Malawi tested these possibilities (Carr, MacLachlan, & Chipande, 1998). Lecturers at the time were paid and benefited, from Figure 28.1., as civil servants (largely locals) or aid workers (expatriates). As predicted, expatriate lecturers on aid salaries reported a combination of guilt and superiority, whilst local lecturers reported perceived unfairness and feelings of disengagement (MacLachlan & Carr, 2005). Because neither self-inflation nor disengagement is conducive to developing capacity, we termed this process "double demotivation." Research on remunerative (pay and benefit) discrepancy is currently being expanded to a multicountry, interdisciplinary, cross-sector project on work performance (see poverty.massey.ac.nz/#addup and, www.esrc.ac.uk/ESRCInfoCentre/Images/Impact%20case%20study%20discrepancies%20in%20aid%20and%20development%20workers%20salaries_tcm6-37066.pdf).

Such research challenges vested interests and is, therefore, difficult to implement (Lefkowitz, 2008). Activist Upton Sinclair remarked, "It is difficult to get a man to understand something when his salary depends on not understanding it." No surprise then that pay discrepancies have been taboo. Harmonizing the initiative with an Agenda for Decent Work may help *break* the taboo: "By presenting the aspirations, facts and experiences on submerged issues and by unearthing ignored concerns, the advocate raises public awareness" (Yiu & Saner, 2005, p. 3). Potential ways of managing pay and benefits dispersion include more outsourcing of aid to international local NGOs and non profits, instead of to aid agencies. The formers' salaries are likely to be more affordable (Werker & Ahmed, 2008). As Werker and Ahmed also suggest, growing professionalism in the volunteer sector includes a "love factor" of people willing to do meaningful grass roots work for less money. NGOs can thus recruit the best of the best, whether they come from higher- or lower-income economies. Policy-wise too, NGOs may realistically have a head start in helping to harmonize and align pay, thereby promoting decent work *and* remuneration.

Gaps in remuneration have a clear potential to fuel "brain drain." Economic theory predicts that the utility of higher earnings abroad will partly motivate international mobility behavior (Brown & Connell, 2006). The sectors most affected by brain drain are typically education and health care (Mullen, 2005; Millennium Development Goals 2–6 in Table 28.1.). Aggressive recruitment from health sectors in wealthier economies exacerbates "capacity stripping" and increases dependence on expatriate aid. The country as a whole suffers, while a few individuals themselves may benefit: extended families at home may also potentially benefit from remittances, return migration ("brain gain"), and diaspora networks (Katseli, Lucas, & Xenogiani, 2006). Skilled immigrants to wealthier economies must first find full employment in the new country. That is not always easy, or possible. Skilled immigrants from lower-income countries often experience employer discrimination resulting in "brain waste" (Mahroum, 2000). Prejudice prevents full employment (*access bias*), and if decent work *is* secured, career development is often blocked (*treatment bias*).

Applied psychologists, in high-income countries, have an awareness-raising responsibility to address brain waste. Reasons for the biases have been researched. They can and do include sociocultural influences like similarity-attraction and social dominance (Coates & Carr, 2003; Lim & Ward, 2003). Those links may be implicit, opening a socio-cultural, -economic and -political function for evidence-based awareness training for job *selectors* (Evers & van der Flier, 1998). Further applications are stock-in-trade to practicing organizational, educational, and health psychologists: Training the selectors in structuring selections, appraisals, and job application protocols might reduce bias as perhaps could awareness training in overcoming group prejudice and counselling for resilience (Evers & van der Flier, 1998).

In the longer term, energy can be directed at reversing brain drain itself. There is need to understand motives for migration in the first place (Katseli & Xenogiani, 2006). This includes kinetic pushes and pulls, personal and structural, in both directions, away from and toward home (Carr, Inkson, & Thorn, 2005). Personality research from Eastern Europe and the Caribbean indicates that achievement motivation is a push factor, while affiliation is more a pull home (Boneva & Frieze, 2001; Tidrick, 1971; also, McClelland, 1961). An underrated factor in retaining "brains" is greater *indigenization* of professional education programs in source countries; indigenization includes integrating traditional conceptions of health and illness in medical training (Bandawe, 2005). Another possibility is the selection and training of a cadre of mid-level health care providers "who perform tasks conventionally associated with more highly trained [yet] internationally mobile workers" (McAuliffe et al., 2009, p. 1).

Achievement motivation was a focus for early attempts by applied psychologists to foster a different form of mobility: socioeconomic. Research by McClelland and associates focused on growing small businesses, by cultivating individual achievement orientation (McClelland & Winter, 1971; McClelland, 1987a). Recent research by Frese and colleagues expands that focus to "entrepreneurial orientation." This includes innovativeness, learning orientation, integrity, and a range of environmental constraints (Frese, Brantjes, & Hoorn, 2002). These can lift organizational performance (Krauss, Frese, Friedrich & Under, 2005). Such models may help boost enterprise capacity, via training or selection into sponsorship programs to start or restart micro-enterprises, for example, in the wake of natural disasters like the 2004 Indian Ocean Boxing Day (December 26) tsunami (de Mel, Mckenzie, & Woodruff, 2007).

Micro-enterprise development is widely seen as a viable means of poverty reduction. Based on the Grameen (village-based) model of community lending, most micro-credit schemes recognize the importance of social context for individual achievement. In the original training programs for achievement motivation, entrepreneurs who managed to retain a sense of community tradition grew their enterprise more than their more "modern" counterparts (McClelland, 1987b). Modern micro-credit schemes utilize group solidarity as a means of guaranteeing and thus securing small individual loans (Schein, 1999). As Schein points out, many of these programs are focused on women in development, and thus Millennium Development Goals 2 and 3 (Table 28.1.).

Programs for the Woman is a micro-credit lending enterprise development project based in Nicaragua. It focuses on providing small loans to women to grow businesses like street-vending and home tailoring. Collectives of 25–30 women form an association, which splits into groups of 4–8, each with a representative in the association. A group meets once a week for 16 weeks to repay loans at a rate of 3%, which goes back to the programs. Once all funds are paid back, the women can double their credit from the sponsoring agency, renewing the cycle. As well as boosting economic activity, such networks foster self-esteem, social inclusion, and capacity development generally in the communities in which they grow (Schein, 2003). Schein uses extended observations in these groups to argue cogently that psychology can do more to help promote these forms of empowerment, and literally engender poverty reduction. She goes on to illustrate how women's solidarity groups generally, for example, in unions and sweat shops and agricultural cooperatives, are a fertile ground for socially responsive psychological research. Similarly, it has been argued that micro-credit schemes can be diversified beyond credit only, for example, to include savings clubs and reciprocal lending (Rugimbana & Spring, 2009). These authors conclude that diversified services may be optimally in tune with consumer demand among local women—and to that extent reduce poverty more.

Budget versus project aid

From Figure 28.1., governments feature prominently in poverty reduction. Should development assistance be channeled through the in-country government, for example, state civil servant, or should it be aimed more directly at smaller-scale, local aid projects (local NGOs)? This debate on "budget support versus project aid" continues (de Renzio, 2006). Harmonization, for instance, would seem to favor budget support (Accra Agenda for Action, 2008). Yet the effectiveness of budget support also depends on the quality of government and on trust in civil servants themselves.

Governance has been analyzed by Ferrinho and van Lerberghe (2002). This World Bank paper focuses on management versus mismanagement in public health systems, although it is not restricted to these (p. 19). Its thesis is that government workers are maligned by imputations that they are corrupt. In their everyday work, however, they face a range of disincentives, ranging from poor salaries compared to the private sector (what psychology would call "distributive injustice"), broken psychological contracts (procedural injustice), and poor performance management (interaction injustice). Budget support can thus to some extent become misaligned with civil servant need, especially for organizational justice.

Granted that unmet need, it would be rational to expect some kind of backlash, a form of justice *restoration*. According to Ferrinho and van Lergberghe, this can entail absenteeism, under-the-counter payments, and "fee-splitting" (e.g., referring to a specialist for a share of the fee or graft). In such work climates, even the most conscientious worker may observe and decide to shrink their "radius of trust" and look after their own (Easterly, 2006). Hence both project aid—which can induce double de-motivation—and budget support—which can induce graft in governance—depend on enabling organizational justice (MacLachlan, Carr, & McAuliffe, 2010). Culture-sensitive psychological theories of justice are apposite but under-utilized (Greenberg, 2007). Nevertheless as Sen and *Voices of the Poor* show, tackling injustice removes a core barrier to human development.

Social responsibility

Governance is not confined to governments. For example in Figure 28.1, aid agencies and collaborating non-profits are subject to public accountability (Werker & Ahmed, 2008). Possibly most accountable of all are corporations. In recent years, the salient ambit for "corporate social responsibility" has grown dramatically (McWilliams & Siegel, 2001). It has expanded beyond ecological ("green") responsibility (Bauer & Aiman-Smith, 1996; Millennium Development Goal 7). It includes not only governance, but also poverty reduction (Jenkins, 2005). One pathway for corporate social responsibility to reduce poverty is through Decent Work (Yiu & Saner, 2005). Another is by good health (Yiu & Saner, 2005, p. 3; Millennium Development Goals 4–6 in Table 28.1.). Thus were major drug corporations shamed into backing down from legally blocking the South African government from importing low-cost HIV medicines (Millennium Development Goal 6, Table 28.1.).

The Millennium Development Goals have elevated corporate social responsibility's leverage (Kolk & van Tulder, 2006). There are now clearer bottom-line incentives for firms to comply (McGuire, Sundgren, & Schneeweis, 1988). Corporate social responsibility does not just flow from financial performance (Waddock & Graves, 1997). Corporate social responsibility also predicts it (Orlitzky, Schmidt, & Rynes, 2003). Commercial, social, and reputational advantages accruing to firms from corporate social responsibility include competitive advantage in recruitment (Turban & Greening, 1996), social capital among local communities (Godfrey, 2005), and overcoming nationalistic barriers in new markets (Gardberg & Fombrun, 2006). Multinational corporations can engage responsively with lower-income populations as consumers (Dowell, Hart & Yeung, 2000). Responsibly managed (Gordon, 2008), multinational corporations, local firms, and employers foster inclusion and employment, raise shareholder profits, and lower poverty (Prahalad & Hart, 2002).

Applied psychologists are uniquely placed to *measure* corporate social responsibility, including its antecedents and consequences (Berry, Reichman, & Schein, 2008). We can also advocate for corporate social responsibility (Lefkowitz, 2008). In 2000, the United Nations created a "Global Compact with business" (www.unglobalcompact.org/). This is a code of conduct to which businesses can be persuaded to adhere, pledging to foster decent work with decent wages, promote collective bargaining, preserve the environment, improve governance, and support community development (Camino, 2003).

Mediation

A key conduit for public awareness about social responsibility is the mass media (Mehryar, 1984). Policy-makers today are increasingly interested in how the media can bolster awareness about the Millennium Development Goals (Banda, 2007). "Mediation" in the aid and development arena does not mean statistical mediation. It means the media act as a conduit for communicating the Millennium Development Goals to the general donor public (www.futureofaid.net/node/337). Mediation may help boost support for the Millennium Development Goals, and thereby contribute to poverty reduction (Fransman & Lecomte, 2004). According to the OECD, a key stakeholder group in such an outcome is the tax payer. Taxes (Figure 28.1) fund national contributions to the Millennium Development Goals through a set percentage of their national income tax levy given over to international aid. This gets channeled through "bilateral" (country-to-country) and "multilateral" (e.g., United Nations) aid agencies. Since the 1970s, the minimum level of gross national product (GNP) contributed towards development assistance has been set at 0.7%. The average figure actually attained, however, is typically only about 0.22%. From Table 28.1., Millennium Development Goal 8 hopes to raise that contribution from taxes to above its current, generally low, level.

Psychology can and should help. Beginning with Feagin (1972), research on attributions (for poverty) has steadily moved from attributions for local poverty in wealthier economies, to local and international attributions for poverty in poorer contexts (Furnham, 2003). Broadly speaking, an overall pattern in this research is that, independently of country of residence, comparative wealth links to making relatively dispositional attributions that blame the poor themselves. Poverty is linked with a tendency to make more situational attributions that blame climate change, natural disasters, and other extrinsic factors. There is an actor–observer difference, in which outsiders blame people more while the impoverished blame the system more. These differences may be exaggerated further by sociocultural and sociopolitical beliefs that stress individual over collective responsibility and equal responsibility over more paternalistic forms of government. Either way an actor–observer difference can undermine donation behavior, because it "shifts the burden" of responsibility and blame (Senge, 1992) away from those most in a position to do something about it (Carr, McAuliffe, & MacLachlan, 1998). Dispositional attributions among observers, for instance, can reduce donation behavior (Cheung & Chan, 2000).

The link to *mediation* is that aid advertisers often use person-focused rather than context-focused images of poverty in their appeals (Harper, 2003). These risk fueling dispositional attributions, stereotypes, and avoidance. Over the mid to long term they may amplify global exclusion. Psychology has the theory, research, and practical measurement skills to help lower such risks (Panadero & Vázquez, 2008). The debate on *mediation* is therefore a timely opportunity for psychology to help improve aid advertising practice (Bolitho, Carr, & Fletcher, 2007).

According to Figure 28.1., *mediation* can influence opinions not only about taxes and donations, but about shares and investments as well. In 2007, foreign direct investment in "developing" economies was one-third of the global total of US$ 400,000 million (www.unctad.org/Templates/webflyer.asp?docid=9439&intItemID=1528&lang=1). That figure is approximately four times the official global aid budget for 2007, at just over $100,000 million (www.oecd.org/document/8/0,3343,en_2649_33721_40381960_1_1_1_1,00.html).

Some research has charted the psychology of foreign direct investment (Festervand, Jennings, & Mpoyi, 2001). This research employed multidimensional scaling to show how executives' investment decision making is shaped not only by economic considerations like ease of doing business, but also by perceptions about political stability, security, and quality of government (Foo & Sung, 2002). The latter finding, that governance matters, converges with evidence from attributions about poverty. It seems that quality of government is a salient factor for individual decisions (Panadero

& Vázquez, 2008). Media portrayals of lower-income countries, which commonly feature images of poverty, war, corruption, and so on, influence not only the amount of tax and donor aid that wealthier publics give, but also likely behavioral investments.

Similarly, shares are important in Figure 28.1. Their movements tend to affect the poor more than the wealthy, especially during an economic crisis (OECD, 2008). Following the stock market crash of 1987, a behavioral analysis concluded that we need to understand the individual investor, not the market (Eachus, 1988). After the "Asian" crisis of 1997–1998, analysis suggested that investor behavior as a group is important (Aus-Thai Project Team, 2002). After the latest crisis of 2008–2009, psychology might have a role to play in understanding how these individual and group processes are *mediated,* for example, by simulating different types of news reports and aid appeals through agency websites (Burt & Dunham, 2009).

How Can Psychology Be Supplied?

Interdisciplinarity

Process-wise, the Paris Declaration implies that psychology *itself* needs to become harmonized, in both research and application (www.gdnet.org/middle.php?oid=1215). In psychology's own approach to poverty reduction, then, the poor cannot afford psychology to be precious about the purity of theory or its interventions (Turner & Lehning, 2007). Poverty reduction is interdisciplinary (Ortigas, 2000). Our record on alignment, also, has been poor; a "poverty of psychology" (Pearl, 1970). This may spring in part from not appreciating cultural relativism within psychology and its preferred methods themselves (Mohanty & Mistra, 2000). Fundamentally too, it may stem from a failure to appreciate what it is like to live in socioeconomic poverty, another possible instance of actor–observer difference.

Poverty is a real, lived experience for many in the developing world where a day-to-day struggle for economic survival is a way of life. Applied psychology has the mandate to throw in its contribution in addressing the issue of poverty reduction. In Africa, where rampant poverty prevails, psychology has struggled to become relevant. Nigerian psychologist Akin-Ogundeji argued nearly two decades ago that psychologists had yet to justify the existence of the discipline and that it was confined to academia. There was the need "to change and refocus psychology in a pulsating society of sporadic social and economic changes" (Akin-Ogundeji, 1991, p. 3). At that time, a rather staid version of the empiricist approach to psychology, not focused on local issues and using methods that seemed alien, was still ostensibly practiced in Africa. The "essence of psychology which is arguably relating meaningfully to human values, social realities and whole-life issues" (Akin-Ogundeji, 1991, p. 4) had, ironically, been overlooked.

This is *not* to say that empirical psychology is naturally so inclined. Far from it. More recently, for example, psychology in Africa appears to have changed its approach, especially with research output emanating from South Africa. Research there focuses on abused women in the context of poverty (Boonzaier, 2003), on African adolescent identity (Stevens & Lockhat, 2003), and on adherence to taking antiretroviral medication for HIV infection (Kagee, 2008). Encouragingly, steps are also being taken by applied, empirical psychologists to facilitate greater inclusion of people with disabilities (MacLachlan, 2005, 2008). A key in such strategies is to position applied psychology so that it allows itself to observe and crucially, to respect the indigenous psychologies that emanate from the people it is studying (Nsameneng, 2006). These psychologies have adaptively stood the test of eons of time, including the vagaries of colonial and neo-colonial oppression. They are incredibly resilient (MacLachlan, 2005). Indigenous, economically robust psychologies existed long before colonization (Ivory, 2003). It is ironic then that "culture" is often positioned as some sort of culprit in poverty—a cultural attribution error—when the roots of poverty are so often socioeconomic and sociopolitical (MacLachlan et al., 2010). Poverty reduction actually needs to move in concordance with culture not against it, in order to be aligned.

According to the principle of alignment, it is within the epistemological framework of indigenous psychologies, and by respecting the latter, that the idiosyncratic features that facilitate poverty reduction may be found. A start for this process of alignment might occur, for example, at the level of households. Investigations into meaning and application for the local community can be spelled out. A health psychology that seeks to address the dire health indicators of, say, Malawi, where half of the children under five years are stunted due to poor nutrition (National Statistical Office, 2005), can position itself behind an indigenous psychology (Allwood & Berry, 2006). An indigenous psychology *is* applied psychology (Danziger, 2006). It is unique to a local situation and embedded in the community practices, institutions, relationships, and rituals. Within it lies indigenous knowledge; an epistemology coming from the people themselves, in their land, culture, memory, and linguistic heritage (Higgs & van Niekerk, 2002). Recognition of this is the seedbed for an effective and meaningful contribution that applied psychology can make to poverty reduction.

Does this mean that we have to choose between indigenization of modern psychology and adopting an existing indigenous psychology? The answer is: No. Some modern psychology, as we have seen, is relevant to poverty reduction; some is not. Some is more relevant in resource-deprived settings: some is less. Some will require restatement to include the moderating influences of culture, for example, on the process of individual achievement striving in a relatively collectivistic setting (MacLachlan & Carr, 1994). The *process*, however, is invariably one of progressive, pragmatic, and pluralistic alignment. Similarly, the psychological level is not the only process that matters. Poverty is perpetuated and potentially reduced at micro, mezzanine, and macro levels. Interventions can include, for example, direct cash transfers to household decision-makers to pay for child health care and education (Hirata, 2008; Moore, 2008), and individual, business-focused as well as social and community-focused entrepreneurs (www.ashoka.org/fellows/social_entrepreneur.cfm). In that sense, poverty reduction can be harmonized and aligned across the behavioral system in a fruitful *collaboration*, not competition, between new and old, micro and macro.

To sum up, respecting indigenous psychology is a necessary but not necessarily a sufficient condition for poverty reduction. In a globally connected community no culture on earth is an island. Respecting a range of contributions is crucial. In years gone by, psychology may have tended to import rather esoteric theoretical frameworks, grounded in a somewhat universalistic orientation (Mkhize, 2004). Contemporary applied psychology is not following the same process. It cannot for instance assume that the consumer in Figure 28.1. is an individual rather than a collective. We are arguing that the framework needs to be grounded in local as well as global factors, and to include counteracting poverty indigenously (Lever & Martínez, 2008). This creates a tremendous opportunity for psychology, as a discipline and a profession, to contribute meaningfully to poverty reduction.

Experimental evaluation

At the same time as harmonizing and aligning ourselves, making a contribution will mean differentiating psychology from other disciplines (Reichman et al., 2008). One of our distinctive, value-adding knowledge-skills-ability sets is reliance on evidence, including experiments. Experimentation can be compatible with local aspirations and interests (Carr, 2004). A decade ago, researchers in childhood poverty reduction said, "We urge program funders and developers to continue demanding that high-quality experimental research be part of any new program or policy. Without such research, we cannot know what about a program works, or doesn't work" (St. Pierre & Layzer, 1998, p. 20). That argument today is even stronger. To meet demand, various umbrella networks, often research-focused, are implementing experimental evaluations of local poverty initiatives. In keeping with the Paris Declaration, the networks are interdisciplinary (harmonized) and focused on need (alignment). They conduct ethically appropriate field experiments (Duflo, 2009). These evaluate impacts of aid and community interventions against no-treatment controls with the criteria being consequent enablement.

One example is the Comparative Research Programme on Poverty (www.crop.org). This is supported by the International Social Science Council. Another is Innovations for Poverty Action (www.poverty-action.org/). An example is teacher absenteeism, which, as we have seen, can rise in civil service positions. A monitoring and salary incentives program was introduced. Teachers took a picture of themselves and students at the start and end of each day. They received a bonus over and above base salary for each day pictured. Teacher absenteeism decreased from 43% (no treatment control) to 24% in treatment schools. A year later, student test scores in treatment schools were 0.17 standard deviations above controls. Children were 43% more likely to enrol in the next school level. Following the evaluation, according to the IPA, the NGO adopted the system across all its schools.

S.m.a.r.t. and evaluated interventions like these are not confined to education in the formal sense. They apply as well to, say, education about health. They might simply gauge whose advice about HIV/AIDS prevention is actually most heeded by youth, or, to take another example, whether instructional board games can be used to effectively communicate good advice (MacLachlan, Chimombo, & Mpemba, 1997). Whatever the case, experimental evaluation can be interdisciplinary and cross-contextual, thereby addressing more than one of the Millennium Development Goals in Table 28.1.

At this point, a sceptical reader might be asking whether improving education is tantamount to reducing poverty. In other words, we might have lost sight of the criterion, poverty reduction. Where is the evidence linking psychology to poverty reduction? Without it, the chapter may be invalid. To answer this pivotal question, we can return to the empirical thesis in Laureate Sen's (1999) *Development as freedom*: Poverty reduction is a medium- to long-term goal. Investments in education and gender empowerment, for instance, may take years before showing up (Clemens, Radelet, & Bhavnani, 2004). Psychology often perhaps prefers rather shorter-term and individual criteria, like school performance and teacher attendance. Yet according to the basic capabilities approach these are legitimate precursors of poverty reduction: They actually *mediate* between intervention and poverty reduction, over developmental time. Provided applied psychology accepts such interdisciplinary perspectives—in effect working collaboratively with economists, other social sciences, and above all local communities—then facilitating school performance, or work of any kind, is a perfectly valid way to proceed (as well as encouraging us to take a more longitudinal perspective in general).

Conclusion

Psychology currently has little or no profile within poverty reduction initiatives. Demand has not framed our supply. Demand is interdisciplinary, creating opportunities to strategize engagement. Applied psychology can align with the Millennium Development Goals, focus on harmonization and alignment, and emphasize its uniqueness. That includes theoretical depth, rigor in measurement, and experimental evaluation. To capitalize on strengths we can develop an applied psychology of Poverty Reduction Strategy Papers, capacity development (including mobility), budget support versus project aid, social responsibility, mediation, and household health. Promising starts have been made. Applying psychology to poverty is not just an exercise for science and practice. We can also articulate our professional and ethical values, build capacity, boost awareness of what we do, and become more interdisciplinary (Lefkowitz, 2008). We should retain empiricism but focus more on problems of immediate need in the local population.

Notes

1 Unless indicated, the chief source for most of these statistics is A. Shah's website, "Global Issues: Social, political, economic, and environmental issues that affect us all." www.globalissues.org/article/26/poverty-facts-and-stats (accessed November 8, 2008). A secondary source is article/4/, which is from the same website.

2 A further policy concept is the sector-wide approach, or "SWAp." SWAps harmonize and align poverty reduction initiatives within sectors, and with local demand. Funding supports a single sector policy, under local government leadership, e.g., a coordinated program to roll out HIV retroviral medicines, under Millennium Development Goal 6, within a particular country's health sector.

3 The model is not a geographical representation. "poorer," "wealthier," "demand" and "supply" can be found in "developing" and "developed" countries, alike. Hence taxes, donations and shares & investments are not necessarily mediated through aid agencies, not profits, and corporations: they can also go directly to governments, local NGOs, and local firms.

References

Accra Agenda for Action. (2008). *Third high-level forum on aid effectiveness.* Accra, Ghana: September 2–4.

Akin-Ogundeji, O. (1991). Asserting psychology in Africa. *The Psychologist: Bulletin of the British Psychological Society, 4,* 2–4.

Allwood, C., & Berry, J. (2006). Origins and development of indigenous psychologies: An international analysis. *International Journal of Psychology, 41,* 243–268.

Annan, K. A. (2000). *We the peoples: The role of the United Nations in the 21st century.* New York: UN Department of Public Information.

Ardila, R. (2004). Latin American psychology: The first half-century. *Revista Interamericana de Psicologia, 38,* 317–322 (Text in Spanish, abstract only in English).

Aus-Thai Project Team. (2002). Managing economic crisis: A human factors approach. *Psychology and Developing Societies, 14,* 277–309.

Banda, F. (2007, September). *Mediating the Paris Declaration on Aid Effectiveness,* Forum on Ownership in Practice, OECD Global Forum on Development: Financing Development Effectively 2006–9, Paris.

Bandawe, C. R. (2000). *A schistosomiasis health education intervention among rural Malawian school children: Lessons learned.* Cape Town: University of Cape Town.

Bandawe, C. R. (2005). Psychology brewed in an African pot: Indigenous philosophies and the quest for relevance. *Higher Education Policy, 18,* 289–300.

Barnes, R. L. (1985). Across cultures: The Peace Corps training model. *Training & Development Journal, 10,* 46–49.

Basu, K. (2007). *Participatory equity, identity, and productivity: Policy implications for promoting development.* World Bank/Conference on New Frontiers of Social Policy, Arusha, Tanzania. Cornell/Harvard University: CAE Working Paper no. 06-06.

Bauer, T. N., & Aiman-Smith, L. (1996). Green career choices: The influence of ecological stance on recruiting. *Journal of Business and Psychology, 10,* 445–458.

Berry, M. O., Reichman, W., & Schein, V. (2008). The United Nations Global Compact needs I/O psychology participation. *The Industrial Psychologist, 45,* 33–37.

Bloom, M. (1999). The performance effects of pay dispersion on individuals and organizations. *Academy of Management Journal, 42,* 25–40.

Bolitho, F. H., Carr, S. C., & Fletcher, R. B. (2007). Public thinking about poverty: Why it matters and how to measure it. *International Journal of Non-Profit and Voluntary Sector Marketing, 12,* 13–22.

Boneva, B., & Frieze, I. (2001). Toward a concept of migrant personality. *Journal of Social Issues, 57,* 477–491.

Boonzaier, F. (2003). Women abuse: A critical review. In K. Ratele & N. Duncan (Eds.), *Social psychology: Identities and relationships* (pp. 177–197). Cape Town: UCT Press.

Brown, R. P. C., & Connell, J. (2006). The migration of doctors and nurses from South Pacific Island Nations. *Social Science and Medicine, 58,* 2193–2210.

Burt, C. D., & Dunham, A. H. (2009). Trust generated by aid agency web page design. *International Journal of Non-profit and Voluntary Sector Marketing, 14*(2), 125–136.

Camino, A. (2003). Ancash Association helps one of Peru's most diverse regions. *Dialogue, June*, 16–18.

Carr, S. C. (2004). *Globalization and culture at work: Exploring their combined glocality.* New York: Springer.

Carr, S. C. (2007). I/O psychology and poverty reduction. *The Industrial Psychologist, 45*, 43–50.

Carr, S. C., Inkson, K., & Thorn, K. J. (2005). From brain drain to talent flow. *Journal of World Business, 40*, 386–98.

Carr, S. C., & MacLachlan, M. (1998). Psychology in developing countries: Reassessing its impact. *Psychology and Developing Societies, 10*, 1–20.

Carr, S. C., MacLachlan, M., & Chipande, R. (1998). Expatriate aid salaries in Malawi: A doubly de-motivating influence? *International Journal of Educational Development, 18*, 133–143.

Carr, S. C., MacLachlan, M., Reichman, W., Klobas, J., O'Neill Berry, M., & Furnham, A. (2008). Organizational psychology and poverty reduction: Where supply meets demand. *Journal of Organizational Behavior, 29*, 843–851.

Carr, S. C., McAuliffe, E., & MacLachlan, M. (1998). *Psychology of aid.* London: Routledge.

Cheung, C. K., & Chan, C. M. (2000). Social-cognitive factors of donating money to charity, with special attention to an international relief organization. *Evaluation and Program Planning, 23*, 241–523.

Clemens, M. A., Radelet, S., & Bhavnani, R. (2004). *Counting chickens when they hatch: The effect of aid on growth.* Working Paper No. 44. Washington, DC: Center for Global Development.

Coates, K., & Carr, S. C. (2005). Skilled immigrants and selection bias. *International Journal of Intercultural Relations, 29*, 577–599.

Colquitt, J. A., Conlon, D. E., Wesson, M. J., Porter, C. O., and Ng, K. Y. (2001). Justice at the millennium: A meta-analytic review of 25 years of organizational justice research. *Journal of Applied Psychology, 86*, 425–445.

Danziger, K. (2006). Comment. *International Journal of Psychology, 41*, 269–275.

De Mel, S., McKenzie, D., & Woodruff, C. (2007). Returns to capital in micro-enterprises: Evidence from a field experiment. World Bank Policy Research Working Paper No. 4230. Washington, DC: World Bank.

De Renzio, P. (2006). Aid, budgets and accountability: A survey article. *Development Policy Review, 24*, 627–45.

Dowell, G., Hart, S., & Yeung, B. (2000). Do corporate global environmental standards create or destroy market value? *Management Science, 46*, 1059–1074.

Drucker, P. F. (1986). *The frontiers of management: Where tomorrow's decisions are being shaped today.* New York: J. P. Dutton.

Duflo, E. (2009). Fighting poverty efficiently. 21 solutions to save the world. *Forbes.com Leadership News, May* (1st). Retrieved January 16, 2009 from http://goliath.ecnext.com/coms2/gi_0199-6532752/21-solutions-to-save-the.html

Eachus, P. (1988). The psychology of the stock market. *The Psychologist, March*, 100–103.

Easterly, W. (2006). *The white man's burden: Why the West's efforts to aid the rest have done so much ill and so little good.* London: Penguin Books.

Easterly, W., & Pfutze, T. (2008). Where does the money go? Best and worst practices in foreign aid. *Journal of Economic Perspectives, 22*, 29–52.

Evers, A., & van der Flier, H. (1998). Ethnic minorities on the labour market. In P. J. D. Drenth, H. Thierry, & C. J. de Wolff (Eds.), *Handbook of work and organizational psychology* (pp. 229–259). Hove, UK: Psychology press.

Eyben, R. (2005). Donors' learning difficulties: Results, relationships and responses. Institute of Development Studies *IDS Bulletin*, *36*, 98–107.

Fakuda-Parr, S. (2008). *Are the MDGs priority in development strategies and aid programmes? Only few are!* International Poverty Centre Working Paper 28, October. Brasilia, Brazil: International Poverty Centre/UNDP.

Feagin, J. R. (1972). God helps those who help themselves. *Psychology Today*, *11*, 101–129.

Festervand, T. A., Jennings, A., & Mpoyi, R. T. (2001). U.S. executives' perceptions of emerging nations as FDI options. *Journal of Business in Developing Nations*, *5*, 1–12.

Ferrinho, P., & van Lergberghe, W. (2002, December). *Managing health professionals in the context of limited resources: A fine line between corruption and the need for moonlighting.* Washington, DC: World Bank Working Paper, Report No. 26941.

Foo, J. P. N., & Sung, J. C. H. (2002). The impact of governance obstacles and state capture of transition countries on foreign direct investment. *Journal of Business in Developing Nations*, *6*, 1–27.

Fransman, J., & Lecomte, J. B. S. (2004). Mobilizing public opinion against global poverty. *OECD Policy Insights*, *2*, 1–5.

Freire, P. (1972). *Pedagogy of the oppressed.* New York: Herder & Herder.

Frese, M., Brantjes, A., & Hoorn, R. (2002). Psychological success factors of small scale businesses in Namibia: The roles of strategy process, entrepreneurial orientation, and the environment. *Journal of Developmental Entrepreneurship*, *7*, 259–282.

Fryer, D., & Fagan, R. (2003). Poverty and unemployment. In S. C. Carr & T. S. Sloan (Eds.), *Poverty and psychology: From global perspective to local practice* (pp. 87–102). New York: Springer.

Furnham, A. (2003). Poverty and wealth. In S. C. Carr & T. S. Sloan (Eds.), *Poverty and psychology: From global perspective to local practice* (pp. 163–184). New York: Springer.

Furnham, A., & Bochner, S. (1986). *Culture shock: Psychological reactions to unfamiliar environments.* London: Methuen.

Gardberg, N. A., & Fombrun, C. J. (2006). Corporate citizenship: Creating intangible assets across institutional environments. *Academy of Management Review*, *31*, 329–346.

Godfrey, P. C. (2005). The relationship between corporate philanthropy and shareholder wealth: A risk management perspective. *Academy of Management Review*, *30*, 777–798.

Gordon, M. D. (2008). Management education and the base of the pyramid. *Journal of Management Education*, *32*, 767–781.

Greenberg, J. (2007). The top ten reasons why everyone should know about, and study, organizational justice. In A. I. Glendon, B. M. Thompson, & B. Myros (Eds.), *Advances in organizational psychology* (pp. 323–346). Brisbane, Australia: Australian Academic Press (AAP).

Greenberg, J. (2008). Everybody talks about organizational justice, but nobody does anything about it. *Industrial and Organizational Psychology: Perspectives on Science and Practice*, *2*(2), 1–36.

Harper, D. (2003). Poverty and discourse. In S. C. Carr & T. S. Sloan (Eds.), *Poverty and psychology: From global perspective to local practice* (pp. 185–203). New York: Springer.

Harris, J. G. (1973). A science of the South Pacific: Analysis of the character structure of the Peace Corps Volunteer. *American Psychologist*, *28*, 232–47.

Higgs, P., & van Niekerk, M. (2002). The programme for Indigenous Knowledge Systems (IKS) and higher educational discourse in South Africa: A critical reflection. *SAJHE/SATHO*, *16*, 38–49.

Hirata, G. I. (2008). *Cash transfers and child labour.* International Poverty Centre, One Pager. Brasilia, Brazil: International Poverty Centre.

Iceland, J. (2005). Measuring poverty: Theoretical and empirical considerations. *Measurement, 2*, 199–235.

Ivory, B. (2003). Poverty and enterprise. In S. C. Carr & T. S. Sloan (Eds.), *Poverty and psychology: From global perspective to local practice* (pp. 251–266). New York: Springer.

Jenkins, R. (2005). Globalization, corporate social responsibility, and poverty. *International Affairs, 81*, 525–540.

Kagee, A. (2008), Adherence to antiretroviral therapy in the context of the national roll-out in South Africa: Defining a research agenda for psychology. *South African Journal of Psychology, 38*, 413–428.

Kakwani, N., & Silber, J. (2007). *The many dimensions of poverty.* Basingstoke, UK: Palgrave-Macmillan/UNDP.

Katseli, L. T., Lucas, R. E. B., & Xenogiani, T. (2006). *Effects of migration on sending countries: What do we know?* OECD Working Paper 250. Paris: OECD Development Centre.

Katseli, L .T., & Xenogiani, T. (2006). Migration: A positive or a negative driver for development? *OECD Policy Insights, 29*, 1–2.

Kealey, D. J. (1989). A study of cross-cultural effectiveness: Theoretical issues, practical applications. *International Journal of Intercultural Relations, 13*, 387–428.

Kolk, A., & van Tulder, R. (2006). Poverty alleviation as business strategy: Evaluating commitments of frontrunner multinational corporations. *World Development, 34*, 789–801.

Krauss, S. I., Frese, M., Friedrich, C., & Unger, J. M. (2005). Entrepreneurial orientation: A psychological model of success among southern African small business owners. *European Journal of Work & Organizational Psychology, 14*, 315–44.

Latham, G. P. (2006). *Work motivation: History, theory, research and practice.* London: Sage.

Lefkowitz, J. (2008). Expand the values of organizational psychology to match the quality of its ethics. *Journal of Organizational Behavior, 29*, 439–453.

Lever, J. P. (2007). The subjective dimensions of poverty: A psychological viewpoint. In N. Kakwani & J. Silber (Eds.), *The many dimensions of poverty* (pp. 75–86). Basingstoke, UK: Palgrave-Macmillan/UNDP.

Lever, J. P. L., & Martínez, Y. I. C. (2007). Poverty and social support: A comparative study in three socio-economic levels. *Revista Interamericana de Psicología, 41*, 177–188 (Text in Spanish, abstract only in English).

Lever, J. P., Pĩnol, N. L., & Uralde, J. H. (2005). Poverty, psychological resources, and subjective well-being. *Social Indicators Research, 73*, 375–408.

Lewin, K. (1947). Group decision and social change. In G. E. Swanson, T. M. Newcomb, & E. L. Hartley (Eds.), *Readings in social psychology* (pp. 340–344). New York: Holt.

Lewis, O. (1959). *Five families: Mexican case studies in the culture of poverty.* New York: Basic Books.

Lim, A., & Ward, C. (2003). The effects of nationality, length of residence and occupational demand on the perceptions of "foreign talent" in Singapore. In K.-S. Yang & K.-K. Hwang (Eds.), *Progress in Asian social psychology* (pp. 247–259). Westport, CT: Praeger.

Locke, E. A., & Latham, G. P. (2002). Building a practically useful theory of goal-setting and task motivation: A 35-year odyssey. *American Psychologist, 57*, 705–717.

MacLachlan, M. (2005). *Culture and health* (2nd ed.). Chichester, UK: Wiley.

MacLachlan, M. (2008). How can I/O Psychology assist with the global promotion of human rights to health and social inclusion? *The Industrial Psychologist, 4*, 79–81.

MacLachlan, M., & Carr, S. C. (1994). Pathways to a psychology for development: Reconstituting, refuting, restating, and realising. *Psychology and Developing Societies, 6*(1), 21–28.

MacLachlan, M., & Carr, S. C. (2005). The human dynamics of aid. *OECD Policy Insights, 10.* Retrieved from www.oecd.org/dev/insights

MacLachlan, M., Carr, S. C., & McAuliffe, E. (2010). *The aid triangle: Recognizing the human dynamics of dominance, justice and identity.* London/New York: Zed Books.

MacLachlan, M., Chimombo, M., & Mpemba, N. (1997). AIDS education for youth through active learning: A school-based approach from Malawi. *International Journal of Educational Development, 17*, 41–50.

MacLachlan, M., & McAuliffe, E. (2003). Poverty and process skills. In S. C. Carr & T. S. Sloan (Eds.), *Poverty and psychology: From global perspective to local practice* (pp. 267–284). New York: Springer.

Mahroum, S. (2000). High skilled globetrotters: Mapping the international migration of human capital. *R & D Management, 30*, 23–32.

Manning, R. (2006). Technical cooperation. *The Development Assistance Committee Journal, 7*, 111–138.

Marsella, A. J. (1998). Toward a global community psychology: Meeting the needs of a changing world. *American Psychologist, 53*, 1282–1291.

McAuliffe, E., Bowie, C., Manafa, O., Maseko, F., MacLachlan, M., Hevey, D., Normand, C., & Chirwa, M. (2009). Measuring and managing the work environment of the mid-level provider—the neglected human resource. *Human Resources for Health, 7*, 1–9.

McClelland, D. C. (1961). *The achieving society.* New York: Free Press.

McClelland, D. C. (1987a). Characteristics of successful entrepreneurs. *Journal of Creative Behavior, 21*, 219–233.

McClelland, D. C. (1987b). *Human motivation.* Cambridge, UK: Cambridge University Press.

McClelland, D. C, & Winter, D. (1971). *Motivating economic achievement.* New York: Free Press.

McFarlane, C. A. (2004). Risks associated with the psychological adjustment of humanitarian aid workers. *The Australasian Journal of Disaster and Trauma Studies, 1*, online journal. Retrieved January 20, 2009 from www.massey.ac.nz/~trauma/issues/2004-1/mcfarlane.htm

McGuire, J. B., Sundgren, A., & Schneeweis, T. (1988). Corporate social responsibility and firm financial performance. *Academy of Management Review, 31*, 854–872.

McWilliams, A., & Siegel, D. (2001). Corporate social responsibility: A theory of the firm perspective. *Academy of Management Review, 26*, 117–127.

Mehryar, A. H. (1984). The role of psychology in national development: Wishful thinking and reality. *International Journal of Psychology, 19*, 159–167.

Miller, G. A. (1969). Psychology as a means of promoting human welfare. *American Psychologist, 24*, 1063–1075.

Mkhize, N. (2004). Psychology: An African perspective. In D. Hook (Ed.), *Critical Psychology* (pp. 24–52). Cape Town: UCT Press.

Mohanty, A. K., & Mistra, G. (Eds.) (2000). *Psychology of poverty and disadvantage.* New Delhi: Concept Publishing Company.

Moore, C. (2008). Nicaragua's Red de Protección social: An exemplary but short-lived conditional cash transfer programme. UNDP: International Policy Centre for Inclusive Growth. Retrieved from http://ideas.repec.org/p/ipc/cstudy/17.html#provider

Moreira, V. (2007). Critical phenomenology of depression in Brazil, Chile, and the United States. *Latin American Journal of Fundamental Psychopathology on Line, 7*, 193–218.

Mullen, F. (2005). The metrics of the physician brain drain. *New England Journal of Medicine, 353*, 1810–1018.

Musa, S. A., & Hamid, A. R. M. (2008). Psychological problems among aid workers operating in Darfur. *Social Behavior and Personality, 36*, 407–416.

Narayan, D., Patel, R., Schafft, K., Rademacher, A., Koch-Schulte, S. (2000). *Voices of the poor: Can anyone hear us?* Oxford, UK: Oxford University Press.

Narayan, D., Chambers, R., Shah, M. K., & Petesch, P. (2000). *Voices of the poor: Crying out for change.* Oxford, UK: Oxford University Press.

Narayan, D., & Petesch, P. (Eds.). (2002). *Voices of the poor: From many lands.* Oxford, UK: Oxford University Press.

National Statistical Office [Malawi] & ORC Macro. (2005). *Malawi demographic and health survey 2004.* National Statistical Office & ORC Macro: Zomba, Malawi & Calverton, Maryland, USA.

Nickerson, R. S. (1999). How we know—and sometimes misjudge—what others know: Imputing one's own knowledge to others. *Psychological Bulletin, 125*, 737–759.

Nsamenang, B. (2006). Human ontogenesis: An indigenous African view on development and intelligence. *International Journal of Psychology, 41*, 293–297.

OECD. (Organization for Economic Cooperation and Development). (2003). *Harmonising donor practices for effective aid delivery: Good practice papers.* Paris: OECD.

OECD. (2008). The financial crisis: Implications for aid and development finance. *OECD News, November*, 1–2.

Orlitzky, M., Schmidt, F. L., & Rynes, S. L. (2003). Corporate social and financial performance: A meta-analysis. *Organization Studies, 24*, 403–441.

Ortigas, C. D. (2000). *Poverty revisited: A social psychological approach to community empowerment.* Quezon City, Manila: Philippines.

Panadero, S., & Vázquez, J. J. (2008). Perceived causes of poverty in developing nations: Causes of third world poverty questionnaire in Spanish-speaking samples. *Social Behavior and Personality, 36*, 571–576.

Pastor, S. (1997). The distinctiveness of cross-cultural training in the Northern Territory. *Northern Radius, 4*, 3–8.

Pearl, A. (1970). The poverty of psychology: An indictment. In V. L. Allen (Ed.), *Psychological factors in poverty* (pp. 348–364). Chicago, IL: Markham Publishing Company.

Porter, D., Allen, B. J., & Thompson, G. (1991). *Development in practice: Paved with good intentions.* London: Routledge.

Prahalad, C. K., & Hart, S. (2002). The fortune at the bottom of the pyramid. *Strategy and Competition, 26*, 55–67.

Prilleltensky, I. (2003). Poverty and power. In S. C. Carr & T. S. Sloan (Eds.), *Poverty and psychology: From global perspective to local practice* (pp. 19–44). New York: Springer.

Reichman, W., Frese, M., Schein, V., Carr, S. C., MacLachlan, M., & Landy, F. J. (2008, April). *Organizational psychologists and world poverty: Our roles and obligations.* Society for Industrial and Organizational Psychology (SIOP), 23rd Annual Conference, San Francisco, USA.

Riddell, R. C. (2007). Effective aid requires new structures. *Poverty in Focus, October*, 3–5.

Rugimbana, R. O., & Spring, A. (2009). Marketing micro-finance to women: Integrating global with local. *International Journal of Nonprofit and Voluntary Sector Marketing, 14*, 149–154.

Sachs, J. (2005). *The end of poverty: Economic possibilities for our time.* New York: Penguin Books.

Sánchez, E., Cronick, K., & Wiesenfeld, E. (2003). Poverty and community. In S. C. Carr & T. S. Sloan (Eds.), *Poverty and psychology: From global perspective to local practice* (pp. 123–145). New York: Springer.

Schein, V. E. (1999). Poor women and work in the Third World: A research agenda for organisational psychologists. *Psychology and Developing Societies, 11*, 105–117.

Schein, V. E. (2003). The functions of work-related group participation for poor women in developing countries: An exploratory look. *Psychology and Developing Societies, 15*, 123–142.

Scisleski, A. C. C., Maraschin, C., & Tittoni, J. (2006). The social psychology of the work in communities: Limits and possibilities. *Revista Interamericana de Psicologia, 40*, 51–58 (Text in Spanish, abstract only in English).

Sen, A. (1999). *Development as freedom.* Oxford, UK: Oxford University Press.

Senge, P. (1992). *The fifth discipline.* Sydney: Random House.

Sinha, D., & Holtzman, W. H. (Eds.). (1984). The impact of psychology on "Third World" development. *International Journal of Psychology, 19*, 3–192 [Special Issue].

Sloan, T. S. (2003). Poverty and psychology: A call to arms. In S. C. Carr & T. S. Sloan (Eds.), *Poverty and psychology: From global perspective to local practice* (pp. 301–314). New York: Springer.

Smith, P. B. (2006). When elephants fight, the grass gets trampled: The GLOBE and Hofstede projects. *Journal of International Business Studies 37*, 915–921.

Stevens, G., & Lockhat, R. (2003). Black adolescent identity during and after apartheid. In K. Ratele & N. Duncan (Eds). *Social psychology: Identities and relationships* (pp. 130–147). Cape Town: UCT Press.

St. Pierre, R. G., & Layzer, J. I. (1998). Improving the life chances of children in poverty: Assumptions and what we have learned. *Social Policy Report, XII*, 1–25.

Tidrick, K. (1971). Need for achievement, social class, and intention to emigrate in Jamaican students. *Social & Economic Studies, 20*, 52–60.

Turban, D. B., & Greening, D. W. (1996). Corporate social performance and organizational attractiveness to prospective employees. *Academy of Management Journal, 40*, 658–672.

Turner, K., & Lehning, A. J. (2007). Psychological theories of poverty. *Journal of Human Behavior in the Social Environment, 16*, 57–72.

United Nations. (2006). *The Millennium Development Goals Report.* New York: United Nations.

United Nations. (2008). *Follow-up international conference on financing for development to deliver the implementation of the Monterrey Consensus.* Doha, Qatar, 29th November-2nd December.

Waddock, S. A., & Graves, S. B. (1997). The corporate social performance–financial performance link. *Strategic Management Journal, 18*, 303–319.

Ward, C., Bochner, S., & Furnham, A. (2001). *The psychology of culture shock* (2nd ed.). London: Routledge.

Werker, E., & Ahmed, F. Z. (2008). What do non-governmental organizations do? *Journal of Economic Perspectives, 22*, 73–92.

Wigley, B. (2005). Not off the hook: Relationships between aid organisation culture and climate and the experience of workers in volatile environments. In V. Bowie (Ed.), *Workplace violence: Issues, trends, strategies* (pp. 141–60). Uffculme, UK: Willan Publishing.

World Bank. (2000). *Attacking poverty: Opportunity, empowerment, and security.* World Development Report 2000/2001. Washington, DC: World Bank/Oxford University Press.

World Bank. (2003). *Making services work for poor people.* World Development Report 2004. Washington, DC: World Bank/Oxford University Press.

Yiu, L., & Saner, R. (2005). *Decent work and poverty reduction strategies (PRS): An ILO advocacy guidebook.* Geneva: ILO.

29

Psychology Applied to Terrorism

Psychological Treatment for Victims of Terrorist Attacks

María Paz García-Vera and Jesús Sanz

In recent years, terrorism has become one of the most severe and alarming problems worldwide. According to the data of the National Counterterrorism Center (NCTC) of the United States of America, in the past four years (2005–2008), a yearly average of 12,933 terrorist attacks have occurred, causing approximately 18,406 deaths, 35,338 injured, and 15,141 hostages each year (NCTC, 2006, 2007, 2008, 2009). Although during this interval most of the terrorist attacks have been concentrated in the Near East (approximately 46%) and in South Asia (approximately 30%), and, specifically, in countries like Iran, Afghanistan, Pakistan, or India, the plague of terrorism affects all regions of the world to a greater or lesser degree (NCTC, 2006, 2007, 2008, 2009).

Research on the psychopathological consequences of traumatic events such as war has a long history in psychiatry and psychology, concerning both soldiers (e.g., Miller, 1920) and civilians (e.g., Baumgarten-Tramer, 1948). This tradition is very recent in the case of terrorism, although for some time the psychopathological consequences of terrorist attacks and the need for their treatment have been pointed out in the psychiatric and psychological literature (Curran, 1988). However, until almost 10–15 years ago, no systematic investigation programs for either of these issues were developed. In fact, the most solid information available about the mental health problems derived from terrorist attacks and their treatment is practically limited to that obtained after investigating a much smaller number of attacks. Specifically, these attacks are those that have been carried out in developed countries, and particularly those that have occurred in the past 15 years in the USA, Israel, and Western Europe (Spain, France, Ireland, and the United Kingdom) and caused a large number of deaths and injuries, such as, for example, the April 19th attack in Oklahoma, the August 15th attack in Omagh (Northern Ireland), the attacks of September 11th, 2001 in

IAAP Handbook of Applied Psychology, First Edition. Edited by Paul R. Martin, Fanny M. Cheung, Michael C. Knowles, Michael Kyrios, Lyn Littlefield, J. Bruce Overmier, and José M. Prieto.

New York and Washington DC, and the attacks of March 11th, 2004 in Madrid, or the attacks of July 7th, 2005 in London.

On the other hand, bearing this limitation in mind, it must be acknowledged that in recent years, such research has grown rapidly and fruitfully so that if, at the beginning of this century, a large part of the knowledge of the mental disorders caused by terrorism and, in particular, of the treatment of people affected by such disorders, came from the more extensive scientific literature on traumatic events (i.e., rape, physical and sexual abuse, car accidents, robbery with violence), including that dedicated to all kinds of disasters (i.e., wars, serious train, plane, or boat accidents, flash floods, fires, earthquakes), currently the knowledge of mental health problems derived specifically from terrorism has led to various meta-analyses (DiMaggio & Galea, 2006; DiMaggio, Galea, & Li, 2009). Consequently the literature on the treatment of such mental problems now includes more than half a dozen empirical studies with group designs, including some experimental ones (Difede, Malta, et al., 2007; Duffy, Gillespie, & Clark, 2007).

The purpose of this chapter is to review the empirical studies on the psychological treatment of people affected by the attacks, with the conviction that any strategy or plan to attend to the mental health of the victims of terrorist attacks must use the intervention methods that receive the most empirical support concerning their efficacy and effectiveness.

Psychological Treatment of the Psychopathological Repercussions of Terrorist Attacks

From meta-analytic (e.g., DiMaggio & Galea, 2006; DiMaggio, Galea, & Li, 2009) and narrative reviews (e.g., Bills et al., 2008; García-Vera & Sanz, 2008) on the psychopathological repercussions of terrorist attacks, it emerges that after terrorist attacks an important percentage of direct victims (around 20-30%) will develop a posttraumatic stress disorder (PTSD) as well as other mental disorders, mainly, major depression disorder, panic disorder, generalized anxiety disorder, agoraphobia, and alcohol and other substance dependence/abuse disorders. The percentage of indirect victims who will develop those disorders will be lower, but nonetheless over the habitual prevalence of the above-mentioned disorders in the general population before the terrorist attacks. Consequently, both direct and indirect victims will need short-, medium-, and long-term psychological attention.

This psychological attention should take into account the diverse needs and characteristics of the affected individuals, the fact that such needs have different priorities and can vary at different moments or phases after the attacks, and the commitment and suitability of integrating psychological interventions within a global response plan (National Institute of Mental Health [NIMH], 2002).

Taking this global action context into account, the following sections will focus on the treatment of the victims with psychological disorders derived from terrorist attacks, and on the psychological action phases known as recovery phase (1–4 weeks) and return to life (2 weeks–2 years) (NIMH, 2002). The reader is referred to other works (Foa et al., 2005; Institute of Medicine Committee on Responding to the

Psychological Consequences of Terrorism, 2003; NIMH, 2002) for a more detailed presentation of other kinds of psychological actions and of the most suitable interventions and psychological treatments in earlier action phases.

Treatment of Posttraumatic Stress Disorder

PTSD is the most frequent disorder after the experience of a traumatic event, including a terrorist attack (DiMaggio & Galea, 2006; García-Vera & Sanz, 2008; Norris et al., 2002). Consequently, most research on the psychological treatment of the victims of terrorism has focused on this disorder.

Until about 7–8 years ago, there were practically no published empirical studies on the specific psychological treatment of PTSD derived from terrorist acts, so the recommendations of the treatments that should be applied to the victims of terrorism were based on the literature about the efficacy of the psychological treatments of PTSD in people who had experienced other types of traumatic events, including war veterans, victims of physical violence or rape, refugees, or traffic-accident survivors.

Fortunately, this empirical literature is now abundant and has allowed researchers to carry out numerous narrative and meta-analytical reviews of experimental studies with control group (or randomized controlled clinical trials), which provide solid conclusions about the treatments with the greatest empirical support regarding their efficacy for PTSD (Australian Centre for Posttraumatic Mental Health, 2007; Bisson & Andrew, 2007; Bisson et al., 2007; Bradley, Greene, Russ, Dutra, & Westen, 2005; Cloitre, 2009; Institute of Medicine Committee on Treatment of Posttraumatic Stress Disorder, 2007; National Institute for Health and Clinical Excellence [NICE], 2005). On the basis of these conclusions, various scientific societies and panels of experts have been able to elaborate guidelines of clinical practice that coincide to a great extent in their therapeutic recommendations of psychological treatments for PTSD (American Psychiatric Association, 2004; Australian Centre for Posttraumatic Mental Health, 2007; Institute of Medicine Committee on Treatment of Posttraumatic Stress Disorder, 2007; NICE, 2005; NIMH, 2002).

Specifically, according to this empirical literature and these guidelines of clinical practice, the treatments with the greatest empirical guarantees are currently: exposure therapies, trauma-focused cognitive-behavioral therapies (which include cognitive restructuring techniques and exposure techniques), anxiety control training (or stress-inoculation training), and eye movement desensitization and reprocessing (EMDR), although there is some debate about the last therapy with regard to whether its efficacy is mainly due to the exposure and cognitive restructuring components included in it, and whether the other, not strictly cognitive-behavioral, components of the therapy, including the eye movement, are unnecessary (Australian Centre for Posttraumatic Mental Health, 2007; Lohr, Hooke, Gist, & Tolin, 2004).

In fact, most of those guidelines of clinical practice suggest that, on the basis of current scientific knowledge, these psychological therapies should be considered the treatments of choice for PTSD (Australian Centre for Posttraumatic Mental Health, 2007; Institute of Medicine Committee on Treatment of Posttraumatic Stress

Disorder, 2007; NICE, 2005; NIMH, 2002), over and above other popular psychological therapies (e.g., psychological debriefing) or psychopharmacological therapies.

Efficacy of the psychological treatments for PTSD in victims of terrorism

Recently, the results of two experimental studies with control group were published that suggest that the level of efficacy of trauma-focused cognitive-behavioral therapy for the direct or indirect victims of terrorist attacks who suffer from PTSD is similar to the efficacy of this therapy with patients who suffer from PTSD due to other kinds of traumatic situations. The main characteristics and the most important results of both studies are displayed in Table 29.1.

The first of the experimental studies was carried out by Duffy et al. (2007) with a sample of 59 patients that included people injured in terrorist acts and other civil conflicts in Northern Ireland, as well as people who had experienced these events but who had not been injured in them (direct witnesses) and indirect witnesses of these traumatic situations, all of them diagnosed with chronic PTSD. The authors randomly assigned these patients either to a group that received trauma-focused cognitive-behavioral therapy following the cognitive model of Ehlers and Clark (2000) of persistent PTSD, or to a waiting-list control group, which, after posttreatment assessment, also received the cognitive-behavioral therapy.

The therapy based on Ehlers and Clark's model is essentially cognitive, as its final goals, in accordance with the assumptions of the model, are to: (1) elaborate and integrate the traumatic memory within the context of the individual's experience and thus reduce its intrusive experience; (2) modify the negative appraisals of the traumatic situation or of its sequelae, and (3) abandon the cognitive and behavioral strategies (i.e., avoidance of situations or thoughts) that prevent elaboration of the memory, exacerbate the symptoms, or hinder reassessment of the negative appraisals (Gillespie, Duffy, Hackmann, & Clark, 2002). For this purpose the therapy includes various cognitive strategies to evoke and reappraise the patients' negative evaluations and dysfunctional attitudes, especially strategies of cognitive restructuring based on designing behavioral experiments in which the patients test their negative appraisals of the trauma and its consequences and their beliefs about the usefulness of their dysfunctional strategies. But, as is usual with cognitive-behavioral therapies for PTSD, in order to achieve the goals, the treatment applied by Duffy et al. (2007) also used imaginal exposure (visualizing the attack and reliving it in the present, including thoughts and feelings) intensively, and even, when considered necessary, in vivo exposure (direct exposure to the real situations and stimuli associated with the attack), so it could be better conceptualized as a cognitive-behavioral therapy rather than a purely cognitive one.

The results of the study of Duffy et al. (2007) confirmed the efficacy of this kind of cognitive-behavioral therapy for the treatment of the direct and indirect victims of terrorist attacks, because at posttreatment, the patients of the group that received this therapy showed statistically significant improvement in comparison to the patients from the waiting-list control group, revealing pre-posttreatment changes with a large

Table 29.1. Group Studies on Psychological Treatment of Victims of Terrorism

Reference	*Terrorist incident*	*Victims*	*Main psychological disorders (% of victims)*	*Psychological treatment*	*Measures*	*Short-term results*	*Medium-and long-term results*
			Between-group design with randomized assignment to treatment (TG) and control groups (CG)				
Duffy, Gillespie & Clark (2007)	Terrorist attacks and related civil conflicts in Northern Ireland	58 victims: 32 direct witnesses 15 indirect witnesses 11 injured	PTSD: 100% MDD: 63.8% Panic disorder: 20.7% Alcohol or substance use disorder: 13.8% Specific phobias: 10.3% GAD: 5.2%	TG (29 patients): CBT (12 weekly sessions; mean number = 5.9) with additional follow-up sessions (mean number = 2) CG (29 patients): wait-list for 12 weeks followed by cognitive therapy	PDS BDI-IA SDS-W, SDS-S, and SDS-F	At 12 weeks, significant between-group differences on all measures, with the TG improving significantly on all measures and CG not improving on any measure. Within-group ES for all patients who received CBT (intention-to-treat $n = 58$): 1.25 (PDS), 1.05 (BDI-IA), 0.97 (SDS-W), 1.03 (SDS-S), and 0.70 (SDS-F). For all patients who received CBT (intention-to-treat $n = 59$), 56.1% improved (at least 50% reduction in PDS)	Treatment gains were well maintained: no significant differences or further significant improvements were found in scores from after treatment to follow-up (1-, 4-, or 12-month follow-up)

Continued

Table 29.1. *Contiued*

Reference	*Terrorist incident*	*Victims*	*Main psychological disorders (% of victims)*	*Psychological treatment*	*Measures*	*Short-term results*	*Medium-and long-term results*
Difede, Malta, et al. (2007)	New York September 11, 2001, World Trade Center plane crashes	31 disaster workers	PTSD: 67.7% Subthreshold PTSD criteria: 32.3%	TG (15 patients; completers = 7): CBT (12 weekly sessions) CG (16 patients; completers = 14): treatment as usual (assessment feedback and advice and help to obtain treatment for PTSD: none sought treatment)	CAPS PCL BDI BSI-GSI MAST	At 12 weeks, no significant between-group differences on any measure for intention-to-treat sample. Significant between-group differences on CAPS and PCL for completers. Between-group ES for completers: 1.37 (CAPS) and 1.66 (PCL). For completers, 78.1% (TG) vs. 28.6% (CG) improved in CAPS	At 3-month follow-up, treatment gains seem to be well maintained on PCL, BDI, GSI and MAST for TG completers ($n = 6$), but clear statistical results were not reported

Between-group design with nonrandomized assignment to treatment (TG) and control groups (CG)							
Difede, Cukor, et al. (2007)	New York September 11, 2001, World Trade Center plane crashes	21 disaster workers and civilians	PTSD: 100%	TG (13 patients; completers = 10): CBT with virtual reality exposure (8-14 weekly sessions) CG (8 patients): wait-list	CAPS PCL BDI BSI-GSI	At post-treatment, significant between-group differences on CAPS for completers. Between-group ES for completers: 1.54 (CAPS). For completers, 90% improved in CAPS	At 6-month follow-up, treatment gains were well maintained on CAPS for completers ($n = 9$), with significant within-group differences on CAP from pretreatment to follow-up
Within-group design							
Gillespie et al. (2002)	Omagh bombing (Northern Ireland)	91 victims: - 33% injured - 42% direct witnesses - 12% emergency personnel - 13% other victims	- PTSD: 100% - MDD: 47.3% - Alcohol abuse or dependence: 5.5% - Panic disorder and/or agoraphobia: 4.4%	CBT (median number of sessions = 8; range: 2-73)	- PDS - RIES - BDI-IA - GHQ	At post-treatment, significant within-group differences on PDS ($n = 78$ patients), BDI ($n = 33$) and GHQ ($n = 37$). Within-group ES for PDS: 2.47 ($n = 78$ patients). For $n = 78$, 73.1% improved (at least 50% reduction in PDS)	No follow-up

Continued

Table 29.1. *Contiued*

Reference	*Terrorist incident*	*Victims*	*Main psychological disorders (% of victims)*	*Psychological treatment*	*Measures*	*Short-term results*	*Medium-and long-term results*
García-Vera & Romero Colino (2004)	Madrid, March 11, 2004, train bombings	40 victims: 7.5% injured 55% relatives of dead victims 17.5% rescue volunteers 12.5% direct witnesses 7.5% indirect witnesses	PTSD: 22.5% Acute stress disorder: 22.5% Adjustment disorder: 37.5% MDD: 2.5% Grief: 15%	CBT (mean number of sessions = 5; range = 2-16)	ESEA EI BDI-II STAI	For all patients: 5% dropouts 90% recovered (not meeting diagnostic criteria + scores on symptom measures falling within the normal range) 5% not recovered For patients with PTSD: 22% dropouts 67% recovered 11% not recovered For patients with acute stress disorder: 100% recovered For patients with adjustment disorders: 100% recovered	No follow-up

Levitt et al. (2007)	New York September 11, 2001, World Trade Center plane crashes	59 victims: 83% direct witnesses 7% injured 10% indirect witnesses	PTSD symptoms: 100%	CBT: 16 weekly sessions plus additional sessions until maximum of 25 (mean number of sessions = 19; range = 12-25)	MPSS-SR BDI NMR SAS-SR BSI-H and BSI-IS COPE-AD and COPE-SS	At post-treatment, significant within-group differences on all measures for completers (n = 38 patients). Within-group ES for completers: 1.79 (MPSS-SR), 1.23 (BDI), -.70 (NMR), .64 (SAS-SR), .82 (BSI-H), .67 (BSI-IS), .59 (COPE-AD), -.43 (COPE-SS)	No follow-up

Continued

Table 29.1. *Contiued*

Reference	*Terrorist incident*	*Victims*	*Main psychological disorders (% of victims)*	*Psychological treatment*	*Measures*	*Short-term results*	*Medium-and long-term results*
Brewin et al. (2008)	London July 7, 2005, bombings	75 survivors	DSM-IV PTSD or ICD-10 PTSD: 100%	CBT: 80% patients EMDR: 10% patients CBT + EMDR: 10% patients. Modal number of sessions = 9 (range = 1-29)	PDS BDI	At post-treatment, significant within-group differences on all measures for intention-to-treat sample. Within-group ES for patients with DSM-IV PTSD: 2.53 (PDS) and 1.90 (BDI). Within-group ES for patients with ICD-10 PTSD: 1.99 (PDS) and 1.04 (BDI). For n = 53, 87% and 79% improved in PDS (score < 24) and BDI (score < 15), respectively	No follow-up

Note: Psychological disorders: GAD = Generalized anxiety disorder. MDD = Major depression disorder. PTSD = Posttraumatic stress disorder.
Psychological treatments: CBT = Cognitive-behavioral treatment. EMDR = Eye movement desensitization and reprocessing.
Measures: BDI, BDI-IA and BDI-II = First edition, first edition amended and second edition of the Beck Depression Inventory. BSI-H and BSI-IS = Hostility and Interpersonal sensitivity subscales of the Brief Symptom Inventory. BSI-GSI = Global severity index of the Brief Symptom Inventory. CAPS = Clinician-Administered PTSD Scale. COPE-AD and COPE-SS = Alcohol and drug use and Social support subscales of the Coping Orientation to Problems Experienced Inventory. ESEA = Scale of Acute Stress Symptoms. EI = Maladjustment Scale. GHQ = General Health Questionnaire. MAST = Michigan Alcohol Screening Test. MPSS-SR = Modified PTSD Symptom Scale Self-Report. NMR = General Expectancy for Negative Mood Regulation Scale. PCL = PTSD Checklist. PDS = Post-trauma Diagnosis Scale.
RIES = Revised Impact of Events Scale. SAS-SR = Social Adjustment Scale Self-Report. SDS-W, SDS-S and SDS-F: Work, Social, and Family subscales of the Sheehan Disability Scale. STAI = State-Trait Anxiety Inventory.
Results: ES = Effect size.

effect size (that is, with a within-group effect size > .80) in practically all the measures of symptomatology and dysfunctionality applied, including a measure of symptoms of posttraumatic stress: the Posttraumatic Stress Diagnostic Scale (PDS; Foa, Cashman, Jaycox, & Perry, 1997). In fact, these changes were maintained in the treatment group at the 1-month, 4-month and 1-year follow-ups (see Table 29.1.).

Moreover, taking into account the results of both groups of patients once the control group had also received trauma-focused cognitive-behavioral therapy, and defining clinically significant improvement as a reduction of at least 50% of the posttraumatic stress symptomatology assessed at pretreatment with the PDS, it could be estimated that 56.1% of the patients presented a clinically significant improvement after the therapy.

In line with these results, the second experimental study (Difede, Malta, et al., 2007) corroborated the efficacy of trauma-focused cognitive-behavioral therapy in the specific case of the disaster workers who helped in the 9/11 terrorist attacks on the World Trade Center and who suffered a diagnosable PTSD or high levels of posttraumatic stress symptomatology. In this study the cognitive-behavioral therapy that the 15 patients who were randomly assigned to the treatment group received included breathing training, cognitive reprocessing, imaginal exposure, and gradual in vivo exposure, with particular emphasis on the latter two components. In contrast, the 16 patients randomly assigned to the control group received the habitual intervention for this type of worker, which, in this case, consisted of providing information about the results of the pretreatment psychological assessment, advising them to seek treatment for PTSD, and remitting them to the appropriate professionals to help them obtain this treatment through community resources (which, in the course of the study, none of these patients sought).

Although at posttreatment, the patients who received cognitive-behavioral therapy showed lower levels of posttraumatic stress symptomatology than the patients of the control group, these differences were not statistically significant when taking into account the data of all the patients who initiated the study, both those who completed the treatment and those who dropped out of the study prematurely. However, when only considering the data of the patients who completed the treatment, the results indicate that the patients who received cognitive-behavioral therapy showed—statistically significantly—lower levels of posttraumatic stress symptoms than the patients from the control group in the two standardized measures of PTSD, and the group differences in these measures were of a magnitude that was much higher than the value conventionally considered a large effect size (effect size > .80; see Table 29.1.). In fact, considering a 10-point reduction in the Clinician Administered PTSD Scale (CAPS; Blake et al., 1995) to be a clinically significant improvement, 78.1% of the patients who completed the cognitive-behavioral therapy improved in a clinically significant way versus only 28.6% of the patients from the control group (see Table 29.1.).

Summing up, the results of the two experimental studies carried out to date on the treatment of victims of terrorism who suffer from PTSD suggest that trauma-focused cognitive-behavioral therapy is efficacious for this kind of disorder and, therefore, it would be the therapy of choice in the absence of studies on the specific efficacy in victims of terrorism of the other psychological therapies that have been shown to be efficacious for PTSD derived from other traumatic events (exposure therapy, anxiety control training, and EMDR). This is, of course, above and beyond other psychological or psychopharmacological therapies that not only have not been tested with victims of terrorism, but that also lack adequate empirical support for their efficacy in PTSD produced by other traumatic situations.

Nevertheless, this recommendation should be taken with due caution, not only because it is based on a very reduced number of studies, but also because in one of the studies, that of Difede, Malta et al. (2007), a high rate of drop-outs was found in the group that received the cognitive-behavioral therapy (53.3%), at least in comparison with the usual drop-out rate in studies of psychological therapy of PTSD, which, in the meta-analysis of Bradley et al. (2005), was estimated at 21%, precisely the rate also found for all the patients of the study by Duffy et al. (2007) when they started the cognitive-behavioral therapy (20%).

On the other hand, on the basis of the literature on PTSD due to other traumatic situations, it could be expected that future experimental research will confirm that some of the other psychological treatments, if not all of them, that have proven their efficacy for victims of these other situations, will also be effective for the victims of terrorism.

Clinical effectiveness of psychological treatments for PTSD in victims of terrorism

The two studies cited in the previous section were designed to assess the efficacy of cognitive-behavioral therapy, not their clinical effectiveness (or clinical utility). As with other experimental studies with control group, such studies are characterized by lending priority to internal validity in their designs and thus, allowing them to infer the existence of a causal relation between the therapies and the positive results observed upon completion. For this purpose, researchers prepare the most optimum and controlled conditions possible to allow them to detect any minimal positive effect that can be attributed exclusively to the treatment (e.g., strict inclusion and exclusion criteria, homogeneous samples, random assignation of the patients to a treatment group or to a control group, therapists with very similar training, university or research therapeutic contexts, treatment manuals, defined therapeutic protocols with regard to the number of sessions and their duration, assessment of the degree of fidelity to the protocols and manuals). As they lend priority to internal validity, such studies partially sacrifice external validity and, therefore, it is unclear whether the positive effects found in these ideal and controlled conditions are at all generalizable to the habitual clinical practice in which one intervenes on a much more heterogeneous population that has some capacity to choose the type of treatment it will receive, and in which the administration of treatments is flexible, self-corrective, as well as being in the charge of clinical professionals who vary much more in their degree of training and clinical experience.

Studies that directly address the clinical utility of an intervention that has previously proved its efficacy by examining its effects in conditions similar to those found in the habitual clinical practice are known as effectiveness studies. The main characteristics of such studies is that they give priority to external validity and, therefore, they examine the effects of treatments in conditions as similar as possible to those of the habitual clinical practice (e.g., natural therapeutic contexts, clinical professionals who work in such contexts, samples of more heterogeneous patients who are selected with hardly any exclusion or inclusion criteria from among the people who normally come to consultation or are remitted to such contexts).

Although there are not many studies that have addressed the clinical effectiveness of psychological treatment for PTSD, strangely enough, with regard to the victims of terrorism, four studies have been published to date (Brewin et al., 2008; García-Vera & Romero Colino, 2004; Gillespie et al., 2002; Levitt, Malta, Martin, Davis, & Cloitre, 2007) that meet many of the characteristics of clinical effectiveness studies. These four studies are also displayed in Table 29.1. All of them used a pre-posttreatment within-group design and analyzed the results of the administration of trauma-focused cognitive-behavioral therapy for PTSD with heterogeneous samples of direct and indirect victims of terrorist attacks.

In two of them the clinical effectiveness of two specific cognitive-behavioral therapies was analyzed. In the study of Gillespie et al. (2002), with a sample of victims of the car bomb that exploded in Omagh (Northern Ireland), the effectiveness of the cognitive-behavioral therapy developed from the cognitive model of Ehlers and Clark (2000) was examined. This therapy has been analyzed with regard to its efficacy with victims of terrorism, in the above-mentioned experimental study of Duffy et al. (2007). In the study of Levitt et al. (2007), the clinical effectiveness with direct and indirect victims of the 9/11 terrorist attacks at the World Trade Center of the cognitive-behavioral therapy called Skills Training in Affective and Interpersonal Regulation/Modified Prolonged Exposure (STAIR) was examined. The efficacy of this treatment had been previously demonstrated for PTSD derived from infant abuse in a randomized and controlled clinical trial carried out by Cloitre, Koenen, Cohen, and Han (2002).

In the remaining two studies, researchers did not test specific cognitive-behavioral therapies, but in both of them, with most of the patients, if not all of them, programs were applied that included the basic components of trauma-focused cognitive-behavioral therapy. Thus, in the study of García-Vera and Romero Colino (2004) with direct and indirect victims of the Madrid March 11 terrorist attacks, the patients received therapies that included diaphragmatic breathing training, distraction techniques and stop-thinking, self-statement training, cognitive restructuring, and imaginal and in vivo exposure to the memories and stimuli associated with the attacks, whereas in the study of Brewin et al. (2008) with direct victims of the bombs that exploded on July 7, 2005, in the transportation system of London, 80% of the patients received a trauma-focused cognitive-behavioral therapy that included cognitive therapy along with imaginal and in vivo exposure to the memories and stimuli related to the explosions.

In general, the results of the four studies were positive (see Table 29.1.), with rates of clinically significant improvement for PTSD of 67% (García-Vera & Romero Colino, 2004), 73% (Gillespie et al., 2002), and 87% (Brewin et al., 2008), rates that, with the precautions due to the different definitions of improvement used, are similar to those found in the studies reviewed in the above section on the efficacy of trauma-focused cognitive-behavioral therapy (56 and 78%; see Table 29.1.). Likewise, the therapeutic results in terms of the magnitude of the pre-posttreatment differences in the measures of posttraumatic stress symptomatology were, overall, similar to those found in the studies of efficacy (see Table 29.1.). Strange to say, however, the rates of treatment drop-out for the patients with PTSD were lower in the studies of effectiveness (4% in Brewin et al., 2008; 22% in García-Vera & Romero Colino, 2004; and 24% in Levitt et al., 2007—including 5% who refused to continue with exposure although they remained in treatment to complete the other components of the treatment) than in one of the efficacy studies (53% in Difede, Malta et al., 2007), and similar or also lower than in the other study (20% in Duffy et al., 2007).

Summing up, the results of the studies on the clinical effectiveness or clinical utility of trauma-focused cognitive-behavioral therapy for victims of terrorism who suffer from PTSD allow us to conclude that this therapy is not only efficacious but it is also clinically useful in habitual psychotherapeutic practice. These results corroborate the recommendation to use trauma-focused cognitive-behavioral therapy as the first choice for the victims of terrorism with PTSD, especially as there is no study published to date about the clinical effectiveness of other types of psychological treatment, including the treatments that have shown their efficacy and clinical effectiveness with victims of other traumatic events.

Innovative treatments

The use of virtual reality in exposure therapy is being investigated in the treatment of victims of terrorism with PTSD (Difede & Hoffman, 2002; Josman et al., 2006). In fact, a study with a group design, but nonexperimental (no randomization of patients to groups) has been published that compared, in a sample of volunteers and professionals who helped to rescue the victims of the September 11 attacks and who had a diagnosis of PTSD, the efficacy of cognitive-behavioral therapy with exposure using virtual reality versus a waiting-list control group (Difede, Cukor et al., 2007). The results of this study, that are summarized in Table 29.1., are quite promising, as the patients who completed the cognitive-behavioral therapy with virtual reality exposure showed significantly lower levels of posttraumatic stress symptomatology at posttreatment than the waiting-list patients. In fact, considering a 10-point reduction in the CAPS as clinically significant improvement, 90% of the patients who completed the therapy showed clinically significant improvement at posttreatment. Moreover, the therapeutic benefits were maintained at the 6-month follow-up with a mean reduction of approximately 35 points in the CAPS from pretreatment to follow-up, a reduction that was statistically significant (see Table 29.1.).

Although the conclusions that can be reached from this study should be taken with caution because of its quasi-experimental design, the small number of patients that finally completed treatment (n = 10), and the lack of information about the results of the group of patients who initiated therapy (not only the results of those who completed it), its results are nonetheless promising and they offer a very encouraging therapeutic alternative, especially for patients who have difficulties in engaging emotionally in imaginal exposure and for whom this type of exposure may therefore not be effective. In this sense, Difede, Cukor et al. (2007) indicated that 5 of the patients who had made up the treatment group in their study had not managed to improve previously with imaginal exposure therapy, possibly because of their difficulties in engaging emotionally in the exposure, as they had reported scores of 0 in the Subjective Units of Distress Scale (SUDS) across several sessions of imaginal exposure. In contrast, after receiving the cognitive-behavioral therapy with virtual reality exposure, 3 of these patients had shown a posttreatment reduction of at least 25% in their CAPS scores with regard to their pretreatment scores, whereas the 2 remaining patients showed a reduction of more than 50%.

Treatment of Other Mental Disorders

Up until now, no experimental or quasi-experimental study has been published that has tested the efficacy or clinical effectiveness of the psychological treatments applied specifically to direct or indirect victims of terrorist attacks who suffer from mental disorders other than PTSD. As commented on above, after a terrorist attack the onset of major depressive disorder, agoraphobia, panic disorder, generalized anxiety disorder, or alcohol and substance dependence disorders is frequent, and, for all these disorders, there is currently a large number of therapies, mainly cognitive-behavioral, that have proved their efficacy and clinical effectiveness in samples of patients extracted from hospitals, mental health centers, or primary care centers, and who have not necessarily undergone either terrorist attacks or any other kind of traumatic event (NICE 2007a, 2007b; Pérez Álvarez, Fernández Hermida, Fernández Rodríguez, & Amigo Vázquez, 2003).

There is clearly a gap in current research on the treatment of the psychopathological consequences of terrorism, because the number of people affected by mental disorders other than PTSD is quite significant. In fact, the presence of comorbidity among the victims of terrorist attacks is very frequent, particularly among the victims who seek or receive psychological aid. Especially, the simultaneous presence of PTSD and major depressive disorder or of PTSD and other anxiety disorders or alcohol or substance abuse/dependence is very frequent. Thus, for example, among the victims of terrorism with chronic PTSD of the study of Gillespie et al. (2002), 54% were found to suffer simultaneously from another Axis I clinical disorder, mainly major depressive disorder (47.3%), whereas in the study of Duffy et al. (2007), 63.8% of the patients with chronic PTSD also suffered from major depressive disorder (see Table 29.1.).

In the current state of research the treatment of choice that should be administered to the victims of terrorist attacks who present psychological disorders other than PTSD would be the therapy or therapies with the greatest empirical support to treat such disorders in other kinds of psychopathological populations. In fact, this is the strategy that has been followed in the studies displayed in Table 29.1. to address the presence of other disorders in the victims (García-Vera & Romero Colino, 2004) or the presence of comorbid disorders in victims with PTSD (Brewin et al., 2008; Duffy et al., 2007; Gillespie et al., 2002). For example, Duffy et al. (2007) used behavioral activation in the first sessions of therapy when the initial levels of depression interfered with processing the trauma (in their sample, approximately 64% of the victims presented PTSD comorbidly with major depressive disorder), whereas

García-Vera and Romero Colino (2004) applied techniques of gradual planning of activities and planning of pleasant activities for the victims who presented relevant depressive symptoms (in their sample of victims, 10% presented adaptive disorder with mixed anxiety and depressed mood, 2.5% presented adaptive disorder with depressed mood, 2.5% presented major depressive disorder, and 15% grief). All these techniques are a part of the behavioral and cognitive-behavioral therapies whose efficacy is supported by the empirical literature (NICE, 2007a; Pérez & García, 2003).

It is not possible to carry out a specific analysis of the role of these techniques in the efficacy or effectiveness of the therapies or in the differential efficacy or effectiveness in the victims who present other disorders or other disorders comorbidly with PTSD. However, the data in Table 29.1. show that the trauma-focused cognitive-behavioral therapies which, in some cases, included these antidepressive techniques had positive effects both on the victims with depressive disorders (approximately 92% of the patients with depression spectrum disorders recovered in García-Vera & Romero Colino, 2004) and on the victims who showed comorbidity (in Brewin et al., 2008, 79% of the victims improved in a clinically significant way with regard to their scores on the Beck Depression Inventory -BDI- whereas in Duffy et al., 2007, a mean pre-posttreatment reduction was reached of about one standard deviation –ES = 1.05– with regard to the depressive symptomatology measured by the BDI).

In any case, the presence of other mental disorders in the victims, especially if it is comorbid, is a challenge from the therapeutic viewpoint. In the victims of terrorism with PTSD, comorbidity is usually associated with a longer duration of the trauma-focused cognitive-behavioral therapy (Duffy et al., 2007; Gillespie et al., 2002), partly because the therapists must introduce additional techniques to address the other disorders.

In this sense the treatment of people who have lost a loved one in the attacks deserves special mention. In these cases, the habitual reactions after a situation of loss (i.e., certain depressive reactions) are exacerbated by the symptoms of posttraumatic stress that make up a specific syndrome. For example, the images and memories of the deceased may generate a mixture of feelings of sadness and traumatic suffering so that even the positive memories of the loved one are doubly avoided: in the first place, because they produce sadness and longing for the deceased, and secondly, because they also trigger painful and anxious memories of the loved one's traumatic and violent death. In fact, as shown in the results of Shear, Jackson, Essock, Donahue, and Felton (2006), it is likely that many of these cases fall into the category of traumatic grief proposed by Prigerson et al. (1999). This category, which replaces the one that has sometimes been called complicated or pathological grief, refers to a different disorder from PTSD, depression, or other anxiety disorders, in which, after the death of a loved one, which was not necessarily violent or the product of a traumatic event, there are concurrent symptoms of separation distress (e.g., yearning, searching for the deceased, excessive loneliness resulting from the loss) and symptoms of traumatic distress (i.e., intrusive thoughts about the deceased, disbelief about the loss, a sense of futility about the future, being dazed and feeling numbness, and loss of the feeling of security and trust in others). This condition requires a specific therapeutic approach, for example, the one developed by Shear et al. (2001) that combines strategies from cognitive-behavioral therapy for PTSD and interpersonal therapy for depression. Future research should address the administration of this kind of treatment to the direct and indirect victims of terrorism who have lost loved ones in the attacks.

Lastly, a therapeutic approach that is still in the experimental phase in its administration to the victims of terrorism who present mental disorders other than PTSD is the application of cognitive-behavioral techniques via the internet, an approach that has already produced positive results in patients who suffer from depression, panic, alcohol abuse, or anxiety, or even PTSD as a result of other traumatic events (see the review of Amstadter, Broman-Fulks, Zinzowa, Ruggiero, & Cercone, 2009). Ruggiero et al. (2006) have developed an intervention program for victims of terrorism made up of seven modules targeting, respectively, the following disorders and problems: PTDS/panic, depression, generalized anxiety, alcohol abuse, marihuana abuse, abuse of other drugs, and smoking. Each one of these modules includes psychoeducation and information about coping techniques based on the cognitive-behavioral therapies whose efficacy for each one of these disorders and problems has more empirical support. Thus, for example, the module of PTSD/panic includes recommendations for exposure, reduction of avoidance behaviors, and learning control of breathing. Although no data have yet been published on the efficacy or effectiveness of this kind of intervention, there are data with a sample of 285 residents of New York after the September 11 attacks that indicate that the intervention is feasible, in terms of, for example, users' time and effort, acquisition of knowledge about PTSD, panic, and depression, or degree of satisfaction (Ruggiero et al., 2006). As the internet offers the possibility of reaching a large number of people quickly and cheaply, this kind of intervention, if finally efficacious, could be a therapeutic alternative to be considered both by itself and used conjointly with the traditional therapies.

Conclusions

In the last few decades terrorism has become one of the most severe and alarming problems worldwide. In response, in the past 10–15 years, psychology has developed systematic research programs about the psychopathological repercussions of terrorist attacks and their treatment, although those programs have been practically limited to the massive terrorist attacks that have occurred in developed countries.

After a terrorist attack, an important percentage of the direct victims (around 20–30%) will develop PTSD and other mental disorders (depression, other anxiety disorders, alcohol and other substance abuse/dependence disorders). The number of indirect victims who will develop these disorders will be lower, but, even so, it will be higher than the habitual prevalence of such disorders in the general population before the attacks. Consequently, both the direct and indirect victims will need psychological attention at the short, medium, and long term, which should be provided within a framework of a global response to terrorism, especially in the case of terrorist attacks that cause a very high number of dead and injured, as well as important material destruction. Moreover, the psychological intervention should take into account the diverse needs and characteristics of the affected and the fact that such needs have different priorities and can vary at different moments or phases after the attacks.

In the phases of this global response known as recovery and return to life, the victims who present PTSD and other mental disorders should be provided with the psychological treatments that have the greatest empirical guarantees regarding their efficacy and clinical effectiveness. Although still scarce, in recent years, some experimental and quasi-experimental group studies have been published about the efficacy and clinical effectiveness of trauma-focused cognitive-behavioral therapy for the victims of terrorism who present PTSD. This kind of therapy combines cognitive techniques with in vivo and imaginal exposure, and in some cases also with stress control techniques. The results of these studies allow us to recommend this therapy above and beyond other therapeutic alternatives, including therapies that have proved their efficacy and effectiveness in the treatment for PTSD derived from other traumatic events (e.g., exposure therapy alone, anxiety control training, eye movement desensitization and reprocessing).

Future research should precisely determine whether these other psychological treatments that have proved their efficacy with victims of other traumatic events (i.e., war veterans, victims of physical violence or rape, refugees, or traffic-accident survivors) can also be efficacious with victims of terrorism. Likewise, another challenge for psychological research in the sphere of terrorism is the development and testing of specific therapies for the other mental disorders that victims of terrorism may present because, currently, the recommendations to address them are based on the data about the efficacy and effectiveness of diverse psychological treatments when applied to other kinds of psychopathological patients, who have not necessarily suffered terrorist attacks or any other kind of traumatic event.

References

American Psychiatric Association. (2004). Practice guideline for the treatment of patients with acute stress disorder and posttraumatic stress disorder. Retrieved December 17, 2010 from: www.psychiatryonline.com/pracGuide/PracticePDFs/ASD_PTSD_Inactivated_04-16-09.pdf

Amstadter, A. B., Broman-Fulks, J., Zinzowa, H., Ruggiero, K. J., & Cercone, J. (2009). Internet-based interventions for traumatic stress-related mental health problems: a review and suggestion for future research. *Clinical Psychology Review*, *29*, 410–420.

Australian Centre for Posttraumatic Mental Health. (2007). *Australian guidelines for the treatment of adults with acute stress disorder and posttraumatic stress disorder.* Melbourne, Victoria: ACPMH.

Baumgarten-Tramer, F. (1948). Zur Psychologie der Ausgebombten [The psychology of the bombed-out]. *Gesundheit und Wohlfahrt*, *28*, 158–163.

Bills, C. B., Levy, N. A., Sharma, V., Charney, D. S., Herbert, R., Moline, J., & Katz, C. L. (2008). Mental health of workers and volunteers responding to events of 9/11: Review of the literature. *The Mount Sinai Journal of Medicine*, *75*, 115–127.

Bisson, J., & Andrew, M. (2007). Psychological treatment of post-traumatic stress disorder (PTSD). *Cochrane Database of Systematic Reviews 2007*, *3*. Art. No.: CD003388.

Bisson, J. I., Ehlers, A., Matthews, R., Pilling, S., Richards, D., & Turner, S. (2007). Psychological treatments for chronic post-traumatic stress disorder: systematic review and meta-analysis. *British Journal of Psychiatry*, *190*, 97–104.

Blake, D. D., Weathers, F. W., Nagy, L. M., Kalopek, D. G., Charney, D. S., & Keane, T. M. (1995). *Clinician-Administered PTSD Scale for DSM-IV (CAPS-DX).* Boston, MA: Boston VA Medical Center, National Center for Posttraumatic Stress Disorder, Behavioral Science Division.

Bradley, R., Greene, J., Russ, E., Dutra, L., & Westen, D. (2005). A multidimensional meta-analysis of psychotherapy for PTSD. *American Journal of Psychiatry, 162*, 214–227.

Brewin, C. R., Scragg, P., Robertson, M., Thompson, M., d'Ardenne, P., & Ehlers, A., on behalf of the Psychosocial Steering Group, London Bombings Trauma Response Programme (2007). Promoting mental health following the London bombings: a screen and treat approach. *Journal of Traumatic Stress, 21*, 3–8.

Cloitre, M. (2009). Effective psychotherapies for posttraumatic stress disorder: A review and critique. *CNS Spectrums, 14*(Suppl. 1), 32–43.

Cloitre, M., Koenen, K. C., Cohen, L. R., & Han, H. (2002). Skills training in affective and interpersonal regulation followed by exposure: a phase-based treatment for PTSD related to childhood abuse. *Journal of Consulting and Clinical Psychology, 70*, 1067–1074.

Curran, P. S. (1988) Psychiatric aspects of terrorist violence: Northern Ireland 1969–1987. *British Journal of Psychiatry, 153*, 470–475.

Difede, J., Cukor, J., Jayasinghe, N., Patt, I., Jedel, S., Spielman, L. ... Hoffman, H. G. (2007). Virtual reality exposure therapy for the treatment of posttraumatic stress disorder following September 11, 2001. *Journal of Clinical Psychiatry, 68*, 1639–1647.

Difede, J., Malta, L., Best, S., Henn-Haase, C., Metzler, T., Bryant, R., & Marmar, C. (2007). A randomized controlled clinical treatment trial for World Trade Center attack-related PTSD in disaster workers. *The Journal of Nervous and Mental Disease, 195*, 861–865.

Difede, J., & Hoffman, H. G. (2002). Virtual reality exposure therapy for World Trade Center post-traumatic stress disorder: A case report. *Cyberpsychology & Behavior, 5*, 529–535.

DiMaggio, C., & Galea, S. (2006). The behavioral consequences of terrorism: a meta-analysis. *Academic Emergency Medicine, 13*, 559–566.

DiMaggio, C., Galea, S., & Li, G. (2009). Substance use and misuse in the aftermath of terrorism. A Bayesian meta-analysis. *Addiction, 104*, 894–904.

Duffy, M., Gillespie, K., & Clark, D. M. (2007). Post-traumatic stress disorder in the context of terrorism and other civil conflict in Northern Ireland: randomised controlled trial. *British Medical Journal, 334*, 1147–1150.

Ehlers, A., & Clark, D. M. (2000). A cognitive model of posttraumatic stress disorder. *Behaviour Research and Therapy, 38*, 319–345.

Foa, E. B., Cashman, L., Jaycox, L., & Perry, K. (1997). The validation of a self-report measure of posttraumatic stress disorder: The Posttraumatic Diagnostic Scale. *Psychological Assessment, 9*, 445–451.

Foa, E. B., Cahill, S. P., Boscarino, J. A., Hobfoll, S. E., Lahad, M., McNally, R. J., & Solomon, Z. (2005). Social, psychological, and psychiatric interventions following terrorist attacks: recommendations for practice and research. *Neuropsychopharmacology, 30*, 1806–1817.

García-Vera, M. P., & Sanz, J. (2008). El papel de las guías de auto-ayuda y las pautas de intervención psicológica para los afectados por los atentados del 11-M [The role of self-help guides and psychological intervention guidelines for people affected by the March 11th terrorist attacks]. In M. P. García-Vera, F. J. Labrador, & C. Larroy (Eds.), *Ayuda psicológica a las víctimas de atentados y catástrofes [Psychological help for victims of terrorist attacks and disasters,* pp. 1–34*]*. Madrid: Editorial Complutense.

García-Vera, M. P., & Romero Colino, L. (2004). Tratamiento psicológico de los trastornos por estrés derivados de los atentados del 11-M: De la psicología clínica basada en la evidencia a la práctica profesional [Psychological treatment of stress dissorders caused by Madrid March 11 attacks. From evidence-based clinical psychology to professional practice]. *Clínica y Salud, 15*, 355–385.

Gillespie, K., Duffy, M., Hackmann, A., & Clark, D. M. (2002). Community based cognitive therapy in the treatment of posttraumatic stress disorder following the Omagh bomb. *Behaviour Research and Therapy, 40*, 345–357.

Institute of Medicine Committee on Responding to the Psychological Consequences of Terrorism with Butler, A. S., Panzer, A. M., & Goldfrank, L. R. (Eds.). (2003). *Preparing for the psychological consequences of terrorism: A public health strategy.* Washington, DC: National Academies Press.

Institute of Medicine Committee on Treatment of Posttraumatic Stress Disorder. (2007). *Treatment of posttraumatic stress disorder: an assessment of the evidence.* Washington, DC: National Academies Press.

Josman, N., Somer, E., Reisberg, A., Weiss, P. L., García-Palacios, A., & Hoffman, H. (2006). BusWorld: Designing a virtual environment for post-traumatic stress disorder in Israel: A protocol. *Cyberpsychology & Behavior, 9*, 241–244.

Levitt, J. T., Malta, L. S., Martin, A., Davis, L., & Cloitre, M. (2007). The flexible application of a manualized treatment for PTSD symptoms and functional impairment related to the 9/11 World Trade Center attack. *Behaviour Research and Therapy, 45*, 1419–1433.

Lohr, J. M., Hooke, W., Gist, R., & Tolin, D. F. (2004). Novel and controversial treatments for trauma-related stress disorders. In S. O. Lilienfeld, S. J. Lynn & J. M. Lohr (Eds.), *Science and pseudoscience in clinical psychology* (pp. 243–272). New York: Guilford.

Miller, H. C. (Ed.). (1920). *Functional nerve disease: an epitome of war experience for the practitioner.* London: Henry Frowde, Hodder & Stoughton.

National Counterterrorism Center. (2006). NCTC Report on incidents of terrorism 2005. Retrieved June 19, 2009 from National Counterterrorism Center's Worldwide Incidents Tracking System web site: http://wits.nctc.gov/reports/crot2005nctcannexfinal.pdf

National Counterterrorism Center. (2007). NCTC Report on terrorist incidents—2006. Retrieved June 19, 2009 from National Counterterrorism Center's Worldwide Incidents Tracking System web site: http://wits.nctc.gov/reports/crot2006nctcannexfinal.pdf

National Counterterrorism Center. (2008). NCTC 2007 Report on terrorism. Retrieved June 19, 2009 from National Counterterrorism Center's Worldwide Incidents Tracking System web site: http://wits.nctc.gov/reports/crot2007nctcannexfinal.pdf

National Counterterrorism Center. (2009). NCTC 2008 Report on terrorism. Retrieved June 19, 2009 from National Counterterrorism Center's Worldwide Incidents Tracking System web site: http://wits.nctc.gov/Reports.do?f=crt2008nctcannexfinal.pdf

National Institute of Mental Health. (2002). *Mental health and mass violence: Evidence-based early psychological intervention for victims/survivors of mass violence. A workshop to reach consensus on best practices.* NIH Publication No. 02-5138, Washington, DC: U.S. Government Printing Office.

National Institute for Health and Clinical Excellence. (NICE) (2005). Post-traumatic stress disorder (PTSD): the management of PTSD in adults and children in primary and secondary care. Clinical guideline 26. Retrieved February 19, 2008 from NICE web site: www.nice.org.uk/CG026NICEguideline

National Institute for Health and Clinical Excellence. (NICE) (2007a). Depression: management of depression in primary and secondary care. Clinical guideline 23 (amended 2003). Retrieved June 10, 2009 from NICE web site: www.nice.org.uk/CG023NICEguideline

National Institute for Health and Clinical Excellence. (NICE) (2007b). Anxiety: management of generalised anxiety disorder and panic disorder (with or without agoraphobia) in adults in primary, secondary and community care. Clinical guideline 22 (amended 2007). Retrieved June 10, 2009 from NICE web site: www.nice.org.uk/CG022NICEguideline

Norris, F. H., Friedman, M. J., Watson, P. J., Byrne, C. M., Diaz, E., Kaniasty, K. (2002). 60,000 disaster victims speak: Part I. An empirical review of the empirical literature, 1981–2001. *Psychiatry, 65,* 207–239.

Pérez Álvarez, M., Fernández Hermida, J. R., Fernández Rodríguez, C., & Amigo Vázquez, I. (Eds.). (2003). *Guía de tratamientos psicológicos eficaces I. Adultos* [Guide to efficacious psychological treatments I. Adults]. Madrid: Pirámide.

Pérez, M., & García, J. M. (2003). Guía de tratamientos psicológicos eficaces para la depresión [Guide to efficacious psychological treatments for depression]. In M. Pérez Álvarez, J. R. Fernández Hermida, C. Fernández Rodríguez, & I. Amigo Vázquez (Eds.), *Guía de tratamientos psicológicos eficaces I. Adultos* [Guide to efficacious psychological treatments I. Adults] (pp. 161–195). Madrid: Pirámide.

Prigerson, H. G., Shear, M. K., Jacobs, S. C., Reynolds, C. F., III, Maciejewski, P. K., Davidson, J. R. T., ... Zisook, S. (1999). Consensus criteria for traumatic grief: a preliminary empirical test. *British Journal of Psychiatry, 174,* 67–73.

Ruggiero, K. J., Resnick, H. S., Acierno, R., Carpenter, M. J., Kilpatrick, D. J., Coffey, S. F., Ruscio, A. M., ... Galea, S. (2006). Internet-based intervention for mental health and substance use problems in disaster-affected populations: a pilot feasibility study. *Behaviour Research and Therapy, 37,* 190–205.

Shear, K. M., Jackson, C. T., Essock, S. M., Donahue, S. A., & Felton, C. J. (2006). Screening for complicated grief among Project Liberty service recipients 18 months after September 11, 2001. *Psychiatric Services, 57,* 1291–1297.

Shear, M. K., Frank, E., Foa, E., Cherry, C., Reynolds , C. F., III, Vander Bilt, J., & Masters, S. (2001). Traumatic grief treatment: A pilot study. *American Journal of Psychiatry, 158,* 1506–1508.

30

Psychology and Forced Migrants

Zachary Steel and Catherine Robina Bateman Steel

Forced migration is commonly associated with extreme mental stressors. Violence, conflict, social and economic degradation, dislocation, loss, and instability all create a picture of immense vulnerability for affected persons and populations. The mental health consequences of such conditions have made it incumbent on psychology to play a multitude of roles in documenting, assessing, and intervening to support those affected at all stages of the process of forced migration.

This chapter outlines the historical development of the complex relationship between psychology and the experience of forced migration. The evolution and ongoing role of the trauma model in allowing psychologists and mental health professionals to engage in the mental health consequences of forced migration are described. Refugee resettlement in Western countries and the resultant policies of deterrence that became popular amongst Western governments are discussed from the perspective of mental health professionals. One particularly complex aspect of the asylum process for psychologists, the refugee determination process, is considered. The cultural critique of the trauma model and its relevance to practitioners is also discussed. In conclusion, a model that may provide a valuable tool for continued engagement in supporting forced migrant mental health is proposed.

Refugees, Asylum Seekers, and Displaced Populations

At the end of 2009, it was estimated that there were 43 million displaced persons as a result of persecution and conflict, including 15 million refugees outside their country of origin and 28 million internally displaced persons (IDPs) (UNHCR, 2010). This represents an overall increase in global displacement after a period of

IAAP Handbook of Applied Psychology, First Edition. Edited by Paul R. Martin, Fanny M. Cheung, Michael C. Knowles, Michael Kyrios, Lyn Littlefield, J. Bruce Overmier, and José M. Prieto.

steady decline in the early 2000s, reflecting the effects of prolonged conflict and instability in the Middle East and Southern Asia. The vast majority of refugees are displaced to adjacent countries with between 83 and 90% of refugees remaining within their region of displacement and the vast majority residing within developing countries. A comparatively small number of displaced persons proceed to seek protection from industrialized countries with 300–350,000 new asylum applications being lodged per year over the period from 2004–2008. In 2009, new asylum applications to industrialized nations increased by 5% from 2008 (UNHCR, 2010), an increase largely accounted for by applications from citizens of Afghanistan, Somalia and other countries experiencing current conflict. The five largest recipient countries for asylum seekers in recent years have been the USA, the UK, France, Canada, and Germany (UNHCR, 2008b). In addition to seeking asylum a minority of displaced persons successfully apply to the UNHCR to obtain permanent resettlement with 112,400 being resettled during 2009, the majority to the three major resettlement countries of the US (79,900), Canada (12,500), and Australia (11,100) (UNHCR, 2010).

Forced Migrants and Mental Health

Early mental health research and intervention with refugees—The rise in prominence of the trauma model

The trauma, losses and deprivations associated with forced migration would clearly be expected to enhance the risk of mental health problems for refugee communities. The first attempts to document these effects followed the mass displacement and resettlement following World War II. Murphy (1955) examined rates of psychiatric admissions amongst refugees resettled in England and found that newly settled refugees exhibited higher than expected rates of admissions for psychosis. He showed that admission rates appeared to be associated with levels of exposure to persecution and trauma and that the most common diagnoses were schizophrenia and depression. Psychiatric admissions were also investigated by Eitinger (1959) who highlighted admission rates of five times the national average amongst 1816 refugees resettled in Norway following World War II. The majority of admissions (77%) were classified as reactive psychoses, with 23% diagnosed with paranoid schizophrenia. Murphy's earlier findings (1955) were supported by a study of World War II refugees in Australia in 1973 by Krupinski and colleagues (1973) where, not only were higher admission rates found among East European refugees compared with the Australian-born or British migrants, but there was also a strong association between the extent of war trauma, admission rates and severity of psychotic and neurotic symptoms.

The lack of standardized diagnostic systems at the time and a tendency to rely on hospital data and admission rates as an index of psychopathology (Dohrenwend & Dohrenwend, 1982) created difficulties in drawing generalizable conclusions. Notwithstanding these limitations, the early psychiatric research appeared to broadly suggest that refugees were at increased risk of mental disorder. Indeed, the evidence was compelling enough for lead researchers and clinicians, such as Henry Krystal and

William Niederland, working with World War II refugees, to forge a path towards greater recognition of psychopathology related to traumatic experiences associated with migration. In the case of Krystal and Niederland the route to this recognition was through fostering support for the diagnosis of post-traumatic stress disorder (PTSD) and they were both instrumental in ensuring inclusion of the diagnosis in the third edition of the Diagnostic and Statistical Manual of Mental Disorders (DSM-III; Scott, 1990).

The delineation of the diagnosis of PTSD was a key development in the intersecting histories of forced migration and mental health. Although stress-related responses and trauma-related conditions had appeared in some form in the earlier editions of the DSM it was not until the third edition that PTSD itself was formally introduced as a subcategory of anxiety disorders (American Psychiatric Association, 1980).

Prior to formal delineation of PTSD, published reports on the psychological effects of torture began to appear in the late 1970s (Allodi, 1979; Amnesty International, 1977). The Danish Medical Group (Lunde, 1982; Rasmussen & Lunde, 1980) found that 75% of 135 torture survivors experienced severe psychological reactions including irritability, memory disturbance, poor concentration, nightmares, fear and anxiety, depressive symptoms, social isolation, and chronic fatigue. These clinical symptom profiles were similarly described in relation to other early samples of torture survivors collected during this period (Allodi & Cowgill, 1982; Domovitch, Berger, Wawer, Etlin, & Marshall, 1984; Petersen et al., 1985), and also in relation to newly arrived Indochinese and Latin American refugee populations (Allodi, 1980; Kinzie, Tran, Breckenridge, & Bloom, 1980).

Although psychiatric documentation of the effects of torture predated the introduction of the diagnosis of PTSD, the codification of that diagnostic category provided a conceptual framework that gave impetus to the field. While other psychiatric disorders had consistently been identified in trauma-affected populations (de Jong, 2005; Fazel, Wheeler, & Danesh, 2005) the category of PTSD provided a focus for research in the field that gathered momentum. Unlike other psychiatric disorders, PTSD specifically identified the traumatic stressor as the proximate cause of psychiatric impairment and disability (Breslau, Chase, & Anthony, 2002), thus offering a tool by which mental health researchers could document and quantify psychological consequences associated with exposure to human rights abuse and organized violence.

Pivotal to the history of psychiatric traumatology, of which PTSD became central, was the mass flight of Indochinese refugees since it occurred just as PTSD was being introduced into DSM-III. Hence Southeast Asian refugees were the first non-Western population to be examined within the context of the new model of traumatic stress. Descriptions of posttraumatic symptom presentations amongst Indochinese refugees began to appear during the mid 1980s particularly in relation to experiences of Cambodian survivors of the Pol Pot genocide, a population that began to be resettled in sizeable numbers at the beginning of the 1980s (Kinzie, Fredrickson, Ben, Fleck, & Karls, 1984; Mollica, Wyshak, & Lavelle, 1987). Similarly, clear evidence of PTSD presentations were concurrently identified in clinical surveys of torture victims (Goldfeld, Mollica, Pesavento, & Faraone, 1988; Weisaeth, 1989). Even in this early phase, however, concerns were raised that the PTSD constellation was not sufficiently comprehensive to account for the full range of symptoms experienced by torture survivors (Petersen, 1989).

Convergence of mental health and human rights

The rise of the trauma model occurred at a time of increasing awareness and attention to human rights particularly in relation to the human rights abuses associated with violent conflict. The mental health consequences of violent conflict, as seen through the impacts on refugees, saw mental health and human rights converge, moving mental health professionals into the center of the human rights arena. Political and philosophical discourse had been considering the importance of human rights since as early as the 17th century (Cmiel, 2004), but the end of World War II and the recognition of the scale of the atrocities committed in that conflict represented a watershed. The response was a global human rights movement that was intent on creating durable and effective international structures for the protection of rights at a universal level. In 1948, the adoption of the Universal Declaration of Human Rights represented a milestone in advancing that process (Twiss, 2004). Since then, an expanding body of international instruments, conventions and treaties have enshrined a comprehensive range of rights within international law (Gruskin, Mills, & Tarantola, 2007).

PTSD, and the modern trauma model, emerged during this period of increased international developments in advancing human rights (Steel, Bateman-Steel, & Silove, 2009). Lawyers and medical personnel became involved in activities aimed at prohibiting state abuses such as torture, and in 1975, the United Nations issued the *Declaration on the Protection of All Persons from Torture* which explicitly prohibited the use of this inhumane practice under any circumstances (United Nations, 1975). The World Medical Association concurrently adopted the *Declaration of Tokyo* which explicitly forbade doctors from participating in torture in any circumstances (World Medical Association, 1975). These developments culminated in the 1986 UN Convention against Torture and Other Cruel, Inhuman or Degrading Treatments (United Nations, 1987).

Whilst the movement to document mental health consequences gathered momentum from the focus provided by PTSD, the human rights movement also gained an impetus and focus through the development of human rights instruments. The two processes became intertwined as PTSD and other psychiatric disorders such as depression provided an avenue to quantify the impact of human rights abuses such as torture. As such, psychologists and mental health professionals found themselves, at times unintentionally, simultaneously advocating for mental health and for human rights. The coinciding of these two processes provided grounds for a general claim that the delineation of PTSD was a product of the development of a psychiatric activism that motivated the growing international awareness of gross human rights abuses and mass trauma (Bracken, Giller, & Summerfield, 1995; Breslau, 2004; Summerfield, 1999; Young, 1995). However, it is important to note that the international impetus to document the psychiatric consequences of torture predated and to a large extent occurred independently of the process that lead to the delineation and inclusion of PTSD within DSM-III (Allodi, 1991). The two processes gained momentum from each other, but it would be to simplify the case to suggest that PTSD developed as an instrument of the torture and trauma movement.

The emergence of a trauma-focused psychiatric epidemiology

Since these first studies, a comprehensive body of research has developed documenting elevated rates of mental disorder, particularly PTSD and major depression. Early research focused primarily on the mental health of refugee populations resettled to Western countries (Kinzie et al., 1984; Mollica et al., 1987; Westermeyer, Vang, & Neider, 1983). Research, however, was soon extended to displaced and resident populations in conflict-affected regions of the world (Cardozo, Vergara, Agani, & Gotway, 2000; de Jong et al., 2001; de Jong, Mulhern, Ford, van der Kam, & Kleber, 2000; Modvig et al., 2000; Mollica et al., 1993; Mollica et al., 1999; Turner, Bowie, Dunn, Shapo, & Yule, 2003). Within this context, Miller and colleagues (Miller, Kulkarni, & Kushner, 2006) note the dominance of what they refer to as a trauma-focused psychiatric epidemiology with a particular focus on the prevalence of PTSD and depression.

A recent systematic review and meta-analysis of the field (Steel et al., 2009) identified 181 epidemiological surveys reporting the prevalence of PTSD and/or depression undertaken with refugee and conflict-affected populations over the period from 1980 until 2009 covering a total population of 81,866 persons from 40 source countries. The surveys reviewed demonstrated substantial heterogeneity in prevalence rates with PTSD rates ranging from 0% in a low-intensity conflict region of Iran (Hashemian et al., 2006) to 99% in Sierra Leone (de Jong et al. 2000) and depression rates ranging between 3 and 86% (Fox & Tang, 2000; Steel et al., 2005). The findings of this review build on and extend the results of two previous meta-analytic reviews by Porter and Haslam (Porter, 2007; Porter & Haslam, 2005) and Fazel and colleagues (Fazel et al., 2005). As with these earlier reviews methodological factors emerged as being highly salient accounting for 12.9% of inter-survey variance in reported rates of PTSD and 27.7% of variance in depression. However, the review additionally identified a series of substantive population risk factors associated with inter-survey rates of PTSD and depression after adjusting for the above methodological factors. Notably, the review confirmed a dose-effect between reports of torture and other potentially traumatic events and the reported prevalence of PTSD and depression identified by a survey, a finding that had only previously been identified in individual surveys (Mollica, McInnes, Pham, et al., 1998; Mollica, McInnes, Poole, & Tor, 1998). For PTSD, the prevalence of reported torture was the single strongest predictor, while for depression, exposure to potentially traumatic events emerged as the strongest risk factor. Prevalence rates of PTSD and depression also showed a pattern of gradual decline with increasing time since conflict or resettlement to a safe third country. Conditions of the recovery environment emerged as salient. Surveys undertaken in countries with higher levels of political terror as derived from Amnesty International and US State Department country reports (Gibney & Dalton, 1996) retuned higher rates of PTSD than surveys in countries with less severe political terror.

Displaced populations within or external to the source country or living in a refugee camp had higher rates of depression than those that were permanently resettled in another country.

These studies have cemented a growing field of trauma-focused psychiatric epidemiology and highlighted the importance of engaging with the question of how the experience of forced migration impacts on mental well-being. These impacts appear significant and will clearly draw psychologists and other mental health professionals into working closely with displaced and conflict-affected populations. Their role may range from documentation of effects, to treatment, and at times advocacy. However, the field, and the role of mental health professionals, remains at times contested and controversial. It is to two of the most complex arenas within the forced migration and mental health field that we now turn our attention: the process of seeking asylum in western countries, and the cross-cultural relevance of the trauma model.

Asylum seekers, policies of deterrence and mental health

Internationally, the situation facing asylum seekers over the past two decades is a context in which mental health professionals have found themselves practicing in a turbulent arena (Steel & Silove, 2004). The roles in which they can be cast vary greatly and at times have seen them brought into contentious relationships with their own governments (Steel, Mares, Newman, Blick, & Dudley, 2004).

In order to be granted asylum, an applicant must meet the definition of refugee status based on proving an individual fear of persecution as set out in Article 1A(2) of the Refugee Convention: "any person who … owing to a well-founded fear of being persecuted for reasons of race, religion, nationality, membership of a particular social group or political opinion, is outside the country of his nationality and is unable or unwilling to avail himself of the protection of that country"; … The process of determining whether the applicant meets the definition can be long and arduous.

Many Western countries, in response to fears of perceived "floods" of asylum seekers, have implemented broad policies of "humane deterrence," commonly including a range of restrictions affecting asylum seekers during the refugee determination process (Silove, Austin, & Steel, 2007). These affect their social and economic lives substantially and often include limited access, if any, to work rights, welfare support, housing, healthcare, and legal support. In Australia, for example, it was not uncommon for asylum seekers to be denied work rights and welfare support during the full duration of the refugee determination process which could take two or more years to be finalized. Asylum seekers often find themselves highly dependent on charitable organizations for daily living needs for all or part of this time.

The Australian case illustrates the multiple points of convergence between forced migration and mental health concerns, in relation to the restrictions imposed during the process of refugee determination. Australian government representatives disputed claims that the restrictions in access to social resources were harmful or associated with negative consequences for asylum seekers. Consistent with the broad approach, established earlier by trauma-focused psychiatric epidemiology, mental health researchers began to systematically document the consequences of these policies (Silove, Sinnerbrink, Field, Manicavasagar, & Steel, 1997; Silove et al., 2006; Steel et al., 2009; Steel, Silove, Bird, McGorry, & Mohan, 1999). Similar research was also carried out in other jurisdictions, particularly the Netherlands and Sweden (Laban, Gernaat, Komproe, Schreuders, & de Jong, 2004; Laban, Gernaat, Komproe, van der Tweel, & De Jong, 2005). Early research documented the extent to which cumulative exposure to postmigration stressors caused by the asylum process was associated with negative mental health outcomes, adjusting for the impact of premigration trauma experiences. While a number of these studies documented an association between the length of time spent in an indeterminate legal state and poor mental health, these findings were limited by the cross-sectional nature of the surveys. More recent surveys have applied more rigorous methodologies to ensure the implementation of representative sampling designs and prospective cohort designs, nevertheless, documenting similar findings to those generated by previous research (Silove et al., 2006). This body of research has collectively established the importance of the postmigration recovery environment as a major factor mediating psycho-social recovery of refugee and asylum seeking populations. This has helped advance the understanding of the process of recovery amongst refugee populations as well as establishing an evidence base for advocating for more humane policies for the processing of asylum seekers.

The context in which disputes over mental health consequences of migration experiences have been most volatile is in relation to the use of immigration detention for asylum seekers. In 1992 the Australian Federal Government introduced a policy of mandatory detention that was not subject to judicial review. The policy was applied to all persons, including asylum seekers, who arrived in Australia without valid visas. Periods of detention could last for as long as seven years with the policy applied to all categories of unauthorized arrivals including women and children. The policy was associated with a high level of controversy from the outset; mental health professionals in particular created unease by identifying the mental health risks associated with such an approach. However, the government argued that detention was a key element in their strategy of border protection and was highly reluctant to give credence to the concerns being raised about mental health damage that would result from such a harsh policy.

As the mental health of detainees deteriorated, mental health professionals increasingly found themselves inextricably drawn into the frontline of debate as they were confronted by mental health consequences of detention in their daily practice (Silove et al., 2007; Steel, Mares, et al., 2004; Steel & Silove, 2004). In the context of ongoing government denial of the apparent mental health consequences, a natural impetus arose to document the perceived harm to detainees associated with this policy. A series of studies commencing in 2001 began to document extraordinarily high levels of psychiatric impairment amongst immigration detainees (Silove et al., 2007). This evidence base, along with the testimony of health professionals from within the centers, was pivotal in creating a consensus amongst the health community that immigration detention was particularly harmful to children and needed comprehensive review. This led to the largest alliance of health professionals in Australian history. While the government of the day continued to be highly resistant to the process of recommended reform and review, continued scandals in the management and implementation of immigration detention ultimately led to a process of comprehensive reform that continues until today.

The Australian example illustrates not only the complexity of mental health research and practice in such a contested arena, but also the ongoing intersecting relationship between mental health and human rights. In terms of a rights-based model, the asylum process established in many Western countries thus excludes asylum seekers from the majority of rights enshrined in the International Covenant on Economic, Social and Cultural Rights (ICESCR). Policies of mandatory detention appear to also result in multiple breaches of international law affecting rights enshrined in the International Covenant on Civil and Political Rights. In this context mental health professionals advocating for mental health find themselves by necessity also advocating for the protection of human rights.

Refugee determination process

As the trauma model has gained in ascendancy, despite the initial lack of consensus between governments and mental health professionals, mental health expertise is increasingly relied on in the process of determining an applicant's refugee status (Herlihy, Ferstman, & Turner, 2004; Steel, Frommer, & Silove, 2004). This raises an important cautionary note for the psychologist providing evidence in the refugee determination process. Whilst the value of documenting psychological outcomes has been demonstrated as a powerful form of advocacy, an overreliance on psychological sequelae to demonstrate the impact of human rights violations risks overlooking those for whom the effects of abuses do not manifest themselves as psychological symptoms (Steel et al., 2009). There may be a broad range of responses to trauma (an issue that is raised in relation to cross-cultural psychiatric evaluation in the next section) and there is potential danger in the over-dominance of western medical concepts when addressing validity of claims of persecution (Bogner, Herlihy, & Brewin, 2007; Herlihy, Scragg, & Turner, 2002; Herlihy & Turner, 2006). Great caution should also be taken to respect each individual's personal, cultural, and social world so as to understand their own responses to human rights violations. An absence of psychological trauma symptoms should not automatically lead to assumptions that the abuses did not occur.

Psychology, anthropology, and refugees

It is important to draw attention to the growing critique that has surrounded the trauma model's gain in ascendancy in the psychiatric literature, and its application particularly amongst non-Western populations. The commonly attested concern is that the uncritical application of a Western-derived psychiatric model, with its focus on the individual and "trauma," may undermine premises on which many indigenous societies are built, such as a collectivist notion of suffering and recovery (Breslau, 2004; Kleinman, 1995; Summerfield, 1999).

It has been argued that views and experiences of distress amongst culturally diverse societies can differ substantially, potentially invalidating diagnostic constructs devised and primarily researched in advanced industrialized societies. In relation to the trauma model, for instance, critics have argued that the very concept of trauma and in particular the category of PTSD may not have universal validity or equivalence of meaning (Bracken, et al., 1995). The ensuing debate has become fiercely polarized in a way that risks obscuring the important humanitarian value of the opposing arguments. Nevertheless, it is important to consider whether and to what extent the trauma model may inadvertently exacerbate difficulties facing forced migrants in order for the field to adapt appropriately to any legitimate concerns.

PTSD–like syndromes are often not distinguished from other mental health syndromes in indigenous cultures (Kleinman, 1995). In Timor–Leste for example, where our team has worked for a number of years, terms used by the Timorese to describe mental illness do not map in any direct way to Western diagnostic categories such as PTSD (Silove et al., 2008). At the same time it has been our experience that the Timorese can readily endorse symptoms of PTSD if asked and while those symptoms are associated with ongoing functional impairment (Silove et al., 2008), they do not define their suffering categorically in way that could be related to PTSD. Similarly treatment approaches developed within the context of the western trauma model differ substantially from traditional indigenous healing systems. The introduction of such models of care risk undervaluing indigenous approaches to understanding and healing locally recognised forms of distress.

There has been a subsequent call for mental health practitioners to be mindful of the immense power differentials between the well-resourced evidence-based models available to Western researchers and forms of traditional knowledge that may be vulnerable due to the fracture of surrounding social structures caused by conflict. Mental health practitioners are urged to give central attention to the values of the local world, accord genuine and deep respect for established cultural knowledge, and develop strategies to work in an effective relationship with indigenous healing systems.

In practice, this does not preclude applying Western psychiatric methods, but calls for a complementary or integrative process of incorporating local understandings and approaches that strives for a synthesis of knowledge that is consistent with the historical, cultural, and political context. The form that this will take will depend in part on each social context. Miller and colleagues (2006) provide some examples of how this synthesis might be reflected in practice. They urge the mental health professional to go beyond issues of individual morbidity to consider broader questions whose answers will increase the value gained by communities and local services, and where possible strengthen local healing worlds. One important procedure is to seek to understand and document local idioms of distress and explanatory models of illness (Patel, Gwanzura, Simunyu, Mann, & Lloyd, 1995). Also important is defining functioning and impairment in terms of the context of local lives (Bolton, Neugebauer, & Ndogoni, 2002). In considering models of service delivery, it is vital to examine culturally specific patterns that shape help-seeking behavior, expectations of treatment, and the nature of the healer–patient relationship. In so doing, it is important to map all the local resources that people access to address problems in order to deal with their social and emotional wellbeing. Many of these essentially ethnographic strategies build on a long tradition of anthropological methods that privileges and values the lived experiences of each cultural context. These types of approaches may offer creative ways for researchers and clinicians to highlight suffering and advocate for those affected, whilst attending to the broader issue of protecting fragile social and cultural fabric that is vital for recovery.

Psychology and forced migrants: Future directions—the ADAPT model

The ADAPT (Adaptation and Development after Persecution and Trauma) model emphasizes that posttraumatic stress disorder is not the only stress response observed in survivors of mass disasters (Silove, 1999; Silove & Steel, 2006). Displaced populations are vulnerable to a range of problems, including complicated grief, depression, somatoform disorders, drug and alcohol abuse, as well as a complex array of social problems. These outcomes have a complex relationship to a range of challenges faced by disaster-affected societies. The ADAPT model proposes that the key psychosocial domains that are threatened by disasters include: security and safety; interpersonal bonds and networks (the family, kinship groups, community, society); justice and protection from abuse; identities and roles (parent, worker, student, citizen, social leader, etc.); and institutions that confer existential meaning and coherence: traditions, religion, spiritual practices, political and social participation. Repairing these damaged systems and the institutions that support them forms the basis for building a framework of recovery for both individual survivors and their collectives. Successful humanitarian programs achieve this by creating durable conditions of safety and security; reuniting families, kinship groups, and communities; establishing effective systems of justice; creating the foundations for work, and the re-establishment of livelihoods, the pursuit of education, training, and other opportunities, and the establishment of national and other identities; and re-creating institutions that facilitate the practice of religion, cultural traditions, and participation in the governance of emerging societies, thereby establishing a sense of social coherence and meaning.

None of these recovery processes are easily achieved, however, with several obstacles (social, political, economic) retarding progress in many postconflict and resettlement settings. The less successful such processes are, the more prevalent will be community-wide distress. In particular, if conditions of danger and insecurity persist, then it is expectable that more members of the survivor community will continue to experience PTSD symptoms. Conversely, where conditions of durable safety are achieved, then the numbers with chronic conditions such as PTSD will be smaller. In that sense, social stability may be the best psychotherapist at the population level.

At the same time, it is inevitable that even in optimal recovery environments, there will be a minority of persons who, because of special vulnerabilities or the overwhelming nature of their trauma, will continue to experience chronic PTSD and other stress-related disorders, and their needs should not be overlooked. A series of randomized controlled trials have investigated the effectiveness of trauma-focused exposure therapies for symptoms of PTSD amongst displaced populations resettled to the West (Hinton et al., 2005; Hinton et al., 2004; Otto et al., 2003) and in low- and middle-income countries (Neuner, Schauer, Klaschik, Karunakara, & Elbert, 2004; Neuner et al., 2008) with encouraging findings. The extent to which these findings can be generalized to the provision of routine clinical care is uncertain with Carlsson, Mortensen, and Kastrup (2005) reporting little clinical benefit amongst 55 refugees with extensive trauma backgrounds receiving an average of 35 treatment sessions over an eight-month period. The development and evaluation of effective and practical interventions to assist survivors who have ongoing mental health problems remains a major challenge for the field in the coming decades.

Concluding Comments

The field of refugee and postconflict mental health has developed significantly over the previous few decades. The mental health effects of organized violence have been extensively documented across multiple populations from multiple source countries. While Miller and colleagues (2006) are correct to identify a need for the field to develop beyond an epidemiological focus, it is likely that the humanitarian and human rights imperative of documenting the consequences of mass conflict and organized violence will continue. The importance of the recovery environment has also been a major focus of research with an increasing body of evidence supporting the need for governments to adopt more humane policies of managing irregular asylum seekers as well as the imperative to provide a secure environment for populations affected by conflict as a part of mental health recovery. The evaluation of models of intervention remains in its infancy with formidable ongoing challenges to the field in identifying approaches that allow clinicians to address the needs of trauma-affected refugees at an individual level while also working towards addressing psychosocial stressors at the community level. An important ongoing challenge to the field relates to the need for researchers and clinicians from Western backgrounds to value and privilege the traditional knowledge and beliefs of refugee communities in our work.

References

Allodi, F. A. (1979, September). *Psychiatric effects of torture: A Canadian study.* Paper presented at the annual meeting of the Canadian Psychiatric Association, Vancouver, BC.

Allodi, F. A. (1980). The psychiatric effects in children and families of victims of political persecution and torture. *Danish Medical Bulletin*, *27*(5), 229–232.

Allodi, F. A. (1991). Assessment and treatment of torture victims: A critical review. *Journal of Nervous and Mental Disease*, *179*(1), 4–11.

Allodi, F. A., & Cowgill, G. (1982). Ethical and psychiatric aspects of torture: A Canadian study. *Canadian Journal of Psychiatry*, *27*, 98–102.

American Psychiatric Association. (1980). *Diagnostic and Statistical Manual of Mental Disorders* (3rd ed.). Washington, DC: American Psychiatric Association Press.

Amnesty International. (1977). *Evidence of torture: Studies of the Amnesty International Danish medical group* (No. PUB 72/00/77). London: Amnesty International Publications.

Bogner, D., Herlihy, J., & Brewin, C. R. (2007). Impact of sexual violence on disclosure during Home Office interviews. *British Journal of Psychiatry*, *191*, 75–81.

Bolton, P., Neugebauer, R., & Ndogoni, L. (2002). Prevalence of depression in rural Rwanda based on symptom and functional criteria. *Journal of Nervous & Mental Disease, 190*(9), 631–637.

Bracken, P. J., Giller, J. E., & Summerfield, D. (1995). Psychological responses to war and atrocity: The limitations of current concepts. *Social Science & Medicine, 40*(8), 1073–1082.

Breslau, J. (2004). Cultures of trauma: Anthropological views of posttraumatic stress disorder in international health. *Culture, Medicine, & Psychiatry, 28*(2), 113–126.

Breslau, N., Chase, G. A., & Anthony, J. C. (2002). The uniqueness of the DSM defnition of post-traumatic stress disorder: Implications for research. *Psychological Medicine, 32*, 573–576.

Cardozo, B. L., Vergara, A., Agani, F., & Gotway, C. A. (2000). Mental health, social functioning and attitudes of Kosovar Albanians following the war in Kosovo. *Journal of the American Medical Association, 284*, 569–577.

Carlsson, J. M., Mortensen, E. L., & Kastrup, M. (2005). A follow-up study of mental health and health-related quality of life in tortured refugees in multidiscipilinary treatment. *The Journal of Nervous and Mental Disease, 193*(10), 651–657.

Cmiel, K. (2004). The recent history of human rights. *The American Historical Review.*

de Jong, J. T. (2005). Deconstructing critiques on the internationalization of PTSD. *Culture, Medicine, & Psychiatry, 29*(3), 361–370.

de Jong, J. T., Komproe, I. H., Van Ommeren, M., El Masri, M., Araya, M., Khaled, N., … Somasundaram, D. (2001). Lifetime events and posttraumatic stress disorder in 4 post-conflict settings. *Journal of the American Medical Association, 286*(5), 555–562.

de Jong, K., Mulhern, M., Ford, N., van der Kam, S., & Kleber, R. (2000). The trauma of war in Sierra Leone. *Lancet, 355*, 2067–2068.

Dohrenwend, B., & Dohrenwend, B. S. (1982). Perspectives on the past and future of psychiatric epidemiology: The 1981 Rema Lapouse lecture. *American Journal of Public Health, 72*(11), 1271–1279.

Domovitch, E., Berger, P. B., Wawer, M. J., Etlin, D. D., & Marshall, J. C. (1984). Human torture: Description and sequelae of 104 cases. *Candian Family Physician, 30*, 827–830.

Eitinger, L. (1959). The incidence of mental disorders among refugees in Norway. *Journal of Mental Science, 105*, 326–338.

Fazel, M., Wheeler, J., & Danesh, J. (2005). Prevalence of serious mental disorder in 7000 refugees resettled in western countries: A systematic review. *Lancet, 365*, 1309–1314.

Fox, S. H., & Tang, S. S. (2000). The Sierra Leonean refugee experience: Traumatic events and psychiatric sequelae. *Journal of Nervous & Mental Disease, 188*(8), 490–495.

Gibney, M., & Dalton, M. (1996). The political terror scale. *Policy Studies and Developing Nations, 4*, 73–84.

Goldfeld, A. E., Mollica, R. F., Pesavento, B. H., & Faraone, S. V. (1988). The physical and psychological sequelae of torture: Symptomatology and diagnosis. *Journal of the American Medical Association, 259*(18), 2725–2729.

Gruskin, S., Mills, E. J., & Tarantola, D. (2007). History, principles, and practice of human rights. *The Lancet, 370*, 449–455.

Hashemian, F., Khoshnood, K., Desai, M. M., Falahati, F., Kasl, S., & Southwick, S. (2006). Anxiety, depression, and posttraumatic stress in Iranian survivors of chemical warfare. *Journal of the American Medical Association, 296*(5), 560–566.

Herlihy, J., Ferstman, C., & Turner, S. W. (2004). Legal isues in work with asylum seekers. In J. Wilson & B. Drozdek (Eds.), *Broken spirits: The treatment of traumatised asylum seekers, refugees, war and torture survivors* (pp. 641–658). New York: Brunner Routledge.

Herlihy, J., Scragg, P., & Turner, S. (2002). Discrepancies in autobiographical memories: Implications for the assessment of asylum seekers: Repeated interviews study. *British Medical Journal, 324*(Feb. 9), 324–327.

Herlihy, J., & Turner, S. (2006). Should discrepant accounts given by asylum seekers be taken as proof of deceit? *Torture, 16*(2), 81–92.

Hinton, D., Chhean, D., Pich, V., Safren, S., Hofmann, S., & Pollack, M. (2005). A randomized controlled trial of cognitive-behavior therapy for Cambodian refugees with treatment-resistant PTSD and panic attacks: A cross-over design. *Journal of Traumatic Stress, 18*(6), 617–629.

Hinton, D., Pham, T., Tran, M., Safren, S., Otto, M., & Pollack, M. (2004). CBT for Vietnamese refugees with treatment-resistant PTSD and panic attacks: A pilot study. *Journal of Traumatic Stress, 17*(5), 429–433.

Kinzie, J. D., Fredrickson, R. H., Ben, R., Fleck, J., & Karls, W. (1984). Posttraumatic stress disorder among survivors of Cambodian concentration-camps. *American Journal of Psychiatry, 141*(5), 645–650.

Kinzie, J. D., Tran, K. A., Breckenridge, A., & Bloom, J. D. (1980). An Indochinese refugee psychiatric clinic: Culturally accepted treatment approaches. *American Journal of Psychiatry, 137*(11), 1429–1432.

Kleinman, A. (1995). Violence, culture, and the politics of trauma. In A. Kleinman (Ed.), *Writing at the margin* (pp. 173–189). Berkeley, CA: University of California Press.

Krupinski, J., Stoller, A., & Wallace, L. (1973). Psychiatric disorders in East European refugees now in Australia. *Social Science & Medicine, 7*(1), 31–49.

Laban, C. J., Gernaat, H. B., Komproe, I. H., Schreuders, B. A., & de Jong, J. T. (2004). Impact of a long asylum procedure on the prevalence of psychiatric disorders in Iraqi asylum aeekers in the Netherlands. *Journal of Nervous & Mental Disease, 192*(12), 843–851.

Laban, C. J., Gernaat, H. B. P. E., Komproe, I. H., van der Tweel, I., & De Jong, J. T. V. M. (2005). Postmigration living problems and common psychiatric disorders in Iraqi asylum seekers in the Netherlands. *Journal of Nervous & Mental Disease, 193*(12), 825–832.

Lunde, I. (1982). Psykiske folger has torturofet [Mental sequelae to torture]. *ManedssKrift Praktisk Laegegerning* [Danish Medical Journal], *60*, 476–488.

Miller, K. E., Kulkarni, M., & Kushner, H. (2006). Beyond trauma-focused psychiatric epidemiology: Bridging research and practice with war-affected populations. *American Journal of Orthopsychiatry, 76*(4), 409–422.

Modvig, J., Pagaduan-Lopez, J., Rodenburg, J., Salud, C. M., Cabigon, R. V., & Panelo, C. I. (2000). Torture and trauma in post-conflict East Timor. *Lancet, 356*(9243), 1763.

Mollica, R. F., Donelan, K., Tor, S., Lavelle, J., Elias, C., Frankel, M., & Blendon, R. J. (1993). The effect of trauma and confinement on functional health and mental health status of Cambodians living in Thailand-Cambodia border camps. *Journal of the American Medical Association, 270*(5), 581–586.

Mollica, R. F., McInnes, K., Pham, T., Smith Fawzi, M. C., Murphy, E., & Lin, L. (1998). The dose-effect relationships between torture and psychiatric symptoms in Vietnamese ex-political detainees and a comparison group. *Journal of Nervous & Mental Disease., 186*(9), 543–553.

Mollica, R. F., McInnes, K., Poole, C., & Tor, S. (1998). Dose-effect relationships of trauma to symptoms of depression and post-traumatic stress disorder among Cambodian survivors of mass violence. *British Journal of Psychiatry, 173*, 482–488.

Mollica, R. F., McInnes, K., Sarajlic, N., Lavelle, J., Sarajlic, I., & Massagli, M. P. (1999). Disability associated with psychiatric comorbidity and health status in Bosnian refugees living in Croatia. *Journal of the American Medical Association*, *282*(5), 433–439.

Mollica, R. F., Wyshak, G., & Lavelle, J. (1987). The psychosocial impact of war trauma and torture on Southeast Asian refugees. *American Journal of Psychiatry*, *144*(12), 1567–1572.

Murphy, H. B. M. (1955). *Flight and resettlement*. Paris: UNESCO.

Neuner, F., Onyut, P. L., Ertl, V., Odenwald, M., Schauer, E., & Elbert, T. (2008). Treatment of posttraumatic stress disorder by trained lay counselors in an African refugee settlement: A randomized controlled trial. *Journal of Consulting and Clinical Psychology*, *76*(4), 686–694.

Neuner, F., Schauer, M., Klaschik, C., Karunakara, U., & Elbert, T. (2004). A comparison of narrative exposure therapy, supportive counseling, and psycheducation for treating post-traumatic stress disorder in an African refugee settlement. *Journal of Consulting and Clinical Psychology*, *72*(4), 579–587.

Otto, M., Hinton, D., Korbly, N., Chea, A., Ba, P., Gershuny, B., & Pollack, M. H. (2003). Treatment of pharmacotherapy-refractory posttraumatic stress disorder among Cambodian refugees: A pilot study of combination treatment with cognitive-behavior therapy vs sertraline alone. *Behaviour Research and Therapy*, *41*(11), 1271–1276.

Patel, V., Gwanzura, F., Simunyu, E., Mann, A., & Lloyd, K. (1995). The explanatory models and phenomenology of common mental disorder in Harare, Zimbabwe. *Psychological Medicine*, *25*, 1191–1199.

Petersen, H. D. (1989). The controlled study of torture victims: Epidemiological considerations and some future aspects. *Scandinavian Journal of Social Medicine*, *17*(1), 13–20.

Petersen, H. D., Abildgaard, U., Daugaard, G., Jess, P., Marcussen, H., & Wallach, M. (1985). Psychological and physical long term effects of torture. *Scandinavian Journal of Social Medicine*, *13*, 89–93.

Porter, M. (2007). Global evidence for a biopsychosocial understanding of refugee adaptation. *Transcultural Psychiatry*, *44*(3), 418–439.

Porter, M., & Haslam, N. (2005). Predisplacement and postdisplacement factors associated with mental health of refugees and internally displaced persons: A meta-analysis. *Journal of the American Medical Association*, *294*(5), 602–612.

Rasmussen, O. V., & Lunde, I. (1980). Evaluation of investigation of 200 torture victims. *Danish Medical Bulletin*, *27*(5), 241–243.

Scott, W. L. (1990). PTSD in DSM-III: A case in the politics of diagnosis and disease. *Social Problems*, *37*(3), 294–310.

Silove, D. (1999). The psychosocial effects of torture, mass human rights violations, and refugee trauma: Toward an integrated conceptual framework. *Journal of Nervous & Mental Disease*, *187*(4), 200–207.

Silove, D., Austin, P., & Steel, Z. (2007). No refuge from terror: The impact of detention on the mental health of trauma-affected refugees seeking asylum in Australia. *Transcultural Psychiatry*, *44*(3), 359–393.

Silove, D., Bateman, C., Brooks, R., Zulmira, F. C. A., Steel, Z., Rodger, J., … Bauman, A. (2008). Estimating clinically relevant mental disorders in a rural and urban setting in post-conflict Timor Leste. *Archives of General Psychiatry*, *65*(10), 1205–1212.

Silove, D., Sinnerbrink, I., Field, A., Manicavasagar, V., & Steel, Z. (1997). Anxiety, depression and PTSD in asylum seekers: associations with pre-migration trauma and post-migration stressors. *British Journal of Psychiatry*, *170*, 351–357.

Silove, D., & Steel, Z. (2006). Understanding community psychosocial needs after disasters: Implications for mental health services. *Journal of Postgraduate Medicine*, *52*(2), 121–125.

Silove, D., Steel, Z., Susljik, I., Frommer, N., Loneragan, C., Brooks, R., ... Harris, E. (2006). Torture, mental health status and the outcomes of refugee applications among recently arrived asylum seekers in Australia. *International Journal of Migration, Health and Social Care*, *2*(1), 4–14.

Steel, Z., Bateman-Steel, C. R., & Silove, D. (2009). Human rights and the trauma model: Genuine partners or uneasy allies? *Journal of Traumatic Stress Studies*, *22*(5), 358–365.

Steel, Z., Chey, T., Silove, D., Marnane, C., Bryant, R. A., & van Ommeren, M. (2009). Association of torture and other potentially traumatic events with mental health outcomes among populations exposed to mass conflict and displacement: A systematic review and meta-analysis. *Journal of the American Medical Association*, *302*(5), 537–549.

Steel, Z., Frommer, N., & Silove, D. (2004). Failing to understand: Refugee determination and the traumatized applicant. *International Journal of Law & Psychiatry*, *27*(6), 511–528.

Steel, Z., Mares, S., Newman, L., Blick, B., & Dudley, M. (2004). The politics of asylum and immigration detention: Advocacy, ethics and the professional role of the therapist. In J. P. Wilson & B. Drozdek (Eds.), *Broken spirits: The treatment of traumatised asylum seekers, refugees, war and torture survivors* (pp. 659–687). New York: Brunner-Routledge.

Steel, Z., & Silove, D. (2004). Science and the common good: Indefinite, non-reviewable mandatory detention of asylum seekers and the research imperative. [Peer-Reviewed]. *Monash Bioethics Review*, *23*(4), 93–103.

Steel, Z., Silove, D., Bird, K., McGorry, P., & Mohan, P. (1999). Pathways from war trauma to posttraumatic stress symptoms among Tamil asylum seekers, refugees, and immigrants. *Journal of Traumatic Stress*, *12*(3), 421–435.

Steel, Z., Silove, D., Chey, T., Bauman, A., Phan, T., & Phan, T. (2005). Mental disorders, disability and health service use amongst Vietnamese refugees and the host Australian population. *Acta Psychiatrica Scandinavica*, *111*(4), 300–309.

Summerfield, D. (1999). A critique of seven assumptions behind psychological trauma programmes in war-affected areas. *Social Science & Medicine*, *48*(10), 1449–1462.

Turner, S. W., Bowie, C., Dunn, G., Shapo, L., & Yule, W. (2003). Mental health of Kosovan Albanian refugees in the UK. *British Journal of Psychiatry*, *182*, 444–448.

Twiss, S. B. (2004). History, human rights and globalization. *Journal of Religious Ethics*, *32.1*, 39–70.

UNHCR. (2008). Asylum levels and trends in industralized countries 2008. Retrieved August, 2003 from www.unhcr.org/49c796572.html

UNHCR. (2010). *2009 Global trends: Refugees, asylum-seekers, returnees, internally displaced and stateless persons.* Geneva: United Nations High Commission for Refugees.

United Nations. (1975). *Declaration on the protection of all persons from torture and other cruel, inhumane, or degrading treatment or punishment.* General Assembly Resolution 3452, December 9, 1975 Geneva: United Nations.

United Nations. (1987). *Convention against torture and other cruel, inhuman or degrading treatment or punishment.* General Assembly Resolution. 39/46 June 26, 1987. Geneva: United Nations.

Weisaeth, L. (1989). Torture of a Norwegian ship's crew: The torture, stress reactions and psychiatric after-effects. *Acta Psychiatrica Scandinavica, Supplementum*, *355*, 63–72.

Westermeyer, J., Vang, T. F., & Neider, J. (1983). Refugees who do and do not seek psychiatric care. An analysis of premigratory and postmigratory characteristics. *Journal of Nervous & Mental Disease.*, *171*(2), 86–91.

World Medical Association. (1975). *Guidelines for medical doctors concerning torture and other cruel, inhuman or degrading treatment or punishment in relation to detention and imprisonment.* Adopted by the 29th World Medical Assembly, Tokyo, Japan, October 1975. Geneva: WMA.

Young, A. (1995). *The harmony of illusions: Inventing post-traumatic stress disorder.* Princeton: Princeton University Press.

31

The Evolution of Ethics in Psychology

Going International and Global

Janel Gauthier and Jean L. Pettifor

Psychologists live in a globalizing world where traditional boundaries are fading and, therefore, they increasingly work with persons from diverse cultural backgrounds within their own country or in other countries. Although human societies across the globe have been in a process of transformation since ancient times, the pace of transformation has increased dramatically since World War II. The economic, political, social, and technological developments that are accelerating in the early 21st century represent macro-level forces that are moving psychology toward a science and profession without borders *vis-à-vis* dialogue, understanding, and integration of knowledge across countries and cultures. In their book *Toward a Global Psychology*, Stevens and Gielen (2007) offer rich and varied evidence for the globalizing of psychology.

Ethics is at the core of psychology as a scientific discipline and a profession providing services to the public. The development of codes of ethics and ethical guidelines for psychologists is influenced by the phenomenon of globalization, as are many other professions. It takes a conscious effort to understand the implications for psychology of the cultural differences that exist, especially since most of us have not been nurtured or socialized in the multicultural aspects of today's changing world. It is helpful also to have knowledge of how ethics for psychologists is influenced by political and economic developments such as, for example, the creation of powerful regional trade treaties, or countries operating on a wartime status. The globalization of psychology provides new opportunities in research, education, practice, and social advocacy. The ideals and challenges for psychologists are to use their knowledge and skills to contribute to a more respectful, peaceful, just, and harmonious world, and to do so in ways that are ethically and morally sound.

The purpose of this chapter is twofold: (1) to review formally adopted regional and international ethics documents and discuss their meaning in terms of the evolu-

---

IAAP Handbook of Applied Psychology, First Edition. Edited by Paul R. Martin, Fanny M. Cheung, Michael C. Knowles, Michael Kyrios, Lyn Littlefield, J. Bruce Overmier, and José M. Prieto.

tion of ethics in psychology; and (2) to review the research literature on ethics from an international perspective and highlight important questions to consider for the advancement of international ethics.

Ethics Documents in Psychology: Regional and International Development

Historical context

Codes that determine desired professional and societal behaviors have been around since antiquity (e.g., Code of Hammurabi, Hippocratic Oath). Prior to World War II, however, ethics codes for psychologists did not exist. The convergence of several factors following the war contributed to the development of codes of ethics for psychologists.

In 1945–1946, the Nuremberg Trials disclosed to the world the extent of torture carried out by credible professionals in Nazi Germany. The public demanded greater scrutiny of the professions and stricter standards (Sinclair, Simon, & Pettifor, 1996). The *Nuremberg Code of Ethics on Medical Research* (1947) was developed and had tremendous influence on the subsequent development of professional codes of ethics. The *Nuremberg Code* (1947), the World Medical Association (WMA) *Declaration of Geneva* (WMA, 1948), and the WMA *Declaration of Helsinki* (WMA, 1964) formed the foundation for modern psychological research ethics in many Western countries.

In 1948, the United Nations adopted the *Universal Declaration of Human Rights* (United Nations, 1948) which required nations to commit to protecting the rights and entitlements of their citizens.

In 1945, the first legislation in North America for the regulation of psychological practice for the purpose of protecting the public from harm was passed in Connecticut (Pettifor, Estay, & Paquet, 2002). The remaining states in the United States and provincial/territorial jurisdictions in Canada all followed suit. Psychological practice gained credibility during World War II. With legislated regulation, it was also essential to develop codes of ethics and the means for handling disciplinary complaints. In 1948, the American Psychological Association (APA) began working on the first code of ethics for psychologists, again to protect the public from harm. In the development of its first code of ethics, the APA depended heavily on consultation with its members on the kinds of ethical dilemmas that they encountered in practice. A final draft was adopted on a trial basis by APA in 1952 and published in 1953 (APA, 1953; Fisher, 2003). Since then, the code has been revised nine times. The latest revision was adopted by the APA Council of Representatives in 2002 (APA, 2002). Over the years, the APA Ethics Code has been used as model for the development of codes in other psychology jurisdictions, albeit with modifications consistent with local needs.

Since the development of the first APA Ethics Code, there have been over 50 national codes of ethics developed globally (see www.am.org/iupsys/ethics/ethic-com-natl-list.html for a list), with the majority being developed in the past quarter-century. Within the last decade, many psychological organizations have been developing or revising their codes. For example, in the past five years, Iran and Turkey have developed their own codes, while China has revised its code of ethics for counseling and clinical practice.

The following provides an overview of the development of formally adopted ethics documents in psychology intended to be applied across national boundaries. As shown below, ethics codes have been developed by regional (i.e., groups of countries) and international psychological associations.

Regional development

In the 60-year history of ethics codes for psychologists, the consideration of ethics from a regional perspective is relatively new. In 1988, the Nordic countries (Denmark, Finland, Iceland, Norway, and Sweden) were among the first psychology regions to adopt a common code of ethics (Aanonsen, 2003). In 1996 and 1997, they revised their code to be consistent with the *Meta-Code of Ethics* of the European Federation of Psychologists' Associations (EFPA, formerly EFPPA—European Federation of Professional Psychologists Associations) (EFPPA, 1995). The revised version was adopted in 1998. Entitled *Etiske Prinsipper for Nordiske Psykologer* [Ethical Principles for Nordic Psychologists] (1998), it is organized around four main ethical principles: (a) respect for individual rights and dignity, (b) professional competence, (c) professional and scientific responsibilities, and (d) professional integrity. All the members of the Nordic psychological associations are obliged to follow these principles in their professional practice. The individual country associations or governments are responsible for the regulatory systems that include the investigation and adjudication of disciplinary complaints.

The development of the EFPA *Meta-Code of Ethics* (EFPPA, 1995; EFPA, 2005) is of interest as it is an example of how a regional association of psychologists with members from different countries can promote common high standards for ethical practice (Lindsay, Koene, Øvreeide & Lang, 2008). An EFPA Task Force on Ethics had been set up in 1990 with the aim of producing a common ethical code for psychologists in Europe. However, it was evident at the first meeting of the Task Force that this aspiration was unrealistic. Instead, the Task Force devised a meta-code that set out what each member association should address in their codes of ethics, but left it to the member associations to produce their own specific codes. Since EFPA adopted the *Meta-Code* in 1995, national associations with existing codes have revised their codes of ethics, as needed, to be consistent with the *Meta-Code*. European psychologists' associations without codes or in the process of developing a code have used or are using the *Meta-Code* as a template. The template comprises four ethical principles: (a) respect for a person's rights and dignity, (b) competence, (c) responsibility, and (d) integrity.

Another regional initiative is the development of the *Protocolo de Acuerdo Marco de Principios Éticos para el Ejercicio Profesional de los Psicólogos en el Mercosur y Paises Asociados* [*Protocol of the Framework Agreement of Ethical Principles for the Professional Practice of Psychology in the Mercosur and Associated Countries*] (1997) by the Comité

Coordinador de Psicólogos del Mercosur y Paises Asociados [Coordinating Committee of Psychologists of the Mercosur and Associated Countries] in South America. It was endorsed in 1997 by six southeast countries of South America that had formed in 1991 a common market called "Mercado Común del Sur" or "Mercosur" with Argentina, Brazil, Paraguay, and Uruguay as full members, and Chile and Bolivia as associated countries. The development of the document represents an example of how psychologists from different countries without a regional association were able to develop an ethical framework for the professional practice of psychology across several countries. The framework includes five "general" ethical principles: (a) respect for people's rights and dignity, (b) professional competence, (c) professional and scientific commitment, (d) integrity, and (e) social responsibility. The Coordinating Committee of Psychologists is responsible for the implementation of the *Protocol.*

International development

The interest of international psychology organizations in providing guidance regarding the ethical conduct of psychologists is not new. For example, in 1976, the General Assembly of the International Union of Psychological Science (IUPsyS) adopted a statement that requested each national member to enact a code of ethics that would enable taking action against any member guilty of human rights violations (IUPsyS, 1976). However, the development of international psychology organization ethics documents is quite recent.

The International School Psychology Association (ISPA) was among the first international psychology organizations to develop a code of ethics for its members. It adopted its code in 1990 (ISPA, 1990). The ISPA expects all school psychologists to exemplify the values and principles articulated in the code. The code addresses issues important to professional responsibilities, confidentiality, professional growth, professional limitations, professional relationships, assessment and research (Oakland, Goldman, & Bischoff, 1997).

The International Society of Sport Psychology (ISSP) developed ethical standards explicitly to ensure respect for the dignity and welfare of individuals, athletes, professionals, volunteers, administrators, teams, and the general public in the provision of services by its members (ISSP, n.d.). These standards are grouped according to seven "general principles": (a) competence, (b) consent and confidentiality, (c) integrity, (d) personal conduct, (e) professional and scientific responsibility, (f) research ethics, and (g) social responsibility. The ethical standards are expressed in general terms so that they can be applied to sport psychologists engaged in varied roles (Henschen, Ripoll, Hackfort, & Mohan, 1995). The code states that the application of the ethical standards may vary depending upon the context (e.g., country and organization).

The International Association of Marriage and Family Counselors (IAMFC) adopted ethical standards for practice by its members in 2002 and approved a revision of those standards in 2005 (IAMFC, 2005). The revised ethics document is divided into eight sections: (a) client well-being, (b) confidentiality, (c) competence, (d) assessment, (e) private practice, (f) research and publications, (g) supervision, and (h) media and public statement. Members are required not to impose personal values on the families with whom they work, to become multiculturally competent, and to use indigenous healing practices when appropriate.

The most recent international development in psychology ethics is the unanimous adoption of the *Universal Declaration of Ethical Principles for Psychologists* (2008) by the International Union of Psychological Science (IUPsyS) General Assembly and the International Association of Applied Psychology (IAAP) Board of Directors in 2008 (Gauthier, 2008a, 2008b, 2009; Ferrero & Gauthier, 2009). The rationale for developing a universal declaration of ethical principles for psychologists was threefold: (a) to ensure psychology's universal recognition and promotion of fundamental ethical principles, (b) to encourage the development of codes of ethics across the globe, and (c) to provide a shared moral framework for psychology to speak with a collective voice on matters of ethical concern. The task of the Ad Hoc Joint Committee was to develop a universal declaration of ethical principles for psychologists, not a worldwide code of ethics or code of conduct. A declaration of ethical principles reflects the moral principles and values that are expected to be addressed in a code of ethics or a code of conduct. Codes of conduct define what you must or must not do as a psychologist, whereas codes of ethics tend to be more aspirational, articulating ethical principles and values, as well as standards of behavior.

The *Universal Declaration of Ethical Principles for Psychologists* (2008) describes ethical principles based on shared human values across cultures. It includes a preamble followed by four sections, each relating to a different ethical principle: (a) respect for the dignity of persons and peoples, (b) competent caring for the well-being of persons and peoples, (c) integrity, and (d) professional and scientific responsibilities to society. Each section includes a statement defining the ethical principle and outlining fundamental ethical values contained in the principle.

The *Universal Declaration of Ethical Principles for Psychologists* (2008) is the product of a multiyear process involving careful research, broad international consultation, and numerous revisions in response to feedback and suggestions from the international psychology community. The development of the *Universal Declaration* is noteworthy inasmuch as it reflects a successful process that attained maximum generalizability and acceptance. The most important components of that strategy involved inclusiveness, research, consultation, and respect for cultural diversity:

- The *Universal Declaration* was developed by a working group that included distinguished scientists and practitioners in psychology representing major regions and cultures of the world. No attempt was made to have representation from all countries because a smaller group appeared more effective than a larger group for drafting a document. However, all countries that have membership in IUPsyS were given the opportunity to review and discuss progress reports and drafts of the *Declaration*. IUPsyS is an organization composed of national member organizations, not more than one national member per country. It is to psychology what the United Nations is to the world.
- Research results helped to identify the principles and values that would be considered for the framework to be used to draft the *Universal Declaration*. For example, comparisons were made among existing codes of ethics for psychologists from around the world to identify commonalities in ethical principles and values

(Gauthier, 2002, 2003, 2004, 2005); ethical principles and values espoused by other disciplines and communities also were examined (Gauthier, 2005); internationally accepted documents such as the *Universal Declaration of Human Rights* (United Nations, 1948) were reviewed to delineate their underlying moral imperatives (Gauthier, 2003, 2004); Eastern and Western history of modern-day ethical principles and values were explored (Gauthier, 2006; Sinclair, 2005a, 2005b, 2005c).

- The research-based framework and the draft document were presented for review and discussion at many international conferences and in many parts of the world. For example, focus groups of psychologists were held at international meetings in Asia, Europe, India, North America, South America, and the Middle East; international symposia were organized in Singapore, Vienna, Beijing, Granada, Athens, Prague, Kolkata, and Berlin. Further information regarding its development (e.g., background papers, progress reports and discussions on important issues) is available at the IUPsyS website (www.iupsys.org/ethics/univdecl2008.html).

Comments

This overview indicates that ethics documents have evolved considerably since the publication of the first code of ethics in psychology in 1953.

Ethics documents in psychology are becoming international and more global. The *Universal Declaration of Ethical Principles for Psychologists* (2008) represents the latest expression of this movement and the largest international effort of psychologists to establish an explicit moral framework of ethical principles that are based on shared human values across cultures. These ethical principles can serve as a universal guide in the initial development of a code of ethics or in a review of an established code of ethics, and in helping to develop culture-specific standards of behavior. Gauthier, Pettifor, and Ferrero (2010) have proposed a culture-sensitive model for creating and reviewing a code of ethics.

Another major development in ethics documents is the articulation of a moral ethical framework or philosophical foundation that is not only aspirational, but is clearly demonstrated in all value and standards statements that may follow. In the *Universal Declaration of Ethical Principles for Psychologists* (2008), for example, the ethical principle of Respect for Persons and Peoples is demonstrated in such values as confidentiality, consent, and privacy, which may be defined further in specific behaviors or standards according to local or regional cultures, customs, beliefs, and laws. Linking the moral framework directly to the standards has been embraced in countries such as Canada (Canadian Psychological Association CPA, 1986, 1991, 2000), Ireland (Psychological Society of Ireland, 1999), New Zealand (New Zealand Psychological Society, 2000), and Mexico (Sociedad Mexicana de Psicología, 2002, 2007). The EFPA *Meta-Code of Ethics* (EFPPA, 1995; EFPA, 2005) is another example of this recent development. In order to link behavior to ethical principles internationally and globally, it is essential to seek universal principles and shared values. The *Universal Declaration of Ethical Principles for Psychologists* (2008) has built on the growing practice of defining a moral or philosophical foundation of what have been identified as universally shared values.

Language has changed and definitions and themes have evolved. For example, the definitions provided by the *Canadian Code of Ethics for Psychologists* for respect for the dignity of persons (CPA, 1986, 1991, 2000) and by the APA Ethics Code for respect for people's rights and dignity (APA, 1992, 2002) are similar in content with an emphasis on moral rights. Furthermore, both the APA and CPA codes reflect Western societies' emphasis on individual rights and well-being more than on the collective good. In the *Universal Declaration of Ethical Principles for Psychologists* (2008), respect for the dignity of persons and peoples is described as "the most fundamental and universally found ethical principle" and is inclusive of non-Western and indigenous beliefs:

> All human beings, as well as being individuals, are interdependent social beings that are born into, live in, and are a part of the history and ongoing evolution of their peoples. The different cultures, ethnicities, religions, histories, social structures and other such characteristics of peoples are integral to the identity of their members and give meaning to their lives. The continuity of peoples and cultures over time connects the peoples of today with the peoples of past generations and the need to nurture future generations. As such, respect for the dignity of persons includes moral consideration of and respect for the dignity of peoples.

The meaning of words varies across cultures. It will continue to be a challenge to the global acceptance and implementation of ethical principles shared across cultures. One of the lessons learned in developing the *Universal Declaration* was the meaning of language: differences in meaning across cultures are not always immediately visible and how to cope with those differences is not always obvious (Gauthier et al., 2010). The importance of the meaning of language in a global society, without a global language, cannot be overemphasized.

The history of regional and international ethics documents reveals not only how ethics documents in psychology have evolved, it also highlights factors that have influenced their evolution over the last 65 years. For example, it shows that the development of regional ethical guidelines is often driven by politics and economics resulting from the creation of a common market. In Europe, for example, the EFPA *Meta-Code of Ethics* was first adopted in 1995, which is 38 years after the creation of a common market called the European Economic Community and two years after the Single Market was completed with the "four freedoms" of: movement of goods, services, people and money (see the "Maastricht" Treaty on European Union signed in 1993). In South America, the *Protocol of the Framework Agreement of Ethical Principles* was endorsed six years after the Mercosur was formed. The Nordic countries adopted their regional code of ethics in 1988, which is 34 years after the Common Nordic Labour Market was established (see the 1954 Common Nordic Labour Market Agreement) and seven years after the agreement on the common Nordic labour market in health care was signed (see the 1981 Common Nordic Labour Market Agreement in Health Care).

The history also shows that ethics documents tend to reflect concerns of the day and evolve according to changing world conditions. A huge concern after World War

II was the protection of people from harm. We have already mentioned the convergence of events in the late 1940s that led to the development of ethics codes for psychologists, namely the Nuremberg Trials, the United Nations' *Universal Declaration of Human Rights*, the legislated regulation of psychological practice, and the APA beginning to develop a code of ethics.

The *Universal Declaration of Ethical Principles for Psychologists* (2008) was developed some 55 years after the first APA Code of Ethics (APA, 1953). The rapid globalization of today's world means that isolation is impossible, that traditional national borders are rapidly fading, and that many countries are increasingly multicultural. On the one hand technology has opened the possibilities for global peace and harmony, while on the other hand it has increased the potential for universal suffering and destruction. The *Universal Declaration* was developed at a time when, for the sake of the future of our world, global consensus on what constitutes "good" is urgently needed. Looking for universality also means that the *Universal Declaration* does not address specific behaviors and rules for psychologists, for the simple reason that these are not universal, and hence must be culturally specific in their articulation, interpretation, and application. Today's world needs a renewed emphasis on ethical principles as a foundation for ethical standards, and a moral foundation that applies to individual professionals, professions and organizations as much as to governments.

Ethics Research in Psychology: Review from an International Perspective

Overview

This section provides an overview of significant ethics research in psychology from an international perspective.

Schuler (1982) conducted one of the first investigations examining ethical standards across national ethics codes. A comparison of standards for psychological research across nine national codes allowed him to identify three basic standards themes in all of them: protection from physical harm, protection from psychological harm, and confidentiality of data. More recently, Kimmel (1996) surveyed ethics codes from 11 countries. However, his survey did not include a comparative analysis of the specific standards within each code. Building on these two studies, Leach and Harbin (1997) reviewed 19 codes representing 24 countries and compared them with the APA's 1992 Ethics Code. The mean coverage of the APA principles across countries was 70.2%. The mean coverage of the standards was 34.4%, highlighting the existence of both common and culturally specific standards. Leach, Glosoff, and Overmier (2001) conducted a follow-up study to examine the inconsistencies and found eight standards unique to the APA code. Leach and his colleagues concluded that there are more common features among standards than differences, suggesting that psychology as a profession shares some common ethical concerns and standards regardless of geographical region.

Recently, comparisons of national organizations' ethics codes have been assessed for other ethics topics. For example, Leach and Oakland (2007) examined international ethics codes to determine specific test use and development standards in 35 countries. They found that approximately one-third of the codes did not specifically include test use at all. The most common standards found were those that required psychologists to explain test results to the appropriate parties, use tests properly, and restrict their use to qualified individuals only. Conversely, test construction and restricting the use of obsolete tests was rarely included in codes.

More recently, Leach (2009) examined the extent to which national codes of ethics prescribe a duty to disclose confidential information in order to protect persons from serious and imminent harm. He found specific duty-to-protect standards in approximately 70% of the codes referenced.

Another research area of interest for international ethics involves the study of the similarities and differences in ethical dilemmas among psychologists in different countries based on a methodology used by Pope and Vetter (1992). In the Pope and Vetter study, a sample of APA members were asked to "describe, in a few words or more detail, an incident that you or a colleague have faced in the past year or two that was ethically challenging or troubling to you" (p. 398). This same question was asked in nine, primarily Western, countries by various authors in the late 1990s, for which Pettifor and Sawchuk (2006) summarized the results. They found significant commonalities in the types of ethical dilemmas encountered by psychologists across the nine countries, with confidentiality being the most common. They concluded that country-specific differences were influenced less by cultural values and beliefs and more by workplace conditions and specific types of clientele seen for assessment and treatment.

A new research area is the examination of historical documents to identify the origin and history of ethical principles and values in current codes of ethics. The first study was conducted by Sinclair (2003, 2004, 2005a) and involved the examination of the following documents: the *Code of Hammurabi*, 18th century B.C.E.; the *Hippocratic Oath*, 5th century B.C.E.; the first American Medical Association code of ethics, 1847; the *Nuremberg Code of Ethics for Medical Research*, 1948; and the first APA code of ethics, 1953. Each document was examined to determine attitudes and expectations regarding confidentiality and informed consent, trying to be of benefit and doing no harm, staying within the limits of one's competence, truth-telling, and accountability. Although their emphases, application, and interpretation varied, the conclusion was that the ethical principles and values (with the exception of clear statements about consent) had been consistent over many centuries in the Western world.

Later, Sinclair (2005b) extended her research to eight further documents, this time from Eastern countries and cultures (e.g., China, Egypt, India, Japan, Persia). The documents varied from formal oaths taken by new physicians, to sets of instructions for physicians, to, in one case, a physician's prayer. Chronologically, they ranged from circa 300–500 BCE to 1770 CE. Each of the documents was examined for statements regarding the following: inherent worth of each human being, equality, and non-discrimination; consent; privacy/confidentiality; being of benefit and doing no harm; competence; truthfulness and honesty, avoiding conflict of interest; development of knowledge; contribution to humanity and concern for societal well-being; and respect for society, including accountability to society. Again, although the documents reviewed were from several different cultures and geographical locations, considerable consistency could be found across the many cultures, locations, and times represented.

Another research area in psychology ethics that has just begun to receive attention is the identification of ethical principles based on shared human values across cultures. Gauthier (2002, 2003, 2004, 2005) conducted the first series of studies specifically designed to identify "universal" ethical principles. In his first study, he compared codes of ethics from different countries and continents to identify the ethical principles having the strongest commonality across national and continental boundaries in psychology (Gauthier, 2002, 2003, 2004). He found the principles being most common to be: (a) respect for the dignity and rights of persons, (b) caring for others and concerns for their welfare, (c) competence, (d) integrity, and (e) professional and scientific responsibilities to society.

Studies comparing codes of ethics across countries can help to identify commonalities in ethical principles between codes of ethics. However, such studies have serious limitations when it comes to the identification of universal principles because codes of ethics from the West are more prevalent and hence tend to be overrepresented in these studies. As a result, ethical principles based on non-Western or indigenous cultures may be underrepresented.

Being cognizant of the limitations of his original study, Gauthier conducted further research to assess the "universality" of the ethical principles having the highest level of commonality in codes of ethics in psychology. He first reviewed internationally recognized documents such as the *Universal Declaration of Human Rights* (United Nations, 1948) and the *Universal Declaration of a Global Ethic* (Center for Global Ethics, 1998) (Gauthier, 2002, 2003, 2004). He then reviewed codes of ethics in disciplines dissimilar to psychology (e.g., sports coaching, martial arts) (Gauthier, 2004, 2005). Finally, he invited Carole Sinclair to review historical documents from Eastern civilizations (Sinclair, 2005c). Together, all three methodological approaches yielded results showing that the ethical principles most commonly used to articulate codes of ethics in psychology are based on human values shared across communities, disciplines and cultures throughout human history. Even where there are differences in the emphasis on individualism versus collectivism, science versus traditional healing, secular versus religious authority, and authoritarian versus democratic governance, there is a meeting ground in terms of respect, caring and competence, integrity, and the collective well-being of society.

Comments

The brief overview of the research literature on ethics from an international perspective confirms that there are universal ethical principles based on shared human values across cultures, and that they have roots in ancient times. There are, however, also important differences between codes of ethics and types of ethical dilemmas across countries. With this information, one can understand the cultural sensitivity required to develop meaningful regional and international codes of ethics.

The research providing an international perspective on ethics in psychology is small but currently is gaining momentum. As psychology goes international with the prospects of globalization, there are important questions to consider. Let us briefly highlight some of them. One major question is psychology's role as an agent of social change and social justice on an international and global level. Societal challenges are acute and life-threatening in many parts of the world and include such issues as: hunger, poverty, racism, violence, abuse of children and women, intergroup conflict, war, genocide, crime, torture, and terrorism. Many challenges have political implications. Psychologists in Western societies are committed to serving the public good, but have placed greatest emphasis on serving identified clients (persons, families, groups, including organizations or communities) rather than addressing the destructive forces in society that contribute to individual problems. Arguments have been made that psychologists are not trained to be agents of social change and that there is insufficient empirical evidence to support actions that are socially and politically controversial. Those who treat suffering individuals cannot avoid being concerned about the societal causes of human suffering. Psychologists who wish to be relevant globally may also find it necessary to learn new skills in addressing the serious social problems that exist. Are codes of ethics appropriately reflecting the need to protect people from harm? If not, what adjustments are required to address global issues? Are psychologists whose codes of ethics are based on an explicit moral framework more likely to engage in social action activities? To what extent will the application of the *Universal Declaration of Ethical Principles for Psychologists* (2008) influence psychology's involvement in social change and social justice activities? How will research on ethics be affected?

Another major question is the nature of indigenous psychology and the indigenization of psychology, and what is considered competent and credible within a discipline that is based on Western scientific concepts. Are codes of ethics from Western societies with their cultural emphasis on individualism, science, democracy, and secularism reflecting the needs and standards of non-Western and indigenous societies? If not, what adjustments are required, including how psychologists define psychology and what is competent and credible research, education, and practice?

Ethical guidelines can be local (state, province, or territory), national, regional or international. However, requirements for registration as a psychologist with a regulatory body, which is established to protect the public from harm, are usually local or national. Are those requirements able to accommodate international and global mobility and, at the same time, ensure the protection of the public from harm? If not, how can the issue of regulation be addressed?

International ethics documents, approved by international associations, often address such issues as respect for individuals, informed consent, confidentiality, privacy, and conflict of interest, all of which are subject to differences in cultural interpretations. Do international codes of ethics provide guidance on how to recognize and address beliefs and practices in different cultures? Do they provide guidance for situations in which one's own values are irrelevant or inconsistent with the local cultures or when one must consider what is meant by indigenization?

The *Universal Declaration of Ethical Principles for Psychologists* (2008) describes four ethical principles based on shared values across cultures (respect for the dignity of persons and peoples, competent caring for the well-being of persons and peoples, integrity, and professional and scientific responsibilities to society). If the broad field of psychology is one global profession, then these principles may be the cornerstone of the discipline. A fundamental question is whether these principles will result in better practices from an international perspective. Gauthier et al. (2010) have proposed a culture-sensitive model for applying the *Universal Declaration of Ethical Principles for Psychologists* in the creation and review of a code of ethics. Another question arises as to whether such models will result in the development of more culture-sensitive codes of ethics.

The *Universal Declaration of Ethical Principles for Psychologists* (2008) does not provide a model for ethical decision-making, and it is not the purpose of a universal declaration to do so. However, such models can be valuable tools for making ethical decisions because psychologists frequently face ethical dilemmas that are difficult to resolve. Dilemmas that involve cultural diversity are often among the more difficult to resolve in ways that respect and protect the well-being of all parties. Several models of ethical decision making are available in the literature (e.g., CPA, 2000; Fisher, 2003; Koocher & Keith-Spiegel, 2008). To what extent are decision-making practices related to ethical principles? Will decision-making practices become widely adopted regardless of country or culture? How will they differ across countries or cultures?

A greater understanding of life and times across national boundaries can only lead to a reduction in the perceived barriers to meeting physical and psychological needs, which in turn may lead to a major review and revision of our definitions of psychology and our approach to ethics in the past half century. We focus on the issues for psychology because that is the structure in which we exist, but we suggest that the issues are relevant to all allied professions and all professional activities that may impact on the well-being of persons and peoples.

Conclusion

In this chapter, we have reviewed the evolution of ethics codes for psychologists from their appearance in the mid 1900s to the present time. Standards of behavior have been a major concern in psychology. Over time, ethics codes have included explicit statements of overarching or underlying philosophical moral ethical principles. Research studies have supported the observation that many values are shared worldwide. This development was essential for the consideration of a universal set of ethical principles.

For the first time in the history of psychology, a universal set of ethical principles has been unanimously adopted by major international psychology organizations. It is important that as many psychologists as possible worldwide have the opportunity to consider its usefulness within their own cultural venue. It is equally important to learn how well it can help various countries, cultures, and organizations to develop or revise their own codes. In this process, there is promise of developing global ethical principles while still respecting local and regional differences in cultures, customs, beliefs, and laws. To be united on ethical principles promotes respect, understanding, peace, freedom, justice, humanity, and harmony in a world that at present is very fragmented and violent. Hopes for psychology's contribution to a better world require the promotion of aspirational ethical principles. There is promise of worldwide benefit for psychologists and those whom they serve in expanding our international horizons and global perspective.

References

Aanonsen, A. (2003). EFPA Metacode on ethics and the Nordic Code. In J. B. Overmier & J. A. Overmier (Eds.), *Psychology: IUPsyS global resource* [CD-ROM] (4th ed.). Hove, UK: Psychology Press.

American Psychological Association. (1953). *Ethical standards of psychologists.* Washington, DC: American Psychological Association.

American Psychological Association. (1992). Ethical principles of psychologists and code of conduct. *American Psychologist, 47,* 1597–1611.

American Psychological Association. (2002). Ethical principles of psychologists and code of conduct. *American Psychologist, 57,* 1060–1073.

Canadian Psychological Association. (1986). *Canadian code of ethics for psychologists.* Ottawa, ON: Canadian Psychological Association.

Canadian Psychological Association. (1991). *Canadian code of ethics for psychologists* (2nd ed.). Ottawa, ON: Canadian Psychological Association.

Canadian Psychological Association. (2000). *Canadian code of ethics for psychologists* (3rd ed.). Ottawa, ON: Canadian Psychological Association.

Center for Global Ethics. (1998). Toward a universal declaration of a global ethic. Retrieved June 20, 2009 from http://astro.temple.edu/~dialogue/Center/declarel.htm

European Federation of Professional Psychologists' Associations. (1995). *Meta-code of ethics.* Brussels: European Federation of Professional Psychologists' Associations.

European Federation of Psychologists' Associations. (2005). *Meta-code of ethics* (2nd ed.). Brussels: European Federation of Psychologists' Associations.

Etiske Prinsipper for Nordiske Psykologer [Ethical Code for Nordic Psychologists]. (1998). Oslo Norsk Psykologforening. Retrieved June 20, 2009 from www.finndegselv.no/Etiske_Retningslinjer_Psykologer.pdf Also retrieved June 20, 2009 (English translation) from www.psykologi.aau.dk/filer/praktik_ethical_guidance_for_nordic_psychologists.doc

Ferrero, A., & Gauthier, J. (2009). Desarrollo y adopción de la Declaración Universal de Principios Éticos para Psicólogas y Psicólogos [The development and adoption of the Universal Declaration of Ethical Principles for Psychologists]. *Boletín SIP, 90, March, n.d.* Retrieved June 20, 2009 from http://boletin.sipsych.org/index.php?id_page=12&todo=showpage&idtxt=87

Fisher, C. (2003). *Decoding the ethics code: A practical guide for psychologists.* Thousand Oaks, CA: Sage.

Gauthier, J. (2002, July). Ethics and human rights: Toward a universal declaration of ethical principles for psychologists. In J. L. Pettifor (Chair), *Professional codes of ethics across national boundaries: Seeking common grounds.* Symposium conducted at the 25th International Congress of Applied Psychology, Singapore.

Gauthier, J. (2003). Toward a universal declaration of ethical principles for psychologists. In J. B. Overmier & J. A. Overmier (Eds.). *Psychology: IUPsyS Global Resource* [CD-ROM] (4th ed.). Hove, UK: Psychology Press.

Gauthier, J. (2004). Toward a universal declaration of ethical principles for psychologists. *International Association of Applied Psychology/Newsletter, 16*(4), 10–24.

Gauthier, J. (2005). Toward a universal declaration of ethical principles for psychologists: A progress report. In M. J. Stevens & D. Wedding (Eds.), *Psychology: IUPsyS global resource* [CD-ROM] (6th ed.). Hove, UK: Psychology Press.

Gauthier, J. (2006). Onward toward a universal declaration of ethical principles for psychologists: Draft and progress report. In M. J. Stevens & D. Wedding (Eds.). *Psychology: IUPsyS global resource* [CD-ROM] (7th ed.). Hove, UK: Psychology Press.

Gauthier, J. (2008a). IAAP adopts the Universal Declaration of Ethical Principles for Psychologists. *The IAAP Bulletin: The International Association of Applied Psychology, 20*(4), 110–112.

Gauthier, J. (2008b). The Universal Declaration of Ethical Principles for Psychologists presented at the United Nations DPI/NGO Conference in Paris. *Psychology International, 19*(4), October. Retrieved June 20, 2009 from www.apa.org/international/pi/1008gauthier.html

Gauthier, J. (2009). Ethical principles and human rights: Building a better world globally. *Counselling Psychology Quarterly, 22*, 25–32.

Gauthier, J., Pettifor, J., & Ferrero, A. (2010). The Universal Declaration of Ethical Principles for Psychologists: A culture-sensitive model for creating and reviewing a code of ethics. *Ethics and Behavior, 20*(3&4), 179–196.

Henschen, K., Ripoll, H., Hackfort, D., & Mohan, J. (1995). Ethical principles of the International Society of Sport Psychology (ISSP). *International Journal of Sport Psychology, 26*, 588–591.

International Association of Marriage and Family Counsellors. (2005). Ethical code. Retrieved June 20, 2009 from www.iamfc.com/revised_ethical_codes.doc

International School Psychology Association. (1990). Codul etic al ISPA [ISPA Code of Ethics]. Retrieved June 20, 2009 from www.ispaweb.org/Documents/Codul%20etic%20al%20ISPA.doc

International Society of Sport Psychology. (n.d.). Ethical principles of the International Society of Sport Psychology. Retrieved May 30, 2009 from www.issponline.org/p_codeofethics.asp?ms=3

International Union of Psychological Science. (1976). Statement by the International Union of Psychological Science. Retrieved May 25, 2005 from www.amnesty.org/pages/health-ethics6-eng

Kimmel, A. J. (1996). *Ethical issues in behavioural research: A survey.* Cambridge, MA: Blackwell Publishers.

Koocher, G. P., & Keith-Spiegel, P. (2008). *Ethics in psychology: Professional standards and cases* (3rd ed.). New York: Oxford University Press.

Leach, M. M. (2009). International ethics codes and the duty to protect. In J. Werth, E. L. Welfel, & A. Benjamin (Eds.). *The duty to protect: Ethical, legal, and professional considerations in risk assessment and intervention* (pp. 41–58). Washington, DC: American Psychological Association.

Leach, M. M., Glosoff, H., & Overmier, J. B. (2001). *International ethics codes: A follow-up study of previously unmatched standards and principles.* In J. B. Overmier & J. A. Overmier (Eds.), *Psychology: IUPsyS global resource* [CD-ROM] (2nd ed.). Hove, UK: Psychology Press.

Leach, M. M., & Harbin, J. J. (1997). Psychological ethics codes: A comparison of twenty-four countries. *International Journal of Psychology, 32*, 181–192.

Leach, M. M., & Okland, T. (2007). Ethics and standards impacting test development and use: A review of 31 ethics codes impacting practices in 35 countries. *International Journal of Testing, 7*, 71–88.

Lindsay, G., Koene, C., Øvreeide, H., & Lang, F. (2008). *Ethics for European psychologists.* Cambridge, MA: Hogrefe & Huber Publishers.

New Zealand Psychological Society. (2002). *Code of Ethics for Psychologists Working in Aotearoa/New Zealand.* Wellington: Author. Also available online from www.psychology.org.nz/Code_of_Ethics

Nuremberg Code (1947). *Trials of War Criminals before the Nuremberg Military Tribunals under Control Council Law No. 10: Vol. 2* (pp. 181-182). Washington, DC: U.S.

Government Printing Office. Also available online from www.hhs.gov/ohrp/references/nurcode.htm

Oakland, T., Goldman, S., & Bischoff, H. (1997). Code of ethics of the International School Psychology Association. *School Psychology International, 18*, 291–298.

Pettifor, J. L., Estay, I., & Paquet, S. (2002). Preferred strategies for learning ethics in the practice of a discipline. *Canadian Psychology, 42*, 260–269.

Pettifor, J. L., & Sawchuk, T. R. (2006). Psychologists' perceptions of ethically troubling incidents across international borders. *International Journal of Psychology, 41*, 216–225.

Pope, K. S., & Vetter, V. (1992). Ethical dilemmas encountered by members of the American Psychological Association: A national survey. *American Psychologist, 47*, 397–411.

Protocolo de Acuerdo Marco de Principios Éticos para el Ejercicio Profesional de los Psicólogos en el Mercosur y Paises Asociados [Ethical Principles Framework for professional practice of psychology in the Mercosur and Associated States]. (1997), Santiago, Chile.

Psychological Society of Ireland. (1999). *Code of professional ethics.* Dublin: Psychological Society of Ireland.

Schuler, H. (1982). *Ethical problems in psychological research.* New York: Academic Press.

Sinclair, C. (2003, 2004, 2005a). A brief history of ethical principles in professional codes of ethics. In J. B. Overmier & J. A. Overmier (Eds.), *Psychology: IUPsyS global resource* [CD-ROM] (4th, 5th, and 6th eds.). Hove, UK: Psychology Press.

Sinclair, C. (2005b). The eastern roots of ethical principles and values. In M. J. Stevens & D. Wedding (Eds.), *Psychology: IUPsyS global resource* [CD-ROM] (6th ed.). Hove, UK: Psychology Press.

Sinclair, C. (2005c, July). The roots of ethical principles and values in codes of ethics. In J. L. Pettifor (Chair), *Cultural implications for a Universal Declaration of Ethical Principles.* Symposium conducted at the 9th European Congress of Psychology, Granada, Spain.

Sinclair, C., Simon, N. P., & Pettifor, J. L. (1996). The history of ethical codes and licensure. In L. J. Bass, S. T. DeMers, J. R. P. Ogloff, C. Peterson, & J. L. Pettifor (Eds.), *Professional conduct and discipline in psychology* (pp. 1–15). Washington, DC: American Psychological Association.

Sociedad Mexicana de Psicología. (2002). *Código Ético del Psicólogo* [Psychologist's code of ethics] (3rd ed.). México, DF: Editorial Trillas.

Sociedad Mexicana de Psicología. (2007). *Código Ético del Psicólogo* [Psychologist's code of ethics] (4th ed.) México, DF: Editorial Trillas.

Stevens, M. J., & Gielen, U. P. (Eds.). (2007). *Toward a global psychology: Theory, research, intervention, and pedagogy.* Mahwah, NJ: Lawrence Erlbaum Associates.

United Nations. (1948). Universal Declaration of Human Rights. Retrieved June 20, 2009 from www.un.org/en/documents/udhr

Universal Declaration of Ethical Principles for Psychologists (2008). Retrieved June 20, 2009 from www.iupsys.net/index.php/policy/113-universal-declaration-of-ethical-principles-for-psychologists

World Medical Association. (1948). Declaration of Geneva. Retrieved June 20, 2009 from www.wma.net/e/policy/c8.htm

World Medical Association. (1964). Declaration of Helsinki. Retrieved June 20, 2009 from www.wma.net/e/policy/b3.htm

Part IV
Conclusions

32

Applied Psychology in the International Context

What More Needs to Be Done?

Paul R. Martin

Anyone reading this Handbook with a knowledge of the development of applied psychology over the last century will marvel at the progress that has been made. A few examples of the changes will be offered. Most ancient scientists were "polymaths," people whose expertise filled a significant number of subject areas. Leonardo Da Vinci (1452–1519) is usually considered the ultimate "Renaissance man," as he was one of the world's great artists on the one hand, and a great anatomist, scientist, and engineer on the other (and his paintings are considered masterpieces at depicting a variety of psychological states). The man most often considered to be the founder of applied psychology was Hugo Münsterberg (1863–1916), a German-American student of Wilhelm Wundt, and whilst his capacity in the arts has not been documented, the breadth of his contributions in applied psychology are breathtaking. In a 10-year period, he wrote nine books in English (not his first language) applying psychology to law (eyewitness testimony was a particular interest—see Chapter 15), mental health, education, industrial efficiency, business, teaching, and films. The field of applied psychology has developed to a point where it is unimaginable that one individual could write books pertaining to most of the main professional specializations of applied psychology—and all in a decade.

In the early days of applied psychology, even the terminology was different. The international congresses of applied psychology were referred to as the "Psychotechnics Congresses." When I first saw the term "psychotechnics," I thought of fireworks but realized that I was confusing the term with "pyrotechnics," and consultation of an online dictionary revealed that it actually meant "the practical or technological application of psychology, as in analysis of social or economic problems."

Applied psychology in its early days was dominated by Europe and North America. This domination continues and will be discussed subsequently, but other regions of

IAAP Handbook of Applied Psychology, First Edition. Edited by Paul R. Martin, Fanny M. Cheung, Michael C. Knowles, Michael Kyrios, Lyn Littlefield, J. Bruce Overmier, and José M. Prieto.

the world are becoming more involved. For example, the first international congress of applied psychology was organized in Geneva in 1920. During the four decades 1920 to 1960, 16 international congresses of applied psychology were held of which 14 were in Europe (mainly Western Europe) and two were in North America. In contrast, in the four decades 1974–2014, 11 international congresses of applied psychology have been held or are planned, and of these, five were or will be in Europe, two in North America, two in East Asia, and one each in the Middle East and the Pacific Rim. Inspection of the editors/authors of this Handbook supports the observation of the continuing dominance of psychologists from North America and Europe, but 20 out of the 78 editors/authors (25.6%) are from other regions of the world.

The global expansion of psychology has been remarkable. Lunt and Poortinga (1996) made the comical observation "In the 1980s, it was said that all the inhabitants of Spain would be psychologists somewhere in the early decades of the next century if the exponential growth of students registering for psychology continued" (p. 504). Sexton and Hogan (1992) commented upon the record increase in the number of psychologists worldwide through the early 1990s, with marked expansion in Brazil, Israel, Spain, and South America. In their *Handbook of International Psychology*, Stevens and Wedding (2004a) sampled 27 countries and reported evidence of growth in psychology in all of them. For example, Brazil has over 10,000 psychologists joining its workforce every year. Israel increased its number of psychologists by more than 100% between the late 1990s and the publication of their Handbook in 2004. Psychology attracts more students than any other academic discipline in many countries including the UK and Australia. In heavily industrialized countries the expansion of psychology has not plateaued. In Germany, for example, the number of students studying psychology more than doubled in less than 30 years. In developing countries, the number of universities with psychology programs and the number of psychologists with advanced degrees is growing. The Philippines reported, for example, that 32% of its 249 psychology programs were inaugurated in the last decade.

In this concluding chapter of the Handbook, five related questions will be addressed:

- Where has psychology contributed and where could it contribute more?
- What do different regions of the world contribute to the advancement of psychology, and what are the problems with the current situation?
- What organizations are contributing to international psychology and what do they do?
- What more could be done by international psychology organizations?
- How could international psychology organizations achieve more?

Where Has Psychology Contributed and Where Could It Contribute More?

This Handbook is testimony to the extremely wide range of applications of psychology. We have included all the major professional specializations and substantive areas of applied psychology. With respect to the major challenges faced by the world, we have included chapters specifically focused on these challenges such as the chapters on poverty, terrorism, and refugees. Many of the other major challenges are addressed in the earlier chapters such as the environment, climate change, and aging populations.

Nevertheless, it is hard to escape the impression that psychologists have, for whatever reason, tended to focus their research efforts on a subset of potential applications, committing relatively little effort to many issues of global significance. As an illustration of this point, the American Psychological Association (APA) has established "Research in Action" (formerly "Psychology Matters"), which is a web-based compendium of psychological research that demonstrates the application and value of psychology in our everyday lives (www.apa.org/research/action/index.aspx). It is a sampling of the many successful and promising research areas in psychology, and is an exciting read for all of us who are passionate about applied psychology. Twenty-one topics are listed and resources are included under each. One topic listed is "Health and Well-Being" and 38 resources are included under this topic. This is twice as many resources as any other topic. The next four topics with the most resources included are: "Children" (19), "Education" (18), "Parenting" (15), and "Testing and Assessment" (11). Environmental sustainability is considered a global challenge for humanity, whatever source is consulted, and yet the topic "Environmentally Friendly Behaviors" includes only one resource.

In pondering the place of psychology in forwarding society's agenda, the Australian experience of setting national research priorities provides food for thought. In 2001, the Australian Government produced a strategy called "Backing Australia's Ability" that was focused on science, engineering, and technology as the key drivers of technological change, competitiveness, and prosperity. Four research priorities were identified: Nano-Materials and Biomaterials; Genome/Phoneme Research; Photonics; and Complex/Intelligent Systems. Over the next two or three years, the crucial role of the social sciences and the humanities as contributors to national research knowledge and innovation was increasingly recognized, which in turn led to recognition of additional domains that needed to be incorporated into the national research priorities such as health, environment, and security. The result was a new set of four national research priorities: An Environmentally Sustainable Australia; Promoting and Maintaining Good Health; Frontier Technologies for Building and Transforming Australian Industries; and Safeguarding Australia.

The "Academy of Social Sciences in Australia" is an autonomous, nongovernmental organization, devoted to the advancement of knowledge and research in the various social sciences (www.assa.edu.au), and it commissioned a series of papers in response to the new research priorities at the invitation of the responsible government minister (Academy of Social Sciences in Australia, 2003). One of the recommendations in the papers was that a fifth national research priority be added entitled "Building Australia's Creative and Innovative Capability." It was argued that "research into fostering and developing capable, skilled, educated, creative and innovative people is essential to greatly increase the likelihood that the national research effort and its nominated priority areas will actually deliver novel, smart, timely, and implementable solutions" (p. 22). Unfortunately, this recommendation was not taken up, although there is now a goal listed under "Frontier Technologies" called "Promoting an Innovation Culture and Economy."

The Academy report promotes the contribution of the social sciences, including psychology (at the time of the report, the President of the Academy was a psychologist), to the research priorities as listed. For example, it starts its response to "Safeguarding Australia" by pointing out that most people probably think of attacks on our lives and property when they see this research priority, but that we are far more likely to fall prey to accidents, mismanagement, or natural occurrences. It illustrates this point in various ways including that our harbors and coastal waterways are in more danger from ships flushing their bilges than from acts of terrorism. The report argues that "Research in the social sciences can, and should, move 'Safeguarding Australia' from being centered on, or wholly enveloped by, defensive/reactive postures to a position where rational and necessary defence mechanisms work cooperatively with anticipatory, flexible, engaging and adaptive policies that are guided by social science research" (p. 25).

The Academy report pointed out that the research priorities constituted a policy intervention and hence should be evaluated, and that it was social scientists who had the most expertise in this domain. The report also argued that the national research priorities were an exercise in bringing together researchers in new multidisciplinary projects, and social scientists had the expertise in promoting mechanisms to build cooperation, coordination, and trust.

Consideration of the above suggests the following tentative conclusions in the Australian context. First, when the government thinks of national research priorities its initial reaction is to consider the physical sciences, engineering, and technology, rather than person- and community-orientated goals. Second, with much lobbying by psychology and related disciplines, the agenda can be broadened out, but it will still fall short of what most psychologists would argue for. Third, there is a lack of recognition that psychology has much to offer even to the research priorities that they designate. And finally, psychology must accept the blame for some of these problems because many significant research goals that psychology could contribute to do not get a lot of attention. With respect to this last point, one would suspect that the amount of research by psychologists related to the research priority "Promoting and Maintaining Good Health" would be far greater than the amount of research related to the other three priorities combined.

Pawlik and d'Ydewalle (1996) have argued that future challenges for society will increasingly require the behavioral sciences and the adoption of an international approach. They point out, for example, that global climatic change is a worldwide phenomenon with causes (e.g., greenhouse gas emission), effects (e.g., ozone depletion and global warming), and impacts (e.g., on human lifestyles), that reach far beyond national boundaries, necessitating international cooperation on a scale far beyond mere linkage of laboratories or networking of scholars. Another example they give relates to behavioral science contributions to the development of multi-ethnic living, as increased opportunities for travel and demographic pressures lead to increased migration, resulting in population changes that humankind will not adapt to easily.

What Do Different Regions of the World Contribute to the Advancement of Psychology, and What Are the Problems with the Current Situation?

Simonton (1992) has argued that, during the 20th century, the discipline of psychology underwent a transformation that included a shift away from the European-influenced philosophical psychology of the late 19th century to the empirical, research-based, American-dominated psychology of today. This may be true, but Wilhelm Wundt, a German psychologist, is widely regarded as the "Father of Experimental Psychology," and is credited with establishing the first laboratory for psychological research in Leipzig in 1879. The first experimental psychology laboratory in the USA was established by G. Stanley Hall, a student of Wundt, in 1883. G. Stanley Hall went on to found the APA in 1892 and serve as its first President. In 1917, he established the *Journal of Applied Psychology*, the oldest and largest top-tier journal publishing theory and research relevant to industrial and organizational psychology. Van de Vijver and Lonner (1995) argued that world events during the 1930s saw the center of gravity in Western psychology shift from Europe to the USA.

I analyzed country of origin of psychology publications using ISI Web of Science and the top 10 countries were: (i) USA, 39.7%; (ii) England, 7.8%; (iii) Canada, 4.6%; (iv) Germany, 3.1%; (v) Australia, 2.9%; (vi) The Netherlands, 1.8%; (vii) France, 1.5%; (viii) Spain, 1.0%; (ix) Scotland, 1.0%; and (x) The People's Republic of China, 0.9%. The contribution of the USA seems large given that their population represents only 4.5% of the world's population; and it was estimated in 1999 that approximately 20–25% of the world's psychologists worked in the USA (Rosenzweig, 1999), a percentage that is probably smaller a decade later. However, most bibliometric analyses have estimated the proportion of publications from the USA as even higher, although it has been falling over the years. For example, Bauserman (1997) examined the national affiliations of first authors in all PsycLIT abstracts and reported that authors with US affiliations dropped from 75% in 1975 to 54% in 1994. Adair, Coelho, and Luna (2002) used a similar methodology to assess the years 1990, 1994, and 1998 combined, and reported that 55% of first authors had an American affiliation. Arnett (2008) analyzed the authorship of articles in six leading APA journals between 2003 and 2007. He reported the following percentages of first authors: (i) USA, 73%; (ii) English-speaking countries, 14%; (iii) Europe, 11%; (iv) Asia, 1%; and (v) Israel, 1%. There was one publication from Latin America and none from Africa or the Middle East. The pattern was substantially the same for other authors.

Haggbloom et al. (2002) published a list of the 100 most eminent psychologists of the 20th century (99 were actually listed). This list was compiled by combining the following four measures: journal citation frequency; introductory psychology textbook citation frequency; a survey of members of the American Psychological Society; and a qualitative measure of eminence which took account of: (i) whether the psychologist was elected a member of the National Academy of Science; (ii) whether he or she was a recipient of the APA Distinguished Scientific Contributions Award or elected APA President or both; and (iii) whether his or her surname was used as an eponym (e.g., Skinner Box, Pavlovian conditioning). Lists were published for each criterion separately as well as the composite list. Not surprisingly, names such as Skinner, Piaget, Freud, and Bandura, dominated the lists.

Of the 99 most eminent psychologists listed, 72 were born and had worked in the USA, 15 were born and had worked in Europe (including the UK), and 5 were born in Europe and moved to the USA to work. Canada was the only other country with multiple entries. Haggbloom et al. (2002) acknowledged that their eminent list does have an American and an English-language bias as all their sources were American. In PsycINFO, languages other than English make up less than 6% of the data base, with German, French, and Spanish, each contributing around 1%.

Parenthetically, inspection of the list of most eminent psychologists reveals other ways in which this list is hardly representative of the world or even of psychologists. For example, 39% of psychologists on the list are Jewish (including individuals of half- or three-quarters Jewish descent) (www.jinfo.org/Psychologists_100_Most_Eminent.html). Jewish people make up less than 0.2% of the world population. There are no females in the top 50 most eminent psychologists and only six in the top 100, despite the roughly equal balance in the world population and the predominance of women in the psychology workforce (Stevens & Wedding, 2004b).

So what are the problems of the discipline of psychology being dominated by North America with Europe as the other main contributor? In a provocative article entitled "The neglected 95%: Why American psychology needs to become less American," Arnett (2008) argued that American psychology was based on American samples, and it was therefore debatable the degree to which the findings could be generalized to the rest of the world. In developing this argument he pointed out that in the six APA journals that he analyzed, 67% of the samples were American undergraduate students, which led to the tongue-in-cheek suggestion that APA journals should be renamed along the lines of the *Journal of American Abnormal Psychology*. He articulated demographic contrasts between the economically developed countries and the developing countries that comprise the majority of the world's population, including the huge differences in income, education, and health, which raised doubts about whether the psychology that was emerging from studies on such a small and unrepresentative sample of the world's population could be considered a human science.

Arnett went on to argue that a major problem with American psychology was that it had adopted a philosophy of science focused on experimental methods where the primary goal was "to control the experiment so that the distracting variables of real life could be stripped away in order to reveal the essence of the phenomenon" (2008, p. 610). This emphasis on fundamental processes ignores or strips away cultural context.

Stevens and Wedding (2004c) have criticized Western psychology for its focus on interpersonal causation, which has yielded incomplete accounts of phenomena in the non-Western world. They argued that it has limited transnational usefulness because it is relatively decontextualized and psychologists often fail to appreciate the significance of the domains in which human functioning is embedded. They also argued that Western psychology leans toward reductionism and as a result psychologists frequently dismantle the unity that provides a more accurate, complete and meaningful view of psychological phenomenon. In summary, they suggest that Western psychology has limited utility when applied to complex and contextual global issues.

What Organizations are Contributing to International Psychology and What Do They Do?

Organizations that contribute directly to international psychology fall into three categories: international organizations with interests across the spectrum of psychology; international organizations with interests in specific domains of psychology; and national associations with constituent units that focus on the international arena. There are also regional associations with agendas that go beyond national frontiers. Stevens and Wedding (2004c) have estimated that there are over 250 international and regional associations, so only the larger ones will be considered here.

The oldest organization in the first category is the International Association of Applied Psychology (IAAP) (www.iaapsy.org/) founded in 1920 as the Association International de Psychotechnique. Its mission is to promote the science and practice of applied psychology and to facilitate interaction and communication about applied psychology around the world. It has over 1,500 members from more than 90 countries, and has 17 Divisions that represent the interests of its members, such as the Division of Work and Organizational Psychology and the Division of Health Psychology. It publishes two journals (*Applied Psychology: An International Review* and *Applied Psychology: Health and Well-Being*), and holds Congresses every four years. The IAAP has relationships with a number of agencies of the United Nations (UN). It is a non-governmental organization (NGO) accredited to the UN Department of Public Information, and has been accredited with Special Consultative Status to the UN Economic and Social Council (ECOSOC). It is an associate member of the International Social Science Council (ISSC), which is under the auspice of the United Nations Educational, Scientific and Cultural Organization (UNESCO).

Also in this category is the International Union of Psychological Science (IUPsyS) (www.iupsys.org), founded in 1951, but having evolved from a committee that organized international congresses dating back to the International Congress of Physiological Psychology held in Paris in 1889. This organization works to promote the development, representation, and advancement of psychology as a basic and applied science nationally, regionally, and internationally. Whilst the missions of IAAP and IUPsyS have much in common, their structures are quite different as IUPsyS is an organization composed of national member organizations, with not more than one per country. Some national members are psychological associations whilst others are national academies of science. There are currently 71 national members representing over 500,000 psychologists. Thirteen organizations have affiliate status with IUPsyS and two organizations have special liaison status, and these organizations include all the international associations discussed here. IUPsyS publishes a journal (*International Journal of Psychology*) and an annual CD ROM (*Psychology: IUPsyS Global resource*), and holds Congresses every four years. IUPsyS is linked with a number of UN agencies including UNESCO, ISSC and WHO. It is also a member of the International Council for Science (ICSU), an NGO devoted to international co operation in the advancement of science.

The International Council of Psychologists (ICP) (www.iupsys.org) was founded in 1941 with a mission to advance scientific psychology and its global application. It has members from over 80 countries. ICP publishes the *International Psychologist* and hosts thematic annual conferences. It has NGO status at ECOSOC.

In the second category are organizations like the International Test Commission (ITC) and International Association for Cross-Cultural Psychology (IACCP). ITC (www.intestcom.org/) is an association of national psychological associations, test commissions, test publishers, and other organizations committed to effective testing and assessment policies and to the development, evaluation, and proper use of psychometric instruments. IACCP (www.iaccp.org/) was founded in 1972 and has 800 members from more than 65 countries. The aim of the association is to facilitate communication among persons interested in a diverse range of issues involving the intersection of culture and psychology.

With respect to the third category, not all national psychology associations have a unit focusing on the international arena, and the units of those that do vary in scope from small, such as the Standing Committee on International Relations of the Australian Psychological Society, to large, such as the Division of International Psychology of the American Psychological Association (APA52) (http://orgs.tamu-commerce.edu/div52/). The APA has a long-standing commitment to international psychology reflected in having a Director of International Affairs who oversees the activities of its Committee on International Relations in Psychology (CIRP). In 1997, this commitment was taken a step further by the foundation of APA52, which serves psychologists interested in collaborating with colleagues from around the world in teaching, research, and the practice of psychology. Its activities include maintaining a list of psychologists who represent 74 countries for the purpose of facilitating international communication, and providing a web technology which permits conversion of text to and from languages. APA52 publishes the *International Psychology Reporter*.

In addition to these international organizations, there are regional associations such as the European Federation of Psychologists' Associations (EFPA) (www.efpa.eu/), the Interamerican Society of Psychology (SIP) (www.sipsych.org/english/home.htm), and the Asian Psychological Association. EFPA was founded in 1981, has 35 member European national psychology associations representing about 250,000 psychologists, and publishes *The European Psychologist*. SIP (the acronym relates to the Spanish translation of the Interamerican Society of Psychology) was established in 1951 and provides a means of communication among psychologists in North, Central, and South America, and the Caribbean. Its publications include the *Interamerican Journal of Psychology*. The Asian Psychological Association is of more recent origin, having been formed in Indonesia in 2005. These associations sometimes cosponsor events with the international organizations or hold satellite conferences in association with international congresses.

As mentioned above, IAAP and IUPsyS organize international congresses every four years, and they are scheduled such that there is an international congress organized by one or the other organization every two years. IACCP organizes satellite conferences to occur in association with the biennial international congresses. IAAP, IUPsyS, and IACCP also organize or cosponsor regional conferences that are especially important for younger psychologists and colleagues from less developed countries who may not be able to afford the travel cost and congress fees for world congresses. In addition to the regional conferences, these associations organize the Advanced Research Training Seminars (ARTS) for psychologists from low-income countries, and these events are held in conjunction with the biennial international congresses.

These associations make important contributions through working with international organizations, in particular, agencies of the UN. The role of psychologists representing psychological associations accredited at the UN includes acting as advocates for issues relevant to the field of psychology. This involves identifying issues relevant to the UN, taking initiative to demonstrate how psychologists can be effective, and actions such as presenting research, organizing workshops, and writing statements. One mechanism for pursuing these goals is to attend weekly briefings at the UN in New York on topics from poverty to human rights. To give an example of how this works, one briefing meeting was on disaster risk reduction and, following the briefing, the IAAP representative approached the presenter to discuss how psychologists could contribute. This resulted in a series of events unfolding including conference presentations and the submission of a written statement that was endorsed by a number of international psychology organizations including the IAAP, IUPsyS, and ICP. This resulted in recognition that psychosocial/mental health interventions are an integral part of any comprehensive program of disaster preparedness and risk reduction. IUPsyS is involved in international projects that include revision of the International Classification of Diseases, coordination of interdisciplinary projects (e.g., "Psychological Dimensions of Global Change" and "Human Perceptions and Behavior in Sustainable Water Use"), and development of international networks (e.g., "International Network of Psychology and the Developing World" and "Healthnet").

What More Could Be Done by International Psychology Organizations?

International psychology organizations have achieved much through organizing congresses/conferences/workshops/seminars, publishing journals, working with various UN agencies, and completing international projects. More could be achieved by increasing the quantity and quality of their activities. Before trying to articulate what this means, it is relevant to point out that the time is perhaps right for international psychology to proceed to its next stage of development, as there have been signs of national psychology associations adopting a more international perspective since the late 1990s. For example, in the last decade the Australian Psychological Society has signed Memoranda of Understanding that articulate collaborative mechanisms with the Psychological Society of South Africa, the New Zealand Psychological Society, the British Psychological Society, and the APA; it is currently in the final stages of negotiating agreements with the Japanese Psychological Association, the Canadian

Psychological Association, and the Indonesian Psychological Association (Montgomery, 2010). A quite different example is provided by the British Psychological Society, which is currently involved in a partnership that will benchmark the quality and impact of UK psychology against international standards, with a view to identifying ways of enhancing performance, capacity, and future research agendas. A number of Canadians have been prominent in international psychology for many years and the Canadian Psychological Association has supported the recent development of the "Universal Declaration of Ethical Principles for Psychologists," which provides a common moral framework that guides and inspires psychologists worldwide toward the highest ethical ideals in their professional and scientific work (see Chapter 31). The final session of the 4th International Congress on Licensure, Certification and Credentialing of Psychologists to be held in Sydney, Australia, in July 2010, will be used to initiate a process for developing "cross-border global psychology standards" to encourage mutual recognition of qualifications and mobility.

International congresses and the associated satellite conferences and ARTS Workshops are held every two years—there would be advantages to such events being held annually, as occurs with the conferences of national psychological associations. Momentum can be lost over a two-year period. Just as most psychologists know that their national association holds a conference at a certain time of the year every year, it would be advantageous for psychologists to know that their international association(s) holds a congress at a certain time of the year every year.

The organization of international congresses could be improved by IAAP and IUPsyS developing detailed congress organizing manuals, updated on a regular basis. For example, the agenda of international psychology would be served by a system that ensured psychologists from all regions of the world contributed, including presenting the more prestigious Keynote, State-of-the-Art, and Invited Addresses. How to do this is complex as decisions need to be made as to what constitutes appropriate regional participation and how to determine who should be invited. Such decisions should not be left to a Congress Organizing Committee with advice from the relevant association. It would make more sense for the organization to invest time in developing a detailed set of guidelines that would be available to the congress organizers from the commencement of their planning. On a personal note, in 2001 as President of the Australian Psychological Society, I led the bid to hold the 27th International Congress of Applied Psychology in Melbourne in 2010, and subsequently was appointed Congress President. I feel I reached the point of knowing how to organize an international congress about six months before the congress opened, well after all the important decisions had been made, a situation that could have been avoided if a comprehensive congress organizing manual had been available.

The work that international psychology organizations do with UN agencies is excellent, but the UN is so large and diverse on the one hand, and the range of potential contributions of psychology so wide on the other, that much more could be achieved. Also, the goal should be to work more "upstream" with these agencies—that is, to increase knowledge of how these agencies operate and develop relationships with individuals working for them, so that the international psychology organizations find out about initiatives at an earlier stage when it is easier to influence them. The APA has a Congressional Fellowship Program whereby a Fellow spends one year working as a special legislative assistant on the staff of a member of Congress or a Congressional Committee, and this scheme contributes to the more effective use of psychological knowledge in government. A similar scheme placing Fellows in UN agencies would potentially have many advantages.

The international psychology organizations are well aware of the need for capacity building for national psychology associations and have various mechanisms for achieving this goal. However, much more could be done in this domain. Most of the current initiatives are aimed at psychology associations in developing countries, which is very worthy, but psychology associations in developed countries could also benefit from capacity building. Every national psychology association has had its successes and failures sometimes within the same project, and could learn from the experience of other associations. Take for example, the "Decade of Behavior (2000–2010)," designed mainly as a public education opportunity, following on from the Decade of the Brain. This initiative was led by the APA but was intended as a broad-based, collaborative activity of many professional and academic associations. It was designed to focus on how the behavioral and social sciences could: (i) improve education and health care; (ii) enhance safety in homes and communities; (iii) address the needs of an aging population; and (iv) help to curb drug abuse, crime, high-risk behaviors, poverty, racism, and cynicism toward government.

This initiative was launched with much fanfare on Capitol Hill and some impressive achievements were accomplished. These included: (i) a Distinguished Lecture Program—support for major addresses on Decade themes; (ii) Exploring Behavior Week—an annual outreach program that brings the excitement of the behavioral and social sciences to secondary schools; (iii) Policy Seminars—an effort to translate frontier research into action by informing key individuals in the government and media about the importance of the behavioral and social sciences; (iv) Fundsource—a web search tool for locating funding opportunities in the behavioral and social sciences; and (v) Special Publications—scientific conference proceedings and journals published for the Decade effort. However, the initiative ran into problems mainly because the partners from the other disciplines did not contribute as much as hoped, and, as the decade wore on, the APA decided that the resources that it was putting into the initiative could be better spent in developing psychology specifically rather than all of the behavioral and social sciences (S. Breckler, personal communication, January 20, 2010). The point of including this example here is merely to argue that national and international psychology organizations could learn from the APA experience—an initiative with an exemplary set of goals and some excellent programs but one that did not ultimately evolve as hoped.

How Could International Psychology Organizations Achieve More?

For international psychology organizations to become more effective, they need more resources, more standing as the indisputable representatives of international psychology, and for their activities to be driven by well-developed strategic and business plans. Perhaps the obvious starting point is to consider whether these organizations need structural reform individually or collectively. For example, IUPsyS claims to represent over 500,000 psychologists, but its national members consist of psychological associations on the one hand and academies of science on the other. The problem with the latter category of membership is that the representatives of the academies may not be elected by a significant number of psychologists and hence may not be viewed as national representatives of psychology. In Australia, for example, until recently the national member was the National Committee for Psychology, a committee of the Australian Academy of Science. This committee was not an elected committee and only two psychologists were Fellows of the Australian Academy of Science, so not too many of the approximately 22,000 psychologists in Australia would have seen their national member as representing their interests. Allowing national members to be academies of science reduces input from psychologists at large, decreases the opportunities for raising funds, and cuts across the capacity to claim that the organization truly represents psychology/psychologists worldwide.

Just focusing on the revenue issue, national members of IUPsyS pay annual dues based on the number of psychologists they represent, currently ranging from US$125 to US$15,500. It is easy to imagine that national members may be reluctant to pay more, particularly the academies of science. If the dues are broken down into the amount per psychologist represented, however, they come out at around 15 cents per psychologist. If the national members were national psychology associations and they could be persuaded to add to their annual membership subscription an "international levy," an optional or mandatory, fixed or variable amount, the potential to increase the income to the international organization by a large multiple is obvious. If psychologists in developed countries were convinced that an international organization had any merit whatsoever, a levy of say $4 does not seem excessive (about the price of a cup of coffee, a tiny percentage of the national subscription, and probably tax-deductable), which would result in an increase in revenue of over 20-fold.

One way forward is for there to be greater unity between the international psychology organizations perhaps including a merger between IAAP and IUPsyS. Sabourin (2001) posed the question as to whether "greater unification [could] be promoted in the short to middle term? Or, on the contrary, should the science and profession develop separately, but still continue to collaborate?" (p. 80). Stevens and Wedding (2004c) subsequently argued that the time is ripe for greater unity within international psychology and went on to suggest that the integration of international psychological organizations has already begun. They offered as an example the fact that the officers of IAAP and IUPsyS meet yearly to coordinate existing relationships and identify new areas of cooperation. Stevens and Wedding suggested that "the benefits of a more unified international psychology include a stronger voice, pooled resources, and greater efficiency in carrying out projects that address various global problems" (p. 17). Further examples of how IAAP and IUPsyS have increased their cooperative activities in the last two decades are given in Chapter 33.

An international organization that included individual members with a structure to cater for their subdiscipline/professional specialty interests on the one hand, and national members that represented psychologists in their countries on the other hand, would have a standing that would provide a platform for going forward. It would facilitate annual international congresses and associated events. It would bring "new blood" into leadership roles as offices in IAAP and IUPsyS currently span four years, this being the period between their congresses.

A single international organization representing psychology would have more opportunities for raising funds by, for example, developing new income streams. Most national psychology associations have recognized that earning a high percentage of their income through subscriptions places them at risk, and have developed new revenue streams. The Australian Psychological Society, for example, has progressively reduced the proportion of its income derived from subscriptions from 85% in 1994 to 41% in 2009 by introducing new revenue streams including introducing a new membership benefit package (e.g., lower rates for professional indemnity insurance, credit cards, hotel accommodation, car hire, etc), providing professional development activities in Australia and overseas, and establishing an online publication for advertising vacant positions for psychologists. Variations of initiatives such as these could provide additional resources for an international psychology organization.

There has been increasing recognition over some years for all organizations to become more strategically focused and IUPsyS has a strategic plan for the quadrennium 2008–2012 on its web site. In this plan under "enablers," the need for increased financial resources is recognized and some progress has been made by the establishment of new publishing arrangements. In the same section, an intention to increase the human resources necessary for expanding its activities is stated, and this has been achieved towards the end of 2009 by the appointment of an Executive Officer who will have responsibility for implementing the strategic plan in collaboration with the IUPsyS Officers and Executive Committee. This seems a very significant development.

Other international psychology organizations would do well to follow the lead of IUPsyS. However, the strategic plan of IUPsyS looks like a beginning to strategic planning rather than a sophisticated example of the latter. For example, the plan does not include a vision statement, and includes "strategic priorities and strategic activities" rather than specific goals and strategies to achieve each goal. It is not associated with a business or operational plan that includes items such as time lines and person(s) responsible. There is no apparent linkage between the plan and budget process.

Conclusions

This chapter will conclude by summarizing the positives for applied psychology followed by the challenges, and finally by discussing ways forward. Psychology is a growth discipline and profession throughout the world. This reflects the interest in psychology and its growing acceptance, and provides great opportunities for making a difference. IUPsyS represents over 500,000 psychologists, but not all psychologists would be included in this figure as: (i) not all countries have national members of IUPsyS—Brazil does not, for example; (ii) not all psychologists are members of the national associations that IUPsyS uses in deriving the figure of 500,000; and (iii) because the number of psychologists is growing so rapidly, any figure quickly becomes out of date. Given these considerations, it seems likely that the total number of psychologists in the world is closer to one million than half a million.

Other positives include the huge progress that has been made in developing psychology as a discipline and a profession over the last century, including the large range of applications, as testified by this Handbook. Psychology clearly can make a contribution to the major challenges facing the world, and there are signs that this will be even more the case in the future. There are also indications that national psychology associations are becoming less insular and more international in their outlooks.

With respect to challenges, psychology has been dominated by contributions from North America and Europe and there is a need for increasing contributions from other regions of the world. This is necessary from the perspective of making psychology a true science but also because this will assist psychology to meet global challenges. The application of psychology has tended to focus on certain areas, in particular health, but also children/education and testing/assessment; and more attention needs to be given to the big global issues. Governing bodies, both national and international, need to be persuaded to make their priorities/goals more oriented around the well-being of individuals and the community.

A number of international and regional psychology organizations have made important contributions since the first international psychology congress over 120 years ago. Perhaps after all these years it is time for a major review of the structure of these organizations individually and also with a view to whether there should be mergers or at least more collaboration. International psychology needs more resources if it is to achieve greater things, and this can be achieved via increasing subscriptions/dues and/or developing new income streams. Surely, with perhaps a million psychologists worldwide, it must be possible to raise a significant amount of annual revenue! International psychology needs to become more strategic and more sophisticated politically. National capacity building in psychology should be a priority for all countries.

In summary, psychology has achieved much since its origins in the late 19th century but it could achieve so much more. It is an exciting time to be a psychologist.

References

Adair, J. G., Coelho, A. E. L., & Luna, J. R. (2002). How international is psychology? *International Journal of Psychology*, *37*, 160–170.

Arnett, J. J. (2008). Why American psychology needs to become less American. *American Psychologist*, *63*, 602–614.

Academy of Social Sciences in Australia. (2003). *Social science in Australia's national research priorities*. Canberra, Australia: Academy of Social Sciences in Australia.

Bauserman, R. (1997). International representation in the psychological literature. *International Journal of Psychology*, *32*, 107–112.

Haggbloom, S. J., Warnick, R., Warnick, J. E., Jones, V. K., Yarbrough, G. L., Russell, T. M. ... Monte, E. (2002). The 100 most eminent psychologists of the 20th century. *Review of General Psychology*, *6*, 139–152.

Lunt, I., & Poortinga, Y. H. (1996). Internationalizing psychology: The case of Europe. *American Psychologist*, *51*, 504–508.

Montgomery, B. (2010). The internationalisation of psychology. *InPsych*, *32*, 5.

Pawlik, K., & d'Ydewalle, G. (1996). Psychology and the global commons: Perspectives of international psychology. *American Psychologist, 51*, 488–495.

Rosenzweig, M. R. (1999). Continuity and change in the development of psychology around the world. *American Psychologist, 53*, 252–259.

Sabourin, M. (2001). International psychology: Is the whole greater than the sum of its parts? *Canadian Psychology, 42*, 74–81.

Sexton, V. S., & Hogan, J. D. (Eds.). (1992). *International psychology: Views from around the world*. Lincoln, NE: University of Nebraska Press.

Simonton, D. K. (1992). Leaders of American psychology, 1879–1967: Career development, creative output, and professional achievement. *Journal of Personality and Social Psychology, 62*, 5–17.

Stevens, M. J., & Wedding, D. (Eds.). (2004a). *Handbook of international psychology*. New York: Brunner-Routledge.

Stevens, M. J., & Wedding, D. (2004b). International psychology: A synthesis. In M. J. Stevens & D. Wedding (Eds.), *Handbook of international psychology* (pp. 481–500). New York: Brunner-Routledge.

Stevens, M. J., & Wedding, D. (2004c). International psychology: An overview. In M. J. Stevens & D. Wedding (Eds.), *Handbook of international psychology* (pp. 1–21). New York: Brunner-Routledge.

Van de Vijver, F., & Lonner, W. J. (1995). A bibliometric analysis of the *Journal of Cross-Cultural Psychology*. *Journal of Cross-Cultural Psychology, 26*, 591–602.

33

Applied Psychology, Epilogue

Michael C. Knowles

As this wonderfully informative, interesting, and absorbing Handbook wends its way toward its conclusion, this final chapter aims to provide a brief review of where applied psychology has come from, the manner in which it has developed, and some of the most urgent challenges that will shape its future. Not many other disciplines would be characterized by such a long history, not many other disciplines have spawned so many areas of specialization, and not many other disciplines have the intense innate appeal of applied psychology, all of which make it such an attractive field of research, study, and occupation.

To start at the beginning. It may be said that the origins of applied psychology lie in the accumulated wisdom of every culture on earth and are exemplified most of all in those cultures with a rich written history such as India and China. While these insights into the nature of human nature sustained these cultures for centuries and indeed millennia, they have had little impact upon mainstream applied psychology, and much needs to be done to rectify this situation. Instead, the roots of mainstream psychology as they are recognized today lie in ancient Hellenic thought, which has given psychology not only its name but also many of its applied foci as well. These include the integration and development of personality, relationships among citizens, and a range of other aspects of social and political life including welfare, human rights, education and legislation (Georgas, 2005).

The biggest turning point for the development of applied psychology, just as it has been for the evolution of psychology itself, was the establishment of Wilhelm Wundt's laboratory in Leipzig in 1879 with its emphasis upon measurement. This paved the way for the introduction of scientific psychology into the USA by Hugo Münsterberg at Harvard and Edward Titchener at Cornell, and from there to many other parts of the world. Wundt's influence continued apace during the early part of the 20th century into both of the two major fields in the bifurcation of applied psychology, one dealing with normal behavior and the other with the abnormal (Carpintero, 1992). For example, Binet in France and Burt in England undertook pioneering

IAAP Handbook of Applied Psychology, First Edition. Edited by Paul R. Martin, Fanny M. Cheung, Michael C. Knowles, Michael Kyrios, Lyn Littlefield, J. Bruce Overmier, and José M. Prieto.

research into testing and evaluating school children for their suitability for mainstream education, and the study and assessment of mental illness became the province of clinical psychologists, in many cases working in medical faculties in cooperation with psychiatrists. Paradoxically, both world wars contributed hugely to the growth of applied psychology in improving selection, placement, adjustment to institutional life, and leadership, giving rise to industrial and organizational psychology as the third cornerstone upon which the applied discipline rested. Consumer psychology, media psychology, and human factors or engineering psychology also arose in this era.

The second half of the 20th century witnessed an unforeseeably large expansion of applied psychology spawned by a number of factors including:

- diversification into a wide range of areas of specialization;
- further specialization within each field of applied psychology;
- cooperation with other disciplines and professions; and
- an increasing interest in specific problems facing contemporary society such as aging and crime.

Each of these topics may now be briefly discussed, with the last section of the chapter discussing some of the pressing challenges facing the discipline.

Specialization and Diversification

Apart from applied psychology's contribution to education, health, and work embodying educational psychology, psychological assessment and evaluation, clinical psychology, health psychology, and industrial and organizational psychology, the social and political trends of the second half of the 20th century have created their own demands, which have fed into the discipline and profoundly affected its content and structure. Examples, and a few only, include increases in the general standard of living and the rise of leisure; the increasing participation of women in the workforce; the heightening centrality of work and its effect on the balance between work and family; advances in technology; the rise of the knowledge economy; the need to develop "smart" systems of human decision making; and the internationalization and globalization of business and its huge consequences both positive and negative.

Irrespective of the direction from which these influences have come, what they have meant for applied psychology is the development of a large number of areas of specialization, all for the purpose of either acting proactively to prevent problems occurring or reactively to help solve problems of the day. Using the framework of the Handbook these areas of specialization may be listed and grouped as follows:

- Psychology applied to health and well-being including child and adolescent clinical psychology, adult clinical psychology, clinical health psychology, clinical neuropsychology, health promotion, and counseling psychology;
- Psychology applied to education and work including educational and school psychology, vocational psychology, work psychology, personnel/human resource psychology, occupational health psychology, and organizational psychology;

- Psychology applied to individuals and groups including psychological assessment and evaluation, applied cognitive psychology, human factors and ergonomics, forensic psychology, sport psychology, and applied gerontology;
- Psychology applied to the community including environmental psychology, traffic and transportation psychology, community psychology, economic psychology, psychology and societal development, political psychology, and cross-cultural psychology;
- Other applications of psychology including media and consumer psychology, rehabilitation psychology, psychology and poverty, psychology of religion, psychology and terrorism, psychology and refugees, and applied psychology and ethics.

This list of areas of specialization, which is indicative rather than definitive, illustrates the richness and range of the proliferation of applied psychology. As it emphatically shows, applied psychology has diversified enormously over the past 50 years and there is no indication that this rate of development in the discipline is to abate.

Further Specialization within Each Field of Applied Psychology

Apart from the diversification of applied psychology into these kinds of areas of specialization there has also been a high degree of specialization within each field in its own right. For example, to pick one at random, in the area of Educational and School Psychology particular areas of concentration include the following:

- helping every student achieve the highest possible degree of maturity, both intellectually, emotionally, physically and socially
- examining the factors which contribute to educational attainment
- examining the role that family, school, community, society, and culture play in promoting high achievement
- examining those adolescents who are not able to achieve satisfactorily and
  - suffer from psychological and social problems
  - become either a bully or a victim of school violence
  - engage in truancy, delinquency
  - or drop out from the school system
- examining diverse teaching methods, curricula and school environments that promote curiosity and encourage creativity.

Most fields of applied psychology are characterized by a similarly high degree of internal diversification.

Cooperation with other Disciplines and Professions

Although, as has been mentioned above, clinical psychologists have had a typical history of working hand in glove with psychiatrists, it has been a relationship affected by asymmetrical views of the professional distinction between health and mental health, and as a consequence in a number of quarters in competing claims with respect to "turf." Curiously enough, the same conflict of interest has not arisen between doctors and dentists. Be this as it may, perhaps the strongest case of cooperation has been between the disciplines of psychology and engineering, which has produced the field of ergonomics or human factors engineering. This has been a highly productive relationship with spectacular contributions to the design of cockpits and car cabins as well as countless other applications.

Increasingly, interprofessional relationships have been established with other disciplines including architecture, law, accounting, finance, human resource management, industrial relations, social work, nursing, physiotherapy, speech therapy, optometry, occupational therapy, physical education, and many others. In this context perhaps one of the positive outcomes of the global financial crisis has been an increasing recognition of the importance of behavioral economics.

This emerging network of interdisciplinary relationships illustrates that, in addition to a high degree of internal specialization, applied psychology has adopted an open outlook and actively sought professional connections that have been mutually beneficial to the disciplines concerned. Among other things this has helped tremendously in enhancing interdisciplinary awareness and understanding.

Specific Problems Facing Contemporary Society

While applied psychology has contributed substantially to the betterment of society globally, a host of other problems lie in the wake of social "progress" such as road accidents, poverty, drug addiction, crime, and marriage breakdown, to mention only some among a plethora of others. Population growth, the migration of rural workers to cities, the rising levels of immigrant employment, too, have all bred their own families of issues and problems. To these may be added global challenges arising from pollution of the environment, international terrorism, climate change, and increases in the magnitude and frequency of natural disasters.

As this Handbook has demonstrated, in every one of these areas and more applied psychologists have been at the forefront in advancing research to deepen understanding of these problems and developing interventions to help remedy them. While the discipline and the profession can feel proud of these achievements, one major regret is that all too frequently there has been a gap between what is known within the discipline and what is actually practiced in society. The need to do something about this is so pressing and so important that this issue will be addressed separately and more fully in the next section.

Demanding Challenges Facing the Discipline

Thus, despite the enormous and continuing advances that applied psychology has made over the past century, in its shadow lies persistent challenges with which the discipline has yet to come to grips fully. Two crucial ones are visibility and impact, and political influence at both the national and international level.

Visibility and impact: Public awareness

As mentioned above, although the extensive relationships that applied psychology has established with other disciplines and professions has substantially increased its visibility and impact within these neighboring fields, the same cannot be said for the general public and business and community leaders. Hence one of the most crucial challenges facing the field today is to increase public awareness of both the breadth and depth of applied psychology as exemplified in this Handbook and demonstrate what applied psychology can do to help in addressing many of the critical issues facing contemporary society. The following examples, again to name only a few, attest to this poverty of awareness.

The legal system, especially in criminal cases, has always relied on the testimony of eyewitnesses. Although eyewitness evidence can be helpful in developing leads and identifying criminals, few people are aware that psychological research has provided ample empirical evidence that it is not infallible. As Chapter 15 on Psychology and the Law shows, the malleability of eyewitness testimony has long been of interest to cognitive psychologists, and it is through this line of inquiry that research has investigated the effect of eyewitness testimony on juries. However great these research contributions have been, they have rarely found their way into the practices of law enforcement officers or instructions to jurors. Advising judges on the handling of vexatious litigants is another example.

Similarly, few members of the general public know that traffic psychology has contributed substantially to the *what* and the *why* of road safety and the *how to fix it* as well (T. Triggs, 7/10/2008). Psychology also gets heavily involved in the field of evaluation of countermeasures, including work in simulators where research is often multidisciplinary in nature involving engineers and statisticians. Specific areas in which traffic psychology is particularly visible include seat belts, behavioral measures relating to enforcement, the development of road signage, speed limits, driver distraction, and the older driver licensing question (when should people quit?). One of the most notable studies in this connection deals with high-mounted brake lights at the back of cars which have been shown to reduce front-on road accidents by up to 60% (Voevodsky, 1974).

Another laudable example of applied psychology's contribution to world peace at the time were the workshops organized by Herb Kelman and his colleagues. These played a huge role in facilitating the signing of the Oslo agreement between Israel and the Palestinians which eventually led to Rabin, Peres, and Arafat winning a Nobel Peace Prize. Were it not for the lamentable assassination of Rabin, the world today would be a totally different place and applied psychology's service to it arguably the greatest in the discipline's history.

As these few examples highlight, and there are many more embodied in the Handbook's chapters, one of the most immediate needs of psychology and applied psychology alike is to increase awareness among not only the public in general but also leaders in business and government in particular about the vast range of knowledge, experience, and skill that both academics and practitioners can provide and bring to bear in improving organizations, communities, and societies. This they may do by either helping to solve their most pressing problems or, more importantly, improving the situations in which people live and work so that these problems do not occur in the first place.

Political influence at the national level

Disaster management is another area in which it has been demonstrated that applied psychology can make an invaluable contribution, and this is to the way catastrophe is handled. An excellent example is the support provided by Chinese psychologists in the immediate aftermath of the 7.8 earthquake that struck the Sichuan Province in 2008. Within five hours the Chinese Psychological Society (CPS) sent a report containing psychological trauma relief guidelines, based upon domestic and international sources, to central government officials (B. Han, 24/5/2008).

Meanwhile, a small team of psychologists in Beijing met to develop training programs for psychologists and prepare instructional materials for disaster recovery crews, onsite victims (especially surviving children), and local organizers. Some 12 hours later a television interview was broadcast nationwide with a psychologist describing psychological approaches to disaster relief. Viewers were also referred to websites for materials for public reference. Twenty-four hours later the CPS opened a training program on post-traumatic psychological support techniques for candidate teams and announced a call for participation on its website. As a result requests for participation poured into the CPS. Thirty-six hours later the first group of psychologists were sent to Sichuan at the request of the local government.

Not all nations are in a position to accord with this model, however, and thus for the majority there is a special need for applied psychology to increase substantially its involvement in governmental decision making and the political process in which this occurs. This is especially important on account of the central and critical role that politicians play in making vital decisions affecting the course of national and societal development. For those politicians whose interests lie not merely in gaining and retaining political power but in improving human welfare, two requirements are of predominant importance.

One, is to make readily available research-based evidence upon which public policy can be developed. Although there is a wealth of data in every field of specialization of applied psychology as all the previous chapters of this Handbook illustrate, there is a need for this to be coordinated and presented in a user-friendly fashion so that its relevance and potential can be easily recognized and understood. For example, given that terrorism is one of the most serious threats to national and international security, what would be helpful would be a clear statement of the frequency and magnitude of terrorism across the world and the extent of its human and economic consequences, the historical context in which terrorism develops and the manner in which its organizational capacity grows, and the psychological profile of those who become terrorists and the process leading to them becoming terrorists.

The other and arguably the most important need of all is to provide similar readily available strategies by means of which such problems can be remedied. Again using terrorism as the example, the requirement here over and above everything else is to manage convicted terrorists so that the cycle of violence is broken. Despite the existing evidence of the efficacy of such programs, the general practice is to emphasize incarceration and punishment instead of rehabilitation, meaning that the cycle of violence is intensified rather than ruptured. In other words, documented evidence on each of these facets of terrorism would facilitate a deepening understanding of this problem and place the decision maker in a position to handle the issue constructively rather than destructively.

A third necessity for the discipline of applied psychology involves establishing relations with politicians through lobbying and other means. These of course would involve interventions that were targeted to specific issues and another excellent example of this is provided by the experience of the Australian Psychological Society in facilitating the introduction of rebates for psychological services into Medicare (the national publicly funded healthcare system) in 2004 ("Medicare Plus") and 2006 ("Better Access") (Meadows & Martin, 2007).

Political influence at the international level

In addition to the continuing work along the lines just mentioned that is being done by national societies and associations of psychology in order to raise the profile and effectiveness of applied psychology within their respective countries, huge advances have also been achieved at the international level in establishing and facilitating the growth of the discipline. As described in the previous chapter the principal organizations operating at the international level are the International Union of Psychological Science (IUPsyS), the International Association of Applied Psychology (IAAP), the International Association of Cross-Cultural Psychology (IACCP), and the International Council of Psychologists (ICP), while at the regional level the major organizations are the European Federation of Psychologists' Associations (EFPA), the Interamerican Society of Psychology [Sociedad Interamericana de Psicología] (SIP) and the Asian Psychological Association (APsyA).

It is gratifying to note that the origins of cooperation at the international level can be traced back to the 1st International Congress of Psychology, which took place in Paris in 1889 and was held in conjunction with the Paris International Exhibition. One of the aims of the Congress was to establish psychology as a science in the same way as other disciplines, and a permanent international committee was formed to ensure the continuation of such congresses. The foresight of these pioneers was rewarded insofar as international congresses were held more or less every three to five years until 1952, when the International Union of Psychological Science was founded to formalize the organization of psychology internationally.

The International Association of Applied Psychology has a similarly long tradition of organizing international congresses dating back to 1920. This being the year of its foundation also makes IAAP the world's oldest international association of psychology. This long institutional history and its well-preserved institutional memory has made IAAP a potent force in fostering the development of applied psychology, and the diversification of the field as described above has been mirrored in the divisionalization of the Association within which there are now 18 Divisions as well as an equally large number of active Committees and Task Forces.

For most of their histories IAAP and IUPsyS functioned independently of one another, but over the last two decades they have increasingly sought ways to cooperate. This has been achieved by integrating their congress calendars so that a major congress is held every two years, organizing the Advanced Research and Training Seminars (ARTS) which provide intensive training to facilitate the development of research skills of early career psychologists working in low-income countries, and sponsoring Regional Conferences of Psychology (RCPs). The general idea of the RCPs is to foster the development of psychology in selected regions of the world by increasing communication between scientific researchers and professionals, disseminating psychological knowledge and expertise, and supporting the organization of psychology within the region. These Regional Conferences are primarily capacity-building activities where the focus is on the development of individual competence and systems. Their achievements in terms of the strength of their scientific programs and the scope of their emerging regional activities are impressive (Knowles & Sabourin, 2008).

The cooperation between IAAP and IUPsyS, and especially the spirit of cooperation that underlies it, augers well for the future development of psychology internationally, particularly since this partnership in supporting the ARTS and RCP initiatives has been joined by the International Association of Cross-Cultural Psychology. Altogether there have now been 10 ARTS and 8 RCPs which have already contributed hugely not only in responding to needs for particular knowledge and skills in countries with developing economies or in particular regions of the world but also in encouraging the establishment of organized ways of addressing these needs.

Summary

As the present Handbook shows, applied psychology is a field characterized by a long gestation and a relatively short history. The latter has been characterized by a high rate of specialization and diversification, with each field tending to develop its own theory, research methods, and applications. Because of this, the field as a whole encompasses many theoretical orientations, research paradigms, and applied strategies. In addition to its internal growth, applied psychology has established strong external relationships with a wide range of other disciplines, all of which have been mutually beneficial. Currently it is in the process of forging stronger relationships with the general public and with leaders in organizations, communities, and governments, particularly at the national level. This progress has been aided and abetted by the development of coordination and cooperation institutionally, especially at the international level. Because of the excitement inherent in all these areas of growth and development it is no wonder that the discipline has such widespread popularity both as a course of study and as a profession.

References

Carpintero, H. (1992). Spain. In V. S. Sexton & J. D. Hogan (Eds.), *International psychology: Views from around the world* (pp. 364–372). Lincoln, NE: University of Nebraska Press.

Georgas, J. (2005). The education of psychologists in Greece. *International Journal of Psychology*, *40*, 1–6.

Knowles, M. C., & Sabourin, M. (2008). Psychology and modern life challenges: The 2nd Middle East and North Africa Regional Conference of Psychology, Amman, Jordan. *International Journal of Psychology*, *43*, 2, 130–139.

Meadows, G., & Martin, P. R. (2007). When to refer to a psychologist. *Medicine Today*, *8*, 61–65.

Voevodsky, J. (1974). Evaluation of a deceleration warning light for reducing rear-end automobile collisions. *Journal of Applied Psychology*, *59*, 270–273.

Name Index

IAAP Handbook of Applied Psychology, First Edition. Edited by Paul R. Martin, Fanny M. Cheung, Michael C. Knowles, Michael Kyrios, Lyn Littlefield, J. Bruce Overmier, and José M. Prieto.

Subject Index

IAAP Handbook of Applied Psychology, First Edition. Edited by Paul R. Martin, Fanny M. Cheung, Michael C. Knowles, Michael Kyrios, Lyn Littlefield, J. Bruce Overmier, and José M. Prieto.

Index compiled by Frank Pert